Map pages s

by
119
egness
ston
04 105
Cromer
106 107
King's Lynn
Norwich
gh
90 91 92 93
hetford
Cambridge
76 77 78 79
Ipswich
0 61 62 63
ford
N
45 46 47
Maidstone
noaks
33 34 35
Dover
Folkestone
Hastings
20 21

Atlas contents

Scale 1:250,000 or 3.95 miles to 1 inch

Map pages south	inside front cover
Route planner	**II–VII**
Mileage chart	**VIII**
Atlas Symbols	**1**
Road maps 1:250,000 scale	**2–237**
Western Isles 1:700,000 scale	232–233
Orkney Islands 1:636,000 scale	234
Shetland Islands 1:636,000 scale	235
Channel Islands 1:150,000 scale	236
Isle of Man 1:317,000 scale	237
Restricted junctions	**238–239**
Index to place names	**240–319**
County, administrative area map	240–241
Place name index	242–319
Ireland	endpaper
Map pages north	inside back cover

11th edition June 2012

Cartography:

Now fully updated, the 1st edition of this atlas won the British Cartographic Society - Ordnance Survey Award for innovation in the design and presentation of spatial information.

All cartography in this atlas edited, designed and produced by the Mapping Services Department of AA Publishing (A04863).

Publisher's notes:
Published by AA Publishing (a trading name of AA Media Limited, whose registered office is Fanum House, Basing View, Basingstoke, Hampshire RG21 4EA, UK. Registered number 06112600).

ISBN: 978 0 7495 7348 5 (flexibound)

A CIP catalogue record for this book is available from The British Library.

Disclaimer:
The contents of this atlas are believed to be correct at the time of the latest revision, it will not contain any subsequent amended, new or temporary information including diversions and traffic control or enforcement systems. The publishers cannot be held responsible or liable for any loss or damage occasioned to any person acting or refraining from action as a result of any use or reliance on material in this atlas, nor for any errors, omissions or changes in such material. This does not affect your statutory rights.

The publishers would welcome information to correct any errors or omissions and to keep this atlas up to date. Please write to the Atlas Editor, AA Publishing, The Automobile Association, Fanum House, Basing View, Basingstoke, Hampshire RG21 4EA, UK.
E-mail: *roadatlasfeedback@theaa.com*

Acknowledgements:
AA Publishing would like to thank the following for their assistance in producing this atlas:

RoadPilot® Information on fixed speed camera locations provided by and © 2012 RoadPilot® Driving Technology. Crematoria database provided by Cremation Society of Great Britain. Cadw, English Heritage, Forestry Commission, Historic Scotland, Johnsons, National Trust and National Trust for Scotland, RSPB, The Wildlife Trust, Scottish Natural Heritage, Natural England, The Countryside Council for Wales.

Printer:
Printed in Italy by Rotolito Lombarda, Milan. Paper: 100gsm matt coated.

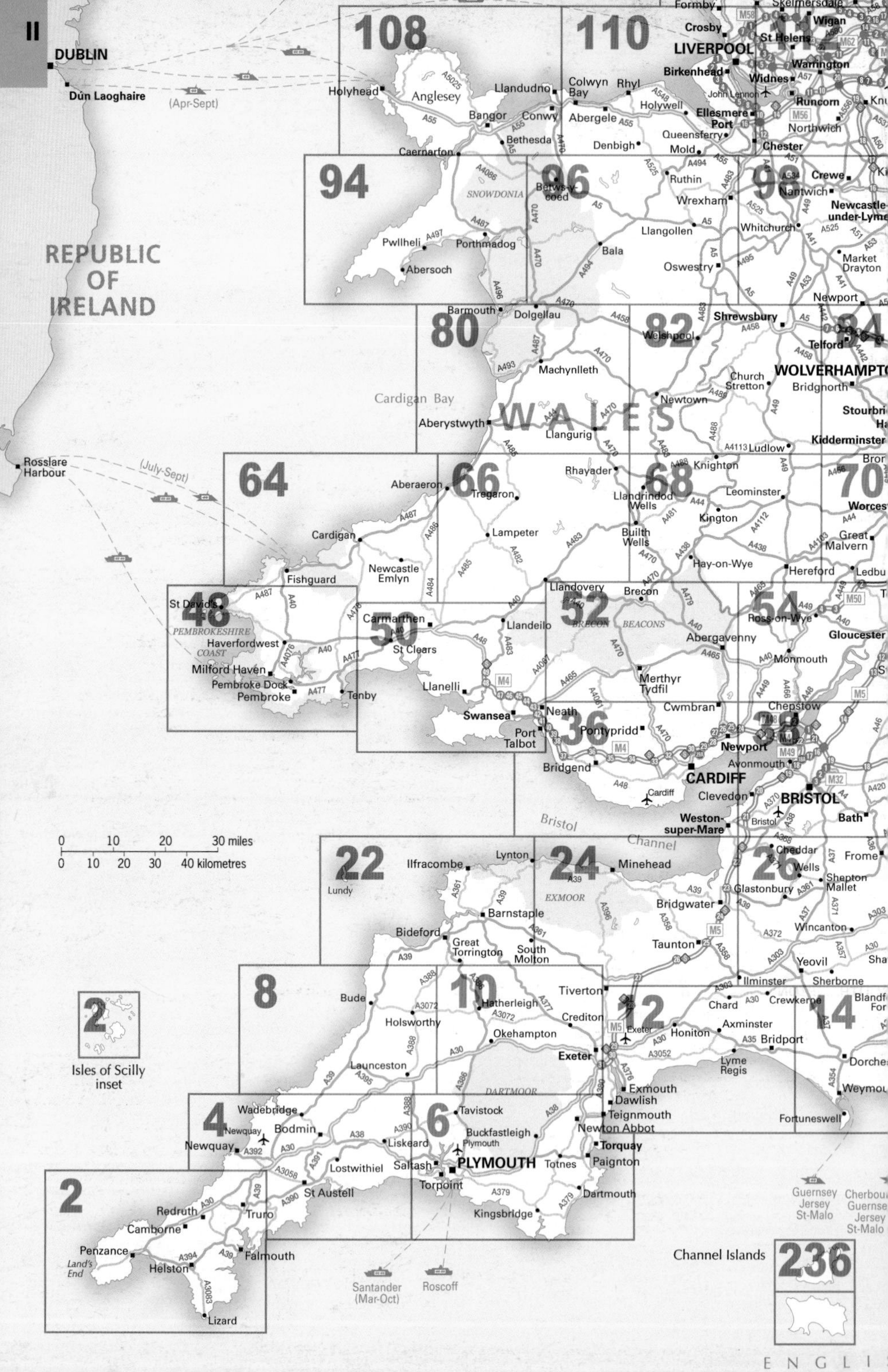
DUBLIN
Dún Laoghaire
(Apr-Sept)
REPUBLIC
OF
IRELAND
Rosslare
Harbour
(July-Sept)
108
110
112
Holyhead
Anglesey
Llandudno
Colwyn
Bay
Rhyl
Bangor
Conwy
Abergele
Holywell
Bethesda
Denbigh
Caernarfon
Formby
Ormskirk
Skelmersdale
Bolton
Crosby
Wigan
LIVERPOOL
St Helens
Birkenhead
Warrington
Widnes
John Lennon
Runcorn
Ellesmere
Port
Northwich
Queensferry
Mold
Chester
94
96
98
SNOWDONIA
Betws-y-
coed
Ruthin
Crewe
Nantwich
Wrexham
Newcastle-
under-Lyme
Llangollen
Whitchurch
Pwllheli
Porthmadog
Bala
Abersoch
Oswestry
Market
Drayton
Newport
Barmouth
Dolgellau
80
82
84
Shrewsbury
Welshpool
Telford
Machynlleth
WOLVERHAMPTON
Church
Stretton
Bridgnorth
Cardigan Bay
Newtown
Aberystwyth
WALES
Llangurig
Stourbridge
Kidderminster
Ludlow
64
66
68
70
Rhayader
Knighton
Aberaeron
Tregaron
Llandrindod
Wells
Leominster
Worcester
Kington
Cardigan
Lampeter
Builth
Wells
Great
Malvern
Newcastle
Emlyn
Hay-on-Wye
Hereford
Ledbury
Fishguard
Llandovery
Brecon
48
50
52
54
St David's
PEMBROKESHIRE
COAST
Carmarthen
Llandeilo
BRECON
BEACONS
Ross-on-Wye
Haverfordwest
St Clears
Abergavenny
Gloucester
Milford Haven
Monmouth
Pembroke Dock
Pembroke
Tenby
Llanelli
Merthyr
Tydfil
Cwmbran
Chepstow
Swansea
Neath
36
38
Port
Talbot
Pontypridd
Newport
Bridgend
CARDIFF
Avonmouth
Cardiff
Clevedon
BRISTOL
Weston-
super-Mare
Bristol
Bath
Bristol
Channel
0 10 20 30 miles
0 10 20 30 40 kilometres
22
24
26
Lundy
Ilfracombe
Lynton
Minehead
EXMOOR
Cheddar
Wells
Frome
Shepton
Mallet
Glastonbury
Barnstaple
Bridgwater
Bideford
Great
Torrington
South
Molton
Taunton
Wincanton
Yeovil
Sherborne
Ilminster
8
10
12
14
Bude
Hatherleigh
Tiverton
Chard
Crewkerne
Holsworthy
Crediton
Exeter
Honiton
Axminster
Bridport
Okehampton
Lyme
Regis
Exeter
Dorchester
2
Isles of Scilly
inset
Launceston
DARTMOOR
Exmouth
Dawlish
Weymouth
4
6
Wadebridge
Tavistock
Teignmouth
Newquay
Bodmin
Buckfastleigh
Newton Abbot
Fortuneswell
Newquay
Liskeard
Plymouth
Torquay
Lostwithiel
Saltash
PLYMOUTH
Totnes
Paignton
Torpoint
St Austell
Dartmouth
Guernsey
Jersey
St-Malo
Cherbourg
Guernsey
Jersey
St-Malo
Redruth
Truro
Camborne
Kingsbridge
Penzance
Falmouth
Channel Islands
236
Land's
End
Helston
Santander
(Mar-Oct)
Roscoff
Lizard
ENGLI

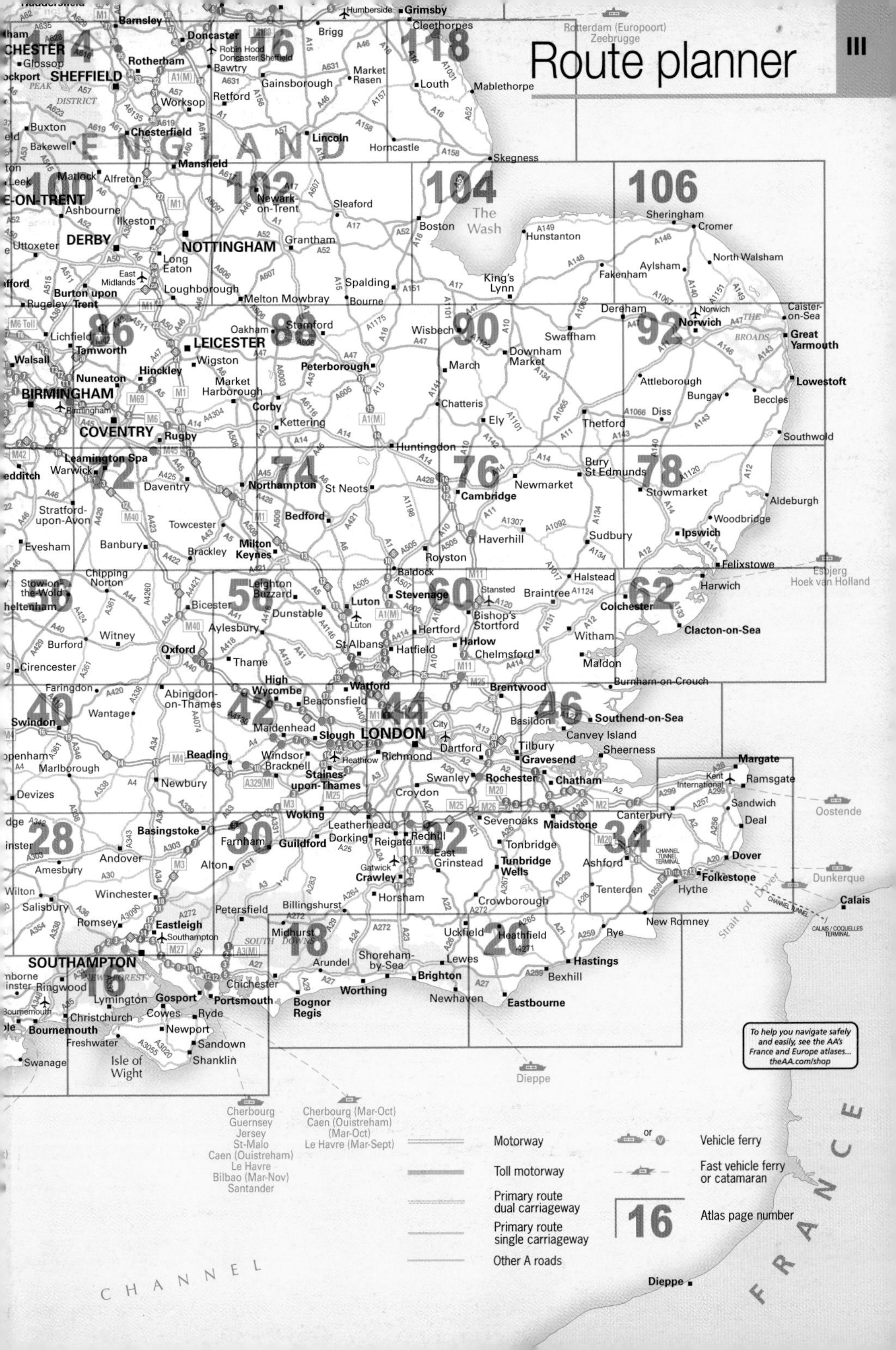

Route planner

Cherbourg
Guernsey
Jersey
St-Malo
Caen (Ouistreham)
Le Havre
Bilbao (Mar-Nov)
Santander

Cherbourg (Mar-Oct)
Caen (Ouistreham)
(Mar-Oct)
Le Havre (Mar-Sept)

Motorway

Toll motorway

Primary route
dual carriageway

Primary route
single carriageway

Other A roads

Vehicle ferry

Fast vehicle ferry
or catamaran

16 Atlas page number

To help you navigate safely and easily, see the AA's France and Europe atlases... theAA.com/shop

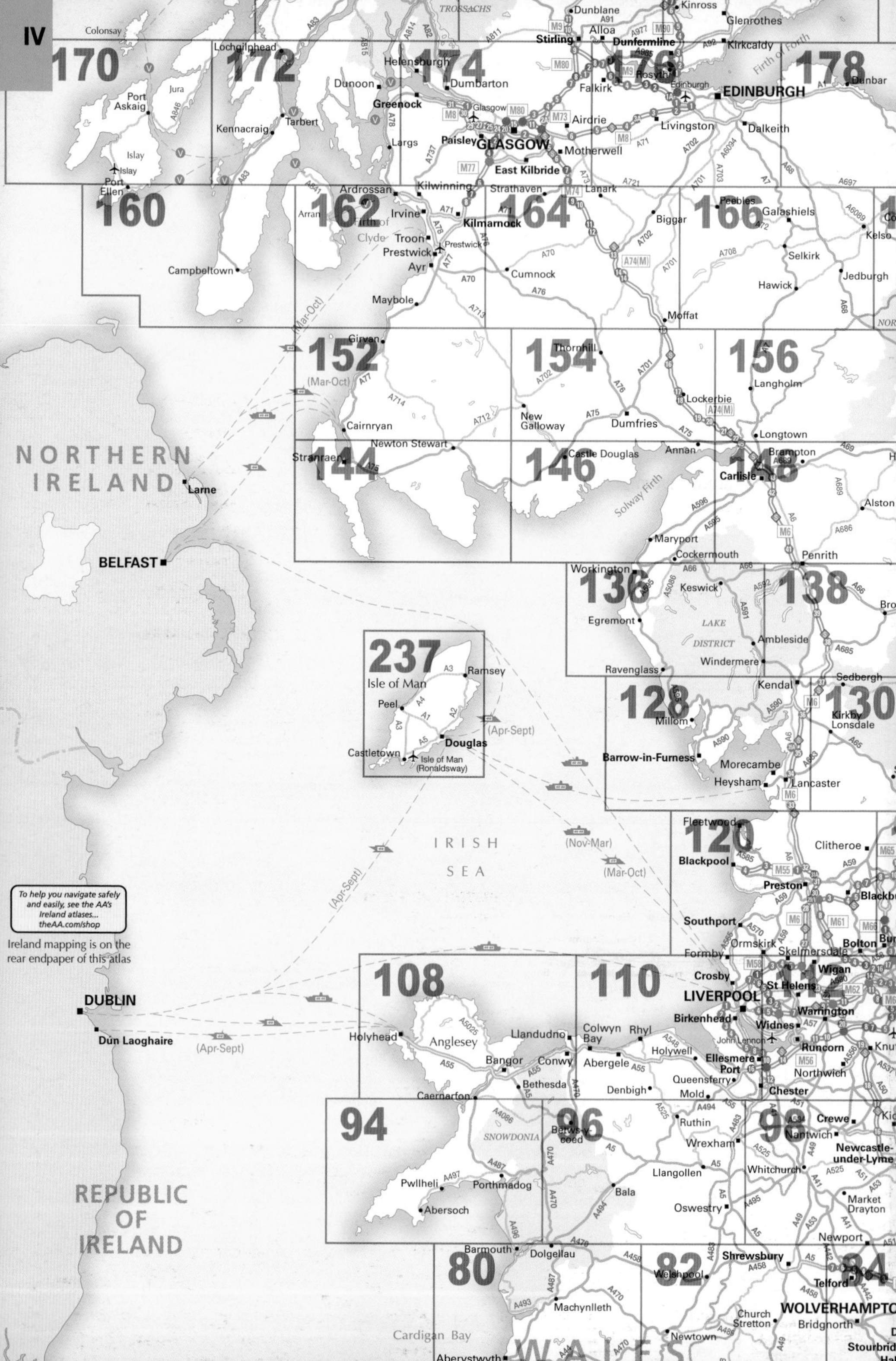

170
172
174
176
178
160
162
164
166
152
154
156
144
146
148
136
138
237
128
130
120
108
110
112
94
96
98
80
82
84
TROSSACHS
Colonsay
Lochgilphead
Helensburgh
Dunoon
Greenock
Dumbarton
Glasgow
GLASGOW
Paisley
Airdrie
Motherwell
East Kilbride
Stirling
Dunblane
Alloa
Dunfermline
Kinross
Glenrothes
Kirkcaldy
Firth of Forth
Falkirk
Rosyth
Edinburgh
EDINBURGH
Dunbar
Livingston
Dalkeith
Port Askaig
Jura
Islay
Port Ellen
Kennacraig
Tarbert
Largs
Campbeltown
Arran
Ardrossan
Kilwinning
Irvine
Firth of Clyde
Troon
Prestwick
Ayr
Kilmarnock
Strathaven
Lanark
Biggar
Peebles
Galashiels
Kelso
Selkirk
Jedburgh
Hawick
Cumnock
Maybole
Moffat
Girvan
(Mar-Oct)
Thornhill
Langholm
Lockerbie
Cairnryan
New Galloway
Dumfries
Longtown
Newton Stewart
Stranraer
Castle Douglas
Annan
Brampton
Carlisle
Solway Firth
Alston
NORTHERN IRELAND
Larne
BELFAST
Maryport
Cockermouth
Penrith
Workington
Keswick
Egremont
LAKE DISTRICT
Ambleside
Windermere
Ravenglass
Isle of Man
Ramsey
Peel
Douglas
Castletown
Isle of Man (Ronaldsway)
(Apr-Sept)
Kendal
Sedbergh
Millom
Kirkby Lonsdale
Barrow-in-Furness
Morecambe
Heysham
Lancaster
IRISH SEA
(Nov-Mar)
(Mar-Oct)
Fleetwood
Clitheroe
Blackpool
Preston
Southport
Ormskirk
Skelmersdale
Formby
Wigan
Bolton
Crosby
St Helens
LIVERPOOL
Birkenhead
Warrington
Widnes
John Lennon
Runcorn
Ellesmere Port
Northwich
Chester
To help you navigate safely and easily, see the AA's Ireland atlases... theAA.com/shop
Ireland mapping is on the rear endpaper of this atlas
DUBLIN
Dún Laoghaire
Holyhead
Anglesey
Llandudno
Colwyn Bay
Rhyl
Holywell
Bangor
Conwy
Abergele
Bethesda
Queensferry
Denbigh
Mold
Caernarfon
SNOWDONIA
Betws-y-coed
Ruthin
Crewe
Nantwich
Wrexham
Newcastle-under-Lyme
Llangollen
Whitchurch
Pwllheli
Porthmadog
Abersoch
Bala
Oswestry
Market Drayton
REPUBLIC OF IRELAND
Barmouth
Dolgellau
Newport
Shrewsbury
Welshpool
Telford
Machynlleth
Church Stretton
WOLVERHAMPTON
Bridgnorth
Cardigan Bay
Newtown
Aberystwyth
WALES

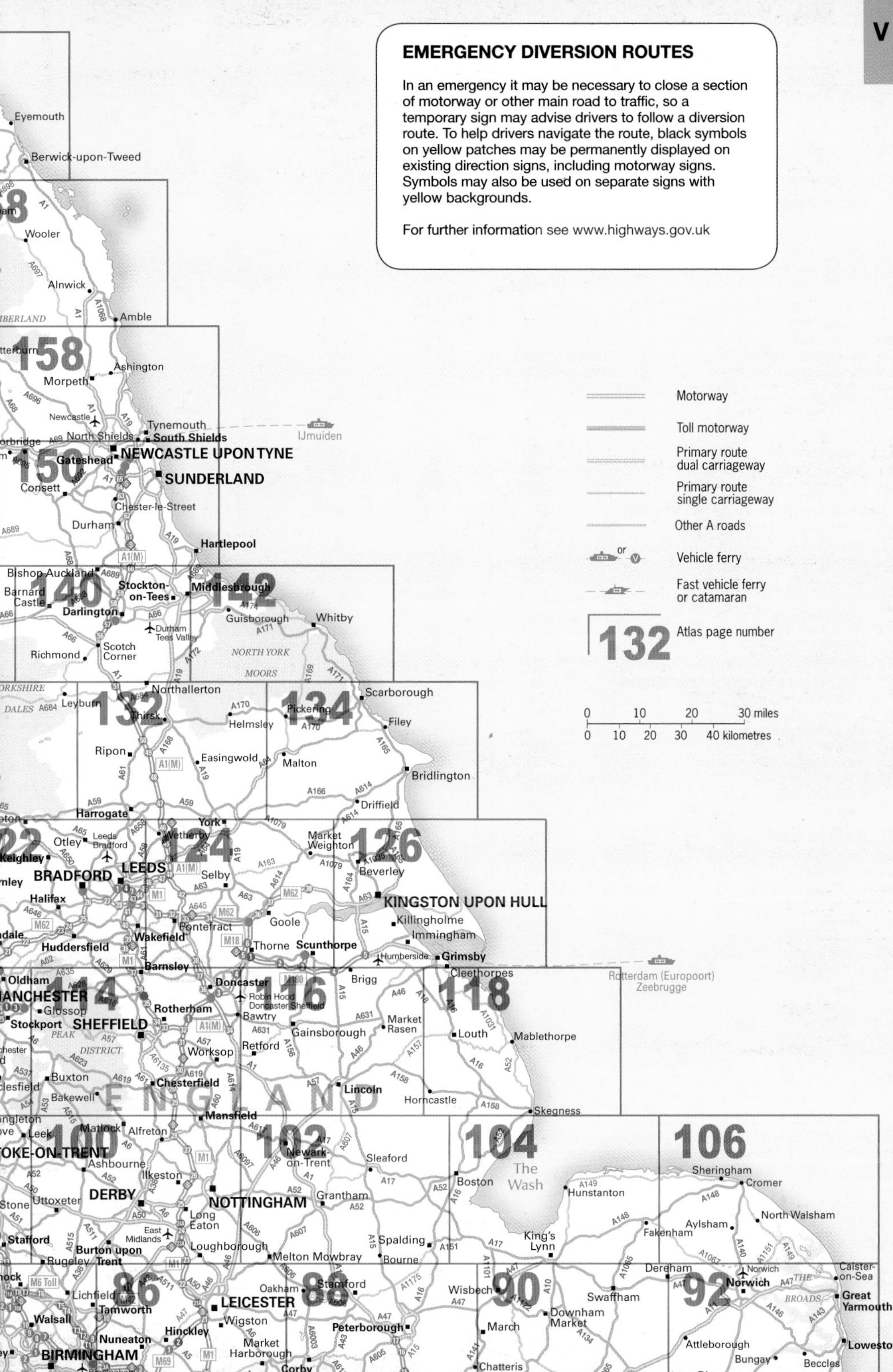
EMERGENCY DIVERSION ROUTES
In an emergency it may be necessary to close a section of motorway or other main road to traffic, so a temporary sign may advise drivers to follow a diversion route. To help drivers navigate the route, black symbols on yellow patches may be permanently displayed on existing direction signs, including motorway signs. Symbols may also be used on separate signs with yellow backgrounds.
For further information see www.highways.gov.uk
Motorway
Toll motorway
Primary route dual carriageway
Primary route single carriageway
Other A roads
Vehicle ferry
Fast vehicle ferry or catamaran
132
Atlas page number
0 10 20 30 miles
0 10 20 30 40 kilometres
ENGLAND

FERRY INFORMATION

Hebrides and west coast Scotland

calmac.co.uk	0800 066 5000
skyeferry.co.uk	01599 522 756
western-ferries.co.uk	01369 704 452

Orkney and Shetland

northlinkferries.co.uk	0845 6000 449
pentlandferries.co.uk	01856 831 226
orkneyferries.co.uk	01856 872 044
shetland.gov.uk/ferries	01595 693 535

Isle of Man

steam-packet.com	08722 992 992

Ireland

irishferries.com	08717 300 400
poferries.com	08716 642 020
stenaline.co.uk	08447 70 70 70

North Sea (Scandinavia and Benelux)

dfdsseaways.co.uk	08715 229 955
poferries.com	08716 642 020
stenaline.co.uk	08447 70 70 70

Isle of Wight

wightlink.co.uk	0871 376 1000
redfunnel.co.uk	0844 844 9988

Channel Islands

condorferries.co.uk	0845 609 1024

Channel hopping (France and Belgium)

brittany-ferries.co.uk	0871 244 0744
condorferries.co.uk	0845 609 1024
eurotunnel.com	08443 35 35 35
ldlines.co.uk	0844 576 8836
dfdsseaways.co.uk	08715 229 955
poferries.com	08716 642 020
transeuropaferries.com	01843 595 522
transmancheferries.co.uk	0844 576 8836

Northern Spain

brittany-ferries.co.uk	0871 244 0744
poferries.com	08716 642 020

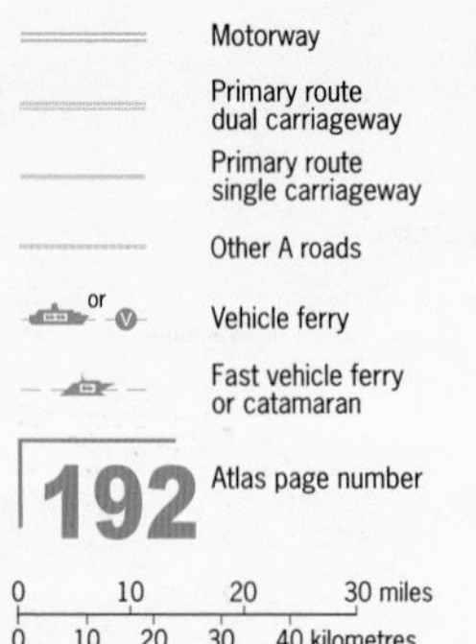

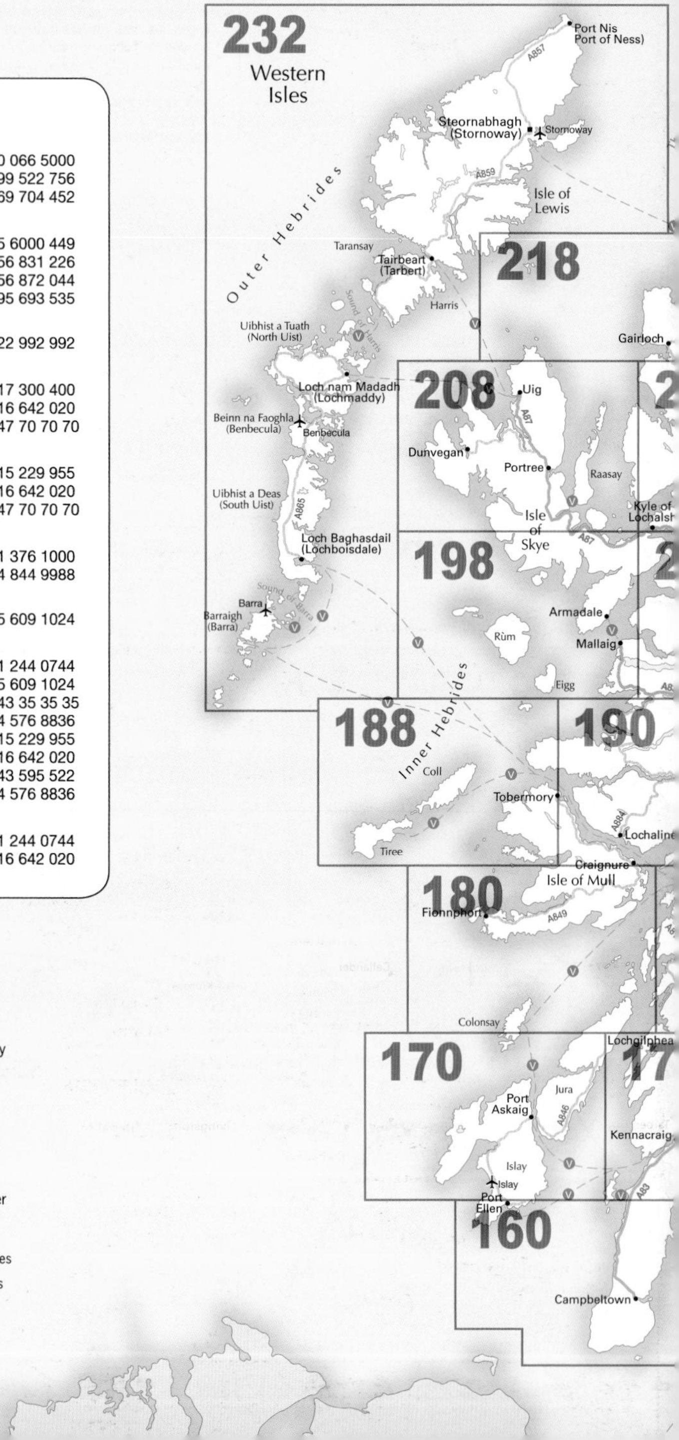

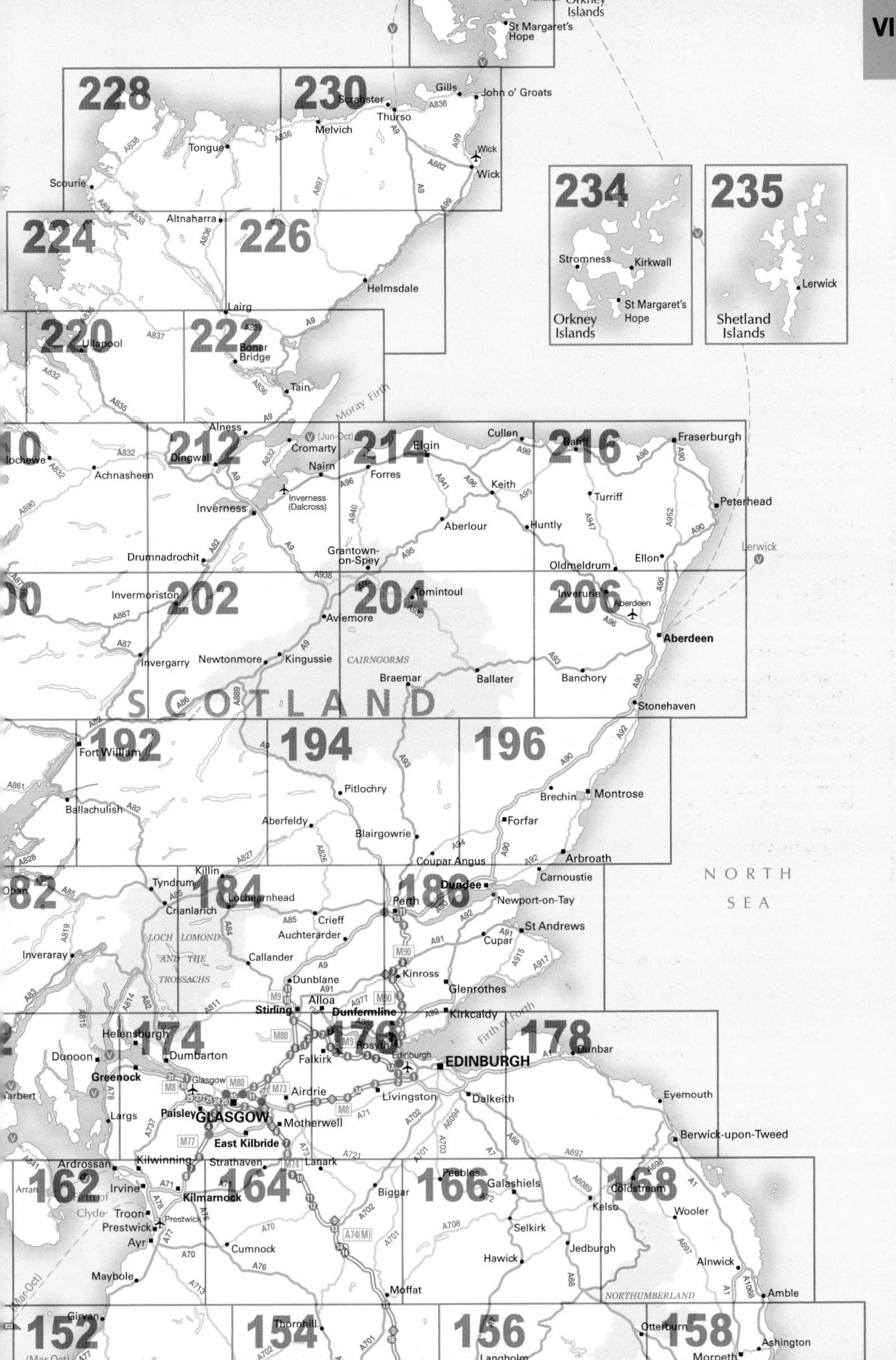

Orkney Islands
Kirkwall
St Margaret's Hope
228
230
Scrabster
Thurso
Gills
John o' Groats
Melvich
Tongue
Wick
Scourie
234
235
Stromness
Kirkwall
St Margaret's Hope
Orkney Islands
Lerwick
Shetland Islands
224
226
Altnaharra
Helmsdale
Lairg
220
222
Ullapool
Bonar Bridge
Tain
Moray Firth
Alness
212
214
216
Cullen
Banff
Fraserburgh
Cromarty
Elgin
Dingwall
Nairn
Forres
Achnasheen
Keith
Turriff
Peterhead
Inverness
Inverness (Dalcross)
Aberlour
Huntly
Drumnadrochit
Grantown-on-Spey
Ellon
Oldmeldrum
Lerwick
202
204
206
Invermoriston
Tomintoul
Inverurie
Aberdeen
Aviemore
Aberdeen
Invergarry
Newtonmore
Kingussie
CAIRNGORMS
Braemar
Ballater
Banchory
SCOTLAND
Stonehaven
192
194
196
Fort William
Pitlochry
Brechin
Montrose
Ballachulish
Aberfeldy
Forfar
Blairgowrie
Coupar Angus
Arbroath
Killin
Tyndrum
184
186
Dundee
Carnoustie
NORTH SEA
Oban
Crianlarich
Lochearnhead
Perth
Newport-on-Tay
Crieff
Auchterarder
St Andrews
Cupar
LOCH LOMOND AND THE TROSSACHS
Inveraray
Callander
Kinross
Dunblane
Glenrothes
Stirling
Alloa
Dunfermline
Kirkcaldy
Helensburgh
174
176
178
Firth of Forth
Dunoon
Dumbarton
Falkirk
Rosyth
Edinburgh
EDINBURGH
Dunbar
Greenock
Glasgow
Airdrie
Livingston
Dalkeith
Eyemouth
Largs
Paisley
GLASGOW
Motherwell
East Kilbride
Berwick-upon-Tweed
Ardrossan
Kilwinning
Strathaven
Lanark
Peebles
Galashiels
162
164
166
168
Arran
Irvine
Kilmarnock
Biggar
Coldstream
Kelso
Firth of Clyde
Troon
Prestwick
Wooler
Ayr
Selkirk
Cumnock
Jedburgh
Hawick
Alnwick
Maybole
Moffat
NORTHUMBERLAND
Amble
Girvan
152
154
156
158
Thornhill
Otterburn
Ashington
Langholm
Morpeth

Mileage chart

The mileage chart shows distances in miles between two towns along AA-recommended routes. Using motorways and other main roads this is normally the fastest route, though not necessarily the shortest.

The journey times, shown in hours and minutes, are average off-peak driving times along AA-recommended routes. These times should be used as a guide only and do not allow for unforeseen traffic delays, rest breaks or fuel stops.

For example, the 378 miles (608 km) journey between Glasgow and Norwich should take approximately 7 hours 28 minutes.

journey times

Town	Journey times to the following towns in order (Aberystwyth, Barnstaple, Birmingham, Brighton, Bristol, Cambridge, Cardiff, Carlisle, Carmarthen, Dorchester, Dover, Edinburgh, Exeter, Fort William, Glasgow, Gloucester, Guildford, Hereford, Holyhead, Hull, Inverness, Kendal, Leeds, Lincoln, Liverpool, Maidstone, Manchester, Middlesbrough, Newcastle, Northampton, Norwich, Nottingham, Oxford, Penzance, Perth, Peterborough, Plymouth, Portsmouth, Preston, Salisbury, Sheffield, Shrewsbury, Southampton, Stoke-on-Trent, Stranraer, Taunton, Wick, York, LONDON)
Aberdeen	906 1052 750 1051 913 907 936 426 1020 1047 1108 236 1027 357 301 836 1007 850 843 735 240 517 655 753 636 1029 632 545 510 840 1007 757 907 1246 151 837 1114 1039 558 1009 721 747 1024 703 505 950 513 643 955
Aberystwyth	436 249 538 301 431 229 444 115 432 612 647 412 901 624 251 443 158 234 436 959 359 345 430 244 533 304 456 527 340 554 339 354 631 720 419 459 455 317 412 350 154 439 252 713 335 1231 410 455
Barnstaple	326 423 200 501 234 629 335 206 513 832 115 1047 810 227 339 303 636 547 1144 544 529 507 456 434 448 628 700 409 624 422 319 233 906 452 145 324 503 232 500 403 307 400 858 109 1417 543 403
Birmingham	310 147 154 210 327 311 321 334 530 301 745 507 110 226 125 334 233 842 242 216 157 153 255 146 315 346 102 316 108 126 520 604 142 348 258 200 243 146 101 243 058 556 224 1115 229 217
Brighton	301 213 336 628 436 232 154 831 351 1045 808 301 102 348 635 451 1143 543 436 353 454 116 447 535 606 223 320 329 200 610 905 248 438 109 501 151 406 402 127 359 857 319 1416 449 128
Bristol	315 059 451 159 144 337 654 134 908 631 048 206 124 457 408 1005 405 351 328 317 258 310 450 521 224 439 243 134 353 727 313 221 217 324 128 321 224 202 221 720 057 1238 404 218
Cambridge	347 448 448 345 210 637 438 906 628 247 200 302 516 248 1003 422 242 149 336 131 319 335 407 112 135 144 201 657 721 044 525 252 342 254 221 243 244 240 717 401 1236 250 129
Cardiff	514 116 230 413 717 210 931 654 117 241 117 455 431 1029 429 414 351 340 334 333 513 544 257 511 307 210 429 751 337 257 253 347 210 345 239 237 245 743 133 1302 428 254
Carlisle	558 625 649 207 605 422 145 414 545 429 421 316 519 056 237 334 214 610 210 200 125 418 549 338 445 824 241 418 652 618 136 547 300 326 602 241 233 528 752 225 533
Carmarthen	330 513 756 310 1011 734 217 341 200 349 531 1108 508 454 451 359 434 414 605 637 357 611 407 310 529 830 436 357 353 427 310 444 249 337 344 822 233 1341 520 354
Dorchester	345 828 123 1042 805 222 208 258 631 542 1139 539 525 454 451 306 444 624 655 315 503 417 222 342 901 356 210 135 458 102 455 358 118 355 854 104 1412 538 242
Dover	838 445 1106 829 337 145 424 656 449 1204 604 442 350 515 046 508 536 607 241 318 345 236 704 922 245 532 238 522 254 422 423 244 420 918 411 1436 450 145
Edinburgh	807 311 057 616 747 630 623 505 332 257 426 523 416 759 412 315 240 620 738 527 647 1026 049 607 854 819 338 749 455 527 804 442 301 730 605 414 735
Exeter	1022 745 202 311 238 611 522 1119 519 504 442 431 406 423 603 635 344 559 357 254 225 841 427 057 254 438 203 435 338 237 335 833 044 1352 518 338
Fort William	242 831 1002 845 838 733 140 512 653 751 631 1027 627 615 541 835 1005 754 902 1241 234 835 1109 1034 552 1004 716 742 1019 657 441 945 413 641 950
Glasgow	554 725 609 601 456 353 235 417 514 354 750 350 340 305 558 728 518 625 1004 115 558 832 757 316 727 440 506 742 421 207 708 625 404 713
Gloucester	208 053 420 331 928 328 314 251 240 258 232 413 444 155 410 206 110 421 650 236 249 219 247 147 244 147 204 144 643 125 1201 327 217
Guildford	254 551 410 1059 459 352 314 410 106 403 451 523 139 310 245 116 530 821 210 358 058 418 120 323 318 106 315 813 238 1332 406 052
Hereford	353 345 943 343 328 305 254 345 247 427 458 211 425 221 156 457 704 251 325 306 301 233 258 122 250 159 657 201 1215 341 303
Holyhead	412 935 335 321 426 221 617 241 432 503 424 638 351 451 830 657 457 658 623 254 553 327 239 608 247 649 534 1208 347 539
Hull	831 249 109 105 217 410 148 200 234 239 332 143 326 740 549 219 608 458 209 447 115 312 443 229 545 444 1103 058 349
Inverness	609 751 848 728 1124 724 642 607 932 1102 852 959 1338 243 932 1206 1131 650 1101 814 840 1116 755 556 1042 237 738 1047
Kendal	158 308 129 526 125 149 205 333 522 300 400 739 332 352 607 532 050 502 214 240 517 155 324 443 843 209 448
Leeds	129 124 405 054 124 155 223 343 127 310 722 510 213 550 442 116 431 048 224 427 139 506 426 1024 040 338
Lincoln	236 311 205 221 253 151 227 057 238 701 607 117 529 407 228 359 108 242 355 200 603 405 1122 136 250
Liverpool	437 046 237 308 244 450 211 311 650 450 317 518 444 047 413 142 137 428 107 443 354 1001 152 359
Maidstone	429 457 528 201 239 306 157 625 843 206 453 159 443 215 343 343 205 341 839 332 1357 411 106
Manchester	208 239 236 419 146 304 642 446 249 510 436 045 405 106 144 420 059 439 346 957 122 352
Middlesbrough	048 321 436 225 408 822 359 306 650 540 226 529 153 338 525 253 429 526 914 109 436
Newcastle	351 506 256 438 853 324 336 721 611 244 559 223 408 555 323 354 557 839 142 506
Northampton	234 114 058 604 653 100 432 231 250 219 152 150 215 147 646 308 1204 235 123
Norwich	253 324 820 823 154 648 400 444 413 324 406 403 355 820 524 1338 352 245
Nottingham	201 615 611 115 443 333 218 322 056 151 318 108 607 319 1125 139 229
Oxford	514 721 152 342 136 318 125 238 218 120 215 714 217 1232 321 115
Penzance	1100 646 148 514 657 423 654 557 457 554 1053 303 1611 737 558
Perth	652 928 853 412 823 535 601 838 517 318 804 516 458 809
Peterborough	514 303 313 306 152 232 255 214 648 350 1206 221 146
Plymouth	341 525 250 522 425 324 422 920 131 1439 605 425
Portsmouth	450 054 410 350 030 347 846 222 1404 453 145
Preston	420 134 159 435 114 405 401 923 144 406
Salisbury	359 320 037 317 816 130 1334 442 150
Sheffield	224 356 124 529 357 1047 107 307
Shrewsbury	335 102 554 301 1112 251 306
Southampton	332 830 205 1349 437 140
Stoke-on-Trent	509 258 1028 206 302
Stranraer	757 829 453 802
Taunton	1315 441 301
Wick	1011 1320
York	352

distances in miles (one mile equals 1.6093 km)

Town	Distances to the following towns in order (Aberdeen, Aberystwyth, Barnstaple, Birmingham, Brighton, Bristol, Cambridge, Cardiff, Carlisle, Carmarthen, Dorchester, Dover, Edinburgh, Exeter, Fort William, Glasgow, Gloucester, Guildford, Hereford, Holyhead, Hull, Inverness, Kendal, Leeds, Lincoln, Liverpool, Maidstone, Manchester, Middlesbrough, Newcastle, Northampton, Norwich, Nottingham, Oxford, Penzance, Perth, Peterborough, Plymouth, Portsmouth, Preston, Salisbury, Sheffield, Shrewsbury, Southampton, Stoke-on-Trent, Stranraer, Taunton, Wick, York)
Aberystwyth	472
Barnstaple	608 214
Birmingham	436 124 180
Brighton	613 288 210 171
Bristol	518 130 100 90 169
Cambridge	463 215 267 97 120 170
Cardiff	537 111 128 109 202 44 203
Carlisle	236 236 371 199 376 281 256 300
Carmarthen	520 48 190 172 264 107 266 68 284
Dorchester	600 206 94 172 119 62 184 120 364 182
Dover	587 326 272 208 82 205 124 239 381 301 200
Edinburgh	126 336 471 299 476 381 333 400 100 386 463 458
Exeter	593 198 44 165 178 84 259 113 356 175 57 248 455
Fort William	156 435 570 398 576 480 456 499 199 485 562 580 137 554
Glasgow	150 332 467 295 472 377 353 396 96 382 459 477 47 451 102
Gloucester	484 113 126 56 155 36 150 63 248 125 118 192 346 110 445 343
Guildford	571 224 175 128 44 106 96 139 335 201 97 97 433 150 532 430 99
Hereford	487 79 144 59 189 54 153 59 250 85 136 225 349 129 448 346 34 133
Holyhead	464 102 339 167 345 249 259 202 228 150 331 369 326 323 425 323 215 302 156
Hull	376 227 320 139 258 230 138 250 170 311 312 262 247 304 367 266 196 239 198 218
Inverness	106 496 631 459 637 541 517 561 260 546 623 641 157 616 66 176 507 595 510 488 430
Kendal	283 189 324 153 330 234 251 254 47 240 316 354 145 309 245 143 200 288 203 181 164 307
Leeds	329 173 301 120 262 211 146 230 123 224 293 271 200 285 321 219 177 220 179 165 59 383 110
Lincoln	388 199 275 98 216 185 95 205 182 267 246 220 258 260 379 277 151 173 154 204 44 441 176 74
Liverpool	362 110 272 101 278 182 193 202 126 158 264 302 224 257 324 222 148 236 151 102 128 386 79 74 139
Maidstone	545 284 234 166 50 167 82 200 339 262 161 41 416 209 537 435 153 58 186 327 220 599 313 231 178 261
Manchester	357 134 261 89 266 171 160 190 120 184 253 290 219 245 318 216 136 224 139 125 97 380 74 44 85 34 248
Middlesbrough	276 244 357 176 318 267 197 286 95 294 349 322 146 341 283 190 232 276 235 235 89 308 84 64 122 145 280 114
Newcastle	235 275 388 207 349 298 229 317 60 325 380 353 106 372 242 153 264 307 266 266 142 267 102 95 154 176 311 145 39
Northampton	486 174 212 56 133 115 56 162 249 224 159 155 348 196 447 345 79 90 111 217 152 509 203 136 94 151 113 139 189 220
Norwich	488 278 329 160 168 233 63 266 282 328 241 172 359 313 480 378 212 160 215 321 147 542 276 174 103 240 130 185 223 254 118
Nottingham	395 162 232 51 193 142 86 161 189 223 224 210 266 216 387 285 107 151 110 178 93 449 164 77 39 112 168 71 130 161 64 119
Oxford	510 160 170 68 109 73 82 107 274 169 115 146 373 154 472 370 48 67 81 242 190 534 228 174 132 176 107 164 227 258 44 146 102
Penzance	702 308 108 274 287 193 368 222 466 284 167 357 564 109 663 562 220 259 238 434 415 726 419 403 370 367 318 356 451 482 326 433 326 265
Perth	86 388 523 351 529 433 378 453 152 438 515 503 42 507 102 64 399 486 401 379 291 114 199 245 303 278 461 275 192 150 400 404 310 426 617
Peterborough	435 204 263 86 158 173 37 193 229 255 204 162 306 248 427 325 139 115 142 225 110 489 223 121 51 159 120 132 170 201 45 78 58 86 357 351
Plymouth	633 239 62 205 218 124 299 153 397 215 98 288 495 44 594 493 151 190 169 365 346 657 350 334 301 298 249 287 382 413 257 364 257 196 78 544 288
Portsmouth	596 244 162 154 53 125 137 158 360 220 73 141 458 132 558 456 118 45 152 328 276 620 314 260 215 262 102 250 313 344 130 204 188 85 241 508 157 172
Preston	326 146 281 110 287 191 209 211 89 197 273 311 188 266 287 185 157 245 160 138 122 349 43 69 134 36 269 35 103 139 159 235 121 184 375 237 180 306 270
Salisbury	549 184 118 121 90 52 145 98 313 160 39 160 411 93 511 409 72 62 105 281 261 573 267 244 202 215 121 203 298 329 115 212 173 70 203 461 165 134 44 223
Sheffield	397 166 272 91 233 182 122 201 161 263 264 247 236 256 359 257 148 191 150 157 66 421 115 38 47 79 205 39 100 131 104 148 45 142 366 309 93 297 228 73 212
Shrewsbury	417 75 220 48 226 130 140 111 181 110 212 250 279 205 379 277 96 184 52 105 162 441 135 119 124 65 208 71 190 221 98 203 87 123 314 329 129 245 209 92 161 88
Southampton	578 225 142 135 66 106 136 140 342 201 53 152 440 111 539 437 100 49 133 309 258 601 295 241 199 243 113 232 294 325 111 204 169 67 221 489 157 152 20 252 23 209 191
Stoke-on-Trent	392 112 220 48 226 130 140 150 156 211 212 250 254 205 353 251 96 184 99 123 129 415 109 93 91 57 208 46 164 195 98 172 54 123 314 303 99 245 209 66 161 50 38 191
Stranraer	235 342 477 305 482 387 363 406 106 392 469 487 132 461 181 86 352 440 355 333 276 261 153 229 288 232 445 229 201 163 354 388 295 380 571 149 333 502 466 195 418 267 287 447 261
Taunton	560 165 50 132 160 51 226 80 323 142 45 224 422 34 521 419 77 126 96 291 272 583 277 261 228 225 185 213 309 340 183 291 184 123 144 471 215 75 114 234 70 224 172 94 172 429
Wick	207 597 732 560 738 642 618 662 361 647 724 742 258 716 166 277 608 695 610 588 531 104 408 484 543 487 700 484 409 367 609 644 550 635 826 215 589 757 721 451 673 523 542 702 516 362 684
York	323 201 314 133 275 224 154 243 116 251 306 279 193 298 314 212 189 233 192 192 38 376 91 24 79 102 237 71 51 89 146 180 87 184 408 239 125 339 269 96 254 57 146 251 120 223 265 477
LONDON	550 239 216 121 54 120 59 153 314 215 125 78 413 200 512 410 102 31 136 282 186 574 268 201 143 216 39 204 254 285 68 118 129 56 310 462 86 241 75 225 85 169 163 77 161 420 167 675 211

Atlas symbols

M4	Motorway with number
T4 Toll Toll	Toll motorway with toll station
3	Restricted motorway junctions
S Fleet	Motorway service area
	Motorway and junction under construction
A3	Primary route single/dual carriageway
1	Primary route junction with and without number
3	Restricted primary route junctions
S	Primary route service area
BATH	Primary route destination
A1123	Other A road single/dual carriageway
B2070	B road single/dual carriageway
	Minor road, more than 4 metres wide, less than 4 metres wide
	Roundabout
	Interchange/junction
	Narrow primary/other A/B road with passing places (Scotland)
	Road under construction/ approved
	Road tunnel
Toll	Road toll, steep gradient (arrows point downhill)
5	Distance in miles between symbols
	Railway line, in tunnel
	Railway station and level crossing
	Tourist railway
628 637 Lecht Summit	Height in metres, mountain pass
30	Speed camera site (fixed location) with speed limit in mph
40	Section of road with two or more fixed speed cameras, with speed limit in mph
50 50	Average speed (SPECS™) camera system with speed limit in mph
V	Fixed speed camera site with variable speed limit
or V	Vehicle ferry
	Fast vehicle ferry or catamaran
H F	Airport, heliport, international freight terminal
H	24-hour Accident & Emergency hospital
C	Crematorium
P+R	Park and Ride (at least 6 days per week)
	City, town, village or other built-up area
	National boundary, administrative boundary

- Scenic route
- Tourist Information Centre (all year/seasonal)
- Visitor or heritage centre
- Picnic site
- Caravan site (AA inspected)
- Camping site (AA inspected)
- Caravan & camping site (AA inspected)
- Abbey, cathedral or priory
- Ruined abbey, cathedral or priory
- Castle
- Historic house or building
- Museum or art gallery
- Industrial interest
- Aqueduct or viaduct
- Garden, arboretum
- Vineyard
- Country park
- Agricultural showground
- Theme park
- Farm or animal centre
- Zoological or wildlife collection
- Bird collection, aquarium
- RSPB site
- National Nature Reserve (England, Scotland, Wales)
- Local nature reserve
- Wildlife Trust reserve
- Forest drive
- National trail
- Viewpoint
- Hill-fort
- Prehistoric monument, Roman antiquity
- 1066 Battle site with year
- Steam railway centre
- Cave
- Windmill, monument
- Golf course
- County cricket ground
- Rugby Union national stadium
- International athletics stadium
- Horse racing, show jumping
- Air show venue, motor-racing circuit
- Ski slope (natural, artificial)
- National Trust property (England & Wales, Scotland)
- English Heritage site
- Historic Scotland site
- Cadw (Welsh heritage) site
- Major shopping centre, other place of interest
- Attraction within urban area
- World Heritage Site (UNESCO)
- National Park and National Scenic Areas
- Forest Park
- Heritage coast

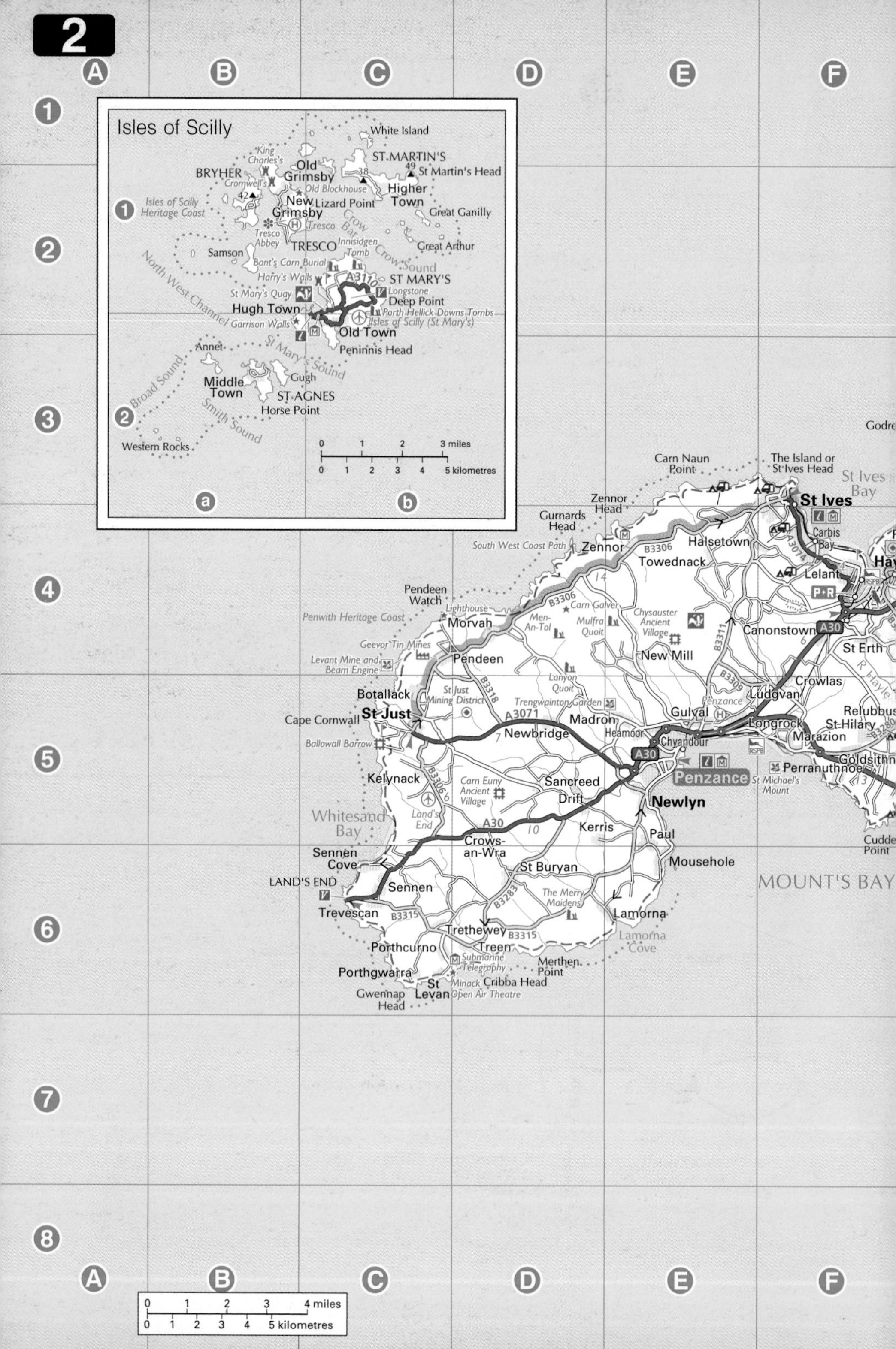

Isles of Scilly
White Island
ST MARTIN'S
St Martin's Head
King Charles's
BRYHER
Old Grimsby
Cromwell's
Old Blockhouse
Higher Town
Isles of Scilly Heritage Coast
New Grimsby
Lizard Point
Great Ganilly
Tresco
Tresco Abbey
Crow Bar
Innisidgen Tomb
Samson
TRESCO
Great Arthur
North West Channel
Bant's Carn Burial
Crow Sound
Harry's Walls
ST MARY'S
St Mary's Quay
Longstone
Deep Point
Hugh Town
Porth Hellick Downs Tombs
Isles of Scilly (St Mary's)
Garrison Walls
Old Town
Annet
Peninnis Head
St Mary's Sound
Broad Sound
Gugh
Middle Town
ST AGNES
Horse Point
Smith Sound
Western Rocks
0 1 2 3 miles
0 1 2 3 4 5 kilometres
Carn Naun Point
The Island or St Ives Head
St Ives Bay
Zennor Head
St Ives
Gurnards Head
Carbis Bay
South West Coast Path
Zennor
Halsetown
Towednack
Lelant
Pendeen Watch
Lighthouse
Carn Galver
Men-An-Tol
Mulfra Quoit
Chysauster Ancient Village
Penwith Heritage Coast
Morvah
Canonstown
Geevor Tin Mines
New Mill
St Erth
Levant Mine and Beam Engine
Pendeen
Lanyon Quoit
Crowlas
Botallack
St Just Mining District
Trengwainton Garden
Penzance
Ludgvan
Relubbus
St Just
Madron
Gulval
Longrock
St Hilary
Cape Cornwall
Newbridge
Heamoor
Marazion
Ballowall Barrow
Chyandour
Goldsithney
Perranuthnoe
Kelynack
Sancreed
Penzance
St Michael's Mount
Carn Euny Ancient Village
Drift
Newlyn
Whitesand Bay
Land's End
Kerris
Paul
Crows-an-Wra
Sennen Cove
Mousehole
Cudden Point
St Buryan
LAND'S END
MOUNT'S BAY
Sennen
The Merry Maidens
Trevescan
Lamorna
Trethewey
Lamorna Cove
Porthcurno
Treen
Submarine Telegraphy
Merthen Point
Porthgwarra
Minack Open Air Theatre
Cribba Head
Gwennap Head
St Levan
0 1 2 3 4 miles
0 1 2 3 4 5 kilometres

G
H
J
K
L
M
1
2
3
4
5
6
7
8
4
Ligger or
Perran Bay
Newlyn
East
Lappa Valley
Enodoc
A30
Summercourt
St Columb Road
Downs
Rose
A3075
A3076
Scarcewater
A3058
Perranporth
Cligga Point
Fiddlers
Green
Mitchell
Goonhavern
World in Miniature
Bolingey
B3285
St Agnes
Heritage Coast
Trevellas
Downs
ST AGNES HEAD
St
Agnes
Perranzabuloe
Penhallow
Zelah
St
Allen
A39
Trispen
Ladock
Mithian
Barkla Shop
Callestick
Wheal Coates
Goonvrea
Goonbell
St Agnes
Mining District
St Erme
B3275
Probus
B3277
B3284
Porthtowan
Mount
Hawke
Shortlanesend
Idless
South West
Coast Path
Mawla
Tresillian
Godrevy-Portreath
Heritage Coast
Portreath
Cambrose
Wheal
Peevor
Blackwater
A390
Threemilestone
Kenwyn
B3300
Truro
Navax
Point
Illogan
Chacewater
Higher
Town
St Clement
Scorrier
Gwennap
Mining District
Malpas
Tehidy
Mount
Ambrose
P+R
Kea
South
Tehidy
St Day
Twelveheads
St Michael
Penkevil
Ruan
Lanihorne
A3078
B3301
Reskadinnick
Cornish
Engines
Redruth
Playing
Place
Lamorran
Tuckingmill
Pool
A3047
Carn Brea
Carharrack
Bissoe
Carnon
Downs
Kehelland
Carn
Brea
B3298
Trelissick
Garden
Camborne
Carnkie
Gwennap
Devoran
Philleigh
Penponds
Lanner
A393
Perranwell
Connor Downs
B3297
Perranarworthal
A39
Angarrack
Barripper
B3303
Troon
Four
Lanes
Penhalvean
Kennall
Vale
Devoran
& Perran
Feock
B3289
Trewithian
Copperhouse
Carnhell
Green
Ponsanooth
Gwinear
Realwa
Mylor
Bridge
St Just-in-
Roseland
Portscatho
St Erth
Praze
Stithians
Gerrans
Nare
Head
B3280
Praze-an-
Beeble
Mylor
Carrick Roads
Gerrans
Carnkie
Longdowns
Leedstown
Crowan
Porkellis
Rame
Mabe
Burnthouse
Penryn
Flushing
Greeb Point
Godolphin
House
Castle
St Mawes
Budock
Water
Argal & College
Water Park
Pendennis
Castle
Bohortha
Wendron
Mining District
Godolphin
Cross
Tregonning, Gwinear
& Trewavas
Mining District
Trenear
Poldark Mine
Treverva
Falmouth
A394
Pendennis
Point
South West Coast Path
Prospidnick
Trescowe
Crowntown
Wendron
Seworgan
ZONE
POINT
Carleen
Trevarno
Penjerrick
Falmouth Bay
Sithney
Coverack
Bridges
Brill
Ashton
Breage
Constantine
Mawnan Smith
Trebah
Carwinion
ROSEMULLION HEAD
Helston
Porth Navas
A394
Gweek
Glendurgan
Garden
Rinsey
Head
Helford Passage
Durgan
Mawnan
B3304
Seal
Sanctuary
Helford River
Trewavas
Head
Flambards
Helford
Porthleven
A3083
St Anthony
Mawgan
Manaccan
Nare Point
Garras
St Martin
Halliggye
Fogou
Gunwalloe
Porthallow
White
Cross
B3293
Porthoustock
Manacle Point
Cury
Futureworld
@ Goonhilly
St Keverne
Poldhu Point
Marconi Memorial
GOONHILLY
DOWNS
B3296
Lowland Point
Mullion Cove
Mullion
B3294
Mullion
Island
Coverack
Ruan
Major
Kuggar
Predannack Head
Black Head
Ruan Minor
Vellan Head
Cadgwith
The Lizard Heritage Coast
South West
Coast Path
Devil's Frying Pan
Lizard Head
Kynance Cove
Church Cove
Lizard
Lighthouse
LIZARD POINT
Bass Point

4
A
B
C
8
D
E
F
1
2
3
4
5
6
7
8
Port Isaac Bay
Rumps Point
Port Quin Bay
Kelland Head
Varley Head
Port Quin
Port Isaac
Pentire Point
Padstow Bay
Bee Centre
Hayle Bay
Stepper Point
Polzeath
Trelights
Trebetherick
B3314
St Endellion
St Minver
Trevose Head Heritage Coast
Mother Ivey's Bay
Gunver Head
TREVOSE HEAD
Harlyn Bay
Dinas Head
Prideaux Place
Trevone
Rock
Constantine Bay
Harlyn
Padstow
Chapel Amble
Windmill
Constantine Bay
St Merryn
A389
B3276
St Issey
Wadebridge
Egloshayle
Porthcothan
Little Petherick
St Breock
Penrose
Trenance
Royal Cornwall
Park Head
Rumford
Burlawn
St Ervan
St Jidgey
St Breock Downs Monolith
Bedruthan Steps
St Eval
Creely Great Adventure Park
Trenance
Nine Maidens
B3274
Ruthernbridge
Berryls Point
Mawgan Porth
A39
Griffins Point
Trevarrian
St Mawgan
Talskiddy
Rosenannon
Vale of Mawgan
St Wenn
Withiel
Watergate Bay
Newquay
Towan Head
Newquay Bay
A3059
St Columb Major
Tregonetha
St Columb Minor
Newquay
Porth
Fistral Bay
Colan
Victoria
Higher Town
West Pentire
A3058
Ruthvoes
Kelsey Head
Pentire
Mountjoy
Goss Moor
Roche
Crantock
Quintrell Downs
A392
Holywell Bay
Lane
St Columb Road
B3279
Bugle
Penhale Point
Tresean
Kestle Mill
Fraddon
Indian Queens
Holywell
Treveal
Dairyland
Ligger Point
Trerice
Whitemoor
Cubert
Newlyn East
St Dennis
B3274
St Enoder
Stenalees
Lappa Valley
A30
Carthew
Ligger or Perran Bay
Summercourt
Nanpean
Treviscoe
Wheal Martyn Heritage Centre
Rose
A3076
A3075
Fiddlers Green
Scarcewater
Foxhole
Perranporth
Goonhavern
Mitchell
B3285
World in Miniature
A3058
High Street
St Austell
Cligga Point
Bolingey
St Stephen
Trewoon
St Agnes Heritage Coast
Trevellas Downs
B3285
ST AGNES HEAD
Perranzabuloe
Zelah
Penhallow
A39
Coombe
Charlestown
St Agnes
St Allen
Ladock
Mithian
Callestick
Trispen
Polgooth
Tregorrick
Wheal Coates
Barkla Shop
Grampound Road
Goonvrea
Goonbell
St Erme
Sticker
St Agnes Mining District
B3275
Hewas Water
B3273
B3277
A390
Porthtowan
Shortlanesend
B3284
Probus
Grampound
Mount Hawke
Idless
Creed
Lost Gardens of Heligan
Mawla
Tresillian
River Fal
St Ewe
Cambrose
B3287
Kenwyn
A390
Threemilestone
Blackwater
Kestle
B3300
Truro
Polmassick
Wheal Peevor
Chacewater
Tregony
A30
Higher Town
Scorrier
St Clement
Mount Ambrose
Gwennap Mining District
P+R
Kea
Malpas
Cornish Engines
3
St Day
St Michael Penkevil
Ruan Lanihorne
St Michael Caerhays
Gorran
Redruth
Twelveheads
A3078
A3047
Playing Place
Lamorran
Carn Brea
Carharrack
Bissoe
Carnon Downs
Boswinger
B3298
Camborne
Carnkie
Gwennap
Trelissick Garden
Philleigh
Veryan Bay
Lanner
A393
Perranwell
Devoran
Veryan
Portloe
B3297
Perranarworthal
A39
DODMAN POINT
Four Lanes
Kennall Vale
Devoran & Perran
Feock
B3289
Penhalvean
The Roseland Heritage Coast
Ponsanooth
Trewithian
Gerrans Bay
Stithians
Mylor Bridge
Nare Head
St Just-in-Roseland
B3280
Portscatho
Mylor
Carrick Roads
Percuil
Carnkie
Longdowns
Gerrans
Mabe Burnthouse
Penryn
St Mawes
Rame
Flushing
Greeb Point
A39
Wendron Mining District
Budock
Castle
Pendennis Castle
Bohortha
0 1 2 3 4 miles
Trenear
0 1 2 3 4 5 kilometres
Poldark Mine
A394
Seworgan
Falmouth
Pendennis
South West Coast Path

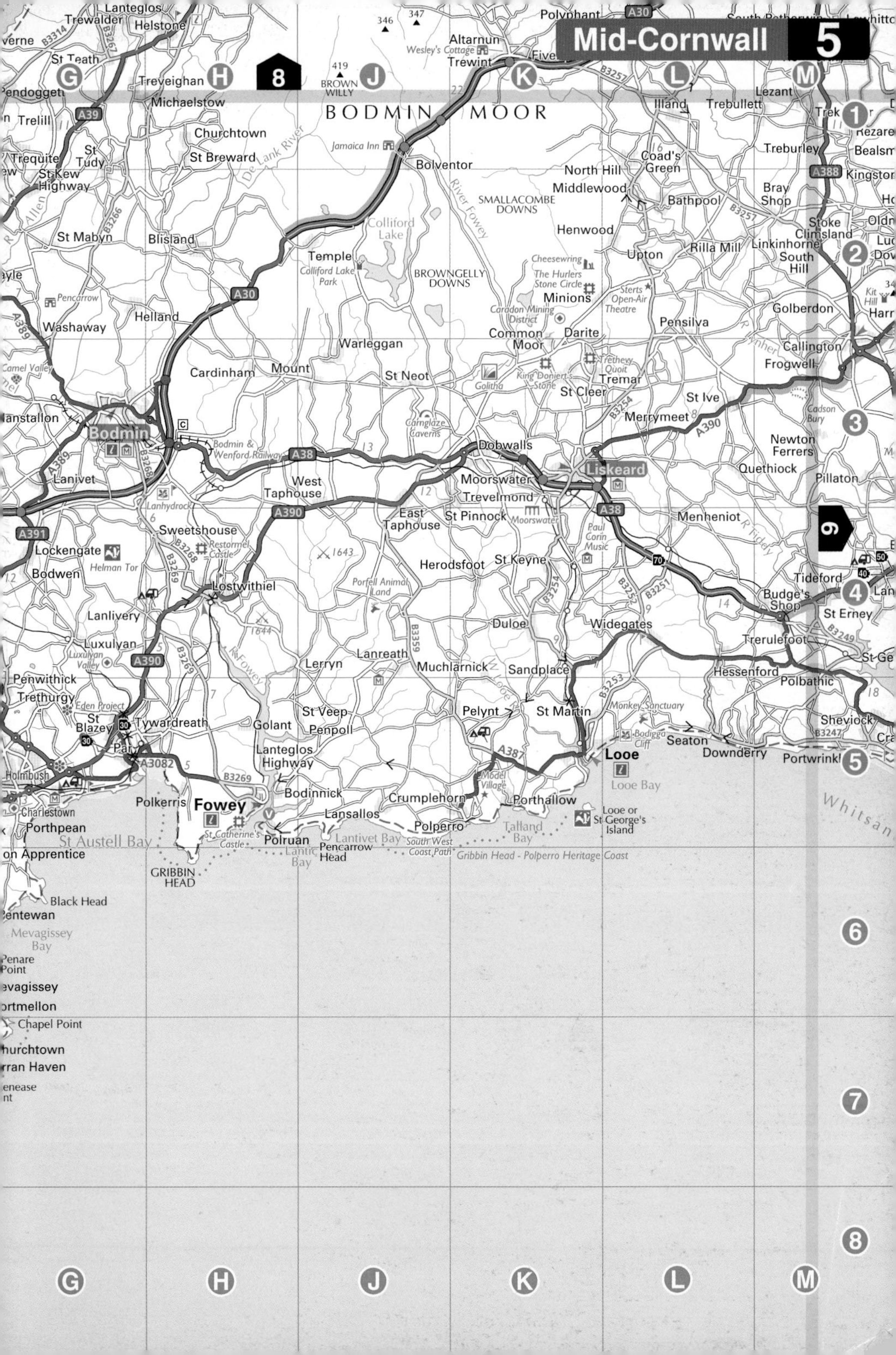
BODMIN MOOR
Bodmin
Liskeard
Lostwithiel
Fowey
Looe
Polperro
St Austell Bay
Looe Bay
Whitsand
Mevagissey Bay
Gribbin Head - Polperro Heritage Coast
South West Coast Path
Jamaica Inn
Colliford Lake
Eden Project
Bodmin & Wenford Railway
Lanhydrock
Restormel Castle
Carnglaze Caverns
Monkey Sanctuary
Callington
St Cleer
St Neot
Dobwalls
Lanreath
Pelynt
Polruan
Lansallos
Crumplehorn
Seaton
Downderry
Hessenford
Tideford
St Germans
Menheniot
Pensilva
Minions
Upton
Rilla Mill
Altarnun
Bolventor
Blisland
St Mabyn
St Breward
Washaway
Lanivet
Tywardreath
Par
Charlestown
Porthpean
Golant
Lerryn
Duloe
Sandplace
St Martin
St Keyne
Herodsfoot
Widegates
Trerulefoot
Polbathic
Sheviock
Portwrinkle
G H J K L M
1 2 3 4 5 6 7 8

9
10
5
A
B
C
D
E
F
1
2
3
4
5
6
7
8
DARTMOOR
FOREST
DARTMOOR
NATIONAL
PARK
Lawhitton
Meadwell
Kelly
Chillaton
North Brentor
Bradstone
Milton Abbot
Lezant
Trekenner
Dunterton
Chaddlehanger
Mary Tavy
Cudliptown
Rezare
Treburley
Bealsmill
Lamerton
Peter Tavy
Kingston
Sydenham Damerel
Bray Shop
Horsebridge
Tavistock
Stoke Climsland
Oldmill
Luckett
Downgate
Latchley
South Hill
Chilsworthy
Gulworthy
Gunnislake
Whitchurch
Sampford Spiney
Princetown
Hexworthy
Golberdon
Harrowbarrow
St Ann's Chapel
Callington
Frogwell
Metherell
St Dominick
Albaston
Calstock
Cotehele
Morwellham Quay
Horrabridge
Walkhampton
Dousland
Yelverton
Sheepstor
Burrator Reservoir
Buckland Monachorum
Buckland Abbey
Bere Alston
Milton Combe
Sowton
Meavy
Clearbrook
Cadson Bury
Tamar Valley Mining District
St Mellion
Newton Ferrers
Quethiock
Pillaton
Cotts
Weir Quay
Maristow
Dewerstone
Shaugh Prior
Cargreen
Hatt
Landulph
Bere Ferrers
Tamerton Foliot
Roborough
Bickleigh
Botusfleming
Carkeel
Tideford
Landrake
Saltash
Crownhill
Boringdon
Dartmoor Wildlife Park
Lutton
Cornwood
Harford
St Erney
Trematon
South Pill
Toll
St Budeaux
Eggbuckland
PLYMOUTH
Hemerdon
Sparkwell
Venton
Trerulefoot
Trehan
St Stephens
St Germans
Antony House
Churchtown Farm Community
Plympton
Ivybridge
Woodland
Bittaford
Polbathic
Lee Mill
Sheviock
Antony
Crafthole
St John
Torpoint
St John's Lake
Devonport
Stonehouse
Cremyll
Saltram
Plymstock
Elburton
Brixton
Westlake
Worston
Ermington
Modbury
Portwrinkle
Mount Edgcumbe
Plymouth Dome
Hooe
Spriddlestone
Yealmpton
Dunstone
Flete
Whitsand Bay
Freathy
Millbrook
South West Coast Path
Kingsand
Cawsand
Cawsand Bay
The Sound
Down Thomas
Staddiscombe
Holbeton
Rame
RAME HEAD
Penlee Point
Heybrook Bay
Wembury
West Wembury
Newton Ferrers
The Old Mill
Bridgend
Wembury Bay
Noss Mayo
Mothecombe
Kingston
Bigbury
Ringmore
Gara Point
Rame Head Heritage Coast
Stoke Point
Erme Mouth
Beacon Point
Bigbury-on-Sea
Burgh Island
Bantham
Thurlestone
Bigbury Bay
Bolt Tail
Santander (Mar-Oct)
Roscoff
517
501 COCKS HILL
539 GREAT MIS TOR
442 COXTOR
Merrivale
Wistman's Wood
Clapper Bridge
406 ROYAL HILL
516 RYDERS HILL
480
471 SHELL TOP
BUTTERDON HILL
Upper Plym Valley
347
Kit Hill
Dupath Well
Calstock Viaduct
The Garden House
A388
A38
A386
A390
A374
A379
B3257
B3362
B3357
B3212
B3267
B3249
B3247
B3373
B3432
B3417
B3214
B3186
B3392
0 1 2 3 4 miles
0 1 2 3 4 5 kilometres

Bovey Tracey
Newton Abbot
Kingsteignton
Ashburton
Buckfastleigh
Dawlish
Teignmouth
Kingskerswell
TORQUAY
Paignton
Tor Bay
Totnes
Brixham
Dartmouth
Kingswear
Kingsbridge
Salcombe
Babbacombe Bay
Start Bay
South Devon Heritage Coast
South West Coast Path
Start Point
Prawle Point
Bolt Head
Berry Head
Hopes Nose
Sharkham Point
Scabbacombe Head
Widecombe in the Moor
Haytor Vale
Buckland in the Moor
Chudleigh
Dartington
Stoke Fleming
Slapton
Torcross
East Prawle

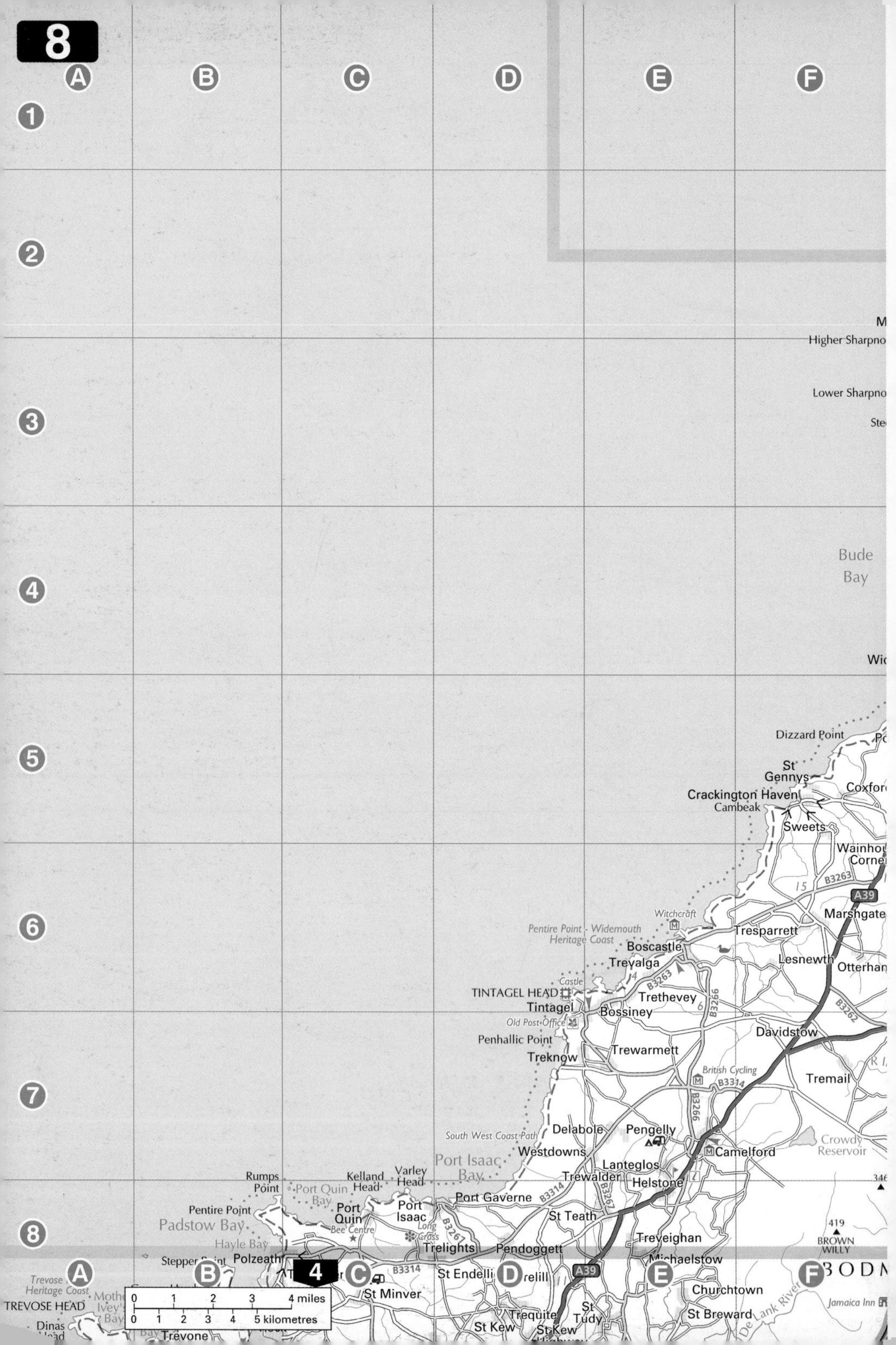
Higher Sharpno
Lower Sharpno
Bude
Bay
Dizzard Point
St
Gennys
Crackington Haven
Cambeak
Sweets
Wainhou
Corne
B3263
A39
Marshgate
Witchcraft
Pentire Point - Widemouth
Heritage Coast
Tresparrett
Boscastle
Trevalga
Lesnewth
Otterhan
Castle
TINTAGEL HEAD
Tintagel
Bossiney
Trethevey
B3266
B3262
Old Post Office
Davidstow
Penhallic Point
Trewarmett
Treknow
British Cycling
B3314
Tremail
South West Coast Path
Delabole
Pengelly
Westdowns
Camelford
Crowdy
Reservoir
Port Isaac
Bay
Lanteglos
Rumps
Point
Kelland
Head
Varley
Head
Port Quin
Bay
Trewalder
Helstone
Port Gaverne
B3267
Pentire Point
Port
Quin
Port
Isaac
St Teath
Padstow Bay
Bee Centre
Long
Cross
419
BROWN
WILLY
Hayle Bay
Trelights
Pendoggett
Treveighan
Stepper Point
Polzeath
Michaelstow
Trevose
Heritage Coast
St Endellion
St Minver
Churchtown
TREVOSE HEAD
Mother
Ivey's
Bay
0 1 2 3 4 miles
0 1 2 3 4 5 kilometres
Dinas
Head
Trevone
St Kew
Trequite
St
Tudy
St Breward
De Lank River
Jamaica Inn
BODM
4

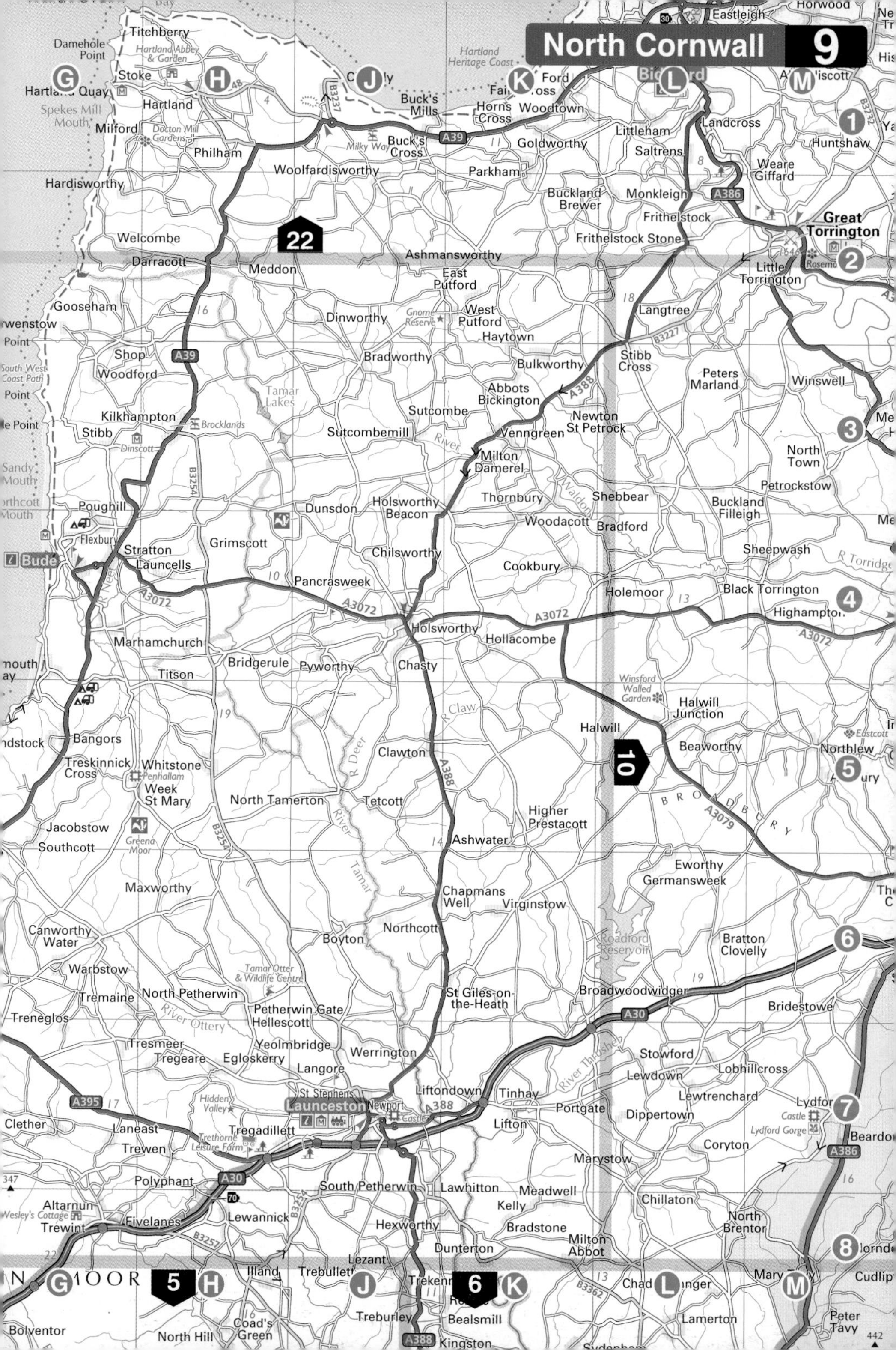
North Cornwall
9
Titchberry
Dameholе Point
Hartland Abbey & Garden
Hartland Heritage Coast
Hartland Quay
Stoke
Hartland
Spekes Mill Mouth
Milford
Docton Mill Gardens
Philham
Buck's Mills
Horns Cross
Woodtown
Ford
Bideford
Eastleigh
Horwood
Landcross
Huntshaw
Littleham
Saltrens
Weare Giffard
Goldworthy
Buck's Cross
Milky Way
Woolfardisworthy
Parkham
Hardisworthy
Buckland Brewer
Monkleigh
Frithelstock
Great Torrington
Frithelstock Stone
Welcombe
22
Darracott
Meddon
Ashmansworthy
East Putford
Little Torrington
Gooseham
Dinworthy
Gnome Reserve
West Putford
Langtree
Haytown
Shop
Bradworthy
Bulkworthy
Stibb Cross
Peters Marland
Winswell
Woodford
Tamar Lakes
Abbots Bickington
Kilkhampton
Brocklands
Sutcombe
Newton St Petrock
Stibb
Dinscott
Sutcombemill
Venngreen
Milton Damerel
North Town
Sandy Mouth
Thornbury
Shebbear
Petrockstow
Poughill
Dunsdon
Holsworthy Beacon
Buckland Filleigh
Flexbury
Woodacott
Bradford
Bude
Stratton
Launcells
Grimscott
Chilsworthy
Cookbury
Sheepwash
R Torridge
Pancrasweek
Holemoor
Black Torrington
A3072
Holsworthy
Hollacombe
Highampton
Marhamchurch
Bridgerule
Pyworthy
Chasty
Titson
Winsford Walled Garden
Halwill Junction
R Claw
Halwill
Bangors
Clawton
Beaworthy
Northlew
Eastcott
10
Treskinnick Cross
Whitstone
Penhallam
Week St Mary
North Tamerton
Tetcott
R Deer
BROADBURY
Higher Prestacott
Jacobstow
Greena Moor
Southcott
Ashwater
Eworthy
Germansweek
Maxworthy
River Tamar
Chapmans Well
Virginstow
Canworthy Water
Northcott
Boyton
Roadford Reservoir
Bratton Clovelly
Warbstow
Tamar Otter & Wildlife Centre
St Giles-on-the-Heath
Broadwoodwidger
Bridestowe
Tremaine
North Petherwin
Treneglos
River Ottery
Petherwin Gate
Hellescott
A30
Tresmeer
Tregeare
Egloskerry
Yeolmbridge
Werrington
River Thrushel
Stowford
Lewdown
Lobhillcross
Langore
St Stephens
Liftondown
Tinhay
Lewtrenchard
Hidden Valley
Launceston
Newport
Castle
Lifton
Portgate
Dippertown
Lydford
Lydford Gorge
Clether
Laneast
Tregadillett
Trethorne Leisure Farm
Coryton
A386
Trewen
Marystow
Polyphant
South Petherwin
Lawhitton
Meadwell
Kelly
Chillaton
Altarnun
Wesley's Cottage
Lewannick
Trewint
Fivelanes
Hexworthy
Bradstone
North Brentor
Milton Abbot
Dunterton
Lezant
Illand
Trebullett
Trekenner
Chadlanger
Mary Tavy
Cudlip
Coad's Green
Treburley
Bealsmill
Lamerton
Peter Tavy
Bolventor
North Hill
Kingston
A39
A388
A3079
A395
B3254
B3227
B3237
B3257
B3362
A386
5
6

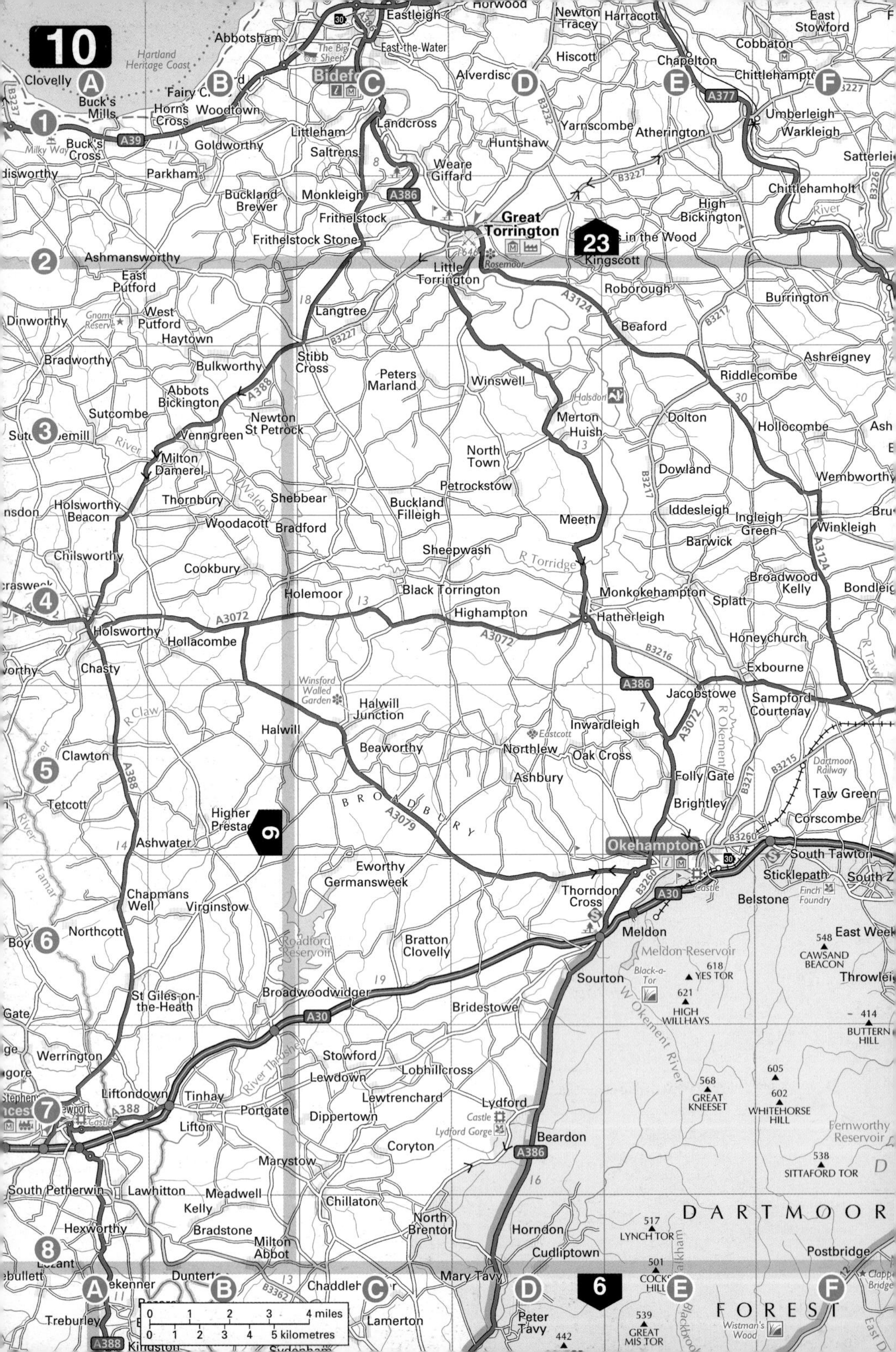
10
Clovelly
Hartland Heritage Coast
Abbotsham
Fairy Cross
Buck's Mills
Horns Cross
Woodtown
Bideford
The Big Sheep
Eastleigh
East-the-Water
Horwood
Newton Tracey
Harracott
Hiscott
East Stowford
Cobbaton
Chapelton
Chittlehampton
Alverdiscott
Umberleigh
Warkleigh
Satterleigh
Yarnscombe
Atherington
Landcross
Littleham
Saltrens
Huntshaw
Weare Giffard
Goldworthy
Parkham
Buck's Cross
Milky Way
Hartland
Woolfardisworthy
Buckland Brewer
Monkleigh
Frithelstock
Frithelstock Stone
Great Torrington
Little Torrington
Rosemoor
Kingscott
St Giles in the Wood
High Bickington
Chittlehamholt
River Taw
Ashmansworthy
East Putford
West Putford
Gnome Reserve
Dinworthy
Haytown
Bradworthy
Langtree
Stibb Cross
Bulkworthy
Roborough
Beaford
Burrington
Ashreigney
Riddlecombe
Peters Marland
Winswell
Halsdon
Abbots Bickington
Newton St Petrock
Sutcombe
Sutcombemill
Venngreen
Milton Damerel
Merton
Huish
Dolton
Hollocombe
North Town
Dowland
Wembworthy
Petrockstow
Thornbury
Shebbear
River Waldon
Holsworthy Beacon
Woodacott
Bradford
Buckland Filleigh
Meeth
Iddesleigh
Ingleigh Green
Winkleigh
Barwick
Chilsworthy
Sheepwash
R Torridge
Cookbury
Broadwood Kelly
Bondleigh
Holemoor
Black Torrington
Monkokehampton
Splatt
Highampton
Hatherleigh
Holsworthy
Hollacombe
Honeychurch
Chasty
Exbourne
R Taw
Jacobstowe
Sampford Courtenay
Winsford Walled Garden
Halwill Junction
Halwill
R Claw
Eastcott
Inwardleigh
Northlew
Oak Cross
R Okement
Beaworthy
Clawton
Ashbury
Folly Gate
Dartmoor Railway
Tetcott
Broadbury
Higher Prestacott
Brightley
Taw Green
Corscombe
Ashwater
Okehampton
South Tawton
Sticklepath
South Zeal
River Tamar
Eworthy
Germansweek
Thorndon Cross
Castle
Belstone
Finch Foundry
Chapmans Well
Virginstow
Meldon
Northcott
East Week
Roadford Reservoir
Bratton Clovelly
Meldon Reservoir
Cawsand Beacon
Throwleigh
Sourton
Black-a-Tor
Yes Tor
High Willhays
W Okement River
St Giles-on-the-Heath
Broadwoodwidger
Bridestowe
Buttern Hill
Werrington
River Thrushel
Stowford
Lobhillcross
Lewdown
Great Kneeset
Whitehorse Hill
Liftondown
Tinhay
Lewtrenchard
Launceston
Newport
Portgate
Dippertown
Lydford
Lydford Gorge
Fernworthy Reservoir
Lifton
Beardon
Coryton
Marystow
Sittaford Tor
South Petherwin
Lawhitton
Meadwell
Kelly
Chillaton
North Brentor
Dartmoor
Hexworthy
Bradstone
Horndon
Lynch Tor
Milton Abbot
Cudliptown
Postbridge
Lezant
Rebullett
Polyphant
Dunterton
Chaddlehanger
Mary Tavy
Cocks Hill
Clapper Bridge
Treburley
Lamerton
Peter Tavy
Great Mis Tor
Forest
Wistman's Wood
Blackbrook
East Dart
Kingston
Sydenham
Walkham
0 1 2 3 4 miles
0 1 2 3 4 5 kilometres
A39
A386
A377
A388
A3072
A3079
A3124
A3260
A30
B3227
B3232
B3237
B3217
B3216
B3215
B3260
B3226
B3362
23
9
6

South Molton
Quince Honey Farm
Aller
East Anstey
Battleton
Bury
Bish Mill
Bishop's Nympton
George Nympton
Crooked Oak
Knowstone
Exbridge
Morebath
Shillingford
Petton
Bampton
Ash Mill
Alswear
River Mole
Mariansleigh
Rose Ash
A361
Oakford
Huntsham
Yard
Romansleigh
Meshaw
Creacombe
Cove
Staple Cross
Rackenford
Stoodleigh
Exe Valley
A396
R Lowman
Little Dart River
Loxbeare
Washfield
Knightshayes Court
Chevithorne
Uplowman
Lurley
Bolham
Chulmleigh
Witheridge
Calverleigh
Sampford Peverell
Cheldon
Worlington
Nomansland
Templeton
B3137
Chawleigh
Washford Pyne
Withleigh
Tiverton
Halberton
B3042
B3096
Pennymoor
R Dart
River Exe
R Dalch
Puddington
Way Village
Nymet Rowland
Eastington
Black Dog
Poughill
Upham
Devon Railway Centre
Butterleigh
Lapford
Morchard Bishop
Woolfardisworthy
Cadeleigh
Bickleigh Mill
Bickleigh
Cullompton
Coldridge
Kennerleigh
Stockleigh English
Cheriton Fitzpaine
Knowle
Colebrook
B3220
R Yeo
A377
East Village
Fursdon
A3072
Cadbury
Down St Mary
Newbuildings
Stockleigh Pomeroy
Bradninch
Zeal Monachorum
Copplestone
Upton Hellions
Up Exe
Silverton
Sandford
Hele
West Sandford
Thorverton
Bow
Coleford
Knowle
Shobrooke
Killerton
Nymet Tracey
Colebrooke
Crediton
Shute
Brampford Speke
Westwood
Ashclyst Forest
Yeoford
Sweetham
Rewe
Stoke Canon
M5
R Clyst
North Down Farm
Uton
Hookway
Upton Pyne
Huxham
Marker's Cottage
Newton St Cyres
Broadclyst
Spreyton
River Troney
Cowley
Hittisleigh
Tedburn St Mary
Pinhoe
Cheriton Bishop
Whitestone Cross
Clyst Honiton
Rockbeare
Exeter
EXETER
Whipton
Blackhorse
A30
Exwick
Heavitree
Sowton
Whiddon Down
Crockernwell
Drewsteignton
Longdown
Wonford
P+R
Spinster's Rock
B3212
Ide
Clyst St Mary
Crealy Adventure Park
West Point
Sandy Park
Castle Drogo
R Teign
Prestonbury Castle
Dunsford
Alphington
A379
Shillingford Abbot
Countess Wear
Clyst St George
Murchington
Easton
Cranbrook Castle
Shillingford St George
Topsham
Great Weeke
Dunchideock
Ebford
Chagford
Manstree
Exminster
Kennford
Doccombe
Bridford
Doddiscombsleigh
A38
Exton
Sloncombe
Moretonhampstead
Woodmanton
Hayne
Christow
B3193
Kenn
Powderham
Lympstone
A376
River Exe
North Bovey
Miniature Pony Centre
Ashton
Lower Ashton
DARTMOOR
R Bovey
Lustleigh Cleave
A382
Canonteign Falls & Country Park
Trusham
Kenton
A La Ronde
Hulham
Grimspound
529
Manaton
Harcombe
Starcross
HAMELDOWN TOR
Lustleigh
Hennock
Lower Upcott
Cofton
Water
Becky Falls
Southcott
Bovey Tracey
Chudleigh
Cockwood
Exmouth
NATIONAL PARK
Hound Tor Medieval Village
Ashcombe
Widecombe in the Moor
Haytor
454
B3387
Chudleigh Knighton
Ideford
Dawlish Warren
B3344
Haytor Vale
Church House
Luton
Dunstone
Ilsington
Brimley
A380
Dawlish
B3192
A3015
B3181
B3179
B3178
B3184
B3226
B3227
B3137
24
12
7

12
25
11
7
Lurley
Bolham
Whitnage
Appledore
Woodgate
Rosemary Lane
Clayhidon
Templeton
Calverleigh
A361
Sampford Peverell
Prescott
Culmstock
Hemyock
Stapley
Withleigh
R Dart
Tiverton
Halberton
Canal
Ash Thomas
Coldharbour Mill
Craddock
Bolham Water
Churchinford
Bolham R
Willand
Ashill
Way Village
Diggerland
Blackborough
Smeatharpe
Madford River
Upham
Devon Railway Centre
Butterleigh
River Exe
Bradfield
Kentisbeare
Sheldon
Cadeleigh
Bickleigh Mill
Bickleigh
Cullompton
River Culm
Upottery
Cheriton Fitzpaine
Knowle
Colebrook
Dunkeswell
Luppitt
Rawridge
Fursdon
Dulford
Kerswell
Wolford Chapel
Cadbury
A3072
Westcott
A373
Broadhembury
Beacon
Upton Hellions
Stockleigh Pomeroy
Bradninch
Norman's Green
Colliton
Hembury
Up Exe
Silverton
Langford
Upton
Combe Raleigh
A30
Hele
Plymtree
Luton
Thorverton
B3181
Payhembury
Awliscombe
Buckerell
Weston
Shute
Killerton
Clyst Hydon
Talaton
Feniton
Offwell
Honiton
Brampford Speke
Rewe
Stoke Canon
Ashclyst Forest
M5
Westwood
Clyst St Lawrence
Newtown
Escot
Fenny Bridges
Gittisham
R Clyst
Marker's Cottage
Alfington
Upton Pyne
Huxham
Whimple
Fairmile
Newton St Cyres
Poltimore
Broadclyst
Hand and Pen
Taleford
Church Green
Cadhay
Ottery St Mary
Cowley
Jack-in-the-Green
Pinhoe
Clyst Honiton
Rockbeare
Allercombe
A375
Whitestone Cross
Exeter
Whipton
West Hill
Southleigh
Exwick
Blackhorse
Marsh Green
Fluxton
Wiggaton
Blackbury Camp
B3212
Heavitree
P+R
Sowton
A377
Aylesbeare
B3183
Farringdon
B3184
B3180
Tipton St John
Coombe
Longdown
Wonford
Venn Ottery
Sidbury
A3052
Perkins Village
West Point
Crealy Adventure Park
Harpford
Bowd
Harcombe
Ide
A3015
Southerton
Sidford
Alphington
Clyst St Mary
A379
Shillingford Abbot
Countess Wear
Woodbury Salterton
The Donkey Sanctuary
Woolbrook
Shillingford St George
Clyst St George
Newton Poppleford
B3178
B3176
Salcombe Regis
Weston
Street
Dunchideock
Topsham
B3179
Ebford
Colaton Raleigh
South West Coast Path
Manstree
Exminster
Woodbury
Sidmouth
Kennford
Exton
Yettington
Bicton Park
Pinn
A38
Woodmanton
Otterton
East Devon Heritage Coast
Kenn
Powderham
A376
East Budleigh
Otterton Mill
Ashton
Lower Ashton
Lympstone
Bystock
River Otter
Ladram Bay
Kenton
A La Ronde
Dalditch
Bystock
Knowle
Kersbrook
Hulham
Harcombe
Starcross
Lower Upcott
Littleham
Budleigh Salterton
Cofton
Exmouth
Cockwood
The Model Railway
World of Country Life
Ashcombe
Ugbrooke Park
B3192
Dawlish Warren
Ideford
Luton
A380
Dawlish
Sandygate
Holcombe
Bishopsteignton
Coombe
A381
Teignmouth
Coombe Cellars
R Teign
Ringmore
Shaldon
Netherton
Combeinteignhead
Stokeinteignhead
Middle Rocombe
Lower Gabwell
Higher Gabwell
Abbotskerswell
Coffinswell
Maidencombe
Daccombe
Barton
Coombe
Pafford
Babbacombe Bay
St Marychurch
Babbacombe
Ellacombe
Compton
Cockington
Marldon
TORQUAY
0 1 2 3 4 miles
0 1 2 3 4 5 kilometres

Chard
Axminster
Crewkerne
Bridport
Lyme Regis
Seaton
Ilminster
LYME BAY
Jurassic Coast World Heritage Site
Charmouth
Beaminster
Honiton

14
Brympton
Sherborne
North Wootton
Allweston
Stourton Caundle
Lydlinch
Sturminster Newton
St Mary
Manston
Fontmell Parva
Bradford Abbas
Barwick
Bishop's Caundle
Bagber
Hammoon
26
Thornford
Folke
A3030
Caundle Marsh
A357
Manor
Harding Moor
East Coker
Stof
Fiddleford
Okeford
Hamble Hill
Hardington
Mandeville
Beer Hackett
Yetminster
Longburton
Holwell
Fifehead Neville
Sturminster Common
Okeford Fitzpaine
Shillingstone
Belchalwell
Knighton
Crouch Hill
King's Stag
Kingston
Fifehead St Quintin
A352
Ryme Intrinseca
Pendomer
Hardington Marsh
Closworth
A37
Hamlet
Leigh
Hazelbury Bryan
B3146
Pulham
Durweston
Turnworth
182
BIRTS HILL
Halstock
Glanvilles Wootton
Middlemarsh
Wonston
Droop
Ibberton
Melbury Osmond
Chetnole
Stockwood
Hermitage
Woolland
B3143
East Chelborough
Melbury Bubb
Lyon's Gate
Duntish
Bulbarrow Hill
Blandford
Corscombe
Mappowder
Winterborne Houghton
A356
Buckland Newton
Evershot
Holywell
Minterne Magna
Henley
Higher Ansty
Lower Ansty
Benville
Uphall
Batcombe
Alton Pancras
Hilton
Winterborne Clenston
Melcombe Bingham
B3163
Rampisham
Frome St Quintin
The Giant
Milton
Plush
Lower Wraxhall
Higher Wraxhall
Cerne Abbas
Milton Abbas
Beaminster
Hooke
Mapperton
Cattistock
Sydling St Nicholas
Cheselbourne
Piddletrenthide
Bingham
North Poorton
Chilfrome
Nether Cerne
White Lackington
PUDDLETON DOWN
Dewlish
A354
Toller Porcorum
Maiden Newton
Godmanstone
R Cerne
Piddlehinton
Milborne St Andrew
13
South Poorton
Toller Fratrum
Hog Cliff
Powerstock
Higher Waterston
Bere Regis
Nettlecombe
West Compton Abbas
Wynford Eagle
Frampton
Athelhampton
Tolpuddle
EGGARDON HILL
Charlton Down
B3142
Puddletown
A35
Loders
Southover
Grimstone
YELLOWHAM HILL
Burleston
Affpuddle
Uploders
Compton Valence
Stratton
Athelhampton
Spyway
Charminster
Hardy's Cottage
Briantspuddle
Askerswell
Bradford Peverell
Tincleton
Higher Bockhampton
Pallington
Kingston Russell
B3390
Dorchester
Winterbourne Abbas
Stinsford
Chilcombe
Barrows
B3150
Woodsford
Clouds Hill
Litton Cheney
Long Bredy
Nine Stones
B3159
Kingston Maurward
West Stafford
R Bride
Winterbourne Steepleton
Martinstown
B3147
Winterborne Came
River Frome
Burton Bradstock
B3157
Littlebredy
Maiden Castle
Whitcombe
Moreton
Swyre
Puncknowle
Valley of Stones
Winterborne Monkton
West Knighton
Crossways
Tank
West Bexington
Abbotsbury Castle
Kingston Russell
Hardy Monument
WHITE HILL
Portesham
A354
Broadmayne
Warmwell
A352
Wool
South West Coast Path
Abbotsbury
Owermoigne
Abbey Remains
Bincombe
White Horse
East Knighton
Jurassic Coast World Heritage Site
Chapel
Rodden
Poxwell
Winfrith Newburgh
Swannery
Osmington
B3071
A353
Langton Herring
Overcombe
Preston
Upton
West Chaldon
East Chaldon (Chaldon Herring)
Lulworth Castle
Buckland Ripers
P+R
Jordan Hill
Osmington Mills
CHALDON DOWN
B3155
RSPB
Chesil Beach
The Fleet
Chickerell
Weymouth Bay
Ringstead Bay
West Lulworth
B3070
BINDON HILL
Fleet
Lulworth Cove
Water Gardens
Durdle Door
Chesil Bank & The Fleet
Weymouth
Westham
Deep Sea Adventure
B3156
Nothe Fort
Wyke Regis
Portland Harbour
A354
Portland Castle
West Bay
Fortuneswell
PORTLAND
Easton
Portland Museum & Shipwreck Centre
Guernsey
Jersey
St-Malo
Portland Bill Lighthouse
PORTLAND BILL
0 1 2 3 4 miles
0 1 2 3 4 5 kilometres

Dorset Coast
15
27
28
16
G
H
J
K
L
M
1
2
3
4
5
6
7
8
Waldron
New Town
Farnham
Boveridge
Iwerne Minster
Chettle
Gussage St Andrew
Cranborne
Alderholt
North Gorley
South Gorley
Ibsley
Ibsley Common
Rockford Common
Tarrant Hinton
Gussage St Michael
Edmondsham
Dorset Heavy Horse Centre
Stourpaine
Pimperne
Tarrant Launceston
Tarrant Monkton
Long Crichel
Gussage All Saints
Moor Crichel
Romford
Verwood
Woodlands
Horton
Royal Signals
Manswood
Tarrant Rawston
Witchampton
Forum
Mannington
Three Legged Cross
Ringwood
Poulner
Moors Valley
Tarrant Rushton
Hinton Martell
Charlton Marshall
Charlton on the Hill
Tarrant Keyneston
St Leonards
Liberty's Raptor & Reptile Centre
Kingston Great Common
Tarrant Crawford
Badbury Rings
Honeybrook
Holt
West Moors
Avon Heath
Thornicombe
Spetisbury
Kingston Lacy
Hillbutts
Shapwick
Abbott Street
Colehill
Ferndown
FOXBURY HILL
Sandford
Bisterne
Sturminster Marshall
Pamphill
Wimborne Minster
Leigh Park
Hampreston
Knoll
Ripley
Avon
Bransgore
Winterborne Zelston
Merley
Longham
Dudsbury
Bournemouth
Hurn
Sopley
West Parley
Kinson
Bearwood
Corfe Mullen
West Howe
Cudnell
Ensbury
Red Hill
Adventure Wonderland
West Morden
Morden
Broadstone
Upton Heath
East Howe
Throop
Burton
East Morden
Lytchett Matravers
Moordown
Canford Heath
Wallisdown
Winton
Somerford
Iford
Christchurch
Newtown
Branksome
Organford
Lytchett Minster
Upton
Morden Bog
Pokesdown
Tuckton
Mudeford
Castle
Wick
Boscombe
Southbourne
Christchurch Bay
Hamworthy
Lake
Lower Hamworthy
Parkstone
Lilliput
Westbourne
Branksome Park
BOURNEMOUTH
HENGISTBURY
Piddle or River Trent
POOLE
Canford Cliffs
Sandford
Northport
Arne
Poole Harbour
Brownsea Island
Sandbanks
RSPB
Binnegar
Wareham
POOLE BAY
Stoborough
Ridge
Toll
East Stoke
West Holme
East Holme
Stoborough Heath
Purbeck Heritage Coast
Studland Bay
Hartland Moor
Blue Pool
ISLE OF PURBECK
THE FORELAND
East Lulworth
Studland
(Apr-Oct)
Purbeck Hills
Corfe Castle
Swanage Railway
Church Knowle
Harman's Cross
Ulwell
Ballard Point
Tyneham Village
Swanage Bay
Kingston
Kimmeridge
Swanage
Kimmeridge Bay
Cherbourg
Guernsey
Jersey
St-Malo (May-Sept)
South West Coast Path
Langton Matravers
Durlston
DURLSTON HEAD
Jurassic Coast World Heritage Site
Chapman's Pool
Worth Matravers
Anvil Point
ST ALDHELM'S OR ST ALBAN'S HEAD
A350
A354
A31
A35
A351
A338
A341
A349
A348
A347
A3049
A3060
B3078
B3081
B3072
B3082
B3075
B3074
B3073
B3347
B3068
B3061
B3065
B3369
B3069
B3070
B3351

28
15
A
B
C
D
E
F
1
2
3
4
5
6
7
8
Fritham
Brook Hill
Brook
Copythorne
Cadnam
Winsor
Calmore
Testwood
M271
Millbrook
Shirley
Portswood
West End
Bitterne
Hedge End
Rufus Stone
Netley Marsh
Bartley
Woodlands
Furzey
Minstead
Ashurst
Eling
Totton
SOUTHAMPTON
Northam
Sholing
Woolston
Isle of Wight Ferry Terminal
Netley Abbey
Bursledon
North Gorley
South Gorley
Ibsley Common
Rockford Common
NEW FOREST
NATIONAL PARK
Emery Down
Lyndhurst
Longdown Activity Farm
Otter, Owl & Wildlife Park
Marchwood
Dibden
Netley
Sarisbury
Beaulieu River
Bank
Dibden Purlieu
Langdown
Southampton Water
Royal Victoria
Hythe
Hamble-le-Rice
Warsash
Hardley
Fawley
Holbury
Blackfield
Calshot Castle
Calshot
Langley
Exbury
Stanswood Bay
A31
A35
A337
A326
B3056
B3054
B3055
B3053
B3058
B3397
Liberty's Raptor & Reptile Centre
Burley Street
Rhinefield Ornamental Drive
Kingston Great Common
MARKWAY HILL
Burley
Brockenhurst
National Motor Museum
Beaulieu
Bucklers Hard
North Solent
Sandford
Bisterne
Thorney Hill
East Boldre
Ripley
Bransgore
Sway
Boldre
Pilley
Norleywood
South Baddesley
Needs Ore Point
Cowes
Spinners
East End
Burton
New Milton
Hordle
Lymington
Walkford
Ashley
Everton
Highcliffe
Highcliffe Castle
Somerford
Christchurch
Mudeford
Barton-on-Sea
Braxton
Wick
Southbourne
Christchurch Bay
HENGISTBURY HEAD
Keyhaven
Milford on Sea
Hurst Castle
Sconce Point
Yarmouth
THE SOLENT
Gurnard Bay
Gurnard
Rew Street
Thorness Bay
Hamstead Heritage Coast
Newtown Bay
Northwood
Porchfield
Newtown
Old Town Hall
Colwell Bay
Totland
Totland Bay
Norton Green
Thorley Street
Ningwood
Shalfleet
A3054
Carisbrooke
Carisbrooke Castle
Newbridge
B3401
Wellow
Freshwater
Afton
Watermill
Chessell Pottery
B3399
Calbourne
Bowcombe
BRIGHSTONE DOWN
ISLE OF WIGHT
Blackwater
Alum Bay
Dimbola Lodge
B3322
THE NEEDLES
Needles Old Battery
West Wight
Afton, Compton & Brook Downs
Compton Bay
Hanover Point
Brook
Hulverstone
Manor Garden
Museum
Gatcombe
Chillerton
B3323
Mottistone
Limerstone
Shorwell
Tennyson Heritage Coast
Brighstone
Chilton Chine
Kingston
Chale Green
Brighstone Bay
A3055
A3020
Atherfield Point
St Catherine's Oratory
Whale Chine
Chale
Niton
Blackgang Chine
Rocken End
ST CATHERINE'S POINT
0 1 2 3 4 miles
0 1 2 3 4 5 kilometres

Isle of Wight
17
Waltham Chase
Shirrell Heath
Soberton Heath
Hambledon
Catherington
Blendworth
Chalton
Curdridge
Shedfield
Newtown
Wickham
Forestside
Singleton
West Dean
Weald & Downland Air Museum
29
30
G
H
J
K
L
M
Curbridge
Worlds End
Anmore
Soake
Cowplain
Stoughton
Bow Hill
Kingley Vale
North Boarhunt
Rowland's Castle
Walderton
Burridge
Whiteley
Swanwick
WATERLOOVILLE
Southwick
Stakes
Staunton
Funtington
Woodend
West Stoke
Mid Lavant
Westbourne
Boarhunt
Ports Down
Purbrook
HAVANT
Woodmancote
West Ashling
East Ashling
Summersdale
M27
Titchfield Abbey
Wallington
Catisfield
Royal Armouries
Bedhampton
Hambrook
Cosham
Drayton
Southbourne
Broadbridge
Titchfield
FAREHAM
Portchester
Castle
Farlington
Brockhampton
Langstone
Emsworth
Nutbourne
Walton
Fishbourne
Palace
Portsmouth Harbour
Whale Island
Hilsea
RSPB
Northney
Chidham
Bosham
Stubbingston
Bridgemary
M275
North Hayling
THORNEY ISLAND
Dell Quay
Apuldram
Hill Head
Fort Brockhurst
Elson
Continental Ferry Terminal
North End
Stoke
HAYLING ISLAND
West Thorney
Donnington
Rowner
Hardway
Langstone Harbour
Hunston
GOSPORT
Portsea
Fratton
West Itchenor
Birdham
Lee-on-the-Solent
Chichester Harbour
Spinnaker Tower
Shipton Green
Isle of Wight Ferry Terminal
Southsea
West Town
South Hayling
Street Side
Stokes Bay
Alverstoke
Eastney
Fort Cumberland
Somerley
Highleigh
PORTSMOUTH
Hayling Bay
West Wittering
Gilkicker Point
East Wittering
Earnley
Osborne
Spitbank Fort
Bracklesham
18
East Cowes
Osborne House
Bay
SPITHEAD
Bracklesham Bay
Whippingham
Fishbourne
Ryde
Wootton Bridge
Puckpool Point
Selsey
Binstead
Brickfields Horse Country
Flamingo Park
Nettlestone Point
Seaview
(Mar-Oct)
Rosemary
World
Cross Lane
Isle of Wight Steam Railway
Havenstreet
Little Whitefield
Nettlestone
St Helens
Robin Hill
The Duver
Newport
East Ashey
Bembridge
Bembridge Windmill
Lifeboat Station
FORELAND
Nunwell
Brading
Cherbourg
Guernsey
Jersey
St-Malo
Caen (Ouistreham)
Bilbao (Mar-Nov)
Le Havre
Santander
Cherbourg
Caen (Ouistreham)
Le Havre (Mar-Sept)
Maritime
WIGHT
Arreton
Haseley Manor
Alverstone
Bembridge Down
Whitecliff Bay
Newchurch
Dinosaur Isle
Yaverland
Culver Cliff
Merstone
Queen's Bower
Rookley
Winford
Lake
Sandown
Branstone
Sandown Bay
Apse Heath
Sandford
Godshill
Whiteley Bank
Shanklin
Old Smithy & Gardens
Shanklin Chine
Luccombe Village
Wroxall
Luccombe Chine
Appuldurcombe House
Ventnor Down
DUNNOSE
Whitwell
Ventnor
IOW Glass
Botanic Garden
St Lawrence
The Undercliffe
Binnel Bay
A3
A32
A27
A334
A3051
A3(M)
A2030
A3023
A259
A286
A288
A3054
A3055
A3056
A3020
B2177
B2150
B2149
B2148
B2146
B2147
B2178
B3385
B3334
B3333
B3330
B3395
B3327
B2179
B2198
B2145
B2201
1
2
3
4
5
6
7
8

18
30
17
Liphook
Linchmere
Kingsley Green
Fernhurst
Milland
Woodmansgreen
Redford
Henley
Lickfold
Lurgashall
Northchapel
Plaistow
Ifold
Loxwood
Black Down
BLACKDOWN HILL
Kirdford
Balls Cross
Wisborough Green
Billingshurst
Five Oaks
Barns Green
Broadbridge Heath
SOUTH DOWNS NATIONAL PARK
Fyning
Chithurst
Iping
Woolbeding
Lodsworth
River
Upperton
Trotton
Stedham
Easebourne
Midhurst
Tillington
Petworth
Byworth
Little Bognor
Codmore Hill
Adversane
Coneyhurst Common
Broadford Bridge
Coolham
Nyewood
Selham
Elsted
Cocking Causeway
West Lavington
South Ambersham
Fittleworth
Stopham
Pulborough
Nutbourne
Dial Post
Didling
Treyford
Bepton
Cocking
Upper Norwood
Duncton
Coates
Marehill
West Chiltington
Thakeham
Heyshott
Graffham
Barlavington
Coldwaltham
Hardham
Greatham
Abingworth
Ashington
East Lavington
Sutton
Watersfield
Chilgrove
East Marden
Bignor
Rackham
Storrington
Singleton
West Dean
Upwaltham
Bury
Amberley
Washington
Charlton
East Dean
Houghton
Stoughton
Bow Hill
Halnaker Hill
North Stoke
South Stoke
Walderton
West Stoke
Eartham
Burpham
Wepham
Offham
East Lavant
Waterbeach
Slindon
Findon
Mid Lavant
Strettington
Fontwell
Arundel
Warningcamp
Patching
Clapham
East Ashling
West Ashling
Boxgrove
Halnaker
Binsted
Poling Corner
High Salvington
Summersdale
Tangmere
Norton
Nyton
Walberton
Broadbridge
Westhampnett
Aldingbourne
Eastergate
Poling
Angmering
Durrington
Salvington
Walton
Fishbourne
Oving
Westergate
Woodgate
North End
Lyminster
Chichester
Bosham
Dell Quay
Apuldram
Merston
Colworth
Barnham
Yapton
Ford
Wick
Rustington
East Preston
Ferring
West Tarring
Goring-by-Sea
West Worthing
Shripney
Climping
Littlehampton
Donnington
Runcton
North Bersted
Bilsham
Hunston
North Mundham
South Mundham
Birdham
Flansham
South Bersted
Middleton-on-Sea
Felpham
Street End
Sidlesham
Rose Green
Somerley
Highleigh
Nyetimber
Aldwick
BOGNOR REGIS
Earnley
Pagham Harbour
Pagham
Bracklesham Bay
Church Norton
Selsey
SELSEY BILL
A B C D E F
1 2 3 4 5 6 7 8
0 1 2 3 4 miles
0 1 2 3 4 5 kilometres

Horsham
St Leonards Forest
Handcross
Balcombe
Staplefield
Slaugham
Lower Beeding
Mannings Heath
Monk's Gate
Southwater
Widening in progress
Warninglid
Nuthurst
Copsale
Maplehurst
Crabtree
Cuckfield
Haywards Heath
Ansty
Bolney
West Grinstead
Cowfold
Hickstead
Twineham
Partridge Green
Sayers Common
Hurstpierpoint
Burgess Hill
Henfield
Blackstone
Albourne
Keymer
Ditchling
Hassocks
Clayton
Woodmancote
Pyecombe
Small Dole
Poynings
Upper Beeding
Edburton
Fulking
Pangdean
Saddlescombe
Bramber
Botolphs
Coombes
Lancing College Chapel
Patcham
Coldean
Withdean
Hollingbury
Hangleton
West Blatchington
Mile Oak
Portslade
Old Shoreham
Shoreham
Lancing
Shoreham-by-Sea
Southwick
Portslade-by-Sea
HOVE
BRIGHTON
WORTHING
Preston
Moulsecoomb
Kemp Town
Ovingdean
Woodingdean
Rottingdean
Saltdean
Peacehaven
Telscombe
Southease
Piddinghoe
Rodmell
Iford
Kingston near Lewes
Falmer
Stanmer
Lewes
South Malling
Offham
Hamsey
Barcombe
Barcombe Cross
Upper Wellingham
Wivelsfield
Wivelsfield Green
North Chailey
Chailey
South Chailey
Plumpton Green
Plumpton
East Chiltington
Streat
Westmeston
DITCHLING BEACON
MOUNT HARRY
SOUTH DOWNS NATIONAL PARK
NEWMARKET HILL
Newick
Fletching
Scayne's Hill
Lindfield
Horsted Keynes
Danehill
Nutley
Fairwarp
Maresfield
Splayne's Green
Piltdown
Uckfield
Isfield
Little Horsted
Ringmer
Glynde
Beddingham
Firle
FIRLE BEACON
Tarring Neville
South Heighton
Denton
Newhaven
Norton
Bishopstone
East Blatchington
Sutton
Seaford
Seaford Head
Seaford Bay
Dieppe
Halland
Shortgate
Laughton
Buxted
Ardingly Reservoir
Wakehurst Place
Nymans Garden
Borde Hill
Leonardslee
Sheffield Park
Bluebell Railway
Bentley Wildfowl & Motor Museum
Charleston Farmhouse
Monk's House
Paradise Park
Devil's Dyke
TRULEIGH HILL

A
B
C
D
E
F
1
2
3
4
5
6
7
8
32
33
19
Cross
Three Legged Cross
Flimwell
A268
Highgate
Hawkhurst
The Moor
B2100
Tidebrook
Rotherfield
Ticehurst
River Limden
Pashley Manor
Merriments
Kent Ditch
Hurst Green
Sweethaws
Fairwarp
A26
B2101
Stonegate
Witherenden Hill
Etchingham
B2244
A21
Bodiam
A267
Mayfield
High Hurstwood
River Rother
Five Ash Down
Pound Green
Five Ashes
A265
Maresfield
Salehurst
Burwash
Bateman's
Buxted
A272
Hadlow Down
Broad Oak
Burwash Common
Burwash Weald
Robertsbridge
Staple Cross
Cross in Hand
Heathfield
Cade St
R Dudwell
Uckfield
Blackboys
B2102
Framfield
Brightling
Darwell Reservoir
Mountfield
Punnett's Town
New Town
Three Cups Corner
Wood's Corner
B2203
Little London
Ridgewood
East Sussex National
Waldron
Maynard's Green
B2096
Dallington
Netherfield
A2100
Lavender Line
Whatlington
B2192
Little Horsted
Rushlake Green
Warbleton
Sed
Battle
Halland
East Hoathly
Horam
Vines Cross
Wildfowl Motor Museum
A22
Gun Hill
1066
Shortgate
Chiddingly
Bodle Street Green
Cowbeech
A271
B2204
B2095
Whitesmith
Catsfield
Muddles Green
A2100
Laughton
B2124
Herstmonceux
A269
Crowhurst
RSPB
Ringmer
Hellingly
The Truggery
Windmill Hill
Ninfield
Henley's Down
Lower Dicker
Horsebridge
Magham Down
Boreham Street
Lunsford's Cross
Ripe
Upper Dicker
Knockhatch
Leap Cross
Hailsham
Herstmonceux Castle & Observatory
Hooe
Glynde Place
Chalvington
Michelham Priory
Wartling
Little Common
Sidley
A2036
St Leonards
Pevensey Levels
Firle
A27
Selmeston
Arlington
Cooden
B2182
Firle Place
219
Charleston Farmhouse
Cuckmere R
B2104
A259
Bexhill
Alciston
FIRLE BEACON
Polegate
Berwick
Drusillas
Pevensey
Westham
Castle
Tarring Neville
Wilmington
A2270
Wannock
Lower Willingdon
South Heighton
Folkington
Pevensey Bay
Alfriston
The Long Man of Wilmington
Willingdon
Hampden Park
Langney
Clergy House
Ratton Village
A2280
Norton
Litlington
Jevington
St Anthony's Hill
Bishopstone
Roselands
East Blatchington
Lullington Heath
South Downs Way
A2021
Langney Point
Seaford Bay
Westdean
Sutton
Old Town
Seaford
Friston
EASTBOURNE
Seven Sisters
East Dean
B2103
Seaford Head
South Downs Way
Beachy Head Countryside Centre
Dieppe
BEACHY HEAD
Sussex Heritage Coast
0 1 2 3 4 miles
0 1 2 3 4 5 kilometres

Rolvenden
Small Hythe
Reading Street
Rolvenden Layne
Tenterden Vineyard Park
Kent & East Sussex Railway
Newenden
ISLE OF OXNEY
Wittersham
The Stocks
Stone in Oxney
Snargate
Brenzett
Ivychurch
St Mary in the Marsh
St Mary's Bay
Brookland
Old Romney
New Romney
Littlestone-on-Sea
Greatstone-on-Sea
Northiam
Beckley
Rye Foreign
Iden
Clayhill
Peasmarsh
Playden
Houghton Green
WALLAND MARSH
Rye
East Guldeford
Lydd
Broad Oak
Cock Marling
Camber
Broadland Row
Udimore
Brede
Camber Castle
Castle Water
Rye Harbour
Broad Street
Winchelsea
Icklesham
Rye Bay
DUNGENESS
Old Lighthouse
Three Oaks
Guestling Thorn
Guestling Green
Pett
Cliff End
Ore
Fairlight
HASTINGS
Royal Military Canal
River Rother
Rother Levels
River Brede
Romney Marsh
Aeronautical
Martello
A259
A268
A28
A2070
B2080
B2082
B2088
B2165
B2089
B2071
B2075
34
G
H
J
K
L
M
1
2
3
4
5
6
7
8

A
B
C
D
E
F
1
2
3
4
5
6
7
8
North West Point
Lundy Heritage Coast
LUNDY
142
Marisco
Surf Point
Shutter Point
Baggy Poin
Croyde
BARNSTAPLE
OR
BIDEFORD BAY
Westward
HARTLAND POINT
Shipload Bay
Titchberry
Dameholе Point
Hartland Abbey & Garden
Stoke
Hartland Quay
Hartland
B3248
Spekes Mill Mouth
Milford
Docton Mill Gardens
Philham
Clovelly
B3237
Buck's Mills
Hartland Heritage Coast
Abbotsha
Ford
Fairy Cross
Horns Cross
Woodtown
A39
Milky Way
Buck's Cross
Goldworthy
Woolfardisworthy
Parkham
Hardisworthy
Bucklan
Brewe
Welcombe
Frit
Darracott
Ashmansworthy
9
East Putford
Gooseham
Morwenstow
Dinworthy
Gnome Reserve
West Putford
Haytown
Higher Sharpnose Point
Shop
Bradworthy
South West Coast Path
Woodford
Bulkworthy
Lower Sharpnose Point
Tamar Lakes
Abbots Bickington
A388
Kilkhampton
Sutcombe
New St Pe
Steeple Point
Dinscott
Milton Damerel
B3254
0 1 2 3 4 miles
0 1 2 3 4 5 kilometres
Northcott
Holsworthy
Thornbury

Ilfracombe
Barnstaple
Braunton
Bideford
Northam
Great Torrington
South Molton
Lynton
Lynmouth
Combe Martin
EXMOOR FOREST
Foreland Point
Lynmouth Bay
Woody Bay
Elwill Bay
Martinhoe
Trentishoe
Countisbury
Brendon
Rockford
Watersmeet House
Barbrook
Toll Dean
Parracombe
Kentisbury
Berrynarbor
Watermouth Castle
Water Mouth
Combe Martin Bay
Hele Bay
Hele
Lee Bay
Bull Point
Rockham Bay
Mortehoe
Lee
Slade
Chambercombe Manor
The Old Corn Mill
Wildlife & Dinosaur Park
Lynton & Barnstaple Railway
Hoaroak Hill 474
Challacombe
Barton Town
River Barle
Simonsbath
Kinsford Water
Span Head
Wistlandpound Reservoir
Exmoor Zoological Park
Arlington
Arlington Court
Loxhore
Lower Loxhore
Bratton Fleming
Clifton
Bittadon
West Down
Trimstone
North Buckland
Georgeham
Croyde
Darracott
Saunton
Knowle
Boode
Marwood
Marwood Hill
Higher Muddiford
Muddiford
Milltown
Guineaford
Shirwell
Prixford
Heanton Punchardon
Wrafton
Braunton Burrows
Chivenor
River Taw
Ashford
Bradiford
Pilton
Derby
Goodleigh
Stoke Rivers
Brayford
High Bray
Bentwichen
Charles
Gunn
Stoodleigh
West Buckland
East Buckland
Heasley Mill
North Molton
Upcott
Fremington
Bickington
Landkey
Swimbridge Newland
Swimbridge
Crow Point
Appledore
Instow
Tapeley Park
Westleigh
Tawstock
St John's Chapel
Bishop's Tawton
Hannaford
Castle Hill
Filleigh
Eastleigh
Horwood
Newton Tracey
Harracott
East Stowford
Quince Honey Farm
Aller
East-the-Water
The Big Sheep
Hiscott
Chapelton
Cobbaton
Chittlehampton
Bish Mill
Alverdiscott
Umberleigh
Warkleigh
George Nympton
Landcross
Yarnscombe
Atherington
Huntshaw
Weare Giffard
Satterleigh
River Mole
Alswear
Mariansleigh
Yard
Ash Mill
Chittlehamholt
Kings Nympton
Romansleigh
Meshaw
High Bickington
Frithelstock
St Giles in the Wood
Kingscott
Rosemoor
Little Torrington
Roborough
Burrington
Langtree
Beaford
Ashreigney
Chulmleigh
Cheldon
Worlington
Chawleigh
Riddlecombe
Peters Marland
Winswell
Halsdon
Merton
Huish
Dolton
Hollocombe
Ashley
Eggesford
North Town
Dowland
Wembworthy
Petrockstow
Buckland
Nymet Rowland
Eastington
River Dalch
A39
A399
A361
A3123
A377
A386
A3124
A3125
B3343
B3231
B3233
B3230
B3229
B3358
B3223
B3226
B3227
B3232
B3137
B3217
B3096
B3042
B3236
10
24

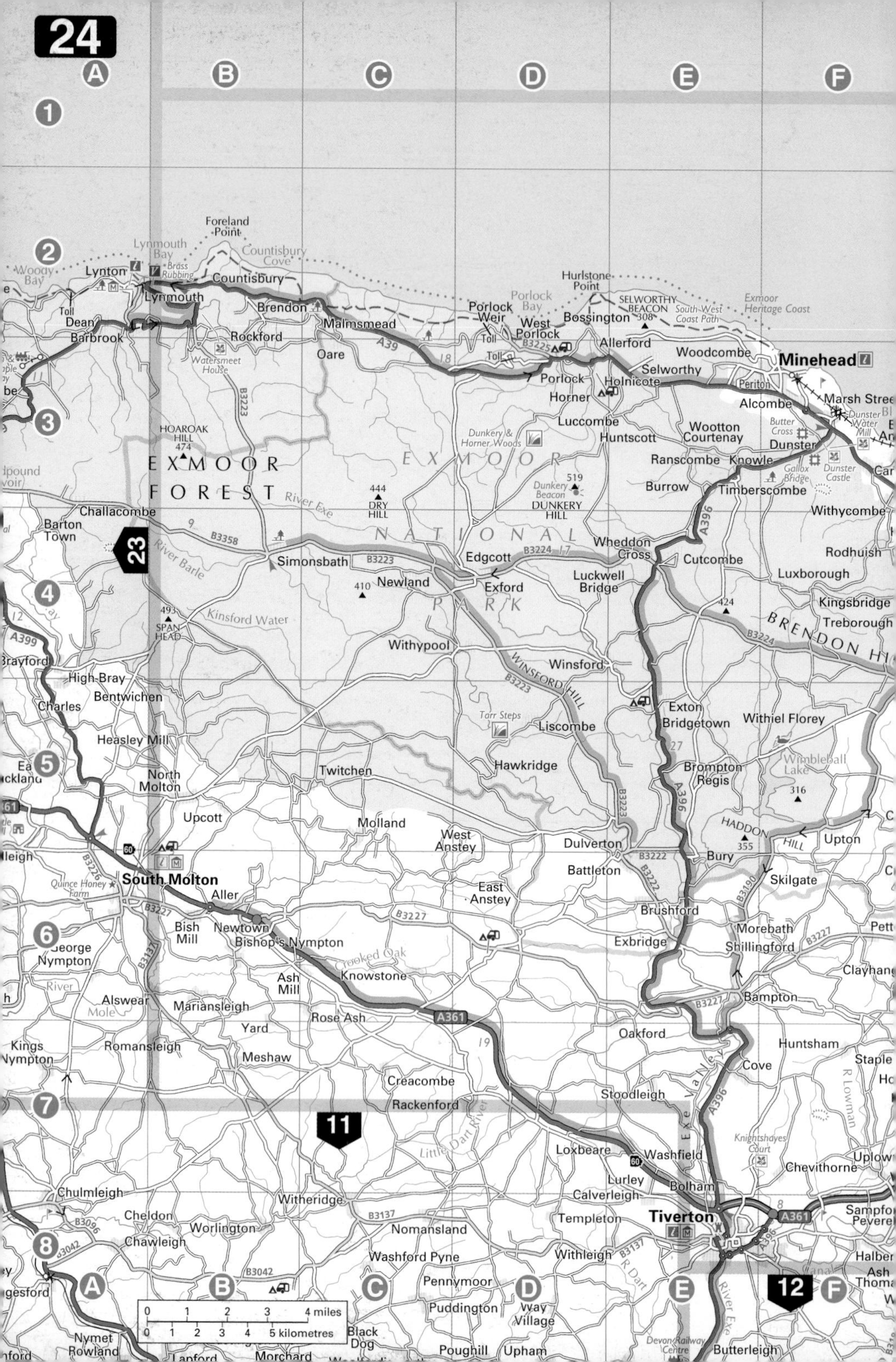

24
A
B
C
D
E
F
1
2
3
4
5
6
7
8
Foreland Point
Lynmouth Bay
Countisbury Cove
Woody Bay
Lynton
Brass Rubbing
Countisbury
Lynmouth
Brendon
Toll
Dean
Barbrook
Rockford
Malmsmead
Watersmeet House
Oare
A39
18
Porlock Bay
Porlock Weir
Hurlstone Point
SELWORTHY BEACON 308
South West Coast Path
Exmoor Heritage Coast
West Porlock
Bossington
B3225
Allerford
Woodcombe
Minehead
Toll
Porlock
Selworthy
Horner
Holnicote
Periton
Alcombe
Marsh Street
Dunster Water Mill
Butter Cross
Dunster
Luccombe
Huntscott
Wootton Courtenay
Dunkery & Horner Woods
HOAROAK HILL 474
B3223
EXMOOR FOREST
EXMOOR NATIONAL PARK
Ranscombe
Knowle
Gallox Bridge
Dunster Castle
519
Dunkery Beacon
DUNKERY HILL
Burrow
Timberscombe
444 DRY HILL
River Exe
Challacombe
Barton Town
Withycombe
9
B3358
River Barle
23
Simonsbath
B3223
Edgcott
B3224
17
Wheddon Cross
Cutcombe
Rodhuish
Luxborough
410
Newland
Exford
Luckwell Bridge
A396
Kingsbridge
424
Treborough
BRENDON HILLS
B3224
493 SPAN HEAD
Kinsford Water
A399
12
Brayford
Withypool
Winsford
WINSFORD HILL
B3223
High Bray
Bentwichen
Charles
Heasley Mill
Tarr Steps
Liscombe
Exton
Bridgetown
Withiel Florey
27
Wimbleball Lake
Hawkridge
Brompton Regis
North Molton
Twitchen
316
A361
Upcott
Molland
West Anstey
B3223
A396
HADDON HILL
355
Upton
Dulverton
B3222
Bury
Battleton
B3190
Skilgate
B3226
Quince Honey Farm
South Molton
Aller
East Anstey
B3227
B3227
Brushford
Bish Mill
Newtown
Morebath
Shillingford
B3227
George Nympton
Bishop's Nympton
Exbridge
B3137
Crooked Oak
Ash Mill
Knowstone
Clayhanger
River Mole
Alswear
Mariansleigh
Bampton
B3227
Yard
Rose Ash
A361
Oakford
Huntsham
Kings Nympton
Romansleigh
Meshaw
19
Cove
Staple
Creacombe
Exe Valley
R Lowman
Stoodleigh
Rackenford
A396
11
Little Dart River
Knightshayes Court
Loxbeare
Washfield
Chevithorne
Lurley
Chulmleigh
Witheridge
Calverleigh
Bolham
Cheldon
B3137
Templeton
Tiverton
8
A361
B3096
Worlington
Nomansland
A396
Chawleigh
B3042
Withleigh
B3137
R Dart
Washford Pyne
B3042
Pennymoor
12
Puddington
Way Village
0 1 2 3 4 miles
0 1 2 3 4 5 kilometres
Black Dog
Nymet Rowland
Poughill
Upham
Devon Railway Centre
River Exe
Butterleigh
Lapford
Morchard

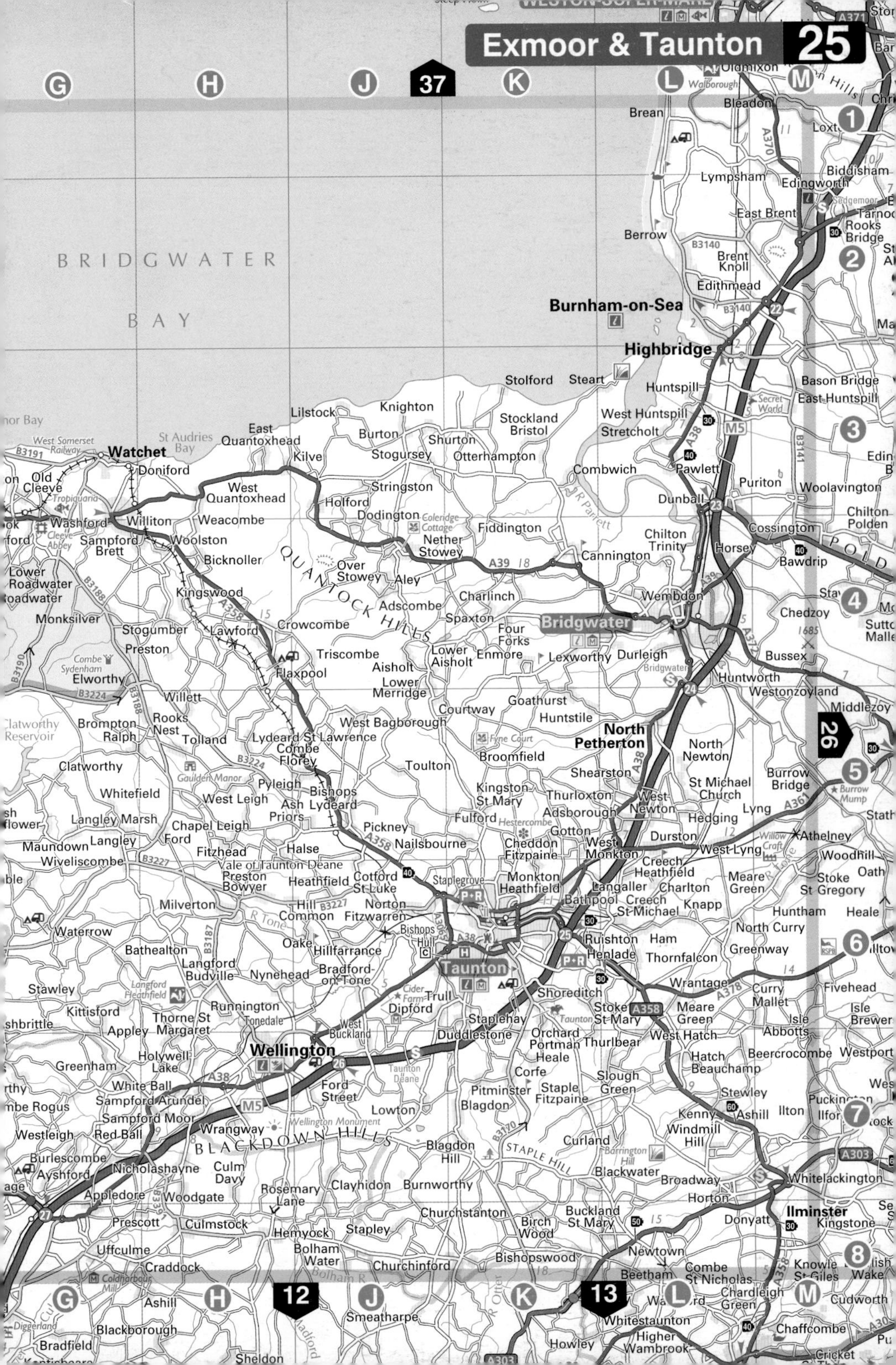
Exmoor & Taunton
25
G
H
J
37
K
L
M
1
2
3
4
5
6
7
8
26
12
13
BRIDGWATER
BAY
Brean
Bleadon
Oldmixon
Walborough
Lympsham
Biddisham
Edingworth
East Brent
Sedgemoor
Rooks Bridge
Berrow
Brent Knoll
Edithmead
Burnham-on-Sea
Highbridge
Stolford
Steart
Huntspill
Bason Bridge
East Huntspill
Secret World
West Huntspill
Stretcholt
Stockland Bristol
Lilstock
Knighton
Burton
Shurton
Stogursey
Otterhampton
Combwich
Pawlett
Puriton
Woolavington
Dunball
Chilton Polden
Cossington
Bawdrip
Horsey
Chilton Trinity
Cannington
Wembdon
Bridgwater
Chedzoy
Sutton Mallet
Bussex
Huntworth
Westonzoyland
Middlezoy
Durleigh
Lexworthy
Enmore
Four Forks
Spaxton
Charlinch
Fiddington
Nether Stowey
Coleridge Cottage
Dodington
Holford
Stringston
Kilve
East Quantoxhead
St Audries Bay
West Quantoxhead
Watchet
Doniford
West Somerset Railway
Old Cleeve
Tropiquaria
Washford
Cleeve Abbey
Williton
Weacombe
Sampford Brett
Woolston
Bicknoller
QUANTOCK HILLS
Over Stowey
Aley
Adscombe
Kingswood
Lower Roadwater
Roadwater
Monksilver
Stogumber
Lawford
Crowcombe
Preston
Combe Sydenham
Elworthy
Triscombe
Aisholt
Lower Aisholt
Lower Merridge
Flaxpool
Willett
Goathurst
Courtway
Huntstile
North Petherton
Clatworthy Reservoir
Brompton Ralph
Rooks Nest
Tolland
Lydeard St Lawrence
West Bagborough
Fyne Court
Combe Florey
Broomfield
North Newton
Clatworthy
Gaulden Manor
Toulton
Shearston
Burrow Bridge
Burrow Mump
St Michael Church
Whitefield
Pyleigh
West Leigh
Bishops Lydeard
Ash Priors
Kingston St Mary
Thurloxton
West Newton
Adsborough
Lyng
Hedging
Langley Marsh
Chapel Leigh
Pickney
Fulford
Hestercombe
Gotton
Durston
Athelney
Langley
Ford
Maundown
Wiveliscombe
Fitzhead
Halse
Nailsbourne
Cheddon Fitzpaine
West Monkton
Creech Heathfield
West Lyng
Willow Craft
Woodhill
Oath
Vale of Taunton Deane
Preston Bowyer
Heathfield
Cotford St Luke
Staplegrove
Monkton Heathfield
Langaller
Bathpool
Charlton
Meare Green
Stoke St Gregory
Milverton
Hill Common
Norton Fitzwarren
Creech St Michael
Knapp
Huntham
Heale
R Tone
Waterrow
Bishops Hull
North Curry
Oake
Ruishton
Ham
Henlade
Greenway
Bathealton
Langford Budville
Hillfarrance
Taunton
Thornfalcon
Nynehead
Bradford-on-Tone
Stawley
Langford Heathfield
Cider Farm
Trull
Dipford
Shoreditch
Wrantage
Curry Mallet
Fivehead
Kittisford
Runnington
Tonedale
Thorne St Margaret
Appley
Staplehay
Stoke St Mary
Meare Green
Isle Abbotts
Isle Brewers
West Buckland
Duddlestone
Orchard Portman
Thurlbear
West Hatch
Holywell Lake
Wellington
Heale
Hatch Beauchamp
Beercrocombe
Westport
Greenham
Taunton Deane
Corfe
Slough Green
White Ball
Ford Street
Pitminster
Staple Fitzpaine
Stewley
Sampford Arundel
Blagdon
Lowton
Kenny
Ashill
Ilton
Puckington
Ilford
Sampford Moor
Wrangway
Wellington Monument
Westleigh
Red Ball
Windmill Hill
Curland
BLACKDOWN HILLS
Blagdon Hill
Barrington Hill
STAPLE HILL
Burlescombe
Ayshford
Nicholashayne
Culm Davy
Blackwater
Broadway
Whitelackington
Rosemary Lane
Clayhidon
Burnworthy
Horton
Appledore
Woodgate
Ilminster
Kingstone
Prescott
Culmstock
Churchstanton
Birch Wood
Buckland St Mary
Donyatt
Hemyock
Stapley
Uffculme
Bolham Water
Newtown
Craddock
Churchinford
Bishopswood
Beetham
Combe St Nicholas
Knowle St Giles
Coldharbour Mill
Bolham R
Chardleigh Green
Cudworth
Ashill
Smeatharpe
R Otter
Whitestaunton
Diggerland
Blackborough
Higher Wambrook
Chaffcombe
Bradfield
Howley
Cricket
Sheldon
A38
A39
A358
A370
A371
A372
A378
A303
A361
M5
B3140
B3141
B3191
B3188
B3190
B3224
B3227
B3187
B3170

26
Stonebridge
Sandford
Churchill
Lower Langford
Rickford
Blagdon Lake
Nempnett Thrubwell
Chew Valley Lake
Bishop Sutton
Stowey
Clutton Hill
Clutton
Banwell
Upper Langford
Burrington
Blagdon
North Widcombe
Sutton Wick
High Littleton
Oldmixon
Star
Rowberrow
Yarborough
Winscombe
Sidcot
Shipham
West Harptree
38
South Widcombe
Temple Cloud
Hallatrow
Bleadon
Christon
Compton Martin
Cameley
Hinton Blewett
Paulton
Loxton
Compton Bishop
King John's Hunting Lodge
Charterhouse
East Harptree
Coley
Farrington Gurney
Cross
Cheddar Caves & Gorge
Litton
Sherborne
Midsomer Norton
Biddisham
Lower Weare
Axbridge
Ubley Warren
MENDIP HILLS
Edingworth
Sedgemoor
Cheddar Res
Cheddar
Badgworth
Weare
Chewton Mendip
Ston Easton
Clapton
East Brent
Tarnock
Rooks Bridge
Alston Sutton
Bathway
Chilcompton
Brent Knoll
Stone Allerton
Draycott
Emborough
Chapel Allerton
Clewer
Priddy
Green Ore
Gurney Slade
Downside
Cocklake
Ebbor Gorge
Rodney Stoke
Binegar
Nettlebridge
Mark
Westbury-sub-Mendip
Wookey Hole
R Axe
Wedmore
Blackford
Walcombe
West Horrington
Ashwick
Oakhill
Theale
Easton
East Horrington
Bagley
Westham
Wookey
Stoke St Michael
Bason Bridge
Secret World
Henton
Burcott Mill
Dulcote
Dinder
East Huntspill
Westhay Moor
Bleadney
Yarley
Coxley Wick
Wells
Darshill
Croscombe
Shepton Mallet
Doulting
Catcott Burtle
Lower Godney
Upper Godney
West Compton
Edington Burtle
Coxley
North Town
Cranmore
Puriton
Woolavington
Westhay
Godney
Meare Fish House
North Wootton
Pilton
Chesterblade
Chilton Polden
Catcott
Oxenpill
Meare
East Compton
Prestleigh
Cossington
Edington
Shapwick Heath
Ham Wall
Glastonbury
Royal Bath and West Showground
Stoney Stratton
POLDEN HILLS
Bawdrip
Catcott
Glastonbury Tor
Street on the Fosse
Shapwick
West Pennard
Pylle
Stawell
Ashcott
West Bradley
East Pennard
Evercreech
Chedzoy
Moorlinch
Sutton Mallet
Walton
Street
Parbrook
1685
Greinton
Pedwell
Butleigh Wootton
Tilham Street
Lamyatt
Bussex
Overleigh
Wraxall
Ditcheat
Westonzoyland
Baltonsborough
Ham Street
Alhampton
Wyke Champflower
Middlezoy
25
Compton Dundon
Hornblotton Green
Clanville
Ansford
River Cary
Butleigh
Henley
West Lydford
Pitcombe
National Animal Welfare Trust
Dundon
Barton St David
East Lydford
Alford
Castle Cary
Othery
BRADLEY HILL
Lovington
Burrow Bridge
Beer
High Ham
Littleton
Kingweston
Keinton Mandeville
Lydford on Fosse
Burrow Mump
Stembridge Tower Mill
Charlton Mackrell
Foddington
Galhampton
Lyng
Stathe
Aller
Low Ham
Bramwell
Somerton
Babcary
North Barrow
Athelney
Pitney
Charlton Adam
South Barrow
Willow Craft
Woodhill
Wearne
Haynes Motor Museum
Brookhampton
Oath
Langport
Upton
North Cadbury
Meare Green
Stoke St Gregory
Lytes Cary Manor
Curry Rivel
Huish Episcopi
Pibsbury
Catsgore
Kingsdon
Downhead
Sparkford
Little Weston
Blackford
Huntham
Heale
Long Sutton
West Camel
Compton Pauncefoot
North Curry
Abbey
Muchelney
Knole
Podimore
Queen Camel
South Cadbury
Willtown
Drayton
Little Load
Wales
Sutton Montis
RSPB
Long Load
Bridgehampton
Curry Mallet
Fivehead
Thorney
Muchelney Ham
Ilchester
RNAS Yeovilton
Fleet Air Arm
Chilton Cantelo
Marston Magna
Yeovilton
Corton Denham
Isle Brewers
Hambridge
Kingsbury Episcopi
Milton
Witcombe
Limington
Ashington
Isle Abbotts
Stapleton Coat
Rimpton
Beercrocombe
Westport
Ash
Tintinhull Garden
West Mudford
Adber
Sandford Orcas
Milborne
Treasurer's House
Chilthorne Domer
Mudford Sock
New Cross
Stembridge
Mudford
Poyntington
West Lambrook
Martock
Yeovil Marsh
Barrington
East Lambrook
Tintinhull
Up Mudford
Trent
Puckington
Priory
Stoke sub Hamdon
Ilton
Ilford
Barrington Court
Compton Durville
Nether Compton
Stocklinch
Shepton Beauchamp
South Petherton
Montacute
Yeovil
Goathill
Over Compton
Stallen
Old Castle
Norton sub Hamdon
Montacute House
Odcombe
Preston Plucknett
Castle
Whitelackington
Seavington St Michael
Wigborough
Little Norton
Sherborne
North Wootton
Over Stratton
Chiselborough
Brympton
Ilminster
Seavington St Mary
Kingstone
West Coker
Barwick
Bradford Abbas
Allowenshay
Lopen
West Chinnock
East Chinnock
Thornford
Folke
Dinnington
Middle Chinnock
Stoford
Knowle St Giles
Dowlish Wake
Ludney
Hinton St George
Merriott
Hardington Mandeville
Hardington Moor
East Coker
Lillington
Longburton
Cudworth
13
Haselbury Plucknett
Beer Hackett
14
Knighton
Crewkerne
Pendomer
Ryme Intrinseca
Yetminster
North Perrott
Hardington Marsh
Closworth
Chaffcombe
Cricket
Hewish
Hamlet
Leigh
0 1 2 3 4 miles
0 1 2 3 4 5 kilometres
182

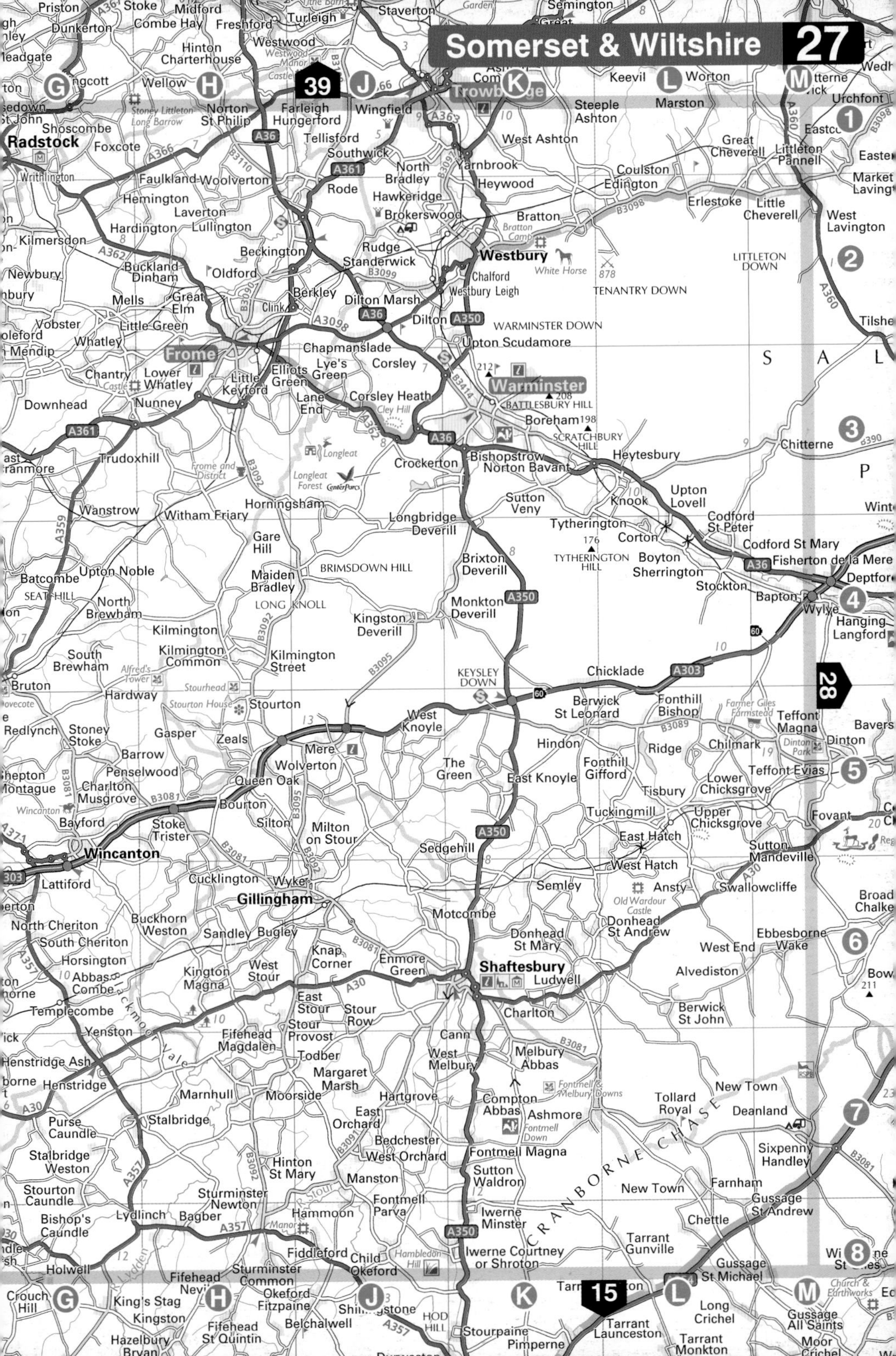

Somerset & Wiltshire
27
39
28
15
G
H
J
K
L
M
1
2
3
4
5
6
7
8
Priston
Stoke
Midford
Dunkerton
Combe Hay
Freshford
Turleigh
Staverton
Semington
Hinton Charterhouse
Westwood
Westwood Manor
Wellow
Farleigh Hungerford
Wingfield
Trowbridge
Keevil
Worton
Urchfont
Norton St Philip
Stoney Littleton Long Barrow
Steeple Ashton
Marston
Shoscombe
Radstock
Foxcote
Tellisford
Southwick
West Ashton
Great Cheverell
Littleton Pannell
Writhlington
Faulkland
Woolverton
Rode
North Bradley
Yarnbrook
Heywood
Coulston
Edington
Erlestoke
Little Cheverell
Market Lavington
West Lavington
Hemington
Laverton
Hawkeridge
Brokerswood
Bratton
Bratton Camp
Hardington
Lullington
Kilmersdon
Beckington
Rudge
Westbury
White Horse
878
LITTLETON DOWN
Newbury
Buckland Dinham
Oldford
Standerwick
Chalford
Westbury Leigh
TENANTRY DOWN
Mells
Great Elm
Berkley
Clink
Dilton Marsh
Dilton
Vobster
Little Green
WARMINSTER DOWN
Upton Scudamore
Whatley
Mendip
Frome
Chapmanslade
Corsley
Lye's Green
Elliots Green
S
A
L
P
Chantry
Lower Whatley
Little Keyford
Castle
Warminster
212
208
BATTLESBURY HILL
Downhead
Nunney
Lane End
Corsley Heath
Cley Hill
Boreham
198
SCRATCHBURY HILL
Chitterne
Trudoxhill
Longleat
Crockerton
Bishopstrow
Norton Bavant
Heytesbury
Cranmore
Frome and District
Longleat Forest
Center Parcs
Sutton Veny
Knook
Upton Lovell
Wanstrow
Horningsham
Witham Friary
Longbridge Deverill
Tytherington
Codford St Peter
Codford St Mary
Corton
Gare Hill
176
TYTHERINGTON HILL
Brixton Deverill
Boyton
Sherrington
Fisherton de la Mere
Batcombe
Upton Noble
Maiden Bradley
BRIMSDOWN HILL
Stockton
Bapton
Deptford
SEAT HILL
North Brewham
LONG KNOLL
Monkton Deverill
Wylye
Hanging Langford
Kingston Deverill
Kilmington
South Brewham
Kilmington Common
Kilmington Street
Chicklade
Alfred's Tower
KEYSLEY DOWN
Bruton
Stourhead
Hardway
Stourton House
Stourton
Berwick St Leonard
Fonthill Bishop
Farmer Giles Farmstead
Teffont Magna
Bavers
Redlynch
Stoney Stoke
Gasper
West Knoyle
Dinton
Dinton Park
Zeals
Mere
Hindon
Ridge
Chilmark
Barrow
Wolverton
The Green
Fonthill Gifford
Teffont Evias
Penselwood
Queen Oak
East Knoyle
Tisbury
Lower Chicksgrove
Charlton Musgrove
Wincanton
Bourton
Silton
Milton on Stour
Tuckingmill
Upper Chicksgrove
Fovant
Bayford
Stoke Trister
East Hatch
Wincanton
Sedgehill
West Hatch
Sutton Mandeville
Lattiford
Cucklington
Wyke
Gillingham
Semley
Ansty
Swallowcliffe
Old Wardour Castle
Broad Chalke
North Cheriton
Buckhorn Weston
Motcombe
Donhead St Andrew
South Cheriton
Sandley
Bugley
Donhead St Mary
Ebbesborne Wake
Horsington
Knap Corner
Enmore Green
West End
Abbas Combe
Kington Magna
West Stour
Shaftesbury
Ludwell
Alvediston
211
Templecombe
East Stour
Stour Row
Charlton
Berwick St John
Yenston
Fifehead Magdalen
Stour Provost
Cann
Todber
West Melbury
Melbury Abbas
Henstridge Ash
Henstridge
Margaret Marsh
Marnhull
Moorside
Hartgrove
Compton Abbas
Fontmell & Melbury Downs
Tollard Royal
New Town
Deanland
Purse Caundle
Stalbridge
East Orchard
Ashmore
Fontmell Down
Bedchester
Stalbridge Weston
West Orchard
Fontmell Magna
Sixpenny Handley
Hinton St Mary
Manston
Sutton Waldron
Stourton Caundle
Sturminster Newton
Fontmell Parva
New Town
Farnham
Gussage St Andrew
Bishop's Caundle
Lydlinch
Bagber
Hammoon
Iwerne Minster
Chettle
Manor
CRANBORNE CHASE
Fiddleford
Child Okeford
Hambledon Hill
Iwerne Courtney or Shroton
Tarrant Gunville
Holwell
Gussage St Michael
Fifehead Neville
Sturminster Common
Church & Earthworks
Crouch Hill
King's Stag
Okeford Fitzpaine
Shillingstone
Long Crichel
Gussage All Saints
Kingston
Belchalwell
HOD HILL
Stourpaine
Tarrant Launceston
Fifehead St Quintin
Hazelbury Bryan
Pimperne
Tarrant Monkton
Moor Crichel
A36
A361
A363
A366
A362
A3098
A350
B3414
A303
B3089
B3081
A371
A357
A30
A359
A360
B3098
B3090
B3092
B3095
B3099
B3110
B3097
B3390

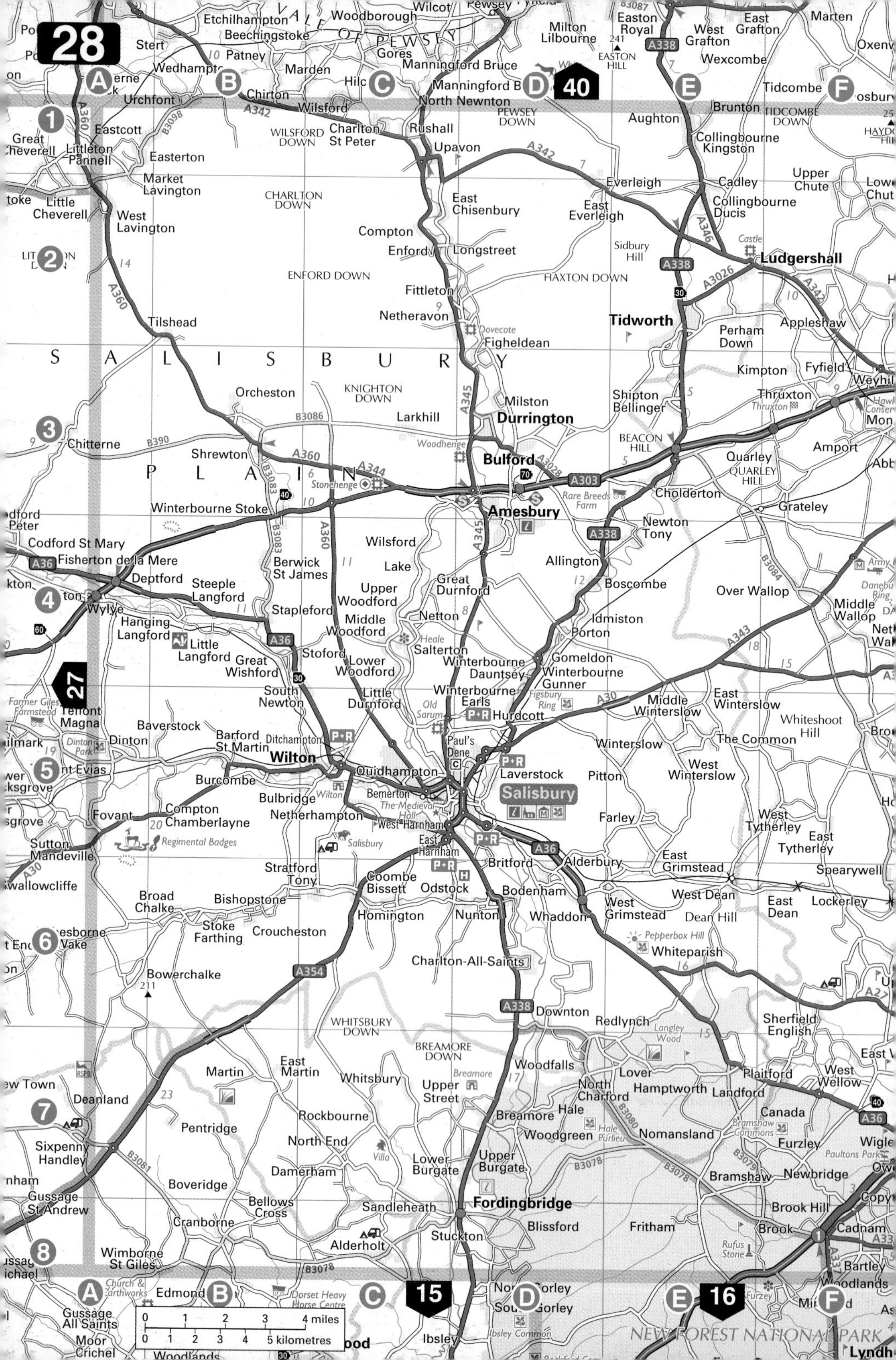
28
Etchilhampton
VALE OF PEWSEY
Woodborough
Wilcot
Pewsey
Milton Lilbourne
Easton Royal
241
EASTON HILL
West Grafton
East Grafton
Marten
Beechingstoke
Stert
Patney
Gores
Wedhampton
Marden
Manningford Bruce
Wexcombe
A338
Chirton
Hilcot
Manningford Bohune
40
Tidcombe
Urchfont
Wilsford
North Newnton
A
B
C
D
E
F
1
A360
Eastcott
B3098
A342
WILSFORD DOWN
Charlton St Peter
Rushall
PEWSEY DOWN
Brunton
TIDCOMBE DOWN
Aughton
Great Cheverell
Littleton Pannell
Easterton
Upavon
Collingbourne Kingston
Market Lavington
CHARLTON DOWN
Everleigh
Cadley
Upper Chute
Little Cheverell
West Lavington
East Chisenbury
East Everleigh
Collingbourne Ducis
A346
2
Compton
Enford
Longstreet
Sidbury Hill
Castle
Ludgershall
ENFORD DOWN
HAXTON DOWN
A3026
Fittleton
Netheravon
Dovecote
Figheldean
Tidworth
Tilshead
Perham Down
Appleshaw
S A L I S B U R Y
Kimpton
Fyfield
Weyhill
Orcheston
KNIGHTON DOWN
A345
Milston
Shipton Bellinger
Thruxton
Larkhill
Durrington
B3086
3
Chitterne
B390
Woodhenge
BEACON HILL
Amport
Shrewton
A360
Bulford
A3028
Quarley
QUARLEY HILL
P L A I N
A344
A303
Stonehenge
B3083
Cholderton
Rare Breeds Farm
Winterbourne Stoke
Amesbury
Grateley
Codford St Mary
Newton Tony
A36
Fisherton de la Mere
Wilsford
A338
Berwick St James
Lake
Allington
B3084
Deptford
Steeple Langford
Great Durnford
Boscombe
4
Wylye
Upper Woodford
Over Wallop
Middle Wallop
Hanging Langford
Stapleford
Middle Woodford
Netton
Idmiston
Porton
Little Langford
Great Wishford
Heale
Salterton
Stoford
Lower Woodford
A343
Gomeldon
Winterbourne Dauntsey
Winterbourne Gunner
27
Farmer Giles Farmstead
Teffont Magna
South Newton
Little Durnford
Winterbourne Earls
Figsbury Ring
A30
Middle Winterslow
East Winterslow
Whiteshoot Hill
Old Sarum
P+R
Hurdcott
Baverstock
Barford St Martin
Ditchampton
Dinton Park
Dinton
Paul's Dene
Winterslow
The Common
5
Wilton
Quidhampton
Laverstock
Pitton
West Winterslow
Burcombe
Bemerton
Salisbury
Bulbridge
Wilton
The Medieval Hall
Netherhampton
Farley
West Tytherley
Fovant
Compton Chamberlayne
West Harnham
East Tytherley
Regimental Badges
Salisbury
East Harnham
A36
Sutton Mandeville
Britford
Alderbury
East Grimstead
Spearywell
Swallowcliffe
Stratford Tony
Coombe Bissett
Odstock
Bodenham
West Dean
Broad Chalke
Bishopstone
Homington
Nunton
Whaddon
West Grimstead
Dean Hill
East Dean
Lockerley
Stoke Farthing
6
Croucheston
Pepperbox Hill
Whiteparish
Charlton-All-Saints
Bowerchalke
211
A354
A338
Downton
Redlynch
Sherfield English
WHITSBURY DOWN
Langley Wood
BREAMORE DOWN
Breamore
Woodfalls
East Martin
Martin
Whitsbury
Lover
Upper Street
North Charford
Hamptworth
Landford
Plaitford
West Wellow
Deanland
7
Rockbourne
Breamore
Hale
Canada
Pentridge
Woodgreen
Hale Purlieu
Nomansland
Bramshaw Commons
B3080
Sixpenny Handley
North End
Villa
Furzley
Paultons Park
B3081
Lower Burgate
Upper Burgate
B3078
Damerham
Bramshaw
Newbridge
Gussage St Andrew
Boveridge
Bellows Cross
Fordingbridge
Brook Hill
Cranborne
Sandleheath
Blissford
Fritham
Brook
Cadnam
Stuckton
8
Alderholt
Rufus Stone
Bartley
Wimborne St Giles
A337
Woodlands
Church & Earthworks
Edmondsham
Dorset Heavy Horse Centre
15
North Gorley
South Gorley
Furzey
16
Minstead
Gussage All Saints
Ibsley Common
NEW FOREST NATIONAL PARK
Moor Crichel
Ibsley
Lyndhurst
Woodlands
0 1 2 3 4 miles
0 1 2 3 4 5 kilometres

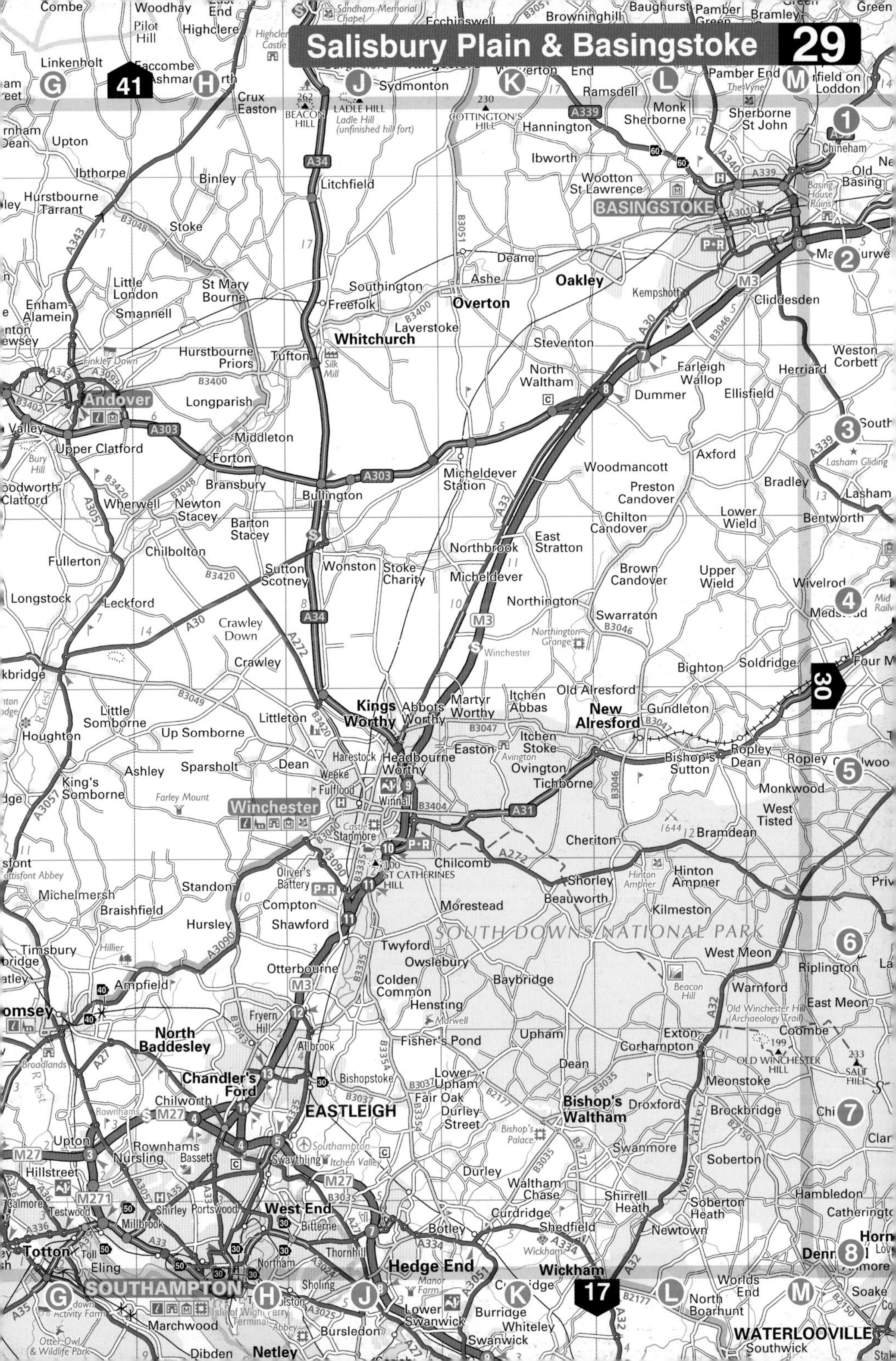
41
Linkenholt
Woodhay
Highclere
Sydmonton
Crux Easton
BEACON HILL
LADLE HILL
Ladle Hill (unfinished hill fort)
COTTINGTON'S HILL
Hannington
Ramsdell
Monk Sherborne
Sherborne St John
The Vyne
Chineham
Old Basing
Basing House Ruins
BASINGSTOKE
Wootton St Lawrence
Ibworth
Upton
Ibthorpe
Binley
Litchfield
Hurstbourne Tarrant
Stoke
Little London
St Mary Bourne
Enham Alamein
Smannell
Southington
Freefolk
Overton
Ashe
Deane
Oakley
Kempshott
Cliddesden
Laverstoke
Whitchurch
Steventon
Hurstbourne Priors
Tufton
Silk Mill
Finkley Down
Andover
Longparish
North Waltham
Dummer
Farleigh Wallop
Ellisfield
Herriard
Weston Corbett
Upper Clatford
Middleton
Forton
Bury Hill
Bransbury
Bullington
Micheldever Station
Woodmancott
Axford
Preston Candover
Bradley
Lasham
Lasham Gliding
Wherwell
Newton Stacey
Barton Stacey
Chilton Candover
Lower Wield
Bentworth
Chilbolton
Fullerton
Sutton Scotney
Wonston
Stoke Charity
Northbrook
East Stratton
Micheldever
Brown Candover
Upper Wield
Longstock
Leckford
Crawley Down
Northington
Swarraton
Northington Grange
Winchester
Crawley
Bighton
Soldridge
Four Marks
30
Houghton
Little Somborne
Up Somborne
Littleton
Kings Worthy
Abbots Worthy
Martyr Worthy
Itchen Abbas
Old Alresford
New Alresford
Gundleton
Easton
Avington
Itchen Stoke
Ovington
Tichborne
Bishop's Sutton
Ropley
Ropley Dean
Monkwood
King's Somborne
Ashley
Sparsholt
Dean
Harestock
Headbourne Worthy
Weeke
Fulflood
Winnall
Farley Mount
Winchester
Castle
Stanmore
West Tisted
Bramdean
Cheriton
Chilcomb
ST CATHERINES HILL
Oliver's Battery
Shorley
Hinton Ampner
Beauworth
Kilmeston
Michelmersh
Braishfield
Standon
Compton
Hursley
Shawford
Morestead
SOUTH DOWNS NATIONAL PARK
Timsbury
Twyford
Owslebury
West Meon
Riplington
Hillier
Ampfield
Otterbourne
Colden Common
Baybridge
Beacon Hill
Warnford
East Meon
Old Winchester Hill (Archaeology Trail)
Romsey
Hensting
Marwell
Fryern Hill
North Baddesley
Allbrook
Fisher's Pond
Upham
Exton
Corhampton
Coombe
OLD WINCHESTER HILL
SALT HILL
Broadlands
Chandler's Ford
Bishopstoke
Lower Upham
Dean
Meonstoke
Chilworth
Fair Oak
EASTLEIGH
Durley Street
Bishop's Waltham
Droxford
Brockbridge
Rownhams
Upton
Nursling
Bassett
Southampton
Swaythling
Itchen Valley
Bishop's Palace
Swanmore
Soberton
Hillstreet
Durley
Waltham Chase
Shirrell Heath
Hambledon
Calmore
Testwood
Shirley
Portswood
West End
Bitterne
Curdridge
Soberton Heath
Catherington
Millbrook
Botley
Shedfield
Newtown
Totton
Toll
Eling
Northam
Thornhill
Hedge End
Wickham
Denmead
SOUTHAMPTON
Sholing
Manor Farm
17
Worlds End
North Boarhunt
Marchwood
Isle of Wight Ferry Terminal
Lower Swanwick
Burridge
Whiteley
Bursledon
Swanwick
Netley
Dibden
Otter, Owl & Wildlife Park
WATERLOOVILLE
Southwick
Meon Valley
M3
M27
M271
A34
A303
A30
A31
A33
A339
A343
A3057
A3090
A272
A32
A27
A335
A334
B3400
B3420
B3048
B3049
B3047
B3046
B3404
B3335
B3354
B3037
B3035
B2177
B2150
B3051

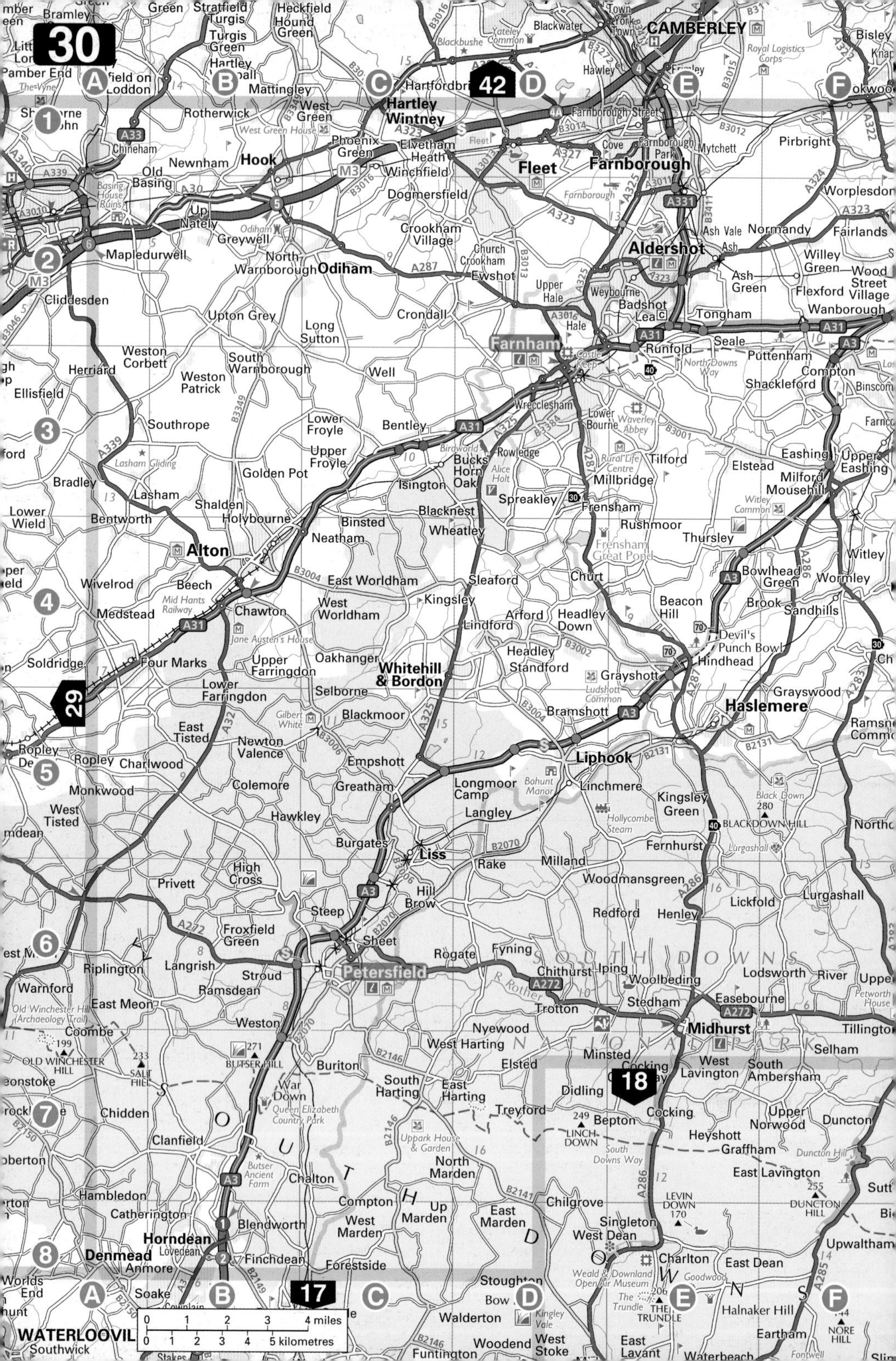
30
42
29
18
17
A
B
C
D
E
F
1
2
3
4
5
6
7
8
Bramley
Stratfield Turgis
Heckfield
Hound Green
Turgis Green
Hartley Wespall
Pamber End
Stratfield on Loddon
The Vyne
Sherborne St John
Mattingley
Rotherwick
West Green
West Green House
Blackbushe
Yateley Common
Blackwater
York Town
CAMBERLEY
Royal Logistics Corps
Bisley
Hawley
Frimley
Hartfordbridge
Hartley Wintney
Phoenix Green
Elvetham Heath
Winchfield
Farnborough Street
Cove
Farnborough Park
Mytchett
Pirbright
Chineham
Newnham
Hook
Old Basing
Basing House (Ruins)
Fleet
Farnborough
Worplesdon
Up Nately
Greywell
Odiham
Dogmersfield
Crookham Village
Church Crookham
Ash Vale
Normandy
Fairlands
Ash
Aldershot
Willey Green
Wood Street Village
Mapledurwell
North Warnborough
Odiham
Ewshot
Upper Hale
Weybourne
Badshot Lea
Ash Green
Flexford
Wanborough
Cliddesden
Upton Grey
Crondall
Hale
Tongham
Long Sutton
Farnham
Castle Keep
Runfold
Seale
Puttenham
North Downs Way
Compton
Weston Corbett
Herriard
South Warnborough
Weston Patrick
Well
Shackleford
Binscombe
Ellisfield
Wrecclesham
Lower Bourne
Waverley Abbey
Southrope
Lower Froyle
Bentley
Upper Froyle
Birdworld
Bucks Horn Oak
Rowledge
Alice Holt
Rural Life Centre
Tilford
Elstead
Eashing
Upper Eashing
Lasham Gliding
Bradley
Golden Pot
Isington
Millbridge
Milford
Mousehill
Lasham
Shalden
Spreakley
Frensham
Witley Common
Lower Wield
Bentworth
Holybourne
Binsted
Blacknest
Wheatley
Rushmoor
Thursley
Alton
Neatham
Frensham Great Pond
Witley
Wivelrod
Beech
East Worldham
Sleaford
Churt
Bowlhead Green
Wormley
Mid Hants Railway
Medstead
Chawton
West Worldham
Kingsley
Arford
Headley Down
Beacon Hill
Brook
Sandhills
Lindford
Jane Austen's House
Devil's Punch Bowl
Soldridge
Four Marks
Upper Farringdon
Oakhanger
Whitehill & Bordon
Headley
Standford
Grayshott
Hindhead
Lower Farringdon
Selborne
Ludshott Common
Grayswood
Gilbert White
Blackmoor
Bramshott
Haslemere
East Tisted
Newton Valence
Ropley
Ropley Dean
Charlwood
Empshott
Liphook
Linchmere
Colemore
Greatham
Longmoor Camp
Bohunt Manor
Kingsley Green
Monkwood
West Tisted
Black Down
BLACKDOWN HILL
Hawkley
Langley
Hollycombe Steam
Burgates
Liss
Rake
Milland
Fernhurst
Lurgashall
High Cross
Privett
Hill Brow
Woodmansgreen
Lickfold
Steep
Redford
Henley
Froxfield Green
Sheet
Rogate
Fyning
SOUTH DOWNS
Ripplington
Langrish
Stroud
Petersfield
Chithurst
Iping
Woolbeding
Lodsworth
River
Warnford
Ramsdean
R. Rother
Trotton
Stedham
Easebourne
East Meon
Petworth House
Old Winchester Hill (Archaeology Trail)
Weston
Nyewood
Midhurst
Tillington
Coombe
NATIONAL PARK
OLD WINCHESTER HILL
SALT HILL
BUTSER HILL
West Harting
Minsted
Selham
Buriton
Elsted
West Lavington
South Ambersham
Cocking Causeway
South Harting
East Harting
Didling
War Down
Queen Elizabeth Country Park
Treyford
Bepton
Cocking
Upper Norwood
Duncton
Chidden
LINCH DOWN
South Downs Way
Heyshott
Graffham
Duncton Hill
Clanfield
Uppark House & Garden
North Marden
Butser Ancient Farm
East Lavington
Chalton
DUNCTON HILL
Hambledon
Compton
Chilgrove
LEVIN DOWN
Catherington
West Marden
Up Marden
East Marden
Singleton
Horndean
Lovedean
Blendworth
West Dean
Upwaltham
Denmead
Anmore
Finchdean
Forestside
Charlton
East Dean
Worlds End
Soake
Stoughton
Weald & Downland Open Air Museum
Goodwood
Bow Hill
Kingley Vale
The Trundle
THE TRUNDLE
Halnaker Hill
NORE HILL
Walderton
Earltham
WATERLOOVILLE
Southwick
Woodend
West Stoke
East Lavant
Funtington
0 1 2 3 4 miles
0 1 2 3 4 5 kilometres
M3
A33
A339
A30
A323
A3013
A327
A3011
A331
A325
A287
A31
A3016
A3
A322
A324
A32
A272
A286
A283
A285
B3349
B3016
B3013
B3014
B3012
B3004
B3002
B3006
B2131
B2070
B2146
B2141
B2149
B2150
B3384
B3001
B3046

Cobham
Oxshott
Epsom
Sheerwater
Maybury
Pyrford
WOKING
Painshill Park
Semaphore Tower
Downside
Wisley
43
44
Stoke d'Abernon
Ripley
Old Woking
Send
Ockham
Leatherhead
Fetcham
Tadworth
Chipstead
Hooley
Kingswood
Netherne-on-the-Hill
Chaldon
Caterham
Headley
Walton on the Hill
Sutton Green
West Horsley
Little Bookham
Great Bookham
Bocketts
Headley Common
Walton Heath
West Clandon
East Horsley
Norbury Park
Mickleham
Merstham
South Merstham
Hatchlands Park
Effingham
Polesden Lacey
Reigate Hill
Redhill
Burpham
Clandon Park
East Clandon
Westhumble
Box Hill
Buckland
Holmethorpe
Nutfield
Merrow
Newlands Corner
Denbies
Pixham
Betchworth
Brockham
Reigate
Earlswood
GUILDFORD
Westcott
Dorking
South Park
Doversgreen
Gomshall
Abinger Hammer
Shalford Mill
Chilworth
Shalford
Shere
Albury
Blackheath
Albury Heath
North Holmwood
Dawesgreen
Leigh
Abinger Common
Salfords
32
Bramley
Wonersh
Farley Green
Peaslake
South Holmwood
Coldharbour
Outwood
Norwood Hill
Horley
Shamley Green
Holmbury St Mary
Leith Hill Tower
Beare Green
Parkgate
Godalming
HOLMBURY HILL
PITCH HILL
LEITH HILL
Newdigate
Charlwood
Povey Cross
Grafham
Forest Green
Burstow
Winkworth Arboretum
Gatwick
Rowly
Ewhurst
Ockley
Capel
Lowfield Heath
Russ Hill
Tinsley Green
Shipley Bridge
Ewhurst Green
Cranleigh
Loxhill
Ifield
Wattlehurst Farm
Lambs Green
Three Bridges
Pound Hill
Okewood Hill
Rusper
Turner's Hill
Dunsfold
Alfold Crossways
Ellen's Green
Kingsfold
CRAWLEY
Maidenbower
Worth
Faygate
Tilgate
Tilgate Park
Alfold
Rudgwick
Warnham
Buchan Country Park
Pease Pottage
Bucks Green
Littlehaven
Roffey
Colgate
Loxwood
Ifold
Slinfold
St Leonards Forest
Toyhorse Int Stud Farm
Broadbridge Heath
Horsham
Balcombe
Handcross
Nymans Garden
Staplefield
Itchingfield
Five Oaks
Barns Green
Manning's Heath
Lower Beeding
Slaugham
Widening in progress
Kirdford
Monk's Gate
Southwater
Leonardslee
Billingshurst
Fishers
Balls Cross
Wisborough Green
Nuthurst
Warninglid
Copsale
Maplehurst
Crabtree
Cuckfield
Coneyhurst Common
Bookers
Ansty
Adversane
Bolney
Broadford Bridge
Coolham
Shipley
West Grinstead
Cowfold
Petworth
Byworth
Little Bognor
Codmore Hill
Wineham
Hickstead
Worlds End
Stopham
Nutbourne
Dial Post
Partridge Green
Twineham
19
Fittleworth
Pulborough
Marehill
Holly Gate Cactus Garden
Sayers Common
West Chiltington
Thakeham
Hardham
Coldwaltham
Greatham
Abingworth
Ashington
Henfield
Blackstone
Albourne
Hurstpierpoint
Keymer
Watersfield
Ashurst
Hassocks
Rackham
Parham
Wiston
Woodmancote
Clayton
Storrington
Washington
Small Dole
Pyecombe
Amberley
Bury
KITHURST HILL
Chanctonbury Ring
Amberley Museum
Poynings
Houghton
South Downs Way
Steyning
Upper Beeding
Edburton
Devil's Dyke
Saddlescombe
North Stoke
South Stoke
TRULEIGH HILL
Bramber
HARROW HILL
Offham
Burpham
Findon
Botolphs
Patcham

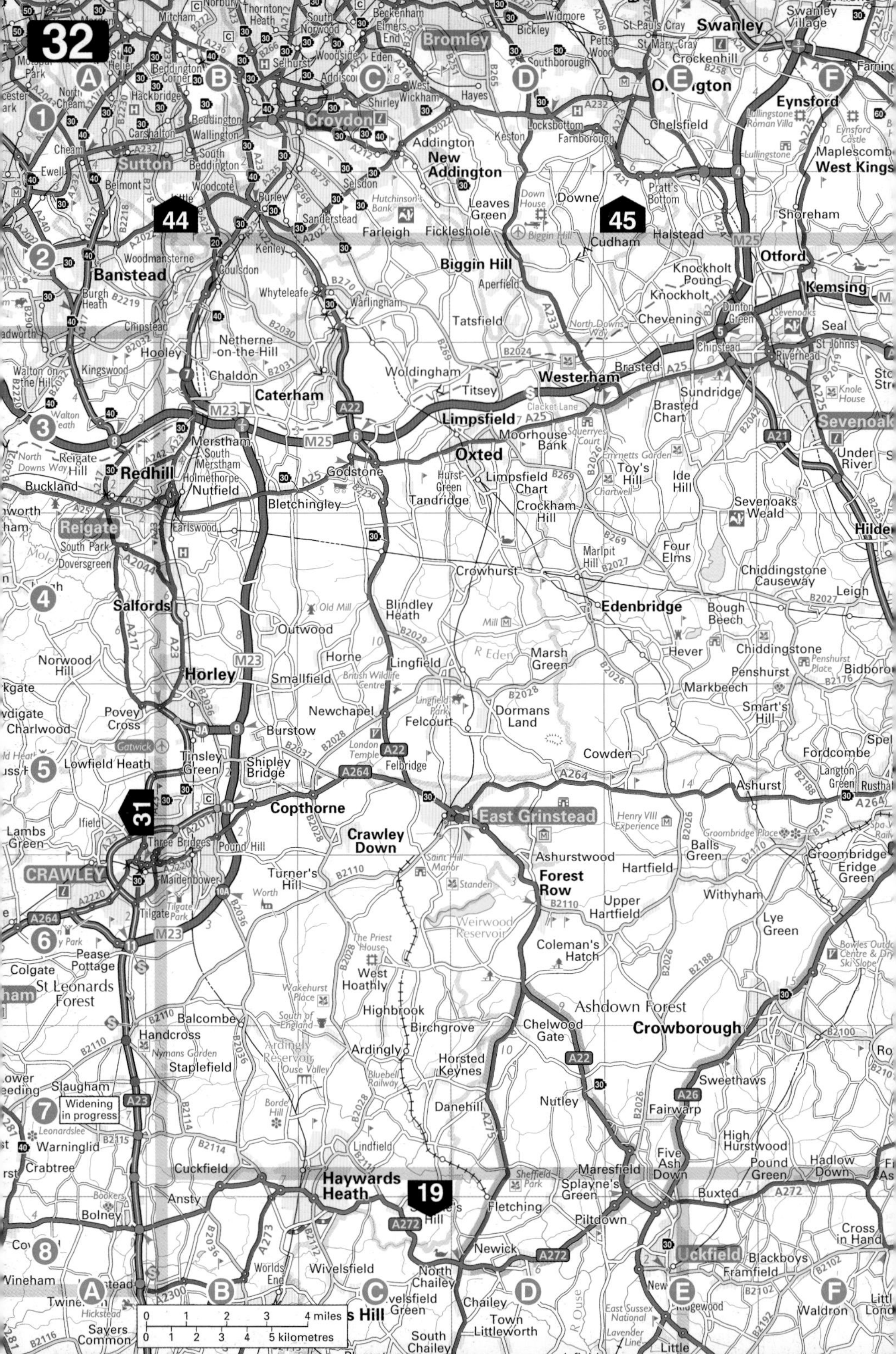
Croydon
Sutton
Bromley
Redhill
Reigate
Oxted
Westerham
Caterham
Horley
Edenbridge
CRAWLEY
East Grinstead
Forest Row
Crowborough
Haywards Heath
Uckfield
Sevenoaks
Swanley
Banstead
Biggin Hill
Gatwick
Ashdown Forest
Widening in progress
0 1 2 3 4 miles
0 1 2 3 4 5 kilometres

Longfield
New Barn
Cobham
Strood
ROCHESTER
CHATHAM
Hartley
Meopham
Sole Street
Luddesdown
New Ash Green
Ash
Hodsoll Street
Culverstone Green
Harvel
Paddlesworth
Stansted
Fairseat
Vigo
Snodland
Birling
Trottiscliffe
Ryarsh
Wrotham
Halling
Wouldham
Burham
Walderslade
Lords Wood
Bredhurst
Rainham
Wigmore
Hartlip
Newington
Bobbing
Milton Regis
Chalkwell
Borden
Bapchild
Tunstall
Highsted
Hill Green
Oad St
Stockbury
South Green
Bredgar
Eccles
Aylesford
Addington
Leybourne
Larkfield
Ditton
West Malling
Offham
Kings Hill
Herne Pound
Boxley
Detling
Thurnham
Bicknor
Hucking
Broad Street
Wormshill
Milstead
Frinsted
Doddington
East Malling
British Legion Village
MAIDSTONE
Bearsted
Hollingbourne
Eyhorne Street
Harrietsham
Lenham
Mereworth
Wateringbury
Teston
East Barming
Tovil
Willington
Shepway
Otham
Leeds
Broomfield
Plaxtol
Dunk's Green
West Peckham
Nettlestead
Nettlestead Green
East Farleigh
West Farleigh
Loose
Boughton Green
Langley
Sandway
Hadlow
East Peckham
Yalding
Coxheath
Linton
Boughton Monchelsea
Chart Sutton
Grafty Green
Parkers Green
Golden Green
Hale Street
Benover
Hunton
Chainhurst
Sutton Valence
Ulcombe
Egerton
Barnes Street
Laddingford
Mockbeggar
Tonbridge
Five Oak Green
Whetsted
Fowlhall
Collier Street
Cross-at-Hand
Tudeley
Rhoden Grn
Capel
Colt's Hill
Paddock Wood
Claygate
Marden
Wanshurst Green
Headcorn
Marden Thorn
Staplehurst
Smarden Bell
Smarden
Maltman's Hill
Matfield
Lower Green
High Brooms
Pembury
Brenchley
Horsmonden
Winchet Hill
Curtisden Green
Knox Bridge
Frittenden
Standen
Kipping's Cross
TUNBRIDGE WELLS
Marle Place
Three Chimneys
Sissinghurst Castle Garden
Biddenden
Goudhurst
Iden Green
Sissinghurst
High Halden
Owl House
Bayham Old Abbey
Lamberhurst
Finchcocks
Scotney Castle
Union Mill
East End
Bells Yew Green
Hook Green
Kilndown
Cranbrook
St Michaels
Lamberhurst Down
Cousley Wood
Goddard's Green
Wood's Green
National Pinetum & Garden
Hartley
Benenden
Tenterden
Bewl Water
Sparrows Green
Wadhurst
Three Leg Cross
Stonecrouch
Flimwell
Iden Green
Mark Cross
Historic Vehicles Collection
Rolvenden
Small Hythe
Highgate
Tidebrook
Hawkhurst
Tenterden Vineyard Park
Smallhythe Place
Ticehurst
The Moor
Four Throws
Rolvenden Layne
Sandhurst
Kent & East Sussex Railway
Pashley Manor
Stonegate
River Limden
Merriments
Hurst Green
Kent Ditch
Newenden
ISLE OF OXNEY
Witherenden Hill
Mayfield
Etchingham
River Rother
Great Dixter
Bodiam
Bodiam Castle
Ewhurst Green
Northiam
Rother Levels
Rye Foreign
Burwash
Bateman's
Salehurst
Robertsbridge
Staple Cross
Millcorner
Beckley
Clayhill
Peasmarsh
Broad Oak
Heathfield
Burwash Common
Burwash Weald
Cade St
R Dudwell
Darwell Reservoir
Brightling
Punnett's Town
Three Cups Corner
Wood's Corner
Mountfield
Cock Marling
Maynard's Green
Dallington
Netherfield
Whatlington
Broadland Row
Udimore
Rushlake Green
Sedlescombe
Brede
River Brede
Winchelsea
Camber Castle

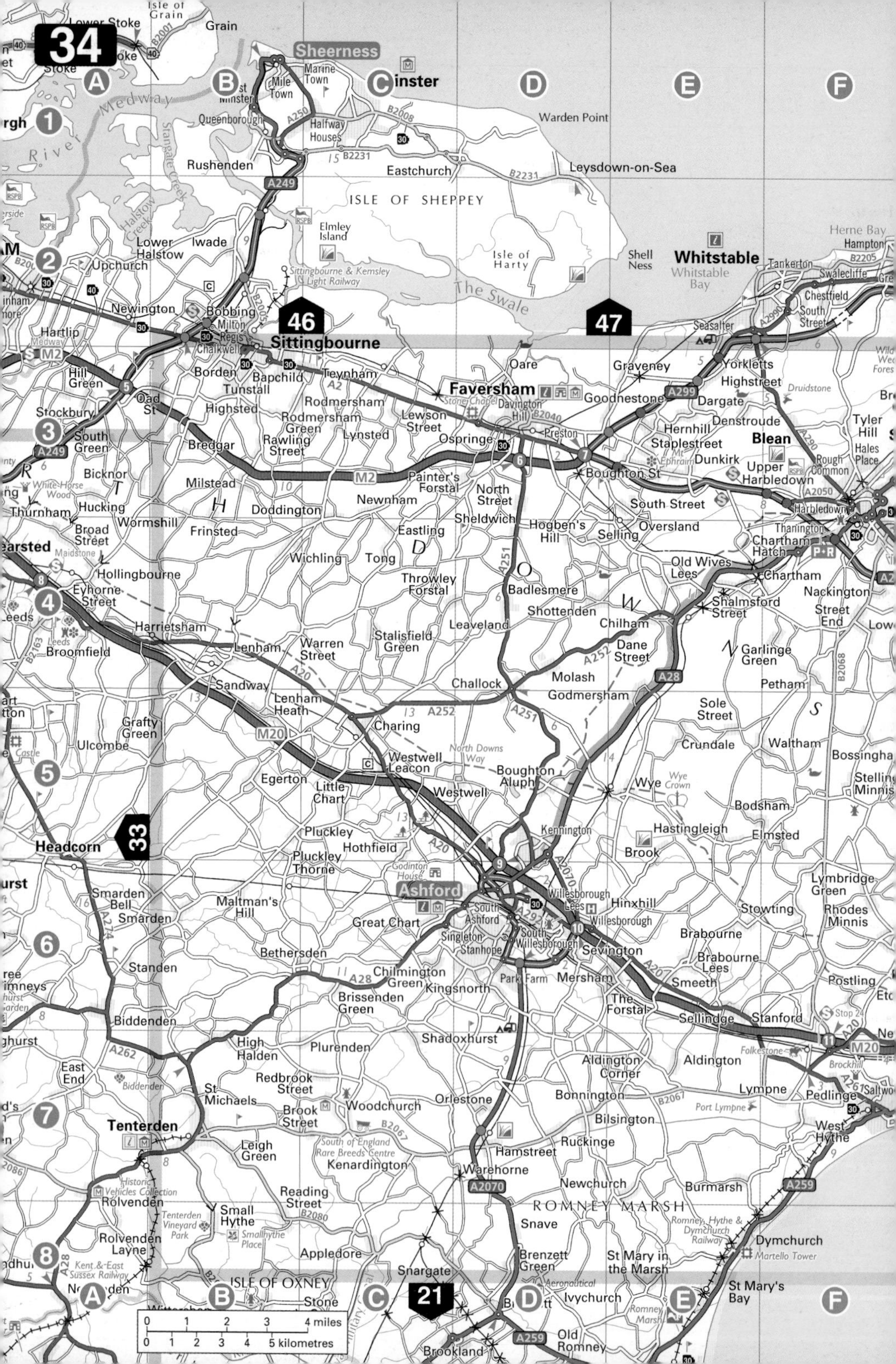
34
Isle of Grain
Grain
Lower Stoke
Stoke
River Medway
Sheerness
Marine Town
Mile Town
Minster
Queenborough
Halfway Houses
Warden Point
Eastchurch
Leysdown-on-Sea
Rushenden
ISLE OF SHEPPEY
Elmley Island
Isle of Harty
Shell Ness
Whitstable
Whitstable Bay
Herne Bay
Hampton
Tankerton
Swalecliffe
Chestfield
South Street
The Swale
Stangate Creek
Halstow Creek
Lower Halstow
Iwade
Upchurch
Sittingbourne & Kemsley Light Railway
Newington
Bobbing
Milton Regis
Chalkwell
Sittingbourne
46
47
Seasalter
Hartlip
Hill Green
Borden
Bapchild
Teynham
Tunstall
Oad St
Stockbury
South Green
Highsted
Rodmersham
Rodmersham Green
Bredgar
Rawling Street
Lynsted
Lewson Street
Faversham
Stone Chapel
Davington Hill
Oare
Graveney
Goodnestone
Yorkletts
Highstreet
Dargate
Druidstone
Preston
Ospringe
Hernhill
Denstroude
Staplestreet
Blean
Tyler Hill
Hales Place
Mt Ephraim
Dunkirk
Upper Harbledown
Rough Common
Boughton St
Painter's Forstal
North Street
Bicknor
Milstead
Newnham
South Street
Harbledown
Thurnham
White Horse Wood
Hucking
Broad Street
Wormshill
Frinsted
Doddington
Sheldwich
Hogben's Hill
Selling
Oversland
Thanington
Chartham Hatch
Bearsted
Maidstone
Hollingbourne
Eastling
Wichling
Tong
Throwley Forstal
Badlesmere
Old Wives Lees
Chartham
Nackington
Eyhorne Street
Leeds
Shottenden
Chilham
Shalmsford Street
Street End
Harrietsham
Leaveland
Stalisfield Green
Warren Street
Lenham
Dane Street
Garlinge Green
Broomfield
Molash
Challock
Godmersham
Petham
Sandway
Lenham Heath
Charing
Sole Street
Grafty Green
Ulcombe
North Downs Way
Westwell Leacon
Crundale
Waltham
Bossingham
Egerton
Little Chart
Boughton Aluph
Westwell
Wye
Wye Crown
Stelling Minnis
Bodsham
Headcorn
33
Pluckley
Hothfield
Kennington
Hastingleigh
Brook
Elmsted
Pluckley Thorne
Godinton House
Ashford
Willesborough Lees
Hinxhill
Lymbridge Green
Smarden Bell
Smarden
Maltman's Hill
South Ashford
Great Chart
Willesborough
Stowting
Rhodes Minnis
Singleton
Stanhope
South Willesborough
Sevington
Brabourne
Bethersden
Standen
Chilmington Green
Kingsnorth
Park Farm
Mersham
Brabourne Lees
Smeeth
Postling
Brissenden Green
The Forstal
Sellindge
Stanford
Stop 24
Biddenden
Shadoxhurst
High Halden
Plurenden
Aldington Corner
Aldington
Folkestone
Brockhill
East End
Redbrook Street
St Michaels
Orlestone
Bonnington
Lympne
Pedlinge
Saltwood
Port Lympne
Tenterden
Brook Street
Woodchurch
Bilsington
West Hythe
Leigh Green
South of England Rare Breeds Centre
Hamstreet
Ruckinge
Kenardington
Warehorne
Newchurch
Burmarsh
Rolvenden
Historic Vehicles Collection
Reading Street
ROMNEY MARSH
Small Hythe
Tenterden Vineyard Park
Smallhythe Place
Snave
Romney, Hythe & Dymchurch Railway
Dymchurch
Rolvenden Layne
Appledore
Brenzett Green
St Mary in the Marsh
Martello Tower
Kent & East Sussex Railway
Snargate
ISLE OF OXNEY
Aeronautical
Ivychurch
St Mary's Bay
Stone
21
Old Romney
Brookland
0 1 2 3 4 miles
0 1 2 3 4 5 kilometres
A
B
C
D
E
F
1
2
3
4
5
6
7
8

MARGATE
Foreness Point
Cliftonville
Kingsgate
Westgate on Sea
Westbrook
Northdown
NORTH FORELAND
Minnis Bay
Reading Street
Lighthouse
Herne Bay
Reculver Towers
Reculver
Bishopstone
Birchington
Garlinge
Salmestone Grange
Beltinge
ISLE OF THANET
Lydden
Westwood
St Peter's
Broadstairs
Broomfield
Herne
St Nicholas at Wade
Acol
RAF Manston
Manston
Dumpton
Boyden Gate
Sarre
Monkton
Kent International
Hereson
Chislet
Durlock
St Lawrence
Ramsgate
Hoath
Upstreet
West Stourmouth
Minster
St Augustine's Cross
Viking Ship 'Hugin'
Pegwell
Pegwell Bay
Hersden
R Stour
East Stourmouth
Westmarsh
Oostende
Westbere
Stodmarsh
Preston
Elmstone
Cop Street
Hoaden
Richborough Roman Fort
Prince's
Sandwich Bay
Old Town Hall
Wickhambreaux
Littlebourne
Seaton
Ickham
Ash
Sandwich
Royal St George's
Durlock
Wingham
Marshborough
Stone Cross
Toll
Howletts
Bramling
Staple
Woodnesborough
Bekesbourne
Statenborough
Worth
Goodnestone
Eastry
Patrixbourne
Ham
Hacklinge
Adisham
Ratling
Chillenden
Finglesham
Higham Park
Aylesham
Nonington
Sholden
The Downs
Castle
North Downs Way
Betteshanger
Northbourne
Deal
Kingston
Tilmanstone
Great Mongeham
Upper Deal
Womenswold
Elvington
Elham Valley
Barham
Lower Eythorne
Ripple
Walmer
Castle
Barfrestone
Eythorne
Sutton
Woolage Green
East Studdal
Ringwould
East Kent Railway
Shepherdswell
Ashley
Sutton Downs
Kingsdown
North Downs Way
West Langdon
Martin
Denton
Coldred
Lydden
East Langdon
Wootton
Lydden
Whitfield
Guston
St Margaret's at Cliffe
St Margaret's Bay
Selsted
Temple Ewell
Ewell Minnis
Kearsney
River
West Cliffe
Pines
SOUTH FORELAND
Swingfield Minnis
Swingfield Street
Lighthouse
South Foreland Heritage Coast
Butterfly Centre
Buckland
Castle
Gateway to the White Cliffs
Alkham
St Radigund's
Densole
South Alkham
Maxton
Upper Standen
Drellingore
Hawkinge
West Hougham
Dunkerque Calais
DOVER
Lower Standen
Channel Tunnel Terminal
Battle of Britain
Capel-le-Ferne
Samphire Hoe
Dover - Folkestone Heritage Coast
Channel Tunnel (Rail)
Cheriton
Morehall
East Wear Bay
STRAIT OF DOVER
FOLKESTONE
Sandgate
Seabrook
Hythe

36
52
51
Rhydyfro
Craig Llangiwg
Cilybebyll
Gellinudd
Alltwen
Mynydd March Hywel
Crynant
Fynydd
Blaengwrach
Rhigos
Hirwaun
Penywaun
Cwmdare
Llwydcoed
Aber-nant
Trecynon
Aberdare (Aberdâr)
Aberaman
Cwmaman
Abercwmboi
Vale of Neath
River Neath
River Dulais
Resolven
Melin Cwrt Waterfalls
RESOLVEN MOUNTAIN
CRAIG-Y-LLYN
Mynydd Ystradffernol
Blaenrhondda
Glais
Bryn-côch
Cilfrew
Cadoxton Juxta-Neath
Aberdulais Falls
Aberdulais
Clyne
MOEL-YR HYRDDAD
Birchgrove
Llansamlet
Tonna
Cefn Mawr
Glyncorrwg
Treherbert
Maerdy
Neath (Castell-nedd)
Cefn Morfydd
Afan Forest Park
Blaengwynfi
Rhondda Valley
Treorchy
Ferndale
Winshwen
Skewen
Cimla
Tonmawr
Abercregan
Cynonville
Duffryn
Cymer
Abergwynfi
Cwmparc
Pentre
Ystrad
Pentre-chwyth
Crymlyn Bog
Efail-fach
Pont-rhyd-y-fen
Afan Argoed
Croeserw
Caerau
MYNYDD CAERAU
WERFA
Tylorstown
Briton Ferry
FOEL MYNYDDAU
MOEL TRAWSNANT
Nant-y-moel
Clydach Vale
Llwynypia
Trealaw
Pwll-y-glaw
National Waterfront
Baglan
Blaengarw
Mynydd Llangeinwyr
Cwmafan
Bryn
Pontycymer
Garw Fechan Woodland Park
Tonypandy
Penygraig
Maesteg
Glanllynfi
Aberavon
Port Talbot
Swansea Bay
Mynydd Margam
Cwmfelin
Ogmore Vale
Gilfach Goch
Taibach
Llangynwyd
Lewistown
Margam
Stones Museum
MOEL TON-MAWR
Margam Park
Llangeinor
Betws
Blackmill
Bryngarw
Coytrahen
Brynmenyn
Mynydd Maendy
Tondu
Heol-y-Cyw
Brynna Woods
Afon Kenfig
Cefn Cribwr
Aberkenfig
Sarn Park
Pant-ffrwyth
Brynna
Llanharan
Pyle
Pencoed
Mawdlam
North Cornelly
Bridgend (Pen-y-Bont-ar-Ogwr)
Castle
Coity
Llanilid
Llanharry
Dragon International Studios
Brynsadler
Kenfig
South Cornelly
Laleston
Coychurch
Rest Bay
NEWTON DOWN
Tythegston
Nottage
Merthyr Mawr
Treoes
Llangan
Newton
Corntown
Ewenny
Ystradowen
Trerhyngyll
Porthcawl
Porthcawl Point
Ogmore
St Bride's Major
Penllyn
Maendy
Ogmore-by-Sea
Colwinston
Pentre Meyrick
St Quentin's Castle
Aberthin
Cowbridge
Llysworney
Southerndown
Llandow
Llanblethian
Llandough
St Hilary
Old Beaupre
Wick
Sigingstone
St Mary Church
Broughton
Flemingston
Monknash
Llanmaes
Marcross
St Donats
St Athan
Nash Point
Llantwit Major
Gileston
Glamorgan Heritage Coast
Limpert Bay
A B C D E F
1 2 3 4 5 6 7 8
0 1 2 3 4 miles
0 1 2 3 4 5 kilometres

Merthyr Tydfil
(Merthyr Tudful)
Pentrebach
Troedyrhiw
New Tredegar
Tirphil
Deri
Bedlinog
Brithdir
Cwmfelin
Aberfan
Merthyr Vale
Bargoed
(Bargod)
Manmoel
Markham
Bedwellty
Argoed
Cwmtillery
Abertillery
(Abertyleri)
Llanhilleth
Garnclochdy
Penperlleni
Kemeys
Monkswood
Pontypool
(Pont-y-Pŵl)
Llandegfedd Reservoir
Usk
Llanbadoc
Llanllowell
Griffithstown
New Inn
Coed-y-paen
Llangybi
Llantrisant
Oakdale
Crumlin
Penmaen
Blackwood
Pontllanfraith
Pengam
Newbridge
Mynydd Maen
Treharris
Gelligaer
Trelewis
Nelson
Hengoed
Maesycwmmer
Pentwynmawr
Greenmeadow Community Farm
Pontnewydd
Forge Hammer
Croesyceiliog
Llandegveth
Tredunnock
Abercarn
Cwmcarn
Cwmcarn Forest Drive
Cwmbran
(Cwmbrân)
Llantarnam
Llanfrechfa
Llanhennock
Ponthir
Ynysboeth
Abercynon
Ynysybwl
Ystrad Mynach
Ynysddu
Pontywaun
Crosskeys
Mynydd Eglwysilan
Senghenydd
Cwmfelinfach
Wattsville
Risca
Henllys
Malpas
Caerleon
Celtic Manor
Bettws
Llanbradach
Bedwas
Machen
Cilfynydd
Rhondda Heritage Park
Trehafod
Pontypridd
Abertridwr
Trefforest
Lower Machen
Rogerstone
Rhiwderyn
Bassaleg
Cefn
Maindee
Christchurch
Liswerry
Llanwern
Pen-y-coedcae
Llantwit Fardre
Groes-Wen
Caerphilly
(Caerffili)
Rudry
Draethen
Newport
(Casnewydd-ar-Wysg)
Beddau
Church Village
Tyn-y-nant
Efail Isaf
Michaelstone-y-Fedw
Tredegar
Nash
Goldcliff
Solutia
Llantrisant
Park Cefn Onn
Castell Coch
Taff's Well
Tongwynlais
Lisvane
Cardiff Gate
Castleton
Marshfield
Rhiwbina
Llanishen
Llanedeyrn
St Mellons
St Brides Wentlooge
Creigiau
Pentyrch
Groes-faen
Miskin
Radyr
Whitchurch
Birchgrove
Llanrumney
Rumney
Peterstone Wentlooge
Cardiff West
Clawdd-coch
St Fagans
Llandaff
Roath
Pengam
St Brides super-Ely
National History
Fairwater
Canton
Splottlands
Pendoylan
Peterston-super-Ely
St George's
Ely
Caerau
Cardiff
(Caerdydd)
Severn Estuary
St Nicholas
Bonvilston
Tinkinswood
Michaelston-le-Pit
Llandough
Penarth Head
Llantrithyd
St Lythans
Wenvoe
Burial Chamber
St Andrew's Major
Cogan
Penarth
Dinas Powys
Lower Penarth
Moulton
Penmark
Cadoxton
Cosmeston Lakes & Medieval Village
Lavernock
Lavernock Point
Sully
Barry
(Y Barri)
Rhoose
Porthkerry
Cold Knap Point
Barry Island
Sully Island
Flat Holm
Steep Holm
Clevedon
Woodspring Bay
Sand Point
Wick St Lawrence
Sand Bay
Kewstoke
West Hewish
St Georges
Worle
Milton
Toll
Ashcombe
Weston-super-Mare
Locking
Hutton
Brean Down
Tropical Bird Garden
Uphill
Oldmixon
Walborough
Bleadon
Brean
Loxton
Lympsham
Edingworth
Biddisham
53
25
38

38
Kemeys Commander
Kingcoed
Trellech
Harold's Stones
St Briavels
Bream
Allaston
Llandenny
Wye Valley
Llandogo
Lydney
Monkswood
Llanishen
Llansoy
Forest Park
Offa's Dyke Path
Hewelsfield
Aylburton
Usk
Gwernesney
Brockweir
Woolaston Common
Alvington
Gwent Rural Life
Pentre
Tintern Parva
Tintern Abbey
Llanbadoc
Llangwm
Wolvesnewton
Chapel Hill
Netherend
Llanllowell
Springdale Farm
Kilgwrrwg Common
Devauden
54
Woolaston
Coed-y-paen
Newchurch
Stroat
Llangybi
Llantrisant
Gaerllwyd
Itton Common
St Arvans
Tidenham
Woodcroft
Itton
Tutshill
Tredunnock
Mynydd-bach
Sedbury
Llanfrechfa
Llanhennock
Llanvair Discoed
Mounton
Shirenewton
Pwllmeyric
Chepstow
(Cas-Gwent)
River Severn
Oldbury-on-Severn
Rockhampton
Lower Morton
Hill
Caerleon
Parc Seymour
Llanvaches
Runston Chapel
Newton Green
Caerwent
Bulwark
Cowhill
Kington
Whitfield
Llanbeder
Penhow
Celtic Manor
Llandevaud
St Pierre
Mathern
M48
Severn Bridge
Littleton-on-Severn
Severn View
Milbury Heath
Thornbury
Christchurch
Llanmartin
Bishton
Roman Town
Caldicot
(Cil-y-coed)
Magor
Llanfihangel Rogiet
Ifton
Portskewett
Aust
Elberton
Alveston
Llanwern
Liswerry
Rogiet
Toll
Sudbrook
Ingst
Olveston
Rudgeway
NEWPORT
(CASNEWYDD-AR-WYSG)
Llandevenny
Magor
Undy
M4
Redwick
Tockington
Second Severn Crossing
Magor Marsh
Pilning
Almondsbury
Severn Beach
Latteridge
Nash
Goldcliff
Whitson
Redwick
Iron Acton
Easter Compton
Compton Greenfield
Frampton Cotterell
SEVERN ESTUARY
Patchway
Bradley Stoke
Great Stoke
Winterbourne
Hallen
Cribbs Causeway
A403
M49
Blaise
Filton
Stoke Gifford
Battery Point
Avonmouth
Kings Weston
Westbury-on-Trym
Frenchay
Downend
37
Shirehampton
Horfield
Portishead
Mangotsfield
Gordano
BRISTOL
Weston-in-Gordano
Clapton-in-Gordano
Portbury
Easton-in-Gordano
Abbots Leigh
Redland
Fishponds
Eastville
Soundwell
Walton-in-Gordano
Clifton
Warmley
Noah's Ark
Lower Failand
Walton Park
Clevedon Court
Failand
Leigh Woods
Kingswood
Hanham
Cadbury Camp
Tyntesfield
Ashton Court
Oldland
Clevedon
Tickenham
Wraxall
Bedminster
Nailsea
Long Ashton
Knowle
Brislington
Flax Bourton
Bedminster Down
Stockwood
Kenn
West End
Chelvey
Farleigh
Backwell
Bishopsworth
Keynsham
Woodspring Bay
Kingston Seymour
West Town
Barrow Gurney
Withywood
Queen Charlton
Wick St Lawrence
Claverham
Brockley
Dundry
East Dundry
Maes Knoll
Whitchurch
Chewton Keynsham
Lulsgate Bottom
Upper Town
Maiden Head
Norton Malreward
Yatton
Cleeve
Felton
Bristol
Winford
Norton Hawkfield
Kewstoke
West Hewish
Congresbury
St Georges
Worle
Puxton
Redhill
Belluton
Publow
Compton Dando
Chew Magna
Wrington
Regil
Stanton Drew
Pensford
Hunstrete
Stone Circle
Ashcombe
Stock
Blackmoor
Butcombe
Chew Stoke
Stanton Wick
Chelwood
Cowslip Green
Havyat
Blagdon Lake
Chew Valley Lake
Locking
Stonebridge
Sandford
Churchill
Lower Langford
Nempnett Thrubwell
Bishop Sutton
Stowey
Clutton Hill
Farmborough
Hutton
Rickford
Banwell
Upper Langford
Burrington
Blagdon
North Widcombe
Clutton
Timsbury
Oldmixon
Bleadon Hills
Star
Rowberrow
Sutton Wick
High Littleton
Yarborough
Sidcot
Ubley
West Harptree
Temple Cloud
Winscombe
Shipham
Compton Martin
South Widcombe
Cameley
Hallatrow
Bleadon
Christon
Hinton Blewett
Loxton
Compton Bishop
King John's Hunting Lodge
26
Farrington Gurney
Charterhouse
East Harptree
Cheddar Caves & Gorge
Ubley Warren
Sherborne
Litton
Midsomer Norton
Bidd
Weare
Edingworth
0 1 2 3 4 miles
0 1 2 3 4 5 kilometres

Stonehouse
Ebley
Eastington
Cambridge
Slimbridge
Purton
Wildfowl & Wetlands Trust
Frocester
King's Stanley
Leonard Stanley
Chalford
Frampton
Coaley
Gossington
Nympsfield
Woodchester Park
St Chloe
Brimscombe
Amberley
Burleigh
Windsoredge
Box
Minchinhampton
Coates
Tarlton
Chesterton
Amphitheatre
Siddington
Wanswell
Cam
Nympsfield
Uley Long Barrow
Nailsworth
55
Cherington
Stinchcombe
Uley
Downend
Avening
Rodmarton
Newport
Dursley
Woodmancote
Owlpen Manor
Horsley
Barton End
Ewen
Kemble
South Cerney
Kingscote
Tiltups End
Windmill Tump Long Barrow
Tyndale
North Nibley
Michaelwood
Culkerton
Chavenage
Poole Keynes
Ashton Keynes
Wotton-under-Edge
Coombe
Beverston
Ashley
Tetbury
Crudwell
Oaksey
Lower Moor Farm
Tortworth
Newark Park
Charfield
Kingswood
Abbey Gatehouse
Tresham
Leighterton
Long Newnton
Upper Minety
Minety
Westonbirt
Shipton Moyne
Hankerton
Cloatley
Alderley
Hillesley
Willesley
Westonbirt
Brokenborough
Perry Green
Wickwar
Hawkesbury
Oldbury on the Hill
Malmesbury
Charlton
Lower Woods
Knockdown
Garsdon
Hawkesbury Upton
Didmarton
Easton Grey
Milbourne
Bagstone
Hawkesbury
Sopworth
Sherston
Lea
Cleverton
Rangeworthy
Dunkirk
Horton Court
Engine Common
Horton
Little Badminton
Norton
Luckington
Corston
Little Somerford
Brinkworth
Badminton
Rodbourne
Great Somerford
Little Sodbury
Great Badminton
Alderton
Hullavington
Startley
Dauntsey
Yate
Chipping Sodbury
Old Sodbury
Lower Stanton St Quintin
Littleton Drew
Stanton St Quintin
Upper Seagry
Lower Seagry
Westerleigh
Dodington
Acton Turville
Grittleton
Leigh Delamere
Cotswold Way
Tormarton
Burton
M4
Bradenstoke
Codrington
Nettleton
Christian Malford
Sutton Benger
Hinton
West Kington
Castle Combe
Kington St Michael
Kington Langley
Catcomb
Pucklechurch
Dyrham Park
Dyrham
West Littleton
Yatton Keynell
Langley Burrell
Charlcutt
Abson
North Wraxall
Ford
Allington
Hardenhuish
East Tytherton
Doynton
Upper Wraxall
Slaughterford
Tytherton Lucas
Chippenham
Bremhill
Wick
Marshfield
Biddestone
Compton Bassett
Thickwood
Cold Ashton
Sir Bevil Grenville's Monument 1643
Studley
Colerne
Corsham Court
Calne
Upton Cheyney
Rudloe
Easton
Derry Hill
North Stoke
Ditteridge
Lackham
Bowood
Notton
Corsham
Langridge
Swainswick
Middlehill
Gastard
Sandy Lane
Woolley
Box
Neston
Lacock Abbey
Fox Talbot Museum
Lacock
Batheaston
Ashley
Beckford's Tower
Bowden Hill
Chittoe
Stockley
Kelston
Weston
Charlcombe
Kingsdown
Toll
Bathford
Whitley
Beanacre
Heddington
BATH
Monkton Farleigh
Atworth
Bathampton
Shaw
Bishops Cannings
Newton St Loe
Claverton
Bromham
White Horse
Twerton
South Wraxall
Great Chalfield Manor
Melksham
Prior Park
Great Chalfield
Broughton Gifford
Rowde
Roundway
Englishcombe
Combe Down
Monkton Combe
Sells Green
Dundas
Bradford-on-Avon
Bradford Leigh
Odd Down
Inglesbatch
Limpley Stoke
Winsley
Holt
Whaddon
Seend Cleeve
Seend
Devizes
The Courts Garden
South Stoke
Semington
Priston
Tithe Barn
Staverton
Midford
Great Hinton
Dunkerton
Combe Hay
Freshford
Turleigh
The Strand
Poulshot
Westwood
Hilperton
Bulkington
Hinton Charterhouse
Westwood Manor
Potterne
Potterne Wick
Ashton Common
Carlingcott
Wellow
Keevil
Worton
Castle
A366
Trowbridge
Stoney Littleton Long Barrow
Norton St Philip
Farleigh Hungerford
Wingfield
Steeple Ashton
Marston
Urchfont
27
Radstock
Foxcote
Tellisford
West Ashton
Great Cheverell
Littleton Pannell
Southwick
North Bradley
Yarnbrook
Coulston
Writhlington
Faulkland
Woolverton
Heywood
40

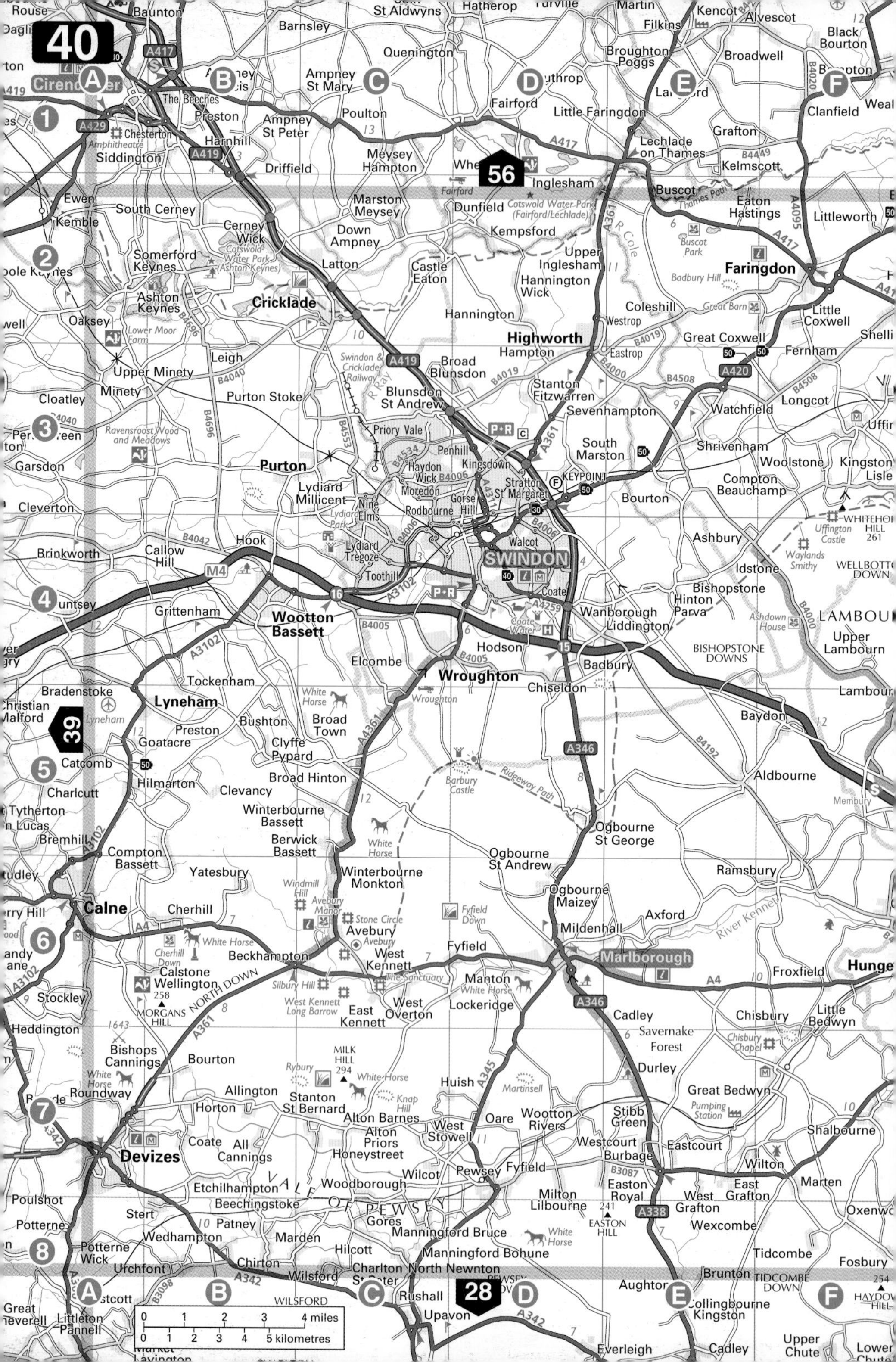
40
Rouse
Baunton
St Aldwyns
Hatherop
Martin
Kencot
Alvescot
Barnsley
Filkins
Black Bourton
A417
Quenington
Broughton Poggs
Broadwell
Cirencester
Ampney Crucis
Ampney St Mary
Southrop
Langford
Bampton
A419
The Beeches
Poulton
Fairford
Little Faringdon
Clanfield
A429
Chesterton
Amphitheatre
Preston
Ampney St Peter
Grafton
Siddington
Harnhill
Meysey Hampton
Lechlade on Thames
Driffield
56
Kelmscott
Inglesham
Buscot
Thames Path
Fairford
Ewen
South Cerney
Marston Meysey
Dunfield
Cotswold Water Park (Fairford/Lechlade)
Eaton Hastings
Littleworth
Kemble
Cerney Wick
Kempsford
Down Ampney
Buscot Park
Somerford Keynes
Cotswold Water Park (Ashton Keynes)
Upper Inglesham
Poole Keynes
Latton
Castle Eaton
Hannington Wick
Faringdon
Ashton Keynes
Cricklade
Badbury Hill
Coleshill
Great Barn
Little Coxwell
Oaksey
Hannington
Westrop
Lower Moor Farm
Swindon & Cricklade Railway
Highworth
Great Coxwell
Fernham
Leigh
Hampton
Eastrop
Upper Minety
Broad Blunsdon
Stanton Fitzwarren
Watchfield
Longcot
Minety
Purton Stoke
Blunsdon St Andrew
Sevenhampton
Cloatley
Priory Vale
South Marston
Shrivenham
Woolstone
Kingston Lisle
Ravensroost Wood and Meadows
Penhill
Haydon Wick
Kingsdown
Garsdon
Purton
Moredon
Stratton St Margaret
Keypoint
Bourton
Compton Beauchamp
Lydiard Millicent
Nine Elms
Rodbourne
Gorse Hill
Cleverton
Lydiard Park
Walcot
Ashbury
Whitehorse Hill 261
Uffington Castle
Hook
Lydiard Tregoze
Swindon
Waylands Smithy
Brinkworth
Callow Hill
Toothill
Idstone
Wellbottom Down
M4
Coate
Bishopstone
Hinton Parva
Grittenham
Wootton Bassett
Wanborough
Liddington
Ashdown House
Lambourn
Upper Lambourn
Elcombe
Hodson
Coate Water
Bishopstone Downs
Badbury
Bradenstoke
Tockenham
Wroughton
Chiseldon
Christian Malford
Lyneham
White Horse
Lambourn
39
Bushton
Broad Town
Baydon
Preston
Goatacre
Clyffe Pypard
Catcomb
Broad Hinton
Barbury Castle
Ridgeway Path
Aldbourne
Charlcutt
Hilmarton
Clevancy
Membury
Tytherton Lucas
Winterbourne Bassett
Ogbourne St George
Bremhill
Berwick Bassett
Compton Bassett
Ogbourne St Andrew
Yatesbury
Winterbourne Monkton
Ramsbury
Windmill Hill
Avebury Manor
Ogbourne Maizey
Calne
Cherhill
Fyfield Down
Axford
Stone Circle
Avebury
Mildenhall
River Kennet
White Horse
Cherhill Down
Beckhampton
West Kennett
Fyfield
Marlborough
Sandy Lane
Calstone Wellington
Silbury Hill
The Sanctuary
Manton
Froxfield
Hungerford
Stockley
258 Morgans Hill
North Down
West Kennett Long Barrow
East Kennett
West Overton
Lockeridge
Cadley
Chisbury
Little Bedwyn
Heddington
Savernake Forest
Chisbury Chapel
Bishops Cannings
Milk Hill 294
Bourton
Rybury
Durley
Huish
Martinsell
Roundway
Allington
Stanton St Bernard
Knap Hill
Great Bedwyn
Horton
Alton Barnes
Oare
Wootton Rivers
Stibb Green
Pumping Station
Devizes
Coate
All Cannings
Alton Priors
Honeystreet
West Stowell
Westcourt
Burbage
Eastcourt
Shalbourne
Wilcot
Pewsey
Fyfield
Wilton
Poulshot
Etchilhampton
Vale of Pewsey
Woodborough
Milton Lilbourne
Easton Royal
East Grafton
Marten
Beechingstoke
West Grafton
Oxenwood
Stert
Patney
Gores
Manningford Bruce
241 Easton Hill
Wexcombe
Potterne
Wedhampton
Marden
Hilcott
Manningford Bohune
Tidcombe
Potterne Wick
Urchfont
Chirton
Charlton St Peter
North Newnton
Fosbury
Wilsford
Brunton
Tidcombe Down
254 Haydown Hill
Eastcott
Rushall
28
Pewsey Down
Aughton
Collingbourne Kingston
Great Cheverell
Littleton Pannell
Wilsford
Upavon
Everleigh
Cadley
Upper Chute
Lower Chute
Market Lavington
0 1 2 3 4 miles
0 1 2 3 4 5 kilometres

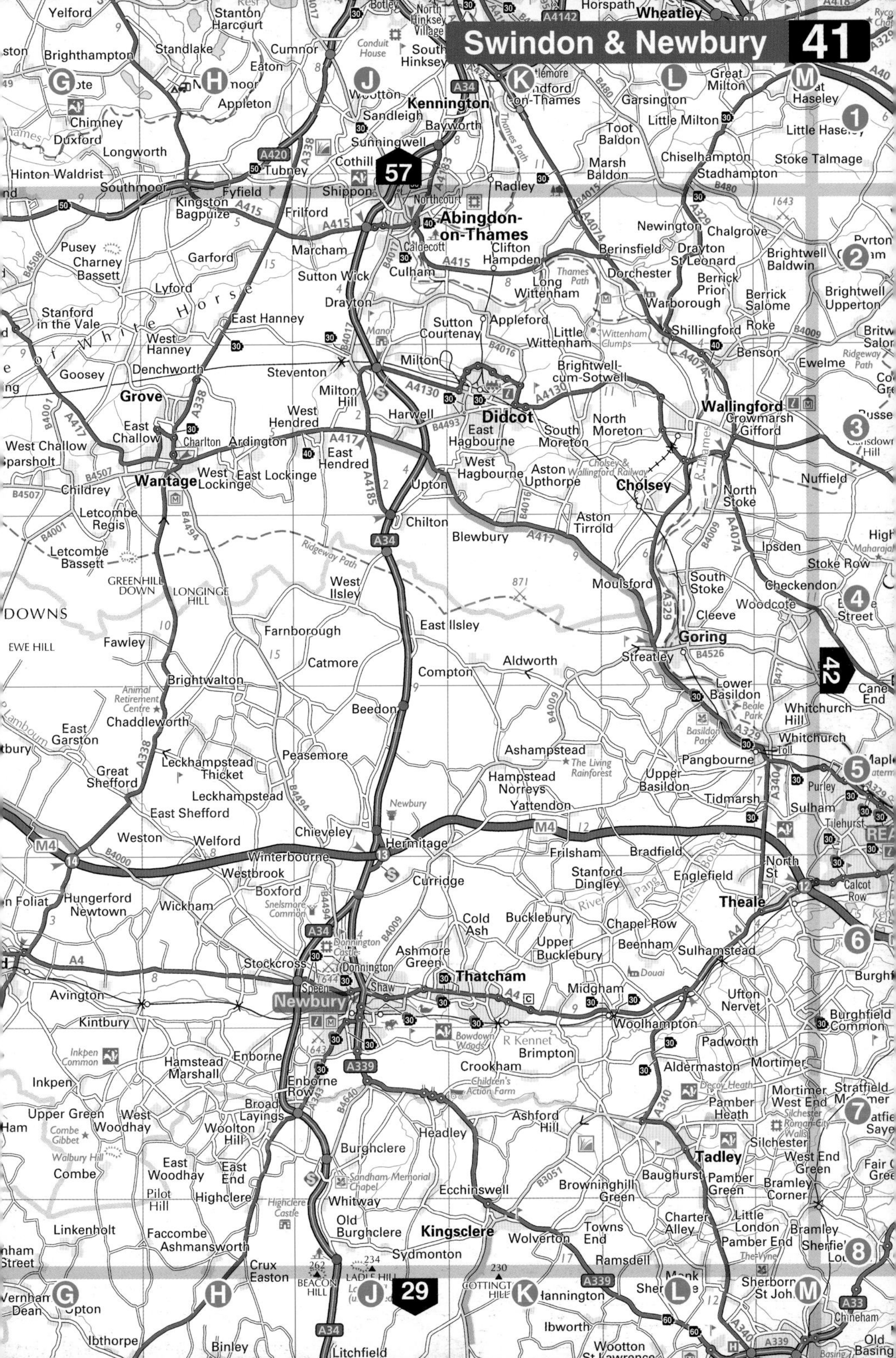
Yelford
Stanton Harcourt
Standlake
Cumnor
Eaton
Botley
North Hinksey Village
South Hinksey
Conduit House
Horspath
Wheatley
Brighthampton
Appleton
Wootton
Sandleigh
Kennington
Bayworth
Sunningwell
Cothill
Shippon
Sandford-on-Thames
Garsington
Great Milton
Great Haseley
Little Milton
Little Haseley
Toot Baldon
Marsh Baldon
Chiselhampton
Stadhampton
Stoke Talmage
Chimney
Duxford
Longworth
Hinton Waldrist
Tubney
Southmoor
Fyfield
Kingston Bagpuize
Frilford
Radley
Northcourt
Abingdon-on-Thames
Caldecott
Culham
Clifton Hampden
Newington
Chalgrove
Berinsfield
Drayton St Leonard
Brightwell Baldwin
Dorchester
Berrick Prior
Berrick Salome
Brightwell Upperton
Warborough
Shillingford
Roke
Benson
Ewelme
Pusey
Charney Bassett
Garford
Marcham
Sutton Wick
Lyford
Drayton
Long Wittenham
Little Wittenham
Wittenham Clumps
Sutton Courtenay
Appleford
Stanford in the Vale
East Hanney
West Hanney
Goosey
Denchworth
Steventon
Milton
Milton Hill
Brightwell-cum-Sotwell
Grove
East Challow
West Challow
Sparsholt
Charlton
Ardington
West Hendred
East Hendred
Harwell
Didcot
East Hagbourne
West Hagbourne
South Moreton
North Moreton
Wallingford
Crowmarsh Gifford
Wantage
West Lockinge
East Lockinge
Upton
Aston Upthorpe
Cholsey & Wallingford Railway
Cholsey
North Stoke
Nuffield
Childrey
Letcombe Regis
Letcombe Bassett
Chilton
Blewbury
Aston Tirrold
Ipsden
Ridgeway Path
Greenhill Down
Longinge Hill
Downs
Ewe Hill
West Ilsley
East Ilsley
Moulsford
South Stoke
Checkendon
Woodcote
Stoke Row
Cleeve
Goring
Streatley
Farnborough
Catmore
Compton
Aldworth
Fawley
Brightwalton
Lower Basildon
Beale Park
Basildon Park
Whitchurch Hill
Whitchurch
Cane End
Animal Retirement Centre
Chaddleworth
East Garston
Beedon
Ashampstead
The Living Rainforest
Pangbourne
Purley
Great Shefford
Leckhampstead Thicket
Leckhampstead
Peasemore
Hampstead Norreys
Upper Basildon
Tidmarsh
Sulham
Tilehurst
East Shefford
Weston
Welford
Chieveley
Newbury
Yattendon
Hermitage
Frilsham
Bradfield
Winterbourne
Westbrook
Curridge
Stanford Dingley
Englefield
North St
Theale
Calcot Row
Hungerford Newtown
Wickham
Boxford
Snelsmore Common
Cold Ash
Bucklebury
Chapel Row
Beenham
Sulhamstead
Upper Bucklebury
Donnington Castle
Donnington
Ashmore Green
Thatcham
Stockcross
Speen
Shaw
Midgham
Douai
Ufton Nervet
Burghfield
Avington
Kintbury
Newbury
Woolhampton
Burghfield Common
Bowdown Woods
R Kennet
Brimpton
Padworth
Inkpen Common
Hamstead Marshall
Enborne
Crookham
Aldermaston
Mortimer
Inkpen
Enborne Row
Children's Action Farm
Decoy Heath
Mortimer West End
Stratfield Mortimer
Upper Green
West Woodhay
Broad Layings
Woolton Hill
Headley
Ashford Hill
Pamber Heath
Silchester Roman City Walls
Combe Gibbet
Walbury Hill
Burghclere
Tadley
Silchester
West End Green
Combe
East Woodhay
East End
Sandham Memorial Chapel
Browninghill Green
Baughurst
Pamber Green
Bramley Corner
Pilot Hill
Highclere
Highclere Castle
Whitway
Ecchinswell
Linkenholt
Faccombe
Ashmansworth
Old Burghclere
Kingsclere
Wolverton
Towns End
Charter Alley
Little London
Pamber End
Bramley
Sherfield on Loddon
Sydmonton
Ramsdell
The Vyne
Crux Easton
Beacon Hill
Ladle Hill
Cottington Hill
Hannington
Monk Sherborne
Sherborne St John
Vernham Dean
Upton
Ibthorpe
Binley
Litchfield
Ibworth
Wootton St Lawrence
Chineham
Old Basing
57
42
29

42
A
B
C
D
E
F
1
2
3
4
5
6
7
8
Haseley
Little Haseley
Stoke Talmage
Moreton
Tetsworth
Emmington
Sydenham
Postcombe
Hent
Bledlow
Chinnor
Chinnor & Princes Risborough Railway
Crowell
Kingston Blount
Aston Rowant
LODGE HILL
Ilmer
Towersey
Longwick
Monks Risborough
Askett
Pitch Green
Princes Risborough
Whiteleaf
Saunderton
Great Hampden
Loosley Row
Lacey Green
Dunsmore
The Lee
Lee Clump
Prestwood
Great Missenden
Bellingdon
Asheridge
Chartridge
Ballinger Common
South Heath
Hyde Heath
Chesham Bois
58
Walter's Ash
Hughenden Valley
Little Kingshill
Great Kingshill
Little Missenden
Amersham
Amersham Old Town
Cryers Hill
Holmer Green
Widmer End
Hazlemere
Penn Street
Winchmore Hill
Coleshill
Radnage
The City
Bledlow Ridge
Bradenham
Naphill
Hughenden Manor
Beacon's Bottom
Hell Fire Caves
Downley
West Wycombe Park
HIGH WYCOMBE
Cressex
Booker
Wycombe Marsh
Loudwater
Penn
Bekonscot Model Village
Beaconsfield
South Weston
Lewknor
Pyrton
Cuxham
Shirburn
Watlington
Stokenchurch
Brightwell Baldwin
Berrick Salome
Brightwell Upperton
Roke
Benson
Britwell Salome
Ewelme
Ridgeway Path
Cookley Green
Ibstone
Cadmore End
Turville
Fingest
Lane End
Skirmett
Frieth
Flackwell Heath
Wooburn Green
Rare Breeds Centre
Bourne End
Wooburn
Hedgerley
Russell's Water
Pishill
Stonor Park
Park Corner
Stonor
Warburg
Gangsdown Hill
Nuffield
Nettlebed
Crocker End
Rockwell End
Marlow Bottom
Marlow
Little Marlow
Fawley
Hambleden
Mill End
Cookham
Hedsor
Egypt
Cliveden
Burnham Beeches
Highmoor
Maharajah's Well
Bix
Ipsden
Stoke Row
Checkendon
Highmoor Cross
Greys Court
Lower Assendon
Remenham
Aston
Medmenham
Bisham
Hurley
Cookham Dean
Cookham Rise
River & Rowing
Remenham Hill
Maidenhead
Taplow
Burnham
Farnham Royal
Greys Green
Rotherfield Greys
Henley-on-Thames
Cockpole Gn
Warren Row
Burchett's Green
North Town
Exlade Street
Rotherfield Peppard
Sonning Common
The Herb Farm
Lower Shiplake
Wargrave
Knowl Hill
Littlewick Green
Braywick
Bray
Dorney
Dorney Court
Cippenham
Eton Wick
Eton
Cane End
Kidmore End
Whitchurch
Beale Park
41
Tokers Green
Dunsden Green
Binfield Heath
Shiplake
Thames Path
Hare Hatch
Ruscombe
Waltham St Lawrence
White Waltham
Woodlands Park
Holyport
Fifield
Dedworth
Windsor
Mapledurham
Watermill
Purley
Sulham
Play Hatch
Charvil
Sonning
Twyford
Caversham
Paley Street
Shurlock Row
Legoland
Tilehurst
READING
Whistley Green
Woodley
Maiden's Green
Cranbourne
Great Park
North St
Calcot Row
Kennet & Avon
Whitley
Earley
Winnersh
Dinton Pastures
Hurst
Binfield
Warfield
Newell Green
Winkfield
Winkfield Row
Woodside
Guards Polo Club
Virginia Water
Reading
Sindlesham
Shinfield
Wokingham
North Ascot
Bullbrook
Ascot
Burghfield
Three Mile Cross
Arborfield
Great Hollands
BRACKNELL
Sunninghill
Sunningdale
Burghfield Common
Spencers Wood
Arborfield Cross
REME
Barkham
Gardeners Green
TOWER HILL
Swallowfield
Farley Hill
California
Wellingtonia Avenue
Look Out Discovery Centre
Mortimer
Mortimer West End
Stratfield Mortimer
Beech Hill
Riseley
Wellington
Finchampstead
Crowthorne
Wildmoor Heath
Bagshot
Windlesham
Lightwater
Silchester
Stratfield Saye
Blackwater R
Eversley
Eversley Cross
Owlsmoor
Sandhurst
West End
West End Green
Fair Oak Green
Stratfield Turgis
Heckfield
Hound Green
Yateley
College Town
York Town
CAMBERLEY
Bisley
Bramley Corner
Turgis Green
Blackwater
Blackbushe
Yateley Common
Royal Logistics Corps
Little London
Bramley
Hartley Wespall
Sherfield on Loddon
Mattingley
Hartfordbridge
Hawley
Frimley
Brookwood
Sherborne St John
Rotherwick
West Green
West Green House
Hartley Wintney
30
Farnborough Street
Elvetham Heath
Phoenix Green
Winchfield
Fleet
Cove
Farnborough Park
Farnborough
Mytchett
Pirbright
Chineham
Basing
0 1 2 3 4 miles
0 1 2 3 4 5 kilometres
M40
M4
M3
A40
A4010
A404
A4155
A4130
A329(M)
A404(M)
A33
A30
A322
A327

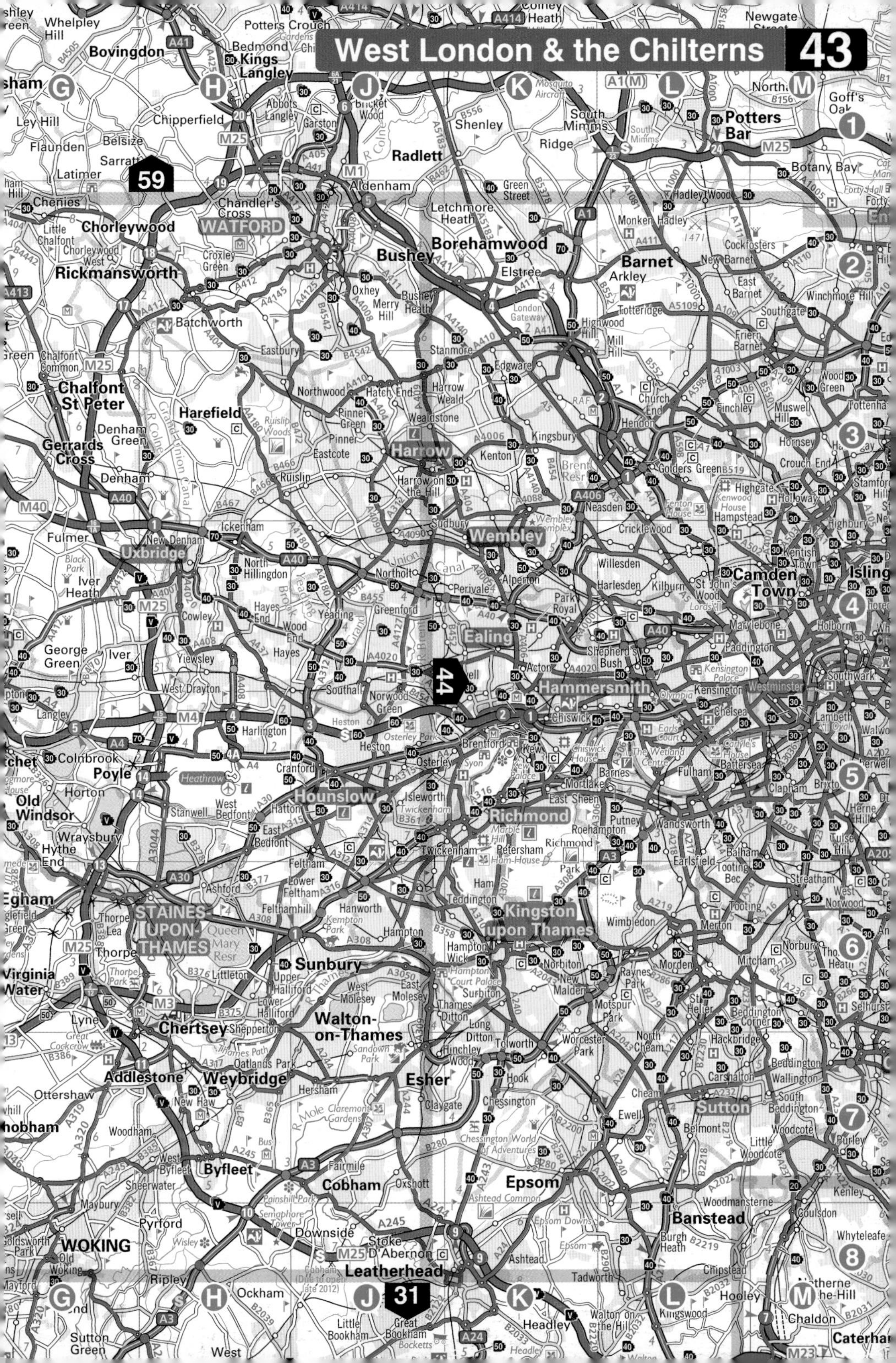
WATFORD
Bushey
Borehamwood
Barnet
Rickmansworth
Chorleywood
Chalfont St Peter
Gerrards Cross
Harefield
Uxbridge
Harrow
Wembley
Ealing
Hammersmith
Camden Town
Hounslow
Richmond
Kingston upon Thames
STAINES UPON-THAMES
Sunbury
Walton-on-Thames
Esher
Chertsey
Addlestone
Weybridge
Byfleet
Cobham
Epsom
Sutton
Banstead
WOKING
Leatherhead
Potters Bar
Radlett
Bovingdon
Kings Langley
59
44
31

44
59
43
31
Kings Langley
Colney
Park
Cuffley
Abbots Langley
Bricket Wood
Mosquito Aircraft
South Mimms
Potters Bar
Northaw
Chipperfield
Belsize
Sarratt
Latimer
Radlett
Ridge
Botany Bay
Chenies
Amersham Common
Chandler's Cross
Aldenham
Green Street
Hadley Wood
Little Chalfont
Chorleywood
WATFORD
Letchmore Heath
Monken Hadley
Chorleywood West
Croxley Green
Bushey
Borehamwood
Cockfosters
Rickmansworth
Oxhey
Merry Hill
Bushey Heath
Elstree
Barnet
Arkley
New Barnet
East Barnet
Batchworth
London Gateway
Totteridge
Highwood Hill
Mill Hill
Southgate
Friern Barnet
Chalfont St Giles
Seer Green
Chalfont Common
Eastbury
Stanmore
Edgware
Chalfont St Peter
Northwood
Hatch End
Harrow Weald
Church End
Finchley
Muswell Hill
Wood Green
Harefield
Pinner Green
Wealdstone
Hendon
Denham Green
Ruislip Woods
Pinner
Kingsbury
Hornsey
Gerrards Cross
Eastcote
Harrow
Kenton
Golders Green
Crouch End
Denham
Ruislip
Harrow on the Hill
Brent Resr
Highgate
Holloway
Neasden
Hampstead
Ickenham
Sudbury
Wembley
Cricklewood
Fulmer
New Denham
Uxbridge
North Hillingdon
Northolt
Willesden
Camden Town
Stoke Poges
Black Park
Iver Heath
Perivale
Alperton
Harlesden
Kilburn
St John's Wood
Hayes End
Yeading
Greenford
Park Royal
Cowley
Wood End
Ealing
Marylebone
Paddington
George Green
Iver
Yiewsley
Hayes
Shepherd's Bush
Acton
West Drayton
Southall
Hanwell
Kensington
Westminster
Upton
Norwood Green
Hammersmith
Chelsea
Langley
Harlington
Heston
Chiswick
Brentford
Kew
Datchet
Colnbrook
Cranford
Osterley
Barnes
Battersea
Poyle
Heathrow
Syon
Kew Palace
Mortlake
Fulham
Brixton
Horton
West Bedfont
Hatton
Hounslow
Isleworth
East Sheen
Clapham
Old Windsor
Stanwell
Twickenham
Richmond
Putney
Wandsworth
Wraysbury
East Bedfont
Marble Hill
Petersham
Roehampton
Hythe End
Feltham
Twickenham
Ham House
Earlsfield
Balham
Runnymede
Tooting Bec
Egham
Ashford
Lower Feltham
Ham
Streatham
Englefield Green
Thorpe Lea
STAINES-UPON-THAMES
Hanworth
Teddington
Kingston upon Thames
Wimbledon
Tooting
Feltham Hill
Kempton Park
Hampton
Merton
Thorpe
Queen Mary Resr
Sunbury
Hampton Wick
Norbiton
Morden
Mitcham
Virginia Water
Thorpe Park
Littleton
Upper Halliford
West Molesey
East Molesey
Hampton Court Palace
Surbiton
New Malden
Raynes Park
Lower Halliford
Thames Ditton
Motspur Park
St Helier
Beddington Corner
Lyne
Chertsey
Shepperton
Walton-on-Thames
Long Ditton
Worcester Park
North Cheam
Hackbridge
Sandown Park
Hinchley Wood
Tolworth
Carshalton
Beddington
Wallington
Addlestone
Oatlands Park
Weybridge
Esher
Hook
Ottershaw
Hersham
Claygate
Chessington
Cheam
Sutton
South Beddington
New Haw
Ewell
Burrowhill
Claremont Gardens
Belmont
Chobham
Woodham
Chessington World of Adventures
Woodcote
Little Woodcote
West Byfleet
Byfleet
Fairmile
Sheerwater
Cobham
Oxshott
Epsom
Maybury
Painshill Park
Ashtead Common
Woodmansterne
Coulsdon
Horsell
Semaphore Tower
Epsom Downs
Banstead
Pyrford
Downside
Goldsworth Park
WOKING
Wisley
Stoke D'Abernon
Ashtead
Burgh Heath
St Johns
Mayford
Old Woking
Ripley
Leatherhead
Tadworth
Chipstead
Netherne-on-the-Hill
Hooley
Send
Ockham
Fetcham
Walton on the Hill
Kingswood
Headley
Chaldon
Sutton Green
Little Bookham
Great Bookham
Bocketts
Headley Common
West
Norbury Park
Effingham
Mickleham
Polesden Lacey
Walton Heath
Reigate
Merstham
0 1 2 3 4 miles
0 1 2 3 4 5 kilometres

Cheshunt
Waltham Abbey
Upshire
Epping
Bassett
Chipping Ongar
Stondon Massey
Fryerning
Doddinghurst
Heybridge
Ingatestone
Theydon Bois
Kelvedon Hatch
Navestock Side
Navestock
Mountnessing
High Beach
Epping Forest
Abridge
Lambourne End
Loughton
Buckhurst Hill
Chigwell
Bournebridge
Stapleford Abbotts
Pilgrims Hatch
Coxtie Green
South Weald
BRENTWOOD
Shenfield
Hutton
Little Burstead
Ingrave
Havering-atte-Bower
Chigwell Row
Harold Hill
Brook Street
Chingford
Woodford Wells
Woodford
Highams Park
Grange Hill
Hainault
Collier Row
Woodford Bridge
Clayhall
Barkingside
Gidea Park
Harold Wood
Great Warley
Edmonton
Higham Hill
Walthamstow
Snaresbrook
Newbury Park
Chadwell Heath
Romford
West Horndon
Upper Clapton
Leytonstone
Wanstead
Seven Kings
Goodmayes
Rush Green
Hornchurch
Upminster
Bulphan
Leyton
Forest Gate
Ilford
Manor Park
Becontree
Elm Park
Corbets Tey
Lower Clapton
Stratford
Barking
Dagenham
South Hornchurch
Horndon on the Hill
Dalston
Hackney
West Ham
East Ham
Bethnal Green
Bow
Plaistow
Canning Town
Beckton
Creekmouth
Rainham
South Ockendon
Orsett
Stepney
Poplar
Whitechapel
Wennington
North Stifford
LONDON
Isle of Dogs
Thamesmead
Aveley
Thames Barrier
Woolwich
Abbey Wood
Rainham Marshes
Bermondsey
Greenwich
Charlton
Plumstead
Belvedere
Erith
Purfleet
West Thurrock
Grays
Chadwell St Mary
West Tilbury
Little Thurrock
Deptford
East Wickham
Slade Green
Dartford Crossing
Queen Elizabeth Bridge
Tilbury
Peckham
New Cross
Blackheath
Kidbrooke
Welling
Bexleyheath
Crayford
Greenhithe
Tilbury Fort
Nunhead
East Dulwich
Lee
Lewisham
Eltham
Red House
Hall Place
Dartford
Swanscombe
Northfleet
Hither Green
Blackfen
Bexley
Bluewater Park
Swanscombe Skull
Ebbsfleet International
Chalk
GRAVESEND
Dulwich
Catford
Forest Hill
New Eltham
Sydenham
Grove Park
Mottingham
Sidcup
Joyden's Wood
Wilmington
Green Street Green
Betsham
Hook Green
Southfleet
Singlewell
Crystal Palace
Downham
Hextable
Darenth
South Darenth
Istead Rise
Sutton at Hone
Penge
Anerley
Chislehurst
Swanley Village
Dean Bottom
Beckenham
Elmers End
Widmore
Bickley
St Pauls Cray
Swanley
Longfield
New Barn
Cobham
Bromley
Petts Wood
St Mary Cray
Horton Kirby
South Norwood
Woodside
Eden Park
Addiscombe
Southborough
Crockenhill
Hartley
Shirley
West Wickham
Hayes
Farningham
Fawkham Green
Meopham
Orpington
Eynsford
Lullingstone Roman Villa
Croydon
Locksbottom
Chelsfield
Brands Hatch
New Ash Green
Addington
Keston
Farnborough
Eynsford Castle
New Addington
Lullingstone
Maplescombe
West Kingsdown
Ash
Harvel
Selsdon
Pratt's Bottom
Hodsoll Street
Culverstone Green
Paddlesworth
Hutchinson's Bank
Down House
Downe
Leaves Green
Shoreham
Stansted
Fairseat
Vigo
Sanderstead
Farleigh
Fickleshole
Biggin Hill
Halstead
Trottiscliffe
Ryarsh
Otford
Wrotham
Addington
Leybourne
Cudham
Knockholt Pound
Kemsing
Heaverham
Aperfield
Knockholt
Dunton Green
Borough Green
West Malling
Warlingham
Tatsfield
Chevening
Sevenoaks
Seal
Ightham
Platt
Offham
North Downs Way
Chipstead
St Johns
Riverhead
Oldbury
Woldingham
Westerham
Brasted
Stone Street
Kings Hill
Titsey
Sundridge
Knole House
Ivy Hatch
Mereworth
Wateringbury
Limpsfield
Clacket Lane
Chart
Sevenoaks
Plaxtol
Moorhouse Bank
Squerryes Court
Ightham Mote
Dunk's Green
Oxted
Emmetts Garden
Shipbourne
West
Nettlestead

46
Margaretting
Margaretting Tye
Galleywood
Ingatestone
Stock
West Hanningfield
Hanningfield Reservoir
South Hanningfield
East Hanningfield
Bicknacre
Cock Clarks
Purleigh
Rudley Green
Mundon Hill
Maylandsea
Steeple
Mayland
Howe Green
Woodham Ferrers
Stow Maries
Cold Norton
Althorne
Hyde Hall
Coalhill
61
Tropical Wings
South Woodham Ferrers
North Fambridge
Bridgemarsh Island
Marsh Farm
River Crouch
South Fambridge
Canewdon
Hullbridge
Downham
Ramsden Bellhouse
Runwell
Battlesbridge
Hutton
Billericay
South Green
Wickford
Rawreth
Shotgate
Little Burstead
Great Burstead
Crays Hill
Ingrave
Hockley
Hawkwell
Ashingdon
Paglesham
Eastend
Wallasea Island
Great Stambridge
Potton Is
Rayleigh
Rochford
Barling
North Benfleet
BASILDON
Bowers Gifford
Pitsea
Thundersley
Laindon
Lee Chapel
Vange
Langdon
Westley Heights
Southend
R Roach
Little Wakering
Great Wakering
Eastwood
Prittlewell
Bournes Green
North Shoebury
Hadleigh
Hadleigh Castle
Leigh-on-Sea
Westcliff-on-Sea
Southchurch
Thorpe Bay
Shoeburyness
Bulphan
One Tree Hill
Wat Tyler
South Benfleet
Holehaven Creek
Fobbing
Horndon on the Hill
Corringham
Orsett
Stanford le Hope
Coryton
Canvey Island
Leigh Beck
Canvey Point
SOUTHEND-ON-SEA
Shoebury Ness
THAMES ESTUARY
45
Chadwell St Mary
West Tilbury
Little Thurrock
Grays
East Tilbury
Tilbury
Tilbury Fort
Coalhouse Fort
Cliffe
Cooling
St Mary's Hoo
Allhallows
Isle of Grain
Lower Stoke
Grain
High Halstow
Fenn Street
Middle Stoke
Stoke
Sheerness
Marine Town
Mile Town
West Minster
Queenborough
Halfway Houses
Rushenden
Church Street
Milton
Chalk
GRAVESEND
Higham
Cliffe Woods
Chattenden
Hoo St Werburgh
River Medway
Stangate Creek
Southfleet
Singlewell
Shorne
Shorne Wood
Wainscott
Upnor Castle
Frindsbury
The Historic Dockyard Chatham
Istead Rise
New Barn
Cobham
Strood
ROCHESTER
Diggerland
Fort Amherst
Brompton
Grange
Riverside
Halstow Creek
Lower Halstow
Iwade
ISLE OF SHEPPEY
Elmley Island
Sole Street
Rochester Castle
CHATHAM
GILLINGHAM
Upchurch
Sittingbourne & Kemsley Light Railway
Meopham
Luddesdown
Cuxton
Borstal
Luton
North Downs Way
Rainham
Wigmore
Newington
Bobbing
Milton Regis
Sittingbourne
Wouldham
Walderslade
Hartlip
Chalkwell
Harvel
Halling
Buckmore Park
Lords Wood
Hill Green
Borden
Bapchild
Teynham
Culverstone Green
Paddlesworth
Bredhurst
Tunstall
Snodland
Burham
Blue Bell Hill
Oad St
Stockbury
Highsted
Rodmersham
Rodmersham Green
Lynsted
Vigo
Birling
Kit's Coty
Tyland Barn
South Green
Bredgar
Rawling Street
Ryarsh
Eccles
Aylesford
33
Lunsford
Addington
Leybourne
Larkfield
Boxley
Kent County
White Horse Wood
Bicknor
Milstead
Newnham
West Malling
Ditton
Detling
Thurnham
Hucking
Wormshill
Frinsted
Doddington
Tower
British Legion Village
Offham
East Malling
Bearsted
Broad Street
Kings Hill
Herne Pound
MAIDSTONE
Maidstone
Hollingbourne
Wichling
Tong
Mereworth
Wateringbury
East Barming
Tovil
Willington
Eyhorne Street
Otham
Shepway
Leeds
Harrietsham
Lenham
Warren Street
Nettlestead
Broomfield
West
0 1 2 3 4 miles
0 1 2 3 4 5 kilometres

Dengie
G
H
J
K
L
M
62
Holliwell Point
Foulness Point
Courtsend
Churchend
FOULNESS ISLAND
Warden Point
Leysdown-on-Sea
B2231
Isle of Harty
Shell Ness
The Swale
Whitstable
Whitstable Bay
Herne Bay
Hampton
Tankerton
Swalecliffe
Greenhill
Beltinge
Bishopstone
Reculver
Reculver Towers
Broomfield
Herne
Chestfield
South Street
Seasalter
Minnis Bay
Westgate on Sea
Birchington
St Nicholas at Wade
Boyden Gate
Sarre
Chislet
Acol
Monkton
Minster
34
35
Faversham
Goodnestone
Oare
Davington Hill
Ospringe
Preston
Yorkletts
Highstreet
Dargate
Druidstone
Denstroude
Hernhill
Staplestreet
Dunkirk
Boughton St
Blean
Upper Harbledown
Rough Common
Harbledown
Tyler Hill
Hales Place
Sturry
Broad Oak
Wildwood Wealden Forest Park
Hoath
Hersden
Westbere
Stodmarsh
Fordwich
Old Town Hall
Wickhambreaux
Littlebourne
Canterbury
West Stourmouth
East Stourmouth
Westmarsh
Preston
Elmstone
Cop Street
Hoaden
Ash
Seaton
Ickham
Durlock
Wingham
Marshborough
North Street
Sheldwich
South Street
Hogben's Hill
Selling
Oversland
Thanington
Chartham Hatch
Chartham
Old Wives Lees
Shalmsford Street
Bekesbourne
Bramling
Patrixbourne
Bridge
Adisham
Howletts
Staple
Goodnestone
Chillenden
Statenborough
Eastry
Stone Cross
Badlesmere
Shottenden
Leaveland
Chilham
Dane Street
Garlinge Green
Street End
Lower Hardres
Bishopsbourne
Higham Park
Aylesham
Nonington
Betteshanger
North Downs Way
A299
A28
A253
A257
A2050
A2
A290
A291
A251
B2040
B2205
B2190
B2046
R Stour

A B C D E F
1 2 3 4 5 6 7 8
Pen Brush
Pembrokeshire Coast Path
St Nicholas
Trefasser
Manorowen
Goodwick
Ynys Daullyn
Granston
Carreg Sampson
64
Jordanston
Porthgain
Trefin
Mathry
Abereiddy
Llanrhian
A487
Llangloffan Fen
B4331
Berea
Croes-goch
Letterston
Treglemais
Treleddyd-fawr
ST DAVID'S HEAD
Rhodiad-y-brenin
Caer Farchell
River Solva
B4330
Llandeloy
Whitesand Bay
B4583
Bishop's Palace
Whitchurch
Treffgarne Owen
Hayscastle
Hayscastle Cross
St David's
RAMSEY ISLAND
RSPB
Ramsey Sound
Solva
A487
Pen-y-cwm
178
DUDWELL MT
Leweston
St David's Peninsula Heritage Coast
Newgale
Roch
Wolfsdale
PEMBROKESHIRE COAST NATIONAL PARK
Simpson Cross
Rickets Head
Nolton Haven
Nolton
A487
Keeston
St Brides Bay
St Brides Bay Heritage Coast
Druidston
Haroldston West
Portfield Gate
B4341
Broad Haven
Broadway
B4327
Dreen Hill
A4076
Little Haven
Walton West
Pembrokeshire Coast Path
Talbenny
Tiers Cross
Walwyn's Castle
SKOMER ISLAND
Wooltack Point
Marloes
B4327
St Ishmael's
Herbrandston
Steynton
A477
Broad Sound
Hubberston
Hakin
Waterston
Marloes and Dale Heritage Coast
Dale
Westdale Bay
Great Castle Head
Dale Point
Milford Haven
Milford Haven (Aberdaugleddau)
Llanstadwell
SKOKHOLM ISLAND
Pembroke Dock (Doc Penfro)
Angle
Angle Bay
St Anns Head
Rhoscrowther
B4320
Rosslare Harbour
Castlemartin Brook
B4320
Freshwater West
B4319
Castlemartin
Warren
Merrion
Linney Head
PEMBROKESHIRE COAST NATIONAL PARK
Pembrokeshire Coast Path
0 1 2 3 4 miles
0 1 2 3 4 5 kilometres

Fishguard
(Abergwaun)
Newport
Nevern
Felindre Farchog
Dinas
Newcastle
Rhoshill
Pen-rhiw
Blaenffos
Crosswell
Brynberian
Crymmych
Bwlch-y-groes
Star
Tegryn
Hermon
Llanfyrnach
Trelech
MYNYDD PRESELI
PEMBROKESHIRE COAST NATIONAL PARK
Pontfaen
Llanychaer Bridge
Trecwn
Puncheston
Rosebush
Mynachlog ddu
Tufton
Castlebythe
Maenclochog
Llandre Isaf
Glandwr
Hebron
Blaenwaun
Henry's Moat (Castell Hendre)
Llangolman
Llanglydwen
Cefn-y-pant
Cwmbach
Llanwinio
Rinaston
Ambleston
New Moat
Llys-y-frân
Efailwen
Llanycefn
Login
Llanboidy
Gellywen
Spittal
Walton East
Pen-ffordd
Clarbeston
Clarbeston Road
Bletherston
Llandissilio
Llanfallteg
Clunderwen
Llanfallteg West
Cwmfelin Boeth
Llangynin
Meidrim
Wiston
Bethesda
Llawhaden
Robeston Wathen
Haverfordwest
(Hwlffordd)
Whitland
Llanddewi Velfrey
Pwll Trap
St Clears
Uzmaston
Narberth
Crinow
Lampeter Velfrey
Llanddowror
Tavernspite
Templeton
Red Roses
Hook
Martletwy
Ludchurch
Llanteg
Crunwear
Llansadurnen
Llangwm
Loveston
Reynalton
Begelly
Stepaside
Amroth
Pendine
Llanmiloe
Lawrenny
Cresswell
Jeffreyston
Kilgetty
Summerhill
Burton
Cresselly
Broadmoor
Wiseman's Bridge
West Williamston
Carew Newton
Neyland
Redberth
East Williamston
Saundersfoot
Carew
Milton
Cosheston
Sageston
Carew Cheriton
New Hedges
Monkstone Point
Gumfreston
St Florence
Tenby
(Dinbych-y-Pysgod)
Lamphey
Manorbier Newton
Penally
CARMARTHEN BAY
Hodgeston
Jameston
Lydstep
Giltar Point
Manorbier
Lydstep Point
Trewent Point
Cheriton or Stackpole Elidor
CALDEY ISLAND
Stackpole
South Pembrokeshire Heritage Coast
Barafundle Bay
Stackpole Head
St Govan's Head
65
50

50
65
49
A
B
C
D
E
F
1
2
3
4
5
6
7
8
Llanfyrnach
Trelech
Llanpumsaint
Glandwr
Hebron
Blaenwaun
Cynwyl Elfed
Rhydargaeau
Llanglydwen
Cefn-y-pant
The Welsh Chocolate Farm
Cwmbach
Llanwinio
Blaen-y-Coed
Talog
Gwili Railway
River Gwili
Efailwen
Login
Llanboidy
Gellywen
Abernant
Bronwydd
Felingwm
Afon Cynin
Meidrim
Carmarthen
(Caerfyrddin)
Abergwili
Nantgaredig
Llangunnor
Tre-gynwr
Johnstown
Llanllwch
United Counties
Cwmfelin Boeth
Llanfallteg West
Whitland Abbey
Llangynin
Bancyfelin
Llanddewi Velfrey
Whitland
Pwll Trap
St Clears
Croesyceiliog
Cwmffrwd
Lampeter Velfrey
Llanddowror
River Taf
Afon Cywyn
Llangynog
Idole
Bancycapel
Llangendeirne
Tavernspite
Pontantwn
Crwbin
Bancffosfelen
Red Roses
Laugharne
Llanybri
Llansteffan
Llandyfaelog
Llanteg
Crunwear
Llansadurnen
Ferryside
River Towy
Meinciau
Four Roads
Pontyates
Colby Woodland Garden
Amroth
Pendine
Museum of Speed
Llanmiloe
Wharley Point
Ginst Point
Llansaint
Mynyddgarreg
Summerhill
R Gwendraeth
Castle
Kidwelly
(Cydweli)
Carway
Ffos Las
Five Roads
Wiseman's Bridge
Saundersfoot
Trimsaran
Pen-y-Mynydd
Monkstone Point
Pembrey
Ffrwd Farm Mire
Archddu
Burry Port
Pwll
Tenby
(Dinbych-y-Pysgod)
CARMARTHEN
BAY
CALDEY ISLAND
Burry Inlet
Broughton Bay
Llanmadoc
Landimore
Burry Holms
Cheriton
Llangennith
Burry Green
Oldwalls
Rhossili Bay
Rhossili Downs
Reynoldston
Llanddewi
Knelston
Rhossili
Visitor Centre
WORMS HEAD
Middleton
Paviland
Port Eynon
Overton
Culver Hole
Port Einon Point
A40
A48
A477
A4066
A484
A485
B4299
B4298
B4312
B4300
B4306
B4309
B4317
B4308
B4311
B4328
B4314
B4301
A4118
B4247
0 1 2 3 4 miles
0 1 2 3 4 5 kilometres

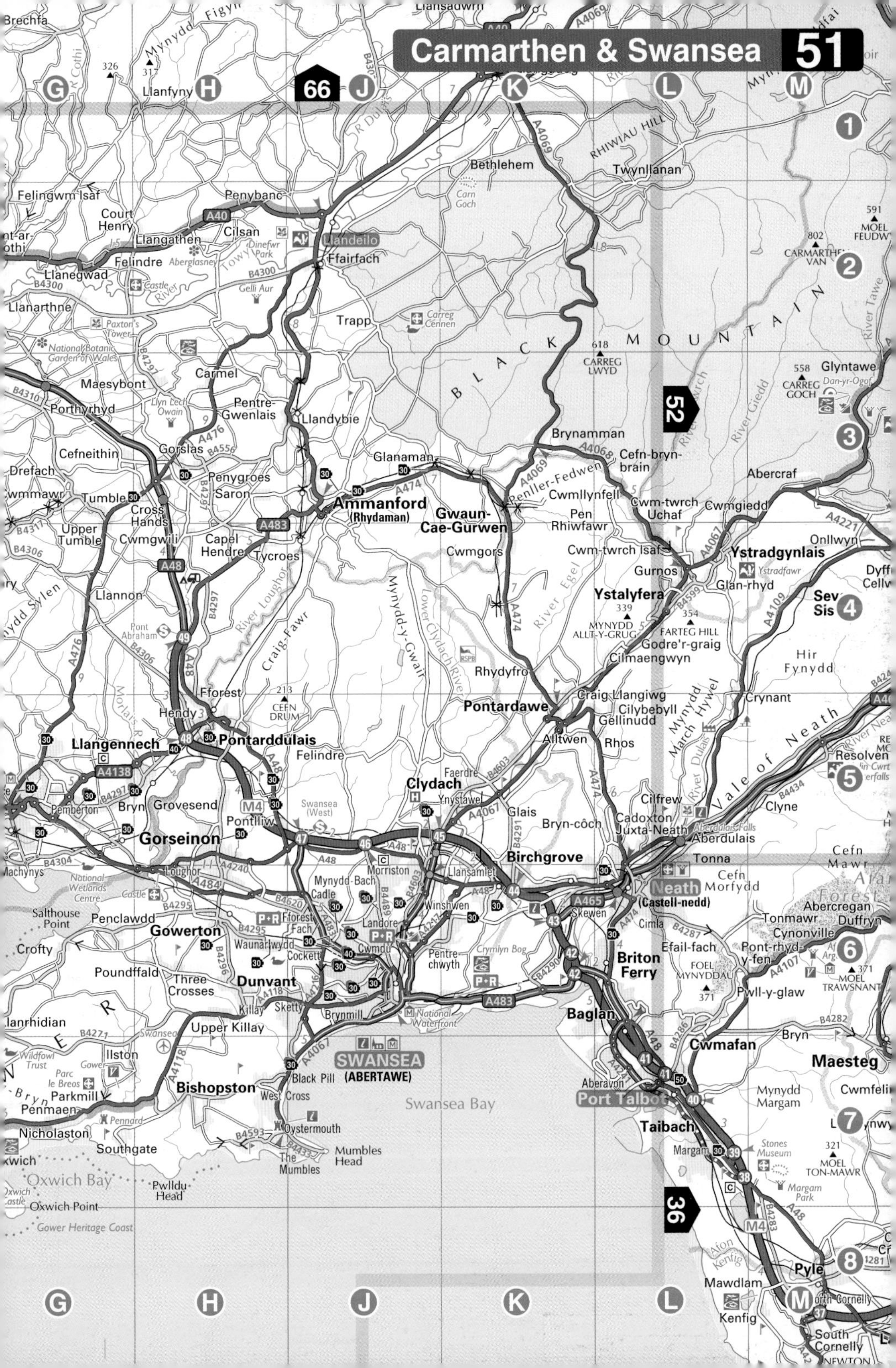

Llandeilo
Ffairfach
Trapp
Carreg Cennen
BLACK MOUNTAIN
Brynamman
Glanaman
Ammanford (Rhydaman)
Gwaun-Cae-Gurwen
Ystalyfera
Ystradgynlais
Pontardawe
Pontarddulais
Llangennech
Gorseinon
Clydach
Birchgrove
Neath (Castell-nedd)
Briton Ferry
Baglan
Port Talbot
Taibach
Cwmafan
Maesteg
Pyle
Kenfig
SWANSEA (ABERTAWE)
Swansea Bay
The Mumbles
Mumbles Head
Oystermouth
Bishopston
Gowerton
Dunvant
Penclawdd
Oxwich Bay
Gower Heritage Coast
Vale of Neath
Resolven
Aberdulais
Cross Hands
Tumble
Gorslas
Carmel
Llanarthne
National Botanic Garden of Wales
Penybanc
Llangathen
Felindre
Bethlehem
Twynllanan
CARREG LWYD
CARMARTHEN VAN
Glyntawe
Abercraf
Cwmgiedd
Onllwyn
Crynant
Glais
Morriston
Llansamlet
Skewen
Cimla
Margam
Mawdlam
North Cornelly
South Cornelly

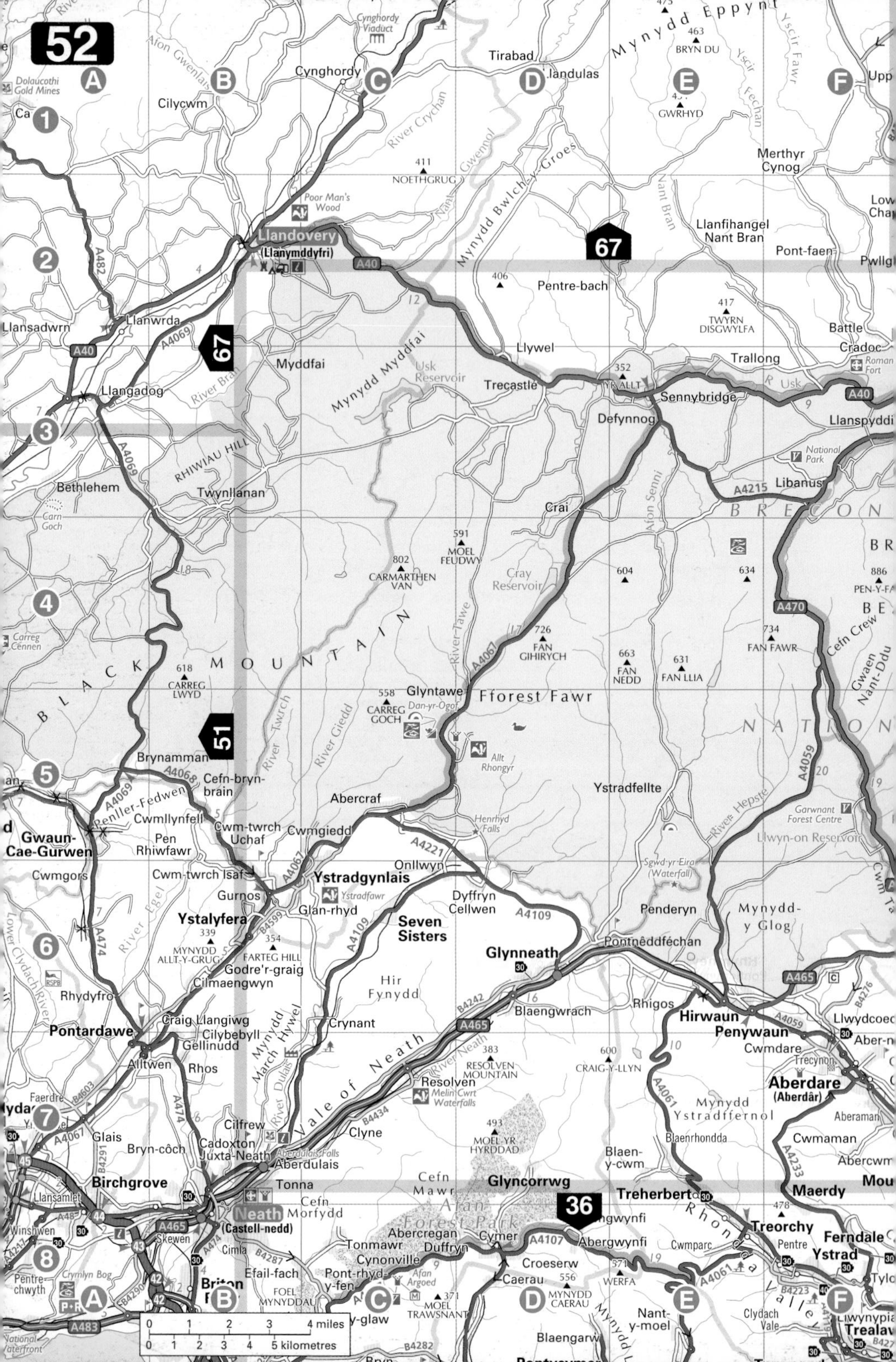
52
Dolaucothi Gold Mines
Afon Gwenlais
Cilycwm
Cynghordy Viaduct
Cynghordy
Tirabad
Llandulas
Mynydd Eppynt
BRYN DU
GWRHYD
Yscir Fechan
Yscir Fawr
Merthyr Cynog
River Crychan
411 NOETHGRUG
Nant Gwennol
Mynydd Bwlch-y-Groes
Nant Bran
Poor Man's Wood
Llandovery
(Llanymddyfri)
A40
A482
Llanfihangel Nant Bran
Pont-faen
Pwllgl
67
406
Pentre-bach
417 TWYRN DISGWYLFA
Battle
Cradoc
Roman Fort
Llansadwrn
Llanwrda
A4069
Myddfai
Mynydd Myddfai
Usk Reservoir
Llywel
Trecastle
352 YR ALLT
Trallong
Sennybridge
Usk
Llangadog
River Bran
Defynnog
Llanspyddid
RHIWIAU HILL
National Park
Bethlehem
Twynllanan
Libanus
A4215
Carn Goch
Crai
Afon Senni
BRECON
591 MOEL FEUDWY
802 CARMARTHEN VAN
Cray Reservoir
604
634
886 PEN-Y-FA
A470
Carreg Cennen
726 FAN GIHIRYCH
734 FAN FAWR
Cefn Crew
Gwaen Nant-Ddu
BLACK MOUNTAIN
618 CARREG LWYD
River Tawe
A4067
663 FAN NEDD
631 FAN LLIA
558 CARREG GOCH
Glyntawe
Dan-yr-Ogof
Fforest Fawr
NATIONAL
51
River Twrch
River Giedd
Allt Rhongyr
Brynamman
A4068
Cefn-bryn-brain
A4059
Abercraf
Ystradfellte
River Hepste
Penller-Fedwen
Cwmllynfell
Gwaun-Cae-Gurwen
Pen Rhiwfawr
Cwm-twrch Uchaf
Cwmgiedd
Henrhyd Falls
Garwnant Forest Centre
Llwyn-on Reservoir
A4221
Onllwyn
Sgwd-yr-Eira (Waterfall)
Cwmgors
Cwm-twrch Isaf
Ystradgynlais
Ystradfawr
Gurnos
Dyffryn Cellwen
Glan-rhyd
A4109
Penderyn
Mynydd-y Glog
Ystalyfera
B4599
Seven Sisters
River Egel
339 MYNYDD ALLT-Y-GRUG
354 FARTEG HILL
Glynneath
Pontneddfechan
Lower Clydach River
Godre'r-graig
Cilmaengwyn
A474
Hir Fynydd
A465
Rhydyfro
Mynydd March Hywel
Blaengwrach
Rhigos
Hirwaun
Penywaun
A4059
Llwydcoed
Crynant
B4242
Pontardawe
Craig Llangiwg
Cilybebyll
Gellinudd
River Neath
383 RESOLVEN MOUNTAIN
600 CRAIG-Y-LLYN
Cwmdare
Aber-nant
Trecynon
Alltwen
Rhos
Vale of Neath
River Dulais
Resolven
Melin Cwrt Waterfalls
Aberdare
(Aberdâr)
A4061
Faerdre
B4603
B4434
Mynydd Ystradffernol
Cilfrew
Clyne
493 MOEL-YR-HYRDDAD
Aberaman
A4067
Glais
Bryn-côch
Cadoxton Juxta-Neath
Aberdulais Falls
Aberdulais
Blaenrhondda
Cwmaman
B4291
Blaen-y-cwm
Abercwm
Birchgrove
Tonna
Cefn Mawr
Glyncorrwg
Treherbert
A4233
Maerdy
Llansamlet
Cefn Morfydd
Afan Forest Park
36
478
Neath
(Castell-nedd)
Abercregan
Cymer
Rhondda Valley
Treorchy
Ferndale
Winshwen
Skewen
Tonmawr
Duffryn
A4107
Abergwynfi
Pentre
Ystrad
Cimla
B4287
Cynonville
Croeserw
571 WERFA
Cwmparc
Pentre-chwyth
Efail-fach
Pont-rhyd-y-fen
Afan Argoed
Caerau
556 MYNYDD CAERAU
Crymlyn Bog
Briton Ferry
FOEL MYNYDDAU
371 MOEL TRAWSNANT
B4223
A4061
Clydach Vale
Llwynypia
Trealaw
A483
Nant-y-moel
Blaengarw
B4282
0 1 2 3 4 miles
0 1 2 3 4 5 kilometres
National Waterfront

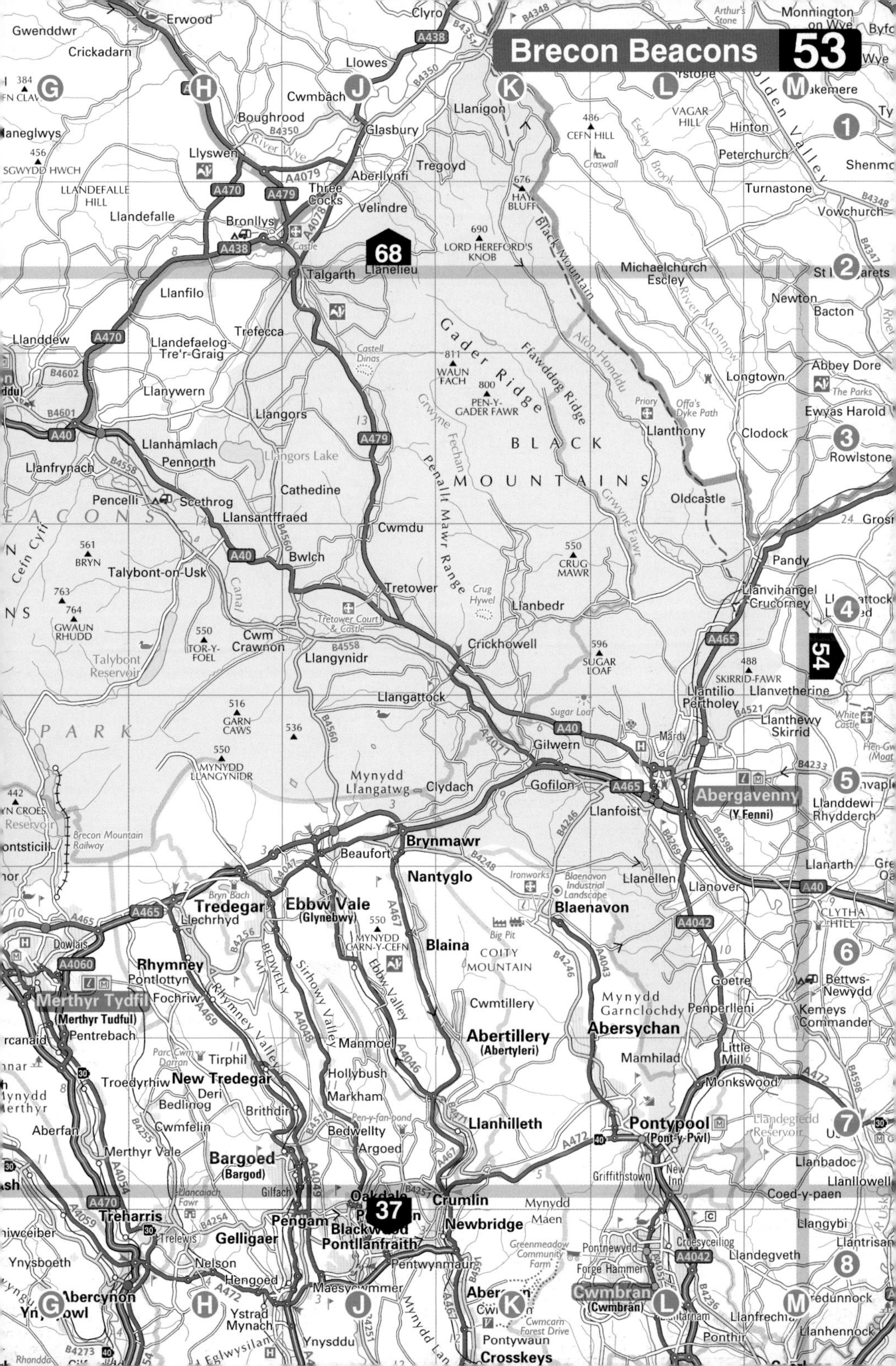
Brecon Beacons
53
68
54
37
Erwood
Clyro
Gwenddwr
Crickadarn
Llowes
Cwmbâch
Boughrood
Glasbury
Llyswen
Llanigon
Three Cocks
Aberllynfi
Velindre
Bronllys
Talgarth
Llanelieu
Tregoyd
Llandefalle
Llanfilo
Trefecca
Llanddew
Llandefaelog-Tre'r-Graig
Llanywern
Llangors
Llanhamlach
Pennorth
Llanfrynach
Llangors Lake
Cathedine
Pencelli
Scethrog
Llansantffraed
Cwmdu
Bwlch
Talybont-on-Usk
Tretower
Cwm Crawnon
Llangynidr
Crickhowell
Llanbedr
Llangattock
Gilwern
Gofilon
Clydach
Llanfoist
Abergavenny
(Y Fenni)
Brynmawr
Beaufort
Nantyglo
Tredegar
Ebbw Vale
(Glynebwy)
Blaenavon
Blaina
Rhymney
Merthyr Tydfil
(Merthyr Tudful)
Abertillery
(Abertyleri)
Abersychan
New Tredegar
Bargoed
(Bargod)
Pontypool
(Pont-y-Pŵl)
Crumlin
Newbridge
Blackwood
Pontllanfraith
Gelligaer
Treharris
Cwmbran
(Cwmbrân)
Crosskeys
Abercynon
Black Mountains
Gader Ridge
Ffawddog Ridge
Penallt Mawr Range
Black Mountain
Llanthony
Longtown
Oldcastle
Pandy
Llanvihangel Crucorney
Llantilio Pertholey
Llanvetherine
Abbey Dore
Ewyas Harold
Clodock
Rowlstone
Michaelchurch Escley
Peterchurch
Vowchurch
Turnastone
Hinton
Newton
Bacton
Llanover
Llanellen
Goetre
Penperlleni
Little Mill
Monkswood
Mamhilad
Griffithstown
New Inn
Llanbadoc
Coed-y-paen
Llangybi
Llandegveth
Ponthir
Llanfrechfa
Tregaron
Talybont Reservoir
Sugar Loaf
Waun Fach
Pen-y-Gader Fawr
Hay Bluff
Lord Hereford's Knob
Crug Mawr
Skirrid-Fawr
Coity Mountain
Mynydd Llangatwg
Brecon Mountain Railway

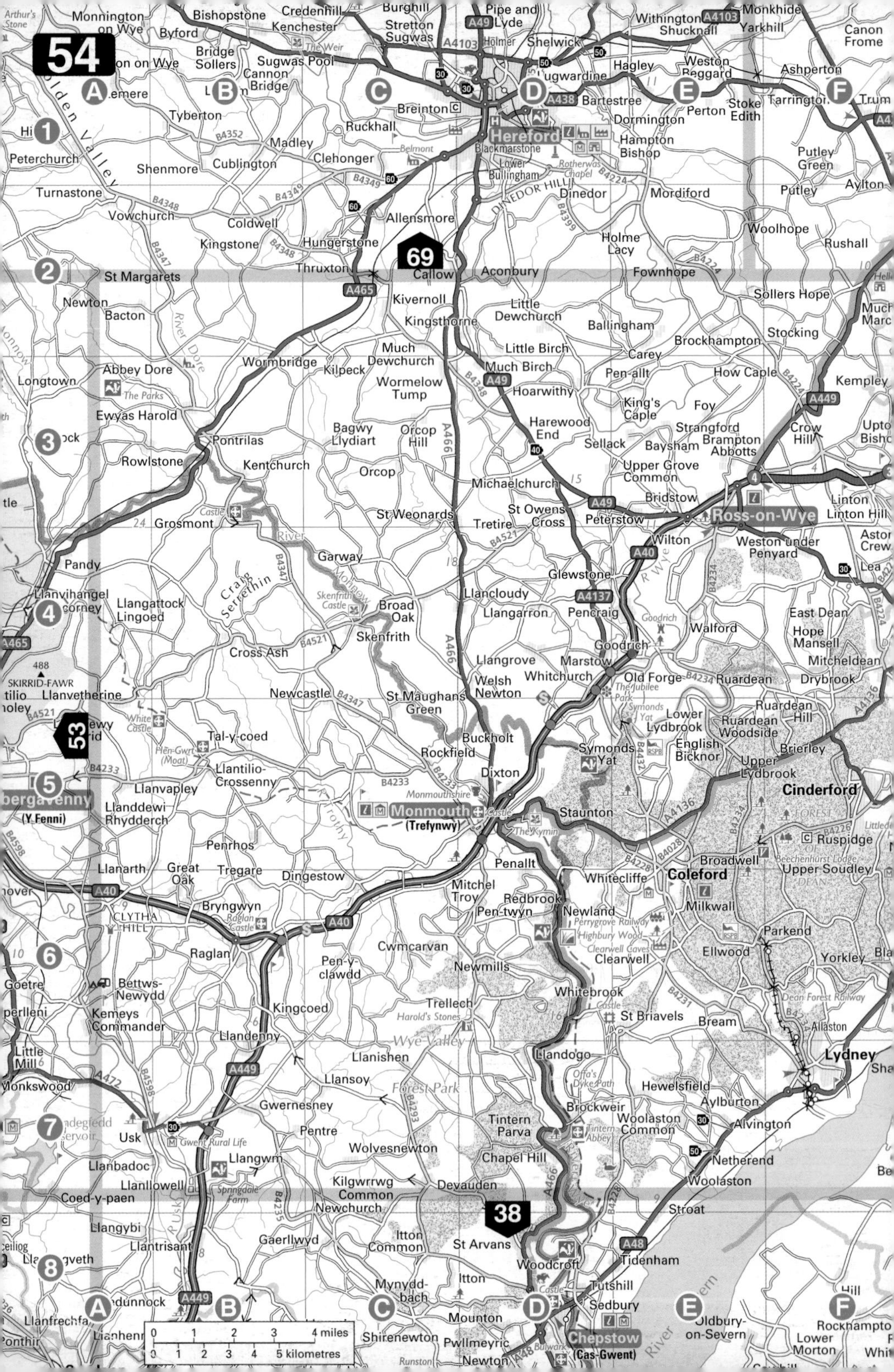
54
69
53
38
A
B
C
D
E
F
1
2
3
4
5
6
7
8
Monnington on Wye
Bishopstone
Credenhill
Burghill
Pipe and Lyde
Withington
A4103
Monkhide
Byford
Kenchester
Stretton Sugwas
Holmer
Shelwick
Shucknall
Yarkhill
Canon Frome
Bridge Sollers
Sugwas Pool
A49
A4103
Hagley
Weston Beggard
Ashperton
Cannon Bridge
Lugwardine
Breinton
Bartestree
Tarrington
Trumpet
Tyberton
Ruckhall
Dormington
Perton
Stoke Edith
Hereford
Hampton Bishop
Peterchurch
Shenmore
Cublington
Madley
Clehonger
Belmont
Blackmarstone
Lower Bullingham
Rotherwas Chapel
Putley Green
Turnastone
Golden Valley
B4352
B4349
B4348
B4224
Dinedor
DINEDOR HILL
Mordiford
Putley
Aylton
Vowchurch
Coldwell
Allensmore
B4399
Woolhope
Kingstone
Hungerstone
Holme Lacy
Rushall
B4347
St Margarets
Thruxton
Callow
Aconbury
Fownhope
A465
Newton
Kivernoll
Little Dewchurch
Sollers Hope
Bacton
Kingsthorne
Ballingham
Much Marcle
River Dore
Stocking
Little Birch
Carey
Brockhampton
Longtown
Abbey Dore
Wormbridge
Kilpeck
Much Dewchurch
Much Birch
Pen-allt
How Caple
Kempley
The Parks
Wormelow Tump
Hoarwithy
King's Caple
A449
Ewyas Harold
Foy
Harewood End
Crow Hill
Upton Bishop
Pontrilas
Bagwy Llydiart
Orcop Hill
A466
Sellack
Strangford
Baysham
Brampton Abbotts
Rowlstone
Kentchurch
Orcop
Upper Grove Common
Michaelchurch
Bridstow
Linton
Linton Hill
Castle
Grosmont
St Weonards
St Owens Cross
Tretire
A49
Peterstow
Ross-on-Wye
Aston Crews
Wilton
Weston under Penyard
River Monnow
Pandy
Garway
B4521
Glewstone
A40
R Wye
B4234
Lea
Craig Serrerthin
Llancloudy
A4137
Llanvihangel Crucorney
Llangattock Lingoed
Skenfrith Castle
Broad Oak
Llangarron
Pencraig
Goodrich
Walford
East Dean
Hope Mansell
Skenfrith
Goodrich
A465
Cross Ash
Llangrove
Marstow
Mitcheldean
488
SKIRRID-FAWR
Llanvetherine
Newcastle
St Maughans Green
Welsh Newton
Whitchurch
Old Forge
Ruardean
Drybrook
B4347
The Jubilee Park
Symonds Yat
Lower Lydbrook
Ruardean Hill
A4136
White Castle
Buckholt
Ruardean Woodside
Tal-y-coed
English Bicknor
Brierley
Symonds Yat
Hen Gwrt (Moat)
Rockfield
B4432
RSPB
Upper Lydbrook
B4233
Llantilio-Crossenny
Dixton
Cinderford
Abergavenny (Y Fenni)
Llanvapley
B4233
Monmouthshire
Llanddewi Rhydderch
Monmouth (Trefynwy)
Castle
The Kymin
Staunton
FOREST OF DEAN
Ruspidge
B4598
Penrhos
River Trothy
B4028
Broadwell
Beechenhurst Lodge
Upper Soudley
Llanarth
Great Oak
Tregare
Dingestow
Penallt
B4228
Whitecliffe
Coleford
Mitchel Troy
A40
Redbrook
Pen-twyn
Newland
Milkwall
CLYTHA HILL
Bryngwyn
Raglan Castle
Perrygrove Railway
Highbury Wood
Parkend
A40
Cwmcarvan
Clearwell Caves
Raglan
Clearwell
Ellwood
Yorkley
Pen-y-clawdd
Newmills
Goetre
Bettws-Newydd
Whitebrook
B4231
Dean Forest Railway
Kemeys Commander
Kingcoed
Trellech
Castle
St Briavels
Bream
Allaston
Harold's Stones
Llandenny
Wye Valley
Little Mill
Llandogo
Lydney
Llanishen
A449
A472
Monkswood
B4598
Llansoy
Offa's Dyke Path
Hewelsfield
Forest Park
Gwernesney
Brockweir
Aylburton
Usk
Gwent Rural Life
Tintern Parva
Woolaston Common
Alvington
Tintern Abbey
Pentre
B4293
Llanbadoc
Wolvesnewton
Netherend
Llangwm
Chapel Hill
River Wye
Llanllowell
Springdale Farm
Kilgwrrwg Common
Devauden
Woolaston
Coed-y-paen
B4235
A466
B4228
Newchurch
Stroat
Llangybi
Itton Common
St Arvans
A48
Llantrisant
Gaerllwyd
Tidenham
Woodcroft
R Usk
Itton
Tutshill
Mynydd-bach
Sedbury
Hill
A449
Llanfrechfa
Mounton
Castle
Oldbury-on-Severn
Rockhampton
Shirenewton
Chepstow (Cas-Gwent)
Lower Morton
Pwllmeyric
River Severn
Runston
Newton
Bulwark
A48
0 1 2 3 4 miles
0 1 2 3 4 5 kilometres

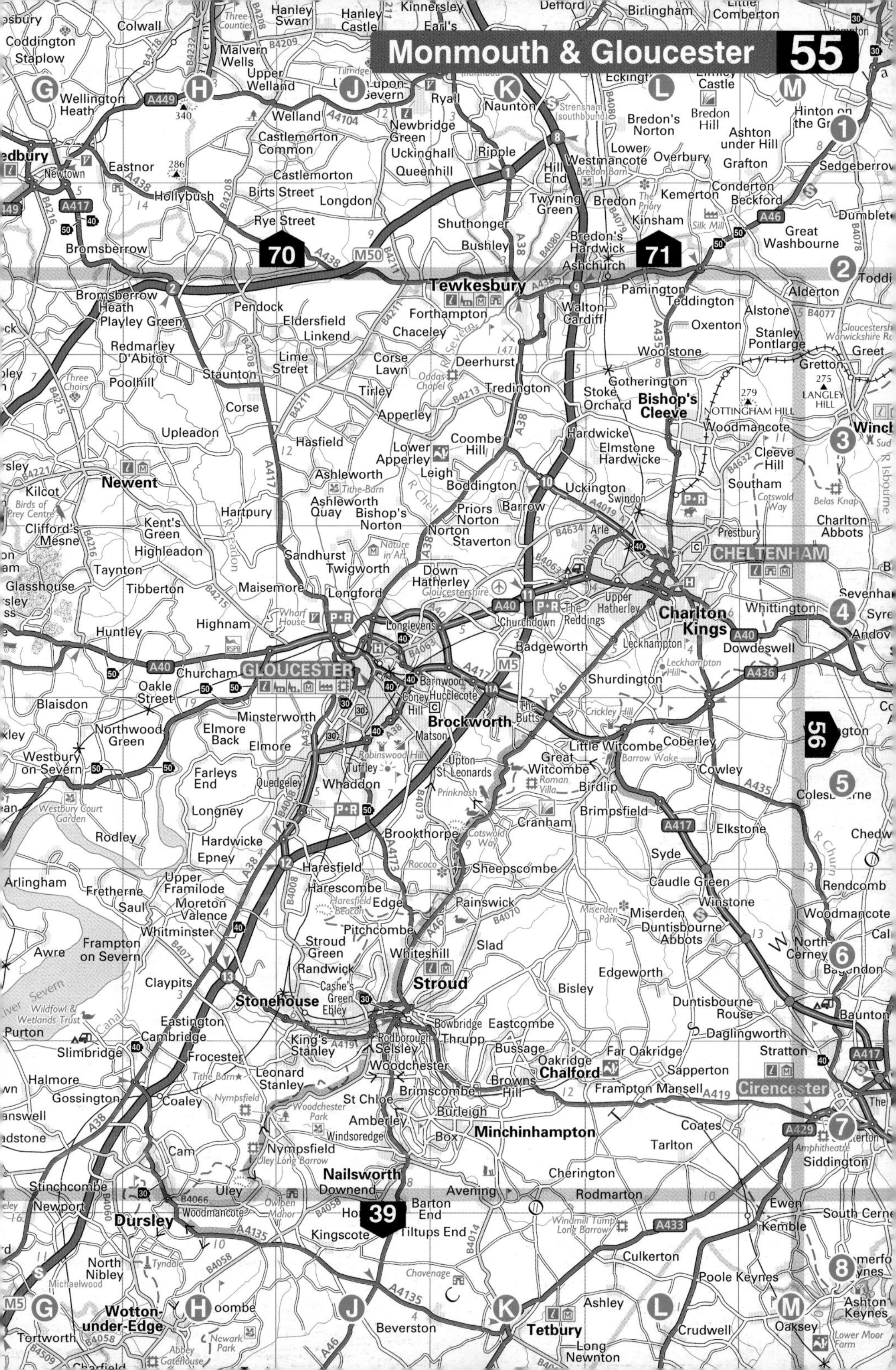
Colwall
Coddington
Staplow
Wellington Heath
Hanley Swan
Hanley Castle
Kinnersley
Earl's Croome
Defford
Birlingham
Little Comberton
Malvern Wells
Upper Welland
Welland
Upton upon Severn
Ryall
Naunton
Eckington
Elmley Castle
Bredon Hill
Strensham (southbound)
Bredon's Norton
Hinton on the Green
Ashton under Hill
Newbridge Green
Castlemorton Common
Uckinghall
Ripple
Lower Westmancote
Overbury
Grafton
Sedgeberrow
Eastnor
Hollybush
Castlemorton
Birts Street
Longdon
Queenhill
Hill End
Twyning Green
Bredon
Kemerton
Conderton
Beckford
Kinsham
Dumbleton
Great Washbourne
Rye Street
Shuthonger
Bushley
Bredon's Hardwick
Ashchurch
Bromsberrow
Bromsberrow Heath
Playley Green
Pendock
Eldersfield
Linkend
Tewkesbury
Forthampton
Chaceley
Walton Cardiff
Pamington
Teddington
Alderton
Alstone
Oxenton
Stanley Pontlarge
Greet
Gretton
Woolstone
Redmarley D'Abitot
Poolhill
Staunton
Lime Street
Corse Lawn
Deerhurst
Tredington
Gotherington
Stoke Orchard
Bishop's Cleeve
Nottingham Hill
Langley Hill
Woodmancote
Winchcombe
Corse
Tirley
Apperley
Upleadon
Hasfield
Coombe Hill
Lower Apperley
Leigh
Hardwicke
Elmstone Hardwicke
Cleeve Hill
Southam
Newent
Kilcot
Birds of Prey Centre
Clifford's Mesne
Ashleworth
Ashleworth Quay
Hartpury
Bishop's Norton
Boddington
Uckington
Swindon
Barrow
Priors Norton
Norton
Staverton
Arle
Prestbury
Belas Knap
Charlton Abbots
Kent's Green
Highleadon
Taynton
Tibberton
Glasshouse
Sandhurst
Twigworth
Maisemore
Longford
Down Hatherley
Cheltenham
Upper Hatherley
Charlton Kings
Whittington
Sevenhampton
Syreford
Andoversford
Dowdeswell
Huntley
Highnam
Longlevens
Churchdown
The Reddings
Badgeworth
Leckhampton
Leckhampton Hill
Gloucester
Churcham
Oakle Street
Blaisdon
Barnwood
Hucclecote
Coney Hill
Brockworth
The Butts
Shurdington
Crickley Hill
Little Witcombe
Coberley
Minsterworth
Northwood Green
Elmore Back
Elmore
Matson
Westbury on Severn
Westbury Court Garden
Farleys End
Quedgeley
Tuffley
Robinswood Hill
Whaddon
Upton St Leonards
Prinknash
Great Witcombe
Roman Villa
Barrow Wake
Birdlip
Cowley
Colesbourne
Longney
Rodley
Hardwicke
Epney
Brookthorpe
Cranham
Brimpsfield
Elkstone
Chedworth
Arlingham
Fretherne
Saul
Upper Framilode
Moreton Valence
Harescombe
Haresfield
Rococo
Sheepscombe
Syde
Caudle Green
Rendcomb
Whitminster
Awre
Frampton on Severn
Haresfield Beacon
Edge
Painswick
Miserden
Miserden Park
Winstone
Duntisbourne Abbots
Woodmancote
Pitchcombe
Stroud Green
Randwick
Whiteshill
Slad
North Cerney
Bagendon
Claypits
Stonehouse
Cashe's Green
Ebley
Stroud
Bisley
Edgeworth
Duntisbourne Rouse
Baunton
Wildfowl & Wetlands Trust
Purton
Slimbridge
Eastington
Cambridge
King's Stanley
Rodborough
Selsley
Bowbridge
Thrupp
Eastcombe
Bussage
Daglingworth
Stratton
Frocester
Leonard Stanley
Woodchester
Oakridge
Far Oakridge
Chalford
Sapperton
Cirencester
Halmore
Gossington
Coaley
Nympsfield
Woodchester Park
St Chloe
Brimscombe
Browns Hill
Frampton Mansell
Burleigh
Amberley
Box
Minchinhampton
Coates
Tarlton
Siddington
Amphitheatre
Cam
Uley Long Barrow
Windsoredge
Nailsworth
Downend
Cherington
Stinchcombe
Newport
Uley
Owlpen Manor
Woodmancote
Avening
Rodmarton
Ewen
Kemble
South Cerney
Dursley
Barton End
Horsley
Kingscote
Tiltups End
Windmill Tump Long Barrow
Culkerton
Tyndale
North Nibley
Michaelwood
Chavenage
Poole Keynes
Ashley
Ashton Keynes
Oaksey
Wotton-under-Edge
Coombe
Beverston
Tetbury
Long Newnton
Crudwell
Lower Moor Farm
Tortworth
Newark Park
Abbey Gatehouse
Charfield
Cotswold Way
River Severn
R Leadon
R Chelt
R Churn
Three Choirs
Tithe Barn
Nature in Art
Gloucestershire
Silk Mill
The Priory
Bredon Barn
Three Counties
RSPB
Wharf House
Oddas Chapel
70
71
56
39

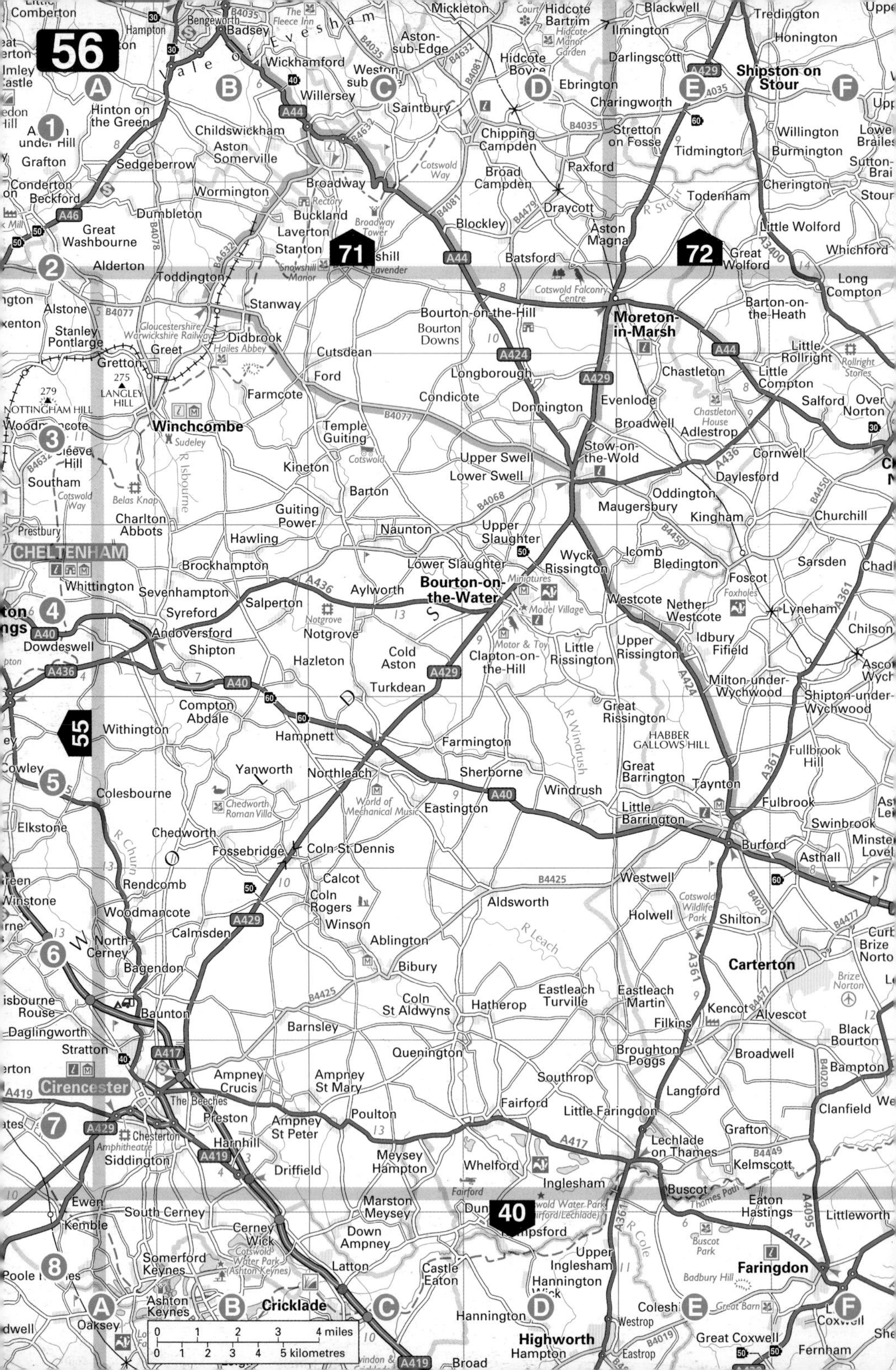

56
Comberton
Hampton
Bengeworth
Badsey
Vale of Evesham
The Fleece Inn
Aston-sub-Edge
Mickleton
Hidcote Bartrim
Hidcote Manor Garden
Blackwell
Ilmington
Tredington
Honington
Darlingscott
Shipston on Stour
Hinton on the Green
Wickhamford
Weston sub Edge
Willersey
Saintbury
Hidcote Boyce
Ebrington
Charingworth
Stretton on Fosse
Willington
Burmington
Tidmington
Ashton under Hill
Grafton
Childswickham
Aston Somerville
Sedgeberrow
Chipping Campden
Cotswold Way
Broad Campden
Paxford
Conderton
Beckford
Wormington
Broadway
Rectory
Buckland
Broadway Tower
Draycott
Todenham
Cherington
Dumbleton
Great Washbourne
Laverton
Stanton
Blockley
Aston Magna
Little Wolford
Whichford
Alderton
Toddington
Snowshill Manor
Snowshill
Lavender
Batsford
Great Wolford
Long Compton
Stanway
Cotswold Falconry Centre
Moreton-in-Marsh
Barton-on-the-Heath
Alstone
Gloucestershire Warwickshire Railway
Didbrook
Bourton-on-the-Hill
Bourton Downs
Stanley Pontlarge
Greet
Hailes Abbey
Cutsdean
Little Rollright
Rollright Stones
Gretton
Ford
Longborough
Chastleton
Little Compton
Langley Hill
Nottingham Hill
Farmcote
Condicote
Donnington
Evenlode
Chastleton House
Salford
Over Norton
Woodmancote
Winchcombe
Sudeley
Temple Guiting
Cotswold
Broadwell
Adlestrop
Cleeve Hill
Upper Swell
Lower Swell
Stow-on-the-Wold
Cornwell
Daylesford
Southam
Kineton
Barton
Oddington
Maugersbury
Belas Knap
Charlton Abbots
Guiting Power
Naunton
Upper Slaughter
Kingham
Churchill
Prestbury
Hawling
Icomb
Bledington
Cheltenham
Brockhampton
Lower Slaughter
Wyck Rissington
Sarsden
Whittington
Sevenhampton
Aylworth
Bourton-on-the-Water
Miniatures
Model Village
Foscot
Foxholes
Syreford
Salperton
Notgrove
Westcote
Nether Westcote
Lyneham
Chilson
Dowdeswell
Andoversford
Shipton
Hazleton
Cold Aston
Motor & Toy
Clapton-on-the-Hill
Little Rissington
Upper Rissington
Idbury
Fifield
Milton-under-Wychwood
Shipton-under-Wychwood
Turkdean
Compton Abdale
Great Rissington
Withington
Hampnett
Habber Gallows Hill
Farmington
Fullbrook Hill
Cowley
Yanworth
Northleach
Sherborne
Windrush
R Windrush
Great Barrington
Taynton
Colesbourne
Chedworth Roman Villa
World of Mechanical Music
Eastington
Little Barrington
Fulbrook
Swinbrook
Elkstone
Chedworth
Burford
Asthall
Fossebridge
Coln St Dennis
Westwell
Calcot
Rendcomb
Coln Rogers
Winson
Aldsworth
Holwell
Cotswold Wildlife Park
Shilton
Winstone
Woodmancote
Calmsden
Ablington
North Cerney
R Leach
Carterton
Brize Norton
Bagendon
Bibury
Eastleach Turville
Eastleach Martin
Coln St Aldwyns
Hatherop
Kencot
Alvescot
Baunton
Barnsley
Filkins
Black Bourton
Daglingworth
Stratton
Quenington
Broughton Poggs
Broadwell
Bampton
Ampney Crucis
Ampney St Mary
Southrop
Langford
Cirencester
The Beeches
Preston
Fairford
Little Faringdon
Clanfield
Ampney St Peter
Poulton
Amphitheatre
Chesterton
Grafton
Siddington
Harnhill
Lechlade on Thames
Meysey Hampton
Whelford
Kelmscott
Driffield
Inglesham
Buscot
Ewen
Kemble
South Cerney
Marston Meysey
Cotswold Water Park (Fairford/Lechlade)
Thames Path
Eaton Hastings
Littleworth
Cerney Wick
Cotswold Water Park (Ashton Keynes)
Down Ampney
Kempsford
Buscot Park
Somerford Keynes
Upper Inglesham
Poole Keynes
Latton
Castle Eaton
Hannington Wick
Badbury Hill
Faringdon
Ashton Keynes
Cricklade
Coleshill
Great Barn
Coxwell
Oaksey
Hannington
Westrop
Great Coxwell
Highworth
Eastrop
Fernham
Hampton
Broad
0 1 2 3 4 miles
0 1 2 3 4 5 kilometres

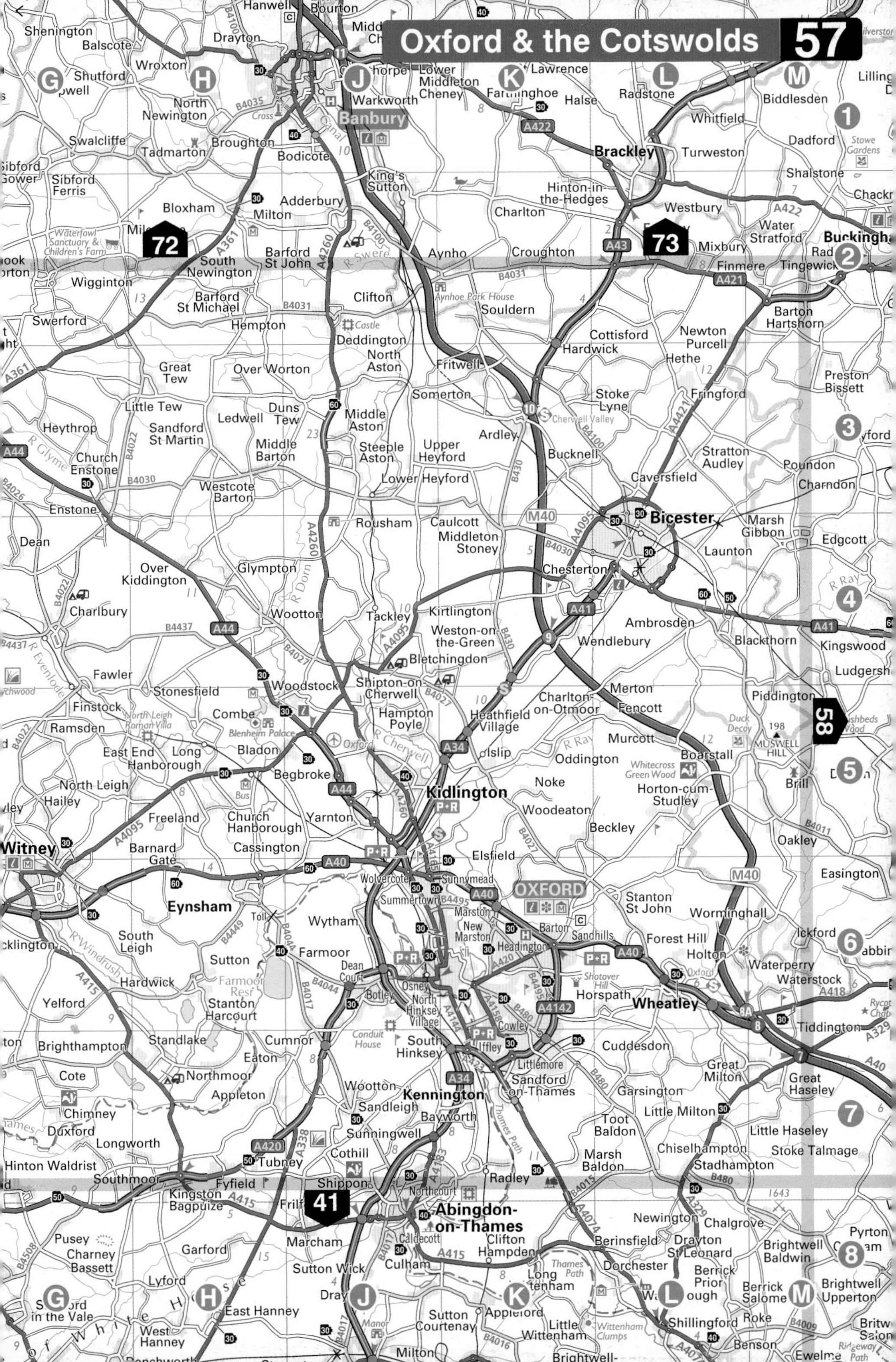
Oxford & the Cotswolds
57
Shenington
Balscote
Hanwell
Bourton
Drayton
Wroxton
Shutford
North Newington
Warkworth
Banbury
Lower Middleton Cheney
Lawrence
Farthinghoe
Halse
Radstone
Biddlesden
Whitfield
Swalcliffe
Tadmarton
Broughton
Bodicote
Brackley
Turweston
Dadford
Stowe Gardens
Sibford Gower
Sibford Ferris
King's Sutton
Hinton-in-the-Hedges
Shalstone
Bloxham
Milton
Adderbury
Charlton
Westbury
Water Stratford
Buckingham
Waterfowl Sanctuary & Children's Farm
72
73
Barford St John
Aynho
Croughton
Mixbury
Finmere
Tingewick
South Newington
Wigginton
Barford St Michael
Clifton
Aynhoe Park House
Souldern
Barton Hartshorn
Swerford
Hempton
Castle
Deddington
Cottisford
Hardwick
Newton Purcell
Hethe
Great Tew
Over Worton
North Aston
Fritwell
Preston Bissett
Little Tew
Somerton
Stoke Lyne
Fringford
Heythrop
Ledwell
Duns Tew
Sandford St Martin
Middle Aston
Ardley
Cherwell Valley
Church Enstone
Middle Barton
Steeple Aston
Upper Heyford
Bucknell
Stratton Audley
Poundon
Charndon
Westcote Barton
Lower Heyford
Caversfield
Enstone
Dean
Rousham
Caulcott
Middleton Stoney
Bicester
Marsh Gibbon
Edgcott
Launton
Over Kiddington
Glympton
Chesterton
Charlbury
Wootton
Tackley
Kirtlington
Weston-on-the-Green
Ambrosden
Wendlebury
Blackthorn
Kingswood
Ludgershall
Bletchingdon
Fawler
Stonesfield
Woodstock
Shipton-on-Cherwell
Merton
Fencott
Charlton-on-Otmoor
Piddington
Finstock
North Leigh Roman Villa
Combe
Blenheim Palace
Hampton Poyle
Heathfield Village
Ramsden
East End
Long Hanborough
Bladon
Oxford
Islip
Oddington
Murcott
Duck Decoy
Muswell Hill
Boarstall
Whitecross Green Wood
Brill
North Leigh
Hailey
Begbroke
Kidlington
Noke
Horton-cum-Studley
Freeland
Church Hanborough
Yarnton
Woodeaton
Beckley
Oakley
Witney
Barnard Gate
Cassington
Elsfield
Easington
Wolvercote
Sunnymead
Summertown
OXFORD
Eynsham
Marston
New Marston
Stanton St John
Worminghall
South Leigh
Wytham
Barton
Headington
Sandhills
Forest Hill
Ickford
Sutton
Farmoor
Dean Court
Holton
Waterperry
Waterstock
Hardwick
Farmoor Resr
Botley
Osney
Shotover Hill
Horspath
Wheatley
Yelford
Stanton Harcourt
North Hinksey Village
Cowley
Tiddington
Brighthampton
Standlake
Cumnor
Conduit House
South Hinksey
Iffley
Littlemore
Cuddesdon
Great Milton
Great Haseley
Cote
Eaton
Northmoor
Sandford-on-Thames
Appleton
Wootton
Kennington
Garsington
Chimney
Sandleigh
Bayworth
Toot Baldon
Little Milton
Duxford
Longworth
Sunningwell
Thames Path
Little Haseley
Cothill
Marsh Baldon
Chiselhampton
Stoke Talmage
Hinton Waldrist
Tubney
Stadhampton
Southmoor
Fyfield
Shippon
Radley
Kingston Bagpuize
41
Northcourt
Abingdon-on-Thames
Newington
Chalgrove
Pusey
Charney Bassett
Marcham
Caldecott
Clifton Hampden
Berinsfield
Drayton St Leonard
Brightwell Baldwin
Pyrton
Garford
Sutton Wick
Culham
Dorchester
Berrick Prior
Berrick Salome
Brightwell Upperton
Lyford
Long Wittenham
Drayton
Stanford in the Vale
East Hanney
Sutton Courtenay
Appleford
Little Wittenham
Wittenham Clumps
Shillingford
Roke
West Hanney
Milton
Benson
Ewelme
Ridgeway Path
Brightwell-
Denchworth
Vale of White Horse
58
M40
A40
A34
A44
A41
A43
A420
A415
A4260
A4095
A4142
A422
A421

58
Silverstone
Potterspury
Haversham
Newport Pagnell
Crawley
Wharley End
Lillingstone Lovell
Lillingston Dayrell
Puxley
Old Stratford
Cosgrove
New Bradwell
Great Linford
Willen
Cranfield
Moulsoe
Biddlesden
Deanshanger
Stony Stratford
Passenham
Wolverton
Bradwell
Xscape
Broughton
Salford
Wicken
Calverton
MILTON KEYNES
Gulliver's Land
Woolstone
Woughton on the Green
Dadford
Stowe Gardens
Shalstone
Akeley
Maids Moreton
Leckhampstead
Beachampton
Shenley Church End
Loughton
Lower End
Wavendon
Aspley Guise
Chackmore
Water Stratford
Buckingham
Radclive
Tingewick
Thornton
Nash
Shenley Brook End
Whaddon
Simpson
Walton
Woburn Sands
Aspley Heath
Bow Brickhill
73
74
Bletchley
Woburn
Thornborough
Gawcott
Barton Hartshorn
Great Horwood
Newton Longville
Little Brickhill
Woburn Abbey
Padbury
Adstock
Little Horwood
Great Brickhill
Stockgrove
King's Wood
Preston Bissett
Hillesden
Addington
Drayton Parslow
Stoke Hammond
Mursley
Winslow
Heath and Reach
Steeple Claydon
Twyford
Middle Claydon
Hollingdon
Hockliffe
Poundon
Charndon
Claydon House
East Claydon
Swanbourne
Soulbury
Clipstone
Stewkley
Hoggeston
Linslade
Leighton Buzzard
Marsh Gibbon
Granborough
Dunton
Botolph Claydon
Burcott
Stanbridge
Edgcott
North Marston
Cublington
Wing
Ascott
Billington
Eaton Green
Little Billington
Finemere Wood
R Ray
186
QUAINTON HILL
Oving
Grendon Underwood
Whitchurch
Ledburn
Slapton
Aston Abbotts
Pitchcott
Mentmore
Northall
Blackthorn
Kingswood
Woodham
Quainton
Buckinghamshire Railway Centre
Hardwick
Wingrave
Horton
Grand Union Canal
Ludgershall
Westcott
Waddesdon
Weedon
Rowsham
Piddington
Duck Decoy
57
Muswell Hill
Rushbeds Wood
Wotton Underwood
Waddesdon Manor
Hulcott
Cheddington
Ivinghoe
Bierton
Long Marston
Brill
Dorton
Upper Winchendon
Ashendon
Pitstone
Marsworth
Aylesbury
Wilstone
R Thame
Buckland
Nether Winchendon
Stone
Lower Hartwell
Aston Clinton
Drayton Beauchamp
Tring
Oakley
Chilton
Southcourt
Cuddington
Upton
Sedrup
Stoke Mandeville
Weston Turville
Dinton
Westlington
Chearsley
Easington
Long Crendon Courthouse
Long Crendon
Bishopstone
Goat Centre
Halton
Dancersend
Wigginton
Haddenham
Ford
North Lee
Ridgeway Path
Hastoe
St Tiggywinkles
Wendover
Buckland Common
Berkhamsted
Ickford
Little Kimble
Shabbington
Thame
St Leonards
Waterperry
Kingsey
Owlswick
Meadle
Ellesborough
Cholesbury
Waterstock
Ilmer
Great Kimble
Askett
Pulpit Hill
Rycote Chapel
Longwick
Monks Risborough
Dunsmore
Lee Clump
Bellingdon
Tiddington
Moreton
Towersey
The Lee
Asheridge
Whiteleaf
Chartridge
Pitch Green
Princes Risborough
Great Hampden
Ballinger Common
Great Haseley
Tetsworth
Emmington
Henton
Sydenham
Bledlow
Saunderton
South Heath
Chinnor & Princes Risborough Railway
Loosley Row
Lacey Green
Hyde Heath
Little Haseley
Postcombe
Chinnor
209
LODGE HILL
Prestwood
Great Missenden
Stoke Talmage
Crowell
Speen
Chesham Bois
Aston Rowant
Kingston Blount
Little Kingshill
Little Missenden
Amersham
South Weston
Radnage
Walter's Ash
Hughenden Valley
Great Kingshill
Lewknor
The City
42
Bradenham
Cryers Hill
Holmer Green
Amersham Old Town
Pyrton
Shirburn
Bledlow Ridge
Naphill
Penn Street
Cuxham
Stokenchurch
Beacon's Bottom
Hell Fire Caves
Hughenden Manor
Widmer End
Hazlemere
Coleshill
Brightwell Baldwin
Watlington
Downley
Winchmore Hill
Berrick Salome
Brightwell Upperton
West Wycombe Park
HIGH WYCOMBE
Penn
Roke
Ibstone
Cadmore End
Cressex
Bekonscot Model Village
Benson
Ewelme
Turville
Lane End
Booker
Wycombe Marsh
0 1 2 3 4 miles
0 1 2 3 4 5 kilometres

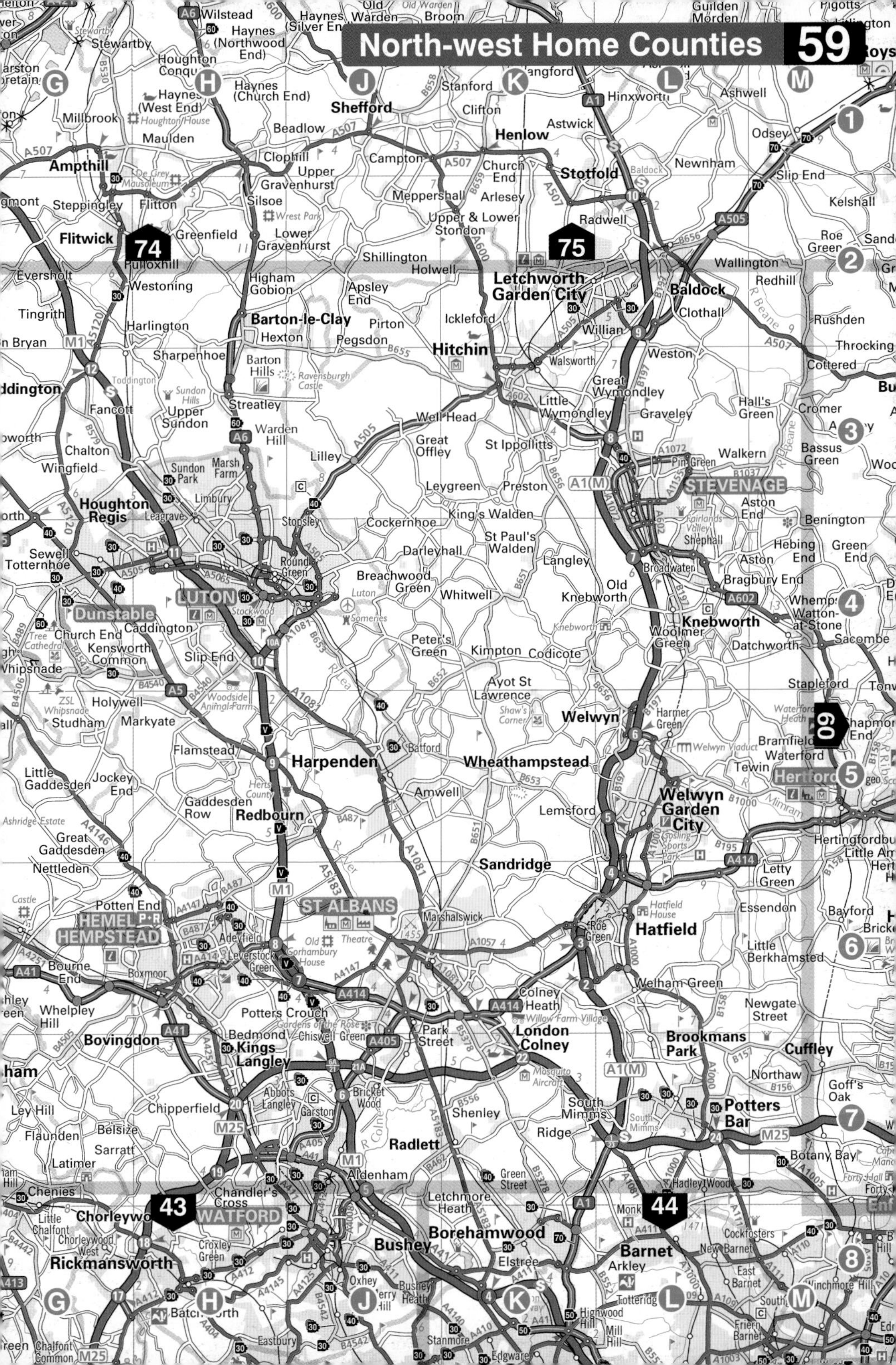
Ampthill
Flitwick
Shefford
Henlow
Stotfold
Baldock
Letchworth Garden City
Hitchin
Barton-le-Clay
Houghton Regis
Dunstable
LUTON
STEVENAGE
Knebworth
Welwyn
Welwyn Garden City
Harpenden
Wheathampstead
Redbourn
Sandridge
ST ALBANS
HEMEL HEMPSTEAD
Hatfield
London Colney
Kings Langley
Bovingdon
Brookmans Park
Potters Bar
Cuffley
Radlett
Borehamwood
Barnet
Bushey
WATFORD
Rickmansworth
Chorleywood
Hertford
74
75
43
44
60

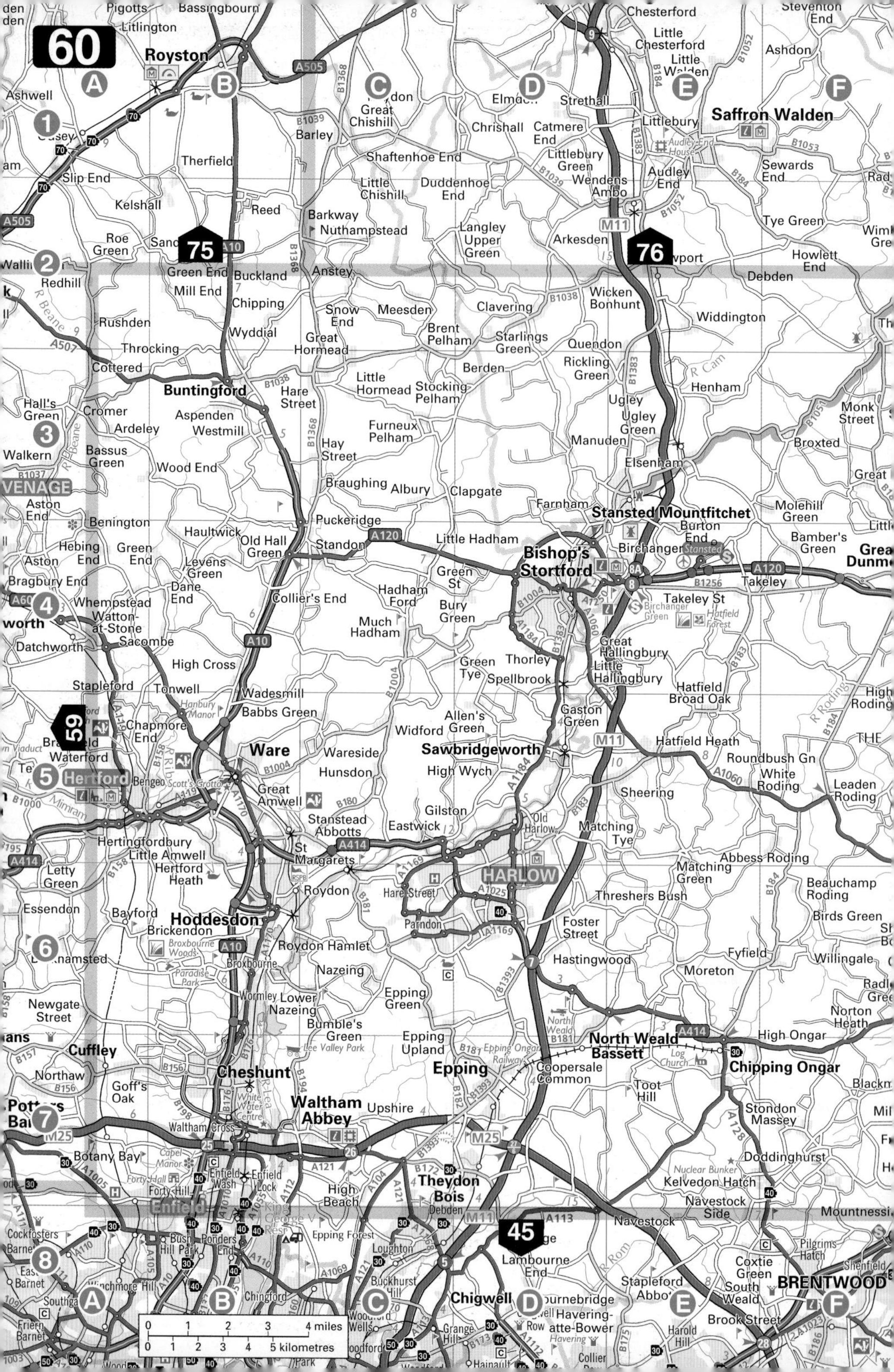
60
Pigotts
Bassingbourn
Litlington
Royston
Chesterford
Little Chesterford
Little Walden
Steventon End
Ashdon
Ashwell
Great Chishill
Elmdon
Strethall
Saffron Walden
Caldecote
Barley
Chrishall
Catmere End
Littlebury
Audley End House
Shaftenhoe End
Littlebury Green
Audley End
Sewards End
Therfield
Slip End
Little Chishill
Duddenhoe End
Wendens Ambo
Kelshall
Reed
Barkway
Nuthampstead
Langley Upper Green
Arkesden
Tye Green
Roe Green
Sandon
75
76
Newport
Howlett End
Wallington
Redhill
Green End
Buckland
Anstey
Debden
Mill End
Chipping
Snow End
Meesden
Clavering
Wicken Bonhunt
Widdington
Rushden
Wyddial
Great Hormead
Brent Pelham
Starlings Green
Quendon
Throcking
Berden
Rickling Green
Cottered
Buntingford
Hare Street
Little Hormead
Stocking Pelham
Henham
Hall's Green
Cromer
Aspenden
Ugley
Ugley Green
Monk Street
Ardeley
Westmill
Furneux Pelham
Manuden
Broxted
Walkern
Bassus Green
Hay Street
Elsenham
Wood End
Braughing
Albury
Clapgate
Great
STEVENAGE
Aston End
Farnham
Stansted Mountfitchet
Molehill Green
Benington
Puckeridge
Burton End
Haultwick
Old Hall Green
Standon
Little Hadham
Birchanger
Bamber's Green
Hebing End
Green End
Levens Green
Bishop's Stortford
Aston
Green St
Takeley
Bragbury End
Dane End
Collier's End
Hadham Ford
Takeley St
Whempstead
Watton-at-Stone
Bury Green
Birchanger Green
Hatfield Forest
Much Hadham
Sacombe
Great Hallingbury
Datchworth
High Cross
Green Tye
Thorley
Little Hallingbury
Spellbrook
Stapleford
Tonwell
Wadesmill
Hatfield Broad Oak
Hanbury Manor
Babbs Green
Allen's Green
Gaston Green
59
Chapmore End
Widford
Brickendon
Waterford
Ware
Wareside
Sawbridgeworth
Hatfield Heath
Roundbush Gn
Hunsdon
High Wych
White Roding
Leaden Roding
Hertford
Bengeo
Scott's Grotto
Great Amwell
Sheering
Mimram
Gilston
Stanstead Abbotts
Eastwick
Old Harlow
Matching Tye
Hertingfordbury
Little Amwell
St Margarets
Abbess Roding
Letty Green
Hertford Heath
HARLOW
Matching Green
Beauchamp Roding
Roydon
Hare Street
Threshers Bush
Essendon
Bayford
Hoddesdon
Foster Street
Birds Green
Brickendon
Parndon
Broxbourne Woods
Roydon Hamlet
Broxbourne
Hastingwood
Fyfield
Willingale
Paradise Park
Nazeing
Moreton
Newgate Street
Wormley
Lower Nazeing
Epping Green
North Weald
Norton Heath
Bumble's Green
Epping Upland
North Weald Bassett
High Ongar
Cuffley
Lee Valley Park
Epping Ongar Railway
Coopersale Common
Log Church
Chipping Ongar
Northaw
Cheshunt
Epping
Goff's Oak
White Water Centre
Toot Hill
Potters Bar
Waltham Abbey
Upshire
Stondon Massey
Waltham Cross
M25
Botany Bay
Capel Manor
Doddinghurst
Nuclear Bunker
Enfield Wash
Enfield Lock
Forty Hall
Forty Hill
High Beach
Theydon Bois
Kelvedon Hatch
Enfield
King George V Res
Debden
Navestock
Navestock Side
Mountnessing
Cockfosters
Bush Hill Park
Ponders End
Epping Forest
Loughton
45
Lambourne End
Pilgrims Hatch
Coxtie Green
Shenfield
East Barnet
Winchmore Hill
Buckhurst Hill
Stapleford Abbotts
South Weald
BRENTWOOD
Southgate
Chingford
Chigwell
Havering-atte-Bower
Brook Street
Friern Barnet
Woodford Wells
Grange Hill
Harold Hill
Collier Row
Hainault
0 1 2 3 4 miles
0 1 2 3 4 5 kilometres
A505
A10
A507
A120
A414
A1169
A1025
A1060
A1184
A1170
A121
A104
A113
A128
A110
A105
A1005
A1010
A1055
A112
A1112
B1368
B1039
B1038
B1383
B1052
B1053
B184
B1004
B183
B180
B181
B1393
B158
B157
B156
B198
B176
B194
B172
B173
B175
B186
B1000
B1037
B1256
M11
M25
Stansted
R Beane
R Cam
R Rib
R Lea
R Roding
R Rom
A
B
C
D
E
F
1
2
3
4
5
6
7
8

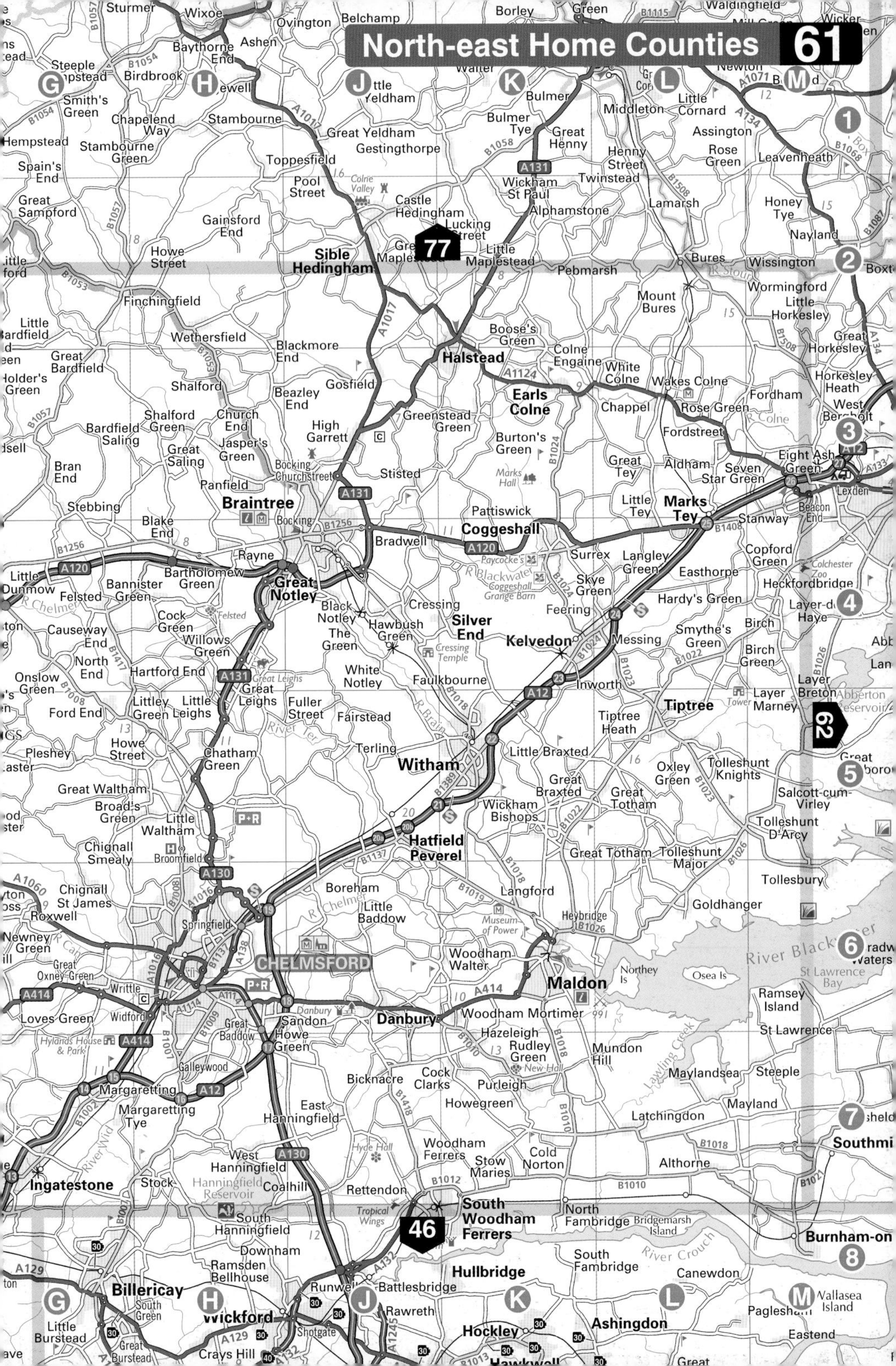

62
77
78
61
47
Hadleigh
Manningtree
COLCHESTER
Wivenhoe
Brightlingsea
West Mersea
MERSEA ISLAND
East Mersea
Jaywick
CLACTON-ON-SEA
Southminster
Burnham-on-Crouch
Harwich
Frinton-
River Blackwater
River Stour
River Orwell
Holbrook Bay
Pennyhole Bay
Colne Point
Sales Point
Shinglehead Point
Holliwell Point
Foulness Point
Courtsend
0 1 2 3 4 miles
0 1 2 3 4 5 kilometres

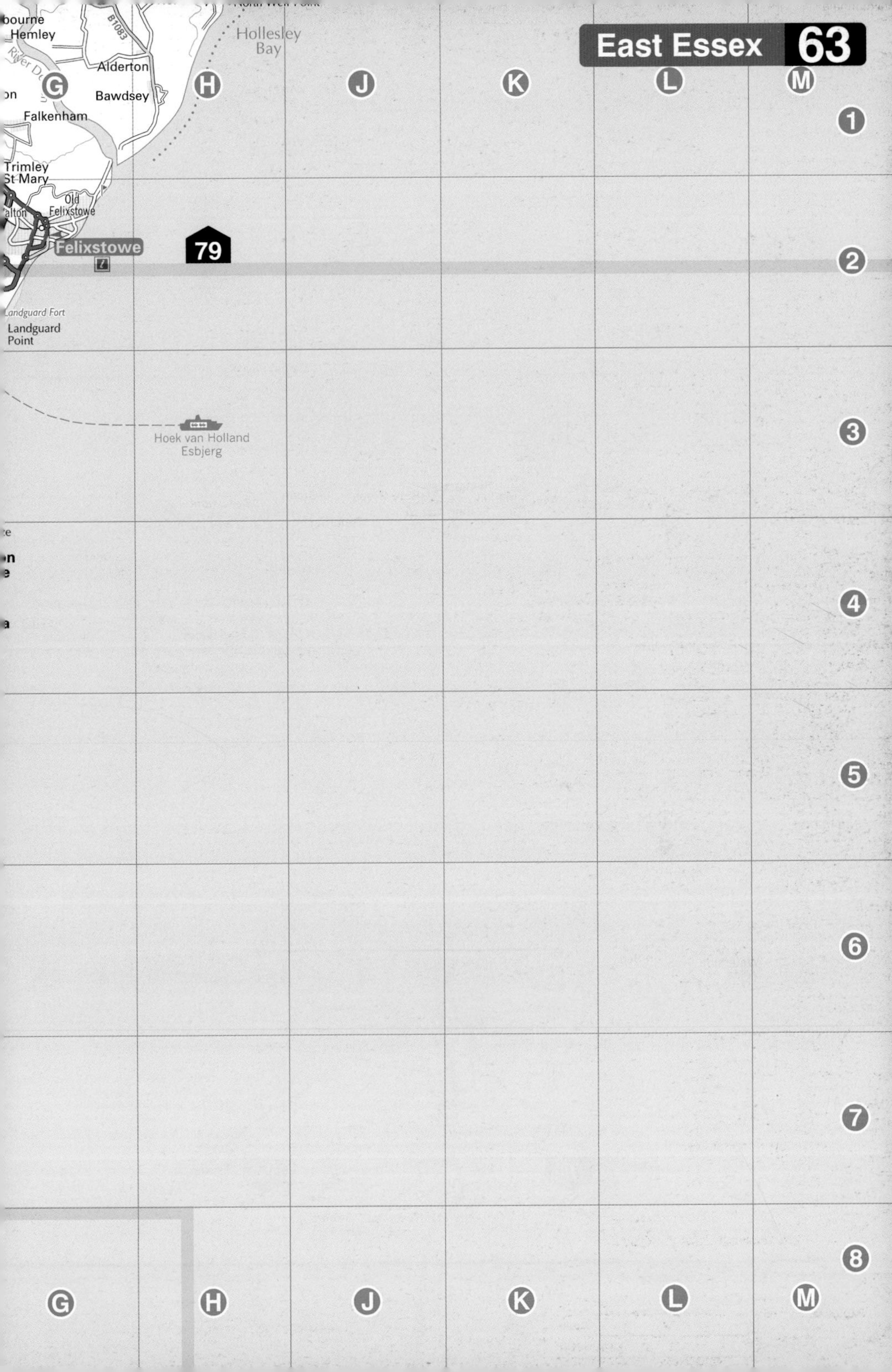

Hollesley Bay
Alderton
Bawdsey
Falkenham
Hemley
Trimley St Mary
Old Felixstowe
Felixstowe
79
Landguard Fort
Landguard Point
Hoek van Holland
Esbjerg
B1083

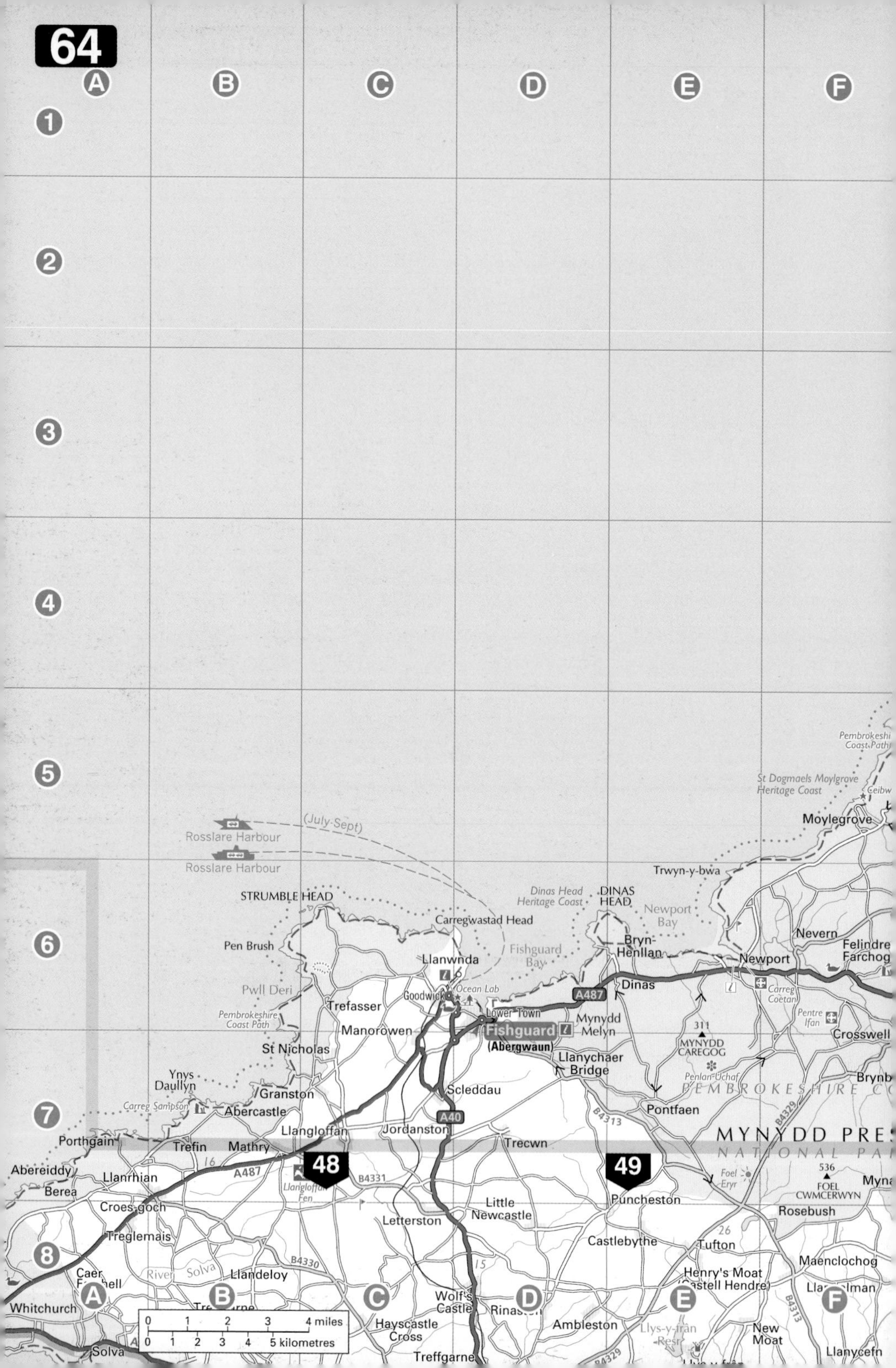

A
B
C
D
E
F
1
2
3
4
5
6
7
8
Rosslare Harbour
(July-Sept)
Rosslare Harbour
Pembrokeshire Coast Path
St Dogmaels Moylgrove Heritage Coast
Moylegrove
Trwyn-y-bwa
STRUMBLE HEAD
Carregwastad Head
Dinas Head Heritage Coast
DINAS HEAD
Newport Bay
Pen Brush
Llanwnda
Fishguard Bay
Bryn-Henllan
Nevern
Newport
Felindre Farchog
Pwll Deri
Goodwick
Ocean Lab
Dinas
A487
Carreg Coetan
Trefasser
Lower Town
Pembrokeshire Coast Path
Manorowen
Fishguard
(Abergwaun)
Mynydd Melyn
311
MYNYDD CAREGOG
Pentre Ifan
Crosswell
St Nicholas
Llanychaer Bridge
Penlan-Uchaf
Ynys Daullyn
Granston
Scleddau
PEMBROKESHIRE CO
Carreg Sampson
Abercastle
A40
B4313
Pontfaen
B4329
Porthgain
Llangloffan
Jordanston
MYNYDD PRES
NATIONAL PA
Trefin
Mathry
Trecwn
Abereiddy
16
A487
48
49
Llanrhian
Berea
Llangloffan Fen
B4331
Foel Eryr
536
FOEL CWMCERWYN
Croes-goch
Little Newcastle
Puncheston
Rosebush
Letterston
Treglemais
Castlebythe
26
Tufton
Maenclochog
River Solva
B4330
15
Llandeloy
Henry's Moat (Castell Hendre)
Wolf's Castle
Whitchurch
Rinaston
B4313
Hayscastle Cross
Ambleston
Llys-y-fran Resr
New Moat
Solva
Treffgarne
B4329
Llanycefn
0 1 2 3 4 miles
0 1 2 3 4 5 kilometres

Aberarth
Aberaeron
New Quay
Llanina
Ceredigion Heritage Coast
Maen-y-groes
Gilfachrheda
Llanarth
Cross Inn
Llwyncelyn
Oakford
Cwmtydu
Nanternis
Caerwedros
Dihewyd
Mydroilyn
Ynys-Lochtyn
Llwyndafydd
Llangranog
Pontgarreg
Plwmp
Penbryn
Pentregat
Aberporth
Sarnau
Brynhoffnant
Talgarreg
Cardigan Island
Mwnt
Felinwynt Rainforest & Butterfly Centre
Cardigan Island Coastal Farm Park
Tresaith
Y Ferwig
Poppit Sands
Tremain
Blaenannerch
Tan-y-groes
Glynarthen
Blaenporth
Penparc
Rhydlewis
Ffostrasol
Cwrt-newydd
Cardigan
(Aberteifi)
Abbey
Dogmaels
Bettws Evan
Beulah
Hawen
Pontshaen
Troedyraur
Penrhiw-pal
Tre-groes
Llanwenog
Ponthirwaun
Brongest
Maesllyn
Pren-gwyn
Rhydowen
Llechryd
Llandygwydd
Croes-lan
Teifi Marshes
Pen-y-bryn
Castle
Afon Teifi
TIVY SIDE
Cilgerran
Rock Mill Woollen & Water Mill
Capel Dewi
Abercych
Cenarth
Cwm-cou
Adpar
Llandyfriog
Penrhiw-llan
Teifi Valley Railway
Llandysul
Rhoshill
Pen-rhiw
Newcastle Emlyn
(Castell Newydd Emlyn)
Henllan
Llanfihangel-ar-arth
Newchapel
Llangeler
Pontwelly
Eglwyswrw
Drefach
Felindre
National Wool
Glynteg
Pentre-cwrt
Boncath
Cwmhiraeth
Blaenffos
Capel Iwan
Pencader
Bwlch-y-groes
Cwmpengraig
Star
Rhos
Gwyddgrug
Crymmych
Tegryn
Hermon
Cwmduad
Alltwalis
Llanfyrnach
FOEL DRYCH
Trelech
Glandwr
Llanpumsaint
River Gwili
Pontarsais
Hebron
Blaen-y-Coed
Cynwyl Elfed
Blaenwaun
Llanglydwen
Cefn-y-pant
Cwmbach
Talog
Gwili Railway
Efailwen
Felingwm
A487
A484
A478
A486
A485
A475
A482
B4342
B4333
B4334
B4321
B4338
B4459
B4571
B4570
B4548
B4546
B4332
B4336
B4476
B4299
B4301
49
50
99

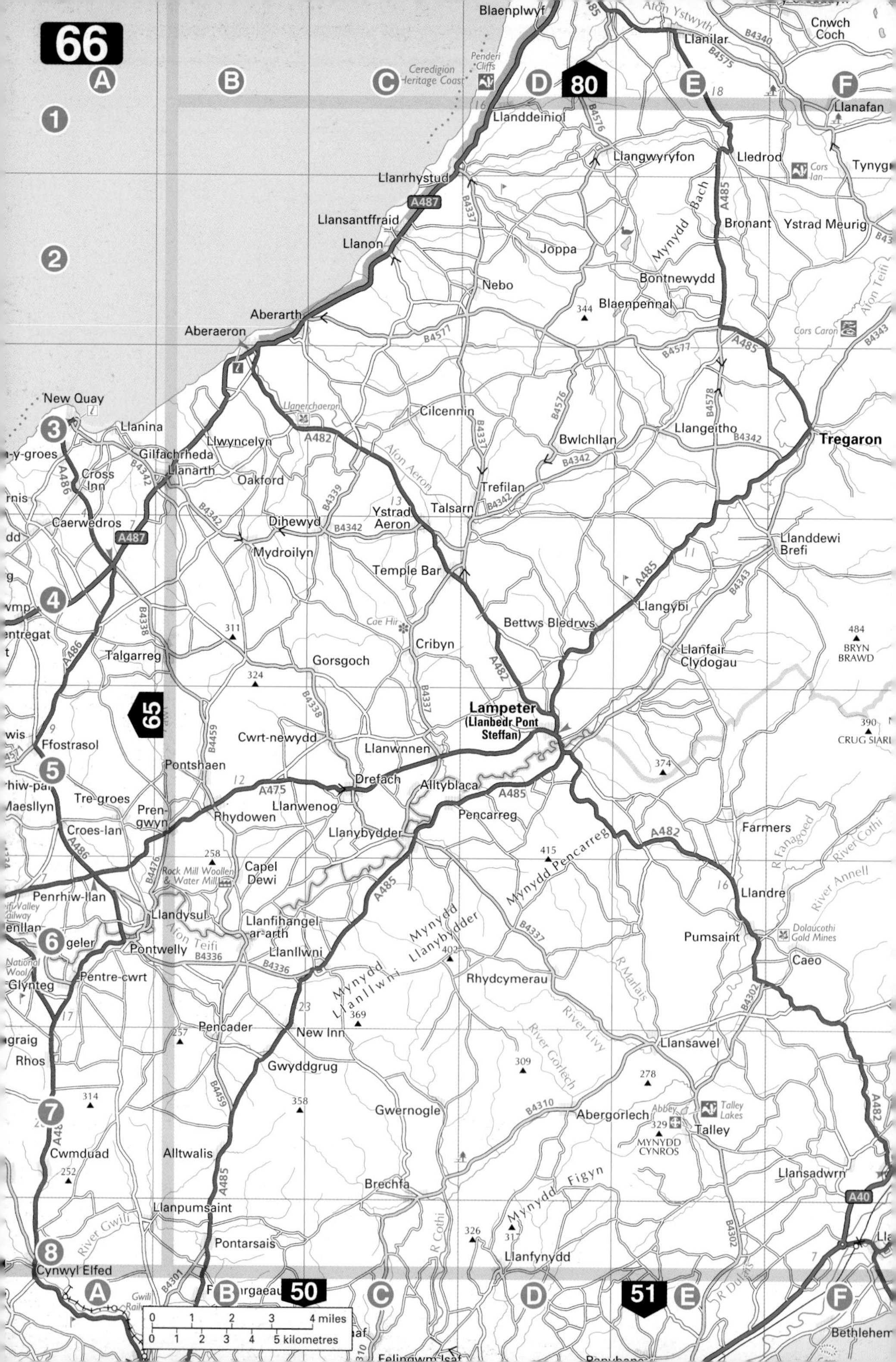
66
A
B
C
D
E
F
1
2
3
4
5
6
7
8
80
65
50
51
Blaenplwyf
Afon Ystwyth
Llanilar
B4340
B4575
Cnwch Coch
Penderi Cliffs
Ceredigion Heritage Coast
Llanafan
Llanddeiniol
B4576
Llangwyryfon
Lledrod
Cors Ian
Tynygr
Llanrhystud
A487
B4337
Llansantffraid
Llanon
Mynydd Bach
A485
Bronant
Ystrad Meurig
Joppa
Nebo
Bontnewydd
Blaenpennal
344
Afon Teifi
Aberarth
Aberaeron
B4577
Cors Caron
B4343
New Quay
Llanerchaeron
Cilcennin
B4578
Llanina
A482
Llwyncelyn
Bwlchllan
Llangeitho
B4342
Tregaron
Gilfachrheda
Llanarth
Cross Inn
A486
Afon Aeron
Oakford
Trefilan
Caerwedros
B4339
Ystrad Aeron
Talsarn
Dihewyd
Mydroilyn
Llanddewi Brefi
Temple Bar
Cae Hir
Llangybi
Bettws Bledrws
B4338
311
Cribyn
Talgarreg
Gorsgoch
Llanfair Clydogau
484
BRYN BRAWD
324
Lampeter
(Llanbedr Pont Steffan)
Cwrt-newydd
B4459
390
CRUG SIARL
Ffostrasol
Llanwnnen
Pontshaen
374
A475
Drefach
Alltyblaca
Tre-groes
Llanwenog
Pencarreg
Pren-gwyn
Rhydowen
Croes-lan
Llanybydder
Farmers
258
415
Mynydd Pencarreg
R Fanagoed
River Cothi
Capel Dewi
Rock Mill Woollen & Water Mill
River Annell
Penrhiw-llan
Llandysul
Mynydd Llanybydder
Llandre
Llanfihangel-ar-arth
B4336
Pumsaint
Dolaucothi Gold Mines
Pontwelly
Afon Teifi
Llanllwni
402
Caeo
Pentre-cwrt
Mynydd Llanllwni
Rhydcymerau
R Marlais
Glynteg
B4302
369
River Livy
Pencader
257
New Inn
Llansawel
River Gorlech
Rhos
Gwyddgrug
309
278
314
358
B4310
Gwernogle
Abergorlech
Abbey
Talley Lakes
Talley
329
MYNYDD CYNROS
Cwmduad
Alltwalis
252
Mynydd Figyn
Llansadwrn
A40
Brechfa
Llanpumsaint
River Gwili
R Cothi
326
317
Pontarsais
Llanfynydd
Cynwyl Elfed
B4301
R Dulais
Gwili Railway
Bethlehem
0
1
2
3
4 miles
5 kilometres

81
52
68
Pontrhydygroes
Ysbyty Ystwyth
Cwmystwyth
GEIFAS
St Harmon
Gilfach Farm
Craig-Goch Resr
Rhayader
Llansantffraed-Cwmdeuddwr
Ffair Rhos
Pontrhydfendigaid
Abbey
Pen-y-Garreg Resr
Nantmel
DIBYN DU
Claerwen Reservoir
Garreg-Ddu Resr
Elan Village
Elan Valley
Caban Coch Resr
Llanwrthwl
Llanyre
Llandrindod
PEN-MAEN-WERN
Howey
CEFN CNWC
DRYGARN FAWR
Newbridge on Wye
River Towi
Esgair Cerrig
Abergwesyn Common
Afon Irfon
Llanafan-Fawr
PEN CARREG-DÂN
CEFN COCH
Cwmbach Llechrhyd
Vicarage Meadows
Abergwesyn
CEFN CRUG
Royal Welsh
Llanelwedd
PEN-Y-GURNOS
CEFN FANNOG
Beulah
Cilmery
Prince Llewelyn
Builth Wells
(Llanfair-ym-Muallt)
Garth
CARCWM
River Doethie
Llyn Brianne
MYNYDD TRAWSNANT
Llanwrtyd Wells
Llangammarch Wells
BANC-Y-CELYN
River Brun
Cefngorwydd
DRUM DDU
Rhandirmwyn
Cynghordy Viaduct
Mynydd Eppynt
BRYN DU
Ysgir Fawr
Gwenddwr
Crickadarn
Tirabad
Llandulas
Upper Chapel
CEFN CLAWDD
Cynghordy
Cilycwm
River Crychan
GWRHYD
Llaneglwys
YSGWYDD HWCH
Merthyr Cynog
NOETHGRUG
Mynydd Bwlch-y-Groes
Nant Bran
Poor Man's Wood
Lower Chapel
Llandovery
(Llanymddyfri)
Llanfihangel Nant Bran
Pont-faen
Pwllgloyw
TWYRN DISGWYLFA
Battle
Llanddew
Cradoc
Roman Fort
Llywel
Trallong
Brecon
(Aberhonddu)
Myddfai
Mynydd Myddfai
Usk Reservoir
Trecastle
YR ALLT
Sennybridge
River Usk
River Bran
Defynnog
Llanspyddid
Llanfrynach
Twynllanan
Libanus
Crai
BRECON BEACONS
A44
A470
A4081
B4358
A483
B4519
B4520
B4567
A40
A4215
B4518
B4343
B4574
B4602
A4069

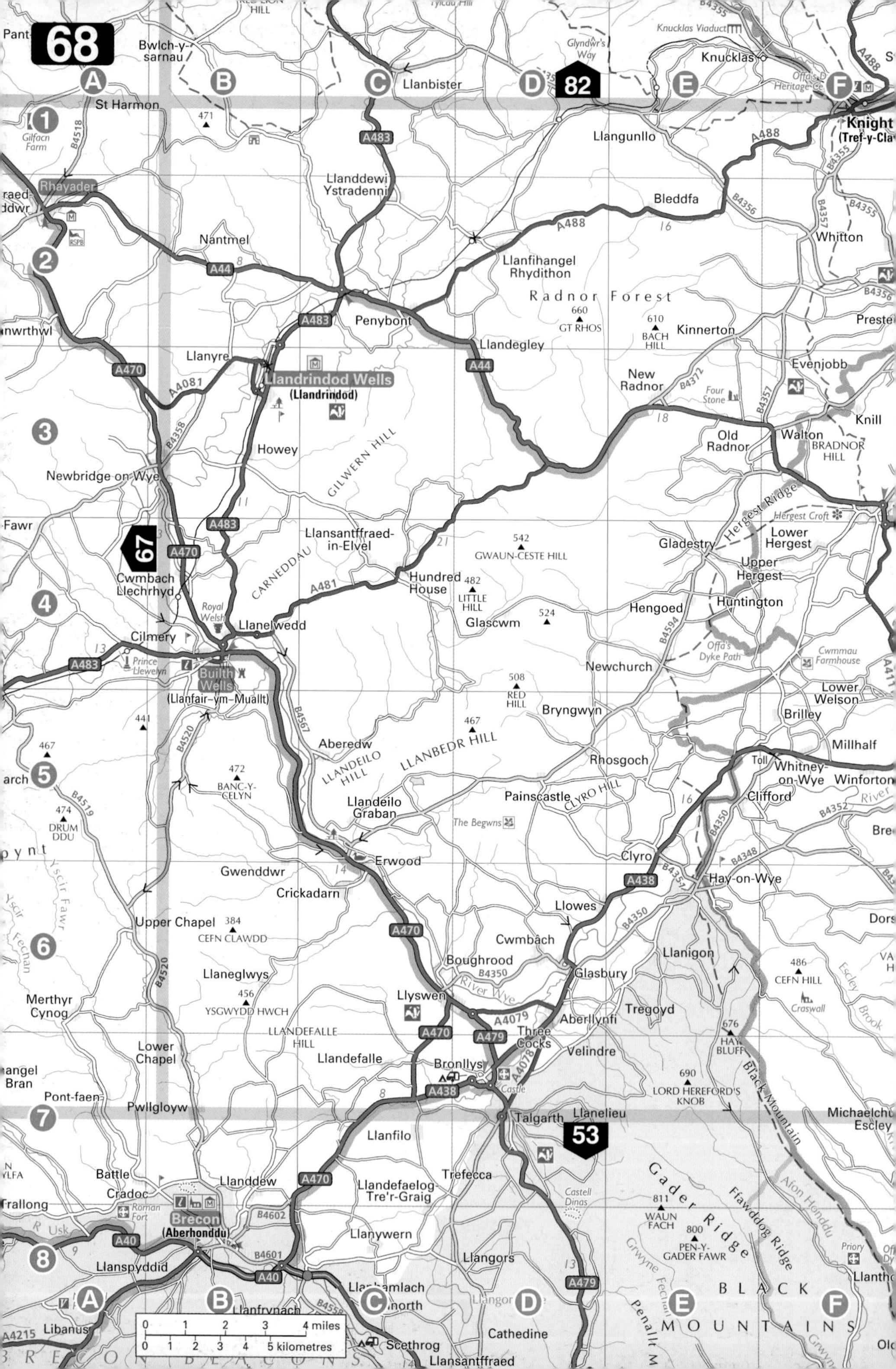
68
82
67
53
A
B
C
D
E
F
1
2
3
4
5
6
7
8
Pant-
Bwlch-y-sarnau
Llanbister
Glyndŵr's Way
Knucklas Viaduct
Knucklas
Offa's Dyke Heritage Centre
St Harmon
Gilfach Farm
471
Knighton
(Tref-y-Clawdd)
Llangunllo
A483
A488
B4518
Rhayader
Llanddewi Ystradenni
Bleddfa
B4356
B4357
B4355
Whitton
RSPB
Nantmel
A44
A488
16
Llanfihangel Rhydithon
Radnor Forest
660
GT RHOS
610
BACH HILL
Kinnerton
Presteigne
Penybont
A483
Llandegley
Llanyre
A470
A4081
Llandrindod Wells
(Llandrindod)
New Radnor
B4372
Four Stone
Evenjobb
Knill
18
Old Radnor
Walton
BRADNOR HILL
Howey
GILWERN HILL
B4358
Newbridge on Wye
11
A483
Hergest Ridge
Hergest Croft
Lower Hergest
Gladestry
Llansantffraed-in-Elvel
21
542
GWAUN-CESTE HILL
A470
Cwmbach Llechrhyd
CARNEDDAU
A481
Hundred House
482
LITTLE HILL
Upper Hergest
Huntington
Hengoed
Royal Welsh
Llanelwedd
Glascwm
524
Cilmery
13
A483
Prince Llewelyn
Builth Wells
(Llanfair-ym-Muallt)
B4594
Offa's Dyke Path
Newchurch
Cwmmau Farmhouse
Lower Welson
508
RED HILL
Bryngwyn
Brilley
441
B4520
B4567
467
467
LLANBEDR HILL
Aberedw
Millhalf
472
BANC-Y-CELYN
LLANDEILO HILL
Rhosgoch
Toll
Whitney-on-Wye
Winforton
5
B4519
474
DRUM DDU
Llandeilo Graban
Painscastle
CLYRO HILL
16
Clifford
B4352
The Begwns
B4350
River Wye
Erwood
14
Gwenddwr
Crickadarn
Clyro
B4348
Hay-on-Wye
B4351
A438
Yscir Fawr
Yscir Fechan
Upper Chapel
384
CEFN CLAWDD
A470
Llowes
B4350
Dorstone
Cwmbâch
Llanigon
486
CEFN HILL
Craswall
Escley Brook
Boughrood
B4350
Glasbury
Llaneglwys
B4520
Merthyr Cynog
456
YSGWYDD HWCH
Llyswen
River Wye
A4079
Aberllynfi
Tregoyd
LLANDEFALLE HILL
A470
A479
Three Cocks
676
HAY BLUFF
Lower Chapel
Llandefalle
Bronllys
A4078
Velindre
Castle
Llanfihangel Bran
Pont-faen
Pwllgloyw
8
A438
690
LORD HEREFORD'S KNOB
Black Mountain
Talgarth
Llanelieu
Michaelchurch Escley
Llanfilo
Battle
Cradoc
Llanddew
A470
Trefecca
Llandefaelog-Tre'r-Graig
Gader Ridge
Ffawddog Ridge
Castell Dinas
Afon Honddu
Trallong
Roman Fort
Brecon
(Aberhonddu)
B4602
811
WAUN FACH
800
PEN-Y-GADER FAWR
R Usk
A40
9
Llanywern
Llanspyddid
B4601
A40
Llangors
Grwyne Fechan
Priory
Llanthony
Libanus
Llanfrynach
B4558
A479
13
BLACK MOUNTAINS
A4215
0 1 2 3 4 miles
0 1 2 3 4 5 kilometres
Scethrog
Cathedine
Llansantffraed
Penallt Mawr
BRECON BEACONS

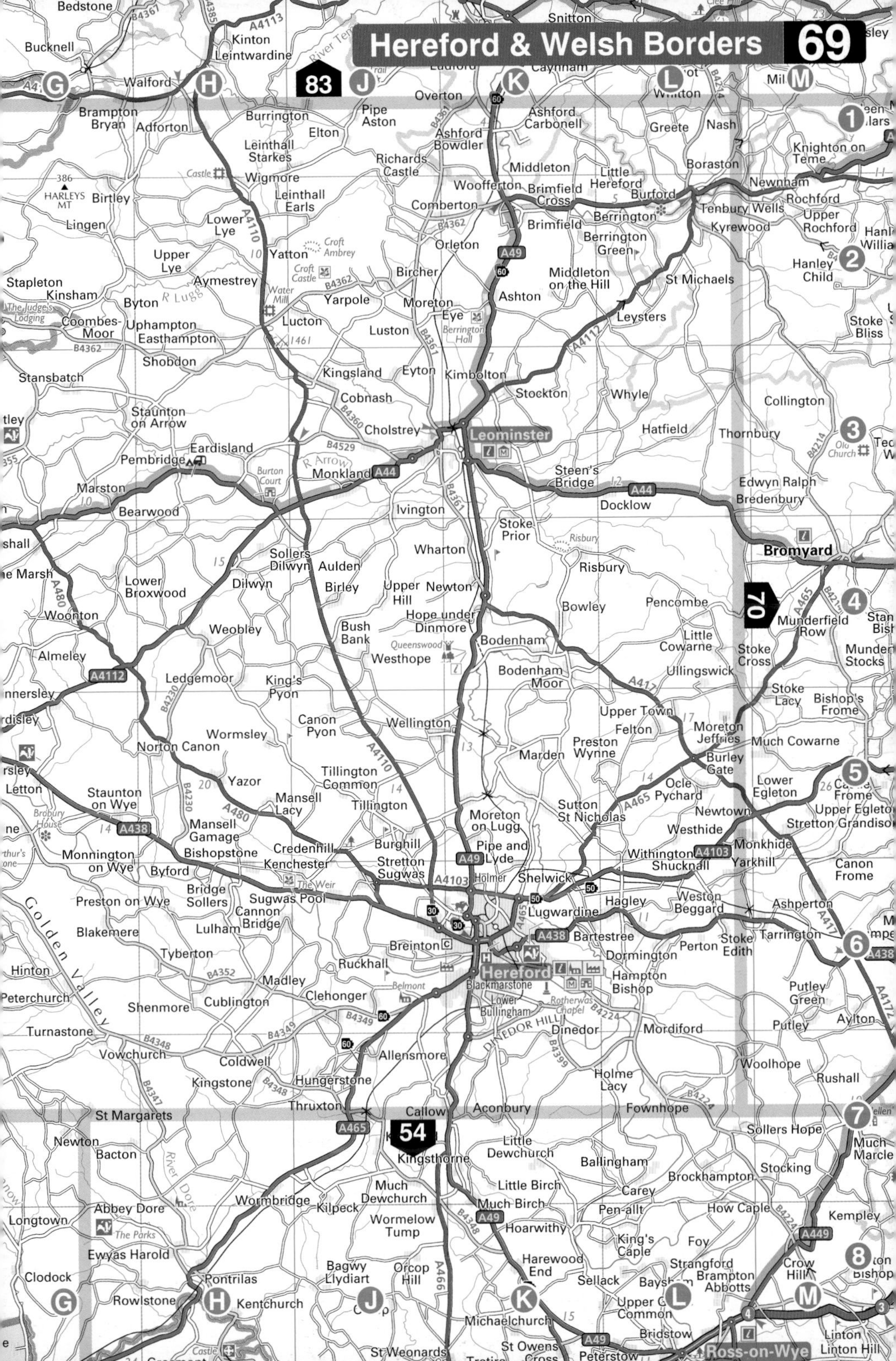
Bedstone
Bucknell
Kinton
Leintwardine
Snitton
Walford
Brampton Bryan
Adforton
Burrington
Pipe Aston
Overton
Ashford Carbonell
Ashford Bowdler
Greete
Nash
Elton
Leinthall Starkes
Richards Castle
Middleton
Little Hereford
Boraston
Knighton on Teme
Newnham
Wigmore
HARLEYS MT
Birtley
Leinthall Earls
Comberton
Woofferton
Brimfield Cross
Burford
Tenbury Wells
Rochford
Upper Rochford
Lingen
Lower Lye
Croft Ambrey
Orleton
Brimfield
Berrington
Kyrewood
Berrington Green
Upper Lye
Yatton
Bircher
Middleton on the Hill
Hanley Child
Stapleton
Kinsham
Aymestrey
Croft Castle
Yarpole
Ashton
St Michaels
Byton
R Lugg
Water Mill
Moreton
Eye
Berrington Hall
Leysters
The Judge's Lodging
Coombes-Moor
Uphampton
Easthampton
Lucton
Luston
Stoke Bliss
Shobdon
Stansbatch
Kingsland
Eyton
Kimbolton
Cobnash
Stockton
Whyle
Collington
Staunton on Arrow
Cholstrey
Leominster
Hatfield
Thornbury
Old Church
Eardisland
Pembridge
Burton Court
R Arrow
Monkland
Steen's Bridge
Edwyn Ralph
Marston
Bredenbury
Bearwood
Ivington
Docklow
Stoke Prior
Risbury
Bromyard
Sollers Dilwyn
Aulden
Wharton
Lower Broxwood
Dilwyn
Birley
Upper Hill
Newton
Bowley
Pencombe
Munderfield Row
Woonton
Hope under Dinmore
Weobley
Bush Bank
Queenswood
Bodenham
Little Cowarne
Almeley
Westhope
Stoke Cross
Bodenham Moor
Ullingswick
Munderfield Stocks
Ledgemoor
King's Pyon
Stoke Lacy
Bishop's Frome
Upper Town
Canon Pyon
Wellington
Felton
Moreton Jeffries
Wormsley
Norton Canon
Marden
Preston Wynne
Much Cowarne
Burley Gate
Yazor
Tillington Common
Ocle Pychard
Lower Egleton
Staunton on Wye
Mansell Lacy
Tillington
Sutton St Nicholas
Newtown
Upper Egleton
Stretton Grandison
Letton
Brobury House
Mansell Gamage
Moreton on Lugg
Westhide
Monkhide
Monnington on Wye
Bishopstone
Credenhill
Burghill
Pipe and Lyde
Withington
Canon Frome
Kenchester
Stretton Sugwas
Shucknall
Yarkhill
Byford
Holmer
Shelwick
Bridge Sollers
The Weir
Preston on Wye
Sugwas Pool
Lugwardine
Hagley
Weston Beggard
Ashperton
Cannon Bridge
Blakemere
Lulham
Bartestree
Tarrington
Breinton
Dormington
Perton
Stoke Edith
Tyberton
Hinton
Golden Valley
Ruckhall
Hereford
Hampton Bishop
Madley
Belmont
Blackmarstone
Peterchurch
Clehonger
Lower Bullingham
Rotherwas Chapel
Putley Green
Shenmore
Cublington
DINEDOR HILL
Dinedor
Mordiford
Putley
Aylton
Turnastone
Vowchurch
Allensmore
Coldwell
Holme Lacy
Woolhope
Kingstone
Hungerstone
Rushall
Thruxton
St Margarets
Callow
Aconbury
Fownhope
Sollers Hope
Little Dewchurch
Newton
Bacton
River Dore
Kingsthorne
Ballingham
Much Marcle
Stocking
Much Dewchurch
Little Birch
Brockhampton
Carey
Wormbridge
Kilpeck
Much Birch
Longtown
Abbey Dore
The Parks
Wormelow Tump
Pen-allt
How Caple
Kempley
Hoarwithy
King's Caple
Foy
Ewyas Harold
Harewood End
Strangford
Crow Hill
Bagwy Llydiart
Orcop Hill
Brampton Abbotts
Clodock
Pontrilas
Sellack
Rowlstone
Kentchurch
Upper Common
Michaelchurch
Bridstow
Linton
Linton Hill
St Weonards
St Owens Cross
Peterstow
Ross-on-Wye

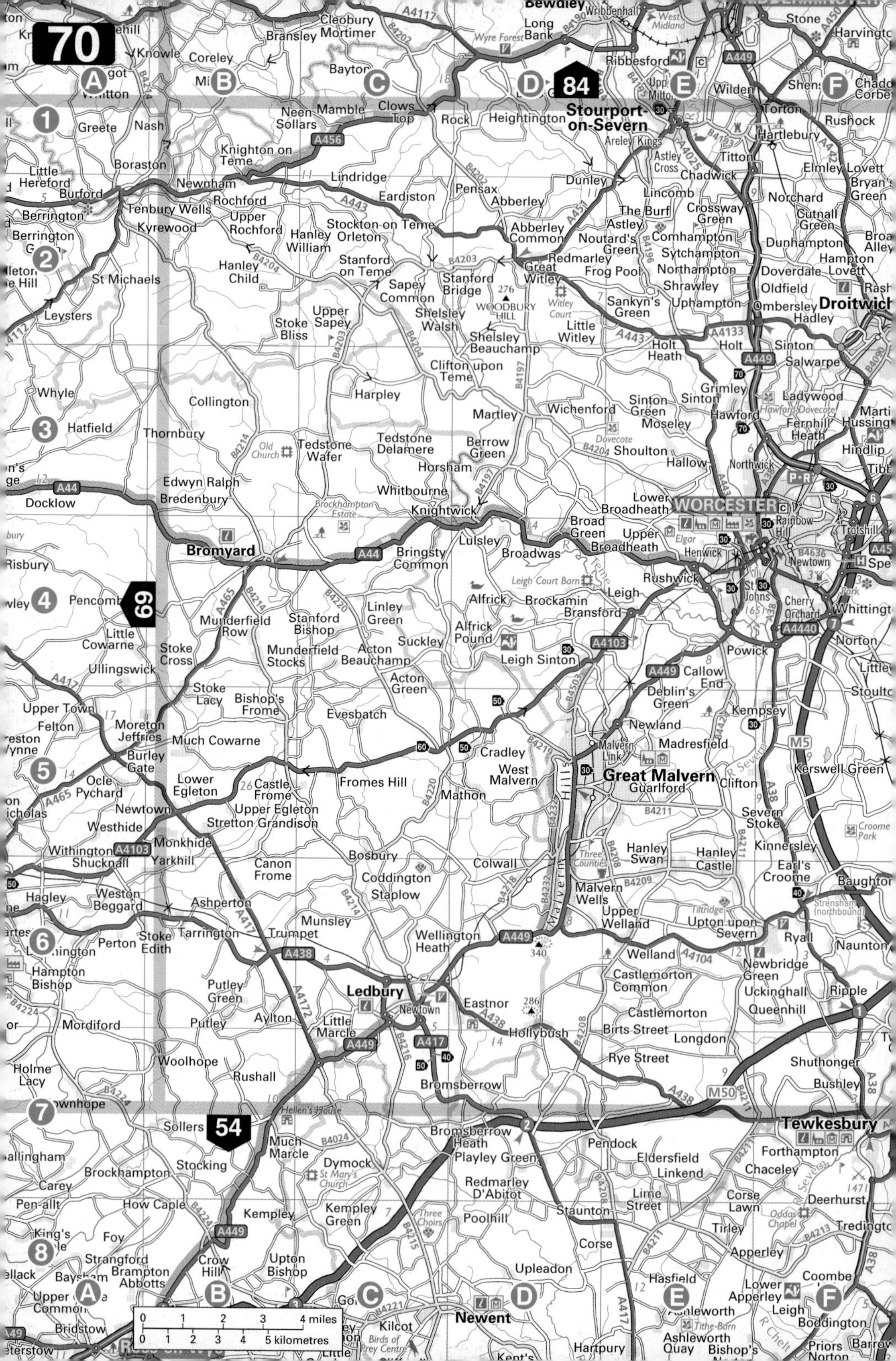
70
84
69
54
A
B
C
D
E
F
1
2
3
4
5
6
7
8
Bewdley
Wribbenhall
Cleobury Mortimer
Bransley
A4117
Long Bank
Wyre Forest
West Midland
Stone
Harvington
Knowle
Coreley
Baytor
Ribbesford
Wilden
Chaddesley Corbett
Whitton
Greete
Nash
Neen Sollars
Mamble
Clows Top
Rock
Heightington
Stourport-on-Severn
Areley Kings
Torton
Rushock
Hartlebury
Astley Cross
Titton
A456
Knighton on Teme
Boraston
Little Hereford
Burford
Newnham
Lindridge
Pensax
Dunley
Chadwick
Elmley Lovett
Bryan's Green
Lincomb
Berrington
Tenbury Wells
Rochford
Upper Rochford
Eardiston
Abberley
Crossway Green
Norchard
Kyrewood
Hanley William
Stockton on Teme
Orleton
Abberley Common
The Burf
Astley
Noutard's Green
Comhampton
Cutnall Green
Dunhampton
Sytchampton
Hampton Lovett
St Michaels
Hanley Child
Stanford on Teme
Sapey Common
Stanford Bridge
Great Witley
Redmarley
Frog Pool
Northampton
Shrawley
Doverdale
Oldfield
Uphampton
Ombersley
Droitwich
Hadley
Leysters
Stoke Bliss
Upper Sapey
Shelsley Walsh
Woodbury Hill
276
Witley Court
Sankyn's Green
Little Witley
Shelsley Beauchamp
Holt Heath
Holt
A4133
Sinton
Salwarpe
A449
Clifton upon Teme
Whyle
Collington
Harpley
Grimley
Sinton Green
Sinton
Ladywood
Hawford Dovecote
Wichenford
Martley
Moseley
Hawford
Fernhill Heath
Hindlip
Hatfield
Thornbury
Old Church
Tedstone Wafer
Tedstone Delamere
Berrow Green
Dovecote
Shoulton
Hallow
Northwick
Horsham
Edwyn Ralph
Bredenbury
Whitbourne
A44
Docklow
Lower Broadheath
WORCESTER
Brockhampton Estate
Knightwick
Rainbow Hill
Broad Green
Upper Broadheath
Elgar
Henwick
Trotshill
Bromyard
Lulsley
Broadwas
Bringsty Common
Risbury
Newtown
Leigh Court Barn
Rushwick
Pencombe
Linley Green
Alfrick
Brockamin
Leigh
St Johns
Cherry Orchard
Whittington
Munderfield Row
Stanford Bishop
Bransford
Alfrick Pound
A4103
A4440
Norton
Little Cowarne
Suckley
Powick
Stoke Cross
Munderfield Stocks
Acton Beauchamp
Leigh Sinton
Callow End
Ullingswick
Acton Green
Deblin's Green
Stoke Lacy
Bishop's Frome
Evesbatch
Kempsey
Upper Town
Felton
Newland
Moreton Jeffries
Much Cowarne
Cradley
Malvern Link
Madresfield
Burley Gate
West Malvern
Great Malvern
Clifton
M5
Kerswell Green
Lower Egleton
Castle Frome
Fromes Hill
Mathon
Guarlford
Ocle Pychard
Newtown
Upper Egleton
Stretton Grandison
Severn Stoke
Westhide
Malvern Hills
Croome Park
Withington
Monkhide
Yarkhill
Shucknall
Canon Frome
Bosbury
Colwall
Three Counties
Hanley Swan
Hanley Castle
Kinnersley
Earl's Croome
Hagley
Weston Beggard
Coddington
Staplow
Malvern Wells
Baughton
Ashperton
Munsley
Upper Welland
Upton upon Severn
Strensham (northbound)
Tarrington
Trumpet
Wellington Heath
Ryall
Perton
Stoke Edith
340
Welland
Naunton
Hampton Bishop
A438
Castlemorton Common
Newbridge Green
Putley Green
Ledbury
Newtown
Eastnor
286
Uckinghall
Ripple
Queenhill
Mordiford
Putley
Aylton
Little Marcle
Castlemorton
Hollybush
Birts Street
Longdon
Holme Lacy
Woolhope
Rushall
Rye Street
Shuthonger
Bromsberrow
Bushley
M50
Fownhope
Sollers
Hellen's House
Tewkesbury
Much Marcle
Bromsberrow Heath
Pendock
Eldersfield
Forthampton
Ballingham
Stocking
Playley Green
Linkend
Chaceley
Brockhampton
Dymock
St Mary's Church
Carey
Redmarley D'Abitot
Lime Street
Corse Lawn
Deerhurst
Pen-allt
How Caple
Kempley
Staunton
Odda's Chapel
Kempley Green
Three Choirs
Poolhill
Tirley
Tredington
King's Caple
Foy
Corse
Apperley
Strangford
Brampton Abbotts
Crow Hill
Upton Bishop
Upleadon
Hasfield
Lower Apperley
Coombe Hill
Upper Common
Ashleworth
Leigh
Boddington
Newent
Kilcot
Birds of Prey Centre
Tithe Barn
Ashleworth Quay
Bridstow
Hartpury
Prior's Norton
0 1 2 3 4 miles
0 1 2 3 4 5 kilometres

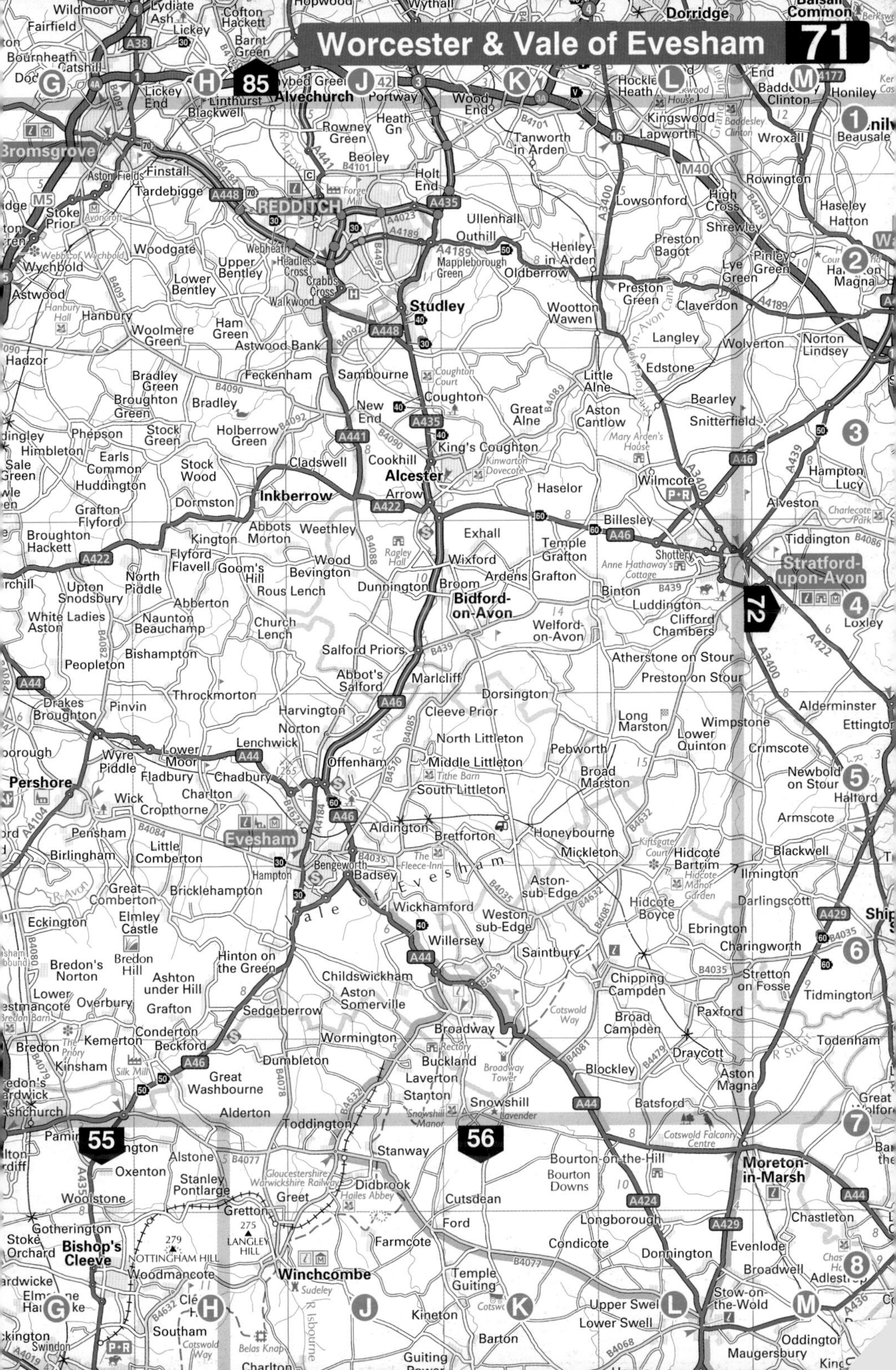
Bromsgrove
Alvechurch
Redditch
Studley
Alcester
Inkberrow
Bidford-on-Avon
Stratford-upon-Avon
Pershore
Evesham
Vale of Evesham
Broadway
Chipping Campden
Moreton-in-Marsh
Winchcombe
Bishop's Cleeve
Stow-on-the-Wold
Henley-in-Arden
Tanworth in Arden
Hockley Heath
Dorridge
Lapworth
Kingswood
Feckenham
Cookhill
Ragley Hall
Coughton Court
Mary Arden's House
Anne Hathaway's Cottage
Hidcote Manor Garden
Kiftsgate Court
Snowshill Manor
Broadway Tower
Cotswold Falconry Centre
Sudeley
Hailes Abbey
Gloucestershire Warwickshire Railway
Cotswold Way
85
72
55
56

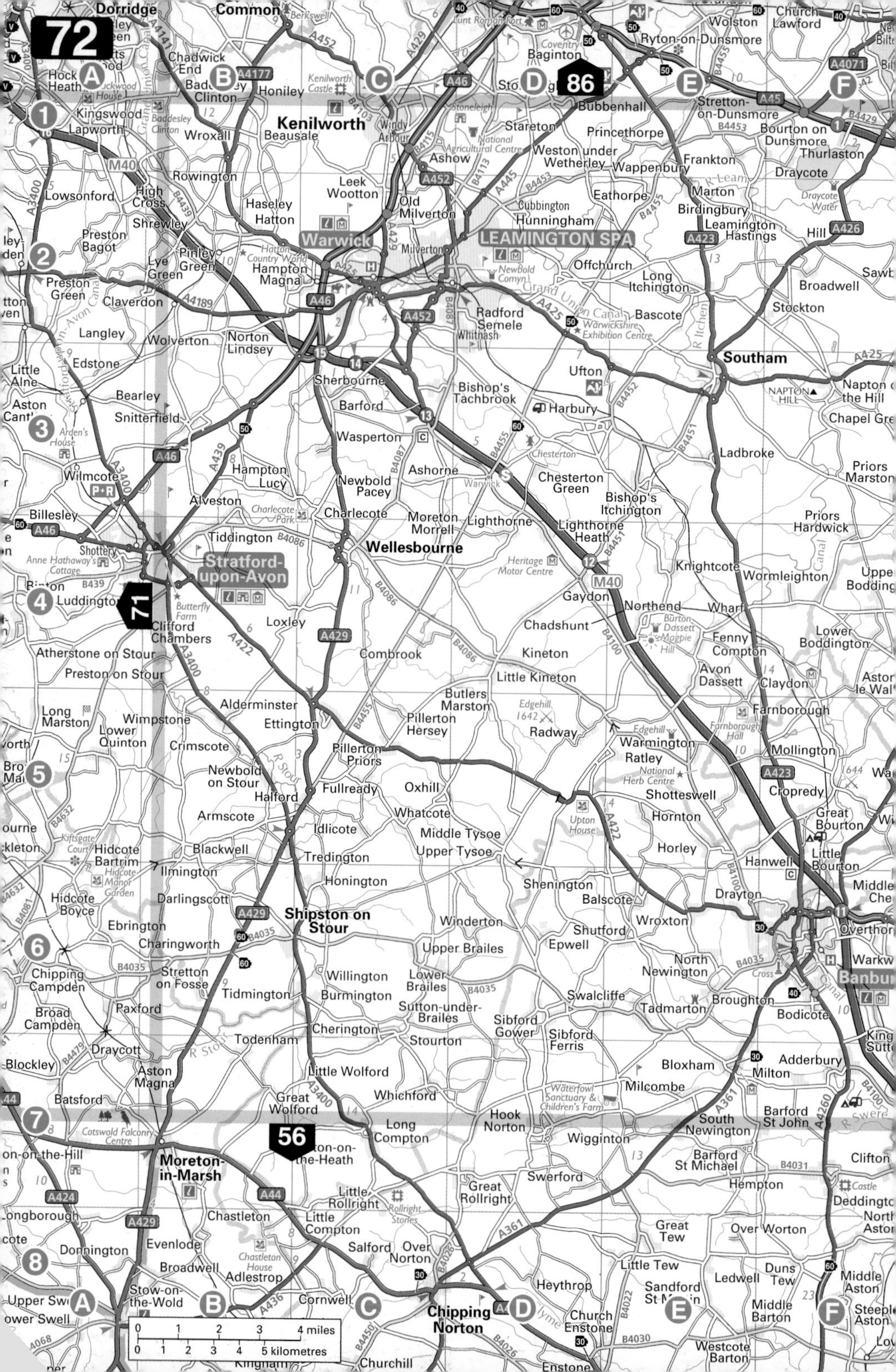
Dorridge
Common
Berkswell
A452
A429
Lunt Roman Fort
Coventry
Baginton
86
Wolston
Church Lawford
Ryton-on-Dunsmore
A4071
Hock Heath
Chadwick End
A4177
Baddesley Clinton
Honiley
Kenilworth Castle
A46
Stoneleigh
B4455
Stretton-on-Dunsmore
A45
Bourton on Dunsmore
Thurlaston
Kingswood
Lapworth
Wroxall
Kenilworth
Beausale
Windy Arbour
Stareton
Bubbenhall
Princethorpe
Frankton
Draycote
M40
Rowington
Ashow
National Agricultural Centre
Weston under Wetherley
Wappenbury
Lowsonford
High Cross
Haseley
Hatton
Leek Wootton
Old Milverton
A452
B4113
A445
Eathorpe
Marton
Birdingbury
Draycote Water
Shrewley
Cubbington
Hunningham
Leamington Hastings
A426
Hill
Preston Bagot
Pinley Green
Lye Green
Hatton Country World
Hampton Magna
Warwick
Milverton
LEAMINGTON SPA
A423
Newbold Comyn
Offchurch
Long Itchington
Broadwell
Preston Green
Claverdon
A4189
A46
A425
A452
B4087
Radford Semele
Whitnash
Grand Union Canal
Bascote
Stockton
Langley
Wolverton
Norton Lindsey
Warwickshire Exhibition Centre
Southam
Edstone
Little Alne
Sherbourne
Bishop's Tachbrook
Ufton
Napton Hill
Napton on the Hill
Aston Cantlow
Bearley
Snitterfield
Barford
Harbury
B4452
B4451
Chapel Green
Arden's House
A46
A439
Wasperton
B4087
Chesterton
Ladbroke
Wilmcote
Hampton Lucy
Newbold Pacey
Ashorne
B4455
Warwick
Chesterton Green
Bishop's Itchington
Priors Marston
A3400
Alveston
Charlecote Park
Charlecote
Moreton Morrell
Lighthorne
Lighthorne Heath
Priors Hardwick
Billesley
Shottery
Tiddington
B4086
Wellesbourne
Heritage Motor Centre
Knightcote
Wormleighton
Upper Boddington
Anne Hathaway's Cottage
Stratford-upon-Avon
B439
Binton
Luddington
71
Butterfly Farm
Clifford Chambers
Gaydon
Northend
Wharf
Chadshunt
Burton Dassett
Magpie Hill
Loxley
A429
B4086
A422
Fenny Compton
Lower Boddington
Atherstone on Stour
Combrook
Kineton
B4100
Preston on Stour
A3400
Little Kineton
Avon Dassett
Claydon
Aston le Walls
Butlers Marston
Edgehill 1642
Long Marston
Alderminster
Ettington
Pillerton Hersey
Farnborough
Farnborough Hall
Wimpstone
Lower Quinton
Crimscote
Pillerton Priors
Radway
Edgehill
Warmington
Ratley
Mollington
Newbold on Stour
National Herb Centre
A423
Halford
Fullready
Oxhill
Shotteswell
Cropredy
Armscote
Whatcote
Upton House
A422
Hornton
Great Bourton
Kiftsgate Court
Hidcote Bartrim
Hidcote Manor Garden
Blackwell
Idlicote
Middle Tysoe
Upper Tysoe
Horley
Little Bourton
Ilmington
Tredington
Hanwell
Honington
Shenington
Drayton
Hidcote Boyce
Darlingscott
Shipston on Stour
A429
Balscote
Ebrington
Winderton
Wroxton
Charingworth
B4035
Shutford
Epwell
Upper Brailes
Overthorpe
Chipping Campden
Stretton on Fosse
Willington
Lower Brailes
North Newington
B4035
Banbury
Cross
Tidmington
Burmington
Sutton-under-Brailes
Swalcliffe
Tadmarton
Broughton
Broad Campden
Paxford
Sibford Gower
Sibford Ferris
Bodicote
Draycott
Cherington
Stourton
Todenham
Blockley
Aston Magna
Little Wolford
Bloxham
Adderbury
Milton
Kings Sutton
Batsford
Great Wolford
Whichford
Waterfowl Sanctuary & Children's Farm
Milcombe
Cotswold Falconry Centre
56
Long Compton
Hook Norton
South Newington
A361
Barford St John
B4100
Moreton-in-Marsh
Barton-on-the-Heath
Wigginton
Barford St Michael
B4031
Clifton
A424
A44
Little Rollright
Rollright Stones
Great Rollright
Swerford
Hempton
Castle
Deddington
Longborough
A429
Chastleton
Little Compton
Great Tew
Over Worton
North Aston
Evenlode
Chastleton House
A361
Donnington
Broadwell
Adlestrop
Salford
Over Norton
B4026
Little Tew
Ledwell
Duns Tew
Middle Aston
Heythrop
Sandford St Martin
B4022
Upper Swell
Stow-on-the-Wold
A436
Cornwell
Chipping Norton
Church Enstone
Middle Barton
Steeple Aston
Lower Swell
B4450
B4026
B4030
Westcote Barton
Churchill
Enstone
Kingham
4 miles
5 kilometres

Banbury & South Midlands
73
Clifton upon Dunsmore
Yelvertoft
Mawsley
Winwick
Hillmorton
Rugby
Crick
West Haddon
DIRFT Logistics Park
Kilsby
87
Cottesbrooke Hall
Hanging Houghton
Old
Orlingbury
Hollowell
Creaton
Scaldwell
Walgrave
Barby
Coton Manor
Coton
Ravensthorpe
Teeton
Brixworth
Hannington
Great Harrowden
Oxford Canal
Ashby St Ledgers
Watford
Spratton
Holcot
Hardwick
East Haddon
Pitsford Reservoir
Brixworth
Northampton & Lamport Railway
Pitsford
Wellingborough
Willoughby
Watford Gap
Long Buckby
Holdenby House
Holdenby
Moulton
Sywell
Mears Ashby
Braunston
Welton
Chapel Brampton
Boughton
Overstone
Great Brington
Church Brampton
Whilton
Little Brington
Althorp Park
Harlestone
Sywell Reservoir
Daventry
Flecknoe
Norton
Kingsthorpe
Kingsley Park
Ecton
Brockhall
New Duston
Dallington
Great Billing
Staverton
Daventry
Northampton
Weston Favell
Little Billing
Harpole
Duston
Abington
Cogenhoe
Dodford
Flore
Upper Heyford
St James's End
Little Houghton
Newnham
Weedon
Kislingbury
Far Cotton
R Nene
Little Everdon
Nether Heyford
Great Houghton
Brafield-on-the-Green
Hellidon
Badby
Eleanor Cross
Denton
Church Stowe
Hunsbury Hill
Hardingstone
Windmill
Great Everdon
Bugbrooke
Northampton
Wootton
Charwelton
Upper Stowe
Rothersthorpe
Collingtree
Preston Capes
Farthingstone
Gayton
Hackleton
Milton Malsor
Quinton
Pattishall
Piddington
Horton
Litchborough
Eastcote
Blisworth
74
Little Preston
Grimscote
Cold Higham
Astcote
Byfield
Woodford Halse
Maidford
Courteenhall
Tiffield
Roade
West Farndon
Adstone
Ravenstone
Canons Ashby House
Hartwell
Blakesley
Eydon
Canons Ashby
Stoke Bruerne
Moreton Pinkney
Shutlanger
Greens Norton
National Waterways
Ashton
Stoke Goldington
Woodend
Stoke Park Pavilions
Chipping Warden
Bradden
Long Street
Plumpton
Towcester
R Tove
Grafton Regis
Culworth
Weedon Lois
Slapton
Alderton
Hanslope
Weston
Milthorpe
Grand Union Canal
Thorpe Mandeville
Abthorpe
Paulerspury
Pury End
Yardley Gobion
Sulgrave
Wappenham
Little Linford
Newport Pagnell
Helmdon
Silverstone
Whittlebury
Castlethorpe
Haversham
Thenford
Potterspury
Greatworth
Syresham
Silverstone
Cosgrove
New Bradwell
Marston St Lawrence
Puxley
Lillingstone Lovell
Old Stratford
Lillingstone Dayrell
Wolverton
Bradwell
Farthinghoe
Radstone
Deanshanger
Stony Stratford
Halse
Biddlesden
Passenham
Wicken
Whitfield
Calverton
Milton Keynes
Brackley
Dadford
Turweston
Stowe Gardens
Leckhampstead
Shalstone
Akeley
Loughton
Hinton-in-the-Hedges
Beachampton
Chackmore
Maids Moreton
Shenley Church End
Charlton
Westbury
Thornton
Evenley
Water Stratford
Shenley Brook End
Buckingham
R Great Ouse
Whaddon
Aynho
Croughton
Mixbury
Radclive
Nash
Finmere
Tingewick
57
58
Thornborough
Bletchley
Aynhoe Park House
Souldern
Barton Hartshorn
Gawcott
Great Horwood
Cottisford
Newton Purcell
Padbury
Little Horwood
Hardwick
Adstock
Fritwell
Hethe
Preston Bissett
Drayton Parslow
Hillesden
Stoke Lyne
Fringford
Addington
Mursley
Winslow
Cherwell Valley
Steeple Claydon
Twyford
Audley
Middle Claydon
Swanbourne
Stewkley
Bucknell
Stratton Audley
Poundon
East Claydon
Claydon House
Hoggeston
Caversfield
Charndon
Granborough
Dunton
Botolph
M1
M45
A5
A428
A5199
A508
A5076
A4500
A45
A43
A361
B4036
B5385
B4037
A413
A422
A421
A4421
B4031
B4100
B430
B4525
B4033
B4032
B526
A509
B4034

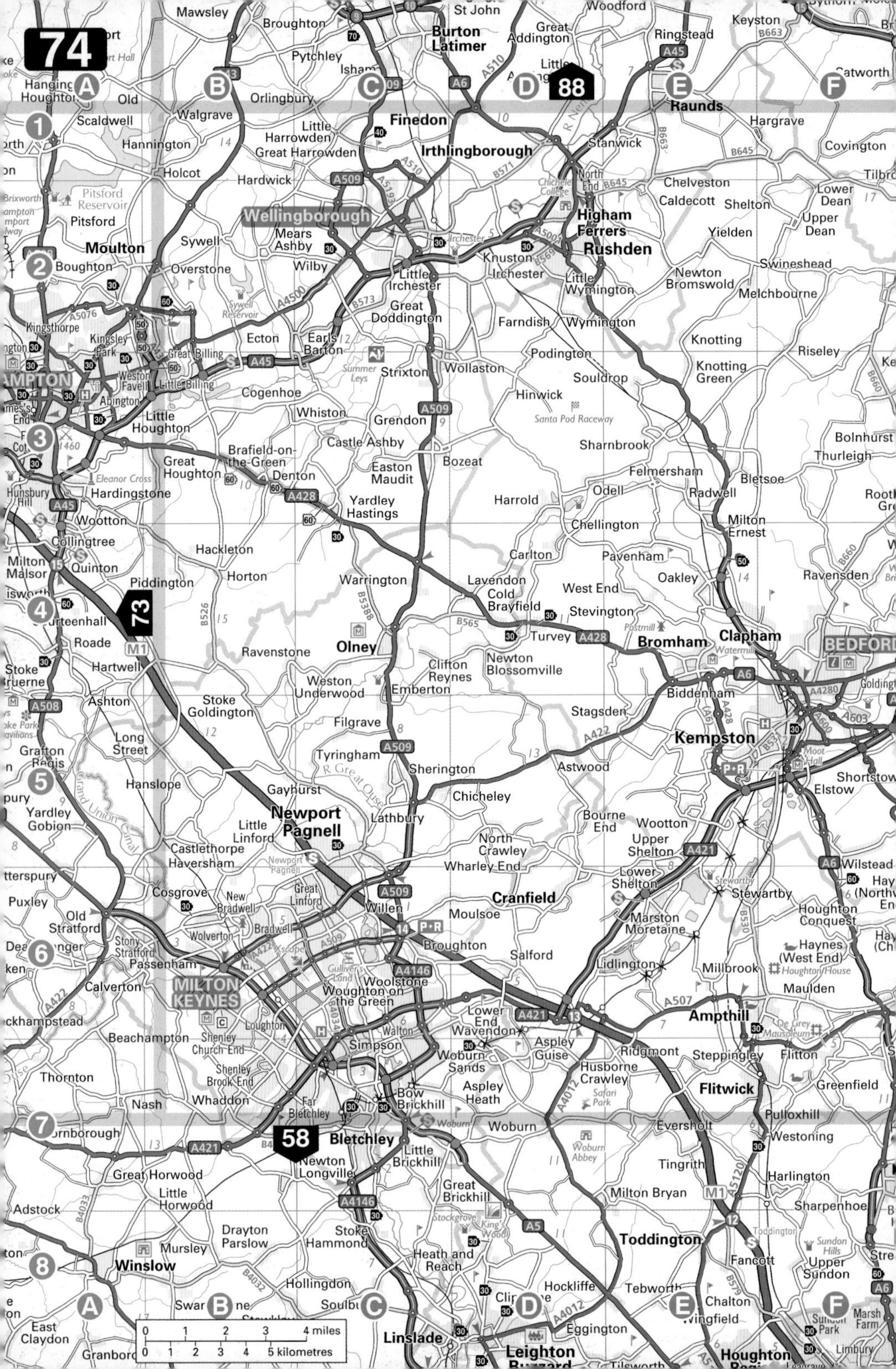

74
88
73
58
A
B
C
D
E
F
1
2
3
4
5
6
7
8
Mawsley
Broughton
St John
Burton Latimer
Woodford
Great Addington
Ringstead
Keyston
Catworth
Pytchley
Isham
Hanging Houghton
Old
Scaldwell
Walgrave
Orlingbury
Finedon
Raunds
Hargrave
Covington
Hannington
Little Harrowden
Great Harrowden
Irthlingborough
Stanwick
Holcot
Hardwick
Pitsford Reservoir
Brixworth
Pitsford
Wellingborough
Mears Ashby
Sywell
Moulton
Boughton
Overstone
Wilby
Irchester
Knuston
Chichele College
North End
Higham Ferrers
Rushden
Chelveston
Caldecott
Shelton
Lower Dean
Upper Dean
Yielden
Swineshead
Newton Bromswold
Melchbourne
Little Irchester
Great Doddington
Little Wymington
Wymington
Farndish
Sywell Reservoir
Kingsthorpe
Kingsley Park
Ecton
Earls Barton
Great Billing
Weston Favell
Little Billing
Abington
Summer Leys
Strixton
Wollaston
Podington
Souldrop
Knotting
Knotting Green
Riseley
Cogenhoe
Whiston
Hinwick
Santa Pod Raceway
Little Houghton
Grendon
Castle Ashby
Sharnbrook
Bolnhurst
Thurleigh
Brafield-on-the-Green
Great Houghton
Denton
Easton Maudit
Bozeat
Eleanor Cross
Hardingstone
Hunsbury Hill
Felmersham
Odell
Radwell
Bletsoe
Yardley Hastings
Harrold
Chellington
Milton Ernest
Wootton
Collingtree
Milton Malsor
Quinton
Hackleton
Horton
Piddington
Carlton
Pavenham
Oakley
Ravensden
Warrington
Lavendon
Cold Brayfield
West End
Stevington
Roade
Hartwell
Ravenstone
Olney
Turvey
Postmill
Bromham
Clapham
BEDFORD
Watermill
Stoke Bruerne
Weston Underwood
Clifton Reynes
Newton Blossomville
Emberton
Biddenham
Ashton
Stoke Goldington
Filgrave
Stagsden
Kempston
Long Street
Tyringham
Sherington
Astwood
Grafton Regis
R Great Ouse
Moot Hall
Elstow
Shortstow
Hanslope
Gayhurst
Chicheley
Yardley Gobion
Grand Union Canal
Newport Pagnell
Little Linford
Lathbury
Bourne End
Wootton
Upper Shelton
North Crawley
Castlethorpe
Haversham
Wharley End
Lower Shelton
Stewartby
Wilstead
Cosgrove
New Bradwell
Great Linford
Willen
Cranfield
Potterspury
Puxley
Old Stratford
Wolverton
Bradwell
Moulsoe
Marston Moretaine
Houghton Conquest
Stony Stratford
Passenham
Broughton
Haynes (West End)
Xscape
Gulliver's Land
Woolstone
Salford
Lidlington
Millbrook
Houghton House
Calverton
MILTON KEYNES
Woughton on the Green
Maulden
Lower End
Wavendon
Ampthill
De Grey Mausoleum
Beachampton
Shenley Church End
Loughton
Walton
Simpson
Woburn Sands
Aspley Guise
Ridgmont
Steppingley
Flitton
Thornton
Shenley Brook End
Husborne Crawley
Safari Park
Flitwick
Greenfield
Nash
Whaddon
Far Bletchley
Bow Brickhill
Aspley Heath
Bletchley
Little Brickhill
Woburn
Woburn Abbey
Eversholt
Pulloxhill
Westoning
Great Horwood
Newton Longville
Tingrith
Harlington
Little Horwood
Great Brickhill
Milton Bryan
Adstock
Stockgrove
King's Wood
Sharpenhoe
Drayton Parslow
Stoke Hammond
Toddington
Mursley
Heath and Reach
Toddington
Fancott
Sundon Hills
Upper Sundon
Winslow
Hollingdon
Hockliffe
Tebworth
Chalton
Soulbury
Wingfield
Marsh Farm
East Claydon
Linslade
Eggington
Leighton Buzzard
Houghton Regis
Limbury
A45
A6
A510
A509
A5193
B571
B645
B663
A5001
B569
A4500
B573
A5076
A43
A428
A508
M1
B526
B5388
B565
A428
A6
A4280
A600
A603
B660
A422
A421
A4146
A4034
A507
A4012
A5
A5120
B579
B4033
B4032
P+R
0 1 2 3 4 miles
0 1 2 3 4 5 kilometres

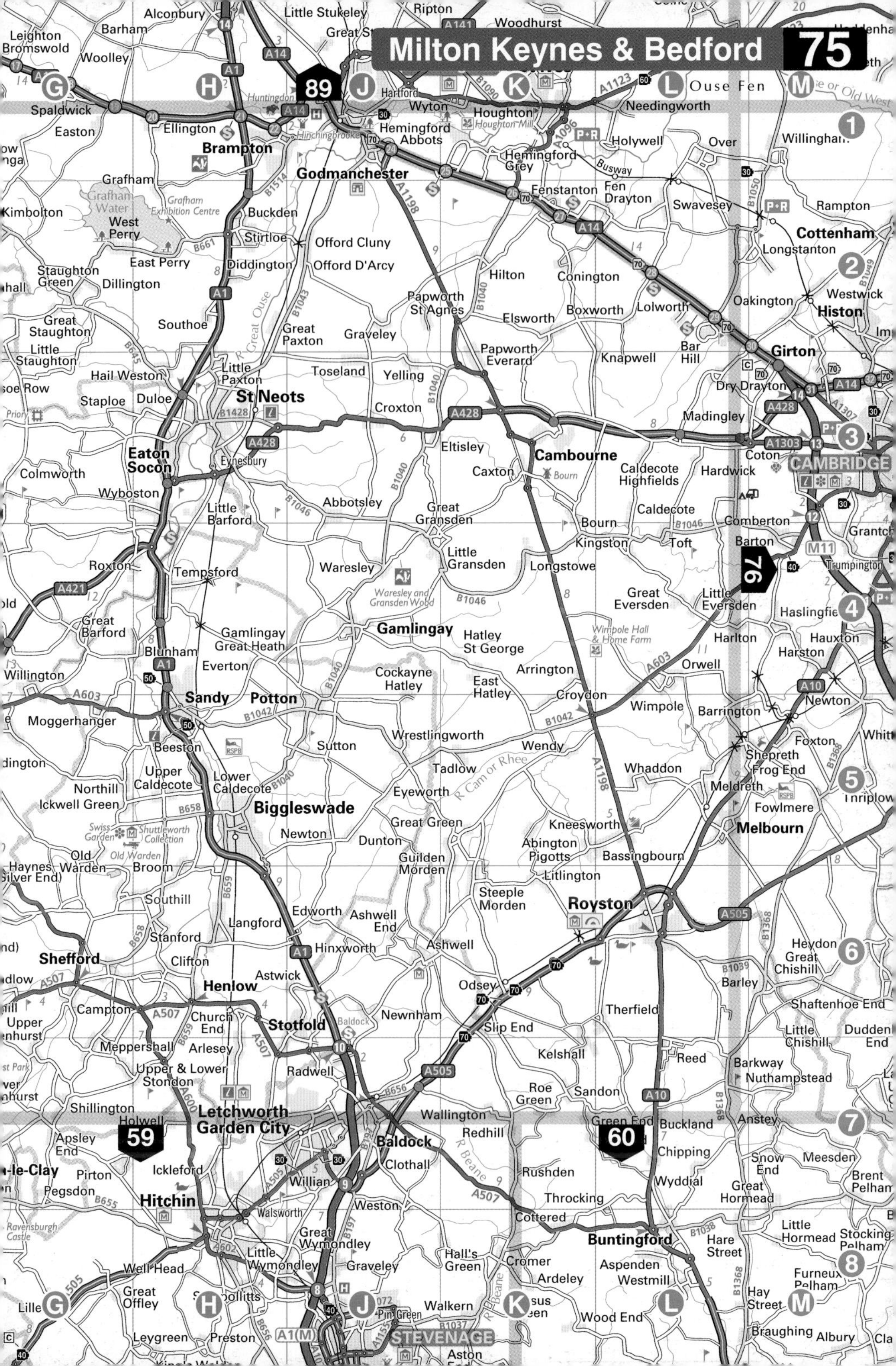
Huntingdon
Godmanchester
St Neots
Eaton Socon
Sandy
Potton
Biggleswade
Gamlingay
Cambourne
Cambridge
Royston
Baldock
Letchworth Garden City
Hitchin
Stevenage
Buntingford
Shefford
Henlow
Stotfold
Melbourn
Cottenham
Histon
Girton
Brampton
Buckden
Papworth Everard
Bassingbourn
Ouse Fen
89
76
59
60

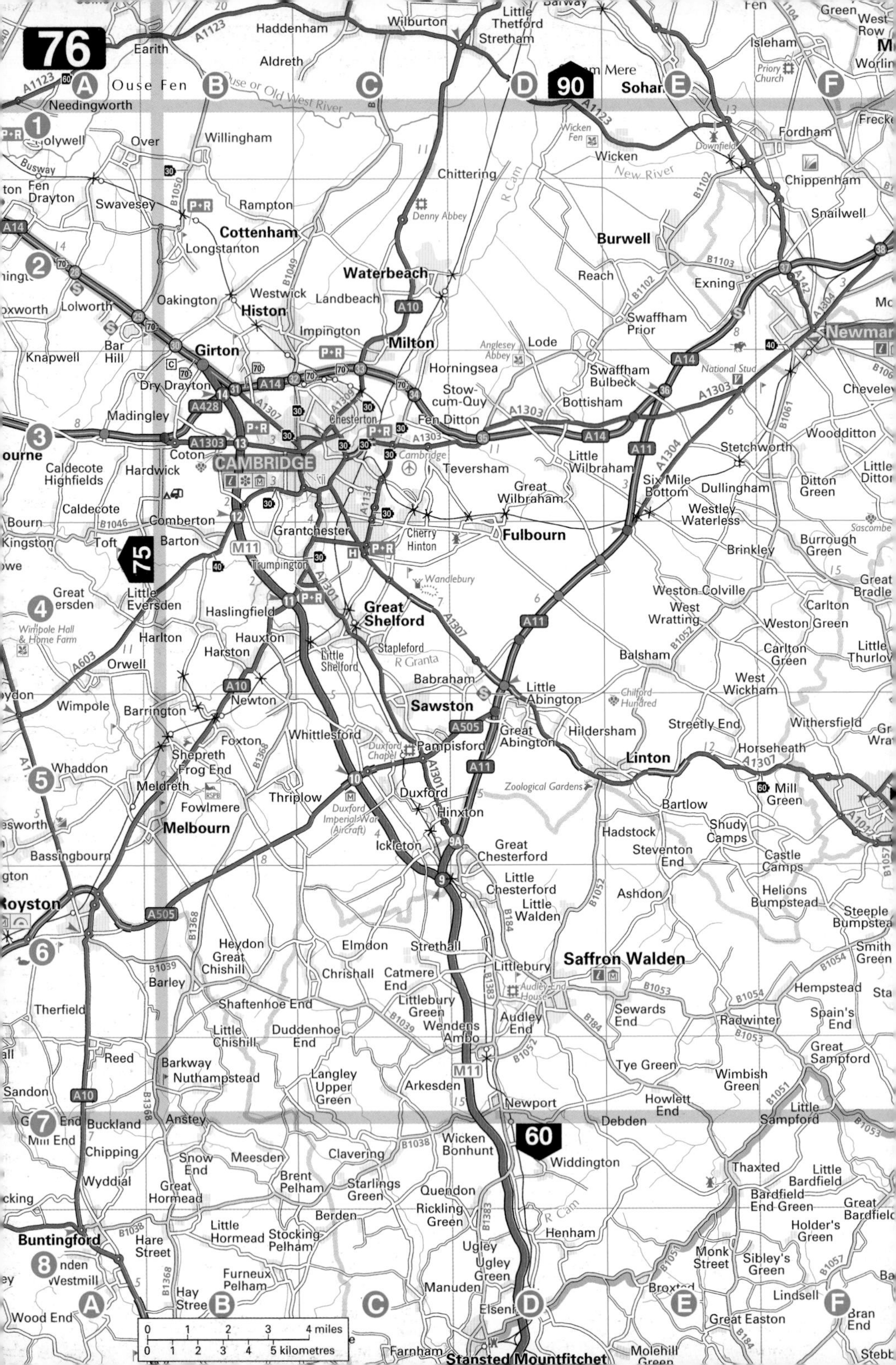

Haddenham
Wilburton
Little Thetford
Stretham
Earith
A1123
Aldreth
Ouse Fen
Ouse or Old West River
Soham Mere
90
Soham
Isleham
Priory Church
Worlington
West Row
Needingworth
Holywell
Over
Willingham
Wicken Fen
Wicken
New River
Fordham
Downfield
Freckenham
Busway
Fen Drayton
Swavesey
Rampton
Chittering
Denny Abbey
R Cam
Chippenham
Snailwell
A14
Cottenham
Longstanton
Burwell
Reach
B1103
Exning
Lolworth
Oakington
Westwick
Histon
Landbeach
Waterbeach
A10
Swaffham Prior
B1102
Knapwell
Bar Hill
Girton
Impington
Milton
Anglesey Abbey
Lode
Newmarket
Dry Drayton
Horningsea
Swaffham Bulbeck
National Stud
Cheveley
A428
Stow-cum-Quy
Bottisham
A1303
Madingley
Chesterton
Fen Ditton
A1307
Coton
CAMBRIDGE
Cambridge
Teversham
Little Wilbraham
A11
A1304
Stetchworth
Woodditton
Caldecote Highfields
Hardwick
Six Mile Bottom
Dullingham
Ditton Green
Little Ditton
Caldecote
Great Wilbraham
Westley Waterless
Bourn
B1046
Comberton
Grantchester
Cherry Hinton
Fulbourn
Kingston
Toft
Barton
M11
75
Trumpington
Wandlebury
Brinkley
Burrough Green
Sascombe
Great Eversden
Little Eversden
Haslingfield
Great Shelford
Weston Colville
Carlton
Great Bradley
Wimpole Hall & Home Farm
Harlton
Hauxton
Stapleford
West Wratting
Weston Green
Harston
Little Shelford
R Granta
Balsham
Carlton Green
Little Thurlow
Orwell
A603
Babraham
B1052
West Wickham
Wimpole
Barrington
Newton
Sawston
Little Abington
Chilford Hundred
Great Abington
Hildersham
Streetly End
Withersfield
A505
Foxton
Whittlesford
Duxford Chapel
Pampisford
Linton
Horseheath
Shepreth
Frog End
B1368
A1301
Whaddon
Meldreth
Thriplow
Duxford
Zoological Gardens
Mill Green
Bartlow
RSPB
Fowlmere
Melbourn
Hinxton
Duxford Imperial War (Aircraft)
Hadstock
Shudy Camps
Bassingbourn
Ickleton
Great Chesterford
Steventon End
Castle Camps
Royston
Little Chesterford
Little Walden
Ashdon
Helions Bumpstead
Steeple Bumpstead
Heydon
Great Chishill
Elmdon
Strethall
Smith Green
B1039
Barley
Chrishall
Catmere End
Saffron Walden
Littlebury
B1383
Audley End House
B1053
Hempstead
Therfield
Shaftenhoe End
Littlebury Green
Wendens Ambo
Audley End
Sewards End
Radwinter
Spain's End
Little Chishill
Duddenhoe End
Great Sampford
Reed
Barkway
Nuthampstead
Langley Upper Green
Arkesden
Tye Green
Wimbish Green
Sandon
Howlett End
Little Sampford
Buckland
Anstey
Newport
Debden
Mill End
Chipping
Snow End
Meesden
Clavering
Wicken Bonhunt
60
Widdington
Wyddial
Great Hormead
Brent Pelham
Starlings Green
Quendon
Thaxted
Little Bardfield
Bardfield End Green
Great Bardfield
Berden
Rickling Green
R Cam
Henham
Buntingford
Hare Street
Little Hormead
Stocking Pelham
Holder's Green
Ugley
Monk Street
Sibley's Green
Westmill
Furneux Pelham
Ugley Green
Manuden
Broxted
Lindsell
Wood End
Hay Street
Elsenham
Great Easton
Bran End
Farnham
Stansted Mountfitchet
Molehill Green
0 1 2 3 4 miles
0 1 2 3 4 5 kilometres

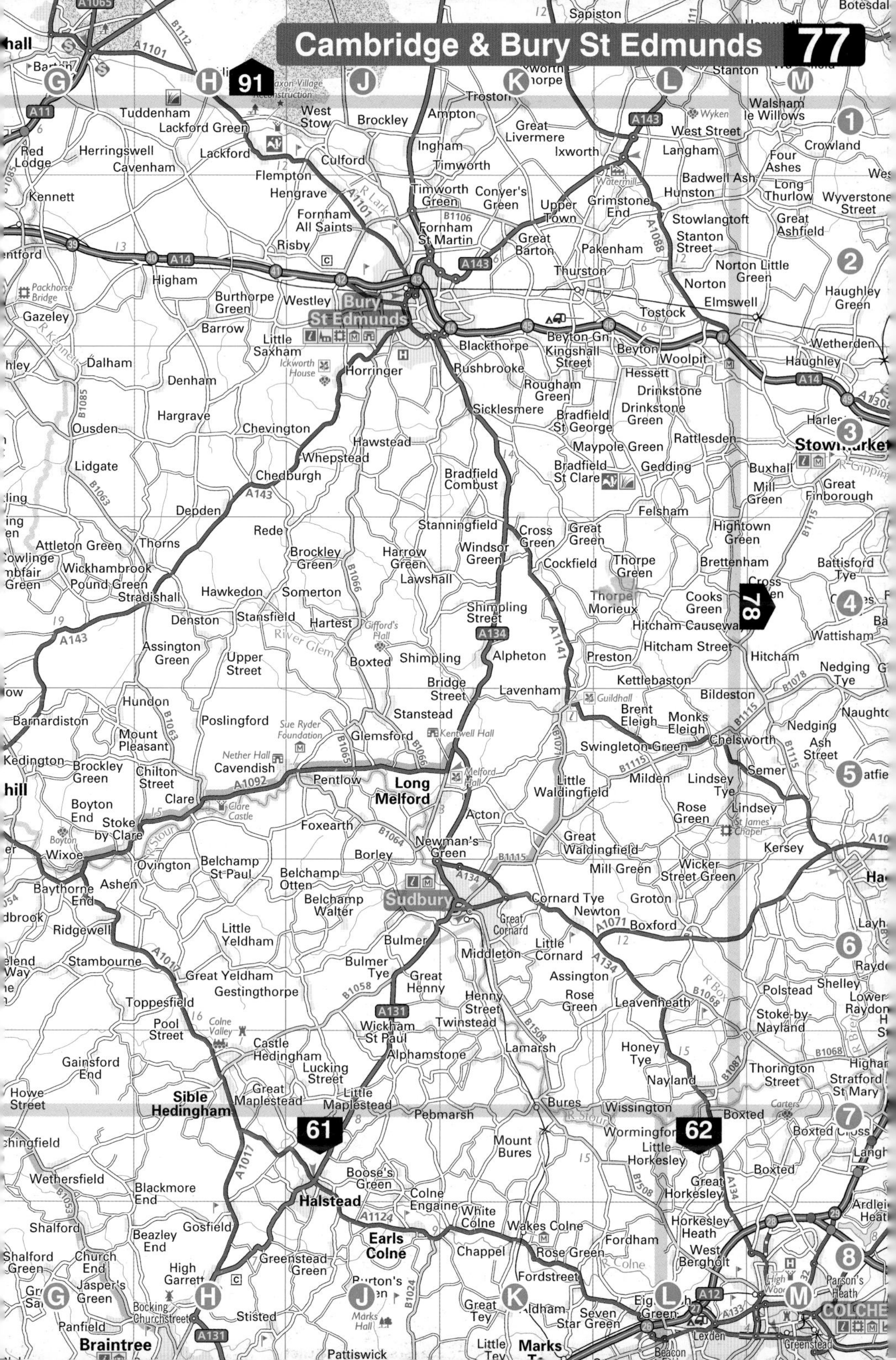
Bury St Edmunds
Sudbury
Long Melford
Halstead
Earls Colne
Sible Hedingham
Braintree
Stowmarket
Lavenham
Ixworth
Woolpit
Glemsford
Cavendish
Clare
Nayland
Boxford
Hadleigh
Colchester

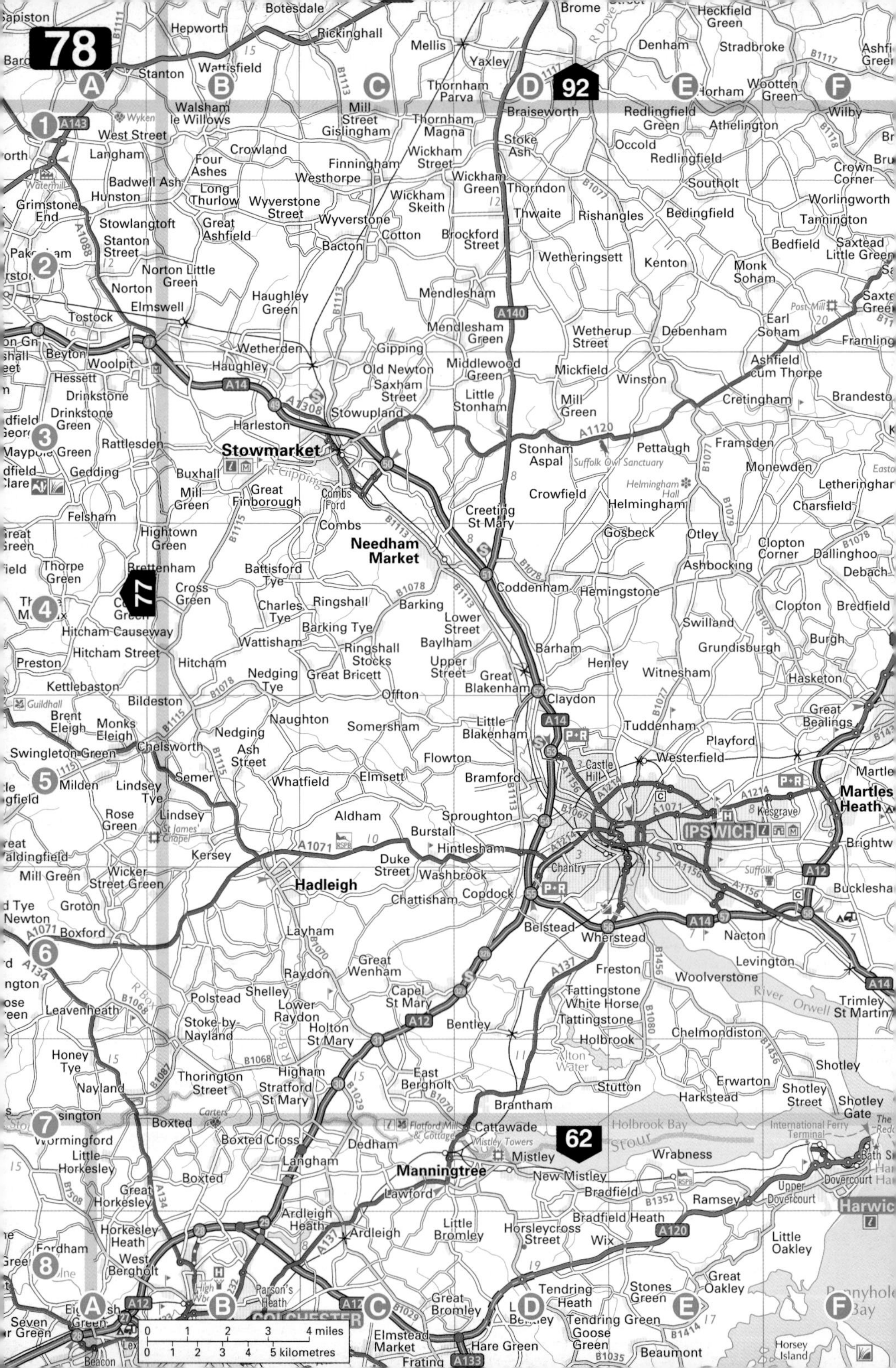
78
92
77
62
A
B
C
D
E
F
1
2
3
4
5
6
7
8
Botesdale
Hepworth
Rickinghall
Mellis
Yaxley
Brome
Heckfield Green
Denham
Stradbroke
Stanton
Wattisfield
Thornham Parva
Horham
Wootten Green
Walsham le Willows
Mill Street
Gislingham
Thornham Magna
Braiseworth
Redlingfield Green
Athelington
Wilby
West Street
Langham
Crowland
Four Ashes
Finningham
Wickham Street
Stoke Ash
Occold
Redlingfield
Crown Corner
Badwell Ash
Long Thurlow
Westhorpe
Wickham Green
Thorndon
Southolt
Hunston
Grimstone End
Wyverstone Street
Wickham Skeith
Worlingworth
Stowlangtoft
Great Ashfield
Wyverstone
Thwaite
Rishangles
Bedingfield
Tannington
Stanton Street
Cotton
Brockford Street
Bedfield
Saxtead Little Green
Bacton
Wetheringsett
Kenton
Monk Soham
Norton Little Green
Norton
Haughley Green
Mendlesham
Elmswell
Tostock
Beyton
Woolpit
Wetherden
Haughley
Gipping
Mendlesham Green
Wetherup Street
Debenham
Earl Soham
Post Mill
Middlewood Green
Mickfield
Winston
Ashfield cum Thorpe
Hessett
Drinkstone
Drinkstone Green
Old Newton
Saxham Street
Little Stonham
Mill Green
Cretingham
Brandeston
Harleston
Stowupland
Stowmarket
Rattlesden
Stonham Aspal
Suffolk Owl Sanctuary
Pettaugh
Framsden
Monewden
Gedding
Buxhall
Mill Green
Great Finborough
Combs Ford
Combs
Crowfield
Helmingham Hall
Helmingham
Letheringham
Charsfield
Felsham
Creeting St Mary
Needham Market
Gosbeck
Otley
Clopton Corner
Dallinghoo
Debach
Hightown Green
Brettenham
Battisford Tye
Coddenham
Hemingstone
Ashbocking
Thorpe Green
Cross Green
Charles Tye
Ringshall
Barking
Lower Street
Clopton
Bredfield
Swilland
Hitcham Causeway
Barking Tye
Baylham
Burgh
Hitcham Street
Wattisham
Ringshall Stocks
Grundisburgh
Preston
Hitcham
Nedging Tye
Great Bricett
Upper Street
Great Blakenham
Barham
Henley
Witnesham
Hasketon
Kettlebaston
Guildhall
Bildeston
Offton
Claydon
Great Bealings
Brent Eleigh
Monks Eleigh
Naughton
Somersham
Little Blakenham
Tuddenham
Playford
Swingleton Green
Chelsworth
Nedging
Ash Street
Flowton
Westerfield
Milden
Lindsey Tye
Semer
Whatfield
Elmsett
Bramford
Castle Hill
Martlesham Heath
Rose Green
Lindsey
St James' Chapel
Aldham
Sproughton
Kesgrave
IPSWICH
Burstall
RSPB
Hintlesham
Brightwell
Kersey
Wicker Street Green
Duke Street
Washbrook
Chantry
Suffolk
Bucklesham
Mill Green
Hadleigh
Chattisham
Copdock
Groton
Boxford
Layham
Belstead
Wherstead
Nacton
Great Wenham
Freston
Levington
Raydon
Woolverstone
Leavenheath
Polstead
Shelley
Capel St Mary
Tattingstone White Horse
Tattingstone
River Orwell
Trimley St Martin
Stoke-by-Nayland
Lower Raydon
Holton St Mary
Bentley
Holbrook
Chelmondiston
Honey Tye
Alton Water
Shotley
Nayland
Thorington Street
Higham
Stratford St Mary
East Bergholt
Stutton
Erwarton
Harkstead
Shotley Street
Shotley Gate
Boxted
Carters
Flatford Mill & Cottages
Cattawade
Brantham
Holbrook Bay
International Ferry Terminal
Wormingford
Boxted Cross
Dedham
Mistley Towers
Mistley
Stour
Wrabness
Little Horkesley
Langham
Manningtree
New Mistley
Dovercourt
Boxted
Great Horkesley
Lawford
Bradfield
Ramsey
Upper Dovercourt
Harwich
Horkesley Heath
Ardleigh Heath
Ardleigh
Little Bromley
Horsleycross Street
Bradfield Heath
Wix
Little Oakley
Fordham
West Bergholt
Parson's Heath
Great Oakley
Tendring Heath
Stones Green
Great Bromley
Tendring Green
Goose Green
COLCHESTER
Elmstead Market
Hare Green
Frating
Beaumont
Horsey Island
Seven Green
0 1 2 3 4 miles
0 1 2 3 4 5 kilometres
A143
A1088
A14
A1308
A140
A1120
B1077
B1078
B1079
B1113
B1115
A1071
A1214
A1156
A12
A137
A134
B1068
B1070
B1029
B1456
B1080
B1352
A120
B1414
B1035
A133
B1087
B1508
B1117
B1118

Southwold
Wenhaston
Blythburgh
Cratfield
Cookley
Blackheath
Huntingfield
Walpole
Walberswick
Thorington
Bramfield
93
Laxfield
Heveningham
Ubbeston Green
Suffolk Coast
Dunwich
Darsham
Sibton
Peasenhall
Yoxford
Westleton
Middleton
Minsmere
RSPB
Badingham
Middleton Moor
Bruisyard
Eastbridge
Theberton
Bruisyard Street
Cransford
Rendham
Kelsale
Leiston Abbey
Shawsgate
Carlton
Saxmundham
Swefling
North Green
Knodishall
Great Glemham
Benhall Street
Benhall Green
Sternfield
Leiston
Aldringham
Thorpe Ness
Stratford St Andrew
Parham
Friday Street
Friston
Knodishall Common
Farnham
Thorpeness
Hacheston
Snape
Easton
Snape Street
Marlesford
Little Glemham
The Maltings
Aldeburgh
Blaxhall
Campsea Ash
Tunstall
Aldeburgh Bay
Rendlesham
River Alde
Ufford
Sudbourne
Chillesford
Eyke
Bromeswell
Butley
Castle
Orford
Orford Ness
Capel St Andrew
RSPB
Sutton
Boyton
Orfordness-Havergate
Waldringfield
Shottisham
River Ore
Suffolk Heritage Coast
Hollesley
North Weir Point
Hemley
Hollesley Bay
River Deben
Alderton
Bawdsey
Falkenham
Trimley St Mary
Walton
Old Felixstowe
Felixstowe
Landguard Fort
Landguard Point
Hoek van Holland
Esbjerg
A12
A144
A1120
A1094
A1152
B1117
B1387
B1125
B1122
B1120
B1119
B1121
B1353
B1069
B1078
B1084
B1083
B1438
G
H
J
K
L
M
1
2
3
4
5
6
7
8

95
A
B
C
D
E
F
1
2
3
4
5
6
7
8
Llanelltyd
Toll
Penmaenpool
Barmouth
Barmouth Bridge
Afon Mawddach
A496
A493
Barmouth
Bay
Fairbourne & Barmouth Steam Railway
Fairbourne
SNOWDONIA
NATIONAL
PARK
CADER
892
621
Tal-y-llyn
Llwyngwril
Castell y Bere
Afon Dysynni
Llangelynin
Abergynolwyn
667
Rhoslefain
Llanegryn
Tal-y-Llyn Railway
Bryncrug
B4405
633
TAREN
HENDRE
Dolgoch Falls
Aber
Dysynni
Tywyn
Pennal
CARDIGAN
BAY
Dovey
Aberdyfi
A493
Afon Dyfi (River Dovey)
RSPB
Dyfi Furnace
A487
B4353
Cwm Clettwr
Tre Taliesin
Borth
Tal-y-bont
Ceredigion
Heritage Coast
Llandre
Rhyd-y pennau
Bont-goch
or Elerch
Bow
Street
B4572
Salem
Clarach
Bay
Garth
Penrhyncoch
Pen-bont
Rhydybeddau
A4159
Capel-
Dewi
Waunfawr
Aberystwyth
Llanbadarn
Fawr
P+R
Capel
Bangor
Goginan
Rheidol
Power Station
Aberystwyth
and District
Capel
Seion
Coed
Penglanowen
A4120
Llanfarian
Llanfihangel-
y-Creuddyn
Blaenplwyf
A485
Afon Ystwyth
Cnwch
Coch
Llanilar
B4340
B4575
Penderi
Cliffs
Ceredigion
Heritage Coast
Llanddeiniol
B4576
Llanafan
66
Llangwyryfon
Lledrod
Cors
Ian
Tynygraig
Llanrhystud
0 1 2 3 4 miles
0 1 2 3 4 5 kilometres

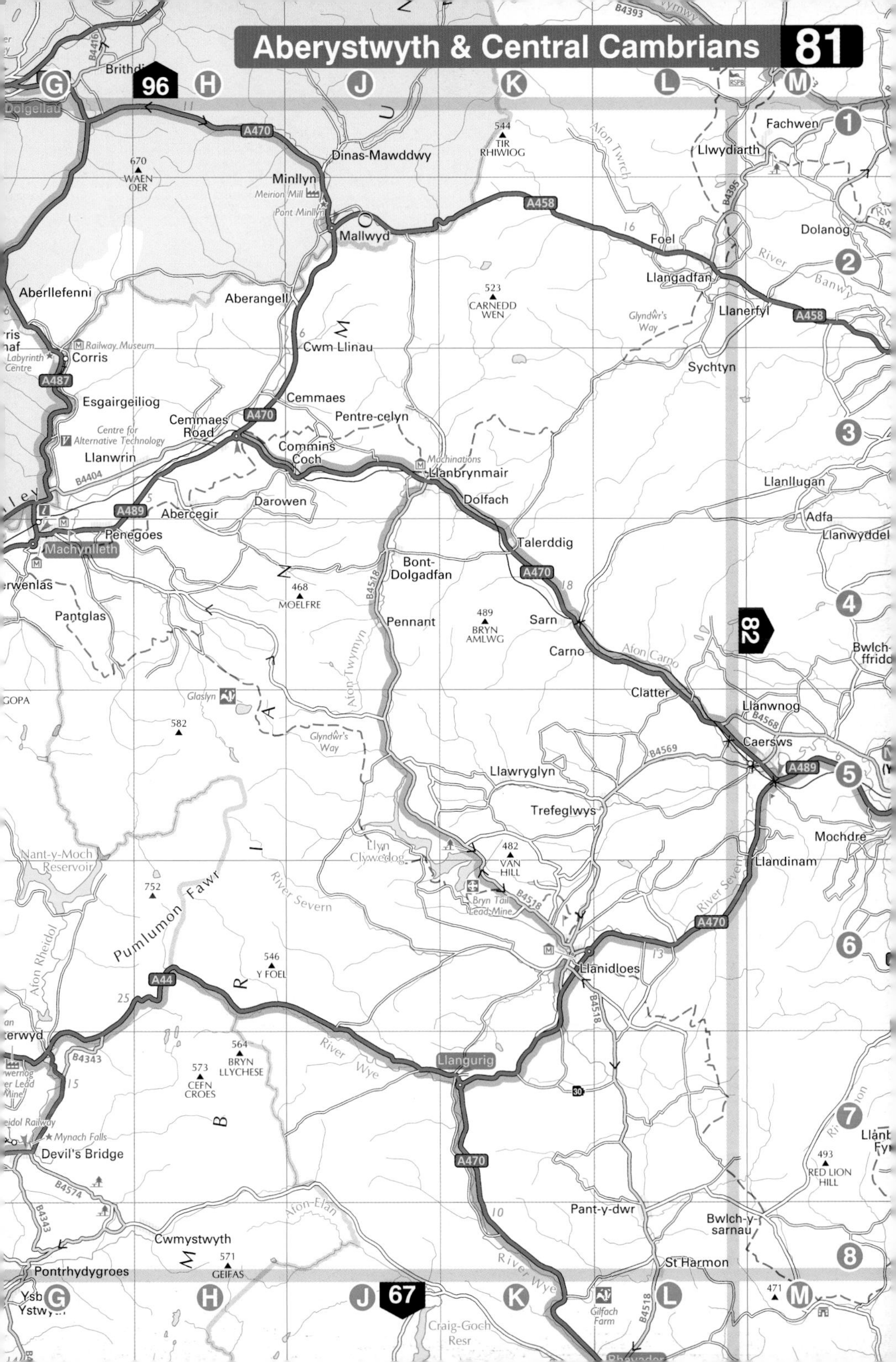
96
67
82
G
H
J
K
L
M
1
2
3
4
5
6
7
8
Dolgellau
Brithdir
B4416
A470
Dinas-Mawddwy
544
TIR
RHIWIOG
Afon Twrch
Fachwen
Llwydiarth
670
WAEN
OER
Minllyn
Meirion Mill
Pont Minllyn
Mallwyd
A458
B4395
Foel
Dolanog
River Banwy
Llangadfan
Llanerfyl
523
CARNEDD
WEN
Glyndŵr's
Way
Aberllefenni
Aberangell
Railway Museum
Labyrinth Centre
Corris
Cwm Llinau
Sychtyn
A487
Esgairgeiliog
Cemmaes
Pentre-celyn
Cemmaes
Road
Centre for
Alternative Technology
Commins
Coch
Machinations
Llanbrynmair
Llanwrin
B4404
Llanllugan
Dolfach
A489
Abercegir
Darowen
Adfa
Penegoes
Machynlleth
Talerddig
Llanwyddelan
Bont-
Dolgadfan
B4518
468
MOELFRE
Pantglas
Pennant
489
BRYN
AMLWG
Sarn
Carno
Afon Carno
Afon Twymyn
Glaslyn
Clatter
Llanwnog
B4568
582
Caersws
B4569
Llawryglyn
Trefeglwys
Mochdre
Nant-y-Moch
Reservoir
Llyn
Clywedog
482
VAN
HILL
Llandinam
752
Pumlumon Fawr
River Severn
Bryn Tail
Lead Mine
Afon Rheidol
546
Y FOEL
Llanidloes
A44
River Wye
564
BRYN
LLYCHESE
573
CEFN
CROES
Llangurig
B4343
Rheidol Railway
Mynach Falls
Devil's Bridge
B4574
493
RED LION
HILL
Pant-y-dwr
Afon Elan
Bwlch-y-
sarnau
Cwmystwyth
571
GEIFAS
St Harmon
Pontrhydygroes
471
Gilfach
Farm
Craig-Goch
Resr
Rhayader

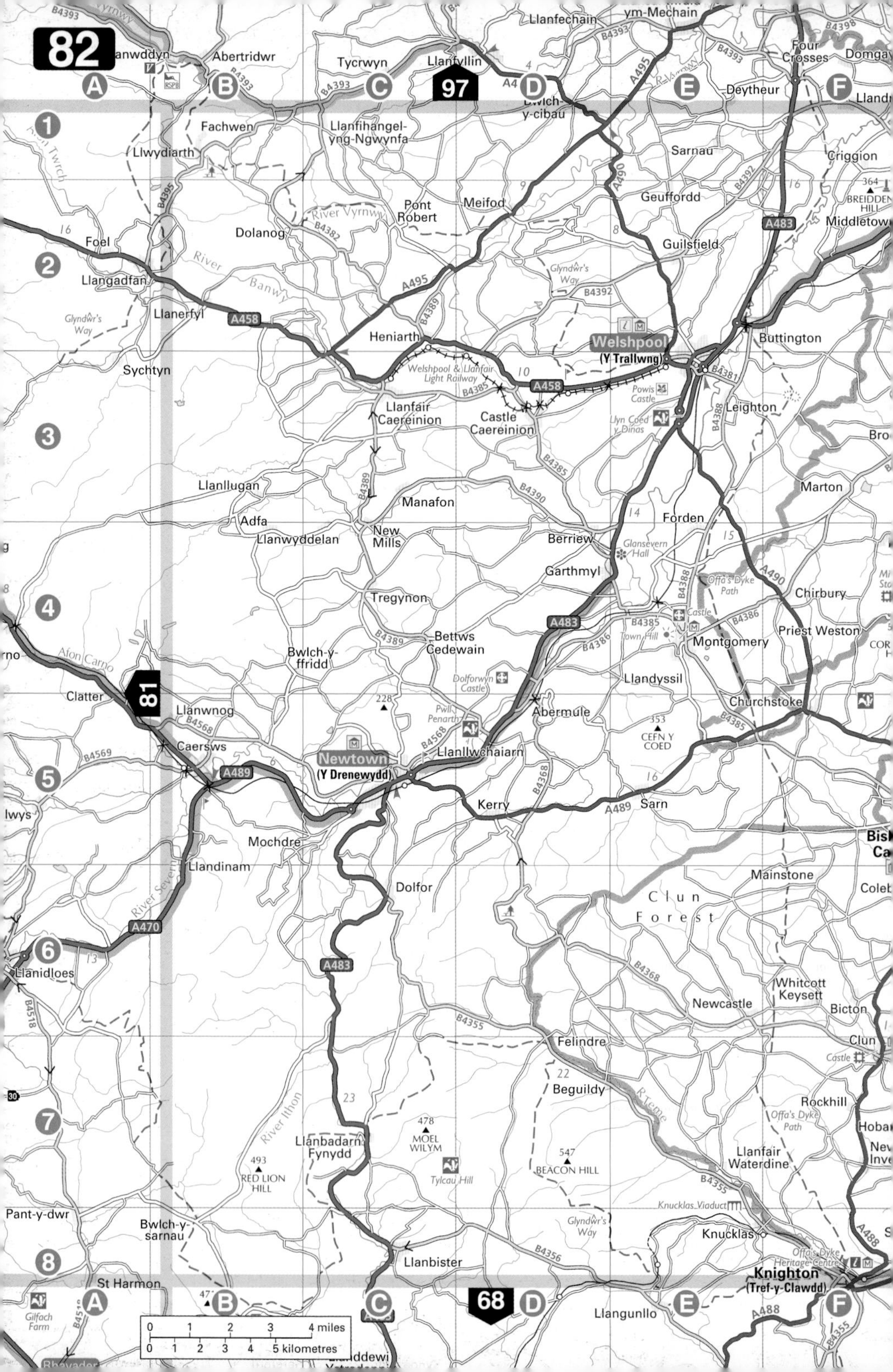

82
97
81
68
A
B
C
D
E
F
1
2
3
4
5
6
7
8
Abertridwr
Tycrwyn
Llanfyllin
Llanfechain
ym-Mechain
Four Crosses
Deytheur
Bwlch-y-cibau
Fachwen
Llanfihangel-yng-Ngwynfa
Llwydiarth
Sarnau
Criggion
BREIDDEN HILL
364
Geufford
Middletown
Pont Robert
Meifod
Dolanog
River Vyrnwy
Foel
Llangadfan
Llanerfyl
River Banwy
Guilsfield
Glyndŵr's Way
A495
A458
A490
A483
A489
A470
A488
B4393
B4395
B4382
B4389
B4392
B4385
B4381
B4388
B4390
B4386
B4568
B4569
B4368
B4355
B4356
B4518
Heniarth
Welshpool
(Y Trallwng)
Buttington
Sychtyn
Welshpool & Llanfair Light Railway
Powis Castle
Llyn Coed y Dinas
Llanfair Caereinion
Castle Caereinion
Leighton
Llanllugan
Manafon
Marton
Adfa
Llanwyddelan
New Mills
Forden
Berriew
Glansevern Hall
Garthmyl
Offa's Dyke Path
Tregynon
Chirbury
Castle
Town Hill
Montgomery
Priest Weston
Bettws Cedewain
Bwlch-y-ffridd
Afon Carno
Dolforwyn Castle
Llandyssil
Clatter
Llanwnog
228
Pwll Penarth
Abermule
Churchstoke
353
CEFN Y COED
Caersws
Newtown
(Y Drenewydd)
Llanllwchaiarn
Kerry
Sarn
Mochdre
Llandinam
River Severn
Dolfor
Mainstone
Clun Forest
Llanidloes
Whitcott Keysett
Newcastle
Bicton
Felindre
Clun
Beguildy
R Teme
Rockhill
River Ithon
Llanbadarn Fynydd
478
MOEL WILYM
493
RED LION HILL
Tylcau Hill
547
BEACON HILL
Llanfair Waterdine
Knucklas Viaduct
Pant-y-dwr
Bwlch-y-sarnau
Knucklas
Llanbister
Offa's Dyke Heritage Centre
Knighton
(Tref-y-Clawdd)
St Harmon
Llangunllo
Gilfach Farm
Llanddewi
0 1 2 3 4 miles
0 1 2 3 4 5 kilometres

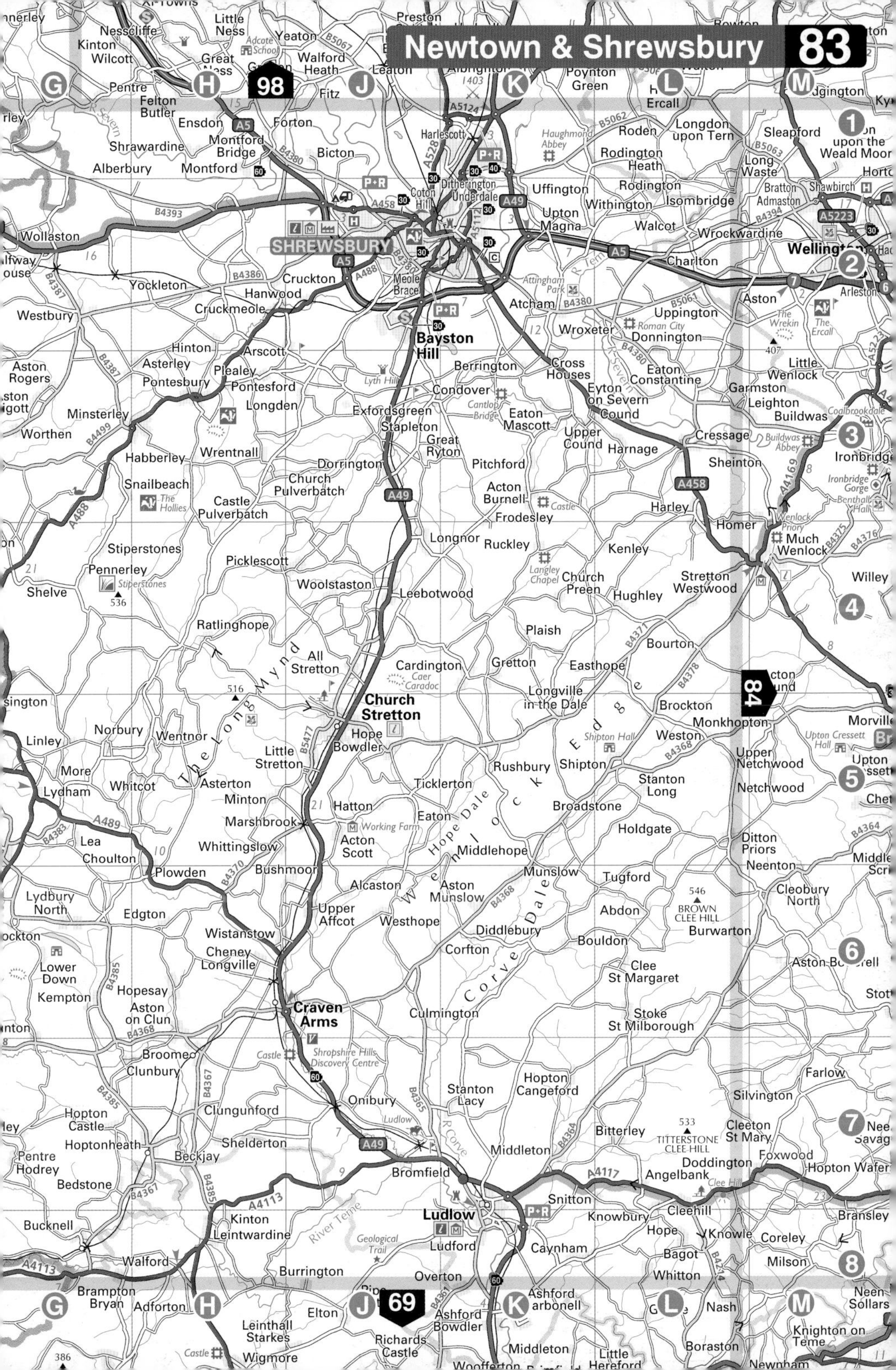

Newtown & Shrewsbury
83
98
84
69
Nesscliffe
Little Ness
Preston
Kinton
Wilcott
Adcote School
Yeaton
Walford Heath
Great Ness
Leaton
Albrighton
Poynton Green
Pentre
Felton Butler
Fitz
Ercall
Ensdon
Forton
Harlescott
Haughmond Abbey
Roden
Longdon upon Tern
Sleapford
upon the Weald Moors
Shrawardine
Montford Bridge
Bicton
Rodington Heath
Long Waste
Alberbury
Montford
Ditherington
Underdale
Coton Hill
Uffington
Rodington
Bratton
Admaston
Shawbirch
Withington
Isombridge
Upton Magna
Walcot
Wrockwardine
Wollaston
SHREWSBURY
Wellington
Charlton
Yockleton
Cruckton
Hanwood
Meole Brace
Attingham Park
Atcham
Aston
Arleston
Westbury
Cruckmeole
Uppington
Wroxeter
Roman City
Donnington
The Wrekin
The Ercall
407
Hinton
Arscott
Bayston Hill
Berrington
Cross Houses
Eaton Constantine
Little Wenlock
Aston Rogers
Asterley
Pontesbury
Pealey
Pontesford
Lyth Hill
Condover
Eyton on Severn
Garmston
Leighton
Buildwas
Coalbrookdale
Minsterley
Longden
Exfordsgreen
Cantlop Bridge
Eaton Mascott
Cound
Worthen
Stapleton
Great Ryton
Upper Cound
Harnage
Cressage
Buildwas Abbey
Ironbridge
Habberley
Wrentnall
Dorrington
Pitchford
Sheinton
Ironbridge Gorge
Benthall Hall
Snailbeach
The Hollies
Church Pulverbatch
Acton Burnell
Castle
Harley
Castle Pulverbatch
Frodesley
Homer
Wenlock Priory
Much Wenlock
Stiperstones
Longnor
Ruckley
Kenley
Picklescott
Langley Chapel
Church Preen
Stretton Westwood
Willey
Pennerley
Stiperstones
536
Shelve
Woolstaston
Leebotwood
Hughley
Ratlinghope
Plaish
Bourton
All Stretton
Cardington
Caer Caradoc
Gretton
Easthope
The Long Mynd
516
Church Stretton
Longville in the Dale
Brockton
Monkhopton
Morville
Norbury
Wentnor
Hope Bowdler
Shipton Hall
Weston
Upton Cressett Hall
Linley
Little Stretton
Rushbury
Shipton
Upper Netchwood
More
Whitcot
Asterton
Wenlock Edge
Stanton Long
Netchwood
Lydham
Minton
Ticklerton
Broadstone
Marshbrook
Hatton
Eaton
Working Farm
Hope Dale
Holdgate
Lea
Choulton
Whittingslow
Acton Scott
Middlehope
Ditton Priors
Plowden
Bushmoor
Munslow
Tugford
Neenton
Lydbury North
Alcaston
Aston Munslow
546
Brown Clee Hill
Cleobury North
Edgton
Upper Affcot
Westhope
Abdon
Wistanstow
Diddlebury
Burwarton
Cheney Longville
Corfton
Bouldon
Corve Dale
Lower Down
Clee St Margaret
Aston Botterell
Kempton
Hopesay
Aston on Clun
Craven Arms
Culmington
Stoke St Milborough
Broome
Shropshire Hills Discovery Centre
Clunbury
Hopton Cangeford
Farlow
Stanton Lacy
Silvington
Hopton Castle
Clungunford
Onibury
Ludlow
Bitterley
533
Titterstone Clee Hill
Cleeton St Mary
Hoptonheath
Shelderton
Middleton
Doddington
Foxwood
Pentre Hodrey
Beckjay
Bromfield
Angelbank
Hopton Wafers
Bedstone
Clee Hill
Snitton
Cleehill
Bransley
Kinton
Knowbury
Bucknell
Leintwardine
River Teme
Geological Trail
Ludlow
Hope
Knowle
Coreley
Caynham
Bagot
Walford
Ludford
Milson
Whitton
Burrington
Overton
Brampton Bryan
Adforton
Elton
Ashford Carbonell
Nash
Neen Sollars
Leinthall Starkes
Ashford Bowdler
Knighton on Teme
Richards Castle
Middleton
Little Hereford
Boraston
Wigmore
Newnham
386
A5
A49
A458
A488
A489
A4113
A4117
A4169
A5124
A528
A5112
A5223
B4380
B4386
B4387
B4393
B4499
B4370
B4383
B4368
B4385
B4367
B4365
B4364
B4361
B4378
B4371
B4376
B4375
B4394
B5062
B5063
B5061
B5067
B4214
B5477
A4113
R. Severn
R. Tern
R. Corve
G
H
J
K
L
M
1
2
3
4
5
6
7
8

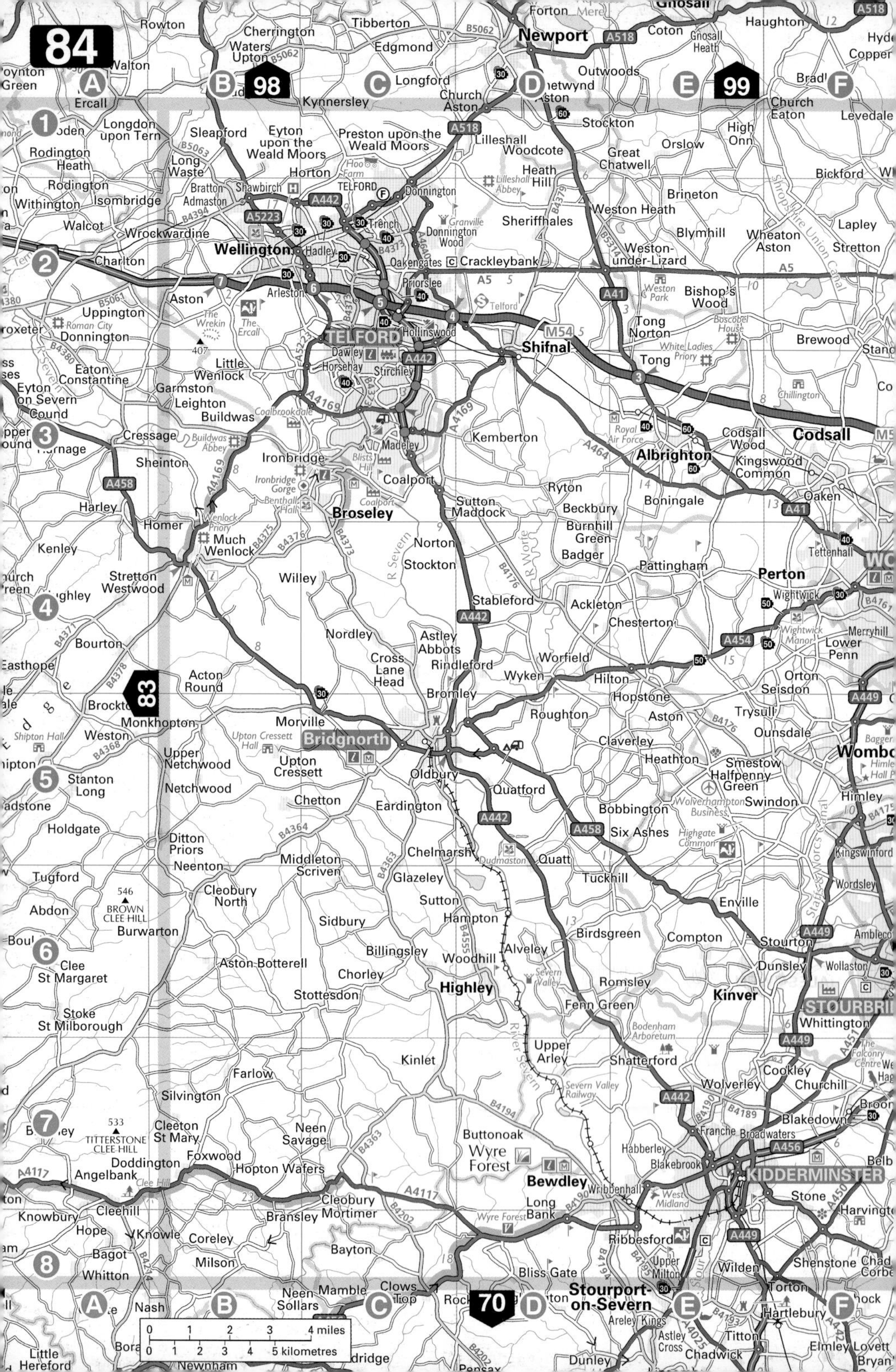
84
98
99
83
70
Rowton
Cherrington
Tibberton
Forton
Newport
Gnosall
Coton
Gnosall Heath
Haughton
Waters Upton
Edgmond
Walton
Longford
Outwoods
Church Aston
Chetwynd Aston
Church Eaton
Bradley
Ercall
Kynnersley
Longdon upon Tern
Sleapford
Eyton upon the Weald Moors
Preston upon the Weald Moors
Lilleshall
Stockton
High Onn
Levedale
Rodington Heath
Long Waste
Horton
Woodcote
Great Chatwell
Orslow
Rodington
Bratton
Admaston
Shawbirch
TELFORD
Donnington
Lilleshall Abbey
Heath Hill
Brineton
Bickford
Withington
Isombridge
Trench
Granville
Donnington Wood
Sheriffhales
Weston Heath
Lapley
Walcot
Wrockwardine
Wellington
Hadley
Oakengates
Crackleybank
Blymhill
Wheaton Aston
Stretton
Charlton
Weston-under-Lizard
Priorslee
Aston
Arleston
Telford
Weston Park
Bishop's Wood
Uppington
Roman City
Wroxeter
Donnington
The Wrekin
The Ercall
407
Hollinswood
TELFORD
Shifnal
Tong Norton
Boscobel House
Brewood
White Ladies Priory
Tong
Dawley
Horsehay
Stirchley
Eaton Constantine
Little Wenlock
Garmston
Eyton on Severn
Leighton
Buildwas
Cound
Coalbrookdale
Chillington
Royal Air Force
Codsall Wood
Codsall
Cressage
Buildwas Abbey
Harnage
Kemberton
Albrighton
Kingswood Common
Madeley
Ironbridge
Blists Hill
Sheinton
Ironbridge Gorge
Coalport
Benthall Hall
Ryton
Oaken
Harley
Broseley
Sutton Maddock
Beckbury
Boningale
Homer
Wenlock Priory
Much Wenlock
Norton
Burnhill Green
Badger
Kenley
Stockton
Pattingham
Perton
Tettenhall
Stretton Westwood
Willey
Stableford
Ackleton
Wightwick
Hughley
Chesterton
Wightwick Manor
Merryhill
Nordley
Astley Abbots
Lower Penn
Bourton
Cross Lane Head
Rindleford
Worfield
Easthope
Acton Round
Wyken
Hilton
Orton
Seisdon
Brockton
Bromley
Hopstone
Trysull
Monkhopton
Morville
Roughton
Aston
Shipton Hall
Weston
Upton Cressett Hall
Bridgnorth
Claverley
Ounsdale
Wombourne
Upper Netchwood
Upton Cressett
Heathton
Smestow
Halfpenny Green
Stanton Long
Oldbury
Netchwood
Quatford
Wolverhampton Business
Swindon
Himley
Chetton
Eardington
Bobbington
Holdgate
Ditton Priors
Six Ashes
Highgate Common
Kingswinford
Neenton
Chelmarsh
Dudmaston
Quatt
Tugford
Middleton Scriven
Glazeley
Tuckhill
Wordsley
546
BROWN CLEE HILL
Cleobury North
Abdon
Sutton
Enville
Burwarton
Sidbury
Hampton
Birdsgreen
Compton
Stourton
Amblecote
Billingsley
Woodhill
Alveley
Clee St Margaret
Aston Botterell
Chorley
Severn Valley
Dunsley
Wollaston
Romsley
Highley
Stottesdon
Kinver
STOURBRIDGE
Stoke St Milborough
Fenn Green
Bodenham Arboretum
Whittington
Upper Arley
River Severn
Kinlet
Shatterford
The Falconry Centre
Farlow
Cookley
Churchill
Wolverley
Silvington
Severn Valley Railway
533
TITTERSTONE CLEE HILL
Cleeton St Mary
Neen Savage
Buttonoak
Blakedown
Broadwaters
Franche
Wyre Forest
Habberley
Doddington
Foxwood
Angelbank
Hopton Wafers
Blakebrook
KIDDERMINSTER
Clee Hill
Bewdley
Cleobury Mortimer
Cleehill
Wribbenhall
West Midland
Stone
Harvington
Long Bank
Knowbury
Hope
Bransley
Knowle
Coreley
Wyre Forest
Ribbesford
Bagot
Milson
Bayton
Upper Milton
Shenstone
Whitton
Bliss Gate
Wilden
Neen Sollars
Mamble
Clows Top
Rock
Stourport-on-Severn
Torton
Nash
Hartlebury
Areley Kings
Astley Cross
Titton
Chadwick
Elmley Lovett
Little Hereford
Dunley
0 1 2 3 4 miles
0 1 2 3 4 5 kilometres
A518
A442
A5223
A5
A41
M54
A4169
A458
A454
A449
A4117
A456
A450
A451
B5062
B5063
B4394
B5061
B4380
B4373
B4375
B4376
B4371
B4378
B4368
B4364
B4363
B4555
B4176
B4379
B5314
B4194
B4190
B4189
B4202
B4214
B4193
A4025
B4195
R Severn
R Worfe
Staffs & Worcs Canal
Shropshire Union Canal
A B C D E F
1 2 3 4 5 6 7 8

West Midlands
85
Penkridge
Hednesford
Rugeley
Cannock Chase
Cannock
Heath Hayes & Wimblebury
Norton Canes
Burntwood
Great Wyrley
Cheslyn Hay
Brownhills
Lichfield
Pelsall
Aldridge
Walsall
Sutton Coldfield
West Bromwich
Dudley
Birmingham
Halesowen
Solihull
Tamworth
Fazeley
Kingsbury
Coleshill
Meriden
Knowle
Dorridge
Balsall Common
Alvechurch
Bromsgrove
Romsley
Yoxall
Elmhurst
Streethay
Whittington
Shenstone
Wednesbury
Tipton
Oldbury
Smethwick
Harborne
Edgbaston
Moseley
Bournville
Northfield
Shirley
Elmdon
Hampton in Arden
Lapworth
Wythall
Hopwood
Rubery
Frankley
Clent
Baddesley Clinton
Kenilworth
M6
M6 Toll
M5
M42
A38(M)
100
98
71

86
Dunstall
Branston
Barton-under-Needwood
Yoxall
Swadlincote
Worthington
Belton
Shepshed
Staunton Harold Church
Lount
Smisby
Osgathorpe
Blackfordby
100
Cauldwell
Rosliston
Wychnor
Norris Hill
Ashby-de-la-Zouch
Thringstone
Linton
Conkers
Castle
Moira
Swannington
Charnwood
Mount St Bernard
Forest
Whitwick
Alrewas
National Memorial
Coton in the Elms
Overseal
Fradley
Donisthorpe
Packington
Ravenstone
Coalville
Lullington
Oakthorpe
Netherseal
Bardon
Edingale
Normanton le Heath
Clifton Campville
Chilcote
R Mease
Measham
Heather
Donington le Heath
Stanton under Bardon
Elford
Streethay
Harlaston
Haunton
Appleby Magna
Swepstone
Snarestone
Ellistown
Ibstock
Thorpe Constantine
No Man's Heath
Appleby Parva
Newton Burgoland
Birmingham & Fazeley Canal
Newton Regis
Norton-Juxta-Twycross
Ashby Canal
Odstone
Bagworth
Thornton
Whittington
Comberford
Seckington
Staffordshire Regiment
Wigginton
Austrey
Barton in the Beans
Nailstone
Shackerstone
Bilstone
Congerstone
Barlestone
Shuttington
Twycross
Hopwas
Amington
Alvecote
Orton-on-the-Hill
Carlton
Osbaston
Tropical Birdland
TAMWORTH
Warton
The Battlefield Line
Market Bosworth
Newbold Verdon
Weeford
Kettlebrook
Glascote
Polesworth
Hints
Sheepy Magna
Market Bosworth
Cadeby
Desford
Drayton Manor
Fazeley
Two Gates
Sheepy Parva
Peckleton
Sutton Cheney
Dordon
Sibson
Kirkby Mallory
Mallory Park
Drayton Bassett
Grendon
Ratcliffe Culey
Upton
Shenton
Bosworth Battlefield
Stapleton
Baddesley Ensor
Whittington
Middleton
Whateley
R Anker
Atterton
Earl Shilton
Ash End House
Middleton Hall
Dadlington
Witherley
Atherstone
Hurley Common
Allen End
Kingsbury
Hurley
Baxterley
Mancetter
Fenny Drayton
Higham on the Hill
Stoke Golding
Barwell
Elmesthorpe
Bentley
Ridge Lane
Hartshill Hayes
Coventry Canal
Foul End
Birchley Heath
Hinckley
Stoney Stanton
Wishaw
85
Lea Marston
Nether Whitacre
Oldbury
Hartshill
Weddington
Burbage Common & Woods
Curdworth
Whiteacre Heath
Hoggrill's End
HAMS HALL
Sapcote
Water Orton
Ansley
NUNEATON
Sketchley
Burbage
Aston Flamville
Stockingford
Castle Bromwich
Shustoke
Over Whitacre
Arley
Attleborough
Burton Hastings
Frolesworth
Wigston Parva
Coleshill
Astley
Arbury Hall
Griff
Maxstoke
Fillongley
Bedworth
Bramcote
Wolvey
Wolvey Heath
Copston Magna
Chelmsley Wood
Bulkington
Marston Green
Exhall
Corley
Ash Green
Little Packington
Sheldon
Birmingham
Keresley
Withybrook
Shilton
Monks Kirby
Newnham Paddox
N.E.C.
Stonebridge
Holbrooks
Longford
Aldermans Green
Ansty
Elmdon
Meriden
Foleshill
Potters Green
Street Ashton
Bickenhill
National Motorcycle
Pickford
Jaguar Daimler
Ricoh Arena
Henley Green
Stretton under Fosse
Lode Heath
Hampton in Arden
Allesley
Radford
Wyken
Walsgrave on Sowe
Coombe Abbey
Easenhall
SOLIHULL
Four Oaks
Eastern Green
COVENTRY
Eastcote
Berkswell
Reeves Green
Tile Hill
Earlsdon
Stoke
Brinklow
Barston
Binley
Bretford
Knowle
Carol Green
Canley
Binley Woods
Long Lawford
Balsall Common
Berkswell
Stivichall
Willenhall
Brandon
Dorridge
Church Lawford
Darley Green
Lunt Roman Fort
Wolston
Chessetts Wood
Chadwick End
Coventry
Baginton
Ryton-on-Dunsmore
Hockley Heath
Packwood House
Baddesley Clinton
Honiley
Kenilworth Castle
Stoneleigh
Ryton Wood
Stretton-on-Dunsmore
Bubbenhall
Kenilworth
72
Princethorpe
Bourton on Dunsmore
Thurlaston
Agricultural Centre
Weston under Wetherley
Wappenbury
Frankton
Ashow
Draycote
R Leam
Leek
R Tame
R Trent
R Sence
0 1 2 3 4 miles
0 1 2 3 4 5 kilometres

Loughborough
Burton on the Wolds
Walton on the Wolds
Shoby
Asfordby
Ragdale
Seagrave
Hoby
Kirby Bellars
Frisby on the Wreake
Thorpe
Freeby
Garthorpe
Stapleford
R Eye
Quorn
Thrussington
Rotherby
Burton Lazars
Teigh
Woodhouse
Sileby
Ratcliffe on the Wreake
Little Dalby
Whissendine
Great Central Railway
Mountsorrel
Rearsby
Great Dalby
Woodhouse Eaves
Rothley
Cossington
East Goscote
Gaddesby
Leesthorpe
Swithland
Queniborough
Ashby Folville
Thorpe Satchville
Burrough Hill
Pickwell
Bradgate Park
Thurcaston
Wanlip
Barsby
Burrough on the Hill
Cold Overton
Newtown Linford
Cropston
Syston
Twyford
Somerby
Barleythorpe
Birstall
Watermead
Thurmaston
Barkby
South Croxton
Anstey
Castle Hill
Knossington
Barkby Thorpe
Beeby
Owston
Oakham
Groby
Belgrave
Hungarton
Lowesby
Braunston
Glenfield
Keyham
Halstead
LEICESTER
Humberstone
Scraptoft
Tilton on the Hill
Prior's Coppice
Thurnby
Houghton on the Hill
River Chater
Kirby Fields
Dane Hills
North Evington
Evington
Leicester Forest East
Braunstone
Stoneygate
Skeffington
Ridlington
Loddington
Stoughton
R Sence
Billesdon
Knighton
Little Stretton
Gaulby
Rolleston
Tugby
Belton
Aylestone
Oadby
King's Norton
Illston on the Hill
East Norton
Allexton
Wardley
Uppingham
Enderby
Glen Parva
Brocks Hill
Great Glen
Burton Overy
Goadby
Leicester Record Office
Wigston
South Wigston
Whetstone
Newton Harcourt
Carlton Curlieu
Stockerston
Horninghold
Blaby
Littlethorpe
Hallaton
Eyebrook Reservoir
Countesthorpe
Cosby
Shangton
Stonton Wyville
Glooston
Cranoe
Foston
Kilby
Kibworth Harcourt
Tur Langton
Kibworth Beauchamp
Slawston
Nevill Holt
Willoughby Waterleys
Fleckney
Church Langton
Medbourne
Great Easton
Peatling Magna
Saddington
Smeeton Westerby
Welham
Drayton
Arnesby
East Langton
Thorpe Langton
Leire
Ashby Magna
Shearsby
Weston by Welland
Ashley
Middleton
Dunton Bassett
Bruntingthorpe
Gumley
Sutton Bassett
East Carlton
Peatling Parva
Mowsley
Foxton
Great Bowden
Ashby Parva
Laughton
Stoke Albany
Wilbarston
Gilmorton
Dingley
Lubenham
Brampton Ash
Walton
Union Canal
Pipewell
Bitteswell
Kimcote
Marston Trussell
Lutterworth
Market Harborough
West Lodge Rural Centre
Grand
Theddingworth
East Farndon
Braybrooke
Misterton
Husbands Bosworth
Desborough
Walcote
North Kilworth
Great Oxendon
Triangular Lodge
Rushton
Cotesbach
Sibbertoft
Arthingworth
South Kilworth
Shawell
Clipston
Rothwell
Welford
Kelmarsh Hall
Harrington
Swinford
Stanford Hall
Newton
Stanford on Avon
R Avon
1645
Kelmarsh
Orton
Loddington
Catthorpe
Naseby
Haselbech
Lilbourne
Clay Coton
Cold Ashby
Great Cransley
Maidwell
Draughton
Clifton upon Dunsmore
Mawsley
Yelvertoft
Broughton
Thornby
Lamport
Hillmorton
Winwick
Cottesbrooke
Cottesbrooke Hall
Lamport Hall
RUGBY
Guilsborough
Hanging Houghton
Old
DIRFT Logistics Park
Crick
West Haddon
Hollowell
Creaton
Kilsby
Walgrave
Barby
Ravensthorpe
Teeton
Brixworth
Hannington
Spratton
Holcot
Ashby
Watford
Oxford
A6
A46
A607
A606
A47
A563
A5199
A426
A4304
A14
A508
A427
A6047
B6047
B664
A43
A428
A5
A4303
M1
101
102
73
88
G
H
J
K
L
M
1
2
3
4
5
6
7
8

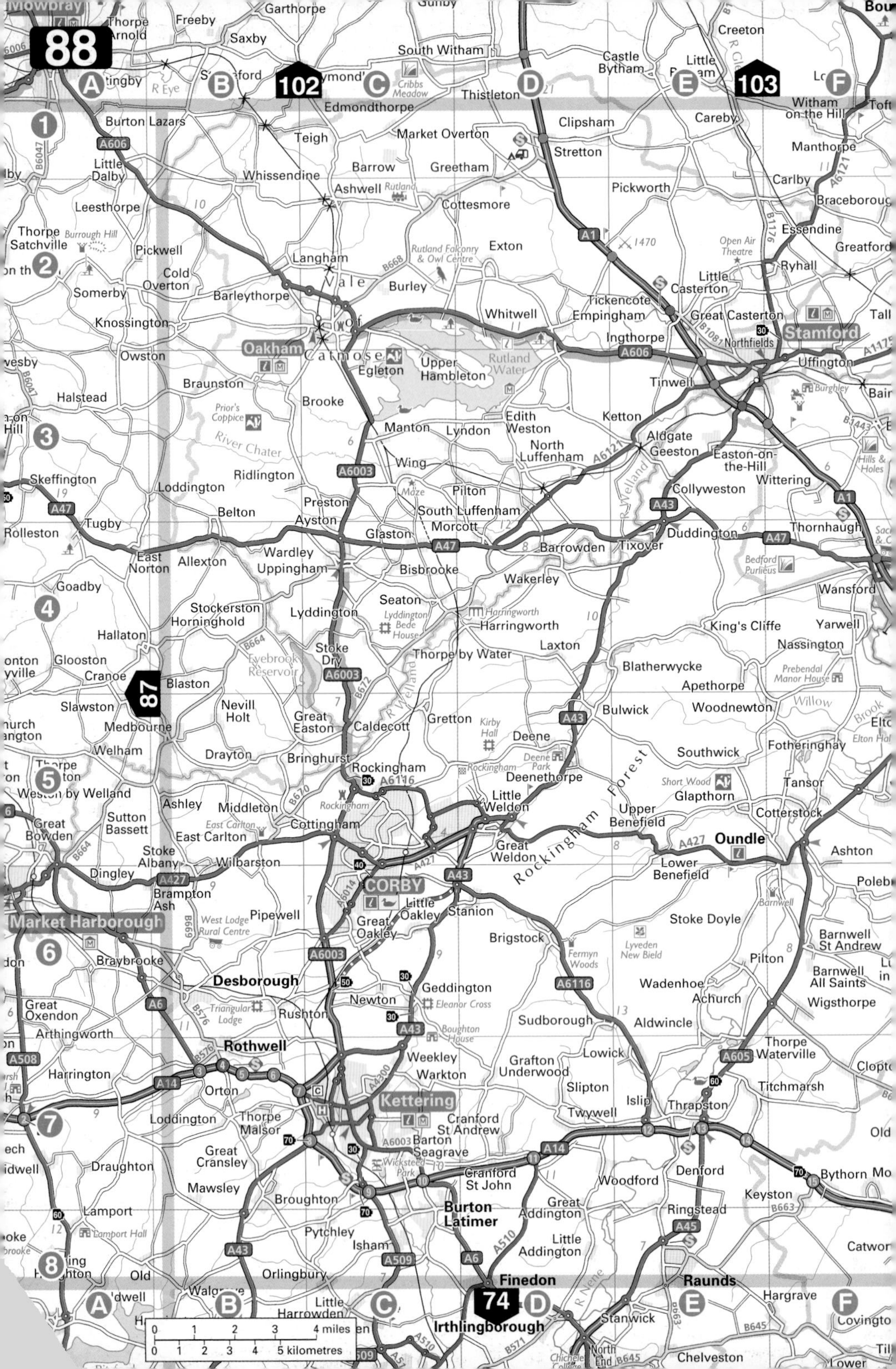
88
102
103
87
74
A
B
C
D
E
F
1
2
3
4
5
6
7
8
Garthorpe
Thorpe Arnold
Freeby
Saxby
South Witham
Castle Bytham
Creeton
Little Bytham
Cribbs Meadow
Thistleton
Edmondthorpe
Witham on the Hill
Burton Lazars
Teigh
Market Overton
Clipsham
Careby
Stretton
Manthorpe
Little Dalby
Whissendine
Barrow
Greetham
Pickworth
Carlby
Ashwell
Rutland
Cottesmore
Braceborough
Leesthorpe
Essendine
Thorpe Satchville
Burrough Hill
Pickwell
Langham
Rutland Falconry & Owl Centre
Exton
Open Air Theatre
Greatford
Ryhall
Cold Overton
Somerby
Barleythorpe
Vale
Burley
Little Casterton
Tickencote
Empingham
Whitwell
Great Casterton
Knossington
Stamford
Northfields
Ingthorpe
Oakham
Owston
Catmose
Egleton
Upper Hambleton
Rutland Water
Uffington
Tinwell
Burghley
Braunston
Halstead
Prior's Coppice
Brooke
Ketton
Edith Weston
Aldgate
Geeston
Easton-on-the-Hill
Manton
Lyndon
North Luffenham
River Chater
Wing
R. Welland
Hills & Holes
Skeffington
Ridlington
Wittering
Collyweston
Loddington
Moze
Pilton
Preston
Rolleston
Tugby
Belton
Ayston
South Luffenham
Morcott
Duddington
Thornhaugh
Glaston
Barrowden
Tixover
East Norton
Allexton
Wardley
Uppingham
Bisbrooke
Wakerley
Bedford Purlieus
Goadby
Wansford
Stockerston
Horninghold
Lyddington
Seaton
Lyddington Bede House
Harringworth
King's Cliffe
Yarwell
Hallaton
Laxton
Nassington
Glooston
Cranoe
Stoke Dry
Eyebrook Reservoir
Thorpe by Water
Blatherwycke
Apethorpe
Prebendal Manor House
Blaston
Slawston
Medbourne
Nevill Holt
Great Easton
Caldecott
Gretton
Kirby Hall
Bulwick
Woodnewton
Willow Brook
Deene
Deene Park
Welham
Drayton
Bringhurst
Rockingham
Southwick
Fotheringhay
Elton Hall
Thorpe Langton
Weston by Welland
Deenethorpe
Short Wood
Glapthorn
Tansor
Little Weldon
Rockingham Forest
Upper Benefield
Cotterstock
Great Bowden
Sutton Bassett
Ashley
Middleton
East Carlton
Cottingham
Great Weldon
Oundle
Ashton
Stoke Albany
Wilbarston
Lower Benefield
Dingley
Brampton Ash
CORBY
Little Oakley
Stanion
Market Harborough
West Lodge Rural Centre
Pipewell
Great Oakley
Brigstock
Stoke Doyle
Barnwell
Barnwell St Andrew
Braybrooke
Fermyn Woods
Lyveden New Bield
Pilton
Barnwell All Saints
Desborough
Geddington
Wadenhoe
Great Oxendon
Triangular Lodge
Newton
Eleanor Cross
Achurch
Wigsthorpe
Rushton
Arthingworth
Boughton House
Sudborough
Aldwincle
Rothwell
Lowick
Thorpe Waterville
Harrington
Weekley
Warkton
Grafton Underwood
Orton
Kettering
Slipton
Titchmarsh
Loddington
Thorpe Malsor
Twywell
Islip
Thrapston
Cranford St Andrew
Barton Seagrave
Great Cransley
Draughton
Wicksteed Park
Cranford St John
Denford
Woodford
Bythorn
Mawsley
Broughton
Keyston
Great Addington
Burton Latimer
Ringstead
Lamport
Lamport Hall
Pytchley
Isham
Little Addington
Old
Orlingbury
Finedon
Raunds
Hargrave
Covington
Little Harrowden
Irthlingborough
Stanwick
Chelveston
Lower
North End
Chichele College
A606
A1
A47
A6003
A43
A6116
A427
A6014
A6
A14
A508
A4300
A509
A510
A605
A45
A6121
A1175
B6047
B668
B1176
B1081
B1443
B664
B672
B670
B669
B576
B663
B645
B571
R Eye
R Nene
0 1 2 3 4 miles
0 1 2 3 4 5 kilometres

Twenty
Deeping St Nicholas
Deeping Fen
Bedford Level
Thurlby
Baston
Market Deeping
Deeping Gate
Deeping St James
Northborough
Frognall
Crowland
Whaplode Drove
Holbeach Drove
Gedney Hill
Sutton St Edmund
Sutton St James
Tydd St Mary
Cowbit
Gorefield
Wisbech St Mary
Parson Drove
Tholomas Drove
Murrow
Morris Fen
Maxey
Etton
Peakirk
Glinton
Helpston
Newborough
Thorney
Eye
Guyhirn
Werrington
Marholm
Castor Hanglands
Upton
Ailsworth
New England
PETERBOROUGH
North Side
West Fen
Westry
Longthorpe
Castor
Ferry Meadows
Nene Valley Railway
New Fletton
Woodston
Old Fletton
Orton Longueville
Orton Waterville
Alwalton
Chesterton
Stanground
Flag Fen Bronze Age Centre
Whittlesey
Coates
Eastrea
Turves
Town End
Farcet
Hampton
East of England
Haddon
Morborne
Yaxley
Farcet Fen
Whittlesey Mere
Pondersbridge
White Fen
Wimblington
Benwick
Doddington
Ramsey Mereside
Folksworth
Stilton
Caldecote
Holme
Holme Fen
Ramsey St Mary's
Lutton
Denton
Glatton
Ramsey Forty Foot
Chatteris
Conington
Woodwalton Fen
Ramsey Heights
Ramsey
Ramsey Abbey Gatehouse
Sawtry
Tick Fen
Bury
Horseley Fen
Great Gidding
Upwood
Steeple Gidding
Hamerton Zoo Park
Coppingford
Monks Wood
Wood Walton
Great Raveley
Wistow
Little Raveley
Warboys
Fenton
Hamerton
Upton
Wennington
Abbots Ripton
Alconbury Weston
Chatteris Fen
Old Hurst
Pidley
Somersham
Buckworth
Broughton
Kings Ripton
Colne
Alconbury
Little Stukeley
Barham
Great Stukeley
Woodhurst
Leighton Bromswold
Woolley
Bluntisham
Earith
Haddenham
Aldreth
Huntingdon
St Ives
Ouse Fen
Spaldwick
Hartford
Wyton
Houghton
Needingworth
Brampton
Hinchingbrooke
Hemingford Grey
Holywell
Over
Godmanchester
Grafham
Fenstanton
103
104
75

Walpole Cross Keys
St Clement
Clenchwarton
African Violet Centre
West Lynn
Gaywood
Fairstead
King's Lynn
Tydd Gote
Tydd St Mary
Sutton St James
Walpole St Andrew
104
Tilney All Saints
Tilney High End
Fair Green
Saddle Bow
West Winch
North Runcton
Four Gotes
Walpole St Peter
Tydd St Giles
Newton
River Nene
Tilney St Lawrence
Wiggenhall St Germans
Setchey
Sutton St Edmund
Holbeach Drove
West Walton
Walpole Highway
Terrington St John
Wiggenhall St Mary the Virgin
West Walton Highway
Gorefield
Leverington
St John's Fen End
Watlington
Wiggenhall St Mary Magdalen
Tottenhill
Walsoken
Wisbech
New Walsoken
Marshland St James
Runcton Holme
South Runcton
Parson Drove
Wisbech St Mary
Emneth
Murrow
Tholomas Drove
Elm
Emneth Hungate
Middle Level Drain
Stowbridge
Stow Bardolph
Wimbotsham
Stradsett
Guyhirn
Friday Bridge
Outwell
Stow Bardolph Fen
Downham Market
Bexwell
Crimplesham
Moreton Leam
Laddus Fen
Upwell
Denver
West Dereham
Fordham
Nordelph
West Fen
Westry
R Nene (Old Course)
Euximoor Fen
Upwell Fen
Old Bedford River
New Bedford River
Hilgay
R Wissey
March
Ten Mile Bank
Turves
Christchurch
Lakesend
Hilgay Fen
Town End
89
Upwell Fen
Welney
Wildfowl & Wetlands Trust
Southery
Great Ouse
Fens
Methwold
White Fen
Wimblington
Benwick
Doddington
Sixteen Foot Drain
Manea
Hockwold cum Wilton Fen
Chatteris
Pymoor
Littleport
Burnt Fen
Little Ouse River
Oxlode
Langwood Fen
Little Downham
Horseley Fen
Outdoor Centre
Coveney
Chettisham
Prickwillow
Wardy Hill
Mepal
Witcham
Queen Adelaide
River Lark
Ely
Kennyhill
Chatteris Fen
Middle Fen
Mildenhall Fen
Sutton
Wentworth
Witchford
Stuntney
Great Fen
Somersham
Colne
Barway
Isleham Fen
Thistley Green
West Row
Haddenham
Wilburton
Little Thetford
Bluntisham
Earith
Stretham
Isleham
Aldreth
Soham Mere
Priory Church
Ouse Fen
Ouse or Old West River
Soham
Needingworth
Holywell
76
Wicken Fen
Downfield
Fordham
Freckenham
Busway
Wicken
New River
Chittering
Cam
Chippenham
0 1 2 3 4 miles
0 1 2 3 4 5 kilometres

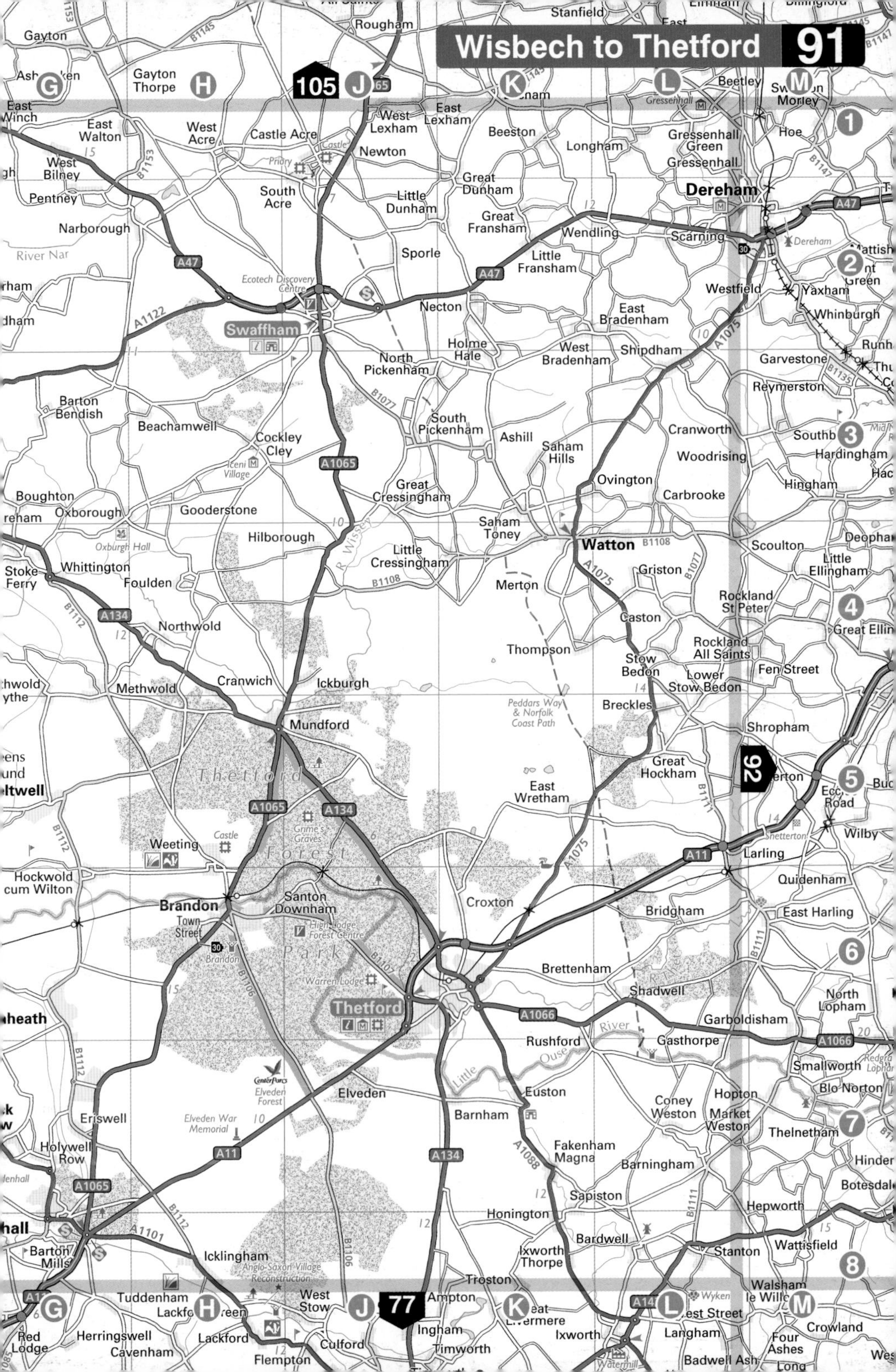
105
77
92
Swaffham
Dereham
Watton
Thetford
Brandon
Mundford
Methwold
Northwold
Stoke Ferry
Necton
Shipdham
Castle Acre
Narborough
Hingham
East Harling
Garboldisham
Elveden
Barnham
Euston
Ixworth
Mildenhall
Barton Mills
Icklingham
Lakenheath
Eriswell
Weeting
Hockwold cum Wilton
Croxton
Larling
Quidenham
Attleborough
Great Hockham
East Wretham
Thompson
Merton
Saham Toney
Ashill
Great Cressingham
Little Cressingham
Hilborough
Gooderstone
Oxborough
Cockley Cley
Beachamwell
Barton Bendish
North Pickenham
South Pickenham
Sporle
Thetford Forest Park
Peddars Way & Norfolk Coast Path
Rushford
Gasthorpe
Coney Weston
Hopton
Market Weston
Thelnetham
Fakenham Magna
Sapiston
Honington
Bardwell
Ixworth Thorpe
Troston
Ampton
Ingham
Culford
West Stow
Flempton
Lackford
Tuddenham
Cavenham
Herringswell
Red Lodge
A47
A1065
A134
A11
A1066
A1075
A1088
A1101
A1122
B1108
B1077
B1106
B1107
B1111
B1112

92
106
91
78
A
B
C
D
E
F
1
2
3
4
5
6
7
8
Bawdeswell
Sparham
Brandiston
Hevingham
Stratton Strawless
B1354
East
Old Beetley
Worthing
B1145
B1147
Norfolk Wildlife Park
Alderford
Swannington
Horstead
A1067
Felthorpe
Hainford
Beetley
Lenwade
Upgate
Gressenhall
Elsing
Morton on the Hill
Attlebridge
Horsford
Newton St Faith
Hillside
Longham
Gressenhall Green
Hoe
Swanton Morley
R Wensum
Thorpe Marriott
A140
Gressenhall
B1147
Weston Longville
Horsham St Faith
Spixworth
North Tuddenham
Aviation
Drayton
Norwich
Dereham
A47
Hockering
Ringland
Taverham
Old Catton
12
P+R
Wendling
Scarning
Dereham
Mattishall Burgh
Honingham
Costessey
Hellesdon
Sprowston
Mattishall
A1042
NORWICH
Clint Green
East Tuddenham
Easton
16
Westfield
Yaxham
South Green
Welborne
Royal Norfolk
New Costessey
East Bradenham
Whinburgh
Colton
Marlingford
A1074
R Yare
B1108
A1242
Brandon Parva
Barford
Bawburgh
Shipdham
Runhall
10
A1075
Garvestone
Thuxton
B1108
Little Melton
Colney
New Lakenham
Whitlingham
Reymerston
B1135
Coston
Barnham Broom
A47
Lynch Green
Cringleford
Eaton
Norfolk
Trowse
Old Lakenham
Carleton Forehoe
High Green
Cranworth
Southburgh
Mid Norfolk Railway
Kimberley
Hethersett
Keswick
Arminghall
Woodrising
Hardingham
B1172
Crownthorpe
Ketteringham
Caistor St Edmund
Ovington
Hingham
Hackford
14
Swardeston
Caistor Roman Town
Upper Stoke
Carbrooke
B1108
Wicklewood
East Carleton
Dunston
Poringland
Mulbarton
Stoke Holy Cross
Watton
B1108
Scoulton
Deopham
Morley St Botolph
Wymondham
Swainsthorpe
A140
Little Ellingham
A11
Wreningham
Bracon Ash
Hawe's Green
Shotesham
Griston
B1077
Deopham Green
Silfield
Newton Flotman
A1075
Rockland St Peter
B1172
Ashwellthorpe
Toprow
Saxlingham Thorpe
Saxlingham Nethergate
Easton
Great Ellingham
Spooner Row
Fundenhall
Flordon
Rockland All Saints
Besthorpe
Hapton
Tasburgh
Saxlingham Green
Stow Bedon
Fen Street
Tacolneston
Low Tharston
Tharston
Upper Tasburgh
Attleborough
Bunwell
Forncett End
Forncett St Mary
Stratton St Michael
Hempnall
Breckles
14
Shropham
Carleton Rode
B1113
Fritton
B1077
Forncett St Peter
Hempnall Green
Great Hockham
Snetterton
Morningthorpe
Old Buckenham
Wacton
Long Stratton
Shelton
B1111
Eccles Road
Great Moulton
Tibenham
Aslacton
New Buckenham
High Green
19
A140
Hardwick
14
Snetterton
Wilby
A11
Larling
B1077
Colegate End
Banham
B1134
Quidenham
Tivetshall St Margaret
Alburgh
Bridgham
East Harling
Banham
Kenninghall
Gissing
Pulham Market
Pulham St Mary
Winfarthing
Tivetshall St Mary
Starston
B1111
Shelfanger
Garlic Street
Shadwell
North Lopham
Fersfield
Shimpling
Rushall
Harleston
15
Garboldisham
Burston
River
South Lopham
B1077
Dickleburgh
Needham
Gasthorpe
A1066
20
Bressingham
Walcot Green
Thelveton
Thorpe Abbotts
Weybread
B1123
Smallworth
Redgrave and Lopham Fen
Diss
Brockdish
Coney Weston
Hopton
Blo Norton
Steam Museum & Gardens
Roydon
Scole
Upper Weybread
Market Weston
River Waveney
Palgrave
A143
B1116
Thelnetham
Redgrave
B1118
Billingford
Stuston
Hoxne
Wingfield
Barningham
Hinderclay
Wortham
Oakley
Brome Street
Cross Street
College
A143
Thrandeston
Brome
Sapiston
B1113
R Dove
Heckfield Green
Botesdale
Hepworth
Rickinghall
Mellis
Denham
Stradbroke
B1111
15
Yaxley
Bardwell
Stanton
Wattisfield
B1117
Eye
B1117
Thornham Parva
Wootten Green
Mill Street
Horham
Walsham le Willows
Braiseworth
Wyken
B1113
Redlingfield Green
West Street
Gislingham
Thornham Magna
Athelington
Wilby
Langham
Occold
Redlingfield
Wickham Street
Crown Corner
Stoke Ash
Badwell Ash
Watermill
Wickham Green
Thorndon
Southolt
0 1 2 3 4 miles
0 1 2 3 4 5 kilometres

Irstead
Potter Heigham
Hoveton
Ludham
107
Martham
Upper Street
A1062
Horning
Upper Street
Repps
Rollesby
Hemsby
Scratby
Ormesby Broad
Ormesby St Margaret
Hemsby Hole
Woodbastwick
Bure Marshes
Broadland Conservation Centre
Thurne
Burgh St Margaret
Ormesby St Michael
California
Salhouse
Ranworth
Pilson Green
Clippesby
Fairhaven
Little Plumstead
Panxworth
Cargate Green
Billockby
Caister-on-Sea
South Walsham
A1064
Filby
Mautby
Caister
A149
Thrigby
Thrigby Hall
West End
West Caister
Upton
Acle
Blofield Heath
Great Plumstead
North Burlingham
Stokesby
Witton
Runham
Stracey Arms Windpump
A47
Blofield
Lingwood
Damgate
Brundall
Beighton
Tunstall
THE BROADS
Postwick
Strumpshaw
South Burlingham
Moulton St Mary
Halvergate
River Yare
GREAT YARMOUTH
Southtown
Buckenham
B1140
Surlingham
Freethorpe
Burgh Castle
Bramerton
Hassingham
Wickhampton
East Port
Rockland St Mary
Cantley
Freethorpe Common
Berney Arms Windmill
Burgh Castle
Bradwell
Gorleston on Sea
Claxton
Limpenhoe
Belton
Carleton St Peter
Langley Street
Ashby St Mary
Pettitts Crafts & Animal Adventure Park
Reedham
Hardley Street
Bergh Apton
Thurton
Fritton
Fritton Lake Countryworld
St Olave's Priory
Hopton on Sea
Chedgrave
Lound
Brooke
R Chet
Loddon
Norton Subcourse
Thurlton
A143
St Olaves
A12
Herringfleet
Mundham
Somerleyton Hall & Gardens
Hales
Blundeston
Corton
Seething
B1136
Kirstead Green
Raveningham
Haddiscoe
Somerleyton
B1074
Pleasurewood Hills
B1385
B1375
Thwaite St Mary
A146
Maypole Green
Toft Monks
Stockton
A1117
Oulton
Woodton
Kirby Cane
Wheatacre
Burgh St Peter
Hedenham
Aldeby
Lowestoft Ness
B1332
Ellingham
Oulton Broad
LOWESTOFT
Street
Gillingham
Kirkley
Ditchingham
Broome
Geldeston
River Waveney
Pakefield
Bungay
Shipmeadow
A1145
B1062
Worlingham
Barnby
Earsham
Mettingham
Barsham
Beccles
North Cove
Carlton Colville
Ringsfield
Gisleham
Ilketshall St Andrew
Mutford
Aviation
Rushmere
Flixton
Kessingland
Winter Flora
Hulver Street
Ringsfield Corner
Black Street
Ilketshall St Margaret
Homersfield
Suffolk Wildlife Park
Henstead
Sotterley
St Margaret South Elmham
A144
Redisham
Benacre Ness
B1127
Benacre
Shadingfield
St Cross South Elmham
A145
Wrentham
Stone Street
Stoven
Covehithe
Rumburgh
Brampton
South Cove
St James South Elmham
Westhall
Suffolk Heritage Coast
Spexhall
Uggeshall
B1124
Wissett
Wangford
B1126
Sole Bay
B1123
Linstead Parva
Chediston
Holton
Reydon
A1095
Blyford
Halesworth
Lighthouse
Hen Reedbeds
Southwold
Cookley
B1123
Wenhaston
Cratfield
Blythburgh
Blackheath
Huntingfield
B1117
Walpole
B1387
Walberswick
Thorington
Bramfield
Suffolk Coast
Laxfield
Heveningham
Ubbeston Green
79
Dunwich
Darsham
Sibton
Peasenhall
Westleton

A
B
C
D
E
F
1
2
3
4
5
6
7
8
Aberffraw Bay Heritage Coast
Malltra
Llanddwy
CAERNARFON
BAY
Lleyn Heritage Coast
Tre
564
YR EIF
Trwyn y Grolech
B4417
Llithfa
Porth Nefyn
Carreg Ddu
Pistyll
Morfa Nefyn
Nefyn
Edern
Bodfuan
Porth Ysgaden
LLEYN
A497
Llanr
Tudweiliog
Efailne
Dinas
371
Carn Fadrum
B4415
Porth Colman
Bryn-mawr
Llaniestyn
Rhyd-y-clafdy
A499
Pen-y-graig
B4417
Penrhos
Llangwnnadl
Meyllteyrn
Llanbedrog
Sarn
Botwnnog
B4413
B4413
Bryncroes
Trwyn Llanbedr
Porthoer
Rhoshirwaun
St Tudwal's Road
Plas yn Rhiw
B4413
Llangian
Y Rhiw
Abersoch
Llanengan
Aberdaron
Llanfaelrhys
Porth Neigwl or Hell's Mouth
Bwlchtocyn
Marchros
St Tudwal's Island East
Porth Ysgo
Aberdaron Bay
St Tudwal's Island West
Bardsey Sound
Porth Geiriad
Lleyn Heritage Coast
St Mary's
BARDSEY ISLAND
0 1 2 3 4 miles
0 1 2 3 4 5 kilometres

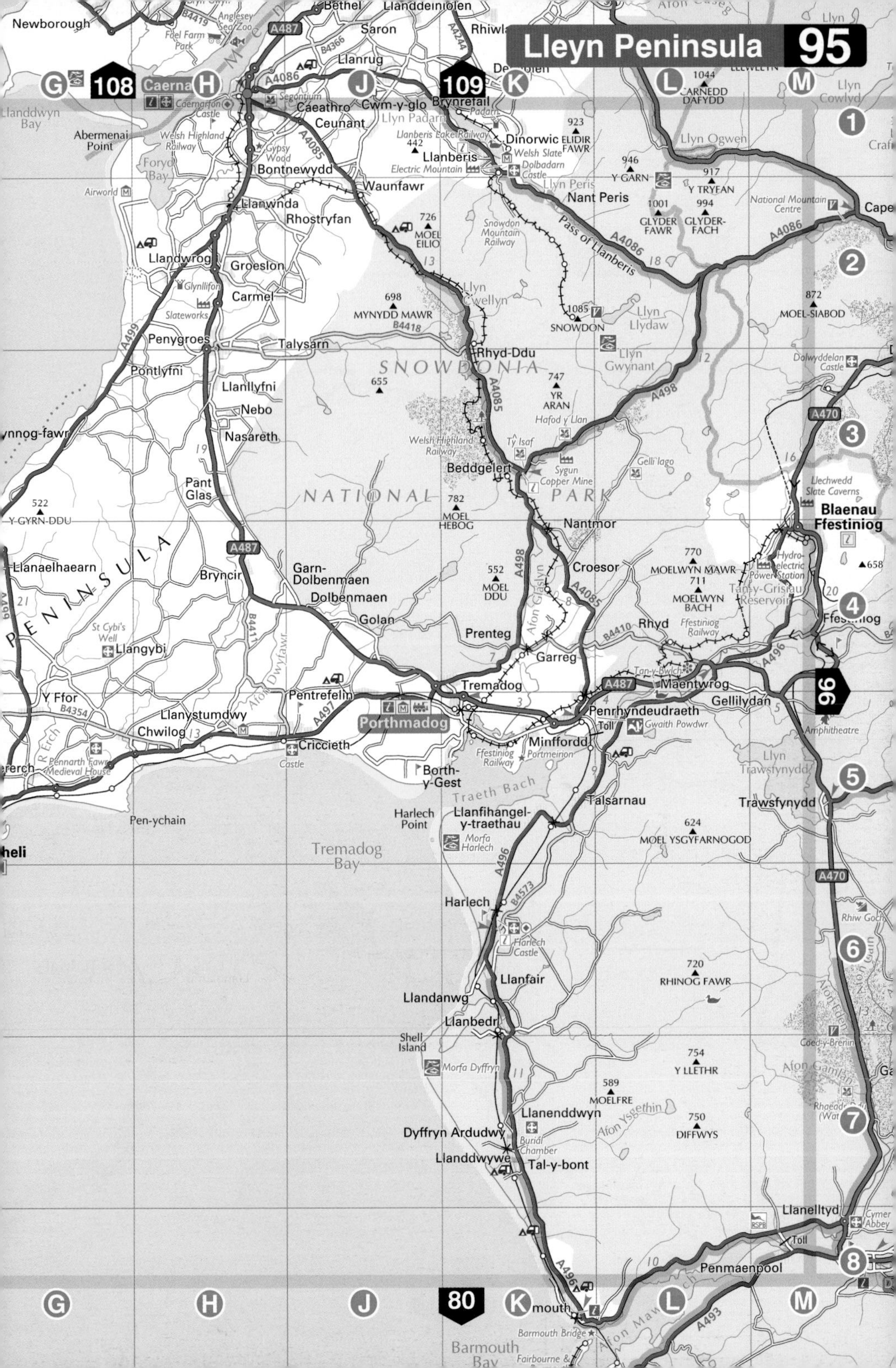
Newborough
Bethel
Llanddeiniolen
Saron
Rhiwlas
Llanrug
Caernarfon
Caeathro
Cwm-y-glo
Brynrefail
Ceunant
Llyn Padarn
Dinorwic
Llanberis
Deiniolen
Abermenai Point
Llanddwyn Bay
Foryd Bay
Bontnewydd
Waunfawr
Llanwnda
Rhostryfan
Llandwrog
Groeslon
Carmel
Penygroes
Talysarn
Pontlyfni
Llanllyfni
Nebo
Nasareth
Pant Glas
Llanaelhaearn
Bryncir
Garn-Dolbenmaen
Dolbenmaen
Golan
Llangybi
Y Ffor
Pentrefelin
Llanystumdwy
Chwilog
Criccieth
Porthmadog
Tremadog
Borth-y-Gest
Pen-ychain
Tremadog Bay
Harlech Point
Llanfihangel-y-traethau
Harlech
Llanfair
Llandanwg
Llanbedr
Shell Island
Llanenddwyn
Dyffryn Ardudwy
Llanddwywe
Tal-y-bont
Barmouth
Barmouth Bay
Barmouth Bridge
Fairbourne
Penmaenpool
Llanelltyd
Cymer Abbey
Trawsfynydd
Llyn Trawsfynydd
Gellilydan
Maentwrog
Penrhyndeudraeth
Minffordd
Portmeirion
Talsarnau
Rhyd
Garreg
Prenteg
Croesor
Nantmor
Beddgelert
Rhyd-Ddu
Llyn Cwellyn
SNOWDON
Nant Peris
Pass of Llanberis
Llyn Ogwen
Blaenau Ffestiniog
Ffestiniog
Tan-y-Grisiau Reservoir
Dolwyddelan Castle
Llyn Cowlyd
SNOWDONIA NATIONAL PARK
LLEYN PENINSULA
1085 SNOWDON
1044 CARNEDD DAFYDD
923 ELIDIR FAWR
946 Y GARN
917 Y TRYFAN
1001 GLYDER FAWR
994 GLYDER-FACH
872 MOEL-SIABOD
726 MOEL EILIO
698 MYNYDD MAWR
655
747 YR ARAN
782 MOEL HEBOG
552 MOEL DDU
522 Y-GYRN-DDU
770 MOELWYN MAWR
711 MOELWYN BACH
624 MOEL YSGYFARNOGOD
720 RHINOG FAWR
754 Y LLETHR
589 MOELFRE
750 DIFFWYS
Welsh Highland Railway
Ffestiniog Railway
Snowdon Mountain Railway
Llanberis Lake Railway
Welsh Slate Museum
Electric Mountain
Dolbadarn Castle
Segontium
Gypsy Wood
Airworld
Glynllifon
Slateworks
St Cybi's Well
Pennarth Fawr Medieval House
Harlech Castle
Morfa Harlech
Morfa Dyffryn
Burial Chamber
Sygun Copper Mine
Hafod y Llan
Ty Isaf
Gelli Iago
Llechwedd Slate Caverns
Hydro-electric Power Station
Coed-y-Brenin
Rhiw Goch
Amphitheatre
Anglesey Sea Zoo
Foel Farm Park
National Mountain Centre
Afon Glaslyn
Afon Dwyfawr
Afon Ysgethin
Afon Mawddach
Afon Gamlan
Traeth Bach
Toll
A487
A499
A4085
A4086
A498
A497
A496
A470
A4244
A493
B4418
B4411
B4410
B4354
B4573
B4366
B4419
108
109
96
80

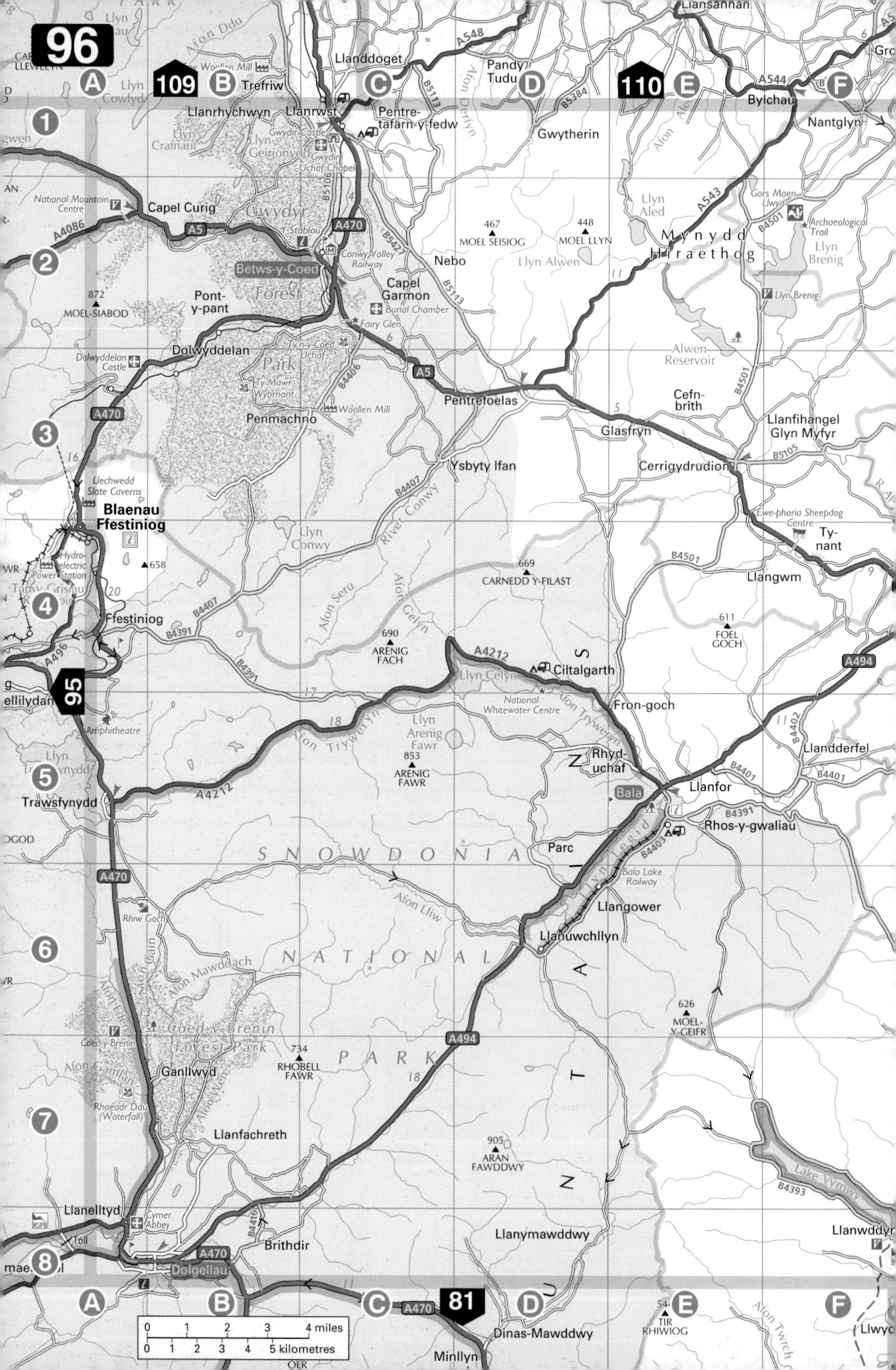

109
110
95
81
Llansannan
Llanddoget
A548
Pandy Tudu
Trefriw
Llyn Cowlyd
Llanrhychwyn
Llanrwst
Pentre-tafarn-y-fedw
Gwytherin
Bylchau
Nantglyn
A544
B5384
B5113
Afon Derfyn
Llyn Crafnant
Llyn Geirionydd
Gwydir Castle
Gwydir Uchaf Chapel
National Mountain Centre
Capel Curig
A4086
A5
Gwydyr
Y Stablau
A470
Conwy Valley Railway
Betws-y-Coed
Forest
B5106
B5427
467
MOEL SEISIOG
448
MOEL LLYN
Llyn Alwen
Nebo
Llyn Aled
A543
Mynydd Hiraethog
Gors Maen Llwyd
B4501
Archaeological Trail
Llyn Brenig
872
MOEL-SIABOD
Pont-y-pant
Capel Garmon
Burial Chamber
Fairy Glen
Alwen Reservoir
Dolwyddelan
Dolwyddelan Castle
Tyn-y-Coed Uchaf
Park
Ty Mawr Wybrnant
B4406
Woollen Mill
Pentrefoelas
Cefn-brith
Penmachno
Glasfryn
Llanfihangel Glyn Myfyr
B5105
Ysbyty Ifan
Cerrigydrudion
Llechwedd Slate Caverns
Blaenau Ffestiniog
B4407
River Conwy
Llyn Conwy
Ewe-phoria Sheepdog Centre
Ty-nant
Hydro-electric Power Station
658
669
CARNEDD Y-FILAST
Tanygrisiau Reservoir
Afon Serw
Afon Gelyn
Llangwm
Ffestiniog
B4391
690
ARENIG FACH
611
FOEL GOCH
A496
A4212
Llyn Celyn
Ciltalgarth
A494
National Whitewater Centre
Afon Tryweryn
Fron-goch
Amphitheatre
Llyn Arenig Fawr
853
ARENIG FAWR
Rhyd-uchaf
B4402
Llandderfel
B4401
Llyn Trawsfynydd
Trawsfynydd
Bala
Llanfor
B4391
Rhos-y-gwaliau
SNOWDONIA
Parc
B4403
Bala Lake Railway
Llyn Tegid
Llangower
Afon Lliw
Rhiw Goch
Llanuwchllyn
NATIONAL
Afon Mawddach
Afon Gain
Afon Eden
626
MOEL-Y-GEIFR
Coed-y-Brenin Forest Park
734
RHOBELL FAWR
PARK
Afon Gamlan
Ganllwyd
Afon Wen
Rhaeadr Ddu (Waterfall)
Llanfachreth
905
ARAN FAWDDWY
Lake Vyrnwy
B4393
Llanelltyd
Cymer Abbey
B4416
Brithdir
Llanymawddwy
Llanwddyn
Toll
Dolgellau
Dinas-Mawddwy
Minllyn
Afon Twrch
TIR RHIWIOG
0 1 2 3 4 miles
0 1 2 3 4 5 kilometres
A B C D E F
1 2 3 4 5 6 7 8

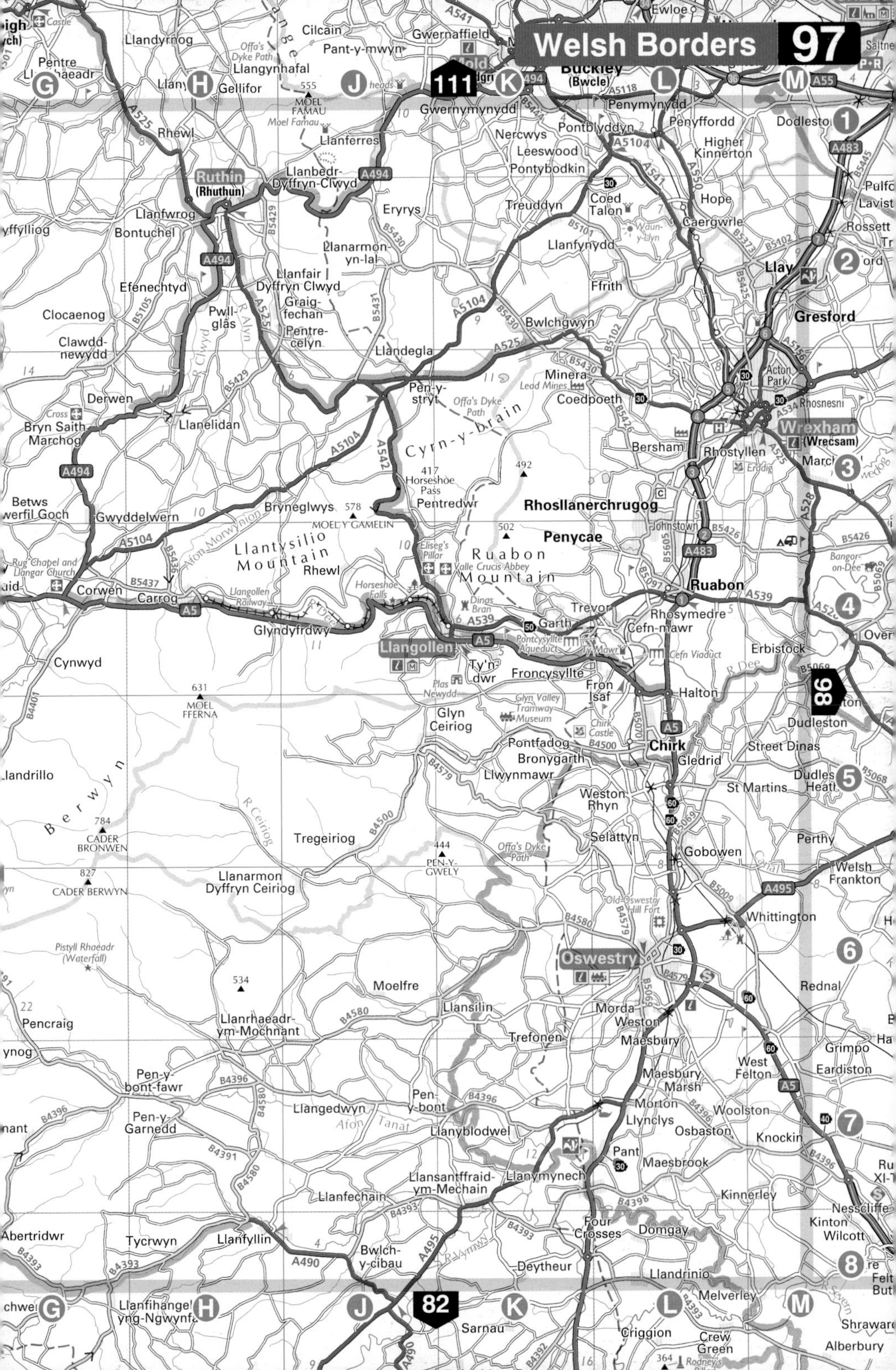
Mold
Buckley (Bwcle)
Ewloe
Cilcain
Gwernaffield
Pant-y-mwyn
Llandyrnog
Llangynhafal
Gellifor
Offa's Dyke Path
Moel Famau
Gwernymynydd
Penymynydd
Penyffordd
Dodleston
Higher Kinnerton
Pontblyddyn
Nercwys
Leeswood
Pontybodkin
Llanferres
Rhewl
Ruthin (Rhuthun)
Llanbedr-Dyffryn-Clwyd
Llanfwrog
Bontuchel
Eryrys
Treuddyn
Coed Talon
Hope
Caergwrle
Llanarmon-yn-Ial
Llanfynydd
Llanfair Dyffryn Clwyd
Efenechtyd
Ffrith
Llay
Rossett
Gresford
Clocaenog
Pwll-glâs
Graig-fechan
Pentre-celyn
Bwlchgwyn
Clawdd-newydd
Llandegla
Minera
Acton Park
Rhosnesni
Derwen
Pen-y-stryt
Coedpoeth
Lead Mines
Offa's Dyke Path
Cross
Bryn Saith Marchog
Llanelidan
Cyrn-y-brain
Wrexham (Wrecsam)
Bersham
Rhostyllen
Erddig
Horseshoe Pass
Pentredwr
Rhosllanerchrugog
Betws Gwerfil Goch
Gwyddelwern
Bryneglwys
Moel y Gamelin
Penycae
Johnstown
Llantysilio Mountain
Ruabon Mountain
Eliseg's Pillar
Valle Crucis Abbey
Bangor-on-Dee
Rug Chapel and Llangar Church
Corwen
Carrog
Rhewl
Llangollen Railway
Horseshoe Falls
Ruabon
Dinas Bran
Trevor
Rhosymedre
Garth
Glyndyfrdwy
Cefn-mawr
Pontcysyllte Aqueduct
Ty Mawr
Cefn Viaduct
Llangollen
Erbistock
Cynwyd
Ty'n-dwr
Froncysyllte
Fron Isaf
Halton
Moel Fferna
Plas Newydd
Glyn Ceiriog
Glyn Valley Tramway Museum
Chirk Castle
Dudleston
Pontfadog
Bronygarth
Chirk
Gledrid
Street Dinas
Llandrillo
Llwynmawr
Weston Rhyn
St Martins
Dudleston Heath
Berwyn
Cader Bronwen
R Ceiriog
Tregeiriog
Selattyn
Gobowen
Perthy
Pen-y-Gwely
Welsh Frankton
Cader Berwyn
Llanarmon Dyffryn Ceiriog
Old Oswestry Hill Fort
Whittington
Pistyll Rhaeadr (Waterfall)
Oswestry
Moelfre
Rednal
Llansilin
Pencraig
Llanrhaeadr-ym-Mochnant
Morda
Weston
Trefonen
Maesbury
Grimpo
West Felton
Eardiston
Pen-y-bont-fawr
Maesbury Marsh
Pen-y-bont
Morton
Llangedwyn
Woolston
Pen-y-Garnedd
Afon Tanat
Llanyblodwel
Llynclys
Osbaston
Knockin
Pant
Maesbrook
Llansantffraid-ym-Mechain
Llanymynech
Llanfechain
Kinnerley
Nesscliffe
Four Crosses
Domgay
Kinton
Abertridwr
Tycrwyn
Llanfyllin
Bwlch-y-cibau
Wilcott
Deytheur
Llandrinio
Llanfihangel yng-Ngwynfa
Melverley
Sarnau
Criggion
Crew Green
Shrawardine
Alberbury
Rodney's Pillar
111
82
98

111
112
97
83
A
B
C
D
E
F
1
2
3
4
5
6
7
8
Saltney
Handbridge
Christleton
Huntington
Castle
Rowton
Eccleston
Saighton
Duddon
Burton
R Gowy
Overton
Hargrave
Clotton
Utkinton
Cotebrook
Little Budworth
Oulton Park
Eaton
Tarporley
Huxley
Dodleston
Higher Kinnerton
Aldford
Pulford
Lavister
Rossett
Trevalyn
Marford
Gresford
Holt
Farndon
Churton
Milton Green
Handley
Shropshire Union Canal
Tattenhall
Newton
Castle
Beeston
Burwardsley
Spurstow
Peckforton
Tilstone Fearnall
Tiverton
Alpraham
Calveley
Bunbury
Haughton Moss
Wardle
Wettenhall
Church Minshull
Worleston
Harthill
Clutton
Barton
Crewe
Water Mill
Bulkeley
Faddiley
Burland
Acton
Nantwich
Cholmondeley Castle
Chorley
Acton Park
Rhosnesni
Wrexham
(Wrecsam)
Erddig
Marchwiel
R Clywedog
Tilston
Horton Green
Shocklach
Ebnal
Chorlton Lane
Hampton Heath
No Man's Heath
Malpas
Bickley
Norbury
Marbury
Wrenbury
Secret Bunker
Sound
Aston
Newhall
Hankelow
Audlem
Dodd's Green
Cuddington Heath
Worthenbury
Bangor-is-y-coed
Bangor-on-Dee
Threapwood
Tallarn Green
Higher Wych
Bell o' th' Hill
Wirswall
Canal
Grindley Brook
Whitchurch
Burleydam
Overton
Erbistock
R Dee
Horseman's Green
Eglwys Cross
Penley
Hanmer
Bronington
Redbrook
Broughall
Wilkesley
Adderley
Ash Magna
Ightfield
Knolton
Dudleston
Street Dinas
Dudleston Heath
Tilstock
Prees Heath
Calverhall
Prees Higher Heath
Ellesmere
Welshampton
Bettisfield
Whixall
Moreton Say
Longford
Perthy
Prees
Bletchley
Welsh Frankton
Tetchill
Lyneal
Northwood
Colemere
Newtown
Edstaston
Fauls
Ternhill
Whittington
Hordley
English Frankton
Prees Green
Hawkstone
Hawkstone Park
Weston-under-Redcastle
Marchamley
Hodnet
Wollerton
Rednal
R Perry
Loppington
Cockshutt
Noneley
Wem
Aston
Hodnet Hall
Bury Walls
Stoke upon Tern
Bagley
Haughton
Grimpo
Lee Brockhurst
West Felton
Eardiston
Wykey
Burlton
Weston Lullingfields
Preston Brockhurst
High Hatton
Ollerton
Myddle
Clive
Stanton upon Hine Heath
Peplow
Child's Ercall
Woolston
Knockin
Eyton
Grinshill
Moreton Corbet
Castle
Ellerdine Heath
Newtown
Baschurch
Harmer Hill
Shawbury
Great Bolas
Kinnerley
Ruyton-XI-Towns
Nesscliffe
Little Ness
Preston Gubbals
Hadnall
Rowton
Kinton
Wilcott
Adcote School
Yeaton
Bomere Heath
Astley
Cherrington
Waters Upton
Great Ness
Grafton
Walford Heath
Leaton
Albrighton
Poynton Green
Walton
Pentre
Felton Butler
Fitz
High Ercall
Crudgington
Forton
Haughmond Abbey
Roden
Longdon upon Tern
Sleapford
Eyton upon the Weald Moors
Rodington Heath
Long Waste
Ditherington
A55
A483
A41
A534
A49
A51
A525
A528
A539
A495
A530
A5
A53
A442
A5124
B5445
B5102
B5130
B5069
B5426
B5068
B5063
B5476
B5065
B4397
B4396
B5067
B5062
B5074
B5341
0 1 2 3 4 miles
0 1 2 3 4 5 kilometres

Middlewich
Green
A54
Eaton
Wincle
Bosley
M6
Brereton Green
113
Arclid Green
Brookhouse Green
Astbury
THE CLOUD
Timbersbrook
Rushton Spencer
GUN HILL
Goldsley
Elworth
Sandbach
Spen Green
A534
A527
A523
Upper Hulme
Meerbrook
Ettiley Heath
Newtown
Bradfield Green
Wheelock
Lakemore
Winterley
Trent & Mersey Canal
Little Moreton Hall
A50
A533
A34
Poolfold
Biddulph Grange Garden
Biddulph
Biddulph Moor
Rudyard Reservoir
Rudyard
Tittesworth Reservoir
Abbey Green
Thorncliffe
Mow Cop
Mow Cop (folly)
Scholar Green
Rode Heath
Brown Lees
Horton
Brindley Mill
Leek
Bradnop
Onecote
CREWE
Haslington
Alsager
Greenway
Ladderedge
Longsdon
A53
B5077
B5078
Crewe Green
A5020
Kidsgrove
Brown Edge
Endon Bank
Endon
Stanley
Flint Mill
Deep Hayes
A520
A523
Shavington
A500
Weston
Barthomley
Parrot's Drumble
Talke
A5011
Hough
Audley
Tunstall
B5051
Cheddleton
Chorlton
Wybunbury
B5500
Ceramica
Burslem
Bagnall
Churnet Valley Railway
Caldon Canal
Wetley Rocks
Consall
Ipstones
Foxt
Walgherton
Betley
Blakenhall
A531
B5071
Wolstanton
Central Forest Park
NEWCASTLE-UNDER-LYME
May Bank
Etruria
Hanley
Bucknall
A52
Cellarhead
Froghall
B5053
Hunsterson
Checkley
Wrinehill
M6
Silverdale
Hartshill
Hulme
Kingsley
Keele
Stoke-upon-Trent
STOKE-ON-TRENT
Fenton
A50074
Weston Coyney
Dilhorne
Cheadle
Oakamoor
B5417
A522
A521
Buerton
Bridgemere Garden World
Madeley
A525
Keele
Longton
B5490
Caverswall
Onneley
Woore
Butterton
A53
A5182
Meir
Foxfield Light Railway
Forsbrook
Mobberley
Draycott in the Moors
Pipe Gate
Aston
Dorrington
Knighton
Bearstone
Whitmore
Acton
Hanchurch
Shelton Under Harley
Trentham
The Wedgwood Story
A5035
B5029
Dorothy Clive
Hill Chorlton
A519
100
Cresswell
Blackbrook
Norton in Hales
Maer
Beech
Barlaston
A520
Fulford
Lower Tean
Upper Tean
Mucklestone
Chapel Chorlton
Ashley
Tittensor
Downs Banks
Knenhall
Upper Leigh
Moddershall
B5415
B5026
Loggerheads
Podmore
Cranberry
Bowers
Standon
Swynnerton
Oulton
Church Leigh
Hilderstone
Dod's Leigh
A53
Chatcull
Wetwood
Millmeece
M6
Stone
Little Stoke
Garshall Green
Hales
Fairoak
Coldmeece
Yarnfield
Slindon
Croxton
B5027
Milwich
Fieldon
Chipnall
Little Sugnall
Sugnall
Stafford (northbound)
Stafford (southbound)
Fradswell
Cheswardine
Bishop's Offley
Pershall
Norton Bridge
Aston-by-Stone
R. Trent
R. Sow
B5066
Sandon
Lockleywood
Great Soudley
Copmere End
Eccleshall
Chebsey
Izaak Walton's Cottage
Sandon Bank
Whitgreave
A34
A51
Gayton
Amerton Railway
A518
Stowe by Chartley
Little Soudley
Adbaston
Tunstall
Knighton
Marston
Salt
Weston
Ellenhall
Great Bridgeford
Hopton
Hinstock
Shebdon
High Offley
Woodseaves
Seighford
Holmcroft
Staffordshire County Showground
Hixon
Weston Jones
Knightley
B5405
Ranton
STAFFORD
Ingestre
Blithfield Reservoir
Sambrook
Norbury
Ranton Green
Coton Clanford
Aston
Littleworth
Tixall
Great Haywood
Little Haywood
A41
R. Meese
Derrington
Forebridge
Shugborough
Colwich
Chetwynd
Sutton
Long Compton
Shut Heath
Rickerscote
A513
Bishton
Forton
Aqualate Mere
Gnosall
A518
Milford
Tibberton
B5062
Haughton
Walton-on-the-Hill
Brocton
Newport
A518
Coton
Gnosall Heath
Hyde Lea
Coppenhall
Wolseley Bridge
Edmond
Acton Trussell
Etchinghill
Outwoods
Bradley
Dunston
CANNOCK CHASE
Longford
Chetwynd Aston
Church Aston
Church Eaton
Levedale
Bednall
Stockton
84
High Onn
85
Slitting Mill
Preston upon the Weald Moors
Lilleshall
Woodcote
Orslow
M6
A34
Birches Valley Forest Centre
Great Chatwell
A449
Heath Hill
Bickford
Whiston
Penkridge
A460

100
A
B
C
D
E
F
114
1
2
3
4
5
6
7
8
Hollinsclough
Longnor
Crowdecote
Pilsbury
Lathkill Dale
Haddon Hall
Rowsley
Arbor Low Stone Circle
Youlgreave
Alport
Stanton in Peak
Darley Dale
Middleton
Birchover
Churchtown
Darley Bridge
Wensley
Oker Side
Peak District
Hartington
Brund
Sheen
Heathcote
Elton
Winster
Market House
Upper Hulme
Tittesworth Reservoir
Upper Elkstone
Hulme End
Biggin
Abbey Green
Thorncliff
Warslow
R Hamps
River Dove
Grangemill
Aldwark
Heights of Abraham
Masson Mills
Bonsall
Matlock
Gulliver's Kingdom
Ible
Cromford
National Park
Butterton
Alstonefield
Alsop en le Dale
Longcliffe
Middleton
National Stone Centre
Bolehill
Bradnop
Onecote
Wetton
Grindon
Hope
Milldale
Parwich
Ballidon
Brassington
Wirksworth
Ford
R Manifold
Dove Dale
Tissington
Hopton
Carsington
Bradbourne
Carsington Water
Cheddleton
Winkhill
Waterfall
Ilam
Fenny Bentley
Hognaston
Kirk Ireton
Churnet
Caldon Canal
Ipstones
Waterhouses
Cauldon
Calton
Ilam Park
Thorpe
Kniveton
Blackwall
Idridgehay
Foxt
Blore
Atlow
Ecclesbourne Valley Railway
Froghall
Whiston
Mapleton
Ashbourne
Hulland Ward
Hillcliff Lane
Shottlegate
Kingsley
Near Cotton
Stanton
Turnditch
Hulland
Cowers Lane
Ramshorn
Mayfield
Middle Mayfield
Clifton
Bradley
Cross o' th' hands
Hazelwood
Oakamoor
Farley
Wootton
Osmaston
Dilhorne
Upper Ellastone
Church Mayfield
Cheadle
Alton Towers
Ellastone
Snelston
Darley Moor
Wyaston
Mugginton
Weston Underwood
Forsbrook
Threapwood
Alton
Mobberley
Bradley in the Moors
Denstone
Norbury
Roston
Shirley
Brailsford
Kedleston
Greatgate
Foston Brk
Rodsley
Yeaveley
Hollington
Upper Tean
Croxden
Abbey
Rocester
Hollington
Kirk Langley
Lower Tean
Marston Montgomery
Great Cubley
Alkmonton
Thurvaston
Longlane
Checkley
Longford
Lees Green
Lees
Mackworth
Upper Leigh
Fole
Little Cubley
Lower Leigh
Withington
Stramshall
Somersal Herbert
Boylestone
Sutton Brook
Radbourne
Church Leigh
Upper Nobut
Harehill
Trusley
Dod's Leigh
Doveridge
Lane Ends
Mickleover
Uttoxeter
Church Broughton
Sutton on the Hill
Milwich
Field
Bramshall
R Dove
Sudbury Hall
Sudbury
Foston
Etwall
Burnaston
Fradswell
Birch Cross
Marchington
Scropton
Hatton
Hilton
Findern
Kingstone
Gorsty Hill
Marston on Dove
Draycott in the Clay
Tutbury
Egginton
Amerton Railway
Stowe by Chartley
Rolleston on Dove
Willington
Drointon
Hanbury
Repton
Weston
Newborough
Stretton
Milton
Hixon
Newton
Abbots Bromley
Anslow
Anslow Gate
Horninglow
Newton Solney
Blithfield Reservoir
BURTON UPON TRENT
Admaston
Newchurch
Rangemore
Winshill
Bretby
Great Haywood
Hoar Cross
Tatenhill
Shugborough
Little Haywood
Colwich
Stapenhill
Bishton
Milford
Colton
Hadley End
Dunstall
Branston
Brocton
Wolseley Bridge
Blithbury
Hamstall Ridware
Olive Green
Woodhouses
Barton-under-Needwood
Swadlincote
Cannock Chase
Etchinghill
Hill Ridware
Rugeley
Morrey
Yoxall
Trent Valley
Walton-on-Trent
Castle Gresley
Cauldwell
Blackfordby
Slitting Mill
Mavesyn Ridware
Nethertown
Hays Valley Forest Centre
Rosliston
Coton in the Elms
Overseal
King's Bromley
Alrewas
National Memorial Arboretum
R Trent
85
86
99
A53
B5053
B5054
B5056
A5012
B5056
A523
B5053
A52
A515
B5035
B5023
A517
A521
A522
B5417
B5032
B5033
B5030
A50
A518
B5027
B5017
A511
B5008
B5234
A51
A513
B5013
B5014
A444
B5353
A514
B5016
A38
A5121
A516
B5020
0 1 2 3 4 miles
0 1 2 3 4 5 kilometres

NOTTINGHAM
DERBY
MANSFIELD
Loughborough
Sutton in Ashfield
Kirkby in Ashfield
Hucknall
Eastwood
Ilkeston
Heanor
Ripley
Alfreton
Belper
Stapleford
Beeston
Long Eaton
West Bridgford
Castle Donington
Melbourne
Shepshed
Kegworth
Ruddington
Keyworth
Cotgrave
Radcliffe on Trent
Burton Joyce
Blidworth
Ravenshead
SHERWOOD FOREST
Clay Cross
North Wingfield
South Normanton
Somercotes
Swanwick
Codnor
Borrowash
Breaston
Ockbrook
Barrow upon Soar
Mountsorrel
Whitwick
Sileby
115
102
87

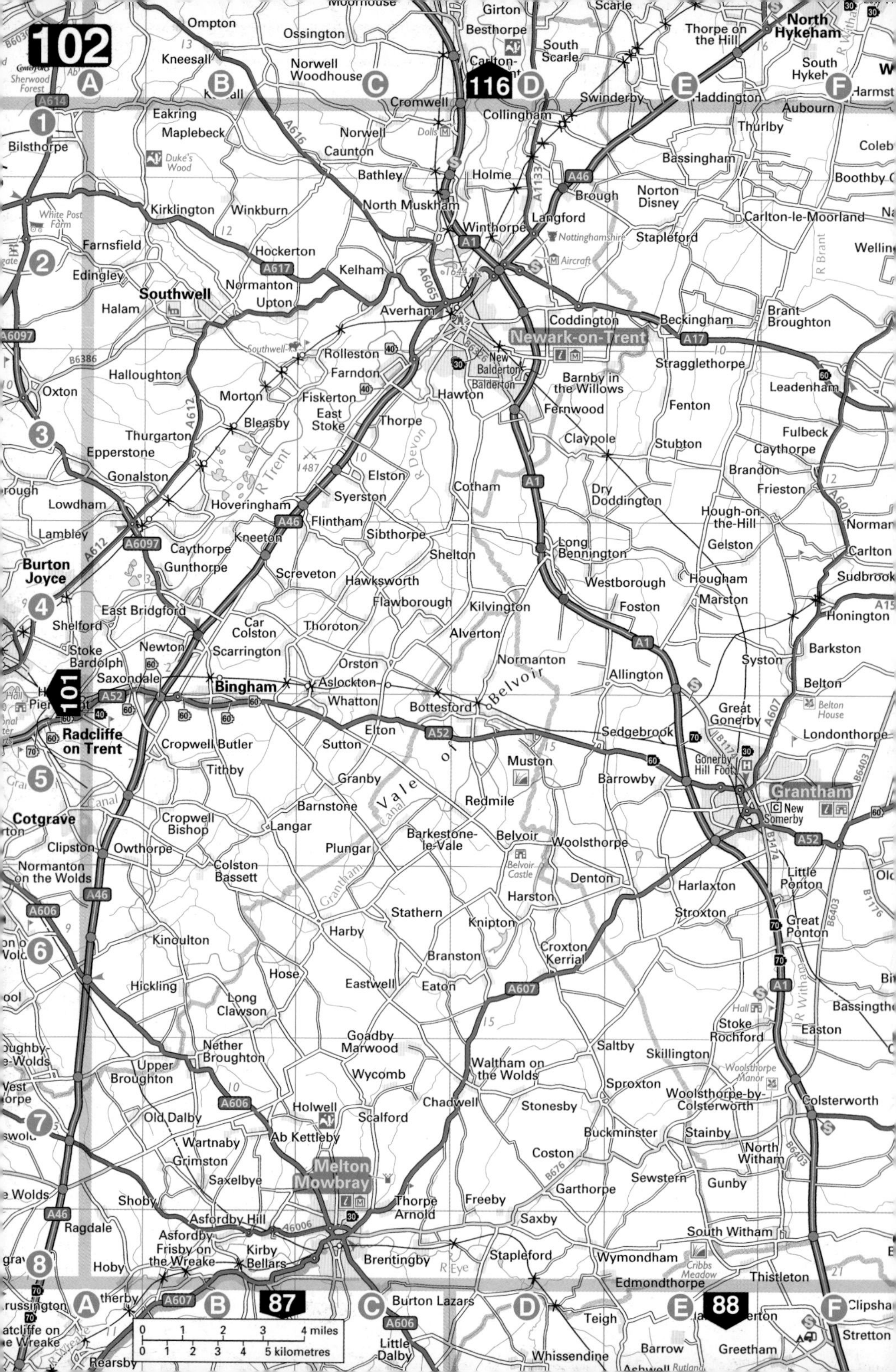

A
B
C
D
E
F
1
2
3
4
5
6
7
8
116
101
87
88
Ompton
Ossington
Girton
Besthorpe
Scarle
Thorpe on the Hill
North Hykeham
South Hykeham
Kneesall
Norwell Woodhouse
Carlton-on-Trent
South Scarle
Sherwood Forest
A614
Eakring
Cromwell
Collingham
Swinderby
Haddington
Aubourn
Thurlby
Maplebeck
Norwell
Caunton
Dolls
Bilsthorpe
Duke's Wood
Bathley
Holme
Bassingham
A616
A46
A1133
Brough
Norton Disney
Boothby
Kirklington
Winkburn
North Muskham
Langford
Carlton-le-Moorland
White Post Farm
Winthorpe
Stapleford
Nottinghamshire
Aircraft
R Brant
Farnsfield
Hockerton
A1
A617
Edingley
Kelham
Normanton
Southwell
Upton
A6065
Halam
Averham
Coddington
Beckingham
Brant Broughton
Newark-on-Trent
A17
A6097
Southwell
Rolleston
Farndon
New Balderton
Balderton
Stragglethorpe
B6386
Halloughton
Oxton
Morton
Fiskerton
Hawton
Barnby in the Willows
Leadenham
East Stoke
Fernwood
Fenton
A612
Bleasby
Thorpe
Thurgarton
Claypole
Fulbeck
Epperstone
R Trent
Stubton
Caythorpe
Elston
R Devon
Brandon
Gonalston
Cotham
Frieston
Syerston
Dry Doddington
Lowdham
Hoveringham
Flintham
Hough-on-the-Hill
A607
Lambley
Kneeton
Sibthorpe
Burton Joyce
Caythorpe
Gelston
Long Bennington
Shelton
Carlton
Gunthorpe
Screveton
Hawksworth
Westborough
Hougham
Sudbrook
Flawborough
Marston
Shelford
East Bridgford
Kilvington
Foston
Honington
Car Colston
Thoroton
Alverton
Stoke Bardolph
Newton
Scarrington
Barkston
Normanton
Orston
Allington
Syston
Saxondale
Bingham
Aslockton
Belvoir
Belton
Whatton
Bottesford
Great Gonerby
Belton House
A52
Radcliffe on Trent
Elton
Sedgebrook
Cropwell Butler
Sutton
Londonthorpe
Vale of Belvoir
Gonerby Hill Foot
B1174
B6403
Tithby
Muston
Granby
Barrowby
Grantham
Cotgrave
Canal
Cropwell Bishop
Barnstone
Redmile
New Somerby
Langar
Clipston
Owthorpe
Plungar
Barkestone-le-Vale
Belvoir
Woolsthorpe
Normanton on the Wolds
Colston Bassett
Grantham Canal
Belvoir Castle
Denton
Harlaxton
Little Ponton
A606
Harston
Stathern
Stroxton
Great Ponton
Knipton
Harby
Kinoulton
Croxton Kerrial
Branston
Hose
Hickling
Eastwell
Eaton
R Witham
Bassingthorpe
Long Clawson
Hall
Stoke Rochford
Easton
Goadby Marwood
Nether Broughton
Saltby
Skillington
Upper Broughton
Waltham on the Wolds
Woolsthorpe Manor
Wycomb
Sproxton
Woolsthorpe-by-Colsterworth
Colsterworth
Chadwell
Stonesby
Holwell
Scalford
Old Dalby
Buckminster
Stainby
Ab Kettleby
North Witham
Wartnaby
Coston
Grimston
Sewstern
Gunby
Melton Mowbray
B676
Saxelbye
Garthorpe
Shoby
Thorpe Arnold
Freeby
Asfordby Hill
Ragdale
Saxby
South Witham
A6006
Asfordby
Frisby on the Wreake
Kirby Bellars
Brentingby
Stapleford
Wymondham
Cribbs Meadow
Hoby
R Eye
Thistleton
Edmondthorpe
Burton Lazars
A607
Teigh
Stretton
Clipsham
Little Dalby
Whissendine
Barrow
Greetham
Ashwell
Rearsby
R Wreake
0 1 2 3 4 miles
0 1 2 3 4 5 kilometres

Potterhanworth
B1178
B1202
Nocton
G
H
117
J
Metheringham Delph
Kirkstead
K
Woodhall Spa
Kirkby on Bain
L
Wood Enderby
118
M
Old Bolingbroke
East Kirkby
Revesby
1
B1188
B1189
Metheringham
Blankney
Martin
B1191
Timberland Delph
Tattershall Thorpe
Tumby
A153
A155
Mareham le Fen
Scopwick
Kirkby Green
Timberland
Tattershall
Coningsby
Tattershall Castle
Tattershall College
Battle of Britain Memorial Flight
Tumby Woodside
New Bolingbroke
A15
Thorpe Tilney
Ashby de la Launde
Rowston
Walcott
Hawthorn Hill
New York
2
Dogdyke
Scrub Hill
Digby
Billinghay
Chapel Hill
West
Fen
North
Bloxholm
Dorrington
North Kyme
B1183
B1192
Ruskington
R Witham
Sibsey Trader Windmill
Holland Fen
Frithville
A153
Anwick
Gipsey Bridge
B1184
Cranwell
R Slea
South Kyme
Fishtoft Drove
3
B1429
Leasingham
B1209
Langrick
B1395
North Rauceby
Holdingham
A17
Evedon
Ewerby
Anton's Gowt
Kirkby la Thorpe
Howell
Sleaford
South Rauceby
Asgarby
East Heckington
Holland Fen
Boston
B1517
Ancaster
Quarrington
Heckington
The Pearoom
A17
A1121
4
A52
Great Hale
Burton Pedwardine
Little Hale
Silk Willoughby
Kelby
Swarby
Scredington
Helpringham
Swineshead
B1391
Culverthorpe
Aswarby
B1394
104
Heydour
Aisby
Aunsby
Osbournby
Spanby
Bicker
Kirton
5
Dembleby
Swaton
Skeldyke
Newton
Northorpe
Haceby
Threekingham
A52
B1181
Donington
Wigtoft
Sutterton
Braceby
Walcot
Horbling
A17
Burtoft
Algarkirk
Billingborough
Quadring Eaudike
Sapperton
Pickworth
B1397
Folkingham
Humby
A15
South Forty Foot Drain
Quadring
A152
A16
Fosdyke
Laughton
Pointon
Westhorpe
Gosberton
R Welland
Aslackby
Lenton
Risegate
6
Ingoldsby
Dowsby
B1397
Rippingale
B1356
Surfleet
Moulton Seas End
Irnham
B1171
B1176
Kirkby Underwood
Dunsby
Pinchbeck
Corby Glen
A151
Hacconby
B1180
Weston
Springfields
A151
Hanthorpe
Morton
Mill Green
Moulton
Elsthorpe
Grimsthorpe
Spalding
Fulney
7
Dyke
A151
Swinstead
Edenham
B1165
A15
B1357
Bourne
A151
Twenty
B1193
Creeton
R Glen
B1172
Little Bytham
Moulton Chapel
A151
Lound
Witham on the Hill
Toft
Cowbit
8
R Welland
R Glen
Thurlby
89
Bedford
Level
Manthorpe
Deeping Fen
A1175
A6121
Carlby
A16

Hundleby
Old Bolingbroke
Bolingbroke Castle
Halton Holegate
Monksthorpe
Great Steeping
Burgh le Marsh
Bratoft
A158
Skegness
Toynton All Saints
Northcote
B1195
118
119
Little Steeping
Firsby
East Kirkby
Lincolnshire Aviation
Revesby
Mareham le Fen
Keal Cotes
Stickford
Croft
Fendike Corner
Thorpe St Peter
Wainfleet Haven
Wainfleet All Saints
Tumby Woodside
New Bolingbroke
Stickney
New Leake
Wainfleet St Mary
A52
Gibraltar Point
Eastville
East Fen
Friskney
A16
West Fen
B1183
Northlands
Leake Common Side
Sibsey Trader Windmill
Sibsey
Frithville
B1184
Wrangle
Fishtoft Drove
Old Leake
Hilldyke
Leverton
Anton's Gowt
Benington
Butterwick
Boston
A1121
Freiston
Fishtoft
Scrane End
Wyberton East
B1391
B1397
103
Frampton
Kirton
The Haven
RSPB
THE WASH
Skeldyke
Sutterton
Algarkirk
Fosdyke
Holbeach St Matthew
R Welland
Holbeach St Mark's
Holbeach Marsh
Gedney Drove End
B1359
A17
B1357
Moulton Seas End
Saracen's Head
Holbeach Bank
Holbeach Hurn
Gedney Dyke
Holbeach Clough
Lutton
Fleet Hargate
B1515
The Wash
Weston
A151
Holbeach
Moulton
Whaplode
Fleet
Gedney
Butterfly & Falconry Park
Gedney Broadgate
Long Sutton
Sutton Bridge
B1165
B1168
B1390
Terrington St Clement
Walpole Cross Keys
Clenchwarton
African Violet Centre
West Lynn
Great Ouse
Moulton Chapel
Tydd Gote
Tilney All Saints
Holbeach St Johns
Sutton St James
Tydd St Mary
Walpole St Andrew
Tilney High End
A47
Four Gotes
Walpole St Peter
Tydd St Giles
Level
Newton
River Nene
Tilney St Lawrence
West
Sutton
0 1 2 3 4 miles
0 1 2 3 4 5 kilometres
89
90

G
H
J
K
L
M
1
2
3
4
5
6
7
8
North Norfolk Heritage Coast
Holkham Bay
Brancaster Bay
Scolt Head Island
Peddars Way & Norfolk Coast Path
Blakeney Point
Holme Dunes
Holme next the Sea
Brancaster
Brancaster Staithe
Burnham Norton
Burnham Overy Staithe
Holkham
Wells-next-the-sea
Old Hunstanton
Hunstanton
Titchwell
Thornham
Branodunum Roman Fort
Burnham Deepdale
Burnham Market
Burnham Overy
Holkham Hall
Warham St Mary
Warham All Saints
Burnham Thorpe
Ringstead
Wighton
Heacham
Norfolk Lavender
Summerfield
Peddars Way & Norfolk Coast Path
North Creake
Creake Abbey
Wells & Walsingham Light Railway
The Shrine of Our Lady
106
Docking
Stanhoe
Little Walsingham
Great Walsingham
Sedgeford
South Creake
North Barsham
Hindringham
Houghton St Giles
Fring
Bircham Newton
Snettisham
Park Farm
West Barsham
East Barsham
Great Snoring
Thursford
Ingoldisthorpe
Shernborne
Syderstone
Great Bircham
Bircham Tofts
Wicken Green Village
Little Snoring
R Stiffkey
Dersingham
Sculthorpe
Kettlestone
Dersingham Bog
Anmer
Dunton
Shereford
Tattersett
Coxford
Fakenham
Hempton
Wolferton
Sandringham
West Newton
Houghton Hall
West Rudham
New Houghton
Little Ryburgh
Tatterford
East Rudham
Toftrees
Babingley River
Flitcham
Great Ryburgh
Helhoughton
East Raynham
Colkirk
Harpley
Castle Rising
Hillington
Little Massingham
West Raynham
South Raynham
Castle
Congham
Horningtoft
Gateley
Roydon
Grimston
Great Massingham
Weasenham St Peter
Whissonsett
Wootton
Wellingham
Brisley
Weasenham All Saints
Tittleshall
North Elmham
Stanfield
Fairstead
Gayton
Rougham
East Bilney
Old Beetley
King's Lynn
Ashwicken
Gayton Thorpe
Mileham
Litcham
Gressenhall
Fair Green
East Winch
West Lexham
East Lexham
East Walton
91
Newton
Longham
Gressenhall Green
Middleton
North Runcton
West Bilney
Blackborough End
Priory
Great Dunham
A149
A148
A47
A1065
A1067
B1155
B1153
B1355
B1105
B1454
B1440
B1439
B1145
B1146
B1110
RSPB

A
B
C
D
E
F
1
2
3
4
5
6
7
8
North Norfolk Heritage Coast
Blakeney Point
Blakeney Point
Morston Marshes
Guildhall
Cley Marshes
Wells-next-the-sea
Morston
Blakeney
Cley next the Sea
Muckleburgh Collection
Sheringham
West Runton
East Runton
Cromer
Salthouse
Weybourne
Sheringham Park
Stiffkey
Cockthorpe
Wiveton
Kelling
Upper Sheringham
Beeston Regis
Norfolk Shire Horse Centre
St Mary
Warham All Saints
Langham
Glandford
North Norfolk Railway
Bodham
A148
Overstrand
Aylmerton
A149
Felbrigg
Sidestrand
Wighton
Binham
Saxlingham
R Glaven
Holt
West Beckham
East Beckham
Felbrigg Hall
Northrepps
Binham Priory & Market Cross
Field Dalling
Letheringsett
Baconsthorpe Castle
Gresham
Crossdale Street
105
Sharrington
Holt Lowes
Bessingham
Sustead
Metton
Great Walsingham
Bale
Hempstead
Southrepps
Hindringham
Thornage
Baconsthorpe
Roughton
Houghton St Giles
Brinton
Hunworth
Plumstead
Hanworth
Thorpe Market
Thursford
Edgefield Green
Thurgarton
A140
Great Snoring
Stody
Matlask
East Barsham
Thursford
Gunthorpe
Briningham
Edgefield
Aldborough
Bradfield
B1354
Little Barningham
Wickmere
Antingham
A148
Barney
Melton Constable
Erpingham
Suffield
Little Snoring
Briston
Calthorpe
Croxton
Swanton Novers
Mannington Gardens
Wolterton Park
North Walsham
Kettlestone
Fulmodeston
Saxthorpe
Itteringham
Pensthorpe Waterfowl Park
R Bure
Banningham
Fakenham
Hindolveston
Corpusty
Ingworth
Little Ryburgh
Stibbard
Thurning
Blickling
Blickling Hall
Felmingham
Oulton
Tuttington
Great Ryburgh
Wood Norton
Oulton Street
Heydon
Aylsham
Wood Dalling
A1067
R Wensum
Guestwick
Burgh next Aylsham
Guist
Salle
B1145
Foulsham
Bure Valley Railway
Swanton Abbott
Gateley
Twyford
Themelthorpe
Oxnead
Cawston
Marsham
Horningtoft
Foxley Wood
Reepham
Lamas
Brampton
Bintree
Eastgate
North Elmham Chapel
Foxley
Whitwell Street
Buxton Heath
Brisley
Buxton
North Elmham
Billingford
Brandiston
R Bure
Stratton Strawless
Bawdeswell
Hevingham
East Bilney
Sparham
Norfolk Wildlife Park
Old Beetley
Worthing
Alderford
Swannington
Horstead
Mileham
Felthorpe
Dinosaur
Hainford
Beetley
Lyng
Lenwade
Frettenham
Swanton Morley
Upgate
Gressenhall
Elsing
Morton on the Hill
92
Horsford
Newton St Faith
Gressenhall
Weston Longville
Vensum
Thorpe Marriott
Horsham St Faith
Spixworth
Dereham
0 1 2 3 4 miles
0 1 2 3 4 5 kilometres

G
H
J
K
L
M
1
2
3
4
5
6
7
8
rimingham
Mundesley
Stow Mill
Paston
B1159
Knapton
Bacton
Edingthorpe
Walcott
Edingthorpe Green
Witton
Ridlington
Happisburgh
Whimpwell Green
Meeting House Hill
Happisburgh Common
Hempstead
Honing
Lessingham
A149
Ingham Corner
Sea Palling
Briggate
East Ruston
B1159
Waxham
Worstead
Ingham
Stalham
Calthorpe Street
Dilham
Hickling
Smallburgh
Barton Turf
Wood Street
Sutton
Hickling Green
Horsey
Tunstead
Barton Broad
Hickling Broad
Horsey Windpump
Neatishead
Catfield
Irstead
A1151
R Ant
Potter Heigham
B1354
Winterton-on-Sea
Hoveton
Ludham
Martham
A1062
Bastwick
R Thurne
Hemsby
Hemsby Hole
Upper Street
Horning
Repps
93
Scratby
Woodbastwick
Bure Marshes
Broadland Conservation Centre
Thurne
B1152
Burgh St Margaret
St Margaret
California
Salhouse
Ranworth
Pilson
Clippesby
Ormesby St Michael
heath

A
B
C
D
E
F
1
2
3
4
5
6
7
8
North Anglesey Heritage Coast
The Skerries
Wylfa Head
Cemaes Bay
Porth Wen
Bull Bay
Amlwch
Cemlyn Bay
Hen Borth
Cemaes
Burwen
CARMEL HEAD
Tregele
A5025
Llanfechell
Bodewryd
Penysarn
Llanfairynghornwy
Dublin
Holyhead Bay
Church Bay
Llanrhyddlad
Carreglefn
Rhosybol
Dublin
Dún Laoghaire
(Apr-Sept)
Llanfaethlu
Capel Parc
Llyn Alaw
Porth Tywynmawr
Llanddeusant
B5111
North Stack
Breakwater Quarry
Llanfwrog
Afon Alaw
Elim
Gogarth Bay
Holyhead
(Caergybi)
Llanerchymedd
RSPB
Holyhead Mountain Hut Group
Capel Coch
South Stack
Penrhos-Feilw
Llanfachraeth
Llyn Llywenan
B5112
Holyhead Mountain Heritage Coast
Kingsland
Llanynghenedl
ANGLESEY
Presaddfed
B5109
Penrhyn Mawr
Porth Dafarch
Trefignath
A55
A5
Valley
Bodedern
B5111
Trearddur Bay
B4545
Caergeiliog
B5112
Llanfihangel yn Nhowyn
Llynfaes
Rhos
HOLY ISLAND
Four Mile Bridge
Bryngwran
Bodffordd
Cefni Reservoir
Oriel Ynys Môn
Llanfair-yn-Neubwll
Gwalchmai
Rhoscolyn
Rhoscolyn Head
RSPB
Anglesey
A4080
A5114
Cymyran Bay
Ty Newydd
Pencarnisiog
Llangristiolus
Rhosneigr
Llanfaelog
Din Dryfol
Hen Blas
Pentre Berw
A4080
Barclodiad y Gawres
B4422
Afon Cefni
Porth Trecastell
Bethel
B4419
Aberffraw
Llangadwaladr
Malltraeth
Bodowyr Burial Chamber
Anglesey Circuit
Llangaffo
A4080
B4421
Aberffraw Bay
Dwyran
Castell Bryn Gwyn
B4419
Newborough
Foel Farm Park
Aberffraw Bay Heritage Coast
Malltraeth Bay
Caernarfon
Llanddwyn Island
Caernarfon Castle
95
Highland Railway
Foryd Bay
0 1 2 3 4 miles
0 1 2 3 4 5 kilometres

Dulas Bay
Seawatch Centre
Moelfre
Llanallgo
Benllech
Red Wharf Bay
Red Wharf Bay
Pentraeth
Llanddona
Puffin Island
Penmon Priory, Cross & Dovecote
Toll
Black Point
Llangoed
Gaol & Courthouse
Beaumaris Castle
Beaumaris
Llansadwrn
Llandegfan
Menai Bridge (Porthaethwy)
Anglesey Column
Llanfair P G
Bryn Celli Ddu
Britannia Bridge
Plas Newydd
Bangor
Penrhyn
Llandygai
Tal-y-bont
Llanllechid
Rachub
Bethesda
Tregarth
Glasinfryn
Rhyd-y-groes
Pentir
Y Felinheli
Green Wood Forest Park
Seion
Bethel
Llanddeiniolen
Saron
Rhiwlas
Llanrug
Deiniolen
Segontium
Caeathro
Cwm-y-glo
Brynrefail
Llyn Padarn
Llanberis Lake Rd
Llanberis
442
Electric Mountain
Welsh Slate
Dolbadarn Castle
Llyn Peris
923 ELIDIR FAWR
946 Y GARN
917
Llyn Ogwen
1044 CARNEDD DAFYDD
1062 CARNEDD LLEWELYN
Afon Caseg
580 MOEL WINION
757 Y DROSGL
942 FOEL-FRAS
Aber Waterfall
Afon Anafon
Abergwyngregyn
Llanfairfechan
Penmaenmawr
Dwygyfylchi
Conwy
Conwy Castle
Capelulo
Henryd
SNOWDONIA NATIONAL PARK
610 TAL-Y-FAN
Rowen
Ty'n-y-Groes
Llanbedr-y-Cennin
Tal-y-Bont
Dolgarrog
Afon Dulyn
Llyn Eigiau
Afon Ddu
Llyn Cowlyd
Trefriw Woollen Mill
Trefriw
Llyn Crafnant
Geirionydd
Gwydir Castle
Gwydir Uchaf Chapel
Llanrwst
Vale of Conwy
Conwy Bay
Great Orme Heritage Coast
GREAT ORMES HEAD
Llandudno
Deganwy
Little Ormes
Penrhyn Bay
Llandrillo-yn-Rhos
Llandudno Junction
Llansanffraid Glan Conwy
Bodnant
Graig
Tal-y-Cafn
Eglwysbach
Llanddoget
Pentre-tafarn-y-fedw
A55
A5
A470
A545
A5025
A4087
A4244
A4547
B5109
B5110
B5108
B5420
B4366
B4409
B5106
B5115
B5113
110
95
96

A
B
C
D
E
F
1
2
3
4
5
6
7
8
109
Little Ormes Head
Penrhyn Bay
Rhôs-on-Sea
Colwyn Bay
(Bae Colwyn)
Abergele Roads
Kinmel Bay
Prestatyn
Rhyl
Gronant
Gwaenysgor
Llanasa
Meliden
Trelawnyd
Dyserth
Cwm
Rhuddlan
Llandudno Junction
Llandrillo-yn-Rhos
Old Colwyn
Llanddulas
Llysfaen
Rhyd-y-foel
Abergele
Pensarn
Towyn
Llanelian-yn-Rhôs
Bryn-y-Maen
Llansanffraid Glan Conwy
Conwy Castle
Dolwen
Betws-yn-Rhos
St George
Bodelwyddan
Rhuallt
St Asaph
Tremeirchion
Caerwys
Afon-w
Bodfari
Trefnant
Llannefydd
Llanfair Talhaiarn
River Elwy
Llangernyw
Llansannan
Henllan
Denbigh Friary
Denbigh
(Dinbych)
Castle
Groes
Pentre Llanrhaeadr
Llandyrnog
Llanynys
Graig
Tal-y-Cafn
Eglwysbach
Bodnant
Vale of Conwy
Vale of Clwyd
River Clwyd
Offa's Dyke
Miniature
Llanddoget
Pandy Tudur
Afon Derfyn
Afon Aled
Bylchau
Llanrwst
Pentre-tafarn-y-fedw
Gwytherin
Gwydir Uchaf Chapel
Gwydir Castle
96
97
A55
A470
A547
A548
A544
A543
A525
A541
A5151
B5115
B5113
B5381
B5383
B5382
B5384
B5428
B5429
B5435
B4501
B5118
B5119
0 1 2 3 4 miles
0 1 2 3 4 5 kilometres

Formby
Formby Point
Great Altcar
Hightown
Ince Blundell
Maghull
Aughton
Skelmersdale
Bickerstaffe
Little Crosby
Sefton
Melling
KIRKBY
Dublin
Douglas
Belfast
LIVERPOOL BAY
Blundellsands
Brighton le Sands
CROSBY
Waterloo
Seaforth
Litherland
BOOTLE
Fazakerley
Croxteth
Knowsley
WALLASEY
New Brighton
Liscard
Egremont
LIVERPOOL
Anfield
Everton
Kirkdale
Hoylake
Moreton
Hilbre Island
West Kirby
Greasby
Frankby
Upton
Claughton
BIRKENHEAD
Tranmere
Rock Ferry
Toxteth
Allerton
Woolton
Halewood
Huyton
WIRRAL
Irby
Thurstaston
Thingwall
Port Sunlight
Bebington
Barnston
Brimstage
Heswall
Bromborough
Garston
Speke
Oglet
Hale
Thornton Hough
Eastham
River Dee
River Mersey
Mostyn
Greenfield
Holywell (Treffynnon)
ELLESMERE PORT
Neston
Parkgate
Willaston
Childer Thornton
Overpool
Ince
Elton
Burton
Flint (Y Fflint)
Bagillt
Capenhurst
Little Stanney
Thornton-le-Moors
Stoak
Puddington
Shotwick
Backford
Wervin
Picton
Connah's Quay
Great Saughall
Mollington
Little Saughall
Halkyn
Northop
Northop Hall
Shotton
Queensferry
Blacon
Upton
Newton
CHESTER
Hawarden
Ewloe
Mancot
Aston
Saltney
Bretton
Broughton
Mold (Yr Wyddgrug)
Buckley (Bwcle)
Huntington
Handbridge
Christleton
Rowton
Eccleston
Saighton
Pontblyddyn
Penyffordd
Higher Kinnerton
Leeswood
Pontybodkin
Aldford
97
98
112
120

120
121
111
98
A
B
C
D
E
F
1
2
3
4
5
6
7
8
Halsall
Burscough
Parbold
Newburgh
Appley Bridge
Blackrod
Standish
Shevington
Ormskirk
Aughton Park
Aughton
Skelmersdale
Up Holland
WIGAN
Scholes
Westhoughton
Ince-in-Makerfield
Hindley
Ince Blundell
Lydiate
Maghull
Lunt
Sefton
Kennessee Green
Bickerstaffe
Orrell
Pemberton
Newtown
Rainford
Billinge
Abram
Bryn Gates
Three Sisters
Melling
KIRKBY
Crank
Moss Bank
Ashton-in-Makerfield
Golborne
Litherland
Aintree
Fazakerley
Knowsley
ST HELENS
Eccleston
Haydock
Blackbrook
Broad Oak
Earlestown
Newton-le-Willows
Croxteth
Norris Green
Croxteth Hall
Knowsley Safari Park
Peasley Cross
Collins Green
Croft
Kirkdale
Anfield
West Derby
Prescot
Burtonwood
Winwick
Risley
Everton
LIVERPOOL
Knotty Ash
Roby
Whiston
Rainhill
Rainhill Stoops
Huyton
Sankey Valley
Hulme
Orford
Woolston
Mersey Tunnels
Albert Dock
Toxteth
Childwall
National Wildflower Centre
WARRINGTON
Dingle
Allerton
Cronton
Upton
Farnworth
Thelwall
Rock Ferry
Aigburth
Woolton
Halewood
Hough Green
Appleton
WIDNES
Higher Walton
Stockton Heath
Grassendale
Garston
Speke
Speke Hall
John Lennon
Oglet
Hale
DITTON
West Bank
Catalyst
Moore
Appleton Thorn
Walton Hall
Hatton
Stretton
Port Sunlight
Bebington
Bromborough
Eastham
River Mersey
RUNCORN
Norton
Halton
Daresbury
Preston on the Hill
Preston Brook
Dutton
Higher Whitley
Lower Whitley
Antrobus
Sutton Weaver
Aston
Frodsham
ELLESMERE PORT
Overpool
Willaston
Childer Thornton
Ince
Elton
Manchester Ship Canal
Mersey View
Comberbach
Little Leigh
Marbury
Acton Bridge
Crowton
Kingsley
Helsby
Alvanley
Hapsford
Thornton-le-Moors
Stoak
Blue Planet
Little Stanney
Capenhurst
Barnton
Anderton Boat Lift
Winnington
Onston
Weaverham
Northwich
Norley
Rudheath
Leftwich
Shotwick
Backford
Picton
Dunham-on-the-Hill
Bridge Trafford
Mouldsworth
Manley
Hatchmere
Blakemere
Delamere
Hartford
Davenham
Cuddington
Great Saughall
Wervin
Mollington
Mickle Trafford
Plemstall
Long Green
Little Barrow
Ashton
Forest Park
Linmere
Moulton
Little Saughall
Upton
Newton
Blacon
Guilden Sutton
Hollowmoor Heath
Kelsall
Whitegate
CHESTER
Littleton
Christleton
Great Barrow
Stamford Bridge
Tarvin
Oscroft
Cotebrook
Little Budworth
Winsford
Hawarden
Bretton
Saltney
Handbridge
Castle
Huntington
Rowton
Duddon
Burton
Utkinton
Clotton
Eaton
Oulton Park
Waverton
Hargrave
Tarporley
Eccleston
Saighton
R Gowy
Shropshire Union Canal
Tilstone Fearnall
Alpraham
Tiverton
Church Minshull
0 1 2 3 4 miles
0 1 2 3 4 5 kilometres
M6
M56
M53
M57
M58
M62
A580
A570
A5300
A557
A56
A49
A54
A51
A55
A483
A41
A550
A494
A556
A533
A50
A57
A58
A579
A5209

114
Moor
Marsden
Meltham
Brockholes
Thurstonland
West
High Hoyland
Darton
Wilshaw
Netherthong
Lower Cumberworth
Scissett
Shepley
New Mill
Cannon Hall Open Farm
Cawthorne
Delph
Diggle
Upperthong
Holmfirth
123
Birds Edge
Upper Cumberworth
Denby Dale
Dobcross
Hepworth
Upper Denby
Silkstone
Holmbridge
Holme
Uppermill
Ingbirchworth
Hoyland Swaine
Saddleworth Moor
Grasscroft
Greenfield
582 BLACK HILL
525
Holme Moss
Crow Edge
Thurlstone
Silkstone Common
Mossley
Winscar Reservoir
Millhouse Green
Townhead
Penistone
Oxspring
Thurgoland
Pennine Way
537 FEATHERBED MOSS
Langsett
450 Woodhead
Crowden
Midhopestones
Stalybridge
PEAK DISTRICT
Garden Village
Deepcar
Stocksbridge
Tintwistle
Howden Moors
Bolsterstone
Hollingworth
Hadfield
Mottram in Longdendale
628 BLEAKLOW HILL
546 MARGERY HILL
Ewden Village
Wharncliffe Side
M67
Hattersley
Glossop
Snake Pass 512
Howden Reservoir
Broadbottom
Werneth Low
R Alport
Bradfield
Oughtibridge
Charlesworth
544 FEATHERBED TOP
NATIONAL PARK
Worrall
Chisworth
ROAD CLOSED SAT/SUN/ BH MON
Derwent Reservoir
Low Bradfield
Mill Brow
HIGH PEAK
Ughill
Stacey Bank
Rowarth
Brookhouses
THE PEAK 631
Ladybower Reservoir
Thornsett
Hayfield
636 KINDER SCOUT
Stannington
Birch Vale
Pennine Way
Edale
Wyming Brook
New Mills
569 BROWN KNOLL
476 LOSE HILL
464 WIN HILL
457 HIGH NEB
Fulwood
Redmires Reservoir
Blue John Cavern
Mam Tor
Treak Cliff Cavern
Hope
Aston
Thornhill
Bamford
113
Furness Vale
Chinley
Castleton
Peveril Castle
Whaley Bridge
Chestnut Centre
Speedwell Cavern
Peak Cavern
Hathersage
Brick Houses
Hathersage Booths
Dore
Tunstead Milton
Sparrowpit
Bradwell
Chapel-en-le-Frith
Abney
Blacka Moor
Totley
Taxal
Cockyard
Kettleshulme
Dove Holes
Peak Forest
Eyam Moor
Longshaw Estate
Dunge Valley
Fernilee
Little Hucklow
Great Hucklow
Nether Padley
Goyt Valley
Combs
Grindlow
Grindleford
501 HOB TOR
Wheston
Foolow
Eyam
Froggatt
Tideswell
Litton
Wardlow
Stoney Middleton
Calver
Curbar
559
Tunstead
Fairfield
Buxton
Wormhill
Miller's Dale
Cressbrook
Rowland
Wye Valley
Hassop
515
Poole's Cavern
Blackwell
Great Longstone
Little Longstone
Baslow
Forest Chapel
Solomon's Temple
551 AXE EDGE
Pilsley
Chatsworth
Wadshelf
Taddington
Chelmorton
Ashford in the Water
Edensor
506
Hob Hurst's House
Flagg
Sheldon
Magpie Mine
Bakewell
Beeley
Earl Sterndale
Flash
R Dove
Monyash
Over Haddon
Allgreave
Rowsley
Hollinsclough
Lathkill Dale
Haddon Hall
Crowdecote
Longnor
Stanton in Peak
Alport
Youlgreave
Arbor Low Stone Circle
Pilsbury
Nine Ladies
Darley Dale
Two Dales
Middleton
505 THE ROACHES
R Derwent
Peak Railway
Stanton Lees
PEAK DISTRICT NATIONAL PARK
Hartington
Birchover
Churchtown
Darley Bridge
Wensley
Oker Side
Brund
100
Elton
Winster
Heathcote
Market House
Hartington
Hulme End
Biggin
Heights of Abraham
0 1 2 3 4 miles
0 1 2 3 4 5 kilometres

Barnsley
Cudworth
South Kirkby
Grimethorpe
Hooton Pagnell
Thurnscoe
Great Houghton
Brodsworth
Hickleton
Doncaster
Armthorpe
Edenthorpe
Dunsville
Arksey
Bentley
Scawsby
Marr
Goldthorpe
Barnburgh
High Melton
Sprotbrough
Mexborough
Wombwell
Darfield
Hoyland Nether
Wath upon Dearne
Swinton
Conisbrough
Denaby
Cadeby
Warmsworth
Bessacarr
Cantley
Branton
Auckley
Finningley
Rossington
New Rossington
Loversall
Wadworth
Edlington
Old Edlington
Tankersley
Wentworth
Rawmarsh
Thrybergh
Hooton Roberts
Ravenfield
Clifton
Braithwell
Stainton
Tickhill
Austerfield
Bawtry
Rotherham
Bramley
Maltby
Wickersley
Thurcroft
Hooton Levitt
Stone
Styrrup
Harworth
Bircotes
Scaftworth
Scrooby
Mattersey
Oldcotes
Blyth
Firbeck
Langold
Letwell
Dinnington
Aughton
Aston
Treeton
Ulley
Catcliffe
Handsworth
Woodhouse
Beighton
Killamarsh
Mosborough
Eckington
Todwick
Kiveton Park
South Anston
North Anston
Woodsetts
Gildingwells
North Carlton
Carlton in Lindrick
Hodsock
Torworth
Sutton cum Lound
Shireoaks
Worksop
Scofton
Ranby
Harthill
Thorpe Salvin
Woodall
Dronfield
Apperknowle
Renishaw
Spinkhill
Barlborough
Whitwell
Hodthorpe
Clowne
Creswell
Staveley
Brimington
Chesterfield
Bolsover
Whaley Thorns
Cuckney
Norton
Meden Vale
Budby
Market Warsop
Edwinstowe
Ollerton
Perlethorpe
Bothamsall
Shirebrook
Langwith
Glapwell
Clipstone
Wellow
Rufford
North Wingfield
Clay Cross
Pilsley
Tibshelf
Teversal
Mansfield
Sutton in Ashfield
Bilsthorpe
Higham
Stonebroom
Newton
124
101
116

116
125
115
102
Scunthorpe
Broughton
Burringham
Althorpe
Sandtoft
Hatfield Woodhouse
Dunsville
Westgate
Belton
Beltoft
East Butterwick
West Butterwick
Bottesford
Yaddlethorpe
Ashby
Brumby
Messingham
Scawby
Sturton
Manton
Epworth
Wroot
Carrhouse
Old Cantley
Branton
Auckley
Blaxton
Finningley
Rossington
Westwoodside
Haxey
Low Burnham
Owston Ferry
East Lound
Susworth
Scotterthorpe
Scotter
Scotton
Kirton in Lindsey
Gainsthorpe Medieval Village
Graiseland
Wildsworth
East Ferry
Laughton
Northorpe
Gunthorpe
West Stockwith
Misterton
East Stockwith
Blyton
Grayingham
Blyborough
Misson
Austerfield
Bawtry
Walkerith
Pilham
Aisby
Willoughton
Walkeringham
Gringley on the Hill
Morton
Corringham
Gainsborough
Hemswell
Hemswell Cliff
Harwell
Everton
Scaftworth
Scrooby
Drakeholes
Wiseton
Beckingham
Springthorpe
Harpswell
Mattersey
Mattersey Abbey
Clayworth
Saundby
Heapham
Glentworth
Ranskill
Torworth
Lound
Bole
Lea
Upton
Fillingham
Sutton cum Lound
Hayton
North Wheatley
Kexby
Knaith
Barnby Moor
Clarborough
Sturton le Steeple
Willingham by Stow
Ingham
Coates
Retford
North Leverton with Habblesthorpe
Fenton
Gate Burton
Welham
Littleborough
Marton
Stow
Cammeringham
Babworth
Ranby
Scofton
Grove
South Leverton
Cottam
Brampton
Sturton by Stow
Scampton
Ordsall
Treswell
Sundown Adventureland
Torksey
Bransby
Eaton
Nether Headon
Rampton
Stokeham
Laneham
Fenton
North Carlton
South Carlton
Headon
Gamston
Upton
East Drayton
Laughterton
Saxilby
Fossdyke Navigation
Elkesley
Rockley
Askham
Kettlethorpe
Burton
Clumber Park
West Drayton
Markham Moor
Dunham
Toll
Bothamsall
Milton
Ragnall
Darlton
North Clifton
Newton on Trent
Burton Waters
Sibthorpe
East Markham
Thorney
Skellingthorpe
Bevercotes
West Markham
Fledborough
Walesby
Tuxford
High Marnham
South Clifton
Harby
Perlethorpe
Wigsley
Lincoln
Skegby
Spalford
Doddington
Birchwood
Hartsholme
Swanpool Garden Suburb
Ollerton
Kirton
Boughton
Egmanton
Normanton on Trent
Low Marnham
New Ollerton
Laxton
Weston
Grassthorpe
Whisby
Eagle
Swallow Beck
Road Transport
Wellow
Sutton on Trent
North Scarle
Moorhouse
Girton
Ompton
Ossington
Besthorpe
Thorpe on the Hill
North Hykeham
Rufford
Rufford Abbey
Kneesall
Norwell Woodhouse
Carlton-on-Trent
South Scarle
South Hykeham
Eakring
Kersall
Swinderby
Haddington
Cromwell
Harmston
Aubourn
Bilsthorpe
Thurlby
Dolls
Bassingham
Bathley
Holme
Boothby
Coleby
Robin Hood Doncaster Sheffield
R Idle
R Trent
R Till
R Eau
R Ryton
Chesterfield Canal
M180
M181
M18
A18
A161
A159
A15
A631
A614
A638
A634
A620
A156
A1500
A1
A57
A6075
A1133
A46
B1396
B1403
B1205
B1206
B1398
B1400
B1241
B1190
B1164
B6387
B6420
B6079
B6045
B6463
B1450
B1378
B1003
A1434
0 1 2 3 4 miles
0 1 2 3 4 5 kilometres
A B C D E F
1 2 3 4 5 6 7 8

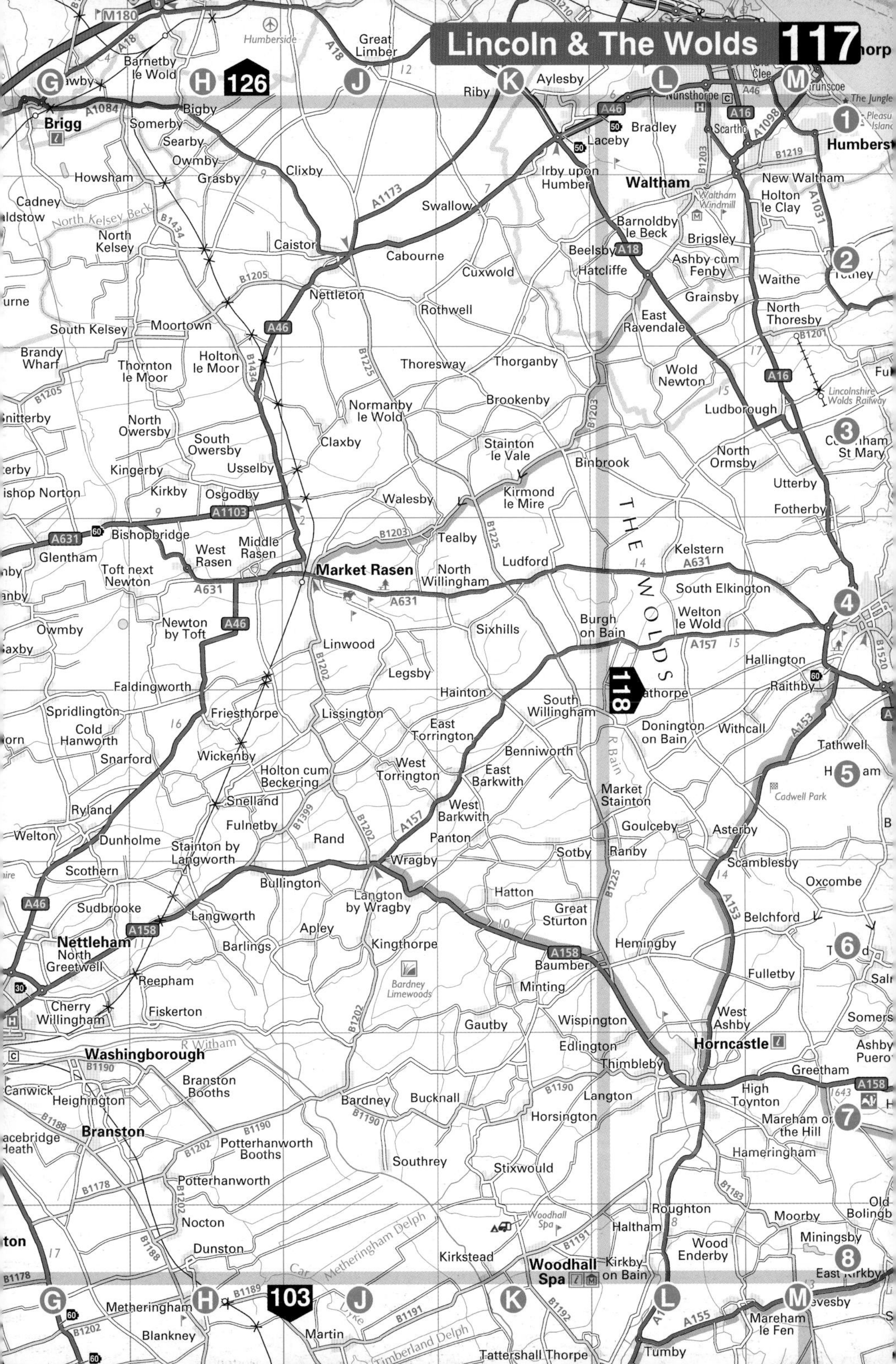
M180
Humberside
Great
Limber
A18
Barnetby
le Wold
126
Aylesby
Riby
Bigby
Brigg
A1084
Somerby
Searby
Owmby
Grasby
Howsham
Clixby
Cadney
North Kelsey Beck
North
Kelsey
B1434
Caistor
A1173
Swallow
Cabourne
Cuxwold
Nettleton
B1205
Rothwell
South Kelsey
Moortown
A46
Brandy
Wharf
Thornton
le Moor
Holton
le Moor
Thoresway
Thorganby
Normanby
le Wold
Brookenby
North
Owersby
South
Owersby
Claxby
Stainton
le Vale
Kingerby
Usselby
Binbrook
Kirkby
Osgodby
Kirmond
le Mire
Walesby
A1103
A631
Bishopbridge
Glentham
West
Rasen
Middle
Rasen
B1203
Tealby
B1225
Market Rasen
North
Willingham
Ludford
Toft next
Newton
Newton
by Toft
Owmby
Linwood
Sixhills
Legsby
Faldingworth
Spridlington
Cold
Hanworth
Friesthorpe
Lissington
Hainton
East
Torrington
Snarford
Wickenby
Holton cum
Beckering
West
Torrington
East
Barkwith
Snelland
B1399
Rand
West
Barkwith
Ryland
Welton
Dunholme
Fulnetby
Panton
Stainton by
Langworth
Wragby
A157
B1202
Scothern
Bullington
Langton
by Wragby
Sudbrooke
Langworth
A158
Apley
Nettleham
North
Greetwell
Barlings
Kingthorpe
Reepham
Bardney
Limewoods
Cherry
Willingham
Fiskerton
Gautby
R Witham
Washingborough
B1190
Branston
Booths
Canwick
Heighington
Bardney
Bucknall
B1188
Branston
Potterhanworth
Booths
Southrey
Stixwould
Potterhanworth
B1178
Nocton
Metheringham Delph
Woodhall
Spa
Dunston
Kirkstead
Woodhall
Spa
B1191
Metheringham
B1189
103
Blankney
Martin
B1191
Timberland Delph
Tattershall Thorpe
Laceby
Bradley
Irby upon
Humber
Waltham
Waltham
Windmill
Barnoldby
le Beck
Brigsley
Beelsby
A18
Hatcliffe
Ashby cum
Fenby
Grainsby
East
Ravendale
Wold
Newton
Ludborough
North
Ormsby
THE WOLDS
Kelstern
South Elkington
Welton
le Wold
Burgh
on Bain
A157
Hallington
118
Raithby
South
Willingham
Donington
on Bain
Withcall
Benniworth
R Bain
Market
Stainton
Goulceby
Asterby
Sotby
Ranby
Scamblesby
Hatton
Great
Sturton
A153
Belchford
Oxcombe
Hemingby
Baumber
Fulletby
Minting
Wispington
West
Ashby
Edlington
Horncastle
Thimbleby
Greetham
High
Toynton
Langton
Horsington
Mareham on
the Hill
Hameringham
B1183
Roughton
Moorby
Haltham
Wood
Enderby
Miningsby
Kirkby
on Bain
East Kirkby
A155
Mareham
le Fen
Tumby
Nunsthorpe
Scartho
A1098
A16
B1203
B1219
New Waltham
Holton
le Clay
A1031
Waithe
North
Thoresby
B1201
Lincolnshire
Wolds Railway
Utterby
Fotherby
A631
Tathwell
Cadwell Park
A1
Humberston
The Jungle
Clee

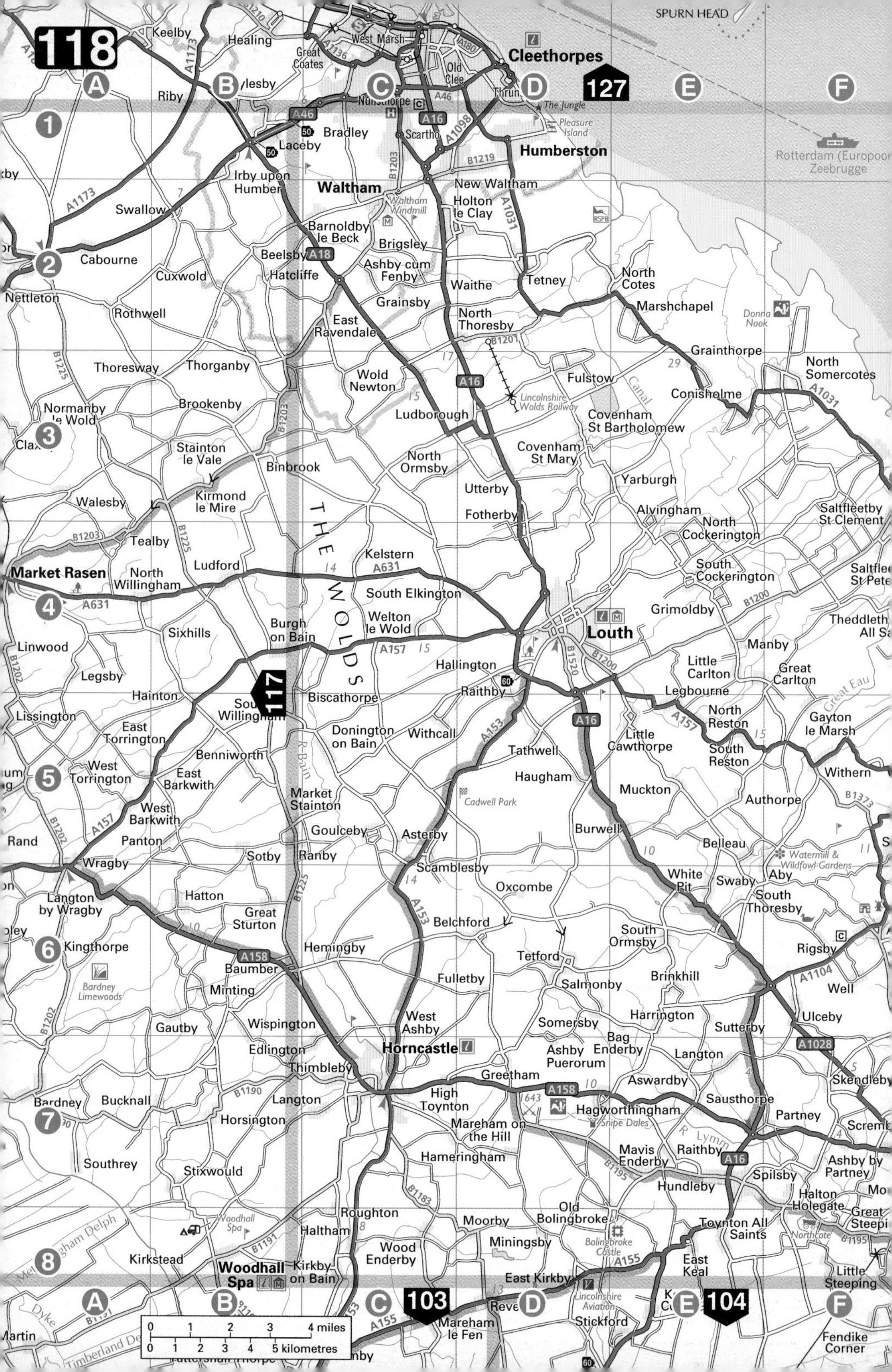
SPURN HEAD
Cleethorpes
127
Keelby
Healing
Great Coates
West Marsh
Old Clee
Riby
Aylesby
Nunsthorpe
Thrunscoe
The Jungle
Pleasure Island
Bradley
Laceby
Scartho
Humberston
Rotterdam (Europoort)
Zeebrugge
Irby upon Humber
Waltham
New Waltham
Swallow
Waltham Windmill
Holton le Clay
Barnoldby le Beck
Brigsley
Cabourne
Beelsby
Cuxwold
Hatcliffe
Ashby cum Fenby
Waithe
Tetney
North Cotes
Nettleton
Rothwell
Grainsby
North Thoresby
Marshchapel
East Ravendale
Donna Nook
Grainthorpe
Thoresway
Thorganby
Wold Newton
Fulstow
Canal
North Somercotes
Normanby le Wold
Brookenby
Ludborough
Lincolnshire Wolds Railway
Conisholme
Covenham St Bartholomew
Stainton le Vale
Covenham St Mary
Binbrook
North Ormsby
Yarburgh
Kirmond le Mire
Utterby
Walesby
Alvingham
Fotherby
Saltfleetby St Clement
North Cockerington
THE WOLDS
Tealby
Kelstern
South Cockerington
Market Rasen
North Willingham
Ludford
South Elkington
Grimoldby
Welton le Wold
Louth
Linwood
Sixhills
Burgh on Bain
Manby
Hallington
Little Carlton
Great Carlton
Legsby
Hainton
Legbourne
South Willingham
117
Biscathorpe
Raithby
North Reston
Gayton le Marsh
Lissington
East Torrington
Donington on Bain
Withcall
Little Cawthorpe
South Reston
Benniworth
Tathwell
Withern
West Torrington
East Barkwith
Haugham
Muckton
Market Stainton
R Bain
Cadwell Park
Authorpe
West Barkwith
Goulceby
Burwell
Rand
Panton
Asterby
Belleau
Wragby
Sotby
Ranby
Watermill & Wildfowl Gardens
Scamblesby
White Pit
Swaby
Aby
Langton by Wragby
Hatton
Oxcombe
South Thoresby
Great Sturton
Belchford
South Ormsby
Kingthorpe
Hemingby
Tetford
Rigsby
Baumber
Bardney Limewoods
Fulletby
Salmonby
Brinkhill
Well
Minting
Harrington
West Ashby
Gautby
Wispington
Somersby
Sutterby
Ulceby
Bag Enderby
Edlington
Horncastle
Ashby Puerorum
Langton
Thimbleby
Greetham
Aswardby
Skendleby
High Toynton
Sausthorpe
Bardney
Bucknall
Langton
Hagworthingham
Partney
Horsington
Mareham on the Hill
Snipe Dales
Scremby
R Lymn
Mavis Enderby
Raithby
Southrey
Hameringham
Ashby by Partney
Stixwould
Spilsby
Hundleby
Halton Holegate
Great Steeping
Roughton
Woodhall Spa
Old Bolingbroke
Toynton All Saints
Northcote
Moorby
Haltham
Miningsby
Bolingbroke Castle
East Keal
Kirkstead
Wood Enderby
Little Steeping
Kirkby on Bain
East Kirkby
Lincolnshire Aviation
Woodhall Spa
103
104
Revesby
Stickford
Mareham le Fen
Martin
Dyke
Timberland
Fendike Corner
0 1 2 3 4 miles
0 1 2 3 4 5 kilometres

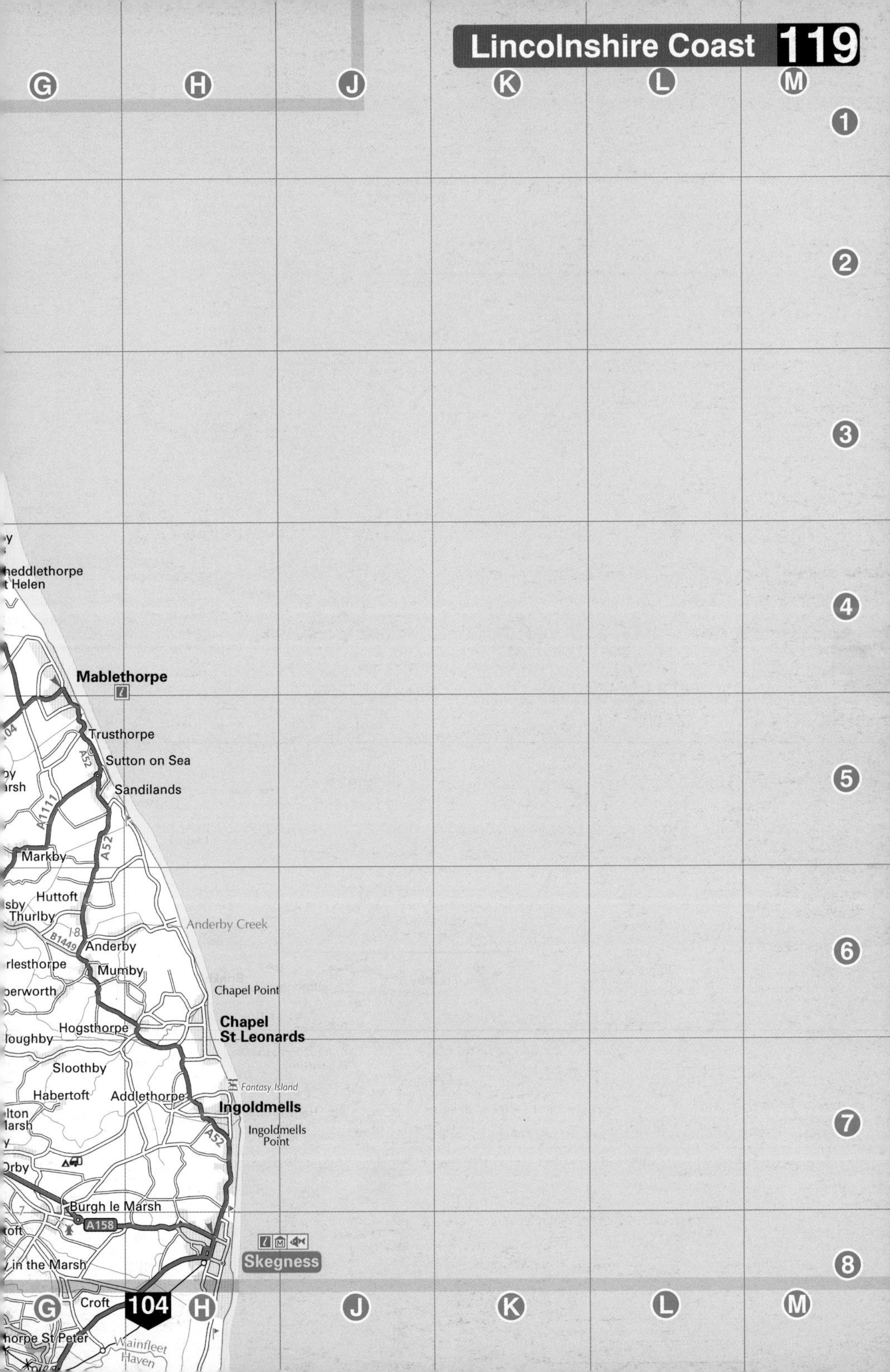
G
H
J
K
L
M
1
2
3
4
5
6
7
8
heddlethorpe
t Helen
Mablethorpe
Trusthorpe
Sutton on Sea
Sandilands
A52
A1111
Markby
Huttoft
Thurlby
B1449
Anderby
Anderby Creek
rlesthorpe
Mumby
Chapel Point
Chapel
St Leonards
Hogsthorpe
loughby
Sloothby
Fantasy Island
Habertoft
Addlethorpe
Ingoldmells
Ingoldmells Point
Orby
Burgh le Marsh
A158
Skegness
in the Marsh
Croft
104
horpe St Peter
Wainfleet Haven

129
111
Sunderland
Glasson
Cockersand
Cockerham
Knott End-on-Sea
Pilling
Preesall
COCKERHAM
Winmarleigh
Fleetwood
Rossall Point
River Wyre
Stalmine
Staynall
Eagland Hill
Cleveleys
Thornton
Hambleton
Out Rawcliffe
Moss Edge
Great Eccleston
Little Singleton
Copp
Poulton-le-Fylde
Singleton
Warbreck
North Shore
Elswick
Thistleton
BLACKPOOL
Esprick
Wharles
Staining
Model Village
Great Marton
Weeton
M55
South Shore
Great Plumpton
Wesham
Treales
Kirkham
Westby
Blackpool
Wrea Green
Newton with Scales
Kellamergh
Freckleton
St Anne's
Royal Lytham & St Annes
Ansdell
Warton
Fairhaven
Lytham St Anne's
River Ribble
Lytham
RSPB Discovery Centre
Hesketh Bank
Becconsall
Banks
Tarleton
SOUTHPORT
New Pleasureland
Mere Brow
Leisure Lakes
Holmeswood
Rufford
Windmill Animal Farm
Birkdale
The Royal Birkdale
Wildfowl & Wetlands Trust
Scarisbrick
Shirdley Hill
Burscough Bridge
Bescar
Ainsdale
Heaton's Bridge
Ainsdale Sand-Dunes
Halsall
Leeds & Liverpool Canal
Burscough
Barton
Haskayne
Ormskirk
Cabin Hill
Freshfield
Formby
Little Altcar
Great Altcar
Aughton Park
Aughton
Skelmersdale
Hightown
0 1 2 3 4 miles
0 1 2 3 4 5 kilometres

Forest of Bowland
130
Abbeystead
Dolphinholme
WHINS BROW
Slaidburn
Newton-in-Bowland
HAWTHORNTHWAITE FELL
Lancaster (Forton)
Scorton
Calder Fell
Dunsop Bridge
TOTRIDGE FELL
BRADFORD FELL
Holden
Bolton by Bowland
Oakenclough
Calder Vale
FAIRSNAPE FELL
PARLICK
Whitewell
Sawley
Grindleton
Rimington
West Bradford
Downham
Bonds
Waddington
Chatburn
Horrocksford
Worston
Bashall Eaves
Chipping
Beacon Fell
Claughton
Clitheroe
PENDLE HILL
White Chapel
Hesketh Lane
Inglewhite
Longridge Fell
Pendleton
Barley
Bilsborrow
Knowle Green
Hurst Green
Cromwell's Bridge
Great Mitton
Barrow
Longridge
Barton
Goosnargh
Wiswell
Sabden
Fence
Newsham
Whalley
Higham
Old Langho
Broughton
Chingle Hall
Ribchester
Little Town
Copster Green
Billington
Read
Simonstone
Padiham
Gawthorpe Hall
Woodplumpton
Grimsargh
Langho
Higher Bartle
Balderstone
Great Harwood
Clayton-le-Moors
Hapton
Habergham
Cadley
Sharoe Green
Fulwood
Brockholes
Samlesbury Hall
Osbaldeston
Ribbleton
Mellor Brook
Wilpshire
Mellor
Rishton
PRESTON
BLACKBURN
Witton
Church
Dill Hall
Accrington
Higher Walton
Walton-le-Dale
Oswaldtwistle
Higher Penwortham
Hoghton
Pleasington
Hoghton Tower
Riley Green
Baxenden
Goodshaw
Hutton
Bamber Bridge
Feniscowles
Belthorn
Crawshawbooth
New Longton
Farington
Brindle
Reeds Holme
Haslingden
Tockholes
Higher Wheelton
Abbey Village
Blackburn with Darwen
Waterside
Leyland
Cuerden Valley
Sunnyhurst
Darwen
Hoddlesden
Helmshore
East Lancashire Railway
Clayton-le-Woods
Whittle-le-Woods
Withnell
Brinscall
Buckshaw Village
Wheelton
Textiles Museum
Euxton
Chatterton
Stubbins
Chorley
Eccleston
Cowling
Ramsbottom
Edgworth
Shuttleworth
Charnock Richard
Camelot
Turton Tower
Turton Bottoms
Belmont
WINTER HILL
Egerton
Chapeltown
Nuttall
Rivington
Summerseat
Jumbles
Greenmount
Coppull
Grimeford Village
Mossy Lea
Adlington
Horwich
Tottington
Chesham
Eagley
Smithills Hall
Astley Bridge
BURY
Parbold
Bolton West
Blackrod
Ainsworth
Appley Bridge
Halliwell
Breightmet
Standish
Shevington
Aspull
BOLTON
Marylebone
Deane
Moses Gate
Daubhill
Radcliffe
Little Lever
Holland
Scholes
Whitefield
Newtown
Ince-in-Makerfield
Hindley
Kearsley
112
113
122
M6
M65
M61
M60
A59
A6
A666
A671
A680
A56
A677
A675
A674
A49
A5209
A58
A673
A676
B6243
B6478
B5269

122
130
131
121
113
A
B
C
D
E
F
1
2
3
4
5
6
7
8
Slaidburn
Halton West
Coniston Cold
Gargrave
Thorlby
Embsay
Eastby
Halton East
Draug
Skipton
Paythorne
East Marton
West Marton
Broughton
Horton
Elslack
Carleton
Low Bradley
Holden
Bolton by Bowland
Gisburn
Bracewell
Thornton-in-Craven
Yorkshire Dales Lead Mining
Cononley
Lothersdale
Silsden
Kildwick
Glusburn
Sutton-in-Craven
Eastburn
Steeton
396
BRADFORD FELL
Sawley
Abbey
Rimington
Newby
Barnoldswick
Bancroft Mill
Salterforth
Earby
Kelbrook
Cowling
Ickornshaw
Grindleton
West Bradford
Downham
Chatburn
Horrocksford
Worston
Clitheroe
382
Foulridge
Lund's Tower
Wainman's Pinnacle
KEIGHLEY
Laycock
557
PENDLE HILL
Blacko
Colne
Pendleton
Barley
Barrowford
Wycoller
443
Keighley Moor
Oakworth
Barrow
Great Mitton
315
Nelson
Trawden
Haworth
Stanbury
Wiswell
Sabden
Fence
Higham
Whalley
Brierfield
The Forest of Trawden
Penistone Hill
518
BOULSWORTH HILL
459
Billington
Langho
Read
Simonstone
R Calder
Padiham
Gawthorpe Hall
Harle Syke
BURNLEY
Oxenhope
Wadsworth Moor
Habergham
Clayton-le-Moors
Hapton
Rose Hill
Worsthorne
Hurstwood
Mereclough
Towneley Hall
447
Rishton
Church
Accrington
Oswaldtwistle
Baxenden
Heptonstall Moor
Pecket Well
Walk Mill
Holme Chapel
Colden
Slack
Blackshaw Head
Heptonstall
Mytholm
Charlestown
Hebden Bridge
Chisley
Wainstalls
Booth
Midgley
Mytholmroyd
Luddenden
Goodshaw
Chapel
Cornholme
Belthorn
Forest of Rossendale
Crawshawbooth
Portsmouth
Weir
Lydgate
Todmorden
Pennine Way
Stoodley Pike
Luddenden Foot
Reeds Holme
Constable Lee
Haslingden
Waterside
Rawtenstall
Bacup
Clough Foot
Steep Lane
Sowerby
Hoddlesden
Helmshore
East Lancashire Railway
Walsden
Textiles Museum
Bottoms
Lumb
Mill Bank
Soyland Town
Ripponden
Chatterton
Stubbins
Edenfield
Whitworth
Rishworth
Ramsbottom
Edgworth
Shuttleworth
Wardle
Rishworth Moor
Turton Tower
Turton Bottoms
Chapeltown
Jumbles
Littleborough
Deanhead
Saddleworth Moor
Hollingworth Lake
381
Nuttall
Summerseat
Greenmount
463
Standedge Experience
Moss Moor
Milnrow
ROCHDALE
Tottington
Eagley
Astley Bridge
Chesham
BURY
Close Moor
Ainsworth
Heywood
Castleton
Denshaw
Breightmet
BOLTON
Shaw
Birch
Tandle Hill
Royton
Delph
Diggle
Moses Gate
Tower
Little Lever
Radcliffe
Whitefield
Chadderton
Dobcross
Farnworth
Uppermill
MIDDLETON
Greenfield
Grasscroft
Lees
Saddleworth Moor
0 1 2 3 4 miles
0 1 2 3 4 5 kilometres

Blubberhouses
Kettlesing
Low Harrogate
Harrogate
Starbeck
Goldsborough
A59
Fewston Reservoir
Fewston
Swinsty Res
132
Pannal Ash
Rossett Green
Little Ribston
Walshford
Timble
Beamsley
A61
Follifoot
A661
North Deighton
A658
Langbar
Pannal
Spofforth
Kirk Deighton
Nesfield
North Rigton
Kirkby Overblow
Middleton
Denton
Askwith
Clifton
Sicklinghall
Farnley
Huby
Wetherby
Ilkley
Ben Rhydding
A65
Weston
Leathley
Dunkeswick
Linton
Burley in Wharfedale
A660
Newall
A658
Weeton
Netherby
Chapel Hill
Boston Spa
Otley
Pool
Castley
Harewood
A659
Collingham
Burley Wood Head
Chevin Forest Park
Arthington
Weardley
East Keswick
Menston
East Carlton
Old Bramhope
Bramhope
Bardsey
East Rigton
East Riddlesden Hall
East Morton
Guiseley
Eccup Reservoir
Wike
A58
A650
Hawksworth
Park Gate
Leeds Bradford
Scarcroft
Bramham Park
Cross Flatts
Yeadon
Alwoodley
Bingley
Baildon
Rawdon
Moortown
Shadwell
Sand Hills
Thorner
Baildon Green
Charlestown
Saltaire
A6120
Moor Allerton
A64
Harden
Thackley
Horsforth
Chapel Allerton
Roundhay
Aberford
Cottingley
Moorhead
Idle
Weetwood
Meanwood
Barwick in Elmet
Wilsden
Shipley
Wrose
Greengates
Kirkstall
Gledhow
Harehills
Scholes
Seacroft
Frizinghall
Eccleshill
Headingley
Heaton
Bramley
Manningham
Undercliffe
Woodhouse
LEEDS
Manston
Denholme
Cross Gates
Thornton
Allerton
Thornbury
Fartown
Sheepscar
Halton
Laisterdyke
Armley
Osmondthorpe
Whitkirk
Garforth
BRADFORD
Pudsey
Farnley
Wortley
Colton
Great Horton
Clayton
Little Horton
Bowling
West Bowling
Tong
Beeston
Cross Green
Temple Newsam
Swillington
Kippax
Mountain
Queensbury
Hunslet
Wibsey
Gildersome
Churwell
M621
Great Preston
Ambler Thorn
Shibden Head
Buttershaw
Odsal
Drighlington
White Rose
Middleton Railway
Middleton
Rothwell
124
Oakenshaw
Birkenshaw
Bower's Row
Northowram
Wyke
Hunsworth
M606
Morley
Carlton
Oakwell Hall
Ouzlewell Green
Methley Junction
A58
Shibden Hall
M62
Ardsley East
Lofthouse
Hipperholme
Birstall
Lofthouse Gate
Cleckheaton
Heckmondwike
Woodkirk
Carr Gate
Wakefield Europort
Hartshead Moor
Liversedge
Norristhorpe
Chidswell
Southowram
Clifton
Batley
Hanging Heaton
Kirkhamgate
Normanton
Roberttown
Dewsbury
Brighouse
Rastrick
Hartshead
WAKEFIELD
Woodhouse
Alverthorpe
Earlsheaton
A638
Flanshaw
Kirkthorpe
Warmfield
Featherstone
Elland
Northorpe
Ravensthorpe
Savile Town
A644
Mirfield
Ossett
Lupset
Heath
New Sharlston
Broad Carr
Netheroyd Hill
Sheepridge
Belle Vue
Sharlston
Nostell Priory
Clough Head
Fartown
Upper Heaton
Upper Hopton
Thornhill
Horbury
Sandal Magna
Crofton
Lindley
HUDDERSFIELD
Kirkheaton
Whitley Lower
Middlestown
Calder Grove
Edgerton
Hill Side
Scapegoat Hill
National Coal Mining Museum
Walton
New Crofton
Moldgreen
Houses Hill
Grange Moor
Overton
Netherton
Crigglestone
Golcar
Greenside
Flockton Green
Hill Top
Lower Houses
Almondbury
Newmillerdam
Linthwaite
Lepton
Flockton
Midgley
Ryhill
Kinsley
Newsome
West Bretton
Netherton
Blackmoorfoot
Highburton
Emley
Woolley Edge
Notton
Hemsworth
Woolley
Yorkshire Sculpture Park
Helme
Honley
Farnley Tyas
Kirkburton
Kirklees Light Railway
Royston
Staincross
Shafton
Shelley
Skelmanthorpe
Clayton West
Thurstonland
Brockholes
High Hoyland
Darton
Carlton
Meltham
A637
Scissett
Wilshaw
Lower Cumberworth
Netherthong
New Mill
Shepley
Mapplewell
New Lodge
Cannon Hall Open Farm
Upperthong
Denby Dale
Cawthorne
Cudworth
Upper Cumberworth
Holmfirth
Scholes
Birds Edge
BARNSLEY
Hepworth
114
Upper Denby
Silkstone
Higham
Little Houghton
A628
Dodworth
Ingbirchworth
Hoyland Swaine
Crow Edge
Darfield
Thurlstone
Silkstone Common
Worsbrough
G
H
J
K
L
M
1
2
3
4
5
6
7
8

124
132
133
123
115
Goldsborough
Kirk Hammerton
Cattal
Overton
Nether Poppleton
Upper Poppleton
Hessay
Tockwith
Cowthorpe
Follifoot
North Deighton
Kirk Deighton
Spofforth
Pannal
Kirkby Overblow
Sicklinghall
Bickerton
Long Marston
Rufforth
Hutton Wandesley
Knapton
Acomb
Holgate
South Bank
Nunthorpe
Dringhouses
Fulford
Osbaldwick
YORK
Wetherby
Bilton
Askham Bryan
Angram
Askham Richard
Healaugh
Walton
Dunkeswick
Netherby
Chapel Hill
Linton
Boston Spa
Thorp Arch
R Wharfe
Wighill
Bilbrough
Catterton
Bishopthorpe
Copmanthorpe
Harewood
Collingham
Newton Kyme
Acaster Malbis
Naburn
East Keswick
Bardsey
East Rigton
Clifford
Tadcaster
Colton
Oxton
Appleton Roebuck
Escrick
Eccup Reservoir
Wike
Bramham
Bramham Park
Bolton Percy
Acaster Selby
Scarcroft
Stutton
Kirkby Wharfe
Thorner
Towton
Ulleskelf
Ryther
Stillingfleet
Shadwell
Sand Hills
Moor Allerton
Chapel Allerton
Roundhay
Aberford
R Cock
Barwick in Elmet
Cawood
Kelfield
Riccall
Gledhow
Harehills
Scholes
Seacroft
Saxton
Church Fenton
Barkston Ash
Wistow
R Ouse
LEEDS
Manston
Cross Gates
Sheepscar
Lotherton Hall
Little Fenton
Sherburn in Elmet
Barlby
Halton
Whitkirk
Colton
Osmondthorpe
Garforth
Micklefield
Cross Green
Hunslet
Temple Newsam
Swillington
Kippax
Steeton Hall Gatehouse
South Milford
Thorpe Willoughby
Hambleton
Brayton
Middleton Railway
Middleton
Rothwell
Great Preston
Ledsham
Lumby
Monk Fryston
Ledston
Fairburn
Hillam
Gateforth
Bower's Row
Allerton Bywater
Burton Salmon
Birkin
Selby Canal
Burn
Carlton
Oulzewell Green
Mickletown
Chapel Haddlesey
Brotherton
West Haddlesey
Camblesforth
Lofthouse
Lofthouse Gate
Castleford
Beal
Temple Hirst
Carr Gate
Sutton
Kellington
Hirst Courtney
WAKEFIELD EUROPORT
Xscape
Knottingley
Hensall
Normanton
Ferrybridge
Eggborough
Snaith
Ackton
Featherstone
Pontefract
Gowdall
Alverthorpe
Flanshaw
WAKEFIELD
Woodhouse
Kirkthorpe
Warmfield
Heath
New Sharlston
Whitley
Great Heck
Darrington
Belle Vue
Sharlston
Nostell Priory
High Ackworth
East Hardwick
Womersley
Polling
Horbury
Sandal Magna
Crofton
Low Ackworth
Balne
Calder Grove
Hessle
Little Smeaton
Walden Stubbs
R Went
New Crofton
Wentbridge
Kirk Smeaton
Crigglestone
Walton
Wragby
Ackworth Moor Top
Sykehouse
Fenwick
Norton
Hill Top
Newmillerdam
Fitzwilliam
Thorpe Audlin
Ryhill
Kinsley
Badsworth
Moss
Woolley Edge
Havercroft
Upton
Askern
Notton
South Hiendley
Hemsworth
Campsall
Woolley
North Elmsall
Kirk Bramwith
Staincross
Royston
Shafton
Brierley
South Elmsall
Skelbrooke
Haywood
Darton
Carlton
Moorthorpe
Burghwallis
Owston
South Bramwith
Hampole
Skellow
Thorpe in Balne
Barnby Dun
Mapplewell
New Lodge
Grimethorpe
South Kirkby
Carcroft
Adwick Le Street
Cudworth
Clayton
Hooton Pagnell
Toll Bar
Kirk Sandall
Woodlands
BARNSLEY
Pickburn
Little Houghton
Great Houghton
Thurnscoe
Brodsworth
Arksey
Edenth
Dodworth
Hickleton
Scawthorpe
Bentley
Armthorpe
Billingley
Marr
Scawsby
Wheatley Hills
DONCASTER
Worsbrough
Goldthorpe
0 1 2 3 4 miles
0 1 2 3 4 5 kilometres

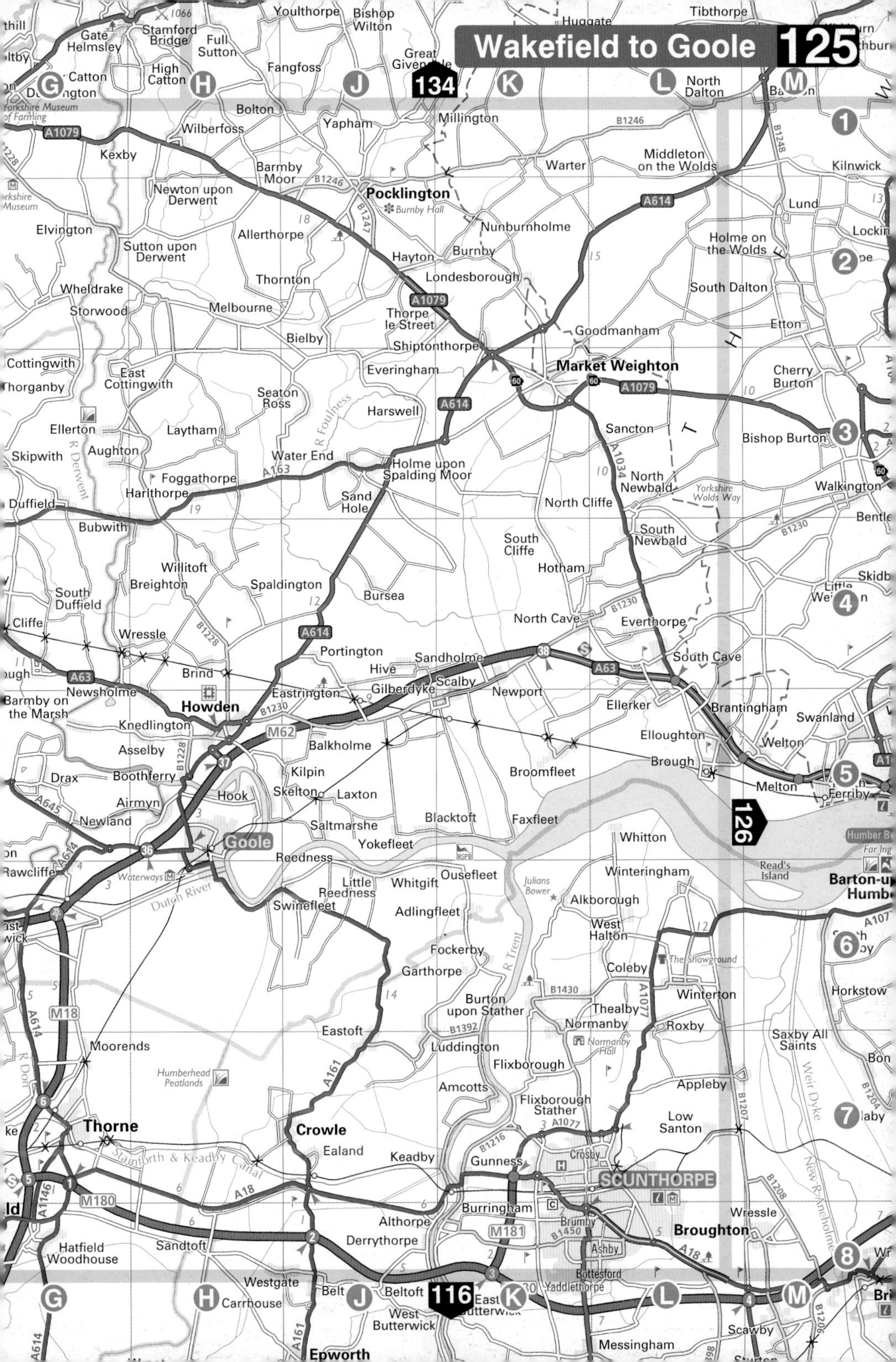
Youlthorpe
Bishop Wilton
Tibthorpe
Huggate
Gate Helmsley
Stamford Bridge
Full Sutton
Great Givendale
134
Catton
High Catton
Fangfoss
North Dalton
Yorkshire Museum of Farming
Bolton
Yapham
Millington
B1246
Wilberfoss
A1079
Kexby
Barmby Moor
Pocklington
Burnby Hall
Warter
Middleton on the Wolds
Kilnwick
Newton upon Derwent
A614
Lund
Elvington
Allerthorpe
Nunburnholme
Holme on the Wolds
Sutton upon Derwent
Hayton
Burnby
Londesborough
South Dalton
Wheldrake
Thornton
Storwood
Melbourne
Thorpe le Street
Goodmanham
Etton
Bielby
Shiptonthorpe
Market Weighton
Cottingwith
Thorganby
East Cottingwith
Everingham
Cherry Burton
Seaton Ross
R Foulness
Harswell
Ellerton
Laytham
Sancton
Bishop Burton
Aughton
Skipwith
Water End
Holme upon Spalding Moor
A163
Foggathorpe
Harlthorpe
North Newbald
Yorkshire Wolds Way
Walkington
A1034
Duffield
Sand Hole
North Cliffe
Bubwith
R Derwent
South Newbald
B1230
South Cliffe
Hotham
Willitoft
Breighton
Spaldington
Bursea
South Duffield
North Cave
Everthorpe
Little Weighton
Cliffe
Wressle
A614
B1228
Portington
Sandholme
South Cave
Hive
Brind
A63
Newsholme
Eastrington
Gilberdyke
Scalby
Newport
Ellerker
Brantingham
Swanland
Barmby on the Marsh
Howden
Knedlington
M62
Balkholme
Elloughton
Welton
Asselby
Brough
Kilpin
Broomfleet
Drax
Boothferry
Melton
Ferriby
Skelton
Laxton
Hook
Airmyn
A645
Newland
Blacktoft
Faxfleet
Saltmarshe
126
Goole
Yokefleet
Whitton
Reedness
RSPB
Read's Island
Rawcliffe
Waterways
Little Reedness
Whitgift
Ousefleet
Julians Bower
Winteringham
Barton-upon-Humber
Dutch River
Swinefleet
Alkborough
Adlingfleet
West Halton
Fockerby
R Trent
Coleby
Garthorpe
The Showground
M18
A614
B1430
Burton upon Stather
Thealby
Winterton
Horkstow
Normanby
Normanby Hall
Roxby
A1077
B1392
Eastoft
Saxby All Saints
Moorends
Luddington
Flixborough
Humberhead Peatlands
A161
Weir Dyke
Amcotts
Appleby
Flixborough Stather
B1207
Thorne
Crowle
Low Santon
Stainforth & Keadby Canal
Ealand
Keadby
Crosby
Gunness
SCUNTHORPE
New R Ancholme
B1208
M180
A18
Burringham
A1146
Wressle
Althorpe
Brumby
Broughton
M181
Hatfield Woodhouse
Sandtoft
Derrythorpe
B1450
Ashby
Bottesford
Westgate
Yaddlethorpe
Belt
Beltoft
116
East Butterwick
Carrhouse
West Butterwick
Scawby
Messingham
Epworth

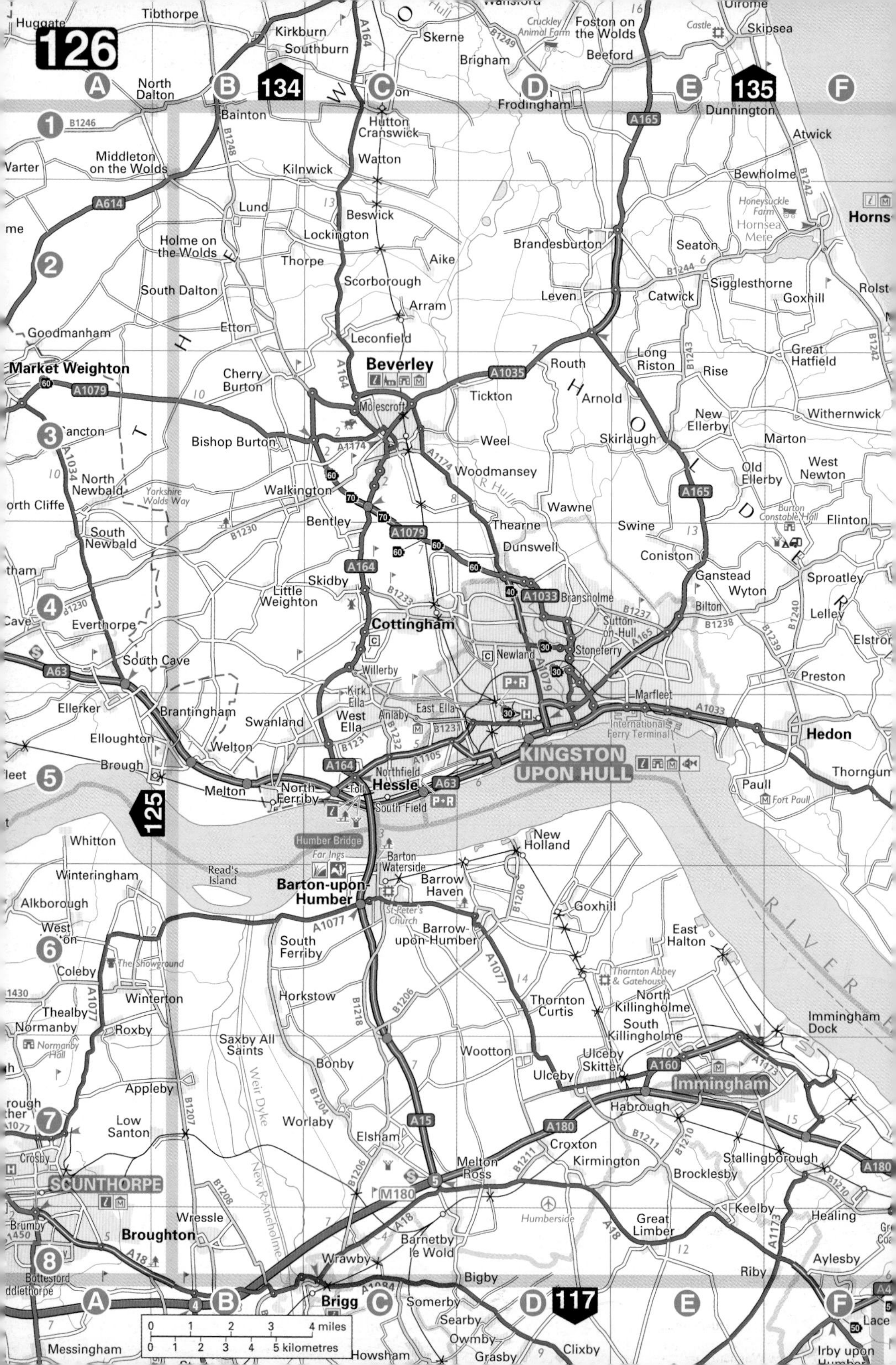

126
Huggate
Tibthorpe
Kirkburn
Southburn
Skerne
Cruckley Animal Farm
Foston on the Wolds
Brigham
Beeford
Castle
Skipsea
North Dalton
134
Bainton
Hutton Cranswick
Frodingham
A165
Dunnington
135
Atwick
B1246
Middleton on the Wolds
Warter
Watton
Kilnwick
Bewholme
A614
B1248
Lund
Beswick
Lockington
Honeysuckle Farm
Hornsea Mere
Holme on the Wolds
Thorpe
Aike
Brandesburton
Seaton
South Dalton
Scorborough
B1244
Sigglesthorne
Goxhill
Arram
Leven
Catwick
Goodmanham
Etton
Leconfield
Long Riston
Great Hatfield
Market Weighton
Cherry Burton
A164
Beverley
A1035
Routh
Rise
A1079
Tickton
Arnold
Molescroft
Withernwick
Bishop Burton
A1174
Weel
Skirlaugh
New Ellerby
Marton
North Newbald
Yorkshire Wolds Way
Walkington
Woodmansey
R Hull
Old Ellerby
West Newton
A1034
Bentley
Thearne
Wawne
Swine
A165
Burton Constable Hall
Flinton
South Newbald
B1230
Dunswell
Coniston
Skidby
Little Weighton
A1033
Bransholme
Ganstead
Wyton
Sproatley
Everthorpe
Cottingham
B1233
Sutton-on-Hull
Bilton
B1238
Lelley
B1237
B1240
B1239
South Cave
Newland
Stoneferry
A63
Willerby
Kirk Ella
West Ella
Anlaby
East Ella
P+R
Marfleet
Preston
Ellerker
Brantingham
Swanland
B1231
B1232
International Ferry Terminal
Hedon
Elloughton
Welton
A1105
KINGSTON UPON HULL
Brough
Northfield
Hessle
Thorngumbald
Melton
North Ferriby
Toll
South Field
Paull
Fort Paull
125
Whitton
Humber Bridge
Far Ings
Barton Waterside
New Holland
Winteringham
Read's Island
Barrow Haven
Alkborough
Barton-upon-Humber
St Peter's Church
Goxhill
West Halton
A1077
South Ferriby
Barrow-upon-Humber
East Halton
RIVER HUMBER
B1206
Coleby
The Showground
Thornton Abbey & Gatehouse
Winterton
Horkstow
Thornton Curtis
North Killingholme
Thealby
Normanby
Normanby Hall
Roxby
B1218
South Killingholme
Immingham Dock
Saxby All Saints
Wootton
Ulceby Skitter
A160
Bonby
Ulceby
Immingham
A1173
Appleby
Weir Dyke
B1204
Habrough
Low Santon
B1207
Worlaby
A15
A180
Croxton
Elsham
B1211
B1210
Stallingborough
Crosby
Melton Ross
Kirmington
Brocklesby
SCUNTHORPE
New R Ancholme
M180
B1208
Humberside
Keelby
Healing
Brumby
Wressle
A18
Barnetby le Wold
Great Limber
Broughton
Wrawby
Aylesby
Bottesford
Riby
Bigby
Brigg
A1084
Somerby
117
Searby
Owmby
Messingham
Howsham
Grasby
Clixby
Irby upon Humber
0 1 2 3 4 miles
0 1 2 3 4 5 kilometres

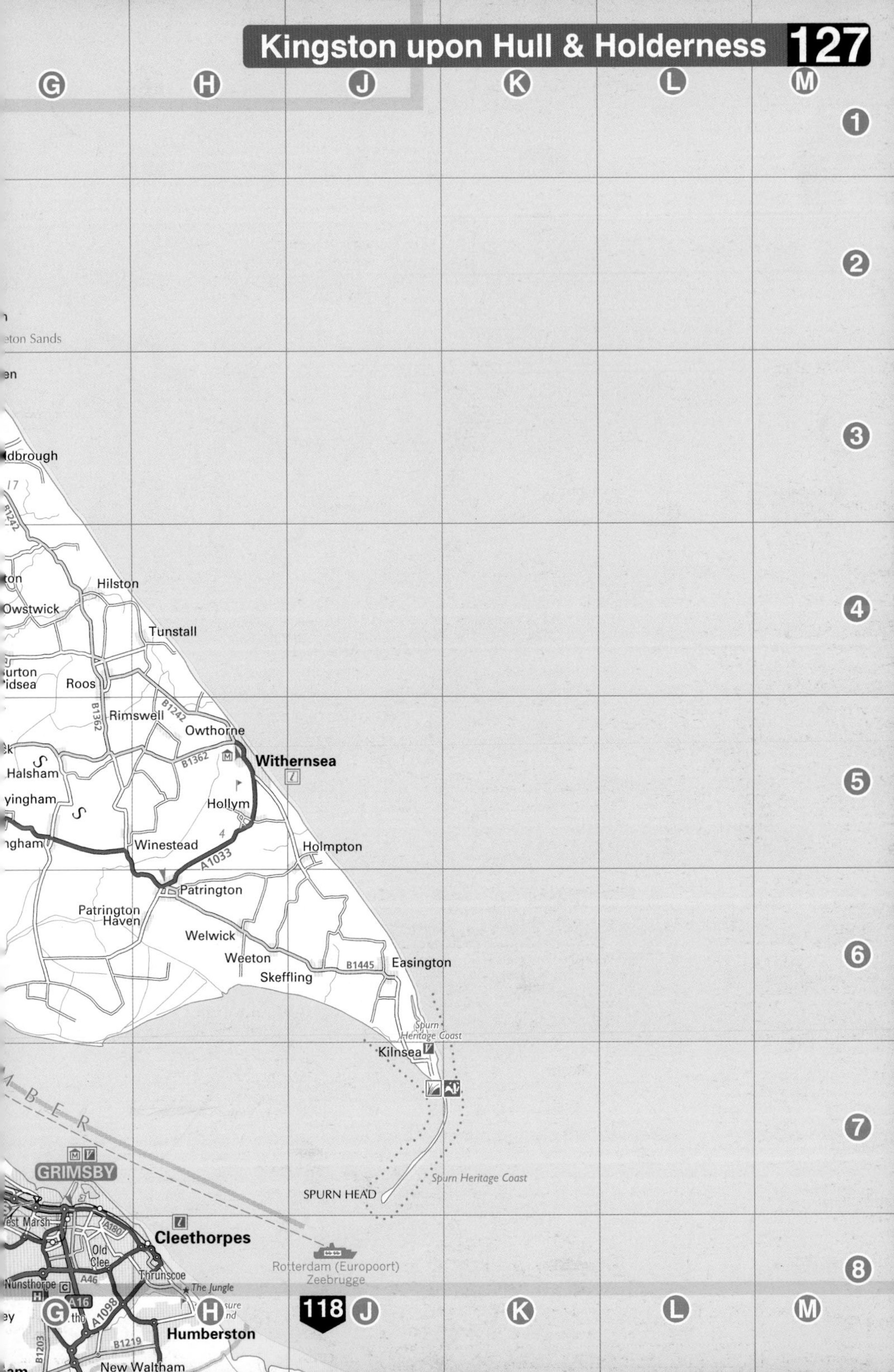
G
H
J
K
L
M
1
2
3
4
5
6
7
8
Hilston
Owstwick
Tunstall
Roos
Rimswell
B1242
B1362
Owthorne
Withernsea
Halsham
Hollym
Winestead
A1033
Holmpton
Patrington
Patrington Haven
Welwick
Weeton
Skeffling
B1445
Easington
Spurn Heritage Coast
Kilnsea
SPURN HEAD
GRIMSBY
Cleethorpes
Old Clee
A46
A180
Thrunscoe
The Jungle
A16
A1098
B1219
B1203
Humberston
New Waltham
Rotterdam (Europoort)
Zeebrugge
118

A
B
C
D
E
F
1
2
3
4
5
6
7
8
Seascale
Hallsenna Moor
Drigg
Holmrook
Eskdale Green
Eskdale
652
HARTER FELL
Muncaster Mill
Ravenglass and Eskdale Railway
River Esk
Devoke Water
River Duddon
Seathwaite Tarn
Ravenglass
Roman Bath House
Muncaster
A595
Hall Dunnerdale
Seathwaite
136
137
Waberthwaite
573
WHITFELL
Ulpha
LAKE DISTRICT NATIONAL PARK
Broughton Mills
A593
Hycemoor
Selker Bay
Bootle
Swinside Stone Circle
Broughton-in-Fu
A595
Lady Hall
Foxfield
Grize
600
BLACK COMBE
Whitbeck
The Green
Gutterby Spa
A5093
The Hill
Whicham
Silecroft
Kirkby-in-F
Beck Si
Soutergate
Kirksanton
Millom
A595
RSPB
Haverigg
Haverigg Point
Ireleth
Askam in Furness
Lindal in Furness
South Lakes Animal Park
Sandscale Haws
North Walney
Dalton-in-Furness
BARROW-IN-FURNESS
Newton
Furness Abbey
Bow Bridge
Dendron
Vickerstown
Barrow Island
A590
A5087
ISLE OF WALNEY
Ramps
Sheep Island
Piel Castle
Piel Island
Piel Bar
Hilpsford Point
South Walney
0 1 2 3 4 miles
0 1 2 3 4 5 kilometres

Hawkshead
Hawkshead Hill
Outgate
Bowness-on-Windermere
Windermere Steamboats & Museum
Far Sawrey
Near Sawrey
Grizedale
Grizedale Forest Park
Coniston Water
Satterthwaite
Furness Fells
Graythwaite Hall
Thwaite Head
High Nibthwaite
Rusland Cross
Finsthwaite
Stott Park Bobbin Mill
Oxen Park
Colton
Lowick Green
Bouth
Spark Bridge
Haverthwaite
Penny Bridge
Greenodd
Arrad Foot
Barrow Monument
Swarthmoor
Conishead Priory
Great Urswick
Bardsea
Baycliff
Aldingham
Lakeside and Haverthwaite Railway
Lakeland Motor Museum
Newby Bridge
Staveley
Fell Foot Park
Gummers How
Blackwell
Winster
Crosthwaite
Witherslack
Ayside
High Newton
Row
Whitbarrow
Brigsteer
Underbarrow
Ings
Garth Row
Grayrigg
Burneside
Kendal
Oxenholme
Natland
Middleshaw
Killington
Killington Lake (southbound only)
Old Hutton
New Hutton
Firbank
Sizergh Castle
Levens
Sedgwick
Stainton
Hincaster
Levens Hall
Leasgill
Heversham
Westmorland
Crooklands
Endmoor
Preston Patrick
Old Town
Nook
Lupton
Milnthorpe
Meathop
Lindale
Brown Robin
Hampsfell
Priory Gatehouse
Cartmel
Holker
Cark
Allithwaite
Flookburgh
Grange-over-Sands
Arnside
Arnside Knott
River Kent
Storth
Beetham
Whasset
Farleton
Holme
Holme Park Fell
Hale
Lakeland Wildlife Oasis
Burton-in-Kendal
Burton-in-Kendal (northbound only)
Kearstwick
Hutton Roof
High Biggins
Low Biggins
Park Wood
Whittington
Silverdale
Yealand Redmayne
Leighton Hall
Jack Scout
Yealand Conyers
Priest Hutton
Humphrey Head
Heald Brow
Warton
Old Rectory
Borwick
Arkholme
Carnforth
Gressingham
Wennington
Over Kellet
Nether Kellet
Hornby
Wray
MORECAMBE BAY
Bolton le Sands
Hest Bank
Slyne
Aughton
Claughton
Farleton
Morecambe
Bare
Torrisholme
Halton
Caton Green
Brookhouse
Caton
River Lune Millennium Park
Crossgill
Skerton
Sandylands
Lancaster
Heysham
Higher Heysham
Aldcliffe
Scotforth
R Roeburn
Ward's Stone
Douglas
Overton
Ellel
Sunderland
Glasson
River Lune
Galgate
Lancaster Canal
Cockersand
R Wyre
Abbeystead
Dolphinholme
Cockerham
Hawthorn Fell
Knott End
Calder Fell
A591
A6
A685
M6
A684
A592
B5284
A5074
B5285
A5084
A5092
B5278
B5281
A590
B5277
B5282
B6385
B6384
A6070
A65
B6254
A683
A5105
B5321
B5273
A589
A588
B5272
137
138
130
120
121

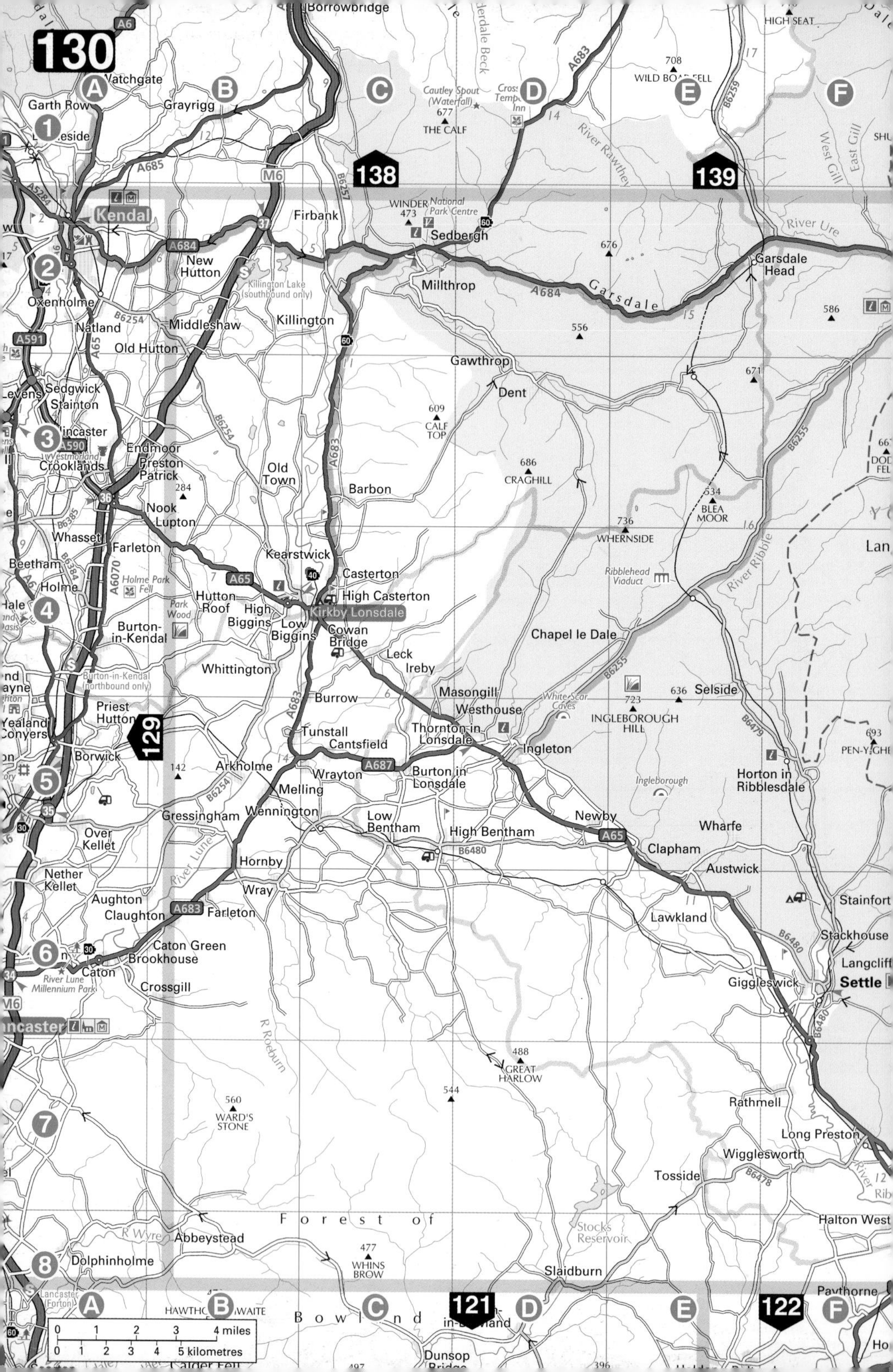
Borrowbridge
A6
Watchgate
Garth Row
Grayrigg
Cautley Spout (Waterfall)
677 THE CALF
Cross Keys Temperance Inn
A683
708 WILD BOAR FELL
HIGH SEAT
B6259
West Gill
East Gill
River Rawthey
A685
M6
138
139
B6257
A5284
Kendal
WINDER 473
National Park Centre
Firbank
Sedbergh
River Ure
A684
New Hutton
Killington Lake (southbound only)
Millthrop
676
Garsdale Head
Garsdale
Oxenholme
B6254
Middleshaw
Killington
556
586
A591
Natland
A65
Old Hutton
Gawthrop
Dent
671
Sedgwick
Levens
Stainton
609 CALF TOP
Lincaster
A590
Westmorland
Crooklands
Endmoor
Preston Patrick
B6254
Old Town
686 CRAGHILL
Barbon
A683
534 BLEA MOOR
284
Nook
Lupton
B6385
Whasset
Farleton
736 WHERNSIDE
Beetham
B6384
A6070
Kearstwick
Casterton
Holme Park Fell
Holme
Hutton Roof
High Casterton
Ribblehead Viaduct
River Ribble
B6255
Hale
High Biggins
Low Biggins
Kirkby Lonsdale
Park Wood
Burton-in-Kendal
Cowan Bridge
Chapel le Dale
Leck
Ireby
Whittington
Burton-in-Kendal (northbound only)
Priest Hutton
Burrow
Masongill
Westhouse
White Scar Caves
723 INGLEBOROUGH HILL
636
Selside
B6479
Yealand Conyers
129
Tunstall
Cantsfield
Thornton-in-Lonsdale
Ingleton
693 PEN-Y-GHENT
Borwick
142
Arkholme
A687
Wrayton
Burton in Lonsdale
Horton in Ribblesdale
Ingleborough
Melling
B6254
Gressingham
Wennington
Low Bentham
High Bentham
Newby
A65
Wharfe
Over Kellet
B6480
Clapham
Hornby
Austwick
Nether Kellet
River Lune
Wray
Stainforth
Aughton
Claughton
A683
Farleton
Lawkland
Stackhouse
B6480
Caton Green
Brookhouse
Langcliffe
Caton
River Lune Millennium Park
Giggleswick
Settle
Crossgill
M6
Lancaster
B6480
R Roeburn
488 GREAT HARLOW
544
560 WARD'S STONE
Rathmell
Long Preston
Wigglesworth
Tosside
B6478
River Ribble
Forest of
Stocks Reservoir
Halton West
R Wyre
Abbeystead
477 WHINS BROW
Dolphinholme
Slaidburn
Lancaster (Forton)
Paythorne
HAWTHORNTHWAITE
Bowland
121
122
Newton-in-Bowland
Dunsop Bridge
0 1 2 3 4 miles
0 1 2 3 4 5 kilometres

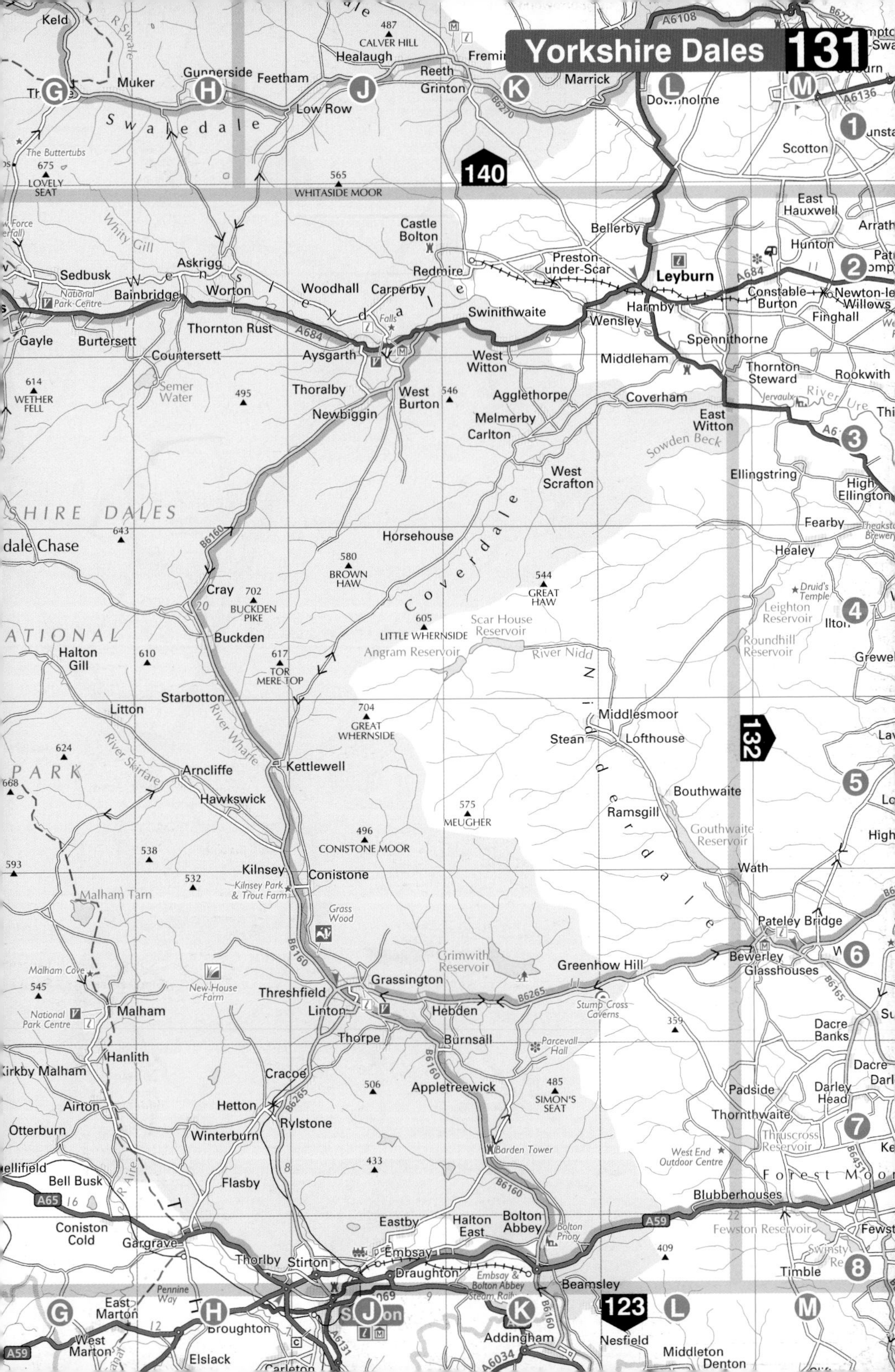
Keld
487
CALVER HILL
Healaugh
Fremington
Muker
Gunnerside
Feetham
Reeth
Grinton
Marrick
Downholme
Low Row
Swaledale
The Buttertubs
675
LOVELY SEAT
565
WHITASIDE MOOR
140
Scotton
East Hauxwell
Arrathorne
Hunton
Bellerby
Castle Bolton
Whity Gill
Askrigg
Redmire
Preston-under-Scar
Leyburn
Sedbusk
Bainbridge
National Park Centre
Worton
Woodhall
Carperby
Wensleydale
Harmby
Constable Burton
Newton-le-Willows
Finghall
Swinithwaite
Wensley
Gayle
Burtersett
Thornton Rust
Falls
Aysgarth
Spennithorne
Countersett
West Witton
Middleham
Thornton Steward
Rookwith
Semer Water
614
WETHER FELL
495
Thoralby
West Burton
546
Agglethorpe
Coverham
Jervaulx
River Ure
Newbiggin
Melmerby
Carlton
East Witton
Sowden Beck
West Scrafton
Ellingstring
High Ellington
YORKSHIRE DALES
643
Langstrothdale Chase
Horsehouse
Fearby
Theakston Brewery
580
BROWN HAW
Healey
544
GREAT HAW
Druid's Temple
Cray
702
BUCKDEN PIKE
Coverdale
Leighton Reservoir
Ilton
NATIONAL
605
LITTLE WHERNSIDE
Scar House Reservoir
Buckden
Roundhill Reservoir
Halton Gill
610
617
TOR MERE TOP
Angram Reservoir
River Nidd
Grewelthorpe
Starbotton
Litton
River Wharfe
704
GREAT WHERNSIDE
Middlesmoor
Stean
Lofthouse
132
624
PARK
River Skirfare
Arncliffe
Kettlewell
668
Hawkswick
Bouthwaite
Nidderdale
575
MEUGHER
Ramsgill
Gouthwaite Reservoir
496
CONISTONE MOOR
538
593
Kilnsey
Conistone
Wath
532
Kilnsey Park & Trout Farm
Malham Tarn
Grass Wood
Pateley Bridge
Malham Cove
Grimwith Reservoir
Greenhow Hill
Bewerley
Glasshouses
545
New House Farm
Grassington
Threshfield
B6265
Stump Cross Caverns
National Park Centre
Malham
Linton
Hebden
359
Thorpe
Burnsall
Parcevall Hall
Dacre Banks
Hanlith
Kirkby Malham
Cracoe
Dacre
Darley Head
506
Appletreewick
485
SIMON'S SEAT
Padside
Airton
Hetton
Thornthwaite
Otterburn
Rylstone
Winterburn
Barden Tower
Thruscross Reservoir
Hellifield
West End Outdoor Centre
Bell Busk
433
Flasby
Forest Moor
A65
Blubberhouses
Coniston Cold
Gargrave
Eastby
Halton East
Bolton Abbey
Bolton Priory
A59
Fewston Reservoir
Fewston
Thorlby
Stirton
Embsay
409
Swinsty Reservoir
Draughton
Timble
Pennine Way
Embsay & Bolton Abbey Steam Railway
Beamsley
East Marton
Skipton
123
Broughton
West Marton
Addingham
Nesfield
Middleton
Denton
Elslack
Carleton
A6108
A6136
A684
B6270
B6160
A6034
A6131
A629
B6265
B6165
B6451
1
2
3
4
5
6
7
8
G
H
J
K
L
M

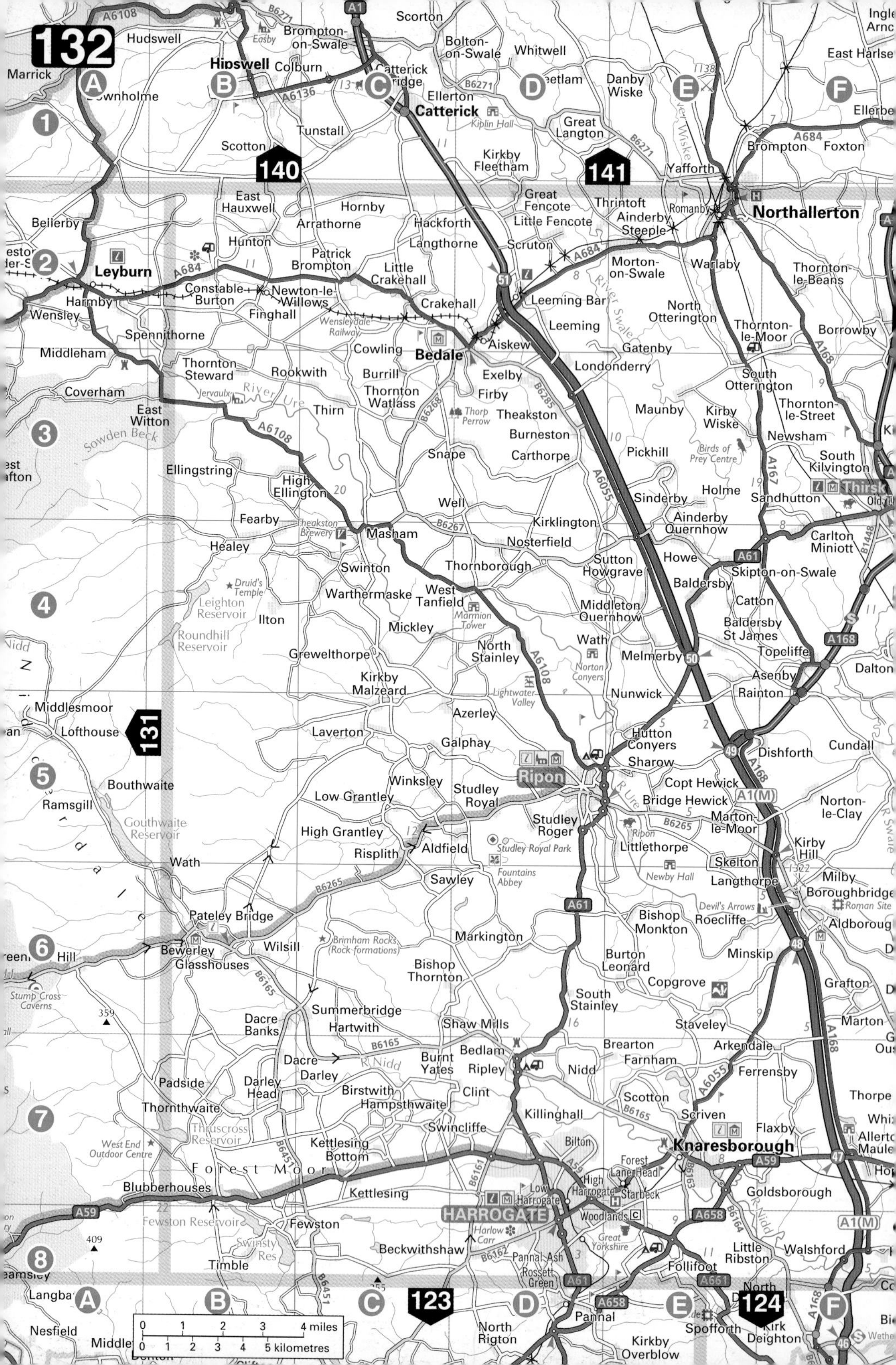
132
140
141
131
123
124
A
B
C
D
E
F
1
2
3
4
5
6
7
8
Hudswell
Marrick
Downholme
Easby
Brompton-on-Swale
Scorton
Hipswell
Colburn
Catterick Bridge
Bolton-on-Swale
Whitwell
Danby Wiske
East Harlsey
Ellerton
Catterick
Kiplin Hall
Tunstall
Scotton
Great Langton
Kirkby Fleetham
Yafforth
Brompton
Foxton
Bellerby
East Hauxwell
Hornby
Arrathorne
Hackforth
Great Fencote
Little Fencote
Thrintoft
Ainderby Steeple
Romanby
Northallerton
Hunton
Patrick Brompton
Langthorne
Scruton
Leyburn
Constable Burton
Newton-le-Willows
Little Crakehall
Crakehall
Morton-on-Swale
Warlaby
Thornton-le-Beans
Harmby
Wensley
Finghall
Leeming Bar
North Otterington
Thornton-le-Moor
Borrowby
Spennithorne
Wensleydale Railway
Leeming
River Swale
Middleham
Cowling
Bedale
Aiskew
Gatenby
Londonderry
Thornton Steward
Rookwith
Burrill
Exelby
South Otterington
Coverham
Jervaulx
River Ure
Thornton Watlass
Firby
Thirn
Maunby
Kirby Wiske
Thornton-le-Street
East Witton
Thorp Perrow
Theakston
Burneston
Newsham
Sowden Beck
Birds of Prey Centre
A6108
Snape
Carthorpe
Pickhill
South Kilvington
Ellingstring
High Ellington
Sinderby
Holme
Sandhutton
Thirsk
Well
Ainderby Quernhow
Fearby
Theakston Brewery
Masham
Kirklington
Carlton Miniott
Healey
Nosterfield
Howe
Swinton
Thornborough
Sutton Howgrave
Baldersby
Skipton-on-Swale
Druid's Temple
West Tanfield
Warthermaske
Catton
Leighton Reservoir
Ilton
Middleton Quernhow
Marmion Tower
Baldersby St James
Mickley
Roundhill Reservoir
Wath
Norton Conyers
North Stanley
Melmerby
Topcliffe
Grewelthorpe
Dalton
Asenby
Kirkby Malzeard
Nunwick
Rainton
Lightwater Valley
Middlesmoor
Lofthouse
Azerley
Laverton
Hutton Conyers
Galphay
Dishforth
Cundall
Sharow
Bouthwaite
Winksley
Ripon
Copt Hewick
Ramsgill
Low Grantley
Studley Royal
Bridge Hewick
Norton-le-Clay
Goutbwaite Reservoir
Studley Roger
Marton-le-Moor
High Grantley
Studley Royal Park
Littlethorpe
Kirby Hill
Risplith
Aldfield
Fountains Abbey
Skelton
Wath
Newby Hall
Langthorpe
Milby
Sawley
Boroughbridge
Roman Site
Pateley Bridge
Devil's Arrows
Bishop Monkton
Roecliffe
Aldborough
Bewerley
Wilsill
Markington
Brimham Rocks (Rock formations)
Glasshouses
Burton Leonard
Minskip
Bishop Thornton
Copgrove
Grafton
Stump Cross Caverns
South Stainley
Summerbridge
Hartwith
Dacre Banks
Shaw Mills
Staveley
Marton
Brearton
Arkendale
Bedlam
Burnt Yates
Dacre
Darley
Ripley
Nidd
Farnham
Ferrensby
Padside
Darley Head
Birstwith
Clint
Scotton
Thorpe
Thornthwaite
Hampsthwaite
Killinghall
Scriven
Flaxby
Thruscross Reservoir
Swincliffe
Bilton
Knaresborough
Allerton Mauleverer
West End Outdoor Centre
Kettlesing Bottom
Forest Lane Head
Forest Moor
High Harrogate
Blubberhouses
Kettlesing
Low Harrogate
Starbeck
Goldsborough
HARROGATE
Woodlands
Fewston Reservoir
Fewston
Harlow Carr
Great Yorkshire
Swinsty Res
Beckwithshaw
Pannal Ash
Rossett Green
Little Ribston
Walshford
Follifoot
Timble
Langbar
Pannal
North Deighton
Kirk Deighton
Spofforth
Nesfield
North Rigton
Kirkby Overblow
Middleton
0 1 2 3 4 miles
0 1 2 3 4 5 kilometres

NORTH YORK MOORS NATIONAL PARK
Howardian Hills
Osmotherley
Thimbleby
Over Silton
Nether Silton
Cowesby
Kirby Knowle
Upsall
Boltby
Thirlby
Hawnby
Old Byland
Rievaulx
Cold Kirby
Scawton
Helmsley
Carlton
Beadlam
Pockley
Nawton
Wombleton
Kirkbymoorside
Gillamoor
Fadmoor
Hutton-le-Hole
Spaunton
Appleton-le-Moors
Lastingham
Cropton
Wrelton
Aislaby
Middleton
Sinnington
Marton
Pickering
Rosedale Abbey
Thorgill
Low Mill
Fangdale Beck
Chop Gate
Seave Green
Sproxton
Harome
Normanby
Salton
West Ness
East Ness
Great Barugh
Brawby
Kirby Misperton
Butterwick
Great Habton
Nunnington
Stonegrave
Oswaldkirk
Ampleforth
Wass
High Kilburn
Oldstead
Kilburn
Bagby
Thirkleby
Hutton Sessay
Carlton Husthwaite
Birdforth
Husthwaite
Coxwold
Newburgh Priory
Gilling East
Hovingham
Yearsley
Oulston
Thormanby
Slingsby
Barton-le-Street
Amotherby
Broughton
Swinton
Malton
Appleton-le-Street
Coulton
Scackleton
Brandsby
Raskelf
Crayke
Stearsby
Skewsby
Dalby
Terrington
Coneysthorpe
Whenby
Ganthorpe
Castle Howard
Easingwold
Welburn
Bulmer
High Hutton
Low Hutton
Stillington
Farlington
Tholthorpe
Sheriff Hutton
Thornton-le-Clay
Whitwell-on-the-Hill
Foston
Firby
Kirkham
Kennythorpe
Huby
West Lilling
Flawith
Alne
Crambe
Westow
Tollerton
Youlton
Sutton-on-the-Forest
Sutton Park
Howsham
Barton-le-Willows
Flaxton
Linton-on-Ouse
Aldwark
Strensall
Harton
Bossall
Acklam
Leppington
Claxton
Scrayingham
Newton on Ouse
Shipton
Beningbrough Hall
Nun Monkton
Beningbrough
Wigginton
Towthorpe
Sand Hutton
Buttercrambe
Haxby
Green Hammerton
Moor Monkton
Skelton
Stockton on the Forest
Upper Helmsley
Skirpenbeck
Huntington
Overton
New Earswick
Kirk Hammerton
Nether Poppleton
Upper Poppleton
Rawcliffe
Hopgrove
Warthill
Gate Helmsley
Stamford Bridge
Full Sutton
Youlthorpe
Holtby
Hessay
Clifton
Murton
Low Catton
High Catton
Fangfoss
Tockwith
Dunnington
Yorkshire Museum of Farming
YORK
Osbaldwick
Long Marston
Rufforth
Acomb
South Bank
Nunthorpe
Heslington
Kexby
Wilberfoss
Bolton
Hutton Wandesley
Bilton
Askham
Dringhouses
Barmby Moor
Newton upon
A170
A19
A59
A64
A166
A1237
A1036
A1079
B1257
B1363
B1228
B1224
142
134
124
125

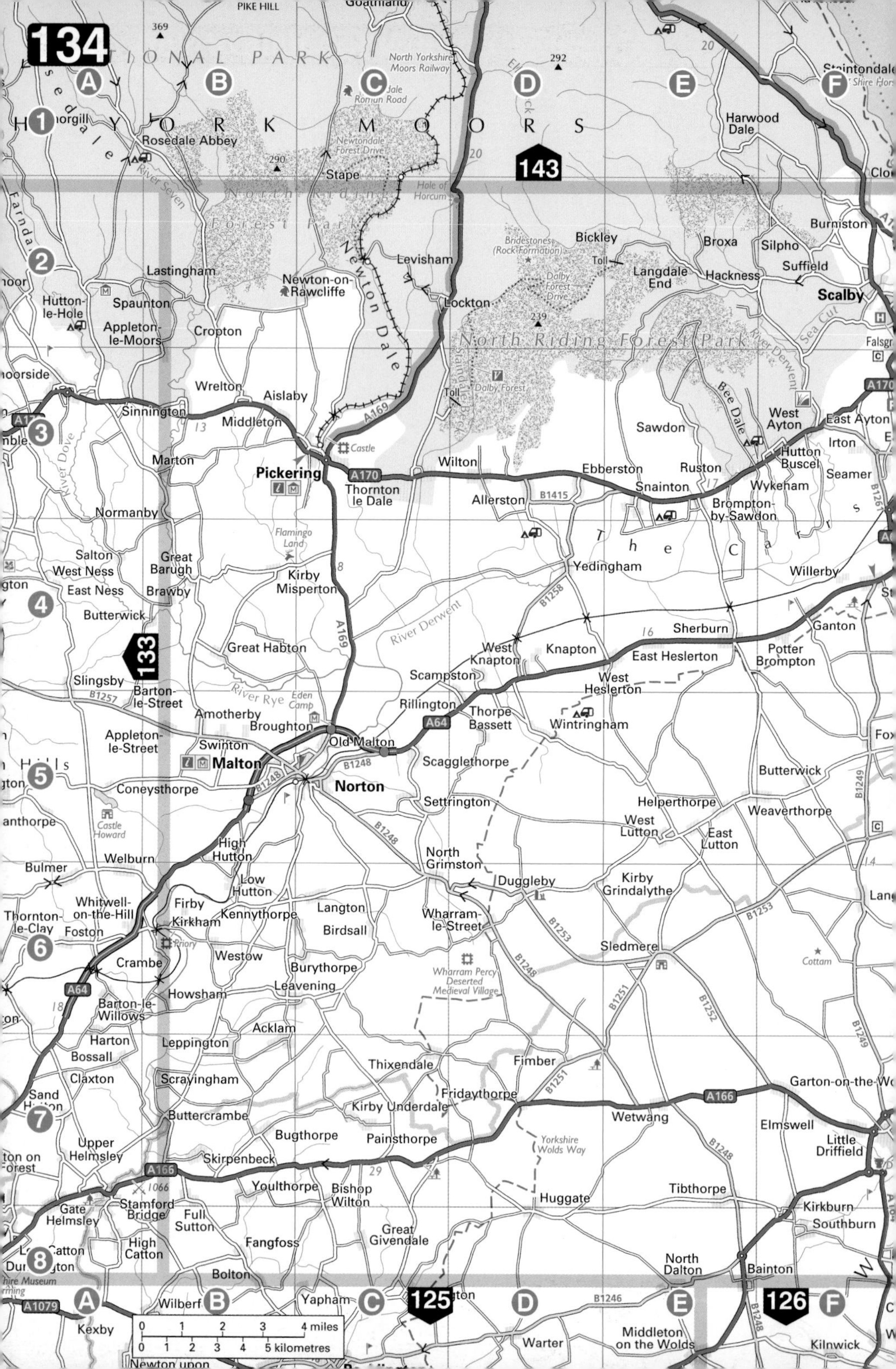

134
NORTH YORK MOORS NATIONAL PARK
PIKE HILL
369
A
B
C
D
E
F
1
2
3
4
5
6
7
8
Rosedale Abbey
Rosedale
River Seven
North Yorkshire Moors Railway
Newtondale Forest Drive
Roman Road
292
290
Stape
Hale of Horcum
143
Harwood Dale
Staintondale
Shire Horse
Farndale
North Riding Forest Park
Newton Dale
Levisham
Lockton
Bridestones (Rock Formation)
Bickley
Toll
Langdale End
Dalby Forest Drive
239
Broxa
Silpho
Burniston
Suffield
Hackness
Scalby
Sea Cut
River Derwent
Falsgrave
Lastingham
Spaunton
Hutton-le-Hole
Appleton-le-Moors
Cropton
Newton-on-Rawcliffe
Staindale Beck
Dalby Forest
Bee Dale
Wrelton
Aislaby
Sinnington
Middleton
A170
13
River Dove
Marton
Pickering
Castle
Thornton le Dale
Wilton
Ebberston
Allerston
B1415
Snainton
Ruston
Sawdon
West Ayton
East Ayton
Irton
Hutton Buscel
Wykeham
Brompton-by-Sawdon
Seamer
17
20
The Carrs
B1261
Normanby
Salton
West Ness
East Ness
Great Barugh
Brawby
Butterwick
Flamingo Land
Kirby Misperton
8
A169
Yedingham
B1258
Willerby
River Derwent
16
Sherburn
Ganton
West Knapton
Knapton
East Heslerton
Potter Brompton
West Heslerton
Great Habton
133
Slingsby
Barton-le-Street
B1257
River Rye
Eden Camp
Amotherby
Broughton
Scampston
Rillington
Thorpe Bassett
Wintringham
A64
Appleton-le-Street
Swinton
Malton
Old Malton
Norton
B1248
Scagglethorpe
Settrington
Coneysthorpe
Castle Howard
Butterwick
Helperthorpe
Weaverthorpe
West Lutton
East Lutton
B1249
High Hutton
Low Hutton
Welburn
Bulmer
Whitwell-on-the-Hill
Thornton-le-Clay
Foston
Firby
Kirkham
Priory
Kennythorpe
Langton
Birdsall
North Grimston
Duggleby
Kirby Grindalythe
Wharram-le-Street
B1253
14
Sledmere
Cottam
Crambe
Westow
Burythorpe
Wharram Percy Deserted Medieval Village
B1251
B1252
Howsham
Leavening
Barton-le-Willows
Acklam
18
Harton
Bossall
Leppington
Claxton
Scrayingham
Thixendale
Fimber
Sand Hutton
Fridaythorpe
Garton-on-the-Wolds
A166
Wetwang
Elmswell
Little Driffield
Buttercrambe
Kirby Underdale
Bugthorpe
Painsthorpe
Yorkshire Wolds Way
Upper Helmsley
Skirpenbeck
29
Youlthorpe
Bishop Wilton
Huggate
Tibthorpe
Kirkburn
Southburn
1066
Gate Helmsley
Stamford Bridge
Full Sutton
Fangfoss
Great Givendale
High Catton
Low Catton
Bolton
North Dalton
Bainton
A1079
Wilberfoss
Yapham
125
B1246
126
Kexby
Warter
Middleton on the Wolds
Kilnwick
0 1 2 3 4 miles
0 1 2 3 4 5 kilometres

G
H
J
K
L
M
1
2
3
4
5
6
7
8
Cloughton Wyke
omer Point
eveland Way
Scarborough
Castle
Hatherleigh Deep Sea Trawler
Oliver's Mount
A165
P+R
Osgodby
Cayton Bay
B1261
gates
Cayton
The Wyke
Lebberston
Gristhorpe
A1039
Filey Brigg
R Hertford
Filey
Folkton
Muston
A1039
Flixton
Filey Bay
hire Way
Hunmanby
Fordon
Reighton
Speeton
Flamborough Head Heritage Coast
Bempton Cliffs
RSPB
Thornwick Bay
B1229
Wold Newton
Burton Fleming
Buckton
Bempton
North Landing
B1229
Selwicks Bay
Grindale
A165
B1259
FLAMBOROUGH HEAD
Lighthouse
hwing
B1255
Flamborough
Sewerby
Bondville Miniature Village
B1253
Boynton
Rudston
Monolith
A1038
Bridlington
Bessingby
Hilderthorpe
BRIDLINGTON BAY
Carnaby
Haisthorpe
Thornholme
Kilham
Burton Agnes
Norman Manor House
A165
Harpham
uston Parva
Lowthorpe
A614
Fraisthorpe
Nafferton
Gransmoor
ield
Great Kelk
Lissett
Barmston
B1242
R Hull
Ulrome
Wansford
Gembling
Cruckley Animal Farm
Foston on the Wolds
Castle
Skipsea
Skerne
B1249
Beeford
Brigham
North Frodingham
Dunnington
A165
126
Atwick
Bewholme
B1242

136
A
B
C
D
E
F
1
2
3
4
5
6
7
8
Crosscanonby
Crosby
Fort
River Ellen
Maryport
Dearham
Gilcru
Tallenti
A594
Bridekirk
Flimby
Broughton Moor
147
Standingstone
Dovenby
A595
Great Broughton
Papcastle
Camerton
Seaton
Great Clifton
A66
Brigham
Greysouthen
Stainburn
Little Clifton
Eaglesfield
Workington
Moss Bay
Mossbay
Westfield
Salterbeck
A596
A595
Deanscales
Harrington
A597
Branthwaite
Dean
Ullock
Pardshaw
Distington
Common End
B5306
Gilgarran
Mockerkin
A5086
Lowca
Howgate
Low Moresby
Parton
R Keekle
Loweswater
Lamplugh
572
A595
Asby
Arlecdon
Rowrah
Kirkland
Whitehaven
High Leys
Saltom Bay
Hensingham
Frizington
B5295
B5294
615
Cleator Moor
Ennerdale Bridge
Ennerdale Water
Sandwith
Mirehouse
B5345
River Ehen
Rottington
Cleator
River Calder
St Bees Head
RSPB
St Bees Head Heritage Coast
Bigrigg
St Bees
Egremont
533
LANK RIGG
Worm Gill
Thornhill
Haile
River Bleng
Nethertown
Beckermet
Calder Bridge
R Ehen
Cross
Wellington
Gosforth
B5343
Santon
Seascale
Hallsenna Moor
Drigg
Holmrook
Muncaster Mill
River Esk
Ravenglass
Roman Bath House
Muncaster
A595
128
Waberthw
0 1 2 3 4 miles
0 1 2 3 4 5 kilometres
Hycemoor
Selker Bay
Bootle

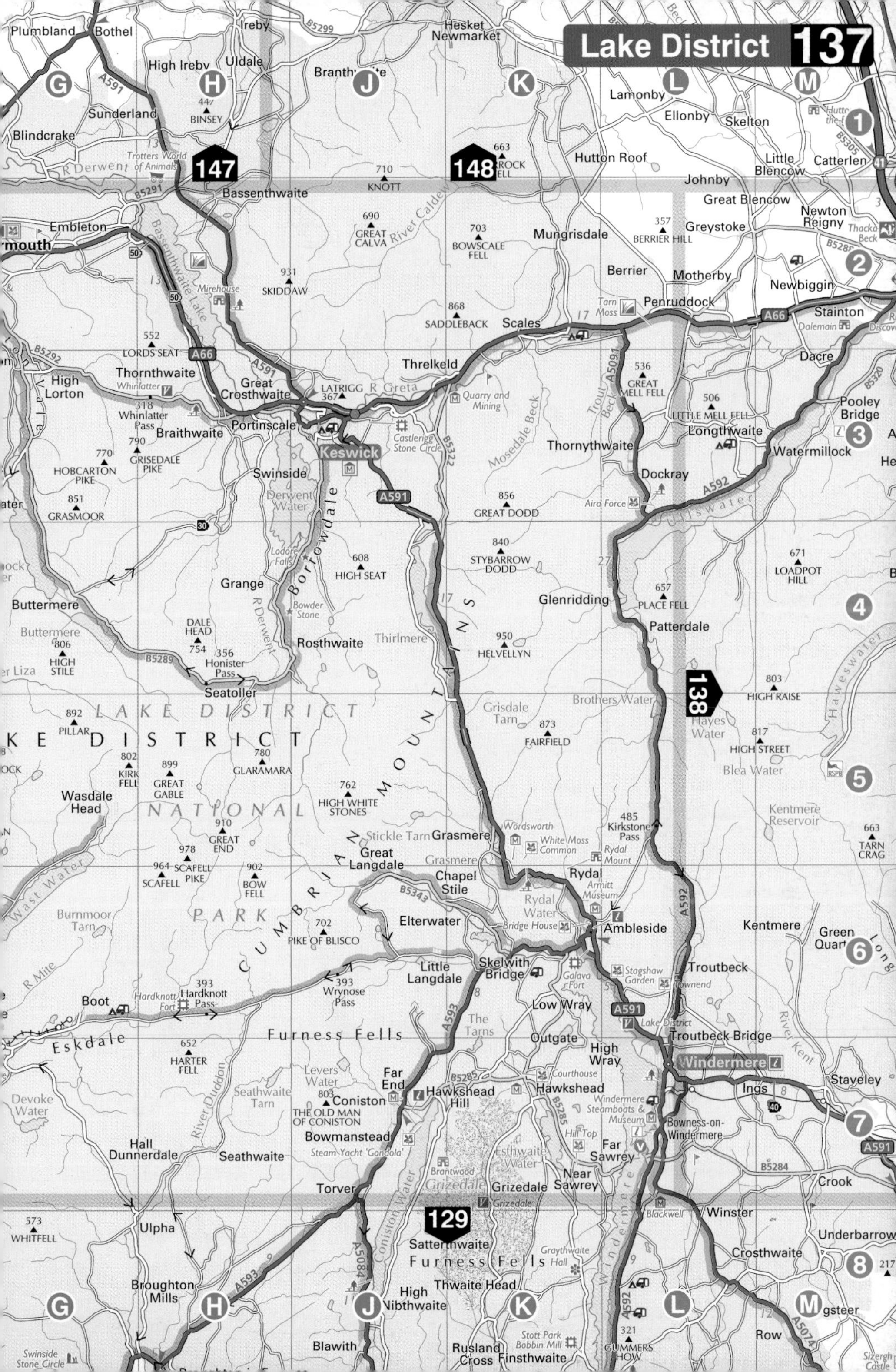
Plumbland
Bothel
Ireby
Hesket Newmarket
High Ireby
Uldale
Lamonby
Ellonby
Skelton
Sunderland
Blindcrake
BINSEY
Trotters World of Animals
147
148
KNOTT
Hutton Roof
Little Blencow
Catterlen
Johnby
Bassenthwaite
Great Blencow
Newton Reigny
Embleton
GREAT CALVA
BOWSCALE FELL
Mungrisdale
BERRIER HILL
Greystoke
Berrier
Motherby
Newbiggin
Mirehouse
SKIDDAW
Bassenthwaite Lake
Penruddock
SADDLEBACK
Scales
Stainton
Dalemain
LORDS SEAT
Thornthwaite
Threlkeld
Dacre
High Lorton
Whinlatter
Great Crosthwaite
LATRIGG
R Greta
GREAT MELL FELL
Pooley Bridge
Whinlatter Pass
Braithwaite
Portinscale
Quarry and Mining
LITTLE MELL FELL
Longthwaite
Watermillock
GRISEDALE PIKE
HOBCARTON PIKE
Castlerigg Stone Circle
Keswick
Mosedale Beck
Thornythwaite
Swinside
Dockray
Derwent Water
Borrowdale
GRASMOOR
GREAT DODD
Aira Force
Ullswater
STYBARROW DODD
LOADPOT HILL
Lodore Falls
HIGH SEAT
Grange
Glenridding
PLACE FELL
Buttermere
Bowder Stone
DALE HEAD
Patterdale
Rosthwaite
Thirlmere
HELVELLYN
HIGH STILE
Honister Pass
Seatoller
HIGH RAISE
LAKE DISTRICT NATIONAL PARK
PILLAR
Grisdale Tarn
Brothers Water
138
Hayes Water
Haweswater
FAIRFIELD
HIGH STREET
GLARAMARA
KIRK FELL
GREAT GABLE
Blea Water
Wasdale Head
HIGH WHITE STONES
Kentmere Reservoir
CUMBRIAN MOUNTAINS
Wordsworth
White Moss Common
Kirkstone Pass
Stickle Tarn
Grasmere
TARN CRAG
GREAT END
Great Langdale
Rydal Mount
SCAFELL PIKE
Rydal
SCAFELL
BOW FELL
Chapel Stile
Armitt Museum
Wast Water
Rydal Water
Burnmoor Tarn
Elterwater
Bridge House
Ambleside
Kentmere
Green Quarter
PIKE OF BLISCO
Little Langdale
Skelwith Bridge
Galava Fort
Stagshaw Garden
Troutbeck
Townend
Hardknott Fort
Hardknott Pass
Wrynose Pass
Boot
Low Wray
R Mite
The Tarns
Lake District
Troutbeck Bridge
Eskdale
Furness Fells
Outgate
River Kent
HARTER FELL
High Wray
Windermere
Staveley
Ings
Levers Water
Courthouse
Hawkshead
Far End
Hawkshead Hill
Devoke Water
Seathwaite Tarn
River Duddon
Coniston
THE OLD MAN OF CONISTON
Windermere Steamboats & Museum
Bowness-on-Windermere
Hill Top
Hall Dunnerdale
Bowmanstead
Steam Yacht 'Gondola'
Seathwaite
Far Sawrey
Brantwood
Esthwaite Water
Coniston Water
Crook
Torver
Grizedale
Near Sawrey
Blackwell
Winster
129
WHITFELL
Ulpha
Satterthwaite
Underbarrow
Crosthwaite
Graythwaite Hall
Broughton Mills
Thwaite Head
High Nibthwaite
Row
GUMMERS HOW
Stott Park Bobbin Mill
Blawith
Rusland Cross
Finsthwaite
Swinside Stone Circle
Sizergh Castle

138
A
B
C
D
E
F
1
2
3
4
5
6
7
8
Hutton End
247
LAZONBY FELL
Lazonby
Glassonby
Gamblesby
710
MELMERBY FELL
Lamonby
Ellonby
Skelton
Hutton-in-the-Forest
B5305
B6413
Plumpton
Salkeld Dykes
Great Salkeld
Long Meg and her Daughters
Melmerby
740
GREEN FELL
Little Salkeld
Hunsonby
B6412
Winskill
Ousby
663
CARROCK FELL
Hutton Roof
Little Blencow
Catterlen
41
148
Langwathby
Skirwith
Johnby
Great Blencow
Newton Reigny
Thacka Beck
Edenhall
Blencarn
703
BOWSCALE FELL
Mungrisdale
357
BERRIER HILL
Greystoke
Penrith
A686
Castle
R Eamont
B6412
B5288
Culgaith
Berrier
Motherby
Newbiggin
Mayburgh Henge
Brougham Castle
Acorn Bank Garden
Milburn
Newbiggin
Tarn Moss
Penruddock
40
Countess Pillar
Oasis Whinfell Park
220
Scales
A66
Stainton
Dalemain
Rheged Discovery Centre
Eamont Bridge
Yanwath
Temple Sowerby
Kirkby Thore
Center Parcs
Wetheriggs Country Pottery
Clifton Hall
Tirril
Dacre
Clifton
River Eden
Long Marton
Quarry and Mining
536
GREAT MELL FELL
A5091
B5320
Cilburn Moss
Cliburn
Melkinthorpe
Trout Beck
R Lowther
506
LITTLE MELL FELL
Pooley Bridge
Lowther
Mosedale Beck
Longthwaite
Hackthorpe
Askham
13
A66
Thornythwaite
Watermillock
Leisure & Wildlife Park
Great Strickland
Morland
Bolton
Helton
Crackenthorpe
Dockray
A592
Newby
Kings Meaburn
856
GREAT DODD
Aira Force
Ullswater
Colby
Little Strickland
River Lyvennet
Appleby-in-Westmorland
840
STYBARROW DODD
671
LOADPOT HILL
Sleagill
Burrells
Bampton
Bampton Grange
Reagill
657
PLACE FELL
Glenridding
Rosgill
Maulds Meaburn
M6
Patterdale
950
HELVELLYN
Shap Abbey
Shap
Swindale
Haweswater
Crosby Ravensworth
Keld Chapel
B6260
803
HIGH RAISE
137
Brothers Water
Grisdale Tarn
Hayes Water
873
FAIRFIELD
817
HIGH STREET
39
316
Shap Summit
Blea Water
RSPB
Great Asby Scar
LAKE DISTRICT
A6
412
Kentmere Reservoir
485
Kirkstone Pass
663
TARN CRAG
B6261
Orton
Wordsworth
White Moss Common
Rydal Mount
Crookdale Beck
Rydal
Armitt Museum
Tebay
B6260
B6261
R Lune
NATIONAL
Rydal Water
Bridge House
Ambleside
A592
Borrow Beck
38
Kentmere
Green Quarter
Long Sleddale
Tebay
Skelwith Bridge
Galava Fort
Stagshaw Garden
Troutbeck
Townend
Langdale
A685
Low Wray
A591
PARK
River Kent
Low Borrowbridge
The Tarns
Outgate
Lake District
Troutbeck Bridge
A6
High Wray
Windermere
Courthouse
Hawkshead
Ings
Staveley
Watchgate
Windermere Steamboats & Museum
Garth Row
Grayrigg
Cautley Spout (Waterfall)
677
THE CALF
B5285
Hill Top
Bowness-on-Windermere
Far Sawrey
A591
Burneside
Esthwaite Water
B5284
A685
M6
Near Sawrey
Crook
Grizedale
Blackwell
Winster
129
Kendal
130
WINDER
473
National Park Centre
Sedbergh
A5284
Underbarrow
A684
Graythwaite Hall
Crosthwaite
217
New Hutton
Killington Lake (southbound only)
Satterthwaite Head
A592
Windermere
Brigsteer
Oxenholme
Millthrop
Killington
B6254
Middleshaw
Stott Park Bobbin Mill
Natland
Old Hutton
Sizergh Castle
A591
A65
Finsthwaite
0 1 2 3 4 miles
0 1 2 3 4 5 kilometres

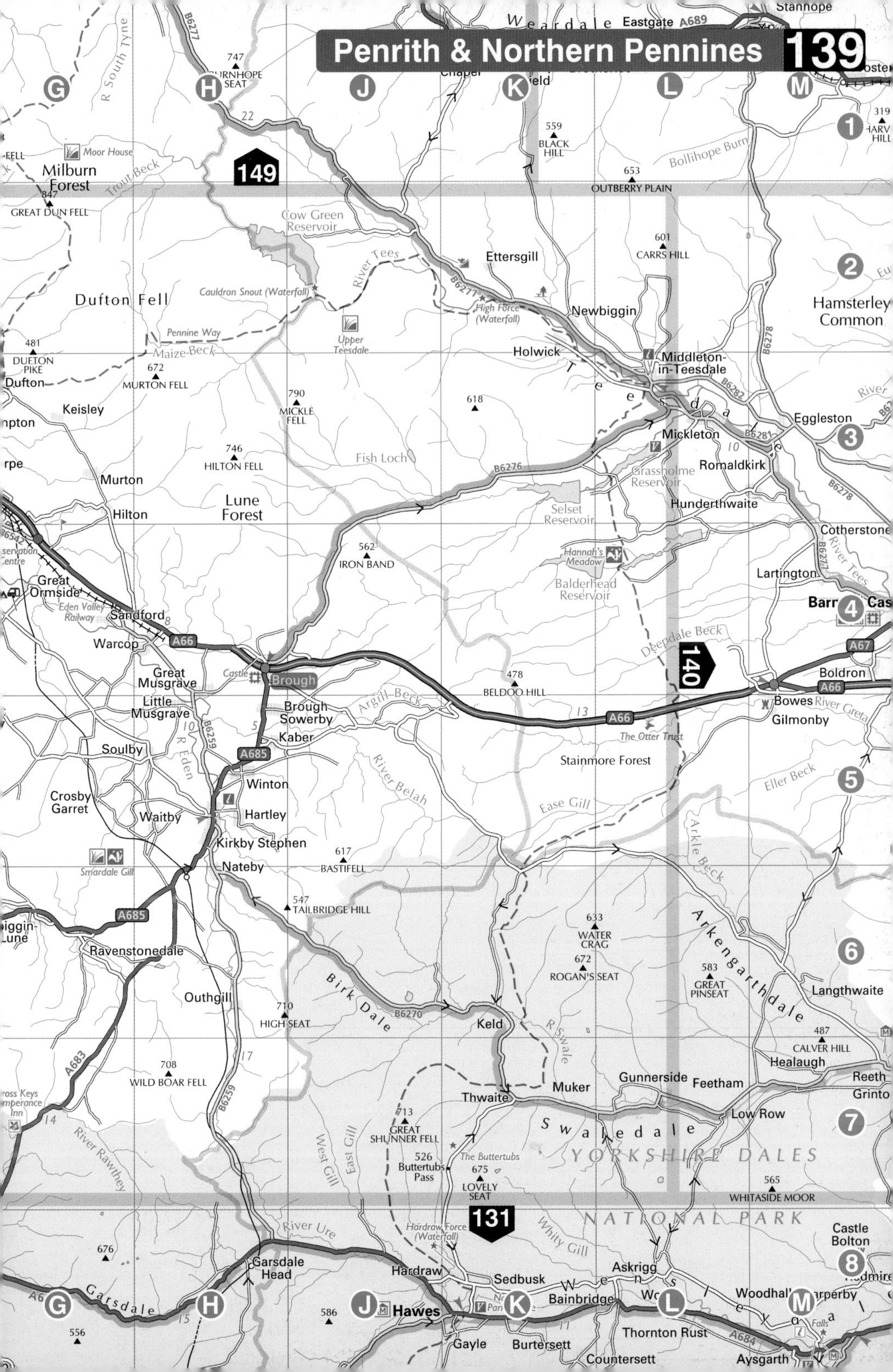
Weardale
Eastgate
Stanhope
BURNHOPE SEAT
Milburn Forest
GREAT DUN FELL
Moor House
Cow Green Reservoir
Cauldron Snout (Waterfall)
River Tees
Dufton Fell
Pennine Way
Maize Beck
DUFTON PIKE
Dufton
MURTON FELL
MICKLE FELL
Keisley
Murton
Hilton
HILTON FELL
Lune Forest
Fish Loch
Upper Teesdale
Ettersgill
High Force (Waterfall)
Newbiggin
Holwick
Middleton-in-Teesdale
Teesdale
Mickleton
Romaldkirk
Eggleston
Hamsterley Common
BLACK HILL
OUTBERRY PLAIN
Bollihope Burn
CARRS HILL
Grassholme Reservoir
Selset Reservoir
Hunderthwaite
Cotherstone
Hannah's Meadow
Balderhead Reservoir
Lartington
IRON BAND
Great Ormside
Eden Valley Railway
Sandford
Warcop
Great Musgrave
Brough
Little Musgrave
Brough Sowerby
Kaber
Argill Beck
BELDOO HILL
Deepdale Beck
Boldron
Bowes
River Greta
Gilmonby
The Otter Trust
Stainmore Forest
Soulby
Crosby Garret
Winton
Hartley
Waitby
River Belah
Ease Gill
Eller Beck
Kirkby Stephen
Nateby
BASTIFELL
Smardale Gill
TAILBRIDGE HILL
Arkle Beck
Arkengarthdale
WATER CRAG
ROGAN'S SEAT
GREAT PINSEAT
Langthwaite
Ravenstonedale
Outhgill
Birk Dale
HIGH SEAT
Keld
R Swale
CALVER HILL
Healaugh
Reeth
WILD BOAR FELL
Thwaite
Muker
Gunnerside
Feetham
Low Row
Swaledale
YORKSHIRE DALES
NATIONAL PARK
GREAT SHUNNER FELL
Buttertubs Pass
The Buttertubs
LOVELY SEAT
WHITASIDE MOOR
River Rawthey
West Gill
East Gill
River Ure
Whity Gill
Hardraw Force (Waterfall)
Castle Bolton
Garsdale Head
Garsdale
Hardraw
Sedbusk
Askrigg
Wensleydale
Hawes
Bainbridge
Woodhall
Carperby
Thornton Rust
Gayle
Burtersett
Countersett
Aysgarth
Falls
A66
A685
A683
A684
A689
B6277
B6276
B6259
B6270
B6278
B6282
B6281
149
140
131

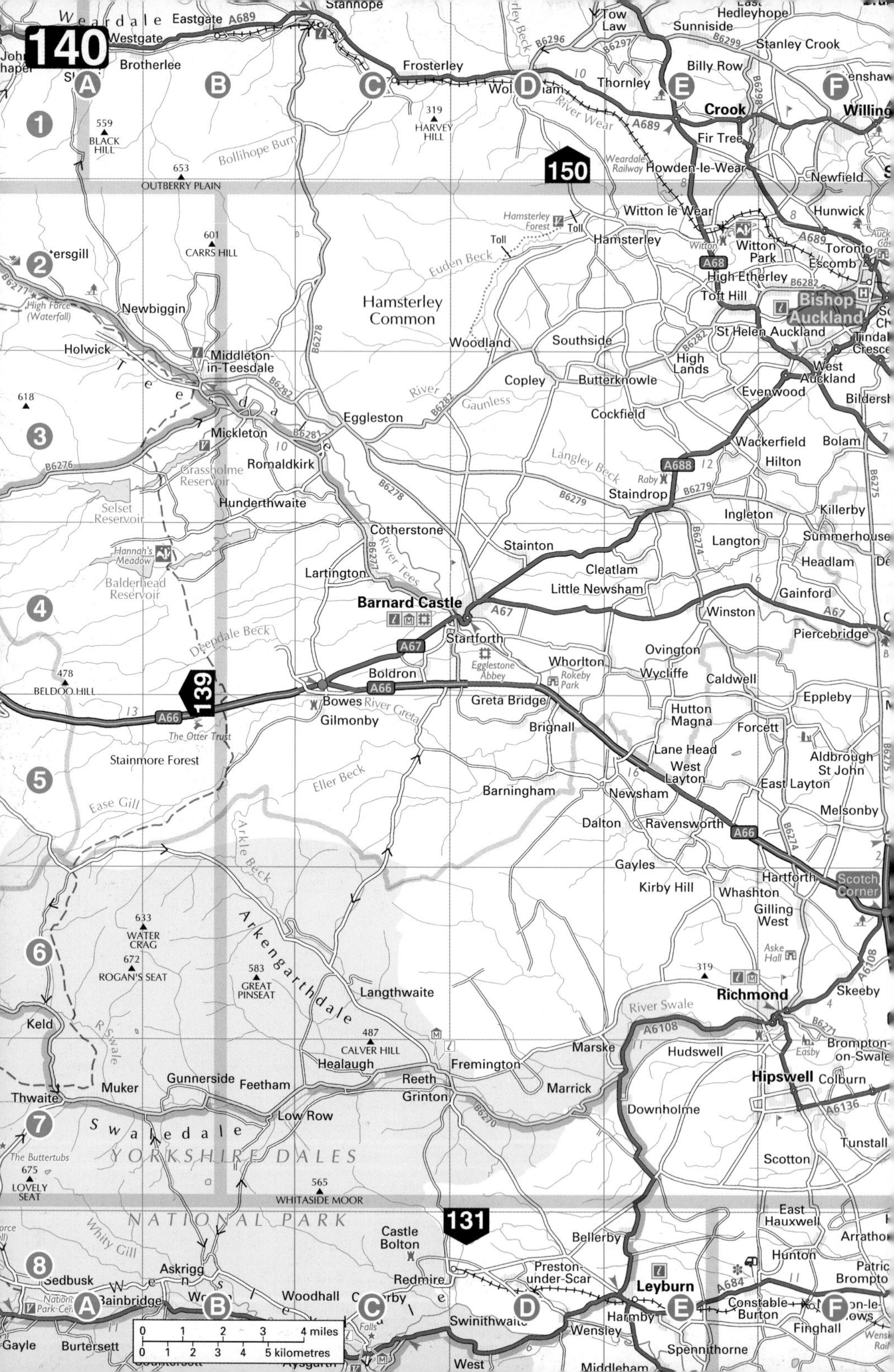
140
150
139
131
Weardale
Eastgate
Westgate
Stanhope
Brotherlee
Frosterley
Wolsingham
Tow Law
Hedleyhope
Sunniside
Stanley Crook
Billy Row
Thornley
Crook
Willington
Fir Tree
Howden-le-Wear
Weardale Railway
River Wear
A689
B6296
B6297
B6299
B6298
559 BLACK HILL
319 HARVEY HILL
653 OUTBERRY PLAIN
Bollihope Burn
Witton le Wear
Hamsterley Forest
Toll
Hamsterley
Witton Park
Newfield
Hunwick
Toronto
Escomb
A68
High Etherley
Toft Hill
B6282
Bishop Auckland
St Helen Auckland
West Auckland
Evenwood
601 CARRS HILL
Euden Beck
Hamsterley Common
Woodland
Southside
High Lands
Copley
Butterknowle
Cockfield
High Force (Waterfall)
B6277
Newbiggin
Holwick
Middleton-in-Teesdale
Teesdale
618
Mickleton
B6281
Eggleston
River Gaunless
B6278
B6276
Grassholme Reservoir
Romaldkirk
Hunderthwaite
Selset Reservoir
Hannah's Meadow
Balderhead Reservoir
Cotherstone
River Tees
Lartington
Barnard Castle
Wackerfield
Bolam
Hilton
Langley Beck
Raby
A688
Staindrop
B6279
Ingleton
Killerby
Stainton
B6274
Langton
Summerhouse
Headlam
Cleatlam
Little Newsham
Gainford
Winston
A67
Piercebridge
B6275
Deepdale Beck
Startforth
Eggleston Abbey
Whorlton
Rokeby Park
Ovington
Wycliffe
Caldwell
Boldron
478 BELDOO HILL
A66
Bowes
River Greta
Gilmonby
Greta Bridge
Brignall
Hutton Magna
Eppleby
Forcett
The Otter Trust
Stainmore Forest
Lane Head
West Layton
Aldbrough St John
East Layton
Eller Beck
Barningham
Newsham
Ease Gill
Dalton
Ravensworth
Melsonby
Arkle Beck
Gayles
Kirby Hill
Hartforth
Whashton
Scotch Corner
Gilling West
633 WATER CRAG
672 ROGAN'S SEAT
583 GREAT PINSEAT
Arkengarthdale
Langthwaite
Aske Hall
319
Richmond
Skeeby
A6108
River Swale
Keld
R Swale
487 CALVER HILL
Healaugh
Fremington
Marske
Hudswell
Easby
Brompton-on-Swale
B6271
Gunnerside
Feetham
Reeth
Grinton
Marrick
Hipswell
Colburn
A6136
Thwaite
Muker
Low Row
B6270
Downholme
Swaledale
YORKSHIRE DALES
Tunstall
The Buttertubs
675 LOVELY SEAT
565 WHITASIDE MOOR
Scotton
NATIONAL PARK
Whity Gill
Castle Bolton
Bellerby
East Hauxwell
Arrathorne
Hunton
Patrick Brompton
Preston-under-Scar
Askrigg
Redmire
Leyburn
A684
Sedbusk
National Park Centre
Bainbridge
Wensleydale
Woodhall
Carperby
Swinithwaite
Harmby
Constable Burton
Finghall
Wensley
Gayle
Burtersett
Aysgarth Falls
Spennithorne
Middleham
West
0 1 2 3 4 miles
0 1 2 3 4 5 kilometres

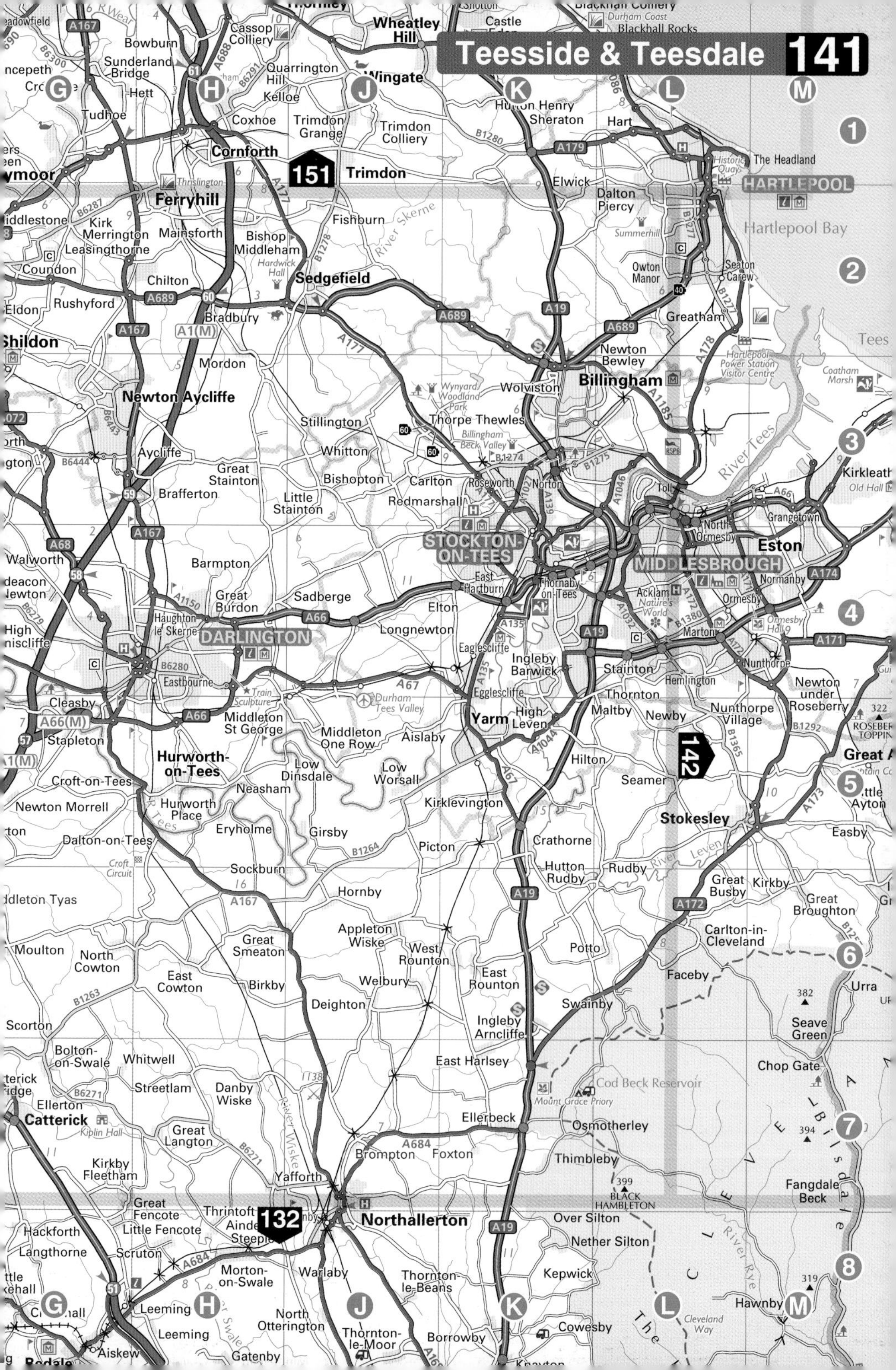
Wheatley Hill
Castle Eden
Blackhall Rocks
Durham Coast
Cassop Colliery
Bowburn
Sunderland Bridge
Quarrington Hill
Wingate
Hett
Kelloe
Hutton Henry
Sheraton
Tudhoe
Coxhoe
Trimdon Grange
Trimdon Colliery
Hart
Cornforth
Trimdon
The Headland
Historic Quay
HARTLEPOOL
Thrislington
Ferryhill
Elwick
Dalton Piercy
Hartlepool Bay
Fishburn
River Skerne
Kirk Merrington
Mainsforth
Bishop Middleham
Summerhill
Leasingthorne
Hardwick Hall
Coundon
Owton Manor
Seaton Carew
Chilton
Sedgefield
Rushyford
Eldon
Bradbury
Greatham
Shildon
Mordon
Newton Bewley
Tees
Hartlepool Power Station Visitor Centre
Coatham Marsh
Billingham
Wynyard Woodland Park
Wolviston
Newton Aycliffe
Stillington
Thorpe Thewles
Billingham Beck Valley
RSPB
River Tees
Aycliffe
Whitton
Great Stainton
Bishopton
Carlton
Roseworth
Norton
Kirkleatham
Old Hall
Brafferton
Little Stainton
Redmarshall
Toll
North Ormesby
Grangetown
STOCKTON-ON-TEES
Eston
Walworth
Barmpton
MIDDLESBROUGH
Heighington
Great Burdon
Sadberge
East Hartburn
Thornaby-on-Tees
Normanby
Ormesby
Acklam
Nature's World
High Coniscliffe
Haughton le Skerne
Elton
DARLINGTON
Longnewton
Ormesby Hall
Marton
Eaglescliffe
Ingleby Barwick
Stainton
Hemlington
Nunthorpe
Eastbourne
Train Sculpture
Egglescliffe
Thornton
Newton under Roseberry
Cleasby
Durham Tees Valley
Maltby
Nunthorpe Village
Middleton St George
Yarm
High Leven
Newby
ROSEBERRY TOPPING
Stapleton
Middleton One Row
Aislaby
Great Ayton
Hurworth-on-Tees
Low Dinsdale
Low Worsall
Hilton
Croft-on-Tees
Neasham
Seamer
Little Ayton
Newton Morrell
Hurworth Place
Kirklevington
Stokesley
Dalton-on-Tees
Eryholme
Girsby
Crathorne
Easby
Picton
Croft Circuit
Sockburn
Hutton Rudby
Rudby
River Leven
Great Busby
Kirkby
Middleton Tyas
Hornby
Great Broughton
Appleton Wiske
Carlton-in-Cleveland
Great Smeaton
Moulton
North Cowton
West Rounton
Potto
East Cowton
Faceby
Birkby
Welbury
East Rounton
Urra
Deighton
Swainby
Scorton
Ingleby Arncliffe
Seave Green
Bolton-on-Swale
Whitwell
East Harlsey
Chop Gate
Catterick Bridge
Streetlam
Danby Wiske
Cod Beck Reservoir
Mount Grace Priory
Ellerton
River Wiske
Catterick
Kiplin Hall
Great Langton
Ellerbeck
Osmotherley
Kirkby Fleetham
Brompton
Foxton
Thimbleby
BLACK HAMBLETON
Fangdale Beck
Yafforth
Great Fencote
Thrintoft
Northallerton
Little Fencote
Ainderby Steeple
Over Silton
Hackforth
Nether Silton
Langthorne
Scruton
Morton-on-Swale
Warlaby
Thornton-le-Beans
Kepwick
River Rye
Bilsdale
Cleveland
Leeming
North Otterington
Hawnby
Cleveland Way
Cowesby
Aiskew
Thornton-le-Moor
Borrowby
Gatenby
151
142
132

142
A
B
C
D
E
F
151
133
141
1
2
3
4
5
6
7
8
Castle Eden
Blackhall Colliery
Durham Coast
Blackhall Rocks
Hutton Henry
Sheraton
Hart
A179
A1086
The Headland
Historic Quay
HARTLEPOOL
Hartlepool Bay
Elwick
Dalton Piercy
Summerhill
Owton Manor
Seaton Carew
B1277
A19
A689
Greatham
A178
Newton Bewley
Billingham
Wolviston
Thorpe Thewles
Hartlepool Power Station Visitor Centre
Tees Bay
Coatham Marsh
Redcar
Marske-by-the-Sea
Saltburn-by-the-Sea
Saltburn Smugglers
A1185
B1274
B1275
Roseworth
Norton
A139
A1027
A1046
River Tees
Toll
A66
Kirkleatham
Old Hall
A1042
B1269
A1085
A174
New Marske
Upleatham
Brotton
Skelton
Kilton
Loftus
STOCKTON-ON-TEES
MIDDLESBROUGH
North Ormesby
Grangetown
Eston
Normanby
Wilton
Dunsdale
B1268
A173
Boosbeck
Lingdale
Kilton Thorpe
Easington
East Hartburn
Thornaby-on-Tees
Acklam
Nature's World
Ormesby
Ormesby Hall
A1032
A172
B1380
Marton
A135
A171
Margrove Park
Woodhill
Stanghow
Liverton
Guisborough
Guisborough Forest
Eaglescliffe
Egglescliffe
Ingleby Barwick
Stainton
Hemlington
Nunthorpe
Thornton
Maltby
Newby
Nunthorpe Village
Newton under Roseberry
Hutton Lowcross
Cleveland Way
Moorsholm
B1366
Scaling
Gerrick
Yarm
High Leven
A1044
A67
Hilton
Seamer
B1365
B1292
322
ROSEBERRY TOPPING
Great Ayton
Captain Cook Monument
Commondale
Little Ayton
Kildale
The Moors Centre
301
Danby
Castleton
Ainthorpe
Lealholm
River Esk
Kirklevington
Crathorne
Stokesley
Easby
Battersby
Hutton Rudby
Rudby
River Leven
Great Busby
Kirkby
Great Broughton
Ingleby Greenhow
Westerdale
Glaisdale
Carlton-in-Cleveland
B1257
Potto
East Rounton
Faceby
382
Urra
454
URRA MOOR
Swainby
Seave Green
Ingleby Arncliffe
East Harlsey
Chop Gate
369
Cod Beck Reservoir
Mount Grace Priory
Church Houses
Ellerbeck
Osmotherley
394
Bilsdale
Thorgill
Rosedale Abbey
Thimbleby
338
Low Mill
Rosedale
399
BLACK HAMBLETON
Fangdale Beck
River Seven
Over Silton
Nether Silton
River Rye
Bransdale
Farndale
Kepwick
319
Lastingham
Hawnby
Gillamoor
Hutton-le-Hole
Spaunton
Fadmoor
Appleton-le-Moors
Cropton
Knayton
CLEVELAND HILLS
NORTH YORK MOORS NATIONAL PARK
0 1 2 3 4 miles
0 1 2 3 4 5 kilometres

Staithes
Heritage Centre
Runswick Bay
Runswick
North Yorkshire and Cleveland Heritage Coast
Goldsborough
Ellerby
Overdale Wyke
Lythe
A174
Mickleby
Sandsend
Sandsend Wyke
West Barnby
East Barnby
Whitby
Saltwick Bay
Abbey
Dunsley
Newholm
Ugthorpe
Ruswarp
Briggswath
Stainsacre
A171
Aislaby
Sneaton
High Hawsker
Sleights
Ugglebarnby
B1447
Egton
Iburndale
Ness Point or North Cheek
Esk Dale
Grosmont
Robin Hood's Bay
A169
Fylingthorpe
Robin Hood's Bay
B1416
Old Peak or South Cheek
A171
Goathland
Ravenscar
292
North Yorkshire Moors Railway
Eller Beck
Staintondale
Shire Horse Centre
Wheeldale Roman Road
Hayburn Wyke
M O O R S
Harwood Dale
Newtondale Forest Drive
Cloughton Wyke
Stape
Cloughton
Hole of Horcum
134
A165
Cromer Point
Burniston
Bridestones (Rock Formation)
Bickley
Broxa
Silpho
Cleveland Way
Levisham
Toll
Langdale End
Suffield
Hackness
Dalby Forest Drive
Scalby
Scarborough
Castle
239
Sea Cut
North Riding Forest Park
Falsgrave
Hatherleigh Deep Sea Trawler
G H J K L M
1 2 3 4 5 6 7 8

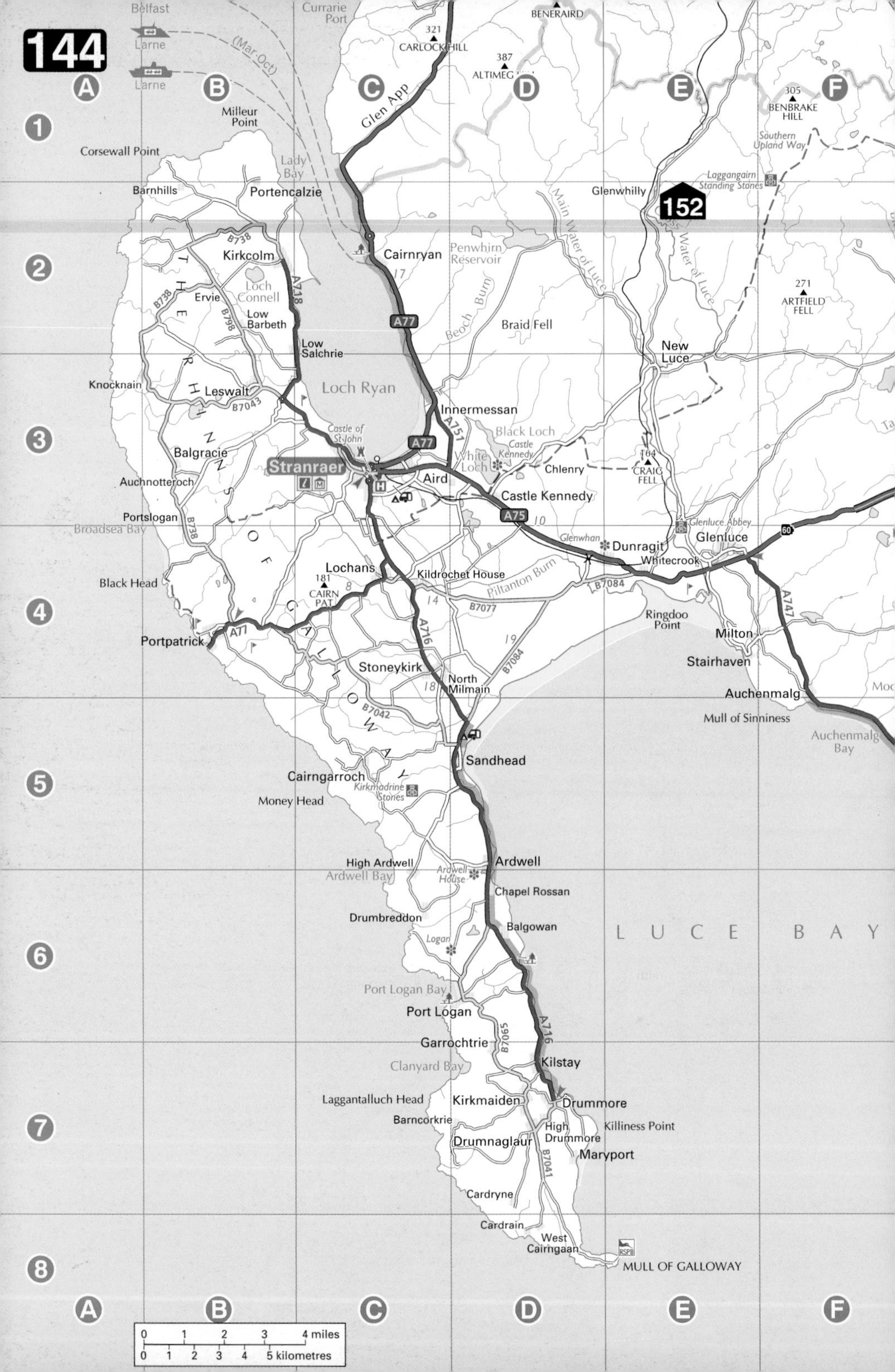

0 1 2 3 4 miles
0 1 2 3 4 5 kilometres

Creebank
Bargrennan
Glen Trool
Drumlamford
716
LAMACHAN HILL
654
Loch
Bruce's
G
H
J
K
L
M
1
2
3
4
5
6
7
8
A712
Black Water of Dee
Loch Ochiltree
440
GARLICK HILL
Galloway Deer Range
402
ROUND FELL
Knowe
River Bladnoch
153
471
FELL OF FLEET
184
FELL
G A L L O W A Y
Loch Grannoch
Loch Fleet
208
AUCHENCLOY HILL
Skerrow
Carseriggan
Challoch
R Cree
Penkill Burn
Minnigaff
710
CAIRNSMORE OF FLEET
Barfad
Newton Stewart
Creebridge
Kirroughtree
214
CULVENNAN FELL
Big Water of Fleet
Little Water of Fleet
335
WHITE TOP OF CULREACH
Shennanton
A714
Palnure
A75
Baltersan
Upper Ruscoe
Craighlaw
Kirkcowan
B733
B735
Causeway End
R Bladnoch
Gem Rock
B796
Fleet Valley
146
Creetown
Gatehouse of Fleet
Clugston
Torhouse Stone Circle
Kirkmabreck
455
CAIRNHARROW
Anwoth
Cardoness Castle
Fell Loch
THE
B7052
B733
Wigtown
Bladnoch
Carsluith
Cairnholy Chambered Cairns
Carsluith Castle
B7005
MACHARS
Kirwaugh
Water of Malzie
Girthon
Braehead
Ravenshall Point
Mossyard
Fleet Bay
Lennox Plunton
B7005
B7052
B7085
Kirkinner
Orchardton Bay
Culshabbin
Margrie
Barrachan
Whauphill
B7004
Culscadden
Islands of Fleet
Chapel Finian (ruin)
Little Airies
A746
Kirkandrews
Elrig
Druchtag Motte
B7085
Sorbie
B7052
Wigtown Bay
Garlieston
Mochrum
Drumtrodden Cup & Ring
Pouton
Borness
Drumtrodden Standing Stones
Drummoddie
Broughton Mains
Cruggleton Bay
Ringdoo Point
Port William
Big Balcraig
B7004
B7063
'Wren's Egg' Standing Stones
B7021
Priory
Barsalloch Fort
Monreith
Whithorn Story
Barsalloch Point
Whithorn
Rispain Camp
Point of Leg
A747
Portyerrock
St Ninian's Cave
B7004
Kidsdale
Isle of Whithorn
St Ninian's Chapel (ruin)
Cutcloy
BURROW HEAD

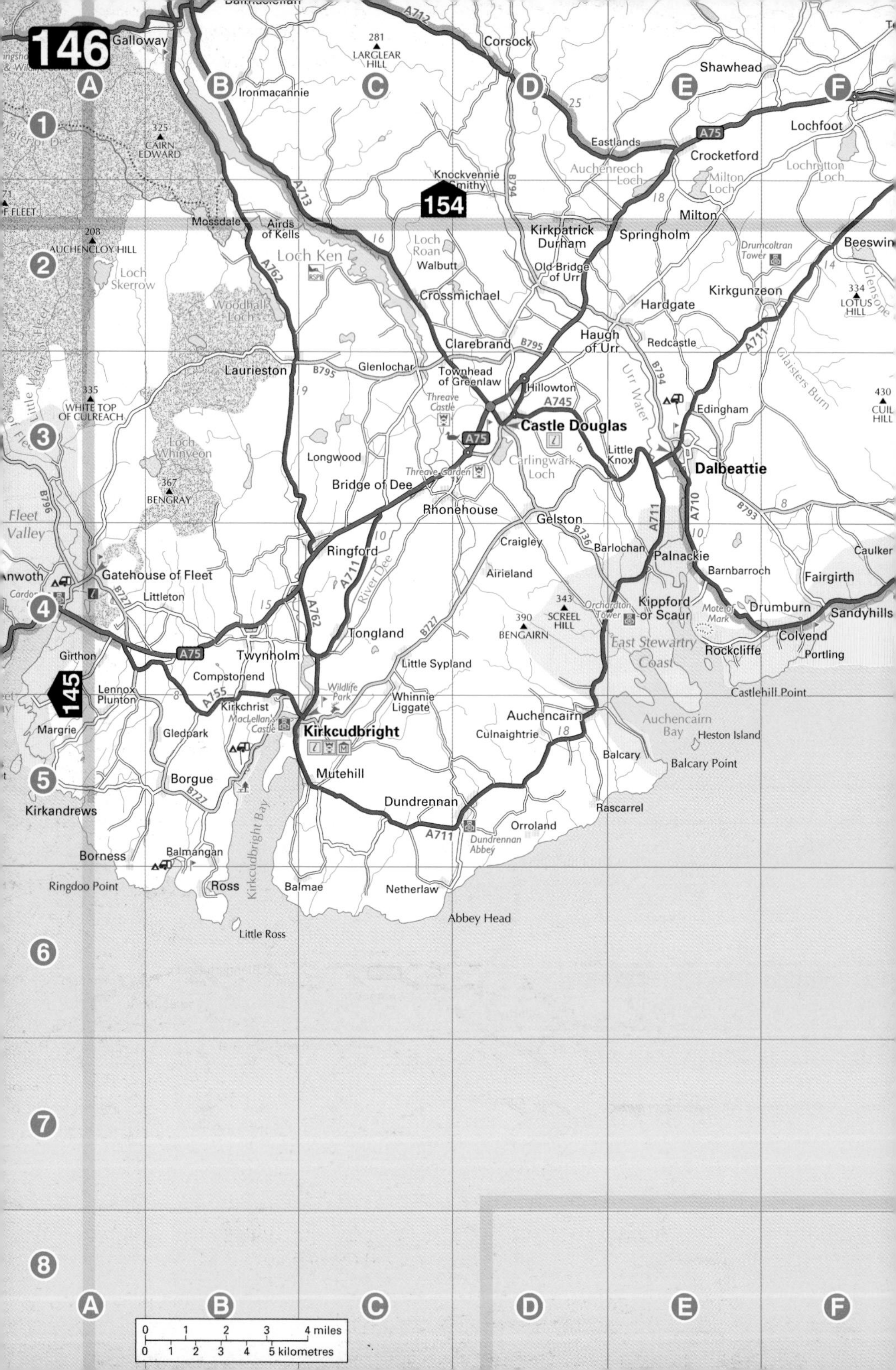

146
154
145
Galloway
Corsock
Shawhead
Ironmacannie
LARGLEAR HILL
CAIRN EDWARD
Lochfoot
Eastlands
Crocketford
Auchenreoch Loch
Milton Loch
Lochrutton Loch
Knockvennie Smithy
Mossdale
Airds of Kells
Milton
Kirkpatrick Durham
Springholm
Beeswing
AUCHENCLOY HILL
Loch Ken
Loch Roan
Walbutt
Drumcoltran Tower
Loch Skerrow
Old Bridge of Urr
Kirkgunzeon
LOTUS HILL
Woodhall Loch
Crossmichael
Hardgate
Haugh of Urr
Clarebrand
Redcastle
Laurieston
Glenlochar
Townhead of Greenlaw
Hillowton
Threave Castle
Urr Water
Glaisters Burn
WHITE TOP OF CULREACH
Edingham
CUIL HILL
Castle Douglas
Loch Whinyeon
Longwood
Carlingwark Loch
Little Knox
Dalbeattie
Threave Garden
Bridge of Dee
BENGRAY
Rhonehouse
Fleet Valley
Gelston
Craigley
Barlochan
Ringford
Palnackie
Caulker
Airieland
Barnbarroch
Fairgirth
Gatehouse of Fleet
River Dee
Littleton
SCREEL HILL
Kippford or Scaur
Orchardton Tower
Drumburn
Sandyhills
BENGAIRN
Mote of Mark
Colvend
Tongland
East Stewartry Coast
Rockcliffe
Portling
Girthon
Twynholm
Little Sypland
Compstonend
Lennox Plunton
Kirkchrist
Wildlife Park
Whinnie Liggate
Castlehill Point
Auchencairn
Auchencairn Bay
MacLellan's Castle
Heston Island
Margrie
Gledpark
Kirkcudbright
Culnaightrie
Balcary
Balcary Point
Mutehill
Borgue
Kirkandrews
Dundrennan
Rascarrel
Kirkcudbright Bay
Orroland
Dundrennan Abbey
Balmangan
Borness
Ringdoo Point
Ross
Balmae
Netherlaw
Abbey Head
Little Ross
A B C D E F
1 2 3 4 5 6 7 8
0 1 2 3 4 miles
0 1 2 3 4 5 kilometres

Roucan
240
CARTHAT HILL
Waterbeck
Roman Camp
Lincluden
Maxwell Town
Dumfries
Kettleholm
Collin
Greenlea
Racks
Dalton
Ecclefechan
Hoddom Cross
Thomas Carlyle's Birthplace
Eaglesfield
Merkland Cross
Islesteps
Kingholm Quay
Mouswald
Carrutherstown
Hoddom Mains
Kirtlebridge
Bonshaw Tower
Robgill Tower
Brydekirk
Kirkconnell Flow
Kelton
Conheath
Kelhead
Creca
Hollee
Glencaple
Bankend
Clarencefield
Ruthwell Cross
Kirkconnell
Annan
Nith Estuary
Ruthwell
Howes
Corn Mill
Sweetheart Abbey
New Abbey
Shearington
Caerlaverock Castle
Bowhouse
Ingleston
Blackshaw
Wildlife & Wetlands Trust Centre
Savings Bank
Cummertrees
Powfoot
Dornock
Eastriggs
Newbie
Loch Kindar
569
CRIFFELL
Torduff Point
Bowness-on-Solway
Port Carlisle
Glasson
Hadrian's Wall Path
Drumburgh
Bowness Common
Drumburgh Moss
Carse Bay
Kirkbean
Carsethorn
Cardurnock
Borron Point
Grune Point
Anthorn
Arbigland
SOLWAY FIRTH
Mainsriddle
Skinburness
Moricambe Bay
Kirkbride
Loaningfoot
Gill Foot Bay
Southerness
Southerness Point
Newton Arlosh
Wedholme Flow
Silloth
Seaville
Biglands
Abbey Town
Holm Cultram
Kelsick
Dundraw
Oulton
Lessonhall
Beckfoot
R Waver
Waverbridge
Wigton
Newtown
Blencogo
Waverton
Holme St Cuthbert
Mawbray
Bromfield
Dubmill Point
Langrigg
Bolton Low Houses
Westnewton
Allonby
Fletchertown
Allonby Bay
Hayton
Aspatria
Blennerhasset
Boltongate
Prospect
Oughterside
Torpenhow
Allerby
Crosscanonby
Crosby
Plumbland
Bothel
Ireby
Gilcrux
High Ireby
Uldale
Fort
River Ellen
Maryport
Dearham
447
BINSEY
Sunderland
Tallentire
Blindcrake
Bridekirk
Trotters World of Animals
Flimby
Broughton Moor
R Derwent
Standingstone
Dovenby
Bassenthwaite
Great Broughton
Papcastle
Camerton
Embleton
Seaton
Great Clifton
Cockermouth
Brigham
Bassenthwaite Lake
Greysouthen
Stainburn
Little Clifton
Eaglesfield
Mirehouse
931
DODD
Workington
Mossbay
Westfield
Moss Bay
Deanscales
552
LORDS SEAT
A75
A709
A780
A710
A725
B725
B7020
B723
B724
B7076
B722
A74(M)
B5307
B5302
B5300
B5301
A596
B5299
A595
A591
A594
A66
B5291
155
136
137
148
G
H
J
K
L
M
1
2
3
4
5
6
7
8

148
156
147
137
138
A
B
C
D
E
F
1
2
3
4
5
6
7
8
Waterbeck
Solwaybank
Hollows
Harelaw
Sleetbeck
Evertown
B6357
B720
Rowanburn
Canonbie
Pentonbridge
Milltown
Woodhouselees
Timpanheck
B7201
B6318
Eaglesfield
Chapelknowe
Merkland Cross
B6357
R Sark
Kirkpatrick-Fleming
Robgill Tower
Creca
Hollee
B7076
Gretna
B6357
Springfield
Longtown
A6071
Gretna Green
A75
Rigg
Gretna
B721
Eastriggs
River Esk
River Lyne
Kirklinton
Boltonfellend
Hethersgill
Kirkcambeck
A7
A6071
Redkirk Point
Torduff Point
Westlinton
Smithfield
Walton
Scalebyhill
Scaleby
Hadrian's Wall Path
Burtholme
Newtown
M6
Laversdale
R Irthing
R Eden
Todhills
Port Carlisle
Glasson
Rockcliffe
Oldwall
Brampton
Irthington
Carlisle
Solway Aviation
Hadrian's Wall Path
Drumburgh
Burgh by Sands
Beaumont
Low Crosby
A689
High Crosby
Newby East
Cargo
Grinsdale
Drumburgh Moss
Monkhill
Kirkandrews upon Eden
Knowlefield
Linstock
Talkin Tarn
Thurstonfield
Moorhouse
Stanwix
CARLISLE
Warwick Bridge
A69
Hayton
Talkin
Finglandrigg Woods
B5307
Castle
Kirkbampton
Belle Vue
How Mill
Little Bampton
Little Orton
A689
Morton
Harraby
Fenton
Heads Nook
Scotby
Castle Carrock
Great Orton
Newby West
Wetheral
Great Corby
Wetheral Priory Gatehouse
Aikton
Wiggonby
Cummersdale
Upperby
Biglands
Blackwell
M6
A595
Cumwhinton
Cumwhitton
B6263
Drumleaning
B6413
River Eden
A596
Thursby
Dalston
Cotehill
Wigton
Buckabank
West Curthwaite
Wreay
B5302
B5299
Gaitsgill
Chalk Beck
Low Hesket
Aiketgate
Ainstable
Rosley
Southwaite
Armathwaite
A595
B5305
Westward
Welton
Southwaite
High Hesket
R Petteril
R Ive
Ivegill
Staffield
A6
Boltongate
343
FAULDS BROW
Sebergham
M6
Kirkoswald
Caldbeck
Calthwaite
Roe Beck
Lazonby
Ireby
B5299
Hesket Newmarket
B5305
Hutton End
247
LAZONBY FELL
Glassonby
Uldale
B6413
Salkeld Dykes
Great Salkeld
Branthwaite
Plumpton
Little Salkeld
Lamonby
Ellonby
Skelton
Hutton-in-the-Forest
B6412
663
CARROCK FELL
B5305
710
KNOTT
Hutton Roof
Little Blencow
Catterlen
Langwathby
Johnby
Bassenthwaite
Great Blencow
Newton Reigny
690
GREAT CALVA
River Caldew
BOWSCALE FELL
Mungrisdale
357
BERRIER HILL
Greystoke
Thacka Beck
Penrith
B5288
Castle
A686
931
DAW
Berrier
Motherby
Newbiggin
Mayburgh Henge
Brougham Castle
Mirehouse
Tarn Moss
Penruddock
Stainton
Eamont Bridge
A66
Dalemain
Rheged Discovery Centre
Yanwath
Clifton Hall
0 1 2 3 4 miles
0 1 2 3 4 5 kilometres

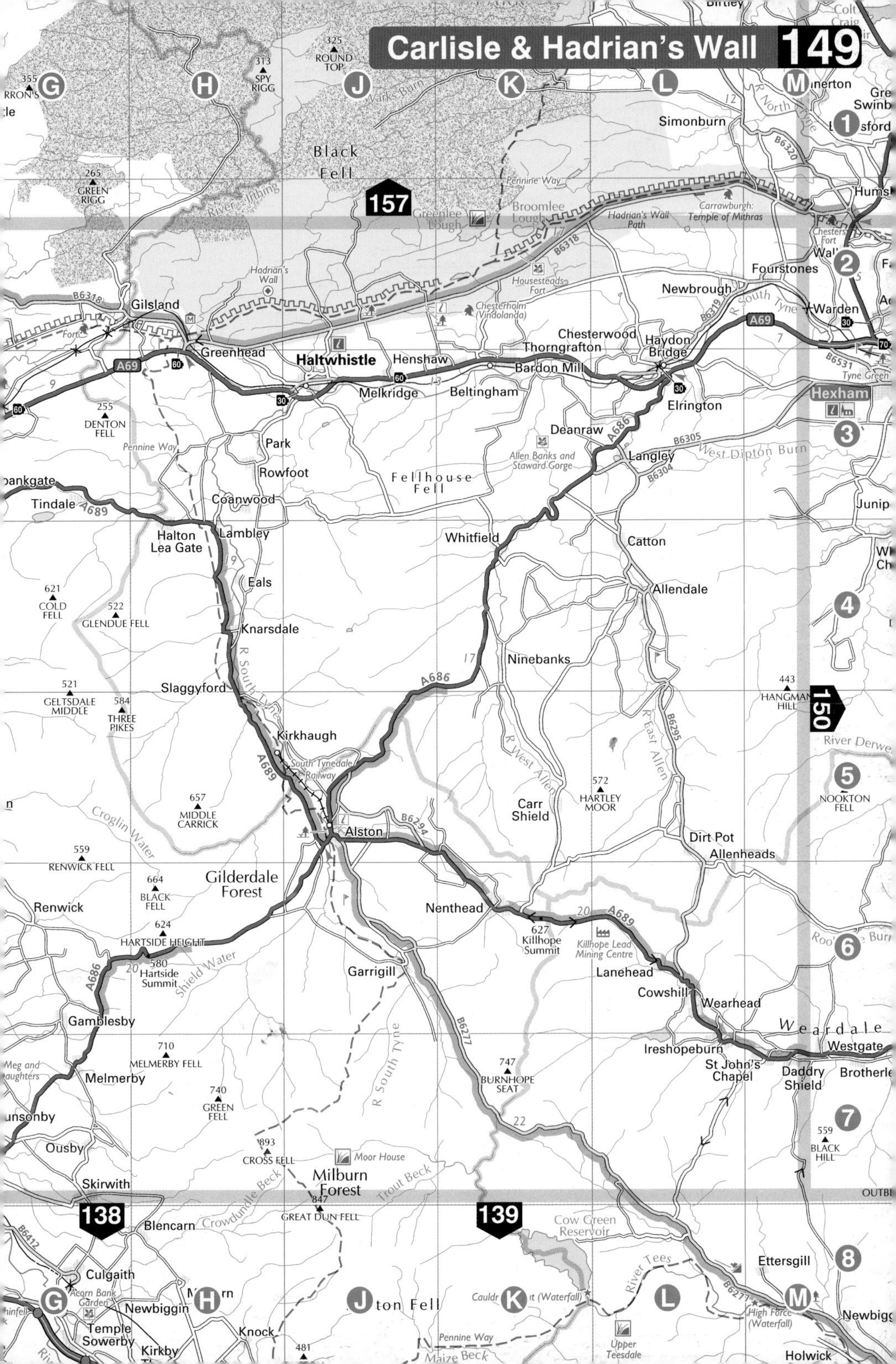
Carlisle & Hadrian's Wall
149
157
150
138
139
G
H
J
K
L
M
1
2
3
4
5
6
7
8
355
313
SPY
RIGG
325
ROUND
TOP
Warks Burn
Simonburn
Black
Fell
265
GREEN
RIGG
River Irthing
Pennine Way
Broomlee
Lough
Greenlee
Lough
B6320
R North Tyne
Humshaugh
Hadrian's Wall
Path
Carrawburgh:
Temple of Mithras
Chesters
Fort
Wall
Fourstones
Newbrough
Warden
Hadrian's
Wall
Housesteads
Fort
Chesterholm
(Vindolanda)
B6318
B6318
B6319
R South Tyne
Gilsland
Fort
Greenhead
Haltwhistle
Henshaw
Thorngrafton
Chesterwood
Haydon
Bridge
Bardon Mill
A69
A69
B6531
Tyne Green
Hexham
Melkridge
Beltingham
Elrington
255
DENTON
FELL
Pennine Way
Park
Deanraw
A686
Allen Banks and
Staward Gorge
Langley
B6305
West Dipton Burn
B6304
Rowfoot
Fellhouse
Fell
Coanwood
Tindale
A689
Halton
Lea Gate
Lambley
Whitfield
Catton
Eals
621
COLD
FELL
522
GLENDUE FELL
Allendale
Knarsdale
Ninebanks
A686
521
GELTSDALE
MIDDLE
584
THREE
PIKES
Slaggyford
R South Tyne
443
HANGMAN
HILL
B6295
R East Allen
River Derwent
Kirkhaugh
R West Allen
South Tynedale
Railway
A689
572
HARTLEY
MOOR
NOOKTON
FELL
Croglin Water
657
MIDDLE
CARRICK
Carr
Shield
Alston
B6294
Dirt Pot
Allenheads
559
RENWICK FELL
664
BLACK
FELL
Gilderdale
Forest
Renwick
Nenthead
A689
624
HARTSIDE HEIGHT
627
Killhope
Summit
Killhope Lead
Mining Centre
580
Hartside
Summit
Shield Water
A686
Garrigill
Lanehead
Cowshill
Wearhead
Gamblesby
Weardale
Westgate
710
MELMERBY FELL
B6277
Ireshopeburn
St John's
Chapel
747
BURNHOPE
SEAT
Daddry
Shield
Brotherlee
Meg and
Daughters
Melmerby
740
GREEN
FELL
R South Tyne
559
BLACK
HILL
Ousby
893
CROSS FELL
Moor House
Milburn
Forest
Trout Beck
Crowdundle Beck
Skirwith
847
GREAT DUN FELL
Blencarn
Cow Green
Reservoir
B6412
Culgaith
Ettersgill
River Tees
Acorn Bank
Garden
Newbiggin
Temple
Sowerby
Kirkby
Knock
Cauldron Snout (Waterfall)
B6277
High Force
(Waterfall)
Newbiggin
481
Pennine Way
Maize Beck
Upper
Teesdale
Holwick

150
158
149
140
Ponteland
Darras Hall
Corbridge
Hexham
Prudhoe
Ryton
Blaydon
Rowland's Gill
Burnopfield
Stanley
Leadgate
Annfield Plain
Consett
Castleside
Lanchester
Stanhope
Crook
Bishop Auckland
Hamsterley
Frosterley
Wolsingham
Tow Law
Blanchland
Edmundbyers
Hunstanworth
Rookhope
Westgate
Eastgate
Weardale
Slaley
Riding Mill
Stocksfield
Wylam
Ovingham
Horsley
Heddon-on-the-Wall
Matfen
Stamfordham
Humshaugh
Chollerton
Barrasford
Acomb
Sandhoe
Halton
Aydon
Dilston
Bywell
Ebchester
Shotley Bridge
Medomsley
Dipton
Tanfield
Witton le Wear
Howden-le-Wear
Toft Hill
Hamsterley Common
Allenheads
High Force (Waterfall)
Hadrian's Wall
Derwent Reservoir
River Derwent
River Wear
A68
A69
A695
A689
A692
A693
A691
A6076
A694
A696
0 1 2 3 4 miles
0 1 2 3 4 5 kilometres

Whitley Bay
Tynemouth
159
North Shields
Longbenton
Wallsend
Jarrow
SOUTH SHIELDS
Hebburn
Felling
GATESHEAD
Cleadon
Whitburn
Souter Point
East Boldon
Birtley
WASHINGTON
SUNDERLAND
Seaham
Houghton-le-Spring
Hetton-le-Hole
Chester-le-Street
Great Lumley
Murton
Easington Colliery
Easington
Peterlee
Durham
Shotton Colliery
Haswell
Thornley
Wheatley Hill
Blackhall Colliery
Wingate
Cornforth
Trimdon
Ferryhill
141
142
HARTLEPOOL
The Headland
Sedgefield
IJmuiden
Durham Heritage Coast

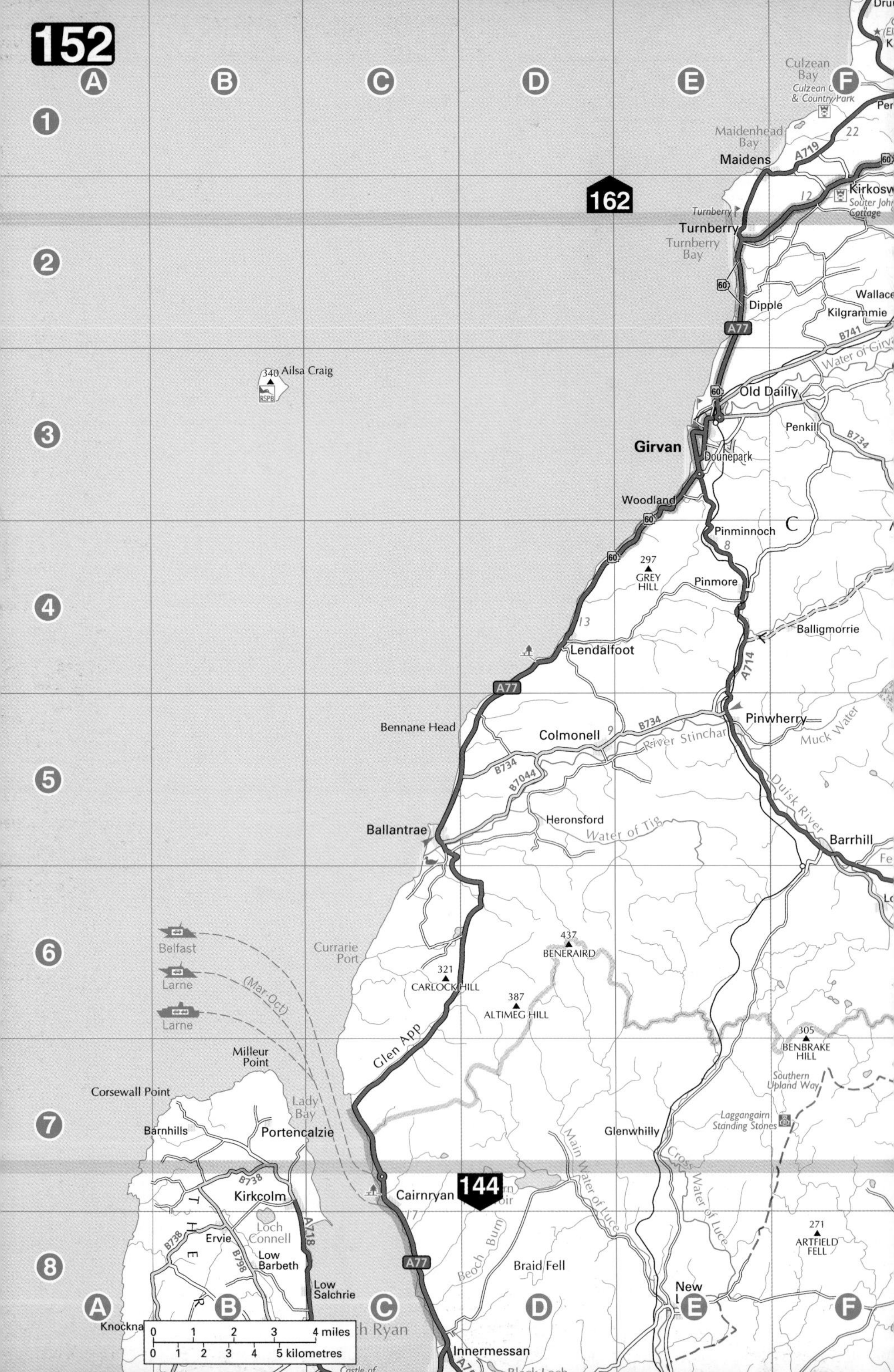

162
144
Ailsa Craig
340
RSPB
Culzean Bay
Culzean Castle & Country Park
Maidenhead Bay
Maidens
A719
Kirkoswald
Souter Johnnie's Cottage
Turnberry
Turnberry Bay
Dipple
Wallacetown
Kilgrammie
B741
Water of Girvan
A77
Old Dailly
Penkill
B734
Girvan
Dounepark
Woodland
Pinminnoch
297
GREY HILL
Pinmore
Balligmorrie
Lendalfoot
A714
Pinwherry
Muck Water
Bennane Head
Colmonell
River Stinchar
B7044
Duisk River
Heronsford
Water of Tig
Ballantrae
Barrhill
437
BENERAIRD
321
CARLOCK HILL
387
ALTIMEG HILL
Currarie Port
Belfast
Larne
(Mar-Oct)
Glen App
305
BENBRAKE HILL
Southern Upland Way
Milleur Point
Corsewall Point
Lady Bay
Laggangairn Standing Stones
Barnhills
Portencalzie
Glenwhilly
Main Water of Luce
Cross Water of Luce
B738
Kirkcolm
Cairnryan
Loch Connell
Ervie
B798
A718
271
ARTFIELD FELL
Low Barbeth
Beoch Burn
Braid Fell
Low Salchrie
New Luce
Innermessan
0 1 2 3 4 miles
0 1 2 3 4 5 kilometres

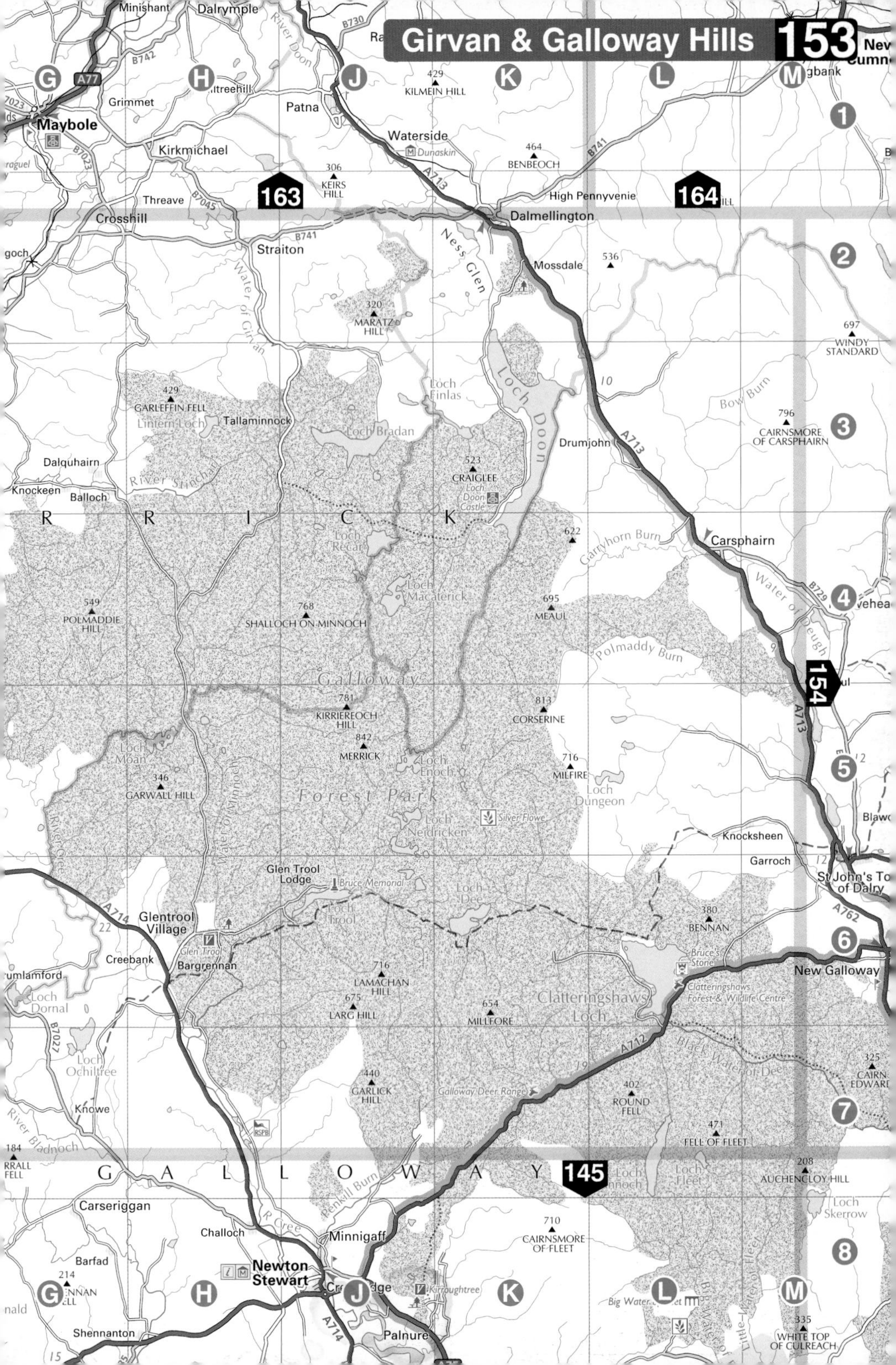

Minishant
Dalrymple
Maybole
Grimmet
Patna
Waterside
Dunaskin
KILMEIN HILL
BENBEOCH
Kirkmichael
KEIRS HILL
Threave
Crosshill
High Pennyvenie
Dalmellington
Straiton
Mossdale
Ness Glen
Water of Girvan
MARATZ HILL
WINDY STANDARD
Loch Doon
Loch Finlas
Loch Bradan
GARLEFFIN FELL
Tallaminnock
Linfern Loch
Drumjohn
CAIRNSMORE OF CARSPHAIRN
Bow Burn
Dalquhairn
CRAIGLEE
Loch Doon Castle
Knockeen
Balloch
River Stinchar
R R I C K
Carsphairn
Garryhorn Burn
Loch Recar
Loch Macaterick
Water of Deugh
POLMADDIE HILL
SHALLOCH ON MINNOCH
MEAUL
Polmaddy Burn
Galloway
KIRRIEREOCH HILL
CORSERINE
MERRICK
Loch Enoch
MILFIRE
Loch Moan
GARWALL HILL
Forest Park
Loch Dungeon
Loch Neldricken
Silver Flowe
Water of Minnoch
River Cree
Knocksheen
Garroch
Glen Trool Lodge
Bruce Memorial
Loch Dee
Loch Trool
St John's Town of Dalry
BENNAN
Glentrool Village
Glen Trool
Creebank
Bargrennan
Bruce's Stone
New Galloway
Loch Dornal
LAMACHAN HILL
LARG HILL
MILLFORE
Clatteringshaws Loch
Clatteringshaws Forest & Wildlife Centre
Loch Ochiltree
Black Water of Dee
GARLICK HILL
Galloway Deer Range
ROUND FELL
FELL OF FLEET
Knowe
River Bladnoch
RSPB
G A L L O W A Y
Loch Fleet
AUCHENCLOY HILL
Loch Skerrow
Carseriggan
Penkill Burn
R Cree
Minnigaff
CAIRNSMORE OF FLEET
Challoch
Barfad
Newton Stewart
Kirroughtree
Big Water of Fleet
Little Water of Fleet
Palnure
Shennanton
WHITE TOP OF CULREACH

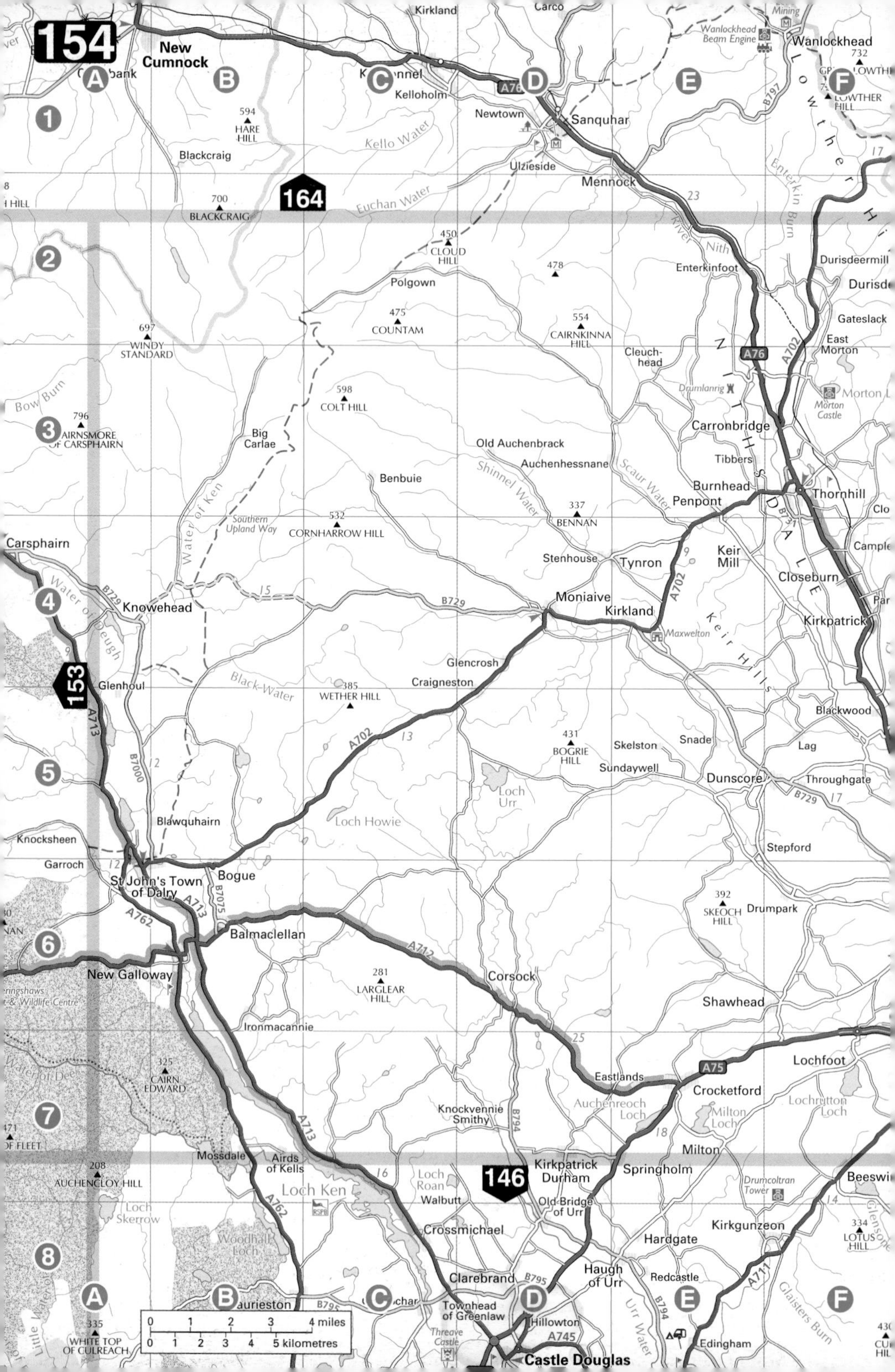
154
New Cumnock
Kirkland
Carco
Wanlockhead Beam Engine
Wanlockhead
Kelloholm
Newtown
Sanquhar
Kello Water
Hare Hill
Blackcraig
Ulzieside
Mennock
164
Blackcraig
Euchan Water
Cloud Hill
Lowther Hills
Enterkinfoot
Durisdeermill
Polgown
Countam
Cairnkinna Hill
Windy Standard
Cleuch-head
Gateslack
East Morton
Drumlanrig
Morton Castle
Colt Hill
Cairnsmore of Carsphairn
Bow Burn
Big Carlae
Old Auchenbrack
Auchenhessnane
Carronbridge
Tibbers
Benbuie
Shinnel Water
Scaur Water
Burnhead
Penpont
Thornhill
Southern Upland Way
Cornharrow Hill
Bennan
Nithsdale
Carsphairn
Water of Ken
Stenhouse
Tynron
Keir Mill
Closeburn
Knowehead
Moniaive
Kirkland
Kirkpatrick
Water of Deugh
Maxwelton
Keir Hills
153
Glenhoul
Glencrosh
Craigneston
Black Water
Wether Hill
Blackwood
Bogrie Hill
Skelston
Snade
Lag
Sundaywell
Dunscore
Throughgate
Loch Urr
Blawquhairn
Loch Howie
Knocksheen
Garroch
Stepford
St John's Town of Dalry
Bogue
Skeoch Hill
Drumpark
Balmaclellan
New Galloway
Corsock
Larglear Hill
Shawhead
Ironmacannie
Cairn Edward
Water of Dee
Lochfoot
Eastlands
Crocketford
Auchenreoch Loch
Lochrutton Loch
Knockvennie Smithy
Milton Loch
Fleet
Milton
Mossdale
Airds of Kells
Kirkpatrick Durham
Springholm
146
Auchencloy Hill
Loch Ken
Loch Roan
Walbutt
Drumcoltran Tower
Beeswing
Loch Skerrow
Old Bridge of Urr
Crossmichael
Woodhall Loch
Kirkgunzeon
Hardgate
Lotus Hill
Clarebrand
Haugh of Urr
Redcastle
Laurieston
Townhead of Greenlaw
Hillowton
Threave Castle
White Top of Culreach
Little Water of Fleet
Urr Water
Glaisters Burn
Edingham
Castle Douglas
0 1 2 3 4 miles
0 1 2 3 4 5 kilometres

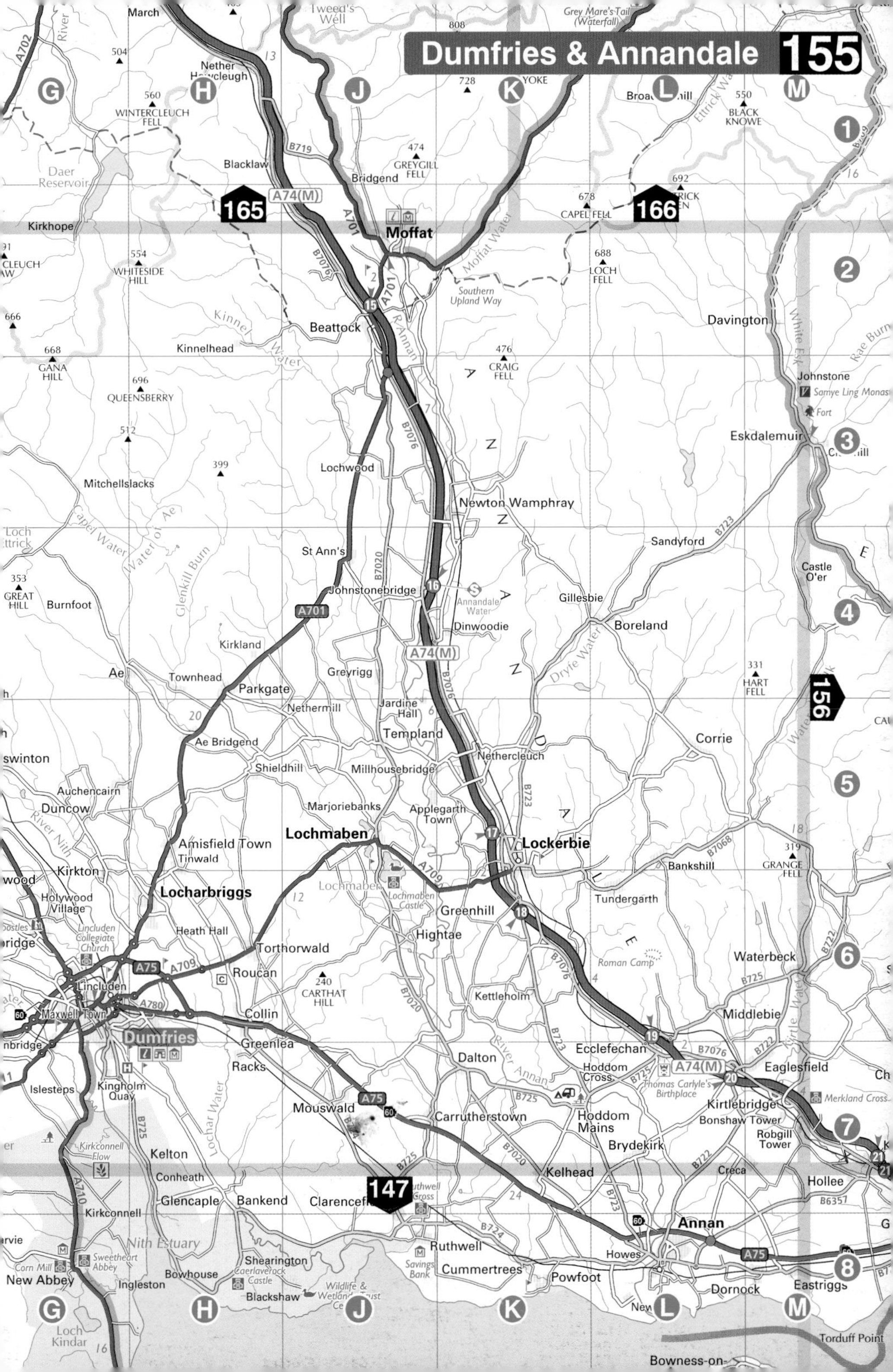
165
166
156
147
Moffat
Beattock
Lochwood
Newton Wamphray
Johnstonebridge
Lochmaben
Lockerbie
Locharbriggs
Dumfries
Annan
Ecclefechan
Eskdalemuir
Boreland
Dalton
Ruthwell
Cummertrees
Powfoot
Eastriggs
Eaglesfield
Middlebie
Waterbeck
Kirtlebridge
Hoddom Mains
Brydekirk
Carrutherstown
Mouswald
Collin
Torthorwald
Tinwald
Amisfield Town
Parkgate
Templand
Greenhill
Hightae
Kelton
Glencaple
Bankend
New Abbey
Southern Upland Way
A74(M)
A701
A75
A709
A710
B7076
B7020
B723
B725
B722
B7068

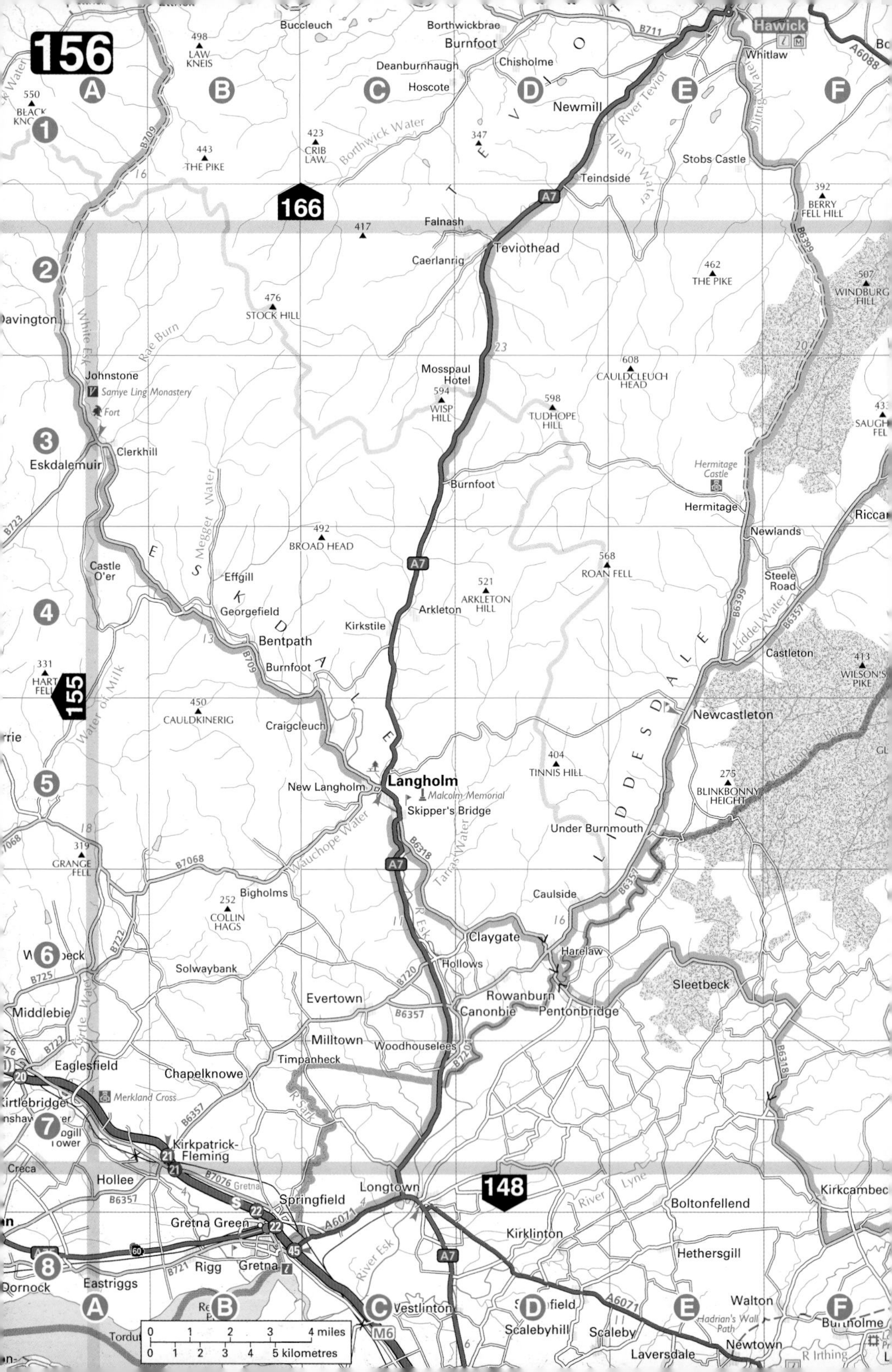
Buccleuch
Borthwickbrae
Burnfoot
Hawick
Whitlaw
A6088
B711
498 LAW KNEIS
Deanburnhaugh
Chisholme
Hoscote
Newmill
550 BLACK KNOWE
River Teviot
Slitrig Water
423 CRIB LAW
Borthwick Water
347
443 THE PIKE
Allan Water
Stobs Castle
Teindside
166
Falnash
417
392 BERRY FELL HILL
Teviothead
Caerlanrig
462 THE PIKE
507 WINDBURGH HILL
476 STOCK HILL
Davington
White Esk
Rae Burn
Mosspaul Hotel
608 CAULDCLEUCH HEAD
Johnstone
Samye Ling Monastery
Fort
594 WISP HILL
598 TUDHOPE HILL
Clerkhill
Eskdalemuir
Hermitage Castle
Burnfoot
Hermitage
Megget Water
492 BROAD HEAD
Newlands
568 ROAN FELL
Castle O'er
Effgill
521 ARKLETON HILL
Steele Road
Georgefield
Arkleton
Kirkstile
Bentpath
Liddel Water
Castleton
331 HART FELL
155
Burnfoot
413 WILSON'S PIKE
450 CAULDKINERIG
Craigcleuch
Water of Milk
Newcastleton
404 TINNIS HILL
275 BLINKBONNY HEIGHT
Kershope Burn
New Langholm
Langholm
Malcolm Memorial
Skipper's Bridge
Wauchope Water
Under Burnmouth
319 GRANGE FELL
B7068
Tarras Water
Bigholms
252 COLLIN HAGS
Caulside
R Esk
Claygate
Harelaw
Solwaybank
Hollows
Sleetbeck
Middlebie
Evertown
Rowanburn
Canonbie
Pentonbridge
Milltown
Woodhouselees
Eaglesfield
Timpanheck
Chapelknowe
Merkland Cross
Kirtlebridge
R Sark
Kirkpatrick-Fleming
Hollee
Gretna
Springfield
Longtown
148
River Lyne
Boltonfellend
Kirkcambeck
Gretna Green
Kirklinton
Hethersgill
Rigg
Gretna
River Esk
Dornock
Eastriggs
Westlinton
Walton
Hadrian's Wall Path
Burtholme
Scalebyhill
Scaleby
Laversdale
Newtown
R Irthing
0 1 2 3 4 miles
0 1 2 3 4 5 kilometres

Camptown
Abbotrule
Jedforest Deer & Farm Park
Chesters
Letham
BROWNDEAN
WOFFEE HEAD
Crag Bank Wood
Carter Bar
Whitelee Moor
HUNGRY LAW
Ramshope
SHILLHOPE LAW
Alwinton
BLACK KIP
NORTHUMBERLAND NATIONAL PARK
CORBY PIKE
CARTER FELL
Catcleugh Reservoir
Byrness
PEEL FELL
OH ME EDGE
Myredykes
Kielder Head
Kielder Burn
River Rede
Rochester
Horsley
HINDHOPE LAW
Pennine Way
MONKSIDE
LOCH KNOWE
Kielder
Kielder Castle
Toll
Otterburn
Elsdon
Otterburn Mill
EARLS SEAT
Kielder Water
Black Middens Bastle House
Gatehouse
WHITE HILL
Falstone
Greenhaugh
West Woodburn
East Woodburn
Tower Knowe
Stannersburn
Charlton
Fort
Risdale
Bellingham
Redesmouth
BOLTS LAW
BLACK KNOWE
SIGHTY CRAG
Chirdon Burn
Birtley
Wark
ROUND TOP
SPY RIGG
Gunnerton
Simonburn
Barrasford
Black Fell
GREEN RIGG
River Irthing
Greenlee Lough
Broomlee Lough
Hadrian's Wall Path
Carrawburgh: Temple of Mithras
Chesters Fort
Wall
Fourstones
Hadrian's Wall
Housesteads Fort
Newbrough
Gilsland
Chesterholm (Vindolanda)
Chesterwood
Thorngrafton
Haydon Bridge
Henshaw
Melkridge
Beltingham
Elrington
Hexham
Tyne Green
R South Tyne
R North Tyne
Lewis Burn
Warks Burn
Tarset Burn
Camp
Hadrian's Wall & Kielder
167
168
158
149

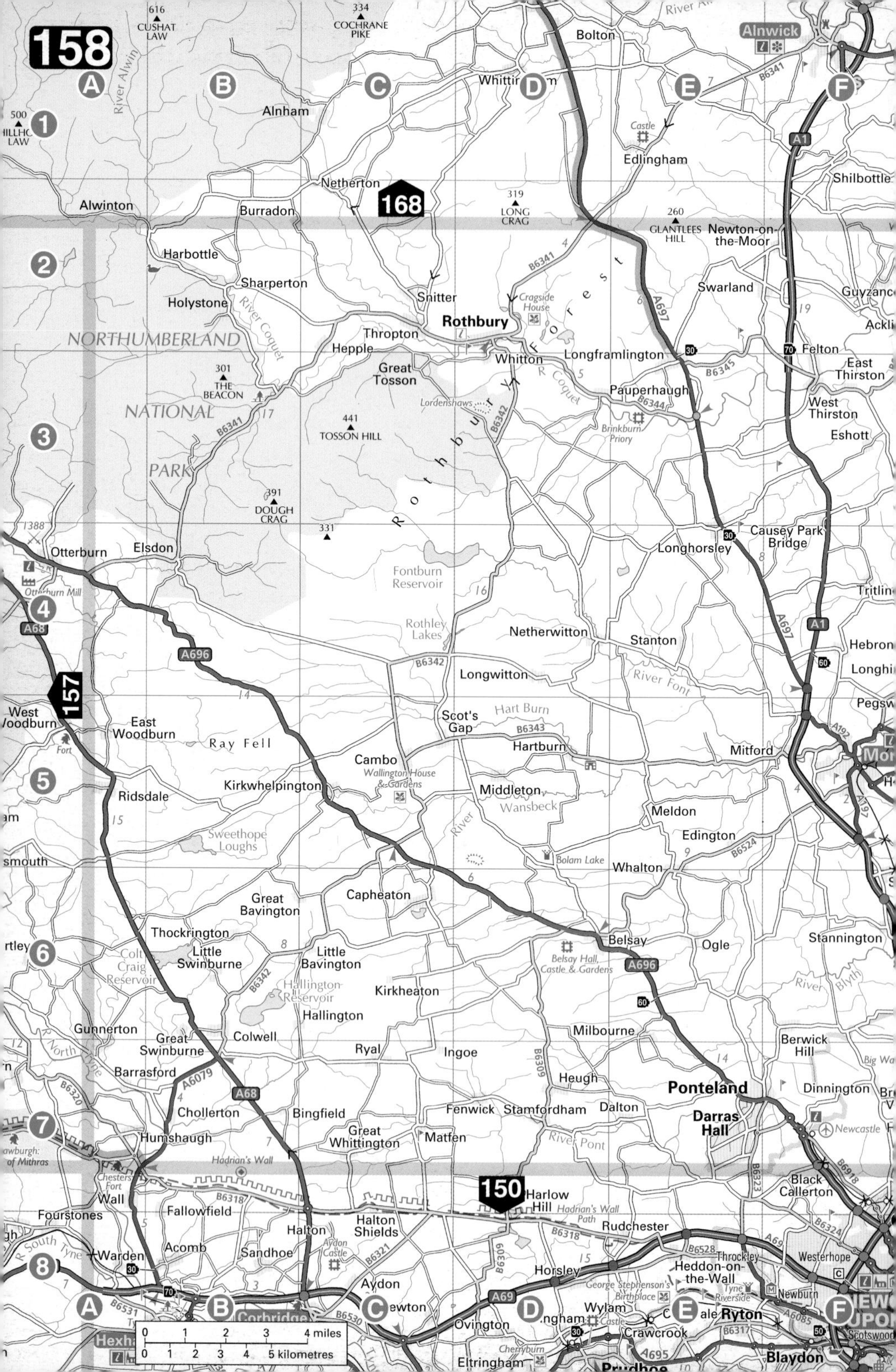

Alnwick
Bolton
Whittingham
Alnham
Edlingham
Shilbottle
Netherton
168
Alwinton
Burradon
Harbottle
Sharperton
Holystone
Snitter
Rothbury
Thropton
Hepple
Great Tosson
Whitton
Longframlington
Pauperhaugh
Felton
NORTHUMBERLAND NATIONAL PARK
Rothbury Forest
Otterburn
Elsdon
Longhorsley
Fontburn Reservoir
Rothley Lakes
Netherwitton
Stanton
Longwitton
Scot's Gap
Cambo
Hartburn
Mitford
Kirkwhelpington
Middleton
Meldon
Edington
Ridsdale
Ray Fell
East Woodburn
West Woodburn
157
Capheaton
Belsay
Whalton
Ogle
Stannington
Great Bavington
Thockrington
Little Swinburne
Little Bavington
Kirkheaton
Hallington
Colwell
Gunnerton
Great Swinburne
Barrasford
Ryal
Ingoe
Milbourne
Heugh
Ponteland
Darras Hall
Berwick Hill
Dinnington
Chollerton
Bingfield
Fenwick
Stamfordham
Dalton
Humshaugh
Great Whittington
Matfen
Hadrian's Wall
150
Harlow Hill
Black Callerton
Wall
Fallowfield
Fourstones
Halton
Halton Shields
Rudchester
Warden
Acomb
Sandhoe
Aydon
Horsley
Heddon-on-the-Wall
Throckley
Westerhope
Newburn
Corbridge
Ovington
Wylam
Ryton
Crawcrook
Blaydon
Eltringham
0 1 2 3 4 miles
0 1 2 3 4 5 kilometres

Seaton Point
Lesbury
Alnmouth
Alnmouth Bay
A1068
169
Warkworth
Amble
Coquet Island
High Hauxley
Togston
Broomhill
B1330
Druridge Bay
Widdrington
North Northumberland Heritage Coast
Widdrington Station
Cresswell
Ulgham
Ellington
Lynemouth
A189
Woodhorn
Beacon Point
Ashington
A197
Hirst
Newbiggin-by-the-Sea
Bothal
Wansbeck Riverside
Stakeford
Guide Post
A196
B1334
Bedlington
B1331
A193
Cowpen
Blyth
Newsham
B1505
A192
A1061
New Hartley
Seaton Sluice
Cramlington
B1326
A190
Seaton
Seaton Delaval
A19
St Mary's Lighthouse
B1322
B1325
Dudley
Wide Open
A1056
Killingworth
Earsdon
A1148
Monkseaton
Whitley Bay
Cullercoats
Shiremoor
A191
Tynemouth
Forest Hall
Tynemouth Priory & Castle
151
IJmuiden
Rising Sun
Longbenton
North Shields
South Gosforth
Jesmond
Wallsend
Willington Quay
A187
SOUTH SHIELDS
Int. Ferry Terminal
Heaton
Toll
Jarrow
Tyne Tunnel
Westoe
A183
Marsden Bay
Walker
Hebburn
A185
Marsden
Souter Lighthouse
Byker
Felling
Monkton
B1298
Cleadon
Souter Point
Whitburn
West Boldon
G H J K L M
1 2 3 4 5 6 7 8

BEINN SHOLUM
Rudha Mòr
171
Eilean a' Chuirn
Port Ellen - Kennacraig
165
MAOL BUIDHE
Port Ellen
A846
Ardbeg
Lagavulin
Laphroaig
Rudha na Gainmhich
Kilnaughton Bay
Texa
ISLAY
THE OA
Lower Killeyan
Risabus
RSPB
Kinnabus
American Monument
Loch Kinnabus
MULL OF OA
Rudha nan Leacan
Earada
MULL OF KINTYR
0 1 2 3 4 miles
0 1 2 3 4 5 kilometres

GIGHA
Ardminish
Achamore
Rhunahaorine Point
Rhunahaorine
Tayinloan
Sound of Gigha
Cara
CRUACH MHIC GOUGAIN
172
264
CNOC-AN SAMHLA
Cour
Lochranza
Grogport
Barmollack
Pirnmill
Penrioch
North Arran
Loch Tanna
715
BEINN BHARRAIN
Whitefarland
Imachar
Balliekine
Glen Iorsa
Iorsa Water
354
CRUACH NAN GABHAR
A83
Muasdale
Glenacardoch Point
Belloch
Barr Water
Glenbarr
MacAlister Clan
Carradale Water
B842
B879
Carradale
Bridgend
Dippen
Carradale House
Carradale Point
Carradale Bay
162
ARRAN
Auchagallon Stone Circle
Machrie
Machrie Bay
Tormore
Machrie Moor Stone Circles
Moss Farm Road Stone Circle
Balmichael
454
BEINN AN TUIRC
319
Cleongart
408
BORD MOR
Saddell
Saddell Bay
Bellochantuy Bay
Bellochantuy
KILBRANNAN SOUND
Torbeg
Shiskine
Blackwaterfoot
Drumadoon Bay
Kilpatrick
Kilpatrick Dun
Brown Head
396
SGREADAN HILL
Ugadale
Tangy Loch
Glen Lussa
Peninver
Ardnacross Bay
Corriecravie
Sliddery
Torr a' Chaisteal Fort
Kilkenzie
Kilmichael
Machrihanish Bay
Machrihanish
Campbeltown
Campbeltown Loch
Island Davarr
B843
Drumlemble
Kilkerran
Kildalloig
352
BEINN GHUILEAN
Achinhoan
385
THE STATE
446
CNOC MOY
Dalsmeran
Ru Stafnish
Conie Glen
Glen Kerran
Glen Breakevie
Strone Glen
Cattadale
Polliwilline Bay
Macharioch
Southend
Carskey
Dunaverty
Carskey Bay
428
Borgadalemore Point
Sanda Sound
Sheep Island
Sanda Island
G
H
J
K
L
M
1
2
3
4
5
6
7
8

162
173
152
161
Lochranza
Catacol
Glen Catacol
Glen Chalmadale
A841
Sannox
North Arran
834
CAISTEAL ABHAIL
Loch Tanna
Penrioch
Pirnmill
715
BEINN BHARRAIN
Glen Iorsa
Corrie
874
GOATFELL
792
BEINN NUIS
Glen Rosa
Merkland Point
Brodick Castle, Garden & Country Club
Brodick Bay
Iorsa Water
Balliekine
ARRAN
Brodick
Strathwhillan
Corriegills
Auchagallon Stone Circle
Machrie
Machrie Bay
512
A'CHRUACH
Machrie Moor Stone Circles
Tormore
B880
Clauchlands Point
Moss Farm Road Stone Circle
Balmichael
503
BEINN BHREAC
Lamlash
Margnaheglish
Lamlash Bay
Holy Island
Cordon
Torbeg
Shiskine
Blackwaterfoot
Drumadoon Bay
Kilpatrick
Kilpatrick Dun
Glen Scorrodale
Auchencairn
Kingscross
Knockenkelly
Carn Ban
Whiting Bay
Brown Head
Glen Ashdale
Largymore
Corriecravie
Torr a' Chaisteal Fort
Sliddery
Kilmory Water
Largybeg
Dippen
Dippen Head
Kilmory
Lagg
Torrylin Cairn
Bennan
Kildonan
Bennan Head
Pladda
FIRTH OF CLYDE
Cumbrae Island
Portencross
Farland Head
B7048
Turnberry
Turnberry Bay
340
Ailsa Craig
RSPB
0 1 2 3 4 miles
0 1 2 3 4 5 kilometres

Dalry
Highfield
Burnhouse
Munnoch
Blackshaw
174
Auchentiber
Dalgarven
High Cross
Stewarton
Crossgates
Kilwinning
Fergushill
Torranyard
Fenwick
Waterside
Benslie
Laigh Fenwick
Eglinton
Cunninghamhead
Stevenston
Saltcoats
Ardeer
Girdle Toll
Kilmaurs
Moscow
Polbaith Burn
Irvine
Maritime
Perceton
Springside
Knockentiber
Knockinlaw
Dean Castle
Dreghorn
Fullarton
Crosshouse
KILMARNOCK
Newmilns
Darvel
Crookedholm
Greenholm
Irvine Bay
R Irvine
Gatehead
Hurlford
Galston
Drybridge
Earlston
Riccarton
Gailes
Shortlees
Dundonald
Castle
Barassie
Middleyard
Symington
Bogend
Craigie
Carnell
Loans
Crosshands
(Mar-Oct)
Troon
Helenton
Wallace Monument Tower
Royal Troon
Auchmillan
Larne
Monkton
Bachelors' Club
Tarbolton
Mauchline
Prestwick
Failford
164
Sorn
Haugh
Catrine
Mossblown
New Prestwick
St Quivox
Whitletts
Annbank
Stair
Ayr Bay
Lugar Water
Wallacetown
Gadgirth
Trabboch
Trabbochburn
Ayr
River Ayr
Ochiltree
Auchinleck
Doonfoot
Joppa
Coylton
Palmerston
Heads of Ayr
Burns Cottage
Belmont
Drongan
Garrallan
Alloway
Skares
Fisherton
Robert Burns Birthplace
Barbieston
Martnaham Loch
Sinclairston
Dunure
Culroy
Hollybush
363 CARSGAILOCH HILL
Drumshang
Minishant
Dalrymple
Croy Brae (Electric Brae)
Knoweside
River Doon
Rankinston
Dalgig
Culzean Bay
Culzean Castle & Country Park
429 KILMEIN HILL
Pennyglen
Grimmet
Guiltreehill
Patna
Whitefaulds
Maybole
Waterside
Dunaskin
464 BENBEOCH
Crossraguel Abbey
Kirkmichael
306 KEIRS HILL
Kirkoswald
Souter Johnnie's Cottage
Threave
High Pennyvenie
568 ENOCH
Crosshill
153
Dalmellington
Straiton
Ness Glen
Roan of Craigoch
Mossdale
536
Wallacetown
Water of Girvan
320 MARATZ HILL
Kilgrammie
Dailly
Loch Finlas
429 GARLEFFIN FELL
A77
A78
A71
A76
A70
A719
A713
A759
A735
B7023

164
175
163
153
154
Strathaven
Stonehouse
Glassford
Chapelton
Kirkmuirhill
Lesmahagow
Newmilns
Darvel
Galston
Drumclog
Muirkirk
Auchinleck
Cumnock
New Cumnock
Sanquhar
Kirkconnel
Dalmellington
Glenbuck
Coalburn
Sorn
Catrine
Lugar
Logan
Priestland
Greenholm
Waterside
Middleyard
Auchmillan
Haugh
Skares
Palmerston
Sinclairston
Garrallan
Roadside
Holmhead
Cronberry
Limmerhaugh
Kames
Carmacoup
Dungavel
Caldermill
Sandford
Blackwood
Draffan
Boghead
New Trows
Auchlochan
Stockbriggs
Carnduff
Knoweglass
Limekilnburn
Shawsburn
Ashgill
Strutherhill
Mansfield
Connel Park
Bankglen
Craigbank
Dalgig
Kelloholm
Newtown
Ulzieside
Mennock
Kirkland
Fingland
Meikle Carco
Blackcraig
High Pennyvenie
Mossdale
Polgown
Laigh Glenmuir
Spirit of Scotland
361 LAIRDS SEAT
335 MILL RIG
383 DISTINKHORN
408 MID HILL
461 AUCHINGILLOCH
522 NUTBERRY HILL
492 PRIESTHILL HEIGHT
466 MIDDLEFIELD LAW
593 CAIRN TABLE
440 DRYRIGS HILL
497 WARDLAW HILL
562
478 MOUNT STEWART
450 HALFMERK HILL
503 COCKER HILL
363 CARSGAILOCH HILL
594 HARE HILL
464
568 ENOCH HILL
700 BLACKCRAIG
450 CLOUD HILL
478
475 COUNTAM
554 CAIRNKINNA
598 COLT HILL
697
536
Glen Water
Avon Water
Kype Water
Logan Water
River Nethan
River Ayr
Gass Water
Glenmuir Water
Spango Water
Lugar Water
River Nith
Kello Water
Euchan Water
Polbaith Burn
A71
A70
A76
A77
A719
A723
B743
B7086
B7078
B7037
B744
B713
B705
B7036
B7083
B7046
B741
B745
B764
0 1 2 3 4 miles
0 1 2 3 4 5 kilometres

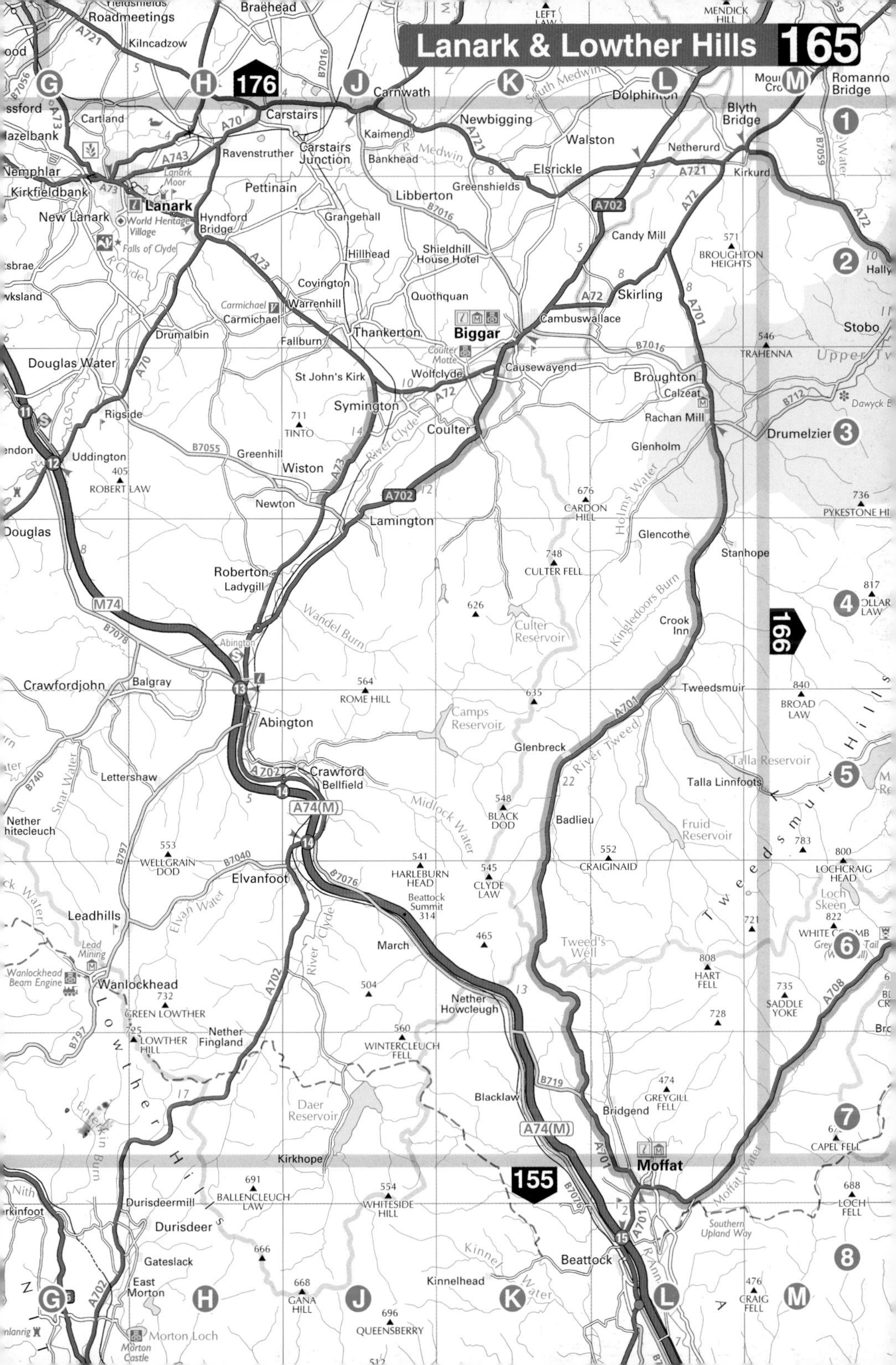
Roadmeetings
Braehead
Kilncadzow
Carnwath
Carstairs
Carstairs Junction
Dolphinton
Newbigging
Walston
Blyth Bridge
Romanno Bridge
Cartland
Ravenstruther
Kaimend
Bankhead
Elsrickle
Netherurd
Kirkurd
Nemphlar
Kirkfieldbank
Lanark
New Lanark
Pettinain
Libberton
Greenshields
Hyndford Bridge
Grangehall
Candy Mill
World Heritage Village
Falls of Clyde
Hillhead
Shieldhill House Hotel
BROUGHTON HEIGHTS
Covington
Skirling
Warrenhill
Quothquan
Carmichael
Cambuswallace
Drumalbin
Thankerton
Biggar
Stobo
Fallburn
Coulter Motte
TRAHENNA
Douglas Water
Wolfclyde
Causewayend
Broughton
St John's Kirk
Calzeat
Rigside
Symington
Rachan Mill
TINTO
Coulter
Drumelzier
Uddington
Greenhill
Glenholm
ROBERT LAW
Wiston
CARDON HILL
PYKESTONE HILL
Newton
Lamington
Douglas
Glencothe
Stanhope
CULTER FELL
Roberton
Ladygill
Wandel Burn
Crook Inn
Culter Reservoir
Kingledoors Burn
Abington
Crawfordjohn
Balgray
ROME HILL
Tweedsmuir
BROAD LAW
Camps Reservoir
Glenbreck
River Tweed
Talla Reservoir
Lettershaw
Crawford
Bellfield
Talla Linnfoots
Midlock Water
BLACK DOD
Badlieu
Fruid Reservoir
Nether Whitecleuch
WELLGRAIN DOD
HARLEBURN HEAD
CLYDE LAW
CRAIGINAID
LOCHCRAIG HEAD
Elvanfoot
Beattock Summit
Leadhills
Elvan Water
Loch Skeen
Lead Mining
March
Tweed's Well
WHITE COOMB
Wanlockhead Beam Engine
Wanlockhead
HART FELL
Nether Howcleugh
SADDLE YOKE
GREEN LOWTHER
LOWTHER HILL
Nether Fingland
WINTERCLEUCH FELL
Blacklaw
GREYGILL FELL
Daer Reservoir
Bridgend
Moffat
CAPEL FELL
Kirkhope
BALLENCLEUCH LAW
WHITESIDE HILL
LOCH FELL
Durisdeermill
Durisdeer
Southern Upland Way
Gateslack
Beattock
East Morton
Kinnelhead
Kinnel Water
GANA HILL
CRAIG FELL
QUEENSBERRY
Morton Loch
Morton Castle
Lowther Hills
Tweedsmuir Hills
Moffat Water
River Clyde
Enterkin Burn
176
155
166

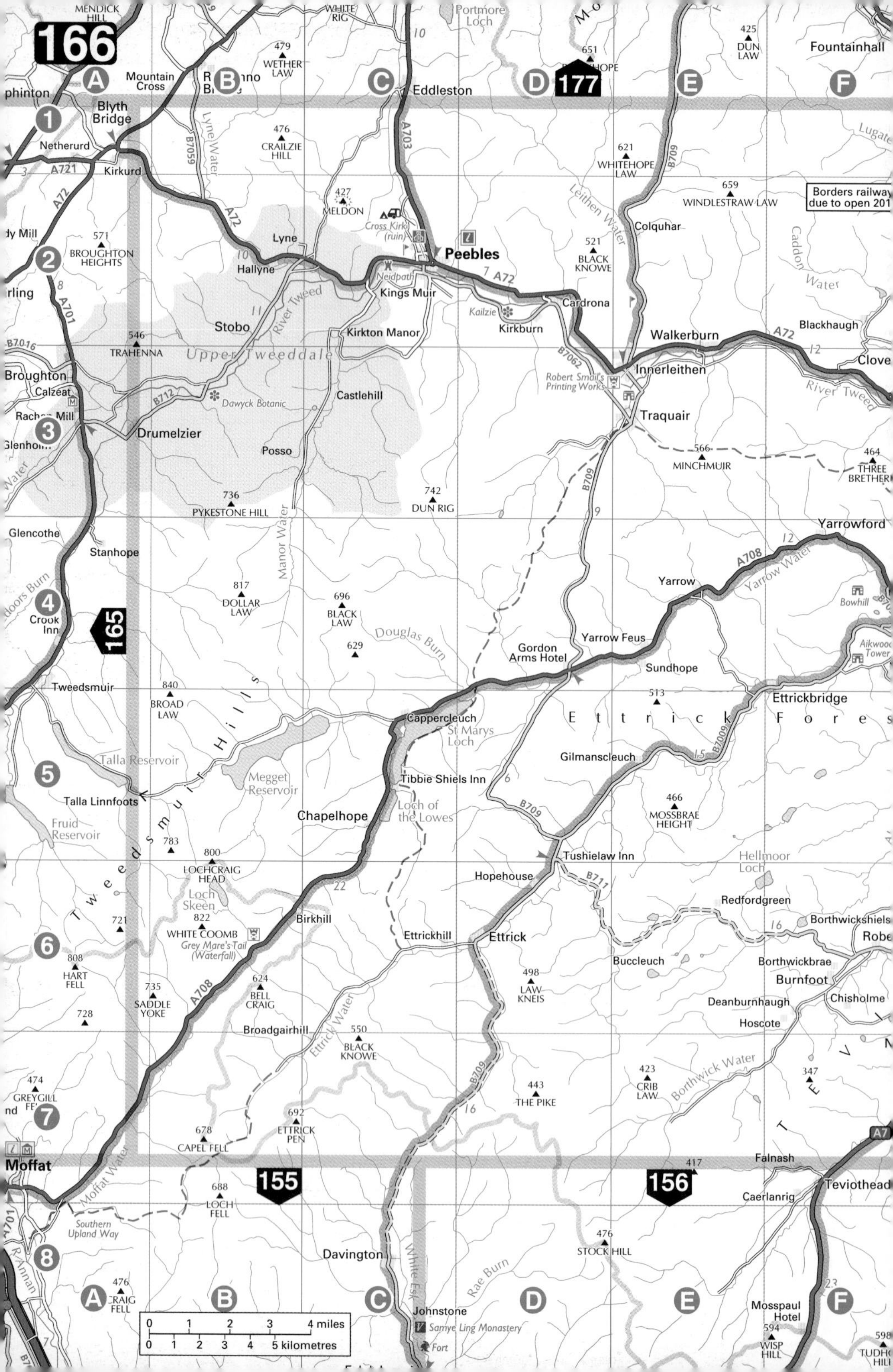

177
165
155
156

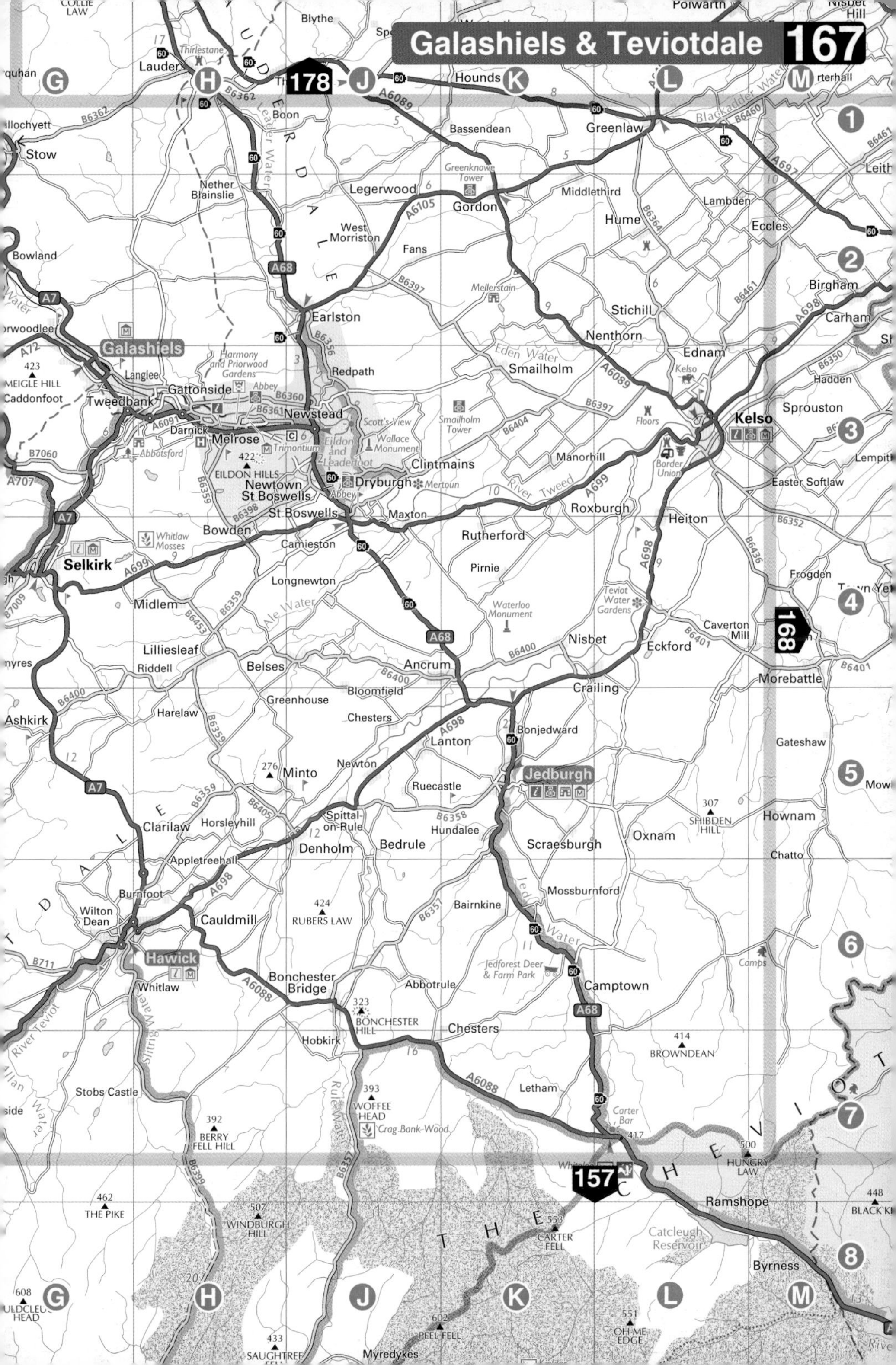
Lauder
Stow
Galashiels
Melrose
Newtown St Boswells
St Boswells
Selkirk
Earlston
Gordon
Greenlaw
Kelso
Jedburgh
Hawick
Denholm
Ancrum
Dryburgh
Smailholm
Stichill
Ednam
Hume
Eccles
Birgham
Sprouston
Morebattle
Hownam
Oxnam
Camptown
Bonchester Bridge
Byrness
Ramshope
Catcleugh Reservoir
CARTER FELL
PEEL FELL
THE CHEVIOT
178
168
157

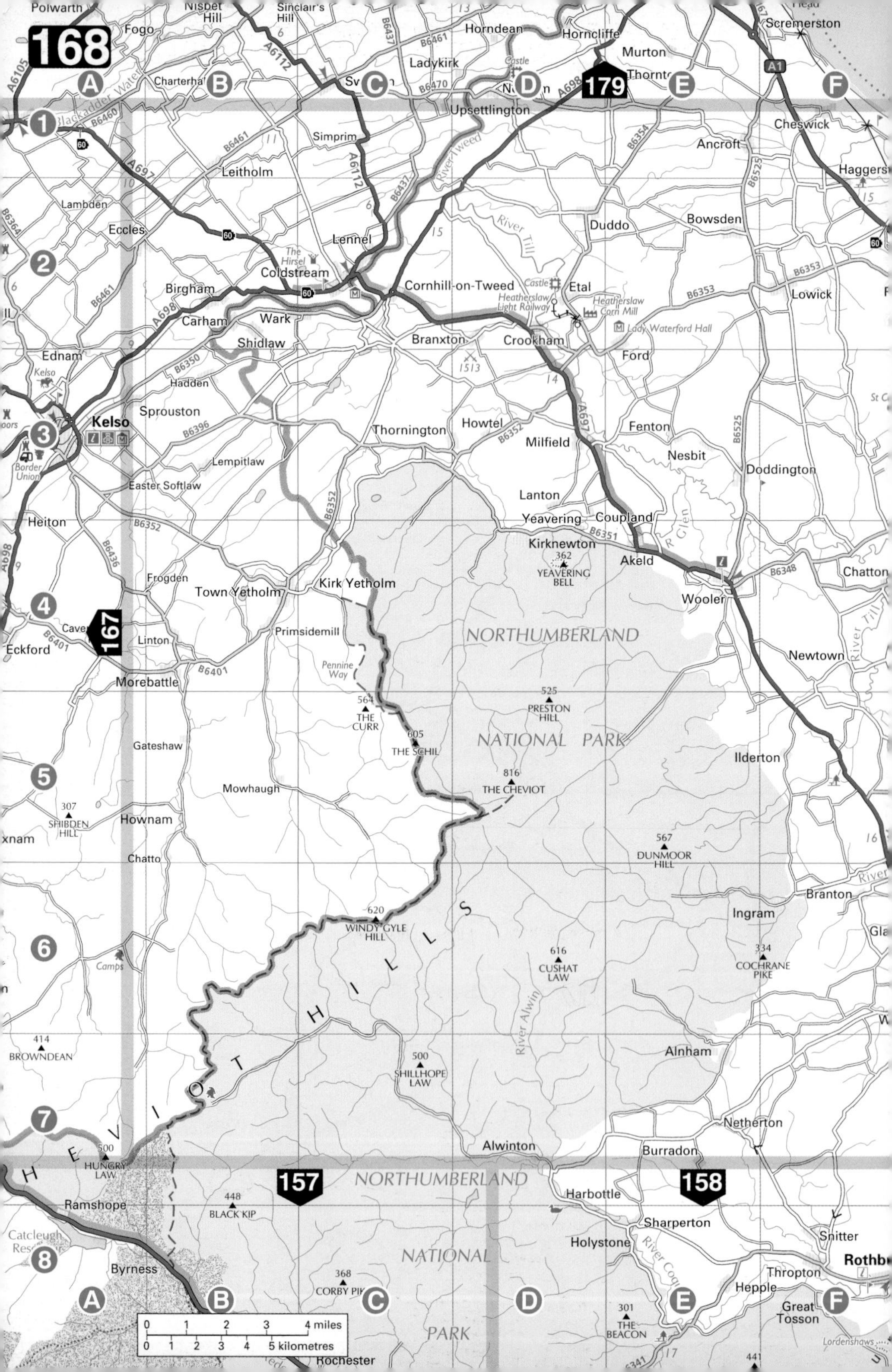
168
Polwarth
Fogo
Nisbet Hill
Sinclair's Hill
Horndean
Horncliffe
Scremerston
Murton
Ladykirk
Charterhall
Blackadder Water
Upsettlington
179
Cheswick
Ancroft
Simprim
Leitholm
River Tweed
River Till
Lambden
Eccles
Duddo
Bowsden
Lennel
The Hirsel
Coldstream
Birgham
Cornhill-on-Tweed
Etal
Lowick
Heatherslaw Light Railway
Heatherslaw Corn Mill
Lady Waterford Hall
Carham
Wark
Shidlaw
Branxton
Crookham
Ford
Ednam
Kelso
Hadden
Sprouston
1513
Border Union
Thornington
Howtel
Milfield
Fenton
Nesbit
Doddington
Lempitlaw
Easter Softlaw
Lanton
Yeavering
Coupland
Heiton
R Glen
Kirknewton
362
YEAVERING BELL
Akeld
Chatton
Frogden
Town Yetholm
Kirk Yetholm
Wooler
Eckford
167
Linton
Primsidemill
NORTHUMBERLAND
Newtown
River Till
Pennine Way
Morebattle
564
THE CURR
525
PRESTON HILL
Gateshaw
605
THE SCHIL
NATIONAL PARK
Ilderton
Mowhaugh
816
THE CHEVIOT
307
SHIBDEN HILL
Hownam
567
DUNMOOR HILL
Chatto
Branton
Ingram
620
WINDY GYLE HILL
616
CUSHAT LAW
334
COCHRANE PIKE
Camps
River Alwin
C H E V I O T H I L L S
414
BROWNDEAN
Alnham
500
SHILLHOPE LAW
Netherton
Alwinton
500
HUNGRY LAW
Burradon
157
NORTHUMBERLAND
158
Harbottle
448
BLACK KIP
Ramshope
Sharperton
Catcleugh Reservoir
Holystone
River Coquet
Snitter
NATIONAL
Thropton
Byrness
368
CORBY PIKE
Hepple
Great Tosson
301
THE BEACON
PARK
Rochester
Lordenshaws
441
0 1 2 3 4 miles
0 1 2 3 4 5 kilometres

CAUSEWAY FLOODED AT HIGH TIDE
HOLY ISLAND
Holy Island
Lindisfarne Castle
Lindisfarne Priory
Castle Point
Guile Point
Longstone Lighthouse
FARNE ISLANDS
Staple Sound
Inner Sound
North Northumberland Heritage Coast
Budle Bay
Bamburgh
Belford
Seahouses
North Sunderland
Lucker
Beadnell
Warenford
Swinhoe
Chathill
Beadnell Bay
Newstead
Tughall
Ellingham
Preston
Ros Castle
Preston Pele Tower
Newton-by-the-Sea
Embleton & Newton Links
Christon Bank
Embleton
Embleton Bay
CATERAN HILL
North Charlton
Fallodon
Dunstanburgh Castle
South Charlton
Dunstan
Craster
Eglingham
Rock
Rennington
Stamford
Howick Hall
Howick
Beanley
Cullernose Point
Longhoughton
Denwick
Boulmer
River Aln
Alnwick
Bolton
Seaton Point
Lesbury
Alnmouth
Alnmouth Bay
Castle
Edlingham
Shilbottle
GLANTLEES HILL
Newton-on-the-Moor
Warkworth Castle & Hermitage
Warkworth
Amble
Coquet Island
159
Gloster Hill
Swarland
Guyzance
High Hauxley
Acklington
Togston
Felton
East Thirston
Broomhill
South Broomhill
West Thirston
Red Row
Druridge Bay
Pauperhaugh
Brinkburn
Coquet
Forest
B6349
B6348
B1342
B1340
B1341
B6347
B1339
B6346
B6341
A1
A1068
A697
B6344

180
Dubh Eile
ISLAY
Nave Island
Ardnave Point
Gortan Poin
Ton Mhòr
Kilnave
Sanaigmore
Loch Gruinart
Eilean Mòr
Loch Gorr
Rudha Lamanais
Lecht Gruinart
RSPB
B8018
B8017
Gruinart
Gleann Mòr
Saligo Bay
Loch Gorm
Coul Point
Sunderland
B8018
Kilchoman
Machir Bay
A847
Loch Indaal
Bruichladdich
Bowmore
Kilchiaran Bay
RHINNS OF ISLAY
15
Port Charlotte
231
BEINN TART A'MHILL
River La
Lossit Bay
Nereabolls
Duich R
A846
Rudha na Faing
Portnahaven
A847
Port Wemyss
Laggan Bay
Islay
Orsay
RHINNS POINT
Rudha Mòr
Kintra
160
165
MAOL BU
THE O
Lower Killevan
Risabus
0 1 2 3 4 miles
0 1 2 3 4 5 kilometres

Scalasaig
Machrins
Garvard
Rudha Bàn
ORONSAY
Eilean Ghurdmail
Colonsay-Port Askaig
JURA
Shian Bay
Corpach Bay
Lussa River
Glen Grundale
466 BEINN BHREAC
453 RAINBERG MÒR
Loch Righ Mòr
Ardlussa
Lussa Point
Lussagiven
A846
Rudh' ant-Sàilein
Loch Tarbert
Rudha' a' Mhàil
Rudha Bholsa
363 SGARBH BREAC
506 SCRINADLE
398 BEINN TARSUINN
Jura Forest
784 BEINN AN OIR
734
Loch a' Chnuic Bhric
Paps of Jura
Bunnahabhain
316 GUIR-BHEINN
Knockrome
Ardfernal
Jura
Sound of Islay
560 GLASS BHEINN
Port Askaig
Finlaggan
Feolin Ferry
Kiells
Loch Finlaggan
529 DUBHA BHEINN
Keils
Craighouse
Small Isles
Ballygrant
Loch Ballygrant
Loch Lossit
342 BRAT BHEINN
Rudha na Gaillich
Cabrach
266 BEINNE DUBH
Am Fraoch Eilean
Brosdale Island
Rudha na Tràille
Gartachossan
429 SGÒRR NAM FAOILEANN
471
Kilennan Burn
McArthur's Head
490 BEINN BHEIGEIR
Port Askaig - Kennacraig
Rudha Liath
Ardtalla
454 BEINN URARAIDH
Loch Uraraidh
Claggain Bay
Kintour
Kildalton Cross
Ardmore Point
346 BEINN SHOLUM
Eilean a' Chuirn
Port Ellen - Kennacraig
Rudha na Gainn
Ardbeg
Lagavulin
Laphroaig
Texa
Sound of Jura
Keills Chapel
Loch Caolisport
St Cormac's Chapel
Kilmory Knap Chapel
Kilmory Bay
Point of Knap
Kilberry Head
Keppoch Point
Kinerara
Tarbert
GIGHA
Rhunahaorine Point
Ardminish
Achamore
Tayinloan
Cara
Sound of Gigha
181
172
160

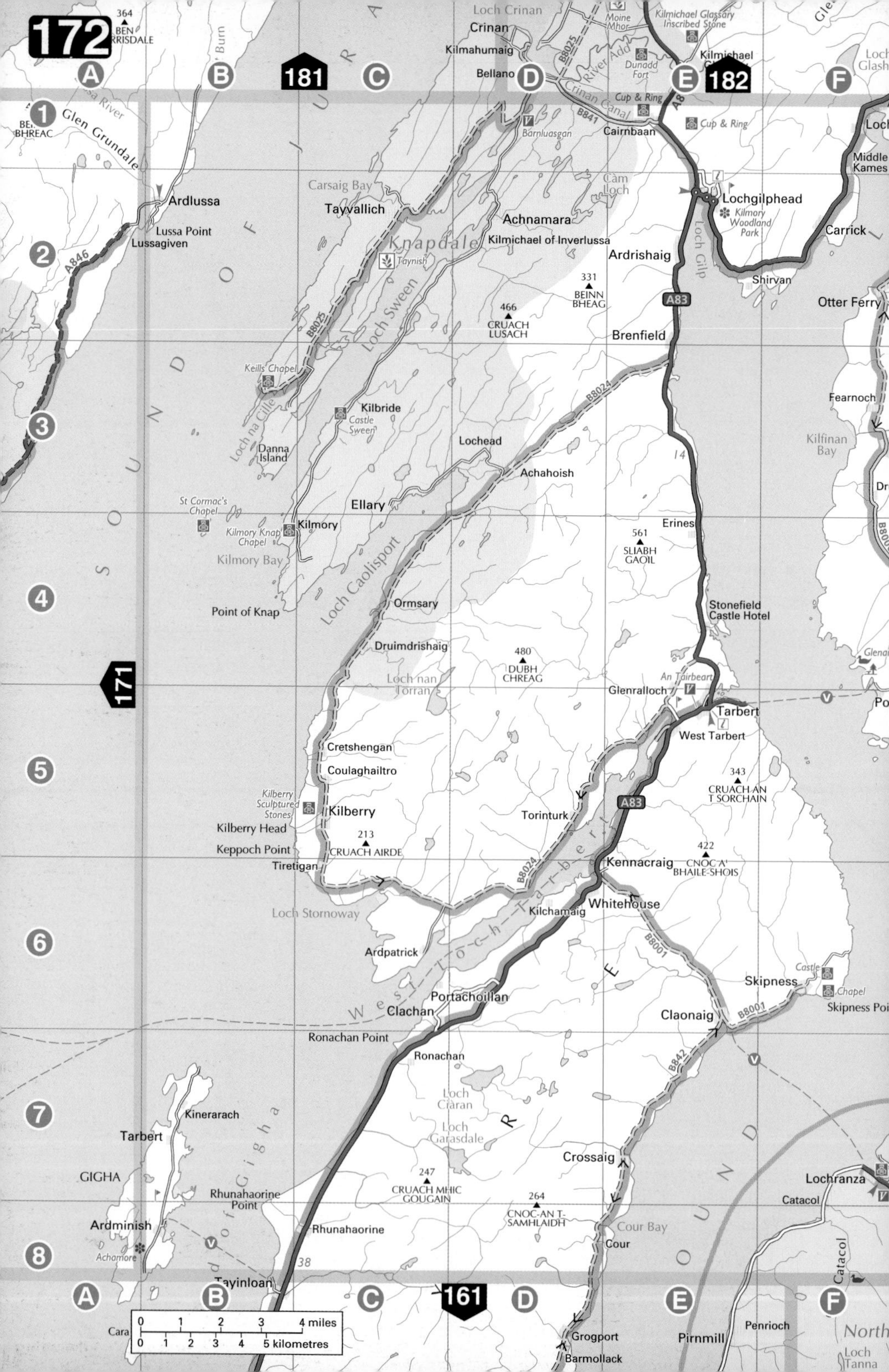

181
182
171
161
Loch Crinan
Crinan
Kilmahumaig
Bellano
Moine Mhor
B8025
River Add
Dunadd Fort
Kilmichael Glassary Inscribed Stone
Kilmichael
Crinan Canal
Cup & Ring
B841
Cairnbaan
Barnluasgan
Carsaig Bay
Tayvallich
Càm Loch
Lochgilphead
Kilmory Woodland Park
Loch Gilp
Achnamara
Knapdale
Kilmichael of Inverlussa
Ardrishaig
Taynish
Loch Sween
331
BEINN BHEAG
466
CRUACH LUSACH
A83
Brenfield
Shirvan
Carrick
Otter Ferry
Middle Kames
Loch Glash
Keills Chapel
Loch na Cille
Kilbride
Castle Sween
B8024
Danna Island
Lochead
Achahoish
Fearnoch
Kilfinan Bay
St Cormac's Chapel
Kilmory Knap Chapel
Kilmory
Ellary
Kilmory Bay
Loch Caolisport
Erines
561
SLIABH GAOIL
Point of Knap
Ormsary
Stonefield Castle Hotel
Druimdrishaig
480
DUBH CHREAG
Loch nan Torran
An Tairbeart
Glenralloch
Tarbert
West Tarbert
Cretshengan
Coulaghailtro
343
CRUACH AN T SORCHAIN
Kilberry Sculptured Stones
Kilberry
Torinturk
Kilberry Head
213
CRUACH AIRDE
Keppoch Point
Tiretigan
422
CNOC A' BHAILE-SHOIS
Kennacraig
Whitehouse
Kilchamaig
Loch Stornoway
B8001
West Loch Tarbert
Ardpatrick
Skipness
Castle
Chapel
Skipness Point
Portachoillan
Clachan
Claonaig
B8001
Ronachan Point
Ronachan
B842
Kinerarach
Loch Ciaran
Loch Garasdale
Tarbert
GIGHA
Crossaig
Lochranza
Catacol
Rhunahaorine Point
247
CRUACH MHIC GOUGAIN
264
CNOC-AN T-SAMHLAIDH
Ardminish
Rhunahaorine
Cour Bay
Cour
Achamore
Tayinloan
Sound of Gigha
Kilbrannan Sound
Sound of Jura
Ardlussa
Lussa Point
Lussagiven
A846
Glen Grundale
Lussa River
364
BEN GARRISDALE
Grogport
Barmollack
Pirnmill
Penrioch
Loch Tanna
North
0 1 2 3 4 miles
0 1 2 3 4 5 kilometres
A B C D E F
1 2 3 4 5 6 7 8

Barnacarry
CRUACH AN LOCHAIN
182
183
174
162
Dunans Castle
Argyll Forest Park
BEINN BHEAG
BEINN MHOR
CREACHAN MOR
Sligrachan
Garelochhead
Rockville
Greenfield
Glen Fruin
River Ruel
Glenmassen
Glen Massen
CLACH BHEINN
BEINN RUADH
Ardentinny
Coulport
Shandon
Gare Loch
CRUACH CHUILCEACHAN
Benmore
STRONCHULLIN HILL
Loch Long
Kilmodan Sculptured Stones
CRUACH NAN CUILEAN
Loch Tarsan
SGORACH MOR
Clynder
Rhu
Glendaruel
B836
Glen Lean
Rashfield
Ardbeg
Blairmore
Rosneath
Cove
Stronafian
Clachaig
Kilmun
Holy Loch
Loch Riddon
Glenkin
Sandbank
Ardnadam
Strone
Kilcreggan
CRUACH NAN CAPULL
Glenstriven
Hunter's Quay
Kirn
Gourock
BEINN BHREAC
BISHOP'S SEAT
Dunoon
Ashton
Cloch Point
Braeside
Larkfield
Chrisswell
Kyles of Bute
Ardentraive
Colintraive
Port Driseach
Rhubodach
Altgaltraig
Loch Striven
Ardyne Burn
Ardhallow
Lunderston Bay
Ardgowan
Loch Thom
Cornalees Bridge
Tighnabruaich
KILMARNOCK HILL
Inverkip
Shielhill
Kames
Dunan
Innellan
Knockdow
Garvock
BUTE
Millhouse
KAMES HILL
Blair's Ferry
CNOC NA CARRAIGE
Ardmaleish
Wemyss Bay
Kilbride
Ardyre Point
Port Bannatyne
St Colmac
Toward
Toward Quay
Skelmorlie
Upper Skelmorlie
REUCH HILL
Kildavanan
B875
Ettrick Bay
Kildavaig
Ardlamont
Ardlamont Bay
Ardlamont Point
Ardbeg
Castle
Bogany Point
Rothesay
B878
St Mary's Chapel (ruin)
Ardencraig
A844
Ascog
Ballanlay
Loch Ascog
Kerrycroy
Noddsdale Water
A78
Knock Castle
HILL OF STAKE
Quarter
Routenburn
Meikle Kilmory
Loch Fada
B881
Mount Stuart
Midpark
Inchmarnock
Skelmorlie Aisle
Vikingar!
Largs
IRISH LAW
Bruchag
GREAT CUMBRAE ISLAND
A760
Ardscalpsie Bay
Kingarth
Kelburn Country Centre
Strayanan Bay
Kilchattan Bay
Millport
B896
B899
Fairlie
Camphill Reservoir
Kilchattan
St Blane's Church
Sound of Bute
COCK LAW
Garrochty
Fairlie Roads
Cock of Arran
Garroch Head
Hunterston Power Station
Drakemyre
Little Cumbrae Island
Glen Chalmadale
A841
Portencross
B7048
Farland Head
Blackshaw
Munnoch
West Kilbride
B781
B780
Seamill
B714
Kilwinning
A737
CAISTEAL ABHAIL
Sannox
A886
A8003
A815
A885
A880
A770
A814
B833
B872
B8000
B7047

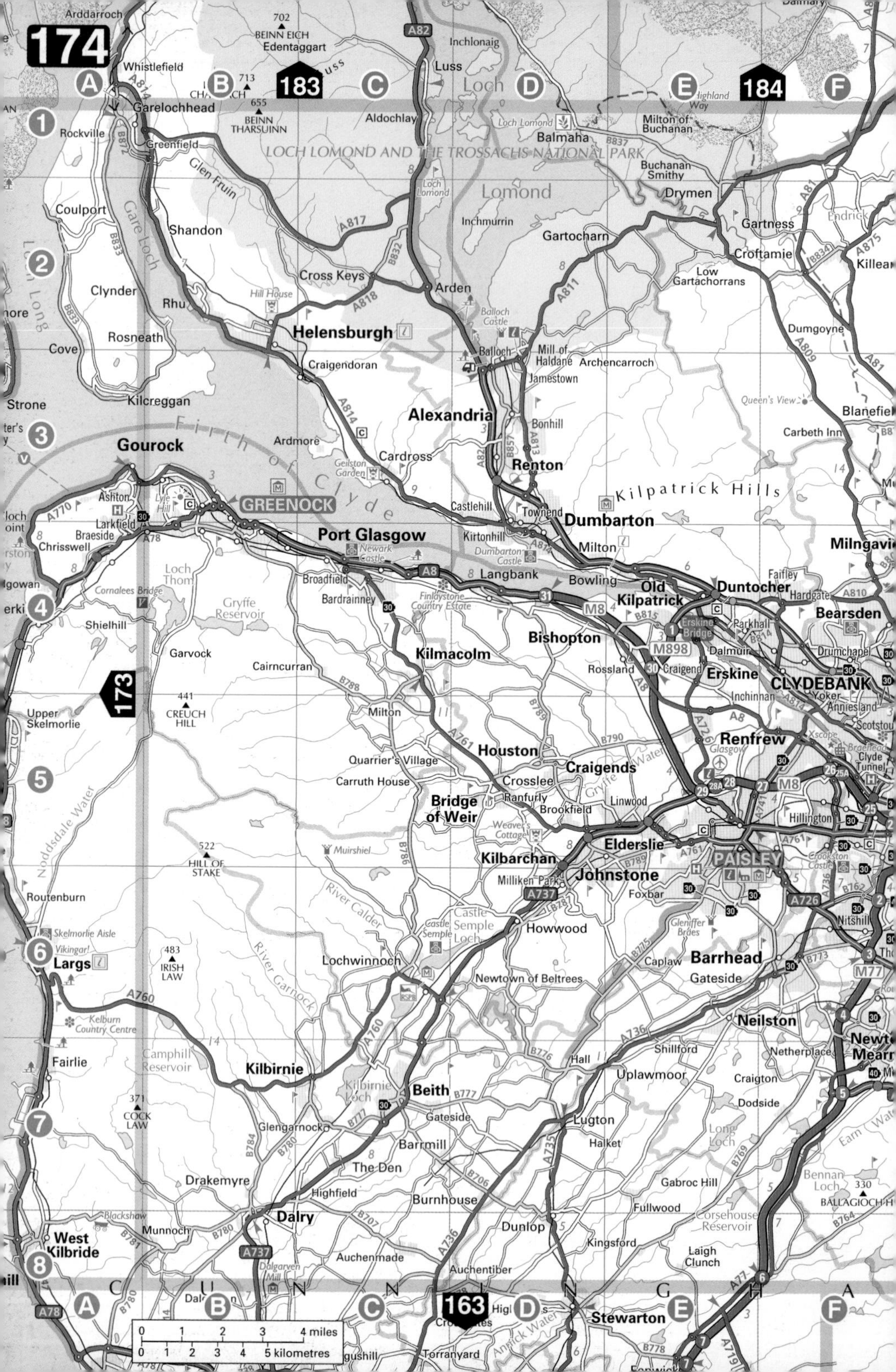

183
184
173
163
Arddarroch
702
BEINN EICH
Edentaggart
Whistlefield
Garelochhead
713
655
BEINN THARSUINN
Luss
Inchlonaig
Loch
Aldochlay
Loch Lomond
Balmaha
Milton of Buchanan
Highland Way
Rockville
Greenfield
LOCH LOMOND AND THE TROSSACHS NATIONAL PARK
Buchanan Smithy
Drymen
Glen Fruin
Lomond
Loch Lomond
Coulport
Shandon
A817
Inchmurrin
Gartocharn
Gartness
Endrick
Croftamie
Killearn
Gare Loch
Clynder
Cross Keys
Arden
Low Gartachorrans
Rhu
Hill House
Balloch Castle
Rosneath
Helensburgh
Dumgoyne
Cove
Craigendoran
Balloch
Mill of Haldane
Archencarroch
Jamestown
Strone
Kilcreggan
Queen's View
Blanefield
Alexandria
Bonhill
Carbeth Inn
Gourock
Firth of Clyde
Ardmore
Cardross
Geilston Garden
Renton
Ashton
Lyle Hill
GREENOCK
Castlehill
Townend
Dumbarton
Kilpatrick Hills
Larkfield
Braeside
Chrisswell
Port Glasgow
Newark Castle
Kirtonhill
Dumbarton Castle
Milton
Milngavie
Loch Thom
Broadfield
Langbank
Bowling
Faifley
Cornalees Bridge
Gryffe Reservoir
Bardrainney
Finlaystone Country Estate
Old Kilpatrick
Duntocher
Hardgate
Bearsden
Shielhill
Bishopton
Erskine Bridge
Parkhall
Garvock
Kilmacolm
M8
M898
Dalmuir
Drumchapel
Cairncurran
Rossland
Craigend
Erskine
CLYDEBANK
441
CREUCH HILL
Inchinnan
Yoker
Anniesland
Upper Skelmorlie
Milton
Scotstoun
Houston
Renfrew
Xscape
Braehead
Clyde Tunnel
Quarrier's Village
Craigends
Gryffe Water
Carruth House
Crosslee
Bridge of Weir
Ranfurly
Brookfield
Linwood
Hillington
Noddsdale Water
Weaver's Cottage
Elderslie
522
HILL OF STAKE
Muirshiel
Kilbarchan
Johnstone
PAISLEY
Crookston Castle
Milliken Park
Foxbar
Routenburn
River Calder
Nitshill
Castle Semple Loch
Howwood
Gleniffer Braes
Skelmorlie Aisle
Vikingar!
Largs
483
IRISH LAW
River Garnock
Lochwinnoch
Caplaw
Barrhead
Gateside
Newtown of Beltrees
Kelburn Country Centre
Neilston
Camphill Reservoir
Hall
Shillford
Netherplace
Newton Mearns
Fairlie
Kilbirnie
Uplawmoor
Craigton
371
COCK LAW
Kilbirnie Loch
Beith
Glengarnock
Gateside
Lugton
Dodside
Halket
Long Loch
Barrmill
The Den
Earn Water
Highfield
Burnhouse
Gabroc Hill
Bennan Loch
330
BALLAGIOCH HILL
Drakemyre
Blackshaw
Dalry
Dunlop
Fullwood
Corsehouse Reservoir
West Kilbride
Munnoch
Kingsford
Laigh Clunch
Auchenmade
Dalgarven Mill
Auchentiber
Stewarton
Annick Water
Torranyard
0 1 2 3 4 miles
0 1 2 3 4 5 kilometres

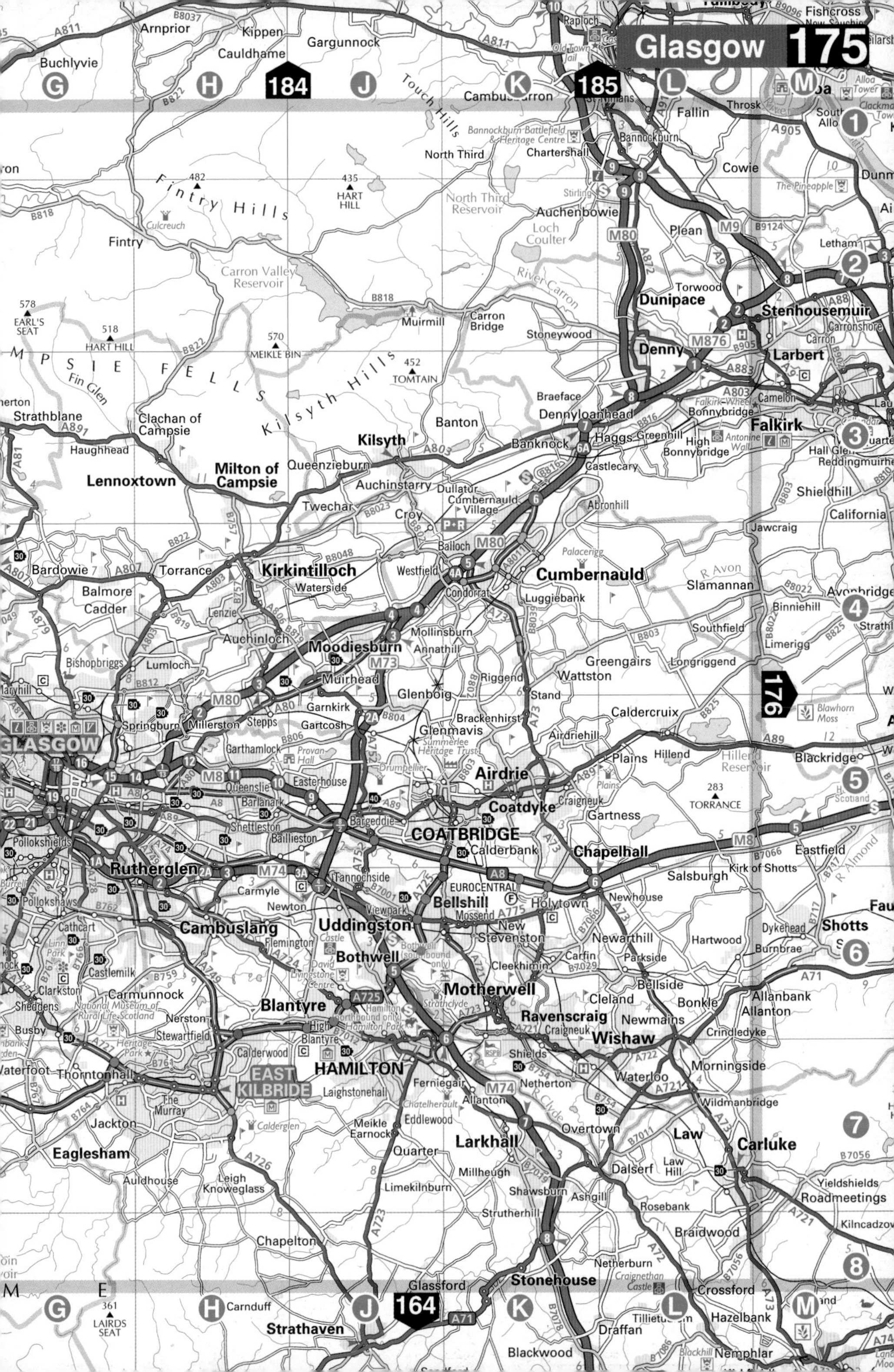
Buchlyvie
Arnprior
Kippen
Gargunnock
Cauldhame
Fintry Hills
Fintry
Carron Valley Reservoir
Campsie Fells
Kilsyth Hills
Strathblane
Clachan of Campsie
Lennoxtown
Milton of Campsie
Kilsyth
Stirling
Bannockburn
Fallin
Cowie
Plean
Dunipace
Denny
Stenhousemuir
Larbert
Falkirk
Bonnybridge
Banknock
Cumbernauld
Kirkintilloch
Bishopbriggs
Moodiesburn
Glenboig
Stepps
GLASGOW
Airdrie
COATBRIDGE
Rutherglen
Cambuslang
Uddingston
Bellshill
Bothwell
Motherwell
Wishaw
Blantyre
HAMILTON
EAST KILBRIDE
Eaglesham
Larkhall
Carluke
Shotts
Stonehouse
Strathaven
Slamannan
Caldercruix
Chapelhall
Holytown
Newmains
Cleland
Law
Carnduff
Glassford
Crossford
Draffan
Blackwood
Nemphlar
184
185
176
164

176
185
175
165
Fishcross
New Sauchie
Coalsnaughton
Gartmorn Dam & Visitor Centre
Forest Mill
Loch Glow
Black Devon
Balgonar
362 KNOCK HILL
Knockhill
Saline
Steelend
Cambus
Norwood
Keilarsbrae
Alloa Tower
Clackmannan Tower
Clackmannan
Throsk
Fallin
South Alloa
Kennet
Bannockburn
Bowershall
227 CRAIGLUSCAR HILL
Kingseat
Cowie
Dunmore
The Pineapple
Kincardine
Kincardine Bridge
Airth
Comrie
Oakley
Carnock
Gowkhall
Townhill
Wellwood
Halbeath
Milesmark
Blairhall
High Valleyfield
Culross Abbey
Culross Palace
Culross
Newmills
Cairneyhill
Low Torry
Torryburn
Crossford
Torry Bay
Crombie
Charlestown
DUNFERMLINE
Rosyth
Limekilns
Plean
Letham
Torwood
Dunipace
Stenhousemuir
Carronshore
Carron
Skinflats
Grangemouth
Denny
Larbert
Bo'ness
Bo'ness & Kinneil Railway
Grangepans
Carriden
Castle
Blackness
House of the Binns
Forth Road Bridge
North Queensferry
Falkirk Wheel
Camelon
Bonnybridge
High Bonnybridge
Antonine Wall
Falkirk
Callendar Park
Laurieston
Dovecot
Westquarter
Hall Glen
Reddingmuirhead
Redding
Kinneil House
Borrowstoun
Birkhill Claymine
Polmont
Rumford
Brightons
Whitecross
Union Canal
Philpstoun
Hopetoun
Newton
Shieldhill
California
Maddiston
Loan
Muiravonside
Linlithgow
Burnside
Bridgend
Three Miletown
Winchburgh
Kirkliston
Royal Highland (Ingliston)
Jawcraig
Standburn
Cockleroy
Beecraigs
Wester Ochiltree
Ecclesmachan
Slamannan
R Avon
Avonbridge
Preceptory
Torphichen
Broxburn
Newbridge
Binniehill
Southfield
Strathloanhead
Westfield
Cairnpapple Hill
Uphall
Ratho Viaduct
Ratho Station
Limerigg
Longriggend
Dechmont
Dechmont Road
Almondell & Calderwood
Ratho
Woodend
Bathgate
Pumpherston
Caldercruix
Blawhorn Moss
Armadale
Bathville
Boghall
Deans
Livingston
Camps
East Calder
Wilkieston
Hillend
Hillend Reservoir
Blackridge
Westrigg
Almond Valley
Mid Calder
Kirknewton
Polkemmet
Livingston Village
Oakbank
283 TORRANCE
Heart of Scotland
East Whitburn
Seafield
Blackburn
Bellsquarry
Harthill
Whitburn
Polbeth
Ainville
Eastfield
Stoneyburn
Loganlea
Salsburgh
Kirk of Shotts
Longridge
West Calder
R Almond
Addiewell
Linhouse Water
Water of Leith
Harperrig Reservoir
Fauldhouse
Greenburn
Breich
Dykehead
Shotts
Hartwood
Stane
Burnbrae
560 EAST CAIRN HILL
562 WEST CAIRN HILL
Cobbinshaw Loch
Bellside
Bonkle
Allanbank
Allanton
Headlesscross
Newmains
Gladsmuir Hills
Crindledyke
342 WORM LAW
Woolfords
Crosswood Reservoir
Tarbrax
Morningside
Wilsontown
West Water
Waterloo
Auchengray
Wildmanbridge
314 HARE HILL
Forth
South Tarbrax
415 HARROWS LAW
Law
Carluke
West Water Reservoir
Law Hill
Dalserf
B7056
Yieldshields
Roadmeetings
Braehead
369 LEFT LAW
451 MENDICK HILL
Rosebank
Medwin
Kilncadzow
Braidwood
Dunsyre
North Medwin
South Medwin
Craignethan Castle
Carnwath
Dolphinton
Mountain Cross
Crossford
Carstairs
Hazelbank
Tillietudlem
Newbigging
Walston
Carstairs Junction
Bankhead
R Medwin
Netherurd
Elsrickle
Kirkurd
Blackhill
Pettinain
Greenshields
0 1 2 3 4 miles
0 1 2 3 4 5 kilometres
M9
M8
M80
M876
M90
A9
A88
A905
A876
A977
A907
A985
A994
A823
A883
A803
A904
A993
A706
A801
A800
A89
A779
A705
A899
A8
A71
A704
A73
A721
A722
A70
A90
B9096
B910
B914
B912
B915
B913
B9037
B9124
B905
B902
B816
B810
B803
B8028
B825
B8022
B8047
B792
B8084
B708
B7002
B718
B7066
B717
B7010
B7015
B7008
B7016
B9156
B980
B916
B800
B903
B9080
B8046
B7030
B7031
B7086
Pentland
A B C D E F
1 2 3 4 5 6 7 8

Cardenden
Cluny
Gallatown
Chapel
Cowdenbeath
Auchtertool
Linktown
Kirkcaldy
Donibristle
Balmule
Kinghorn
Aberdour
Pettycur
Pettycur Bay
Burntisland
Silversands Bay
Dalgety Bay
Inchcolm Abbey
St Bridget's Kirk
Inchkeith
FIRTH OF FORTH
Cramond Island
Dalmeny
Cramond
Lauriston Castle
Granton
Newhaven
Britannia
Leith
EDINBURGH
St Triduana's Chapel
Barnton
Davidson's Mains
Warriston
Blackhall
Dovecot
Castle
Portobello
Musselburgh
Joppa
ARTHUR'S SEAT 251
Duddingston
Newcraighall
Fisherrow
Corstorphine
South Gyle
Craiglockhart
Morningside
Royal Observatory
Craigmillar
Craigmillar Castle
Water of Leith
Blackford Hill
Liberton
Gilmerton
Newton
Danderhall
Millerhill
Juniper Green
Colinton
Currie
Bonaly
Hillend
Straiton
Butterfly Farm
Dalkeith Park
Dalkeith
Eskbank
Lasswade
Malleny Garden
Kinleith
Malleny Mills
493 ALLERMUIR HILL
Boghall
Loanhead
Bilston
Bonnyrigg
Newbattle
Mayfield
Woodhouselee
Castlelaw Hill Fort
Polton
Roslin
Easter Howgate
Milton Bridge
Pentland Hills
448 HARE HILL
579 SCALD LAW
576 CARNETHY HILL
Auchendinny
Mining Museum
Newtonloan
Rosewell
Chesterhill
Newtongrange
Dewarton
Vogrie
Arniston
Newlandrig
Crichton
Crichton Castle
Gorebridge
Silverburn
Penicuik
Pomathorn
Carrington
Howgate
Temple
North Middleton
Mount Lothian
Rosebery Reservoir
Carlops
Leadburn
Craigburn
Gladhouse Reservoir
Heriot
Moorfoot Hills
Heriot Water
Linton
324 WHITE RIG
Waterheads
Portmore Loch
479 WETHER LAW
651 BLACKHOPE SCAR
425 DUN LAW
Fountainhall
Borders railway due to open 2014
Romanno Bridge
Eddleston
Torquhan
476 CRAILZIE HILL
621 WHITEHOPE LAW
Killochyett
Stow
Cockenzie and Port Seton
Seton Collegiate Church
Preston Market Cross
Prestonpans
Heritage Museum
Seton Mains
Longniddry
Tranent
Wallyford
Inveresk
Elphinstone
Ormiston Market Cross
Ormiston
Whitecraig
Crossgatehall
Cousland
Pencaitland
Pathhead
Fala Dam
Fala
Humbie
Blegbie
Soutra Summit 363
394 DUN LAW
Gilston
380 TURF LAW
Oxton
Carfrae
383 COLLIE LAW
Eyebroughy
Dirleton
Gullane Bay
Gullane Point
Muirfield
Gullane
Aberlady Bay
Craigelaw Point
Aberlady
Luffness
Drem
Gosford Bay
Spittal
Ballencrieff
Longniddry
Huntington
Elvingston
Gladsmuir
Macmerry
New Winton
Samuelston
Boggs Holdings
East Saltoun
West Saltoun
Gilchriston
Athelstaneford
186
178
166
G H J K L M
1 2 3 4 5 6 7 8

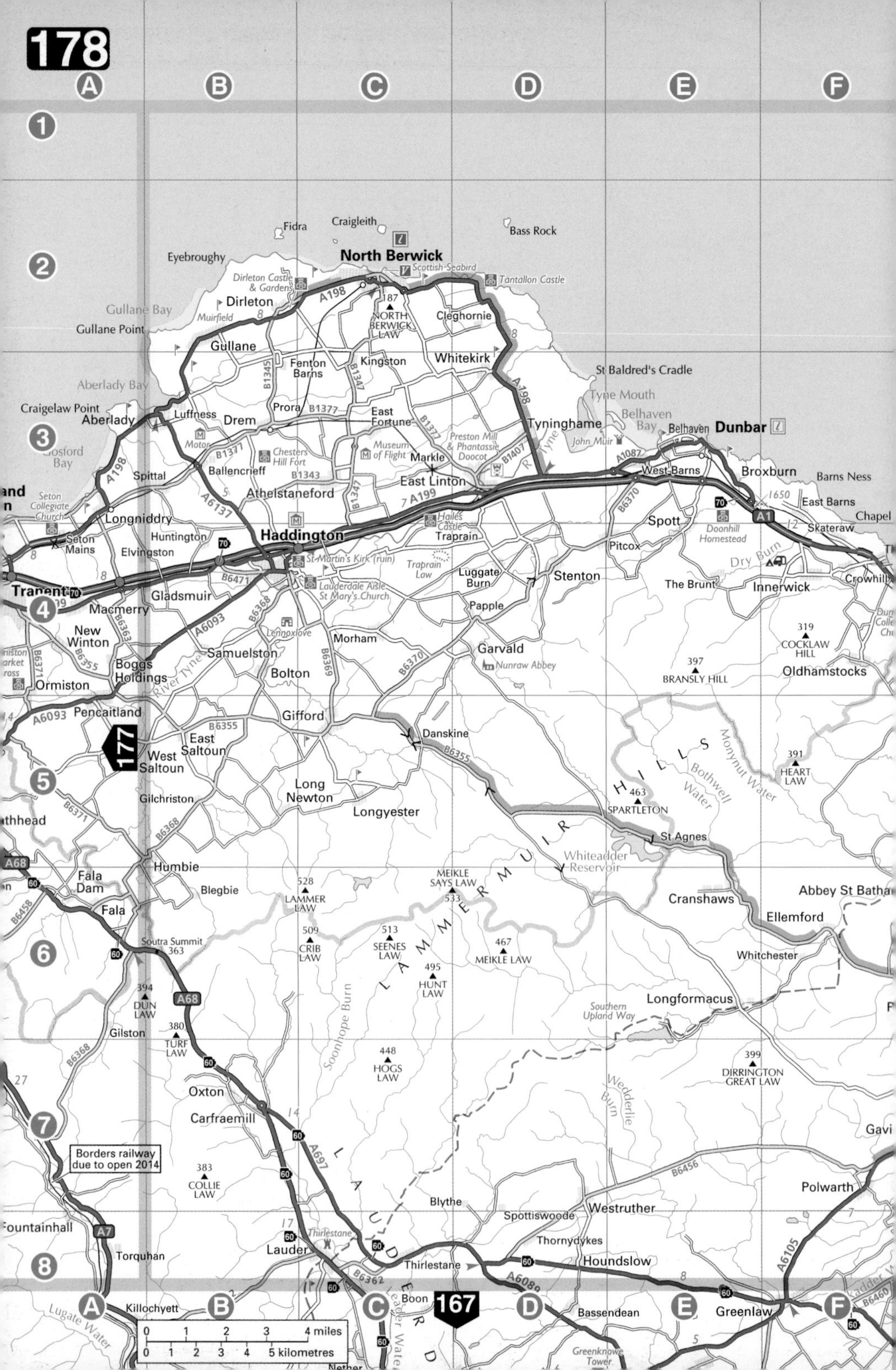

A
B
C
D
E
F
1
2
3
4
5
6
7
8
Fidra
Craigleith
Bass Rock
Eyebroughy
North Berwick
Scottish Seabird
Dirleton Castle & Gardens
Tantallon Castle
Dirleton
Gullane Bay
Muirfield
187 NORTH BERWICK LAW
Cleghornie
Gullane Point
Gullane
Fenton Barns
Kingston
Whitekirk
St Baldred's Cradle
Aberlady Bay
Tyne Mouth
Craigelaw Point
Aberlady
Luffness
Drem
Prora
East Fortune
Tyninghame
Belhaven Bay
Belhaven
Dunbar
Gosford Bay
Motor
Chesters Hill Fort
Museum of Flight
Preston Mill & Phantassie Doocot
John Muir
Spittal
Ballencrieff
Markle
East Linton
West Barns
Broxburn
Barns Ness
Seton Collegiate Church
Athelstaneford
East Barns
Chapel
Longniddry
Hailes Castle
Spott
Skateraw
Seton Mains
Huntington
Haddington
Traprain
Doonhill Homestead
Elvingston
St Martin's Kirk (ruin)
Traprain Law
Pitcox
Dry Burn
Tranent
Gladsmuir
Lauderdale Aisle St Mary's Church
Luggate Burn
Stenton
The Brunt
Innerwick
Crowhill
Macmerry
Papple
New Winton
Lennoxlove
Morham
319 COCKLAW HILL
Samuelston
Garvald
Boggs Holdings
Nunraw Abbey
397 BRANSLY HILL
Ormiston
Bolton
Oldhamstocks
River Tyne
Pencaitland
Gifford
Danskine
East Saltoun
West Saltoun
Monynut Water
Bothwell Water
391 HEART LAW
Long Newton
Longyester
463 SPARTLETON
Gilchriston
LAMMERMUIR HILLS
St Agnes
Whiteadder Reservoir
Humbie
MEIKLE SAYS LAW 533
Fala Dam
Blegbie
528 LAMMER LAW
Cranshaws
Abbey St Bathans
Fala
Ellemford
509 CRIB LAW
513 SEENES LAW
467 MEIKLE LAW
Soutra Summit 363
Whitchester
495 HUNT LAW
394 DUN LAW
Southern Upland Way
Longformacus
Gilston
380 TURF LAW
Soonhope Burn
448 HOGS LAW
399 DIRRINGTON GREAT LAW
Wedderlie Burn
Oxton
Carfraemill
LAUDERDALE
Borders railway due to open 2014
383 COLLIE LAW
Polwarth
Blythe
Westruther
Spottiswoode
Fountainhall
Thirlestane
Thornydykes
Lauder
Torquhan
Thirlestane
Houndslow
Boon
Leader Water
Greenlaw
Killochyett
Lugate Water
Bassendean
Greenknowe Tower
0 1 2 3 4 miles
0 1 2 3 4 5 kilometres
177
167
A198
A1
A1087
A199
A6137
A6093
A68
A697
A7
A6089
A6105
B1345
B1347
B1377
B1371
B1343
B1407
B6370
B6471
B6368
B6363
B6355
B6371
B6369
B6458
B6456
B6362
B6460

Reed Point
Cove
Pease Bay
Siccar Point
Fast Castle Head
A1107
196 BROWN RIG
Coldingham Loch
ST ABB'S HEAD
St Abbs
Coldingham Bay
Grantshouse
Southern Upland Way
Butterdean
Coldingham
Houndwood
Heugh Head
Cairncross
Eyemouth
262 HORSELEY HILL
Reston
Ayton
Burnmouth
Auchencrow
Marygold
Lintlaw
Lamberton
Preston
Chirnside
Marshall Meadows Bay
Cumledge
Edrom Church
Foulden
Chirnsidebridge
North Northumberland Heritage Coast
Edrom
Manderston
Broadhaugh
Edington
Whiteadder Water
Foulden Tithe Barn
1333
Allanton
Hutton
A6105
Berwick-upon-Tweed
Castle
Barracks
Duns
Paxton
Town Ramparts
Blackadder
Tweedmouth
Whitsome
Hilton
Spittal
Huds Head
Nisbet Hill
Sinclair's Hill
Scremerston
Horndean
Horncliffe
Murton
Ladykirk
Castle
Thornton
Swinton
Norham
Cheswick
Upsettlington
168
CAUSEWAY FLOODED AT HIGH TIDE
Simprim
River Tweed
Ancroft
Leitholm
Haggerston
A1
A6112
A6105
B6438
B6355
B6437
B6460
B6461
B6470
A698
B6354
B6525
A1167

A
B
C
D
E
F
1
2
3
4
5
6
7
8
189
171
ULVA
Bac Mòr or Dutchmans Cap
eag
Little Colonsay
Staffa
Fingal's Cave
Loch na Keal,
Isle of Mull
Inch Kenneth
Inchkenneth Chapel
(ruin)
491
CREACH BHEINN
Fossil Tree
Burg
Loch
IONA
Iona Abbey
& Nunnery
Baile Mór
MacLean's Cross
Rudha nan Cearc
Kintra
Loch na Lathaich
Fionnphort
Sound of Iona
Aridhglas
St Columba
Exhibition
Centre
A849
Bunessan
Loch Assapol
ROSS OF MULL
Soa Island
Erraid
Uisken
Ardchiavaig
Rudha
Ardalanish
Torran Rocks
Eilean
Dubh
Balnahard
Kiloran Bay
COLONSAY
Kiloran
Kilchattan
B8087
Scalasaig
B8086
Machrins
Colonsay
B8085
Oronsay
Rudha
Bàn
Dubh Eilean
0 1 2 3 4 miles
0 1 2 3 4 5 kilometres

190
182
171
172

182
A
B
C
D
E
F
1
2
3
4
5
6
7
8
Kilcheran
Kiel Crofts
Scottish Sea Life Sanctuary
BEINN MOLURGAINN
Benderloch
Ledaig
191
BENDERLOCH
B845
BEN MEEAN
Loch Etive
Lynn of Lorn
Ardmucknish Bay
Dunstaffnage Castle
Oban
Ardchattan Priory
Inveresragan
Dunstaffnage Chapel (ruin)
North Connel
Black Crofts
Connel
Achnacloich
Bonawe
River Noe
Dunbeg
Achaleven
A85
Ganavan Bay
Airds Bay
Bonawe Historic Iron Furnace
Gorten
Dunollie Castle
A85
Brochroy
McCaig's Tower
Taynuilt
Ichrachan
1124
BEN CRUACHAN
Oban
(An t-Oban)
Airdeny
Glen Nant
River Awe
Pass of Brander
KERRERA
Clenamacrie
Glen Lonan
River Lonan
Gallanachbeg
Ariogan
Gallanachmore
Sound of Kerrera
Loch Nell
B845
515
BEINN GHLAS
Rudha Seanach
Lerags
Kilmore
Ardanaiseig
Ardanaiseig Hotel
Ardentallen
Loch Feochan
Hayfield
Loch Nant
Kilchrenan
A816
482
BEINN DEARG
Taychreggan Hotel
Cladich
Kilninver
356
AN CREACHAN
Portsonachan Hotel
15
Loch Scamadale
Clachan
B844
Clachan-Seil
SEIL
Balvicar
B840
Inverinan
Loch Tralaig
B8003
24
Lochavich
Loch Avich
589
CRUACH MHOR
181
Melfort
Torsa
Kilmelford
Barnline Stables
Falls of Blarghour
Loch Awe
Degnish
Dalavich
Ardchonnel
A819
Loch Melfort
Newyork
Portinnisherrich
A816
Arduaine
Gleann Domhain
Glen Liever
Inveraray Castle
Inveraray
Inveraray Jail
Shuna Sound
SHUNA
Durran
525
BEINN BHREAC
Braevallich
Douglas Water
Craobh Haven
12
Inverliever Lodge
Shuna Point
Craigdhu
B840
A83
Ardfern
Kintraw
Ford
Fincharn
En Mhic Chrion
Loch Leacann
B8002
En Righ
458
CRUACH MHIC FHIONNLARDH
Auchindrain
433
BEINN LAOIGH
Carnassarie Castle
B840
Furnace
Aird
Loch Craignish
Loch Gaineamhach
A886
Glebe Cairn
Kilmartin
Sandhole
Island Macaskin
Slockavullin
Kilmartin House
Loch Leathan
Newton
Temple Wood Stone Circles
The Nether Largie Cairns
Dunchraigaig Cairn
Crarae
24
Ri Cruin Cairn
Crarae Garden
480
CRUACH NAN CAPULL
Poltalloch
Gleann Airidh
Minard
Castle Lachlan
Loch Crinan
10
Tullochgorm
Kilmichael Glassary Inscribed Stone
Moine Mhor
Crinan
A83
Barnacarry
505
CRUACH AN LOCHAIN
Kilmahumaig
B8025
Kilmichael Glassary
Loch Glashan
Loch Fyne
Dunadd Fort
River Add
Bellanoch
A816
A886
15
Cup & Ring
Crinan Canal
Asknish
B8000
643
B841
172
173
Lochgair
Dunans Castle
River Ruel
Middle Kames
Glenmassan
0 1 2 3 4 miles
0 1 2 3 4 5 kilometres

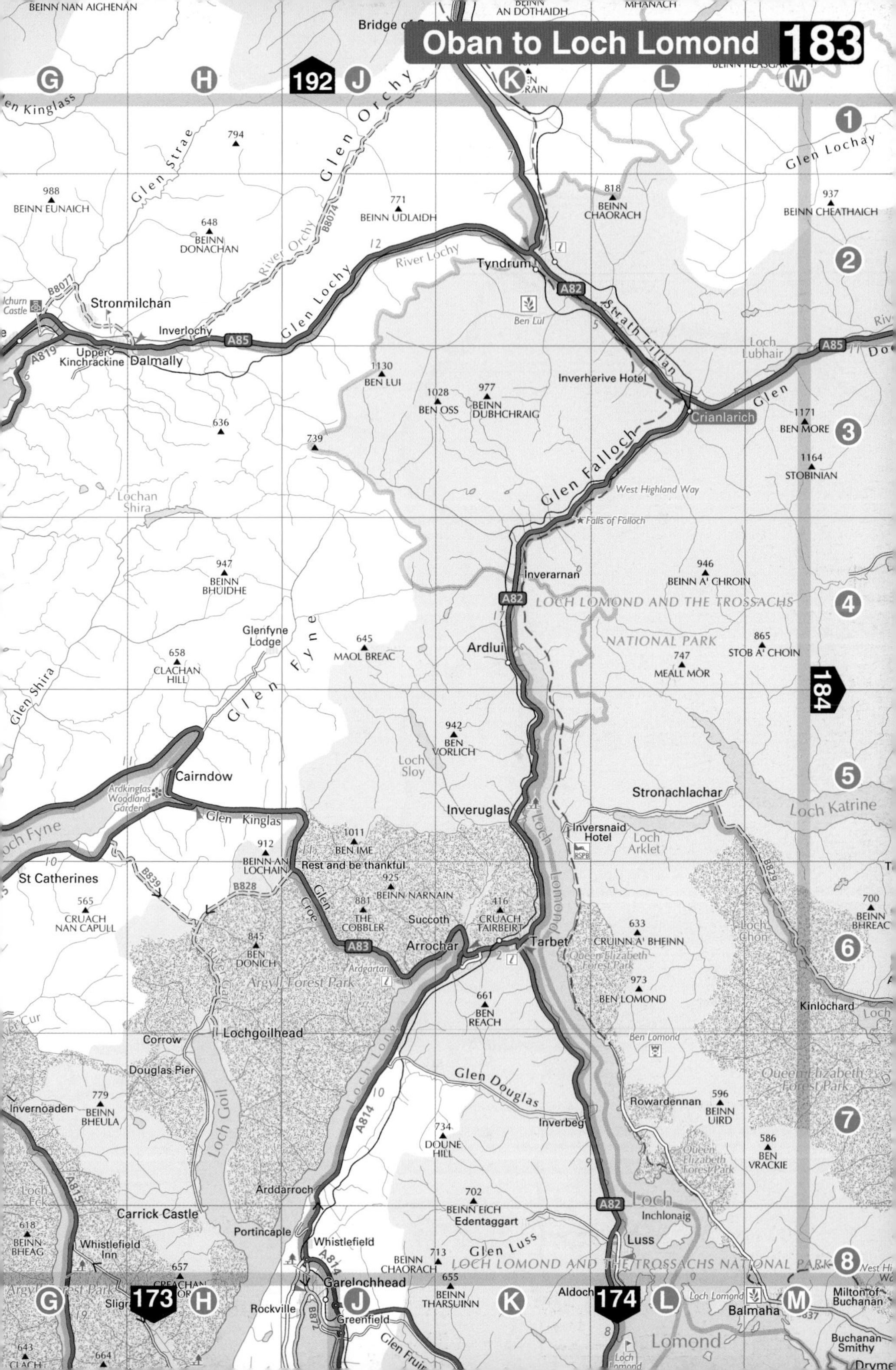
192
184
173
174
BEINN NAN AIGHENAN
Bridge of Orchy
Glen Kinglass
Glen Strae
Glen Orchy
794
988
BEINN EUNAICH
648
BEINN DONACHAN
771
BEINN UDLAIDH
B8074
River Orchy
River Lochy
Glen Lochy
B8077
Stronmilchan
Inverlochy
A85
A819
Upper Kinchrackine
Dalmally
Tyndrum
A82
Strath Fillan
Ben Lui
818
BEINN CHAORACH
937
BEINN CHEATHAICH
Glen Lochay
Loch Lubhair
Inverherive Hotel
Crianlarich
1130
BEN LUI
1028
BEN OSS
977
BEINN DUBHCHRAIG
1171
BEN MORE
1164
STOBINIAN
636
739
Lochan Shira
Glen Falloch
West Highland Way
Falls of Falloch
Inverarnan
947
BEINN BHUIDHE
946
BEINN A' CHROIN
LOCH LOMOND AND THE TROSSACHS NATIONAL PARK
Glenfyne Lodge
Glen Fyne
645
MAOL BREAC
658
CLACHAN HILL
Ardlui
865
STOB A' CHOIN
747
MEALL MÒR
Glen Shira
942
BEN VORLICH
Loch Sloy
Cairndow
Ardkinglas Woodland Garden
Glen Kinglas
Loch Fyne
Inveruglas
Stronachlachar
Loch Katrine
Inversnaid Hotel
Loch Arklet
1011
BEN IME
912
BEINN AN LOCHAIN
Rest and be thankful
St Catherines
B839
B828
925
BEINN NARNAIN
881
THE COBBLER
Succoth
416
CRUACH TAIRBEIRT
Glen Croe
565
CRUACH NAN CAPULL
A83
Arrochar
Tarbet
Loch Lomond
633
CRUINN A' BHEINN
B829
Loch Chon
700
BEINN BHREAC
845
BEN DONICH
Ardgartan
Argyll Forest Park
Queen Elizabeth Forest Park
973
BEN LOMOND
661
BEN REACH
Kinlochard
Lochgoilhead
Corrow
Douglas Pier
Loch Long
Glen Douglas
Loch Goil
779
BEINN BHEULA
Invernoaden
A814
734
DOUNE HILL
Inverbeg
Rowardennan
596
BEINN UIRD
586
BEN VRACKIE
A815
Loch Eck
Arddarroch
702
BEINN EICH
Edentaggart
Carrick Castle
618
BEINN BHEAG
Whistlefield Inn
Portincaple
Whistlefield
Inchlonaig
Luss
Glen Luss
713
BEINN CHAORACH
657
CREACHAN MOR
655
BEINN THARSUINN
Garelochhead
Sligrachan
Rockville
B872
Greenfield
Glen Fruin
Aldochlay
Loch Lomond
Balmaha
B837
Milton of Buchanan
Buchanan Smithy
643
664

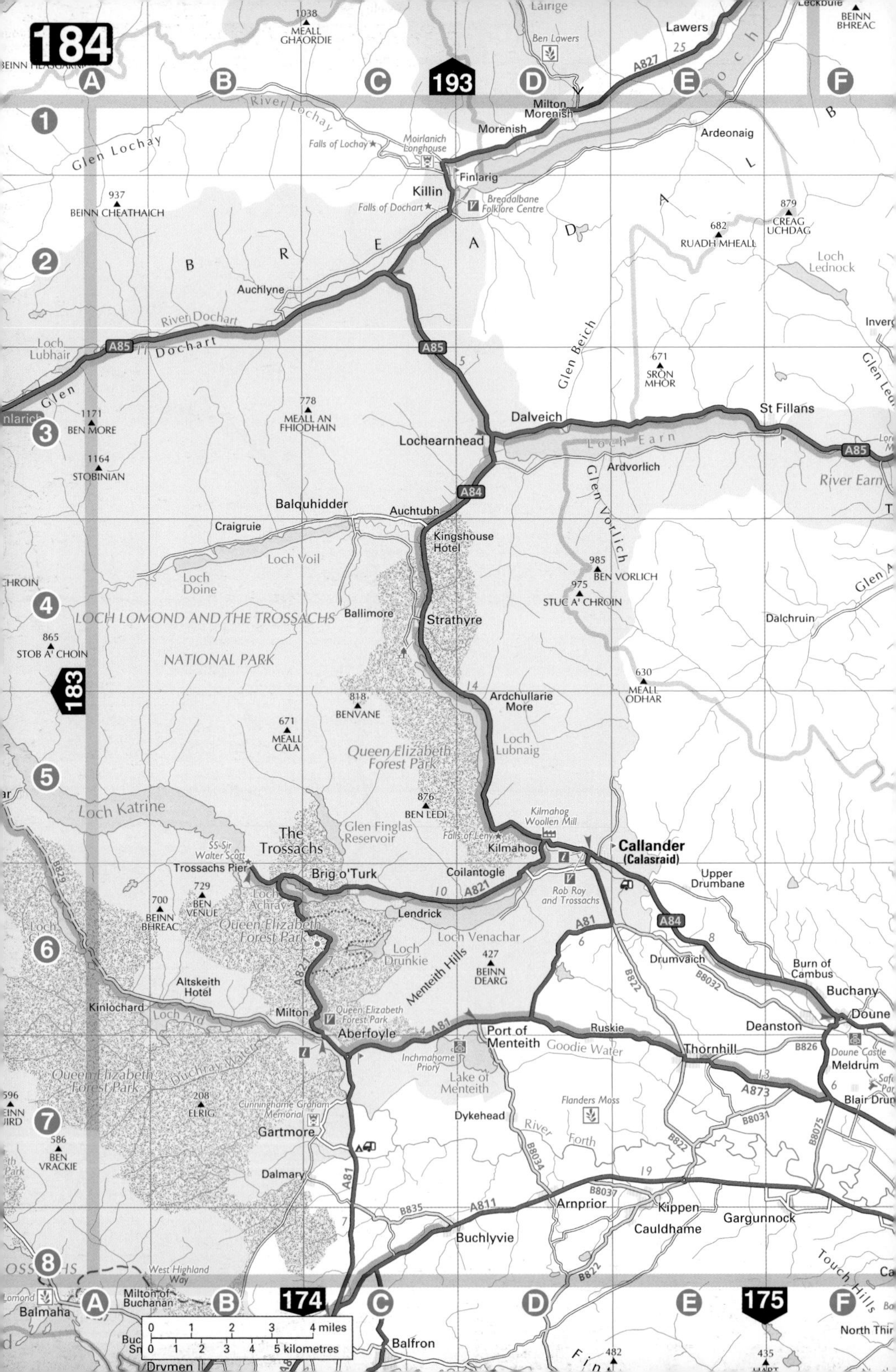
193
183
174
175
A
B
C
D
E
F
1
2
3
4
5
6
7
8
1038 MEALL GHAORDIE
Lawers
A827
25
Loch
BEINN BHREAC
Ben Lawers
River Lochay
Glen Lochay
Falls of Lochay
Moirlanich Longhouse
Milton Morenish
Morenish
Ardeonaig
Finlarig
Killin
Falls of Dochart
Breadalbane Folklore Centre
937 BEINN CHEATHAICH
B R E A D A L B A
879 CREAG UCHDAG
682 RUADH MHEALL
Loch Lednock
Auchlyne
River Dochart
Loch Lubhair
A85
Glen Dochart
5
Glen Beich
671 SRON MHOR
778 MEALL AN FHIODHAIN
1171 BEN MORE
1164 STOBINIAN
Dalveich
St Fillans
Lochearnhead
Loch Earn
Ardvorlich
River Earn
A84
Balquhidder
Auchtubh
Craigruie
Kingshouse Hotel
Loch Voil
Loch Doine
Glen Vorlich
985 BEN VORLICH
975 STUC A' CHROIN
Ballimore
Strathyre
LOCH LOMOND AND THE TROSSACHS NATIONAL PARK
Dalchruin
865 STOB A' CHOIN
630 MEALL ODHAR
14
818 BENVANE
Ardchullarie More
671 MEALL CALA
Queen Elizabeth Forest Park
Loch Lubnaig
Loch Katrine
876 BEN LEDI
Kilmahog Woollen Mill
The Trossachs
Glen Finglas Reservoir
Falls of Leny
Kilmahog
Callander (Calasraid)
SS Sir Walter Scott
Trossachs Pier
Brig o'Turk
Coilantogle
Upper Drumbane
B829
729 BEN VENUE
10
A821
Rob Roy and Trossachs
700 BEINN BHREAC
Loch Achray
Lendrick
A81
Loch Venachar
Loch Drunkie
427 BEINN DEARG
Drumvaich
B8032
Burn of Cambus
Menteith Hills
B822
Altskeith Hotel
Buchany
Kinlochard
Loch Ard
Milton
Queen Elizabeth Forest Park
Doune
Aberfoyle
Port of Menteith
Ruskie
Deanston
Goodie Water
Thornhill
B826
Doune Castle
Meldrum
Duchray Water
Inchmahome Priory
Lake of Menteith
13
A873
Blair Drummond
208 ELRIG
Cunninghame Graham Memorial
Dykehead
Flanders Moss
B8031
596
586 BEN VRACKIE
Gartmore
River Forth
B8034
B8075
Dalmary
19
B8037
B835
A811
Arnprior
Kippen
Gargunnock
Cauldhame
7
Buchlyvie
Touch Hills
West Highland Way
Milton of Buchanan
Balmaha
Balfron
North Third
0 1 2 3 4 miles
0 1 2 3 4 5 kilometres
Drymen
482
435

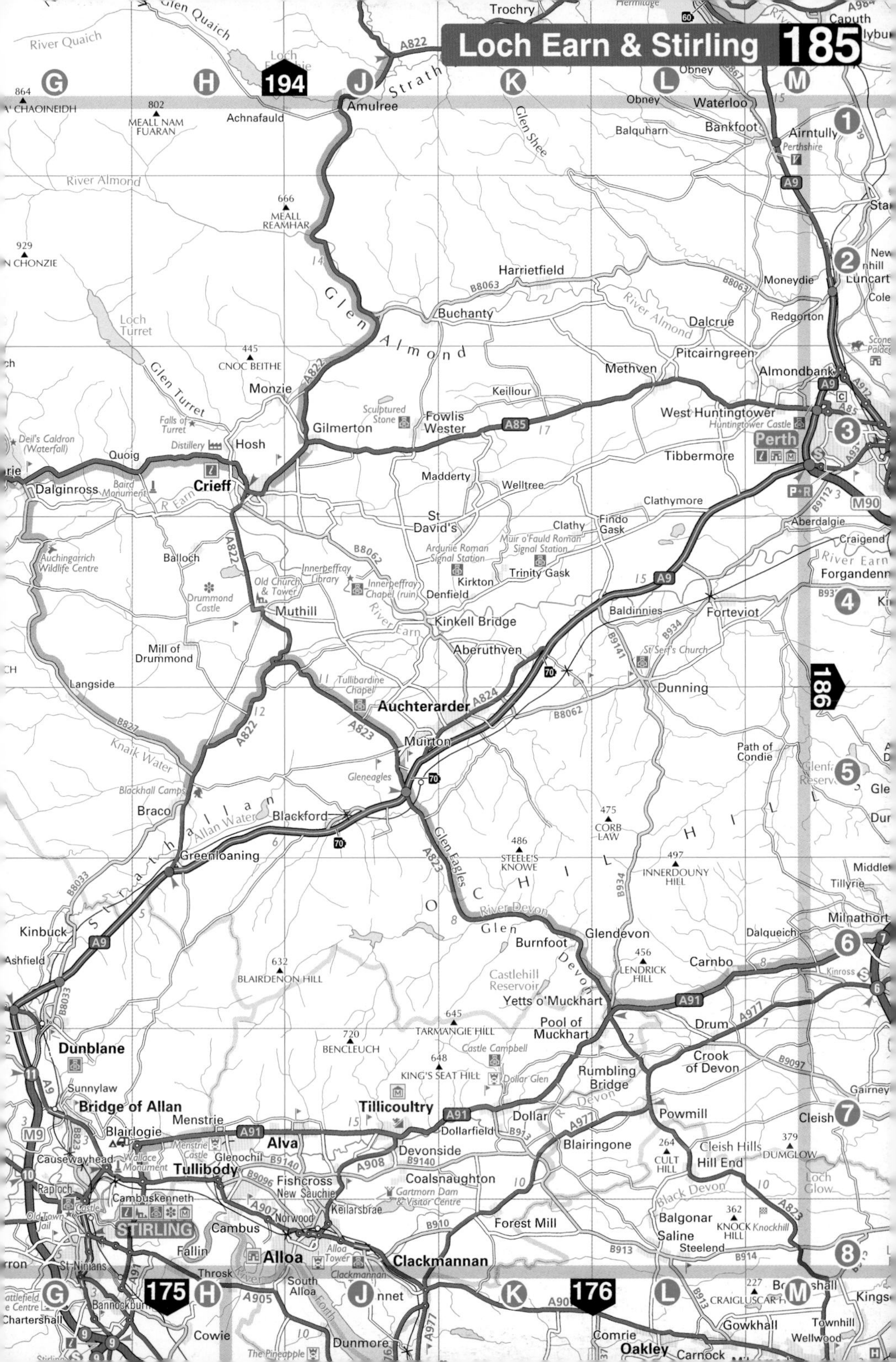
Amulree
Achnafauld
Glen Almond
Harrietfield
Buchanty
Methven
Pitcairngreen
Almondbank
Bankfoot
Perth
Crieff
Gilmerton
Monzie
Hosh
Muthill
Auchterarder
Dunning
Forteviot
Muirton
Blackford
Braco
Greenloaning
Gleneagles
Glendevon
Dunblane
Bridge of Allan
Tillicoultry
Alva
Tullibody
STIRLING
Alloa
Clackmannan
Dollar
Milnathort
Cleish
Saline
Oakley
OCHIL HILLS

186
195
196
185
177
Coupar Angus
Perth
Scone
Dundee
Cupar
Kinross
Loch Leven
Glenrothes
Kirkcaldy
Cowdenbeath
Lochgelly
Methil
Buckhaven
Leslie
Kennoway
Firth of Tay
Sidlaw Hills
Lomond Hills
Newburgh
Auchtermuchty
Falkland
Ladybank
Bridge of Earn
Errol
Inchture
Longforgan
Invergowrie
Stanley
Luncarty
Balbeggie
Abernethy
Glenfarg
Milnathort
Kelty
Cardenden
Lochore
Ballingry
Markinch
Freuchie
Kingskettle
Springfield
Letham
Collessie
Luthrie
Strathmiglo
Gateside
Scotlandwell
Kinnesswood
Auchtermuir
Kinglassie
Thornton
Dysart
Chapel
Gallatown
East Wemyss
West Wemyss
Coaltown of Wemyss
Windygates
Milton of Balgonie
Coaltown of Balgonie
Glenfoot
Aberargie
Dron
Kintillo
Forgandenny
Rhynd
Kinfauns
Glencarse
Glendoick
Kilspindie
Rait
Abernyte
Liff
Benvie
Fowlis
Muirhead
Birkhill
Lundie
Dronley
Kettins
Meikleour
Kinclaven
Caputh
Gellyburn
Airntully
Almondbank
Guildtown
Wolfhill
Kinrossie
Saucher
Collace
Ballindean
Baledgarno
Pitroddie
Grange
Leetown
St Madoes
Inchyra
Fingask
Craigend
Aberdalgie
Balmerino
Gauldry
Kilmany
Rathillet
Brunton
Creich
Glenduckie
Dunbog
Den of Lindores
Grange of Lindores
Monimail
Fernie
Pitlessie
Balmalcolm
Kettlebridge
Langdyke
Star
Baintown
Bonnybank
Muirhead
Balfarg
Cadham
Walkerton
Pitteuchar
Cluny
Auchterderran
Crosshill
Lumphinnans
Auchtertool
Linktown
Pathhead
Kingseat
Gairneybridge
Cleish
Drunzie
Duncrievie
Arngask
Path of Condie
Abbots Deuglie
Middleton
Tillyrie
Dalqueich
Newton of Balcanquhal
Pleasance
Dunshalt
Burnside
Lochieheads
Giffordtown
Charlottetown
Bow of Fife
Cupar Muir
Bridgend
Moonzie
Craigrothie
Struthers
A9
A90
A91
A92
A93
A94
A912
A913
A914
A915
A916
A955
A977
A823
A909
A910
A911
A923
A85
M90
B996
B919
B920
B9097
B921
B922
B981
B912
B914
B915
B917
B936
B937
B9129
B983
B931
B953
B9130
B969
B987
B927
B9157
B9112
B935
B8063
B867
B9099
376 KINGS SEAT
288 POLE HILL
221 MONCREIFFE HILL
285 NORMANS LAW
522 WEST LOMOND
448 EAST LOMOND
248 CLATTO HILL
379 DUMGLOW
362 KNOCK HILL
227 CRAIGLUSCAR HILL
455 CRAIGOWL HILL
0 1 2 3 4 miles
0 1 2 3 4 5 kilometres

Petterden
CARROT HILL
Crombie
Bonnington
Arbirlot
Todhills
Monikie
Kirkton of Monikie
B9128
Monikie
196
Wellbank
Muirdrum
A92
G
H
J
K
L
M
Burnside of Duntrune
Kellas
Newbigging
Carlungie Earth House
Upper Victoria
East Haven
Panbride
Murroes
Ardestie Earth-House
Barry Mill
Barry
West Haven
Carnoustie
Whitfield
B961
Baldovie
B962
A930
Carnoustie
Douglas and Angus
Claypotts Castle
Barnhill
Monifieth
DUNDEE
Broughty Ferry
Broughty Castle
BUDDON NESS
A92
Tay Bridge
Tayport
Newport-on-Tay
Tentsmuir Point
B945
A914
Scottish National Golf Centre
Tentsmuir Point
A919
Leuchars
RAF Leuchars
ST ANDREWS BAY
Balmullo
Guardbridge
River Eden
Kincaple
St Andrews
A91
Castle
St Andrews
Strathkinness
Brownhills
B939
Botanic Garden
Blebocraigs
A917
Craigtoun
Boarhills
Denhead
B9131
Pitscottie
A915
Cameron Reservoir
Kingsbarns
Baldinnie
B940
Dunino
Peat Inn
Radernie
Balcomie Links
FIFE NESS
New Gilston
B941
Kingsmuir
B940
Lathones
Scotland's Secret Bunker
Woodside
Largoward
Lochty
B940
Crail
Carnbee
B9171
Easter Pitkierie
A915
Kellie Castle
A917
Arncroach
Wester Pitkierie
Upper Largo
Kilrenny
B9171
Cellardyke
Colinsburgh
B942
Newton of Balcormo
B9131
Fisheries
Anstruther
Drumeldrie
B941
B942
Lower Largo
Pittenweem
A917
Kilconquhar
St Monans
Largo Bay
Earlsferry
Elie
Isle of May
1
2
3
4
5
6
7
8

A
B
C
D
E
F
1
2
3
4
5
6
7
8
Arnab
Grishipoll
Clabhach
Hogh Bay
Ballyhaugh
Totronald
Coll
Acha
Feall Bay
Arileod
Uig
RSPB
Calgary Point
Crossapol Bay
Loch Breachacha
Rudha Fàsachd
Gunna
Rudha Dubh
Caoles
B8069
Ruaig
Rudha Port Bhiosd
Clachan Mor
Balephetrish Bay
Loch Bhasapoll
Haugh Bay
Ballevullin
Cornoigmore
B8068
Kenovay
Gott Bay
Tiree
Kilkenneth
B8068
Scarinish
Moss
Heylipoll
B8065
Middleton
B8065
Crossapoll
TIREE
Hynish Bay
Barrapoll
B8067
Balemartine
Loch a Phuill
Mannel
Rinn Thorbhais
Hynish
Balephuil Bay
0 1 2 3 4 miles
0 1 2 3 4 5 kilometres

Kildonnan
393
198
Eilean nan Each
MUCK
Port Mor
Sanna Point
Sanna Bay
Portuairk
Achnaha
Ardnamurchan Point
Achosnich
B8007
436
MEALL NAN CON
Kilmory
Ockle
Ockle Point
Branault
ARDNAMU
Loch Mudle
342
BEINN NA SEILG
Kilchoan
Ormsaigmore
Mingary
527
BEN HIANT
Ardslignish
Bagh a Chaisteil (Castlebay)
Loch Baghasdail (Lochboisdale)
Eilean Mòr
Rudha Mòr
Rudha Sgor-innis
Bousd
Sorisdale
B8072
Coll - Oban
COLL
Eilean Ornsay
Ardmore Point
190
Auliston Point
Sorne Point
Glengorm Castle
Quinish Point
Tobermory
Calve Island
Caliach Point
292
'S AIRDE BEINN
Dervaig
B8073
Achnadrish House
Calgary
Calgary Bay
A848
444
SPEINNE MÒR
Loch Frisa
Treshnish Point
Ensay
342
CÀRN MÒR
ISLE OF MULL
Rudh' a' Chaoil
Burg
Glen Aros
Fanmore
390
CNOC AN DÀ CHINN
Glenaros House
Fladda
Loch Tuath
Ballygown
Eas Fors (Waterfall)
333
BEINN NAN CÀRN
Killiechronan
B8035
Lunga
TRESHNISH ISLES
Gometra
Oskamull
B8073
Gruline
Macquarie Mausoleum
ULVA
Bac Mòr or Dutchmans Cap
Loch na Keal, Isle of Mull
Eorsa
Bac Beag
Little Colonsay
591
180
Staffa
Fingal's Cave
Balnahard

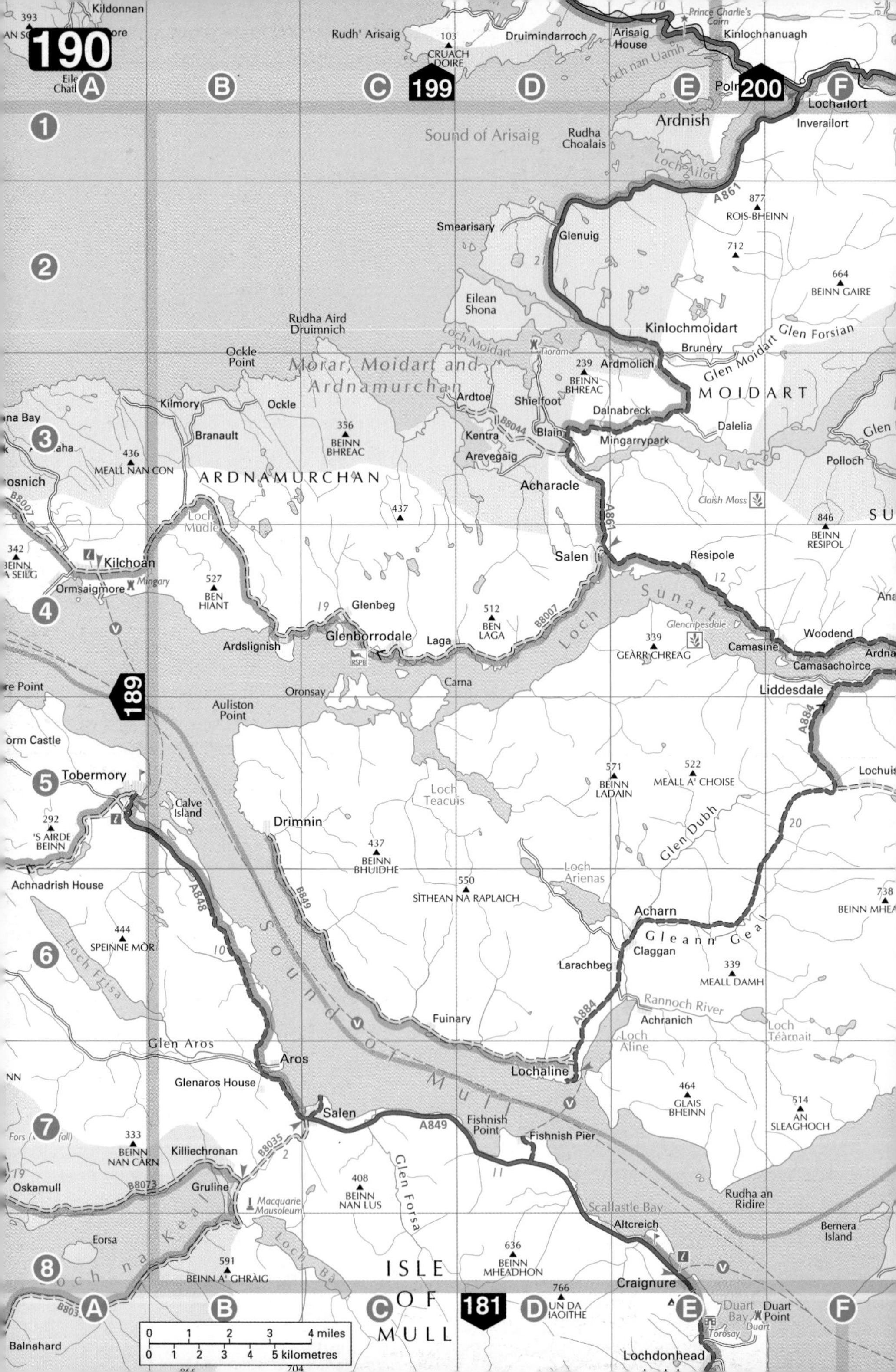
Kildonnan
Rudh' Arisaig
103
CRUACH DOIRE
199
Druimindarroch
Arisaig House
Prince Charlie's Cairn
Kinlochnanuagh
Loch nan Uamh
200
Lochailort
Inverailort
Ardnish
Sound of Arisaig
Rudha Choalais
Loch Ailort
A861
877
ROIS-BHEINN
712
Smearisary
Glenuig
664
BEINN GAIRE
Eilean Shona
Rudha Aird Druimnich
Kinlochmoidart
Glen Forsian
Loch Moidart
Tioram
Brunery
Ockle Point
Morar, Moidart and Ardnamurchan
239
BEINN BHREAC
Ardmolich
Glen Moidart
MOIDART
Kilmory
Ockle
Ardtoe
Shielfoot
Dalnabreck
Dalelia
Branault
356
BEINN BHREAC
B8044
Kentra
Blain
Mingarrypark
Arevegaig
436
MEALL NAN CON
Polloch
ARDNAMURCHAN
Acharacle
Claish Moss
B8007
Loch Mudle
437
846
BEINN RESIPOL
342
Kilchoan
Salen
Resipole
Ormsaigmore
Mingary
527
BEN HIANT
Glenbeg
512
BEN LAGA
Loch Sunart
Glencripesdale
Ardslignish
Glenborrodale
Laga
RSPB
339
GEÀRR CHREAG
Camasine
Woodend
Camasachoirce
189
Oronsay
Carna
Liddesdale
Auliston Point
A884
Tobermory
Calve Island
571
BEINN LADAIN
522
MEALL A' CHOISE
Loch Teacuis
Lochuisge
292
Drimnin
Glen Dubh
437
BEINN BHUIDHE
Achnadrish House
B849
Loch Arienas
550
SÌTHEAN NA RAPLAICH
738
A848
Acharn
444
SPEINNE MÒR
Gleann Geal
Claggan
Loch Frisa
Larachbeg
339
MEALL DAMH
Sound of Mull
Rannoch River
Achranich
Fuinary
Loch Aline
Loch Tèàrnait
Glen Aros
Aros
Lochaline
Glenaros House
464
GLAIS BHEINN
514
AN SLEAGHOCH
Salen
Fishnish Point
A849
Fishnish Pier
333
BEINN NAN CÀRN
Killiechronan
B8035
Oskamull
B8073
Gruline
408
BEINN NAN LUS
Glen Forsa
Macquarie Mausoleum
Rudha an Ridire
Scallastle Bay
Altcreich
Bernera Island
Eorsa
Loch na Keal
Loch Bà
636
BEINN MHEADHON
591
BEINN A' GHRÀIG
ISLE OF MULL
181
766
Craignure
B8035
Duart Bay
Duart Point
Torosay
Duart
Balnahard
Lochdonhead
0 1 2 3 4 miles
0 1 2 3 4 5 kilometres

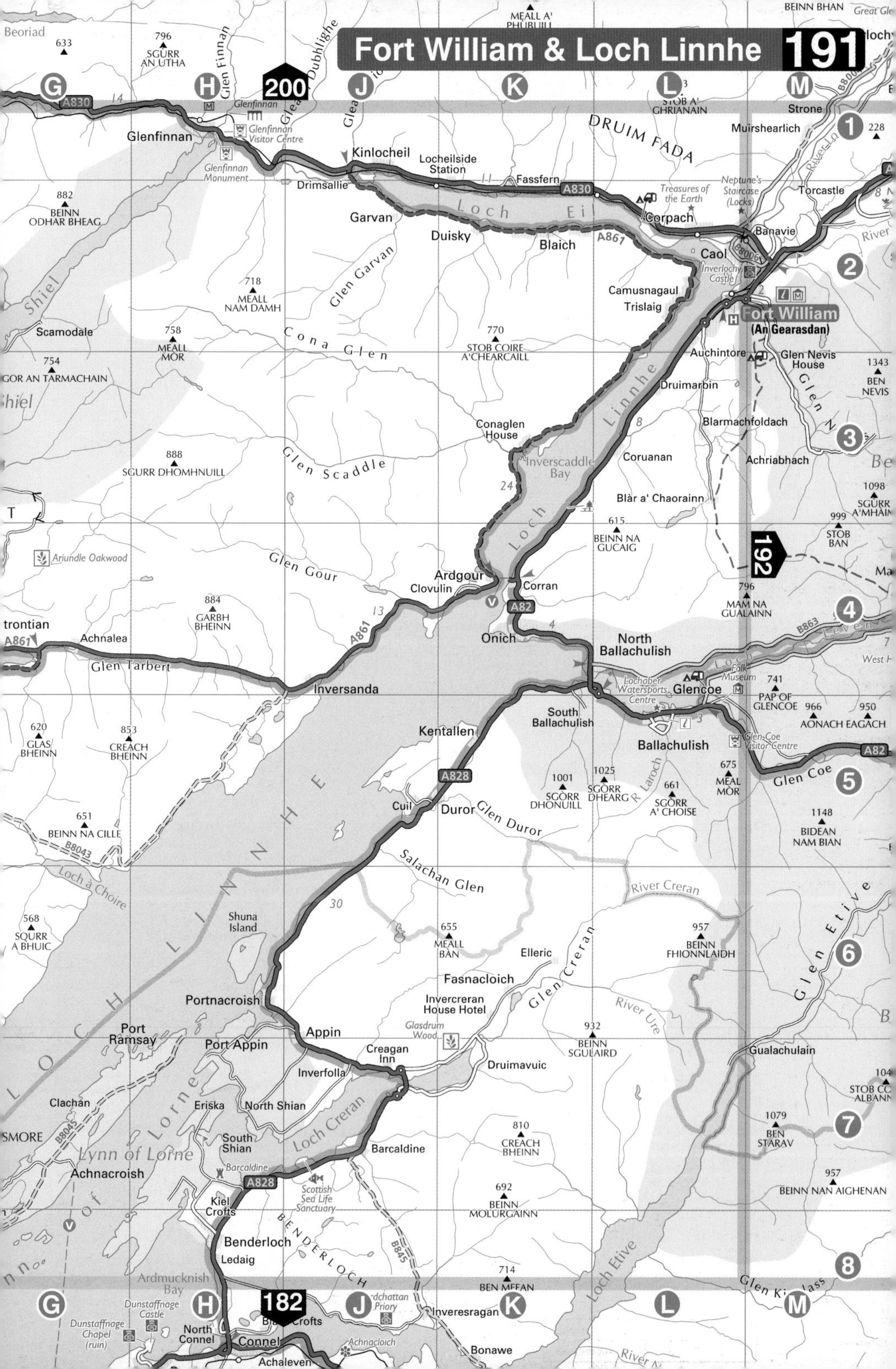
Fort William
(An Gearasdan)
Glenfinnan
Glenfinnan Visitor Centre
Glenfinnan Monument
Kinlocheil
Locheilside Station
Drimsallie
Fassfern
Loch Eil
Corpach
Banavie
Caol
Inverlochy Castle
Treasures of the Earth
Neptune's Staircase (Locks)
Torcastle
Muirshearlich
Strone
Garvan
Duisky
Blaich
Camusnagaul
Trislaig
Auchintore
Glen Nevis House
Druimarbin
Blarmachfoldach
Achriabhach
Coruanan
Blàr a' Chaorainn
Conaglen House
Inverscaddle Bay
Loch Linnhe
Ardgour
Clovulin
Corran
Onich
North Ballachulish
South Ballachulish
Ballachulish
Glencoe
Folk Museum
Lochaber Watersports Centre
Glen Coe Visitor Centre
Glen Coe
Kentallen
Cuil
Duror
Glen Duror
Salachan Glen
River Creran
Glen Creran
River Ure
Elleric
Fasnacloich
Invercreran House Hotel
Glasdrum Wood
Druimavuic
Creagan Inn
Appin
Port Appin
Portnacroish
Port Ramsay
Shuna Island
Inverfolla
North Shian
South Shian
Eriska
Loch Creran
Barcaldine
Scottish Sea Life Sanctuary
Kiel Crofts
Benderloch
Ledaig
Ardmucknish Bay
Dunstaffnage Castle
Dunstaffnage Chapel (ruin)
North Connel
Connel
Achaleven
Achnacloich
Ardchattan Priory
Inveresragan
Bonawe
Loch Etive
Glen Etive
Gualachulain
Glen Kinglass
Lynn of Lorne
Achnacroish
Clachan
Loch à Choire
Inversanda
Glen Tarbert
Achnalea
Strontian
Ariundle Oakwood
Glen Gour
Glen Scaddle
Cona Glen
Glen Garvan
Scamodale
Shiel
Beoriad
Glen Finnan
DRUIM FADA
BENDERLOCH
796 SGURR AN UTHA
633
882 BEINN ODHAR BHEAG
718 MEALL NAM DAMH
758 MEALL MÒR
754
888 SGURR DHOMHNUILL
770 STOB COIRE A'CHEARCAILL
884 GARBH BHEINN
620 GLAS BHEINN
853 CREACH BHEINN
651 BEINN NA CILLE
568 SGURR A BHUIC
615 BEINN NA GUCAIG
796 MAM NA GUALAINN
1343 BEN NEVIS
1098 SGURR A'MHAIM
999 STOB BAN
741 PAP OF GLENCOE
966 AONACH EAGACH
950
1001 SGÒRR DHONUILL
1025 SGÒRR DHEARG
661 SGÒRR A' CHOISE
675 MEAL MÒR
1148 BIDEAN NAM BIAN
655 MEALL BÀN
957 BEINN FHIONNLAIDH
932 BEINN SGULAIRD
1079 BEN STARAV
957 BEINN NAN AIGHENAN
810 CREACH BHEINN
692 BEINN MOLURGAINN
714 BEN MEEAN
228
A830
A861
A82
A828
B8006
B8043
B8045
B845
B863
200
192
182

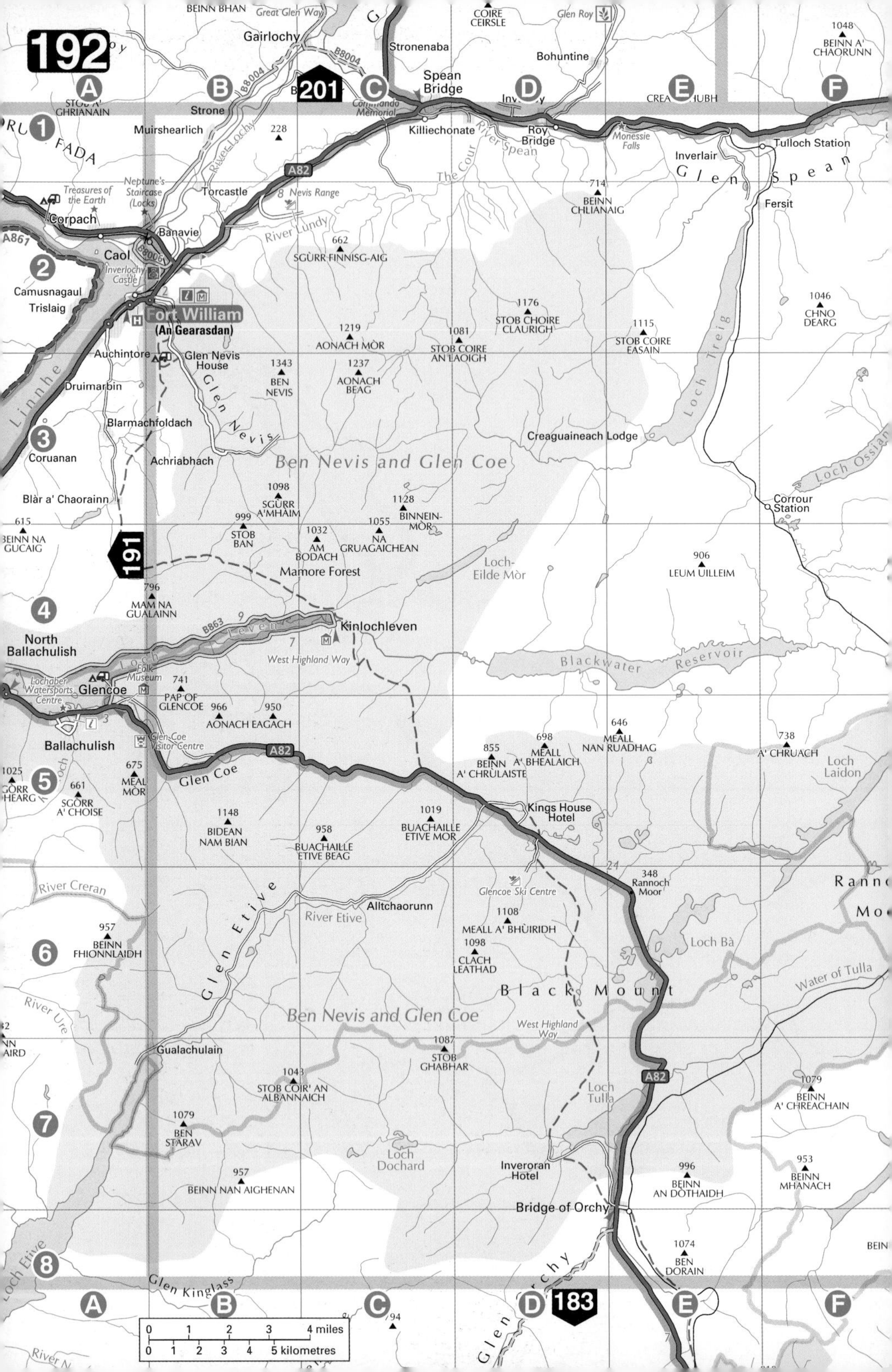
Gairlochy
Stronenaba
Spean Bridge
Commando Memorial
Bohuntine
Glen Roy
Strone
Muirshearlich
Killiechonate
Roy Bridge
Monessie Falls
Tulloch Station
Inverlair
Glen Spean
Fersit
A82
Nevis Range
Treasures of the Earth
Neptune's Staircase (Locks)
Torcastle
Corpach
Banavie
Caol
Inverlochy Castle
Camusnagaul
Trislaig
Fort William
(An Gearasdan)
Auchintore
Glen Nevis House
Druimarbin
Blarmachfoldach
Coruanan
Achriabhach
Glen Nevis
Blàr a' Chaorainn
SGÙRR FINNISG-AIG
AONACH MÒR
AONACH BEAG
BEN NEVIS
STOB CHOIRE CLAURIGH
STOB COIRE AN LAOIGH
STOB COIRE EASAIN
BEINN CHLIANAIG
CHNO DEARG
Loch Treig
Creaguaineach Lodge
Loch Ossian
Corrour Station
Ben Nevis and Glen Coe
SGÙRR A'MHAIM
BINNEIN-MÒR
STOB BAN
AM BODACH
NA GRUAGAICHEAN
Mamore Forest
Loch Eilde Mòr
LEUM UILLEIM
MAM NA GUALAINN
Kinlochleven
North Ballachulish
West Highland Way
Blackwater Reservoir
Lochaber Watersports Centre
Glencoe
Folk Museum
PAP OF GLENCOE
AONACH EAGACH
Ballachulish
Glen Coe Visitor Centre
Glen Coe
MEALL MÒR
SGORR A' CHOISE
BEINN A' CHRÙLAISTE
MEALL A' BHEALAICH
MEALL NAN RUADHAG
A' CHRUACH
Loch Laidon
Kings House Hotel
BIDEAN NAM BIAN
BUACHAILLE ETIVE BEAG
BUACHAILLE ETIVE MOR
Rannoch Moor
Glencoe Ski Centre
River Creran
Glen Etive
Alltchaorunn
River Etive
MEALL A' BHÙIRIDH
CLACH LEATHAD
Loch Bà
BEINN FHIONNLAIDH
Black Mount
Water of Tulla
River Ure
Gualachulain
STOB GHABHAR
STOB COIR' AN ALBANNAICH
Loch Tulla
BEINN A' CHREACHAIN
BEN STARAV
Loch Dochard
Inveroran Hotel
BEINN NAN AIGHENAN
BEINN AN DOTHAIDH
BEINN MHANACH
Bridge of Orchy
BEN DORAIN
Loch Etive
Glen Kinglass
Glen Orchy
201
191
183
0 1 2 3 4 miles
0 1 2 3 4 5 kilometres

A86
747 BINNEIN SHUAS
202
1049 GEAL CHÀRN
896 MEALL CRUAIDH
769 CREAGAN MOR
CÀRN NA CAIM
Loch an Dùin
Loch Pattack
1088 BEINN A' CHLACHAIR
1034 CÀRN DEARG
Loch Ericht
975 A' MHARCONAICH
459 Drumochter Summit
926 GLAS MHEALL MÒR
1008 BEINN UDLAMAIN
991 SGAIRNEACH MHOR
Dalnaspidal
1101 BEINN EIBHINN
1145 BEN ALDER
Loch Garry
Dalnacardoch
Glen Garry
844 MEALL A'BHEALAICH
952 SGÒR GAIBHRE
Loch Con
Loch Errochty
626 SRON A CHLAONAIDH
841 BEINN MHOLACH
864 BEINN PHARIAGAIN
Trinafour
B847
511 TORR DUBH
892 BEINN A' CHUALLAICH
194
R Ericht
Tay Forest Park
B846
Rannoch Station
Bridge of Ericht
Killichonan
Loch Rannoch
Kinloch Rannoch
Drumchastle
Dunalastair
R Tummel
Tummel Bridge
Dunan
Finnart
Inverhadden
Tempar
Dunalastair Water
Loch Eigheach
Bridge of Gaur
Carie
Camghouran
1081 SCHIEHALLION
Glengoulandie Deer Park
Loch Rannoch and Glen Lyon
1042 CÀRN MAIRG
745 MEALL A' MHUIC
824 BEINN DEARG
1027 CÀRN GORM
931 MEALL BUIDHE
860 CAM CHREAG
Fortingall
Loch an Daimh
Glen Lyon
Bridge of Balgie
River Lyon
Kenmore
Fearnan
Acharn
780 MEALL LUAIDHE
924 MEALL A' CHOIRE LEITH
1116 MEALL GARBH
1000 MEALL GREIGH
908 BEINN NAN OIGHREAG
1214 BEN LAWERS
Lochan na Làirige
Leckbuie
713 BEINN BHREAC
1038 MEALL GHAORDIE
Lawers
Ben Lawers
A827
Loch Tay
River Lochay
Milton Morenish
184
Glen Lochay
Falls of Lochay
Finlarig

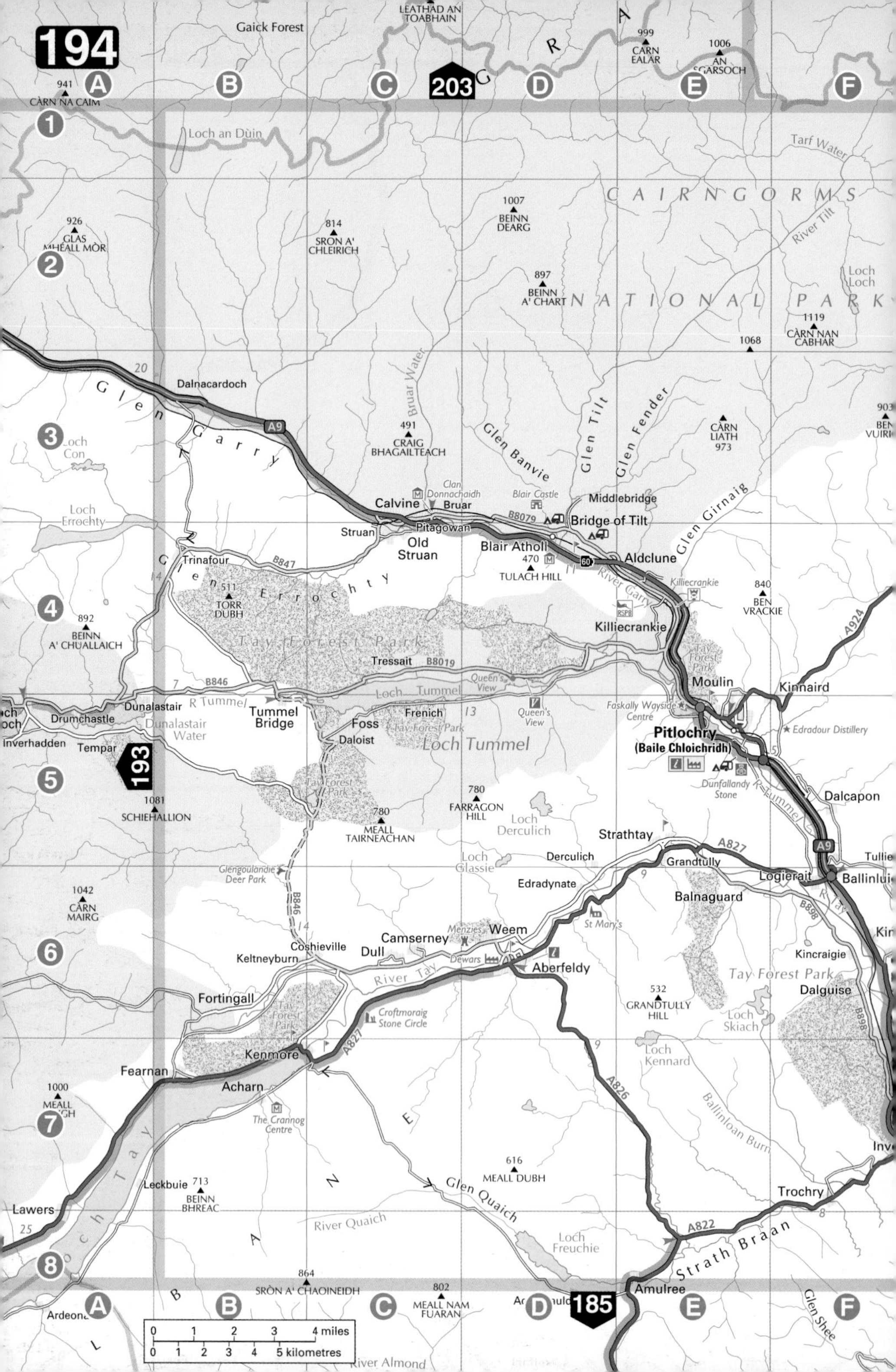
Gaick Forest
LEATHAD AN TOABHAIN
203
999 CÀRN EALAR
1006 AN SGARSOCH
941 CÀRN NA CAIM
Loch an Dùin
Tarf Water
CAIRNGORMS NATIONAL PARK
926 GLAS MHEALL MÒR
814 SRON A' CHLEIRICH
1007 BEINN DEARG
897 BEINN A' CHART
River Tilt
Loch Loch
1119 CÀRN NAN CABHAR
1068
Glen Garry
Dalnacardoch
A9
Bruar Water
491 CRAIG BHAGAILTEACH
Glen Banvie
Glen Tilt
Glen Fender
CÀRN LIATH 973
903
Loch Con
Loch Errochty
Clan Donnachaidh
Blair Castle
Middlebridge
Calvine
Bruar
Glen Girnaig
Struan
Pitagowan
B8079
Bridge of Tilt
Old Struan
Blair Atholl
Aldclune
Trinafour
B847
470 TULACH HILL
River Garry
Killiecrankie
840 BEN VRACKIE
A924
Glen Errochty
511 TORR DUBH
892 BEINN A' CHUALLAICH
Tay Forest Park
Killiecrankie
Tressait
B8019
Queen's View
Moulin
Kinnaird
B846
Loch Tummel
Dunalastair
R Tummel
Tummel Bridge
Frenich
Faskally Wayside Centre
Drumchastle
Dunalastair Water
Foss
Pitlochry (Baile Chloichridh)
Edradour Distillery
Inverhadden
Tempar
Daloist
193
1081 SCHIEHALLION
780 FARRAGON HILL
780 MEALL TAIRNEACHAN
Dunfallandy Stone
Dalcapon
Loch Derculich
Strathtay
A827
Loch Glassie
Derculich
Grandtully
Logierait
Ballinluig
Glengoulandie Deer Park
Edradynate
Balnaguard
B898
1042 CÀRN MAIRG
St Mary's
Camserney
Menzies
Weem
Kincraigie
Coshieville
Keltneyburn
Dull
Dewars
Aberfeldy
River Tay
Tay Forest Park
Fortingall
532 GRANDTULLY HILL
Dalguise
Croftmoraig Stone Circle
Loch Skiach
Kenmore
Loch Kennard
A826
Fearnan
Acharn
1000 MEALL
The Crannog Centre
Ballinloan Burn
616 MEALL DUBH
Glen Quaich
Leckbuie
713 BEINN BHREAC
Trochry
Lawers
River Quaich
A822
Loch Freuchie
Strath Braan
864 SRÒN A' CHAOINEIDH
802 MEALL NAM FUARAN
Amulree
185
Glen Shee
Ardeonaig
0 1 2 3 4 miles
0 1 2 3 4 5 kilometres
River Almond

205
195
186
187
Kirriemuir
Forfar
Carnoustie
Clova
Glen Clova
Glen Prosen
River South Esk
River North Esk
Loch Lee
Invermark
Tarfside
Glen Esk
Glamis
Angus Folk Museum
Edzell Castle & Garden
Brechin Castle & Pictavia
Aberlemno
Letham
Monikie
Tealing
Meigle
Sculptured Stone Museum
Newtyle
Auchterhouse
Barry Mill
0 1 2 3 4 miles
0 1 2 3 4 5 kilometres

Forfar & Angus Coast
197
206
Montrose
Arbroath
Laurencekirk
Inverbervie
Johnshaven
St Cyrus
Gourdon
Ferryden
Lunan Bay
Auchmithie
Inverkeilor
Marykirk
Fordoun
Auchenblae
Drumlithie
Glenbervie
Kinneff
Catterline
Crawton
Arbuthnott

A
B
C
D
E
F
1
2
3
4
5
6
7
8
208
189
Talisker Bay
Talisker
Glen Eynort
447
BEINN BHREAC
Loch Eynort
434
AN CRUACHIN
Glenbrittle House
Bualintur
Loch Brittle
Rudh' an Dùnain
CANNA
210
CÀRN A' GHAILL
Garrisdale Point
A'Chill
Canna Harbour
Sanday
Sound of Canna
Rudha Shamhnan Insir
302
MULLACH MÒR
A Bhrideanach
570
ORVAL
Oigh-sgeir
RÙM
810
ASKIVAL
763
SGÙRR NAN GILLEAN
The Small Isles
Rudha nam Meirleach
Rudha an
Eilean nan Each
0 1 2 3 4 miles
0 1 2 3 4 5 kilometres

Sligachan
GLAMAIG
ISLE
OF
SKYE
Loch Ainort
Dunan
Luib
209
Scalpay
Pabay
Skye Bridge
Kyleakin
A87
564
GLAS BHEIN MHÒRN
965
SGURR NAN GILLEAN
Corry
Broadford Bay
Lower Breakish
Waterloo
Broadford
Harrapool
Skulamus
Upper Breakish
732
BEINN NA CAILLICH
708
BEINN DEORG MHÒR
974
SGURR HEADAIDH
The Cuillin Hills
927
BLAVEN
B8083
732
SGURR NA COINNICH
Otter Haven
1009
SGURR ALASDAIR
Loch Coruisk
Loch na Crèitheach
Torrin
A851
605
BEN ASLAK
894
GARS BHEINN
Kirkibost
Loch Slapin
300
BEINN NAN CÀRN
Heast
561
BEINN NA SEAMRAIG
139
BEINN BHREAC
344
BEN MEABOST
Loch Scavaig
Suisnish
Rudha Suisnish
Loch Eishort
Drumfearn
Loch na Dal
Sandaig Island
Mol-chlach
Elgol
298
SGORACH BREAC
Duisdalemore
Isleornsay
Ornsay
SOAY
Glasnakille
Tokavaig
Ord River
Rudha Buidhe
Strathaird Point
17
Tarskavaig
Teangue
Rudh' Ard Slisneach
Tarskavaig Bay
Achnacloich
Loch nam Uamph
Knock
Ferrindonald
Knock Bay
SOUND OF SLEAT
Kilmore
Inverguseran
Kilbeg
Glen Guseran
Airor
Clan Donald
200
518
DRUIM NA CLUAIN-AIRIDHE
Ardvasar
Armadale
Calligarry
Sandaig
Aird of Sleat
Sandaig Bay
Inverie
Inverie Bay
Ard Thurinish
Rudha Raonuill
Point of Sleat
Courteachan
Mallaigvaig
Mallaig (Malaig)
547
CÀRN A'GHOBHAIR
Glasnacardoch Bay
Loch an Nostaire
437
SGURR BHUIDHE
Beoraidbeg
Morar
Bracorina
Bracora
Tarbet
Swordland
Glenancross
Loch Morar
B8008
A830
Lettermorar
503
CÀRN A' MHÀDAIDH-RUAIDH
Bay of Laig
Cleadale
Eilean Ighe
Bunacaimb
299
AN CRUACHAN
Laig
Back of Keppoch
600
SIDHEAN MOR
EIGG
Arisaig
Luinga Mhòr
Loch nan Ceall
Kildonnan
10
Prince Charlie's Cairn
393
AN SGÙRR
Sandavore
Rudh'-Arisaig
103
CRUACH DOIRE
Druimindarroch
Arisaig House
Kinlochnanuagh
Loch nan Uamh
Eilean Chathastail
Polnish
Lochailort
Ardnish
190
Sound of Arisaig
Rudha Chlolais
Inveraillort
Loch Ailort

Badicaul
Balmacara
Auchtertyre
Conchra
Killilan
SGÙMAN COINNTICH
Loch Long
Camas Luinie
Glen Elchaig
Loch na Leitreach
River Elchaig
Pabay
Kyle of Lochalsh
(Caol Loch Ailse)
Skye Bridge
Nostie
Bundalloch
210
Loch nan Eun
Lochalsh Woodland Garden
Kirkton
Ardelve
Carndu
Eilean Donan
Dornie
Kyleakin
A87
Loch Alsh
Keppoch
Lower Breakish
Upper Breakish
Letterfearn
Loch Duich
732
SGURR NA COINNICH
Otter Haven
Kyle Rhea
603
BEINN A' CHUIRN
840
SGÙRR AN AIRGID
Inverinate
916
A' GHLAS-BHEINN
Morvich
Bernera
Galltair
Kylerhea
(Apr-Oct)
Ratagan
Carn-gorm
Ault a' chruinn
Invershiel
Shiel Bridge
350
Mam Ratagan
605
BEN ASLAK
Glenelg Bay
Glenelg
408
BEINN A' CHAOINICH
Moyle
1031
BEN ATTOW
Eilanreach
Kintail
FIVE SISTERS
561
BEINN NA SEAMRAIG
Glenelg Brochs
Glean Beag
Balvraid
1068
SGURR FHUARAN
Glen Shiel
Loch na Dal
Sandaig Island
1719
SGÙRR
1011
THE SADDLE
974
BEINN SGRITHEAL
773
BEINN NAN CAORACH
Ornsay
Rudha Buidhe
945
SGURR NA SGINE
SOUND OF SLEAT
Loch Hourn
Arnisdale
Rudh' Ard Slisneach
Glen Arnisdale
Corran
614
709
DRUM FADA
Inverguseran
784
BEINN NA CAILLICH
Kinloch Hourn
1026
SGURR A MHAORAICH
Barrisdale Bay
Glen Guseran
199
1019
LADHAR BHEINN
518
DRUIM NA CLUAIN-AIRIDHE
Sandaig
Knoydart
KNOYDART
Loch
940
LUINNE BHEINN
Sandaig Bay
Inverie
Loch an Dubh-Lochain
Inverie Bay
Rudha Raonuill
919
GAIRICH
1003
SGURR MÒR
Mallaigvaig
547
CÀRN A' GHOBHAIR
854
BEINN BHUIDHE
1039
SGURR NA CICHE
Loch Nevis
Loch an Nostaire
437
SGÙRR BHUIDHE
879
SGURR MHURLAGAIN
Morar
Bracorina
Bracora
Kylesmorar
Tarbet
859
SGURR NAH-AIDE
Glen Dessarry
723
SGARR BREAC
Murlaggan
Swordland
Loch Morar
Glen Pean
Lettermorar
716
AN STAC
503
CÀRN A' DAIDH-RUAIDH
Meoble
949
SGURR NAN COIREACHAN
964
SGÙRR THUILM
983
GULVAIN
710
MEITH BHEINN
960
River Meoble
600
SIDHEAN MÒR
Prince Charlie's Cairn
Arisaig House
Kinlochnanuagh
Loch Beoriad
633
796
SGÙRR AN UTHA
Glen Finnan
Gleann Dubhlighe
Gleann Fionnlighe
Polnish
Lochailort
A830
Loch Eilt
Glenfinnan
Glenfinnan Visitor Centre
Rudha Chloalais
190
191
Kinlocheil
Locheilside Station
Glenfinnan Monument
Drimsallie
0 1 2 3 4 miles
0 1 2 3 4 5 kilometres

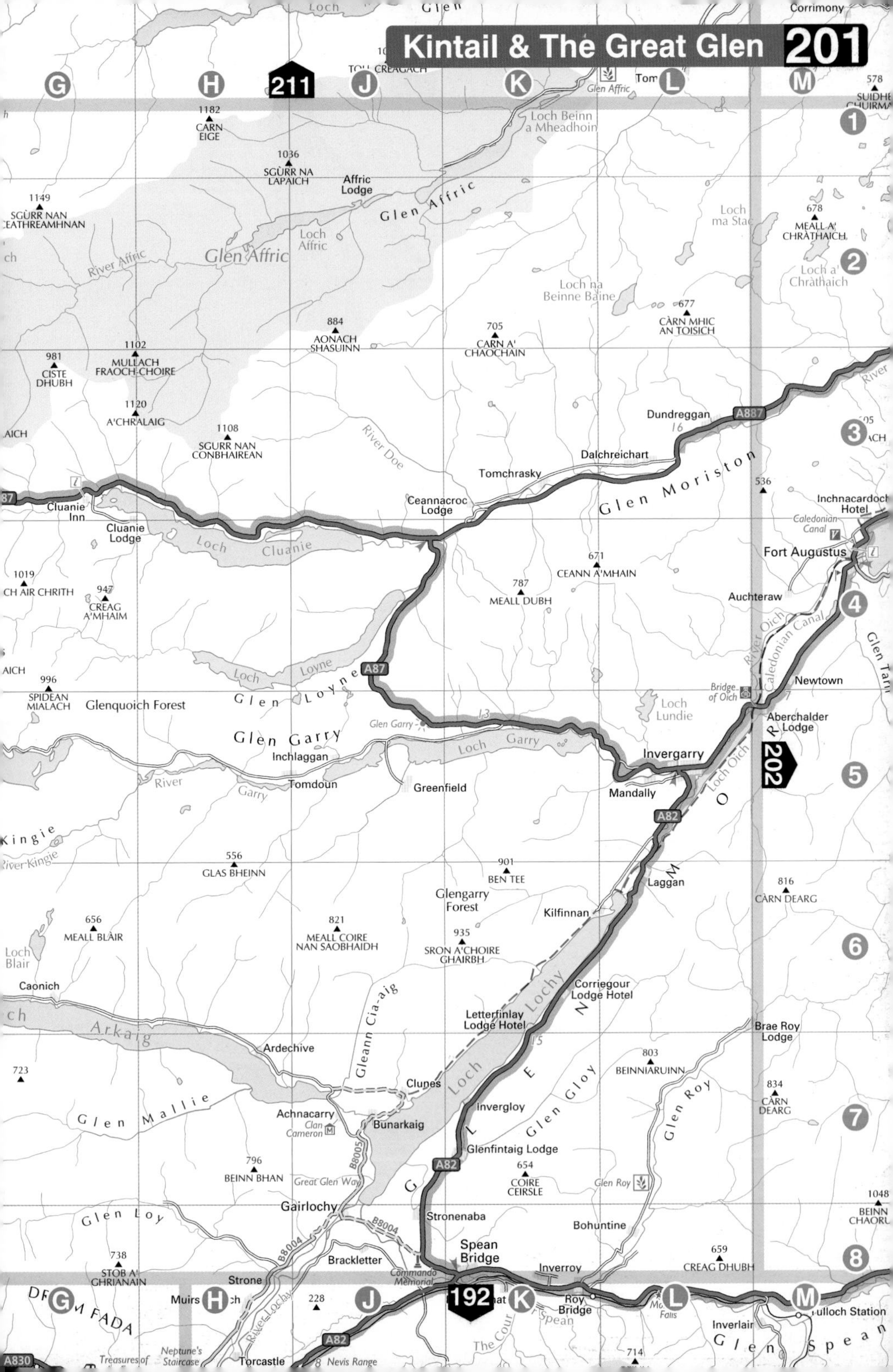

211
202
192
G
H
J
K
L
M
1
2
3
4
5
6
7
8
Glen Affric
Loch Affric
Affric Lodge
River Affric
Loch Beinn a Mheadhoin
CARN EIGE
SGÙRR NA LAPAICH
SGÙRR NAN CEATHREAMHNAN
AONACH SHASUINN
CARN A' CHAOCHAIN
MULLACH FRAOCH-CHOIRE
CISTE DHUBH
A'CHRALAIG
SGURR NAN CONBHAIREAN
Loch ma Stac
MEALL A' CHRATHAICH
Loch a' Chràthaich
Loch na Beinne Baine
CÀRN MHIC AN TOISICH
Dundreggan
A887
Dalchreichart
Tomchrasky
River Doe
Glen Moriston
Ceannacroc Lodge
Cluanie Inn
Cluanie Lodge
Loch Cluanie
Inchnacardoch Hotel
Caledonian Canal
Fort Augustus
CEANN A'MHAIN
MEALL DUBH
Auchteraw
River Oich
Newtown
Glen Tarff
Bridge of Oich
Aberchalder Lodge
Loch Lundie
CREAG A'MHAIM
Loch Loyne
Glen Loyne
A87
SPIDEAN MIALACH
Glenquoich Forest
Glen Garry
Inchlaggan
Loch Garry
Invergarry
Tomdoun
River Garry
Greenfield
Mandally
A82
Loch Oich
Kingie
River Kingie
GLAS BHEINN
BEN TEE
Laggan
Glengarry Forest
Kilfinnan
MEALL BLAIR
MEALL COIRE NAN SAOBHAIDH
SRON A'CHOIRE GHAIRBH
Loch Blair
Caonich
Corriegour Lodge Hotel
Letterfinlay Lodge Hotel
Loch Lochy
Loch Arkaig
Gleann Cia-aig
Ardechive
Brae Roy Lodge
BEINNIARUINN
CÀRN DEARG
Clunes
Glen Mallie
Achnacarry
Clan Cameron
Bunarkaig
Invergloy
Glen Gloy
Glen Roy
Glenfintaig Lodge
BEINN BHAN
Great Glen Way
B8005
COIRE CEIRSLE
Gairlochy
Glen Loy
B8004
Stronenaba
Bohuntine
BEINN CHAORU
Spean Bridge
Brackletter
Commando Memorial
STOB A' GHRIANAIN
Strone
Inverroy
CREAG DHUBH
Roy Bridge
Inverlair
Tulloch Station
Glen Spean
River Lochy
The Cour
Treasures of
Neptune's Staircase
Torcastle
Nevis Range
A830
Corrimony
Glen Affric
Tom

Corrimony
Urquhart
Loch Meiklie
Lewiston
Drum Farm
Falls of Divach
Strone
Urquhart Castle
212
Tomich
578
SUIDHE GHUIRMAIN
Lenie
LOCH NESS
B852
B862
Torness
Loch Ruthven
Aberarder
Inverfarigaig
Aultnagoire
Farigaig
Errogie
Dunmaglass Lodge
Farraline
Loch ma Stac
678
MEALL A' CHRÀTHAICH
Loch a' Chràthaich
Loch nan Breac Deorga
696
A82
Foyers
Gorthleck
686
BEINN DUBHCHARAIOH
677
CÀRN MHIC AN TOISICH
Achnaconeran
Invermoriston
River Moriston
Great Glen Way
Loch Mhor
Glebe
Loch Knockie
Whitebridge
Dundreggan
A887
605
BURACH
810
CÀRN NA SAOBHAIDHE
Glen Moriston
536
Inchnacardoch Hotel
Loch Killin
810
CÀRN NA LARAICHE MAOILE
Caledonian Canal
Glendoe Lodge
Fort Augustus
Glen Doe
Monadhli
Auchteraw
River Oich
Caledonian Canal
Glen Tarff
778
CÀRN EASGANN BÀNA
855
SGARAMAN NAM FIADH
201
Newtown
Loch Lundie
Aberchalder Lodge
816
CÀRN A' CHUILINN
941
Invergarry
Loch Oich
891
CORRIEYAIRACK HILL
861
MEALL NA-H-AISRE
842
CÀRN AN LETH-CHOIN
925
GEAL CHÀRN
881
CÀRN LEAC
Glen Markie
Laggan
816
CÀRN DEARG
River Spey
Blargie
Laggan
Crathie
Loch Spey
Loch Crunachdan
Glenshero Lodge
563
BLACK CRAIG
A86
Catlodge
Strathmashie House
Brae Roy Lodge
803
1005
CÀRN LIATH
Kinlochlaggan
Gallovie
Loch Coaldair
834
CÀRN DEARG
Glen Roy
Creag Meagaidh
Loch Laggan
1128
CREAG MEAGAIDH
River Maghie
Distillery
1048
BEINN A' CHAORUNN
River Pattack
Dalwhinnie
Lochan na h-Earba
747
BINNEIN SHUAS
659
CREAG DHUBH
Moy
1049
GEAL CHÀRN
192
193
Monessie Falls
CREAGAN MOR
0 1 2 3 4 miles
0 1 2 3 4 5 kilometres
Loch Pattack
1088
714

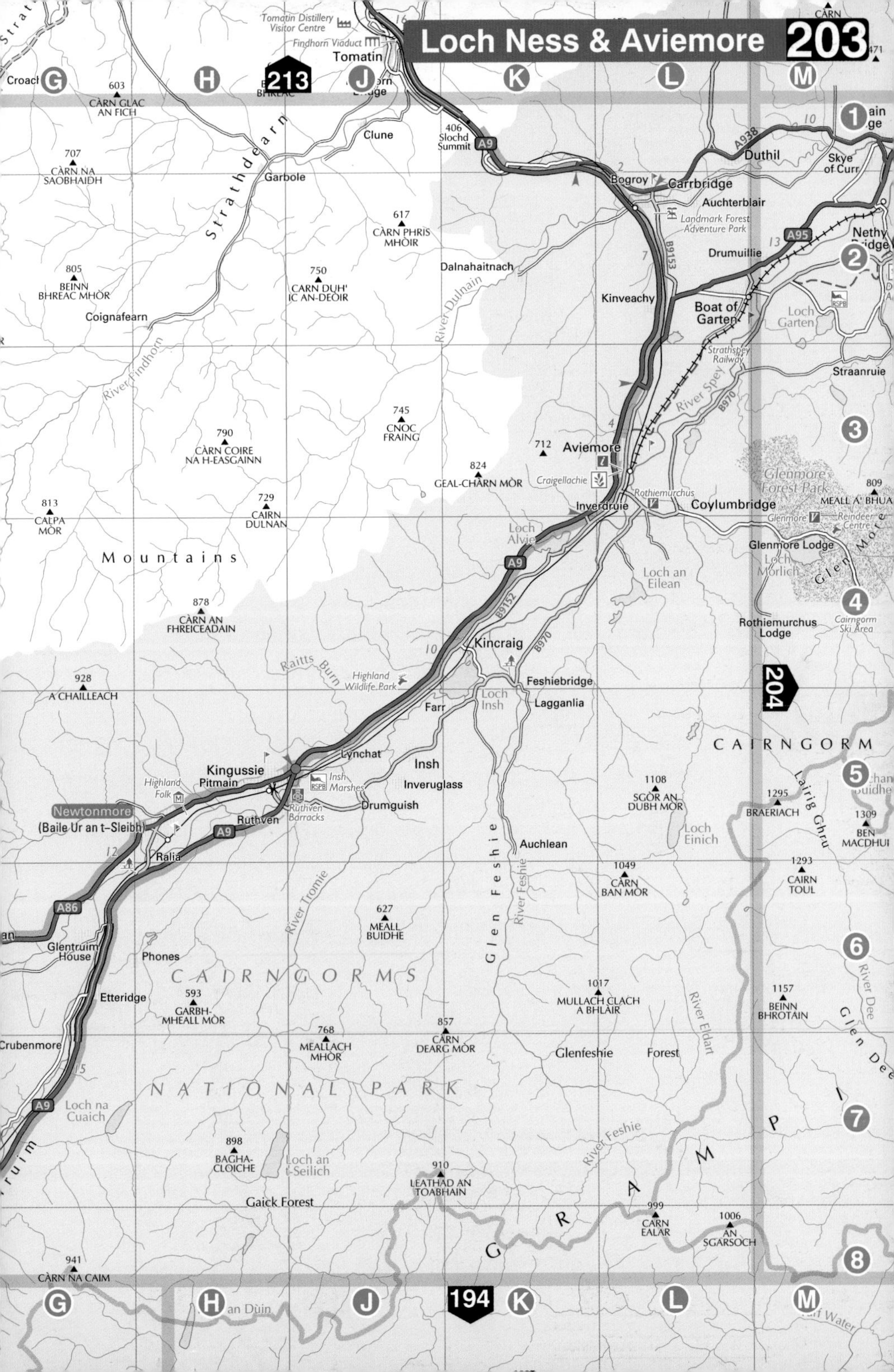
Tomatin Distillery Visitor Centre
Findhorn Viaduct
Tomatin
213
406
Slochd Summit
A9
Clune
Garbole
Strathdearn
603
CÀRN GLAC AN FICH
707
CÀRN NA SAOBHAIDH
805
BEINN BHREAC MHÒR
Coignafearn
River Findhorn
617
CÀRN PHRIS MHÒIR
750
CARN DUH' IC AN-DEOIR
Dalnahaitnach
River Dulnain
745
CNOC FRAING
790
CÀRN COIRE NA H-EASGAINN
813
CALPA MÒR
729
CAIRN DULNAN
824
GEAL-CHÀRN MÒR
Mountains
878
CÀRN AN FHREICEADAIN
928
A CHAILLEACH
A938
Duthil
Skye of Curr
Bogroy
Carrbridge
Auchterblair
Landmark Forest Adventure Park
B9153
A95
Nethy Bridge
Drumuillie
Kinveachy
Boat of Garten
Loch Garten
RSPB
Strathspey Railway
Straanruie
River Spey
B970
712
Aviemore
Craigellachie
Rothiemurchus
Inverdruie
Coylumbridge
Glenmore Forest Park
809
MEALL A' BHUACHAILLE
Glenmore
Reindeer Centre
Glen More
Glenmore Lodge
Loch Alvie
Loch an Eilean
Loch Morlich
Rothiemurchus Lodge
Cairngorm Ski Area
B9152
Kincraig
Raitts Burn
Highland Wildlife Park
Feshiebridge
Loch Insh
Lagganlia
Farr
204
Lynchat
Kingussie
Insh
Inveruglass
Highland Folk
Pitmain
Insh Marshes
Ruthven Barracks
Drumguish
Newtonmore
(Baile Ur an t–Sleibh)
Ruthven
Ralia
A86
CAIRNGORM
1108
SGÒR AN DUBH MÒR
1295
BRAERIACH
Lairig Ghru
1309
BEN MACDHUI
Loch Einich
Auchlean
Glen Feshie
River Feshie
1049
CÀRN BAN MÒR
1293
CAIRN TOUL
River Tromie
627
MEALL BUIDHE
Glentruim House
Phones
CAIRNGORMS
593
GARBH-MHEALL MÒR
1017
MULLACH CLACH A BHLÀIR
River Eidart
1157
BEINN BHROTAIN
River Dee
Glen Dee
Etteridge
768
MEALLACH MHÒR
857
CÀRN DEARG MÒR
Glenfeshie Forest
Crubenmore
NATIONAL PARK
Loch na Cuaich
898
BAGHA-CLOICHE
Loch an t-Seilich
910
LEATHAD AN TOABHAIN
GRAMPIAN
Gaick Forest
999
CARN EALAR
1006
AN SGARSOCH
941
CÀRN NA CAIM
194
G H J K L M
1 2 3 4 5 6 7 8

CÀRN SGRIOB
471
Grantown-on-Spey
Cromdale
214
Hills of Cromdale
Glenlivet
Glenlivet Distillery
Shenval
Auchbreck
Craggan
River Spey
Speybridge
Dulnain Bridge
A938
Duthil
Skye of Curr
Tomnavoulin
Strath Avon
B9136
Glen Livet
Speyside Way
Bogroy
Carrbridge
Auchterblair
Landmark Forest Adventure Park
A95
B9153
Drumuillie
Nethy Bridge
B970
459
CÀRN NA LOINNE
A939
Glen Lochy
Bridge of Brown
Auchnarrow
B9008
Clash
Boat of Garten
Loch Garten
RSPB
Dell Wood (Abernethy)
Lettoch
Glen Brown
Bridge of Avon
Tomintoul
Milton
Strathspey Railway
Straanruie
Dorback Lodge
River Nethy
Delnabo
606
CÀRN TUADHAM
Rothiemurchus
Coylumbridge
Glenmore Forest Park
Glenmore
Reindeer Centre
809
MEALL A' BHUACHAILLE
803
CARN BHEADHAIR
821
GEAL CHÀRN
710
CRAIG VEANN
Lecht Ski Area
792
CARN EALASAID
Glenmore Lodge
Loch Morlich
Glen More
730
MAIM SUIM
Loch an Filean
Rothiemurchus Lodge
Cairngorm Ski Area
741
BIG GARVOUN
River Avon
Glen Avon
Cock
CAIRNGORMS
713
THE BRUACH
203
1245
CAIRN GORM
NATIONAL
Loch Builg
829
BROWN COW HILL
CAIRNGORM
1083
BEINN A CHAORRUINN
1171
BEN AVON
1196
NORTH TOP
Lochan Buidhe
MOUNTAINS
SGOR AN DUBH MOR
1295
BRAERIACH
Lairig Ghru
1309
BEN MACDHUI
Loch Einich
PARK
1084
CARN EAS
1177
SOUTH TOP
900
CULARDOCH
River Gairn
1049
1293
CAIRN TOUL
930
BEINN BHREAC
Glen Derry
MOUNT
618
MEALL GORM
1157
BEINN BHROTAIN
River Dee
Glen Dee
Glen Lui
Linn of Dee
Quoich Water
813
SGOR MOR
Mar Lodge Estate
Allanaquoich
Braemar
Keiloch
A93
Inverey
River Eidart
Forest
859
MORRONE HILL
GRAMPIAN
816
CARN LIATH
Clunie Water
Loch Callater
999
CARN EALAR
1006
AN SGARSOCH
1045
CAIRN TAGGART
919
CARN BHAC
Glen Ey
886
SGOR MOR
Glen Clunie Lodge
195
1018
CÀRN AN TUIRC
Baddoch Burn
Glenshee Ski Area
0 1 2 3 4 miles
0 1 2 3 4 5 kilometres

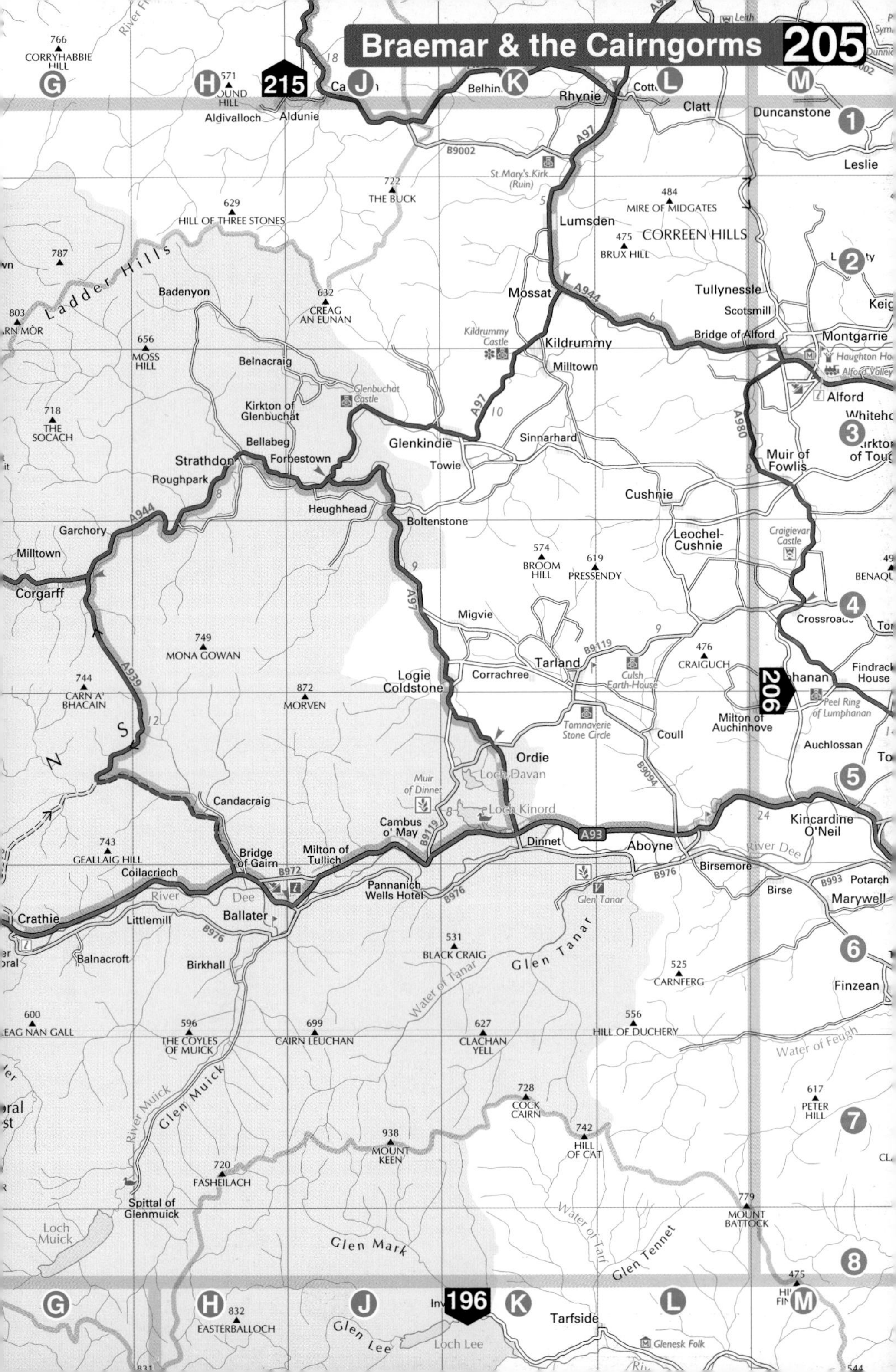

CORRYHABBIE HILL
Aldivalloch
Aldunie
Rhynie
Clatt
Duncanstone
Leslie
THE BUCK
HILL OF THREE STONES
MIRE OF MIDGATES
Lumsden
CORREEN HILLS
BRUX HILL
Ladder Hills
Badenyon
CREAG AN EUNAN
Mossat
Tullynessle
Scotsmill
Bridge of Alford
Montgarrie
Kildrummy Castle
Kildrummy
Milltown
MOSS HILL
Belnacraig
Glenbuchat Castle
Kirkton of Glenbuchat
Alford
THE SOCHAR
Bellabeg
Glenkindie
Sinnarhard
Strathdon
Forbestown
Towie
Muir of Fowlis
Roughpark
Heughhead
Cushnie
Garchory
Boltenstone
Leochel-Cushnie
Craigievar Castle
Milltown
BROOM HILL
PRESSENDY
Corgarff
Migvie
Crossroads
MONA GOWAN
Tarland
CRAIGUCH
Culsh Earth-House
CARN A' BHACAIN
MORVEN
Logie Coldstone
Corrachree
Peel Ring of Lumphanan
Milton of Auchinhove
Tomnaverie Stone Circle
Coull
Auchlossan
Ordie
Loch Davan
Muir of Dinnet
Candacraig
Loch Kinord
Cambus o' May
Kincardine O'Neil
Dinnet
Aboyne
GEALLAIG HILL
Bridge of Gairn
Milton of Tullich
River Dee
Coilacriech
Birsemore
Potarch
Pannanich Wells Hotel
Glen Tanar
Birse
Marywell
Crathie
Littlemill
Ballater
Balnacroft
Birkhall
BLACK CRAIG
Glen Tanar
CARNFERG
Finzean
THE COYLES OF MUICK
CAIRN LEUCHAN
CLACHAN YELL
HILL OF DUCHERY
Water of Tanar
Water of Feugh
Glen Muick
River Muick
COCK CAIRN
PETER HILL
MOUNT KEEN
HILL OF CAT
FASHEILACH
Spittal of Glenmuick
Loch Muick
MOUNT BATTOCK
Water of Tarf
Glen Mark
Glen Tennet
EASTERBALLOCH
Tarfside
Glen Lee
Loch Lee
Glenesk Folk

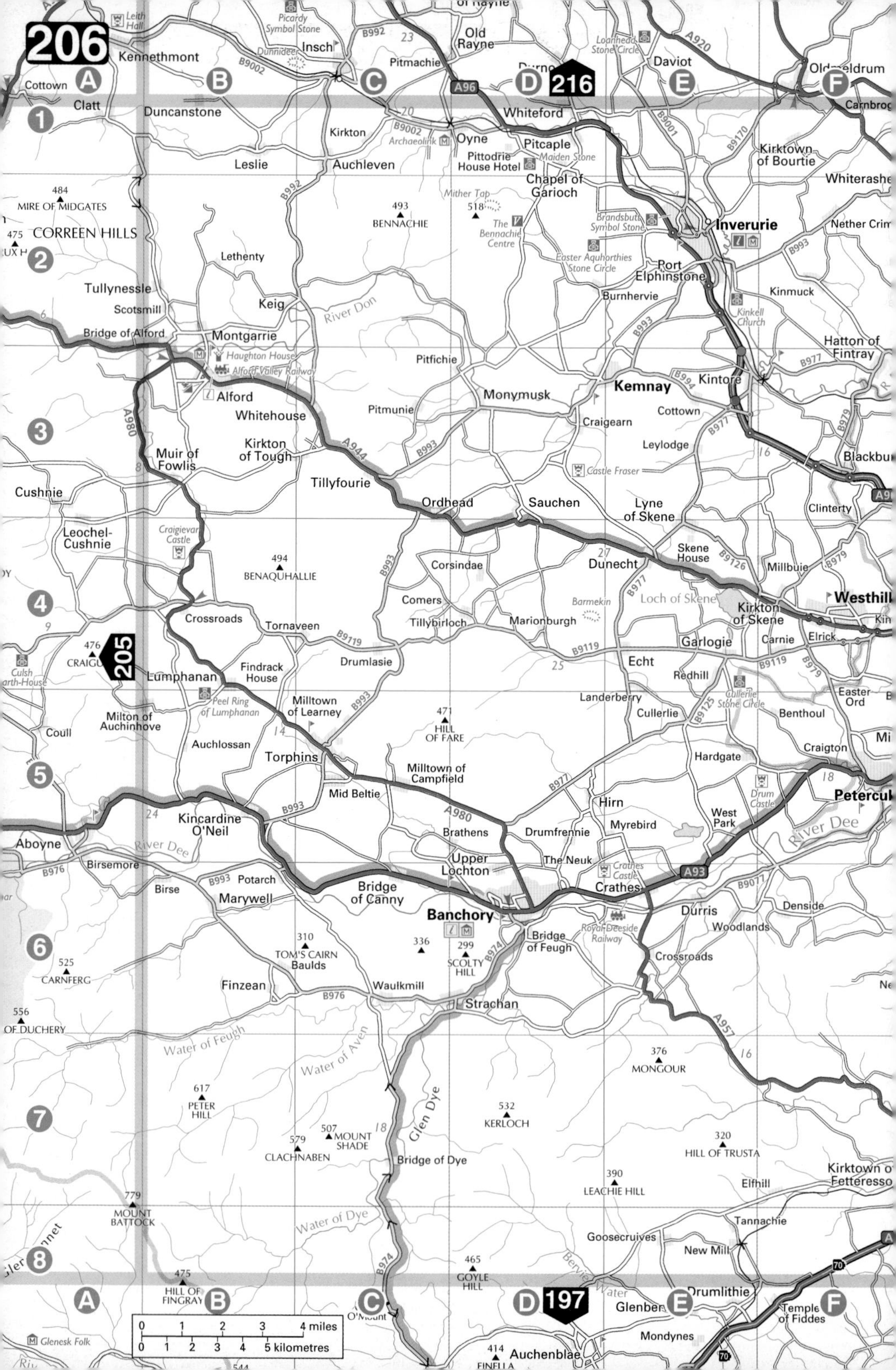
206
216
205
197
Kennethmont
Insch
Old Rayne
Pitmachie
Daviot
Oldmeldrum
Cottown
Clatt
Duncanstone
Whiteford
Kirkton
Oyne
Pitcaple
Leslie
Auchleven
Chapel of Garioch
Inverurie
Port Elphinstone
Kintore
Kemnay
Monymusk
Alford
Whitehouse
Muir of Fowlis
Kirkton of Tough
Tillyfourie
Ordhead
Sauchen
Dunecht
Westhill
Echt
Lumphanan
Torphins
Kincardine O'Neil
Aboyne
Banchory
Crathes
Durris
Peterculter
Strachan
Finzean
Bridge of Dye
Auchenblae
Drumlithie
Glenbervie
CORREEN HILLS
BENNACHIE
BENAQUHALLIE
HILL OF FARE
MOUNT BATTOCK
CLACHNABEN
River Don
River Dee
Water of Feugh
Water of Dye
0 1 2 3 4 miles
0 1 2 3 4 5 kilometres

Ellon
Esslemont
Kirkton of Logie Buchan
Collieston
Pitmedden
Logierieve
217
Forvie
Housieside
Udny Green
Udny Station
Newburgh
Woodland
Pettymuk
Cultercullen
Foveran
Tillygreig
Delfrigs
Reisque
Causeyend
Whitecairns
Belhelvie
Balmedie
Kinmundy
Cothal
Potterton
Blackdog
Dyce
Middleton Park
Denmore
Kirkwall
Lerwick
Stoneywood
Bankhead
Bucksburn
Bridge of Don
Northfield
Old Aberdeen
Kingswells
Kittybrewster
ABERDEEN
Ruthrieston
Torry
Nigg Bay
Mannofield
Cults
Bieldside
Kincorth
Nigg
Milton of Murtle
Banchory-Devenick
Altens Haven
Cove Bay
Kingcausie
Charlestown
Marywell
Hillside
Auchlee
Findon
Portlethen
Cammachmore Bay
Downies
Cammachmore
Newtonhill
Skateraw
Muchalls
Doonie Point
Garron Point
Stonehaven Bay
Stonehaven
Dunnottar
Crawton
Fowlsheugh
Trelong Bay
A90
A920
A975
A956
B9000
B9005
B999
B979
B977
B997
B9119
B9077
G H J K L M
1 2 3 4 5 6 7 8

Duntulm
A855
Lùb Score
Skye Museum of Island Life
Tairbeart (Tarbert)
Borneskitaig
Kilmuir
Kilvaxter
Heribusta
Balgown
218
Linicro
Totscore
Loch nam Madadh (Lochmaddy)
Waternish Point
River Rha
Idrigill
Ascrib Islands
Uig (Uige)
Uig Bay
283 BEN GEARY
Geary
Trumpan
Loch Snizort
Earlish
Ardmore Point
Gillen
Hallin
16
A87
River Hinnisdal
DUNVEGAN HEAD
Isay
Mingay
Stein
Lusta
Loch Bay
Loch Dunvegan
214 BEN DIUBAIG
Greshornish House Hotel
Loch Greshornish
Kingsburgh
Loch Snizort Beag
Claigan
Bay
Boreraig
327 BEINN BHREAC
22
Treaslane
Uig
B886
Flashader
A850
Loch Pooltiel
Upperglen
Feriniquarrie
Totaig
Edinbane
Bernisdale
B8036
Oisgill Bay
Milovaig
Glendale
Colbost
Dunvegan
A850
Tote
Waterstein
Lephin
B884
Colbost Croft
Dunvegan
Skeabost
Toy
Skinidin
Giant Angus MacAskill
Kilmuir
Neist Point
A864
Caroy River
265 BEN AKETIL
271 CRUACHAN BEINN A' CHEARCAILL
Lonmore
Moonen Bay
Roskhill
Uigshader
469 HEALAVAL MORE
Roag
Ramasaig
Orbost
B885
Hoe Rape
Vatten
ISLE OF
Glen Ose
488 HEALAVAL BHEAG
Harlosh
Caroy
A863
Loch Caroy
Ose
Hoe Point
368 BEINN NA BOINEID
Harlosh Island
Colbost Point
Dun Beag
Bracadale
Loch Duagrich
Tarner Island
Loch Bracadale
Ullinish Lodge Hotel
Struan
Coillore
Wiay
23
Idrigill Point
Oronsay
Portnalong
Loch Harport
439 ROINEVAL
Fiskavaig
B8009
Rudha nan Clach
Fernilea
369 ARNAVAL
Carbost
Drynoch
Merkadale
Talisker Bay
Glen Eynort
Talisker
447 BEINN BHREAC
Grula
198
Loch Eynort
0 1 2 3 4 miles
0 1 2 3 4 5 kilometres

Kilmaluag
Flodigarry
Eilean Flodigarry
Staffin Bay
Staffin Island
Digg
Brogaig
Stenscholl
Staffin
218
Kilt Rock Waterfall
Ellishader
Trotternish
Maligar
Marishader
Valtos
Garros
Rudha nam Brathairean
Culnaknock
611
BEINN EDRA
Lealt
Tote
A855
608
CREAG A' LAIN
RONA
Loch a' Bhràige
SOUND OF RAASAY
Old Man of Storr
719
THE STORR
River Romesdal
River Haulton
Loch Leathan
Loch Fada
Eilean Tigh
Eilean Fladday
Manish Point
Loch Arnish
Torran
Arnish
Brochel
Borve
Drumuie
Glengrasco
312
Torvaig
Portree
Seafield
417
BEINN NA GREINE
Penifiler
412
BEN TIANAVAIG
Glenmore
Glenvarragill
Mugeary
A87
Camastianavaig
Tianavaig Bay
Ollach
B883
Glen Varragill
RAASAY
444
DÙN CAAN
Oskaig
Rudha na' Leac
310
BEINN NA LEAC
Clachan
Inverarish
The Braes
444
BEN LEE
Peinchorran
Suisnish Point
Eyre Point
Sconser
773
GLAMAIG
Sligachan
SKYE
A863
INNER SOUND
SCALPAY
396
MULLACH NA CARN
Loch Ainort
Dunan
Luib
Caolas Scalpay
564
GLAS BHEIN MHÒRN
199
965
SGURR NAN GILLEAN
732
Broadford
Corry
Broadford Bay
Waterloo
Lower Breakish
South Erradale
Redpoint
Red Point
Loch Torridon
Rudha na Fearn
Fearnmore
Òb Chuaig
Fearnbeg
Arrina
Kenmore
Cuaig
Callakille
Lonbain
492
AN GARBH-MHEALL
493
CROIC-BHEINN
River Applecross
210
Applecross Bay
Applecross
Milton
626
Pass of the Cattle
774
SGÙRR A' CHAOIRACHAIN
Camusteel
Camusterrach
Bealach-Na-Ba
Aird Dhubh
Culduie
Toscaig
River Toscaig
Caolas Mòr
Eilean Meadhonach
Eilean Mòr
CROWLIN ISLANDS
Loch Carron
67
Longay
Port-an-Eorna
Drumbuie
Badicaul
Kyle of Lochalsh
(Caol Loch Aille)
Skye Bridge
27
Pabay
A87
Kyleakin

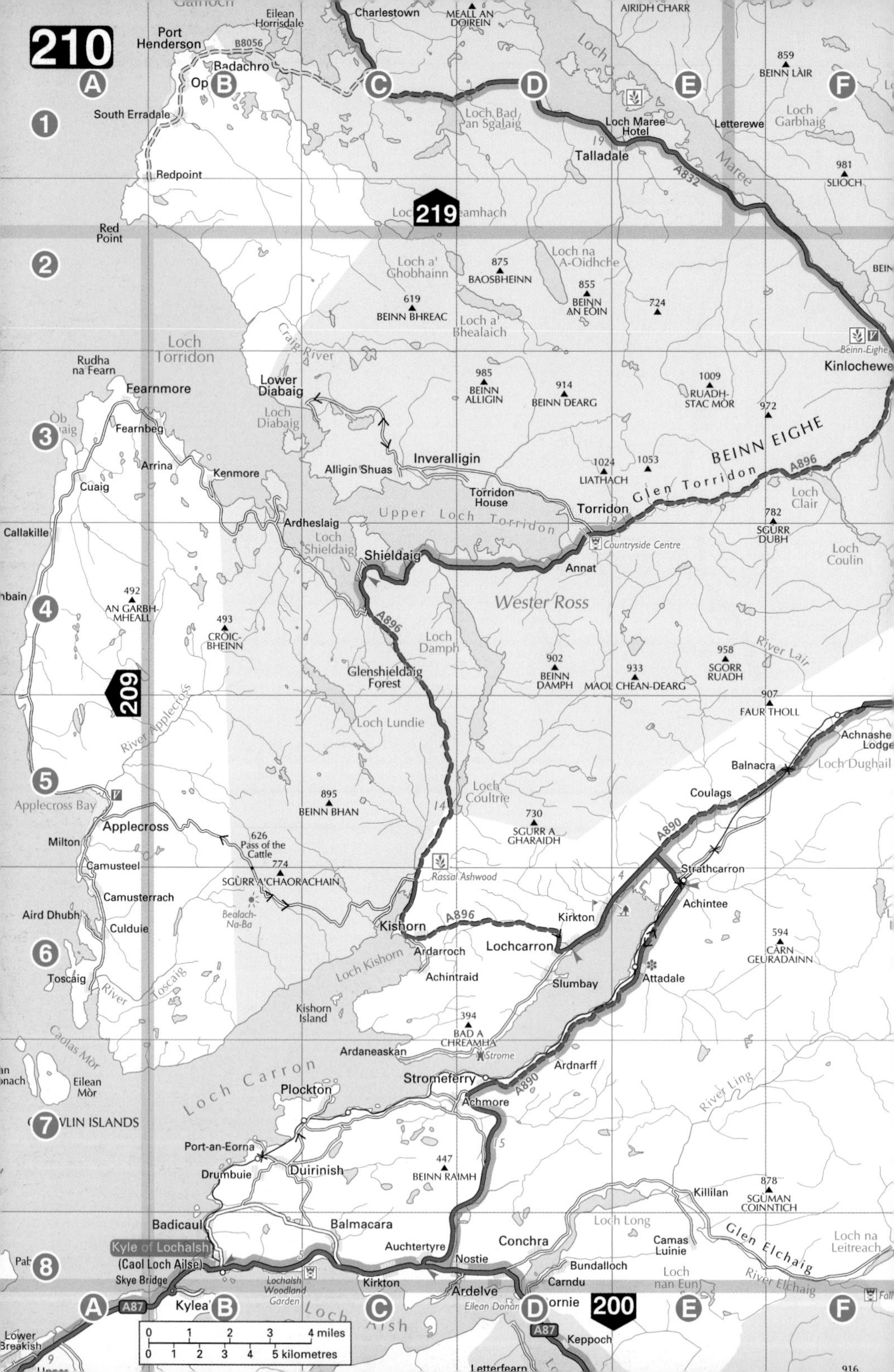

210
Port Henderson
Eilean Horrisdale
Charlestown
MEALL AN DOIREIN
AIRIDH CHARR
B8056
Badachro
Opinan
South Erradale
Loch Bad an Sgalaig
Loch Maree Hotel
Talladale
Letterewe
Loch Garbhaig
BEINN LÀIR
SLIOCH
Loch Maree
A832
Redpoint
Red Point
219
Loch a' Ghobhainn
BAOSBHEINN
Loch na h-Oidhche
BEINN AN EOIN
BEINN BHREAC
Loch a' Bhealaich
Loch Torridon
Craig River
Rudha na Fearn
Fearnmore
Lower Diabaig
Loch Diabaig
BEINN ALLIGIN
BEINN DEARG
RUADH-STAC MÒR
Kinlochewe
Beinn Eighe
Fearnbeg
Arrina
Kenmore
Cuaig
Alligin Shuas
Inveralligin
LIATHACH
BEINN EIGHE
Glen Torridon
A896
Torridon House
Torridon
Loch Clair
Upper Loch Torridon
Ardheslaig
Loch Shieldaig
Shieldaig
Countryside Centre
Annat
SGURR DUBH
Loch Coulin
Callakille
AN GARBH-MHEALL
CROIC-BHEINN
Wester Ross
Loch Damph
River Lair
BEINN DAMPH
MAOL CHEAN-DEARG
SGORR RUADH
Glenshieldaig Forest
209
River Applecross
Loch Lundie
FAUR THOLL
Achnashellach Lodge
Balnacra
Loch Dughaill
Coulags
Applecross Bay
Applecross
Loch Coultrie
BEINN BHAN
SGURR A GHARAIDH
A890
Milton
Pass of the Cattle
SGÙRR A' CHAORACHAIN
Camusteel
Camusterrach
Rassal Ashwood
Strathcarron
Achintee
Bealach-Na-Ba
Aird Dhubh
Culduie
Kishorn
Kirkton
Lochcarron
Ardarroch
CÀRN GEURADAINN
Toscaig
River Toscaig
Loch Kishorn
Achintraid
Slumbay
Attadale
Kishorn Island
BAD A CHREAMHA
Caolas Mòr
Ardaneaskan
Strome
Ardnarff
Eilean Mòr
Loch Carron
Plockton
Stromeferry
Achmore
River Ling
CROWLIN ISLANDS
Port-an-Eorna
Drumbuie
Duirinish
BEINN RAIMH
Killilan
SGÙMAN COINNTICH
Badicaul
Balmacara
Loch Long
Conchra
Camas Luinie
Glen Elchaig
Loch na Leitreach
Kyle of Lochalsh (Caol Loch Ailse)
Auchtertyre
Nostie
Bundalloch
Skye Bridge
Lochalsh Woodland Garden
Kirkton
Ardelve
Carndu
Loch nan Eun
River Elchaig
Kyleakin
A87
Loch Alsh
Eilean Donan
Dornie
200
Lower Breakish
Keppoch
Letterfearn
0 1 2 3 4 miles
0 1 2 3 4 5 kilometres

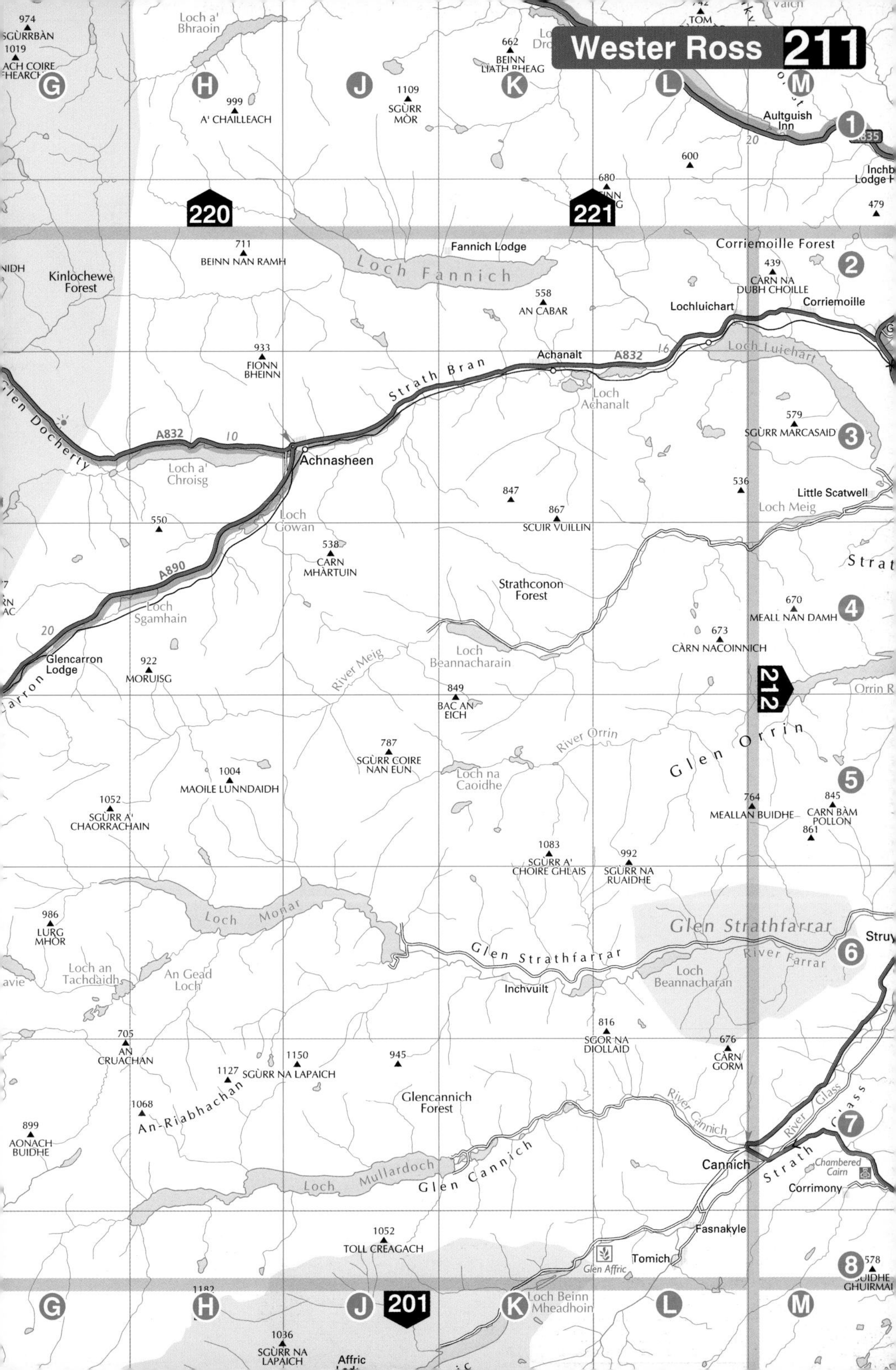

Loch a' Bhraoin
974 SGÙRRBÀN
1019
999 A' CHAILLEACH
1109 SGÙRR MÒR
662 BEINN LIATH BHEAG
Aultguish Inn
A835
600
680
220
221
479
Corriemoille Forest
Fannich Lodge
Loch Fannich
711 BEINN NAN RAMH
Kinlochewe Forest
439 CÀRN NA DUBH CHOILLE
Corriemoille
558 AN CABAR
Lochluichart
Loch Luichart
933 FIONN BHEINN
Achanalt
A832
Strath Bran
Loch Achanalt
Glen Docherty
A832
Loch a' Chroisg
Achnasheen
579 SGÙRR MARCASAID
536
Little Scatwell
Loch Meig
847
867 SCUIR VUILLIN
550
Loch Gowan
538 CARN MHÀRTUIN
A890
Strathconon Forest
Loch Sgamhain
670 MEALL NAN DAMH
673 CÀRN NACOINNICH
Glencarron Lodge
922 MORUISG
River Meig
Loch Beannacharain
212
849 BAC AN EICH
River Orrin
Glen Orrin
787 SGÙRR COIRE NAN EUN
1004 MAOILE LUNNDAIDH
Loch na Caoidhe
1052 SGÙRR A' CHAORRACHAIN
764 MEALLAN BUIDHE
845 CARN BÀM POLLON
861
1083 SGÙRR A' CHOIRE GHLAIS
992 SGÙRR NA RUAIDHE
Loch Monar
986 LURG MHÒR
Glen Strathfarrar
River Farrar
Loch an Tachdaidh
An Gead Loch
Inchvuilt
Loch Beannacharan
816 SGOR NA DIOLLAID
676 CÀRN GORM
705 AN CRUACHAN
1127
1150 SGÙRR NA LAPAICH
945
Glencannich Forest
1068
An-Riabhachan
899 AONACH BUIDHE
River Cannich
River Glass
Strath Glass
Chambered Cairn
Cannich
Corrimony
Loch Mullardoch
Glen Cannich
1052 TOLL CREAGACH
Fasnakyle
Tomich
Glen Affric
578
201
Loch Beinn Mheadhoin
1036 SGÙRR NA LAPAICH
Affric

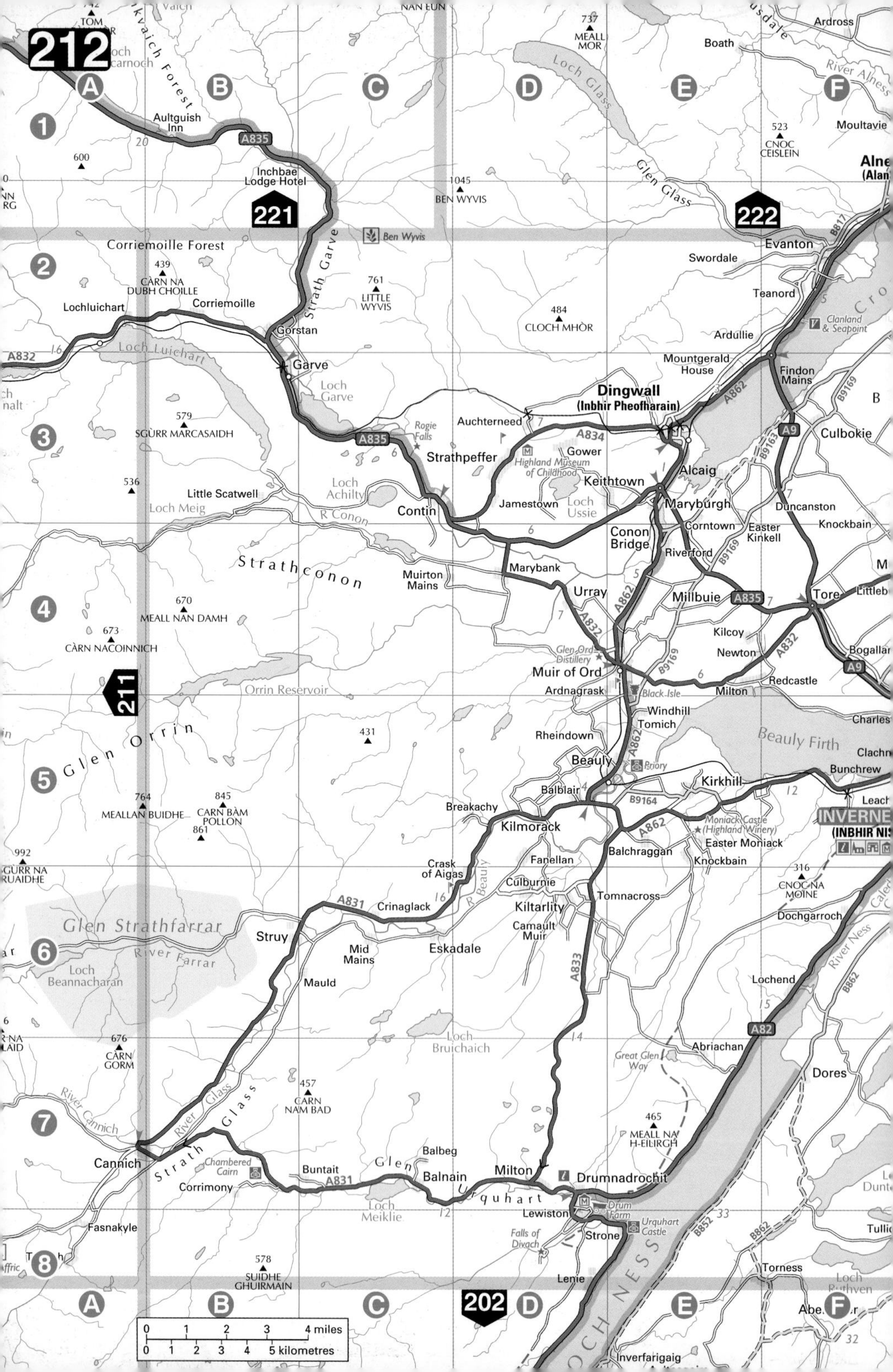

221
222
211
202
Aultguish Inn
Inchbae Lodge Hotel
A835
BEN WYVIS
Ben Wyvis
Loch Glass
Glen Glass
Boath
Ardross
River Alness
Moultavie
CNOC CEISLEIN
Evanton
Swordale
Teanord
Clanland & Seapoint
Corriemoille Forest
CÀRN NA DUBH CHOILLE
Corriemoille
Lochluichart
Loch Luichart
A832
Gorstan
Strath Garve
Garve
Loch Garve
LITTLE WYVIS
CLOCH MHÒR
Ardullie
Mountgerald House
Findon Mains
Dingwall
(Inbhir Pheofharain)
Auchterneed
Rogie Falls
Strathpeffer
Highland Museum of Childhood
Gower
Keithtown
Alcaig
Culbokie
A834
A862
A9
SGÙRR MARCASAIDH
Little Scatwell
Loch Meig
Loch Achilty
R Conon
Contin
Jamestown
Loch Ussie
Maryburgh
Duncanston
Knockbain
Conon Bridge
Corntown
Easter Kinkell
Riverford
Strathconon
Muirton Mains
Marybank
Urray
Millbuie
A835
Tore
MEALL NAN DAMH
CÀRN NACOINNICH
Kilcoy
Newton
Glen Ord Distillery
Muir of Ord
Ardnagrask
Black Isle
Milton
Redcastle
Bogallan
Orrin Reservoir
Glen Orrin
Windhill
Tomich
Rheindown
Beauly Firth
Beauly
Priory
Bunchrew
Kirkhill
Balblair
B9164
Breakachy
Kilmorack
MEALLAN BUIDHE
CARN BÀM POLLON
A862
Moniack Castle (Highland Winery)
Balchraggan
Easter Moniack
Knockbain
INVERNESS
(INBHIR NIS)
Fanellan
Crask of Aigas
R Beauly
Culburnie
Tomnacross
CNOC NA MOINE
A831
Crinaglack
Kiltarlity
Camault Muir
Dochgarroch
Glen Strathfarrar
River Farrar
Struy
Mid Mains
Eskadale
Loch Beannacharan
Mauld
A833
Lochend
River Ness
A82
Loch Bruichaich
Great Glen Way
Abriachan
CÀRN GORM
CARN NAM BAD
River Glass
Strath Glass
River Cannich
Dores
MEALL NA H-EILIRGH
Cannich
Chambered Cairn
Buntait
Glen
Balbeg
Balnain
Milton
Drumnadrochit
Corrimony
Urquhart
Loch Meiklie
Lewiston
Drum Farm
Urquhart Castle
Fasnakyle
Falls of Divach
Strone
B852
B862
SUIDHE GHUIRMAIN
Lenie
Torness
LOCH NESS
Inverfarigaig
0 1 2 3 4 miles
0 1 2 3 4 5 kilometres

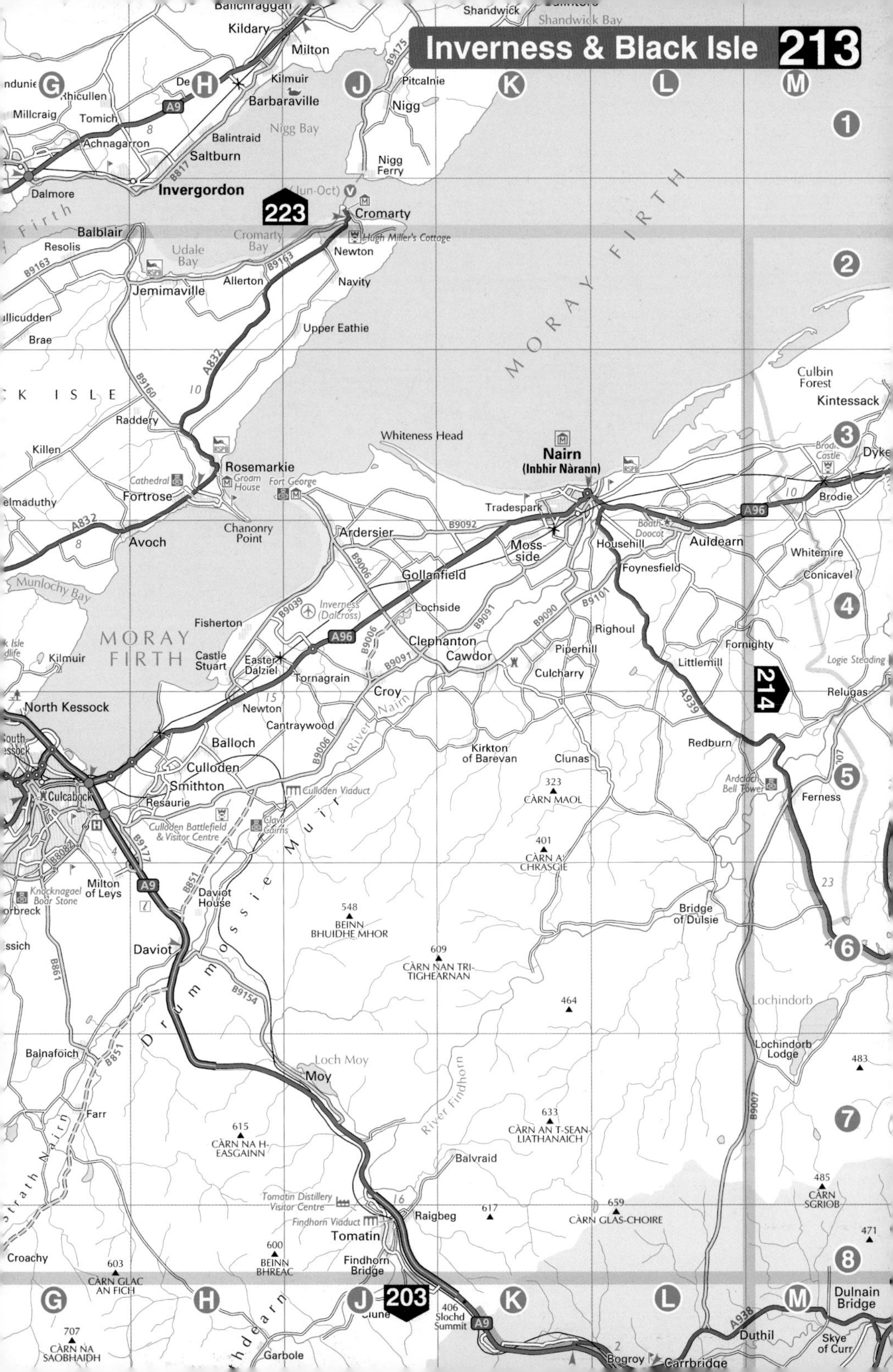
Kildary
Milton
Shandwick
Shandwick Bay
Rhicullen
Millcraig
Tomich
Achnagarron
Barbaraville
Kilmuir
Pitcalnie
Nigg
Nigg Bay
Balintraid
Saltburn
Nigg Ferry
Dalmore
Invergordon
223
Cromarty
Hugh Miller's Cottage
Balblair
Resolis
Cromarty Bay
Udale Bay
Newton
Jemimaville
Allerton
Navity
Upper Eathie
MORAY FIRTH
Culbin Forest
Kintessack
Raddery
Killen
Rosemarkie
Groam House
Cathedral
Fortrose
Fort George
Whiteness Head
Nairn
(Inbhir Nàrann)
Brodie Castle
Dyke
Brodie
Tradespark
Chanonry Point
Avoch
Ardersier
Moss-side
Househill
Boath Doocot
Auldearn
Whitemire
Conicavel
Munlochy Bay
Gollanfield
Foynesfield
Lochside
Inverness (Dalcross)
Fisherton
MORAY FIRTH
Clephanton
Cawdor
Righoul
Piperhill
Culcharry
Fornighty
Littlemill
Logie Steading
Kilmuir
Castle Stuart
Easter Dalziel
Tornagrain
Croy
River Nairn
214
Relugas
North Kessock
Newton
Cantraywood
Balloch
Kirkton of Barevan
Clunas
Redburn
Culloden
Smithton
Resaurie
Culcabock
Culloden Viaduct
Culloden Battlefield & Visitor Centre
Clava Cairns
323
CÀRN MAOL
Ardclach Bell Tower
Ferness
401
CÀRN A' CHRASGIE
Knocknagael Boar Stone
Milton of Leys
Daviot House
548
BEINN BHUIDHE MHOR
Bridge of Dulsie
Daviot
609
CÀRN NAN TRI-TIGHEARNAN
Drummossie Muir
464
Lochindorb
Balnafoich
Loch Moy
Moy
Lochindorb Lodge
483
Farr
River Findhorn
633
CÀRN AN T-SEAN-LIATHANAICH
615
CÀRN NA H-EASGAINN
Balvraid
Strathnairn
Tomatin Distillery Visitor Centre
Findhorn Viaduct
Raigbeg
617
659
CÀRN GLAS-CHOIRE
485
CÀRN SGRIOB
Tomatin
600
BEINN BHREAC
Findhorn Bridge
471
Croachy
603
CÀRN GLAC AN FICH
203
406 Slochd Summit
Dulnain Bridge
707
CÀRN NA SAOBHAIDH
Garbole
Duthil
Skye of Curr
Bogroy
Carrbridge
A9
A96
A832
A939
A938
B817
B9163
B9160
B9175
B9092
B9006
B9039
B9091
B9090
B9101
B9177
B8082
B851
B861
B9154
B9007
G H J K L M
1 2 3 4 5 6 7 8

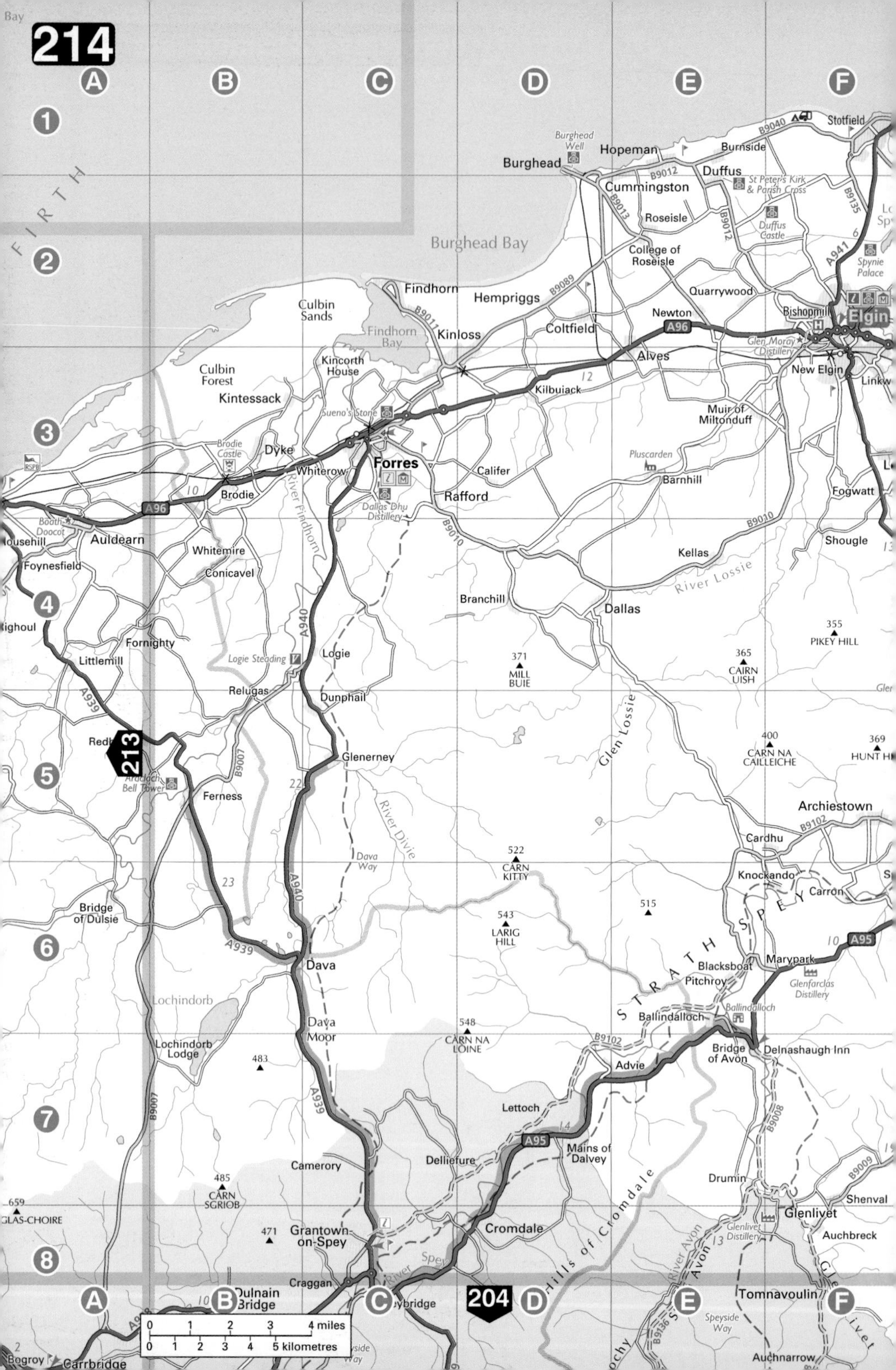

A
B
C
D
E
F
1
2
3
4
5
6
7
8
FIRTH
Burghead Bay
Burghead Well
Hopeman
Burghead
Stotfield
Burnside
Duffus
Cummingston
St Peter's Kirk & Parish Cross
Roseisle
Duffus Castle
College of Roseisle
Spynie Palace
Findhorn
Hempriggs
Quarrywood
Culbin Sands
Findhorn Bay
Kinloss
Coltfield
Newton
Bishopmill
Elgin
Glen Moray Distillery
Alves
New Elgin
Culbin Forest
Kincorth House
Kilbuiack
Muir of Miltonduff
Kintessack
Sueno's Stone
Brodie Castle
Dyke
Forres
Pluscarden
Barnhill
Whiterow
Califer
Brodie
Rafford
Fogwatt
Boath Doocot
Dallas Dhu Distillery
Auldearn
Housefill
Whitemire
Shougle
Kellas
Foynesfield
Conicavel
River Findhorn
River Lossie
Branchill
Dallas
Fornighty
Littlemill
Logie Steading
Logie
371 MILL BUIE
365 CAIRN UISH
355 PIKEY HILL
Relugas
Dunphail
Glen Lossie
400 CARN NA CAILLEICHE
369 HUNT HILL
Glenerney
Ardclach Bell Tower
Ferness
River Divie
Archiestown
Cardhu
Dava Way
522 CARN KITTY
Knockando
Carron
Bridge of Dulsie
515
543 LARIG HILL
STRATH SPEY
Dava
Blacksboat
Marypark
Pitchroy
Glenfarclas Distillery
Lochindorb
Ballindalloch
Dava Moor
548 CARN NA LOINE
Lochindorb Lodge
483
Bridge of Avon
Delnashaugh Inn
Advie
Lettoch
Mains of Dalvey
Dellefure
Camerory
485 CARN SGRIOB
Drumin
Shenval
659 GLAS-CHOIRE
Hills of Cromdale
Glenlivet
471
Grantown-on-Spey
Cromdale
Glenlivet Distillery
Auchbreck
River Spey
River Avon
Craggan
Dulnain Bridge
Tomnavoulin
Speyside Way
Bogroy
Carrbridge
Auchnarrow
0 1 2 3 4 miles
0 1 2 3 4 5 kilometres
213
204
A96
A940
A939
A95
A941
B9040
B9012
B9013
B9089
B9011
B9010
B9007
B9102
B9008
B9009
B9135
B9136

Spey Bay
Buckie
Portknockie
Findochty
Cullen
Cullen Bay
Sandend
Portsoy
Fochabers
Keith
Huntly
Dufftown
Rothes
Craigellachie
Aberlour
Kingston on Spey
Garmouth
Portgordon
Lhanbryde
Mosstodloch
Deskford
Fordyce
Cornhill
Glenbarry
Rothiemay
Ruthven
Cairnie
Drummuir
Maggieknockater
Kirktown of Mortlach
Haugh of Glass
Bridgend
Cabrach
Rhynie
Kennethmont
Gartly
Clatt
Lesmoir
Tap O' Noth
Newmill
Strath Isla
Strath Bogie
River Deveron
River Isla
Glen Fiddich
Speyside Way
Keith and Dufftown Railway
A96
A95
A98
A920
A941
A97
A942
A990
216
205

A
B
C
D
E
F
1
2
3
4
5
6
7
8
Bow Fiddle Rock
Cullen Bay
Cullen
Findlater
Sandend Bay
Sandend
Portsoy
Birkenbog
Tochieneal
A98
Boyndie Bay
Whitehills
Banff
Banff Bay
Macduff
Gamrie Bay
Troup Head
Crovie
Gardenstown
Silverford
Dubford
Protstonhill
Gamrie
B9139
Inver-boyndie
Boyndie
Duff House
Longmanhill
B9031
Milton
Fordyce
Deskford Church
Berryhillock
Windsole
B9022
Mid Culbeuchly
Ella
Ord
Kirktown of Alvah
A97
Clenerty
Minnonie
Netherbrae
221 BRACKLAM HILL
A947
Gorrachie
Danshillock
313 LURG HILL
Cornhill
B9025
B9023
A95
Gordonstown
429 KNOCK HILL
Glenbarry
271 WETHER HILL
Berryhillock
B9121
River Deveron
Muirden
B9105
Fintry
New Byth
Lootcherbrae
Knock
Drumnagorrach
Aberchirder
Garmond
B9027
Farmtown
Bridge of Marnoch
Carnousie
Turriff
Cuminestown
River Isla
B9117
Rothiemay
Muiresk
B9024
B9170
Darra
Howe of Teuchar
Inverkeithny
Auchininna
Ruthven
215
Bogniebrae
Forgue
Fortrie
Birkenhills
Cairnie
Carlincraig
B9001
Glendronach Distillery
Pitglassie
Dykeside
North Millbrex
B992
Auchterless
Nordic Ski Centre
Castle
Affleck
Gourdas
Balgaveny
Cottown of Gight
Drumblade
Lethenty
Logie Newton
Fyvie Castle
Fyvie
R. Ythan
Gordonstown
Huntly
A96
Brideswell
Badenscoth
Woodhead
Strath Bogie
Ythanwells
Thomastown
Rothiebrisbane
Bridgend
Kirkstile
Hillhead
Bainshole
Fisherford
Rothienorman
Glens of Foudland
St Katherines
Earlsford
Culdrain
419 WICHACH HILL
466 HILL OF FOUDLAND
Culsalmond
Rothmaise
Newseat
Barthol Chapel
Gartly
Colpy
Tocher
Folla Rule
Cross of Jackston
Kirkney
Meikle Wartle
Tulloch
Largie
Kirkton of Rayne
Leith Hall
Picardy Symbol Stone
Old Rayne
Loanhead Stone Circle
A920
B992
Kennethmont
Insch
Dunnideer
Pitmachie
Durno
Daviot
Oldmeldrum
B9002
Duncanstone
Clatt
Whiteford
Archaeolink
Pitcaple
Maiden Stone
Pittodrie House Hotel
Chapel of Garioch
206
Kirktown of Bourtie
Carnbre
Whiterash
0 1 2 3 4 miles
0 1 2 3 4 5 kilometres

Castle Lighthouse & Museum
Kinnaird Head
Rosehearty
Sandhaven
Pittulie
Fraserburgh
Peathill
Craigiefold
Fraserburgh Bay
Kirktown
Cairnbulg
Inverallochy
Aberdour Bay
Percyhorner
Pitblae
Maggie's Hoosie
Whitelinks Bay
B9031
Coburby
Mid Ardlaw
B9033
New Aberdour
Boyndlie
B9032
Memsie
St Combs
A90
A98
Memsie Cairn
Rathen
Crofts of Savoch
A981
Newburgh
Lonmay
Rattray Head
Loch of Strathbeg
234
WAUGHTON HILL
Crimond
Blackhill
New Pitsligo
B9093
Strichen
A952
New Leeds
Bonnykelly
Leys
Denhead
Backfolds
Kirktown
St Fergus
Fetterangus
Rora
A950
Deer Abbey
Dunshillock
River Ugie
Maud
B9106
Aden
Mintlaw
Inverugie
New Deer
B9029
Old Deer
Longside
Buchanhaven
Peterhead
Blackhill of Clackriach
Inverquhomery
B9028
A948
Stuartfield
Drymuir
Bulwark
Millbreck
Hillhead of Cocklaw
Peterhead Bay
Nether Kinmundy
A982
Burnhaven
Nethermuir
Knaven
Clola
Buchan Ness
B9030
Kinnadie
Blackhill
Stirling
Boddam
Auchnagatt
Lendrum Terrace
Cairnorrie
Kinknockie
Brownhill
Longhaven
Inkhorn
Coldwells
Ardallie
Bullers of Buchan
Auchiries
Hatton
North Haven
Arthrath
Muirtack
Slains
Cruden Bay
Bogbrae
Chapel Hill
Bay of Cruden
A975
Ythanbank
B9005
Birness
Whinnyfold
The Skares
Auchedly
Altar-Tomb of William Forbes
Artrochie
Kinharrachie
Ythsie
Ellon
P+R
Esslemont
Kirkton of Logie Buchan
Kirktown of Slains
A920
B999
Collieston
Pitmedden Garden
Pitmedden
Logierieve
Forvie
Housieside
207
B9000
Udny Station
Newburgh
Pettymuk
Foveran
Cultercullen

A
B
C
D
E
F
1
2
3
4
5
6
7
8
Fladda-chùain
Eilean Trodday
Rudha Hunish
North Duntulm
Duntulm
Kilmaluag
A855
Tairbeart (Tarbert)
Lùb Score
Skye Museum of Island Life
Flodigarry
Poldorais
Eilean Flodigarry
Borneskitaig
Heribusta
Kilmuir
Kilvaxter
542
MEAL NA SUIREAMACH
Digg
Staffin Bay
Staffin Island
Balgown
Brogaig
Stenscholl
Staffin
Linicro
Totscore
464
BIODA BUIDHE
Trotternish
Kilt Rock Waterfall
Ellishader
208
209
River Rha
Maligar
Idrigill
Loch nam Madadh (Lochmaddy)
Marishader
Valtos
River Conon
Uig (Uige)
611
BEINN EDRA
Garros
Rudha nam Brathairean
Uig Bay
Culnaknock
Loch a' Bhr
Loch Sn…ort
Tote
0 1 2 3 4 miles
0 1 2 3 4 5 kilometres
608

Steornabhagh (Stornoway)
Tanera Beg
Tanera Mòr
Badentarbat Bay
Glas-leac Beag
Eilean Dubh
Priest Island
Greenstone Point
Cailleach Head
Rudha Beag
Scoraig
Stattic Point
Mellon Udrigle
GRUINARD ISLAND
Badluachrach
Gruinard Bay
Laide
A832
Foura
Rudha Reidh
Cove
Mellon Charles
Ormiscaig
Aultbea
Gruinard
296 AN CUAIDH
B8057
ISLE OF EWE
Little Gruinard River
Gruinard River
Melvaig
Aultgrishin
Loch Ewe
Loch Fada
347 CREAG-MHEAL BEAG
220
Inverasdale
293 CNOC BREAC
Naast
Inverewe Garden
681 BEINN A' CHAISGEIN BEAG
B8021
250 MEALL NA MEINE
North Erradale
Poolewe
Londubh
Fionn Loch
Wester Ross
Big Sand
Strath
A832
Smithstown
Lonemore
Auchtercairn
Heritage
Longa Island
Gairloch
Loch Gairloch
Dubh Loch
791 BEINN AIRIDH CHARR
421 MEALL AN DOIREIN
Charlestown
Eilean Horrisdale
Port Henderson
B8056
Badachro
Opinan
Loch Maree
859 BEINN LÀIR
South Erradale
Loch Bad an Sgalaig
Loch Maree Hotel
Letterewe
Loch Garbhaig
Talladale
A832
981 SLIOCH
Redpoint
Loch Ghaineamhach
Red Point
210
Loch na h-Oidhche
Loch Ghobhainn
875 BAOSBHEINN
855 BEINN AN EOIN
619 BEINN BHREAC
724
Loch a' Bhealaich
Loch Torridon
Craig River
Rudha na Fearn
Lower Diabaig
914 BEINN DEARG
1009 RUADH-STAC MÒR
972
Kinlochewe
Loch Diabaig
Òb Chuaig
Fearnbeg
G
H
J
K
L
M
1
2
3
4
5
6
7
8
13
19

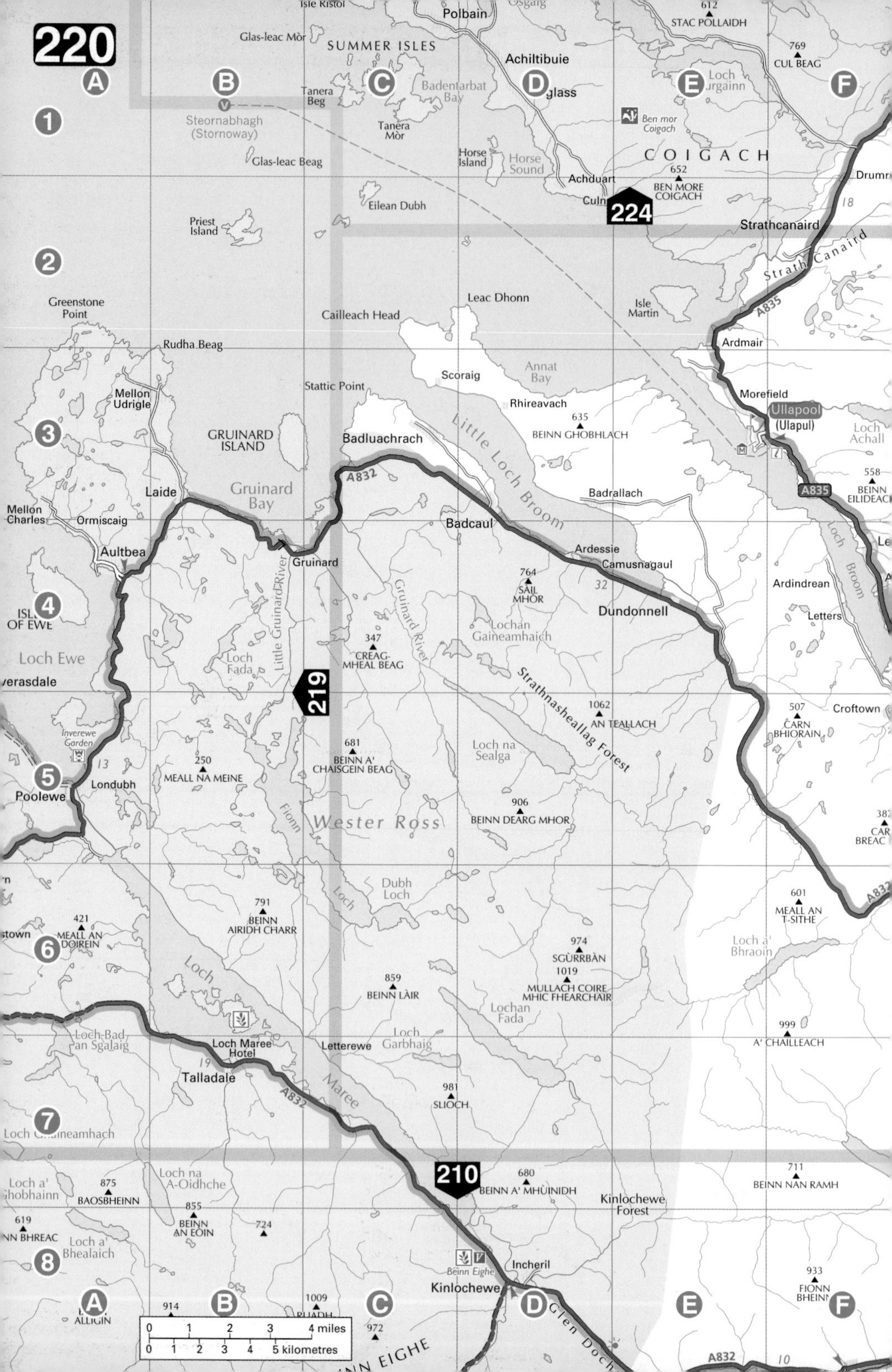

A
B
C
D
E
F
1
2
3
4
5
6
7
8
Isle Ristol
Polbain
Glas-leac Mòr
SUMMER ISLES
Achiltibuie
612
STAC POLLAIDH
769
CUL BEAG
Tanera Beg
Badentarbat Bay
Steornabhagh (Stornoway)
Tanera Mòr
Ben mor Coigach
Glas-leac Beag
Horse Island
Horse Sound
COIGACH
Achduart
652
BEN MORE COIGACH
Drumr
Eilean Dubh
Culn
224
Priest Island
Strathcanaird
18
Strath Canaird
Greenstone Point
Leac Dhonn
Cailleach Head
Isle Martin
A835
Rudha Beag
Ardmair
Scoraig
Annat Bay
Stattic Point
Morefield
Mellon Udrigle
Rhireavach
Ullapool
(Ulapul)
635
BEINN GHOBHLACH
Loch Achall
GRUINARD ISLAND
Badluachrach
Little Loch Broom
558
BEINN EILIDEACH
A832
Gruinard Bay
Laide
Badrallach
A835
Mellon Charles
Ormiscaig
Badcaul
Ardessie
Camusnagaul
Aultbea
Gruinard
764
SAIL MHOR
Ardindrean
Loch Broom
32
ISLE OF EWE
Little Gruinard River
Gruinard River
Dundonnell
Letters
Lochan Gaineamhaich
347
CREAG-MHEAL BEAG
Loch Ewe
Loch Fada
Strathnasheallag Forest
219
1062
AN TEALLACH
507
CARN BHIORAIN
Croftown
Inverewe Garden
681
BEINN A' CHAISGEIN BEAG
Loch na Sealga
250
MEALL NA MEINE
13
Poolewe
Londubh
906
BEINN DEARG MHOR
Fionn
Wester Ross
Dubh Loch
Loch
791
BEINN AIRIDH CHARR
601
MEALL AN T-SITHE
A832
421
MEALL AN DOIREIN
974
SGÙRRBÀN
Loch a' Bhraoin
1019
MULLACH COIRE MHIC FHEARCHAIR
859
BEINN LÀIR
Loch
Lochan Fada
Loch Bad an Sgalaig
Loch Maree Hotel
Letterewe
Loch Garbhaig
999
A' CHAILLEACH
19
Talladale
A832
Maree
981
SLIOCH
Loch Gaineamhach
Loch na A-Oidhche
210
680
BEINN A' MHÙINIDH
711
BEINN NAN RAMH
Loch a' Ghobhainn
875
BAOSBHEINN
Kinlochewe Forest
855
BEINN AN EOIN
724
619
Loch a' Bhealaich
Beinn Eighe
Incheril
933
FIONN BHEIN
Kinlochewe
1009
914
Glen Doch
0
1
2
3
4 miles
0
1
2
3
4
5 kilometres
972
A832
10

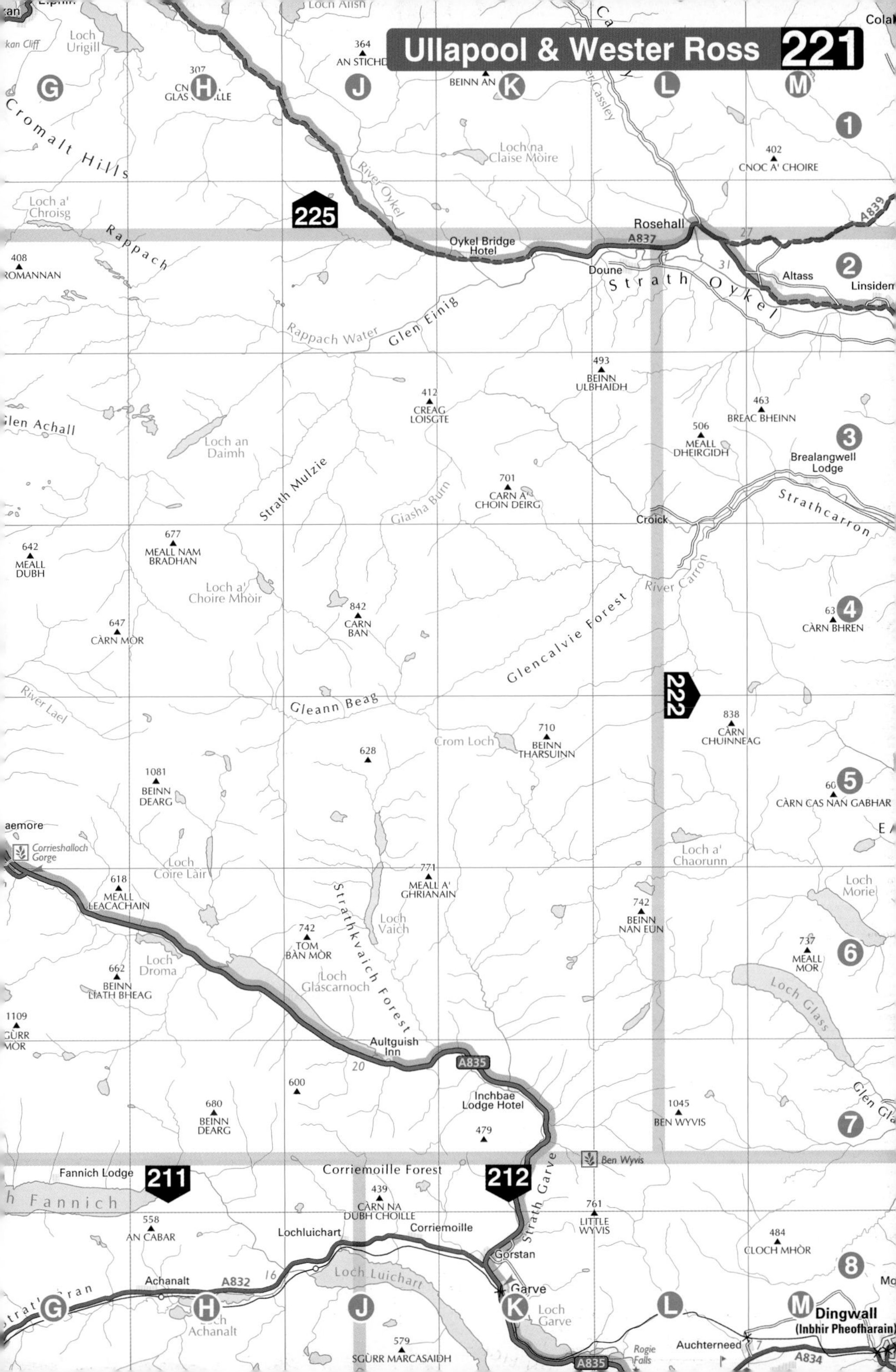
Loch Urigill
Cromalt Hills
364 AN STICHD
BEINN AN
Loch na Claise Mòire
402 CNOC A' CHOIRE
Loch a' Chroisg
225
Rappach
River Oykel
Rosehall
A837
A839
Oykel Bridge Hotel
Doune
Strath Oykel
Altass
Linsidem
408
Rappach Water
Glen Einig
493 BEINN ULBHAIDH
412 CREAG LOISGTE
463 BREAC BHEINN
Glen Achall
Loch an Daimh
506 MEALL DHEIRGIDH
Brealangwell Lodge
Strath Mulzie
Giasha Burn
701 CARN A' CHOIN DEIRG
Strathcarron
Croick
677 MEALL NAM BRADHAN
642 MEALL DUBH
Loch a' Choire Mhòir
River Carron
842 CARN BAN
Glencalvie Forest
647 CÀRN MOR
CÀRN BHREN
222
River Lael
Gleann Beag
838 CÀRN CHUINNEAG
710 BEINN THARSUINN
Crom Loch
628
1081 BEINN DEARG
CÀRN CAS NAN GABHAR
Corrieshalloch Gorge
Loch a' Chaorunn
Loch Coire Làir
618 MEALL LEACACHAIN
771 MEALL A' GHRIANAIN
Strathkvaich Forest
Loch Vaich
Loch Morie
742 BEINN NAN EUN
742 TOM BÀN MÒR
737 MEALL MOR
Loch Droma
662 BEINN LIATH BHEAG
Loch Glascarnoch
Loch Glass
1109
Aultguish Inn
A835
600
Inchbae Lodge Hotel
680 BEINN DEARG
479
1045 BEN WYVIS
Glen Glass
Ben Wyvis
Fannich Lodge
211
Corriemoille Forest
212
Loch Fannich
439 CÀRN NA DUBH CHOILLE
Strath Garve
761 LITTLE WYVIS
558 AN CABAR
Lochluichart
Corriemoille
484 CLOCH MHÒR
Gorstan
Loch Luichart
Achanalt
A832
Garve
Loch Garve
Loch Achanalt
Dingwall (Inbhir Pheofharain)
Auchterneed
A834
579 SGÙRR MARCASAIDH
Rogie Falls

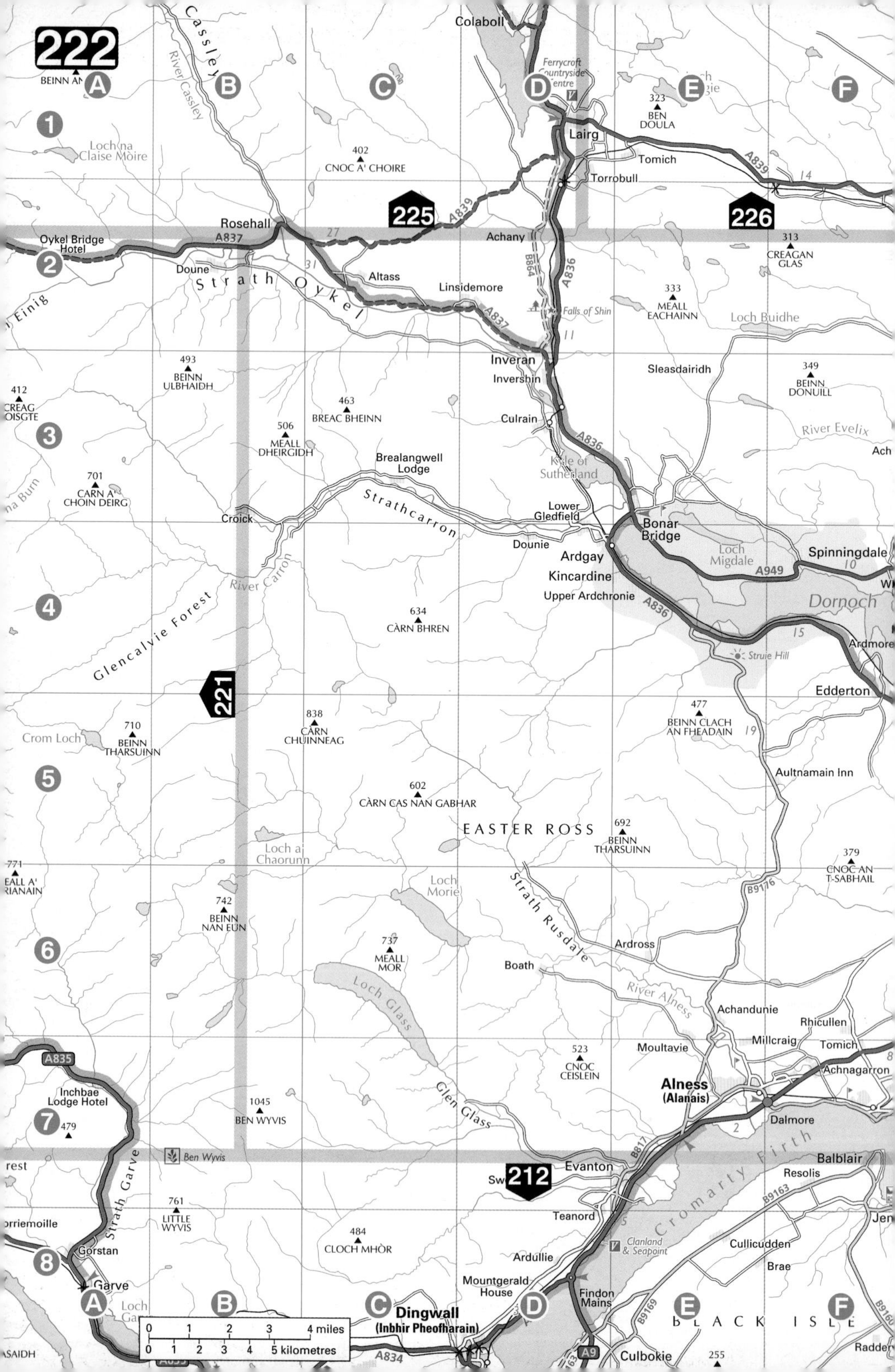
Colaboll
Ferrycroft Countryside Centre
Lairg
Tomich
Torrobull
BEN DOULA
CNOC A' CHOIRE
Loch na Claise Mòire
River Cassley
Cassley
225
226
A839
Rosehall
A837
Oykel Bridge Hotel
Doune
Strath Oykel
Achany
B864
A836
Altass
Linsidemore
Falls of Shin
MEALL EACHAINN
CREAGAN GLAS
Loch Buidhe
Inveran
Invershin
Culrain
Sleasdairidh
BEINN DONUILL
River Evelix
BEINN ULBHAIDH
CREAG
BREAC BHEINN
MEALL DHEIRGIDH
CARN A' CHOIN DEIRG
Brealangwell Lodge
Kyle of Sutherland
Strathcarron
Croick
Lower Gledfield
Bonar Bridge
Dounie
Ardgay
Kincardine
Upper Ardchronie
Loch Migdale
Spinningdale
A949
Dornoch
River Carron
Glencalvie Forest
CÀRN BHREN
Struie Hill
Ardmore
Edderton
221
CÀRN CHUINNEAG
BEINN THARSUINN
Crom Loch
BEINN CLACH AN FHEADAIN
Aultnamain Inn
CÀRN CAS NAN GABHAR
EASTER ROSS
Loch a' Chaorunn
Loch Morie
CNOC AN T-SABHAIL
B9176
Strath Rusdale
BEINN NAN EUN
MEALL MOR
Ardross
Boath
Loch Glass
River Alness
Achandunie
Rhicullen
Millcraig
Tomich
Moultavie
CNOC CEISLEIN
Alness (Alanais)
Achnagarron
A835
Inchbae Lodge Hotel
Glen Glass
BEN WYVIS
Dalmore
Ben Wyvis
B817
Cromarty Firth
Balblair
Evanton
212
Resolis
Strath Garve
LITTLE WYVIS
Teanord
B9163
Cullicudden
Clanland & Seapoint
CLOCH MHÒR
Gorstan
Ardullie
Brae
Garve
Mountgerald House
Findon Mains
B9169
Dingwall (Inbhir Pheofharain)
BLACK ISLE
A834
A9
Culbokie
Raddery
0 1 2 3 4 miles
0 1 2 3 4 5 kilometres

Strath Brora
River Brora
Dalreavoch Lodge
Loch Horn
520 BEN HORN
Golspie Burn
378 CAGAR FEOSAIG
Lothbeg
Dalchalm
Brora
227
Doll
Backies
Carn Liath
A9
446 BEN LUNDIE
383 BEN BHRAGGIE
Rhives
Dunrobin Castle
Golspie
Torboll
Cambusavie Platform
Loch Fleet
Badninish
Skelbo
Skelbo Street
Fourpenny
Embo
Birichin
Embo Street
B9168
Pitgrudy
Evelix
A949
Camore
Dornoch
Historylinks
Cuthill
Dornoch Firth
Tarbat Ness
Wilkhaven
Brucefield
Innis Mhor
Ferry Point
Glenmorangie Distillery
Portmahomack
Morangie
Inver
Rockfield
B9165
Arboll
284
Tain (Baile Dhubhthaich)
Toulvaddie
Lochslin
Loch Eye
Rhynie
Hill of Fearn
Balmuchy
B9165
Hilton of Cadboll Chapel (ruin)
Newfield
Fearn
Tullich
B9166
Hilton
Arabella
Ballchraggan
Balintore
Shandwick
Shandwick Bay
Kildary
Ankerville
Milton
B9175
Kilmuir
Pitcalnie
Barbaraville
Nigg
Nigg Bay
Balintraid
Nigg Ferry
MORAY FIRTH
(Jun-Oct)
Cromarty
Cromarty Bay
Hugh Miller's Cottage
Newton
213
214
Burghead
B9163
Allerton
Navity
Findhorn
Culbin Sands
B9011
Findhorn Bay
Upper Eathie
Kincorth House
Culbin Forest
Kintessack
A832
Sueno's Stone
Whiteness Head

Laxford Bridge
Scourie Bay
A894
Scourie More
Scourie
Badcall
Badcall Bay
Loch a' Mhuilinn
386
BEN AUSKAIRD
Rudh' a' Mhucard
228
Point of Stoer
Old Man of Stoer
OLDANY ISLAND
Eddrachillis Bay
419
BEN STROME
Kylestrome
Kylesku
Culkein Drumbeg
Culkein
Clashnessie Bay
Oldany
Drumbeg
Unapool
Achnacarnin
B869
Clashmore
Nedd
Loch Poll
Glen Leirg
Loch an Leothaid
776
SAIL GHORM
809
QUINAG
Clashnessie
Stoer
A894
Clachtoll
Bay of Clachtoll
Loch Beannach
Achmelvich Bay
Rhicarn
A837
Loch Assynt
Achmelvich
Baddidarrach
Lochinver
539
BEINN GHARBH
Soyea Island
Loch Inver
Strathan
Assynt - Coigach
Inverkirkaig
Loch na Gainimh
847
CANISP
Stronchrubie
River Kirkaig
Fionn Loch
732
SUILVEN
Rhu Coigach
Eilean Mòr
Enard Bay
Loch Awe
Rubha Mòr
Reiff
Achnahaird
Càm Loch
Altandhu
Loch Sionascaig
Loch Veyatie
Eilean Mullagrach
849
CUL MÒR
Ledmore Junction
Elphin
Knockan
Loch Osgaig
Isle Ristol
Polbain
612
STAC POLLAIDH
Knockan Cliff
Loch Urigill
Glas-leac Mòr
SUMMER ISLES
769
CUL BEAG
Achiltibuie
Knockan Crag
Tanera Beg
Badentarbat Bay
Loch Lurgainn
Polglass
Cromalt Hills
Steornabhagh (Stornoway)
Tanera Mòr
Ben mor Coigach
Glas-leac Beag
Horse Island
Horse Sound
COIGACH
652
BEN MORE COIGACH
Drumrunie Lodge
Achduart
Eilean Dubh
Culnacraig
Loch a' Chroisg
Priest Island
Strathcanaird
220
Strath Canaird
408
NA DROMANNAN
A835
Leac Dhonn
Isle Martin
Cailleach Head
Ardmair
Scoraig
Annat Bay
Stattic Point
Morefield
0 1 2 3 4 miles
0 1 2 3 4 5 kilometres
635
BEINN GHOBHLACH
Ullapool (Ulapul)
Glen Achall
Loch Achall
GRUINARD ISLAND
Badluachrach

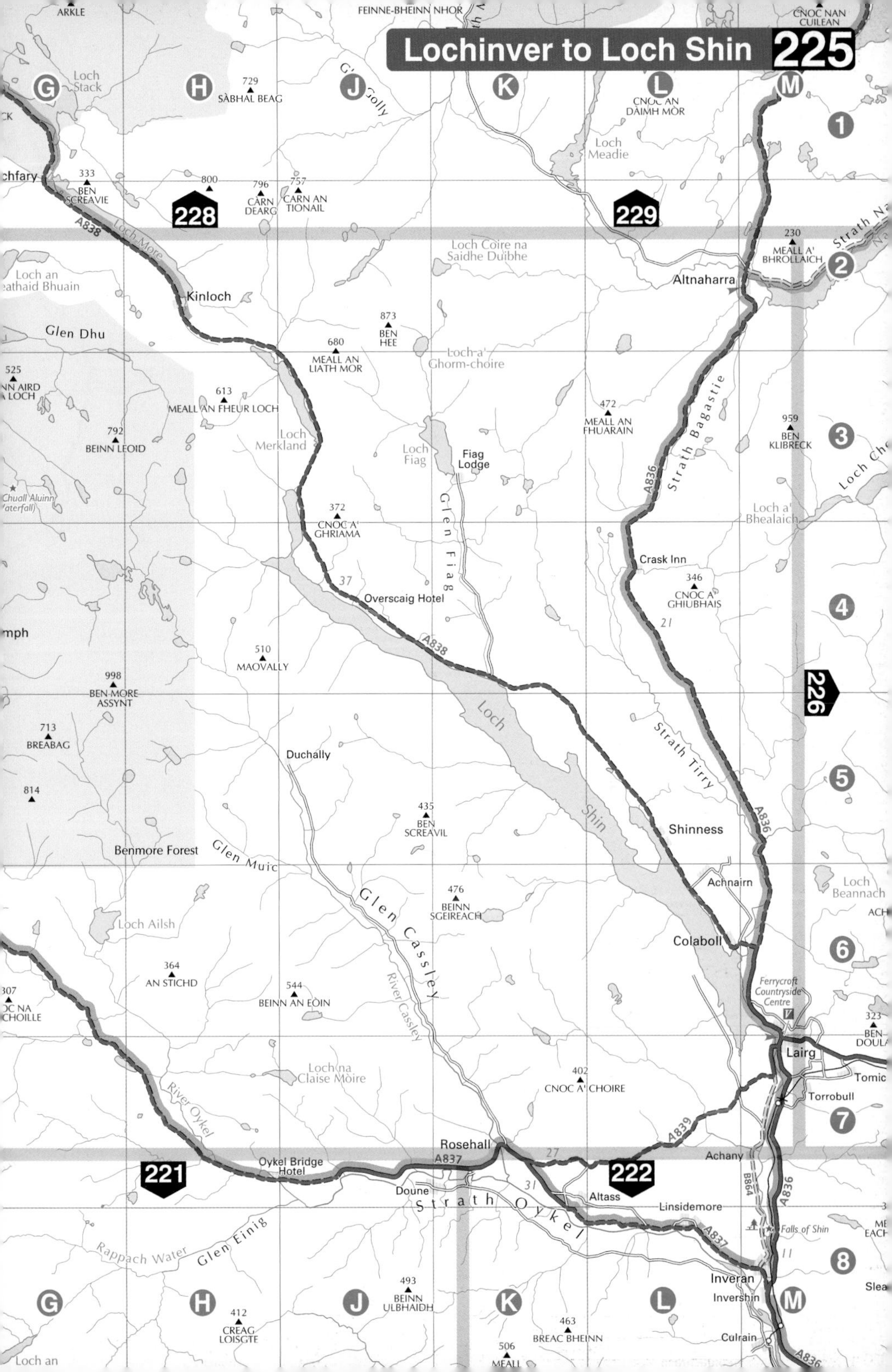
Loch Stack
SÀBHAL BEAG
ARKLE
FEINNE-BHEINN NHOR
CNOC NAN CUILEAN
CNOC AN DÀIMH MÒR
Loch Meadie
BEN SCREAVIE
CARN DEARG
CARN AN TIONAIL
228
229
A838
Loch More
Loch Coire na Saidhe Duibhe
MEALL A' BHROLLAICH
Altnaharra
Loch an Eathaid Bhuain
Kinloch
Glen Dhu
BEN HEE
MEALL AN LIATH MOR
Loch a' Ghorm-choire
MEALL AN FHEUR LOCH
BEINN LEOID
Loch Merkland
Loch Fiag
Fiag Lodge
MEALL AN FHUARAIN
Strath Bagastie
BEN KLIBRECK
Glen Fiag
CNOC A' GHRIAMA
A836
Loch a' Bhealaich
Crask Inn
CNOC A' GHIUBHAIS
Overscaig Hotel
MAOVALLY
BEN MORE ASSYNT
BREABAG
226
Loch Shin
Strath Tirry
Duchally
BEN SCREAVIL
Shinness
Benmore Forest
Glen Muic
Achnairn
Glen Cassley
BEINN SGEIREACH
Loch Beannach
Loch Ailsh
Colaboll
AN STICHD
BEINN AN EOIN
River Cassley
Ferrycroft Countryside Centre
Lairg
Torrobull
Loch na Claise Mòire
CNOC A' CHOIRE
River Oykel
A839
Rosehall
Oykel Bridge Hotel
A837
Achany
221
222
Doune
Altass
Strath Oykel
Linsidemore
B864
Falls of Shin
Rappach Water
Glen Einig
Inveran
Invershin
BEINN ULBHAIDH
CREAG LOISGTE
BREAC BHEINN
Culrain
Loch an

226
229
230
225
223
Strath Naver
Loch Choire Forest
Borrobol Forest
Ben Armine Forest
Strath Skinsdale
Strath Brora
Lairg
Rogart
Golspie
Kinbrace
Dunrobin Castle
Loch Fleet
Learable Hill Cairns, Stone Row & Stone Circles
Ferrycroft Countryside Centre
Falls of Shin
Balnacoil Lodge
Dalreavoch Lodge
0 1 2 3 4 miles
0 1 2 3 4 5 kilometres

Altnabreac Station
Achavanich
Loch Stemster
248 STEMSTER HILL
Loch an Thulachan
Loch Sand
Loch Rangag
CNOC NAN GALL
Rumsdale Water
Strathmore
Dalnawillan Lodge
226 COIRE NA BEINN
Glutt Water
230
348 BEN ALISKY
231
287 BEN-A-CHIELT
Upper Lybster
Glutt Lodge
264 CNOCAN CONACHREAG
Swiney
Houstry
Invershore
Lybster
KNOCKFIN HEIGHTS
Land-hallow
Lybster Bay
Forse
Smerral
Latheron
Dunbeath Water
317 CNOC LOCH MHADADH
Latheronwheel
Janetstown
Berriedale Water
A9
Laidhay Croft
Dunbeath
437
Braemore
484 MAIDEN PAP
Knockally
705 MORVEN
518 CNOC AN EIREANNAICH
Ramscraigs
626 SCARABEN
Borgue
Langwell Forest
Newport
554 CREAG SCALABSDALE
Langwell House
Berriedale
Lodge
401 CNOC NA MAOILE
416 BEINN DUBHAIN
A897
Torrish
River Helmsdale
404 CREAG THORARAIDH
Ord of Caithness
Timespan
Navidale House Hotel
West Helmsdale
East Helmsdale
591 BEINN NA MEILICH
Gartymore
Helmsdale
Portgower
Glen Loth
Lothmore
Lothbeg
G
H
J
K
L
M
1
2
3
4
5
6
7
8

A
B
C
D
E
F
1
2
3
4
5
6
7
8
CAPE WRATH
Cléit Dhubh
Faraid Head
371
SGRIBHIS-BHEINN
297
CNOC A GHIUBHAIS
300
MAOVALLY
Balnakeil Bay
Sango Bay
Balnakeil
THE PARPH
Durness
457
FASHVEN
Sangomore
Smoo
Sandwood Bay
Loch Airigh na Beinne
Kyle of Durness
Keoldale
Sangob
Sandwood Loch
Loch Meadaidh
485
CREAG RIABACH
Strath Shinary
468
BEINN DEARG MHÒR
464
MEALL NA MOINE
423
MEALL MEADHONACH
Rudh' an Fhir Leithe
331
GHLAS-BHEINN
A838
Sheigra
Balchreick
Blairmore
19
Laid
489
MEALL NA CRA
521
FARVEALL
Oldshoremore
355
AN SOCACH
773
BEINN SPIONNAIDH
Kinlochbervie
Loch Clash
Badcall
801
CRANSTACKIE
B801
Loch Inchard
Achriesgill
Strath Dionard
River Dionard
Strath Beag
31
A838
520
AN LEAN-CH
Rhiconich
Loch na Claise Càrnaich
Rudha Ruadh
908
FOINAVEN
Fanagmore
Skerricha
Loch Laxford
Tarbet
A838
HANDA ISLAND
Foindle
North-west Sutherland
Loch na Tuadh
River Laxford
Laxford Bridge
786
ARKLE
FEINN
Scourie Bay
7
A894
Scourie
Scourie More
Loch Stack
729
SÀBHAL BEAG
Glen Golly
721
BEN STACK
Badcall
Badcall Bay
Strath Stack
Loch a' Mhuilinn
386
BEN AUSKAIRD
Achfary
333
BEN SCREAVIE
800
796
CARN DEARG
757
CARN AN TIONAIL
Rudh' a' Mhucard
17
A838
Loch More
224
225
OLDANY ISLAND
Eddrachillis Bay
419
BEN STROME
Loch an Leathaid-Bhuain
Loch a' Chàirn Bhàin
Kinloch
Culkein Drumbeg
Kylestrome
Kylesku
Loch Glendhu
Glen Dhu
Drumbeg
Unapool
680
MEALL AN LIATH MOR
B869
525
BEINN A' DA LOCH
Nedd
Loch Glencoul
613
MEALL AN FHEUR LOCH
Loch Poll
0 1 2 3 4 miles
0 1 2 3 4 5 kilometres
792
Loch Merkland

G
H
J
K
L
M
1
2
3
4
5
6
7
8
Whiten Head
Eilean Hoan
408 BEN HUTIG
Strathan
Talmine
Melness
Midtown
Rabbit Islands
Eilean Nan Ròn
Tongue Bay
Kyle of Tongue
Skerray
Achtoty
Torrisdale
Neave Island
Torrisdale Bay
Farr Bay
Farr
Farr Point
Kirtomy Point
Ardmore Point
Kirtomy
Swordly
Bettyhill
Invernaver
Achina
Borgie
Scullomie
Coldbackie
A838
A836
230 BEN ARNABOLL
262 DRUIM NAN CLIAR
Tongue
310 MEALL LEATHAD NA CRAOIBHE
River Borgie
Loch Meadie
228
Skelpick
Skelpick Burn
Strath Naver
Loch Mòr na Caorach
Loch Hope
318 CNOC CRAGGIE
Loch Craggie
Kinloch
Loch na Seilg
Kyle of Tongue
598 MEALLAN LIATH
927 BEN HOPE
763 BEN LOYAL
527 BEINN STUMANADH
213 CNOC MALPELLY
B871
Loch an Deerie
Loch Loyal
Loyal Lodge
Loch Strathy
335 MEALL BAD NA CUAICHE
557 CNOC NAN CUILEAN
Strath More
Loch Syre
River Naver
Syre
345 CNOC NA TRI-CHLAC
656 CNOC AN DÀIMH MÒR
294 POLE HILL
259 BEINN ROSAIL
404 BEINN MHADADH
Loch Meadie
B873
Strath Naver
Loch Naver
230 MEALL A' BHROLLAICH
270 BEADAIG
Loch Coire na Saidhe Duibhe
225
226
230
Altnaharra
Loch Rimsdale
Loch nan Clàr
Loch Badanloch
Loch a' ...orm-choire
Loch an Altan Fheàrna
Loch Truders
472 MEALL AN FHUARAIN
Bagastie
959 BEN KLIBRECK
...oire Forest
694
434
12
13
16
17

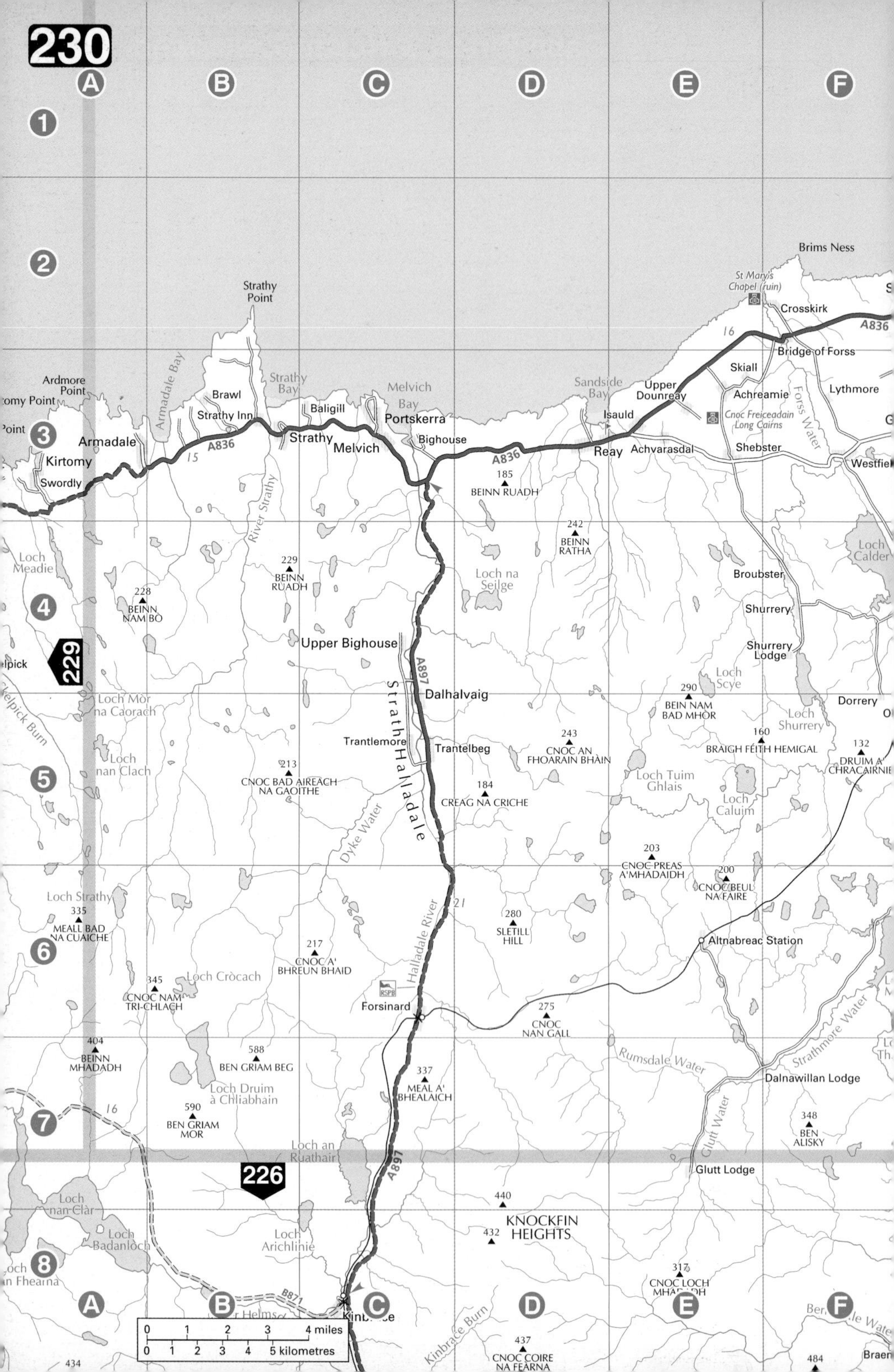
Brims Ness
St Mary's Chapel (ruin)
Crosskirk
A836
Strathy Point
Bridge of Forss
Skiall
Lythmore
Ardmore Point
Armadale Bay
Brawl
Strathy Bay
Melvich Bay
Sandside Bay
Upper Dounreay
Achreamie
Forss Water
Strathy Inn
Baligill
Portskerra
Isauld
Cnoc Freiceadain Long Cairns
Armadale
Strathy
Melvich
Bighouse
Reay
Achvarasdal
Shebster
Westfield
Kirtomy
Swordly
A836
BEINN RUADH
River Strathy
BEINN RATHA
Loch Meadie
BEINN RUADH
Loch na Seilge
Loch Calder
Broubster
BEINN NAM BO
Shurrery
Upper Bighouse
Shurrery Lodge
Loch Scye
229
A897
Strath Halladale
Dalhalvaig
BEIN NAM BAD MHOR
Dorrery
Loch Mòr na Caorach
Loch Shurrery
Halpick Burn
Loch nan Clach
Trantlemore
Trantelbeg
CNOC AN FHOARAIN BHÀIN
BRAIGH FÉITH HEMIGAL
DRUIM A' CHRACAIRNIE
CNOC BAD AIREACH NA GAOITHE
Loch Tuim Ghlais
CREAG NA CRICHE
Loch Caluim
Dyke Water
CNOC PREAS A'MHADAIDH
CNOC BEUL NA FAIRE
Loch Strathy
Halladale River
MEALL BAD NA CUAICHE
SLETILL HILL
Altnabreac Station
CNOC A' BHREUN BHAID
CNOC NAM TRI-CHLACH
Loch Cròcach
RSPB
Forsinard
CNOC NAN GALL
Strathmore Water
BEINN MHADADH
BEN GRIAM BEG
Rumsdale Water
MEAL A' BHEALAICH
Dalnawillan Lodge
Loch Druim à Chliabhain
BEN GRIAM MOR
Glutt Water
BEN ALISKY
Loch an Ruathair
226
A897
Glutt Lodge
Loch nan Clàr
KNOCKFIN HEIGHTS
Loch Badanloch
Loch Arichlinie
CNOC LOCH MHADAIDH
B871
Kinbrace
Kinbrace Burn
CNOC COIRE NA FEÀRNA
Braemore
0 1 2 3 4 miles
0 1 2 3 4 5 kilometres

PENTLAND FIRTH
DUNNET HEAD
Briga Head
Stromness
Holborn Head
DUNNET HILL
Brough
West Dunnet
Dunnet Bay
Dunnet
St John's Loch
Scarfskerry
Rattar
Mey
Loch Mey
Castle of Mey
Gills
Gills Bay
ISLAND OF STROMA
Nethertown
Mell Head
Uppertown
St John's Point
Inner Sound
St Margaret's Hope
DUNCANSBY HEAD
Huna
Kirkstyle
Canisbay
Muckle Stack
John o' Groats
Stacks of Duncansby
Barrock
Inkstack
Brabstermire
Skirza
Thurso Bay
Thurso
Murkle
Castlehill
Castletown
Greenland
Loch Heilen
Gill Burn
Freswick
Freswick Bay
Ness Head
Slickly
Olrig House
Tain
Weydale
Hilliclay
Bowermadden
Auckengill
Kirk Burn
Broch
Nybster
Sortat
Bower
Lyth
Howe
Brough Head
Sordale
Knockdee
Roadside
Loch Scarmclate
Halcro
Mireland
Keiss
Clayock
Burn of Lyth
Kirk
Halkirk
Gillock
Loch of Wester
Georgemas Junction Station
Sinclair Bay
Scotscalder Station
Harpsdale
SPITTAL HILL
Loch Watten
Killimster
Reiss
Castle Girnigoe & Sinclair
Noss Head
Spittal
Watten
Wick River
Winless
Sibster
Ackergill
Staxigoe
Mybster
Loch of Toftingall
Bilbster
Wick
Papigoe
Westerdale
River Thurso
Haster
Milton
Janetstown
Wick Bay
Achairn Burn
Newton
Old Wick
South Head
Castle of Old Wick
Strath Beg
Badlipster
Whiterow
Loch Hempriggs
BEINN CHÀITEAG
Tannach
Thrumster
Loch Ruard
BALLHARN HILL
Grey Cairns of Camster
Sarclet
Achavanich
Loch Stemster
HILL OF YARROWS
Loch of Yarrows
Loch Sand
Loch Rangag
STEMSTER HILL
Ulbster
Cairn o'Get
Whaligoe
COIRE NA BEINN
Whaligoe Steps
Roster
Bruan
Hill o'Many Stanes
Upper Lybster
BEN-A-CHIELT
Mid Clyth
Halberry Head
CNOCAN CONACHREAG
Swiney
Occumster
Clyth Ness
Houstry
Invershore
Lybster
Land-hallow
Lybster Bay
Forse
Smerral
Dunbeath Water
Latheron
Latheronwheel
Janetstown
Laidhay Croft
Dunbeath
A836
A9
A99
A882
B855
B874
B876
B870
234
227

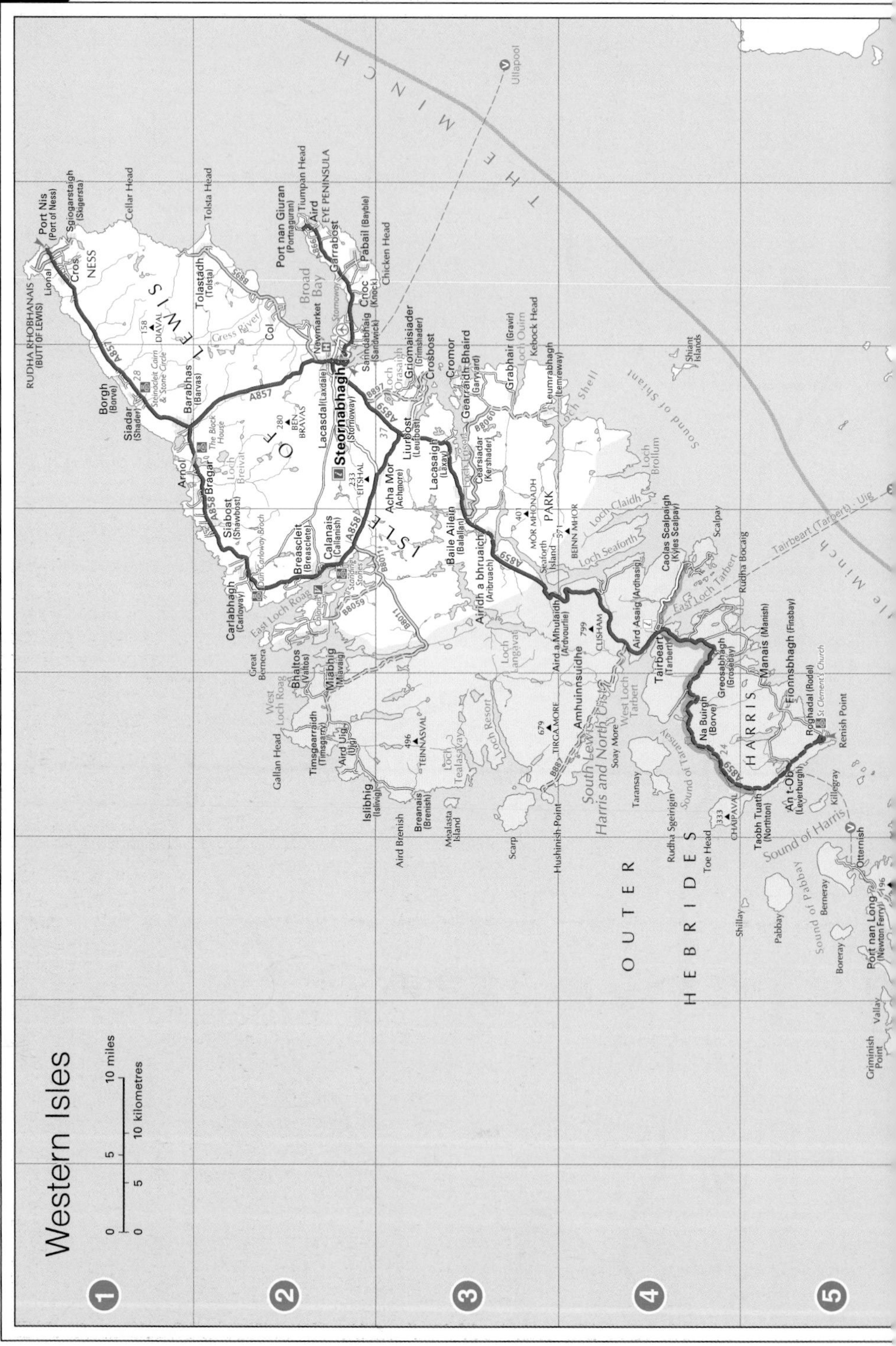

Western Isles

0 5 10 miles

0 5 10 kilometres

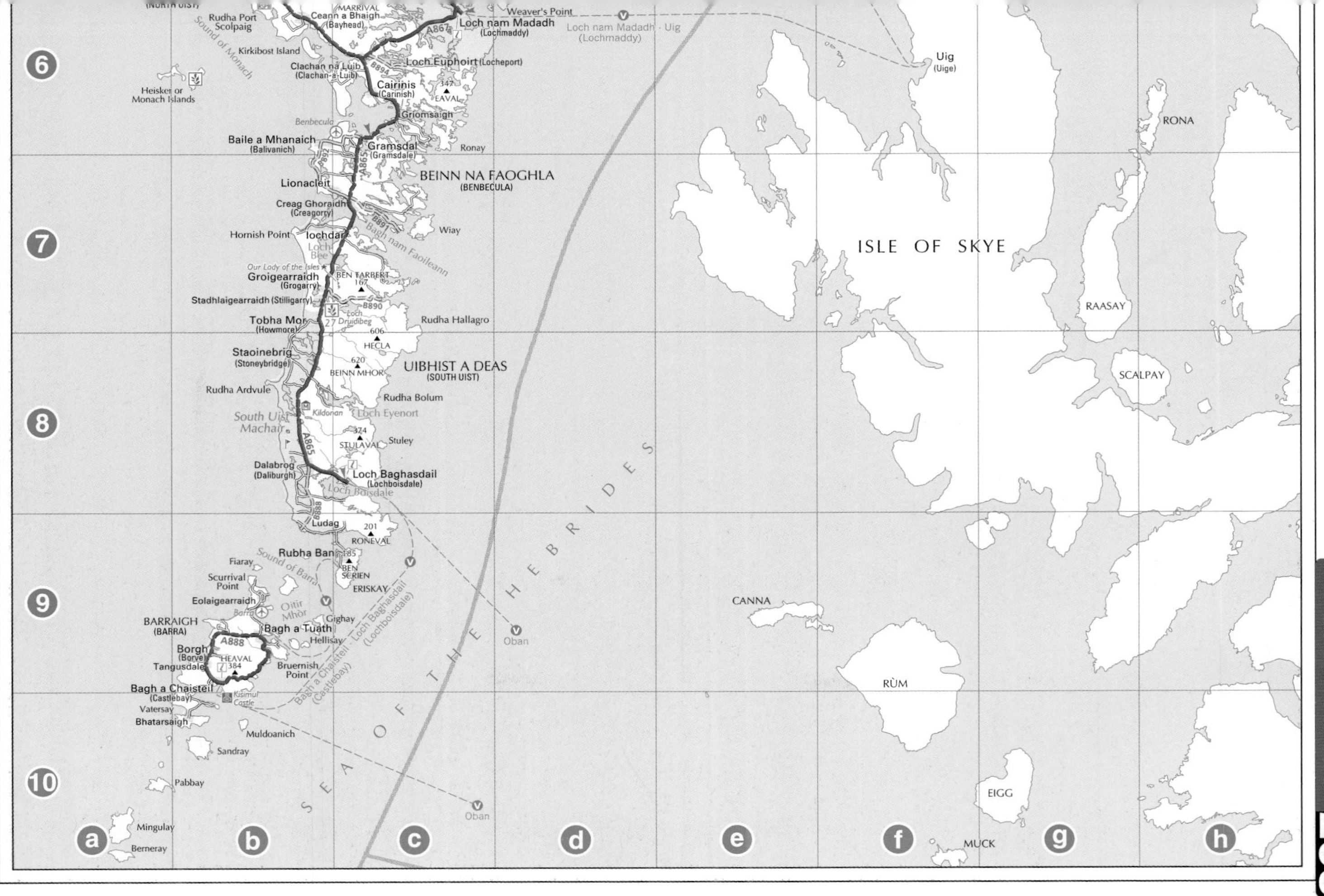
(NORTH UIST)
Rudha Port Scolpaig
Sound of Monach
Kirkibost Island
Heisker or Monach Islands
MARRIVAL
Ceann a Bhaigh
(Bayhead)
Weaver's Point
Loch nam Madadh
(Lochmaddy)
Loch nam Madadh · Uig
(Lochmaddy)
A867
Loch Euphoirt (Locheport)
Clachan na Luib
(Clachan-a-Luib)
B894
Cairinis
(Carinish)
347
EAVAL
Griomsaigh
Benbecula
Baile a Mhanaich
(Balivanich)
Gramsdal
(Gramsdale)
Ronay
B892
A865
Lionacleit
BEINN NA FAOGHLA
(BENBECULA)
Creag Ghoraidh
(Creagorry)
B891
Wiay
Hornish Point
Iochdar
Loch Bee
Bagh nam Faoileann
Our Lady of the Isles
Groigearraidh
(Grogarry)
BEN TARBERT
167
Stadhlaigearraidh (Stilligarry)
B890
Loch Druidibeg
27
Tobha Mor
(Howmore)
Rudha Hallagro
606
HECLA
Staoinebrig
(Stoneybridge)
620
BEINN MHOR
UIBHIST A DEAS
(SOUTH UIST)
Rudha Ardvule
Rudha Bolum
South Uist Machair
Kildonan
Loch Eyenort
374
STULAVAL
Stuley
A865
Dalabrog
(Daliburgh)
Loch Baghasdail
(Lochboisdale)
Loch Boisdale
B888
Ludag
201
RONEVAL
Rubha Ban
185
BEN SCRIEN
ERISKAY
Fiaray
Sound of Barra
Scurrival Point
Eolaigearraidh
Oitir Mhòr
Barra
Gighay
BARRAIGH
(BARRA)
Bagh a Tuath
Hellisay
A888
Borgh
(Borve)
HEAVAL
384
Tangusdale
Bruernish Point
Bagh a Chaisteil · Loch Baghasdail
(Lochboisdale)
(Castlebay)
Bagh a Chaisteil
(Castlebay)
Kisimul Castle
Vatersay
Bhatarsaigh
Muldoanich
Sandray
Pabbay
Mingulay
Berneray
Oban
Oban
SEA OF THE HEBRIDES
Uig
(Uige)
ISLE OF SKYE
RONA
RAASAY
SCALPAY
CANNA
RÙM
EIGG
MUCK
6
7
8
9
10
a
b
c
d
e
f
g
h

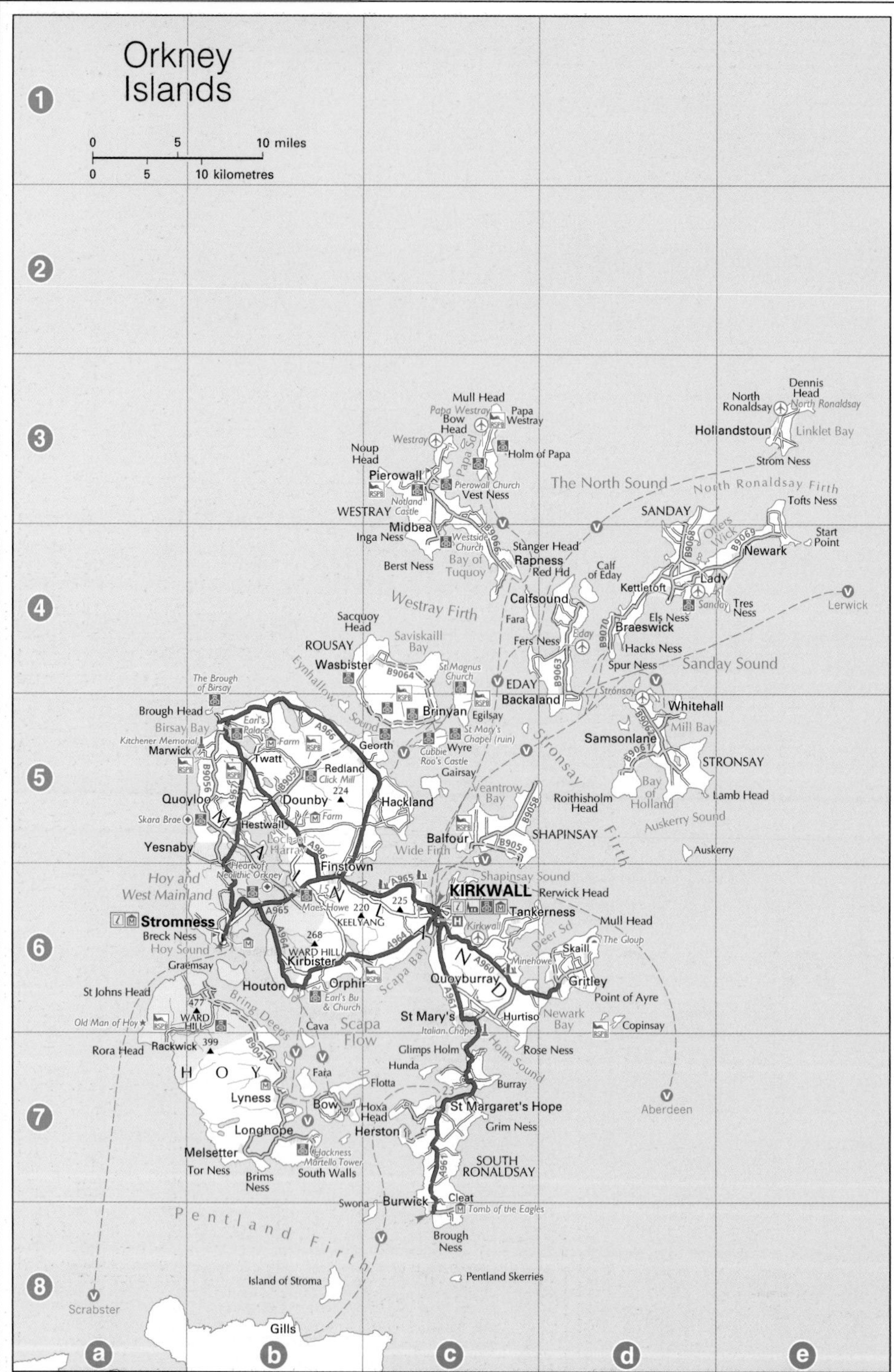
Orkney Islands
0 5 10 miles
0 5 10 kilometres
Mull Head
Papa Westray
Bow Head
Westray
Noup Head
Holm of Papa
Pierowall
Pierowall Church
Notland Castle
Vest Ness
WESTRAY
Midbea
Inga Ness
Westside Church
Bay of Tuquoy
Berst Ness
Stanger Head
Rapness
Red Hd
Calf of Eday
Westray Firth
Calfsound
Fara
Fers Ness
Eday
EDAY
Backaland
Sacquoy Head
ROUSAY
Saviskaill Bay
Wasbister
St Magnus Church
Eynhallow Sound
Brinyan
Egilsay
St Mary's Chapel (ruin)
Wyre
Cubbie Roo's Castle
Gairsay
Georth
The Brough of Birsay
Brough Head
Birsay Bay
Earl's Palace
Kitchener Memorial
Marwick
Farm
Twatt
Redland
Click Mill
224
Quoyloo
Dounby
Hackland
Skara Brae
Hestwall
Farm
Loch of Harray
Yesnaby
Finstown
Heart of Neolithic Orkney
Hoy and West Mainland
Maes Howe
220
225
KIRKWALL
Stromness
KEELYLANG
Breck Ness
268
WARD HILL
Kirbister
Hoy Sound
Graemsay
Houton
Orphir
Earl's Bu & Church
St Johns Head
477
WARD HILL
Old Man of Hoy
Bring Deeps
Cava
Scapa Flow
Scapa Bay
Rora Head
Rackwick
399
HOY
Fara
Lyness
Flotta
Bow
Hoxa Head
Longhope
Herston
Melsetter
Hackness Martello Tower
Tor Ness
Brims Ness
South Walls
MAINLAND
Kirkwall
Quoyburray
St Mary's
Italian Chapel
Glimps Holm
Hunda
Burray
Holm Sound
St Margaret's Hope
Grim Ness
SOUTH RONALDSAY
Swona
Burwick
Cleat
Tomb of the Eagles
Brough Ness
Pentland Skerries
Pentland Firth
Island of Stroma
Gills
Scrabster
Veantrow Bay
Balfour
Wide Firth
SHAPINSAY
Shapinsay Sound
Rerwick Head
Tankerness
Deer Sd
Minehowe
Skaill
Gritley
Point of Ayre
Hurtiso
Newark Bay
Copinsay
Rose Ness
Mull Head
The Gloup
Aberdeen
Stronsay Firth
Roithisholm Head
Bay of Holland
Samsonlane
Mill Bay
Whitehall
STRONSAY
Lamb Head
Auskerry Sound
Auskerry
Stronsay
Spur Ness
Hacks Ness
Sanday Sound
Braeswick
Els Ness
Sanday
Tres Ness
Kettletoft
Lady
Newark
SANDAY
Otters Wick
Start Point
Tofts Ness
The North Sound
North Ronaldsay Firth
Strom Ness
Hollandstoun
Linklet Bay
North Ronaldsay
Dennis Head
Lerwick
A966
A965
A964
A986
A967
A960
A961
B9056
B9057
B9064
B9066
B9068
B9069
B9070
B9063
B9062
B9061
B9058
B9059
B9047
RSPB
a
b
c
d
e
1
2
3
4
5
6
7
8

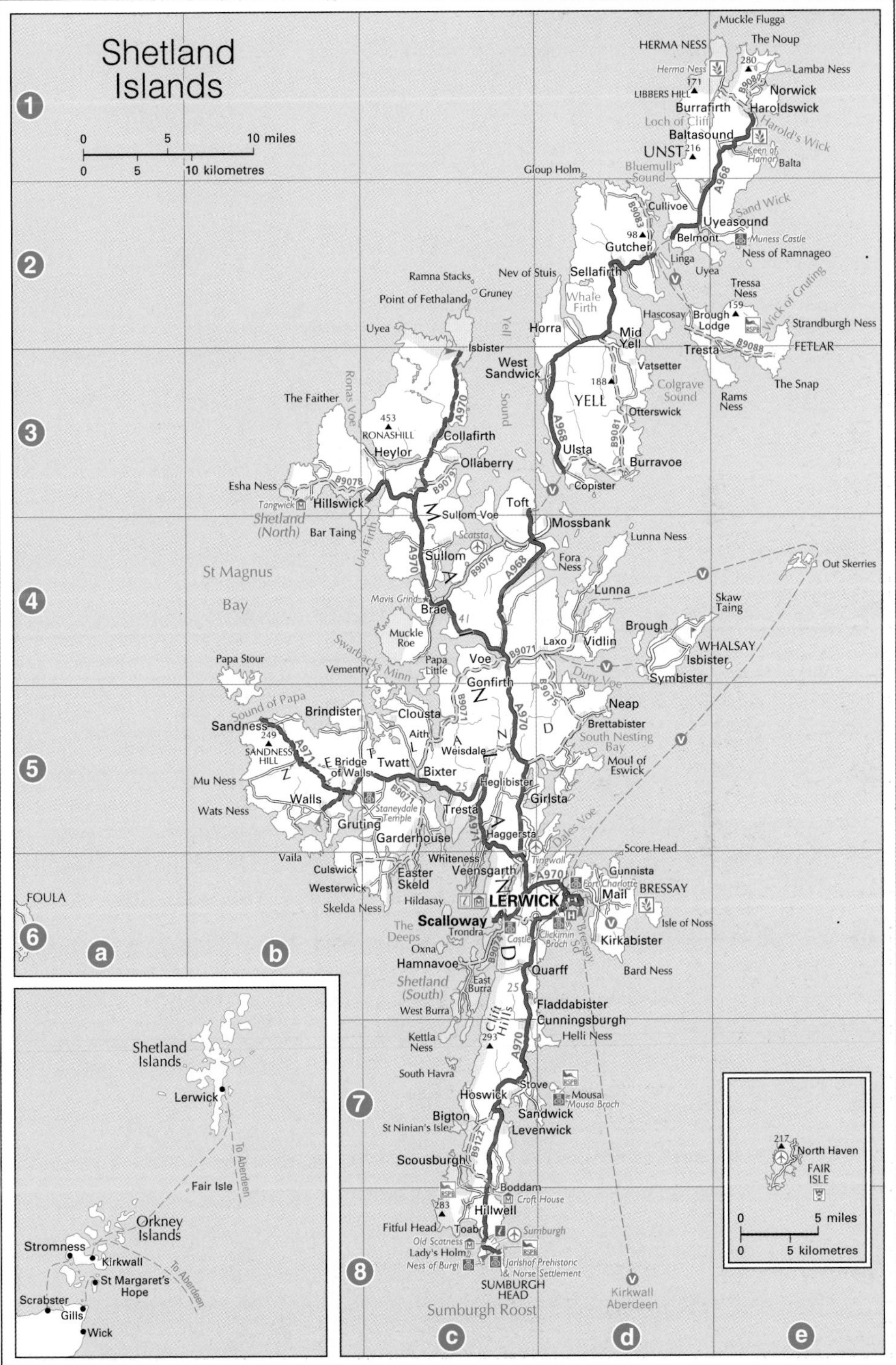
Shetland Islands
0 5 10 miles
0 5 10 kilometres
Muckle Flugga
HERMA NESS
The Noup
Lamba Ness
LIBBERS HILL
Norwick
Burrafirth
Haroldswick
Loch of Cliff
Baltasound
Harold's Wick
UNST
Keen of Hamar
Balta
Gloup Holm
Bluemull Sound
Cullivoe
Sand Wick
Uyeasound
Belmont
Muness Castle
Gutcher
Ness of Ramnageo
Linga
Uyea
Nev of Stuis
Sellafirth
Ramna Stacks
Gruney
Point of Fethaland
Whale Firth
Tressa Ness
Wick of Gruting
Hascosay
Brough Lodge
Strandburgh Ness
Horra
Mid Yell
Uyea
Isbister
Yell Sound
West Sandwick
Tresta
FETLAR
Vatsetter
The Snap
Ronas Voe
Colgrave Sound
The Faither
YELL
Rams Ness
Otterswick
RONAS HILL
Collafirth
Ulsta
Heylor
Ollaberry
Burravoe
Esha Ness
Copister
Hillswick
Tangwick
Toft
Shetland (North)
Sullom Voe
Mossbank
Bar Taing
Lunna Ness
Scatsta
Sullom
Fora Ness
Out Skerries
St Magnus Bay
Ura Firth
Lunna
Mavis Grind
Skaw Taing
Brae
Brough
Muckle Roe
Laxo
Vidlin
WHALSAY
Swarbacks Minn
Isbister
Papa Stour
Vementry
Papa Little
Voe
Symbister
Dury Voe
Gonfirth
Sound of Papa
Neap
Brindister
Clousta
Brettabister
Sandness
Aith
South Nesting Bay
SANDNESS HILL
Weisdale
Moul of Eswick
Bridge of Walls
Twatt
Mu Ness
Bixter
Heglibister
Walls
Wats Ness
Staneydale Temple
Tresta
Girlsta
Gruting
Dales Voe
Garderhouse
Haggersta
Score Head
Vaila
Whiteness
Tingwall
Culswick
Easter Skeld
Veensgarth
Gunnista
Westerwick
Fort Charlotte
BRESSAY
Hildasay
LERWICK
Mail
FOULA
Skelda Ness
Scalloway
Isle of Noss
The Deeps
Trondra
Clickimin Broch
Bressay Sd
Kirkabister
Oxna
Castle
Hamnavoe
Quarff
Bard Ness
Shetland (South)
East Burra
West Burra
Fladdabister
Cunningsburgh
Cliff Hills
Kettla Ness
Helli Ness
South Havra
Stove
Hoswick
Mousa
Mousa Broch
Bigton
Sandwick
St Ninian's Isle
Levenwick
North Haven
FAIR ISLE
Scousburgh
0 5 miles
0 5 kilometres
Boddam
Croft House
Hillwell
Fitful Head
Toab
Sumburgh
Old Scatness
Lady's Holm
Ness of Burgi
Jarlshof Prehistoric & Norse Settlement
SUMBURGH HEAD
Kirkwall Aberdeen
Sumburgh Roost
Shetland Islands
Lerwick
To Aberdeen
Fair Isle
Orkney Islands
Stromness
Kirkwall
St Margaret's Hope
Scrabster
Gills
Wick
To Aberdeen

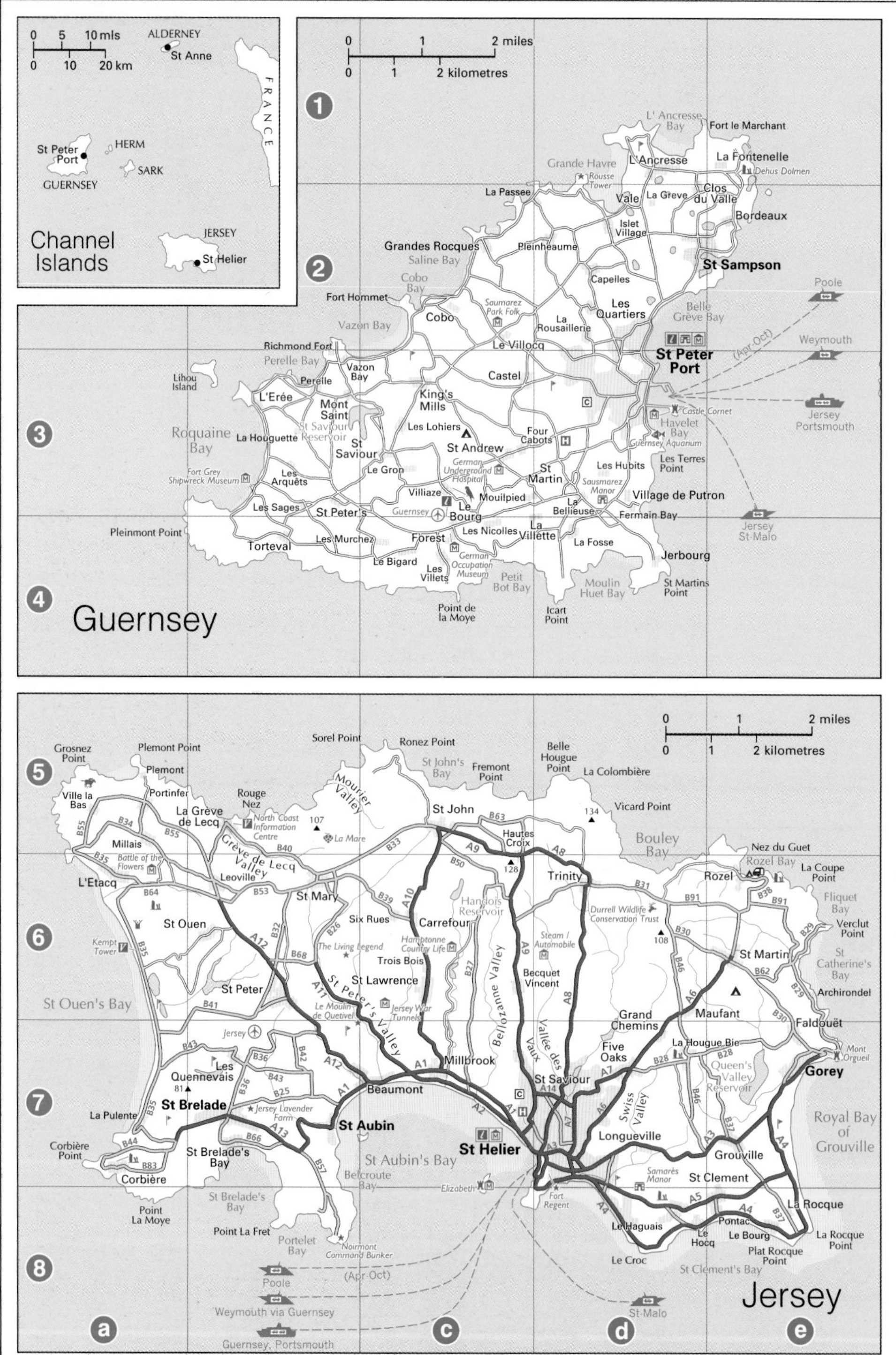
Channel Islands
ALDERNEY
St Anne
FRANCE
St Peter Port
HERM
SARK
GUERNSEY
JERSEY
St Helier
0 5 10 mls
0 10 20 km
Guernsey
0 1 2 miles
0 1 2 kilometres
L' Ancresse Bay
Fort le Marchant
L'Ancresse
La Fontenelle
Dehus Dolmen
Grande Havre
Rousse Tower
La Passee
Vale
La Greve
Clos du Valle
Bordeaux
Islet Village
Grandes Rocques
Saline Bay
Pleinheaume
St Sampson
Cobo Bay
Capelles
Fort Hommet
Saumarez Park Folk
Les Quartiers
Belle Grève Bay
Poole
Vazon Bay
Cobo
La Rousaillerie
Le Villocq
St Peter Port
Weymouth
(Apr-Oct)
Richmond Fort
Perelle Bay
Lihou Island
Perelle
Vazon Bay
Castel
L'Erée
Mont Saint
King's Mills
Castle Cornet
Jersey Portsmouth
Roquaine Bay
St Saviour Reservoir
Havelet Bay
La Houguette
Les Lohiers
Four Cabots
St Saviour
St Andrew
Guernsey Aquarium
Les Terres Point
Fort Grey Shipwreck Museum
Les Arquêts
Le Gron
German Underground Hospital
St Martin
Les Hubits
Sausmarez Manor
Villiaze
Mouilpied
Village de Putron
Les Sages
St Peter's
Guernsey
Le Bourg
La Bellieuse
Fermain Bay
Pleinmont Point
Jersey St-Malo
Les Murchez
Forest
Les Nicolles
La Villette
Torteval
La Fosse
Jerbourg
Le Bigard
German Occupation Museum
Les Villets
Petit Bot Bay
Moulin Huet Bay
St Martins Point
Point de la Moye
Icart Point
Jersey
0 1 2 miles
0 1 2 kilometres
Sorel Point
Ronez Point
Grosnez Point
Plemont Point
Plemont
St John's Bay
Fremont Point
Belle Hougue Point
La Colombière
Mourier Valley
Ville la Bas
Portinfer
Rouge Nez
107
134
Vicard Point
La Grève de Lecq
North Coast Information Centre
St John
La Mare
Hautes Croix
Bouley Bay
Millais
Grève de Lecq Valley
Battle of the Flowers
128
Trinity
Nez du Guet
Rozel Bay
La Coupe Point
L'Etacq
Leoville
St Mary
Handois Reservoir
Rozel
Fliquet Bay
Durrell Wildlife Conservation Trust
Six Rues
Carrefour
Verclut Point
St Ouen
Kempt Tower
Hamptonne Country Life
Steam / Automobile
108
The Living Legend
St Martin
St Catherine's Bay
Trois Bois
Bellozanne Valley
Becquet Vincent
St Lawrence
St Peter's Valley
Archirondel
St Peter
St Ouen's Bay
Maufant
Le Moulin de Quetivel
Jersey War Tunnels
Grand Chemins
Faldouët
Vallée des Vaux
Jersey
Five Oaks
La Hougue Bie
Mont Orgueil
Millbrook
Queen's Valley Reservoir
Les Quennevais
Gorey
81
St Saviour
Beaumont
Swiss Valley
St Brelade
Jersey Lavender Farm
La Pulente
St Aubin
Royal Bay of Grouville
Longueville
St Brelade's Bay
St Helier
Corbière Point
St Aubin's Bay
Grouville
Samarès Manor
Belcroute Bay
St Clement
Corbière
Elizabeth
Fort Regent
St Brelade's Bay
La Rocque
Point La Moye
Le Haguais
Pontac
Point La Fret
Le Hocq
Le Bourg
La Rocque Point
Portelet Bay
Noirmont Command Bunker
Plat Rocque Point
Le Croc
St Clement's Bay
(Apr-Oct)
Poole
Weymouth via Guernsey
St-Malo
Guernsey, Portsmouth
1
2
3
4
5
6
7
8
a
c
d
e

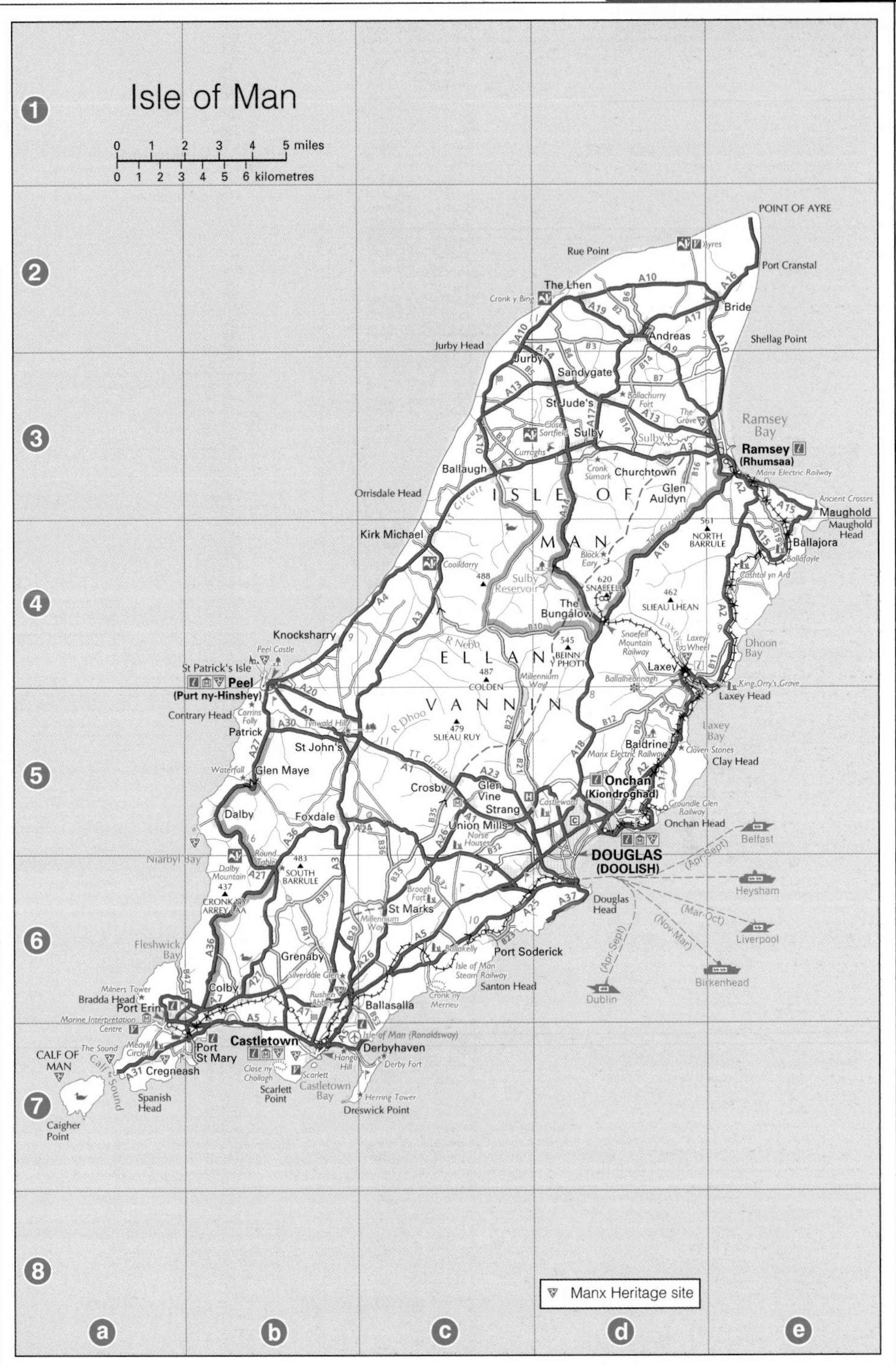
Isle of Man
0 1 2 3 4 5 miles
0 1 2 3 4 5 6 kilometres
POINT OF AYRE
Ayres
Rue Point
Port Cranstal
The Lhen
Cronk y Bing
Bride
Andreas
Shellag Point
Jurby Head
Jurby
Sandygate
Ballachurry Fort
St Jude's
The Grove
Ramsey Bay
Close Sartfield
Sulby
Curraghs
Sulby R.
Ramsey
(Rhumsaa)
Manx Electric Railway
Ballaugh
Cronk Sumark
Churchtown
Glen Auldyn
Orrisdale Head
ISLE OF MAN
Ancient Crosses
Maughold
Maughold Head
561
NORTH BARRULE
Ballajora
Kirk Michael
Ballafayle
Cashtal yn Ard
Black Eary
Cooildarry
488
Sulby Reservoir
620
SNAEFELL
462
SLIEAU LHEAN
The Bungalow
Knocksharry
R. Neb
545
BEINN Y PHOTT
Snaefell Mountain Railway
Laxey Wheel
Dhoon Bay
Peel Castle
St Patrick's Isle
Peel
(Purt ny-Hinshey)
ELLAN VANNIN
487
COLDEN
Millennium Way
Laxey
Ballalheannagh
King Orry's Grave
Laxey Head
Contrary Head
Corrins Folly
Tynwald Hill
R. Dhoo
479
SLIEAU RUY
Laxey Bay
Patrick
Baldrine
St John's
TT Circuit
Cloven Stones
Clay Head
Waterfall
Glen Maye
Manx Electric Railway
Crosby
Glen Vine
Onchan
(Kiondroghad)
Strang
Castleward
Groundle Glen Railway
Dalby
Foxdale
Union Mills
Onchan Head
Norse Houses
Belfast
Niarbyl Bay
Round Table
483
SOUTH BARRULE
DOUGLAS
(DOOLISH)
(Apr-Sept)
Dalby Mountain
437
CRONK NY ARREY LAA
Heysham
Broogh Fort
Douglas Head
St Marks
(Mar-Oct)
Millennium Way
(Nov-Mar)
Liverpool
Fleshwick Bay
Grenaby
Ballakelly
Port Soderick
(Apr-Sept)
Isle of Man Steam Railway
Silverdale Glen
Birkenhead
Santon Head
Milners Tower
Colby
Rushen Abbey
Cronk ny Merrieu
Dublin
Bradda Head
Port Erin
Ballasalla
Marine Interpretation Centre
Isle of Man (Ronaldsway)
Castletown
Derbyhaven
The Sound
Meayll Circle
Port St Mary
Hango Hill
Derby Fort
CALF OF MAN
Calf Sound
Cregneash
Close ny Chollagh
Scarlett
Castletown Bay
Spanish Head
Scarlett Point
Herring Tower
Dreswick Point
Caigher Point
Manx Heritage site
a
b
c
d
e
1
2
3
4
5
6
7
8

Restricted Junctions

Motorway and Primary Route junctions which have access or exit restrictions are shown on the map pages thus:

M1 London - Leeds

Junction	Northbound	Southbound
2	Access only from A1 *(northbound)*	Exit only to A1 *(southbound)*
4	Access only from A41 *(northbound)*	Exit only to A41 *(southbound)*
6A	Access only from M25 (no link from A405)	Exit only to M25 (no link from A405)
7	Access only from A414	Exit only to A414
17	Exit only to M45	Access only from M45
19	Exit only to M6 *(northbound)*	Access only from M6
21A	Exit only, no access	Access only, no exit
23A	Access only from A42	No restriction
24A	Access only, no exit	Exit only, no access
35A	Exit only, no access	Access only, no exit
43	Exit only to M621	Access only from M621
48	Exit only to A1(M) *(northbound)*	Access only from A1(M) *(southbound)*

M2 Rochester - Faversham

Junction	Westbound	Eastbound
1	No exit to A2 *(eastbound)*	No access from A2 *(westbound)*

M3 Sunbury - Southampton

Junction	Northeastbound	Southwestbound
8	Access only from A303, no exit	Exit only to A303, no access
10	Exit only, no access	Access only, no exit
14	Access from M27 only, no exit	No access to M27 *(westbound)*

M4 London - South Wales

Junction	Westbound	Eastbound
1	Access only from A4 *(westbound)*	Exit only to A4 *(eastbound)*
4A	No exit to A4 *(westbound)*	No restriction
21	Exit only to M48	Access only from M48
23	Access only from M48	Exit only to M48
25	Exit only, no access	Access only, no exit
25A	Exit only, no access	Access only, no exit
29	Exit only to A48(M)	Access only from A48(M)
38	Exit only, no access	No restriction
39	Access only, no exit	No access or exit

M5 Birmingham - Exeter

Junction	Northeastbound	Southwestbound
10	Access only, no exit	Exit only, no access
11A	Access only from A417 *(westbound)*	Exit only to A417 *(eastbound)*
18	Exit only, no access	Access only, no exit
18A	Exit only to M49	Access only from M49
29	No restriction	Access only from A30 *(westbound)*

M6 Toll Motorway

Junction	Northwestbound	Southeastbound
T1	Access only, no exit	No access or exit
T2	No access or exit	Exit only, no access
T3	Staggered junction, follow signs - access only from A38 *(northbound)*	Staggered junction, follow signs - access only from A38 *(southbound)*
T5	Access only, no exit	Exit only to A5148 *(northbound)*, no access
T7	Exit only, no access	Access only, no exit
T8	Exit only, no access	Access only, no exit

M6 Rugby - Carlisle

Junction	Northbound	Southbound
3A	Exit only to M6 Toll	Access only from M6 Toll
4A	Access only from M42 *(southbound)*	Exit only to M42
5	Exit only, no access	Access only, no exit
10A	Exit only to M54	Access only from M54
11A	Access only from M6 Toll	Exit only to M6 Toll
with M56 (jct 20A)	No restriction	Access only from M56 *(eastbound)*
20	Access only, no exit	No restriction
24	Access only, no exit	Exit only, no access
25	Exit only, no access	Access only, no exit
29	No direct access, use adjacent slip road to jct 29A	No direct exit, use adjacent slip road from jct 29A
29A	Access only, no exit	Exit only, no access
30	Access only from M61	Exit only to M61
31A	Exit only, no access	Access only, no exit
45	Exit only, no access	Access only, no exit

M8 Edinburgh - Bishopton

Junction	Westbound	Eastbound
8	No access from M73 *(southbound)* or from A8 *(eastbound)* & A89	No exit to M73 *(northbound)* or to A8 *(westbound)* & A89
9	Access only, no exit	Exit only, no access
13	Access only from M80 *(southbound)*	Exit only to M80 *(northbound)*
14	Access only, no exit	Exit only, no access
16	Exit only to A804	Access only from A879
17	Exit only to A82	No restriction
18	Access only from A82 *(eastbound)*	Exit only to A814
19	No access from A814 *(westbound)*	Exit only to A814 *(westbound)*
20	Exit only, no access	Access only, no exit
21	Access only, no exit	Exit only to A8
22	Exit only to M77 *(southbound)*	Access only from M77 *(northbound)*
23	Exit only to B768	Access only from B768
25	No access or exit from or to A8	No access or exit from or to A8
25A	Exit only, no access	Access only, no exit
28	Exit only, no access	Access only, no exit
28A	Exit only to A737	Access only from A737

M9 Edinburgh - Dunblane

Junction	Northwestbound	Southeastbound
1A	Exit only to M9 spur	Access only from M9 spur
2	Access only, no exit	Exit only, no access
3	Exit only, no access	Access only, no exit
6	Access only, no exit	Exit only to A905
8	Exit only to M876 *(southwestbound)*	Access only from M876 *(northeastbound)*

M11 London - Cambridge

Junction	Northbound	Southbound
4	Access only from A406 *(eastbound)*	Exit only to A406
5	Exit only, no access	Access only, no exit
9	Exit only to A11	Access only from A11
13	Exit only, no access	Access only, no exit
14	Exit only, no access	Access only, no exit

M20 Swanley - Folkestone

Junction	Northwestbound	Southeastbound
2	Staggered junction; follow signs - access only	Staggered junction; follow signs - exit only
3	Exit only to M26 *(westbound)*	Access only from M26 *(eastbound)*
5	Access only from A20	For access follow signs - exit only to A20
6	No restriction	For exit follow signs
11A	Access only, no exit	Exit only, no access

M23 Hooley - Crawley

Junction	Northbound	Southbound
7	Exit only to A23 *(northbound)*	Access only from A23 *(southbound)*
10A	Access only, no exit	Exit only, no access

M25 London Orbital Motorway

Junction	Clockwise	Anticlockwise
1B	No direct access, use slip road to Jct 2. Exit only	Access only, no exit
5	No exit to M26 *(eastbound)*	No access from M26
19	Exit only, no access	Access only, no exit
21	Access only from M1 *(southbound)*. Exit only to M1 *(northbound)*	Access only from M1 *(southbound)*. Exit only to M1 *(northbound)*
31	No exit (use slip road via jct 30), access only	No access (use slip road via jct 30), exit only

M26 Sevenoaks - Wrotham

Junction	Westbound	Eastbound
with M25 (jct 5)	Exit only to clockwise M25 *(westbound)*	Access only from anticlockwise M25 *(eastbound)*
with M20 (jct 3)	Access only from M20 *(northwestbound)*	Exit only to M20 *(southeastbound)*

M27 Cadnam - Portsmouth

Junction	Westbound	Eastbound
4	Staggered junction; follow signs - access only from M3 *(southbound)*. Exit only to M3 *(northbound)*	Staggered junction; follow signs - access only from M3 *(southbound)*. Exit only to M3 *(northbound)*
10	Exit only, no access	Access only, no exit
12	Staggered junction; follow signs - exit only to M275 *(southbound)*	Staggered junction; follow signs - access only from M275 *(northbound)*

M40 London - Birmingham

Junction	Northwestbound	Southeastbound
3	Exit only, no access	Access only, no exit
7	Exit only, no access	Access only, no exit
8	Exit only to M40/A40	Access only from M40/A40
13	Exit only, no access	Access only, no exit
14	Access only, no exit	Exit only, no access
16	Access only, no exit	Exit only, no access

M42 Bromsgrove - Measham

Junction	Northeastbound	Southwestbound
1	Access only, no exit	Exit only, no access
7	Exit only to M6 *(northwestbound)*	Access only from M6 *(northwestbound)*
7A	Exit only to M6 *(southeastbound)*	No access or exit
8	Access only from M6 *(southeastbound)*	Exit only to M6 *(northwestbound)*

M45 Coventry - M1

Junction	Westbound	Eastbound
Dunchurch (unnumbered)	Access only from A45	Exit only, no access
with M1 (jct 17)	Access only from M1 *(northbound)*	Exit only to M1 *(southbound)*

M53 Mersey Tunnel - Chester

Junction	Northbound	Southbound
11	Access only from M56 *(westbound)*. Exit only to M56 *(eastbound)*	Access only from M56 *(westbound)*. Exit only to M56 *(eastbound)*

M54 Telford

Junction	Westbound	Eastbound
with M6 (jct 10A)	Access only from M6 *(northbound)*	Exit only to M6 *(southbound)*

M56 North Cheshire

Junction	Westbound	Eastbound
1	Access only from M60 *(westbound)*	Exit only to M60 *(eastbound)* & A34 *(northbound)*
2	Exit only, no access	Access only, no exit
3	Access only, no exit	Exit only, no access
4	Exit only, no access	Access only, no exit
7	Exit only, no access	No restriction
8	Access only, no exit	No access or exit
15	Exit only to M53	Access only from M53

M57 Liverpool Outer Ring Road

Junction	Northwestbound	Southeastbound
3	Access only, no exit	Exit only, no access
5	Access only from A580 *(westbound)*	Exit only, no access

M58 Liverpool - Wigan

Junction	Westbound	Eastbound
1	Exit only, no access	Access only, no exit

M60 Manchester Orbital

Junction	Clockwise	Anticlockwise
2	Access only, no exit	Exit only, no access
3	No access from M56	Access only from A34 *(northbound)*
4	Access only from A34 *(northbound)*. Exit only to M56	Access only from M56 *(eastbound)*. Exit only to A34 *(southbound)*
5	Access and exit only from and to A5103 *(northbound)*	Access and exit only from and to A5103 *(southbound)*
7	No direct access, use slip road to jct 8. Exit only to A56	Access only from A56. No exit - use jct 8
14	Access from A580 *(eastbound)*	Exit only to A580 *(westbound)*
16	Access only, no exit	Exit only, no access
20	Exit only, no access	Access only, no exit
22	No restriction	Exit only, no access
25	Exit only, no access	No restriction
26	No restriction	Exit only, no access
27	Access only, no exit	Exit only, no access

M61 Manchester - Preston

Junction	Northwestbound	Southeastbound
3	No access or exit	Exit only, no access
with M6 (jct 30)	Exit only to M6 *(northbound)*	Access only from M6 *(southbound)*

M62 Liverpool - Kingston upon Hull

Junction	Westbound	Eastbound
23	Access only, no exit	Exit only, no access
32A	No access to A1(M) *(southbound)*	No restriction

M65 Preston - Colne

Junction	Northeastbound	Southwestbound
9	Exit only, no access	Access only, no exit
11	Access only, no exit	Exit only, no access

M66 Bury

Junction	Northbound	Southbound
with A56	Exit only to A56 *(northbound)*	Access only from A56 *(southbound)*
1	Exit only, no access	Access only, no exit

M67 Hyde Bypass

Junction	Westbound	Eastbound
1	Access only, no exit	Exit only, no access
2	Exit only, no access	Access only, no exit
3	Exit only, no access	No restriction

M69 Coventry - Leicester

Junction	Northbound	Southbound
2	Access only, no exit	Exit only, no access

M73 East of Glasgow

Junction	Northbound	Southbound
2	No access from or exit to A89. No access from M8 *(eastbound)*.	No access from or exit to A89. No exit to M8 *(westbound)*

M74 and A74(M) Glasgow - Gretna

Junction	Northbound	Southbound
3	Exit only, no access	Access only, no exit
3A	Access only, no exit	Exit only, no access
7	Access only, no exit	Exit only, no access
9	No access or exit	Exit only, no access
10	No restrictions	Access only, no exit
11	Access only, no exit	Exit only, no access
12	Exit only, no access	Access only, no exit
18	Exit only, no access	Access only, no exit

M77 South of Glasgow

Junction	Northbound	Southbound
with M8 (jct 22)	No exit to M8 *(westbound)*	No access from M8 *(eastbound)*
4	Access only, no exit	Exit only, no access
6	Access only, no exit	Exit only, no access
7	Access only, no exit	No restriction

M80 Glasgow - Stirling

Junction	Northbound	Southbound
4A	Exit only, no access	Access only, no exit
6A	Access only, no exit	Exit only, no access
8	Exit only to M876 *(northeastbound)*	Access only from M876 *(southwestbound)*

M90 Forth Road Bridge - Perth

Junction	Northbound	Southbound
2A	Exit only to A92 *(eastbound)*	Access only from A92 *(westbound)*
7	Access only, no exit	Exit only, no access
8	Exit only, no access	Access only, no exit
10	No access from A912. No exit to A912 *(southbound)*	No access from A912 *(northbound)*. No exit to A912

M180 Doncaster - Grimsby

Junction	Westbound	Eastbound
1	Access only, no exit	Exit only, no access

M606 Bradford Spur

Junction	Northbound	Southbound
2	Exit only, no access	No restriction

M621 Leeds - M1

Junction	Clockwise	Anticlockwise
2A	Access only, no exit	Exit only, no access
4	No exit or access	No restriction
5	Access only, no exit	Exit only, no access
6	Exit only, no access	Access only, no exit
with M1 (jct 43)	Exit only to M1 *(southbound)*	Access only from M1 *(northbound)*

M876 Bonnybridge - Kincardine Bridge

Junction	Northeastbound	Southwestbound
with M80 (jct 5)	Access only from M80 *(northbound)*	Exit only to M80 *(southbound)*
with M9 (jct 8)	Exit only to M9 *(eastbound)*	Access only from M9 *(westbound)*

A1(M) South Mimms - Baldock

Junction	Northbound	Southbound
2	Exit only, no access	Access only, no exit
3	No restriction	Exit only, no access
5	Access only, no exit	No access or exit

A1(M) East of Leeds

Junction	Northbound	Southbound
41	No access to M62 *(eastbound)*	No restriction
43	Access only from M1 *(northbound)*	Exit only to M1 *(southbound)*

A1(M) Scotch Corner - Newcastle upon Tyne

Junction	Northbound	Southbound
57	Exit only to A66(M) *(eastbound)*	Access only from A66(M) *(westbound)*
65	No access Exit only to A194(M) & A1 *(northbound)*	No exit Access only from A194(M) & A1 *(southbound)*

A3(M) Horndean - Havant

Junction	Northbound	Southbound
1	Access only from A3	Exit only to A3
4	Exit only, no access	Access only, no exit

A48(M) Cardiff Spur

Junction	Westbound	Eastbound
29	Access only from M4 *(westbound)*	Exit only to M4 *(eastbound)*
29A	Exit only to A48 *(westbound)*	Access only from A48 *(eastbound)*

A66(M) Darlington Spur

Junction	Westbound	Eastbound
with A1(M) (jct 57)	Exit only to A1(M) *(southbound)*	Access only from A1(M) *(northbound)*

A194(M) Newcastle upon Tyne

Junction	Northbound	Southbound
with A1(M) (jct 65)	Access only from A1(M) *(northbound)*	Exit only to A1(M) *(southbound)*

A12 M25 - Ipswich

Junction	Northeastbound	Southwestbound
13	Access only, no exit	No restriction
14	Exit only, no access	Access only, no exit
20A	Exit only, no access	Access only, no exit
20B	Access only, no exit	Exit only, no access
21	No restriction	Access only, no exit
23	Exit only, no access	Access only, no exit
24	Access only, no exit	Exit only, no access
27	Exit only, no access	Access only, no exit
with A120 (unnumbered)	Exit only, no access	Access only, no exit
29	Access only, no exit	Exit only, no access
Dedham & Stratford St Mary (unnumbered)	Exit only	Access only

A14 M1 - Felixstowe

Junction	Westbound	Eastbound
With M1/M6 (jct19)	Exit only to M6 and M1 *(northbound)*	Access only from M6 and M1 *(southbound)*
4	Exit only, no access	Access only, no exit
31	Access only from A1307	Exit only to A1307
34	Access only, no exit	Exit only, no access
36	Exit only to A11	Access only from A11
38	Access only from A11	Exit only to A11
39	Exit only, no access	Access only, no exit
61	Access only, no exit	Exit only, no access

A55 Holyhead - Chester

Junction	Westbound	Eastbound
8A	Exit only, no access	Access only, no exit
23A	Access only, no exit	Exit only, no access
24A	Exit only, no access	No access or exit
33A	Exit only, no access	No access or exit
33B	Exit only, no access	Access only, no exit
36A	Exit only to A5104	Access only from A5104

Index to place names

This index lists places appearing in the main-map section of the atlas in alphabetical order. The reference before each name gives the atlas page number and grid reference of the square in which the place appears. The map shows counties and administrative areas, together with a list of the abbreviated name forms used in the index. The top 100 places of tourist interest are indexed in **red** (or **green** if a World Heritage site), motorway service areas in **blue** and airports in blue *italic*.

England

BaNES **Bath & N E Somerset (18)**
Barns **Barnsley (19)**
Bed **Bedford**
Birm **Birmingham**
Bl w D **Blackburn with Darwen (20)**
Bmouth **Bournemouth**
Bolton **Bolton (21)**
Bpool **Blackpool**
Br & H **Brighton & Hove (22)**
Br For **Bracknell Forest (23)**
Bristl **City of Bristol**
Bucks **Buckinghamshire**
Bury **Bury (24)**
C Beds **Central Bedfordshire**
C Brad **City of Bradford**
C Derb **City of Derby**
C KuH **City of Kingston upon Hull**
C Leic **City of Leicester**
C Nott **City of Nottingham**
C Pete **City of Peterborough**
C Plym **City of Plymouth**
C Port **City of Portsmouth**
C Sotn **City of Southampton**
C Stke **City of Stoke-on-Trent**
C York **City of York**
Calder **Calderdale (25)**
Cambs **Cambridgeshire**
Ches E **Cheshire East**
Ches W **Cheshire West and Chester**
Cnwll **Cornwall**
Covtry **Coventry**
Cumb **Cumbria**
Darltn **Darlington (26)**
Derbys **Derbyshire**
Devon **Devon**
Donc **Doncaster (27)**
Dorset **Dorset**
Dudley **Dudley (28)**
Dur **Durham**
E R Yk **East Riding of Yorkshire**
E Susx **East Sussex**
Essex **Essex**
Gatesd **Gateshead (29)**
Gloucs **Gloucestershire**
Gt Lon **Greater London**
Halton **Halton (30)**
Hants **Hampshire**
Hartpl **Hartlepool (31)**
Herefs **Herefordshire**
Herts **Hertfordshire**
IoS **Isles of Scilly**
IoW **Isle of Wight**
Kent **Kent**
Kirk **Kirklees (32)**
Knows **Knowsley (33)**
Lancs **Lancashire**
Leeds **Leeds**
Leics **Leicestershire**
Lincs **Lincolnshire**
Lpool **Liverpool**
Luton **Luton**
M Keyn **Milton Keynes**
Manch **Manchester**
Medway **Medway**
Middsb **Middlesbrough**
NE Lin **North East Lincolnshire**
N Linc **North Lincolnshire**
N Som **North Somerset (34)**
N Tyne **North Tyneside (35)**
N u Ty **Newcastle upon Tyne**
N York **North Yorkshire**
Nhants **Northamptonshire**
Norfk **Norfolk**
Notts **Nottinghamshire**
Nthumb **Northumberland**
Oldham **Oldham (36)**
Oxon **Oxfordshire**
Poole **Poole**
R & Cl **Redcar & Cleveland**
Readg **Reading**
Rochdl **Rochdale (37)**
Rothm **Rotherham (38)**
Rutlnd **Rutland**
S Glos **South Gloucestershire (39)**
S on T **Stockton-on-Tees (40)**
S Tyne **South Tyneside (41)**
Salfd **Salford (42)**
Sandw **Sandwell (43)**
Sefton **Sefton (44)**
Sheff **Sheffield**
Shrops **Shropshire**
Slough **Slough (45)**
Solhll **Solihull (46)**
Somset **Somerset**
St Hel **St Helens (47)**
Staffs **Staffordshire**
Sthend **Southend-on-Sea**
Stockp **Stockport (48)**
Suffk **Suffolk**
Sundld **Sunderland**
Surrey **Surrey**
Swindn **Swindon**
Tamesd **Tameside (49)**
Thurr **Thurrock (50)**
Torbay **Torbay**
Traffd **Trafford (51)**
W & M **Windsor and Maidenhead (52)**
W Berk **West Berkshire**
W Susx **West Sussex**
Wakefd **Wakefield (53)**
Warrtn **Warrington (54)**
Warwks **Warwickshire**
Wigan **Wigan (55)**
Wilts **Wiltshire**
Wirral **Wirral (56)**
Wokham **Wokingham (57)**
Wolves **Wolverhampton (58)**
Worcs **Worcestershire**
Wrekin **Telford & Wrekin (59)**
Wsall **Walsall (60)**

Scotland

Abers **Aberdeenshire**
Ag & B **Argyll and Bute**
Angus **Angus**
Border **Scottish Borders**
C Aber **City of Aberdeen**
C Dund **City of Dundee**
C Edin **City of Edinburgh**
C Glas **City of Glasgow**
Clacks **Clackmannanshire (1)**
D & G **Dumfries & Galloway**
E Ayrs **East Ayrshire**
E Duns **East Dunbartonshire (2)**
E Loth **East Lothian**
E Rens **East Renfrewshire (3)**
Falk **Falkirk**
Fife **Fife**
Highld **Highland**
Inver **Inverclyde (4)**
Mdloth **Midlothian (5)**
Moray **Moray**
N Ayrs **North Ayrshire**
N Lans **North Lanarkshire (6)**
Ork **Orkney Islands**
P & K **Perth & Kinross**
Rens **Renfrewshire (7)**
S Ayrs **South Ayrshire**
Shet **Shetland Islands**
S Lans **South Lanarkshire**
Stirlg **Stirling**
W Duns **West Dunbartonshire (8)**
W Isls **Western Isles (Na h-Eileanan an Iar)**
W Loth **West Lothian**

Wales

Blae G **Blaenau Gwent (9)**
Brdgnd **Bridgend (10)**
Caerph **Caerphilly (11)**
Cardif **Cardiff**
Carmth **Carmarthenshire**
Cerdgn **Ceredigion**
Conwy **Conwy**
Denbgs **Denbighshire**
Flints **Flintshire**
Gwynd **Gwynedd**
IoA **Isle of Anglesey**
Mons **Monmouthshire**
Myr Td **Merthyr Tydfil (12)**
Neath **Neath Port Talbot (13)**
Newpt **Newport (14)**
Pembks **Pembrokeshire**
Powys **Powys**
Rhondd **Rhondda Cynon Taff (15)**
Swans **Swansea**
Torfn **Torfaen (16)**
V Glam **Vale of Glamorgan (17)**
Wrexhm **Wrexham**

Channel Islands & Isle of Man

Guern **Guernsey**
Jersey **Jersey**
IoM **Isle of Man**

ORKNEY ISLANDS
SHETLAND ISLANDS
WESTERN ISLES (Na h-Eileanan an Iar)
HIGHLAND
MORAY
SCOTLAND
ABERDEENSHIRE
Aberdeen
ANGUS
PERTH & KINROSS
Dundee
ARGYLL & BUTE
STIRLING
FIFE
1
8
2
FALK
Edinburgh
4
Glasgow
W LOTH
E LOTH
7
6
3
5
NORTH AYRSHIRE
S LANS
SCOTTISH BORDERS
E AYRS
S AYRS
DUMFRIES & GALLOWAY
NORTHUMBERLAND
Newcastle upon Tyne
35
29
41
Sunderland
DURHAM
31
CUMBRIA
26
40
R & CL
Middlesbrough
IoM
NORTH YORKSHIRE
York
EAST RIDING OF YORKSHIRE
Bradford
Blackpool
LANCASHIRE
Leeds
Kingston upon Hull
25
20
53
32
N LINCS
N E LINCS
21
24
37
36
19
27
55
44
47
42
49
Manchester
38
Liverpool
33
54
51
48
Sheffield
56
30
IoA
CONWY
FLINTS
CHES W
CHES E
DERBYS
NOTTS
LINCOLNSHIRE
DENBGS
Stoke-on-Trent
WREXHAM
Nottingham
Derby
GWYNEDD
STAFFS
NORFOLK
59
LEICS
RUTLAND
Leicester
Peterborough
SHROPSHIRE
58
60
28
43
Birmingham
Coventry
46
NHANTS
CAMBS
POWYS
CERDGN
WORCS
WARWKS
Milton Keynes
BED
SUFFOLK
HEREFS
WALES
ENGLAND
PEMBKS
CARMTH
BEDS
Luton
HERTS
ESSEX
12
9
MONS
GLOUCS
OXON
13
15
11
16
Swansea
10
14
Cardiff
BUCKS
Southend-on-Sea
Bristol
39
Swindon
Reading
52
45
GREATER LONDON
50
17
34
18
W BERKS
57
23
MEDWAY
WILTSHIRE
SURREY
KENT
SOMERSET
HAMPSHIRE
W SUSX
E SUSX
22
DEVON
DORSET
Southampton
Portsmouth
Bournemouth
Poole
IoW
Guernsey
CHANNEL ISLANDS
Jersey
CORNWALL
Torbay
Plymouth
IoS

A

27 G6 **Abbas Combe** Somset
70 D2 **Abberley** Worcs
70 D2 **Abberley Common** Worcs
62 B4 **Abberton** Essex
71 H4 **Abberton** Worcs
60 F5 **Abbess Roding** Essex
114 F5 **Abbeydale** Sheff
54 B3 **Abbey Dore** Herefs
99 L2 **Abbey Green** Staffs
178 F6 **Abbey St Bathans** Border
130 B8 **Abbeystead** Lancs
147 L5 **Abbey Town** Cumb
121 J6 **Abbey Village** Lancs
45 J4 **Abbey Wood** Gt Lon
167 J6 **Abbotrule** Border
9 K3 **Abbots Bickington** Devon
100 B7 **Abbots Bromley** Staffs
14 B5 **Abbotsbury** Dorset
186 B5 **Abbots Deuglie** P & K
22 F6 **Abbotsham** Devon
7 K3 **Abbotskerswell** Devon
59 H7 **Abbots Langley** Herts
38 D5 **Abbots Leigh** N Som
75 J3 **Abbotsley** Cambs
71 H4 **Abbots Morton** Worcs
89 J7 **Abbots Ripton** Cambs
71 J4 **Abbot's Salford** Warwks
29 J5 **Abbots Worthy** Hants
29 G3 **Abbotts Ann** Hants
15 J3 **Abbott Street** Dorset
83 L6 **Abdon** Shrops
66 B3 **Aberaeron** Cerdgn
52 F7 **Aberaman** Rhondd
81 J2 **Aberangell** Gwynd
202 F1 **Aberarder** Highld
186 B4 **Aberargie** P & K
66 B2 **Aberarth** Cerdgn
51 L7 **Aberavon** Neath
53 G7 **Abercanaid** Myr Td
37 K2 **Abercarn** Caerph
64 B7 **Abercastle** Pembks
81 H3 **Abercegir** Powys
202 B5 **Aberchalder Lodge** Highld
216 C4 **Aberchirder** Abers
52 C5 **Abercraf** Powys
36 D2 **Abercregan** Neath
52 F7 **Abercwmboi** Rhondd
65 H6 **Abercych** Pembks
37 G2 **Abercynon** Rhondd
185 M4 **Aberdalgie** P & K
52 F7 **Aberdare** Rhondd
94 C7 **Aberdaron** Gwynd
207 H4 **Aberdeen** C Aber
207 G3 *Aberdeen Airport* C Aber
207 G4 **Aberdeen Crematorium** C Aber
177 G2 **Aberdour** Fife
52 B7 **Aberdulais** Neath
80 E4 **Aberdyfi** Gwynd
68 C5 **Aberedw** Powys
48 D2 **Abereiddy** Pembks
95 G5 **Abererch** Gwynd
53 G7 **Aberfan** Myr Td
194 D6 **Aberfeldy** P & K
108 D7 **Aberffraw** IoA
124 C3 **Aberford** Leeds
184 C7 **Aberfoyle** Stirlg
53 L5 **Abergavenny** Mons
110 C6 **Abergele** Conwy
66 D7 **Abergorlech** Carmth
67 J4 **Abergwesyn** Powys
50 F2 **Abergwili** Carmth
36 D2 **Abergwynfi** Neath
109 J6 **Abergwyngregyn** Gwynd
80 F3 **Abergynolwyn** Gwynd
36 D4 **Aberkenfig** Brdgnd
178 B3 **Aberlady** E Loth
196 E5 **Aberlemno** Angus
81 G2 **Aberllefenni** Gwynd
68 D6 **Aberllynfi** Powys
215 G5 **Aberlour** Moray
82 D5 **Abermule** Powys
50 D2 **Abernant** Carmth
52 F7 **Aber-nant** Rhondd
186 C4 **Abernethy** P & K
186 D2 **Abernyte** P & K
65 J4 **Aberporth** Cerdgn
94 E6 **Abersoch** Gwynd
53 K7 **Abersychan** Torfn
36 F5 **Aberthin** V Glam
53 K7 **Abertillery** Blae G
37 H3 **Abertridwr** Caerph
97 G8 **Abertridwr** Powys
185 K4 **Aberuthven** P & K
80 D6 **Aberystwyth** Cerdgn
80 E6 **Aberystwyth Crematorium** Cerdgn
41 J2 **Abingdon-on-Thames** Oxon
31 J3 **Abinger Common** Surrey
31 H2 **Abinger Hammer** Surrey
73 L3 **Abington** Nhants
165 H5 **Abington** S Lans
75 K5 **Abington Pigotts** Cambs
165 H4 **Abington Services** S Lans
18 F3 **Abingworth** W Susx
102 B7 **Ab Kettleby** Leics
56 C6 **Ablington** Gloucs
114 D5 **Abney** Derbys
205 L5 **Aboyne** Abers
112 E2 **Abram** Wigan
212 E7 **Abriachan** Highld
45 J2 **Abridge** Essex
175 K3 **Abronhill** N Lans
39 G5 **Abson** S Glos
73 J5 **Abthorpe** Nhants
118 F5 **Aby** Lincs
124 E2 **Acaster Malbis** C York
124 E3 **Acaster Selby** N York
121 L5 **Accrington** Lancs
121 L5 **Accrington Crematorium** Lancs
188 F5 **Acha** Ag & B
172 D3 **Achahoish** Ag & B
195 H7 **Achalader** P & K
182 D1 **Achaleven** Ag & B
232 f3 **Acha Mor** W Isls
211 K3 **Achanalt** Highld
222 E6 **Achandunie** Highld
222 D2 **Achany** Highld
190 D3 **Acharacle** Highld
190 E6 **Acharn** Highld
194 B7 **Acharn** P & K
231 H6 **Achavanich** Highld
224 C7 **Achduart** Highld
228 D7 **Achfary** Highld
198 D4 **A'Chill** Highld
224 C6 **Achiltibuie** Highld
229 L4 **Achina** Highld
161 J6 **Achinhoan** Ag & B
210 E6 **Achintee** Highld
210 C6 **Achintraid** Highld
224 C4 **Achmelvich** Highld
210 D7 **Achmore** Highld
232 f3 **Achmore** W Isls
224 C3 **Achnacarnin** Highld
201 J7 **Achnacarry** Highld
199 J4 **Achnacloich** Highld
202 C2 **Achnaconeran** Highld
191 G7 **Achnacroish** Ag & B
189 L6 **Achnadrish House** Ag & B
185 J1 **Achnafauld** P & K
222 F7 **Achnagarron** Highld
189 L3 **Achnaha** Highld
224 B5 **Achnahaird** Highld
225 L6 **Achnairn** Highld
191 G4 **Achnalea** Highld
172 D2 **Achnamara** Ag & B
211 J3 **Achnasheen** Highld
210 F5 **Achnashellach Lodge** Highld
215 G7 **Achnastank** Moray
189 K3 **Achosnich** Highld
190 E6 **Achranich** Highld
230 E3 **Achreamie** Highld
192 B3 **Achriabhach** Highld
228 C5 **Achriesgill** Highld
229 K3 **Achtoty** Highld
88 E6 **Achurch** Nhants
222 F3 **Achvaich** Highld
230 E3 **Achvarasdal** Highld
231 L5 **Ackergill** Highld
141 L4 **Acklam** Middsb
134 B7 **Acklam** N York
84 D4 **Ackleton** Shrops
159 G2 **Acklington** Nthumb
124 C6 **Ackton** Wakefd
124 C7 **Ackworth Moor Top** Wakefd
93 J2 **Acle** Norfk
85 K6 **Acock's Green** Birm
35 J2 **Acol** Kent
124 E1 **Acomb** C York
150 B2 **Acomb** Nthumb
54 D2 **Aconbury** Herefs
98 F2 **Acton** Ches E
44 D4 **Acton** Gt Lon
99 J4 **Acton** Staffs
77 K5 **Acton** Suffk
70 C4 **Acton Beauchamp** Herefs
112 E6 **Acton Bridge** Ches W
83 K3 **Acton Burnell** Shrops
70 C4 **Acton Green** Herefs
97 M3 **Acton Park** Wrexhm
84 B4 **Acton Round** Shrops
83 J5 **Acton Scott** Shrops
99 L8 **Acton Trussell** Staffs
39 J4 **Acton Turville** S Glos
99 H6 **Adbaston** Staffs
26 E7 **Adber** Dorset
101 L5 **Adbolton** Notts
72 F7 **Adderbury** Oxon
98 F4 **Adderley** Shrops
176 D5 **Addiewell** W Loth
123 G1 **Addingham** C Brad
58 C3 **Addington** Bucks
45 G7 **Addington** Gt Lon
33 H2 **Addington** Kent
45 G6 **Addiscombe** Gt Lon
43 H7 **Addlestone** Surrey
119 H7 **Addlethorpe** Lincs
59 H6 **Adeyfield** Herts
82 B4 **Adfa** Powys
69 H1 **Adforton** Herefs
35 G4 **Adisham** Kent
56 E3 **Adlestrop** Gloucs
125 K6 **Adlingfleet** E R Yk
121 J7 **Adlington** Lancs
100 B7 **Admaston** Staffs
84 B2 **Admaston** Wrekin
65 J6 **Adpar** Cerdgn
25 L5 **Adsborough** Somset
25 J4 **Adscombe** Somset
58 C3 **Adstock** Bucks
73 H4 **Adstone** Nhants
31 H6 **Adversane** W Susx
214 D7 **Advie** Highld
124 E8 **Adwick Le Street** Donc
115 J2 **Adwick upon Dearne** Donc
155 H4 **Ae** D & G
155 H5 **Ae Bridgend** D & G
36 D2 **Afan Forest Park** Neath
216 B6 **Affleck** Abers
14 F4 **Affpuddle** Dorset
201 J2 **Affric Lodge** Highld
110 F6 **Afon-wen** Flints
16 D5 **Afton** IoW
113 J2 **Agecroft Crematorium** Salfd
131 K3 **Agglethorpe** N York
111 L4 **Aigburth** Lpool
126 C2 **Aike** E R Yk
148 E5 **Aiketgate** Cumb
148 B4 **Aikton** Cumb
89 G4 **Ailsworth** C Pete
132 E4 **Ainderby Quernhow** N York
132 E2 **Ainderby Steeple** N York
62 D4 **Aingers Green** Essex
120 D7 **Ainsdale** Sefton
148 F5 **Ainstable** Cumb
121 L8 **Ainsworth** Bury
142 E5 **Ainthorpe** N York
176 F5 **Ainville** W Loth
181 M7 **Aird** Ag & B
144 D3 **Aird** D & G
232 g2 **Aird** W Isls
232 e3 **Aird a Mhulaidh** W Isls
232 e4 **Aird Asaig** W Isls
209 L6 **Aird Dhubh** Highld
182 E2 **Airdeny** Ag & B
181 H2 **Aird of Kinloch** Ag & B
199 J5 **Aird of Sleat** Highld
175 K5 **Airdrie** N Lans
175 K5 **Airdriehill** N Lans
154 B7 **Airds of Kells** D & G
232 d2 **Aird Uig** W Isls
232 e3 **Airidh a bhruaich** W Isls
146 D4 **Airieland** D & G
195 L6 **Airlie** Angus
125 H5 **Airmyn** E R Yk
186 A1 **Airntully** P & K
199 L4 **Airor** Highld
176 B2 **Airth** Falk
131 G7 **Airton** N York
103 G5 **Aisby** Lincs
116 E3 **Aisby** Lincs
7 G4 **Aish** Devon
7 J4 **Aish** Devon
25 J4 **Aisholt** Somset
132 D2 **Aiskew** N York
134 B3 **Aislaby** N York
143 H5 **Aislaby** N York
141 J5 **Aislaby** S on T
116 F5 **Aisthorpe** Lincs
235 c5 **Aith** Shet
168 E4 **Akeld** Nthumb
73 K6 **Akeley** Bucks
6 B2 **Albaston** Cnwll
83 G1 **Alberbury** Shrops
19 H3 **Albourne** W Susx
84 E3 **Albrighton** Shrops
98 C8 **Albrighton** Shrops
92 F6 **Alburgh** Norfk
60 C3 **Albury** Herts
31 H2 **Albury** Surrey
31 H3 **Albury Heath** Surrey
212 E3 **Alcaig** Highld
83 J6 **Alcaston** Shrops
71 K3 **Alcester** Warwks
20 B5 **Alciston** E Susx
24 F3 **Alcombe** Somset
89 H7 **Alconbury** Cambs
89 H7 **Alconbury Weston** Cambs
132 F6 **Aldborough** N York
106 E5 **Aldborough** Norfk
40 E5 **Aldbourne** Wilts
127 G3 **Aldbrough** E R Yk
140 F5 **Aldbrough St John** N York
58 F5 **Aldbury** Herts
129 K7 **Aldcliffe** Lancs
194 E4 **Aldclune** P & K
79 K3 **Aldeburgh** Suffk
93 J5 **Aldeby** Norfk
43 J2 **Aldenham** Herts

28 D6 **Alderbury** Wilts
106 D8 **Alderford** Norfk
28 C8 **Alderholt** Dorset
39 H3 **Alderley** Gloucs
113 J5 **Alderley Edge** Ches E
86 D6 **Aldermans Green** Covtry
41 L7 **Aldermaston** W Berk
72 B5 **Alderminster** Warwks
30 E2 **Aldershot** Hants
55 M2 **Alderton** Gloucs
73 K5 **Alderton** Nhants
79 H6 **Alderton** Suffk
39 J4 **Alderton** Wilts
132 D5 **Aldfield** N York
98 B2 **Aldford** Ches W
88 E3 **Aldgate** Rutlnd
61 L3 **Aldham** Essex
78 C5 **Aldham** Suffk
18 C5 **Aldingbourne** W Susx
129 G5 **Aldingham** Cumb
34 E7 **Aldington** Kent
71 J5 **Aldington** Worcs
34 E7 **Aldington Corner** Kent
205 H1 **Aldivalloch** Moray
174 C1 **Aldochlay** Ag & B
90 C8 **Aldreth** Cambs
85 J4 **Aldridge** Wsall
79 J3 **Aldringham** Suffk
56 D6 **Aldsworth** Gloucs
215 H8 **Aldunie** Moray
100 E2 **Aldwark** Derbys
133 G6 **Aldwark** N York
18 C6 **Aldwick** W Susx
88 E6 **Aldwincle** Nhants
41 K4 **Aldworth** W Berk
174 D3 **Alexandria** W Duns
25 J4 **Aley** Somset
12 E3 **Alfington** Devon
31 H5 **Alfold** Surrey
31 H4 **Alfold Crossways** Surrey
206 B3 **Alford** Abers
118 F6 **Alford** Lincs
26 E5 **Alford** Somset
118 F6 **Alford Crematorium** Lincs
101 H2 **Alfreton** Derbys
70 D4 **Alfrick** Worcs
70 D4 **Alfrick Pound** Worcs
20 B5 **Alfriston** E Susx
103 M5 **Algarkirk** Lincs
26 F4 **Alhampton** Somset
125 K6 **Alkborough** N Linc
35 H6 **Alkham** Kent
100 D5 **Alkmonton** Derbys
7 J5 **Allaleigh** Devon
204 D6 **Allanaquoich** Abers
175 L6 **Allanbank** N Lans
179 H7 **Allanton** Border
175 L6 **Allanton** N Lans
175 K7 **Allanton** S Lans
54 F6 **Allaston** Gloucs
29 J7 **Allbrook** Hants
40 B7 **All Cannings** Wilts
149 L4 **Allendale** Nthumb
85 L4 **Allen End** Warwks
149 L6 **Allenheads** Nthumb
60 D5 **Allen's Green** Herts
69 J7 **Allensmore** Herefs
101 G6 **Allenton** C Derb
24 B6 **Aller** Devon
26 B5 **Aller** Somset
147 J6 **Allerby** Cumb
12 D4 **Allercombe** Devon
24 D3 **Allerford** Somset
134 D3 **Allerston** N York
125 J2 **Allerthorpe** E R Yk
123 G4 **Allerton** C Brad
213 H2 **Allerton** Highld
111 L4 **Allerton** Lpool
124 C5 **Allerton Bywater** Leeds
132 F7 **Allerton Mauleverer** N York
86 C7 **Allesley** Covtry
101 G5 **Allestree** C Derb
88 B4 **Allexton** Leics
113 L7 **Allgreave** Ches E
46 D4 **Allhallows** Medway
210 C3 **Alligin Shuas** Highld
13 L4 **Allington** Dorset
102 E4 **Allington** Lincs
28 D4 **Allington** Wilts
39 K5 **Allington** Wilts
40 B7 **Allington** Wilts
129 J4 **Allithwaite** Cumb
185 J8 **Alloa** Clacks
147 J6 **Allonby** Cumb
163 J5 **Alloway** S Ayrs
26 B8 **Allowenshay** Somset
83 J4 **All Stretton** Shrops
192 C6 **Alltchaorunn** Highld
66 B7 **Alltwalis** Carmth
51 K5 **Alltwen** Neath
66 C5 **Alltyblaca** Cerdgn
26 F8 **Allweston** Dorset
69 G4 **Almeley** Herefs
99 G5 **Almington** Staffs
185 M3 **Almondbank** P & K
123 H7 **Almondbury** Kirk
38 E4 **Almondsbury** S Glos
133 G6 **Alne** N York
222 E7 **Alness** Highld
168 E7 **Alnham** Nthumb
169 J7 **Alnmouth** Nthumb
169 J6 **Alnwick** Nthumb
44 D4 **Alperton** Gt Lon
77 K7 **Alphamstone** Essex
77 K4 **Alpheton** Suffk
11 L6 **Alphington** Devon
114 E8 **Alport** Derbys
98 E1 **Alpraham** Ches E
62 C4 **Alresford** Essex
85 L1 **Alrewas** Staffs
99 H2 **Alsager** Ches E
100 D2 **Alsop en le Dale** Derbys
149 J5 **Alston** Cumb
13 H2 **Alston** Devon
55 M2 **Alstone** Gloucs
100 C2 **Alstonefield** Staffs
26 B2 **Alston Sutton** Somset
23 L6 **Alswear** Devon
224 B6 **Altandhu** Highld
9 G8 **Altarnun** Cnwll
222 C2 **Altass** Highld
190 D8 **Altcreich** Ag & B
173 H4 **Altgaltraig** Ag & B
61 L7 **Althorne** Essex
125 K8 **Althorpe** N Linc
230 E6 **Altnabreac Station** Highld
225 M2 **Altnaharra** Highld
115 G8 **Alton** Derbys
30 B4 **Alton** Hants
100 B4 **Alton** Staffs
40 C7 **Alton Barnes** Wilts
14 D3 **Alton Pancras** Dorset
40 C7 **Alton Priors** Wilts
100 B4 **Alton Towers** Staffs
113 H4 **Altrincham** Traffd
113 G4 **Altrincham Crematorium** Traffd
184 B6 **Altskeith Hotel** Stirlg
185 J7 **Alva** Clacks
112 D6 **Alvanley** Ches W
101 H5 **Alvaston** C Derb
85 J8 **Alvechurch** Worcs
86 B3 **Alvecote** Warwks
27 L6 **Alvediston** Wilts
84 D6 **Alveley** Shrops
23 H6 **Alverdiscott** Devon
17 H3 **Alverstoke** Hants
17 H5 **Alverstone** IoW
123 L6 **Alverthorpe** Wakefd
102 C4 **Alverton** Notts
214 E3 **Alves** Moray
56 F6 **Alvescot** Oxon
38 F3 **Alveston** S Glos
72 B3 **Alveston** Warwks
118 E4 **Alvingham** Lincs
54 E7 **Alvington** Gloucs
89 G4 **Alwalton** C Pete
168 D7 **Alwinton** Nthumb
123 K3 **Alwoodley** Leeds
195 K6 **Alyth** P & K
101 G3 **Ambergate** Derbys
55 J7 **Amberley** Gloucs
18 D3 **Amberley** W Susx
159 G2 **Amble** Nthumb
84 F6 **Amblecote** Dudley
123 G5 **Ambler Thorn** C Brad
137 K6 **Ambleside** Cumb
49 G3 **Ambleston** Pembks
57 L4 **Ambrosden** Oxon
125 K7 **Amcotts** N Linc
42 F2 **Amersham** Bucks
42 F2 **Amersham Common** Bucks
42 F2 **Amersham Old Town** Bucks
58 F7 **Amersham on the Hill** Bucks
28 D3 **Amesbury** Wilts
232 d4 **Amhuinnsuidhe** W Isls
86 B3 **Amington** Staffs
155 H5 **Amisfield Town** D & G
108 F3 **Amlwch** IoA
51 J3 **Ammanford** Carmth
134 B5 **Amotherby** N York
29 H6 **Ampfield** Hants
133 J4 **Ampleforth** N York
56 B7 **Ampney Crucis** Gloucs
56 C7 **Ampney St Mary** Gloucs
56 B7 **Ampney St Peter** Gloucs
28 F3 **Amport** Hants
74 F6 **Ampthill** C Beds
77 J1 **Ampton** Suffk
49 K6 **Amroth** Pembks
185 J1 **Amulree** P & K
59 K5 **Amwell** Herts
191 G4 **Anaheilt** Highld
103 G4 **Ancaster** Lincs
168 E1 **Ancroft** Nthumb
167 K4 **Ancrum** Border
119 G6 **Anderby** Lincs
29 G3 **Andover** Hants
56 A4 **Andoversford** Gloucs
237 d2 **Andreas** IoM
45 G6 **Anerley** Gt Lon
111 K3 **Anfield** Lpool
111 K3 **Anfield Crematorium** Lpool
3 G4 **Angarrack** Cnwll
83 L7 **Angelbank** Shrops
48 E6 **Angle** Pembks
108 E5 **Anglesey** IoA
18 E5 **Angmering** W Susx
124 D2 **Angram** N York
223 H6 **Ankerville** Highld
126 C5 **Anlaby** E R Yk
105 H6 **Anmer** Norfk
17 J1 **Anmore** Hants
147 L2 **Annan** D & G
155 J4 **Annandale Water Services** D & G
210 D4 **Annat** Highld
175 J4 **Annathill** N Lans
29 G3 **Anna Valley** Hants
163 K5 **Annbank** S Ayrs
71 L4 **Anne Hathaway's Cottage** Warwks
101 J2 **Annesley** Notts
101 J2 **Annesley Woodhouse** Notts
150 F5 **Annfield Plain** Dur
174 F5 **Anniesland** C Glas
120 D5 **Ansdell** Lancs
26 F5 **Ansford** Somset
86 C5 **Ansley** Warwks
100 E7 **Anslow** Staffs
100 D7 **Anslow Gate** Staffs
60 C2 **Anstey** Herts
87 G2 **Anstey** Leics
187 J6 **Anstruther** Fife
19 J2 **Ansty** W Susx
86 E6 **Ansty** Warwks
27 L6 **Ansty** Wilts
147 L4 **Anthorn** Cumb
106 F5 **Antingham** Norfk
232 d5 **An t-Ob** W Isls
103 M3 **Anton's Gowt** Lincs
6 B5 **Antony** Cnwll
112 F5 **Antrobus** Ches W
103 J3 **Anwick** Lincs
145 M4 **Anwoth** D & G
32 D2 **Aperfield** Gt Lon
88 E4 **Apethorpe** Nhants
117 J6 **Apley** Lincs
115 G5 **Apperknowle** Derbys
55 K3 **Apperley** Gloucs
191 J6 **Appin** Ag & B
126 B7 **Appleby** N Linc
139 G3 **Appleby-in-Westmorland** Cumb
86 C2 **Appleby Magna** Leics
86 C2 **Appleby Parva** Leics
209 L5 **Applecross** Highld
23 G5 **Appledore** Devon
25 G8 **Appledore** Devon
34 C8 **Appledore** Kent
41 K2 **Appleford** Oxon
155 J5 **Applegarth Town** D & G
28 F2 **Appleshaw** Hants
112 D4 **Appleton** Halton
57 H7 **Appleton** Oxon
112 F5 **Appleton** Warrtn
133 L3 **Appleton-le-Moors** N York
134 B5 **Appleton-le-Street** N York
124 E3 **Appleton Roebuck** N York
112 F5 **Appleton Thorn** Warrtn
141 J6 **Appleton Wiske** N York
167 H6 **Appletreehall** Border
131 K7 **Appletreewick** N York
25 G6 **Appley** Somset
121 G8 **Appley Bridge** Lancs
17 G5 **Apse Heath** IoW
59 J2 **Apsley End** C Beds
18 A5 **Apuldram** W Susx
223 H6 **Arabella** Highld
196 F7 **Arbirlot** Angus
223 J5 **Arboll** Highld
42 C6 **Arborfield** Wokham
42 C6 **Arborfield Cross** Wokham
197 G7 **Arbroath** Angus
197 K2 **Arbuthnott** Abers
50 F5 **Archddu** Carmth
141 G4 **Archdeacon Newton** Darltn
174 D3 **Archencarroch** W Duns
214 F5 **Archiestown** Moray
99 H1 **Arclid Green** Ches E
217 J6 **Ardallie** Abers
182 F3 **Ardanaiseig Hotel** Ag & B
210 C7 **Ardaneaskan** Highld
210 C6 **Ardarroch** Highld
160 D1 **Ardbeg** Ag & B
173 J5 **Ardbeg** Ag & B
173 K2 **Ardbeg** Ag & B
220 F4 **Ardcharnich** Highld
180 E4 **Ardchiavaig** Ag & B
182 D5 **Ardchonnel** Ag & B
184 D5 **Ardchullarie More** Stirlg
183 J7 **Arddarroch** Ag & B
201 H7 **Ardechive** Highld
163 H2 **Ardeer** N Ayrs
60 A3 **Ardeley** Herts
210 D8 **Ardelve** Highld

174 C2 **Arden** Ag & B
71 K4 **Ardens Grafton** Warwks
182 B3 **Ardentallen** Ag & B
173 L2 **Ardentinny** Ag & B
173 H4 **Ardentraive** Ag & B
184 E1 **Ardeonaig** Stirlg
213 J4 **Ardersier** Highld
220 D4 **Ardessie** Highld
182 A6 **Ardfern** Ag & B
171 K4 **Ardfernal** Ag & B
222 D4 **Ardgay** Highld
191 K4 **Ardgour** Highld
173 L4 **Ardgowan** Inver
173 K4 **Ardhallow** Ag & B
232 e4 **Ardhasig** W Isls
210 B3 **Ardheslaig** Highld
220 F4 **Ardindrean** Highld
32 C7 **Ardingly** W Susx
41 H3 **Ardington** Oxon
173 G5 **Ardlamont** Ag & B
62 C3 **Ardleigh** Essex
62 C2 **Ardleigh Heath** Essex
195 L7 **Ardler** P & K
57 K3 **Ardley** Oxon
183 K4 **Ardlui** Ag & B
172 B2 **Ardlussa** Ag & B
220 E2 **Ardmair** Highld
173 J5 **Ardmaleish** Ag & B
172 B8 **Ardminish** Ag & B
190 E3 **Ardmolich** Highld
174 C3 **Ardmore** Ag & B
222 F4 **Ardmore** Highld
173 K3 **Ardnadam** Ag & B
212 E4 **Ardnagrask** Highld
210 D7 **Ardnarff** Highld
190 F4 **Ardnastang** Highld
172 C6 **Ardpatrick** Ag & B
172 E2 **Ardrishaig** Ag & B
222 E6 **Ardross** Highld
163 G2 **Ardrossan** N Ayrs
123 K5 **Ardsley East** Leeds
190 B4 **Ardslignish** Highld
171 J7 **Ardtalla** Ag & B
190 C3 **Ardtoe** Highld
182 A5 **Arduaine** Ag & B
212 E2 **Ardullie** Highld
199 K5 **Ardvasar** Highld
184 D3 **Ardvorlich** P & K
232 e3 **Ardvourlie** W Isls
144 D5 **Ardwell** D & G
113 J3 **Ardwick** Manch
70 E1 **Areley Kings** Worcs
190 D3 **Arevegaig** Highld
30 D4 **Arford** Hants
53 J7 **Argoed** Caerph
183 J6 **Argyll Forest Park** Ag & B
232 e3 **Aribruach** W Isls
180 D3 **Aridhglas** Ag & B
188 F5 **Arileod** Ag & B
189 G5 **Arinagour** Ag & B
182 C3 **Ariogan** Ag & B
199 K7 **Arisaig** Highld
199 L7 **Arisaig House** Highld
132 F7 **Arkendale** N York
76 C7 **Arkesden** Essex
130 B5 **Arkholme** Lancs
156 C4 **Arkleton** D & G
44 E2 **Arkley** Gt Lon
115 L1 **Arksey** Donc
115 H7 **Arkwright Town** Derbys
55 L4 **Arle** Gloucs
136 E4 **Arlecdon** Cumb
75 H7 **Arlesey** C Beds
84 B2 **Arleston** Wrekin
112 F5 **Arley** Ches E
86 C5 **Arley** Warwks
55 G6 **Arlingham** Gloucs
23 K4 **Arlington** Devon
20 B4 **Arlington** E Susx
199 K5 **Armadale** Highld
230 A3 **Armadale** Highld
176 C5 **Armadale** W Loth
148 E5 **Armathwaite** Cumb
92 F3 **Arminghall** Norfk
85 J1 **Armitage** Staffs
123 K4 **Armley** Leeds
72 B5 **Armscote** Warwks
115 L1 **Armthorpe** Donc
188 F4 **Arnabost** Ag & B
131 H5 **Arncliffe** N York
187 H6 **Arncroach** Fife
215 G5 **Arndilly House** Moray
15 H5 **Arne** Dorset
87 H5 **Arnesby** Leics
186 B5 **Arngask** P & K
200 C3 **Arnisdale** Highld
209 J5 **Arnish** Highld
177 K6 **Arniston** Mdloth
232 f1 **Arnol** W Isls
126 E3 **Arnold** E R Yk
101 L4 **Arnold** Notts
184 D7 **Arnprior** Stirlg
129 K4 **Arnside** Cumb
190 B7 **Aros** Ag & B
129 G4 **Arrad Foot** Cumb
126 C2 **Arram** E R Yk
162 B3 **Arran** N Ayrs
132 C2 **Arrathorne** N York
17 G5 **Arreton** IoW
210 B3 **Arrina** Highld
75 K4 **Arrington** Cambs
183 K6 **Arrochar** Ag & B
71 J3 **Arrow** Warwks
83 J2 **Arscott** Shrops
212 F4 **Artafallie** Highld
123 K2 **Arthington** Leeds
87 L7 **Arthingworth** Nhants
217 H6 **Arthrath** Abers
217 J7 **Artrochie** Abers
18 D4 **Arundel** W Susx
136 E3 **Asby** Cumb
173 J5 **Ascog** Ag & B
42 F6 **Ascot** W & M
56 F4 **Ascott-under-Wychwood** Oxon
132 F4 **Asenby** N York
102 B8 **Asfordby** Leics
102 B8 **Asfordby Hill** Leics
103 J4 **Asgarby** Lincs
35 H3 **Ash** Kent
45 L6 **Ash** Kent
26 C7 **Ash** Somset
30 E2 **Ash** Surrey
41 K5 **Ashampstead** W Berk
78 E4 **Ashbocking** Suffk
100 D3 **Ashbourne** Derbys
25 G6 **Ashbrittle** Somset
7 H2 **Ashburton** Devon
10 D5 **Ashbury** Devon
40 E4 **Ashbury** Oxon
125 L8 **Ashby** N Linc
118 F7 **Ashby by Partney** Lincs
118 C2 **Ashby cum Fenby** NE Lin
103 H2 **Ashby de la Launde** Lincs
86 D1 **Ashby-de-la-Zouch** Leics
87 K2 **Ashby Folville** Leics
87 H5 **Ashby Magna** Leics
87 G5 **Ashby Parva** Leics
118 D7 **Ashby Puerorum** Lincs
73 H2 **Ashby St Ledgers** Nhants
93 G3 **Ashby St Mary** Norfk
55 L2 **Ashchurch** Gloucs
11 L8 **Ashcombe** Devon
37 M7 **Ashcombe** N Som
26 C4 **Ashcott** Somset
76 E6 **Ashdon** Essex
29 K2 **Ashe** Hants
62 A7 **Asheldham** Essex
77 H6 **Ashen** Essex
58 B5 **Ashendon** Bucks
58 F6 **Asheridge** Bucks
185 G6 **Ashfield** Stirlg
78 E3 **Ashfield cum Thorpe** Suffk
92 F8 **Ashfield Green** Suffk
7 G6 **Ashford** Devon
23 H4 **Ashford** Devon
34 D6 **Ashford** Kent
43 H6 **Ashford** Surrey
69 K1 **Ashford Bowdler** Shrops
69 K1 **Ashford Carbonell** Shrops
41 K7 **Ashford Hill** Hants
114 D7 **Ashford in the Water** Derbys
175 K7 **Ashgill** S Lans
30 E2 **Ash Green** Surrey
86 D6 **Ash Green** Warwks
12 E1 **Ashill** Devon
91 K3 **Ashill** Norfk
25 L7 **Ashill** Somset
46 E2 **Ashingdon** Essex
159 G5 **Ashington** Nthumb
26 E6 **Ashington** Somset
18 F3 **Ashington** W Susx
167 G5 **Ashkirk** Border
55 J3 **Ashleworth** Gloucs
55 J3 **Ashleworth Quay** Gloucs
77 G3 **Ashley** Cambs
113 H5 **Ashley** Ches E
10 F3 **Ashley** Devon
39 L2 **Ashley** Gloucs
16 B4 **Ashley** Hants
29 G5 **Ashley** Hants
35 J5 **Ashley** Kent
87 L5 **Ashley** Nhants
99 H5 **Ashley** Staffs
39 J6 **Ashley** Wilts
58 F6 **Ashley Green** Bucks
98 E4 **Ash Magna** Shrops
41 H8 **Ashmansworth** Hants
22 E7 **Ashmansworthy** Devon
24 C6 **Ash Mill** Devon
27 K7 **Ashmore** Dorset
41 J6 **Ashmore Green** W Berk
72 C3 **Ashorne** Warwks
115 G8 **Ashover** Derbys
72 C1 **Ashow** Warwks
70 B6 **Ashperton** Herefs
7 J4 **Ashprington** Devon
25 J5 **Ash Priors** Somset
10 F3 **Ashreigney** Devon
78 B5 **Ash Street** Suffk
44 D8 **Ashtead** Surrey
12 C1 **Ash Thomas** Devon
112 D7 **Ashton** Ches W
3 G5 **Ashton** Cnwll
11 K7 **Ashton** Devon
69 K2 **Ashton** Herefs
173 L3 **Ashton** Inver
73 L5 **Ashton** Nhants
88 F5 **Ashton** Nhants
39 K8 **Ashton Common** Wilts
112 E2 **Ashton-in-Makerfield** Wigan
40 B2 **Ashton Keynes** Wilts
71 H6 **Ashton under Hill** Worcs
113 L2 **Ashton-under-Lyne** Tamesd
16 D1 **Ashurst** Hants
32 F5 **Ashurst** Kent
121 G8 **Ashurst** Lancs
19 G3 **Ashurst** W Susx
32 D5 **Ashurstwood** W Susx
30 E2 **Ash Vale** Surrey
9 K5 **Ashwater** Devon
75 J6 **Ashwell** Herts
88 C2 **Ashwell** Rutlnd
75 J6 **Ashwell End** Herts
92 D4 **Ashwellthorpe** Norfk
26 F2 **Ashwick** Somset
105 H8 **Ashwicken** Norfk
128 F4 **Askam in Furness** Cumb
124 E7 **Askern** Donc
14 A4 **Askerswell** Dorset
58 D6 **Askett** Bucks
138 D3 **Askham** Cumb
116 C6 **Askham** Notts
124 E2 **Askham Bryan** C York
124 E2 **Askham Richard** C York
172 F1 **Asknish** Ag & B
131 H2 **Askrigg** N York
123 H2 **Askwith** N York
103 H6 **Aslackby** Lincs
92 D5 **Aslacton** Norfk
102 C4 **Aslockton** Notts
147 K6 **Aspatria** Cumb
60 B3 **Aspenden** Herts
74 D7 **Aspley Guise** C Beds
74 D7 **Aspley Heath** C Beds
121 J8 **Aspull** Wigan
125 H5 **Asselby** E R Yk
77 L6 **Assington** Suffk
77 H4 **Assington Green** Suffk
99 J1 **Astbury** Ches E
73 J4 **Astcote** Nhants
118 C5 **Asterby** Lincs
83 H3 **Asterley** Shrops
83 H5 **Asterton** Shrops
56 F5 **Asthall** Oxon
56 F5 **Asthall Leigh** Oxon
223 G3 **Astle** Highld
98 D8 **Astley** Shrops
86 C5 **Astley** Warwks
113 G2 **Astley** Wigan
70 D2 **Astley** Worcs
84 C4 **Astley Abbots** Shrops
121 K7 **Astley Bridge** Bolton
70 E1 **Astley Cross** Worcs
98 E3 **Aston** Ches E
112 E5 **Aston** Ches W
114 D5 **Aston** Derbys
111 J7 **Aston** Flints
59 L4 **Aston** Herts
57 G7 **Aston** Oxon
115 J4 **Aston** Rothm
84 E5 **Aston** Shrops
98 D6 **Aston** Shrops
99 H4 **Aston** Staffs
99 K7 **Aston** Staffs
42 C4 **Aston** Wokham
84 B2 **Aston** Wrekin
58 D4 **Aston Abbotts** Bucks
84 B6 **Aston Botterell** Shrops
99 K6 **Aston-by-Stone** Staffs
71 K3 **Aston Cantlow** Warwks
58 E5 **Aston Clinton** Bucks
54 F4 **Aston Crews** Herefs
59 L3 **Aston End** Herts
71 G1 **Aston Fields** Worcs
86 F5 **Aston Flamville** Leics
55 G4 **Aston Ingham** Herefs
72 F4 **Aston le Walls** Nhants
71 L7 **Aston Magna** Gloucs
83 K6 **Aston Munslow** Shrops
83 H6 **Aston on Clun** Shrops
83 G3 **Aston Pigott** Shrops
83 G3 **Aston Rogers** Shrops
58 B7 **Aston Rowant** Oxon
71 J6 **Aston Somerville** Worcs
71 K6 **Aston-sub-Edge** Gloucs
41 K3 **Aston Tirrold** Oxon
101 H6 **Aston-upon-Trent** Derbys
41 K3 **Aston Upthorpe** Oxon
75 J6 **Astwick** C Beds
74 D5 **Astwood** M Keyn
71 G2 **Astwood** Worcs

71 J3 **Astwood Bank** Worcs
70 F3 **Astwood Crematorium** Worcs
103 H4 **Aswarby** Lincs
118 E7 **Aswardby** Lincs
83 K2 **Atcham** Shrops
14 E4 **Athelhampton** Dorset
78 E1 **Athelington** Suffk
25 M5 **Athelney** Somset
178 C3 **Athelstaneford** E Loth
23 J6 **Atherington** Devon
86 C4 **Atherstone** Warwks
72 B4 **Atherstone on Stour** Warwks
113 G2 **Atherton** Wigan
100 E3 **Atlow** Derbys
210 E6 **Attadale** Highld
117 G3 **Atterby** Lincs
115 G4 **Attercliffe** Sheff
86 D4 **Atterton** Leics
92 C4 **Attleborough** Norfk
86 D5 **Attleborough** Warwks
92 D1 **Attlebridge** Norfk
77 G4 **Attleton Green** Suffk
126 F1 **Atwick** E R Yk
39 J7 **Atworth** Wilts
116 F8 **Aubourn** Lincs
214 F8 **Auchbreck** Moray
217 G7 **Auchedly** Abers
197 H1 **Auchenblae** Abers
175 L2 **Auchenbowie** Stirlg
146 D5 **Auchencairn** D & G
155 G5 **Auchencairn** D & G
162 D4 **Auchencairn** N Ayrs
179 H6 **Auchencrow** Border
177 H6 **Auchendinny** Mdloth
176 D7 **Auchengray** S Lans
215 J3 **Auchenhalrig** Moray
164 F2 **Auchenheath** S Lans
154 E3 **Auchenhessnane** D & G
173 G4 **Auchenlochan** Ag & B
174 C8 **Auchenmade** N Ayrs
144 F4 **Auchenmalg** D & G
174 C8 **Auchentiber** N Ayrs
182 E6 **Auchindrain** Ag & B
221 G5 **Auchindrean** Highld
216 C5 **Auchininna** Abers
164 B5 **Auchinleck** E Ayrs
175 H4 **Auchinloch** N Lans
175 J3 **Auchinstarry** N Lans
191 L2 **Auchintore** Highld
217 K6 **Auchiries** Abers
203 K5 **Auchlean** Highld
207 G6 **Auchlee** Abers
206 C1 **Auchleven** Abers
164 F3 **Auchlochan** S Lans
206 B5 **Auchlossan** Abers
184 B2 **Auchlyne** Stirlg
164 A4 **Auchmillan** E Ayrs
197 G7 **Auchmithie** Angus
186 C6 **Auchmuirbridge** Fife
196 D4 **Auchnacree** Angus
217 H6 **Auchnagatt** Abers
204 F2 **Auchnarrow** Moray
144 B3 **Auchnotteroch** D & G
215 H4 **Auchroisk** Moray
185 K5 **Auchterarder** P & K
202 B4 **Auchteraw** Highld
203 L2 **Auchterblair** Highld
219 J6 **Auchtercairn** Highld
186 C7 **Auchterderran** Fife
196 B8 **Auchterhouse** Angus
216 D6 **Auchterless** Abers
186 D5 **Auchtermuchty** Fife
212 D3 **Auchterneed** Highld
177 H1 **Auchtertool** Fife
210 C8 **Auchtertyre** Highld
184 C4 **Auchtubh** Stirlg
231 L3 **Auckengill** Highld
115 M2 **Auckley** Donc
113 K3 **Audenshaw** Tamesd
98 F4 **Audlem** Ches E
99 J3 **Audley** Staffs
76 D6 **Audley End** Essex
76 D6 **Audley End House** Essex
125 G3 **Aughton** E R Yk
111 L1 **Aughton** Lancs
129 L6 **Aughton** Lancs
115 J4 **Aughton** Rothm
28 E1 **Aughton** Wilts
112 B1 **Aughton Park** Lancs
213 L4 **Auldearn** Highld
69 J4 **Aulden** Herefs
154 F5 **Auldgirth** D & G
175 H7 **Auldhouse** S Lans
200 E2 **Ault a' chruinn** Highld
219 K4 **Aultbea** Highld
219 H4 **Aultgrishin** Highld
221 J7 **Aultguish Inn** Highld
115 J7 **Ault Hucknall** Derbys
215 J4 **Aultmore** Moray
202 E2 **Aultnagoire** Highld
222 F5 **Aultnamain Inn** Highld
103 H5 **Aunsby** Lincs
38 E3 **Aust** S Glos
116 A3 **Austerfield** Donc
86 C3 **Austrey** Warwks
130 E5 **Austwick** N York
118 E5 **Authorpe** Lincs
40 C6 **Avebury** Wilts
45 L4 **Aveley** Thurr
39 K2 **Avening** Gloucs
102 C2 **Averham** Notts
7 G6 **Aveton Gifford** Devon
203 L3 **Aviemore** Highld
41 G6 **Avington** W Berk
213 G4 **Avoch** Highld
15 L3 **Avon** Hants
176 B4 **Avonbridge** Falk
72 E4 **Avon Dassett** Warwks
38 D5 **Avonmouth** Bristl
7 G4 **Avonwick** Devon
28 F6 **Awbridge** Hants
12 E3 **Awliscombe** Devon
55 G6 **Awre** Gloucs
101 J4 **Awsworth** Notts
26 B1 **Axbridge** Somset
29 L3 **Axford** Hants
40 E6 **Axford** Wilts
13 H3 **Axminster** Devon
13 G4 **Axmouth** Devon
141 G3 **Aycliffe** Dur
150 C2 **Aydon** Nthumb
54 E7 **Aylburton** Gloucs
12 D4 **Aylesbeare** Devon
58 D5 **Aylesbury** Bucks
126 F8 **Aylesby** NE Lin
33 J2 **Aylesford** Kent
35 H4 **Aylesham** Kent
87 H4 **Aylestone** C Leic
106 E5 **Aylmerton** Norfk
106 E6 **Aylsham** Norfk
70 B6 **Aylton** Herefs
56 C4 **Aylworth** Gloucs
69 H2 **Aymestrey** Herefs
57 K2 **Aynho** Nhants
59 K5 **Ayot St Lawrence** Herts
163 J5 **Ayr** S Ayrs
131 J2 **Aysgarth** N York
25 G7 **Ayshford** Devon
129 J3 **Ayside** Cumb
88 C4 **Ayston** Rutlnd
179 J6 **Ayton** Border
132 C5 **Azerley** N York

B

7 L3 **Babbacombe** Torbay
60 C5 **Babbs Green** Herts
26 E5 **Babcary** Somset
76 D4 **Babraham** Cambs
116 B5 **Babworth** Notts
234 d4 **Backaland** Ork
217 J4 **Backfolds** Abers
111 L6 **Backford** Ches W
223 H2 **Backies** Highld
199 K7 **Back of Keppoch** Highld
38 C6 **Backwell** N Som
106 D5 **Baconsthorpe** Norfk
54 A2 **Bacton** Herefs
107 H5 **Bacton** Norfk
78 C2 **Bacton** Suffk
122 C6 **Bacup** Lancs
219 J6 **Badachro** Highld
40 D4 **Badbury** Swindn
73 H3 **Badby** Nhants
228 B7 **Badcall** Highld
228 C4 **Badcall** Highld
220 D3 **Badcaul** Highld
86 B8 **Baddesley Clinton** Warwks
86 C4 **Baddesley Ensor** Warwks
224 D4 **Baddidarrach** Highld
176 F7 **Baddinsgill** Border
216 D6 **Badenscoth** Abers
205 H2 **Badenyon** Abers
84 D4 **Badger** Shrops
55 K4 **Badgeworth** Gloucs
26 B2 **Badgworth** Somset
210 B8 **Badicaul** Highld
79 G2 **Badingham** Suffk
34 D4 **Badlesmere** Kent
165 K5 **Badlieu** Border
231 J5 **Badlipster** Highld
220 C3 **Badluachrach** Highld
223 G3 **Badninish** Highld
220 D3 **Badrallach** Highld
71 J5 **Badsey** Worcs
30 E2 **Badshot Lea** Surrey
124 C7 **Badsworth** Wakefd
78 B2 **Badwell Ash** Suffk
27 H8 **Bagber** Dorset
133 G4 **Bagby** N York
118 E6 **Bag Enderby** Lincs
56 A6 **Bagendon** Gloucs
233 b9 **Bagh a Chaisteil** W Isls
233 b9 **Bagh a Tuath** W Isls
111 H6 **Bagillt** Flints
86 D8 **Baginton** Warwks
51 L6 **Baglan** Neath
98 B6 **Bagley** Shrops
26 C3 **Bagley** Somset
99 L3 **Bagnall** Staffs
83 L8 **Bagot** Shrops
42 E7 **Bagshot** Surrey
39 G3 **Bagstone** S Glos
86 F2 **Bagworth** Leics
54 C3 **Bagwy Llydiart** Herefs
123 H3 **Baildon** C Brad
123 H3 **Baildon Green** C Brad
232 f3 **Baile Ailein** W Isls
233 b6 **Baile a Mhanaich** W Isls
180 D3 **Baile Mor** Ag & B
175 J5 **Baillieston** C Glas
131 H2 **Bainbridge** N York
216 B7 **Bainshole** Abers
89 G3 **Bainton** C Pete
126 B1 **Bainton** E R Yk
186 F6 **Baintown** Fife
167 K6 **Bairnkine** Border
114 E7 **Bakewell** Derbys
96 E5 **Bala** Gwynd
232 f3 **Balallan** W Isls
212 C7 **Balbeg** Highld
186 C2 **Balbeggie** P & K
212 D5 **Balblair** Highld
213 G2 **Balblair** Highld
115 K2 **Balby** Donc
146 E5 **Balcary** D & G
212 E5 **Balchraggan** Highld
228 B4 **Balchreick** Highld
32 B6 **Balcombe** W Susx
187 K5 **Balcomie Links** Fife
132 E4 **Baldersby** N York
132 E4 **Baldersby St James** N York
121 J4 **Balderstone** Lancs
102 D3 **Balderton** Notts
187 G5 **Baldinnie** Fife
185 L4 **Baldinnies** P & K
75 J7 **Baldock** Herts
75 J6 **Baldock Services** Herts
187 G2 **Baldovie** C Dund
237 d5 **Baldrine** IoM
20 F3 **Baldslow** E Susx
106 B5 **Bale** Norfk
186 D2 **Baledgarno** P & K
188 C7 **Balemartine** Ag & B
177 G5 **Balerno** C Edin
186 D6 **Balfarg** Fife
196 E3 **Balfield** Angus
234 c5 **Balfour** Ork
174 F1 **Balfron** Stirlg
216 C6 **Balgaveny** Abers
185 L8 **Balgonar** Fife
144 D6 **Balgowan** D & G
202 F6 **Balgowan** Highld
218 B7 **Balgown** Highld
144 B3 **Balgracie** D & G
165 H5 **Balgray** S Lans
44 F5 **Balham** Gt Lon
195 L6 **Balhary** P & K
186 B1 **Balholmie** P & K
230 C3 **Baligill** Highld
195 L5 **Balintore** Angus
223 J6 **Balintore** Highld
223 G7 **Balintraid** Highld
233 b6 **Balivanich** W Isls
196 B7 **Balkeerie** Angus
125 J5 **Balkholme** E R Yk
191 L5 **Ballachulish** Highld
237 e4 **Ballajora** IoM
173 H6 **Ballanlay** Ag & B
152 C5 **Ballantrae** S Ayrs
237 b6 **Ballasalla** IoM
205 J6 **Ballater** Abers
237 c3 **Ballaugh** IoM
223 G6 **Ballchraggan** Highld
178 B3 **Ballencrieff** E Loth
188 B6 **Ballevullin** Ag & B
100 D2 **Ballidon** Derbys
161 L2 **Balliekine** N Ayrs
182 F7 **Balliemore** Ag & B
152 F4 **Balligmorrie** S Ayrs
184 C4 **Ballimore** Stirlg
214 E6 **Ballindalloch** Moray
186 D2 **Ballindean** P & K
58 E7 **Ballinger Common** Bucks
54 E2 **Ballingham** Herefs
186 C7 **Ballingry** Fife
194 F6 **Ballinluig** P & K
196 C5 **Ballinshoe** Angus
195 H5 **Ballintuim** P & K
213 H5 **Balloch** Highld
175 K4 **Balloch** N Lans
185 H4 **Balloch** P & K
153 G3 **Balloch** S Ayrs
174 D3 **Balloch** W Duns
31 G6 **Balls Cross** W Susx
32 E6 **Balls Green** E Susx
189 K7 **Ballygown** Ag & B
171 G5 **Ballygrant** Ag & B
188 F5 **Ballyhaugh** Ag & B
154 B6 **Balmaclellan** D & G
146 C6 **Balmae** D & G
174 D1 **Balmaha** Stirlg
186 E5 **Balmalcolm** Fife
146 B5 **Balmangan** D & G
207 H2 **Balmedie** Abers
186 F3 **Balmerino** Fife
162 B3 **Balmichael** N Ayrs
205 G6 **Balmoral Castle Grounds** Abers
175 G4 **Balmore** E Duns
223 J5 **Balmuchy** Highld
177 G2 **Balmule** Fife
187 G4 **Balmullo** Fife
226 E6 **Balnacoil Lodge** Highld
210 F5 **Balnacra** Highld
205 G6 **Balnacroft** Abers

213 G7 **Balnafoich** Highld
194 E6 **Balnaguard** P & K
180 F1 **Balnahard** Ag & B
180 F7 **Balnahard** Ag & B
212 C7 **Balnain** Highld
228 F2 **Balnakeil** Highld
124 F6 **Balne** N York
185 L1 **Balquharn** P & K
184 C3 **Balquhidder** Stirlg
86 B7 **Balsall Common** Solhll
85 J6 **Balsall Heath** Birm
72 E6 **Balscote** Oxon
76 E4 **Balsham** Cambs
235 e1 **Baltasound** Shet
145 J3 **Baltersan** D & G
26 D4 **Baltonsborough** Somset
181 M4 **Balvicar** Ag & B
200 C3 **Balvraid** Highld
213 K7 **Balvraid** Highld
121 H5 **Bamber Bridge** Lancs
60 F4 **Bamber's Green** Essex
169 H3 **Bamburgh** Nthumb
169 H3 **Bamburgh Castle** Nthumb
114 E5 **Bamford** Derbys
138 D4 **Bampton** Cumb
24 E6 **Bampton** Devon
56 F7 **Bampton** Oxon
138 D4 **Bampton Grange** Cumb
191 L2 **Banavie** Highld
72 F6 **Banbury** Oxon
72 F6 **Banbury Crematorium** Oxon
50 F3 **Bancffosfelen** Carmth
206 D6 **Banchory** Abers
207 G5 **Banchory-Devenick** Abers
50 E3 **Bancycapel** Carmth
50 D2 **Bancyfelin** Carmth
186 C2 **Bandirran** P & K
216 D2 **Banff** Abers
109 H6 **Bangor** Gwynd
109 H6 **Bangor Crematorium** Gwynd
98 B4 **Bangor-is-y-coed** Wrexhm
9 G5 **Bangors** Cnwll
92 C6 **Banham** Norfk
16 C2 **Bank** Hants
147 H2 **Bankend** D & G
185 M1 **Bankfoot** P & K
164 C6 **Bankglen** E Ayrs
207 G4 **Bankhead** C Aber
165 J1 **Bankhead** S Lans
175 K3 **Banknock** Falk
120 E6 **Banks** Lancs
155 L5 **Bankshill** D & G
106 F6 **Banningham** Norfk
61 H4 **Bannister Green** Essex
175 L1 **Bannockburn** Stirlg
44 E7 **Banstead** Surrey
6 F6 **Bantham** Devon
175 K3 **Banton** N Lans
38 B8 **Banwell** N Som
34 C3 **Bapchild** Kent
27 M4 **Bapton** Wilts
232 f1 **Barabhas** W Isls
163 J3 **Barassie** S Ayrs
223 G6 **Barbaraville** Highld
163 K5 **Barbieston** S Ayrs
130 C3 **Barbon** Cumb
23 L2 **Barbrook** Devon
73 G1 **Barby** Nhants
191 J7 **Barcaldine** Ag & B
19 L3 **Barcombe** E Susx
19 L3 **Barcombe Cross** E Susx
33 G4 **Barden Park** Kent
61 G2 **Bardfield End Green** Essex
61 G3 **Bardfield Saling** Essex
117 J7 **Bardney** Lincs
86 F2 **Bardon** Leics
149 K3 **Bardon Mill** Nthumb
175 G4 **Bardowie** E Duns
174 C4 **Bardrainney** Inver
129 G5 **Bardsea** Cumb
124 B2 **Bardsey** Leeds
94 B7 **Bardsey Island** Gwynd
91 L8 **Bardwell** Suffk
129 K6 **Bare** Lancs
145 G2 **Barfad** D & G
92 D3 **Barford** Norfk
72 C3 **Barford** Warwks
57 H2 **Barford St John** Oxon
28 B5 **Barford St Martin** Wilts
57 H2 **Barford St Michael** Oxon
35 H5 **Barfrestone** Kent
175 J5 **Bargeddie** N Lans
53 J7 **Bargoed** Caerph
153 H6 **Bargrennan** D & G
89 G7 **Barham** Cambs
35 G5 **Barham** Kent
78 D4 **Barham** Suffk
35 G5 **Barham Crematorium** Kent
75 L2 **Bar Hill** Cambs
88 F2 **Barholm** Lincs
87 J2 **Barkby** Leics
87 J2 **Barkby Thorpe** Leics
102 C5 **Barkestone-le-Vale** Leics
42 C6 **Barkham** Wokham
45 H3 **Barking** Gt Lon
78 C4 **Barking** Suffk
45 H3 **Barkingside** Gt Lon
78 C4 **Barking Tye** Suffk
122 F6 **Barkisland** Calder
3 J2 **Barkla Shop** Cnwll
102 F4 **Barkston** Lincs
124 D4 **Barkston Ash** N York
75 L7 **Barkway** Herts
175 H5 **Barlanark** C Glas
99 K5 **Barlaston** Staffs
18 C3 **Barlavington** W Susx
115 J6 **Barlborough** Derbys
124 F4 **Barlby** N York
86 E3 **Barlestone** Leics
76 B6 **Barley** Herts
122 B3 **Barley** Lancs
88 B2 **Barleythorpe** Rutlnd
46 F3 **Barling** Essex
117 H6 **Barlings** Lincs
146 E4 **Barlochan** D & G
115 G6 **Barlow** Derbys
150 E3 **Barlow** Gatesd
124 F5 **Barlow** N York
125 J2 **Barmby Moor** E R Yk
125 G5 **Barmby on the Marsh** E R Yk
161 K1 **Barmollack** Ag & B
80 E1 **Barmouth** Gwynd
141 H4 **Barmpton** Darltn
135 J7 **Barmston** E R Yk
182 E8 **Barnacarry** Ag & B
88 F3 **Barnack** C Pete
140 D4 **Barnard Castle** Dur
57 H6 **Barnard Gate** Oxon
77 G5 **Barnardiston** Suffk
146 E4 **Barnbarroch** D & G
115 J2 **Barnburgh** Donc
93 K5 **Barnby** Suffk
124 F8 **Barnby Dun** Donc
102 E3 **Barnby in the Willows** Notts
116 A5 **Barnby Moor** Notts
144 D7 **Barncorkrie** D & G
44 E5 **Barnes** Gt Lon
33 H4 **Barnes Street** Kent
44 E2 **Barnet** Gt Lon
126 C8 **Barnetby le Wold** N Linc
106 B6 **Barney** Norfk
91 K7 **Barnham** Suffk
18 C5 **Barnham** W Susx
92 C3 **Barnham Broom** Norfk
197 G5 **Barnhead** Angus
187 H2 **Barnhill** C Dund
214 E3 **Barnhill** Moray
152 B7 **Barnhills** D & G
140 D5 **Barningham** Dur
91 L7 **Barningham** Suffk
118 C2 **Barnoldby le Beck** NE Lin
122 C2 **Barnoldswick** Lancs
31 J6 **Barns Green** W Susx
115 G1 **Barnsley** Barns
56 B6 **Barnsley** Gloucs
115 G1 **Barnsley Crematorium** Barns
23 J5 **Barnstaple** Devon
61 G4 **Barnston** Essex
111 J5 **Barnston** Wirral
102 B5 **Barnstone** Notts
85 H8 **Barnt Green** Worcs
177 G4 **Barnton** C Edin
112 F6 **Barnton** Ches W
88 F6 **Barnwell All Saints** Nhants
88 F6 **Barnwell St Andrew** Nhants
55 K4 **Barnwood** Gloucs
153 G4 **Barr** S Ayrs
233 b9 **Barra** W Isls
233 b9 *Barra Airport* W Isls
145 H5 **Barrachan** D & G
233 b9 **Barraigh** W Isls
188 B7 **Barrapoll** Ag & B
158 A7 **Barrasford** Nthumb
174 F6 **Barrhead** E Rens
152 F5 **Barrhill** S Ayrs
76 B5 **Barrington** Cambs
26 B7 **Barrington** Somset
3 H4 **Barripper** Cnwll
174 C7 **Barrmill** N Ayrs
231 J2 **Barrock** Highld
55 K3 **Barrow** Gloucs
121 L3 **Barrow** Lancs
88 C1 **Barrow** Rutlnd
27 G5 **Barrow** Somset
77 H2 **Barrow** Suffk
102 E5 **Barrowby** Lincs
88 D4 **Barrowden** Rutlnd
122 C3 **Barrowford** Lancs
38 D6 **Barrow Gurney** N Som
126 D6 **Barrow Haven** N Linc
128 E5 **Barrow-in-Furness** Cumb
128 E5 **Barrow Island** Cumb
126 D6 **Barrow-upon-Humber** N Linc
101 L8 **Barrow upon Soar** Leics
101 G6 **Barrow upon Trent** Derbys
187 J1 **Barry** Angus
37 H6 **Barry** V Glam
37 H6 **Barry Island** V Glam
87 K2 **Barsby** Leics
93 H5 **Barsham** Suffk
86 B7 **Barston** Solhll
69 L6 **Bartestree** Herefs
216 F7 **Barthol Chapel** Abers
61 H4 **Bartholomew Green** Essex
99 H3 **Barthomley** Ches E
28 F8 **Bartley** Hants
85 H6 **Bartley Green** Birm
76 E5 **Bartlow** Cambs
76 B4 **Barton** Cambs
98 C2 **Barton** Ches W
56 C3 **Barton** Gloucs
120 E8 **Barton** Lancs
121 G3 **Barton** Lancs
141 G5 **Barton** N York
57 K6 **Barton** Oxon
7 K3 **Barton** Torbay
91 G3 **Barton Bendish** Norfk
39 J2 **Barton End** Gloucs
57 M2 **Barton Hartshorn** Bucks
101 K6 **Barton in Fabis** Notts
86 E3 **Barton in the Beans** Leics
59 H2 **Barton-le-Clay** C Beds
133 L5 **Barton-le-Street** N York
133 L6 **Barton-le-Willows** N York
91 G8 **Barton Mills** Suffk
16 B4 **Barton-on-Sea** Hants
56 E2 **Barton-on-the-Heath** Warwks
26 D5 **Barton St David** Somset
88 C7 **Barton Seagrave** Nhants
29 H3 **Barton Stacey** Hants
23 L4 **Barton Town** Devon
107 H7 **Barton Turf** Norfk
100 D8 **Barton-under-Needwood** Staffs
126 C6 **Barton-upon-Humber** N Linc
126 C6 **Barton Waterside** N Linc
232 f1 **Barvas** W Isls
90 D7 **Barway** Cambs
86 F4 **Barwell** Leics
10 E4 **Barwick** Devon
26 E8 **Barwick** Somset
124 B3 **Barwick in Elmet** Leeds
98 B7 **Baschurch** Shrops
72 E2 **Bascote** Warwks
121 K2 **Bashall Eaves** Lancs
46 B3 **Basildon** Essex
46 C3 **Basildon & District Crematorium** Essex
29 M2 **Basingstoke** Hants
29 K3 **Basingstoke Crematorium** Hants
114 E6 **Baslow** Derbys
25 M3 **Bason Bridge** Somset
37 L3 **Bassaleg** Newpt
167 K1 **Bassendean** Border
137 H2 **Bassenthwaite** Cumb
29 H7 **Bassett** C Sotn
75 K5 **Bassingbourn** Cambs
102 E1 **Bassingham** Lincs
102 F6 **Bassingthorpe** Lincs
60 A3 **Bassus Green** Herts
89 G2 **Baston** Lincs
107 J8 **Bastwick** Norfk
43 H2 **Batchworth** Herts
14 C2 **Batcombe** Dorset
27 G4 **Batcombe** Somset
59 J5 **Batford** Herts
39 H7 **Bath** BaNES
39 H7 **Bathampton** BaNES
25 G6 **Bathealton** Somset
39 H6 **Batheaston** BaNES
39 H6 **Bathford** BaNES
176 D5 **Bathgate** W Loth
102 C2 **Bathley** Notts
5 L2 **Bathpool** Cnwll
25 K6 **Bathpool** Somset
62 F2 **Bath Side** Essex
176 C5 **Bathville** W Loth
26 E2 **Bathway** Somset
123 J5 **Batley** Kirk
71 L7 **Batsford** Gloucs
142 D5 **Battersby** N York
44 F5 **Battersea** Gt Lon
78 B4 **Battisford Tye** Suffk
20 F3 **Battle** E Susx
52 F2 **Battle** Powys
196 D5 **Battledykes** Angus
103 L2 **Battle of Britain Memorial Flight** Lincs
46 C2 **Battlesbridge** Essex
24 E6 **Battleton** Somset

70 F6 **Baughton** Worcs
41 L7 **Baughurst** Hants
206 B6 **Baulds** Abers
40 F3 **Baulking** Oxon
117 L6 **Baumber** Lincs
56 A6 **Baunton** Gloucs
28 B5 **Baverstock** Wilts
92 D2 **Bawburgh** Norfk
106 C7 **Bawdeswell** Norfk
25 M4 **Bawdrip** Somset
79 H6 **Bawdsey** Suffk
115 M3 **Bawtry** Donc
122 B5 **Baxenden** Lancs
86 C4 **Baxterley** Warwks
208 D4 **Bay** Highld
232 g2 **Bayble** W Isls
29 K6 **Baybridge** Hants
129 G5 **Baycliff** Cumb
40 F5 **Baydon** Wilts
60 A6 **Bayford** Herts
27 G5 **Bayford** Somset
233 b6 **Bayhead** W Isls
78 D4 **Baylham** Suffk
54 E3 **Baysham** Herefs
83 J2 **Bayston Hill** Shrops
77 G6 **Baythorne End** Essex
84 C8 **Bayton** Worcs
57 J7 **Bayworth** Oxon
73 L6 **Beachampton** Bucks
91 H3 **Beachamwell** Norfk
20 C6 **Beachy Head** E Susx
12 F2 **Beacon** Devon
62 A3 **Beacon End** Essex
30 E4 **Beacon Hill** Surrey
42 C2 **Beacon's Bottom** Bucks
42 F3 **Beaconsfield** Bucks
42 F3 **Beaconsfield Services** Bucks
133 K3 **Beadlam** N York
75 G6 **Beadlow** C Beds
169 J4 **Beadnell** Nthumb
10 E2 **Beaford** Devon
124 E5 **Beal** N York
169 G2 **Beal** Nthumb
6 A1 **Bealsmill** Cnwll
13 L3 **Beaminster** Dorset
150 F4 **Beamish** Dur
131 K8 **Beamsley** N York
39 K7 **Beanacre** Wilts
169 G5 **Beanley** Nthumb
10 D7 **Beardon** Devon
31 K3 **Beare Green** Surrey
71 L3 **Bearley** Warwks
151 G6 **Bearpark** Dur
174 F4 **Bearsden** E Duns
33 K3 **Bearsted** Kent
99 G5 **Bearstone** Shrops
85 H6 **Bearwood** Birm
69 H4 **Bearwood** Herefs
15 K3 **Bearwood** Poole
155 J2 **Beattock** D & G
60 F6 **Beauchamp Roding** Essex
53 J5 **Beaufort** Blae G
16 E3 **Beaulieu** Hants
16 E2 **Beaulieu House** Hants
212 E5 **Beauly** Highld
109 H6 **Beaumaris** IoA
148 C3 **Beaumont** Cumb
62 E3 **Beaumont** Essex
236 c7 **Beaumont** Jersey
72 B1 **Beausale** Warwks
29 L6 **Beauworth** Hants
10 C5 **Beaworthy** Devon
61 H3 **Beazley End** Essex
111 K5 **Bebington** Wirral
93 J5 **Beccles** Suffk
120 F6 **Becconsall** Lancs
84 D3 **Beckbury** Shrops
45 G6 **Beckenham** Gt Lon
45 G6 **Beckenham Crematorium** Gt Lon
136 E6 **Beckermet** Cumb
147 J5 **Beckfoot** Cumb
71 H7 **Beckford** Worcs
40 C6 **Beckhampton** Wilts
102 E2 **Beckingham** Lincs
116 C4 **Beckingham** Notts
27 J2 **Beckington** Somset
83 H7 **Beckjay** Shrops
21 G2 **Beckley** E Susx
57 K5 **Beckley** Oxon
91 G7 **Beck Row** Suffk
128 F3 **Beck Side** Cumb
45 H4 **Beckton** Gt Lon
132 D8 **Beckwithshaw** N York
45 J3 **Becontree** Gt Lon
132 D2 **Bedale** N York
27 J7 **Bedchester** Dorset
37 G4 **Beddau** Rhondd
95 K3 **Beddgelert** Gwynd
19 L4 **Beddingham** E Susx
44 F6 **Beddington** Gt Lon
44 F6 **Beddington Corner** Gt Lon
78 F2 **Bedfield** Suffk
74 F5 **Bedford** Bed
75 G4 **Bedford Crematorium** Bed
17 K2 **Bedhampton** Hants
78 E2 **Bedingfield** Suffk
132 D7 **Bedlam** N York
159 G5 **Bedlington** Nthumb
53 H7 **Bedlinog** Myr Td
38 E6 **Bedminster** Bristl
38 E6 **Bedminster Down** Bristl
59 J7 **Bedmond** Herts
99 L8 **Bednall** Staffs
167 J5 **Bedrule** Border
83 G7 **Bedstone** Shrops
37 J3 **Bedwas** Caerph
53 J7 **Bedwellty** Caerph
86 D6 **Bedworth** Warwks
87 J2 **Beeby** Leics
30 B4 **Beech** Hants
99 J5 **Beech** Staffs
42 B7 **Beech Hill** W Berk
40 C8 **Beechingstoke** Wilts
41 J5 **Beedon** W Berk
135 H8 **Beeford** E R Yk
114 E7 **Beeley** Derbys
117 K2 **Beelsby** NE Lin
41 L6 **Beenham** W Berk
13 G5 **Beer** Devon
26 B5 **Beer** Somset
25 L7 **Beercrocombe** Somset
14 B1 **Beer Hackett** Dorset
7 J7 **Beesands** Devon
118 F5 **Beesby** Lincs
7 J7 **Beeson** Devon
75 H5 **Beeston** C Beds
98 D2 **Beeston** Ches W
123 K4 **Beeston** Leeds
91 K1 **Beeston** Norfk
101 K5 **Beeston** Notts
106 E4 **Beeston Regis** Norfk
146 F2 **Beeswing** D & G
129 K4 **Beetham** Cumb
25 L8 **Beetham** Somset
106 A8 **Beetley** Norfk
57 J5 **Begbroke** Oxon
49 J6 **Begelly** Pembks
82 D7 **Beguildy** Powys
93 H2 **Beighton** Norfk
115 H5 **Beighton** Sheff
233 c7 **Beinn Na Faoghla** W Isls
174 C7 **Beith** N Ayrs
35 G4 **Bekesbourne** Kent
107 G8 **Belaugh** Norfk
85 G7 **Belbroughton** Worcs
14 E1 **Belchalwell** Dorset
77 J6 **Belchamp Otten** Essex
77 H6 **Belchamp St Paul** Essex
77 J6 **Belchamp Walter** Essex
118 D6 **Belchford** Lincs
169 G3 **Belford** Nthumb
87 H3 **Belgrave** C Leic
178 E3 **Belhaven** E Loth
207 H2 **Belhelvie** Abers
215 K8 **Belhinnie** Abers
205 H3 **Bellabeg** Abers
182 A8 **Bellanoch** Ag & B
195 K4 **Bellaty** Angus
131 G7 **Bell Busk** N York
118 E5 **Belleau** Lincs
85 G7 **Bell End** Worcs
131 L2 **Bellerby** N York
148 C4 **Belle Vue** Cumb
123 L6 **Belle Vue** Wakefd
164 F3 **Bellfield** S Lans
165 J5 **Bellfield** S Lans
58 F6 **Bellingdon** Bucks
157 L5 **Bellingham** Nthumb
161 H2 **Belloch** Ag & B
161 H3 **Bellochantuy** Ag & B
98 D4 **Bell o' th' Hill** Ches W
175 J6 **Bellshill** N Lans
175 L6 **Bellside** N Lans
176 E5 **Bellsquarry** W Loth
33 G6 **Bells Yew Green** E Susx
38 E7 **Belluton** BaNES
213 G3 **Belmaduthy** Highld
121 K7 **Belmont** Bl w D
44 E7 **Belmont** Gt Lon
163 J5 **Belmont** S Ayrs
235 d2 **Belmont** Shet
205 J3 **Belnacraig** Abers
101 G3 **Belper** Derbys
158 D6 **Belsay** Nthumb
167 J4 **Belses** Border
7 H4 **Belsford** Devon
59 G7 **Belsize** Herts
78 D6 **Belstead** Suffk
10 F6 **Belstone** Devon
121 L5 **Belthorn** Lancs
47 K6 **Beltinge** Kent
149 K3 **Beltingham** Nthumb
116 D1 **Beltoft** N Linc
101 H7 **Belton** Leics
102 F4 **Belton** Lincs
116 C1 **Belton** N Linc
93 K3 **Belton** Norfk
88 B3 **Belton** Rutlnd
45 J4 **Belvedere** Gt Lon
102 D5 **Belvoir** Leics
102 D5 **Belvoir Castle** Leics
17 J5 **Bembridge** IoW
28 C5 **Bemerton** Wilts
135 J5 **Bempton** E R Yk
93 K6 **Benacre** Suffk
233 c7 **Benbecula** W Isls
233 c6 *Benbecula Airport* W Isls
154 C3 **Benbuie** D & G
191 H8 **Benderloch** Ag & B
33 K6 **Benenden** Kent
150 D4 **Benfieldside** Dur
60 A5 **Bengeo** Herts
71 J5 **Bengeworth** Worcs
79 H3 **Benhall Green** Suffk
79 H3 **Benhall Street** Suffk
197 K3 **Benholm** Abers
133 H7 **Beningbrough** N York
59 M4 **Benington** Herts
104 C3 **Benington** Lincs
109 G5 **Benllech** IoA
173 K2 **Benmore** Ag & B
162 C5 **Bennan** N Ayrs
192 B3 **Ben Nevis** Highld
117 K5 **Benniworth** Lincs
33 J4 **Benover** Kent
123 H2 **Ben Rhydding** C Brad
163 J2 **Benslie** N Ayrs
41 L3 **Benson** Oxon
206 F5 **Benthoul** C Aber
115 K1 **Bentley** Donc
126 C4 **Bentley** E R Yk
30 C3 **Bentley** Hants
78 D6 **Bentley** Suffk
86 C4 **Bentley** Warwks
45 L2 **Bentley Crematorium** Essex
156 B4 **Bentpath** D & G
24 B5 **Bentwichen** Devon
30 A4 **Bentworth** Hants
186 E2 **Benvie** Angus
14 A2 **Benville** Dorset
89 L5 **Benwick** Cambs
71 J1 **Beoley** Worcs
199 L6 **Beoraidbeg** Highld
18 B3 **Bepton** W Susx
60 D3 **Berden** Essex
48 D2 **Berea** Pembks
6 C3 **Bere Alston** Devon
6 C3 **Bere Ferrers** Devon
14 F4 **Bere Regis** Dorset
93 G4 **Bergh Apton** Norfk
41 L2 **Berinsfield** Oxon
55 G7 **Berkeley** Gloucs
59 G6 **Berkhamsted** Herts
27 J2 **Berkley** Somset
86 B7 **Berkswell** Solhll
45 G4 **Bermondsey** Gt Lon
200 C2 **Bernera** Highld
208 F4 **Bernisdale** Highld
41 L2 **Berrick Prior** Oxon
41 L2 **Berrick Salome** Oxon
227 K4 **Berriedale** Highld
137 L2 **Berrier** Cumb
82 D4 **Berriew** Powys
83 K3 **Berrington** Shrops
69 L2 **Berrington** Worcs
69 L2 **Berrington Green** Worcs
25 L2 **Berrow** Somset
70 D3 **Berrow Green** Worcs
215 L3 **Berryhillock** Moray
215 L4 **Berryhillock** Moray
23 J3 **Berrynarbor** Devon
7 J4 **Berry Pomeroy** Devon
97 L3 **Bersham** Wrexhm
20 B5 **Berwick** E Susx
40 C5 **Berwick Bassett** Wilts
158 F6 **Berwick Hill** Nthumb
28 B4 **Berwick St James** Wilts
27 L6 **Berwick St John** Wilts
27 L5 **Berwick St Leonard** Wilts
179 K7 **Berwick-upon-Tweed** Nthumb
120 E7 **Bescar** Lancs
71 G5 **Besford** Worcs
115 L2 **Bessacarr** Donc
135 J6 **Bessingby** E R Yk
106 E5 **Bessingham** Norfk
92 C4 **Besthorpe** Norfk
116 D8 **Besthorpe** Notts
101 K3 **Bestwood Village** Notts
126 C2 **Beswick** E R Yk
31 K2 **Betchworth** Surrey
62 C3 **Beth Chatto Garden** Essex
109 G7 **Bethel** Gwynd
108 E7 **Bethel** IoA
34 C6 **Bethersden** Kent
109 J7 **Bethesda** Gwynd
49 J4 **Bethesda** Pembks
51 K1 **Bethlehem** Carmth
45 G4 **Bethnal Green** Gt Lon
99 H3 **Betley** Staffs
45 L5 **Betsham** Kent
35 J4 **Betteshanger** Kent
13 K3 **Bettiscombe** Dorset
98 C5 **Bettisfield** Wrexhm
37 L3 **Bettws** Newpt
66 D4 **Bettws Bledrws** Cerdgn
82 C4 **Bettws Cedewain** Powys
65 J5 **Bettws Evan** Cerdgn
54 A6 **Bettws-Newydd** Mons

229 L3 **Bettyhill** Highld
36 D3 **Betws** Brdgnd
97 G3 **Betws Gwerfil Goch** Denbgs
96 C2 **Betws-y-Coed** Conwy
110 C6 **Betws-yn-Rhos** Conwy
65 J5 **Beulah** Cerdgn
67 K4 **Beulah** Powys
116 B6 **Bevercotes** Notts
126 C3 **Beverley** E R Yk
39 K2 **Beverston** Gloucs
156 F7 **Bewcastle** Cumb
84 D7 **Bewdley** Worcs
132 B6 **Bewerley** N York
126 E1 **Bewholme** E R Yk
20 E4 **Bexhill** E Susx
45 J5 **Bexley** Gt Lon
45 J5 **Bexleyheath** Gt Lon
90 F3 **Bexwell** Norfk
77 L2 **Beyton** Suffk
77 L2 **Beyton Green** Suffk
232 d2 **Bhaltos** W Isls
233 b10 **Bhatarsaigh** W Isls
56 C6 **Bibury** Gloucs
57 L4 **Bicester** Oxon
85 L6 **Bickenhill** Solhll
103 L5 **Bicker** Lincs
112 C2 **Bickerstaffe** Lancs
124 C1 **Bickerton** N York
84 F2 **Bickford** Staffs
7 J2 **Bickington** Devon
23 H5 **Bickington** Devon
6 D4 **Bickleigh** Devon
12 B2 **Bickleigh** Devon
98 D3 **Bickley** Ches W
45 H6 **Bickley** Gt Lon
134 E2 **Bickley** N York
61 J7 **Bicknacre** Essex
25 H4 **Bicknoller** Somset
33 L2 **Bicknor** Kent
82 F6 **Bicton** Shrops
83 J1 **Bicton** Shrops
32 F5 **Bidborough** Kent
33 L5 **Biddenden** Kent
74 E4 **Biddenham** Bed
39 K5 **Biddestone** Wilts
26 B2 **Biddisham** Somset
73 J6 **Biddlesden** Bucks
99 K2 **Biddulph** Staffs
99 K2 **Biddulph Moor** Staffs
23 G6 **Bideford** Devon
71 K4 **Bidford-on-Avon** Warwks
125 J2 **Bielby** E R Yk
207 G5 **Bieldside** C Aber
17 G6 **Bierley** IoW
58 D5 **Bierton** Bucks
145 H6 **Big Balcraig** D & G
6 F6 **Bigbury** Devon
6 F6 **Bigbury-on-Sea** Devon
117 H1 **Bigby** Lincs
154 B3 **Big Carlae** D & G
165 K2 **Biggar** S Lans
100 D2 **Biggin** Derbys
32 D2 **Biggin Hill** Gt Lon
45 H7 *Biggin Hill Airport* Gt Lon
75 H5 **Biggleswade** C Beds
156 B6 **Bigholms** D & G
230 C3 **Bighouse** Highld
29 L4 **Bighton** Hants
148 A4 **Biglands** Cumb
18 D3 **Bignor** W Susx
53 K6 **Big Pit Blaenavon** Torfn
136 D5 **Bigrigg** Cumb
219 H5 **Big Sand** Highld
235 c7 **Bigton** Shet
101 K4 **Bilborough** C Nott
25 G3 **Bilbrook** Somset
124 E2 **Bilbrough** N York
231 K5 **Bilbster** Highld
140 F3 **Bildershaw** Dur
78 B5 **Bildeston** Suffk
46 B2 **Billericay** Essex
87 K3 **Billesdon** Leics
71 K3 **Billesley** Warwks
103 J5 **Billingborough** Lincs
112 D2 **Billinge** St Hel
92 E7 **Billingford** Norfk
106 B7 **Billingford** Norfk
141 K3 **Billingham** S on T
103 J2 **Billinghay** Lincs
115 H1 **Billingley** Barns
31 H6 **Billingshurst** W Susx
84 C6 **Billingsley** Shrops
58 F4 **Billington** C Beds
121 L4 **Billington** Lancs
93 J2 **Billockby** Norfk
150 E7 **Billy Row** Dur
121 G3 **Bilsborrow** Lancs
119 G6 **Bilsby** Lincs
18 D5 **Bilsham** W Susx
34 D7 **Bilsington** Kent
101 M1 **Bilsthorpe** Notts
177 H5 **Bilston** Mdloth
85 G4 **Bilston** Wolves
86 D3 **Bilstone** Leics
126 E4 **Bilton** E R Yk
124 D1 **Bilton** N York
132 D7 **Bilton** N York
86 F8 **Bilton** Warwks
117 K3 **Binbrook** Lincs
14 D5 **Bincombe** Dorset
26 E2 **Binegar** Somset
42 D6 **Binfield** Br For
42 C5 **Binfield Heath** Oxon
158 B7 **Bingfield** Nthumb
102 B4 **Bingham** Notts
123 G3 **Bingley** C Brad
106 B5 **Binham** Norfk
86 E7 **Binley** Covtry
29 H2 **Binley** Hants
86 E7 **Binley Woods** Warwks
15 G5 **Binnegar** Dorset
176 B4 **Binniehill** Falk
30 F3 **Binscombe** Surrey
17 H4 **Binstead** IoW
30 C3 **Binsted** Hants
18 D4 **Binsted** W Susx
71 K4 **Binton** Warwks
106 B7 **Bintree** Norfk
61 M4 **Birch** Essex
105 J5 **Bircham Newton** Norfk
105 J6 **Bircham Tofts** Norfk
60 E4 **Birchanger** Essex
60 E4 **Birchanger Green Services** Essex
100 C6 **Birch Cross** Staffs
69 J2 **Bircher** Herefs
61 M4 **Birch Green** Essex
37 J4 **Birchgrove** Cardif
51 K5 **Birchgrove** Swans
32 D7 **Birchgrove** W Susx
35 J2 **Birchington** Kent
86 C5 **Birchley Heath** Warwks
100 E1 **Birchover** Derbys
122 C8 **Birch Services** Rochdl
114 A4 **Birch Vale** Derbys
116 F7 **Birchwood** Lincs
25 K8 **Birch Wood** Somset
112 F4 **Birchwood** Warrtn
115 M3 **Bircotes** Notts
77 G6 **Birdbrook** Essex
133 G4 **Birdforth** N York
17 M3 **Birdham** W Susx
72 E2 **Birdingbury** Warwks
55 L5 **Birdlip** Gloucs
134 C6 **Birdsall** N York
123 J8 **Birds Edge** Kirk
60 F6 **Birds Green** Essex
84 D6 **Birdsgreen** Shrops
13 K3 **Birdsmoorgate** Dorset
115 G2 **Birdwell** Barns
168 B2 **Birgham** Border
223 G3 **Birichin** Highld
141 H6 **Birkby** N York
120 D7 **Birkdale** Sefton
215 L2 **Birkenbog** Abers
111 K4 **Birkenhead** Wirral
216 E5 **Birkenhills** Abers
123 J5 **Birkenshaw** Kirk
205 H6 **Birkhall** Abers
186 F1 **Birkhill** Angus
166 B6 **Birkhill** D & G
124 E5 **Birkin** N York
69 J4 **Birley** Herefs
115 G3 **Birley Carr** Sheff
46 B7 **Birling** Kent
71 G5 **Birlingham** Worcs
85 J6 **Birmingham** Birm
85 L6 *Birmingham Airport* Solhll
195 G7 **Birnam** P & K
217 J7 **Birness** Abers
206 B6 **Birse** Abers
205 L5 **Birsemore** Abers
123 J5 **Birstall** Kirk
87 H2 **Birstall** Leics
132 C7 **Birstwith** N York
151 G4 **Birtley** Gatesd
69 G2 **Birtley** Herefs
157 L6 **Birtley** Nthumb
151 G4 **Birtley Crematorium** Gatesd
70 D7 **Birts Street** Worcs
88 C4 **Bisbrooke** Rutlnd
118 C5 **Biscathorpe** Lincs
42 D4 **Bisham** W & M
71 H4 **Bishampton** Worcs
24 B6 **Bish Mill** Devon
140 F2 **Bishop Auckland** Dur
117 G4 **Bishopbridge** Lincs
175 G4 **Bishopbriggs** E Duns
126 B3 **Bishop Burton** E R Yk
141 H2 **Bishop Middleham** Dur
214 F2 **Bishopmill** Moray
132 E6 **Bishop Monkton** N York
117 G3 **Bishop Norton** Lincs
35 G4 **Bishopsbourne** Kent
40 B7 **Bishops Cannings** Wilts
83 G5 **Bishop's Castle** Shrops
27 G8 **Bishop's Caundle** Dorset
55 L3 **Bishop's Cleeve** Gloucs
70 B5 **Bishop's Frome** Herefs
61 G4 **Bishop's Green** Essex
25 J6 **Bishops Hull** Somset
72 E3 **Bishop's Itchington** Warwks
25 J5 **Bishops Lydeard** Somset
55 J3 **Bishop's Norton** Gloucs
24 B6 **Bishop's Nympton** Devon
99 H6 **Bishop's Offley** Staffs
60 D4 **Bishop's Stortford** Herts
29 L5 **Bishop's Sutton** Hants
72 C3 **Bishop's Tachbrook** Warwks
23 J5 **Bishop's Tawton** Devon
7 K2 **Bishopsteignton** Devon
29 J7 **Bishopstoke** Hants
51 H7 **Bishopston** Swans
58 D6 **Bishopstone** Bucks
19 M5 **Bishopstone** E Susx
69 H5 **Bishopstone** Herefs
47 K6 **Bishopstone** Kent
40 E4 **Bishopstone** Swindn
28 B6 **Bishopstone** Wilts
27 K3 **Bishopstrow** Wilts
38 E7 **Bishop Sutton** BaNES
29 K7 **Bishop's Waltham** Hants
25 K8 **Bishopswood** Somset
84 E2 **Bishop's Wood** Staffs
38 E6 **Bishopsworth** Bristl
132 D6 **Bishop Thornton** N York
124 F2 **Bishopthorpe** C York
141 J3 **Bishopton** Darltn
174 E4 **Bishopton** Rens
134 C7 **Bishop Wilton** E R Yk
38 B3 **Bishton** Newpt
100 A7 **Bishton** Staffs
55 K6 **Bisley** Gloucs
42 F8 **Bisley** Surrey
3 K3 **Bissoe** Cnwll
15 L3 **Bisterne** Hants
103 G6 **Bitchfield** Lincs
23 J3 **Bittadon** Devon
6 F4 **Bittaford** Devon
83 L7 **Bitterley** Shrops
29 J8 **Bitterne** C Sotn
87 G6 **Bitteswell** Leics
39 G6 **Bitton** S Glos
42 B4 **Bix** Oxon
235 c5 **Bixter** Shet
87 H4 **Blaby** Leics
179 H7 **Blackadder** Border
7 J5 **Blackawton** Devon
12 E1 **Blackborough** Devon
90 F1 **Blackborough End** Norfk
56 F6 **Black Bourton** Oxon
20 B2 **Blackboys** E Susx
101 G3 **Blackbrook** Derbys
112 D3 **Blackbrook** St Hel
99 H5 **Blackbrook** Staffs
206 F3 **Blackburn** Abers
121 K5 **Blackburn** Bl w D
176 D5 **Blackburn** W Loth
121 K5 **Blackburn with Darwen Services** Bl w D
150 F2 **Black Callerton** N u Ty
164 C7 **Blackcraig** E Ayrs
182 D1 **Black Crofts** Ag & B
207 H3 **Blackdog** Abers
11 J3 **Black Dog** Devon
13 K2 **Blackdown** Dorset
115 G2 **Blacker Hill** Barns
45 J5 **Blackfen** Gt Lon
16 E3 **Blackfield** Hants
185 J5 **Blackford** P & K
26 B2 **Blackford** Somset
26 F6 **Blackford** Somset
101 G8 **Blackfordby** Leics
177 G4 **Blackhall** C Edin
151 K6 **Blackhall Colliery** Dur
150 E4 **Blackhall Mill** Gatesd
166 F2 **Blackhaugh** Border
45 G5 **Blackheath** Gt Lon
85 H6 **Blackheath** Sandw
93 J8 **Blackheath** Suffk
31 G3 **Blackheath** Surrey
217 K3 **Blackhill** Abers
217 K5 **Blackhill** Abers
150 D5 **Blackhill** Dur
217 H5 **Blackhill of Clackriach** Abers
12 C4 **Blackhorse** Devon
165 K7 **Blacklaw** D & G
113 J2 **Blackley** Manch
113 J2 **Blackley Crematorium** Manch
195 J4 **Blacklunans** P & K
69 K6 **Blackmarstone** Herefs
36 E3 **Blackmill** Brdgnd
30 C5 **Blackmoor** Hants
38 C7 **Blackmoor** N Som
123 G7 **Blackmoorfoot** Kirk
60 F7 **Blackmore** Essex
61 H2 **Blackmore End** Essex
176 E3 **Blackness** Falk
30 D3 **Blacknest** Hants
61 J4 **Black Notley** Essex

122 C3 **Blacko** Lancs
51 J7 **Black Pill** Swans
120 D4 **Blackpool** Bpool
7 K6 **Blackpool** Devon
120 D4 *Blackpool Airport* Lancs
176 B5 **Blackridge** W Loth
121 J7 **Blackrod** Bolton
214 E6 **Blacksboat** Moray
147 J2 **Blackshaw** D & G
122 E5 **Blackshaw Head** Calder
19 H3 **Blackstone** W Susx
93 K6 **Black Street** Suffk
57 L4 **Blackthorn** Oxon
77 K2 **Blackthorpe** Suffk
125 J5 **Blacktoft** E R Yk
207 G4 **Blacktop** C Aber
10 C4 **Black Torrington** Devon
100 E3 **Blackwall** Derbys
3 J3 **Blackwater** Cnwll
42 D7 **Blackwater** Hants
17 G5 **Blackwater** IoW
25 K7 **Blackwater** Somset
162 A4 **Blackwaterfoot** N Ayrs
148 D4 **Blackwell** Cumb
101 H2 **Blackwell** Derbys
114 C6 **Blackwell** Derbys
72 B5 **Blackwell** Warwks
71 H1 **Blackwell** Worcs
37 J2 **Blackwood** Caerph
154 F5 **Blackwood** D & G
164 F1 **Blackwood** S Lans
111 L7 **Blacon** Ches W
145 J4 **Bladnoch** D & G
57 J5 **Bladon** Oxon
65 H5 **Blaenannerch** Cerdgn
96 A4 **Blaenau Ffestiniog** Gwynd
53 K6 **Blaenavon** Torfn
65 H6 **Blaenffos** Pembks
36 D2 **Blaengarw** Brdgnd
52 D6 **Blaengwrach** Neath
36 D2 **Blaengwynfi** Neath
66 E2 **Blaenpennal** Cerdgn
80 D7 **Blaenplwyf** Cerdgn
65 J5 **Blaenporth** Cerdgn
52 E7 **Blaenrhondda** Rhondd
50 B1 **Blaenwaun** Carmth
50 D1 **Blaen-y-Coed** Carmth
52 E7 **Blaen-y-cwm** Rhondd
38 D8 **Blagdon** N Som
25 K7 **Blagdon** Somset
7 K4 **Blagdon** Torbay
25 K7 **Blagdon Hill** Somset
191 K2 **Blaich** Highld
190 D3 **Blain** Highld
53 J6 **Blaina** Blae G
194 D4 **Blair Atholl** P & K
184 F7 **Blair Drummond** Stirlg
195 J7 **Blairgowrie** P & K
176 D2 **Blairhall** Fife
185 K7 **Blairingone** P & K
185 H7 **Blairlogie** Stirlg
173 L2 **Blairmore** Ag & B
228 C4 **Blairmore** Highld
173 G4 **Blair's Ferry** Ag & B
55 G5 **Blaisdon** Gloucs
84 E7 **Blakebrook** Worcs
84 F7 **Blakedown** Worcs
61 H4 **Blake End** Essex
112 D7 **Blakemere** Ches W
69 G6 **Blakemere** Herefs
85 H3 **Blakenall Heath** Wsall
54 F6 **Blakeney** Gloucs
106 B4 **Blakeney** Norfk
99 G3 **Blakenhall** Ches E
85 G4 **Blakenhall** Wolves
73 J4 **Blakesley** Nhants
150 B5 **Blanchland** Nthumb
15 G2 **Blandford Forum** Dorset
15 G2 **Blandford St Mary** Dorset
174 F3 **Blanefield** Stirlg
103 H1 **Blankney** Lincs
175 J6 **Blantyre** S Lans
191 L3 **Blar a' Chaorainn** Highld
202 F6 **Blargie** Highld
191 L3 **Blarmachfoldach** Highld
88 B4 **Blaston** Leics
88 D4 **Blatherwycke** Nhants
129 G2 **Blawith** Cumb
154 B5 **Blawquhairn** D & G
79 H3 **Blaxhall** Suffk
116 A2 **Blaxton** Donc
150 F3 **Blaydon** Gatesd
26 C3 **Bleadney** Somset
25 M1 **Bleadon** N Som
34 F3 **Blean** Kent
102 B3 **Bleasby** Notts
187 G4 **Blebocraigs** Fife
68 E2 **Bleddfa** Powys
56 E4 **Bledington** Gloucs
58 C7 **Bledlow** Bucks
42 D2 **Bledlow Ridge** Bucks
178 B6 **Blegbie** E Loth
138 F2 **Blencarn** Cumb
147 L5 **Blencogo** Cumb
30 B8 **Blendworth** Hants
147 L6 **Blennerhasset** Cumb
57 J4 **Bletchingdon** Oxon
32 B3 **Bletchingley** Surrey
58 E2 **Bletchley** M Keyn
98 F5 **Bletchley** Shrops
49 H4 **Bletherston** Pembks
74 E3 **Bletsoe** Bed
41 K4 **Blewbury** Oxon
106 E6 **Blickling** Norfk
101 L2 **Blidworth** Notts
101 L2 **Blidworth Bottoms** Notts
147 K7 **Blindcrake** Cumb
32 C4 **Blindley Heath** Surrey
5 H2 **Blisland** Cnwll
28 D8 **Blissford** Hants
84 D8 **Bliss Gate** Worcs
73 K4 **Blisworth** Nhants
100 B8 **Blithbury** Staffs
71 L7 **Blockley** Gloucs
93 G2 **Blofield** Norfk
93 G2 **Blofield Heath** Norfk
92 B7 **Blo Norton** Norfk
167 J4 **Bloomfield** Border
100 C3 **Blore** Staffs
72 E7 **Bloxham** Oxon
103 H2 **Bloxholm** Lincs
85 H3 **Bloxwich** Wsall
15 G4 **Bloxworth** Dorset
132 B7 **Blubberhouses** N York
24 F3 **Blue Anchor** Somset
46 C7 **Blue Bell Hill** Kent
114 C5 **Blue John Cavern** Derbys
111 J2 **Blundellsands** Sefton
93 L4 **Blundeston** Suffk
75 H4 **Blunham** C Beds
40 C3 **Blunsdon St Andrew** Swindn
84 F8 **Bluntington** Worcs
89 L8 **Bluntisham** Cambs
116 F3 **Blyborough** Lincs
93 J7 **Blyford** Suffk
84 E2 **Blymhill** Staffs
115 L4 **Blyth** Notts
159 H5 **Blyth** Nthumb
165 M1 **Blyth Bridge** Border
93 J7 **Blythburgh** Suffk
159 H5 **Blyth Crematorium** Nthumb
178 D7 **Blythe** Border
116 D3 **Blyton** Lincs
187 J5 **Boarhills** Fife
17 H2 **Boarhunt** Hants
57 L5 **Boarstall** Bucks
222 D6 **Boath** Highld
203 L2 **Boat of Garten** Highld
46 E6 **Bobbing** Kent
84 E5 **Bobbington** Staffs
61 J4 **Bocking** Essex
61 J3 **Bocking Churchstreet** Essex
217 L6 **Boddam** Abers
235 c7 **Boddam** Shet
55 K3 **Boddington** Gloucs
108 D5 **Bodedern** IoA
110 D6 **Bodelwyddan** Denbgs
69 K4 **Bodenham** Herefs
28 D6 **Bodenham** Wilts
69 K4 **Bodenham Moor** Herefs
108 E4 **Bodewryd** IoA
110 F7 **Bodfari** Denbgs
108 F6 **Bodffordd** IoA
94 F5 **Bodfuan** Gwynd
106 D4 **Bodham** Norfk
33 K7 **Bodiam** E Susx
33 K7 **Bodiam Castle** E Susx
72 F6 **Bodicote** Oxon
5 H5 **Bodinnick** Cnwll
20 D3 **Bodle Street Green** E Susx
5 G3 **Bodmin** Cnwll
5 J1 **Bodmin Moor** Cnwll
109 M6 **Bodnant Garden** Conwy
34 E5 **Bodsham** Kent
5 G4 **Bodwen** Cnwll
212 F4 **Bogallan** Highld
217 J7 **Bogbrae** Abers
163 K3 **Bogend** S Ayrs
177 L4 **Boggs Holdings** E Loth
177 H5 **Boghall** Mdloth
176 D5 **Boghall** W Loth
164 F2 **Boghead** S Lans
215 H2 **Bogmoor** Moray
197 G3 **Bogmuir** Abers
216 B5 **Bogniebrae** Abers
18 C6 **Bognor Regis** W Susx
203 L2 **Bogroy** Highld
154 B6 **Bogue** D & G
3 L5 **Bohortha** Cnwll
201 L8 **Bohuntine** Highld
140 F3 **Bolam** Dur
7 G7 **Bolberry** Devon
85 K5 **Boldmere** Birm
16 C3 **Boldre** Hants
140 C4 **Boldron** Dur
116 C4 **Bole** Notts
100 F2 **Bolehill** Derbys
24 E7 **Bolham** Devon
25 J8 **Bolham Water** Devon
3 K1 **Bolingey** Cnwll
113 L6 **Bollington** Ches E
31 L6 **Bolney** W Susx
74 F3 **Bolnhurst** Bed
197 G6 **Bolshan** Angus
115 J7 **Bolsover** Derbys
114 F3 **Bolsterstone** Sheff
133 G3 **Boltby** N York
205 J3 **Boltenstone** Abers
121 L8 **Bolton** Bolton
138 F3 **Bolton** Cumb
178 B4 **Bolton** E Loth
125 J1 **Bolton** E R Yk
169 G6 **Bolton** Nthumb
131 K8 **Bolton Abbey** N York
122 B1 **Bolton by Bowland** Lancs
148 E2 **Boltonfellend** Cumb
147 M6 **Boltongate** Cumb
129 K6 **Bolton le Sands** Lancs
147 M6 **Bolton Low Houses** Cumb
141 G7 **Bolton-on-Swale** N York
124 E3 **Bolton Percy** N York
115 J2 **Bolton Upon Dearne** Barns
121 J7 **Bolton West Services** Lancs
5 J1 **Bolventor** Cnwll
98 C8 **Bomere Heath** Shrops
222 E3 **Bonar Bridge** Highld
182 E2 **Bonawe** Ag & B
126 C7 **Bonby** N Linc
65 H6 **Boncath** Pembks
167 J6 **Bonchester Bridge** Border
10 F4 **Bondleigh** Devon
121 G2 **Bonds** Lancs
176 D3 **Bo'ness** Falk
85 J2 **Boney Hay** Staffs
174 D3 **Bonhill** W Duns
84 E3 **Boningale** Shrops
167 K5 **Bonjedward** Border
175 L6 **Bonkle** N Lans
196 F7 **Bonnington** Angus
34 E7 **Bonnington** Kent
186 F6 **Bonnybank** Fife
175 L3 **Bonnybridge** Falk
217 G4 **Bonnykelly** Abers
177 J5 **Bonnyrigg** Mdloth
196 B8 **Bonnyton** Angus
100 F2 **Bonsall** Derbys
155 M7 **Bonshaw Tower** D & G
81 J4 **Bont-Dolgadfan** Powys
80 F6 **Bont-goch or Elerch** Cerdgn
66 E2 **Bontnewydd** Cerdgn
95 H1 **Bontnewydd** Gwynd
97 G2 **Bontuchel** Denbgs
37 G5 **Bonvilston** V Glam
23 H4 **Boode** Devon
42 D3 **Booker** Bucks
167 J1 **Boon** Border
142 E4 **Boosbeck** R & Cl
61 K2 **Boose's Green** Essex
137 G6 **Boot** Cumb
122 F5 **Booth** Calder
103 G2 **Boothby Graffoe** Lincs
102 F6 **Boothby Pagnell** Lincs
125 H5 **Boothferry** E R Yk
113 G2 **Boothstown** Salfd
128 D2 **Bootle** Cumb
111 K3 **Bootle** Sefton
70 B1 **Boraston** Shrops
236 e2 **Bordeaux** Guern
34 B3 **Borden** Kent
157 G5 **Border Forest Park**
167 H3 **Borders Crematorium** Border
61 J6 **Boreham** Essex
27 K3 **Boreham** Wilts
20 D4 **Boreham Street** E Susx
44 D2 **Borehamwood** Herts
155 L4 **Boreland** D & G
208 C4 **Boreraig** Highld
232 f1 **Borgh** W Isls
233 b9 **Borgh** W Isls
229 K4 **Borgie** Highld
146 B5 **Borgue** D & G
227 K4 **Borgue** Highld
77 J6 **Borley** Essex
218 B7 **Borneskitaig** Highld
146 A5 **Borness** D & G
132 F6 **Boroughbridge** N York
33 G2 **Borough Green** Kent
101 H5 **Borrowash** Derbys
132 F2 **Borrowby** N York
176 D3 **Borrowstoun** Falk
46 B6 **Borstal** Medway
80 E5 **Borth** Cerdgn
166 F6 **Borthwickbrae** Border
166 F6 **Borthwickshiels** Border
95 K5 **Borth-y-Gest** Gwynd

209 G5 **Borve** Highld
232 d4 **Borve** W Isls
232 f1 **Borve** W Isls
233 b9 **Borve** W Isls
129 L5 **Borwick** Lancs
70 C5 **Bosbury** Herefs
8 E6 **Boscastle** Cnwll
15 L4 **Boscombe** Bmouth
28 D4 **Boscombe** Wilts
17 L2 **Bosham** W Susx
49 G8 **Bosherston** Pembks
113 K7 **Bosley** Ches E
133 L7 **Bossall** N York
8 E6 **Bossiney** Cnwll
34 F5 **Bossingham** Kent
24 D2 **Bossington** Somset
112 F7 **Bostock Green** Ches W
104 B4 **Boston** Lincs
104 A4 **Boston Crematorium** Lincs
124 C2 **Boston Spa** Leeds
4 F7 **Boswinger** Cnwll
2 C5 **Botallack** Cnwll
59 M7 **Botany Bay** Gt Lon
92 C7 **Botesdale** Suffk
159 G5 **Bothal** Nthumb
116 A6 **Bothamsall** Notts
147 L6 **Bothel** Cumb
13 L4 **Bothenhampton** Dorset
175 J6 **Bothwell** S Lans
175 J6 **Bothwell Services** S Lans
59 G7 **Botley** Bucks
29 K8 **Botley** Hants
57 J6 **Botley** Oxon
58 B3 **Botolph Claydon** Bucks
19 G4 **Botolphs** W Susx
102 D5 **Bottesford** Leics
116 E1 **Bottesford** N Linc
76 D3 **Bottisham** Cambs
186 F3 **Bottomcraig** Fife
122 D6 **Bottoms** Calder
6 B4 **Botusfleming** Cnwll
94 E6 **Botwnnog** Gwynd
32 E4 **Bough Beech** Kent
68 C6 **Boughrood** Powys
73 L2 **Boughton** Nhants
91 G3 **Boughton** Norfk
116 B7 **Boughton** Notts
34 D5 **Boughton Aluph** Kent
33 K3 **Boughton Green** Kent
33 K3 **Boughton Monchelsea** Kent
34 E3 **Boughton Street** Kent
83 K6 **Bouldon** Shrops
169 K6 **Boulmer** Nthumb
116 F7 **Boultham** Lincs
75 K3 **Bourn** Cambs
103 H7 **Bourne** Lincs
45 J2 **Bournebridge** Essex
85 J6 **Bournebrook** Birm
42 E3 **Bourne End** Bucks
74 D5 **Bourne End** C Beds
59 G6 **Bourne End** Herts
15 K4 **Bournemouth** Bmouth
15 L3 *Bournemouth Airport* Dorset
15 L4 **Bournemouth Crematorium** Bmouth
46 E3 **Bournes Green** Sthend
85 G8 **Bournheath** Worcs
151 H5 **Bournmoor** Dur
85 J7 **Bournville** Birm
27 H5 **Bourton** Dorset
40 E3 **Bourton** Oxon
83 L4 **Bourton** Shrops
40 B7 **Bourton** Wilts
72 E1 **Bourton on Dunsmore** Warwks
56 D2 **Bourton-on-the-Hill** Gloucs
56 D4 **Bourton-on-the-Water** Gloucs
189 G4 **Bousd** Ag & B
129 H3 **Bouth** Cumb
131 L5 **Bouthwaite** N York
28 B7 **Boveridge** Dorset
7 J1 **Bovey Tracey** Devon
59 G7 **Bovingdon** Herts
14 F5 **Bovington Tank Museum** Dorset
11 G4 **Bow** Devon
45 G4 **Bow** Gt Lon
234 b7 **Bow** Ork
74 C7 **Bow Brickhill** M Keyn
55 J6 **Bowbridge** Gloucs
151 H7 **Bowburn** Dur
16 F5 **Bowcombe** IoW
12 E4 **Bowd** Devon
167 H4 **Bowden** Border
39 L6 **Bowden Hill** Wilts
113 H4 **Bowdon** Traffd
231 J3 **Bower** Highld
28 A6 **Bowerchalke** Wilts
231 J3 **Bowermadden** Highld
99 J5 **Bowers** Staffs
46 C3 **Bowers Gifford** Essex
176 F1 **Bowershall** Fife
124 B5 **Bower's Row** Leeds
140 C4 **Bowes** Dur
121 G2 **Bowgreave** Lancs
147 H2 **Bowhouse** D & G
167 G2 **Bowland** Border
69 K4 **Bowley** Herefs
30 E4 **Bowlhead Green** Surrey
123 H4 **Bowling** C Brad
174 E4 **Bowling** W Duns
137 J7 **Bowmanstead** Cumb
170 F6 **Bowmore** Ag & B
147 L3 **Bowness-on-Solway** Cumb
137 L7 **Bowness-on-Windermere** Cumb
186 E5 **Bow of Fife** Fife
196 E6 **Bowriefauld** Angus
168 E2 **Bowsden** Nthumb
80 E6 **Bow Street** Cerdgn
55 K7 **Box** Gloucs
39 J6 **Box** Wilts
77 L6 **Boxford** Suffk
41 H6 **Boxford** W Berk
18 B4 **Boxgrove** W Susx
33 K2 **Boxley** Kent
59 H6 **Boxmoor** Herts
62 B2 **Boxted** Essex
62 B2 **Boxted** Essex
77 J4 **Boxted** Suffk
62 B2 **Boxted Cross** Essex
75 L2 **Boxworth** Cambs
47 L6 **Boyden Gate** Kent
100 D5 **Boylestone** Derbys
216 C2 **Boyndie** Abers
217 G2 **Boyndlie** Abers
135 H6 **Boynton** E R Yk
197 G6 **Boysack** Angus
9 J6 **Boyton** Cnwll
79 H5 **Boyton** Suffk
27 L4 **Boyton** Wilts
61 G6 **Boyton Cross** Essex
77 G5 **Boyton End** Suffk
74 C3 **Bozeat** Nhants
34 E6 **Brabourne** Kent
34 E6 **Brabourne Lees** Kent
231 K2 **Brabstermire** Highld
208 E6 **Bracadale** Highld
88 F2 **Braceborough** Lincs
117 G7 **Bracebridge Heath** Lincs
116 F7 **Bracebridge Low Fields** Lincs
103 G5 **Braceby** Lincs
122 C2 **Bracewell** Lancs
101 G2 **Brackenfield** Derbys
175 K5 **Brackenhirst** N Lans
17 L3 **Bracklesham** W Susx
201 J8 **Brackletter** Highld
73 H6 **Brackley** Nhants
42 E6 **Bracknell** Br For
185 H5 **Braco** P & K
215 L4 **Bracobrae** Moray
92 E4 **Bracon Ash** Norfk
199 L6 **Bracora** Highld
199 L6 **Bracorina** Highld
100 D3 **Bradbourne** Derbys
141 H2 **Bradbury** Dur
73 J5 **Bradden** Nhants
42 D2 **Bradenham** Bucks
39 M4 **Bradenstoke** Wilts
12 D1 **Bradfield** Devon
62 D2 **Bradfield** Essex
106 F5 **Bradfield** Norfk
114 F3 **Bradfield** Sheff
41 L6 **Bradfield** W Berk
77 K3 **Bradfield Combust** Suffk
99 G2 **Bradfield Green** Ches E
62 D3 **Bradfield Heath** Essex
77 K3 **Bradfield St Clare** Suffk
77 K3 **Bradfield St George** Suffk
123 H4 **Bradford** C Brad
9 L4 **Bradford** Devon
26 E8 **Bradford Abbas** Dorset
39 J7 **Bradford Leigh** Wilts
39 J7 **Bradford-on-Avon** Wilts
25 J6 **Bradford-on-Tone** Somset
14 C4 **Bradford Peverell** Dorset
23 J5 **Bradiford** Devon
17 H5 **Brading** IoW
100 E4 **Bradley** Derbys
29 M3 **Bradley** Hants
118 C1 **Bradley** NE Lin
99 K8 **Bradley** Staffs
85 G4 **Bradley** Wolves
71 H3 **Bradley** Worcs
71 H3 **Bradley Green** Worcs
100 B4 **Bradley in the Moors** Staffs
38 E4 **Bradley Stoke** S Glos
101 L6 **Bradmore** Notts
12 C2 **Bradninch** Devon
100 A2 **Bradnop** Staffs
13 L4 **Bradpole** Dorset
123 G4 **Bradshaw** Calder
9 K8 **Bradstone** Devon
113 H8 **Bradwall Green** Ches E
114 D5 **Bradwell** Derbys
61 J4 **Bradwell** Essex
74 B6 **Bradwell** M Keyn
93 K3 **Bradwell** Norfk
99 J3 **Bradwell Crematorium** Staffs
62 B6 **Bradwell-on-Sea** Essex
62 B6 **Bradwell Waterside** Essex
9 J3 **Bradworthy** Devon
213 G2 **Brae** Highld
235 c4 **Brae** Shet
175 K3 **Braeface** Falk
197 H5 **Braehead** Angus
145 J4 **Braehead** D & G
176 C7 **Braehead** S Lans
204 E6 **Braemar** Abers
221 G5 **Braemore** Highld
227 J3 **Braemore** Highld
201 L6 **Brae Roy Lodge** Highld
173 L4 **Braeside** Inver
195 L5 **Braes of Coul** Angus
215 J3 **Braes of Enzie** Moray
234 d4 **Braeswick** Ork
182 D6 **Braevallich** Ag & B
141 H3 **Brafferton** Darltn
132 F5 **Brafferton** N York
74 B3 **Brafield-on-the-Green** Nhants
232 f2 **Bragar** W Isls
59 L4 **Bragbury End** Herts
175 L8 **Braidwood** S Lans
100 E4 **Brailsford** Derbys
61 J4 **Braintree** Essex
78 D1 **Braiseworth** Suffk
29 G6 **Braishfield** Hants
137 H3 **Braithwaite** Cumb
115 K3 **Braithwell** Donc
19 G4 **Bramber** W Susx
86 E5 **Bramcote** Warwks
101 J5 **Bramcote Crematorium** Notts
29 L5 **Bramdean** Hants
93 G3 **Bramerton** Norfk
59 M5 **Bramfield** Herts
93 H8 **Bramfield** Suffk
78 D5 **Bramford** Suffk
113 K5 **Bramhall** Stockp
124 C2 **Bramham** Leeds
123 K2 **Bramhope** Leeds
41 M8 **Bramley** Hants
123 K4 **Bramley** Leeds
115 J3 **Bramley** Rothm
31 G3 **Bramley** Surrey
41 M8 **Bramley Corner** Hants
35 G4 **Bramling** Kent
11 L5 **Brampford Speke** Devon
75 J1 **Brampton** Cambs
138 F3 **Brampton** Cumb
148 F3 **Brampton** Cumb
116 D5 **Brampton** Lincs
106 F7 **Brampton** Norfk
115 H2 **Brampton** Rothm
93 J6 **Brampton** Suffk
54 E3 **Brampton Abbotts** Herefs
87 L6 **Brampton Ash** Nhants
83 G8 **Brampton Bryan** Herefs
115 J4 **Brampton-en-le-Morthen** Rothm
100 B6 **Bramshall** Staffs
28 F7 **Bramshaw** Hants
30 D5 **Bramshott** Hants
26 B5 **Bramwell** Somset
190 B3 **Branault** Highld
105 J4 **Brancaster** Norfk
105 J4 **Brancaster Staithe** Norfk
150 F7 **Brancepeth** Dur
214 D4 **Branchill** Moray
214 F1 **Branderburgh** Moray
126 E2 **Brandesburton** E R Yk
78 F3 **Brandeston** Suffk
106 D7 **Brandiston** Norfk
151 G6 **Brandon** Dur
102 E3 **Brandon** Lincs
91 H6 **Brandon** Suffk
86 E7 **Brandon** Warwks
92 C2 **Brandon Parva** Norfk
133 J5 **Brandsby** N York
117 G3 **Brandy Wharf** Lincs
61 G3 **Bran End** Essex
15 K4 **Branksome** Poole
15 K4 **Branksome Park** Poole
29 H3 **Bransbury** Hants
116 E5 **Bransby** Lincs
12 F5 **Branscombe** Devon
70 E4 **Bransford** Worcs
16 A3 **Bransgore** Hants
126 D4 **Bransholme** C KuH
84 B7 **Bransley** Shrops

102 D6 **Branston** Leics
117 G7 **Branston** Lincs
100 E7 **Branston** Staffs
117 H7 **Branston Booths** Lincs
17 G5 **Branstone** IoW
102 E2 **Brant Broughton** Lincs
78 D7 **Brantham** Suffk
136 E3 **Branthwaite** Cumb
148 B7 **Branthwaite** Cumb
125 L5 **Brantingham** E R Yk
115 M2 **Branton** Donc
168 F6 **Branton** Nthumb
132 F6 **Branton Green** N York
168 D2 **Branxton** Nthumb
100 E2 **Brassington** Derbys
32 E3 **Brasted** Kent
32 E3 **Brasted Chart** Kent
206 D5 **Brathens** Abers
119 G8 **Bratoft** Lincs
116 F5 **Brattleby** Lincs
27 K2 **Bratton** Wilts
84 B2 **Bratton** Wrekin
10 C6 **Bratton Clovelly** Devon
23 K4 **Bratton Fleming** Devon
26 F5 **Bratton Seymour** Somset
60 C3 **Braughing** Herts
73 G2 **Braunston** Nhants
88 B3 **Braunston** Rutlnd
87 G3 **Braunstone** Leics
23 H4 **Braunton** Devon
134 B4 **Brawby** N York
230 B3 **Brawl** Highld
42 E4 **Bray** W & M
87 L6 **Braybrooke** Nhants
23 L4 **Brayford** Devon
5 M2 **Bray Shop** Cnwll
124 F4 **Brayton** N York
42 E4 **Braywick** W & M
59 J4 **Breachwood Green** Herts
101 G5 **Breadsall** Derbys
55 G7 **Breadstone** Gloucs
3 G5 **Breage** Cnwll
212 D5 **Breakachy** Highld
43 H3 **Breakspear Crematorium** Gt Lon
222 C3 **Brealangwell Lodge** Highld
54 E6 **Bream** Gloucs
28 D7 **Breamore** Hants
25 L1 **Brean** Somset
232 d3 **Breanais** W Isls
132 E7 **Brearton** N York
232 e2 **Breascleit** W Isls
232 e2 **Breasclete** W Isls
101 J5 **Breaston** Derbys
66 C7 **Brechfa** Carmth
196 F4 **Brechin** Angus
91 L5 **Breckles** Norfk
53 G3 **Brecon** Powys
52 F3 **Brecon Beacons National Park**
113 L3 **Bredbury** Stockp
21 G3 **Brede** E Susx
69 L3 **Bredenbury** Herefs
78 F4 **Bredfield** Suffk
34 B3 **Bredgar** Kent
46 D7 **Bredhurst** Kent
71 G6 **Bredon** Worcs
71 G7 **Bredon's Hardwick** Worcs
71 G6 **Bredon's Norton** Worcs
69 G5 **Bredwardine** Herefs
101 H7 **Breedon on the Hill** Leics
176 C6 **Breich** W Loth
121 L8 **Breightmet** Bolton
125 G4 **Breighton** E R Yk
69 J6 **Breinton** Herefs
39 L5 **Bremhill** Wilts
33 H5 **Brenchley** Kent
24 B2 **Brendon** Devon
172 E2 **Brenfield** Ag & B
232 d3 **Brenish** W Isls
77 L5 **Brent Eleigh** Suffk
44 D5 **Brentford** Gt Lon
102 C8 **Brentingby** Leics
25 M2 **Brent Knoll** Somset
7 G4 **Brent Mill** Devon
60 C2 **Brent Pelham** Herts
45 L2 **Brentwood** Essex
21 K1 **Brenzett** Kent
34 D8 **Brenzett Green** Kent
85 J1 **Brereton** Staffs
113 H8 **Brereton Green** Ches E
235 d6 **Bressay** Shet
92 C7 **Bressingham** Norfk
100 F7 **Bretby** Derbys
100 F7 **Bretby Crematorium** Derbys
86 E7 **Bretford** Warwks
71 K5 **Bretforton** Worcs
121 G6 **Bretherton** Lancs
235 d5 **Brettabister** Shet
91 L6 **Brettenham** Norfk
77 L4 **Brettenham** Suffk
111 K8 **Bretton** Flints
84 F2 **Brewood** Staffs
14 F4 **Briantspuddle** Dorset
60 A6 **Brickendon** Herts
59 J7 **Bricket Wood** Herts
114 F5 **Brick Houses** Sheff
71 H6 **Bricklehampton** Worcs
237 e2 **Bride** IoM
147 K7 **Bridekirk** Cumb
10 D6 **Bridestowe** Devon
216 B6 **Brideswell** Abers
11 J7 **Bridford** Devon
35 G4 **Bridge** Kent
26 E6 **Bridgehampton** Somset
132 E5 **Bridge Hewick** N York
150 D5 **Bridgehill** Dur
17 H2 **Bridgemary** Hants
215 L7 **Bridgend** Abers
161 K2 **Bridgend** Ag & B
171 G6 **Bridgend** Ag & B
196 E3 **Bridgend** Angus
36 E4 **Bridgend** Brdgnd
165 L7 **Bridgend** D & G
6 E6 **Bridgend** Devon
186 F5 **Bridgend** Fife
215 J7 **Bridgend** Moray
186 B3 **Bridgend** P & K
176 E3 **Bridgend** W Loth
195 L5 **Bridgend of Lintrathen** Angus
206 B2 **Bridge of Alford** Abers
185 G7 **Bridge of Allan** Stirlg
204 E2 **Bridge of Avon** Moray
214 E7 **Bridge of Avon** Moray
193 J6 **Bridge of Balgie** P & K
195 J4 **Bridge of Brewlands** Angus
204 D2 **Bridge of Brown** Highld
195 J6 **Bridge of Cally** P & K
206 C6 **Bridge of Canny** Abers
195 K5 **Bridge of Craigisla** Angus
146 C3 **Bridge of Dee** D & G
207 H4 **Bridge of Don** C Aber
213 L6 **Bridge of Dulsie** Highld
206 C7 **Bridge of Dye** Abers
186 B4 **Bridge of Earn** P & K
193 H5 **Bridge of Ericht** P & K
206 D6 **Bridge of Feugh** Abers
230 F2 **Bridge of Forss** Highld
205 H6 **Bridge of Gairn** Abers
193 H5 **Bridge of Gaur** P & K
216 B4 **Bridge of Marnoch** Abers
192 E7 **Bridge of Orchy** Ag & B
194 D4 **Bridge of Tilt** P & K
215 J3 **Bridge of Tynet** Moray
235 b5 **Bridge of Walls** Shet
174 D5 **Bridge of Weir** Rens
9 H4 **Bridgerule** Devon
69 H6 **Bridge Sollers** Herefs
77 K5 **Bridge Street** Suffk
24 E5 **Bridgetown** Somset
112 C7 **Bridge Trafford** Ches W
91 L6 **Bridgham** Norfk
84 C5 **Bridgnorth** Shrops
25 L4 **Bridgwater** Somset
25 L4 **Bridgwater Services** Somset
135 J6 **Bridlington** E R Yk
13 L4 **Bridport** Dorset
54 E3 **Bridstow** Herefs
122 C3 **Brierfield** Lancs
124 C7 **Brierley** Barns
54 F5 **Brierley** Gloucs
85 G6 **Brierley Hill** Dudley
117 G1 **Brigg** N Linc
107 G6 **Briggate** Norfk
143 H5 **Briggswath** N York
136 F2 **Brigham** Cumb
135 G8 **Brigham** E R Yk
123 H6 **Brighouse** Calder
16 E5 **Brighstone** IoW
57 G7 **Brighthampton** Oxon
10 E5 **Brightley** Devon
20 D2 **Brightling** E Susx
62 C5 **Brightlingsea** Essex
19 J5 **Brighton** Br & H
111 J2 **Brighton le Sands** Sefton
176 C3 **Brightons** Falk
41 H5 **Brightwalton** W Berk
78 F5 **Brightwell** Suffk
41 M2 **Brightwell Baldwin** Oxon
41 L3 **Brightwell-cum-Sotwell** Oxon
42 A2 **Brightwell Upperton** Oxon
140 D5 **Brignall** Dur
184 C6 **Brig o'Turk** Stirlg
118 C2 **Brigsley** NE Lin
129 K2 **Brigsteer** Cumb
88 D6 **Brigstock** Nhants
58 A5 **Brill** Bucks
3 J5 **Brill** Cnwll
68 F5 **Brilley** Herefs
69 K2 **Brimfield** Herefs
69 K2 **Brimfield Cross** Herefs
115 H6 **Brimington** Derbys
7 J1 **Brimley** Devon
55 L5 **Brimpsfield** Gloucs
41 K7 **Brimpton** W Berk
55 K7 **Brimscombe** Gloucs
111 J5 **Brimstage** Wirral
115 F4 **Brincliffe** Sheff
125 H4 **Brind** E R Yk
235 c5 **Brindister** Shet
121 J5 **Brindle** Lancs
84 E2 **Brineton** Staffs
88 B5 **Bringhurst** Leics
70 C4 **Bringsty Common** Herefs
88 F7 **Brington** Cambs
106 C5 **Briningham** Norfk
118 E6 **Brinkhill** Lincs
76 F4 **Brinkley** Cambs
86 E7 **Brinklow** Warwks
40 A4 **Brinkworth** Wilts
121 J6 **Brinscall** Lancs
101 J3 **Brinsley** Notts
115 H4 **Brinsworth** Rothm
106 C5 **Brinton** Norfk
234 c5 **Brinyan** Ork
105 M7 **Brisley** Norfk
38 F6 **Brislington** Bristl
34 C6 **Brissenden Green** Kent
38 E5 **Bristol** Bristl
38 D7 *Bristol Airport* N Som
38 E5 **Bristol Zoo** Bristl
106 C6 **Briston** Norfk
28 D5 **Britford** Wilts
53 J7 **Brithdir** Caerph
96 B8 **Brithdir** Gwynd
33 J2 **British Legion Village** Kent
51 L6 **Briton Ferry** Neath
42 A2 **Britwell Salome** Oxon
7 L5 **Brixham** Torbay
6 E5 **Brixton** Devon
44 F5 **Brixton** Gt Lon
27 K4 **Brixton Deverill** Wilts
73 L1 **Brixworth** Nhants
56 F6 **Brize Norton** Oxon
56 F6 *Brize Norton Airport* Oxon
70 F2 **Broad Alley** Worcs
40 D3 **Broad Blunsdon** Swindn
113 M3 **Broadbottom** Tamesd
17 M2 **Broadbridge** W Susx
31 J5 **Broadbridge Heath** W Susx
71 L6 **Broad Campden** Gloucs
123 G6 **Broad Carr** Calder
28 B6 **Broad Chalke** Wilts
12 C3 **Broadclyst** Devon
174 C4 **Broadfield** Inver
199 K2 **Broadford** Highld
31 H6 **Broadford Bridge** W Susx
166 C7 **Broadgairhill** Border
70 D4 **Broad Green** Worcs
179 H7 **Broadhaugh** Border
48 E5 **Broad Haven** Pembks
113 H4 **Broadheath** Traffd
12 E2 **Broadhembury** Devon
7 J3 **Broadhempston** Devon
40 C5 **Broad Hinton** Wilts
21 G2 **Broadland Row** E Susx
41 H7 **Broad Layings** Hants
215 J3 **Broadley** Moray
71 K5 **Broad Marston** Worcs
14 D5 **Broadmayne** Dorset
49 J6 **Broadmoor** Pembks
13 K3 **Broadoak** Dorset
20 C2 **Broad Oak** E Susx
21 G2 **Broad Oak** E Susx
54 C4 **Broad Oak** Herefs
35 G3 **Broad Oak** Kent
112 D3 **Broad Oak** St Hel
61 H5 **Broad's Green** Essex
35 K2 **Broadstairs** Kent
15 J4 **Broadstone** Poole
83 K5 **Broadstone** Shrops
21 H3 **Broad Street** E Susx
33 L2 **Broad Street** Kent
40 C5 **Broad Town** Wilts
70 D4 **Broadwas** Worcs
59 L4 **Broadwater** Herts
18 F5 **Broadwater** W Susx
84 E7 **Broadwaters** Worcs
48 E5 **Broadway** Pembks
25 L7 **Broadway** Somset
71 K6 **Broadway** Worcs
54 E5 **Broadwell** Gloucs
56 D3 **Broadwell** Gloucs
56 E6 **Broadwell** Oxon
72 F2 **Broadwell** Warwks
13 K2 **Broadwindsor** Dorset
10 F4 **Broadwood Kelly** Devon

9 K6 **Broadwoodwidger** Devon
209 J5 **Brochel** Highld
182 E2 **Brochroy** Ag & B
70 D4 **Brockamin** Worcs
29 L7 **Brockbridge** Hants
92 E7 **Brockdish** Norfk
16 C3 **Brockenhurst** Hants
164 F2 **Brocketsbrae** S Lans
78 D2 **Brockford Street** Suffk
73 J2 **Brockhall** Nhants
31 K2 **Brockham** Surrey
56 B4 **Brockhampton** Gloucs
17 K2 **Brockhampton** Hants
54 E2 **Brockhampton** Herefs
70 C4 **Brockhampton Estate** Herefs
123 H7 **Brockholes** Kirk
126 E7 **Brocklesby** Lincs
38 C6 **Brockley** N Som
77 J1 **Brockley** Suffk
77 G5 **Brockley Green** Suffk
77 J4 **Brockley Green** Suffk
83 G3 **Brockton** Shrops
83 G6 **Brockton** Shrops
83 L5 **Brockton** Shrops
54 D7 **Brockweir** Gloucs
55 K5 **Brockworth** Gloucs
99 L8 **Brocton** Staffs
162 C3 **Brodick** N Ayrs
214 B3 **Brodie** Moray
115 J1 **Brodsworth** Donc
218 C7 **Brogaig** Highld
39 K3 **Brokenborough** Wilts
113 K6 **Broken Cross** Ches E
27 J2 **Brokerswood** Wilts
111 K5 **Bromborough** Wirral
92 D7 **Brome** Suffk
92 D7 **Brome Street** Suffk
79 G4 **Bromeswell** Suffk
147 L5 **Bromfield** Cumb
83 J7 **Bromfield** Shrops
74 E4 **Bromham** Bed
39 L7 **Bromham** Wilts
45 H6 **Bromley** Gt Lon
84 D4 **Bromley** Shrops
46 C6 **Brompton** Medway
141 J7 **Brompton** N York
134 E3 **Brompton-by-Sawdon** N York
140 F7 **Brompton-on-Swale** N York
25 G5 **Brompton Ralph** Somset
24 E5 **Brompton Regis** Somset
70 D7 **Bromsberrow** Gloucs
55 G2 **Bromsberrow Heath** Gloucs
71 G1 **Bromsgrove** Worcs
70 B4 **Bromyard** Herefs
66 E2 **Bronant** Cerdgn
65 K5 **Brongest** Cerdgn
98 C4 **Bronington** Wrexhm
68 D7 **Bronllys** Powys
50 E2 **Bronwydd** Carmth
97 K5 **Bronygarth** Shrops
110 A5 **Bron-y-Nant Crematorium** Conwy
28 F8 **Brook** Hants
16 E5 **Brook** IoW
34 E6 **Brook** Kent
30 F4 **Brook** Surrey
93 G4 **Brooke** Norfk
88 B3 **Brooke** Rutlnd
117 K3 **Brookenby** Lincs
174 D5 **Brookfield** Rens
26 F5 **Brookhampton** Somset
28 F8 **Brook Hill** Hants
129 L6 **Brookhouse** Lancs
115 K4 **Brookhouse** Rothm
99 J1 **Brookhouse Green** Ches E
114 B4 **Brookhouses** Derbys
21 K1 **Brookland** Kent
113 H4 **Brooklands** Traffd
59 L7 **Brookmans Park** Herts
45 L2 **Brook Street** Essex
34 C7 **Brook Street** Kent
55 J5 **Brookthorpe** Gloucs
42 F8 **Brookwood** Surrey
75 H6 **Broom** C Beds
115 H3 **Broom** Rothm
71 K4 **Broom** Warwks
93 H5 **Broome** Norfk
83 H7 **Broome** Shrops
84 F7 **Broome** Worcs
113 G4 **Broomedge** Warrtn
61 H5 **Broomfield** Essex
33 L3 **Broomfield** Kent
47 K6 **Broomfield** Kent
25 K5 **Broomfield** Somset
125 K5 **Broomfleet** E R Yk
150 C3 **Broomhaugh** Nthumb
115 H2 **Broom Hill** Barns
101 K3 **Broom Hill** Notts
159 G3 **Broomhill** Nthumb
151 G6 **Broompark** Dur
226 F7 **Brora** Highld
84 C3 **Broseley** Shrops
150 A7 **Brotherlee** Dur
124 D5 **Brotherton** N York
142 E4 **Brotton** R & Cl
230 F4 **Broubster** Highld
139 H4 **Brough** Cumb
125 L5 **Brough** E R Yk
231 J2 **Brough** Highld
102 D2 **Brough** Notts
235 d4 **Brough** Shet
98 E4 **Broughall** Shrops
235 d2 **Brough Lodge** Shet
139 H5 **Brough Sowerby** Cumb
165 L3 **Broughton** Border
89 K7 **Broughton** Cambs
111 K8 **Broughton** Flints
28 F5 **Broughton** Hants
121 G4 **Broughton** Lancs
74 C6 **Broughton** M Keyn
126 B8 **Broughton** N Linc
122 D1 **Broughton** N York
134 B5 **Broughton** N York
88 B7 **Broughton** Nhants
72 E6 **Broughton** Oxon
113 J2 **Broughton** Salfd
36 E6 **Broughton** V Glam
87 G5 **Broughton Astley** Leics
39 K7 **Broughton Gifford** Wilts
71 G3 **Broughton Green** Worcs
71 G4 **Broughton Hackett** Worcs
128 F3 **Broughton-in-Furness** Cumb
145 J6 **Broughton Mains** D & G
128 F2 **Broughton Mills** Cumb
147 J7 **Broughton Moor** Cumb
56 E7 **Broughton Poggs** Oxon
187 H2 **Broughty Ferry** C Dund
29 L4 **Brown Candover** Hants
99 K2 **Brown Edge** Staffs
217 G6 **Brownhill** Abers
187 H4 **Brownhills** Fife
85 J3 **Brownhills** Wsall
41 L7 **Browninghill Green** Hants
99 K2 **Brown Lees** Staffs
15 J5 **Brownsea Island** Dorset
55 K7 **Browns Hill** Gloucs
7 G5 **Brownston** Devon
134 E2 **Broxa** N York
60 B6 **Broxbourne** Herts
178 E3 **Broxburn** E Loth
176 E4 **Broxburn** W Loth
60 F3 **Broxted** Essex
231 K7 **Bruan** Highld
194 C3 **Bruar** P & K
223 K4 **Brucefield** Highld
173 J6 **Bruchag** Ag & B
170 E6 **Bruichladdich** Ag & B
79 G2 **Bruisyard** Suffk
79 G2 **Bruisyard Street** Suffk
125 K8 **Brumby** N Linc
100 C1 **Brund** Staffs
93 G2 **Brundall** Norfk
78 F1 **Brundish** Suffk
78 F1 **Brundish Street** Suffk
190 E3 **Brunery** Highld
159 G7 **Brunswick Village** N u Ty
122 F2 **Brunthwaite** C Brad
87 H5 **Bruntingthorpe** Leics
186 E3 **Brunton** Fife
28 E1 **Brunton** Wilts
11 G4 **Brushford** Devon
24 E6 **Brushford** Somset
27 G4 **Bruton** Somset
70 F2 **Bryan's Green** Worcs
15 G2 **Bryanston** Dorset
155 L7 **Brydekirk** D & G
2 a1 **Bryher** IoS
26 D7 **Brympton** Somset
51 G5 **Bryn** Carmth
36 C3 **Bryn** Neath
51 K3 **Brynamman** Carmth
64 F7 **Brynberian** Pembks
95 H4 **Bryncir** Gwynd
51 L5 **Bryn-coch** Neath
94 D6 **Bryncroes** Gwynd
80 E3 **Bryncrug** Gwynd
97 H3 **Bryneglwys** Denbgs
111 G6 **Brynford** Flints
112 E2 **Bryn Gates** Wigan
108 D6 **Bryngwran** IoA
54 B6 **Bryngwyn** Mons
68 D5 **Bryngwyn** Powys
64 E6 **Bryn-Henllan** Pembks
65 K4 **Brynhoffnant** Cerdgn
53 J5 **Brynmawr** Blae G
94 D5 **Bryn-mawr** Gwynd
36 D4 **Brynmenyn** Brdgnd
51 J6 **Brynmill** Swans
36 F4 **Brynna** Rhondd
109 H8 **Brynrefail** Gwynd
37 G4 **Brynsadler** Rhondd
97 G3 **Bryn Saith Marchog** Denbgs
108 F7 **Brynsiencyn** IoA
109 G5 **Brynteg** IoA
110 B6 **Bryn-y-Maen** Conwy
198 F2 **Bualintur** Highld
86 D8 **Bubbenhall** Warwks
125 H4 **Bubwith** E R Yk
166 E6 **Buccleuch** Border
174 E1 **Buchanan Smithy** Stirlg
217 L5 **Buchanhaven** Abers
185 J2 **Buchanty** P & K
184 F6 **Buchany** Stirlg
184 C8 **Buchlyvie** Stirlg
148 C5 **Buckabank** Cumb
75 H2 **Buckden** Cambs
131 H4 **Buckden** N York
93 H3 **Buckenham** Norfk
12 E3 **Buckerell** Devon
7 H3 **Buckfast** Devon
7 H3 **Buckfastleigh** Devon
186 F7 **Buckhaven** Fife
54 D5 **Buckholt** Mons
27 H6 **Buckhorn Weston** Dorset
45 H2 **Buckhurst Hill** Essex
215 J2 **Buckie** Moray
73 K7 **Buckingham** Bucks
58 E5 **Buckland** Bucks
7 G6 **Buckland** Devon
71 J7 **Buckland** Gloucs
75 L7 **Buckland** Herts
35 J6 **Buckland** Kent
41 G2 **Buckland** Oxon
31 K2 **Buckland** Surrey
22 F7 **Buckland Brewer** Devon
58 F6 **Buckland Common** Bucks
27 H2 **Buckland Dinham** Somset
10 C3 **Buckland Filleigh** Devon
7 G2 **Buckland in the Moor** Devon
6 D3 **Buckland Monachorum** Devon
14 D2 **Buckland Newton** Dorset
14 C6 **Buckland Ripers** Dorset
25 L8 **Buckland St Mary** Somset
7 H6 **Buckland-Tout-Saints** Devon
41 K6 **Bucklebury** W Berk
16 E3 **Bucklers Hard** Hants
78 F6 **Bucklesham** Suffk
111 J8 **Buckley** Flints
113 G5 **Bucklow Hill** Ches E
102 E7 **Buckminster** Leics
99 K3 **Bucknall** C Stke
117 K7 **Bucknall** Lincs
57 K3 **Bucknell** Oxon
83 G8 **Bucknell** Shrops
215 J2 **Buckpool** Moray
207 G4 **Bucksburn** C Aber
22 E6 **Buck's Cross** Devon
31 H5 **Bucks Green** W Susx
121 H6 **Buckshaw Village** Lancs
30 D3 **Bucks Horn Oak** Hants
22 E6 **Buck's Mills** Devon
135 J5 **Buckton** E R Yk
169 G2 **Buckton** Nthumb
89 G7 **Buckworth** Cambs
115 L7 **Budby** Notts
9 G4 **Bude** Cnwll
5 M4 **Budge's Shop** Cnwll
12 D6 **Budleigh Salterton** Devon
3 K5 **Budock Water** Cnwll
99 G4 **Buerton** Ches E
73 J3 **Bugbrooke** Nhants
4 F4 **Bugle** Cnwll
27 H6 **Bugley** Dorset
134 B7 **Bugthorpe** E R Yk
84 B3 **Buildwas** Shrops
68 B4 **Builth Wells** Powys
28 C5 **Bulbridge** Wilts
28 D3 **Bulford** Wilts
98 D2 **Bulkeley** Ches E
86 E6 **Bulkington** Warwks
39 L8 **Bulkington** Wilts
9 K3 **Bulkworthy** Devon
42 E6 **Bullbrook** Br For
29 J3 **Bullington** Hants
117 H6 **Bullington** Lincs
77 J6 **Bulmer** Essex
133 L6 **Bulmer** N York
77 J6 **Bulmer Tye** Essex
45 M3 **Bulphan** Thurr
217 H5 **Bulwark** Abers
101 K4 **Bulwell** C Nott
88 D5 **Bulwick** Nhants
60 C6 **Bumble's Green** Essex
199 K7 **Bunacaimb** Highld
201 J7 **Bunarkaig** Highld
98 E2 **Bunbury** Ches E

212 F5 **Bunchrew** Highld
210 D8 **Bundalloch** Highld
180 E3 **Bunessan** Ag & B
93 G5 **Bungay** Suffk
171 H4 **Bunnahabhain** Ag & B
101 L6 **Bunny** Notts
212 C7 **Buntait** Highld
60 B3 **Buntingford** Herts
92 D5 **Bunwell** Norfk
86 F5 **Burbage** Leics
40 E7 **Burbage** Wilts
42 D4 **Burchett's Green** W & M
28 B5 **Burcombe** Wilts
58 E4 **Burcott** Bucks
77 K7 **Bures** Essex
56 E5 **Burford** Oxon
69 L2 **Burford** Shrops
189 J7 **Burg** Ag & B
30 C5 **Burgates** Hants
19 J2 **Burgess Hill** W Susx
78 F4 **Burgh** Suffk
148 B3 **Burgh by Sands** Cumb
93 K3 **Burgh Castle** Norfk
41 J7 **Burghclere** Hants
214 D1 **Burghead** Moray
42 A6 **Burghfield** W Berk
42 A6 **Burghfield Common** W Berk
44 E7 **Burgh Heath** Surrey
69 J5 **Burghill** Herefs
6 F6 **Burgh Island** Devon
119 G7 **Burgh le Marsh** Lincs
106 F7 **Burgh next Aylsham** Norfk
117 L4 **Burgh on Bain** Lincs
93 J2 **Burgh St Margaret** Norfk
93 K5 **Burgh St Peter** Norfk
124 E7 **Burghwallis** Donc
46 B7 **Burham** Kent
30 C7 **Buriton** Hants
98 E2 **Burland** Ches E
4 F2 **Burlawn** Cnwll
55 K7 **Burleigh** Gloucs
25 G7 **Burlescombe** Devon
14 E4 **Burleston** Dorset
16 B2 **Burley** Hants
88 C2 **Burley** Rutlnd
98 E4 **Burleydam** Ches E
69 L5 **Burley Gate** Herefs
123 H2 **Burley in Wharfedale** C Brad
16 B2 **Burley Street** Hants
123 H2 **Burley Wood Head** C Brad
98 C7 **Burlton** Shrops
34 E7 **Burmarsh** Kent
72 C6 **Burmington** Warwks
124 F5 **Burn** N York
113 K3 **Burnage** Manch
100 F6 **Burnaston** Derbys
176 B6 **Burnbrae** N Lans
125 K2 **Burnby** E R Yk
138 D7 **Burneside** Cumb
132 D3 **Burneston** N York
38 F7 **Burnett** BaNES
166 F6 **Burnfoot** Border
167 H6 **Burnfoot** Border
155 G4 **Burnfoot** D & G
156 C3 **Burnfoot** D & G
156 C4 **Burnfoot** D & G
185 K6 **Burnfoot** P & K
42 F4 **Burnham** Bucks
105 J4 **Burnham Deepdale** Norfk
105 K4 **Burnham Market** Norfk
105 K4 **Burnham Norton** Norfk
46 F2 **Burnham-on-Crouch** Essex
25 L2 **Burnham-on-Sea** Somset
105 K4 **Burnham Overy** Norfk
105 K4 **Burnham Overy Staithe** Norfk
105 K4 **Burnham Thorpe** Norfk
217 L5 **Burnhaven** Abers
154 E3 **Burnhead** D & G
206 D2 **Burnhervie** Abers
84 E4 **Burnhill Green** Staffs
150 F5 **Burnhope** Dur
174 D7 **Burnhouse** N Ayrs
134 F2 **Burniston** N York
122 C4 **Burnley** Lancs
122 B4 **Burnley Crematorium** Lancs
179 K6 **Burnmouth** Border
184 F6 **Burn of Cambus** Stirlg
150 F4 **Burnopfield** Dur
131 J7 **Burnsall** N York
196 C4 **Burnside** Angus
196 E6 **Burnside** Angus
186 B5 **Burnside** Fife
214 E1 **Burnside** Moray
176 E3 **Burnside** W Loth
187 G1 **Burnside of Duntrune** Angus
177 H2 **Burntisland** Fife
85 J2 **Burntwood** Staffs
85 J2 **Burntwood Green** Staffs
132 C7 **Burnt Yates** N York
25 J7 **Burnworthy** Somset
31 G2 **Burpham** Surrey
18 E4 **Burpham** W Susx
168 E7 **Burradon** Nthumb
235 e1 **Burrafirth** Shet
235 d3 **Burravoe** Shet
138 F4 **Burrells** Cumb
195 K8 **Burrelton** P & K
13 H2 **Burridge** Devon
17 G1 **Burridge** Hants
132 C3 **Burrill** N York
125 K8 **Burringham** N Linc
10 F2 **Burrington** Devon
69 J1 **Burrington** Herefs
38 C8 **Burrington** N Som
76 F4 **Burrough Green** Cambs
87 L2 **Burrough on the Hill** Leics
130 C4 **Burrow** Lancs
24 E3 **Burrow** Somset
26 A5 **Burrow Bridge** Somset
42 F7 **Burrowhill** Surrey
50 F7 **Burry Green** Swans
50 F5 **Burry Port** Carmth
120 F7 **Burscough** Lancs
120 F7 **Burscough Bridge** Lancs
125 J4 **Bursea** E R Yk
16 F1 **Bursledon** Hants
99 K3 **Burslem** C Stke
78 D5 **Burstall** Suffk
13 K2 **Burstock** Dorset
92 D6 **Burston** Norfk
32 B5 **Burstow** Surrey
126 F5 **Burstwick** E R Yk
131 G2 **Burtersett** N York
148 F3 **Burtholme** Cumb
77 H2 **Burthorpe Green** Suffk
103 L5 **Burtoft** Lincs
111 K6 **Burton** Ches W
112 D8 **Burton** Ches W
15 M4 **Burton** Dorset
116 F6 **Burton** Lincs
49 G6 **Burton** Pembks
25 J3 **Burton** Somset
39 J4 **Burton** Wilts
135 H6 **Burton Agnes** E R Yk
13 L4 **Burton Bradstock** Dorset
103 G7 **Burton Coggles** Lincs
126 F4 **Burton Constable Hall** E R Yk
60 E4 **Burton End** Essex
135 G5 **Burton Fleming** E R Yk
86 E5 **Burton Hastings** Warwks
129 L4 **Burton-in-Kendal** Cumb
129 L4 **Burton-in-Kendal Services** Cumb
130 C5 **Burton in Lonsdale** N York
101 M4 **Burton Joyce** Notts
88 C8 **Burton Latimer** Nhants
87 L1 **Burton Lazars** Leics
132 E6 **Burton Leonard** N York
101 L7 **Burton on the Wolds** Leics
87 J4 **Burton Overy** Leics
103 J4 **Burton Pedwardine** Lincs
127 G4 **Burton Pidsea** E R Yk
124 D5 **Burton Salmon** N York
61 K3 **Burton's Green** Essex
125 K6 **Burton upon Stather** N Linc
100 E7 **Burton upon Trent** Staffs
116 F6 **Burton Waters** Lincs
112 E3 **Burtonwood** Warrtn
112 E4 **Burtonwood Services** Warrtn
98 D2 **Burwardsley** Ches W
84 B6 **Burwarton** Shrops
33 H7 **Burwash** E Susx
20 D2 **Burwash Common** E Susx
20 D2 **Burwash Weald** E Susx
76 E2 **Burwell** Cambs
118 E5 **Burwell** Lincs
108 E3 **Burwen** IoA
234 c8 **Burwick** Ork
122 B7 **Bury** Bury
89 K6 **Bury** Cambs
24 E6 **Bury** Somset
18 D3 **Bury** W Susx
60 D4 **Bury Green** Herts
77 J2 **Bury St Edmunds** Suffk
134 C6 **Burythorpe** N York
175 G6 **Busby** E Rens
40 E2 **Buscot** Oxon
197 J4 **Bush** Abers
69 J4 **Bush Bank** Herefs
85 G3 **Bushbury** Wolves
85 G3 **Bushbury Crematorium** Wolves
43 J2 **Bushey** Herts
43 J2 **Bushey Heath** Herts
45 G2 **Bush Hill Park** Gt Lon
70 F7 **Bushley** Worcs
83 J6 **Bushmoor** Shrops
40 B5 **Bushton** Wilts
55 K7 **Bussage** Gloucs
26 A4 **Bussex** Somset
38 D7 **Butcombe** N Som
173 H4 **Bute** Ag & B
26 D5 **Butleigh** Somset
26 D4 **Butleigh Wootton** Somset
72 D4 **Butlers Marston** Warwks
79 H4 **Butley** Suffk
133 L7 **Buttercrambe** N York
179 G5 **Butterdean** Border
140 E3 **Butterknowle** Dur
12 C2 **Butterleigh** Devon
137 G4 **Buttermere** Cumb
123 H5 **Buttershaw** C Brad
195 G7 **Butterstone** P & K
99 J4 **Butterton** Staffs
100 B2 **Butterton** Staffs
104 C4 **Butterwick** Lincs
133 L4 **Butterwick** N York
134 F5 **Butterwick** N York
82 E2 **Buttington** Powys
84 D7 **Buttonoak** Shrops
78 B3 **Buxhall** Suffk
20 A2 **Buxted** E Susx
114 B6 **Buxton** Derbys
106 F7 **Buxton** Norfk
106 E7 **Buxton Heath** Norfk
53 J4 **Bwlch** Powys
97 K2 **Bwlchgwyn** Wrexhm
66 D3 **Bwlchllan** Cerdgn
94 E7 **Bwlchtocyn** Gwynd
97 J8 **Bwlch-y-cibau** Powys
82 B4 **Bwlch-y-ffridd** Powys
65 H7 **Bwlch-y-groes** Pembks
82 B8 **Bwlch-y-sarnau** Powys
150 F7 **Byers Green** Dur
73 G4 **Byfield** Nhants
43 H7 **Byfleet** Surrey
69 H6 **Byford** Herefs
151 G3 **Byker** N u Ty
110 D8 **Bylchau** Conwy
113 G7 **Byley** Ches W
157 K2 **Byrness** Nthumb
12 D5 **Bystock** Devon
88 F7 **Bythorn** Cambs
69 G2 **Byton** Herefs
150 D3 **Bywell** Nthumb
31 G7 **Byworth** W Susx

C

117 J2 **Cabourne** Lincs
171 J5 **Cabrach** Ag & B
215 J8 **Cabrach** Moray
121 G2 **Cabus** Lancs
11 L4 **Cadbury** Devon
175 G4 **Cadder** E Duns
59 H4 **Caddington** C Beds
167 G3 **Caddonfoot** Border
115 K2 **Cadeby** Donc
86 E3 **Cadeby** Leics
11 L4 **Cadeleigh** Devon
20 C2 **Cade Street** E Susx
3 J7 **Cadgwith** Cnwll
186 D6 **Cadham** Fife
113 G3 **Cadishead** Salfd
51 J6 **Cadle** Swans
121 G4 **Cadley** Lancs
28 E2 **Cadley** Wilts
40 E6 **Cadley** Wilts
42 C3 **Cadmore End** Bucks
28 F8 **Cadnam** Hants
117 G2 **Cadney** N Linc
37 H6 **Cadoxton** V Glam
51 L5 **Cadoxton Juxta-Neath** Neath
95 J1 **Caeathro** Gwynd
117 G4 **Caenby** Lincs
66 F6 **Caeo** Carmth
36 D2 **Caerau** Brdgnd
37 H5 **Caerau** Cardif
48 D3 **Caer Farchell** Pembks
108 D5 **Caergeiliog** IoA
97 L2 **Caergwrle** Flints
156 D2 **Caerlanrig** Border
37 M3 **Caerleon** Newpt
37 M3 **Caerleon Roman Amphitheatre** Newpt
108 F8 **Caernarfon** Gwynd
108 F8 **Caernarfon Castle** Gwynd
37 J3 **Caerphilly** Caerph
82 B5 **Caersws** Powys
65 L4 **Caerwedros** Cerdgn
38 C3 **Caerwent** Mons
110 F6 **Caerwys** Flints
233 c6 **Cairinis** W Isls
172 E1 **Cairnbaan** Ag & B
217 J2 **Cairnbulg** Abers

179 J5 Cairncross Border
174 C4 Cairncurran Inver
183 H5 Cairndow Ag & B
176 E2 Cairneyhill Fife
144 C5 Cairngarroch D & G
204 C5 Cairngorms National Park
215 K5 Cairnie Abers
217 G6 Cairnorrie Abers
144 C2 Cairnryan D & G
215 H4 Cairnty Moray
93 L2 Caister-on-Sea Norfk
117 J2 Caistor Lincs
92 F3 Caistor St Edmund Norfk
232 e2 Calanais W Isls
16 E5 Calbourne IoW
111 G6 Calcot Flints
56 C6 Calcot Gloucs
42 A6 Calcot Row W Berk
215 G2 Calcots Moray
148 B6 Caldbeck Cumb
75 L3 Caldecote Cambs
89 G5 Caldecote Cambs
75 L3 Caldecote Highfields Cambs
74 E2 Caldecott Nhants
41 J2 Caldecott Oxon
88 C5 Caldecott Rutlnd
175 K5 Calderbank N Lans
136 E6 Calder Bridge Cumb
175 L5 Caldercruix N Lans
123 L6 Calder Grove Wakefd
164 D2 Caldermill S Lans
121 G2 Calder Vale Lancs
175 H7 Calderwood S Lans
49 K7 Caldey Island Pembks
38 C3 Caldicot Mons
85 H4 Caldmore Wsall
140 E5 Caldwell N York
237 a7 Calf of Man IoM
234 d4 Calfsound Ork
189 J6 Calgary Ag & B
214 D3 Califer Moray
176 B3 California Falk
93 K1 California Norfk
101 G7 Calke Derbys
209 L4 Callakille Highld
184 D5 Callander Stirlg
232 e2 Callanish W Isls
3 K2 Callestick Cnwll
199 K5 Calligarry Highld
6 A3 Callington Cnwll
69 J7 Callow Herefs
70 E4 Callow End Worcs
40 B4 Callow Hill Wilts
29 G7 Calmore Hants
56 B6 Calmsden Gloucs
39 M6 Calne Wilts
16 F3 Calshot Hants
6 C3 Calstock Cnwll
40 B6 Calstone Wellington Wilts
106 E6 Calthorpe Norfk
107 J7 Calthorpe Street Norfk
148 E6 Calthwaite Cumb
100 C3 Calton Staffs
98 E2 Calveley Ches E
114 E6 Calver Derbys
98 E5 Calverhall Shrops
11 L3 Calverleigh Devon
73 L6 Calverton M Keyn
101 L3 Calverton Notts
194 C3 Calvine P & K
165 L3 Calzeat Border
55 H7 Cam Gloucs
190 F4 Camasachoirce Highld
190 F4 Camasine Highld
210 E8 Camas Luinie Highld
209 H6 Camastianavaig Highld
212 D6 Camault Muir Highld
21 J2 Camber E Susx
42 E7 Camberley Surrey
44 F5 Camberwell Gt Lon
124 F5 Camblesforth N York
158 C5 Cambo Nthumb
3 H4 Camborne Cnwll
75 K3 Cambourne Cambs
76 C3 Cambridge Cambs
55 H7 Cambridge Gloucs
76 C3 *Cambridge Airport* Cambs
76 B3 Cambridge City Crematorium Cambs
3 H3 Cambrose Cnwll
185 H8 Cambus Clacks
223 G3 Cambusavie Platform Highld
185 G8 Cambusbarron Stirlg
185 G8 Cambuskenneth Stirlg
175 H6 Cambuslang S Lans
205 J5 Cambus o' May Abers
165 K2 Cambuswallace S Lans
44 F4 Camden Town Gt Lon
38 E8 Cameley BaNES
8 E7 Camelford Cnwll
176 B3 Camelon Falk
214 C7 Camerory Highld
39 G8 Camerton BaNES
136 E2 Camerton Cumb
193 J5 Camghouran P & K
167 J4 Camieston Border
207 G6 Cammachmore Abers
116 F5 Cammeringham Lincs
223 G4 Camore Highld
161 J5 Campbeltown Ag & B
161 H5 *Campbeltown Airport* Ag & B
154 F4 Cample D & G
195 K8 Campmuir P & K
176 E5 Camps W Loth
124 E7 Campsall Donc
79 G4 Campsea Ash Suffk
75 G6 Campton C Beds
167 K6 Camptown Border
48 F4 Camrose Pembks
194 C6 Camserney P & K
191 L2 Camusnagaul Highld
220 D4 Camusnagaul Highld
209 L6 Camusteel Highld
209 L6 Camusterrach Highld
28 F7 Canada Hants
205 H5 Candacraig Abers
118 F7 Candlesby Lincs
165 L2 Candy Mill Border
42 B4 Cane End Oxon
46 E2 Canewdon Essex
15 K5 Canford Cliffs Poole
38 E5 Canford Crematorium Bristl
15 J4 Canford Heath Poole
231 L2 Canisbay Highld
86 C7 Canley Covtry
86 C7 Canley Crematorium Covtry
27 K7 Cann Dorset
198 C4 Canna Highld
211 L7 Cannich Highld
25 K4 Cannington Somset
45 H4 Canning Town Gt Lon
85 H2 Cannock Staffs
99 M8 Cannock Chase Staffs
69 H6 Cannon Bridge Herefs
156 C6 Canonbie D & G
70 B5 Canon Frome Herefs
69 J5 Canon Pyon Herefs
73 H4 Canons Ashby Nhants
2 F4 Canonstown Cnwll
34 F3 Canterbury Kent
34 F3 Canterbury Cathedral Kent
93 H3 Cantley Norfk
37 J5 Canton Cardif
213 J5 Cantraywood Highld
130 C5 Cantsfield Lancs
46 D4 Canvey Island Essex
117 G7 Canwick Lincs
9 G6 Canworthy Water Cnwll
191 L2 Caol Highld
232 e4 Caolas Scalpaigh W Isls
188 D6 Caoles Ag & B
201 G6 Caonich Highld
33 H4 Capel Kent
31 K4 Capel Surrey
80 E7 Capel Bangor Cerdgn
108 F5 Capel Coch IoA
96 A2 Capel Curig Conwy
50 F2 Capel Dewi Carmth
66 B6 Capel Dewi Cerdgn
80 E6 Capel-Dewi Cerdgn
96 C2 Capel Garmon Conwy
51 H4 Capel Hendre Carmth
65 J7 Capel Iwan Carmth
35 H6 Capel le Ferne Kent
108 F4 Capel Parc IoA
79 H5 Capel St Andrew Suffk
78 C6 Capel St Mary Suffk
80 E7 Capel Seion Cerdgn
109 L6 Capelulo Conwy
111 K6 Capenhurst Ches W
158 C6 Capheaton Nthumb
174 E6 Caplaw E Rens
166 C5 Cappercleuch Border
7 J5 Capton Devon
195 H7 Caputh P & K
174 F3 Carbeth Inn Stirlg
2 F4 Carbis Bay Cnwll
208 F5 Carbost Highld
208 F7 Carbost Highld
115 G4 Carbrook Sheff
91 L3 Carbrooke Norfk
102 B4 Car Colston Notts
124 E8 Carcroft Donc
186 C7 Cardenden Fife
214 F5 Cardhu Moray
37 J5 Cardiff Cardif
37 G6 *Cardiff Airport* V Glam
37 K4 Cardiff Gate Services Cardif
37 H4 Cardiff West Services Cardif
65 G5 Cardigan Cerdgn
74 F5 Cardington Bed
83 K4 Cardington Shrops
5 H3 Cardinham Cnwll
144 D8 Cardrain D & G
166 D2 Cardrona Border
174 C3 Cardross Ag & B
174 C3 Cardross Crematorium Ag & B
144 D7 Cardryne D & G
147 L3 Cardurnock Cumb
88 E1 Careby Lincs
196 E4 Careston Angus
49 H6 Carew Pembks
49 H6 Carew Cheriton Pembks
49 H6 Carew Newton Pembks
54 E2 Carey Herefs
175 K6 Carfin N Lans
178 B7 Carfraemill Border
93 H2 Cargate Green Norfk
155 G6 Cargenbridge D & G
195 J8 Cargill P & K
148 C3 Cargo Cumb
6 C4 Cargreen Cnwll
168 B2 Carham Nthumb
24 F3 Carhampton Somset
3 J3 Carharrack Cnwll
193 K5 Carie P & K
233 c6 Carinish W Isls
16 F5 Carisbrooke IoW
129 H4 Cark Cumb
6 B4 Carkeel Cnwll
232 e2 Carlabhagh W Isls
140 F4 Carlbury Darltn
88 F2 Carlby Lincs
3 G5 Carleen Cnwll
122 E1 Carleton N York
120 D3 Carleton Crematorium Bpool
92 C3 Carleton Forehoe Norfk
92 D5 Carleton Rode Norfk
93 H3 Carleton St Peter Norfk
216 D5 Carlincraig Abers
39 G8 Carlingcott BaNES
148 D4 Carlisle Cumb
148 E3 *Carlisle Airport* Cumb
148 C4 Carlisle Crematorium Cumb
177 G6 Carlops Border
232 e2 Carloway W Isls
124 B7 Carlton Barns
74 D4 Carlton Bed
76 F4 Carlton Cambs
123 L5 Carlton Leeds
86 E3 Carlton Leics
124 F5 Carlton N York
131 K3 Carlton N York
133 J3 Carlton N York
101 L4 Carlton Notts
141 J3 Carlton S on T
79 H2 Carlton Suffk
93 K5 Carlton Colville Suffk
87 K4 Carlton Curlieu Leics
76 F4 Carlton Green Cambs
133 G4 Carlton Husthwaite N York
142 B6 Carlton-in-Cleveland N York
115 L5 Carlton in Lindrick Notts
102 E2 Carlton-le-Moorland Lincs
132 F4 Carlton Miniott N York
116 D8 Carlton-on-Trent Notts
102 F4 Carlton Scroop Lincs
175 L7 Carluke S Lans
164 F4 Carmacoup S Lans
50 E2 Carmarthen Carmth
51 H3 Carmel Carmth
111 G6 Carmel Flints
95 H2 Carmel Gwynd
165 H2 Carmichael S Lans
99 K3 Carmountside Crematorium C Stke
175 G6 Carmunnock C Glas
175 H6 Carmyle C Glas
196 E7 Carmyllie Angus
135 H6 Carnaby E R Yk
187 J6 Carnbee Fife
185 L6 Carnbo P & K
3 H3 Carn Brea Cnwll
216 F8 Carnbrogie Abers
210 D8 Carndu Highld
164 D1 Carnduff S Lans
163 L3 Carnell E Ayrs
129 K5 Carnforth Lancs
200 E2 Carn-gorm Highld
3 G4 Carnhell Green Cnwll
206 F4 Carnie Abers
3 H4 Carnkie Cnwll
3 J4 Carnkie Cnwll
81 K4 Carno Powys
176 E1 Carnock Fife
4 C7 Carnon Downs Cnwll
216 C4 Carnousie Abers
187 J1 Carnoustie Angus
165 J1 Carnwath S Lans
86 C7 Carol Green Solhll
131 J2 Carperby N York
161 K2 Carradale Ag & B
203 L2 Carrbridge Highld
236 c6 Carrefour Jersey
108 E4 Carreglefn IoA
123 L5 Carr Gate Wakefd
116 C1 Carrhouse N Linc
172 F2 Carrick Ag & B
183 H8 Carrick Castle Ag & B
176 D3 Carriden Falk

177 J6 **Carrington** Mdloth
113 H3 **Carrington** Traffd
97 H4 **Carrog** Denbgs
176 B2 **Carron** Falk
214 F6 **Carron** Moray
154 F3 **Carronbridge** D & G
175 K2 **Carron Bridge** Stirlg
176 B2 **Carronshore** Falk
149 K5 **Carr Shield** Nthumb
155 J7 **Carrutherstown** D & G
174 C5 **Carruth House** Inver
151 H6 **Carrville** Dur
181 H3 **Carsaig** Ag & B
145 G2 **Carseriggan** D & G
147 H3 **Carsethorn** D & G
44 F6 **Carshalton** Gt Lon
100 E2 **Carsington** Derbys
161 H7 **Carskey** Ag & B
145 K4 **Carsluith** D & G
153 L4 **Carsphairn** D & G
165 H1 **Carstairs** S Lans
165 J1 **Carstairs Junction** S Lans
56 F6 **Carterton** Oxon
4 F5 **Carthew** Cnwll
132 D3 **Carthorpe** N York
165 G1 **Cartland** S Lans
129 H4 **Cartmel** Cumb
50 F4 **Carway** Carmth
55 J6 **Cashe's Green** Gloucs
57 J5 **Cassington** Oxon
151 J7 **Cassop Colliery** Dur
236 c3 **Castel** Guern
130 C4 **Casterton** Cumb
91 J1 **Castle Acre** Norfk
74 C3 **Castle Ashby** Nhants
233 b9 **Castlebay** W Isls
131 J2 **Castle Bolton** N York
85 K5 **Castle Bromwich** Solhll
103 G8 **Castle Bytham** Lincs
49 H2 **Castlebythe** Pembks
82 D3 **Castle Caereinion** Powys
76 F6 **Castle Camps** Cambs
148 F4 **Castle Carrock** Cumb
175 K3 **Castlecary** Falk
26 F5 **Castle Cary** Somset
39 J5 **Castle Combe** Wilts
101 H6 **Castle Donington** Leics
146 D3 **Castle Douglas** D & G
40 C2 **Castle Eaton** Swindn
151 K7 **Castle Eden** Dur
124 C5 **Castleford** Wakefd
70 C5 **Castle Frome** Herefs
100 F8 **Castle Gresley** Derbys
77 H7 **Castle Hedingham** Essex
166 C3 **Castlehill** Border
231 H2 **Castlehill** Highld
78 D5 **Castle Hill** Suffk
174 D3 **Castlehill** W Duns
144 D3 **Castle Kennedy** D & G
182 E7 **Castle Lachlan** Ag & B
48 F7 **Castlemartin** Pembks
175 G6 **Castlemilk** C Glas
70 E6 **Castlemorton** Worcs
70 E6 **Castlemorton Common** Worcs
156 A4 **Castle O'er** D & G
83 H3 **Castle Pulverbatch** Shrops
137 J3 **Castlerigg Stone Circle** Cumb
105 G7 **Castle Rising** Norfk
150 D5 **Castleside** Dur
213 H4 **Castle Stuart** Highld
74 B5 **Castlethorpe** M Keyn
156 E4 **Castleton** Border
114 D5 **Castleton** Derbys
142 E5 **Castleton** N York
37 K4 **Castleton** Newpt
122 D7 **Castleton** Rochdl
231 H3 **Castletown** Highld
237 b7 **Castletown** IoM
151 J4 **Castletown** Sundld
123 K2 **Castley** N York
91 L4 **Caston** Norfk
89 G4 **Castor** C Pete
172 F7 **Catacol** N Ayrs
115 H4 **Catcliffe** Rothm
40 A5 **Catcomb** Wilts
26 B4 **Catcott** Somset
26 B3 **Catcott Burtle** Somset
32 C3 **Caterham** Surrey
107 H7 **Catfield** Norfk
45 G5 **Catford** Gt Lon
121 G4 **Catforth** Lancs
175 G6 **Cathcart** C Glas
53 H3 **Cathedine** Powys
30 B8 **Catherington** Hants
13 J4 **Catherston Leweston** Dorset
17 G2 **Catisfield** Hants
202 F6 **Catlodge** Highld
76 C6 **Catmere End** Essex
41 J4 **Catmore** W Berk
129 L6 **Caton** Lancs
129 L6 **Caton Green** Lancs
164 B4 **Catrine** E Ayrs
20 E3 **Catsfield** E Susx
26 D6 **Catsgore** Somset
85 G8 **Catshill** Worcs
161 H7 **Cattadale** Ag & B
133 G8 **Cattal** N York
62 D2 **Cattawade** Suffk
121 G3 **Catterall** Lancs
141 G7 **Catterick** N York
141 G7 **Catterick Bridge** N York
148 E7 **Catterlen** Cumb
197 L2 **Catterline** Abers
124 D2 **Catterton** N York
31 G3 **Catteshall** Surrey
87 G7 **Catthorpe** Leics
14 B3 **Cattistock** Dorset
132 E4 **Catton** N York
149 L4 **Catton** Nthumb
126 E2 **Catwick** E R Yk
88 F8 **Catworth** Cambs
55 L6 **Caudle Green** Gloucs
57 K3 **Caulcott** Oxon
197 G6 **Cauldcots** Angus
184 E8 **Cauldhame** Stirlg
167 H6 **Cauldmill** Border
100 B3 **Cauldon** Staffs
86 B1 **Cauldwell** Derbys
147 G4 **Caulkerbush** D & G
156 D6 **Caulside** D & G
27 G8 **Caundle Marsh** Dorset
102 C1 **Caunton** Notts
145 J3 **Causeway End** D & G
61 G4 **Causeway End** Essex
165 K3 **Causewayend** S Lans
185 G7 **Causewayhead** Stirlg
207 H2 **Causeyend** Abers
158 F3 **Causey Park Bridge** Nthumb
77 J5 **Cavendish** Suffk
77 H1 **Cavenham** Suffk
57 L3 **Caversfield** Oxon
42 B5 **Caversham** Readg
99 L4 **Caverswall** Staffs
167 M4 **Caverton Mill** Border
213 K4 **Cawdor** Highld
124 E3 **Cawood** N York
6 C5 **Cawsand** Cnwll
106 D7 **Cawston** Norfk
123 K8 **Cawthorne** Barns
75 K3 **Caxton** Cambs
83 K8 **Caynham** Shrops
102 F3 **Caythorpe** Lincs
102 B4 **Caythorpe** Notts
135 G3 **Cayton** N York
233 b6 **Ceann a Bhaigh** W Isls
201 K3 **Ceannacroc Lodge** Highld
232 f3 **Cearsiadar** W Isls
37 L3 **Cefn** Newpt
96 E3 **Cefn-brith** Conwy
51 L3 **Cefn-bryn-brain** Carmth
36 D4 **Cefn Cribwr** Brdgnd
51 G3 **Cefneithin** Carmth
67 J5 **Cefngorwydd** Powys
97 L4 **Cefn-mawr** Wrexhm
49 K3 **Cefn-y-pant** Carmth
187 J6 **Cellardyke** Fife
99 L3 **Cellarhead** Staffs
108 E3 **Cemaes** IoA
81 H3 **Cemmaes** Powys
81 H3 **Cemmaes Road** Powys
65 J6 **Cenarth** Cerdgn
186 F5 **Ceres** Fife
14 C3 **Cerne Abbas** Dorset
40 B2 **Cerney Wick** Gloucs
96 E3 **Cerrigydrudion** Conwy
95 J1 **Ceunant** Gwynd
55 J2 **Chaceley** Gloucs
3 K3 **Chacewater** Cnwll
73 K7 **Chackmore** Bucks
72 F5 **Chacombe** Nhants
71 H5 **Chadbury** Worcs
113 K1 **Chadderton** Oldham
101 G5 **Chaddesden** C Derb
84 F8 **Chaddesley Corbett** Worcs
6 C1 **Chaddlehanger** Devon
41 H5 **Chaddleworth** W Berk
57 G4 **Chadlington** Oxon
72 D4 **Chadshunt** Warwks
102 C7 **Chadwell** Leics
45 J3 **Chadwell Heath** Gt Lon
45 M4 **Chadwell St Mary** Thurr
70 E2 **Chadwick** Worcs
86 B8 **Chadwick End** Solhll
13 J1 **Chaffcombe** Somset
11 G7 **Chagford** Devon
19 K2 **Chailey** E Susx
33 J4 **Chainhurst** Kent
32 B3 **Chaldon** Surrey
16 F6 **Chale** IoW
16 F6 **Chale Green** IoW
43 G3 **Chalfont Common** Bucks
43 G2 **Chalfont St Giles** Bucks
43 G3 **Chalfont St Peter** Bucks
55 K7 **Chalford** Gloucs
27 K2 **Chalford** Wilts
41 M2 **Chalgrove** Oxon
46 A5 **Chalk** Kent
34 B2 **Chalkwell** Kent
23 L3 **Challacombe** Devon
145 H2 **Challoch** D & G
34 D5 **Challock** Kent
59 G3 **Chalton** C Beds
30 B7 **Chalton** Hants
42 F4 **Chalvey** Slough
20 B4 **Chalvington** E Susx
43 H2 **Chandler's Cross** Herts
29 H7 **Chandler's Ford** Hants
126 D4 **Chanterlands Crematorium** C KuH
27 G3 **Chantry** Somset
78 D5 **Chantry** Suffk
186 D8 **Chapel** Fife
123 L3 **Chapel Allerton** Leeds
26 B2 **Chapel Allerton** Somset
4 F2 **Chapel Amble** Cnwll
73 K2 **Chapel Brampton** Nhants
99 J5 **Chapel Chorlton** Staffs
77 G6 **Chapelend Way** Essex
114 B5 **Chapel-en-le-Frith** Derbys
72 F3 **Chapel Green** Warwks
124 E5 **Chapel Haddlesey** N York
175 K5 **Chapelhall** N Lans
217 K7 **Chapel Hill** Abers
103 K2 **Chapel Hill** Lincs
54 D7 **Chapel Hill** Mons
123 L2 **Chapel Hill** N York
166 C5 **Chapelhope** Border
156 B7 **Chapelknowe** D & G
82 F7 **Chapel Lawn** Shrops
130 E4 **Chapel le Dale** N York
25 H5 **Chapel Leigh** Somset
206 D1 **Chapel of Garioch** Abers
144 D6 **Chapel Rossan** D & G
41 L6 **Chapel Row** W Berk
119 H6 **Chapel St Leonards** Lincs
137 K6 **Chapel Stile** Cumb
197 G6 **Chapelton** Angus
23 J6 **Chapelton** Devon
175 J8 **Chapelton** S Lans
121 L7 **Chapeltown** Bl w D
204 F2 **Chapeltown** Moray
115 G3 **Chapeltown** Sheff
27 J2 **Chapmanslade** Wilts
9 J6 **Chapmans Well** Devon
60 B5 **Chapmore End** Herts
61 L3 **Chappel** Essex
13 H2 **Chard** Somset
13 J2 **Chard Junction** Somset
13 H1 **Chardleigh Green** Somset
13 H2 **Chardstock** Devon
39 G3 **Charfield** S Glos
34 C5 **Charing** Kent
34 C5 **Charing Crematorium** Kent
71 L6 **Charingworth** Gloucs
57 G4 **Charlbury** Oxon
39 H6 **Charlcombe** BaNES
39 M5 **Charlcutt** Wilts
72 C3 **Charlecote** Warwks
85 H5 **Charlemont** Sandw
23 L5 **Charles** Devon
196 C7 **Charleston** Angus
207 H5 **Charlestown** C Aber
123 H3 **Charlestown** C Brad
122 E5 **Charlestown** Calder
5 G5 **Charlestown** Cnwll
176 E2 **Charlestown** Fife
213 G5 **Charlestown** Highld
219 J6 **Charlestown** Highld
113 J2 **Charlestown** Salfd
78 B4 **Charles Tye** Suffk
114 A3 **Charlesworth** Derbys
25 K4 **Charlinch** Somset
186 E5 **Charlottetown** Fife
45 H4 **Charlton** Gt Lon
73 G7 **Charlton** Nhants
157 K5 **Charlton** Nthumb
41 H3 **Charlton** Oxon
25 L6 **Charlton** Somset
27 G2 **Charlton** Somset
18 B3 **Charlton** W Susx
27 K6 **Charlton** Wilts
39 L3 **Charlton** Wilts
71 H5 **Charlton** Worcs
83 L2 **Charlton** Wrekin
56 B3 **Charlton Abbots** Gloucs
26 D5 **Charlton Adam** Somset
28 D6 **Charlton-All-Saints** Wilts
14 D4 **Charlton Down** Dorset
26 F6 **Charlton Horethorne** Somset
55 L4 **Charlton Kings** Gloucs

26 D5 **Charlton Mackrell** Somset
15 G2 **Charlton Marshall** Dorset
27 G5 **Charlton Musgrove** Somset
57 K5 **Charlton-on-Otmoor** Oxon
15 G2 **Charlton on the Hill** Dorset
28 C1 **Charlton St Peter** Wilts
30 A5 **Charlwood** Hants
31 L3 **Charlwood** Surrey
14 D4 **Charminster** Dorset
13 J4 **Charmouth** Dorset
58 A3 **Charndon** Bucks
41 G2 **Charney Bassett** Oxon
121 H7 **Charnock Richard** Lancs
121 H6 **Charnock Richard Crematorium** Lancs
121 H7 **Charnock Richard Services** Lancs
78 F3 **Charsfield** Suffk
41 L8 **Charter Alley** Hants
179 G8 **Charterhall** Border
26 D1 **Charterhouse** Somset
175 K1 **Chartershall** Stirlg
34 E4 **Chartham** Kent
34 E4 **Chartham Hatch** Kent
58 F7 **Chartridge** Bucks
33 K4 **Chart Sutton** Kent
42 C5 **Charvil** Wokham
73 G4 **Charwelton** Nhants
85 J2 **Chase Terrace** Staffs
85 J2 **Chasetown** Staffs
56 E3 **Chastleton** Oxon
9 J4 **Chasty** Devon
121 L2 **Chatburn** Lancs
99 H5 **Chatcull** Staffs
46 C6 **Chatham** Medway
61 H5 **Chatham Green** Essex
169 J4 **Chathill** Nthumb
114 E7 **Chatsworth House** Derbys
46 C5 **Chattenden** Medway
90 B6 **Chatteris** Cambs
122 B6 **Chatterton** Lancs
78 C6 **Chattisham** Suffk
168 B5 **Chatto** Border
168 F4 **Chatton** Nthumb
11 G3 **Chawleigh** Devon
30 B4 **Chawton** Hants
100 A4 **Cheadle** Staffs
113 K4 **Cheadle** Stockp
113 K4 **Cheadle Hulme** Stockp
44 E7 **Cheam** Gt Lon
58 B6 **Chearsley** Bucks
99 J6 **Chebsey** Staffs
42 A4 **Checkendon** Oxon
99 G4 **Checkley** Ches E
100 B5 **Checkley** Staffs
77 H3 **Chedburgh** Suffk
26 C2 **Cheddar** Somset
58 F4 **Cheddington** Bucks
99 L3 **Cheddleton** Staffs
25 K6 **Cheddon Fitzpaine** Somset
93 H4 **Chedgrave** Norfk
13 L2 **Chedington** Dorset
93 H7 **Chediston** Suffk
56 B5 **Chedworth** Gloucs
25 M4 **Chedzoy** Somset
113 J2 **Cheetham Hill** Manch
11 H3 **Cheldon** Devon
113 J6 **Chelford** Ches E
101 G6 **Chellaston** C Derb
74 D4 **Chellington** Bed
84 C5 **Chelmarsh** Shrops
78 E6 **Chelmondiston** Suffk
114 C7 **Chelmorton** Derbys
61 H6 **Chelmsford** Essex
61 H6 **Chelmsford Crematorium** Essex
85 L6 **Chelmsley Wood** Solhll
44 F4 **Chelsea** Gt Lon
45 J7 **Chelsfield** Gt Lon
77 L5 **Chelsworth** Suffk
55 L4 **Cheltenham** Gloucs
55 L4 **Cheltenham Crematorium** Gloucs
74 E1 **Chelveston** Nhants
38 C6 **Chelvey** N Som
38 F7 **Chelwood** BaNES
32 D6 **Chelwood Gate** E Susx
83 H6 **Cheney Longville** Shrops
43 G2 **Chenies** Bucks
38 D2 **Chepstow** Mons
40 B6 **Cherhill** Wilts
55 K7 **Cherington** Gloucs
72 C6 **Cherington** Warwks
29 L5 **Cheriton** Hants
35 G7 **Cheriton** Kent
50 F6 **Cheriton** Swans
11 H6 **Cheriton Bishop** Devon
11 K4 **Cheriton Fitzpaine** Devon
49 G7 **Cheriton or Stackpole Elidor** Pembks
98 F8 **Cherrington** Wrekin
126 B3 **Cherry Burton** E R Yk
76 C3 **Cherry Hinton** Cambs
70 F4 **Cherry Orchard** Worcs
117 G6 **Cherry Willingham** Lincs
43 H6 **Chertsey** Surrey
57 K3 **Cherwell Valley Services** Oxon
14 E3 **Cheselbourne** Dorset
58 F7 **Chesham** Bucks
122 B7 **Chesham** Bury
58 F7 **Chesham Bois** Bucks
60 B7 **Cheshunt** Herts
14 B6 **Chesil Beach** Dorset
85 H3 **Cheslyn Hay** Staffs
85 L8 **Chessetts Wood** Warwks
44 D7 **Chessington** Gt Lon
44 D7 **Chessington World of Adventures** Gt Lon
112 B7 **Chester** Ches W
26 F3 **Chesterblade** Somset
112 B7 **Chester Cathedral** Ches W
111 L7 **Chester Crematorium** Ches W
115 G7 **Chesterfield** Derbys
115 H6 **Chesterfield Crematorium** Derbys
101 H1 **Chesterfield Services** Derbys
177 K5 **Chesterhill** Mdloth
151 G5 **Chester-le-Street** Dur
151 G5 **Chester Moor** Dur
167 J5 **Chesters** Border
167 K7 **Chesters** Border
112 C6 **Chester Services** Ches W
76 C3 **Chesterton** Cambs
89 G4 **Chesterton** Cambs
56 A7 **Chesterton** Gloucs
57 K4 **Chesterton** Oxon
84 D4 **Chesterton** Shrops
72 D3 **Chesterton Green** Warwks
149 L2 **Chesterwood** Nthumb
112 B7 **Chester Zoo** Ches W
47 J6 **Chestfield** Kent
7 G4 **Cheston** Devon
99 G6 **Cheswardine** Shrops
168 F1 **Cheswick** Nthumb
14 B2 **Chetnole** Dorset
90 D6 **Chettisham** Cambs
27 L8 **Chettle** Dorset
84 B5 **Chetton** Shrops
99 G7 **Chetwynd** Wrekin
99 H8 **Chetwynd Aston** Wrekin
76 F3 **Cheveley** Cambs
32 E2 **Chevening** Kent
77 H3 **Chevington** Suffk
168 A7 **Cheviot Hills**
24 F7 **Chevithorne** Devon
38 E7 **Chew Magna** BaNES
38 E7 **Chew Stoke** BaNES
38 F6 **Chewton Keynsham** BaNES
26 E2 **Chewton Mendip** Somset
74 C5 **Chicheley** M Keyn
18 B5 **Chichester** W Susx
18 B4 **Chichester Crematorium** W Susx
14 C6 **Chickerell** Dorset
27 K4 **Chicklade** Wilts
30 A7 **Chidden** Hants
30 F4 **Chiddingfold** Surrey
20 B3 **Chiddingly** E Susx
32 E4 **Chiddingstone** Kent
32 F4 **Chiddingstone Causeway** Kent
13 K4 **Chideock** Dorset
17 L2 **Chidham** W Susx
123 K6 **Chidswell** Kirk
41 J5 **Chieveley** W Berk
61 G6 **Chignall St James** Essex
61 G5 **Chignall Smealy** Essex
45 H2 **Chigwell** Essex
45 J2 **Chigwell Row** Essex
29 H4 **Chilbolton** Hants
29 J5 **Chilcomb** Hants
13 M4 **Chilcombe** Dorset
26 F2 **Chilcompton** Somset
86 C2 **Chilcote** Leics
111 K6 **Childer Thornton** Ches W
27 J8 **Child Okeford** Dorset
41 G3 **Childrey** Oxon
98 F7 **Child's Ercall** Shrops
71 J6 **Childswickham** Worcs
112 B4 **Childwall** Lpool
14 B3 **Chilfrome** Dorset
18 A3 **Chilgrove** W Susx
34 E4 **Chilham** Kent
10 C8 **Chillaton** Devon
35 H4 **Chillenden** Kent
16 F5 **Chillerton** IoW
79 H4 **Chillesford** Suffk
7 J7 **Chillington** Devon
13 K1 **Chillington** Somset
27 L5 **Chilmark** Wilts
34 C6 **Chilmington Green** Kent
56 F4 **Chilson** Oxon
6 B2 **Chilsworthy** Cnwll
9 J4 **Chilsworthy** Devon
42 C2 **Chiltern Hills**
42 F2 **Chilterns Crematorium** Bucks
26 D7 **Chilthorne Domer** Somset
58 B5 **Chilton** Bucks
141 H2 **Chilton** Dur
41 J4 **Chilton** Oxon
29 L4 **Chilton Candover** Hants
26 E6 **Chilton Cantelo** Somset
40 F6 **Chilton Foliat** Wilts
26 B4 **Chilton Polden** Somset
77 H5 **Chilton Street** Suffk
25 L4 **Chilton Trinity** Somset
101 K5 **Chilwell** Notts
29 H7 **Chilworth** Hants
31 G3 **Chilworth** Surrey
57 G7 **Chimney** Oxon
30 A1 **Chineham** Hants
45 G2 **Chingford** Gt Lon
114 B5 **Chinley** Derbys
58 C7 **Chinnor** Oxon
99 G6 **Chipnall** Shrops
76 F1 **Chippenham** Cambs
39 L5 **Chippenham** Wilts
59 H7 **Chipperfield** Herts
60 B2 **Chipping** Herts
121 J2 **Chipping** Lancs
71 L6 **Chipping Campden** Gloucs
56 F3 **Chipping Norton** Oxon
60 E7 **Chipping Ongar** Essex
39 G4 **Chipping Sodbury** S Glos
72 F5 **Chipping Warden** Nhants
25 G6 **Chipstable** Somset
32 E3 **Chipstead** Kent
32 B2 **Chipstead** Surrey
82 F4 **Chirbury** Shrops
97 L5 **Chirk** Wrexhm
179 H6 **Chirnside** Border
179 H7 **Chirnsidebridge** Border
40 B8 **Chirton** Wilts
40 F6 **Chisbury** Wilts
26 C8 **Chiselborough** Somset
40 D4 **Chiseldon** Swindn
57 L7 **Chiselhampton** Oxon
166 F6 **Chisholme** Border
45 H6 **Chislehurst** Gt Lon
47 L6 **Chislet** Kent
122 F5 **Chisley** Calder
59 J6 **Chiswell Green** Herts
44 E4 **Chiswick** Gt Lon
113 M3 **Chisworth** Derbys
30 D6 **Chithurst** W Susx
76 C1 **Chittering** Cambs
27 M3 **Chitterne** Wilts
23 K7 **Chittlehamholt** Devon
23 K6 **Chittlehampton** Devon
39 L6 **Chittoe** Wilts
7 H7 **Chivelstone** Devon
23 H4 **Chivenor** Devon
144 D3 **Chlenry** D & G
42 F7 **Chobham** Surrey
28 E3 **Cholderton** Wilts
58 F6 **Cholesbury** Bucks
158 B7 **Chollerton** Nthumb
41 L3 **Cholsey** Oxon
69 J3 **Cholstrey** Herefs
142 C7 **Chop Gate** N York
159 G5 **Choppington** Nthumb
150 E4 **Chopwell** Gatesd
98 E3 **Chorley** Ches E
121 H6 **Chorley** Lancs
84 C6 **Chorley** Shrops
43 H2 **Chorleywood** Herts
43 G2 **Chorleywood West** Herts
99 G3 **Chorlton** Ches E
113 J3 **Chorlton-cum-Hardy** Manch
98 C3 **Chorlton Lane** Ches W
83 H5 **Choulton** Shrops
76 C6 **Chrishall** Essex
173 L4 **Chrisswell** Inver
90 C4 **Christchurch** Cambs
15 M4 **Christchurch** Dorset
37 M3 **Christchurch** Newpt
39 L5 **Christian Malford** Wilts
112 C7 **Christleton** Ches W
38 B8 **Christon** N Som

169 J5 **Christon Bank** Nthumb
11 J7 **Christow** Devon
11 K8 **Chudleigh** Devon
7 J1 **Chudleigh Knighton** Devon
11 G3 **Chulmleigh** Devon
121 L5 **Church** Lancs
55 H4 **Churcham** Gloucs
99 H8 **Church Aston** Wrekin
73 K2 **Church Brampton** Nhants
100 D5 **Church Broughton** Derbys
3 J8 **Church Cove** Cnwll
30 D2 **Church Crookham** Hants
55 K4 **Churchdown** Gloucs
99 J8 **Church Eaton** Staffs
59 G4 **Church End** C Beds
75 H6 **Church End** C Beds
47 G2 **Churchend** Essex
61 H3 **Church End** Essex
44 E3 **Church End** Gt Lon
57 G3 **Church Enstone** Oxon
124 D3 **Church Fenton** N York
85 H5 **Churchfield** Sandw
12 F3 **Church Green** Devon
57 H5 **Church Hanborough** Oxon
142 E7 **Church Houses** N York
13 H3 **Churchill** Devon
38 C7 **Churchill** N Som
56 F3 **Churchill** Oxon
71 G4 **Churchill** Worcs
84 F7 **Churchill** Worcs
25 K8 **Churchinford** Somset
15 H6 **Church Knowle** Dorset
87 K5 **Church Langton** Leics
86 F7 **Church Lawford** Warwks
100 A5 **Church Leigh** Staffs
71 H4 **Church Lench** Worcs
100 D4 **Church Mayfield** Staffs
98 F1 **Church Minshull** Ches E
18 B6 **Church Norton** W Susx
87 G7 **Churchover** Warwks
83 K4 **Church Preen** Shrops
83 H3 **Church Pulverbatch** Shrops
25 J8 **Churchstanton** Somset
82 F5 **Churchstoke** Powys
7 G6 **Churchstow** Devon
73 J3 **Church Stowe** Nhants
46 B5 **Church Street** Kent
83 J5 **Church Stretton** Shrops
5 H1 **Churchtown** Cnwll
114 E8 **Churchtown** Derbys
237 d3 **Churchtown** IoM
121 G2 **Churchtown** Lancs
37 G3 **Church Village** Rhondd
115 K7 **Church Warsop** Notts
7 K5 **Churston Ferrers** Torbay
30 D4 **Churt** Surrey
98 B2 **Churton** Ches W
123 K5 **Churwell** Leeds
95 G5 **Chwilog** Gwynd
2 E5 **Chyandour** Cnwll
2 E4 **Chysauster** Cnwll
111 G7 **Cilcain** Flints
66 C3 **Cilcennin** Cerdgn
52 B7 **Cilfrew** Neath
37 G3 **Cilfynydd** Rhondd
65 H6 **Cilgerran** Pembks
51 L4 **Cilmaengwyn** Neath
67 L4 **Cilmery** Powys
51 H2 **Cilsan** Carmth
96 D4 **Ciltalgarth** Gwynd
67 G6 **Cilycwm** Carmth
36 B2 **Cimla** Neath
54 F5 **Cinderford** Gloucs
42 F4 **Cippenham** Slough
56 A7 **Cirencester** Gloucs
45 G4 **City** Gt Lon
45 H4 ***City Airport*** *Gt Lon*
45 H3 **City of London Crematorium** Gt Lon
188 F5 **Clabhach** Ag & B
173 J3 **Clachaig** Ag & B
172 C6 **Clachan** Ag & B
182 A4 **Clachan** Ag & B
191 G7 **Clachan** Ag & B
209 H6 **Clachan** Highld
233 c6 **Clachan-a-Luib** W Isls
188 C6 **Clachan Mor** Ag & B
233 c6 **Clachan na Luib** W Isls
175 G3 **Clachan of Campsie** E Duns
181 M4 **Clachan-Seil** Ag & B
213 G5 **Clachnaharry** Highld
224 C3 **Clachtoll** Highld
195 J4 **Clackavoid** P & K
32 D3 **Clacket Lane Services** Surrey
185 J8 **Clackmannan** Clacks
214 F3 **Clackmarras** Moray
62 E5 **Clacton-on-Sea** Essex
182 F3 **Cladich** Ag & B
71 J3 **Cladswell** Worcs
190 E6 **Claggan** Highld
208 C4 **Claigan** Highld
30 B7 **Clanfield** Hants
56 F7 **Clanfield** Oxon
28 F2 **Clanville** Hants
26 F5 **Clanville** Somset
172 E6 **Claonaig** Ag & B
60 C3 **Clapgate** Herts
74 F4 **Clapham** Bed
44 F5 **Clapham** Gt Lon
130 E5 **Clapham** N York
18 F4 **Clapham** W Susx
13 K2 **Clapton** Somset
26 F2 **Clapton** Somset
38 C5 **Clapton-in-Gordano** N Som
56 D4 **Clapton-on-the-Hill** Gloucs
150 E3 **Claravale** Gatesd
49 H3 **Clarbeston** Pembks
49 H4 **Clarbeston Road** Pembks
116 B5 **Clarborough** Notts
77 H5 **Clare** Suffk
146 D2 **Clarebrand** D & G
147 J2 **Clarencefield** D & G
167 H5 **Clarilaw** Border
175 G6 **Clarkston** E Rens
223 G4 **Clashmore** Highld
224 C3 **Clashmore** Highld
224 C3 **Clashnessie** Highld
204 F2 **Clashnoir** Moray
185 K4 **Clathy** P & K
185 L3 **Clathymore** P & K
205 L1 **Clatt** Abers
81 L5 **Clatter** Powys
25 G5 **Clatworthy** Somset
121 G3 **Claughton** Lancs
130 B6 **Claughton** Lancs
111 J4 **Claughton** Wirral
71 L2 **Claverdon** Warwks
38 C6 **Claverham** N Som
60 D2 **Clavering** Essex
84 E5 **Claverley** Shrops
39 H7 **Claverton** BaNES
37 G5 **Clawdd-coch** V Glam
97 G3 **Clawdd-newydd** Denbgs
9 J5 **Clawton** Devon
117 J3 **Claxby** Lincs
133 L7 **Claxton** N York
93 H3 **Claxton** Norfk
86 F5 **Claybrooke Magna** Leics
87 H7 **Clay Coton** Nhants
115 H8 **Clay Cross** Derbys
72 F4 **Claydon** Oxon
78 D5 **Claydon** Suffk
156 D6 **Claygate** D & G
33 J4 **Claygate** Kent
44 D7 **Claygate** Surrey
45 H3 **Clayhall** Gt Lon
24 F6 **Clayhanger** Devon
25 J7 **Clayhidon** Devon
21 G2 **Clayhill** E Susx
231 H4 **Clayock** Highld
55 H6 **Claypits** Gloucs
102 D3 **Claypole** Lincs
123 G4 **Clayton** C Brad
124 C8 **Clayton** Donc
19 J3 **Clayton** W Susx
121 L4 **Clayton-le-Moors** Lancs
121 H6 **Clayton-le-Woods** Lancs
123 K7 **Clayton West** Kirk
116 B4 **Clayworth** Notts
199 G7 **Cleadale** Highld
151 J3 **Cleadon** S Tyne
6 D3 **Clearbrook** Devon
54 E6 **Clearwell** Gloucs
141 G5 **Cleasby** N York
234 c8 **Cleat** Ork
140 E4 **Cleatlam** Dur
136 D4 **Cleator** Cumb
136 E4 **Cleator Moor** Cumb
123 J5 **Cleckheaton** Kirk
83 L7 **Cleehill** Shrops
175 K6 **Cleekhimin** N Lans
83 L6 **Clee St Margaret** Shrops
127 H8 **Cleethorpes** NE Lin
84 B7 **Cleeton St Mary** Shrops
38 C7 **Cleeve** N Som
41 L4 **Cleeve** Oxon
55 M3 **Cleeve Hill** Gloucs
71 J5 **Cleeve Prior** Worcs
178 D2 **Cleghornie** E Loth
69 J6 **Clehonger** Herefs
186 A7 **Cleish** P & K
175 L6 **Cleland** N Lans
182 C2 **Clenamacrie** Ag & B
104 F7 **Clenchwarton** Norfk
216 E3 **Clenerty** Abers
85 G7 **Clent** Worcs
84 C7 **Cleobury Mortimer** Shrops
84 B6 **Cleobury North** Shrops
161 H3 **Cleongart** Ag & B
213 J4 **Clephanton** Highld
156 A3 **Clerkhill** D & G
154 E3 **Cleuch-head** D & G
40 B5 **Clevancy** Wilts
38 B6 **Clevedon** N Som
120 D2 **Cleveleys** Lancs
39 L4 **Cleverton** Wilts
26 C2 **Clewer** Somset
106 C4 **Cley next the Sea** Norfk
138 E3 **Cliburn** Cumb
29 M2 **Cliddesden** Hants
46 C5 **Cliffe** Medway
125 G4 **Cliffe** N York
21 H3 **Cliff End** E Susx
46 C5 **Cliffe Woods** Medway
68 E5 **Clifford** Herefs
124 C2 **Clifford** Leeds
71 L4 **Clifford Chambers** Warwks
55 G4 **Clifford's Mesne** Gloucs
38 E5 **Clifton** Bristl
75 H6 **Clifton** C Beds
101 K5 **Clifton** C Nott
133 J8 **Clifton** C York
123 H6 **Clifton** Calder
138 D2 **Clifton** Cumb
100 D4 **Clifton** Derbys
23 J3 **Clifton** Devon
115 K3 **Clifton** Donc
120 F4 **Clifton** Lancs
123 J2 **Clifton** N York
57 J2 **Clifton** Oxon
70 F5 **Clifton** Worcs
86 B2 **Clifton Campville** Staffs
41 K2 **Clifton Hampden** Oxon
74 C4 **Clifton Reynes** M Keyn
87 G7 **Clifton upon Dunsmore** Warwks
70 C3 **Clifton upon Teme** Worcs
35 K1 **Cliftonville** Kent
18 D5 **Climping** W Susx
27 H2 **Clink** Somset
132 D7 **Clint** N York
206 F3 **Clinterty** C Aber
92 B2 **Clint Green** Norfk
167 J3 **Clintmains** Border
93 J2 **Clippesby** Norfk
88 D1 **Clipsham** Rutlnd
87 K7 **Clipston** Nhants
101 M5 **Clipston** Notts
58 F3 **Clipstone** C Beds
115 L8 **Clipstone** Notts
121 L3 **Clitheroe** Lancs
98 D7 **Clive** Shrops
117 J2 **Clixby** Lincs
39 M3 **Cloatley** Wilts
97 G2 **Clocaenog** Denbgs
215 J3 **Clochan** Moray
53 L3 **Clodock** Herefs
217 J5 **Clola** Abers
74 F6 **Clophill** C Beds
88 F7 **Clopton** Nhants
78 F4 **Clopton** Suffk
78 F4 **Clopton Corner** Suffk
236 d2 **Clos du Valle** Guern
154 F4 **Closeburn** D & G
154 F3 **Closeburnmill** D & G
14 B1 **Closworth** Somset
59 L2 **Clothall** Herts
112 D8 **Clotton** Ches W
122 D5 **Clough Foot** Calder
123 G6 **Clough Head** Calder
143 K7 **Cloughton** N York
235 c5 **Clousta** Shet
196 B2 **Clova** Angus
22 E6 **Clovelly** Devon
167 G3 **Clovenfords** Border
191 K4 **Clovulin** Highld
115 J6 **Clowne** Derbys
70 C1 **Clows Top** Worcs
201 G3 **Cluanie Inn** Highld
201 G3 **Cluanie Lodge** Highld
145 H4 **Clugston** D & G
82 F7 **Clun** Shrops
213 K5 **Clunas** Highld
83 G7 **Clunbury** Shrops
49 J4 **Clunderwen** Carmth
203 J1 **Clune** Highld
201 J7 **Clunes** Highld
83 H7 **Clungunford** Shrops
195 H7 **Clunie** P & K
83 G7 **Clunton** Shrops
186 D7 **Cluny** Fife
38 F8 **Clutton** BaNES
98 C2 **Clutton** Ches W
38 F8 **Clutton Hill** BaNES
53 K5 **Clydach** Mons
51 K5 **Clydach** Swans
36 F2 **Clydach Vale** Rhondd
174 F4 **Clydebank** W Duns
174 E4 **Clydebank Crematorium** W Duns
40 B5 **Clyffe Pypard** Wilts
174 A2 **Clynder** Ag & B
52 C7 **Clyne** Neath
95 G3 **Clynnog-fawr** Gwynd
68 E5 **Clyro** Powys

12 C4 **Clyst Honiton** Devon
12 D3 **Clyst Hydon** Devon
12 C5 **Clyst St George** Devon
12 D3 **Clyst St Lawrence** Devon
12 C4 **Clyst St Mary** Devon
232 g2 **Cnoc** W Isls
80 F8 **Cnwch Coch** Cerdgn
5 L1 **Coad's Green** Cnwll
164 F3 **Coalburn** S Lans
150 E3 **Coalburns** Gatesd
55 H7 **Coaley** Gloucs
61 J7 **Coalhill** Essex
38 F4 **Coalpit Heath** S Glos
84 C3 **Coalport** Wrekin
185 J7 **Coalsnaughton** Clacks
186 E7 **Coaltown of Balgonie** Fife
186 E7 **Coaltown of Wemyss** Fife
86 E2 **Coalville** Leics
149 H3 **Coanwood** Nthumb
26 C7 **Coat** Somset
175 J5 **Coatbridge** N Lans
175 K5 **Coatdyke** N Lans
40 D4 **Coate** Swindn
40 B7 **Coate** Wilts
89 K4 **Coates** Cambs
55 L7 **Coates** Gloucs
116 E5 **Coates** Lincs
18 D3 **Coates** W Susx
23 K6 **Cobbaton** Devon
55 L5 **Coberley** Gloucs
46 A6 **Cobham** Kent
43 J7 **Cobham** Surrey
43 J8 **Cobham Services** Surrey
69 J3 **Cobnash** Herefs
236 c2 **Cobo** Guern
217 H2 **Coburby** Abers
75 J5 **Cockayne Hatley** C Beds
205 G4 **Cock Bridge** Abers
179 G4 **Cockburnspath** Border
61 K7 **Cock Clarks** Essex
177 L4 **Cockenzie and Port Seton** E Loth
120 F1 **Cockerham** Lancs
136 F2 **Cockermouth** Cumb
59 J4 **Cockernhoe** Herts
51 J6 **Cockett** Swans
140 E3 **Cockfield** Dur
77 K4 **Cockfield** Suffk
44 F2 **Cockfosters** Gt Lon
61 H4 **Cock Green** Essex
18 B3 **Cocking** W Susx
18 B2 **Cocking Causeway** W Susx
7 K3 **Cockington** Torbay
26 C2 **Cocklake** Somset
91 H3 **Cockley Cley** Norfk
21 H2 **Cock Marling** E Susx
42 D4 **Cockpole Green** Wokham
98 B6 **Cockshutt** Shrops
106 B4 **Cockthorpe** Norfk
12 C6 **Cockwood** Devon
114 B5 **Cockyard** Derbys
78 D4 **Coddenham** Suffk
70 C6 **Coddington** Herefs
102 D2 **Coddington** Notts
27 L4 **Codford St Mary** Wilts
27 L4 **Codford St Peter** Wilts
59 K4 **Codicote** Herts
31 H7 **Codmore Hill** W Susx
101 H3 **Codnor** Derbys
39 G5 **Codrington** S Glos
84 F3 **Codsall** Staffs
84 F3 **Codsall Wood** Staffs
97 L3 **Coedpoeth** Wrexhm
97 L2 **Coed Talon** Flints
53 M7 **Coed-y-paen** Mons
7 K3 **Coffinswell** Devon
12 C6 **Cofton** Devon
85 H7 **Cofton Hackett** Worcs
37 J6 **Cogan** V Glam
74 B3 **Cogenhoe** Nhants
61 K4 **Coggeshall** Essex
203 H2 **Coignafearn** Highld
205 H6 **Coilacriech** Abers
184 D6 **Coilantogle** Stirlg
208 E6 **Coillore** Highld
36 E4 **Coity** Brdgnd
232 g2 **Col** W Isls
225 L6 **Colaboll** Highld
4 D4 **Colan** Cnwll
12 D5 **Colaton Raleigh** Devon
208 C5 **Colbost** Highld
140 F7 **Colburn** N York
138 F3 **Colby** Cumb
237 b6 **Colby** IoM
62 B3 **Colchester** Essex
62 B4 **Colchester Crematorium** Essex
41 K6 **Cold Ash** W Berk
87 J7 **Cold Ashby** Nhants
39 H6 **Cold Ashton** S Glos
56 C4 **Cold Aston** Gloucs
229 J4 **Coldbackie** Highld
74 D4 **Cold Brayfield** M Keyn
19 J4 **Coldean** Br & H
7 J2 **Coldeast** Devon
122 E5 **Colden** Calder
29 J6 **Colden Common** Hants
117 G5 **Cold Hanworth** Lincs
31 J3 **Coldharbour** Surrey
73 J4 **Cold Higham** Nhants
179 J5 **Coldingham** Border
133 H3 **Cold Kirby** N York
99 J6 **Coldmeece** Staffs
61 K7 **Cold Norton** Essex
88 B2 **Cold Overton** Leics
35 H5 **Coldred** Kent
11 G4 **Coldridge** Devon
168 C2 **Coldstream** Border
18 D3 **Coldwaltham** W Susx
69 H7 **Coldwell** Herefs
217 H6 **Coldwells** Abers
26 F5 **Cole** Somset
83 G6 **Colebatch** Shrops
12 C2 **Colebrook** Devon
11 H5 **Colebrooke** Devon
102 F1 **Coleby** Lincs
125 L6 **Coleby** N Linc
11 H5 **Coleford** Devon
54 E6 **Coleford** Gloucs
27 G2 **Coleford** Somset
92 E6 **Colegate End** Norfk
15 J3 **Colehill** Dorset
32 D6 **Coleman's Hatch** E Susx
98 B6 **Colemere** Shrops
30 B5 **Colemore** Hants
186 B2 **Colenden** P & K
39 J6 **Colerne** Wilts
56 A5 **Colesbourne** Gloucs
42 F2 **Coleshill** Bucks
40 E2 **Coleshill** Oxon
85 L5 **Coleshill** Warwks
26 E1 **Coley** BaNES
31 L5 **Colgate** W Susx
187 H6 **Colinsburgh** Fife
177 H5 **Colinton** C Edin
173 H4 **Colintraive** Ag & B
105 L7 **Colkirk** Norfk
189 G5 **Coll** Ag & B
186 C2 **Collace** P & K
235 c3 **Collafirth** Shet
188 F5 *Coll Airport* Ag & B
7 G7 **Collaton** Devon
7 K4 **Collaton St Mary** Torbay
214 E2 **College of Roseisle** Moray
42 D7 **College Town** Br For
186 E5 **Collessie** Fife
45 J2 **Collier Row** Gt Lon
60 B4 **Collier's End** Herts
33 J4 **Collier Street** Kent
217 K8 **Collieston** Abers
155 H6 **Collin** D & G
28 E2 **Collingbourne Ducis** Wilts
28 E1 **Collingbourne Kingston** Wilts
124 B2 **Collingham** Leeds
102 D1 **Collingham** Notts
70 B3 **Collington** Herefs
73 L4 **Collingtree** Nhants
112 E3 **Collins Green** Warrtn
196 F7 **Colliston** Angus
12 E2 **Colliton** Devon
88 E3 **Collyweston** Nhants
152 D5 **Colmonell** S Ayrs
75 G3 **Colmworth** Bed
43 G5 **Colnbrook** Slough
89 L7 **Colne** Cambs
122 D3 **Colne** Lancs
61 K3 **Colne Engaine** Essex
92 E3 **Colney** Norfk
59 K6 **Colney Heath** Herts
56 B6 **Coln Rogers** Gloucs
56 C6 **Coln St Aldwyns** Gloucs
56 B5 **Coln St Dennis** Gloucs
180 E7 **Colonsay** Ag & B
180 E8 *Colonsay Airport* Ag & B
216 C7 **Colpy** Abers
166 E2 **Colquhar** Border
102 F7 **Colsterworth** Lincs
102 B5 **Colston Bassett** Notts
214 D2 **Coltfield** Moray
106 F8 **Coltishall** Norfk
129 G3 **Colton** Cumb
124 B4 **Colton** Leeds
124 E2 **Colton** N York
92 D2 **Colton** Norfk
100 B7 **Colton** Staffs
33 H4 **Colt's Hill** Kent
146 F4 **Colvend** D & G
70 D6 **Colwall** Herefs
158 B6 **Colwell** Nthumb
100 A7 **Colwich** Staffs
36 E5 **Colwinston** V Glam
18 C5 **Colworth** W Susx
110 B5 **Colwyn Bay** Conwy
13 G4 **Colyford** Devon
13 G4 **Colyton** Devon
57 H5 **Combe** Oxon
41 G7 **Combe** W Berk
39 H7 **Combe Down** BaNES
7 J3 **Combe Fishacre** Devon
25 J5 **Combe Florey** Somset
39 G7 **Combe Hay** BaNES
7 K2 **Combeinteignhead** Devon
23 J3 **Combe Martin** Devon
12 F3 **Combe Raleigh** Devon
112 F6 **Comberbach** Ches W
85 L3 **Comberford** Staffs
75 L4 **Comberton** Cambs
69 K2 **Comberton** Herefs
13 H1 **Combe St Nicholas** Somset
72 C4 **Combrook** Warwks
114 B6 **Combs** Derbys
78 C3 **Combs** Suffk
78 C3 **Combs Ford** Suffk
25 K3 **Combwich** Somset
206 D4 **Comers** Abers
70 E2 **Comhampton** Worcs
81 J3 **Commins Coch** Powys
142 E5 **Commondale** N York
136 D3 **Common End** Cumb
5 K2 **Common Moor** Cnwll
113 L4 **Compstall** Stockp
146 B4 **Compstonend** D & G
7 K3 **Compton** Devon
29 J6 **Compton** Hants
84 E6 **Compton** Staffs
30 F3 **Compton** Surrey
41 K4 **Compton** W Berk
30 C7 **Compton** W Susx
28 C2 **Compton** Wilts
27 K7 **Compton Abbas** Dorset
56 B5 **Compton Abdale** Gloucs
40 B6 **Compton Bassett** Wilts
40 F3 **Compton Beauchamp** Oxon
26 B1 **Compton Bishop** Somset
28 B5 **Compton Chamberlayne** Wilts
38 F7 **Compton Dando** BaNES
26 C5 **Compton Dundon** Somset
26 B7 **Compton Durville** Somset
38 E4 **Compton Greenfield** S Glos
38 D8 **Compton Martin** BaNES
26 F6 **Compton Pauncefoot** Somset
14 B4 **Compton Valence** Dorset
176 D1 **Comrie** Fife
185 G3 **Comrie** P & K
191 K3 **Conaglen House** Highld
210 D8 **Conchra** Highld
195 H7 **Concraigie** P & K
71 G6 **Conderton** Worcs
56 D3 **Condicote** Gloucs
175 K4 **Condorrat** N Lans
83 J3 **Condover** Shrops
55 J4 **Coney Hill** Gloucs
31 J6 **Coneyhurst Common** W Susx
133 L5 **Coneysthorpe** N York
91 L7 **Coney Weston** Suffk
86 D3 **Congerstone** Leics
105 H7 **Congham** Norfk
113 J8 **Congleton** Ches E
38 C7 **Congresbury** N Som
147 H2 **Conheath** D & G
214 B4 **Conicavel** Moray
103 L2 **Coningsby** Lincs
75 K2 **Conington** Cambs
89 H6 **Conington** Cambs
115 K2 **Conisbrough** Donc
118 E3 **Conisholme** Lincs
137 J7 **Coniston** Cumb
126 E4 **Coniston** E R Yk
131 G8 **Coniston Cold** N York
131 J6 **Conistone** N York
111 J7 **Connah's Quay** Flints
182 C1 **Connel** Ag & B
164 C6 **Connel Park** E Ayrs
3 G4 **Connor Downs** Cnwll
212 E4 **Conon Bridge** Highld
122 E2 **Cononley** N York
99 M3 **Consall** Staffs
150 E5 **Consett** Dur
132 B2 **Constable Burton** N York
122 B5 **Constable Lee** Lancs
3 J5 **Constantine** Cnwll
4 D2 **Constantine Bay** Cnwll
212 C3 **Contin** Highld
109 L6 **Conwy** Conwy
77 K2 **Conyer's Green** Suffk
20 E4 **Cooden** E Susx
9 K4 **Cookbury** Devon
42 E4 **Cookham** W & M
42 E4 **Cookham Dean** W & M
42 E4 **Cookham Rise** W & M

71 J3 Cookhill Worcs
93 H7 Cookley Suffk
84 E7 Cookley Worcs
42 B3 Cookley Green Oxon
207 G6 Cookney Abers
62 E4 Cook's Green Essex
77 L4 Cooks Green Suffk
61 G6 Cooksmill Green Essex
31 J6 Coolham W Susx
46 C5 Cooling Medway
4 E5 Coombe Cnwll
7 L2 Coombe Devon
12 E4 Coombe Devon
39 H2 Coombe Gloucs
30 A7 Coombe Hants
28 C6 Coombe Bissett Wilts
7 K2 Coombe Cellars Devon
55 K3 Coombe Hill Gloucs
14 F5 Coombe Keynes Dorset
7 L3 Coombe Pafford Torbay
19 G4 Coombes W Susx
69 G2 Coombes-Moor Herefs
60 D7 Coopersale Common Essex
78 D6 Copdock Suffk
61 L4 Copford Green Essex
132 E6 Copgrove N York
235 d3 Copister Shet
75 G5 Cople Bed
140 D3 Copley Dur
124 E2 Copmanthorpe C York
99 J6 Copmere End Staffs
120 F3 Copp Lancs
99 K8 Coppenhall Staffs
2 F4 Copperhouse Cnwll
89 H7 Coppingford Cambs
11 H4 Copplestone Devon
121 H7 Coppull Lancs
31 K6 Copsale W Susx
121 K4 Copster Green Lancs
86 F5 Copston Magna Warwks
35 J3 Cop Street Kent
132 E5 Copt Hewick N York
32 B5 Copthorne W Susx
86 F2 Copt Oak Leics
28 F8 Copythorne Hants
45 K3 Corbets Tey Gt Lon
236 a7 Corbiere Jersey
150 C3 Corbridge Nthumb
88 C5 Corby Nhants
103 G7 Corby Glen Lincs
162 D4 Cordon N Ayrs
84 B8 Coreley Shrops
25 K7 Corfe Somset
15 H6 Corfe Castle Dorset
15 J3 Corfe Mullen Dorset
83 J6 Corfton Shrops
205 G4 Corgarff Abers
29 L7 Corhampton Hants
86 C6 Corley Warwks
86 C6 Corley Services Warwks
195 L3 Cormuir Angus
77 K6 Cornard Tye Suffk
151 H7 Cornforth Dur
216 B3 Cornhill Abers
168 C2 Cornhill-on-Tweed Nthumb
122 D5 Cornholme Calder
188 C6 Cornoigmore Ag & B
150 E6 Cornsay Dur
150 F6 Cornsay Colliery Dur
212 E3 Corntown Highld
36 E5 Corntown V Glam
56 F3 Cornwell Oxon
6 E4 Cornwood Devon
7 J5 Cornworthy Devon
191 L2 Corpach Highld
106 D6 Corpusty Norfk
205 K4 Corrachree Abers
191 K4 Corran Highld
200 C4 Corran Highld
155 L5 Corrie D & G
162 C2 Corrie N Ayrs
162 B5 Corriecravie N Ayrs
162 D3 Corriegills N Ayrs
201 K6 Corriegour Lodge Hotel Highld
212 B2 Corriemoille Highld
212 B7 Corrimony Highld
116 E4 Corringham Lincs
46 B4 Corringham Thurr
81 G2 Corris Gwynd
81 G2 Corris Uchaf Gwynd
183 H7 Corrow Ag & B
199 K1 Corry Highld
10 F5 Corscombe Devon
13 M2 Corscombe Dorset
55 H3 Corse Gloucs
55 J2 Corse Lawn Gloucs
39 K6 Corsham Wilts
206 D4 Corsindae Abers
27 J3 Corsley Wilts
27 J3 Corsley Heath Wilts
154 D6 Corsock D & G
39 G7 Corston BaNES
39 L4 Corston Wilts
177 G4 Corstorphine C Edin
196 C4 Cortachy Angus
93 L4 Corton Suffk
27 L4 Corton Wilts
26 F6 Corton Denham Somset
191 L3 Coruanan Highld
97 G4 Corwen Denbgs
10 C7 Coryton Devon
46 C4 Coryton Thurr
87 G4 Cosby Leics
85 G5 Coseley Dudley
73 L6 Cosgrove Nhants
17 J2 Cosham C Port
49 G6 Cosheston Pembks
194 C6 Coshieville P & K
101 J4 Cossall Notts
87 H2 Cossington Leics
26 A4 Cossington Somset
92 E2 Costessey Norfk
101 L7 Costock Notts
102 D7 Coston Leics
92 C3 Coston Norfk
57 G7 Cote Oxon
112 E7 Cotebrook Ches W
148 E5 Cotehill Cumb
101 K7 Cotes Leics
87 G6 Cotesbach Leics
25 J6 Cotford St Luke Somset
101 M5 Cotgrave Notts
207 G3 Cothal Abers
102 C3 Cotham Notts
140 C4 Cotherstone Dur
57 J7 Cothill Oxon
13 G3 Cotleigh Devon
101 J4 Cotmanhay Derbys
76 B3 Coton Cambs
73 J1 Coton Nhants
99 J7 Coton Staffs
99 K7 Coton Clanford Staffs
83 J2 Coton Hill Shrops
86 B1 Coton in the Elms Derbys
55 M6 Cotswolds
7 H4 Cott Devon
121 G4 Cottam Lancs
116 D5 Cottam Notts
76 C2 Cottenham Cambs
60 A3 Cottered Herts
88 F5 Cotterstock Nhants
87 K3 Cottesbrooke Nhants
88 C2 Cottesmore Rutlnd
126 C4 Cottingham E R Yk
88 B5 Cottingham Nhants
123 G3 Cottingley C Brad
123 K4 Cottingley Hall Crematorium Leeds
57 L2 Cottisford Oxon
78 C2 Cotton Suffk
206 E3 Cottown Abers
215 L8 Cottown Abers
216 F6 Cottown of Gight Abers
6 C3 Cotts Devon
71 J3 Coughton Warwks
172 C5 Coulaghailtro Ag & B
210 E5 Coulags Highld
205 L5 Coull Abers
173 L2 Coulport Ag & B
32 B2 Coulsdon Gt Lon
27 L2 Coulston Wilts
165 K3 Coulter S Lans
133 K5 Coulton N York
186 F3 Coultra Fife
83 L3 Cound Shrops
141 G2 Coundon Dur
131 H2 Countersett N York
12 B4 Countess Wear Devon
87 H4 Countesthorpe Leics
24 B2 Countisbury Devon
195 K7 Coupar Angus P & K
168 D3 Coupland Nthumb
172 D8 Cour Ag & B
199 L6 Courteachan Highld
73 L4 Courteenhall Nhants
51 H2 Court Henry Carmth
47 G2 Courtsend Essex
25 J5 Courtway Somset
177 K5 Cousland Mdloth
33 H6 Cousley Wood E Susx
173 L2 Cove Ag & B
179 G4 Cove Border
24 E7 Cove Devon
30 E1 Cove Hants
219 J3 Cove Highld
207 H5 Cove Bay C Aber
93 L6 Covehithe Suffk
85 G3 Coven Staffs
90 C6 Coveney Cambs
118 D3 Covenham St Bartholomew Lincs
118 D3 Covenham St Mary Lincs
86 D7 Coventry Covtry
86 D8 Coventry Airport Warwks
3 K7 Coverack Cnwll
3 H5 Coverack Bridges Cnwll
131 L3 Coverham N York
74 F1 Covington Cambs
165 J2 Covington S Lans
130 C4 Cowan Bridge Lancs
20 C3 Cowbeech E Susx
103 L8 Cowbit Lincs
36 F5 Cowbridge V Glam
32 E5 Cowden Kent
177 G1 Cowdenbeath Fife
100 F3 Cowers Lane Derbys
16 F3 Cowes IoW
133 G2 Cowesby N York
31 K6 Cowfold W Susx
38 E3 Cowhill S Glos
175 L1 Cowie Stirlg
11 K5 Cowley Devon
55 L5 Cowley Gloucs
43 H4 Cowley Gt Lon
57 K7 Cowley Oxon
121 H6 Cowling Lancs
122 E2 Cowling N York
132 C3 Cowling N York
77 G4 Cowlinge Suffk
159 H5 Cowpen Nthumb
17 K1 Cowplain Hants
149 L6 Cowshill Dur
38 C7 Cowslip Green N Som
132 F8 Cowthorpe N York
98 F4 Coxbank Ches E
101 G4 Coxbench Derbys
8 F5 Coxford Cnwll
105 K6 Coxford Norfk
33 J3 Coxheath Kent
151 H7 Coxhoe Dur
26 D3 Coxley Somset
26 D3 Coxley Wick Somset
45 K2 Coxtie Green Essex
133 H4 Coxwold N York
36 E4 Coychurch Brdgnd
36 E4 Coychurch Crematorium Brdgnd
163 K5 Coylton S Ayrs
203 L3 Coylumbridge Highld
36 D4 Coytrahen Brdgnd
71 J2 Crabbs Cross Worcs
31 K6 Crabtree W Susx
138 F3 Crackenthorpe Cumb
8 F5 Crackington Haven Cnwll
84 D2 Crackleybank Shrops
131 J7 Cracoe N York
25 G8 Craddock Devon
85 G6 Cradley Dudley
70 D5 Cradley Herefs
85 G6 Cradley Heath Sandw
52 F2 Cradoc Powys
6 B5 Crafthole Cnwll
204 C1 Craggan Highld
150 F5 Craghead Dur
52 D3 Crai Powys
215 L3 Craibstone Moray
196 E6 Craichie Angus
197 H5 Craig Angus
211 G4 Craig Highld
164 C6 Craigbank E Ayrs
177 H7 Craigburn Border
156 C5 Craigcleuch D & G
216 F7 Craigdam Abers
182 B6 Craigdhu Ag & B
206 D3 Craigearn Abers
215 G5 Craigellachie Moray
186 B4 Craigend P & K
174 E4 Craigend Rens
174 C3 Craigendoran Ag & B
174 D5 Craigends Rens
145 G3 Craighlaw D & G
171 K5 Craighouse Ag & B
195 H7 Craigie P & K
163 K3 Craigie S Ayrs
217 H2 Craigiefold Abers
146 D4 Craigley D & G
51 K4 Craig Llangiwg Neath
177 H4 Craiglockhart C Edin
177 J4 Craigmillar C Edin
154 D5 Craigneston D & G
175 K5 Craigneuk N Lans
175 K6 Craigneuk N Lans
190 E8 Craignure Ag & B
197 H4 Craigo Angus
186 F5 Craigrothie Fife
184 B4 Craigruie Stirlg
196 E8 Craigton Angus
206 F5 Craigton C Aber
174 F7 Craigton E Rens
174 F5 Craigton Crematorium C Glas
196 B6 Craigton of Airlie Angus
187 K5 Crail Fife
167 L4 Crailing Border
116 C2 Craiselound N Linc
132 C2 Crakehall N York
133 L6 Crambe N York
159 G6 Cramlington Nthumb
177 G3 Cramond C Edin
177 G4 Cramond Bridge C Edin
113 H7 Cranage Ches E
99 J5 Cranberry Staffs
28 B8 Cranborne Dorset
42 F5 Cranbourne Br For
33 K6 Cranbrook Kent
74 D6 Cranfield C Beds
43 J5 Cranford Gt Lon
88 D7 Cranford St Andrew Nhants
88 D7 Cranford St John Nhants
55 K5 Cranham Gloucs

112 D2 Crank St Hel
31 H4 Cranleigh Surrey
26 F3 Cranmore Somset
87 L4 Cranoe Leics
79 G2 Cransford Suffk
178 E6 Cranshaws Border
4 C4 Crantock Cnwll
103 G3 Cranwell Lincs
91 H4 Cranwich Norfk
92 B3 Cranworth Norfk
182 A6 Craobh Haven Ag & B
182 E7 Crarae Ag & B
225 L4 Crask Inn Highld
212 D6 Crask of Aigas Highld
169 K5 Craster Nthumb
93 G7 Cratfield Suffk
206 E6 Crathes Abers
206 D6 Crathes Castle Abers
205 G6 Crathie Abers
202 E6 Crathie Highld
141 K5 Crathorne N York
83 H6 Craven Arms Shrops
150 E3 Crawcrook Gatesd
165 J5 Crawford S Lans
165 G5 Crawfordjohn S Lans
29 H4 Crawley Hants
57 G5 Crawley Oxon
31 L4 Crawley W Susx
32 C5 Crawley Down W Susx
122 B5 Crawshawbooth Lancs
197 L1 Crawton Abers
131 H4 Cray N York
45 K5 Crayford Gt Lon
133 H5 Crayke N York
46 B2 Crays Hill Essex
24 C7 Creacombe Devon
191 J7 Creagan Inn Ag & B
233 c7 Creag Ghoraidh W Isls
233 c7 Creagorry W Isls
192 E3 Creaguaineach Lodge Highld
73 K1 Creaton Nhants
155 M7 Creca D & G
69 J5 Credenhill Herefs
11 J5 Crediton Devon
153 H6 Creebank D & G
145 J2 Creebridge D & G
25 L6 Creech Heathfield Somset
25 L6 Creech St Michael Somset
4 E6 Creed Cnwll
45 J4 Creekmouth Gt Lon
78 D3 Creeting St Mary Suffk
103 G8 Creeton Lincs
145 K3 Creetown D & G
237 a7 Cregneash IoM
186 E3 Creich Fife
37 G4 Creigiau Cardif
6 C5 Cremyll Cnwll
83 L3 Cressage Shrops
114 D6 Cressbrook Derbys
49 H6 Cresselly Pembks
42 D3 Cressex Bucks
61 J4 Cressing Essex
159 H4 Cresswell Nthumb
49 H6 Cresswell Pembks
99 L5 Cresswell Staffs
115 K6 Creswell Derbys
78 F3 Cretingham Suffk
172 C5 Cretshengan Ag & B
99 G2 Crewe Ches E
98 B2 Crewe Ches W
99 G2 Crewe Crematorium Ches E
99 G2 Crewe Green Ches E
83 G1 Crew Green Powys
13 K1 Crewkerne Somset
101 G5 Crewton C Derb
183 L3 Crianlarich Stirlg
66 C4 Cribyn Cerdgn
95 J5 Criccieth Gwynd
101 G2 Crich Derbys
177 K6 Crichton Mdloth
87 H8 Crick Nhants
68 C6 Crickadarn Powys
13 J2 Cricket St Thomas Somset
53 K4 Crickhowell Powys
40 C2 Cricklade Wilts
44 E3 Cricklewood Gt Lon
185 H3 Crieff P & K
82 F1 Criggion Powys
123 L7 Crigglestone Wakefd
217 K3 Crimond Abers
90 F3 Crimplesham Norfk
72 B5 Crimscote Warwks
212 C6 Crinaglack Highld
182 A8 Crinan Ag & B
175 L6 Crindledyke N Lans
92 E3 Cringleford Norfk
49 J5 Crinow Pembks
213 G8 Croachy Highld
45 J6 Crockenhill Kent
42 B3 Crocker End Oxon
11 H6 Crockernwell Devon
27 K3 Crockerton Wilts
154 E7 Crocketford D & G
32 D3 Crockham Hill Kent
36 D2 Croeserw Neath
48 D2 Croes-goch Pembks
65 L5 Croes-lan Cerdgn
95 L4 Croesor Gwynd
50 E3 Croesyceiliog Carmth
37 L2 Croesyceiliog Torfn
87 G4 Croft Leics
104 E1 Croft Lincs
112 F3 Croft Warrtn
174 E2 Croftamie Stirlg
124 B6 Crofton Wakefd
141 H5 Croft-on-Tees N York
220 F5 Croftown Highld
215 G4 Crofts Moray
215 H3 Crofts of Dipple Moray
217 K3 Crofts of Savoch Abers
51 G6 Crofty Swans
181 L3 Croggan Ag & B
148 F5 Croglin Cumb
222 B3 Croick Highld
223 H7 Cromarty Highld
176 E2 Crombie Fife
214 D8 Cromdale Highld
59 M3 Cromer Herts
106 F4 Cromer Norfk
100 F2 Cromford Derbys
39 G3 Cromhall S Glos
232 f3 Cromor W Isls
102 D1 Cromwell Notts
164 C5 Cronberry E Ayrs
30 C2 Crondall Hants
112 C4 Cronton Knows
138 C7 Crook Cumb
150 E7 Crook Dur
163 L3 Crookedholm E Ayrs
168 D2 Crookham Nthumb
41 K7 Crookham W Berk
30 C2 Crookham Village Hants
165 L4 Crook Inn Border
129 L3 Crooklands Cumb
185 L7 Crook of Devon P & K
72 F5 Cropredy Oxon
87 G2 Cropston Leics
71 H5 Cropthorne Worcs
134 B2 Cropton N York
102 B5 Cropwell Bishop Notts
102 B5 Cropwell Butler Notts
232 g1 Cros W Isls
232 f3 Crosbost W Isls
147 J7 Crosby Cumb
237 c5 Crosby IoM
125 K7 Crosby N Linc
111 J2 Crosby Sefton
139 G5 Crosby Garret Cumb
138 F4 Crosby Ravensworth Cumb
26 E3 Croscombe Somset
26 B1 Cross Somset
172 E7 Crossaig Ag & B
188 C7 Crossapoll Ag & B
54 B4 Cross Ash Mons
33 K4 Cross-at-Hand Kent
147 J6 Crosscanonby Cumb
106 F5 Crossdale Street Norfk
123 G3 Cross Flatts C Brad
176 E2 Crossford Fife
175 L8 Crossford S Lans
177 K5 Crossgatehall E Loth
163 J1 Crossgates E Ayrs
176 F1 Crossgates Fife
124 B4 Cross Gates Leeds
134 F3 Crossgates N York
129 L6 Crossgill Lancs
123 L4 Cross Green Leeds
77 K4 Cross Green Suffk
78 B4 Cross Green Suffk
51 H3 Cross Hands Carmth
163 L4 Crosshands E Ayrs
186 C7 Crosshill Fife
163 J7 Crosshill S Ayrs
163 K2 Crosshouse E Ayrs
83 K3 Cross Houses Shrops
20 B2 Cross in Hand E Susx
65 L3 Cross Inn Cerdgn
174 C2 Cross Keys Ag & B
37 K3 Crosskeys Caerph
230 F2 Crosskirk Highld
17 G4 Cross Lane IoW
84 C4 Cross Lane Head Shrops
174 D5 Crosslee Rens
146 C2 Crossmichael D & G
216 E7 Cross of Jackston Abers
100 F4 Cross o' th' hands Derbys
206 B4 Crossroads Abers
206 E6 Crossroads Abers
92 E7 Cross Street Suffk
196 E5 Crosston Angus
113 H5 Cross Town Ches E
70 E2 Crossway Green Worcs
14 E5 Crossways Dorset
64 F6 Crosswell Pembks
129 J2 Crosthwaite Cumb
121 G6 Croston Lancs
92 F1 Crostwick Norfk
44 F3 Crouch End Gt Lon
28 B6 Croucheston Wilts
14 D1 Crouch Hill Dorset
73 G7 Croughton Nhants
216 F2 Crovie Abers
3 H4 Crowan Cnwll
32 F6 Crowborough E Susx
25 H4 Crowcombe Somset
114 C7 Crowdecote Derbys
114 B2 Crowden Derbys
114 D2 Crow Edge Barns
58 C7 Crowell Oxon
78 D3 Crowfield Suffk
178 F4 Crowhill E Loth
54 F3 Crow Hill Herefs
20 F3 Crowhurst E Susx
32 D4 Crowhurst Surrey
89 J2 Crowland Lincs
78 B1 Crowland Suffk
2 F5 Crowlas Cnwll
125 J7 Crowle N Linc
71 G4 Crowle Worcs
71 G3 Crowle Green Worcs
41 L3 Crowmarsh Gifford Oxon
78 F1 Crown Corner Suffk
6 C4 Crownhill C Plym
74 B6 Crownhill Crematorium M Keyn
92 C3 Crownthorpe Norfk
3 H5 Crowntown Cnwll
2 D5 Crows-an-Wra Cnwll
42 D7 Crowthorne Wokham
112 E6 Crowton Ches W
151 G7 Croxdale Dur
100 B5 Croxden Staffs
43 H2 Croxley Green Herts
111 L3 Croxteth Lpool
75 J3 Croxton Cambs
126 D7 Croxton N Linc
91 K6 Croxton Norfk
106 B6 Croxton Norfk
99 H6 Croxton Staffs
102 D6 Croxton Kerrial Leics
213 J4 Croy Highld
175 J3 Croy N Lans
23 G4 Croyde Devon
75 K5 Croydon Cambs
44 F6 Croydon Gt Lon
44 F6 Croydon Crematorium Gt Lon
203 G7 Crubenmore Highld
83 H2 Cruckmeole Shrops
83 H2 Cruckton Shrops
217 K6 Cruden Bay Abers
98 F8 Crudgington Wrekin
39 L2 Crudwell Wilts
37 K2 Crumlin Caerph
5 K5 Crumplehorn Cnwll
113 J2 Crumpsall Manch
34 E5 Crundale Kent
49 K5 Crunwear Pembks
29 H1 Crux Easton Hants
50 F3 Crwbin Carmth
42 E2 Cryers Hill Bucks
65 G7 Crymmych Pembks
52 C6 Crynant Neath
45 G5 Crystal Palace Gt Lon
209 L3 Cuaig Highld
181 L4 Cuan Ag & B
72 D2 Cubbington Warwks
4 C4 Cubert Cnwll
58 D4 Cublington Bucks
69 H6 Cublington Herefs
32 B7 Cuckfield W Susx
27 H6 Cucklington Somset
115 K7 Cuckney Notts
57 L7 Cuddesdon Oxon
58 C5 Cuddington Bucks
112 E7 Cuddington Ches W
98 C3 Cuddington Heath Ches W
32 D2 Cudham Gt Lon
10 D8 Cudliptown Devon
15 K3 Cudnell Bmouth
124 B8 Cudworth Barns
13 J1 Cudworth Somset
59 M7 Cuffley Herts
191 J5 Cuil Highld
212 F3 Culbokie Highld
212 D6 Culburnie Highld
213 G5 Culcabock Highld
213 K4 Culcharry Highld
112 F3 Culcheth Warrtn
215 L7 Culdrain Abers
209 L6 Culduie Highld
77 J1 Culford Suffk
138 E2 Culgaith Cumb
41 J2 Culham Oxon
224 C2 Culkein Highld
224 D2 Culkein Drumbeg Highld
39 L2 Culkerton Gloucs
215 L2 Cullen Moray
159 J7 Cullercoats N Tyne
206 E5 Cullerlie Abers
213 G2 Cullicudden Highld
123 G3 Cullingworth C Brad
199 G2 Cuillin Hills Highld
181 L5 Cullipool Ag & B
235 d2 Cullivoe Shet
213 H5 Culloden Highld
12 C2 Cullompton Devon
12 D2 Cullompton Services Devon
25 H7 Culm Davy Devon
83 J6 Culmington Shrops
25 H8 Culmstock Devon
224 C7 Culnacraig Highld

146 D5 **Culnaightrie** D & G
209 H2 **Culnaknock** Highld
222 D3 **Culrain** Highld
176 D2 **Culross** Fife
163 H6 **Culroy** S Ayrs
216 C7 **Culsalmond** Abers
145 K5 **Culscadden** D & G
145 G5 **Culshabbin** D & G
235 b6 **Culswick** Shet
207 H1 **Cultercullen** Abers
207 G5 **Cults** C Aber
45 M7 **Culverstone Green** Kent
103 G4 **Culverthorpe** Lincs
73 G5 **Culworth** Nhants
163 G7 **Culzean Castle & Country Park** S Ayrs
175 K4 **Cumbernauld** N Lans
175 K3 **Cumbernauld Village** N Lans
119 G6 **Cumberworth** Lincs
216 F4 **Cuminestown** Abers
179 G6 **Cumledge** Border
148 D4 **Cummersdale** Cumb
147 K2 **Cummertrees** D & G
214 E1 **Cummingston** Moray
164 B5 **Cumnock** E Ayrs
57 J7 **Cumnor** Oxon
148 F5 **Cumrew** Cumb
155 J5 **Cumrue** D & G
148 D4 **Cumwhinton** Cumb
148 E4 **Cumwhitton** Cumb
132 F5 **Cundall** N York
163 J2 **Cunninghamhead** N Ayrs
235 c7 **Cunningsburgh** Shet
186 F4 **Cupar** Fife
186 F5 **Cupar Muir** Fife
114 E6 **Curbar** Derbys
17 G1 **Curbridge** Hants
57 G6 **Curbridge** Oxon
29 K8 **Curdridge** Hants
85 L5 **Curdworth** Warwks
25 L7 **Curland** Somset
41 J6 **Curridge** W Berk
177 G5 **Currie** C Edin
25 L6 **Curry Mallet** Somset
26 B6 **Curry Rivel** Somset
33 J5 **Curtisden Green** Kent
7 H5 **Curtisknowle** Devon
3 H6 **Cury** Cnwll
205 L3 **Cushnie** Abers
145 J7 **Cutcloy** D & G
24 E4 **Cutcombe** Somset
223 G4 **Cuthill** Highld
70 F2 **Cutnall Green** Worcs
56 C3 **Cutsdean** Gloucs
115 G6 **Cutthorpe** Derbys
42 A2 **Cuxham** Oxon
46 B6 **Cuxton** Medway
117 K2 **Cuxwold** Lincs
110 E6 **Cwm** Denbgs
36 B3 **Cwmafan** Neath
52 F7 **Cwmaman** Rhondd
50 B1 **Cwmbach** Carmth
68 D6 **Cwmbach** Powys
52 F7 **Cwmbach** Rhondd
68 B4 **Cwmbach Llechrhyd** Powys
37 L2 **Cwmbran** Torfn
37 K2 **Cwmcarn** Caerph
54 C6 **Cwmcarvan** Mons
65 J6 **Cwm-cou** Cerdgn
53 H4 **Cwm Crawnon** Powys
52 F7 **Cwmdare** Rhondd
53 J4 **Cwmdu** Powys
51 J6 **Cwmdu** Swans
65 L7 **Cwmduad** Carmth
36 D3 **Cwmfelin** Brdgnd
53 H7 **Cwmfelin** Myr Td
49 K4 **Cwmfelin Boeth** Carmth
37 J3 **Cwmfelinfach** Caerph
50 E3 **Cwmffrwd** Carmth
52 C5 **Cwmgiedd** Powys
51 K4 **Cwmgorse** Carmth
51 H4 **Cwmgwili** Carmth
65 K6 **Cwmhiraeth** Carmth
81 J2 **Cwm Llinau** Powys
51 L3 **Cwmllynfell** Neath
51 G3 **Cwmmawr** Carmth
36 E2 **Cwmparc** Rhondd
65 K6 **Cwmpengraig** Carmth
53 K6 **Cwmtillery** Blae G
52 B6 **Cwm-twrch Isaf** Powys
51 L4 **Cwm-twrch Uchaf** Powys
109 H8 **Cwm-y-glo** Gwynd
81 H8 **Cwmystwyth** Cerdgn
66 C5 **Cwrt-newydd** Cerdgn
51 L5 **Cylibebyll** Neath
36 D2 **Cymer** Neath
36 F3 **Cymmer** Rhondd
67 H6 **Cynghordy** Carmth
36 C2 **Cynonville** Neath
97 G4 **Cynwyd** Denbgs
65 L8 **Cynwyl Elfed** Carmth

D

7 K3 **Daccombe** Devon
138 C2 **Dacre** Cumb
132 B7 **Dacre** N York
132 B6 **Dacre Banks** N York
149 M7 **Daddry Shield** Dur
73 G5 **Dadford** Bucks
86 E4 **Dadlington** Leics
45 J3 **Dagenham** Gt Lon
55 M6 **Daglingworth** Gloucs
59 G5 **Dagnall** Bucks
152 F2 **Dailly** S Ayrs
187 G4 **Dairsie** Fife
233 b8 **Dalabrog** W Isls
182 D5 **Dalavich** Ag & B
146 E3 **Dalbeattie** D & G
237 b5 **Dalby** IoM
133 K5 **Dalby** N York
194 F5 **Dalcapon** P & K
226 F7 **Dalchalm** Highld
201 L3 **Dalchreichart** Highld
184 F4 **Dalchruin** P & K
185 L2 **Dalcrue** P & K
12 D5 **Dalditch** Devon
175 J6 **Daldowie Crematorium** C Glas
101 H5 **Dale** Derbys
48 D6 **Dale** Pembks
190 E3 **Dalelia** Highld
163 H1 **Dalgarven** N Ayrs
177 G2 **Dalgety Bay** Fife
164 B6 **Dalgig** E Ayrs
185 G3 **Dalginross** P & K
194 F6 **Dalguise** P & K
230 C5 **Dalhalvaig** Highld
77 G3 **Dalham** Suffk
233 b8 **Daliburgh** W Isls
177 K5 **Dalkeith** Mdloth
214 D4 **Dallas** Moray
78 F4 **Dallinghoo** Suffk
20 D2 **Dallington** E Susx
73 K3 **Dallington** Nhants
183 H3 **Dalmally** Ag & B
184 C7 **Dalmary** Stirlg
153 K2 **Dalmellington** E Ayrs
176 F3 **Dalmeny** C Edin
222 F7 **Dalmore** Highld
174 E4 **Dalmuir** W Duns
190 E3 **Dalnabreck** Highld
194 B3 **Dalnacardoch** P & K
203 K2 **Dalnahaitnach** Highld
193 K2 **Dalnaspidal** P & K
230 F7 **Dalnawillan Lodge** Highld
194 C5 **Daloist** P & K
186 A6 **Dalqueich** P & K
153 G3 **Dalquhairn** S Ayrs
226 D6 **Dalreavoch Lodge** Highld
174 B7 **Dalry** N Ayrs
163 J6 **Dalrymple** E Ayrs
175 L7 **Dalserf** S Lans
161 G6 **Dalsmeran** Ag & B
148 C5 **Dalston** Cumb
45 G3 **Dalston** Gt Lon
155 G5 **Dalswinton** D & G
155 K7 **Dalton** D & G
132 F4 **Dalton** N York
140 E5 **Dalton** N York
158 E7 **Dalton** Nthumb
128 F5 **Dalton-in-Furness** Cumb
151 K5 **Dalton-le-Dale** Dur
141 H5 **Dalton-on-Tees** N York
141 L2 **Dalton Piercy** Hartpl
184 D3 **Dalveich** Stirlg
202 F7 **Dalwhinnie** Highld
13 G3 **Dalwood** Devon
28 C7 **Damerham** Hants
93 J2 **Damgate** Norfk
61 J6 **Danbury** Essex
142 F5 **Danby** N York
141 H7 **Danby Wiske** N York
215 G5 **Dandaleith** Moray
177 J4 **Danderhall** Mdloth
113 L7 **Danebridge** Ches E
60 B4 **Dane End** Herts
32 D7 **Danehill** E Susx
87 H3 **Dane Hills** C Leic
34 E4 **Dane Street** Kent
216 D3 **Danshillock** Abers
178 C5 **Danskine** E Loth
45 K5 **Darenth** Kent
112 E5 **Daresbury** Halton
115 H1 **Darfield** Barns
34 E3 **Dargate** Kent
5 K3 **Darite** Cnwll
85 H4 **Darlaston** Wsall
85 H4 **Darlaston Green** Wsall
132 C7 **Darley** N York
101 G5 **Darley Abbey** C Derb
100 E1 **Darley Bridge** Derbys
114 F8 **Darley Dale** Derbys
85 L8 **Darley Green** Solhll
59 J4 **Darleyhall** Herts
132 B7 **Darley Head** N York
72 B6 **Darlingscott** Warwks
141 H4 **Darlington** Darltn
141 G4 **Darlington Crematorium** Darltn
116 C6 **Darlton** Notts
167 H3 **Darnick** Border
81 H3 **Darowen** Powys
216 E5 **Darra** Abers
9 G2 **Darracott** Devon
23 G4 **Darracott** Devon
158 E7 **Darras Hall** Nthumb
124 D6 **Darrington** Wakefd
79 J1 **Darsham** Suffk
26 E3 **Darshill** Somset
45 K5 **Dartford** Kent
7 H4 **Dartington** Devon
11 G8 **Dartmoor National Park** Devon
7 K5 **Dartmouth** Devon
123 L7 **Darton** Barns
164 B2 **Darvel** E Ayrs
121 K6 **Darwen** Bl w D
43 G5 **Datchet** W & M
59 L4 **Datchworth** Herts
121 K8 **Daubhill** Bolton
214 F6 **Daugh of Kinermony** Moray
39 M4 **Dauntsey** Wilts
214 C6 **Dava** Highld
112 F7 **Davenham** Ches W
73 H3 **Daventry** Nhants
177 G4 **Davidson's Mains** C Edin
8 F7 **Davidstow** Cnwll
155 M2 **Davington** D & G
34 D3 **Davington Hill** Kent
216 E8 **Daviot** Abers
213 H6 **Daviot** Highld
213 H6 **Daviot House** Highld
215 K4 **Davoch of Grange** Moray
31 K3 **Dawesgreen** Surrey
84 C2 **Dawley** Wrekin
12 B6 **Dawlish** Devon
12 C6 **Dawlish Warren** Devon
101 L4 **Daybrook** Notts
56 E3 **Daylesford** Gloucs
35 K4 **Deal** Kent
136 E3 **Dean** Cumb
7 H3 **Dean** Devon
23 L2 **Dean** Devon
29 K7 **Dean** Hants
57 G4 **Dean** Oxon
26 F3 **Dean** Somset
45 L6 **Dean Bottom** Kent
166 F6 **Deanburnhaugh** Border
7 G3 **Deancombe** Devon
57 J6 **Dean Court** Oxon
121 K8 **Deane** Bolton
29 K2 **Deane** Hants
122 F7 **Deanhead** Kirk
27 M7 **Deanland** Dorset
7 H3 **Dean Prior** Devon
149 L3 **Deanraw** Nthumb
176 D5 **Deans** W Loth
136 F2 **Deanscales** Cumb
73 L6 **Deanshanger** Nhants
215 H4 **Deanshaugh** Moray
184 F6 **Deanston** Stirlg
147 J7 **Dearham** Cumb
78 F4 **Debach** Suffk
45 H2 **Debden** Essex
60 E2 **Debden** Essex
78 E2 **Debenham** Suffk
70 E5 **Deblin's Green** Worcs
176 E4 **Dechmont** W Loth
176 D4 **Dechmont Road** W Loth
57 J2 **Deddington** Oxon
62 C2 **Dedham** Essex
42 F5 **Dedworth** W & M
88 D5 **Deene** Nhants
88 D5 **Deenethorpe** Nhants
114 F3 **Deepcar** Sheff
89 G2 **Deeping Gate** C Pete
89 H2 **Deeping St James** Lincs
89 J1 **Deeping St Nicholas** Lincs
55 K3 **Deerhurst** Gloucs
71 G5 **Defford** Worcs
52 E3 **Defynnog** Powys
109 L5 **Deganwy** Conwy
182 A5 **Degnish** Ag & B
124 F2 **Deighton** C York
141 J6 **Deighton** N York
109 H8 **Deiniolen** Gwynd
8 E7 **Delabole** Cnwll
112 E7 **Delamere** Ches W
207 H2 **Delfrigs** Abers
214 D7 **Delliefure** Highld
18 A5 **Dell Quay** W Susx
204 E3 **Delnabo** Moray
214 E7 **Delnashaugh Inn** Moray
223 G6 **Delny** Highld
122 E8 **Delph** Oldham
150 E5 **Delves** Dur
103 H5 **Dembleby** Lincs
115 J2 **Denaby** Donc
110 E7 **Denbigh** Denbgs
186 F4 **Denbrae** Fife
7 J3 **Denbury** Devon
101 H4 **Denby** Derbys
123 J8 **Denby Dale** Kirk
41 G3 **Denchworth** Oxon
128 F5 **Dendron** Cumb
185 K4 **Denfield** P & K
88 E7 **Denford** Nhants
62 B7 **Dengie** Essex
43 H3 **Denham** Bucks
77 H3 **Denham** Suffk

92 E8 **Denham** Suffk
43 H3 **Denham Green** Bucks
217 J4 **Denhead** Abers
187 G5 **Denhead** Fife
186 F2 **Denhead of Gray** C Dund
167 J5 **Denholm** Border
123 G4 **Denholme** C Brad
30 A8 **Denmead** Hants
207 H3 **Denmore** C Aber
79 G2 **Dennington** Suffk
175 L2 **Denny** Falk
175 L3 **Dennyloanhead** Falk
186 D4 **Den of Lindores** Fife
122 E7 **Denshaw** Oldham
206 F6 **Denside** Abers
35 G6 **Densole** Kent
77 H4 **Denston** Suffk
100 C4 **Denstone** Staffs
34 E3 **Denstroude** Kent
130 D3 **Dent** Cumb
89 G6 **Denton** Cambs
140 F4 **Denton** Darltn
19 L5 **Denton** E Susx
35 G5 **Denton** Kent
102 E6 **Denton** Lincs
123 H2 **Denton** N York
74 B3 **Denton** Nhants
93 G5 **Denton** Norfk
113 L3 **Denton** Tamesd
90 E3 **Denver** Norfk
169 J6 **Denwick** Nthumb
92 C4 **Deopham** Norfk
92 C4 **Deopham Green** Norfk
77 H3 **Depden** Suffk
45 G4 **Deptford** Gt Lon
28 A4 **Deptford** Wilts
101 G5 **Derby** C Derb
23 J5 **Derby** Devon
237 b7 **Derbyhaven** IoM
194 D5 **Derculich** P & K
92 B2 **Dereham** Norfk
53 H7 **Deri** Caerph
35 G5 **Derringstone** Kent
99 K7 **Derrington** Staffs
39 L6 **Derry Hill** Wilts
125 J8 **Derrythorpe** N Linc
105 H6 **Dersingham** Norfk
189 K6 **Dervaig** Ag & B
97 G3 **Derwen** Denbgs
80 F4 **Derwenlas** Powys
137 J3 **Derwent Water** Cumb
88 B6 **Desborough** Nhants
86 F3 **Desford** Leics
215 L3 **Deskford** Moray
33 K2 **Detling** Kent
54 C7 **Devauden** Mons
81 G7 **Devil's Bridge** Cerdgn
40 A7 **Devizes** Wilts
6 C5 **Devonport** C Plym
185 J7 **Devonside** Clacks
4 C7 **Devoran** Cnwll
177 K5 **Dewarton** Mdloth
14 E3 **Dewlish** Dorset
123 K6 **Dewsbury** Kirk
123 J6 **Dewsbury Moor Crematorium** Kirk
97 K8 **Deytheur** Powys
18 F2 **Dial Post** W Susx
16 E2 **Dibden** Hants
16 E2 **Dibden Purlieu** Hants
92 E6 **Dickleburgh** Norfk
56 B2 **Didbrook** Gloucs
41 K3 **Didcot** Oxon
41 K3 **Didcot Railway Centre** Oxon
75 H2 **Diddington** Cambs
83 K6 **Diddlebury** Shrops
18 A3 **Didling** W Susx
39 J3 **Didmarton** Gloucs
113 J3 **Didsbury** Manch
103 H2 **Digby** Lincs
218 C7 **Digg** Highld
122 F8 **Diggle** Oldham
112 C1 **Digmoor** Lancs
66 C4 **Dihewyd** Cerdgn
107 G7 **Dilham** Norfk
99 L4 **Dilhorne** Staffs
121 L4 **Dill Hall** Lancs
75 G2 **Dillington** Cambs
150 B3 **Dilston** Nthumb
27 K2 **Dilton** Wilts
27 J2 **Dilton Marsh** Wilts
69 H4 **Dilwyn** Herefs
94 E5 **Dinas** Gwynd
64 E6 **Dinas** Pembks
81 J1 **Dinas-Mawddwy** Gwynd
37 J6 **Dinas Powys** V Glam
26 E3 **Dinder** Somset
69 K6 **Dinedor** Herefs
54 C6 **Dingestow** Mons
111 K4 **Dingle** Lpool
87 L6 **Dingley** Nhants
212 E3 **Dingwall** Highld
205 K5 **Dinnet** Abers
158 F7 **Dinnington** N u Ty
115 K4 **Dinnington** Rothm
26 B8 **Dinnington** Somset
95 K1 **Dinorwic** Gwynd
58 C5 **Dinton** Bucks
28 A5 **Dinton** Wilts
155 K4 **Dinwoodie** D & G
9 J2 **Dinworthy** Devon
25 J6 **Dipford** Somset
161 K2 **Dippen** Ag & B
162 D5 **Dippen** N Ayrs
10 C7 **Dippertown** Devon
215 H3 **Dipple** Moray
152 E2 **Dipple** S Ayrs
7 G4 **Diptford** Devon
150 E4 **Dipton** Dur
178 B2 **Dirleton** E Loth
149 L5 **Dirt Pot** Nthumb
101 J7 **Diseworth** Leics
132 F5 **Dishforth** N York
113 L5 **Disley** Ches E
92 D7 **Diss** Norfk
136 D3 **Distington** Cumb
136 E3 **Distington Hall Crematorium** Cumb
28 C5 **Ditchampton** Wilts
26 F4 **Ditcheat** Somset
93 G5 **Ditchingham** Norfk
19 J3 **Ditchling** E Susx
83 K2 **Ditherington** Shrops
39 J6 **Ditteridge** Wilts
7 K5 **Dittisham** Devon
33 J2 **Ditton** Kent
76 F3 **Ditton Green** Cambs
83 L5 **Ditton Priors** Shrops
54 D5 **Dixton** Mons
113 M1 **Dobcross** Oldham
5 K3 **Dobwalls** Cnwll
11 H7 **Doccombe** Devon
212 F6 **Dochgarroch** Highld
105 J5 **Docking** Norfk
69 L3 **Docklow** Herefs
137 L3 **Dockray** Cumb
60 F7 **Doddinghurst** Essex
90 B5 **Doddington** Cambs
34 C4 **Doddington** Kent
116 E7 **Doddington** Lincs
168 E3 **Doddington** Nthumb
84 B7 **Doddington** Shrops
11 K7 **Doddiscombsleigh** Devon
98 E4 **Dodd's Green** Ches E
73 H3 **Dodford** Nhants
85 G8 **Dodford** Worcs
39 H4 **Dodington** S Glos
25 J4 **Dodington** Somset
98 A1 **Dodleston** Ches W
174 F7 **Dodside** E Rens
100 A5 **Dod's Leigh** Staffs
114 F1 **Dodworth** Barns
103 K2 **Dogdyke** Lincs
30 C2 **Dogmersfield** Hants
82 B2 **Dolanog** Powys
95 J4 **Dolbenmaen** Gwynd
81 K3 **Dolfach** Powys
82 C6 **Dolfor** Powys
109 L7 **Dolgarrog** Conwy
96 B8 **Dolgellau** Gwynd
226 F7 **Doll** Highld
185 K7 **Dollar** Clacks
185 K7 **Dollarfield** Clacks
111 H6 **Dolphin** Flints
129 L8 **Dolphinholme** Lancs
176 F8 **Dolphinton** S Lans
10 E3 **Dolton** Devon
110 B6 **Dolwen** Conwy
96 B3 **Dolwyddelan** Conwy
97 L8 **Domgay** Powys
115 L2 **Doncaster** Donc
125 G7 **Doncaster North Services** Donc
27 K6 **Donhead St Andrew** Wilts
27 K6 **Donhead St Mary** Wilts
177 G2 **Donibristle** Fife
25 G3 **Doniford** Somset
103 K5 **Donington** Lincs
118 C5 **Donington on Bain** Lincs
101 J7 **Donington Park Services** Leics
86 C2 **Donisthorpe** Leics
56 D3 **Donnington** Gloucs
83 L2 **Donnington** Shrops
41 J6 **Donnington** W Berk
18 B5 **Donnington** W Susx
84 C2 **Donnington** Wrekin
84 C2 **Donnington Wood** Wrekin
25 M8 **Donyatt** Somset
163 H5 **Doonfoot** S Ayrs
204 D3 **Dorback Lodge** Highld
14 D4 **Dorchester** Dorset
41 L2 **Dorchester** Oxon
86 C4 **Dordon** Warwks
114 F5 **Dore** Sheff
212 F7 **Dores** Highld
31 K2 **Dorking** Surrey
32 D5 **Dormans Land** Surrey
69 L6 **Dormington** Herefs
71 H3 **Dormston** Worcs
42 F5 **Dorney** Bucks
200 D1 **Dornie** Highld
223 H4 **Dornoch** Highld
147 M2 **Dornock** D & G
230 F5 **Dorrery** Highld
85 L8 **Dorridge** Solhll
103 H2 **Dorrington** Lincs
83 J3 **Dorrington** Shrops
99 G4 **Dorrington** Shrops
71 K4 **Dorsington** Warwks
69 G6 **Dorstone** Herefs
58 B5 **Dorton** Bucks
237 d6 **Douglas** IoM
165 G4 **Douglas** S Lans
187 G2 **Douglas and Angus** C Dund
237 d5 **Douglas Borough Crematorium** IoM
183 H7 **Douglas Pier** Ag & B
196 C6 **Douglastown** Angus
165 G3 **Douglas Water** S Lans
164 F3 **Douglas West** S Lans
26 F3 **Doulting** Somset
234 b5 **Dounby** Ork
221 L2 **Doune** Highld
184 F6 **Doune** Stirlg
152 E3 **Dounepark** S Ayrs
222 D4 **Dounie** Highld
6 D3 **Dousland** Devon
114 B6 **Dove Holes** Derbys
147 J7 **Dovenby** Cumb
35 J6 **Dover** Kent
35 J6 **Dover Castle** Kent
62 F2 **Dovercourt** Essex
70 F2 **Doverdale** Worcs
100 C5 **Doveridge** Derbys
31 L2 **Doversgreen** Surrey
194 F6 **Dowally** P & K
55 M4 **Dowdeswell** Gloucs
53 G6 **Dowlais** Myr Td
10 E3 **Dowland** Devon
26 A8 **Dowlish Wake** Somset
40 C2 **Down Ampney** Gloucs
5 L5 **Downderry** Cnwll
45 H7 **Downe** Gt Lon
39 J2 **Downend** Gloucs
38 F5 **Downend** S Glos
186 F2 **Downfield** C Dund
6 A2 **Downgate** Cnwll
46 B2 **Downham** Essex
45 H5 **Downham** Gt Lon
122 B2 **Downham** Lancs
90 E3 **Downham Market** Norfk
55 K4 **Down Hatherley** Gloucs
26 E6 **Downhead** Somset
27 G3 **Downhead** Somset
186 A2 **Downhill** P & K
140 E7 **Downholme** N York
207 H6 **Downies** Abers
42 D2 **Downley** Bucks
11 H4 **Down St Mary** Devon
19 J4 **Downs Crematorium** Br & H
43 J8 **Downside** Surrey
6 D6 **Down Thomas** Devon
28 D6 **Downton** Wilts
103 J6 **Dowsby** Lincs
39 G5 **Doynton** S Glos
37 K3 **Draethen** Caerph
164 F1 **Draffan** S Lans
116 B4 **Drakeholes** Notts
174 B7 **Drakemyre** N Ayrs
71 G5 **Drakes Broughton** Worcs
131 K8 **Draughton** N York
87 L7 **Draughton** Nhants
125 G5 **Drax** N York
72 F1 **Draycote** Warwks
101 H6 **Draycott** Derbys
71 L7 **Draycott** Gloucs
26 C2 **Draycott** Somset
100 D6 **Draycott in the Clay** Staffs
99 M4 **Draycott in the Moors** Staffs
17 J2 **Drayton** C Port
88 B5 **Drayton** Leics
92 E2 **Drayton** Norfk
41 J2 **Drayton** Oxon
72 E6 **Drayton** Oxon
26 B6 **Drayton** Somset
85 G7 **Drayton** Worcs
85 L4 **Drayton Bassett** Staffs
58 E5 **Drayton Beauchamp** Bucks
85 L4 **Drayton Manor Park** Staffs
58 D3 **Drayton Parslow** Bucks
41 L2 **Drayton St Leonard** Oxon
48 F5 **Dreen Hill** Pembks
51 G3 **Drefach** Carmth
65 K6 **Drefach** Carmth
66 C5 **Drefach** Cerdgn
163 J2 **Dreghorn** N Ayrs
35 H6 **Drellingore** Kent
178 B3 **Drem** E Loth
11 H6 **Drewsteignton** Devon
134 F7 **Driffield** E R Yk
56 B7 **Driffield** Gloucs
2 D5 **Drift** Cnwll
136 E7 **Drigg** Cumb
123 J5 **Drighlington** Leeds
190 B5 **Drimnin** Highld
13 K2 **Drimpton** Dorset
191 J1 **Drimsallie** Highld

124 E2 Dringhouses C York
77 L3 Drinkstone Suffk
77 L3 Drinkstone Green Suffk
100 A6 Drointon Staffs
70 F2 Droitwich Worcs
186 B4 Dron P & K
115 G5 Dronfield Derbys
163 K5 Drongan E Ayrs
186 E1 Dronley Angus
14 E2 Droop Dorset
29 L7 Droxford Hants
113 K2 Droylsden Tamesd
97 G4 Druid Denbgs
48 E4 Druidston Pembks
191 L3 Druimarbin Highld
191 K7 Druimavuic Ag & B
172 C4 Druimdrishaig Ag & B
199 L7 Druimindarroch Highld
172 F3 Drum Ag & B
185 L7 Drum P & K
165 H2 Drumalbin S Lans
224 D3 Drumbeg Highld
216 B6 Drumblade Abers
144 C6 Drumbreddon D & G
210 B7 Drumbuie Highld
148 A3 Drumburgh Cumb
146 F4 Drumburn D & G
174 F4 Drumchapel C Glas
193 L5 Drumchastle P & K
164 C2 Drumclog S Lans
187 G6 Drumeldrie Fife
165 M3 Drumelzier Border
199 L3 Drumfearn Highld
206 D5 Drumfrennie Abers
196 C6 Drumgley Angus
203 J5 Drumguish Highld
214 E7 Drumin Moray
153 L3 Drumjohn D & G
153 G6 Drumlamford S Ayrs
206 C4 Drumlasie Abers
148 A5 Drumleaning Cumb
161 H5 Drumlemble Ag & B
197 J1 Drumlithie Abers
145 H6 Drummoddie D & G
144 D7 Drummore D & G
215 J5 Drummuir Moray
212 D7 Drumnadrochit Highld
144 D7 Drumnaglaur D & G
215 L4 Drumnagorrach Moray
154 F6 Drumpark D & G
224 E7 Drumrunie Lodge Highld
163 G6 Drumshang S Ayrs
209 G5 Drumuie Highld
204 B2 Drumuillie Highld
184 E6 Drumvaich Stirlg
186 B5 Drunzie P & K
138 F4 Drybeck Cumb
215 K2 Drybridge Moray
163 J3 Drybridge N Ayrs
54 F4 Drybrook Gloucs
167 J3 Dryburgh Border
102 D3 Dry Doddington Lincs
75 L3 Dry Drayton Cambs
174 E2 Drymen Stirlg
217 G5 Drymuir Abers
208 F7 Drynoch Highld
216 F2 Dubford Abers
225 J5 Duchally Highld
57 G6 Ducklington Oxon
76 C7 Duddenhoe End Essex
177 J4 Duddingston C Edin
88 E4 Duddington Nhants
25 K7 Duddlestone Somset
168 D2 Duddo Nthumb
112 D8 Duddon Ches W
97 M5 Dudleston Shrops
98 A5 Dudleston Heath Shrops
85 G5 Dudley Dudley
159 G7 Dudley N Tyne
85 G5 Dudley Port Sandw
15 K3 Dudsbury Dorset
101 G4 Duffield Derbys
36 C2 Duffryn Neath
215 H6 Dufftown Moray
214 E2 Duffus Moray
139 G3 Dufton Cumb
134 D6 Duggleby N York
210 B7 Duirinish Highld
199 L3 Duisdalemore Highld
191 K2 Duisky Highld
78 C6 Duke Street Suffk
113 L2 Dukinfield Tamesd
113 L2 Dukinfield Crematorium Tamesd
26 E3 Dulcote Somset
12 D2 Dulford Devon
194 C6 Dull P & K
175 K3 Dullatur N Lans
76 F3 Dullingham Cambs
204 B1 Dulnain Bridge Highld
75 H3 Duloe Bed
5 K4 Duloe Cnwll
24 E5 Dulverton Somset
45 G5 Dulwich Gt Lon
174 D4 Dumbarton W Duns
71 H7 Dumbleton Gloucs
155 G6 Dumfries D & G
174 F2 Dumgoyne Stirlg
29 L3 Dummer Hants
35 K2 Dumpton Kent
197 G4 Dun Angus
193 L5 Dunalastair P & K
173 K4 Dunan Ag & B
209 J8 Dunan Highld
193 G5 Dunan P & K
161 H7 Dunaverty Ag & B
25 L3 Dunball Somset
178 E3 Dunbar E Loth
227 L3 Dunbeath Highld
182 C2 Dunbeg Ag & B
185 G6 Dunblane Stirlg
186 E4 Dunbog Fife
212 F3 Duncanston Highld
216 B8 Duncanstone Abers
11 K7 Dunchideock Devon
72 F1 Dunchurch Warwks
155 G5 Duncow D & G
186 B5 Duncrievie P & K
18 C3 Duncton W Susx
186 F2 Dundee C Dund
186 F2 *Dundee Airport* C Dund
186 F2 Dundee Crematorium C Dund
26 C5 Dundon Somset
163 J3 Dundonald S Ayrs
220 E4 Dundonnell Highld
147 L5 Dundraw Cumb
201 L3 Dundreggan Highld
146 D5 Dundrennan D & G
38 E6 Dundry N Som
206 E4 Dunecht Abers
176 F2 Dunfermline Fife
176 F2 Dunfermline Crematorium Fife
40 C2 Dunfield Gloucs
164 D3 Dungavel S Lans
21 L3 Dungeness Kent
116 D6 Dunham Notts
112 C6 Dunham-on-the-Hill Ches W
70 F2 Dunhampton Worcs
113 H4 Dunham Town Traffd
113 G4 Dunham Woodhouses Traffd
117 G5 Dunholme Lincs
187 J5 Dunino Fife
175 L2 Dunipace Falk
195 G7 Dunkeld P & K
39 G8 Dunkerton BaNES
12 E2 Dunkeswell Devon
123 L2 Dunkeswick N York
34 E3 Dunkirk Kent
39 H4 Dunkirk S Glos
33 G3 Dunk's Green Kent
196 F3 Dunlappie Angus
70 E2 Dunley Worcs
174 D8 Dunlop E Ayrs
202 F2 Dunmaglass Highld
176 B1 Dunmore Falk
231 J2 Dunnet Highld
196 E6 Dunnichen Angus
185 L4 Dunning P & K
133 K8 Dunnington C York
126 E1 Dunnington E R Yk
71 J4 Dunnington Warwks
173 K3 Dunoon Ag & B
214 C5 Dunphail Moray
144 E4 Dunragit D & G
179 G7 Duns Border
103 J6 Dunsby Lincs
154 F5 Dunscore D & G
124 F8 Dunscroft Donc
142 D4 Dunsdale R & Cl
42 C5 Dunsden Green Oxon
9 J3 Dunsdon Devon
31 G4 Dunsfold Surrey
11 J6 Dunsford Devon
186 D5 Dunshalt Fife
217 J5 Dunshillock Abers
101 J1 Dunsill Notts
143 H5 Dunsley N York
84 F6 Dunsley Staffs
58 E6 Dunsmore Bucks
121 K1 Dunsop Bridge Lancs
59 G4 Dunstable C Beds
100 D7 Dunstall Staffs
169 K5 Dunstan Nthumb
24 F3 Dunster Somset
57 J3 Duns Tew Oxon
151 G3 Dunston Gatesd
117 H8 Dunston Lincs
92 F3 Dunston Norfk
99 L8 Dunston Staffs
6 E5 Dunstone Devon
7 G2 Dunstone Devon
124 F8 Dunsville Donc
126 D4 Dunswell E R Yk
176 E8 Dunsyre S Lans
6 B1 Dunterton Devon
55 L6 Duntisbourne Abbots Gloucs
55 M6 Duntisbourne Rouse Gloucs
14 D2 Duntish Dorset
174 E4 Duntocher W Duns
58 D3 Dunton Bucks
75 J5 Dunton C Beds
105 L6 Dunton Norfk
87 G5 Dunton Bassett Leics
32 F2 Dunton Green Kent
218 C6 Duntulm Highld
163 G6 Dunure S Ayrs
51 H6 Dunvant Swans
208 D5 Dunvegan Highld
79 K1 Dunwich Suffk
3 K5 Durgan Cnwll
151 G6 Durham Dur
151 G6 Durham Cathedral Dur
151 G6 Durham Crematorium Dur
151 H7 Durham Services Dur
141 J5 *Durham Tees Valley Airport* S on T
154 F2 Durisdeer D & G
154 F2 Durisdeermill D & G
25 L4 Durleigh Somset
29 K7 Durley Hants
40 E7 Durley Wilts
29 K7 Durley Street Hants
35 H3 Durlock Kent
35 J2 Durlock Kent
228 F3 Durness Highld
216 D8 Durno Abers
191 K5 Duror Highld
182 D5 Durran Ag & B
18 F5 Durrington W Susx
28 D3 Durrington Wilts
206 E6 Durris Abers
39 H2 Dursley Gloucs
55 G4 Dursley Cross Gloucs
25 L5 Durston Somset
15 G2 Durweston Dorset
73 K3 Duston Nhants
203 L1 Duthil Highld
112 E5 Dutton Ches W
76 C5 Duxford Cambs
57 G7 Duxford Oxon
76 C5 Duxford Aircraft Museum Cambs
109 L6 Dwygyfylchi Conwy
108 F7 Dwyran IoA
207 G3 Dyce C Aber
95 K7 Dyffryn Ardudwy Gwynd
52 D6 Dyffryn Cellwen Neath
103 J7 Dyke Lincs
214 B3 Dyke Moray
195 K5 Dykehead Angus
196 C4 Dykehead Angus
176 B6 Dykehead N Lans
184 D7 Dykehead Stirlg
197 H3 Dykelands Abers
195 K5 Dykends Angus
216 D5 Dykeside Abers
34 E8 Dymchurch Kent
55 G2 Dymock Gloucs
39 H5 Dyrham S Glos
186 E8 Dysart Fife
110 E5 Dyserth Denbgs

E

120 F2 Eagland Hill Lancs
116 E7 Eagle Lincs
141 K4 Eaglescliffe S on T
136 F2 Eaglesfield Cumb
155 M7 Eaglesfield D & G
175 G7 Eaglesham E Rens
121 L7 Eagley Bolton
102 A1 Eakring Notts
125 J7 Ealand N Linc
44 D4 Ealing Gt Lon
149 H4 Eals Nthumb
138 D2 Eamont Bridge Cumb
122 D2 Earby Lancs
84 C5 Eardington Shrops
69 H3 Eardisland Herefs
68 F5 Eardisley Herefs
98 A7 Eardiston Shrops
70 C2 Eardiston Worcs
89 L8 Earith Cambs
112 E3 Earlestown St Hel
42 C6 Earley Wokham
92 E2 Earlham Crematorium Norfk
208 F3 Earlish Highld
74 C2 Earls Barton Nhants
61 K3 Earls Colne Essex
71 G3 Earls Common Worcs
70 F6 Earl's Croome Worcs
86 D7 Earlsdon Covtry
187 H7 Earlsferry Fife
44 E5 Earlsfield Gt Lon
216 F7 Earlsford Abers
123 K6 Earlsheaton Kirk
86 F4 Earl Shilton Leics
78 F2 Earl Soham Suffk
114 C7 Earl Sterndale Derbys
167 J2 Earlston Border
163 K3 Earlston E Ayrs
32 B4 Earlswood Surrey
85 K8 Earlswood Warwks
17 M3 Earnley W Susx
159 H7 Earsdon N Tyne
93 G5 Earsham Norfk
18 C4 Eartham W Susx
142 C5 Easby N York
181 L4 Easdale Ag & B
30 E6 Easebourne W Susx
86 F7 Easenhall Warwks
30 F3 Eashing Surrey
58 B6 Easington Bucks
151 K6 Easington Dur

127 J6 **Easington** E R Yk
142 F4 **Easington** R & Cl
151 K6 **Easington Colliery** Dur
151 J5 **Easington Lane** Sundld
133 H5 **Easingwold** N York
196 B7 **Eassie and Nevay** Angus
37 G6 **East Aberthaw** V Glam
7 H6 **East Allington** Devon
24 D6 **East Anstey** Devon
17 H5 **East Ashey** IoW
17 M2 **East Ashling** W Susx
134 F3 **East Ayton** N York
117 K5 **East Barkwith** Lincs
33 J3 **East Barming** Kent
143 G5 **East Barnby** N York
44 F2 **East Barnet** Gt Lon
178 F3 **East Barns** E Loth
105 L5 **East Barsham** Norfk
106 E4 **East Beckham** Norfk
43 H5 **East Bedfont** Gt Lon
78 C7 **East Bergholt** Suffk
106 A8 **East Bilney** Norfk
20 A5 **East Blatchington** E Susx
151 J3 **East Boldon** S Tyne
16 D3 **East Boldre** Hants
141 H4 **Eastbourne** Darltn
20 C5 **Eastbourne** E Susx
20 D5 **Eastbourne Crematorium** E Susx
91 L2 **East Bradenham** Norfk
25 M2 **East Brent** Somset
79 J2 **Eastbridge** Suffk
102 B4 **East Bridgford** Notts
23 L5 **East Buckland** Devon
12 D5 **East Budleigh** Devon
122 F2 **Eastburn** C Brad
43 J2 **Eastbury** Herts
41 G5 **Eastbury** W Berk
116 D1 **East Butterwick** N Linc
131 J8 **Eastby** N York
176 E5 **East Calder** W Loth
92 E3 **East Carleton** Norfk
123 J2 **East Carlton** Leeds
88 B5 **East Carlton** Nhants
14 E5 **East Chaldon (Chaldon Herring)** Dorset
41 G3 **East Challow** Oxon
7 H7 **East Charleton** Devon
14 A2 **East Chelborough** Dorset
19 K3 **East Chiltington** E Susx
26 C8 **East Chinnock** Somset
28 C2 **East Chisenbury** Wilts
47 G5 **Eastchurch** Kent
31 H2 **East Clandon** Surrey
58 C3 **East Claydon** Bucks
26 D8 **East Coker** Somset
55 K6 **Eastcombe** Gloucs
26 E3 **East Compton** Somset
7 J5 **East Cornworthy** Devon
43 J3 **Eastcote** Gt Lon
73 K4 **Eastcote** Nhants
85 L7 **Eastcote** Solhll
28 A1 **Eastcott** Wilts
125 G3 **East Cottingwith** E R Yk
40 E7 **Eastcourt** Wilts
16 F4 **East Cowes** IoW
125 G6 **East Cowick** E R Yk
141 H6 **East Cowton** N York
27 G3 **East Cranmore** Somset
20 B6 **East Dean** E Susx
54 F4 **East Dean** Gloucs
28 F6 **East Dean** Hants
18 B3 **East Dean** W Susx
12 D4 **East Devon Crematorium** Devon
116 C6 **East Drayton** Notts
45 G5 **East Dulwich** Gt Lon
38 E7 **East Dundry** N Som
126 C5 **East Ella** C KuH
46 F2 **Eastend** Essex
16 D3 **East End** Hants
41 H7 **East End** Hants
33 L6 **East End** Kent
57 H5 **East End** Oxon
26 F3 **East End** Somset
205 G6 **Easter Balmoral** Abers
38 E4 **Easter Compton** S Glos
213 H4 **Easter Dalziel** Highld
18 C5 **Eastergate** W Susx
175 J5 **Easterhouse** C Glas
177 H5 **Easter Howgate** Mdloth
212 E4 **Easter Kinkell** Highld
212 E5 **Easter Moniack** Highld
86 C7 **Eastern Green** Covtry
206 F4 **Easter Ord** Abers
187 J6 **Easter Pitkierie** Fife
235 c6 **Easter Skeld** Shet
168 A3 **Easter Softlaw** Border
28 A1 **Easterton** Wilts
28 D2 **East Everleigh** Wilts
33 J3 **East Farleigh** Kent
87 K6 **East Farndon** Nhants
116 D2 **East Ferry** Lincs
176 B5 **Eastfield** N Lans
135 G3 **Eastfield** N York
178 C3 **East Fortune** E Loth
41 G5 **East Garston** W Berk
150 B7 **Eastgate** Dur
106 D7 **Eastgate** Norfk
87 J2 **East Goscote** Leics
40 E7 **East Grafton** Wilts
28 E5 **East Grimstead** Wilts
32 D5 **East Grinstead** W Susx
21 J2 **East Guldeford** E Susx
73 J2 **East Haddon** Nhants
41 K3 **East Hagbourne** Oxon
126 E6 **East Halton** N Linc
45 H4 **East Ham** Gt Lon
42 D6 **Easthampstead Park Crematorium** Br For
69 H2 **Easthampton** Herefs
41 H2 **East Hanney** Oxon
61 J7 **East Hanningfield** Essex
124 C6 **East Hardwick** Wakefd
92 B6 **East Harling** Norfk
141 K7 **East Harlsey** N York
28 C5 **East Harnham** Wilts
26 E1 **East Harptree** BaNES
141 K4 **East Hartburn** S on T
30 D7 **East Harting** W Susx
27 L5 **East Hatch** Wilts
75 K4 **East Hatley** Cambs
132 B2 **East Hauxwell** N York
187 J1 **East Haven** Angus
103 K4 **East Heckington** Lincs
150 E6 **East Hedleyhope** Dur
227 H5 **East Helmsdale** Highld
41 J3 **East Hendred** Oxon
134 E4 **East Heslerton** N York
20 B3 **East Hoathly** E Susx
15 G5 **East Holme** Dorset
83 L4 **Easthope** Shrops
61 L4 **Easthorpe** Essex
26 E3 **East Horrington** Somset
31 H2 **East Horsley** Surrey
15 K4 **East Howe** Bmouth
25 M3 **East Huntspill** Somset
41 J4 **East Ilsley** W Berk
11 H3 **Eastington** Devon
55 H6 **Eastington** Gloucs
56 C5 **Eastington** Gloucs
118 E8 **East Keal** Lincs
40 C6 **East Kennett** Wilts
124 B2 **East Keswick** Leeds
175 H7 **East Kilbride** S Lans
118 D8 **East Kirkby** Lincs
14 F5 **East Knighton** Dorset
27 K5 **East Knoyle** Wilts
26 B7 **East Lambrook** Somset
122 B8 **East Lancashire Crematorium** Bury
154 E7 **Eastlands** D & G
35 J5 **East Langdon** Kent
87 K5 **East Langton** Leics
18 B4 **East Lavant** W Susx
18 C3 **East Lavington** W Susx
140 E5 **East Layton** N York
56 D6 **Eastleach Martin** Gloucs
56 D6 **Eastleach Turville** Gloucs
101 K7 **East Leake** Notts
23 H5 **Eastleigh** Devon
29 J7 **Eastleigh** Hants
105 K8 **East Lexham** Norfk
34 C4 **Eastling** Kent
178 D3 **East Linton** E Loth
41 H3 **East Lockinge** Oxon
45 H4 **East London Crematorium** Gt Lon
116 C2 **East Lound** N Linc
15 G6 **East Lulworth** Dorset
134 E5 **East Lutton** N York
26 E5 **East Lydford** Somset
33 J2 **East Malling** Kent
30 D8 **East Marden** W Susx
116 C6 **East Markham** Notts
28 B7 **East Martin** Hants
122 D1 **East Marton** N York
30 B6 **East Meon** Hants
62 C5 **East Mersea** Essex
101 J7 *East Midlands Airport* Leics
43 J6 **East Molesey** Surrey
15 G4 **East Morden** Dorset
123 G3 **East Morton** C Brad
154 F3 **East Morton** D & G
133 L4 **East Ness** N York
17 J3 **Eastney** C Port
70 D6 **Eastnor** Herefs
87 L4 **East Norton** Leics
125 J7 **Eastoft** N Linc
7 J2 **East Ogwell** Devon
75 G1 **Easton** Cambs
11 G6 **Easton** Devon
14 D7 **Easton** Dorset
29 K5 **Easton** Hants
102 F6 **Easton** Lincs
92 D2 **Easton** Norfk
26 D3 **Easton** Somset
79 G3 **Easton** Suffk
39 K6 **Easton** Wilts
39 K3 **Easton Grey** Wilts
38 D5 **Easton-in-Gordano** N Som
74 C3 **Easton Maudit** Nhants
88 E3 **Easton-on-the-Hill** Nhants
40 D7 **Easton Royal** Wilts
27 J7 **East Orchard** Dorset
33 H4 **East Peckham** Kent
49 G6 **East Pennar** Pembks
26 E4 **East Pennard** Somset
75 G2 **East Perry** Cambs
7 H7 **East Portlemouth** Devon
7 H8 **East Prawle** Devon
18 E5 **East Preston** W Susx
9 K2 **East Putford** Devon
25 H3 **East Quantoxhead** Somset
151 H5 **East Rainton** Sundld
118 C2 **East Ravendale** NE Lin
105 L7 **East Raynham** Norfk
89 K4 **Eastrea** Cambs
134 F5 **East Riding Crematorium** E R Yk
147 M2 **Eastriggs** D & G
124 B2 **East Rigton** Leeds
125 J4 **Eastrington** E R Yk
40 D2 **Eastrop** Swindn
141 K6 **East Rounton** N York
105 K6 **East Rudham** Norfk
106 E4 **East Runton** Norfk
107 H6 **East Ruston** Norfk
35 J4 **Eastry** Kent
178 B5 **East Saltoun** E Loth
44 D5 **East Sheen** Gt Lon
41 H5 **East Shefford** W Berk
116 C3 **East Stockwith** Lincs
15 G5 **East Stoke** Dorset
102 C3 **East Stoke** Notts
27 J6 **East Stour** Dorset
35 H3 **East Stourmouth** Kent
23 K6 **East Stowford** Devon
29 K4 **East Stratton** Hants
35 J5 **East Studdal** Kent
5 J3 **East Taphouse** Cnwll
23 G6 **East-the-Water** Devon
158 F3 **East Thirston** Nthumb
46 B5 **East Tilbury** Thurr
30 B5 **East Tisted** Hants
117 J5 **East Torrington** Lincs
92 C2 **East Tuddenham** Norfk
28 F5 **East Tytherley** Hants
39 L5 **East Tytherton** Wilts
11 J4 **East Village** Devon
38 E5 **Eastville** Bristl
104 C2 **Eastville** Lincs
91 G1 **East Walton** Norfk
10 F6 **East Week** Devon
102 C6 **Eastwell** Leics
28 F7 **East Wellow** Hants
186 E7 **East Wemyss** Fife
176 C5 **East Whitburn** W Loth
60 C5 **Eastwick** Herts
45 J5 **East Wickham** Gt Lon
49 J6 **East Williamston** Pembks
91 G1 **East Winch** Norfk
28 E5 **East Winterslow** Wilts
17 L3 **East Wittering** W Susx
131 L3 **East Witton** N York
101 J3 **Eastwood** Notts
46 D3 **Eastwood** Sthend
158 A5 **East Woodburn** Nthumb
41 H7 **East Woodhay** Hants
30 C4 **East Worldham** Hants
91 K5 **East Wretham** Norfk
9 H2 **East Youlstone** Devon
72 E2 **Eathorpe** Warwks
113 K7 **Eaton** Ches E
112 E8 **Eaton** Ches W
102 D6 **Eaton** Leics
92 E3 **Eaton** Norfk
116 B6 **Eaton** Notts
57 H7 **Eaton** Oxon
83 K5 **Eaton** Shrops
58 F4 **Eaton Bray** C Beds
83 L3 **Eaton Constantine** Shrops
58 F4 **Eaton Green** C Beds
56 E7 **Eaton Hastings** Oxon
83 K3 **Eaton Mascott** Shrops

75 H3 **Eaton Socon** Cambs
98 F7 **Eaton upon Tern** Shrops
134 D3 **Ebberston** N York
27 M6 **Ebbesborne Wake** Wilts
53 J6 **Ebbw Vale** Blae G
150 D4 **Ebchester** Dur
12 C5 **Ebford** Devon
55 J6 **Ebley** Gloucs
98 C3 **Ebnal** Ches W
71 L6 **Ebrington** Gloucs
41 J8 **Ecchinswell** Hants
178 F5 **Ecclaw** Border
155 L7 **Ecclefechan** D & G
168 A2 **Eccles** Border
46 B7 **Eccles** Kent
113 H2 **Eccles** Salfd
114 F5 **Ecclesall** Sheff
113 H3 **Eccles Crematorium** Salfd
115 G3 **Ecclesfield** Sheff
99 J6 **Eccleshall** Staffs
123 H4 **Eccleshill** C Brad
176 E4 **Ecclesmachan** W Loth
92 B5 **Eccles Road** Norfk
112 B8 **Eccleston** Ches W
121 G6 **Eccleston** Lancs
112 C3 **Eccleston** St Hel
206 E4 **Echt** Abers
167 L4 **Eckford** Border
115 H5 **Eckington** Derbys
71 G6 **Eckington** Worcs
74 B2 **Ecton** Nhants
114 C4 **Edale** Derbys
234 d4 **Eday** Ork
234 d4 *Eday Airport* Ork
19 H4 **Edburton** W Susx
222 F4 **Edderton** Highld
177 H8 **Eddleston** Border
175 J7 **Eddlewood** S Lans
32 D4 **Edenbridge** Kent
122 B6 **Edenfield** Lancs
138 E2 **Edenhall** Cumb
103 H7 **Edenham** Lincs
45 G6 **Eden Park** Gt Lon
5 G5 **Eden Project** Cnwll
114 E7 **Edensor** Derbys
183 K8 **Edentaggart** Ag & B
115 L1 **Edenthorpe** Donc
94 E5 **Edern** Gwynd
85 J6 **Edgbaston** Birm
58 B4 **Edgcott** Bucks
24 D4 **Edgcott** Somset
55 J6 **Edge** Gloucs
106 C5 **Edgefield** Norfk
106 D5 **Edgefield Green** Norfk
123 H6 **Edgerton** Kirk
55 L6 **Edgeworth** Gloucs
99 G8 **Edgmond** Wrekin
83 H6 **Edgton** Shrops
44 D2 **Edgware** Gt Lon
121 L6 **Edgworth** Bl w D
208 E4 **Edinbane** Highld
177 H4 **Edinburgh** C Edin
176 F4 *Edinburgh Airport* C Edin
177 H4 **Edinburgh Castle** C Edin
177 H4 **Edinburgh Royal Botanic Gardens** C Edin
177 G4 **Edinburgh Zoo** C Edin
86 B2 **Edingale** Staffs
146 E3 **Edingham** D & G
102 A2 **Edingley** Notts
107 G6 **Edingthorpe** Norfk
107 G6 **Edingthorpe Green** Norfk
179 J7 **Edington** Border
158 E5 **Edington** Nthumb
26 B4 **Edington** Somset
27 L2 **Edington** Wilts
26 B3 **Edington Burtle** Somset
26 A2 **Edingworth** Somset
25 L2 **Edithmead** Somset
88 D3 **Edith Weston** Rutlnd
58 F4 **Edlesborough** Bucks
169 G7 **Edlingham** Nthumb
118 C7 **Edlington** Lincs
15 K1 **Edmondsham** Dorset
151 G5 **Edmondsley** Dur
102 E8 **Edmondthorpe** Leics
45 G2 **Edmonton** Gt Lon
150 C5 **Edmundbyers** Dur
167 L2 **Ednam** Border
194 D6 **Edradynate** P & K
179 H7 **Edrom** Border
98 D6 **Edstaston** Shrops
71 L3 **Edstone** Warwks
101 L5 **Edwalton** Notts
115 L7 **Edwinstowe** Notts
75 J6 **Edworth** C Beds
70 B3 **Edwyn Ralph** Herefs
196 F3 **Edzell** Angus
197 G3 **Edzell Woods** Abers
36 B2 **Efail-fach** Neath
37 G4 **Efail Isaf** Rhondd
94 F5 **Efailnewydd** Gwynd
49 K3 **Efailwen** Carmth
97 H2 **Efenechtyd** Denbgs
156 B4 **Effgill** D & G
31 J2 **Effingham** Surrey
6 D4 **Efford Crematorium** C Plym
121 K7 **Egerton** Bolton
34 B5 **Egerton** Kent
124 E5 **Eggborough** N York
6 D4 **Eggbuckland** C Plym
11 G3 **Eggesford** Devon
58 F3 **Eggington** C Beds
100 E6 **Egginton** Derbys
141 K4 **Egglescliffe** S on T
140 C3 **Eggleston** Dur
43 G6 **Egham** Surrey
88 C3 **Egleton** Rutlnd
169 G5 **Eglingham** Nthumb
4 F2 **Egloshayle** Cnwll
9 H7 **Egloskerry** Cnwll
109 M7 **Eglwysbach** Conwy
98 C4 **Eglwys Cross** Wrexhm
65 G6 **Eglwyswrw** Pembks
116 B7 **Egmanton** Notts
136 D5 **Egremont** Cumb
111 K3 **Egremont** Wirral
143 G6 **Egton** N York
143 G6 **Egton Bridge** N York
42 F3 **Egypt** Bucks
199 G7 **Eigg** Highld
61 M3 **Eight Ash Green** Essex
200 C2 **Eilanreach** Highld
67 J2 **Elan Valley** Powys
67 K2 **Elan Village** Powys
38 E3 **Elberton** S Glos
6 D5 **Elburton** C Plym
40 C4 **Elcombe** Swindn
55 H2 **Eldersfield** Worcs
174 E5 **Elderslie** Rens
141 G2 **Eldon** Dur
206 F7 **Elfhill** Abers
85 L2 **Elford** Staffs
214 F2 **Elgin** Moray
199 H3 **Elgol** Highld
35 G6 **Elham** Kent
187 H7 **Elie** Fife
108 D4 **Elim** IoA
29 G8 **Eling** Hants
116 B6 **Elkesley** Notts
55 L5 **Elkstone** Gloucs
216 C3 **Ella** Abers
7 L3 **Ellacombe** Torbay
123 G6 **Elland** Calder
172 C3 **Ellary** Ag & B
100 C4 **Ellastone** Staffs
129 K7 **Ellel** Lancs
178 F6 **Ellemford** Border
181 L4 **Ellenabeich** Ag & B
99 J7 **Ellenhall** Staffs
31 H4 **Ellen's Green** Surrey
141 K7 **Ellerbeck** N York
143 G4 **Ellerby** N York
98 F7 **Ellerdine Heath** Wrekin
191 K6 **Elleric** Ag & B
125 L5 **Ellerker** E R Yk
125 G3 **Ellerton** E R Yk
141 G7 **Ellerton** N York
58 D6 **Ellesborough** Bucks
98 B5 **Ellesmere** Shrops
111 L6 **Ellesmere Port** Ches W
93 H5 **Ellingham** Norfk
169 H4 **Ellingham** Nthumb
132 B3 **Ellingstring** N York
75 H1 **Ellington** Cambs
159 G4 **Ellington** Nthumb
27 J3 **Elliots Green** Somset
29 M3 **Ellisfield** Hants
209 H2 **Ellishader** Highld
86 E2 **Ellistown** Leics
217 H7 **Ellon** Abers
148 D7 **Ellonby** Cumb
126 B5 **Elloughton** E R Yk
54 E6 **Ellwood** Gloucs
90 C3 **Elm** Cambs
70 F2 **Elmbridge** Worcs
76 C6 **Elmdon** Essex
85 L6 **Elmdon** Solhll
45 G6 **Elmers End** Gt Lon
112 D1 **Elmer's Green** Lancs
86 F4 **Elmesthorpe** Leics
85 K2 **Elmhurst** Staffs
71 H6 **Elmley Castle** Worcs
70 F1 **Elmley Lovett** Worcs
55 H5 **Elmore** Gloucs
55 H5 **Elmore Back** Gloucs
45 K3 **Elm Park** Gt Lon
78 C5 **Elmsett** Suffk
62 C3 **Elmstead Market** Essex
34 F5 **Elmsted** Kent
35 H3 **Elmstone** Kent
55 K3 **Elmstone Hardwicke** Gloucs
134 F7 **Elmswell** E R Yk
78 B2 **Elmswell** Suffk
115 J6 **Elmton** Derbys
224 F6 **Elphin** Highld
177 K4 **Elphinstone** E Loth
206 F4 **Elrick** Abers
145 G5 **Elrig** D & G
149 L3 **Elrington** Nthumb
158 B4 **Elsdon** Nthumb
60 E3 **Elsenham** Essex
57 K6 **Elsfield** Oxon
126 C7 **Elsham** N Linc
92 C1 **Elsing** Norfk
122 D2 **Elslack** N York
17 H3 **Elson** Hants
165 K2 **Elsrickle** S Lans
30 E3 **Elstead** Surrey
30 D7 **Elsted** W Susx
103 H7 **Elsthorpe** Lincs
102 C3 **Elston** Notts
74 F5 **Elstow** Bed
44 D2 **Elstree** Herts
126 F4 **Elstronwick** E R Yk
120 F3 **Elswick** Lancs
151 G3 **Elswick** N u Ty
75 K2 **Elsworth** Cambs
137 K6 **Elterwater** Cumb
45 H5 **Eltham** Gt Lon
45 J5 **Eltham Crematorium** Gt Lon
75 J3 **Eltisley** Cambs
88 F5 **Elton** Cambs
112 C6 **Elton** Ches W
100 E1 **Elton** Derbys
69 J1 **Elton** Herefs
102 C5 **Elton** Notts
141 J4 **Elton** S on T
150 D3 **Eltringham** Nthumb
165 J6 **Elvanfoot** S Lans
101 H6 **Elvaston** Derbys
91 J7 **Elveden** Suffk
30 D1 **Elvetham Heath** Hants
178 A4 **Elvingston** E Loth
125 G2 **Elvington** C York
35 H5 **Elvington** Kent
141 K2 **Elwick** Hartpl
99 H1 **Elworth** Ches E
25 G4 **Elworthy** Somset
90 D7 **Ely** Cambs
37 H5 **Ely** Cardif
74 C5 **Emberton** M Keyn
137 G2 **Embleton** Cumb
169 J5 **Embleton** Nthumb
223 H3 **Embo** Highld
26 E2 **Emborough** Somset
223 H3 **Embo Street** Highld
131 J8 **Embsay** N York
16 C2 **Emery Down** Hants
123 K7 **Emley** Kirk
58 C7 **Emmington** Oxon
90 C3 **Emneth** Norfk
90 D3 **Emneth Hungate** Norfk
88 D2 **Empingham** Rutlnd
30 C5 **Empshott** Hants
83 K2 **Emstrey Crematorium** Shrops
17 K2 **Emsworth** Hants
41 H7 **Enborne** W Berk
41 H7 **Enborne Row** W Berk
87 G4 **Enderby** Leics
129 L3 **Endmoor** Cumb
99 L2 **Endon** Staffs
99 L2 **Endon Bank** Staffs
60 B7 **Enfield** Gt Lon
60 B7 **Enfield Crematorium** Gt Lon
60 B7 **Enfield Lock** Gt Lon
60 B7 **Enfield Wash** Gt Lon
28 C2 **Enford** Wilts
39 G4 **Engine Common** S Glos
41 L6 **Englefield** W Berk
43 G6 **Englefield Green** Surrey
54 E5 **English Bicknor** Gloucs
39 G7 **Englishcombe** BaNES
98 C6 **English Frankton** Shrops
29 G2 **Enham-Alamein** Hants
25 K4 **Enmore** Somset
27 J6 **Enmore Green** Dorset
136 E4 **Ennerdale Bridge** Cumb
195 G4 **Enochdhu** P & K
189 J6 **Ensay** Ag & B
15 K3 **Ensbury** Bmouth
83 H1 **Ensdon** Shrops
57 G3 **Enstone** Oxon
154 E2 **Enterkinfoot** D & G
84 E6 **Enville** Staffs
233 b9 **Eolaigearraidh** W Isls
55 H5 **Epney** Gloucs
101 M3 **Epperstone** Notts
60 D7 **Epping** Essex
60 C6 **Epping Green** Essex
60 C6 **Epping Upland** Essex
140 F5 **Eppleby** N York
44 E7 **Epsom** Surrey
72 D6 **Epwell** Oxon
116 C2 **Epworth** N Linc
97 M4 **Erbistock** Wrexhm
85 K5 **Erdington** Birm
32 F6 **Eridge Green** E Susx
172 E4 **Erines** Ag & B
191 H7 **Eriska** Ag & B
233 c9 **Eriskay** W Isls
91 G7 **Eriswell** Suffk
45 K4 **Erith** Gt Lon
27 L2 **Erlestoke** Wilts
6 F5 **Ermington** Devon
106 E6 **Erpingham** Norfk
202 E2 **Errogie** Highld
186 D3 **Errol** P & K

174 E4 **Erskine** Rens
144 B2 **Ervie** D & G
78 F7 **Erwarton** Suffk
68 C6 **Erwood** Powys
141 H5 **Eryholme** N York
97 J2 **Eryrys** Denbgs
140 F2 **Escomb** Dur
124 F2 **Escrick** N York
81 G3 **Esgairgeiliog** Powys
150 F6 **Esh** Dur
43 J7 **Esher** Surrey
158 F3 **Eshott** Nthumb
150 F6 **Esh Winning** Dur
212 C6 **Eskadale** Highld
177 J5 **Eskbank** Mdloth
137 G6 **Eskdale Green** Cumb
156 A3 **Eskdalemuir** D & G
120 E3 **Esprick** Lancs
88 F2 **Essendine** Rutlnd
59 L6 **Essendon** Herts
213 G6 **Essich** Highld
85 G3 **Essington** Staffs
217 H7 **Esslemont** Abers
142 C4 **Eston** R & Cl
168 D2 **Etal** Nthumb
40 B7 **Etchilhampton** Wilts
33 J7 **Etchingham** E Susx
34 F6 **Etchinghill** Kent
100 B8 **Etchinghill** Staffs
42 F5 **Eton** W & M
42 F5 **Eton Wick** W & M
99 K3 **Etruria** C Stke
203 G6 **Etteridge** Highld
139 K2 **Ettersgill** Dur
99 G1 **Ettiley Heath** Ches E
85 G4 **Ettingshall** Wolves
72 C5 **Ettington** Warwks
89 G3 **Etton** C Pete
126 B2 **Etton** E R Yk
166 D6 **Ettrick** Border
166 F4 **Ettrickbridge** Border
166 C6 **Ettrickhill** Border
100 F6 **Etwall** Derbys
91 K7 **Euston** Suffk
121 H6 **Euxton** Lancs
212 F2 **Evanton** Highld
103 H3 **Evedon** Lincs
223 G4 **Evelix** Highld
68 F3 **Evenjobb** Powys
73 H7 **Evenley** Nhants
56 E3 **Evenlode** Gloucs
140 E3 **Evenwood** Dur
26 F4 **Evercreech** Somset
125 J3 **Everingham** E R Yk
28 D2 **Everleigh** Wilts
59 G2 **Eversholt** C Beds
14 B2 **Evershot** Dorset
42 C7 **Eversley** Hants
42 C7 **Eversley Cross** Hants
125 L4 **Everthorpe** E R Yk
75 H4 **Everton** C Beds
16 C4 **Everton** Hants
111 K3 **Everton** Lpool
116 B4 **Everton** Notts
156 C6 **Evertown** D & G
70 C5 **Evesbatch** Herefs
71 J5 **Evesham** Worcs
87 J3 **Evington** C Leic
114 F3 **Ewden Village** Sheff
44 E7 **Ewell** Surrey
35 H6 **Ewell Minnis** Kent
41 M3 **Ewelme** Oxon
40 A2 **Ewen** Gloucs
36 D5 **Ewenny** V Glam
103 J3 **Ewerby** Lincs
31 H4 **Ewhurst** Surrey
20 F2 **Ewhurst Green** E Susx
31 H4 **Ewhurst Green** Surrey
111 J7 **Ewloe** Flints
10 C6 **Eworthy** Devon
30 D2 **Ewshot** Hants
54 B3 **Ewyas Harold** Herefs
10 E4 **Exbourne** Devon
24 E6 **Exbridge** Somset
16 E3 **Exbury** Hants
132 D3 **Exelby** N York
11 L6 **Exeter** Devon
12 C4 *Exeter Airport* Devon
12 B4 **Exeter & Devon Crematorium** Devon
12 C4 **Exeter Services** Devon
24 D4 **Exford** Somset
83 J3 **Exfordsgreen** Shrops
71 K4 **Exhall** Warwks
86 D6 **Exhall** Warwks
42 A4 **Exlade Street** Oxon
12 B5 **Exminster** Devon
24 D4 **Exmoor National Park**
12 C6 **Exmouth** Devon
76 E2 **Exning** Suffk
12 C5 **Exton** Devon
29 L7 **Exton** Hants
88 D2 **Exton** Rutlnd
24 E5 **Exton** Somset
11 K6 **Exwick** Devon
114 E6 **Eyam** Derbys
73 G4 **Eydon** Nhants
89 J3 **Eye** C Pete
69 J2 **Eye** Herefs
92 D8 **Eye** Suffk
179 K5 **Eyemouth** Border
75 J5 **Eyeworth** C Beds
33 L3 **Eyhorne Street** Kent
79 G4 **Eyke** Suffk
75 H3 **Eynesbury** Cambs
45 K6 **Eynsford** Kent
57 H6 **Eynsham** Oxon
13 L4 **Eype** Dorset
208 F4 **Eyre** Highld
35 H5 **Eythorne** Kent
69 J3 **Eyton** Herefs
98 C7 **Eyton** Shrops
83 L3 **Eyton on Severn** Shrops
84 B1 **Eyton upon the Weald Moors** Wrekin

F

41 H8 **Faccombe** Hants
141 L6 **Faceby** N York
82 B1 **Fachwen** Powys
98 E3 **Faddiley** Ches E
133 K2 **Fadmoor** N York
51 K5 **Faerdre** Swans
174 F4 **Faifley** W Duns
38 D6 **Failand** N Som
163 L4 **Failford** S Ayrs
113 K2 **Failsworth** Oldham
80 E2 **Fairbourne** Gwynd
124 D5 **Fairburn** N York
114 B6 **Fairfield** Derbys
85 G7 **Fairfield** Worcs
56 D7 **Fairford** Gloucs
146 F4 **Fairgirth** D & G
90 F1 **Fair Green** Norfk
120 D5 **Fairhaven** Lancs
235 e7 **Fair Isle** Shet
30 F2 **Fairlands** Surrey
173 L7 **Fairlie** N Ayrs
21 G4 **Fairlight** E Susx
12 E3 **Fairmile** Devon
43 J7 **Fairmile** Surrey
167 G3 **Fairnilee** Border
29 J7 **Fair Oak** Hants
99 H6 **Fairoak** Staffs
42 A7 **Fair Oak Green** Hants
45 L7 **Fairseat** Kent
61 J5 **Fairstead** Essex
105 G8 **Fairstead** Norfk
32 E7 **Fairwarp** E Susx
37 H5 **Fairwater** Cardif
22 F6 **Fairy Cross** Devon
105 L6 **Fakenham** Norfk
91 K7 **Fakenham Magna** Suffk
177 L6 **Fala** Mdloth
177 L6 **Fala Dam** Mdloth
117 H5 **Faldingworth** Lincs
236 e7 **Faldouet** Jersey
39 G2 **Falfield** S Glos
79 G6 **Falkenham** Suffk
176 B3 **Falkirk** Falk
176 B3 **Falkirk Crematorium** Falk
186 D6 **Falkland** Fife
165 J2 **Fallburn** S Lans
185 H8 **Fallin** Stirlg
169 J5 **Fallodon** Nthumb
113 J3 **Fallowfield** Manch
150 B2 **Fallowfield** Nthumb
182 E5 **Falls of Blarghour** Ag & B
19 K4 **Falmer** E Susx
3 K5 **Falmouth** Cnwll
156 D2 **Falnash** Border
134 F2 **Falsgrave** N York
157 J5 **Falstone** Nthumb
228 B5 **Fanagmore** Highld
59 G3 **Fancott** C Beds
212 D5 **Fanellan** Highld
142 C7 **Fangdale Beck** N York
134 B8 **Fangfoss** E R Yk
189 K7 **Fanmore** Ag & B
211 K2 **Fannich Lodge** Highld
167 J2 **Fans** Border
74 C7 **Far Bletchley** M Keyn
89 H5 **Farcet** Cambs
73 L3 **Far Cotton** Nhants
17 H2 **Fareham** Hants
137 J7 **Far End** Cumb
85 J2 **Farewell** Staffs
40 F2 **Faringdon** Oxon
121 H5 **Farington** Lancs
148 F3 **Farlam** Cumb
38 D6 **Farleigh** N Som
32 C2 **Farleigh** Surrey
39 J8 **Farleigh Hungerford** Somset
29 L3 **Farleigh Wallop** Hants
119 G6 **Farlesthorpe** Lincs
129 L4 **Farleton** Cumb
130 B6 **Farleton** Lancs
100 B4 **Farley** Staffs
28 E5 **Farley** Wilts
31 H3 **Farley Green** Surrey
42 C7 **Farley Hill** Wokham
55 H5 **Farleys End** Gloucs
17 J2 **Farlington** C Port
133 J6 **Farlington** N York
84 B7 **Farlow** Shrops
38 F7 **Farmborough** BaNES
56 B3 **Farmcote** Gloucs
66 E5 **Farmers** Carmth
56 C5 **Farmington** Gloucs
57 J6 **Farmoor** Oxon
112 D2 **Far Moor** Wigan
215 L4 **Farmtown** Moray
45 H7 **Farnborough** Gt Lon
30 E2 **Farnborough** Hants
41 H4 **Farnborough** W Berk
72 E5 **Farnborough** Warwks
30 E1 **Farnborough Park** Hants
30 E1 **Farnborough Street** Hants
31 G3 **Farncombe** Surrey
74 D2 **Farndish** Bed
98 B2 **Farndon** Ches W
102 C3 **Farndon** Notts
169 K2 **Farne Islands** Nthumb
197 G5 **Farnell** Angus
27 L7 **Farnham** Dorset
60 D3 **Farnham** Essex
132 E7 **Farnham** N York
79 H3 **Farnham** Suffk
30 D3 **Farnham** Surrey
42 F4 **Farnham Common** Bucks
42 F4 **Farnham Royal** Bucks
45 K6 **Farningham** Kent
123 K4 **Farnley** Leeds
123 J2 **Farnley** N York
123 H7 **Farnley Tyas** Kirk
101 M2 **Farnsfield** Notts
113 G1 **Farnworth** Bolton
112 D4 **Farnworth** Halton
55 L7 **Far Oakridge** Gloucs
203 K5 **Farr** Highld
213 G7 **Farr** Highld
229 L3 **Farr** Highld
202 E2 **Farraline** Highld
12 C4 **Farringdon** Devon
26 F1 **Farrington Gurney** BaNES
137 K7 **Far Sawrey** Cumb
73 G6 **Farthinghoe** Nhants
73 H4 **Farthingstone** Nhants
123 H6 **Fartown** Kirk
123 J4 **Fartown** Leeds
191 K6 **Fasnacloich** Ag & B
211 L8 **Fasnakyle** Highld
191 K2 **Fassfern** Highld
151 H4 **Fatfield** Sundld
176 C6 **Fauldhouse** W Loth
61 J5 **Faulkbourne** Essex
27 H1 **Faulkland** Somset
98 E6 **Fauls** Shrops
34 D3 **Faversham** Kent
132 F5 **Fawdington** N York
151 G2 **Fawdon** N u Ty
45 L6 **Fawkham Green** Kent
57 G4 **Fawler** Oxon
42 C3 **Fawley** Bucks
16 F2 **Fawley** Hants
41 H4 **Fawley** W Berk
125 K5 **Faxfleet** E R Yk
31 K5 **Faygate** W Susx
111 K3 **Fazakerley** Lpool
85 L3 **Fazeley** Staffs
132 B4 **Fearby** N York
223 H6 **Fearn** Highld
194 B7 **Fearnan** P & K
210 B3 **Fearnbeg** Highld
209 L3 **Fearnmore** Highld
172 F3 **Fearnoch** Ag & B
85 G3 **Featherstone** Staffs
124 C6 **Featherstone** Wakefd
71 H3 **Feckenham** Worcs
61 L4 **Feering** Essex
140 C7 **Feetham** N York
32 C5 **Felbridge** Surrey
106 E5 **Felbrigg** Norfk
32 C5 **Felcourt** Surrey
51 G2 **Felindre** Carmth
65 K6 **Felindre** Carmth
82 D7 **Felindre** Powys
51 J5 **Felindre** Swans
64 F6 **Felindre Farchog** Pembks
51 G2 **Felingwm Isaf** Carmth
51 G1 **Felingwm Uchaf** Carmth
133 G3 **Felixkirk** N York
79 G7 **Felixstowe** Suffk
151 G3 **Felling** Gatesd
74 E3 **Felmersham** Bed
106 F6 **Felmingham** Norfk
18 C5 **Felpham** W Susx
77 L3 **Felsham** Suffk
61 G4 **Felsted** Essex
43 J5 **Feltham** Gt Lon
43 H6 **Felthamhill** Surrey
106 E8 **Felthorpe** Norfk
69 L5 **Felton** Herefs
38 D7 **Felton** N Som
158 F3 **Felton** Nthumb
98 B8 **Felton Butler** Shrops
91 G5 **Feltwell** Norfk
122 C3 **Fence** Lancs
115 H4 **Fence** Rothm
57 L5 **Fencott** Oxon
104 D1 **Fendike Corner** Lincs
76 C3 **Fen Ditton** Cambs
75 L2 **Fen Drayton** Cambs
121 J5 **Feniscowles** Bl w D

12 E3 **Feniton** Devon
90 B5 **Fenland Crematorium** Cambs
84 D6 **Fenn Green** Shrops
46 D5 **Fenn Street** Medway
100 D3 **Fenny Bentley** Derbys
12 E3 **Fenny Bridges** Devon
72 E4 **Fenny Compton** Warwks
86 D4 **Fenny Drayton** Leics
75 K2 **Fenstanton** Cambs
92 B4 **Fen Street** Norfk
99 K4 **Fenton** C Stke
89 K7 **Fenton** Cambs
148 E4 **Fenton** Cumb
102 E3 **Fenton** Lincs
116 D6 **Fenton** Lincs
116 C5 **Fenton** Notts
168 E3 **Fenton** Nthumb
178 B3 **Fenton Barns** E Loth
124 F7 **Fenwick** Donc
163 L2 **Fenwick** E Ayrs
158 D7 **Fenwick** Nthumb
169 G2 **Fenwick** Nthumb
4 C7 **Feock** Cnwll
171 H4 **Feolin Ferry** Ag & B
163 J2 **Fergushill** N Ayrs
208 B4 **Feriniquarrie** Highld
196 D4 **Fern** Angus
36 F2 **Ferndale** Rhondd
15 K3 **Ferndown** Dorset
214 B5 **Ferness** Highld
40 F3 **Fernham** Oxon
70 F3 **Fernhill Heath** Worcs
30 E5 **Fernhurst** W Susx
186 E4 **Fernie** Fife
175 K7 **Ferniegair** S Lans
208 F7 **Fernilea** Highld
114 A5 **Fernilee** Derbys
102 D3 **Fernwood** Notts
132 E7 **Ferrensby** N York
199 K4 **Ferrindonald** Highld
18 F5 **Ferring** W Susx
124 D6 **Ferrybridge Services** Wakefd
197 H5 **Ferryden** Angus
141 H2 **Ferryhill** Dur
223 G4 **Ferry Point** Highld
50 D4 **Ferryside** Carmth
223 G4 **Ferrytown** Highld
92 C6 **Fersfield** Norfk
192 F2 **Fersit** Highld
203 K4 **Feshiebridge** Highld
31 J1 **Fetcham** Surrey
235 e2 **Fetlar** Shet
217 J4 **Fetterangus** Abers
197 G2 **Fettercairn** Abers
132 B8 **Fewston** N York
51 J2 **Ffairfach** Carmth
67 G2 **Ffair Rhos** Cerdgn
96 A4 **Ffestiniog** Gwynd
95 L4 **Ffestiniog Railway** Gwynd
51 H5 **Fforest** Carmth
51 J6 **Fforest Fach** Swans
65 L5 **Ffostrasol** Cerdgn
97 L2 **Ffrith** Flints
111 G5 **Ffynnongroyw** Flints
225 K3 **Fiag Lodge** Highld
32 C2 **Fickleshole** Surrey
25 K4 **Fiddington** Somset
27 J8 **Fiddleford** Dorset
4 C5 **Fiddlers Green** Cnwll
100 A5 **Field** Staffs
106 B5 **Field Dalling** Norfk
86 F2 **Field Head** Leics
27 H6 **Fifehead Magdalen** Dorset
14 E1 **Fifehead Neville** Dorset
14 E1 **Fifehead St Quintin** Dorset
215 J4 **Fife Keith** Moray
56 E4 **Fifield** Oxon
42 E5 **Fifield** W & M
28 D3 **Figheldean** Wilts
93 K2 **Filby** Norfk
135 H4 **Filey** N York
74 C5 **Filgrave** M Keyn
56 E6 **Filkins** Oxon
23 K5 **Filleigh** Devon
116 F4 **Fillingham** Lincs
86 C6 **Fillongley** Warwks
38 E5 **Filton** S Glos
134 D7 **Fimber** E R Yk
196 D5 **Finavon** Angus
91 G3 **Fincham** Norfk
42 D7 **Finchampstead** Wokham
182 C6 **Fincharn** Ag & B
30 C8 **Finchdean** Hants
61 G2 **Finchingfield** Essex
44 F2 **Finchley** Gt Lon
100 F6 **Findern** Derbys
214 C2 **Findhorn** Moray
213 J8 **Findhorn Bridge** Highld
215 K2 **Findochty** Moray
185 L4 **Findo Gask** P & K
207 H6 **Findon** Abers
18 F4 **Findon** W Susx
212 F3 **Findon Mains** Highld
206 B4 **Findrack House** Abers
74 D1 **Finedon** Nhants
186 C4 **Fingask** P & K
42 C3 **Fingest** Bucks
132 B2 **Finghall** N York
164 E6 **Fingland** D & G
35 J4 **Finglesham** Kent
62 B4 **Fingringhoe** Essex
184 C1 **Finlarig** Stirlg
57 M2 **Finmere** Oxon
193 H5 **Finnart** P & K
78 C1 **Finningham** Suffk
116 A2 **Finningley** Donc
232 d5 **Finsbay** W Isls
71 H1 **Finstall** Worcs
129 H2 **Finsthwaite** Cumb
57 G5 **Finstock** Oxon
234 b6 **Finstown** Ork
216 E4 **Fintry** Abers
175 H2 **Fintry** Stirlg
206 B6 **Finzean** Abers
180 D3 **Fionnphort** Ag & B
232 d5 **Fionnsbhagh** W Isls
130 C2 **Firbank** Cumb
115 K4 **Firbeck** Rothm
132 D3 **Firby** N York
134 B6 **Firby** N York
19 M4 **Firle** E Susx
118 F8 **Firsby** Lincs
150 E7 **Fir Tree** Dur
17 G4 **Fishbourne** IoW
18 A5 **Fishbourne** W Susx
18 A5 **Fishbourne Roman Palace** W Susx
141 J2 **Fishburn** Dur
185 J7 **Fishcross** Clacks
216 C7 **Fisherford** Abers
177 K4 **Fisherrow** E Loth
29 J7 **Fisher's Pond** Hants
213 H4 **Fisherton** Highld
163 H6 **Fisherton** S Ayrs
27 M4 **Fisherton de la Mere** Wilts
64 D6 **Fishguard** Pembks
125 G7 **Fishlake** Donc
190 D7 **Fishnish Pier** Ag & B
38 F5 **Fishponds** Bristl
104 B4 **Fishtoft** Lincs
104 A3 **Fishtoft Drove** Lincs
208 E7 **Fiskavaig** Highld
117 H6 **Fiskerton** Lincs
102 C3 **Fiskerton** Notts
28 D2 **Fittleton** Wilts
18 D2 **Fittleworth** W Susx
98 C8 **Fitz** Shrops
25 H5 **Fitzhead** Somset
124 C7 **Fitzwilliam** Wakefd
19 M2 **Five Ash Down** E Susx
32 F7 **Five Ashes** E Susx
26 A6 **Fivehead** Somset
9 G8 **Fivelanes** Cnwll
33 H4 **Five Oak Green** Kent
236 d7 **Five Oaks** Jersey
31 H5 **Five Oaks** W Susx
50 F4 **Five Roads** Carmth
42 E3 **Flackwell Heath** Bucks
71 H5 **Fladbury** Worcs
235 c6 **Fladdabister** Shet
114 C7 **Flagg** Derbys
135 K5 **Flamborough** E R Yk
135 K5 **Flamborough Head** E R Yk
134 B4 **Flamingo Land Theme Park** N York
59 H5 **Flamstead** Herts
18 C5 **Flansham** W Susx
123 L6 **Flanshaw** Wakefd
131 H7 **Flasby** N York
114 A7 **Flash** Staffs
208 E4 **Flashader** Highld
59 G7 **Flaunden** Herts
102 C4 **Flawborough** Notts
133 G6 **Flawith** N York
38 D6 **Flax Bourton** N Som
132 F7 **Flaxby** N York
55 G5 **Flaxley** Gloucs
25 H4 **Flaxpool** Somset
133 K6 **Flaxton** N York
87 J5 **Fleckney** Leics
73 G2 **Flecknoe** Warwks
116 D6 **Fledborough** Notts
14 C6 **Fleet** Dorset
30 D2 **Fleet** Hants
104 C7 **Fleet** Lincs
104 C7 **Fleet Hargate** Lincs
30 D1 **Fleet Services** Hants
120 D2 **Fleetwood** Lancs
36 F6 **Flemingston** V Glam
175 H6 **Flemington** S Lans
77 J1 **Flempton** Suffk
147 L6 **Fletchertown** Cumb
19 L2 **Fletching** E Susx
9 G4 **Flexbury** Cnwll
30 F2 **Flexford** Surrey
147 H7 **Flimby** Cumb
33 J6 **Flimwell** E Susx
111 H6 **Flint** Flints
102 C4 **Flintham** Notts
126 F4 **Flinton** E R Yk
105 H6 **Flitcham** Norfk
74 F7 **Flitton** C Beds
74 F7 **Flitwick** C Beds
125 K7 **Flixborough** N Linc
125 K7 **Flixborough Stather** N Linc
135 G4 **Flixton** N York
93 G6 **Flixton** Suffk
113 H3 **Flixton** Traffd
123 J7 **Flockton** Kirk
123 K7 **Flockton Green** Kirk
218 C6 **Flodigarry** Highld
129 H4 **Flookburgh** Cumb
92 E4 **Flordon** Norfk
73 J3 **Flore** Nhants
78 C5 **Flowton** Suffk
3 L4 **Flushing** Cnwll
12 E4 **Fluxton** Devon
71 H4 **Flyford Flavell** Worcs
46 B4 **Fobbing** Thurr
215 H3 **Fochabers** Moray
53 H6 **Fochriw** Caerph
125 K6 **Fockerby** N Linc
26 E5 **Foddington** Somset
81 L2 **Foel** Powys
125 H3 **Foggathorpe** E R Yk
179 G8 **Fogo** Border
214 F3 **Fogwatt** Moray
228 B5 **Foindle** Highld
195 J4 **Folda** Angus
100 B5 **Fole** Staffs
86 D6 **Foleshill** Covtry
26 F8 **Folke** Dorset
35 H7 **Folkestone** Kent
103 H5 **Folkingham** Lincs
20 B5 **Folkington** E Susx
89 G5 **Folksworth** Cambs
135 G4 **Folkton** N York
216 D7 **Folla Rule** Abers
132 E8 **Follifoot** N York
10 E5 **Folly Gate** Devon
27 L5 **Fonthill Bishop** Wilts
27 L5 **Fonthill Gifford** Wilts
27 K7 **Fontmell Magna** Dorset
27 J8 **Fontmell Parva** Dorset
18 C4 **Fontwell** W Susx
114 D6 **Foolow** Derbys
205 H3 **Forbestown** Abers
140 F5 **Forcett** N York
182 C6 **Ford** Ag & B
58 C6 **Ford** Bucks
115 H5 **Ford** Derbys
22 F6 **Ford** Devon
56 C3 **Ford** Gloucs
168 E2 **Ford** Nthumb
25 H5 **Ford** Somset
100 B2 **Ford** Staffs
18 D5 **Ford** W Susx
39 J5 **Ford** Wilts
32 F5 **Fordcombe** Kent
177 G2 **Fordell** Fife
82 E4 **Forden** Powys
61 G5 **Ford End** Essex
7 H3 **Forder Green** Devon
76 F1 **Fordham** Cambs
61 L3 **Fordham** Essex
90 E4 **Fordham** Norfk
28 D8 **Fordingbridge** Hants
135 G4 **Fordon** E R Yk
197 J2 **Fordoun** Abers
61 L3 **Fordstreet** Essex
25 J7 **Ford Street** Somset
35 G3 **Fordwich** Kent
216 B2 **Fordyce** Abers
99 L7 **Forebridge** Staffs
236 c4 **Forest** Guern
113 L6 **Forest Chapel** Ches E
45 H3 **Forest Gate** Gt Lon
31 J3 **Forest Green** Surrey
151 G2 **Forest Hall** N Tyne
45 G5 **Forest Hill** Gt Lon
57 L6 **Forest Hill** Oxon
132 E7 **Forest Lane Head** N York
185 K8 **Forest Mill** Clacks
54 F5 **Forest of Dean** Gloucs
45 J2 **Forest Park Crematorium** Gt Lon
32 D6 **Forest Row** E Susx
30 C8 **Forestside** W Susx
196 D6 **Forfar** Angus
186 A4 **Forgandenny** P & K
37 L2 **Forge Hammer** Torfn
215 J4 **Forgie** Moray
215 J4 **Forgieside** Moray
216 B5 **Forgue** Abers
111 J1 **Formby** Sefton
92 D5 **Forncett End** Norfk
92 E5 **Forncett St Mary** Norfk
92 E5 **Forncett St Peter** Norfk
77 J2 **Fornham All Saints** Suffk
77 J2 **Fornham St Martin** Suffk
213 L4 **Fornighty** Highld
214 C3 **Forres** Moray
99 L4 **Forsbrook** Staffs
227 M2 **Forse** Highld
230 C6 **Forsinard** Highld
202 B4 **Fort Augustus** Highld
185 L4 **Forteviot** P & K
176 C7 **Forth** S Lans
55 K2 **Forthampton** Gloucs
194 B6 **Fortingall** P & K
29 H3 **Forton** Hants

121 G1 **Forton** Lancs
83 H1 **Forton** Shrops
13 J2 **Forton** Somset
99 H7 **Forton** Staffs
216 C5 **Fortrie** Abers
213 H3 **Fortrose** Highld
14 D7 **Fortuneswell** Dorset
191 L2 **Fort William** Highld
60 B7 **Forty Hill** Gt Lon
40 F8 **Fosbury** Wilts
56 E4 **Foscot** Oxon
104 A5 **Fosdyke** Lincs
194 C5 **Foss** P & K
56 B5 **Fossebridge** Gloucs
60 D6 **Foster Street** Essex
100 D6 **Foston** Derbys
87 H4 **Foston** Leics
102 E4 **Foston** Lincs
133 L6 **Foston** N York
135 H7 **Foston on the Wolds** E R Yk
118 D3 **Fotherby** Lincs
88 F5 **Fotheringhay** Nhants
235 a6 **Foula** Shet
179 J7 **Foulden** Border
91 H4 **Foulden** Norfk
86 B4 **Foul End** Warwks
47 G2 **Foulness Island** Essex
236 d3 **Foulon Vale Crematorium** Guern
122 D3 **Foulridge** Lancs
106 B7 **Foulsham** Norfk
177 L8 **Fountainhall** Border
78 B1 **Four Ashes** Suffk
97 K8 **Four Crosses** Powys
32 E4 **Four Elms** Kent
25 K4 **Four Forks** Somset
90 C1 **Four Gotes** Cambs
3 J4 **Four Lanes** Cnwll
30 A4 **Four Marks** Hants
108 C5 **Four Mile Bridge** IoA
86 B7 **Four Oaks** Solhll
223 H3 **Fourpenny** Highld
50 F4 **Four Roads** Carmth
149 M2 **Fourstones** Nthumb
33 K7 **Four Throws** Kent
28 A5 **Fovant** Wilts
207 H2 **Foveran** Abers
5 H5 **Fowey** Cnwll
33 J4 **Fowlhall** Kent
186 E2 **Fowlis** Angus
185 J3 **Fowlis Wester** P & K
76 B5 **Fowlmere** Cambs
69 L7 **Fownhope** Herefs
174 E6 **Foxbar** Rens
27 G1 **Foxcote** Somset
237 b5 **Foxdale** IoM
77 J5 **Foxearth** Essex
128 F3 **Foxfield** Cumb
4 F5 **Foxhole** Cnwll
134 F5 **Foxholes** N York
106 C7 **Foxley** Norfk
100 B3 **Foxt** Staffs
76 B5 **Foxton** Cambs
87 K5 **Foxton** Leics
141 K7 **Foxton** N York
84 B7 **Foxwood** Shrops
54 E3 **Foy** Herefs
202 D2 **Foyers** Highld
213 L4 **Foynesfield** Highld
4 E4 **Fraddon** Cnwll
85 L2 **Fradley** Staffs
99 M6 **Fradswell** Staffs
135 J7 **Fraisthorpe** E R Yk
20 A2 **Framfield** E Susx
92 F3 **Framingham Earl** Norfk
92 F3 **Framingham Pigot** Norfk
79 G2 **Framlingham** Suffk
14 C4 **Frampton** Dorset
104 B5 **Frampton** Lincs
38 F4 **Frampton Cotterell** S Glos
55 L7 **Frampton Mansell** Gloucs
55 H6 **Frampton on Severn** Gloucs
78 E3 **Framsden** Suffk
151 G6 **Framwellgate Moor** Dur
84 E7 **Franche** Worcs
111 H4 **Frankby** Wirral
85 H7 **Frankley** Worcs
85 H7 **Frankley Services** Worcs
72 E1 **Frankton** Warwks
33 G6 **Frant** E Susx
217 J2 **Fraserburgh** Abers
62 C4 **Frating** Essex
62 C4 **Frating Green** Essex
17 J3 **Fratton** C Port
6 B5 **Freathy** Cnwll
76 F1 **Freckenham** Suffk
120 F5 **Freckleton** Lancs
102 D7 **Freeby** Leics
29 J2 **Freefolk** Hants
57 H5 **Freeland** Oxon
93 J3 **Freethorpe** Norfk
93 J3 **Freethorpe Common** Norfk
104 B4 **Freiston** Lincs
23 H5 **Fremington** Devon
140 D7 **Fremington** N York
38 F5 **Frenchay** S Glos
194 C5 **Frenich** P & K
30 D3 **Frensham** Surrey
120 C8 **Freshfield** Sefton
39 H7 **Freshford** Wilts
16 D5 **Freshwater** IoW
92 F7 **Fressingfield** Suffk
78 E6 **Freston** Suffk
231 L3 **Freswick** Highld
55 G6 **Fretherne** Gloucs
106 F8 **Frettenham** Norfk
186 E6 **Freuchie** Fife
49 G5 **Freystrop** Pembks
85 H4 **Friar Park** Sandw
90 C3 **Friday Bridge** Cambs
79 H3 **Friday Street** Suffk
134 D7 **Fridaythorpe** E R Yk
44 F2 **Friern Barnet** Gt Lon
117 H5 **Friesthorpe** Lincs
102 F3 **Frieston** Lincs
42 D3 **Frieth** Bucks
41 H2 **Frilford** Oxon
41 K5 **Frilsham** W Berk
42 E8 **Frimley** Surrey
46 C6 **Frindsbury** Medway
105 H5 **Fring** Norfk
57 L3 **Fringford** Oxon
34 B4 **Frinsted** Kent
62 F4 **Frinton-on-Sea** Essex
196 F6 **Friockheim** Angus
102 B8 **Frisby on the Wreake** Leics
104 D2 **Friskney** Lincs
20 B6 **Friston** E Susx
79 J3 **Friston** Suffk
101 G3 **Fritchley** Derbys
28 E8 **Fritham** Hants
23 G7 **Frithelstock** Devon
23 G7 **Frithelstock Stone** Devon
104 A3 **Frithville** Lincs
33 K5 **Frittenden** Kent
7 J6 **Frittiscombe** Devon
92 F5 **Fritton** Norfk
93 K4 **Fritton** Norfk
57 K3 **Fritwell** Oxon
123 H4 **Frizinghall** C Brad
136 E4 **Frizington** Cumb
55 H7 **Frocester** Gloucs
83 K3 **Frodesley** Shrops
112 D6 **Frodsham** Ches W
168 B4 **Frogden** Border
76 B5 **Frog End** Cambs
114 E6 **Froggatt** Derbys
100 A3 **Froghall** Staffs
7 H7 **Frogmore** Devon
89 H2 **Frognall** Lincs
70 E2 **Frog Pool** Worcs
6 A3 **Frogwell** Cnwll
87 G5 **Frolesworth** Leics
27 H2 **Frome** Somset
14 B2 **Frome St Quintin** Dorset
70 C5 **Fromes Hill** Herefs
97 K4 **Froncysyllte** Denbgs
96 D5 **Fron-goch** Gwynd
97 L4 **Fron Isaf** Wrexhm
150 C7 **Frosterley** Dur
40 F6 **Froxfield** Wilts
30 B6 **Froxfield Green** Hants
29 H7 **Fryern Hill** Hants
61 G7 **Fryerning** Essex
190 C6 **Fuinary** Highld
102 F3 **Fulbeck** Lincs
76 D4 **Fulbourn** Cambs
56 E5 **Fulbrook** Oxon
29 J5 **Fulflood** Hants
124 F2 **Fulford** C York
25 K5 **Fulford** Somset
99 L5 **Fulford** Staffs
44 E5 **Fulham** Gt Lon
19 H4 **Fulking** W Susx
163 H2 **Fullarton** N Ayrs
61 H5 **Fuller Street** Essex
29 G4 **Fullerton** Hants
118 D6 **Fulletby** Lincs
72 C5 **Fullready** Warwks
134 B7 **Full Sutton** E R Yk
174 E7 **Fullwood** E Ayrs
43 G4 **Fulmer** Bucks
106 B6 **Fulmodeston** Norfk
117 H5 **Fulnetby** Lincs
103 L7 **Fulney** Lincs
118 D3 **Fulstow** Lincs
151 J3 **Fulwell** Sundld
121 H4 **Fulwood** Lancs
114 F4 **Fulwood** Sheff
92 D4 **Fundenhall** Norfk
17 L2 **Funtington** W Susx
184 F3 **Funtullich** P & K
13 H2 **Furley** Devon
182 E7 **Furnace** Ag & B
51 G5 **Furnace** Carmth
114 A5 **Furness Vale** Derbys
60 C3 **Furneux Pelham** Herts
28 F7 **Furzley** Hants
60 F6 **Fyfield** Essex
28 F3 **Fyfield** Hants
57 H7 **Fyfield** Oxon
40 C6 **Fyfield** Wilts
40 D7 **Fyfield** Wilts
143 J6 **Fylingthorpe** N York
30 D6 **Fyning** W Susx
216 E6 **Fyvie** Abers

G

174 E7 **Gabroc Hill** E Ayrs
87 K2 **Gaddesby** Leics
59 H5 **Gaddesden Row** Herts
163 K5 **Gadgirth** S Ayrs
38 C2 **Gaer-llwyd** Mons
108 F7 **Gaerwen** IoA
163 H3 **Gailes** N Ayrs
85 G2 **Gailey** Staffs
140 F4 **Gainford** Dur
116 D4 **Gainsborough** Lincs
77 G7 **Gainsford End** Essex
219 J6 **Gairloch** Highld
201 J8 **Gairlochy** Highld
186 B7 **Gairneybridge** P & K
148 C5 **Gaitsgill** Cumb
167 G3 **Galashiels** Border
129 K7 **Galgate** Lancs
26 F5 **Galhampton** Somset
182 B2 **Gallanachbeg** Ag & B
182 B3 **Gallanachmore** Ag & B
186 E8 **Gallatown** Fife
61 H7 **Galleywood** Essex
202 E7 **Gallovie** Highld
153 J5 **Galloway Forest Park**
196 D7 **Gallowfauld** Angus
186 B1 **Gallowhill** P & K
200 C2 **Galltair** Highld
7 G7 **Galmpton** Devon
7 K5 **Galmpton** Torbay
132 C5 **Galphay** N York
163 L3 **Galston** E Ayrs
149 G6 **Gamblesby** Cumb
75 J4 **Gamlingay** Cambs
75 J4 **Gamlingay Great Heath** Cambs
216 F2 **Gamrie** Abers
101 L5 **Gamston** Notts
116 B6 **Gamston** Notts
182 B2 **Ganavan Bay** Ag & B
96 B7 **Ganllwyd** Gwynd
196 F3 **Gannachy** Angus
126 E4 **Ganstead** E R Yk
133 L5 **Ganthorpe** N York
134 F4 **Ganton** N York
215 H4 **Garbity** Moray
92 B7 **Garboldisham** Norfk
203 H1 **Garbole** Highld
205 G4 **Garchory** Abers
42 D6 **Gardeners Green** Wokham
216 F2 **Gardenstown** Abers
114 E2 **Garden Village** Sheff
235 c5 **Garderhouse** Shet
27 H4 **Gare Hill** Somset
173 L1 **Garelochhead** Ag & B
41 H2 **Garford** Oxon
124 B4 **Garforth** Leeds
131 H8 **Gargrave** N York
184 F8 **Gargunnock** Stirlg
92 E6 **Garlic Street** Norfk
145 K5 **Garlieston** D & G
35 J2 **Garlinge** Kent
34 F4 **Garlinge Green** Kent
206 E4 **Garlogie** Abers
216 F4 **Garmond** Abers
215 H2 **Garmouth** Moray
83 L3 **Garmston** Shrops
95 J4 **Garn-Dolbenmaen** Gwynd
175 J5 **Garnkirk** N Lans
232 g2 **Garrabost** W Isls
164 B5 **Garrallan** E Ayrs
3 J6 **Garras** Cnwll
95 K4 **Garreg** Gwynd
149 J6 **Garrigill** Cumb
153 M6 **Garroch** D & G
144 D7 **Garrochtrie** D & G
173 J7 **Garrochty** Ag & B
209 H2 **Garros** Highld
130 E2 **Garsdale Head** Cumb
39 L3 **Garsdon** Wilts
99 L5 **Garshall Green** Staffs
57 L7 **Garsington** Oxon
121 G2 **Garstang** Lancs
59 J7 **Garston** Herts
112 B5 **Garston** Lpool
171 G6 **Gartachossan** Ag & B
175 J5 **Gartcosh** N Lans
67 K5 **Garth** Powys
97 K4 **Garth** Wrexhm
175 H5 **Garthamlock** C Glas
82 E4 **Garthmyl** Powys
102 D7 **Garthorpe** Leics
125 K6 **Garthorpe** N Linc
80 E6 **Garth Penrhyncoch** Cerdgn
138 D7 **Garth Row** Cumb
215 L7 **Gartly** Abers
184 C7 **Gartmore** Stirlg
175 K5 **Gartness** N Lans
174 F2 **Gartness** Stirlg
174 D2 **Gartocharn** W Duns
134 F7 **Garton-on-the-Wolds** E R Yk
227 H5 **Gartymore** Highld
178 D4 **Garvald** E Loth
191 J2 **Garvan** Highld

171 G1 **Garvard** Ag & B
212 B3 **Garve** Highld
181 K5 **Garvellachs** Ag & B
92 B3 **Garvestone** Norfk
174 B4 **Garvock** Inver
54 C4 **Garway** Herefs
232 f3 **Garyvard** W Isls
27 H5 **Gasper** Wilts
39 K6 **Gastard** Wilts
91 L7 **Gasthorpe** Norfk
60 D5 **Gaston Green** Essex
16 F5 **Gatcombe** IoW
116 D5 **Gate Burton** Lincs
124 E5 **Gateforth** N York
163 K3 **Gatehead** E Ayrs
133 L7 **Gate Helmsley** N York
157 K4 **Gatehouse** Nthumb
145 M4 **Gatehouse of Fleet** D & G
106 A7 **Gateley** Norfk
132 E3 **Gatenby** N York
168 B5 **Gateshaw** Border
151 G3 **Gateshead** Gatesd
196 D7 **Gateside** Angus
174 E6 **Gateside** E Rens
186 C5 **Gateside** Fife
174 C7 **Gateside** N Ayrs
154 F2 **Gateslack** D & G
113 J4 **Gatley** Stockp
167 H3 **Gattonside** Border
32 B5 *Gatwick Airport* W Susx
87 K4 **Gaulby** Leics
186 F3 **Gauldry** Fife
195 K6 **Gauldswell** P & K
117 K6 **Gautby** Lincs
179 G7 **Gavinton** Border
58 B2 **Gawcott** Bucks
113 K7 **Gawsworth** Ches E
130 D3 **Gawthrop** Cumb
129 G3 **Gawthwaite** Cumb
72 D4 **Gaydon** Warwks
74 B5 **Gayhurst** M Keyn
131 G2 **Gayle** N York
140 E5 **Gayles** N York
73 K4 **Gayton** Nhants
105 H8 **Gayton** Norfk
99 M6 **Gayton** Staffs
118 F5 **Gayton le Marsh** Lincs
105 H8 **Gayton Thorpe** Norfk
105 G7 **Gaywood** Norfk
77 G2 **Gazeley** Suffk
232 f3 **Gearraidh Bhaird** W Isls
208 D3 **Geary** Highld
77 L3 **Gedding** Suffk
88 C6 **Geddington** Nhants
101 L4 **Gedling** Notts
104 C7 **Gedney** Lincs
104 C7 **Gedney Broadgate** Lincs
104 D6 **Gedney Drove End** Lincs
104 C7 **Gedney Dyke** Lincs
89 L2 **Gedney Hill** Lincs
88 E3 **Geeston** Rutlnd
93 H5 **Geldeston** Norfk
110 F8 **Gellifor** Denbgs
37 H2 **Gelligaer** Caerph
95 M4 **Gellilydan** Gwynd
51 K5 **Gellinudd** Neath
195 H8 **Gellyburn** P & K
50 C2 **Gellywen** Carmth
146 D3 **Gelston** D & G
102 E4 **Gelston** Lincs
135 H7 **Gembling** E R Yk
85 J2 **Gentleshaw** Staffs
156 B4 **Georgefield** D & G
43 G4 **George Green** Bucks
23 G4 **Georgeham** Devon
231 H4 **Georgemas Junction Station** Highld
23 L6 **George Nympton** Devon
234 b5 **Georth** Ork
10 C6 **Germansweek** Devon
4 D8 **Gerrans** Cnwll
43 G3 **Gerrards Cross** Bucks
142 E5 **Gerrick** R & Cl
77 J6 **Gestingthorpe** Essex
82 E2 **Geuffordd** Powys
45 K3 **Gidea Park** Gt Lon
175 G6 **Giffnock** E Rens
178 C5 **Gifford** E Loth
186 E5 **Giffordtown** Fife
130 F6 **Giggleswick** N York
171 L7 **Gigha** Ag & B
125 K5 **Gilberdyke** E R Yk
178 B5 **Gilchriston** E Loth
147 K7 **Gilcrux** Cumb
123 K5 **Gildersome** Leeds
115 K4 **Gildingwells** Rothm
151 H6 **Gilesgate Moor** Dur
36 F6 **Gileston** V Glam
53 J7 **Gilfach** Caerph
36 F3 **Gilfach Goch** Brdgnd
65 L3 **Gilfachrheda** Cerdgn
136 E3 **Gilgarran** Cumb
133 K2 **Gillamoor** N York
208 D3 **Gillen** Highld
155 K4 **Gillesbie** D & G
133 J4 **Gilling East** N York
27 J6 **Gillingham** Dorset
46 C6 **Gillingham** Medway
93 J5 **Gillingham** Norfk
140 F6 **Gilling West** N York
231 J4 **Gillock** Highld
231 K2 **Gills** Highld
166 E5 **Gilmanscleuch** Border
177 J5 **Gilmerton** C Edin
185 J3 **Gilmerton** P & K
140 C5 **Gilmonby** Dur
87 H6 **Gilmorton** Leics
87 H3 **Gilroes Crematorium** C Leic
149 G2 **Gilsland** Nthumb
177 L6 **Gilston** Border
60 D5 **Gilston** Herts
53 K5 **Gilwern** Mons
107 G5 **Gimingham** Norfk
78 C2 **Gipping** Suffk
103 M3 **Gipsey Bridge** Lincs
163 J2 **Girdle Toll** N Ayrs
235 c5 **Girlsta** Shet
141 J5 **Girsby** N York
146 A4 **Girthon** D & G
76 B3 **Girton** Cambs
116 D7 **Girton** Notts
152 E3 **Girvan** S Ayrs
122 C2 **Gisburn** Lancs
93 K5 **Gisleham** Suffk
78 C1 **Gislingham** Suffk
92 D6 **Gissing** Norfk
12 E3 **Gittisham** Devon
68 E4 **Gladestry** Powys
177 M4 **Gladsmuir** E Loth
51 K5 **Glais** Swans
143 G6 **Glaisdale** N York
196 C6 **Glamis** Angus
51 J3 **Glanaman** Carmth
106 C4 **Glandford** Norfk
49 K2 **Glandwr** Pembks
80 F4 **Glandyfi** Cerdgn
36 D3 **Glanllynfi** Brdgnd
52 B6 **Glan-rhyd** Powys
169 G6 **Glanton** Nthumb
14 D2 **Glanvilles Wootton** Dorset
111 G5 **Glan-y-don** Flints
88 E5 **Glapthorn** Nhants
115 J7 **Glapwell** Derbys
68 D6 **Glasbury** Powys
68 D4 **Glascwm** Powys
96 E3 **Glasfryn** Conwy
175 G5 **Glasgow** C Glas
174 E5 *Glasgow Airport* Rens
175 G5 **Glasgow Science Centre** C Glas
109 H7 **Glasinfryn** Gwynd
199 L6 **Glasnacardoch Bay** Highld
199 H3 **Glasnakille** Highld
175 J8 **Glassford** S Lans
55 G4 **Glasshouse** Gloucs
132 B6 **Glasshouses** N York
148 A3 **Glasson** Cumb
129 K7 **Glasson** Lancs
149 G7 **Glassonby** Cumb
196 F6 **Glasterlaw** Angus
88 C4 **Glaston** Rutlnd
26 D4 **Glastonbury** Somset
89 H6 **Glatton** Cambs
113 G3 **Glazebrook** Warrtn
112 F3 **Glazebury** Warrtn
84 C5 **Glazeley** Shrops
128 F5 **Gleaston** Cumb
202 D2 **Glebe** Highld
123 L3 **Gledhow** Leeds
146 B5 **Gledpark** D & G
97 L5 **Gledrid** Shrops
77 J5 **Glemsford** Suffk
215 G6 **Glenallachie** Moray
199 K6 **Glenancross** Highld
190 B7 **Glenaros House** Ag & B
237 d3 **Glen Auldyn** IoM
161 H3 **Glenbarr** Ag & B
216 B4 **Glenbarry** Abers
190 C4 **Glenbeg** Highld
197 J1 **Glenbervie** Abers
175 J5 **Glenboig** N Lans
190 C4 **Glenborrodale** Highld
183 G7 **Glenbranter** Ag & B
165 K5 **Glenbreck** Border
198 F2 **Glenbrittle House** Highld
164 E4 **Glenbuck** E Ayrs
196 B4 **Glencally** Angus
147 H2 **Glencaple** D & G
211 G4 **Glencarron Lodge** Highld
186 C3 **Glencarse** P & K
204 E8 **Glen Clunie Lodge** Abers
191 L5 **Glencoe** Highld
165 L4 **Glencothe** Border
186 C7 **Glencraig** Fife
154 D4 **Glencrosh** D & G
208 B4 **Glendale** Highld
173 G2 **Glendaruel** Ag & B
185 K6 **Glendevon** P & K
202 C4 **Glendoe Lodge** Highld
186 C3 **Glendoick** P & K
186 D4 **Glenduckie** Fife
170 F7 **Glenegedale** Ag & B
200 C2 **Glenelg** Highld
214 C5 **Glenerney** Moray
186 B5 **Glenfarg** P & K
87 G3 **Glenfield** Leics
191 H1 **Glenfinnan** Highld
201 K7 **Glenfintaig Lodge** Highld
186 C4 **Glenfoot** P & K
183 H4 **Glenfyne Lodge** Ag & B
174 C7 **Glengarnock** N Ayrs
231 G3 **Glengolly** Highld
189 K5 **Glengorm Castle** Ag & B
209 G5 **Glengrasco** Highld
165 L3 **Glenholm** Border
154 A5 **Glenhoul** D & G
195 K4 **Glenisla** Angus
173 K3 **Glenkin** Ag & B
205 K3 **Glenkindie** Abers
214 F8 **Glenlivet** Moray
146 C3 **Glenlochar** D & G
186 C6 **Glenlomond** P & K
144 E4 **Glenluce** D & G
173 J2 **Glenmassen** Ag & B
175 K5 **Glenmavis** N Lans
237 b5 **Glen Maye** IoM
209 G6 **Glenmore** Highld
204 B4 **Glenmore Lodge** Highld
192 B3 **Glen Nevis House** Highld
185 H7 **Glenochil** Clacks
87 H4 **Glen Parva** Leics
196 C4 **Glenquiech** Angus
172 E5 **Glenralloch** Ag & B
137 L4 **Glenridding** Cumb
186 D7 **Glenrothes** Fife
202 E6 **Glenshero Lodge** Highld
173 J3 **Glenstriven** Ag & B
117 G4 **Glentham** Lincs
153 J6 **Glen Trool Lodge** D & G
153 H6 **Glentrool Village** D & G
203 G6 **Glentruim House** Highld
116 F4 **Glentworth** Lincs
190 D2 **Glenuig** Highld
209 G6 **Glenvarragill** Highld
237 c5 **Glen Vine** IoM
152 E7 **Glenwhilly** D & G
164 F4 **Glespin** S Lans
54 E4 **Glewstone** Herefs
89 H3 **Glinton** C Pete
87 L4 **Glooston** Leics
114 B3 **Glossop** Derbys
159 G2 **Gloster Hill** Nthumb
55 J4 **Gloucester** Gloucs
55 J5 **Gloucester Crematorium** Gloucs
55 K4 *Gloucestershire Airport* Gloucs
122 F2 **Glusburn** N York
227 H2 **Glutt Lodge** Highld
57 H4 **Glympton** Oxon
65 K5 **Glynarthen** Cerdgn
97 J5 **Glyn Ceiriog** Wrexhm
52 D7 **Glyncorrwg** Neath
19 L4 **Glynde** E Susx
97 J4 **Glyndyfrdwy** Denbgs
52 D6 **Glynneath** Neath
5 H3 **Glynn Valley Crematorium** Cnwll
37 H3 **Glyntaff Crematorium** Rhondd
52 D5 **Glyntawe** Powys
65 K6 **Glynteg** Carmth
99 J7 **Gnosall** Staffs
99 J7 **Gnosall Heath** Staffs
87 L4 **Goadby** Leics
102 C7 **Goadby Marwood** Leics
40 A5 **Goatacre** Wilts
26 F7 **Goathill** Dorset
143 H6 **Goathland** N York
25 K5 **Goathurst** Somset
97 L5 **Gobowen** Shrops
30 F3 **Godalming** Surrey
33 L6 **Goddard's Green** Kent
75 J1 **Godmanchester** Cambs
14 C3 **Godmanstone** Dorset
34 E5 **Godmersham** Kent
26 C3 **Godney** Somset
3 G5 **Godolphin Cross** Cnwll
51 L4 **Godre'r-graig** Neath
17 G6 **Godshill** IoW
32 C3 **Godstone** Surrey
53 L6 **Goetre** Mons
60 B7 **Goff's Oak** Herts
53 K5 **Gofilon** Mons
177 G4 **Gogar** C Edin
80 F7 **Goginan** Cerdgn
95 J4 **Golan** Gwynd
5 H5 **Golant** Cnwll
5 M2 **Golberdon** Cnwll
112 E3 **Golborne** Wigan
123 G7 **Golcar** Kirk
38 A4 **Goldcliff** Newpt
33 H4 **Golden Green** Kent
30 B3 **Golden Pot** Hants

44 E3 Golders Green Gt Lon
44 E3 Golders Green Crematorium Gt Lon
61 L6 Goldhanger Essex
74 F4 Goldington Bed
132 F7 Goldsborough N York
143 H4 Goldsborough N York
2 F5 Goldsithney Cnwll
43 G8 Goldsworth Park Surrey
115 J2 Goldthorpe Barns
22 F6 Goldworthy Devon
213 J4 Gollanfield Highld
223 H2 Golspie Highld
28 D4 Gomeldon Wilts
31 H2 Gomshall Surrey
102 B3 Gonalston Notts
102 E5 Gonerby Hill Foot Lincs
235 c4 Gonfirth Shet
60 F5 Good Easter Essex
91 H3 Gooderstone Norfk
23 J5 Goodleigh Devon
125 K2 Goodmanham E R Yk
45 J3 Goodmayes Gt Lon
34 D3 Goodnestone Kent
35 H4 Goodnestone Kent
54 E4 Goodrich Herefs
54 E4 Goodrich Castle Herefs
7 K4 Goodrington Torbay
122 B5 Goodshaw Lancs
64 C6 Goodwick Pembks
29 G3 Goodworth Clatford Hants
125 H5 Goole E R Yk
71 H4 Goom's Hill Worcs
3 J2 Goonbell Cnwll
3 K1 Goonhavern Cnwll
3 J2 Goonvrea Cnwll
206 E8 Goosecruives Abers
11 G6 Gooseford Devon
62 D3 Goose Green Essex
38 F5 Goose Green S Glos
9 G2 Gooseham Cnwll
41 G3 Goosey Oxon
121 H3 Goosnargh Lancs
113 H7 Goostrey Ches E
38 D5 Gordano Services N Som
167 K2 Gordon Border
166 D4 Gordon Arms Hotel Border
216 B3 Gordonstown Abers
216 D6 Gordonstown Abers
177 K6 Gorebridge Mdloth
90 B2 Gorefield Cambs
40 C8 Gores Wilts
236 e7 Gorey Jersey
41 L4 Goring Oxon
18 F5 Goring-by-Sea W Susx
93 L3 Gorleston on Sea Norfk
85 G5 Gornal Wood Crematorium Dudley
216 E3 Gorrachie Abers
4 F7 Gorran Churchtown Cnwll
4 F7 Gorran Haven Cnwll
111 G6 Gorsedd Flints
40 D3 Gorse Hill Swindn
51 H5 Gorseinon Swans
66 C4 Gorsgoch Cerdgn
51 H3 Gorslas Carmth
55 G3 Gorsley Gloucs
54 F3 Gorsley Common Herefs
212 B2 Gorstan Highld
100 C6 Gorsty Hill Staffs
181 L2 Gorten Ag & B
202 E2 Gorthleck Highld
113 K3 Gorton Manch
78 D4 Gosbeck Suffk
103 L6 Gosberton Lincs
61 J3 Gosfield Essex
136 E6 Gosforth Cumb
151 G2 Gosforth N u Ty
84 F5 Gospel End Staffs
17 H3 Gosport Hants
55 H7 Gossington Gloucs
101 K6 Gotham Notts
55 L3 Gotherington Gloucs
25 K5 Gotton Somset
33 J5 Goudhurst Kent
118 C5 Goulceby Lincs
216 E6 Gourdas Abers
186 F2 Gourdie C Dund
197 K3 Gourdon Abers
173 L3 Gourock Inver
174 F5 Govan C Glas
7 H6 Goveton Devon
124 F6 Gowdall E R Yk
212 D3 Gower Highld
51 G7 Gower Swans
51 H6 Gowerton Swans
176 E1 Gowkhall Fife
126 F2 Goxhill E R Yk
126 D6 Goxhill N Linc
232 f3 Grabhair W Isls
18 C3 Graffham W Susx
75 H2 Grafham Cambs
31 G3 Grafham Surrey
132 F6 Grafton N York
56 F7 Grafton Oxon
98 B8 Grafton Shrops
71 H6 Grafton Worcs
71 G4 Grafton Flyford Worcs
73 L5 Grafton Regis Nhants
88 D7 Grafton Underwood Nhants
34 B5 Grafty Green Kent
109 M6 Graig Conwy
97 J2 Graig-fechan Denbgs
46 E5 Grain Medway
118 C2 Grainsby Lincs
118 E3 Grainthorpe Lincs
4 E6 Grampound Cnwll
4 E5 Grampound Road Cnwll
233 c6 Gramsdal W Isls
233 c6 Gramsdale W Isls
58 C3 Granborough Bucks
102 C5 Granby Notts
72 F2 Grandborough Warwks
236 d7 Grand Chemins Jersey
236 c2 Grandes Rocques Guern
101 H7 Grand Prix Collection Donington Leics
194 E5 Grandtully P & K
137 H4 Grange Cumb
46 D6 Grange Medway
186 D3 Grange P & K
215 K4 Grange Crossroads Moray
214 C3 Grange Hall Moray
165 J2 Grangehall S Lans
45 H2 Grange Hill Essex
100 E2 Grangemill Derbys
123 J7 Grange Moor Kirk
176 C3 Grangemouth Falk
186 D4 Grange of Lindores Fife
129 J4 Grange-over-Sands Cumb
176 D3 Grangepans Falk
142 C3 Grangetown R & Cl
151 K4 Grangetown Sundld
151 G4 Grange Villa Dur
135 H7 Gransmoor E R Yk
64 C7 Granston Pembks
76 B4 Grantchester Cambs
102 E5 Grantham Lincs
102 F5 Grantham Crematorium Lincs
177 H3 Granton C Edin
214 C8 Grantown-on-Spey Highld
179 G5 Grantshouse Border
117 H1 Grasby Lincs
137 K5 Grasmere Cumb
113 L1 Grasscroft Oldham
111 L4 Grassendale Lpool
131 J6 Grassington N York
115 H7 Grassmoor Derbys
116 C7 Grassthorpe Notts
28 F3 Grateley Hants
75 J2 Graveley Cambs
59 L3 Graveley Herts
34 E3 Graveney Kent
46 A5 Gravesend Kent
232 f3 Gravir W Isls
116 F3 Grayingham Lincs
138 E7 Grayrigg Cumb
45 L4 Grays Thurr
30 E4 Grayshott Hants
30 E4 Grayswood Surrey
115 H3 Greasbrough Rothm
111 H4 Greasby Wirral
76 D5 Great Abington Cambs
88 D7 Great Addington Nhants
71 K3 Great Alne Warwks
111 K1 Great Altcar Lancs
60 B5 Great Amwell Herts
138 F5 Great Asby Cumb
78 B2 Great Ashfield Suffk
142 C5 Great Ayton N York
61 H6 Great Baddow Essex
39 J4 Great Badminton S Glos
61 G2 Great Bardfield Essex
75 G4 Great Barford Bed
85 J4 Great Barr Sandw
56 E5 Great Barrington Gloucs
112 C7 Great Barrow Ches W
77 K2 Great Barton Suffk
134 B4 Great Barugh N York
158 C6 Great Bavington Nthumb
78 F5 Great Bealings Suffk
40 F7 Great Bedwyn Wilts
62 D4 Great Bentley Essex
74 B3 Great Billing Nhants
105 J6 Great Bircham Norfk
78 D4 Great Blakenham Suffk
138 C2 Great Blencow Cumb
98 F7 Great Bolas Wrekin
31 J1 Great Bookham Surrey
72 F5 Great Bourton Oxon
87 L5 Great Bowden Leics
76 F4 Great Bradley Suffk
61 K5 Great Braxted Essex
78 C4 Great Bricett Suffk
58 E3 Great Brickhill Bucks
99 K6 Great Bridgeford Staffs
73 J2 Great Brington Nhants
62 C3 Great Bromley Essex
136 E2 Great Broughton Cumb
142 C6 Great Broughton N York
112 F6 Great Budworth Ches W
141 H4 Great Burdon Darltn
46 B2 Great Burstead Essex
142 B6 Great Busby N York
118 E4 Great Carlton Lincs
88 E2 Great Casterton Rutlnd
39 K7 Great Chalfield Wilts
34 C6 Great Chart Kent
84 E1 Great Chatwell Staffs
76 D6 Great Chesterford Essex
27 M1 Great Cheverell Wilts
76 B6 Great Chishill Cambs
62 E5 Great Clacton Essex
136 E2 Great Clifton Cumb
126 F8 Great Coates NE Lin
71 G6 Great Comberton Worcs
148 E4 Great Corby Cumb
77 K6 Great Cornard Suffk
126 F3 Great Cowden E R Yk
40 F2 Great Coxwell Oxon
88 B7 Great Cransley Nhants
91 J3 Great Cressingham Norfk
137 J3 Great Crosthwaite Cumb
100 D5 Great Cubley Derbys
173 K6 Great Cumbrae Island N Ayrs
87 L2 Great Dalby Leics
74 C2 Great Doddington Nhants
91 K1 Great Dunham Norfk
61 G4 Great Dunmow Essex
28 C4 Great Durnford Wilts
60 F3 Great Easton Essex
88 B5 Great Easton Leics
120 F3 Great Eccleston Lancs
92 B4 Great Ellingham Norfk
27 H2 Great Elm Somset
73 H3 Great Everdon Nhants
75 L4 Great Eversden Cambs
132 D2 Great Fencote N York
78 B3 Great Finborough Suffk
88 F2 Greatford Lincs
91 K2 Great Fransham Norfk
59 G5 Great Gaddesden Herts
100 B4 Greatgate Staffs
89 G6 Great Gidding Cambs
134 C8 Great Givendale E R Yk
79 H3 Great Glemham Suffk
87 J4 Great Glen Leics
102 E5 Great Gonerby Lincs
75 J4 Great Gransden Cambs
75 K5 Great Green Cambs
77 K4 Great Green Suffk
134 B4 Great Habton N York
103 J4 Great Hale Lincs
60 E4 Great Hallingbury Essex
30 C5 Greatham Hants
141 L2 Greatham Hartpl
18 E3 Greatham W Susx
58 D7 Great Hampden Bucks
74 C1 Great Harrowden Nhants
121 L4 Great Harwood Lancs
57 M7 Great Haseley Oxon
126 F3 Great Hatfield E R Yk
99 M7 Great Haywood Staffs
124 E6 Great Heck N York
77 K6 Great Henny Essex
39 K8 Great Hinton Wilts
91 L5 Great Hockham Norfk
62 E4 Great Holland Essex
42 E6 Great Hollands Br For
62 B2 Great Horkesley Essex
60 C3 Great Hormead Herts
123 H4 Great Horton C Brad
58 C2 Great Horwood Bucks
115 H1 Great Houghton Barns
73 L3 Great Houghton Nhants
114 D6 Great Hucklow Derbys

135 H7 **Great Kelk** E R Yk
58 D6 **Great Kimble** Bucks
42 E2 **Great Kingshill** Bucks
137 J6 **Great Langdale** Cumb
141 H7 **Great Langton** N York
61 H4 **Great Leighs** Essex
126 E8 **Great Limber** Lincs
74 C6 **Great Linford** M Keyn
77 K1 **Great Livermere** Suffk
114 D6 **Great Longstone** Derbys
151 H5 **Great Lumley** Dur
70 D5 **Great Malvern** Worcs
77 J7 **Great Maplestead** Essex
120 D4 **Great Marton** Bpool
105 J7 **Great Massingham** Norfk
57 L7 **Great Milton** Oxon
58 E7 **Great Missenden** Bucks
121 K3 **Great Mitton** Lancs
35 K4 **Great Mongeham** Kent
92 E5 **Great Moulton** Norfk
139 H4 **Great Musgrave** Cumb
98 B8 **Great Ness** Shrops
61 H4 **Great Notley** Essex
54 B6 **Great Oak** Mons
62 E3 **Great Oakley** Essex
88 C6 **Great Oakley** Nhants
59 J3 **Great Offley** Herts
139 G4 **Great Ormside** Cumb
148 B4 **Great Orton** Cumb
133 G6 **Great Ouseburn** N York
87 K6 **Great Oxendon** Nhants
61 G6 **Great Oxney Green** Essex
75 H2 **Great Paxton** Cambs
120 E4 **Great Plumpton** Lancs
93 G2 **Great Plumstead** Norfk
102 F6 **Great Ponton** Lincs
124 B5 **Great Preston** Leeds
89 J7 **Great Raveley** Cambs
56 D5 **Great Rissington** Gloucs
56 F2 **Great Rollright** Oxon
106 A6 **Great Ryburgh** Norfk
83 J3 **Great Ryton** Shrops
61 H3 **Great Saling** Essex
148 F7 **Great Salkeld** Cumb
76 F7 **Great Sampford** Essex
111 K7 **Great Saughall** Ches W
41 G5 **Great Shefford** W Berk
76 C4 **Great Shelford** Cambs
141 H6 **Great Smeaton** N York
105 M5 **Great Snoring** Norfk
39 L4 **Great Somerford** Wilts
99 G6 **Great Soudley** Shrops
141 H3 **Great Stainton** Darltn
46 E2 **Great Stambridge** Essex
75 G2 **Great Staughton** Cambs
118 F8 **Great Steeping** Lincs
38 F4 **Great Stoke** S Glos
21 L2 **Greatstone-on-Sea** Kent
138 D3 **Great Strickland** Cumb
89 J8 **Great Stukeley** Cambs
117 K6 **Great Sturton** Lincs
158 B6 **Great Swinburne** Nthumb
57 H3 **Great Tew** Oxon
61 L3 **Great Tey** Essex
76 F4 **Great Thurlow** Suffk
23 H7 **Great Torrington** Devon
158 C3 **Great Tosson** Nthumb
61 K5 **Great Totham** Essex
61 L5 **Great Totham** Essex
129 G5 **Great Urswick** Cumb
46 F3 **Great Wakering** Essex
77 K5 **Great Waldingfield** Suffk
105 M5 **Great Walsingham** Norfk
61 H5 **Great Waltham** Essex
45 L2 **Great Warley** Essex
71 H7 **Great Washbourne** Gloucs
11 G7 **Great Weeke** Devon
88 D5 **Great Weldon** Nhants
78 C6 **Great Wenham** Suffk
158 C7 **Great Whittington** Nthumb
62 A5 **Great Wigborough** Essex
76 D3 **Great Wilbraham** Cambs
28 B4 **Great Wishford** Wilts
55 K5 **Great Witcombe** Gloucs
70 D2 **Great Witley** Worcs
72 B7 **Great Wolford** Warwks
73 G6 **Greatworth** Nhants
77 G5 **Great Wratting** Suffk
59 K3 **Great Wymondley** Herts
85 H3 **Great Wyrley** Staffs
93 L3 **Great Yarmouth** Norfk
93 K3 **Great Yarmouth Crematorium** Norfk
77 H6 **Great Yeldham** Essex
176 C6 **Greenburn** W Loth
60 B2 **Green End** Herts
60 B4 **Green End** Herts
173 M1 **Greenfield** Ag & B
74 F7 **Greenfield** C Beds
111 H6 **Greenfield** Flints
201 J5 **Greenfield** Highld
113 M2 **Greenfield** Oldham
43 J4 **Greenford** Gt Lon
175 K4 **Greengairs** N Lans
123 J3 **Greengates** C Brad
25 G7 **Greenham** Somset
133 G7 **Green Hammerton** N York
157 K5 **Greenhaugh** Nthumb
149 H3 **Greenhead** Nthumb
85 H2 **Green Heath** Staffs
155 J6 **Greenhill** D & G
175 L3 **Greenhill** Falk
47 K6 **Greenhill** Kent
165 H3 **Greenhill** S Lans
45 L5 **Greenhithe** Kent
164 B3 **Greenholm** E Ayrs
167 H5 **Greenhouse** Border
131 L6 **Greenhow Hill** N York
231 J3 **Greenland** Highld
115 H4 **Greenland** Sheff
167 L1 **Greenlaw** Border
155 H6 **Greenlea** D & G
185 H6 **Greenloaning** P & K
122 B7 **Greenmount** Bury
174 B3 **Greenock** Inver
174 B3 **Greenock Crematorium** Inver
129 G3 **Greenodd** Cumb
26 E2 **Green Ore** Somset
138 C6 **Green Quarter** Cumb
165 K2 **Greenshields** S Lans
150 E3 **Greenside** Gatesd
123 H7 **Greenside** Kirk
73 J4 **Greens Norton** Nhants
62 B3 **Greenstead** Essex
61 K3 **Greenstead Green** Essex
59 K7 **Green Street** Herts
60 D4 **Green Street** Herts
45 L6 **Green Street Green** Kent
60 C4 **Green Tye** Herts
25 L6 **Greenway** Somset
45 G4 **Greenwich** Gt Lon
56 B3 **Greet** Gloucs
69 L1 **Greete** Shrops
118 D7 **Greetham** Lincs
88 D2 **Greetham** Rutlnd
123 G6 **Greetland** Calder
26 B4 **Greinton** Somset
237 b6 **Grenaby** IoM
74 C3 **Grendon** Nhants
86 C4 **Grendon** Warwks
58 B4 **Grendon Underwood** Bucks
115 G3 **Grenoside** Sheff
114 F3 **Grenoside Crematorium** Sheff
232 e4 **Greosabhagh** W Isls
97 M2 **Gresford** Wrexhm
106 E5 **Gresham** Norfk
208 E4 **Greshornish House Hotel** Highld
91 L1 **Gressenhall** Norfk
91 L1 **Gressenhall Green** Norfk
130 B5 **Gressingham** Lancs
140 D5 **Greta Bridge** Dur
148 B2 **Gretna** D & G
148 B2 **Gretna Green** D & G
148 B2 **Gretna Services** D & G
56 A2 **Gretton** Gloucs
88 C5 **Gretton** Nhants
83 K4 **Gretton** Shrops
132 C4 **Grewelthorpe** N York
155 J4 **Greyrigg** D & G
42 B4 **Greys Green** Oxon
136 E2 **Greysouthen** Cumb
138 B2 **Greystoke** Cumb
196 E7 **Greystone** Angus
30 B2 **Greywell** Hants
86 D5 **Griff** Warwks
53 L7 **Griffithstown** Torfn
121 J7 **Grimeford Village** Lancs
115 G4 **Grimesthorpe** Sheff
124 C8 **Grimethorpe** Barns
70 E3 **Grimley** Worcs
163 H7 **Grimmet** S Ayrs
118 E4 **Grimoldby** Lincs
98 A7 **Grimpo** Shrops
121 H4 **Grimsargh** Lancs
127 G7 **Grimsby** NE Lin
118 C1 **Grimsby Crematorium** NE Lin
73 J4 **Grimscote** Nhants
9 H4 **Grimscott** Cnwll
232 f3 **Grimshader** W Isls
103 H7 **Grimsthorpe** Lincs
102 B7 **Grimston** Leics
105 H7 **Grimston** Norfk
14 C4 **Grimstone** Dorset
77 L2 **Grimstone End** Suffk
135 H5 **Grindale** E R Yk
114 E6 **Grindleford** Derbys
121 L2 **Grindleton** Lancs
98 D4 **Grindley Brook** Shrops
114 D6 **Grindlow** Derbys
100 B2 **Grindon** Staffs
116 C4 **Gringley on the Hill** Notts
148 C4 **Grinsdale** Cumb
98 D7 **Grinshill** Shrops
140 D7 **Grinton** N York
232 f3 **Griomaisiader** W Isls
233 c6 **Griomsaigh** W Isls
188 F4 **Grishipoll** Ag & B
135 H3 **Gristhorpe** N York
91 L4 **Griston** Norfk
234 d6 **Gritley** Ork
40 B4 **Grittenham** Wilts
39 K4 **Grittleton** Wilts
128 F3 **Grizebeck** Cumb
137 K7 **Grizedale** Cumb
87 G3 **Groby** Leics
110 D8 **Groes** Conwy
37 G4 **Groes-faen** Rhondd
95 H2 **Groeslon** Gwynd
37 H3 **Groes-Wen** Caerph
233 b7 **Grogarry** W Isls
161 K1 **Grogport** Ag & B
233 b7 **Groigearraidh** W Isls
110 F5 **Gronant** Flints
32 F5 **Groombridge** E Susx
232 e4 **Grosebay** W Isls
54 B3 **Grosmont** Mons
143 H6 **Grosmont** N York
77 L6 **Groton** Suffk
236 e7 **Grouville** Jersey
116 C5 **Grove** Notts
41 H3 **Grove** Oxon
33 K3 **Grove Green** Kent
45 H5 **Grove Park** Gt Lon
51 H5 **Grovesend** Swans
219 L4 **Gruinard** Highld
170 F5 **Gruinart** Ag & B
208 F8 **Grula** Highld
190 B7 **Gruline** Ag & B
78 F4 **Grundisburgh** Suffk
235 c5 **Gruting** Shet
192 B7 **Gualachulain** Highld
187 G4 **Guardbridge** Fife
70 E5 **Guarlford** Worcs
194 F6 **Guay** P & K
236 c3 *Guernsey Airport* Guern
21 G3 **Guestling Green** E Susx
21 G3 **Guestling Thorn** E Susx
106 C6 **Guestwick** Norfk
159 G5 **Guide Post** Nthumb
75 K5 **Guilden Morden** Cambs
112 C7 **Guilden Sutton** Ches W
31 G2 **Guildford** Surrey
31 G3 **Guildford Crematorium** Surrey
186 B2 **Guildtown** P & K
87 J8 **Guilsborough** Nhants
82 E2 **Guilsfield** Powys
163 J7 **Guiltreehill** S Ayrs
23 J4 **Guineaford** Devon
142 D4 **Guisborough** R & Cl
123 J3 **Guiseley** Leeds
106 B7 **Guist** Norfk
56 C3 **Guiting Power** Gloucs
178 B2 **Gullane** E Loth
2 E5 **Gulval** Cnwll
6 C2 **Gulworthy** Devon
49 J7 **Gumfreston** Pembks
87 K5 **Gumley** Leics
102 E7 **Gunby** Lincs
118 F7 **Gunby** Lincs
29 L5 **Gundleton** Hants
20 C3 **Gun Hill** E Susx
23 K5 **Gunn** Devon
139 L7 **Gunnerside** N York
158 A7 **Gunnerton** Nthumb
125 K7 **Gunness** N Linc
6 C2 **Gunnislake** Cnwll
235 d6 **Gunnista** Shet
116 D3 **Gunthorpe** N Linc
106 B5 **Gunthorpe** Norfk
102 B4 **Gunthorpe** Notts
3 H6 **Gunwalloe** Cnwll
16 F4 **Gurnard** IoW
26 F2 **Gurney Slade** Somset
52 B6 **Gurnos** Powys
15 J1 **Gussage All Saints** Dorset

27 L8 **Gussage St Andrew** Dorset
15 J1 **Gussage St Michael** Dorset
35 J5 **Guston** Kent
235 d2 **Gutcher** Shet
196 F6 **Guthrie** Angus
90 B3 **Guyhirn** Cambs
158 F2 **Guyzance** Nthumb
110 F5 **Gwaenysgor** Flints
108 E6 **Gwalchmai** IoA
51 K3 **Gwaun-Cae-Gurwen** Carmth
3 J6 **Gweek** Cnwll
68 B6 **Gwenddwr** Powys
3 J4 **Gwennap** Cnwll
37 L2 **Gwent Crematorium** Mons
111 H7 **Gwernaffield** Flints
54 B7 **Gwernesney** Mons
66 C7 **Gwernogle** Carmth
111 H8 **Gwernymynydd** Flints
110 F5 **Gwespyr** Flints
3 G4 **Gwinear** Cnwll
3 G3 **Gwithian** Cnwll
97 G3 **Gwyddelwern** Denbgs
66 B7 **Gwyddgrug** Carmth
96 D1 **Gwytherin** Conwy

H

83 H3 **Habberley** Shrops
84 E7 **Habberley** Worcs
122 B4 **Habergham** Lancs
119 G7 **Habertoft** Lincs
126 E7 **Habrough** NE Lin
103 J7 **Hacconby** Lincs
103 G5 **Haceby** Lincs
79 G3 **Hacheston** Suffk
44 F6 **Hackbridge** Gt Lon
115 H5 **Hackenthorpe** Sheff
92 C3 **Hackford** Norfk
132 C2 **Hackforth** N York
234 c5 **Hackland** Ork
74 B4 **Hackleton** Nhants
35 J4 **Hacklinge** Kent
134 F2 **Hackness** N York
45 G3 **Hackney** Gt Lon
117 G5 **Hackthorn** Lincs
138 D3 **Hackthorpe** Cumb
168 B3 **Hadden** Border
58 C6 **Haddenham** Bucks
90 C7 **Haddenham** Cambs
178 B4 **Haddington** E Loth
116 E8 **Haddington** Lincs
93 J4 **Haddiscoe** Norfk
216 F6 **Haddo** Abers
89 G5 **Haddon** Cambs
114 A3 **Hadfield** Derbys
60 C4 **Hadham Ford** Herts
46 D3 **Hadleigh** Essex
78 B6 **Hadleigh** Suffk
70 F2 **Hadley** Worcs
84 C2 **Hadley** Wrekin
100 C7 **Hadley End** Staffs
44 E1 **Hadley Wood** Gt Lon
33 H3 **Hadlow** Kent
20 B2 **Hadlow Down** E Susx
98 D7 **Hadnall** Shrops
150 B2 **Hadrian's Wall** Nthumb
76 D5 **Hadstock** Essex
71 G3 **Hadzor** Worcs
235 c5 **Haggersta** Shet
168 F2 **Haggerston** Nthumb
175 L3 **Haggs** Falk
69 L6 **Hagley** Herefs
85 G7 **Hagley** Worcs
118 D7 **Hagworthingham** Lincs
136 E5 **Haile** Cumb
57 G5 **Hailey** Oxon
20 C4 **Hailsham** E Susx
75 H3 **Hail Weston** Cambs
45 J2 **Hainault** Gt Lon
106 F8 **Hainford** Norfk
117 K5 **Hainton** Lincs
135 H6 **Haisthorpe** E R Yk
48 F6 **Hakin** Pembks
102 B2 **Halam** Notts
176 F1 **Halbeath** Fife
24 F8 **Halberton** Devon
231 J4 **Halcro** Highld
129 K4 **Hale** Cumb
112 C5 **Hale** Halton
28 D7 **Hale** Hants
30 D2 **Hale** Surrey
113 H4 **Hale** Traffd
113 H4 **Halebarns** Traffd
93 H4 **Hales** Norfk
99 G5 **Hales** Staffs
85 G6 **Halesowen** Dudley
34 F3 **Hales Place** Kent
33 H4 **Hale Street** Kent
93 H7 **Halesworth** Suffk
112 C4 **Halewood** Knows
7 J2 **Halford** Devon
72 C5 **Halford** Warwks
84 E5 **Halfpenny Green** Staffs
83 G2 **Halfway House** Shrops
46 F5 **Halfway Houses** Kent
123 G5 **Halifax** Calder
231 G4 **Halkirk** Highld
111 H7 **Halkyn** Flints
174 D7 **Hall** E Rens
20 A3 **Halland** E Susx
87 L4 **Hallaton** Leics
38 F8 **Hallatrow** BaNES
149 G3 **Hallbankgate** Cumb
137 H7 **Hall Dunnerdale** Cumb
38 D4 **Hallen** S Glos
151 H6 **Hallgarth** Dur
176 B3 **Hall Glen** Falk
85 K7 **Hall Green** Birm
208 D3 **Hallin** Highld
46 B7 **Halling** Medway
118 D4 **Hallington** Lincs
158 C6 **Hallington** Nthumb
121 K7 **Halliwell** Bolton
102 B3 **Halloughton** Notts
70 E3 **Hallow** Worcs
59 L3 **Hall's Green** Herts
166 B2 **Hallyne** Border
55 G7 **Halmore** Gloucs
18 B4 **Halnaker** W Susx
120 E7 **Halsall** Lancs
73 H6 **Halse** Nhants
25 H5 **Halse** Somset
2 E4 **Halsetown** Cnwll
127 G5 **Halsham** E R Yk
61 K2 **Halstead** Essex
45 J7 **Halstead** Kent
87 L3 **Halstead** Leics
14 A2 **Halstock** Dorset
126 C4 **Haltemprice Crematorium** E R Yk
118 C8 **Haltham** Lincs
58 E6 **Halton** Bucks
112 D5 **Halton** Halton
129 K6 **Halton** Lancs
123 L4 **Halton** Leeds
150 C2 **Halton** Nthumb
97 L4 **Halton** Wrexhm
131 K8 **Halton East** N York
131 G4 **Halton Gill** N York
118 F7 **Halton Holegate** Lincs
149 H4 **Halton Lea Gate** Nthumb
150 C2 **Halton Shields** Nthumb
130 F8 **Halton West** N York
149 J3 **Haltwhistle** Nthumb
93 J3 **Halvergate** Norfk
7 H5 **Halwell** Devon
10 C5 **Halwill** Devon
10 C5 **Halwill Junction** Devon
13 G3 **Ham** Devon
55 G7 **Ham** Gloucs
44 D5 **Ham** Gt Lon
35 J4 **Ham** Kent
25 L6 **Ham** Somset
41 G7 **Ham** Wilts
42 C3 **Hambleden** Bucks
29 M7 **Hambledon** Hants
30 F4 **Hambledon** Surrey
16 F2 **Hamble-le-Rice** Hants
120 E3 **Hambleton** Lancs
124 E4 **Hambleton** N York
26 B6 **Hambridge** Somset
17 L2 **Hambrook** W Susx
118 D7 **Hameringham** Lincs
89 G7 **Hamerton** Cambs
71 H2 **Ham Green** Worcs
175 J7 **Hamilton** S Lans
175 J6 **Hamilton Services** S Lans
14 B2 **Hamlet** Dorset
44 E4 **Hammersmith** Gt Lon
85 J3 **Hammerwich** Staffs
27 J8 **Hammoon** Dorset
235 c6 **Hamnavoe** Shet
20 C5 **Hampden Park** E Susx
56 C5 **Hampnett** Gloucs
124 D7 **Hampole** Donc
15 K3 **Hampreston** Dorset
44 E3 **Hampstead** Gt Lon
41 K5 **Hampstead Norreys** W Berk
132 C7 **Hampsthwaite** N York
89 H5 **Hampton** C Pete
43 J6 **Hampton** Gt Lon
47 K6 **Hampton** Kent
84 D6 **Hampton** Shrops
40 D3 **Hampton** Swindn
71 H5 **Hampton** Worcs
69 L6 **Hampton Bishop** Herefs
44 D6 **Hampton Court Palace & Gardens** Gt Lon
98 D3 **Hampton Heath** Ches W
86 B7 **Hampton in Arden** Solhll
70 F2 **Hampton Lovett** Worcs
72 B3 **Hampton Lucy** Warwks
72 C2 **Hampton Magna** Warwks
57 J5 **Hampton Poyle** Oxon
44 D6 **Hampton Wick** Gt Lon
28 E7 **Hamptworth** Wilts
19 L3 **Hamsey** E Susx
100 C8 **Hamstall Ridware** Staffs
41 H7 **Hamstead Marshall** W Berk
140 E2 **Hamsterley** Dur
150 E4 **Hamsterley** Dur
34 D7 **Hamstreet** Kent
26 D4 **Ham Street** Somset
15 J4 **Hamworthy** Poole
100 D6 **Hanbury** Staffs
71 G2 **Hanbury** Worcs
99 J4 **Hanchurch** Staffs
228 A6 **Handa Island** Highld
12 D4 **Hand and Pen** Devon
112 B7 **Handbridge** Ches W
31 L5 **Handcross** W Susx
113 J5 **Handforth** Ches E
98 C2 **Handley** Ches W
101 G1 **Handley** Derbys
85 J5 **Handsworth** Birm
115 H4 **Handsworth** Sheff
123 K6 **Hanging Heaton** Kirk
87 L8 **Hanging Houghton** Nhants
28 B4 **Hanging Langford** Wilts
19 H4 **Hangleton** Br & H
38 F6 **Hanham** S Glos
98 F4 **Hankelow** Ches E
39 L3 **Hankerton** Wilts
99 K3 **Hanley** C Stke
70 E6 **Hanley Castle** Worcs
70 B2 **Hanley Child** Worcs
70 E6 **Hanley Swan** Worcs
70 C2 **Hanley William** Worcs
131 G7 **Hanlith** N York
98 C4 **Hanmer** Wrexhm
23 J5 **Hannaford** Devon
29 K1 **Hannington** Hants
74 B1 **Hannington** Nhants
40 D2 **Hannington** Swindn
40 D2 **Hannington Wick** Swindn
74 B5 **Hanslope** M Keyn
103 H7 **Hanthorpe** Lincs
44 D4 **Hanwell** Gt Lon
72 E5 **Hanwell** Oxon
83 J2 **Hanwood** Shrops
43 J6 **Hanworth** Gt Lon
106 E5 **Hanworth** Norfk
165 G3 **Happendon** S Lans
107 H6 **Happisburgh** Norfk
107 H6 **Happisburgh Common** Norfk
112 C6 **Hapsford** Ches W
122 B4 **Hapton** Lancs
92 E4 **Hapton** Norfk
7 H4 **Harberton** Devon
7 H5 **Harbertonford** Devon
34 F3 **Harbledown** Kent
85 H6 **Harborne** Birm
86 F7 **Harborough Magna** Warwks
158 B2 **Harbottle** Nthumb
7 G4 **Harbourneford** Devon
72 D3 **Harbury** Warwks
102 C6 **Harby** Leics
116 E7 **Harby** Notts
11 K8 **Harcombe** Devon
12 F4 **Harcombe** Devon
13 J4 **Harcombe Bottom** Devon
123 G3 **Harden** C Brad
85 H4 **Harden** Wsall
39 K5 **Hardenhuish** Wilts
206 E5 **Hardgate** Abers
146 E2 **Hardgate** D & G
174 F4 **Hardgate** W Duns
18 E3 **Hardham** W Susx
92 C3 **Hardingham** Norfk
73 L3 **Hardingstone** Nhants
27 H2 **Hardington** Somset
13 M1 **Hardington Mandeville** Somset
13 M1 **Hardington Marsh** Somset
26 D8 **Hardington Moor** Somset
22 C7 **Hardisworthy** Devon
16 E2 **Hardley** Hants
93 H4 **Hardley Street** Norfk
131 G2 **Hardraw** N York
115 H8 **Hardstoft** Derbys
17 H3 **Hardway** Hants
27 G5 **Hardway** Somset
58 D4 **Hardwick** Bucks
75 L3 **Hardwick** Cambs
74 B1 **Hardwick** Nhants
92 F5 **Hardwick** Norfk
57 G6 **Hardwick** Oxon
57 L3 **Hardwick** Oxon
55 H5 **Hardwicke** Gloucs
55 K3 **Hardwicke** Gloucs
61 M4 **Hardy's Green** Essex
123 G4 **Hare Croft** C Brad
43 H3 **Harefield** Gt Lon
62 D3 **Hare Green** Essex
42 D5 **Hare Hatch** Wokham
100 D5 **Harehill** Derbys

123 L4 **Harehills** Leeds
167 H5 **Harelaw** Border
156 D6 **Harelaw** D & G
55 J6 **Harescombe** Gloucs
55 J6 **Haresfield** Gloucs
29 J5 **Harestock** Hants
60 C6 **Hare Street** Essex
60 C3 **Hare Street** Herts
123 L2 **Harewood** Leeds
54 D3 **Harewood End** Herefs
6 F4 **Harford** Devon
98 C1 **Hargrave** Ches W
74 F1 **Hargrave** Nhants
77 H3 **Hargrave** Suffk
78 E7 **Harkstead** Suffk
86 B2 **Harlaston** Staffs
102 E6 **Harlaxton** Lincs
95 K6 **Harlech** Gwynd
83 K1 **Harlescott** Shrops
44 E4 **Harlesden** Gt Lon
115 J6 **Harlesthorpe** Derbys
7 J6 **Harleston** Devon
92 F6 **Harleston** Norfk
78 B3 **Harleston** Suffk
73 K2 **Harlestone** Nhants
122 C4 **Harle Syke** Lancs
115 G2 **Harley** Rothm
83 L3 **Harley** Shrops
59 G2 **Harlington** C Beds
115 J2 **Harlington** Donc
43 H5 **Harlington** Gt Lon
208 D6 **Harlosh** Highld
60 D6 **Harlow** Essex
150 D2 **Harlow Hill** Nthumb
125 H3 **Harlthorpe** E R Yk
76 B4 **Harlton** Cambs
4 D2 **Harlyn** Cnwll
15 J6 **Harman's Cross** Dorset
131 L2 **Harmby** N York
59 L5 **Harmer Green** Herts
98 C7 **Harmer Hill** Shrops
116 F8 **Harmston** Lincs
83 L3 **Harnage** Shrops
56 B7 **Harnhill** Gloucs
45 K2 **Harold Hill** Gt Lon
48 E4 **Haroldston West** Pembks
235 e1 **Haroldswick** Shet
45 K3 **Harold Wood** Gt Lon
133 K3 **Harome** N York
59 J5 **Harpenden** Herts
12 E4 **Harpford** Devon
135 H7 **Harpham** E R Yk
105 J7 **Harpley** Norfk
70 C3 **Harpley** Worcs
73 K3 **Harpole** Nhants
231 G4 **Harpsdale** Highld
116 F4 **Harpswell** Lincs
113 K2 **Harpurhey** Manch
148 D4 **Harraby** Cumb
23 J6 **Harracott** Devon
199 K2 **Harrapool** Highld
185 K2 **Harrietfield** P & K
33 L3 **Harrietsham** Kent
44 F3 **Harringay** Gt Lon
136 D3 **Harrington** Cumb
118 E6 **Harrington** Lincs
87 L7 **Harrington** Nhants
88 D4 **Harringworth** Nhants
232 d4 **Harris** W Isls
132 D8 **Harrogate** N York
132 E8 **Harrogate Crematorium** N York
74 D3 **Harrold** Bed
44 D3 **Harrow** Gt Lon
6 B2 **Harrowbarrow** Cnwll
77 J4 **Harrow Green** Suffk
44 D3 **Harrow on the Hill** Gt Lon
44 D2 **Harrow Weald** Gt Lon
76 B4 **Harston** Cambs
102 D6 **Harston** Leics
125 J3 **Harswell** E R Yk
151 L7 **Hart** Hartpl
158 D5 **Hartburn** Nthumb
77 J4 **Hartest** Suffk
32 E6 **Hartfield** E Susx
89 J8 **Hartford** Cambs
112 F6 **Hartford** Ches W
42 C8 **Hartfordbridge** Hants
61 G4 **Hartford End** Essex
140 F6 **Hartforth** N York
27 J7 **Hartgrove** Dorset
98 D2 **Harthill** Ches W
176 B5 **Harthill** N Lans
115 J5 **Harthill** Rothm
100 C1 **Hartington** Derbys
22 D6 **Hartland** Devon
22 C6 **Hartland Quay** Devon
70 E1 **Hartlebury** Worcs
151 L7 **Hartlepool** Hartpl
142 B2 **Hartlepool Crematorium** Hartpl
139 H5 **Hartley** Cumb
33 K6 **Hartley** Kent
45 L6 **Hartley** Kent
42 B8 **Hartley Wespall** Hants
30 C1 **Hartley Wintney** Hants
46 D7 **Hartlip** Kent
133 L6 **Harton** N York
151 J2 **Harton** S Tyne
55 J3 **Hartpury** Gloucs
123 J6 **Hartshead** Kirk
123 H5 **Hartshead Moor Services** Calder
99 K4 **Hartshill** C Stke
86 D5 **Hartshill** Warwks
100 F7 **Hartshorne** Derbys
73 L4 **Hartwell** Nhants
132 C4 **Hartwith** N York
175 L6 **Hartwood** N Lans
166 F4 **Hartwoodmyres** Border
46 A7 **Harvel** Kent
71 J5 **Harvington** Worcs
84 F8 **Harvington** Worcs
116 B3 **Harwell** Notts
41 J3 **Harwell** Oxon
62 F2 **Harwich** Essex
143 K7 **Harwood Dale** N York
59 L4 **Harwood Park Crematorium** Herts
115 L3 **Harworth** Notts
85 G6 **Hasbury** Dudley
31 G4 **Hascombe** Surrey
87 K7 **Haselbech** Nhants
13 L1 **Haselbury Plucknett** Somset
72 B2 **Haseley** Warwks
71 K3 **Haselor** Warwks
55 J3 **Hasfield** Gloucs
120 E8 **Haskayne** Lancs
78 F4 **Hasketon** Suffk
30 E5 **Haslemere** Surrey
122 B6 **Haslingden** Lancs
76 B4 **Haslingfield** Cambs
99 G2 **Haslington** Ches E
93 H3 **Hassingham** Norfk
19 J3 **Hassocks** W Susx
114 E6 **Hassop** Derbys
231 K5 **Haster** Highld
34 E5 **Hastingleigh** Kent
21 G4 **Hastings** E Susx
21 G3 **Hastings Borough Crematorium** E Susx
60 D6 **Hastingwood** Essex
58 F6 **Hastoe** Herts
151 J6 **Haswell** Dur
151 J6 **Haswell Plough** Dur
25 L7 **Hatch Beauchamp** Somset
43 J3 **Hatch End** Gt Lon
112 D6 **Hatchmere** Ches W
117 K2 **Hatcliffe** NE Lin
125 G8 **Hatfield** Donc
69 L3 **Hatfield** Herefs
59 L6 **Hatfield** Herts
60 E5 **Hatfield Broad Oak** Essex
60 E5 **Hatfield Heath** Essex
61 J5 **Hatfield Peverel** Essex
125 G8 **Hatfield Woodhouse** Donc
41 G2 **Hatford** Oxon
29 G2 **Hatherden** Hants
10 D4 **Hatherleigh** Devon
101 J7 **Hathern** Leics
56 D6 **Hatherop** Gloucs
114 E5 **Hathersage** Derbys
114 E5 **Hathersage Booths** Derbys
99 G3 **Hatherton** Ches E
85 G2 **Hatherton** Staffs
75 K4 **Hatley St George** Cambs
6 B4 **Hatt** Cnwll
113 M3 **Hattersley** Tamesd
217 K6 **Hatton** Abers
196 D7 **Hatton** Angus
100 E6 **Hatton** Derbys
43 J5 **Hatton** Gt Lon
117 K6 **Hatton** Lincs
83 J5 **Hatton** Shrops
112 E5 **Hatton** Warrtn
72 B2 **Hatton** Warwks
206 F3 **Hatton of Fintray** Abers
163 L4 **Haugh** E Ayrs
118 D5 **Haugham** Lincs
175 G3 **Haughhead** E Duns
78 B3 **Haughley** Suffk
78 B2 **Haughley Green** Suffk
215 J6 **Haugh of Glass** Moray
146 E2 **Haugh of Urr** D & G
197 G5 **Haughs of Kinnaird** Angus
98 B6 **Haughton** Shrops
99 K7 **Haughton** Staffs
141 H4 **Haughton le Skerne** Darltn
98 E2 **Haughton Moss** Ches E
60 B4 **Haultwick** Herts
86 B2 **Haunton** Staffs
76 B4 **Hauxton** Cambs
17 K2 **Havant** Hants
17 G4 **Havenstreet** IoW
124 B7 **Havercroft** Wakefd
48 F4 **Haverfordwest** Pembks
76 F5 **Haverhill** Suffk
128 E4 **Haverigg** Cumb
45 K2 **Havering-atte-Bower** Gt Lon
74 B6 **Haversham** M Keyn
129 H3 **Haverthwaite** Cumb
38 C7 **Havyat** N Som
111 J7 **Hawarden** Flints
61 J4 **Hawbush Green** Essex
65 K5 **Hawen** Cerdgn
131 G2 **Hawes** N York
92 F4 **Hawe's Green** Norfk
70 E3 **Hawford** Worcs
167 G6 **Hawick** Border
13 J3 **Hawkchurch** Devon
77 H4 **Hawkedon** Suffk
27 K2 **Hawkeridge** Wilts
39 H3 **Hawkesbury** S Glos
39 H3 **Hawkesbury Upton** S Glos
33 K6 **Hawkhurst** Kent
35 G6 **Hawkinge** Kent
35 G6 **Hawkinge Crematorium** Kent
30 C5 **Hawkley** Hants
24 D5 **Hawkridge** Somset
137 K7 **Hawkshead** Cumb
137 K7 **Hawkshead Hill** Cumb
165 G2 **Hawksland** S Lans
98 E6 **Hawkstone** Shrops
131 H5 **Hawkswick** N York
123 H3 **Hawksworth** Leeds
102 C4 **Hawksworth** Notts
46 E2 **Hawkwell** Essex
42 E8 **Hawley** Hants
56 B4 **Hawling** Gloucs
133 H2 **Hawnby** N York
122 F3 **Haworth** C Brad
77 J3 **Hawstead** Suffk
151 K5 **Hawthorn** Dur
103 K2 **Hawthorn Hill** Lincs
102 C3 **Hawton** Notts
133 J7 **Haxby** C York
116 C2 **Haxey** N Linc
39 G7 **Haycombe Crematorium** BaNES
112 E3 **Haydock** St Hel
149 L3 **Haydon Bridge** Nthumb
40 C3 **Haydon Wick** Swindn
43 J4 **Hayes** Gt Lon
45 H6 **Hayes** Gt Lon
43 H4 **Hayes End** Gt Lon
182 F3 **Hayfield** Ag & B
114 B4 **Hayfield** Derbys
196 E7 **Hayhillock** Angus
2 F4 **Hayle** Cnwll
85 G6 **Hayley Green** Dudley
17 K3 **Hayling Island** Hants
11 H7 **Hayne** Devon
74 F6 **Haynes (Church End)** C Beds
75 G6 **Haynes (Northwood End)** C Beds
75 G6 **Haynes (Silver End)** C Beds
74 F6 **Haynes (West End)** C Beds
68 E6 **Hay-on-Wye** Powys
48 F3 **Hayscastle** Pembks
48 F3 **Hayscastle Cross** Pembks
60 C3 **Hay Street** Herts
147 K6 **Hayton** Cumb
148 E4 **Hayton** Cumb
125 J2 **Hayton** E R Yk
116 B5 **Hayton** Notts
7 H1 **Haytor Vale** Devon
9 K3 **Haytown** Devon
19 J2 **Haywards Heath** W Susx
124 E7 **Haywood** Donc
165 G1 **Hazelbank** S Lans
14 E2 **Hazelbury Bryan** Dorset
61 K7 **Hazeleigh** Essex
113 L4 **Hazel Grove** Stockp
186 E3 **Hazelton Walls** Fife
101 G4 **Hazelwood** Derbys
42 E2 **Hazlemere** Bucks
159 G7 **Hazlerigg** N u Ty
56 B4 **Hazleton** Gloucs
105 G5 **Heacham** Norfk
29 J5 **Headbourne Worthy** Hants
33 L4 **Headcorn** Kent
123 K4 **Headingley** Leeds
57 K6 **Headington** Oxon
140 F4 **Headlam** Dur
176 B6 **Headlesscross** N Lans
71 J2 **Headless Cross** Worcs
30 D4 **Headley** Hants
41 K7 **Headley** Hants
31 K1 **Headley** Surrey
30 D4 **Headley Down** Hants
116 C6 **Headon** Notts
148 E4 **Heads Nook** Cumb
101 G3 **Heage** Derbys
124 D2 **Healaugh** N York
140 C7 **Healaugh** N York
113 J4 **Heald Green** Stockp
25 K7 **Heale** Somset
26 B6 **Heale** Somset
132 B4 **Healey** N York
150 D5 **Healeyfield** Dur
126 F7 **Healing** NE Lin

2 E5 **Heamoor** Cnwll
101 H3 **Heanor** Derbys
23 H4 **Heanton Punchardon** Devon
116 E4 **Heapham** Lincs
86 E5 **Heart of England Crematorium** Warwks
176 B5 **Heart of Scotland Services** N Lans
24 B5 **Heasley Mill** Devon
199 K2 **Heast** Highld
115 J7 **Heath** Derbys
123 L6 **Heath** Wakefd
58 F3 **Heath and Reach** C Beds
100 D1 **Heathcote** Derbys
86 E2 **Heather** Leics
20 C2 **Heathfield** E Susx
25 J6 **Heathfield** Somset
71 J1 **Heath Green** Worcs
155 H6 **Heath Hall** D & G
85 H2 **Heath Hayes & Wimblebury** Staffs
84 D2 **Heath Hill** Shrops
43 H5 *Heathrow Airport* Gt Lon
84 E5 **Heathton** Shrops
85 G4 **Heath Town** Wolves
113 G4 **Heatley** Warrtn
123 H4 **Heaton** C Brad
151 G2 **Heaton** N u Ty
113 L8 **Heaton** Staffs
120 E7 **Heaton's Bridge** Lancs
33 G2 **Heaverham** Kent
12 B4 **Heavitree** Devon
151 H3 **Hebburn** S Tyne
131 J6 **Hebden** N York
122 E5 **Hebden Bridge** Calder
60 A4 **Hebing End** Herts
49 K3 **Hebron** Carmth
158 F4 **Hebron** Nthumb
42 B7 **Heckfield** Hants
92 E7 **Heckfield Green** Suffk
61 M4 **Heckfordbridge** Essex
103 J4 **Heckington** Lincs
123 J5 **Heckmondwike** Kirk
39 M6 **Heddington** Wilts
150 E2 **Heddon-on-the-Wall** Nthumb
93 G5 **Hedenham** Norfk
29 J8 **Hedge End** Hants
42 F3 **Hedgerley** Bucks
25 L5 **Hedging** Somset
150 D3 **Hedley on the Hill** Nthumb
85 H2 **Hednesford** Staffs
126 F5 **Hedon** E R Yk
42 E3 **Hedsor** Bucks
235 c5 **Heglibister** Shet
141 G3 **Heighington** Darltn
117 G7 **Heighington** Lincs
70 D1 **Heightington** Worcs
167 L4 **Heiton** Border
12 C2 **Hele** Devon
23 H3 **Hele** Devon
174 B2 **Helensburgh** Ag & B
163 K3 **Helenton** S Ayrs
3 K6 **Helford** Cnwll
3 K6 **Helford Passage** Cnwll
105 K7 **Helhoughton** Norfk
76 F6 **Helions Bumpstead** Essex
5 G2 **Helland** Cnwll
9 H6 **Hellescott** Cnwll
92 E2 **Hellesdon** Norfk
73 G3 **Hellidon** Nhants
131 G7 **Hellifield** N York
20 C4 **Hellingly** E Susx
73 H5 **Helmdon** Nhants
123 G7 **Helme** Kirk
78 E3 **Helmingham** Suffk
227 H5 **Helmsdale** Highld
122 B6 **Helmshore** Lancs
133 J3 **Helmsley** N York
133 G5 **Helperby** N York
134 E5 **Helperthorpe** N York
103 J4 **Helpringham** Lincs
89 G3 **Helpston** C Pete
112 C6 **Helsby** Ches W
3 H5 **Helston** Cnwll
8 E8 **Helstone** Cnwll
138 D3 **Helton** Cumb
59 H6 **Hemel Hempstead** Herts
6 E4 **Hemerdon** Devon
125 G4 **Hemingbrough** N York
118 C6 **Hemingby** Lincs
75 K1 **Hemingford Abbots** Cambs
75 K1 **Hemingford Grey** Cambs
78 D4 **Hemingstone** Suffk
101 J6 **Hemington** Leics
88 F6 **Hemington** Nhants
27 G2 **Hemington** Somset
79 G6 **Hemley** Suffk
142 B4 **Hemlington** Middsb
92 F5 **Hempnall** Norfk
92 F5 **Hempnall Green** Norfk
214 D2 **Hempriggs** Moray
76 F6 **Hempstead** Essex
106 D5 **Hempstead** Norfk
107 J6 **Hempstead** Norfk
105 L6 **Hempton** Norfk
57 H2 **Hempton** Oxon
107 K8 **Hemsby** Norfk
116 F4 **Hemswell** Lincs
116 F4 **Hemswell Cliff** Lincs
124 C7 **Hemsworth** Wakefd
25 H8 **Hemyock** Devon
44 E3 **Hendon** Gt Lon
151 K4 **Hendon** Sundld
44 E2 **Hendon Crematorium** Gt Lon
51 H5 **Hendy** Carmth
19 G3 **Henfield** W Susx
37 J2 **Hengoed** Caerph
68 E4 **Hengoed** Powys
77 J2 **Hengrave** Suffk
60 E3 **Henham** Essex
82 C2 **Heniarth** Powys
25 L6 **Henlade** Somset
14 D2 **Henley** Dorset
26 B5 **Henley** Somset
78 E4 **Henley** Suffk
30 E6 **Henley** W Susx
71 L2 **Henley-in-Arden** Warwks
42 C4 **Henley-on-Thames** Oxon
20 E3 **Henley's Down** E Susx
65 K6 **Henllan** Cerdgn
110 E7 **Henllan** Denbgs
37 K3 **Henllys** Torfn
75 H6 **Henlow** C Beds
11 J8 **Hennock** Devon
77 K6 **Henny Street** Essex
109 L6 **Henryd** Conwy
49 H3 **Henry's Moat (Castell Hendre)** Pembks
124 F5 **Hensall** N York
149 K3 **Henshaw** Nthumb
136 D4 **Hensingham** Cumb
93 K6 **Henstead** Suffk
29 J6 **Hensting** Hants
27 G7 **Henstridge** Somset
27 G7 **Henstridge Ash** Somset
58 C7 **Henton** Oxon
26 C3 **Henton** Somset
70 E4 **Henwick** Worcs
5 L2 **Henwood** Cnwll
36 E4 **Heol-y-Cyw** Brdgnd
158 C2 **Hepple** Nthumb
158 F5 **Hepscott** Nthumb
122 E5 **Heptonstall** Calder
114 D1 **Hepworth** Kirk
92 B8 **Hepworth** Suffk
48 E6 **Herbrandston** Pembks
69 K6 **Hereford** Herefs
69 J6 **Hereford Crematorium** Herefs
35 K2 **Hereson** Kent
218 B7 **Heribusta** Highld
177 L7 **Heriot** Border
177 G4 **Hermiston** C Edin
156 E3 **Hermitage** Border
14 C2 **Hermitage** Dorset
41 J5 **Hermitage** W Berk
65 K7 **Hermon** Carmth
49 L2 **Hermon** Pembks
47 K6 **Herne** Kent
47 K6 **Herne Bay** Kent
44 F5 **Herne Hill** Gt Lon
33 H3 **Herne Pound** Kent
34 E3 **Hernhill** Kent
5 K4 **Herodsfoot** Cnwll
152 D5 **Heronsford** S Ayrs
30 A3 **Herriard** Hants
93 K4 **Herringfleet** Suffk
77 G1 **Herringswell** Suffk
115 J3 **Herringthorpe** Rothm
151 J4 **Herrington** Sundld
35 G3 **Hersden** Kent
43 J7 **Hersham** Surrey
20 D3 **Herstmonceux** E Susx
234 c7 **Herston** Ork
60 B5 **Hertford** Herts
60 B5 **Hertford Heath** Herts
60 A5 **Hertingfordbury** Herts
120 F5 **Hesketh Bank** Lancs
121 J3 **Hesketh Lane** Lancs
148 C7 **Hesket Newmarket** Cumb
151 K7 **Hesleden** Dur
124 F1 **Heslington** C York
133 H8 **Hessay** C York
5 L4 **Hessenford** Cnwll
77 L3 **Hessett** Suffk
126 C5 **Hessle** E R Yk
124 C6 **Hessle** Wakefd
129 K6 **Hest Bank** Lancs
43 J5 **Heston** Gt Lon
43 J5 **Heston Services** Gt Lon
234 b5 **Hestwall** Ork
111 J5 **Heswall** Wirral
57 L3 **Hethe** Oxon
92 D3 **Hethersett** Norfk
148 E2 **Hethersgill** Cumb
151 G7 **Hett** Dur
131 H7 **Hetton** N York
151 J5 **Hetton-le-Hole** Sundld
158 D7 **Heugh** Nthumb
205 J3 **Heughhead** Abers
179 H6 **Heugh Head** Border
93 G8 **Heveningham** Suffk
32 E4 **Hever** Kent
129 K3 **Heversham** Cumb
106 E7 **Hevingham** Norfk
4 F6 **Hewas Water** Cnwll
54 E7 **Hewelsfield** Gloucs
13 K2 **Hewish** Somset
13 J2 **Hewood** Dorset
150 B3 **Hexham** Nthumb
45 K6 **Hextable** Kent
115 K2 **Hexthorpe** Donc
59 J2 **Hexton** Herts
9 K8 **Hexworthy** Cnwll
6 F2 **Hexworthy** Devon
61 G7 **Heybridge** Essex
61 K6 **Heybridge** Essex
6 D6 **Heybrook Bay** Devon
76 B6 **Heydon** Cambs
106 D6 **Heydon** Norfk
103 G5 **Heydour** Lincs
188 C7 **Heylipoll** Ag & B
235 c3 **Heylor** Shet
129 J7 **Heysham** Lancs
18 B3 **Heyshott** W Susx
27 L3 **Heytesbury** Wilts
57 G3 **Heythrop** Oxon
122 C7 **Heywood** Rochdl
27 K2 **Heywood** Wilts
116 F2 **Hibaldstow** N Linc
115 J1 **Hickleton** Donc
107 J7 **Hickling** Norfk
102 B6 **Hickling** Notts
107 J7 **Hickling Green** Norfk
31 L7 **Hickstead** W Susx
71 L6 **Hidcote Bartrim** Gloucs
71 L6 **Hidcote Boyce** Gloucs
124 C6 **High Ackworth** Wakefd
114 F1 **Higham** Barns
101 H2 **Higham** Derbys
33 G4 **Higham** Kent
46 B5 **Higham** Kent
122 B3 **Higham** Lancs
77 H2 **Higham** Suffk
78 B7 **Higham** Suffk
74 D2 **Higham Ferrers** Nhants
59 J2 **Higham Gobion** C Beds
45 G3 **Higham Hill** Gt Lon
86 E4 **Higham on the Hill** Leics
10 C4 **Highampton** Devon
45 H2 **Highams Park** Gt Lon
144 C6 **High Ardwell** D & G
154 F5 **High Auldgirth** D & G
148 F6 **High Bankhill** Cumb
60 C7 **High Beach** Essex
130 C5 **High Bentham** N York
23 J7 **High Bickington** Devon
130 B4 **High Biggins** Cumb
175 J6 **High Blantyre** S Lans
175 L3 **High Bonnybridge** Falk
23 L5 **High Bray** Devon
25 L3 **Highbridge** Somset
32 C7 **Highbrook** W Susx
33 G5 **High Brooms** Kent
123 J7 **Highburton** Kirk
44 F3 **Highbury** Gt Lon
27 G2 **Highbury** Somset
130 C4 **High Casterton** Cumb
133 L8 **High Catton** E R Yk
41 H8 **Highclere** Hants
16 B4 **Highcliffe** Dorset
141 G4 **High Coniscliffe** Darltn
148 E3 **High Crosby** Cumb
163 K1 **High Cross** E Ayrs
30 B6 **High Cross** Hants
60 B4 **High Cross** Herts
71 L2 **High Cross** Warwks
144 D7 **High Drummore** D & G
60 F5 **High Easter** Essex
132 B3 **High Ellington** N York
14 E2 **Higher Ansty** Dorset
121 G4 **Higher Bartle** Lancs
14 D4 **Higher Bockhampton** Dorset
7 L5 **Higher Brixham** Torbay
98 E8 **High Ercall** Wrekin
13 K1 **Higher Chillington** Somset
113 G2 **Higher Folds** Wigan
7 L3 **Higher Gabwell** Devon
129 J7 **Higher Heysham** Lancs
113 G3 **Higher Irlam** Salfd
97 L1 **Higher Kinnerton** Flints
23 J4 **Higher Muddiford** Devon
121 G5 **Higher Penwortham** Lancs

9 K5 **Higher Prestacott** Devon
4 C6 **Higher Town** Cnwll
4 F4 **Higher Town** Cnwll
2 b1 **Higher Town** IoS
121 H5 **Higher Walton** Lancs
112 E4 **Higher Walton** Warrtn
13 H2 **Higher Wambrook** Somset
14 D4 **Higher Waterston** Dorset
121 J6 **Higher Wheelton** Lancs
112 F5 **Higher Whitley** Ches W
113 G6 **Higher Wincham** Ches W
14 B3 **Higher Wraxhall** Dorset
98 C4 **Higher Wych** Ches W
140 F2 **High Etherley** Dur
150 E3 **Highfield** Gatesd
174 C7 **Highfield** N Ayrs
61 J3 **High Garrett** Essex
44 F3 **Highgate** Gt Lon
132 C5 **High Grantley** N York
92 D3 **High Green** Norfk
92 E5 **High Green** Norfk
115 G3 **High Green** Sheff
34 B7 **High Halden** Kent
46 C5 **High Halstow** Medway
26 B5 **High Ham** Somset
132 D7 **High Harrogate** N York
98 E7 **High Hatton** Shrops
159 G2 **High Hauxley** Nthumb
143 J5 **High Hawsker** N York
148 E6 **High Hesket** Cumb
123 K8 **High Hoyland** Barns
32 E7 **High Hurstwood** E Susx
134 B5 **High Hutton** N York
147 M7 **High Ireby** Cumb
133 H4 **High Kilburn** N York
140 E3 **High Lands** Dur
203 J4 **Highland Wildlife Park** Highld
115 H5 **Highlane** Derbys
113 L4 **High Lane** Stockp
3 G4 **High Lanes** Cnwll
55 H4 **Highleadon** Gloucs
113 G5 **High Legh** Ches E
18 A6 **Highleigh** W Susx
141 K5 **High Leven** S on T
84 D6 **Highley** Shrops
38 F8 **High Littleton** BaNES
137 G3 **High Lorton** Cumb
116 D7 **High Marnham** Notts
115 K2 **High Melton** Donc
150 D3 **High Mickley** Nthumb
42 B4 **Highmoor** Oxon
42 B4 **Highmoor Cross** Oxon
55 H4 **Highnam** Gloucs
151 J4 **High Newport** Sundld
129 J3 **High Newton** Cumb
129 G2 **High Nibthwaite** Cumb
99 H7 **High Offley** Staffs
60 E7 **High Ongar** Essex
84 E1 **High Onn** Staffs
62 C4 **High Park Corner** Essex
163 L7 **High Pennyvenie** E Ayrs
60 F4 **High Roding** Essex
18 F4 **High Salvington** W Susx
150 E3 **High Spen** Gatesd
34 B3 **Highsted** Kent
4 F5 **High Street** Cnwll
34 E3 **Highstreet** Kent
31 G4 **Highstreet Green** Surrey
155 J6 **Hightae** D & G
111 J2 **Hightown** Sefton
77 L4 **Hightown Green** Suffk
118 C7 **High Toynton** Lincs
176 D2 **High Valleyfield** Fife
7 J2 **Highweek** Devon
44 E2 **Highwood Hill** Gt Lon
40 D2 **Highworth** Swindn
137 K7 **High Wray** Cumb
60 D5 **High Wych** Herts
42 E2 **High Wycombe** Bucks
91 J4 **Hilborough** Norfk
40 C8 **Hilcott** Wilts
32 F4 **Hildenborough** Kent
33 G4 **Hilden Park** Kent
76 D5 **Hildersham** Cambs
99 L5 **Hilderstone** Staffs
135 J6 **Hilderthorpe** E R Yk
90 E4 **Hilgay** Norfk
38 F2 **Hill** S Glos
72 F2 **Hill** Warwks
124 D5 **Hillam** N York
30 C6 **Hill Brow** Hants
15 J3 **Hillbutts** Dorset
99 H5 **Hill Chorlton** Staffs
100 F3 **Hillcliffane** Derbys
25 H6 **Hill Common** Somset
104 B3 **Hilldyke** Lincs
176 F2 **Hillend** Fife
185 L7 **Hill End** Fife
70 F6 **Hill End** Gloucs
177 H5 **Hillend** Mdloth
175 L5 **Hillend** N Lans
58 B3 **Hillesden** Bucks
39 H3 **Hillesley** Gloucs
25 J6 **Hillfarrance** Somset
46 D7 **Hill Green** Kent
216 B7 **Hillhead** Abers
17 G2 **Hill Head** Hants
165 J2 **Hillhead** S Lans
217 K5 **Hillhead of Cocklaw** Abers
231 H3 **Hilliclay** Highld
43 H4 **Hillingdon** Gt Lon
174 F5 **Hillington** C Glas
105 H7 **Hillington** Norfk
87 G8 **Hillmorton** Warwks
176 F1 **Hill of Beath** Fife
223 H5 **Hill of Fearn** Highld
146 D3 **Hillowton** D & G
100 B8 **Hill Ridware** Staffs
207 H5 **Hillside** Abers
197 H4 **Hillside** Angus
123 H6 **Hill Side** Kirk
115 J7 **Hills Town** Derbys
29 G7 **Hillstreet** Hants
235 c3 **Hillswick** Shet
123 L7 **Hill Top** Wakefd
235 c8 **Hillwell** Shet
40 A5 **Hilmarton** Wilts
39 K8 **Hilperton** Wilts
17 J2 **Hilsea** C Port
127 G4 **Hilston** E R Yk
179 H7 **Hilton** Border
75 K2 **Hilton** Cambs
139 G3 **Hilton** Cumb
100 E6 **Hilton** Derbys
14 E2 **Hilton** Dorset
140 F3 **Hilton** Dur
223 J6 **Hilton** Highld
141 K5 **Hilton** S on T
84 D4 **Hilton** Shrops
85 G3 **Hilton Park Services** Staffs
71 G3 **Himbleton** Worcs
84 F5 **Himley** Staffs
129 L3 **Hincaster** Cumb
44 D6 **Hinchley Wood** Surrey
86 E5 **Hinckley** Leics
92 B7 **Hinderclay** Suffk
143 G4 **Hinderwell** N York
30 E4 **Hindhead** Surrey
112 F1 **Hindley** Wigan
70 F3 **Hindlip** Worcs
106 C6 **Hindolveston** Norfk
27 K5 **Hindon** Wilts
106 B5 **Hindringham** Norfk
92 B3 **Hingham** Norfk
99 G7 **Hinstock** Shrops
78 C5 **Hintlesham** Suffk
69 G6 **Hinton** Herefs
39 G5 **Hinton** S Glos
83 H2 **Hinton** Shrops
29 L6 **Hinton Ampner** Hants
26 E1 **Hinton Blewett** BaNES
39 H8 **Hinton Charterhouse** BaNES
73 H6 **Hinton-in-the-Hedges** Nhants
15 J2 **Hinton Martell** Dorset
71 H6 **Hinton on the Green** Worcs
40 E4 **Hinton Parva** Swindn
26 B8 **Hinton St George** Somset
27 H7 **Hinton St Mary** Dorset
57 G7 **Hinton Waldrist** Oxon
85 L3 **Hints** Staffs
74 D3 **Hinwick** Bed
34 D6 **Hinxhill** Kent
76 C5 **Hinxton** Cambs
75 J6 **Hinxworth** Herts
123 H5 **Hipperholme** Calder
140 F7 **Hipswell** N York
206 D5 **Hirn** Abers
97 G7 **Hirnant** Powys
159 G5 **Hirst** Nthumb
124 F5 **Hirst Courtney** N York
52 E6 **Hirwaun** Rhondd
23 J6 **Hiscott** Devon
76 B2 **Histon** Cambs
78 B4 **Hitcham** Suffk
78 B4 **Hitcham Causeway** Suffk
78 B4 **Hitcham Street** Suffk
59 K3 **Hitchin** Herts
45 H5 **Hither Green** Gt Lon
11 H5 **Hittisleigh** Devon
125 J4 **Hive** E R Yk
100 A7 **Hixon** Staffs
35 H3 **Hoaden** Kent
100 C7 **Hoar Cross** Staffs
54 D3 **Hoarwithy** Herefs
47 K7 **Hoath** Kent
82 F7 **Hobarris** Shrops
167 J7 **Hobkirk** Border
150 F4 **Hobson** Dur
102 A8 **Hoby** Leics
92 C2 **Hockering** Norfk
102 B2 **Hockerton** Notts
46 D2 **Hockley** Essex
85 L8 **Hockley Heath** Solhll
58 F3 **Hockliffe** C Beds
91 G6 **Hockwold cum Wilton** Norfk
25 G7 **Hockworthy** Devon
60 B6 **Hoddesdon** Herts
121 L6 **Hoddlesden** Bl w D
155 L7 **Hoddom Cross** D & G
155 K7 **Hoddom Mains** D & G
49 H7 **Hodgeston** Pembks
98 E6 **Hodnet** Shrops
115 L4 **Hodsock** Notts
45 M7 **Hodsoll Street** Kent
40 D4 **Hodson** Swindn
115 K6 **Hodthorpe** Derbys
92 B1 **Hoe** Norfk
34 D4 **Hogben's Hill** Kent
58 D3 **Hoggeston** Bucks
86 B5 **Hoggrill's End** Warwks
121 J5 **Hoghton** Lancs
100 E3 **Hognaston** Derbys
119 H6 **Hogsthorpe** Lincs
104 B7 **Holbeach** Lincs
104 B6 **Holbeach Bank** Lincs
104 B6 **Holbeach Clough** Lincs
89 K2 **Holbeach Drove** Lincs
104 C6 **Holbeach Hurn** Lincs
104 B8 **Holbeach St Johns** Lincs
104 B6 **Holbeach St Mark's** Lincs
104 C6 **Holbeach St Matthew** Lincs
115 K6 **Holbeck** Notts
71 H3 **Holberrow Green** Worcs
6 F5 **Holbeton** Devon
44 F4 **Holborn** Gt Lon
101 G4 **Holbrook** Derbys
78 E6 **Holbrook** Suffk
86 D6 **Holbrooks** Covtry
16 E2 **Holbury** Hants
12 B7 **Holcombe** Devon
26 F2 **Holcombe** Somset
25 G7 **Holcombe Rogus** Devon
73 L1 **Holcot** Nhants
122 B1 **Holden** Lancs
73 K2 **Holdenby** Nhants
61 G3 **Holder's Green** Essex
83 L5 **Holdgate** Shrops
103 H3 **Holdingham** Lincs
13 J2 **Holditch** Dorset
10 B4 **Holemoor** Devon
25 J3 **Holford** Somset
124 E1 **Holgate** C York
129 H4 **Holker** Cumb
105 L4 **Holkham** Norfk
105 L4 **Holkham Hall** Norfk
9 K4 **Hollacombe** Devon
103 L3 **Holland Fen** Lincs
62 E5 **Holland-on-Sea** Essex
234 e3 **Hollandstoun** Ork
148 A2 **Hollee** D & G
79 H5 **Hollesley** Suffk
7 K4 **Hollicombe** Torbay
33 L3 **Hollingbourne** Kent
19 J4 **Hollingbury** Br & H
58 E3 **Hollingdon** Bucks
100 E5 **Hollington** Derbys
100 B5 **Hollington** Staffs
114 A3 **Hollingworth** Tamesd
114 B7 **Hollinsclough** Staffs
115 G5 **Hollins End** Sheff
113 G4 **Hollins Green** Warrtn
84 C2 **Hollinswood** Wrekin
113 K2 **Hollinwood Crematorium** Oldham
10 F3 **Hollocombe** Devon
100 F2 **Holloway** Derbys
44 F3 **Holloway** Gt Lon
73 K1 **Hollowell** Nhants
112 C7 **Hollowmoor Heath** Ches W
156 C6 **Hollows** D & G
53 J7 **Hollybush** Caerph
163 K6 **Hollybush** E Ayrs
70 D6 **Hollybush** Herefs
127 H5 **Hollym** E R Yk
114 C1 **Holmbridge** Kirk
31 J3 **Holmbury St Mary** Surrey
5 G5 **Holmbush** Cnwll
99 K7 **Holmcroft** Staffs
89 H6 **Holme** Cambs
129 L4 **Holme** Cumb
114 C1 **Holme** Kirk
132 E3 **Holme** N York
102 D2 **Holme** Notts
122 C5 **Holme Chapel** Lancs
91 K3 **Holme Hale** Norfk
69 L7 **Holme Lacy** Herefs
69 G4 **Holme Marsh** Herefs
105 H4 **Holme next the Sea** Norfk
126 B2 **Holme on the Wolds** E R Yk
101 L5 **Holme Pierrepont** Notts
69 K6 **Holmer** Herefs
42 E2 **Holmer Green** Bucks

147 J5 **Holme St Cuthbert** Cumb
113 H7 **Holmes Chapel** Ches E
114 F6 **Holmesfield** Derbys
120 F6 **Holmeswood** Lancs
32 B3 **Holmethorpe** Surrey
125 J3 **Holme upon Spalding Moor** E R Yk
115 H7 **Holmewood** Derbys
123 H8 **Holmfirth** Kirk
164 B5 **Holmhead** E Ayrs
127 J5 **Holmpton** E R Yk
136 E7 **Holmrook** Cumb
163 J2 **Holmsford Bridge Crematorium** N Ayrs
150 F5 **Holmside** Dur
7 G3 **Holne** Devon
24 E3 **Holnicote** Somset
9 J4 **Holsworthy** Devon
9 K3 **Holsworthy Beacon** Devon
15 J2 **Holt** Dorset
106 C5 **Holt** Norfk
39 K7 **Holt** Wilts
70 E3 **Holt** Worcs
98 B2 **Holt** Wrexhm
133 K8 **Holtby** C York
71 J1 **Holt End** Worcs
70 E2 **Holt Heath** Worcs
57 L6 **Holton** Oxon
27 G6 **Holton** Somset
93 J7 **Holton** Suffk
117 J5 **Holton cum Beckering** Lincs
118 C2 **Holton le Clay** Lincs
117 H3 **Holton le Moor** Lincs
78 C6 **Holton St Mary** Suffk
14 D1 **Holwell** Dorset
59 K2 **Holwell** Herts
102 B7 **Holwell** Leics
56 E6 **Holwell** Oxon
139 K2 **Holwick** Dur
30 B4 **Holybourne** Hants
108 C5 **Holyhead** IoA
108 C5 **Holy Island** IoA
169 H2 **Holy Island** Nthumb
169 H2 **Holy Island** Nthumb
115 G7 **Holymoorside** Derbys
42 E5 **Holyport** W & M
158 B2 **Holystone** Nthumb
175 K6 **Holytown** N Lans
175 K6 **Holytown Crematorium** N Lans
59 G5 **Holywell** C Beds
75 L1 **Holywell** Cambs
4 B4 **Holywell** Cnwll
14 B2 **Holywell** Dorset
111 G6 **Holywell** Flints
123 G6 **Holywell Green** Calder
25 H7 **Holywell Lake** Somset
91 G7 **Holywell Row** Suffk
155 G6 **Holywood** D & G
155 G6 **Holywood Village** D & G
84 B3 **Homer** Shrops
111 K2 **Homer Green** Sefton
93 G6 **Homersfield** Suffk
28 C6 **Homington** Wilts
71 K5 **Honeybourne** Worcs
10 F4 **Honeychurch** Devon
40 C7 **Honeystreet** Wilts
77 L7 **Honey Tye** Suffk
86 B8 **Honiley** Warwks
107 G6 **Honing** Norfk
92 D2 **Honingham** Norfk
102 F4 **Honington** Lincs
91 K8 **Honington** Suffk
72 C6 **Honington** Warwks
12 F3 **Honiton** Devon
123 H7 **Honley** Kirk
45 G5 **Honor Oak Crematorium** Gt Lon
6 D5 **Hooe** C Plym
20 E4 **Hooe** E Susx
113 G5 **Hoo Green** Ches E
120 D3 **Hoohill** Bpool
125 H5 **Hook** E R Yk
44 D7 **Hook** Gt Lon
30 B1 **Hook** Hants
49 G5 **Hook** Pembks
40 B4 **Hook** Wilts
14 A3 **Hooke** Dorset
33 H6 **Hook Green** Kent
45 L6 **Hook Green** Kent
57 G2 **Hook Norton** Oxon
11 K5 **Hookway** Devon
32 B3 **Hooley** Surrey
46 C5 **Hoo St Werburgh** Medway
115 K3 **Hooton Levitt** Rothm
124 D8 **Hooton Pagnell** Donc
115 J3 **Hooton Roberts** Rothm
114 D5 **Hope** Derbys
7 G7 **Hope** Devon
97 L2 **Hope** Flints
83 L8 **Hope** Shrops
100 C2 **Hope** Staffs
83 J5 **Hope Bowdler** Shrops
166 D6 **Hopehouse** Border
214 E1 **Hopeman** Moray
54 F4 **Hope Mansell** Herefs
83 H6 **Hopesay** Shrops
69 K4 **Hope under Dinmore** Herefs
133 K8 **Hopgrove** C York
132 F7 **Hopperton** N York
84 D5 **Hopstone** Shrops
100 E2 **Hopton** Derbys
99 L7 **Hopton** Staffs
92 B7 **Hopton** Suffk
83 K7 **Hopton Cangeford** Shrops
83 G7 **Hopton Castle** Shrops
83 H7 **Hoptonheath** Shrops
93 L4 **Hopton on Sea** Norfk
84 B7 **Hopton Wafers** Shrops
85 L3 **Hopwas** Staffs
85 J7 **Hopwood** Worcs
85 J8 **Hopwood Park Services** Worcs
20 C3 **Horam** E Susx
103 J5 **Horbling** Lincs
123 K6 **Horbury** Wakefd
151 K6 **Horden** Dur
16 C4 **Hordle** Hants
98 B6 **Hordley** Shrops
38 E5 **Horfield** Bristl
92 E8 **Horham** Suffk
62 B3 **Horkesley Heath** Essex
126 B6 **Horkstow** N Linc
72 E5 **Horley** Oxon
32 B5 **Horley** Surrey
26 E5 **Hornblotton Green** Somset
130 B5 **Hornby** Lancs
132 C2 **Hornby** N York
141 J6 **Hornby** N York
118 C7 **Horncastle** Lincs
45 K3 **Hornchurch** Gt Lon
179 J7 **Horncliffe** Nthumb
179 J8 **Horndean** Border
30 B8 **Horndean** Hants
10 D8 **Horndon** Devon
46 A4 **Horndon on the Hill** Thurr
32 C4 **Horne** Surrey
24 D3 **Horner** Somset
107 H8 **Horning** Norfk
88 B4 **Horninghold** Leics
100 E7 **Horninglow** Staffs
76 C3 **Horningsea** Cambs
27 J3 **Horningsham** Wilts
105 M7 **Horningtoft** Norfk
22 F6 **Horns Cross** Devon
126 F2 **Hornsea** E R Yk
44 F3 **Hornsey** Gt Lon
72 E5 **Hornton** Oxon
235 d2 **Horra** Shet
6 D2 **Horrabridge** Devon
77 J3 **Horringer** Suffk
121 L2 **Horrocksford** Lancs
6 B2 **Horsebridge** Devon
20 C4 **Horsebridge** E Susx
29 G5 **Horsebridge** Hants
84 C3 **Horsehay** Wrekin
76 E5 **Horseheath** Cambs
131 K4 **Horsehouse** N York
43 G8 **Horsell** Surrey
98 C4 **Horseman's Green** Wrexhm
107 K7 **Horsey** Norfk
25 L4 **Horsey** Somset
92 E1 **Horsford** Norfk
123 J3 **Horsforth** Leeds
31 K5 **Horsham** W Susx
70 D3 **Horsham** Worcs
92 E1 **Horsham St Faith** Norfk
117 K7 **Horsington** Lincs
27 G6 **Horsington** Somset
101 G4 **Horsley** Derbys
39 J2 **Horsley** Gloucs
150 D2 **Horsley** Nthumb
157 L3 **Horsley** Nthumb
62 D3 **Horsleycross Street** Essex
167 H5 **Horsleyhill** Border
101 H4 **Horsley Woodhouse** Derbys
33 J5 **Horsmonden** Kent
57 L6 **Horspath** Oxon
106 F8 **Horstead** Norfk
32 C7 **Horsted Keynes** W Susx
58 F4 **Horton** Bucks
15 J2 **Horton** Dorset
122 C1 **Horton** Lancs
74 B4 **Horton** Nhants
39 H4 **Horton** S Glos
25 L7 **Horton** Somset
99 L2 **Horton** Staffs
50 F7 **Horton** Swans
43 G5 **Horton** W & M
40 B7 **Horton** Wilts
84 C1 **Horton** Wrekin
57 L5 **Horton-cum-Studley** Oxon
98 C3 **Horton Green** Ches W
130 F5 **Horton in Ribblesdale** N York
45 K6 **Horton Kirby** Kent
121 J7 **Horwich** Bolton
23 H6 **Horwood** Devon
166 F6 **Hoscote** Border
102 B6 **Hose** Leics
185 H3 **Hosh** P & K
235 c7 **Hoswick** Shet
125 L4 **Hotham** E R Yk
34 C5 **Hothfield** Kent
101 L7 **Hoton** Leics
99 G3 **Hough** Ches E
102 E4 **Hougham** Lincs
112 C4 **Hough Green** Halton
102 F3 **Hough-on-the-Hill** Lincs
75 K1 **Houghton** Cambs
29 G5 **Houghton** Hants
49 G6 **Houghton** Pembks
18 D4 **Houghton** W Susx
74 F6 **Houghton Conquest** C Beds
21 H2 **Houghton Green** E Susx
151 H5 **Houghton-le-Spring** Sundld
87 J3 **Houghton on the Hill** Leics
59 G4 **Houghton Regis** C Beds
105 L5 **Houghton St Giles** Norfk
42 B8 **Hound Green** Hants
178 D8 **Houndslow** Border
179 H5 **Houndwood** Border
43 J5 **Hounslow** Gt Lon
213 L4 **Househill** Highld
123 J6 **Houses Hill** Kirk
207 G1 **Housieside** Abers
174 D5 **Houston** Rens
227 K2 **Houstry** Highld
234 b6 **Houton** Ork
19 J5 **Hove** Br & H
102 B3 **Hoveringham** Notts
107 G8 **Hoveton** Norfk
133 K4 **Hovingham** N York
54 E3 **How Caple** Herefs
125 H5 **Howden** E R Yk
150 E7 **Howden-le-Wear** Dur
231 K3 **Howe** Highld
132 E4 **Howe** N York
92 F4 **Howe** Norfk
112 F2 **Howe Bridge Crematorium** Wigan
61 J7 **Howe Green** Essex
61 K7 **Howegreen** Essex
103 J4 **Howell** Lincs
216 E5 **Howe of Teuchar** Abers
147 L2 **Howes** D & G
61 H5 **Howe Street** Essex
77 G7 **Howe Street** Essex
68 B3 **Howey** Powys
136 D3 **Howgate** Cumb
177 H6 **Howgate** Mdloth
169 K5 **Howick** Nthumb
76 E7 **Howlett End** Essex
13 H1 **Howley** Somset
148 E4 **How Mill** Cumb
233 b7 **Howmore** W Isls
168 B5 **Hownam** Border
117 H2 **Howsham** N Linc
133 L6 **Howsham** N York
168 D3 **Howtel** Nthumb
174 D6 **Howwood** Rens
92 E7 **Hoxne** Suffk
234 b7 **Hoy** Ork
111 H4 **Hoylake** Wirral
115 G2 **Hoyland Nether** Barns
114 E1 **Hoyland Swaine** Barns
48 E6 **Hubberston** Pembks
123 K2 **Huby** N York
133 J6 **Huby** N York
55 K4 **Hucclecote** Gloucs
33 L2 **Hucking** Kent
101 K3 **Hucknall** Notts
123 H7 **Huddersfield** Kirk
123 H6 **Huddersfield Crematorium** Kirk
71 G3 **Huddington** Worcs
140 E7 **Hudswell** N York
134 D7 **Huggate** E R Yk
42 E2 **Hughenden Valley** Bucks
83 L4 **Hughley** Shrops
2 b2 **Hugh Town** IoS
10 D3 **Huish** Devon
40 C7 **Huish** Wilts
25 G5 **Huish Champflower** Somset
26 B6 **Huish Episcopi** Somset
58 D5 **Hulcott** Bucks
12 C5 **Hulham** Devon
100 E3 **Hulland** Derbys
100 E3 **Hulland Ward** Derbys
39 K4 **Hullavington** Wilts
46 D2 **Hullbridge** Essex
126 D5 **Hull, Kingston upon** C KuH
113 J3 **Hulme** Manch
99 L4 **Hulme** Staffs
112 E4 **Hulme** Warrtn
100 C2 **Hulme End** Staffs
113 J7 **Hulme Walfield** Ches E
16 E5 **Hulverstone** IoW

93 K6 **Hulver Street** Suffk
126 D7 *Humberside Airport* N Linc
118 D1 **Humberston** NE Lin
87 J3 **Humberstone** C Leic
178 B5 **Humbie** E Loth
126 F4 **Humbleton** E R Yk
103 G6 **Humby** Lincs
167 L2 **Hume** Border
158 A7 **Humshaugh** Nthumb
231 L2 **Huna** Highld
87 G4 **Huncote** Leics
167 K5 **Hundalee** Border
140 C3 **Hunderthwaite** Dur
118 E7 **Hundleby** Lincs
49 G7 **Hundleton** Pembks
77 G5 **Hundon** Suffk
68 C4 **Hundred House** Powys
87 K3 **Hungarton** Leics
25 G4 **Hungerford** Somset
41 G6 **Hungerford** W Berk
41 G6 **Hungerford Newtown** W Berk
69 J7 **Hungerstone** Herefs
135 H4 **Hunmanby** N York
72 D2 **Hunningham** Warwks
73 K3 **Hunsbury Hill** Nhants
60 C5 **Hunsdon** Herts
132 F8 **Hunsingore** N York
123 L4 **Hunslet** Leeds
149 G7 **Hunsonby** Cumb
105 G4 **Hunstanton** Norfk
150 B5 **Hunstanworth** Dur
99 G4 **Hunsterson** Ches E
77 L2 **Hunston** Suffk
18 B5 **Hunston** W Susx
38 F7 **Hunstrete** BaNES
123 J5 **Hunsworth** Kirk
173 K3 **Hunter's Quay** Ag & B
25 M6 **Huntham** Somset
196 D3 **Hunthill Lodge** Angus
89 J8 **Huntingdon** Cambs
93 G8 **Huntingfield** Suffk
133 J7 **Huntington** C York
112 B8 **Huntington** Ches W
178 B4 **Huntington** E Loth
68 E4 **Huntington** Herefs
85 H2 **Huntington** Staffs
55 G4 **Huntley** Gloucs
215 L6 **Huntly** Abers
33 J4 **Hunton** Kent
132 B2 **Hunton** N York
24 E3 **Huntscott** Somset
24 F7 **Huntsham** Devon
23 H6 **Huntshaw** Devon
25 L3 **Huntspill** Somset
25 K5 **Huntstile** Somset
25 L4 **Huntworth** Somset
140 F2 **Hunwick** Dur
106 C5 **Hunworth** Norfk
28 D5 **Hurdcott** Wilts
113 L6 **Hurdsfield** Ches E
42 D4 **Hurley** W & M
86 B4 **Hurley** Warwks
86 B4 **Hurley Common** Warwks
163 L3 **Hurlford** E Ayrs
15 L3 **Hurn** Dorset
29 H6 **Hursley** Hants
42 C5 **Hurst** Wokham
29 H3 **Hurstbourne Priors** Hants
29 G2 **Hurstbourne Tarrant** Hants
33 J7 **Hurst Green** E Susx
62 C5 **Hurst Green** Essex
121 K3 **Hurst Green** Lancs
32 D3 **Hurst Green** Surrey
19 J3 **Hurstpierpoint** W Susx
122 C4 **Hurstwood** Lancs
234 c6 **Hurtiso** Ork
141 H5 **Hurworth-on-Tees** Darltn
141 H5 **Hurworth Place** Darltn
87 J6 **Husbands Bosworth** Leics
74 D7 **Husborne Crawley** C Beds
133 H4 **Husthwaite** N York
115 G5 **Hutcliffe Wood Crematorium** Sheff
101 J2 **Huthwaite** Notts
119 G6 **Huttoft** Lincs
179 J7 **Hutton** Border
134 F8 **Hutton** E R Yk
45 M2 **Hutton** Essex
121 G5 **Hutton** Lancs
37 M8 **Hutton** N Som
134 F3 **Hutton Buscel** N York
132 E5 **Hutton Conyers** N York
126 C1 **Hutton Cranswick** E R Yk
148 D7 **Hutton End** Cumb
151 K7 **Hutton Henry** Dur
133 L2 **Hutton-le-Hole** N York
142 D4 **Hutton Lowcross** R & Cl
140 E5 **Hutton Magna** Dur
130 B4 **Hutton Roof** Cumb
148 C7 **Hutton Roof** Cumb
141 K6 **Hutton Rudby** N York
133 G4 **Hutton Sessay** N York
124 D1 **Hutton Wandesley** N York
12 B3 **Huxham** Devon
98 D1 **Huxley** Ches W
112 C4 **Huyton** Knows
128 D2 **Hycemoor** Cumb
113 L3 **Hyde** Tamesd
58 F7 **Hyde Heath** Bucks
99 K8 **Hyde Lea** Staffs
165 H2 **Hyndford Bridge** S Lans
188 C8 **Hynish** Ag & B
82 F5 **Hyssington** Powys
16 E2 **Hythe** Hants
34 F7 **Hythe** Kent
43 G6 **Hythe End** W & M

I

14 E2 **Ibberton** Dorset
100 E2 **Ible** Derbys
15 L1 **Ibsley** Hants
86 E2 **Ibstock** Leics
42 C2 **Ibstone** Bucks
29 G2 **Ibthorpe** Hants
143 H5 **Iburndale** N York
29 K1 **Ibworth** Hants
182 E2 **Ichrachan** Ag & B
91 J4 **Ickburgh** Norfk
43 H3 **Ickenham** Gt Lon
57 M6 **Ickford** Bucks
35 G3 **Ickham** Kent
59 K2 **Ickleford** Herts
21 H3 **Icklesham** E Susx
76 C5 **Ickleton** Cambs
91 H8 **Icklingham** Suffk
122 E2 **Ickornshaw** N York
75 G5 **Ickwell Green** C Beds
77 J3 **Ickworth** Suffk
56 E4 **Icomb** Gloucs
56 E4 **Idbury** Oxon
10 E3 **Iddesleigh** Devon
11 K6 **Ide** Devon
7 K1 **Ideford** Devon
32 E3 **Ide Hill** Kent
21 H2 **Iden** E Susx
33 J5 **Iden Green** Kent
33 K6 **Iden Green** Kent
123 H3 **Idle** C Brad
4 C6 **Idless** Cnwll
72 C5 **Idlicote** Warwks
28 D4 **Idmiston** Wilts
50 E3 **Idole** Carmth
100 F3 **Idridgehay** Derbys
208 F2 **Idrigill** Highld
40 E4 **Idstone** Oxon
57 K7 **Iffley** Oxon
31 L4 **Ifield** W Susx
31 G5 **Ifold** W Susx
15 L4 **Iford** Bmouth
19 L4 **Iford** E Susx
38 C3 **Ifton** Mons
98 E5 **Ightfield** Shrops
33 G2 **Ightham** Kent
100 C3 **Ilam** Staffs
26 D6 **Ilchester** Somset
168 F5 **Ilderton** Nthumb
45 H3 **Ilford** Gt Lon
26 A7 **Ilford** Somset
23 H2 **Ilfracombe** Devon
101 J4 **Ilkeston** Derbys
93 H6 **Ilketshall St Andrew** Suffk
93 H6 **Ilketshall St Margaret** Suffk
123 G2 **Ilkley** C Brad
5 L1 **Illand** Cnwll
85 H7 **Illey** Dudley
3 H3 **Illogan** Cnwll
87 K4 **Illston on the Hill** Leics
58 C6 **Ilmer** Bucks
72 B5 **Ilmington** Warwks
26 A8 **Ilminster** Somset
7 H2 **Ilsington** Devon
51 H7 **Ilston** Swans
132 B4 **Ilton** N York
25 M7 **Ilton** Somset
161 L2 **Imachar** N Ayrs
126 F7 **Immingham** NE Lin
126 F7 **Immingham Dock** NE Lin
76 C2 **Impington** Cambs
112 C6 **Ince** Ches W
111 K2 **Ince Blundell** Sefton
112 E1 **Ince-in-Makerfield** Wigan
221 K7 **Inchbae Lodge Hotel** Highld
196 F4 **Inchbare** Angus
215 G4 **Inchberry** Moray
211 G3 **Incheril** Highld
174 E5 **Inchinnan** Rens
201 J5 **Inchlaggan** Highld
186 D3 **Inchmichael** P & K
202 B3 **Inchnacardoch Hotel** Highld
224 F4 **Inchnadamph** Highld
186 D2 **Inchture** P & K
211 K6 **Inchvuilt** Highld
186 C4 **Inchyra** P & K
4 E4 **Indian Queens** Cnwll
61 G7 **Ingatestone** Essex
114 E1 **Ingbirchworth** Barns
99 L7 **Ingestre** Staffs
116 F5 **Ingham** Lincs
107 H7 **Ingham** Norfk
77 J1 **Ingham** Suffk
107 H6 **Ingham Corner** Norfk
101 G6 **Ingleby** Derbys
141 K6 **Ingleby Arncliffe** N York
141 K4 **Ingleby Barwick** S on T
142 C6 **Ingleby Greenhow** N York
10 E4 **Ingleigh Green** Devon
39 G7 **Inglesbatch** BaNES
56 D7 **Inglesham** Swindn
147 G2 **Ingleston** D & G
140 F3 **Ingleton** Dur
130 D5 **Ingleton** N York
121 H3 **Inglewhite** Lancs
158 C7 **Ingoe** Nthumb
121 G4 **Ingol** Lancs
105 G6 **Ingoldisthorpe** Norfk
119 H7 **Ingoldmells** Lincs
103 G6 **Ingoldsby** Lincs
168 F6 **Ingram** Nthumb
45 M2 **Ingrave** Essex
122 F3 **Ingrow** C Brad
138 C7 **Ings** Cumb
38 E3 **Ingst** S Glos
88 E2 **Ingthorpe** Rutlnd
106 E6 **Ingworth** Norfk
71 H3 **Inkberrow** Worcs
217 H6 **Inkhorn** Abers
41 G7 **Inkpen** W Berk
231 J2 **Inkstack** Highld
173 K4 **Innellan** Ag & B
166 E3 **Innerleithen** Border
186 F7 **Innerleven** Fife
144 C3 **Innermessan** D & G
178 F4 **Innerwick** E Loth
215 G2 **Innesmill** Moray
216 C8 **Insch** Abers
203 J5 **Insh** Highld
120 F3 **Inskip** Lancs
23 G5 **Instow** Devon
115 H5 **Intake** Sheff
204 F6 **Inver** Abers
223 J5 **Inver** Highld
194 F7 **Inver** P & K
190 F1 **Inverailort** Highld
210 C3 **Inveralligin** Highld
217 K2 **Inverallochy** Abers
222 D2 **Inveran** Highld
182 F5 **Inveraray** Ag & B
209 J7 **Inverarish** Highld
196 D7 **Inverarity** Angus
183 K4 **Inverarnan** Stirlg
219 J4 **Inverasdale** Highld
183 K7 **Inverbeg** Ag & B
197 K2 **Inverbervie** Abers
216 C2 **Inver-boyndie** Abers
191 K6 **Invercreran House Hotel** Ag & B
203 L3 **Inverdruie** Highld
177 K4 **Inveresk** E Loth
182 E1 **Inveresragan** Ag & B
219 K5 **Inverewe Garden** Highld
204 D7 **Inverey** Abers
202 D2 **Inverfarigaig** Highld
191 J7 **Inverfolla** Ag & B
201 L5 **Invergarry** Highld
184 F2 **Invergeldie** P & K
201 K7 **Invergloy** Highld
222 F7 **Invergordon** Highld
186 F2 **Invergowrie** P & K
200 B4 **Inverguseran** Highld
193 L5 **Inverhadden** P & K
183 L3 **Inverherive Hotel** Stirlg
200 B5 **Inverie** Highld
182 E4 **Inverinan** Ag & B
200 E2 **Inverinate** Highld
197 G6 **Inverkeilor** Angus
176 F2 **Inverkeithing** Fife
216 C5 **Inverkeithny** Abers
173 L4 **Inverkip** Inver
224 C4 **Inverkirkaig** Highld
220 F4 **Inverlael** Highld
192 E1 **Inverlair** Highld
182 C6 **Inverliever Lodge** Ag & B
183 H2 **Inverlochy** Ag & B
196 D1 **Invermark** Angus
202 C3 **Invermoriston** Highld
229 L4 **Invernaver** Highld
213 G5 **Inverness** Highld
212 F5 **Inverness Crematorium** Highld
213 J4 *Inverness Dalcross Airport* Highld
183 G7 **Invernoaden** Ag & B
192 D7 **Inveroran Hotel** Ag & B
196 C5 **Inverquharity** Angus
217 J5 **Inverquhomery** Abers
201 K8 **Inverroy** Highld
191 J4 **Inversanda** Highld
200 E2 **Invershiel** Highld
222 D3 **Invershin** Highld
231 J8 **Invershore** Highld

183 K5 **Inversnaid Hotel** Stirlg
217 L5 **Inverugie** Abers
183 K5 **Inveruglas** Ag & B
203 J5 **Inveruglass** Highld
206 E2 **Inverurie** Abers
10 E5 **Inwardleigh** Devon
61 L4 **Inworth** Essex
233 b7 **Iochdar** W Isls
180 D3 **Iona** Ag & B
30 D6 **Iping** W Susx
7 J3 **Ipplepen** Devon
41 M4 **Ipsden** Oxon
100 A3 **Ipstones** Staffs
78 E5 **Ipswich** Suffk
78 E5 **Ipswich Crematorium** Suffk
111 J5 **Irby** Wirral
118 F8 **Irby in the Marsh** Lincs
117 K1 **Irby upon Humber** NE Lin
74 D2 **Irchester** Nhants
147 M7 **Ireby** Cumb
130 C4 **Ireby** Lancs
128 F4 **Ireleth** Cumb
149 L7 **Ireshopeburn** Dur
113 G3 **Irlam** Salfd
103 G7 **Irnham** Lincs
39 G4 **Iron Acton** S Glos
84 C3 **Ironbridge** Wrekin
84 C3 **Ironbridge Gorge** Shrops
154 B6 **Ironmacannie** D & G
101 H3 **Ironville** Derbys
107 H7 **Irstead** Norfk
148 E3 **Irthington** Cumb
74 D1 **Irthlingborough** Nhants
134 F3 **Irton** N York
163 H2 **Irvine** N Ayrs
163 H2 **Irvine Maritime Centre** N Ayrs
230 E3 **Isauld** Highld
235 c2 **Isbister** Shet
235 d4 **Isbister** Shet
19 L3 **Isfield** E Susx
88 C8 **Isham** Nhants
30 C3 **Isington** Hants
171 G4 **Islay** Ag & B
170 F7 *Islay Airport* Ag & B
26 A7 **Isle Abbotts** Somset
26 A7 **Isle Brewers** Somset
90 F8 **Isleham** Cambs
45 G4 **Isle of Dogs** Gt Lon
46 E5 **Isle of Grain** Medway
232 f2 **Isle of Lewis** W Isls
237 c4 **Isle of Man** IoM
237 b7 *Isle of Man Ronaldsway Airport* IoM
181 J1 **Isle of Mull** Ag & B
15 J5 **Isle of Purbeck** Dorset
46 F6 **Isle of Sheppey** Kent
208 F6 **Isle of Skye** Highld
35 J2 **Isle of Thanet** Kent
128 E6 **Isle of Walney** Cumb
145 K7 **Isle of Whithorn** D & G
17 G5 **Isle of Wight** IoW
17 G4 **Isle of Wight Crematorium** IoW
199 L3 **Isleornsay** Highld
2 b2 *Isles of Scilly St Mary's Airport* IoS
155 G7 **Islesteps** D & G
44 D5 **Isleworth** Gt Lon
101 H7 **Isley Walton** Leics
232 d3 **Islibhig** W Isls
44 F3 **Islington** Gt Lon
44 F2 **Islington Crematorium** Gt Lon
88 E7 **Islip** Nhants
57 K5 **Islip** Oxon
232 d3 **Islivig** W Isls
83 L2 **Isombridge** Wrekin
29 K5 **Itchen Abbas** Hants
29 K5 **Itchen Stoke** Hants
31 J5 **Itchingfield** W Susx
106 D6 **Itteringham** Norfk
38 C2 **Itton** Mons
38 C2 **Itton Common** Mons
148 D6 **Ivegill** Cumb
43 G4 **Iver** Bucks
43 G4 **Iver Heath** Bucks
150 E5 **Iveston** Dur
58 F5 **Ivinghoe** Bucks
58 F4 **Ivinghoe Aston** Bucks
69 J3 **Ivington** Herefs
6 F5 **Ivybridge** Devon
21 K1 **Ivychurch** Kent
33 G3 **Ivy Hatch** Kent
46 E6 **Iwade** Kent
27 K8 **Iwerne Courtney or Shroton** Dorset
27 K8 **Iwerne Minster** Dorset
77 L1 **Ixworth** Suffk
91 K8 **Ixworth Thorpe** Suffk

J

12 C4 **Jack-in-the-Green** Devon
175 G7 **Jackton** S Lans
9 G5 **Jacobstow** Cnwll
10 E4 **Jacobstowe** Devon
49 H7 **Jameston** Pembks
212 D3 **Jamestown** Highld
174 D3 **Jamestown** W Duns
227 L3 **Janetstown** Highld
231 L5 **Janets-town** Highld
155 J5 **Jardine Hall** D & G
151 H3 **Jarrow** S Tyne
61 H3 **Jasper's Green** Essex
175 L4 **Jawcraig** Falk
62 D5 **Jaywick** Essex
167 K5 **Jedburgh** Border
49 J6 **Jeffreyston** Pembks
213 H2 **Jemimaville** Highld
236 d4 **Jerbourg** Guern
236 b7 *Jersey Airport* Jersey
236 c7 **Jersey Crematorium** Jersey
151 G2 **Jesmond** N u Ty
20 B5 **Jevington** E Susx
59 H5 **Jockey End** Herts
148 D7 **Johnby** Cumb
112 B5 *John Lennon Airport* Lpool
231 L2 **John o' Groats** Highld
197 J3 **Johnshaven** Abers
48 F5 **Johnston** Pembks
155 M3 **Johnstone** D & G
174 D5 **Johnstone** Rens
155 J4 **Johnstonebridge** D & G
50 E2 **Johnstown** Carmth
97 L4 **Johnstown** Wrexhm
177 J4 **Joppa** C Edin
66 D2 **Joppa** Cerdgn
163 K5 **Joppa** S Ayrs
64 C7 **Jordanston** Pembks
45 K5 **Joyden's Wood** Kent
150 B3 **Juniper** Nthumb
177 G5 **Juniper Green** C Edin
171 J2 **Jura** Ag & B
237 c2 **Jurby** IoM

K

139 H5 **Kaber** Cumb
165 J1 **Kaimend** S Lans
173 G4 **Kames** Ag & B
164 D4 **Kames** E Ayrs
4 C7 **Kea** Cnwll
125 K7 **Keadby** N Linc
104 B1 **Keal Cotes** Lincs
113 H1 **Kearsley** Bolton
35 H6 **Kearsney** Kent
130 B4 **Kearstwick** Cumb
77 G5 **Kedington** Suffk
100 F4 **Kedleston** Derbys
126 E8 **Keelby** Lincs
99 J4 **Keele** Staffs
99 J4 **Keele Services** Staffs
123 G4 **Keelham** C Brad
48 F4 **Keeston** Pembks
39 L8 **Keevil** Wilts
101 J7 **Kegworth** Leics
3 G3 **Kehelland** Cnwll
206 B2 **Keig** Abers
122 F3 **Keighley** C Brad
122 F3 **Keighley Crematorium** C Brad
185 J8 **Keilarsbrae** Clacks
185 K3 **Keillour** P & K
204 E6 **Keiloch** Abers
171 K5 **Keils** Ag & B
26 D5 **Keinton Mandeville** Somset
154 E4 **Keir Mill** D & G
139 G3 **Keisley** Cumb
231 L4 **Keiss** Highld
215 J4 **Keith** Moray
195 K8 **Keithick** P & K
196 F4 **Keithock** Angus
212 E3 **Keithtown** Highld
122 D2 **Kelbrook** Lancs
103 G4 **Kelby** Lincs
139 K6 **Keld** N York
124 F3 **Kelfield** N York
102 C2 **Kelham** Notts
147 K2 **Kelhead** D & G
120 E5 **Kellamergh** Lancs
187 G1 **Kellas** Angus
214 E4 **Kellas** Moray
7 J7 **Kellaton** Devon
106 C4 **Kelling** Norfk
124 E5 **Kellington** N York
151 J7 **Kelloe** Dur
164 E6 **Kelloholm** D & G
9 K8 **Kelly** Devon
87 K7 **Kelmarsh** Nhants
56 E7 **Kelmscott** Oxon
79 H2 **Kelsale** Suffk
112 D7 **Kelsall** Ches W
75 K7 **Kelshall** Herts
147 L5 **Kelsick** Cumb
167 L3 **Kelso** Border
115 G8 **Kelstedge** Derbys
118 C4 **Kelstern** Lincs
39 G6 **Kelston** BaNES
194 B6 **Keltneyburn** P & K
155 H7 **Kelton** D & G
186 B8 **Kelty** Fife
61 K4 **Kelvedon** Essex
60 F7 **Kelvedon Hatch** Essex
2 C5 **Kelynack** Cnwll
187 G4 **Kemback** Fife
84 D3 **Kemberton** Shrops
39 M2 **Kemble** Gloucs
71 G6 **Kemerton** Worcs
53 M6 **Kemeys Commander** Mons
206 E3 **Kemnay** Abers
54 F3 **Kempley** Gloucs
55 G3 **Kempley Green** Gloucs
70 F5 **Kempsey** Worcs
40 D2 **Kempsford** Gloucs
29 L2 **Kempshott** Hants
74 F5 **Kempston** Bed
83 G6 **Kempton** Shrops
19 J5 **Kemp Town** Br & H
32 F2 **Kemsing** Kent
34 C7 **Kenardington** Kent
69 J6 **Kenchester** Herefs
56 E6 **Kencot** Oxon
129 L2 **Kendal** Cumb
36 C4 **Kenfig** Brdgnd
72 C1 **Kenilworth** Warwks
32 B2 **Kenley** Gt Lon
83 L4 **Kenley** Shrops
210 B3 **Kenmore** Highld
194 B7 **Kenmore** P & K
11 L7 **Kenn** Devon
38 B6 **Kenn** N Som
172 D5 **Kennacraig** Ag & B
11 J4 **Kennerleigh** Devon
111 L2 **Kennessee Green** Sefton
176 C1 **Kennet** Clacks
215 L8 **Kennethmont** Abers
77 G2 **Kennett** Cambs
11 L7 **Kennford** Devon
92 C6 **Kenninghall** Norfk
34 D5 **Kennington** Kent
57 K7 **Kennington** Oxon
186 F6 **Kennoway** Fife
25 L7 **Kenny** Somset
90 F7 **Kennyhill** Suffk
134 C6 **Kennythorpe** N York
188 C6 **Kenovay** Ag & B
208 F4 **Kensaleyre** Highld
44 E4 **Kensington** Gt Lon
59 G4 **Kensworth Common** C Beds
191 K5 **Kentallen** Highld
33 G5 **Kent and Sussex Crematorium** Kent
54 B3 **Kentchurch** Herefs
77 G2 **Kentford** Suffk
35 J2 *Kent International Airport* Kent
12 D2 **Kentisbeare** Devon
23 K3 **Kentisbury** Devon
44 F3 **Kentish Town** Gt Lon
138 C6 **Kentmere** Cumb
12 B5 **Kenton** Devon
44 D3 **Kenton** Gt Lon
150 F2 **Kenton** N u Ty
78 E2 **Kenton** Suffk
190 D3 **Kentra** Highld
55 H4 **Kent's Green** Gloucs
28 F6 **Kent's Oak** Hants
4 C6 **Kenwyn** Cnwll
228 F3 **Keoldale** Highld
200 D1 **Keppoch** Highld
133 G2 **Kepwick** N York
86 D6 **Keresley** Covtry
182 B2 **Kerrera** Ag & B
2 D5 **Kerris** Cnwll
82 D5 **Kerry** Powys
173 J6 **Kerrycroy** Ag & B
116 B8 **Kersall** Notts
12 D5 **Kersbrook** Devon
78 B5 **Kersey** Suffk
232 f3 **Kershader** W Isls
12 D2 **Kerswell** Devon
70 F5 **Kerswell Green** Worcs
78 F5 **Kesgrave** Suffk
93 L6 **Kessingland** Suffk
4 F6 **Kestle** Cnwll
4 D4 **Kestle Mill** Cnwll
45 H7 **Keston** Gt Lon
137 J3 **Keswick** Cumb
92 E3 **Keswick** Norfk
88 C7 **Kettering** Nhants
88 C7 **Kettering Crematorium** Nhants
92 E3 **Ketteringham** Norfk
195 K8 **Kettins** P & K
77 L4 **Kettlebaston** Suffk
186 E6 **Kettlebridge** Fife
86 B3 **Kettlebrook** Staffs
78 F3 **Kettleburgh** Suffk
155 K6 **Kettleholm** D & G
113 M5 **Kettleshulme** Ches E
132 C7 **Kettlesing** N York
132 C7 **Kettlesing Bottom** N York
106 A6 **Kettlestone** Norfk
116 D6 **Kettlethorpe** Lincs
234 d4 **Kettletoft** Ork
131 H5 **Kettlewell** N York
88 E3 **Ketton** Rutlnd
44 D5 **Kew** Gt Lon
37 M7 **Kewstoke** N Som
125 G1 **Kexby** C York

116 E4 **Kexby** Lincs
113 K8 **Key Green** Ches E
87 J3 **Keyham** Leics
16 C4 **Keyhaven** Hants
127 G5 **Keyingham** E R Yk
19 J3 **Keymer** W Susx
38 F6 **Keynsham** BaNES
74 F3 **Keysoe** Bed
74 F3 **Keysoe Row** Bed
88 F7 **Keyston** Cambs
101 L6 **Keyworth** Notts
151 G4 **Kibblesworth** Gatesd
87 K5 **Kibworth Beauchamp** Leics
87 K5 **Kibworth Harcourt** Leics
45 H5 **Kidbrooke** Gt Lon
84 E7 **Kidderminster** Worcs
57 J5 **Kidlington** Oxon
42 B5 **Kidmore End** Oxon
145 J7 **Kidsdale** D & G
99 J2 **Kidsgrove** Staffs
50 E4 **Kidwelly** Carmth
191 H8 **Kiel Crofts** Ag & B
157 G4 **Kielder** Nthumb
171 H5 **Kiells** Ag & B
174 D5 **Kilbarchan** Rens
199 K4 **Kilbeg** Highld
172 C5 **Kilberry** Ag & B
174 C7 **Kilbirnie** N Ayrs
172 C3 **Kilbride** Ag & B
173 H5 **Kilbride** Ag & B
214 D3 **Kilbuiack** Moray
101 G4 **Kilburn** Derbys
44 E4 **Kilburn** Gt Lon
133 H4 **Kilburn** N York
87 J4 **Kilby** Leics
172 D6 **Kilchamaig** Ag & B
173 J7 **Kilchattan** Ag & B
180 E7 **Kilchattan** Ag & B
191 G8 **Kilcheran** Ag & B
189 L4 **Kilchoan** Highld
170 D5 **Kilchoman** Ag & B
182 E3 **Kilchrenan** Ag & B
187 H6 **Kilconquhar** Fife
55 G3 **Kilcot** Gloucs
212 E4 **Kilcoy** Highld
173 L3 **Kilcreggan** Ag & B
142 D5 **Kildale** N York
161 J5 **Kildalloig** Ag & B
223 G6 **Kildary** Highld
173 G5 **Kildavaig** Ag & B
173 H5 **Kildavanan** Ag & B
227 G4 **Kildonan** Highld
162 D5 **Kildonan** N Ayrs
226 F4 **Kildonan Lodge** Highld
199 G7 **Kildonnan** Highld
144 C4 **Kildrochet House** D & G
205 K2 **Kildrummy** Abers
122 F2 **Kildwick** N York
172 F3 **Kilfinan** Ag & B
201 K6 **Kilfinnan** Highld
49 J6 **Kilgetty** Pembks
152 F2 **Kilgrammie** S Ayrs
38 C2 **Kilgwrrwg Common** Mons
135 G6 **Kilham** E R Yk
188 B7 **Kilkenneth** Ag & B
161 H4 **Kilkenzie** Ag & B
161 J5 **Kilkerran** Ag & B
9 H3 **Kilkhampton** Cnwll
115 J5 **Killamarsh** Derbys
51 H6 **Killay** Swans
174 F2 **Killearn** Stirlg
213 G3 **Killen** Highld
140 F3 **Killerby** Darltn
12 C3 **Killerton** Devon
193 J5 **Killichonan** P & K
192 D1 **Killiechonate** Highld
190 B7 **Killiechronan** Ag & B
194 E4 **Killiecrankie** P & K
210 E7 **Killilan** Highld
231 K4 **Killimster** Highld
184 C2 **Killin** Stirlg
132 D7 **Killinghall** N York
130 C2 **Killington** Cumb
130 B2 **Killington Lake Services** Cumb
159 G7 **Killingworth** N Tyne
167 G1 **Killochyett** Border
174 C4 **Kilmacolm** Inver
184 D5 **Kilmahog** Stirlg
182 A8 **Kilmahumaig** Ag & B
218 C6 **Kilmaluag** Highld
186 F3 **Kilmany** Fife
163 K2 **Kilmarnock** E Ayrs
182 B7 **Kilmartin** Ag & B
163 K2 **Kilmaurs** E Ayrs
182 B5 **Kilmelford** Ag & B
27 G2 **Kilmersdon** Somset
29 L6 **Kilmeston** Hants
161 H5 **Kilmichael** Ag & B
182 B8 **Kilmichael Glassary** Ag & B
172 D2 **Kilmichael of Inverlussa** Ag & B
13 H3 **Kilmington** Devon
27 H4 **Kilmington** Wilts
27 H4 **Kilmington Common** Wilts
27 H4 **Kilmington Street** Wilts
212 D5 **Kilmorack** Highld
182 C3 **Kilmore** Ag & B
199 K4 **Kilmore** Highld
172 C4 **Kilmory** Ag & B
190 B3 **Kilmory** Highld
162 B5 **Kilmory** N Ayrs
208 D5 **Kilmuir** Highld
213 G4 **Kilmuir** Highld
218 B7 **Kilmuir** Highld
223 G6 **Kilmuir** Highld
173 K3 **Kilmun** Ag & B
170 F4 **Kilnave** Ag & B
176 B8 **Kilncadzow** S Lans
33 J6 **Kilndown** Kent
182 B3 **Kilninver** Ag & B
127 J7 **Kilnsea** E R Yk
131 H6 **Kilnsey** N York
126 C1 **Kilnwick** E R Yk
180 E7 **Kiloran** Ag & B
162 A4 **Kilpatrick** N Ayrs
54 C3 **Kilpeck** Herefs
125 J5 **Kilpin** E R Yk
187 J6 **Kilrenny** Fife
73 H1 **Kilsby** Nhants
186 C3 **Kilspindie** P & K
144 D7 **Kilstay** D & G
175 J3 **Kilsyth** N Lans
212 D6 **Kiltarlity** Highld
142 E4 **Kilton** R & Cl
142 E4 **Kilton Thorpe** R & Cl
218 B7 **Kilvaxter** Highld
25 H3 **Kilve** Somset
102 D4 **Kilvington** Notts
163 H2 **Kilwinning** N Ayrs
92 C3 **Kimberley** Norfk
101 J4 **Kimberley** Notts
115 H3 **Kimberworth** Rothm
151 G5 **Kimblesworth** Dur
75 G2 **Kimbolton** Cambs
69 K3 **Kimbolton** Herefs
87 H6 **Kimcote** Leics
15 H6 **Kimmeridge** Dorset
28 F3 **Kimpton** Hants
59 K4 **Kimpton** Herts
226 F3 **Kinbrace** Highld
185 G6 **Kinbuck** Stirlg
187 G4 **Kincaple** Fife
176 C2 **Kincardine** Fife
222 E4 **Kincardine** Highld
206 B5 **Kincardine O'Neil** Abers
195 J8 **Kinclaven** P & K
207 H5 **Kincorth** C Aber
214 C3 **Kincorth House** Moray
203 K4 **Kincraig** Highld
194 F6 **Kincraigie** P & K
194 F6 **Kindallachan** P & K
172 B7 **Kinerarach** Ag & B
56 C3 **Kineton** Gloucs
72 D4 **Kineton** Warwks
186 C3 **Kinfauns** P & K
173 J6 **Kingarth** Ag & B
81 G3 **King Arthur's Labyrinth** Gwynd
207 G5 **Kingcausie** Abers
54 B6 **Kingcoed** Mons
117 H3 **Kingerby** Lincs
56 E3 **Kingham** Oxon
155 G7 **Kingholm Quay** D & G
177 H2 **Kinghorn** Fife
186 D7 **Kinglassie** Fife
196 B5 **Kingoldrum** Angus
186 E2 **Kingoodie** P & K
6 C5 **Kingsand** Cnwll
187 K5 **Kingsbarns** Fife
7 H6 **Kingsbridge** Devon
24 F4 **Kingsbridge** Somset
85 K1 **King's Bromley** Staffs
208 F4 **Kingsburgh** Highld
44 D3 **Kingsbury** Gt Lon
86 B4 **Kingsbury** Warwks
26 B7 **Kingsbury Episcopi** Somset
54 E3 **King's Caple** Herefs
41 K8 **Kingsclere** Hants
88 E4 **King's Cliffe** Nhants
39 J2 **Kingscote** Gloucs
23 H7 **Kingscott** Devon
71 J3 **King's Coughton** Warwks
162 D4 **Kingscross** N Ayrs
26 D6 **Kingsdon** Somset
35 K5 **Kingsdown** Kent
40 D3 **Kingsdown** Swindn
39 J6 **Kingsdown** Wilts
40 D3 **Kingsdown Crematorium** Swindn
176 F1 **Kingseat** Fife
58 C6 **Kingsey** Bucks
31 K4 **Kingsfold** W Susx
206 F4 **Kingsford** C Aber
174 E8 **Kingsford** E Ayrs
35 K1 **Kingsgate** Kent
77 K3 **Kingshall Street** Suffk
85 J7 **King's Heath** Birm
33 H3 **Kings Hill** Kent
85 H4 **King's Hill** Wsall
192 D5 **Kings House Hotel** Highld
184 C4 **Kingshouse Hotel** Stirlg
7 K3 **Kingskerswell** Devon
186 E5 **Kingskettle** Fife
69 J3 **Kingsland** Herefs
108 C5 **Kingsland** IoA
59 H7 **Kings Langley** Herts
112 D6 **Kingsley** Ches W
30 C4 **Kingsley** Hants
100 A3 **Kingsley** Staffs
30 E5 **Kingsley Green** W Susx
73 L3 **Kingsley Park** Nhants
104 F8 **King's Lynn** Norfk
138 E3 **Kings Meaburn** Cumb
236 c3 **King's Mills** Guern
196 D6 **Kingsmuir** Angus
166 C2 **Kings Muir** Border
187 J5 **Kingsmuir** Fife
34 D6 **Kingsnorth** Kent
85 J7 **King's Norton** Birm
87 K4 **King's Norton** Leics
23 L7 **Kings Nympton** Devon
69 J4 **King's Pyon** Herefs
89 J7 **Kings Ripton** Cambs
29 G5 **King's Somborne** Hants
14 D1 **King's Stag** Dorset
55 J7 **King's Stanley** Gloucs
72 F7 **King's Sutton** Nhants
85 J4 **Kingstanding** Birm
7 K2 **Kingsteignton** Devon
54 D2 **Kingsthorne** Herefs
73 L2 **Kingsthorpe** Nhants
75 L4 **Kingston** Cambs
6 A2 **Kingston** Cnwll
6 F6 **Kingston** Devon
14 E1 **Kingston** Dorset
15 H6 **Kingston** Dorset
178 C3 **Kingston** E Loth
16 F6 **Kingston** IoW
35 G4 **Kingston** Kent
57 H7 **Kingston Bagpuize** Oxon
58 C7 **Kingston Blount** Oxon
27 J4 **Kingston Deverill** Wilts
69 H7 **Kingstone** Herefs
26 B8 **Kingstone** Somset
100 B6 **Kingstone** Staffs
40 F3 **Kingston Lisle** Oxon
19 K4 **Kingston near Lewes** E Susx
101 J6 **Kingston on Soar** Notts
215 H2 **Kingston on Spey** Moray
14 B4 **Kingston Russell** Dorset
25 K5 **Kingston St Mary** Somset
38 B6 **Kingston Seymour** N Som
126 D5 **Kingston upon Hull** C KuH
44 D6 **Kingston upon Thames** Gt Lon
44 D6 **Kingston upon Thames Crematorium** Gt Lon
59 K4 **King's Walden** Herts
7 K5 **Kingswear** Devon
207 G4 **Kingswells** C Aber
38 D5 **Kings Weston** Bristl
84 F5 **Kingswinford** Dudley
58 B4 **Kingswood** Bucks
39 H3 **Kingswood** Gloucs
38 F5 **Kingswood** S Glos
25 H4 **Kingswood** Somset
31 L1 **Kingswood** Surrey
71 L1 **Kingswood** Warwks
84 E3 **Kingswood Common** Staffs
29 J5 **Kings Worthy** Hants
117 J6 **Kingthorpe** Lincs
68 F3 **Kington** Herefs
38 F3 **Kington** S Glos
71 H4 **Kington** Worcs
39 L5 **Kington Langley** Wilts
27 H6 **Kington Magna** Dorset
39 K5 **Kington St Michael** Wilts
203 H5 **Kingussie** Highld
26 D5 **Kingweston** Somset
217 H7 **Kinharrachie** Abers
147 G2 **Kinharvie** D & G
185 J4 **Kinkell Bridge** P & K
217 J6 **Kinknockie** Abers
177 G5 **Kinleith** C Edin
84 C7 **Kinlet** Shrops
198 F5 **Kinloch** Highld
225 H2 **Kinloch** Highld
229 H5 **Kinloch** Highld
195 J7 **Kinloch** P & K
184 B6 **Kinlochard** Stirlg
228 C4 **Kinlochbervie** Highld
191 J1 **Kinlocheil** Highld
210 F3 **Kinlochewe** Highld
200 E4 **Kinloch Hourn** Highld
202 E7 **Kinlochlaggan** Highld
192 C4 **Kinlochleven** Highld
190 E2 **Kinlochmoidart** Highld
200 B8 **Kinlochnanuagh** Highld
193 L5 **Kinloch Rannoch** P & K

214 C3 **Kinloss** Moray
110 D5 **Kinmel Bay** Conwy
206 F2 **Kinmuck** Abers
207 G2 **Kinmundy** Abers
160 B2 **Kinnabus** Ag & B
217 H5 **Kinnadie** Abers
194 F5 **Kinnaird** P & K
197 K2 **Kinneff** Abers
155 H2 **Kinnelhead** D & G
196 F6 **Kinnell** Angus
97 M7 **Kinnerley** Shrops
69 G5 **Kinnersley** Herefs
70 F5 **Kinnersley** Worcs
68 E2 **Kinnerton** Powys
186 C6 **Kinnesswood** P & K
196 B5 **Kinnordy** Angus
102 B6 **Kinoulton** Notts
186 B6 **Kinross** P & K
186 C2 **Kinrossie** P & K
186 B6 **Kinross Services** P & K
69 G2 **Kinsham** Herefs
71 G7 **Kinsham** Worcs
124 C7 **Kinsley** Wakefd
15 K3 **Kinson** Bmouth
200 F2 **Kintail** Highld
41 G6 **Kintbury** W Berk
214 B3 **Kintessack** Moray
186 B4 **Kintillo** P & K
83 H8 **Kinton** Herefs
98 A8 **Kinton** Shrops
206 E3 **Kintore** Abers
171 H7 **Kintour** Ag & B
170 F8 **Kintra** Ag & B
180 D3 **Kintra** Ag & B
182 B6 **Kintraw** Ag & B
161 J2 **Kintyre** Ag & B
203 L2 **Kinveachy** Highld
84 E6 **Kinver** Staffs
124 C4 **Kippax** Leeds
184 E7 **Kippen** Stirlg
146 E4 **Kippford or Scaur** D & G
33 H5 **Kipping's Cross** Kent
234 b6 **Kirbister** Ork
93 G3 **Kirby Bedon** Norfk
102 B8 **Kirby Bellars** Leics
93 H5 **Kirby Cane** Norfk
62 E4 **Kirby Cross** Essex
87 G3 **Kirby Fields** Leics
134 D6 **Kirby Grindalythe** N York
132 F5 **Kirby Hill** N York
140 E6 **Kirby Hill** N York
133 G3 **Kirby Knowle** N York
62 F4 **Kirby le Soken** Essex
134 B4 **Kirby Misperton** N York
87 G3 **Kirby Muxloe** Leics
134 C7 **Kirby Underdale** E R Yk
132 E3 **Kirby Wiske** N York
31 G6 **Kirdford** W Susx
231 K4 **Kirk** Highld
235 d6 **Kirkabister** Shet
146 A5 **Kirkandrews** D & G
148 C4 **Kirkandrews upon Eden** Cumb
148 B4 **Kirkbampton** Cumb
147 G3 **Kirkbean** D & G
124 F7 **Kirk Bramwith** Donc
147 M4 **Kirkbride** Cumb
196 E7 **Kirkbuddo** Angus
166 D2 **Kirkburn** Border
134 F7 **Kirkburn** E R Yk
123 J7 **Kirkburton** Kirk
111 L2 **Kirkby** Knows
117 H3 **Kirkby** Lincs
142 C6 **Kirkby** N York
141 G7 **Kirkby Fleetham** N York
103 H2 **Kirkby Green** Lincs
101 J2 **Kirkby in Ashfield** Notts
128 F3 **Kirkby-in-Furness** Cumb
103 J4 **Kirkby la Thorpe** Lincs
130 B4 **Kirkby Lonsdale** Cumb
131 G7 **Kirkby Malham** N York
86 F4 **Kirkby Mallory** Leics
132 C5 **Kirkby Malzeard** N York
133 L3 **Kirkbymoorside** N York
118 C8 **Kirkby on Bain** Lincs
123 L2 **Kirkby Overblow** N York
139 H5 **Kirkby Stephen** Cumb
138 F3 **Kirkby Thore** Cumb
103 H6 **Kirkby Underwood** Lincs
124 D3 **Kirkby Wharf** N York
186 D8 **Kirkcaldy** Fife
186 D8 **Kirkcaldy Crematorium** Fife
148 F2 **Kirkcambeck** Cumb
146 B5 **Kirkchrist** D & G
144 B2 **Kirkcolm** D & G
164 E6 **Kirkconnel** D & G
147 G2 **Kirkconnell** D & G
145 G3 **Kirkcowan** D & G
146 B5 **Kirkcudbright** D & G
111 K3 **Kirkdale** Lpool
124 B1 **Kirk Deighton** N York
126 C5 **Kirk Ella** E R Yk
165 G2 **Kirkfieldbank** S Lans
146 F2 **Kirkgunzeon** D & G
101 J4 **Kirk Hallam** Derbys
120 F4 **Kirkham** Lancs
134 B6 **Kirkham** N York
123 K6 **Kirkhamgate** Wakefd
133 G7 **Kirk Hammerton** N York
149 H5 **Kirkhaugh** Nthumb
123 H6 **Kirkheaton** Kirk
158 C6 **Kirkheaton** Nthumb
212 E5 **Kirkhill** Highld
165 J7 **Kirkhope** S Lans
199 H2 **Kirkibost** Highld
195 L7 **Kirkinch** P & K
145 J5 **Kirkinner** D & G
175 H4 **Kirkintilloch** E Duns
100 E3 **Kirk Ireton** Derbys
136 E4 **Kirkland** Cumb
154 E4 **Kirkland** D & G
155 H4 **Kirkland** D & G
164 E6 **Kirkland** D & G
100 F5 **Kirk Langley** Derbys
142 D3 **Kirkleatham** R & Cl
141 K5 **Kirklevington** S on T
93 L5 **Kirkley** Suffk
132 D4 **Kirklington** N York
102 B2 **Kirklington** Notts
148 D2 **Kirklinton** Cumb
176 F4 **Kirkliston** C Edin
145 K4 **Kirkmabreck** D & G
144 D7 **Kirkmaiden** D & G
141 G2 **Kirk Merrington** Dur
237 c4 **Kirk Michael** IoM
195 H4 **Kirkmichael** P & K
163 J7 **Kirkmichael** S Ayrs
164 F2 **Kirkmuirhill** S Lans
168 D4 **Kirknewton** Nthumb
176 F5 **Kirknewton** W Loth
215 L7 **Kirkney** Abers
175 L5 **Kirk of Shotts** N Lans
148 F6 **Kirkoswald** Cumb
163 G7 **Kirkoswald** S Ayrs
154 F4 **Kirkpatrick** D & G
154 D7 **Kirkpatrick Durham** D & G
156 B7 **Kirkpatrick-Fleming** D & G
124 F8 **Kirk Sandall** Donc
128 D4 **Kirksanton** Cumb
124 D7 **Kirk Smeaton** N York
123 K4 **Kirkstall** Leeds
103 K1 **Kirkstead** Lincs
215 L7 **Kirkstile** Abers
156 C4 **Kirkstile** D & G
231 L2 **Kirkstyle** Highld
124 B6 **Kirkthorpe** Wakefd
206 C1 **Kirkton** Abers
155 G6 **Kirkton** D & G
186 F3 **Kirkton** Fife
210 C8 **Kirkton** Highld
210 D6 **Kirkton** Highld
185 K4 **Kirkton** P & K
166 C2 **Kirkton Manor** Border
195 L6 **Kirkton of Airlie** Angus
196 B8 **Kirkton of Auchterhouse** Angus
213 K5 **Kirkton of Barevan** Highld
186 C2 **Kirkton of Collace** P & K
205 J3 **Kirkton of Glenbuchat** Abers
217 J7 **Kirkton of Logie Buchan** Abers
196 E4 **Kirkton of Menmuir** Angus
196 E8 **Kirkton of Monikie** Angus
216 D7 **Kirkton of Rayne** Abers
206 F4 **Kirkton of Skene** Abers
186 F1 **Kirkton of Strathmartine** Angus
196 C8 **Kirkton of Tealing** Angus
206 C3 **Kirkton of Tough** Abers
217 J2 **Kirktown** Abers
217 K4 **Kirktown** Abers
216 D3 **Kirktown of Alvah** Abers
206 F1 **Kirktown of Bourtie** Abers
206 F7 **Kirktown of Fetteresso** Abers
215 H6 **Kirktown of Mortlach** Moray
217 K8 **Kirktown of Slains** Abers
165 M1 **Kirkurd** Border
234 c6 **Kirkwall** Ork
234 c6 *Kirkwall Airport* Ork
158 C5 **Kirkwhelpington** Nthumb
168 C4 **Kirk Yetholm** Border
126 D7 **Kirmington** N Linc
117 K3 **Kirmond le Mire** Lincs
173 K3 **Kirn** Ag & B
196 C5 **Kirriemuir** Angus
93 G4 **Kirstead Green** Norfk
155 M7 **Kirtlebridge** D & G
77 G3 **Kirtling** Cambs
76 F4 **Kirtling Green** Cambs
57 J4 **Kirtlington** Oxon
229 M3 **Kirtomy** Highld
104 A5 **Kirton** Lincs
116 B7 **Kirton** Notts
78 F6 **Kirton** Suffk
174 D4 **Kirtonhill** W Duns
116 F2 **Kirton in Lindsey** N Linc
145 J4 **Kirwaugh** D & G
210 C6 **Kishorn** Highld
73 K3 **Kislingbury** Nhants
25 G6 **Kittisford** Somset
207 H4 **Kittybrewster** C Aber
54 C2 **Kivernoll** Herefs
115 J5 **Kiveton Park** Rothm
116 D5 **Knaith** Lincs
27 J6 **Knap Corner** Dorset
42 F8 **Knaphill** Surrey
25 L6 **Knapp** Somset
124 E1 **Knapton** C York
134 D4 **Knapton** N York
107 G5 **Knapton** Norfk
75 K2 **Knapwell** Cambs
132 E7 **Knaresborough** N York
149 H4 **Knarsdale** Nthumb
217 G5 **Knaven** Abers
132 F2 **Knayton** N York
59 L4 **Knebworth** Herts
125 H5 **Knedlington** E R Yk
116 B8 **Kneesall** Notts
75 L5 **Kneesworth** Cambs
102 B4 **Kneeton** Notts
50 F7 **Knelston** Swans
99 L5 **Knenhall** Staffs
72 E4 **Knightcote** Warwks
99 J7 **Knightley** Staffs
87 H4 **Knighton** C Leic
14 C1 **Knighton** Dorset
82 F8 **Knighton** Powys
25 J3 **Knighton** Somset
99 G4 **Knighton** Staffs
99 H6 **Knighton** Staffs
70 B1 **Knighton on Teme** Worcs
70 D4 **Knightwick** Worcs
68 F3 **Knill** Herefs
102 D6 **Knipton** Leics
100 E3 **Kniveton** Derbys
138 F2 **Knock** Cumb
199 K4 **Knock** Highld
215 L4 **Knock** Moray
232 g2 **Knock** W Isls
227 K3 **Knockally** Highld
224 F6 **Knockan** Highld
214 F6 **Knockando** Moray
212 E5 **Knockbain** Highld
212 F3 **Knockbain** Highld
173 L5 **Knock Castle** N Ayrs
231 H4 **Knockdee** Highld
173 J4 **Knockdow** Ag & B
39 J3 **Knockdown** Wilts
153 G3 **Knockeen** S Ayrs
162 D4 **Knockenkelly** N Ayrs
163 K2 **Knockentiber** E Ayrs
32 E2 **Knockholt** Kent
32 E2 **Knockholt Pound** Kent
97 M7 **Knockin** Shrops
163 K2 **Knockinlaw** E Ayrs
144 B3 **Knocknain** D & G
171 K4 **Knockrome** Ag & B
237 b4 **Knocksharry** IoM
153 M5 **Knocksheen** D & G
154 D7 **Knockvennie Smithy** D & G
79 J3 **Knodishall** Suffk
79 J3 **Knodishall Common** Suffk
26 C6 **Knole** Somset
113 J5 **Knolls Green** Ches E
98 B5 **Knolton** Wrexhm
27 L3 **Knook** Wilts
88 B2 **Knossington** Leics
120 E2 **Knott End-on-Sea** Lancs
74 E2 **Knotting** Bed
74 E3 **Knotting Green** Bed
124 D5 **Knottingley** Wakefd
112 B3 **Knotty Ash** Lpool
83 L7 **Knowbury** Shrops
153 G7 **Knowe** D & G
154 A4 **Knowehead** D & G
163 G6 **Knoweside** S Ayrs
38 E6 **Knowle** Bristl
11 H5 **Knowle** Devon
12 C2 **Knowle** Devon
12 D6 **Knowle** Devon
23 H4 **Knowle** Devon
83 L8 **Knowle** Shrops
85 L7 **Knowle** Solhll
24 E3 **Knowle** Somset
148 D4 **Knowlefield** Cumb
121 J3 **Knowle Green** Lancs
13 J1 **Knowle St Giles** Somset

42 D4 **Knowl Hill** W & M
112 C3 **Knowsley** Knows
112 C3 **Knowsley Safari Park** Knows
24 C6 **Knowstone** Devon
33 K5 **Knox Bridge** Kent
82 F8 **Knucklas** Powys
74 D2 **Knuston** Nhants
113 H5 **Knutsford** Ches E
113 G6 **Knutsford Services** Ches E
122 F6 **Krumlin** Calder
3 J7 **Kuggar** Cnwll
200 B1 **Kyleakin** Highld
210 B8 **Kyle of Lochalsh** Highld
200 B2 **Kylerhea** Highld
224 F2 **Kylesku** Highld
200 C6 **Kylesmorar** Highld
232 e4 **Kyles Scalpay** W Isls
224 F2 **Kylestrome** Highld
84 C1 **Kynnersley** Wrekin
69 L2 **Kyrewood** Worcs

L

232 f3 **Lacasaigh** W Isls
232 f2 **Lacasdal** W Isls
117 K1 **Laceby** NE Lin
58 D7 **Lacey Green** Bucks
113 G6 **Lach Dennis** Ches W
77 H1 **Lackford** Suffk
77 H1 **Lackford Green** Suffk
39 K6 **Lacock** Wilts
72 E3 **Ladbroke** Warwks
33 J4 **Laddingford** Kent
4 D5 **Ladock** Cnwll
234 d4 **Lady** Ork
186 E5 **Ladybank** Fife
165 H4 **Ladygill** S Lans
128 E3 **Lady Hall** Cumb
179 J8 **Ladykirk** Border
85 J6 **Ladywood** Birm
70 F3 **Ladywood** Worcs
236 e1 **La Fontenelle** Guern
154 F5 **Lag** D & G
190 D4 **Laga** Highld
160 C1 **Lagavulin** Ag & B
162 B5 **Lagg** N Ayrs
201 L6 **Laggan** Highld
202 F6 **Laggan** Highld
203 K5 **Lagganlia** Highld
236 b5 **La Greve de Lecq** Jersey
228 F4 **Laid** Highld
219 L3 **Laide** Highld
199 G7 **Laig** Highld
174 E8 **Laigh Clunch** E Ayrs
163 L2 **Laigh Fenwick** E Ayrs
164 C5 **Laigh Glenmuir** E Ayrs
175 J7 **Laighstonehall** S Lans
46 B3 **Laindon** Essex
225 M7 **Lairg** Highld
123 J4 **Laisterdyke** C Brad
17 H5 **Lake** IoW
15 J4 **Lake** Poole
28 C4 **Lake** Wilts
137 H5 **Lake District National Park** Cumb
91 G6 **Lakenheath** Suffk
90 D4 **Lakesend** Norfk
36 D4 **Laleston** Brdgnd
77 K7 **Lamarsh** Essex
106 F7 **Lamas** Norfk
167 L2 **Lambden** Border
33 H6 **Lamberhurst** Kent
33 H6 **Lamberhurst Down** Kent
179 K6 **Lamberton** Border
44 F4 **Lambeth** Gt Lon
44 F5 **Lambeth Crematorium** Gt Lon
77 G4 **Lambfair Green** Suffk
101 M4 **Lambley** Notts
149 H4 **Lambley** Nthumb
40 F5 **Lambourn** W Berk
45 J2 **Lambourne End** Essex
31 L4 **Lambs Green** W Susx
6 C1 **Lamerton** Devon
151 G4 **Lamesley** Gatesd
165 J3 **Lamington** S Lans
162 C3 **Lamlash** N Ayrs
148 D7 **Lamonby** Cumb
2 E6 **Lamorna** Cnwll
4 D7 **Lamorran** Cnwll
66 D5 **Lampeter** Cerdgn
49 K5 **Lampeter Velfrey** Pembks
49 H7 **Lamphey** Pembks
136 F3 **Lamplugh** Cumb
87 L8 **Lamport** Nhants
26 F4 **Lamyatt** Somset
165 G2 **Lanark** S Lans
129 K7 **Lancaster** Lancs
129 K6 **Lancaster & Morecambe Crematorium** Lancs
121 G1 **Lancaster Services (Forton)** Lancs
150 F5 **Lanchester** Dur
19 G5 **Lancing** W Susx
236 d1 **L'Ancresse** Guern
76 C2 **Landbeach** Cambs
23 G6 **Landcross** Devon
206 E4 **Landerberry** Abers
28 E7 **Landford** Wilts
227 L2 **Land-hallow** Highld
111 J4 **Landican Crematorium** Wirral
50 F6 **Landimore** Swans
23 J5 **Landkey** Devon
51 J6 **Landore** Swans
6 B4 **Landrake** Cnwll
2 C6 **Land's End** Cnwll
2 C5 *Land's End Airport* Cnwll
6 C4 **Landulph** Cnwll
4 C4 **Lane** Cnwll
9 G7 **Laneast** Cnwll
42 D3 **Lane End** Bucks
27 J3 **Lane End** Wilts
100 E5 **Lane Ends** Derbys
116 D6 **Laneham** Notts
140 E5 **Lane Head** Dur
149 L6 **Lanehead** Dur
25 K6 **Langaller** Somset
102 B5 **Langar** Notts
174 D4 **Langbank** Rens
123 G1 **Langbar** N York
130 F6 **Langcliffe** N York
134 E2 **Langdale End** N York
16 E2 **Langdown** Hants
186 E6 **Langdyke** Fife
62 B4 **Langenhoe** Essex
75 H6 **Langford** C Beds
12 D2 **Langford** Devon
61 K6 **Langford** Essex
102 D2 **Langford** Notts
56 E7 **Langford** Oxon
25 H6 **Langford Budville** Somset
62 B2 **Langham** Essex
106 B4 **Langham** Norfk
88 B2 **Langham** Rutlnd
77 L1 **Langham** Suffk
121 K4 **Langho** Lancs
156 C5 **Langholm** D & G
167 H3 **Langlee** Border
16 F3 **Langley** Hants
59 K4 **Langley** Herts
33 K3 **Langley** Kent
149 L3 **Langley** Nthumb
43 G5 **Langley** Slough
25 G5 **Langley** Somset
30 D5 **Langley** W Susx
71 L3 **Langley** Warwks
39 L5 **Langley Burrell** Wilts
61 L4 **Langley Green** Essex
25 G5 **Langley Marsh** Somset
150 F6 **Langley Park** Dur
93 H3 **Langley Street** Norfk
76 C7 **Langley Upper Green** Essex
20 D5 **Langney** E Susx
115 L4 **Langold** Notts
9 J7 **Langore** Cnwll
26 B6 **Langport** Somset
103 L3 **Langrick** Lincs
39 H6 **Langridge** BaNES
147 K5 **Langrigg** Cumb
30 B6 **Langrish** Hants
114 E2 **Langsett** Barns
185 G5 **Langside** P & K
17 K2 **Langstone** Hants
132 C2 **Langthorne** N York
132 F6 **Langthorpe** N York
140 C6 **Langthwaite** N York
134 F6 **Langtoft** E R Yk
89 G2 **Langtoft** Lincs
140 F4 **Langton** Dur
118 C7 **Langton** Lincs
118 E7 **Langton** Lincs
134 C6 **Langton** N York
117 J6 **Langton by Wragby** Lincs
32 F5 **Langton Green** Kent
14 C6 **Langton Herring** Dorset
15 J6 **Langton Matravers** Dorset
10 C2 **Langtree** Devon
148 F7 **Langwathby** Cumb
227 K4 **Langwell House** Highld
115 K7 **Langwith** Derbys
115 K7 **Langwith Junction** Derbys
117 H6 **Langworth** Lincs
5 H3 **Lanhydrock House & Gardens** Cnwll
5 G3 **Lanivet** Cnwll
5 G4 **Lanlivery** Cnwll
3 J4 **Lanner** Cnwll
5 J4 **Lanreath** Cnwll
5 J5 **Lansallos** Cnwll
8 E7 **Lanteglos** Cnwll
5 J5 **Lanteglos Highway** Cnwll
167 J5 **Lanton** Border
168 D3 **Lanton** Nthumb
11 H3 **Lapford** Devon
160 C1 **Laphroaig** Ag & B
84 F2 **Lapley** Staffs
71 L1 **Lapworth** Warwks
190 E6 **Larachbeg** Highld
176 B3 **Larbert** Falk
216 B7 **Largie** Abers
172 F2 **Largiemore** Ag & B
187 H5 **Largoward** Fife
173 L6 **Largs** N Ayrs
162 D5 **Largybeg** N Ayrs
162 D4 **Largymore** N Ayrs
173 L4 **Larkfield** Inver
33 J2 **Larkfield** Kent
175 K7 **Larkhall** S Lans
28 C3 **Larkhill** Wilts
92 B5 **Larling** Norfk
236 e8 **La Rocque** Jersey
140 C4 **Lartington** Dur
30 A3 **Lasham** Hants
177 J5 **Lasswade** Mdloth
133 L2 **Lastingham** N York
61 L7 **Latchingdon** Essex
6 B2 **Latchley** Cnwll
74 C5 **Lathbury** M Keyn
227 L2 **Latheron** Highld
227 L3 **Latheronwheel** Highld
187 H5 **Lathones** Fife
59 G7 **Latimer** Bucks
38 F4 **Latteridge** S Glos
27 G6 **Lattiford** Somset
40 C2 **Latton** Wilts
178 C8 **Lauder** Border
50 C4 **Laugharne** Carmth
116 D6 **Laughterton** Lincs
20 A3 **Laughton** E Susx
87 J5 **Laughton** Leics
103 H6 **Laughton** Lincs
116 D3 **Laughton** Lincs
115 K4 **Laughton-en-le-Morthen** Rothm
9 H4 **Launcells** Cnwll
9 J7 **Launceston** Cnwll
57 L4 **Launton** Oxon
197 H3 **Laurencekirk** Abers
146 B3 **Laurieston** D & G
176 B3 **Laurieston** Falk
74 D4 **Lavendon** M Keyn
77 K5 **Lavenham** Suffk
37 J6 **Lavernock** V Glam
148 E3 **Laversdale** Cumb
28 D5 **Laverstock** Wilts
29 J2 **Laverstoke** Hants
71 J7 **Laverton** Gloucs
132 C5 **Laverton** N York
27 H2 **Laverton** Somset
236 d4 **La Villette** Guern
98 A2 **Lavister** Wrexhm
175 L7 **Law** S Lans
193 L7 **Lawers** P & K
62 C2 **Lawford** Essex
25 H4 **Lawford** Somset
175 L7 **Law Hill** S Lans
9 J7 **Lawhitton** Cnwll
130 E6 **Lawkland** N York
123 K3 **Lawns Wood Crematorium** Leeds
49 H6 **Lawrenny** Pembks
77 K4 **Lawshall** Suffk
232 f3 **Laxay** W Isls
232 f2 **Laxdale** W Isls
237 d4 **Laxey** IoM
93 G8 **Laxfield** Suffk
228 C6 **Laxford Bridge** Highld
235 d4 **Laxo** Shet
125 J5 **Laxton** E R Yk
88 D4 **Laxton** Nhants
116 B7 **Laxton** Notts
122 F3 **Laycock** C Brad
61 M4 **Layer Breton** Essex
62 A4 **Layer-de-la-Haye** Essex
61 L4 **Layer Marney** Essex
78 B6 **Layham** Suffk
13 K2 **Laymore** Dorset
125 H3 **Laytham** E R Yk
148 F6 **Lazonby** Cumb
101 G2 **Lea** Derbys
54 F4 **Lea** Herefs
116 D4 **Lea** Lincs
83 G5 **Lea** Shrops
39 L3 **Lea** Wilts
212 F5 **Leachkin** Highld
177 H7 **Leadburn** Border
102 F3 **Leadenham** Lincs
60 F5 **Leaden Roding** Essex
150 E5 **Leadgate** Dur
165 G6 **Leadhills** S Lans
56 F5 **Leafield** Oxon
59 H4 **Leagrave** Luton
104 C3 **Leake Common Side** Lincs
142 F5 **Lealholm** N York
209 H3 **Lealt** Highld
86 B5 **Lea Marston** Warwks
72 F2 **Leamington Hastings** Warwks
72 D2 **Leamington Spa** Warwks
20 C4 **Leap Cross** E Susx
129 K3 **Leasgill** Cumb
103 H3 **Leasingham** Lincs
141 G2 **Leasingthorne** Dur
31 K1 **Leatherhead** Surrey
123 J2 **Leathley** N York
98 C8 **Leaton** Shrops
34 D4 **Leaveland** Kent

77 L6 **Leavenheath** Suffk
134 C6 **Leavening** N York
45 H7 **Leaves Green** Gt Lon
135 G3 **Lebberston** N York
236 c4 **Le Bourg** Guern
56 E7 **Lechlade on Thames** Gloucs
170 E5 **Lecht Gruinart** Ag & B
130 C4 **Leck** Lancs
193 L7 **Leckbuie** P & K
29 G4 **Leckford** Hants
73 K6 **Leckhampstead** Bucks
41 H5 **Leckhampstead** W Berk
41 H5 **Leckhampstead Thicket** W Berk
55 L4 **Leckhampton** Gloucs
220 F4 **Leckmelm** Highld
126 C2 **Leconfield** E R Yk
191 H8 **Ledaig** Ag & B
58 E4 **Ledburn** Bucks
70 C6 **Ledbury** Herefs
69 H4 **Ledgemoor** Herefs
224 F6 **Ledmore Junction** Highld
124 C4 **Ledsham** Leeds
124 C5 **Ledston** Leeds
57 H3 **Ledwell** Oxon
23 H3 **Lee** Devon
45 H5 **Lee** Gt Lon
83 J4 **Leebotwood** Shrops
98 D6 **Lee Brockhurst** Shrops
128 F5 **Leece** Cumb
46 B3 **Lee Chapel** Essex
58 E6 **Lee Clump** Bucks
33 L3 **Leeds** Kent
123 K4 **Leeds** Leeds
123 J3 *Leeds Bradford Airport* Leeds
33 L3 **Leeds Castle** Kent
3 G4 **Leedstown** Cnwll
99 M2 **Leek** Staffs
72 C2 **Leek Wootton** Warwks
6 E5 **Lee Mill** Devon
132 D2 **Leeming** N York
132 D2 **Leeming Bar** N York
17 G3 **Lee-on-the-Solent** Hants
100 E5 **Lees** Derbys
113 L2 **Lees** Oldham
100 E5 **Lees Green** Derbys
87 L2 **Leesthorpe** Leics
97 K1 **Leeswood** Flints
186 C3 **Leetown** P & K
112 F6 **Leftwich** Ches W
118 E5 **Legbourne** Lincs
167 J2 **Legerwood** Border
42 F5 **Legoland** W & M
117 J4 **Legsby** Lincs
87 H3 **Leicester** C Leic
87 G3 **Leicester Forest East** Leics
87 G3 **Leicester Forest East Services** Leics
14 C2 **Leigh** Dorset
55 K3 **Leigh** Gloucs
32 F4 **Leigh** Kent
31 L3 **Leigh** Surrey
112 F2 **Leigh** Wigan
40 B3 **Leigh** Wilts
70 D4 **Leigh** Worcs
46 D4 **Leigh Beck** Essex
39 K5 **Leigh Delamere** Wilts
39 K5 **Leigh Delamere Services** Wilts
34 B7 **Leigh Green** Kent
175 H7 **Leigh Knoweglass** S Lans
46 D3 **Leigh-on-Sea** Sthend
15 J3 **Leigh Park** Dorset
70 D4 **Leigh Sinton** Worcs
85 J3 **Leighswood** Wsall
39 J3 **Leighterton** Gloucs
82 E3 **Leighton** Powys
84 B3 **Leighton** Shrops
89 G7 **Leighton Bromswold** Cambs
58 F3 **Leighton Buzzard** C Beds
27 G3 **Leigh upon Mendip** Somset
38 E6 **Leigh Woods** N Som
69 J2 **Leinthall Earls** Herefs
69 J1 **Leinthall Starkes** Herefs
83 H8 **Leintwardine** Herefs
87 G5 **Leire** Leics
79 J3 **Leiston** Suffk
177 H3 **Leith** C Edin
168 B1 **Leitholm** Border
2 F4 **Lelant** Cnwll
126 F4 **Lelley** E R Yk
168 B3 **Lempitlaw** Border
232 f3 **Lemreway** W Isls
59 L5 **Lemsford** Herts
71 J5 **Lenchwick** Worcs
152 D4 **Lendalfoot** S Ayrs
184 C6 **Lendrick** Stirlg
217 L6 **Lendrum Terrace** Abers
34 B4 **Lenham** Kent
34 B5 **Lenham Heath** Kent
202 D1 **Lenie** Highld
168 C2 **Lennel** Border
146 A5 **Lennox Plunton** D & G
175 H3 **Lennoxtown** E Duns
101 K5 **Lenton** C Nott
103 G6 **Lenton** Lincs
106 D8 **Lenwade** Norfk
175 H4 **Lenzie** E Duns
205 L4 **Leochel-Cushnie** Abers
69 K3 **Leominster** Herefs
55 J7 **Leonard Stanley** Gloucs
208 B4 **Lephin** Highld
134 B7 **Leppington** N York
123 J7 **Lepton** Kirk
182 B3 **Lerags** Ag & B
236 b3 **L'Eree** Guern
5 J4 **Lerryn** Cnwll
235 d6 **Lerwick** Shet
169 J6 **Lesbury** Nthumb
206 B1 **Leslie** Abers
186 D6 **Leslie** Fife
164 F2 **Lesmahagow** S Lans
8 F6 **Lesnewth** Cnwll
236 d2 **Les Quartiers** Guern
236 b7 **Les Quennevais** Jersey
107 H6 **Lessingham** Norfk
147 L5 **Lessonhall** Cumb
144 B3 **Leswalt** D & G
236 a6 **L'Etacq** Jersey
43 J2 **Letchmore Heath** Herts
59 L2 **Letchworth Garden City** Herts
41 G4 **Letcombe Bassett** Oxon
41 G3 **Letcombe Regis** Oxon
196 E6 **Letham** Angus
167 K7 **Letham** Border
176 B2 **Letham** Falk
186 E4 **Letham** Fife
197 G7 **Letham Grange** Angus
195 H7 **Lethendy** P & K
206 B2 **Lethenty** Abers
216 F6 **Lethenty** Abers
78 F3 **Letheringham** Suffk
106 C5 **Letheringsett** Norfk
219 L7 **Letterewe** Highld
200 D2 **Letterfearn** Highld
201 K6 **Letterfinlay Lodge Hotel** Highld
199 M7 **Lettermorar** Highld
220 F4 **Letters** Highld
165 H5 **Lettershaw** S Lans
48 F2 **Letterston** Pembks
204 C2 **Lettoch** Highld
214 D7 **Lettoch** Highld
69 G5 **Letton** Herefs
59 M5 **Letty Green** Herts
115 K4 **Letwell** Rothm
187 G3 **Leuchars** Fife
232 f3 **Leumrabhagh** W Isls
232 f3 **Leurbost** W Isls
84 F1 **Levedale** Staffs
126 D2 **Leven** E R Yk
186 F7 **Leven** Fife
129 K3 **Levens** Cumb
60 B4 **Levens Green** Herts
113 K3 **Levenshulme** Manch
235 c7 **Levenwick** Shet
232 d5 **Leverburgh** W Isls
90 C2 **Leverington** Cambs
59 H6 **Leverstock Green** Herts
104 C3 **Leverton** Lincs
236 c2 **Le Villocq** Guern
78 F6 **Levington** Suffk
134 C2 **Levisham** N York
56 F6 **Lew** Oxon
9 H8 **Lewannick** Cnwll
10 C7 **Lewdown** Devon
19 L4 **Lewes** E Susx
48 F3 **Leweston** Pembks
45 G5 **Lewisham** Gt Lon
45 H5 **Lewisham Crematorium** Gt Lon
212 D8 **Lewiston** Highld
36 E3 **Lewistown** Brdgnd
42 B2 **Lewknor** Oxon
34 C3 **Lewson Street** Kent
10 C7 **Lewtrenchard** Devon
62 A3 **Lexden** Essex
25 K4 **Lexworthy** Somset
33 H2 **Leybourne** Kent
131 L2 **Leyburn** N York
59 K3 **Leygreen** Herts
59 G7 **Ley Hill** Bucks
121 H6 **Leyland** Lancs
206 E3 **Leylodge** Abers
217 J4 **Leys** Abers
195 K8 **Leys** P & K
47 G6 **Leysdown-on-Sea** Kent
196 F6 **Leysmill** Angus
196 C6 **Leys of Cossans** Angus
69 L2 **Leysters** Herefs
45 G3 **Leyton** Gt Lon
45 H3 **Leytonstone** Gt Lon
5 M1 **Lezant** Cnwll
215 G3 **Lhanbryde** Moray
52 F3 **Libanus** Powys
165 J2 **Libberton** S Lans
177 J4 **Liberton** C Edin
85 K2 **Lichfield** Staffs
85 H7 **Lickey** Worcs
85 H8 **Lickey End** Worcs
30 F6 **Lickfold** W Susx
190 F4 **Liddesdale** Highld
40 E4 **Liddington** Swindn
77 G3 **Lidgate** Suffk
74 E6 **Lidlington** C Beds
186 E2 **Liff** Angus
85 J7 **Lifford** Birm
9 K7 **Lifton** Devon
9 K7 **Liftondown** Devon
72 D4 **Lighthorne** Warwks
72 D4 **Lighthorne Heath** Warwks
42 F7 **Lightwater** Surrey
87 H7 **Lilbourne** Nhants
84 D1 **Lilleshall** Wrekin
59 J3 **Lilley** Herts
167 H4 **Lilliesleaf** Border
73 K6 **Lillingstone Dayrell** Bucks
73 K6 **Lillingstone Lovell** Bucks
26 F8 **Lillington** Dorset
15 K4 **Lilliput** Poole
25 J3 **Lilstock** Somset
59 H3 **Limbury** Luton
175 J7 **Limekilnburn** S Lans
176 E2 **Limekilns** Fife
176 B4 **Limerigg** Falk
16 E6 **Limerstone** IoW
55 J2 **Lime Street** Worcs
26 D6 **Limington** Somset
164 C4 **Limmerhaugh** E Ayrs
93 H3 **Limpenhoe** Norfk
39 H7 **Limpley Stoke** Wilts
32 D3 **Limpsfield** Surrey
32 D3 **Limpsfield Chart** Surrey
101 K3 **Linby** Notts
30 E5 **Linchmere** W Susx
155 G6 **Lincluden** D & G
116 F7 **Lincoln** Lincs
117 G7 **Lincoln Crematorium** Lincs
70 E2 **Lincomb** Worcs
129 J4 **Lindale** Cumb
128 F4 **Lindal in Furness** Cumb
32 C7 **Lindfield** W Susx
30 D4 **Lindford** Hants
123 G6 **Lindley** Kirk
70 C2 **Lindridge** Worcs
61 G3 **Lindsell** Essex
77 L5 **Lindsey** Suffk
78 B5 **Lindsey Tye** Suffk
142 E4 **Lingdale** R & Cl
69 G2 **Lingen** Herefs
32 C4 **Lingfield** Surrey
93 H2 **Lingwood** Norfk
218 B7 **Linicro** Highld
55 J2 **Linkend** Worcs
41 G8 **Linkenholt** Hants
5 L2 **Linkinhorne** Cnwll
177 J1 **Linktown** Fife
214 F3 **Linkwood** Moray
83 G5 **Linley** Shrops
70 C4 **Linley Green** Herefs
176 D3 **Linlithgow** W Loth
222 D2 **Linsidemore** Highld
58 E3 **Linslade** C Beds
93 G7 **Linstead Parva** Suffk
148 D4 **Linstock** Cumb
85 H8 **Linthurst** Worcs
123 G7 **Linthwaite** Kirk
179 H6 **Lintlaw** Border
215 L2 **Lintmill** Moray
168 B4 **Linton** Border
76 E5 **Linton** Cambs
86 C1 **Linton** Derbys
54 F3 **Linton** Herefs
33 K3 **Linton** Kent
124 B2 **Linton** Leeds
131 J6 **Linton** N York
54 F3 **Linton Hill** Herefs
133 G7 **Linton-on-Ouse** N York
117 J4 **Linwood** Lincs
174 E5 **Linwood** Rens
233 b7 **Lionacleit** W Isls
232 g1 **Lional** W Isls
30 D5 **Liphook** Hants
111 J3 **Liscard** Wirral
24 D5 **Liscombe** Somset
5 K3 **Liskeard** Cnwll
191 G7 **Lismore** Ag & B
30 C5 **Liss** Hants
135 H7 **Lissett** E R Yk
117 J5 **Lissington** Lincs
37 J4 **Lisvane** Cardif
37 M3 **Liswerry** Newpt
105 L8 **Litcham** Norfk
73 J4 **Litchborough** Nhants
29 J2 **Litchfield** Hants
111 K2 **Litherland** Sefton
75 K6 **Litlington** Cambs
20 B5 **Litlington** E Susx
76 D5 **Little Abington** Cambs

88 D8 **Little Addington** Nhants
145 J5 **Little Airies** D & G
71 K3 **Little Alne** Warwks
111 J1 **Little Altcar** Sefton
60 B5 **Little Amwell** Herts
85 K4 **Little Aston** Staffs
142 C5 **Little Ayton** N York
61 J6 **Little Baddow** Essex
39 J4 **Little Badminton** S Glos
148 A4 **Little Bampton** Cumb
61 G2 **Little Bardfield** Essex
75 H3 **Little Barford** Bed
106 D5 **Little Barningham** Norfk
56 D5 **Little Barrington** Gloucs
112 C7 **Little Barrow** Ches W
158 C6 **Little Bavington** Nthumb
40 F7 **Little Bedwyn** Wilts
62 D3 **Little Bentley** Essex
59 M6 **Little Berkhamsted** Herts
74 B3 **Little Billing** Nhants
58 F4 **Little Billington** C Beds
54 D2 **Little Birch** Herefs
78 D5 **Little Blakenham** Suffk
148 E7 **Little Blencow** Cumb
31 G7 **Little Bognor** W Susx
113 G4 **Little Bollington** Ches E
31 J1 **Little Bookham** Surrey
116 D5 **Littleborough** Notts
122 D7 **Littleborough** Rochdl
35 G3 **Littlebourne** Kent
72 F5 **Little Bourton** Oxon
61 K5 **Little Braxted** Essex
196 F4 **Little Brechin** Angus
14 B5 **Littlebredy** Dorset
58 E2 **Little Brickhill** M Keyn
73 J2 **Little Brington** Nhants
62 C3 **Little Bromley** Essex
112 E7 **Little Budworth** Ches W
212 F4 **Littleburn** Highld
46 A2 **Little Burstead** Essex
76 D6 **Littlebury** Essex
76 C6 **Littlebury Green** Essex
103 G8 **Little Bytham** Lincs
118 E4 **Little Carlton** Lincs
88 E2 **Little Casterton** Rutlnd
118 E5 **Little Cawthorpe** Lincs
43 G2 **Little Chalfont** Bucks
34 C5 **Little Chart** Kent
76 D6 **Little Chesterford** Essex
27 M2 **Little Cheverell** Wilts
76 B6 **Little Chishill** Cambs
62 E4 **Little Clacton** Essex
136 E2 **Little Clifton** Cumb
71 G5 **Little Comberton** Worcs
20 E4 **Little Common** E Susx
56 E3 **Little Compton** Warwks
77 K6 **Little Cornard** Suffk
69 L4 **Little Cowarne** Herefs
40 F2 **Little Coxwell** Oxon
132 C2 **Little Crakehall** N York
91 K4 **Little Cressingham** Norfk
111 K2 **Little Crosby** Sefton
100 D5 **Little Cubley** Derbys
87 L2 **Little Dalby** Leics
54 F5 **Littledean** Gloucs
54 D2 **Little Dewchurch** Herefs
76 F3 **Little Ditton** Cambs
90 D6 **Little Downham** Cambs
134 F7 **Little Driffield** E R Yk
91 K2 **Little Dunham** Norfk
195 G7 **Little Dunkeld** P & K
61 G4 **Little Dunmow** Essex
28 C5 **Little Durnford** Wilts
60 F3 **Little Easton** Essex
101 G4 **Little Eaton** Derbys
92 B4 **Little Ellingham** Norfk
73 H3 **Little Everdon** Nhants
75 L4 **Little Eversden** Cambs
56 E7 **Little Faringdon** Oxon
132 D2 **Little Fencote** N York
124 D4 **Little Fenton** N York
91 K2 **Little Fransham** Norfk
59 G5 **Little Gaddesden** Herts
79 H3 **Little Glemham** Suffk
55 G3 **Little Gorsley** Herefs
75 J4 **Little Gransden** Cambs
27 G2 **Little Green** Somset
60 C4 **Little Hadham** Herts
103 J4 **Little Hale** Lincs
101 J4 **Little Hallam** Derbys
60 D4 **Little Hallingbury** Essex
12 D6 **Littleham** Devon
23 G6 **Littleham** Devon
18 D5 **Littlehampton** W Susx
74 C1 **Little Harrowden** Nhants
57 M7 **Little Haseley** Oxon
48 E5 **Little Haven** Pembks
31 K5 **Littlehaven** W Susx
85 K3 **Little Hay** Staffs
100 A7 **Little Haywood** Staffs
7 J4 **Littlehempston** Devon
69 K2 **Little Hereford** Herefs
62 A2 **Little Horkesley** Essex
60 C3 **Little Hormead** Herts
19 M3 **Little Horsted** E Susx
123 H4 **Little Horton** C Brad
58 C2 **Little Horwood** Bucks
115 H1 **Little Houghton** Barns
74 B3 **Little Houghton** Nhants
114 D5 **Little Hucklow** Derbys
133 G4 **Little Hutton** N York
74 C2 **Little Irchester** Nhants
27 H3 **Little Keyford** Somset
58 D6 **Little Kimble** Bucks
72 D4 **Little Kineton** Warwks
58 E7 **Little Kingshill** Bucks
146 E3 **Little Knox** D & G
137 J6 **Little Langdale** Cumb
28 B4 **Little Langford** Wilts
112 F6 **Little Leigh** Ches W
61 H5 **Little Leighs** Essex
121 L8 **Little Lever** Bolton
74 B5 **Little Linford** M Keyn
26 C6 **Little Load** Somset
20 C2 **Little London** E Susx
29 G2 **Little London** Hants
41 L8 **Little London** Hants
114 D6 **Little Longstone** Derbys
77 J7 **Little Maplestead** Essex
70 C7 **Little Marcle** Herefs
42 E3 **Little Marlow** Bucks
105 J7 **Little Massingham** Norfk
92 E3 **Little Melton** Norfk
205 H6 **Littlemill** Abers
213 L4 **Littlemill** Highld
53 L7 **Little Mill** Mons
57 L7 **Little Milton** Oxon
58 F7 **Little Missenden** Bucks
57 K7 **Littlemore** Oxon
139 H5 **Little Musgrave** Cumb
98 B8 **Little Ness** Shrops
49 G2 **Little Newcastle** Pembks
140 E4 **Little Newsham** Dur
26 C7 **Little Norton** Somset
62 F3 **Little Oakley** Essex
88 C6 **Little Oakley** Nhants
148 C4 **Little Orton** Cumb
101 G5 **Littleover** C Derb
86 B6 **Little Packington** Warwks
75 H3 **Little Paxton** Cambs
4 E2 **Little Petherick** Cnwll
93 G2 **Little Plumstead** Norfk
102 F6 **Little Ponton** Lincs
90 E6 **Littleport** Cambs
73 H4 **Little Preston** Nhants
89 J7 **Little Raveley** Cambs
125 J6 **Little Reedness** E R Yk
132 F8 **Little Ribston** N York
56 D4 **Little Rissington** Gloucs
56 F3 **Little Rollright** Oxon
106 A6 **Little Ryburgh** Norfk
148 F7 **Little Salkeld** Cumb
76 F7 **Little Sampford** Essex
111 K7 **Little Saughall** Ches W
77 H2 **Little Saxham** Suffk
212 B3 **Little Scatwell** Highld
76 C4 **Little Shelford** Cambs
120 E3 **Little Singleton** Lancs
125 G3 **Little Skipwith** N York
124 D6 **Little Smeaton** N York
106 A6 **Little Snoring** Norfk
39 H4 **Little Sodbury** S Glos
29 G5 **Little Somborne** Hants
39 L4 **Little Somerford** Wilts
99 G6 **Little Soudley** Shrops
141 J3 **Little Stainton** Darltn
112 B6 **Little Stanney** Ches W
75 G3 **Little Staughton** Bed
118 F8 **Little Steeping** Lincs
99 K6 **Little Stoke** Staffs
21 L2 **Littlestone-on-Sea** Kent
78 D3 **Little Stonham** Suffk
87 J4 **Little Stretton** Leics
83 J5 **Little Stretton** Shrops
138 E4 **Little Strickland** Cumb
89 H7 **Little Stukeley** Cambs
99 J6 **Little Sugnall** Staffs
158 B6 **Little Swinburne** Nthumb
146 C4 **Little Sypland** D & G
57 G3 **Little Tew** Oxon
61 L4 **Little Tey** Essex
90 D7 **Little Thetford** Cambs
151 K6 **Little Thorpe** Dur
87 G4 **Littlethorpe** Leics
132 E5 **Littlethorpe** N York
76 F4 **Little Thurlow** Suffk
45 L4 **Little Thurrock** Thurr
196 B6 **Littleton** Angus
112 C7 **Littleton** Ches W
146 B4 **Littleton** D & G
29 J5 **Littleton** Hants
26 C5 **Littleton** Somset
43 H6 **Littleton** Surrey
39 J4 **Littleton Drew** Wilts
38 E3 **Littleton-on-Severn** S Glos
27 M2 **Littleton Pannell** Wilts
10 D2 **Little Torrington** Devon
151 H6 **Littletown** Dur
121 K4 **Little Town** Lancs
128 F5 **Little Urswick** Cumb
46 F3 **Little Wakering** Essex
76 D6 **Little Walden** Essex
77 K5 **Little Waldingfield** Suffk
105 M5 **Little Walsingham** Norfk
61 H5 **Little Waltham** Essex
126 B4 **Little Weighton** E R Yk
88 D5 **Little Weldon** Nhants
84 B3 **Little Wenlock** Wrekin
26 F6 **Little Weston** Somset
17 H4 **Little Whitefield** IoW
42 D4 **Littlewick Green** W & M
76 D3 **Little Wilbraham** Cambs
55 K5 **Little Witcombe** Gloucs
70 D2 **Little Witley** Worcs
41 K2 **Little Wittenham** Oxon
72 C7 **Little Wolford** Warwks
44 F7 **Little Woodcote** Gt Lon
40 F2 **Littleworth** Oxon
99 L7 **Littleworth** Staffs
70 F4 **Littleworth** Worcs
74 D2 **Little Wymington** Bed
59 K3 **Little Wymondley** Herts
85 H3 **Little Wyrley** Staffs
77 H6 **Little Yeldham** Essex
61 H4 **Littley Green** Essex
114 D6 **Litton** Derbys
131 G5 **Litton** N York
26 E1 **Litton** Somset
14 A4 **Litton Cheney** Dorset
232 f3 **Liurbost** W Isls
111 K4 **Liverpool** Lpool
123 J5 **Liversedge** Kirk
7 J2 **Liverton** Devon
142 F4 **Liverton** R & Cl
176 E5 **Livingston** W Loth
176 E5 **Livingston Village** W Loth
111 G7 **Lixwm** Flints
3 J8 **Lizard** Cnwll
95 G4 **Llanaelhaearn** Gwynd
66 F1 **Llanafan** Cerdgn
67 L4 **Llanafan-Fawr** Powys
109 G4 **Llanallgo** IoA
97 J6 **Llanarmon Dyffryn Ceiriog** Wrexhm
97 J2 **Llanarmon-yn-Ial** Denbgs
65 L3 **Llanarth** Cerdgn
54 B5 **Llanarth** Mons
51 G2 **Llanarthne** Carmth
110 F5 **Llanasa** Flints
80 E7 **Llanbadarn Fawr** Cerdgn
82 C7 **Llanbadarn Fynydd** Powys
54 B7 **Llanbadoc** Mons
38 B3 **Llanbeder** Newpt
95 K7 **Llanbedr** Gwynd
53 K4 **Llanbedr** Powys
97 H2 **Llanbedr-Dyffryn-Clwyd** Denbgs
109 G5 **Llanbedrgoch** IoA
94 F6 **Llanbedrog** Gwynd
109 L7 **Llanbedr-y-Cennin** Conwy
95 K1 **Llanberis** Gwynd
37 G6 **Llanbethery** V Glam
82 C8 **Llanbister** Powys
36 F5 **Llanblethian** V Glam

49 L3 **Llanboidy** Carmth
37 J3 **Llanbradach** Caerph
81 J3 **Llanbrynmair** Powys
37 G6 **Llancadle** V Glam
37 G6 **Llancarfan** V Glam
54 D4 **Llancloudy** Herefs
37 J5 **Llandaff** Cardif
95 K6 **Llandanwg** Gwynd
109 G7 **Llanddaniel Fab** IoA
51 G3 **Llanddarog** Carmth
66 D1 **Llanddeiniol** Cerdgn
109 H7 **Llanddeiniolen** Gwynd
96 F5 **Llandderfel** Gwynd
108 D4 **Llanddeusant** IoA
53 G2 **Llanddew** Powys
50 F7 **Llanddewi** Swans
66 F4 **Llanddewi Brefi** Cerdgn
53 M5 **Llanddewi Rhydderch** Mons
49 K4 **Llanddewi Velfrey** Pembks
68 C2 **Llanddewi Ystradenni** Powys
109 M8 **Llanddoget** Conwy
109 H5 **Llanddona** IoA
50 B3 **Llanddowror** Carmth
110 C6 **Llanddulas** Conwy
95 K7 **Llanddwywe** Gwynd
109 G5 **Llanddyfnan** IoA
53 H3 **Llandefaelog-Tre'r-Graig** Powys
68 C7 **Llandefalle** Powys
109 H6 **Llandegfan** IoA
97 J3 **Llandegla** Denbgs
68 D2 **Llandegley** Powys
37 M2 **Llandegveth** Mons
51 J2 **Llandeilo** Carmth
68 C5 **Llandeilo Graban** Powys
48 E3 **Llandeloy** Pembks
54 B7 **Llandenny** Mons
38 B3 **Llandevaud** Newpt
38 B3 **Llandevenny** Mons
82 B5 **Llandinam** Powys
49 J3 **Llandissilio** Pembks
54 D7 **Llandogo** Mons
36 F6 **Llandough** V Glam
37 J5 **Llandough** V Glam
67 G7 **Llandovery** Carmth
36 E5 **Llandow** V Glam
66 F6 **Llandre** Carmth
80 E6 **Llandre** Cerdgn
49 J2 **Llandre Isaf** Pembks
97 G5 **Llandrillo** Denbgs
110 B5 **Llandrillo-yn-Rhos** Conwy
68 B3 **Llandrindod Wells** Powys
97 L8 **Llandrinio** Powys
109 L5 **Llandudno** Conwy
109 M6 **Llandudno Junction** Conwy
67 J6 **Llandulas** Powys
95 H2 **Llandwrog** Gwynd
51 J3 **Llandybie** Carmth
50 E3 **Llandyfaelog** Carmth
65 K6 **Llandyfriog** Cerdgn
109 H7 **Llandygai** Gwynd
65 H5 **Llandygwydd** Cerdgn
110 F8 **Llandyrnog** Denbgs
82 E4 **Llandyssil** Powys
65 L6 **Llandysul** Cerdgn
37 K4 **Llanedeyrn** Cardif
68 B6 **Llaneglwys** Powys
80 D3 **Llanegryn** Gwynd
51 G2 **Llanegwad** Carmth
108 F3 **Llaneilian** IoA
110 B6 **Llanelian-yn-Rhôs** Conwy
97 H3 **Llanelidan** Denbgs
68 D7 **Llanelieu** Powys
53 L5 **Llanellen** Mons
51 G5 **Llanelli** Carmth
51 G5 **Llanelli Crematorium** Carmth
96 A8 **Llanelltyd** Gwynd
68 B4 **Llanelwedd** Powys
95 K7 **Llanenddwyn** Gwynd
94 E6 **Llanengan** Gwynd
108 E5 **Llanerchymedd** IoA
82 B2 **Llanerfyl** Powys
108 D5 **Llanfachraeth** IoA
96 B7 **Llanfachreth** Gwynd
108 D6 **Llanfaelog** IoA
94 D6 **Llanfaelrhys** Gwynd
108 D4 **Llanfaethlu** IoA
95 K6 **Llanfair** Gwynd
82 C3 **Llanfair Caereinion** Powys
66 E4 **Llanfair Clydogau** Cerdgn
97 H2 **Llanfair Dyffryn Clwyd** Denbgs
109 K6 **Llanfairfechan** Conwy
109 G6 **Llanfair P G** IoA
110 C7 **Llanfair Talhaiarn** Conwy
82 E7 **Llanfair Waterdine** Shrops
108 D4 **Llanfairynghornwy** IoA
108 C6 **Llanfair-yn-Neubwll** IoA
49 K4 **Llanfallteg** Carmth
49 K4 **Llanfallteg West** Carmth
80 D7 **Llanfarian** Cerdgn
97 J7 **Llanfechain** Powys
108 E3 **Llanfechell** IoA
97 J1 **Llanferres** Denbgs
66 B6 **Llanfihangel-ar-arth** Carmth
96 F3 **Llanfihangel Glyn Myfyr** Conwy
67 K7 **Llanfihangel Nant Bran** Powys
68 D2 **Llanfihangel Rhydithon** Powys
38 C3 **Llanfihangel Rogiet** Mons
80 F7 **Llanfihangel-y-Creuddyn** Cerdgn
82 C1 **Llanfihangel-yng-Ngwynfa** Powys
108 D6 **Llanfihangel yn Nhowyn** IoA
95 K5 **Llanfihangel-y-traethau** Gwynd
53 H2 **Llanfilo** Powys
53 L5 **Llanfoist** Mons
96 E5 **Llanfor** Gwynd
37 L2 **Llanfrechfa** Torfn
53 G3 **Llanfrynach** Powys
97 H2 **Llanfwrog** Denbgs
108 C5 **Llanfwrog** IoA
97 H8 **Llanfyllin** Powys
66 D8 **Llanfynydd** Carmth
97 L2 **Llanfynydd** Flints
49 L2 **Llanfyrnach** Pembks
81 L2 **Llangadfan** Powys
66 F8 **Llangadog** Carmth
108 E7 **Llangadwaladr** IoA
108 F7 **Llangaffo** IoA
67 K5 **Llangammarch Wells** Powys
36 E5 **Llangan** V Glam
54 D4 **Llangarron** Herefs
51 H2 **Llangathen** Carmth
53 K4 **Llangattock** Powys
54 A4 **Llangattock Lingoed** Mons
97 J7 **Llangedwyn** Powys
108 F6 **Llangefni** IoA
36 E3 **Llangeinor** Brdgnd
66 E3 **Llangeitho** Cerdgn
65 L6 **Llangeler** Carmth
80 D3 **Llangelynin** Gwynd
50 F3 **Llangendeirne** Carmth
51 H5 **Llangennech** Carmth
50 E7 **Llangennith** Swans
110 B7 **Llangernyw** Conwy
94 E6 **Llangian** Gwynd
64 C7 **Llangloffan** Pembks
49 K3 **Llanglydwen** Carmth
109 J5 **Llangoed** IoA
97 K4 **Llangollen** Denbgs
49 J3 **Llangolman** Pembks
53 H3 **Llangors** Powys
96 D6 **Llangower** Gwynd
65 K4 **Llangranog** Cerdgn
108 F6 **Llangristiolus** IoA
54 D4 **Llangrove** Herefs
68 E1 **Llangunllo** Powys
50 E2 **Llangunnor** Carmth
81 K7 **Llangurig** Powys
96 F4 **Llangwm** Conwy
54 B7 **Llangwm** Mons
49 G5 **Llangwm** Pembks
94 D6 **Llangwnnadl** Gwynd
66 D1 **Llangwyryfon** Cerdgn
66 E4 **Llangybi** Cerdgn
95 G4 **Llangybi** Gwynd
38 A2 **Llangybi** Mons
110 F8 **Llangynhafal** Denbgs
53 J4 **Llangynidr** Powys
50 B2 **Llangynin** Carmth
50 D3 **Llangynog** Carmth
97 G7 **Llangynog** Powys
36 D3 **Llangynwyd** Brdgnd
53 H3 **Llanhamlach** Powys
36 F4 **Llanharan** Rhondd
36 F4 **Llanharry** Rhondd
38 A2 **Llanhennock** Mons
53 K7 **Llanhilleth** Blae G
81 K6 **Llanidloes** Powys
94 E5 **Llaniestyn** Gwynd
68 E6 **Llanigon** Powys
80 E8 **Llanilar** Cerdgn
36 F4 **Llanilid** Rhondd
65 L3 **Llanina** Cerdgn
37 J4 **Llanishen** Cardif
54 C7 **Llanishen** Mons
109 J7 **Llanllechid** Gwynd
54 B7 **Llanllowell** Mons
82 B3 **Llanllugan** Powys
50 E2 **Llanllwch** Carmth
82 C5 **Llanllwchaiarn** Powys
66 C6 **Llanllwni** Carmth
95 H3 **Llanllyfni** Gwynd
50 F6 **Llanmadoc** Swans
36 F6 **Llanmaes** V Glam
38 B3 **Llanmartin** Newpt
50 B4 **Llanmiloe** Carmth
110 D7 **Llannefydd** Conwy
51 G4 **Llannon** Carmth
94 F5 **Llannor** Gwynd
66 C2 **Llanon** Cerdgn
53 L6 **Llanover** Mons
65 L8 **Llanpumsaint** Carmth
97 H7 **Llanrhaeadr-ym-Mochnant** Powys
48 D2 **Llanrhian** Pembks
50 F6 **Llanrhidian** Swans
96 B1 **Llanrhychwyn** Conwy
108 D4 **Llanrhyddlad** IoA
66 C1 **Llanrhystud** Cerdgn
109 G8 **Llanrug** Gwynd
37 K4 **Llanrumney** Cardif
96 C1 **Llanrwst** Conwy
50 C4 **Llansadurnen** Carmth
66 F7 **Llansadwrn** Carmth
109 H6 **Llansadwrn** IoA
50 E4 **Llansaint** Carmth
51 K6 **Llansamlet** Swans
109 M6 **Llansanffraid Glan Conwy** Conwy
110 C7 **Llansannan** Conwy
53 H4 **Llansantffraed** Powys
67 L2 **Llansantffraed-Cwmdeuddwr** Powys
68 C4 **Llansantffraed-in-Elvel** Powys
66 C2 **Llansantffraid** Cerdgn
97 K7 **Llansantffraid-ym-Mechain** Powys
66 E7 **Llansawel** Carmth
97 K6 **Llansilin** Powys
54 C7 **Llansoy** Mons
52 F3 **Llanspyddid** Powys
48 F6 **Llanstadwell** Pembks
50 D4 **Llansteffan** Carmth
37 L2 **Llantarnam** Torfn
49 K5 **Llanteg** Pembks
53 M5 **Llanthewy Skirrid** Mons
53 L3 **Llanthony** Mons
54 B5 **Llantilio-Crossenny** Mons
53 L5 **Llantilio Pertholey** Mons
38 B2 **Llantrisant** Mons
37 G4 **Llantrisant** Rhondd
37 G6 **Llantrithyd** V Glam
37 G3 **Llantwit Fardre** Rhondd
36 F6 **Llantwit Major** V Glam
96 D6 **Llanuwchllyn** Gwynd
38 B3 **Llanvaches** Newpt
38 C3 **Llanvair Discoed** Mons
54 A5 **Llanvapley** Mons
54 A5 **Llanvetherine** Mons
53 L4 **Llanvihangel Crucorney** Mons
96 F8 **Llanwddyn** Powys
66 C5 **Llanwenog** Cerdgn
38 A3 **Llanwern** Newpt
50 C1 **Llanwinio** Carmth
95 H2 **Llanwnda** Gwynd
64 C6 **Llanwnda** Pembks
66 C5 **Llanwnnen** Cerdgn
82 B5 **Llanwnog** Powys
66 F7 **Llanwrda** Carmth
81 H3 **Llanwrin** Powys
67 L2 **Llanwrthwl** Powys
67 J5 **Llanwrtyd Wells** Powys
82 C4 **Llanwyddelan** Powys
97 K7 **Llanyblodwel** Shrops
50 D3 **Llanybri** Carmth
66 C5 **Llanybydder** Carmth
49 J3 **Llanycefn** Pembks
64 D7 **Llanychaer Bridge** Pembks
96 D8 **Llanymawddwy** Gwynd
97 K7 **Llanymynech** Powys
108 D5 **Llanynghenedl** IoA
110 F8 **Llanynys** Denbgs
68 B3 **Llanyre** Powys
95 H5 **Llanystumdwy** Gwynd
53 H3 **Llanywern** Powys
49 H4 **Llawhaden** Pembks
81 K5 **Llawryglyn** Powys
97 M2 **Llay** Wrexhm
53 H6 **Llechrhyd** Caerph
65 H5 **Llechryd** Cerdgn
66 E1 **Lledrod** Cerdgn
94 E5 **Lleyn Peninsula** Gwynd
94 F4 **Llithfaen** Gwynd
111 G6 **Lloc** Flints
68 D6 **Llowes** Powys
52 F6 **Llwydcoed** Rhondd
52 F6 **Llwydcoed Crematorium** Rhondd
82 B1 **Llwydiarth** Powys
66 B3 **Llwyncelyn** Cerdgn
65 L4 **Llwyndafydd** Cerdgn
80 D2 **Llwyngwril** Gwynd
97 K5 **Llwynmawr** Wrexhm
36 F2 **Llwynypia** Rhondd
97 L7 **Llynclys** Shrops

108 E5 **Llynfaes** IoA
110 B6 **Llysfaen** Conwy
68 C6 **Llyswen** Powys
36 E5 **Llysworney** V Glam
49 H3 **Llys-y-frân** Pembks
52 D3 **Llywel** Powys
176 C3 **Loan** Falk
177 J5 **Loanhead** Mdloth
147 G4 **Loaningfoot** D & G
163 J3 **Loans** S Ayrs
10 C7 **Lobhillcross** Devon
200 B8 **Lochailort** Highld
190 D7 **Lochaline** Highld
144 C4 **Lochans** D & G
155 H6 **Locharbriggs** D & G
182 D4 **Lochavich** Ag & B
183 G2 **Lochawe** Ag & B
233 c8 **Loch Baghasdail** W Isls
233 c8 **Lochboisdale** W Isls
181 J3 **Lochbuie** Ag & B
210 D6 **Lochcarron** Highld
181 L2 **Lochdon** Ag & B
181 L2 **Lochdonhead** Ag & B
172 D3 **Lochead** Ag & B
184 D3 **Lochearnhead** Stirlg
186 F2 **Lochee** C Dund
191 K2 **Locheilside Station** Highld
212 F6 **Lochend** Highld
233 c6 **Locheport** W Isls
233 c6 **Loch Euphoirt** W Isls
154 F7 **Lochfoot** D & G
172 F1 **Lochgair** Ag & B
186 C8 **Lochgelly** Fife
172 E2 **Lochgilphead** Ag & B
183 H6 **Lochgoilhead** Ag & B
186 D5 **Lochieheads** Fife
215 G2 **Lochill** Moray
214 B7 **Lochindorb Lodge** Highld
224 D4 **Lochinver** Highld
184 A5 **Loch Lomond and The Trossachs National Park**
211 L2 **Lochluichart** Highld
155 J5 **Lochmaben** D & G
233 c6 **Lochmaddy** W Isls
219 L7 **Loch Maree Hotel** Highld
233 c6 **Loch nam Madadh** W Isls
202 E1 **Loch Ness** Highld
186 C7 **Lochore** Fife
172 F7 **Lochranza** N Ayrs
197 H4 **Lochside** Abers
155 G6 **Lochside** D & G
213 J4 **Lochside** Highld
223 J5 **Lochslin** Highld
152 F6 **Lochton** S Ayrs
196 E4 **Lochty** Angus
187 H5 **Lochty** Fife
190 F5 **Lochuisge** Highld
174 C6 **Lochwinnoch** Rens
155 J3 **Lochwood** D & G
5 G4 **Lockengate** Cnwll
155 K5 **Lockerbie** D & G
40 C6 **Lockeridge** Wilts
28 F6 **Lockerley** Hants
38 A8 **Locking** N Som
112 F3 **Locking Stumps** Warrtn
126 B2 **Lockington** E R Yk
99 G6 **Lockleywood** Shrops
45 H6 **Locksbottom** Gt Lon
17 G2 **Locks Heath** Hants
134 C2 **Lockton** N York
87 L3 **Loddington** Leics
88 B7 **Loddington** Nhants
7 G6 **Loddiswell** Devon
93 H4 **Loddon** Norfk
76 D3 **Lode** Cambs
85 L7 **Lode Heath** Solhll
13 L4 **Loders** Dorset
85 H6 **Lodge Hill Crematorium** Birm
30 F6 **Lodsworth** W Susx
123 L5 **Lofthouse** Leeds
131 L5 **Lofthouse** N York
123 L5 **Lofthouse Gate** Wakefd
142 F4 **Loftus** R & Cl
164 C5 **Logan** E Ayrs
176 C6 **Loganlea** W Loth
99 G5 **Loggerheads** Staffs
197 H4 **Logie** Angus
186 F4 **Logie** Fife
214 C4 **Logie** Moray
205 K4 **Logie Coldstone** Abers
216 C6 **Logie Newton** Abers
197 G4 **Logie Pert** Angus
194 F6 **Logierait** P & K
217 H8 **Logierieve** Abers
49 K3 **Login** Carmth
75 L2 **Lolworth** Cambs
209 L4 **Lonbain** Highld
125 K2 **Londesborough** E R Yk
44 F4 **London** Gt Lon
4 F6 **London Apprentice** Cnwll
59 K7 **London Colney** Herts
132 D3 **Londonderry** N York
44 D2 **London Gateway Services** Gt Lon
102 F5 **Londonthorpe** Lincs
219 K5 **Londubh** Highld
219 J6 **Lonemore** Highld
38 D6 **Long Ashton** N Som
84 D8 **Long Bank** Worcs
102 D4 **Long Bennington** Lincs
151 G2 **Longbenton** N Tyne
56 D3 **Longborough** Gloucs
14 B4 **Long Bredy** Dorset
85 H7 **Longbridge** Birm
27 K4 **Longbridge Deverill** Wilts
73 J2 **Long Buckby** Nhants
26 F8 **Longburton** Dorset
102 B6 **Long Clawson** Leics
100 E2 **Longcliffe** Derbys
7 J4 **Longcombe** Devon
99 J7 **Long Compton** Staffs
56 F2 **Long Compton** Warwks
40 F3 **Longcot** Oxon
58 B6 **Long Crendon** Bucks
15 J1 **Long Crichel** Dorset
83 J3 **Longden** Shrops
44 D6 **Long Ditton** Surrey
85 J2 **Longdon** Staffs
70 E7 **Longdon** Worcs
85 J2 **Longdon Green** Staffs
84 B1 **Longdon upon Tern** Wrekin
11 K6 **Longdown** Devon
3 J4 **Longdowns** Cnwll
115 H7 **Long Duckmanton** Derbys
101 J5 **Long Eaton** Derbys
45 L6 **Longfield** Kent
86 D6 **Longford** Covtry
100 E5 **Longford** Derbys
55 J4 **Longford** Gloucs
98 F5 **Longford** Shrops
99 G8 **Longford** Wrekin
186 E2 **Longforgan** P & K
178 E6 **Longformacus** Border
158 E3 **Longframlington** Nthumb
112 C7 **Long Green** Ches W
15 K3 **Longham** Dorset
91 L1 **Longham** Norfk
57 H5 **Long Hanborough** Oxon
217 L6 **Longhaven** Abers
158 F4 **Longhirst** Nthumb
55 G4 **Longhope** Gloucs
234 b7 **Longhope** Ork
158 E4 **Longhorsley** Nthumb
169 J6 **Longhoughton** Nthumb
72 E2 **Long Itchington** Warwks
100 E5 **Longlane** Derbys
86 F7 **Long Lawford** Warwks
27 J3 **Longleat Safari Park** Wilts
55 J4 **Longlevens** Gloucs
195 L7 **Longleys** P & K
26 C6 **Long Load** Somset
216 E2 **Longmanhill** Abers
58 E5 **Long Marston** Herts
124 D1 **Long Marston** N York
71 L5 **Long Marston** Warwks
138 F3 **Long Marton** Cumb
77 J5 **Long Melford** Suffk
30 C5 **Longmoor Camp** Hants
214 F3 **Longmorn** Moray
113 K6 **Longmoss** Ches E
39 K3 **Long Newnton** Gloucs
167 J4 **Longnewton** Border
178 B5 **Long Newton** E Loth
141 J4 **Longnewton** S on T
55 H5 **Longney** Gloucs
177 L3 **Longniddry** E Loth
83 J4 **Longnor** Shrops
114 C8 **Longnor** Staffs
29 H3 **Longparish** Hants
130 F7 **Long Preston** N York
121 J3 **Longridge** Lancs
176 C5 **Longridge** W Loth
175 L4 **Longriggend** N Lans
126 E3 **Long Riston** E R Yk
2 E5 **Longrock** Cnwll
99 L2 **Longsdon** Staffs
217 K5 **Longside** Abers
76 B2 **Longstanton** Cambs
29 G4 **Longstock** Hants
75 K4 **Longstowe** Cambs
92 E5 **Long Stratton** Norfk
74 B5 **Long Street** M Keyn
28 C2 **Longstreet** Wilts
30 C3 **Long Sutton** Hants
104 C7 **Long Sutton** Lincs
26 C6 **Long Sutton** Somset
89 H4 **Longthorpe** C Pete
78 B2 **Long Thurlow** Suffk
138 B3 **Longthwaite** Cumb
99 K4 **Longton** C Stke
121 G5 **Longton** Lancs
148 C2 **Longtown** Cumb
53 L3 **Longtown** Herefs
236 d7 **Longueville** Jersey
83 K5 **Longville in the Dale** Shrops
84 B1 **Long Waste** Wrekin
101 J7 **Long Whatton** Leics
58 C6 **Longwick** Bucks
41 K2 **Long Wittenham** Oxon
158 D4 **Longwitton** Nthumb
146 C3 **Longwood** D & G
57 G7 **Longworth** Oxon
178 C5 **Longyester** E Loth
217 J3 **Lonmay** Abers
208 D5 **Lonmore** Highld
5 K5 **Looe** Cnwll
33 K3 **Loose** Kent
58 D7 **Loosley Row** Bucks
216 B4 **Lootcherbrae** Abers
26 B8 **Lopen** Somset
98 C6 **Loppington** Shrops
46 C7 **Lords Wood** Medway
195 J6 **Lornty** P & K
101 H3 **Loscoe** Derbys
214 F1 **Lossiemouth** Moray
4 F6 **Lost Gardens of Heligan** Cnwll
113 G6 **Lostock Gralam** Ches W
113 G6 **Lostock Green** Ches W
5 H4 **Lostwithiel** Cnwll
227 G6 **Lothbeg** Highld
122 E2 **Lothersdale** N York
227 G6 **Lothmore** Highld
42 E3 **Loudwater** Bucks
101 K8 **Loughborough** Leics
101 K8 **Loughborough Crematorium** Leics
51 H6 **Loughor** Swans
45 H2 **Loughton** Essex
74 B6 **Loughton** M Keyn
103 H8 **Lound** Lincs
116 B4 **Lound** Notts
93 K4 **Lound** Suffk
101 G8 **Lount** Leics
118 D4 **Louth** Lincs
30 B8 **Lovedean** Hants
28 E7 **Lover** Wilts
115 L2 **Loversall** Donc
61 G6 **Loves Green** Essex
49 J5 **Loveston** Pembks
26 E5 **Lovington** Somset
124 C6 **Low Ackworth** Wakefd
144 B2 **Low Barbeth** D & G
130 C5 **Low Bentham** N York
130 B4 **Low Biggins** Cumb
138 E6 **Low Borrowbridge** Cumb
114 E3 **Low Bradfield** Sheff
122 F2 **Low Bradley** N York
116 C2 **Low Burnham** N Linc
136 D3 **Lowca** Cumb
133 L8 **Low Catton** E R Yk
148 D3 **Low Crosby** Cumb
102 A3 **Lowdham** Notts
141 J5 **Low Dinsdale** Darltn
25 J4 **Lower Aisholt** Somset
14 E2 **Lower Ansty** Dorset
55 J3 **Lower Apperley** Gloucs
11 J7 **Lower Ashton** Devon
42 C4 **Lower Assendon** Oxon
121 G4 **Lower Bartle** Lancs
41 L5 **Lower Basildon** W Berk
31 L6 **Lower Beeding** W Susx
88 E5 **Lower Benefield** Nhants
71 H2 **Lower Bentley** Worcs
72 F4 **Lower Boddington** Nhants
30 D3 **Lower Bourne** Surrey
72 C6 **Lower Brailes** Warwks
199 L2 **Lower Breakish** Highld
70 E3 **Lower Broadheath** Worcs
69 G4 **Lower Broxwood** Herefs
69 K6 **Lower Bullingham** Herefs
28 D7 **Lower Burgate** Hants
75 H5 **Lower Caldecote** C Beds
68 B7 **Lower Chapel** Powys
27 L5 **Lower Chicksgrove** Wilts
28 F2 **Lower Chute** Wilts
45 G3 **Lower Clapton** Gt Lon
85 G7 **Lower Clent** Worcs
123 J8 **Lower Cumberworth** Kirk
74 F2 **Lower Dean** Bed
210 C3 **Lower Diabaig** Highld
20 B4 **Lower Dicker** E Susx
83 G6 **Lower Down** Shrops
133 G6 **Lower Dunsforth** N York
70 B5 **Lower Egleton** Herefs
74 D6 **Lower End** M Keyn
35 H5 **Lower Eythorne** Kent

38 D5 **Lower Failand** N Som
30 B4 **Lower Farringdon** Hants
43 H6 **Lower Feltham** Gt Lon
30 C3 **Lower Froyle** Hants
7 L2 **Lower Gabwell** Devon
222 D4 **Lower Gledfield** Highld
26 C3 **Lower Godney** Somset
75 G7 **Lower Gravenhurst** C Beds
32 F5 **Lower Green** Kent
33 G5 **Lower Green** Kent
43 H6 **Lower Halliford** Surrey
46 E6 **Lower Halstow** Kent
15 J4 **Lower Hamworthy** Poole
34 F4 **Lower Hardres** Kent
58 C5 **Lower Hartwell** Bucks
68 F4 **Lower Hergest** Herefs
57 J3 **Lower Heyford** Oxon
123 H7 **Lower Houses** Kirk
113 G3 **Lower Irlam** Salfd
160 A2 **Lower Killeyan** Ag & B
38 C7 **Lower Langford** N Som
187 G6 **Lower Largo** Fife
100 A5 **Lower Leigh** Staffs
23 K4 **Lower Loxhore** Devon
54 E5 **Lower Lydbrook** Gloucs
69 H2 **Lower Lye** Herefs
37 K3 **Lower Machen** Newpt
25 J4 **Lower Merridge** Somset
73 G6 **Lower Middleton Cheney** Nhants
71 H5 **Lower Moor** Worcs
38 F3 **Lower Morton** S Glos
60 C6 **Lower Nazeing** Essex
37 J6 **Lower Penarth** V Glam
84 F4 **Lower Penn** Staffs
113 H6 **Lower Peover** Ches E
71 L5 **Lower Quinton** Warwks
78 C6 **Lower Raydon** Suffk
25 G4 **Lower Roadwater** Somset
39 L4 **Lower Seagry** Wilts
74 E6 **Lower Shelton** C Beds
42 C4 **Lower Shiplake** Oxon
72 F3 **Lower Shuckburgh** Warwks
56 D4 **Lower Slaughter** Gloucs
35 H6 **Lower Standen** Kent
39 L4 **Lower Stanton St Quintin** Wilts
46 D5 **Lower Stoke** Medway
38 F2 **Lower Stone** Gloucs
91 L5 **Lower Stow Bedon** Norfk
106 F5 **Lower Street** Norfk
78 D4 **Lower Street** Suffk
16 F1 **Lower Swanwick** Hants
56 D3 **Lower Swell** Gloucs
100 A5 **Lower Tean** Staffs
7 G2 **Lower Town** Devon
64 D6 **Lower Town** Pembks
11 K8 **Lower Upcott** Devon
29 K7 **Lower Upham** Hants
26 B2 **Lower Weare** Somset
68 F4 **Lower Welson** Herefs
71 G6 **Lower Westmancote** Worcs
27 H3 **Lower Whatley** Somset
112 E5 **Lower Whitley** Ches W
29 M4 **Lower Wield** Hants
20 C5 **Lower Willingdon** E Susx
113 J7 **Lower Withington** Ches E
28 C4 **Lower Woodford** Wilts
14 B3 **Lower Wraxhall** Dorset
87 K3 **Lowesby** Leics
93 L5 **Lowestoft** Suffk
137 G3 **Loweswater** Cumb
151 G3 **Low Fell** Gatesd
31 L4 **Lowfield Heath** W Susx
174 E2 **Low Gartachorrans** Stirlg
132 C5 **Low Grantley** N York
26 B5 **Low Ham** Somset
132 D7 **Low Harrogate** N York
148 E5 **Low Hesket** Cumb
134 B6 **Low Hutton** N York
88 E7 **Lowick** Nhants
168 F2 **Lowick** Nthumb
129 G3 **Lowick Green** Cumb
137 G3 **Low Lorton** Cumb
116 D7 **Low Marnham** Notts
142 E7 **Low Mill** N York
151 H5 **Low Moorsley** Sundld
136 D3 **Low Moresby** Cumb
129 J3 **Low Newton** Cumb
149 G3 **Low Row** Cumb
140 B7 **Low Row** N York
144 B2 **Low Salchrie** D & G
125 L7 **Low Santon** N Linc
71 L2 **Lowsonford** Warwks
92 E4 **Low Tharston** Norfk
138 D3 **Lowther** Cumb
135 G7 **Lowthorpe** E R Yk
25 J7 **Lowton** Somset
176 D2 **Low Torry** Fife
141 J5 **Low Worsall** N York
137 K6 **Low Wray** Cumb
11 L2 **Loxbeare** Devon
31 G4 **Loxhill** Surrey
23 K4 **Loxhore** Devon
72 C4 **Loxley** Warwks
26 A1 **Loxton** N Som
31 H5 **Loxwood** W Susx
229 J6 **Loyal Lodge** Highld
87 K6 **Lubenham** Leics
24 E3 **Luccombe** Somset
17 H6 **Luccombe Village** IoW
169 H4 **Lucker** Nthumb
6 B2 **Luckett** Cnwll
77 J7 **Lucking Street** Essex
39 J4 **Luckington** Wilts
187 G3 **Lucklawhill** Fife
24 E4 **Luckwell Bridge** Somset
69 J2 **Lucton** Herefs
233 b9 **Ludag** W Isls
118 D3 **Ludborough** Lincs
6 F5 **Ludbrook** Devon
49 K5 **Ludchurch** Pembks
122 F5 **Luddenden** Calder
122 F5 **Luddenden Foot** Calder
46 A6 **Luddesdown** Kent
125 J7 **Luddington** N Linc
71 L4 **Luddington** Warwks
89 G6 **Luddington in the Brook** Nhants
117 K4 **Ludford** Lincs
83 K8 **Ludford** Shrops
58 A4 **Ludgershall** Bucks
28 E2 **Ludgershall** Wilts
2 E5 **Ludgvan** Cnwll
107 H8 **Ludham** Norfk
83 K7 **Ludlow** Shrops
26 B8 **Ludney** Somset
27 K6 **Ludwell** Wilts
151 J6 **Ludworth** Dur
178 B3 **Luffness** E Loth
164 C5 **Lugar** E Ayrs
178 D4 **Luggate Burn** E Loth
175 K4 **Luggiebank** N Lans
174 D7 **Lugton** E Ayrs
69 K6 **Lugwardine** Herefs
209 J8 **Luib** Highld
181 L5 **Luing** Ag & B
69 H6 **Lulham** Herefs
86 B2 **Lullington** Derbys
27 H2 **Lullington** Somset
38 D7 **Lulsgate Bottom** N Som
70 D4 **Lulsley** Worcs
122 F6 **Lumb** Calder
124 D4 **Lumby** N York
175 H4 **Lumloch** E Duns
206 B4 **Lumphanan** Abers
186 C8 **Lumphinnans** Fife
205 K2 **Lumsden** Abers
197 H6 **Lunan** Angus
196 D6 **Lunanhead** Angus
186 A2 **Luncarty** P & K
126 B2 **Lund** E R Yk
125 G4 **Lund** N York
186 E1 **Lundie** Angus
187 G6 **Lundin Links** Fife
187 G6 **Lundin Mill** Fife
22 B3 **Lundy** Devon
181 L5 **Lunga** Ag & B
235 d4 **Lunna** Shet
33 J2 **Lunsford** Kent
20 E4 **Lunsford's Cross** E Susx
111 K2 **Lunt** Sefton
12 F2 **Luppitt** Devon
123 L6 **Lupset** Wakefd
129 L4 **Lupton** Cumb
30 F6 **Lurgashall** W Susx
11 L2 **Lurley** Devon
7 J4 **Luscombe** Devon
183 L8 **Luss** Ag & B
171 L2 **Lussagiven** Ag & B
208 D3 **Lusta** Highld
11 H8 **Lustleigh** Devon
69 J2 **Luston** Herefs
197 G3 **Luthermuir** Abers
186 E4 **Luthrie** Fife
7 K1 **Luton** Devon
12 D2 **Luton** Devon
59 H4 **Luton** Luton
46 C6 **Luton** Medway
59 J4 *Luton Airport* Luton
87 G6 **Lutterworth** Leics
6 E4 **Lutton** Devon
7 G4 **Lutton** Devon
104 C7 **Lutton** Lincs
89 G6 **Lutton** Nhants
24 F4 **Luxborough** Somset
5 G4 **Luxulyan** Cnwll
231 J7 **Lybster** Highld
83 G6 **Lydbury North** Shrops
21 K2 **Lydd** Kent
21 L2 *Lydd Airport* Kent
35 H5 **Lydden** Kent
35 K2 **Lydden** Kent
88 C4 **Lyddington** Rutlnd
25 H5 **Lydeard St Lawrence** Somset
10 D7 **Lydford** Devon
26 E5 **Lydford on Fosse** Somset
122 D5 **Lydgate** Calder
83 G5 **Lydham** Shrops
40 C3 **Lydiard Millicent** Wilts
40 C4 **Lydiard Tregoze** Swindn
111 K2 **Lydiate** Sefton
85 H7 **Lydiate Ash** Worcs
27 H8 **Lydlinch** Dorset
54 F7 **Lydney** Gloucs
49 J7 **Lydstep** Pembks
85 G6 **Lye** Dudley
32 F6 **Lye Green** E Susx
71 L2 **Lye Green** Warwks
27 J3 **Lye's Green** Wilts
41 H2 **Lyford** Oxon
34 F6 **Lymbridge Green** Kent
13 J4 **Lyme Regis** Dorset
34 F6 **Lyminge** Kent
16 C4 **Lymington** Hants
18 D5 **Lyminster** W Susx
113 G4 **Lymm** Warrtn
34 F7 **Lympne** Kent
25 M1 **Lympsham** Somset
12 C5 **Lympstone** Devon
203 J5 **Lynchat** Highld
92 D3 **Lynch Green** Norfk
16 C2 **Lyndhurst** Hants
88 C3 **Lyndon** Rutlnd
166 B2 **Lyne** Border
43 G7 **Lyne** Surrey
98 C6 **Lyneal** Shrops
56 F4 **Lyneham** Oxon
40 A5 **Lyneham** Wilts
40 A5 *Lyneham Airport* Wilts
159 H4 **Lynemouth** Nthumb
206 E4 **Lyne of Skene** Abers
234 b7 **Lyness** Ork
106 C8 **Lyng** Norfk
25 M5 **Lyng** Somset
23 L2 **Lynmouth** Devon
34 C3 **Lynsted** Kent
23 L2 **Lynton** Devon
14 C2 **Lyon's Gate** Dorset
69 G4 **Lyonshall** Herefs
15 H4 **Lytchett Matravers** Dorset
15 H4 **Lytchett Minster** Dorset
231 K3 **Lyth** Highld
120 E5 **Lytham** Lancs
120 D5 **Lytham St Anne's** Lancs
143 H5 **Lythe** N York
230 F3 **Lythmore** Highld

M

3 K4 **Mabe Burnthouse** Cnwll
119 G4 **Mablethorpe** Lincs
113 K6 **Macclesfield** Ches E
113 K6 **Macclesfield Crematorium** Ches E
216 D2 **Macduff** Abers
161 J7 **Macharioch** Ag & B
37 K3 **Machen** Caerph
162 A3 **Machrie** N Ayrs
161 G5 **Machrihanish** Ag & B
180 E8 **Machrins** Ag & B
81 G4 **Machynlleth** Powys
51 G5 **Machynys** Carmth
100 F5 **Mackworth** Derbys
177 L4 **Macmerry** E Loth
185 K3 **Madderty** P & K
176 C3 **Maddiston** Falk
99 H4 **Madeley** Staffs
84 C3 **Madeley** Wrekin
76 B3 **Madingley** Cambs
69 H6 **Madley** Herefs
70 E5 **Madresfield** Worcs
2 E5 **Madron** Cnwll
49 J3 **Maenclochog** Pembks
36 F5 **Maendy** V Glam
95 L4 **Maentwrog** Gwynd
65 L3 **Maen-y-groes** Cerdgn
99 H5 **Maer** Staffs
36 F2 **Maerdy** Rhondd
97 L7 **Maesbrook** Shrops
97 L7 **Maesbury** Shrops
97 L7 **Maesbury Marsh** Shrops
65 K5 **Maesllyn** Cerdgn
36 D3 **Maesteg** Brdgnd
51 H3 **Maesybont** Carmth
37 J2 **Maesycwmmer** Caerph

215 H5 **Maggieknockater** Moray
20 C4 **Magham Down** E Susx
111 K2 **Maghull** Sefton
87 G6 **Magna Park** Leics
38 B3 **Magor** Mons
38 B3 **Magor Services** Mons
32 B6 **Maidenbower** W Susx
27 J4 **Maiden Bradley** Wilts
7 L3 **Maidencombe** Torbay
13 H4 **Maidenhayne** Devon
38 E6 **Maiden Head** N Som
42 E4 **Maidenhead** W & M
14 B3 **Maiden Newton** Dorset
163 G7 **Maidens** S Ayrs
42 E5 **Maiden's Green** Br For
49 G7 **Maiden Wells** Pembks
73 H4 **Maidford** Nhants
73 K7 **Maids Moreton** Bucks
33 K3 **Maidstone** Kent
33 L3 **Maidstone Services** Kent
87 L7 **Maidwell** Nhants
235 d6 **Mail** Shet
37 L3 **Maindee** Newpt
234 c6 **Mainland** Ork
235 c5 **Mainland** Shet
141 H2 **Mainsforth** Dur
196 E4 **Mains of Balhall** Angus
197 G2 **Mains of Balnakettle** Abers
214 D7 **Mains of Dalvey** Highld
197 H2 **Mains of Haulkerton** Abers
215 K8 **Mains of Lesmoir** Abers
196 E5 **Mains of Melgunds** Angus
147 G4 **Mainsriddle** D & G
82 F6 **Mainstone** Shrops
55 J4 **Maisemore** Gloucs
7 G7 **Malborough** Devon
61 K6 **Maldon** Essex
131 G6 **Malham** N York
209 G2 **Maligar** Highld
199 L6 **Mallaig** Highld
199 L5 **Mallaigvaig** Highld
177 G5 **Malleny Mills** C Edin
108 E7 **Malltraeth** IoA
81 J2 **Mallwyd** Gwynd
39 L3 **Malmesbury** Wilts
24 C2 **Malmsmead** Devon
98 C3 **Malpas** Ches W
4 D7 **Malpas** Cnwll
37 L3 **Malpas** Newpt
115 K3 **Maltby** Rothm
141 L5 **Maltby** S on T
118 F5 **Maltby le Marsh** Lincs
34 B6 **Maltman's Hill** Kent
134 C5 **Malton** N York
70 D5 **Malvern Hills**
70 E5 **Malvern Link** Worcs
70 D6 **Malvern Wells** Worcs
70 C1 **Mamble** Worcs
53 L7 **Mamhilad** Mons
3 K6 **Manaccan** Cnwll
82 C3 **Manafon** Powys
232 d5 **Manais** W Isls
11 H8 **Manaton** Devon
118 E4 **Manby** Lincs
86 D4 **Mancetter** Warwks
113 J3 **Manchester** Manch
113 J5 *Manchester Airport* Manch
111 K7 **Mancot** Flints
201 L5 **Mandally** Highld
179 G7 **Manderston House** Border
90 C5 **Manea** Cambs
85 K4 **Maney** Birm
140 F4 **Manfield** N York
38 F5 **Mangotsfield** S Glos
232 d5 **Manish** W Isls
112 D7 **Manley** Ches W
53 J7 **Manmoel** Caerph
188 C7 **Mannel** Ag & B
40 C8 **Manningford Bohune** Wilts
40 C8 **Manningford Bruce** Wilts
123 H4 **Manningham** C Brad
31 K5 **Manning's Heath** W Susx
15 K2 **Mannington** Dorset
62 D2 **Manningtree** Essex
207 H4 **Mannofield** C Aber
49 H7 **Manorbier** Pembks
49 H7 **Manorbier Newton** Pembks
167 K3 **Manorhill** Border
64 C7 **Manorowen** Pembks
45 H3 **Manor Park** Gt Lon
45 H3 **Manor Park Crematorium** Gt Lon
69 H5 **Mansell Gamage** Herefs
69 H5 **Mansell Lacy** Herefs
164 C6 **Mansfield** E Ayrs
101 K1 **Mansfield** Notts
101 K2 **Mansfield & District Crematorium** Notts
115 K8 **Mansfield Woodhouse** Notts
27 J7 **Manston** Dorset
35 J2 **Manston** Kent
124 B4 **Manston** Leeds
15 J2 **Manswood** Dorset
88 F1 **Manthorpe** Lincs
116 F2 **Manton** N Linc
88 C3 **Manton** Rutlnd
40 D6 **Manton** Wilts
60 D3 **Manuden** Essex
26 F6 **Maperton** Somset
102 B1 **Maplebeck** Notts
42 A5 **Mapledurham** Oxon
30 B2 **Mapledurwell** Hants
31 K6 **Maplehurst** W Susx
45 K7 **Maplescombe** Kent
100 D3 **Mapleton** Derbys
101 H4 **Mapperley** Derbys
101 L4 **Mapperley Park** C Nott
13 L3 **Mapperton** Dorset
71 J2 **Mappleborough Green** Warwks
126 F2 **Mappleton** E R Yk
123 L7 **Mapplewell** Barns
14 E2 **Mappowder** Dorset
4 C5 **Marazanvose** Cnwll
2 F5 **Marazion** Cnwll
98 E4 **Marbury** Ches E
90 B4 **March** Cambs
165 J6 **March** S Lans
41 J2 **Marcham** Oxon
98 E6 **Marchamley** Shrops
100 C6 **Marchington** Staffs
94 F7 **Marchros** Gwynd
98 A3 **Marchwiel** Wrexhm
16 D1 **Marchwood** Hants
36 E6 **Marcross** V Glam
69 K5 **Marden** Herefs
33 J4 **Marden** Kent
40 C8 **Marden** Wilts
33 K5 **Marden Thorn** Kent
53 L5 **Mardy** Mons
103 L1 **Mareham le Fen** Lincs
118 C7 **Mareham on the Hill** Lincs
18 E3 **Marehill** W Susx
19 M2 **Maresfield** E Susx
126 E5 **Marfleet** C KuH
98 A2 **Marford** Wrexhm
36 B3 **Margam** Neath
36 C4 **Margam Crematorium** Neath
27 J7 **Margaret Marsh** Dorset
61 G7 **Margaretting** Essex
61 G7 **Margaretting Tye** Essex
35 K1 **Margate** Kent
162 D3 **Margnaheglish** N Ayrs
145 M5 **Margrie** D & G
142 E4 **Margrove Park** R & Cl
91 G2 **Marham** Norfk
9 G4 **Marhamchurch** Cnwll
89 G3 **Marholm** C Pete
24 B6 **Mariansleigh** Devon
46 F5 **Marine Town** Kent
206 D4 **Marionburgh** Abers
209 H2 **Marishader** Highld
6 C3 **Maristow** Devon
155 J5 **Marjoriebanks** D & G
26 B2 **Mark** Somset
32 E5 **Markbeech** Kent
119 G5 **Markby** Lincs
33 G6 **Mark Cross** E Susx
100 F5 **Markeaton Crematorium** C Derb
86 E3 **Market Bosworth** Leics
89 G2 **Market Deeping** Lincs
98 F5 **Market Drayton** Shrops
87 K6 **Market Harborough** Leics
28 A1 **Market Lavington** Wilts
88 C1 **Market Overton** Rutlnd
117 J4 **Market Rasen** Lincs
118 C5 **Market Stainton** Lincs
115 K7 **Market Warsop** Notts
125 K3 **Market Weighton** E R Yk
92 B7 **Market Weston** Suffk
86 F2 **Markfield** Leics
53 J7 **Markham** Caerph
116 B6 **Markham Moor** Notts
186 E6 **Markinch** Fife
132 D6 **Markington** N York
178 C3 **Markle** E Loth
38 F7 **Marksbury** BaNES
61 L4 **Marks Tey** Essex
59 H5 **Markyate** Herts
40 D6 **Marlborough** Wilts
71 K4 **Marlcliff** Warwks
7 K3 **Marldon** Devon
79 G3 **Marlesford** Suffk
92 D2 **Marlingford** Norfk
48 D5 **Marloes** Pembks
42 D3 **Marlow** Bucks
42 D3 **Marlow Bottom** Bucks
32 D4 **Marlpit Hill** Kent
27 H7 **Marnhull** Dorset
113 L4 **Marple** Stockp
115 K1 **Marr** Donc
140 D7 **Marrick** N York
122 F7 **Marsden** Kirk
151 J3 **Marsden** S Tyne
59 K6 **Marshalswick** Herts
106 E7 **Marsham** Norfk
57 K7 **Marsh Baldon** Oxon
35 J3 **Marshborough** Kent
83 J5 **Marshbrook** Shrops
118 E2 **Marshchapel** Lincs
59 H3 **Marsh Farm** Luton
37 L4 **Marshfield** Newpt
39 H5 **Marshfield** S Glos
8 F6 **Marshgate** Cnwll
57 M4 **Marsh Gibbon** Bucks
12 D4 **Marsh Green** Devon
32 D4 **Marsh Green** Kent
90 D2 **Marshland St James** Norfk
115 H5 **Marsh Lane** Derbys
24 F3 **Marsh Street** Somset
13 J3 **Marshwood** Dorset
140 D6 **Marske** N York
142 D3 **Marske-by-the-Sea** R & Cl
69 G3 **Marston** Herefs
102 E4 **Marston** Lincs
57 K6 **Marston** Oxon
99 L6 **Marston** Staffs
27 L1 **Marston** Wilts
85 L6 **Marston Green** Solhll
26 E6 **Marston Magna** Somset
40 C2 **Marston Meysey** Wilts
100 C5 **Marston Montgomery** Derbys
74 E6 **Marston Moretaine** C Beds
100 E6 **Marston on Dove** Derbys
73 G6 **Marston St Lawrence** Nhants
87 K6 **Marston Trussell** Nhants
54 D4 **Marstow** Herefs
58 F5 **Marsworth** Bucks
40 F7 **Marten** Wilts
107 J8 **Martham** Norfk
28 B7 **Martin** Hants
35 J5 **Martin** Kent
103 J1 **Martin** Lincs
23 L2 **Martinhoe** Devon
70 F3 **Martin Hussingtree** Worcs
14 C5 **Martinstown** Dorset
78 F5 **Martlesham** Suffk
78 F5 **Martlesham Heath** Suffk
49 H5 **Martletwy** Pembks
70 D3 **Martley** Worcs
26 C7 **Martock** Somset
113 J7 **Marton** Ches E
126 F3 **Marton** E R Yk
116 D5 **Marton** Lincs
142 B4 **Marton** Middsb
132 F6 **Marton** N York
134 B3 **Marton** N York
82 F3 **Marton** Shrops
72 E2 **Marton** Warwks
132 E5 **Marton-le-Moor** N York
29 K5 **Martyr Worthy** Hants
234 b5 **Marwick** Ork
23 H4 **Marwood** Devon
212 D4 **Marybank** Highld
212 E3 **Maryburgh** Highld
207 G5 **Maryculter** Abers
179 G6 **Marygold** Border
175 G4 **Maryhill** C Glas
175 G4 **Maryhill Crematorium** C Glas
197 H3 **Marykirk** Abers
44 F4 **Marylebone** Gt Lon
121 H8 **Marylebone** Wigan
214 F6 **Marypark** Moray
147 H7 **Maryport** Cumb
144 D7 **Maryport** D & G
10 C7 **Marystow** Devon
6 D1 **Mary Tavy** Devon
197 H5 **Maryton** Angus
206 B6 **Marywell** Abers
207 H5 **Marywell** Abers
197 G7 **Marywell** Angus
132 C4 **Masham** N York
130 C4 **Masongill** N York
163 J5 **Masonhill Crematorium** S Ayrs
115 J6 **Mastin Moor** Derbys
60 E5 **Matching Green** Essex
60 E5 **Matching Tye** Essex
158 C7 **Matfen** Nthumb
33 H5 **Matfield** Kent
38 D3 **Mathern** Mons
70 D5 **Mathon** Herefs
48 E2 **Mathry** Pembks
106 D5 **Matlask** Norfk
100 F1 **Matlock** Derbys
100 F2 **Matlock Bath** Derbys
55 J5 **Matson** Gloucs

Mattersey - Midhopestones

116 B4 **Mattersey** Notts
42 B8 **Mattingley** Hants
92 C2 **Mattishall** Norfk
92 C2 **Mattishall Burgh** Norfk
163 L4 **Mauchline** E Ayrs
217 H5 **Maud** Abers
236 d6 **Maufant** Jersey
56 D3 **Maugersbury** Gloucs
237 e3 **Maughold** IoM
212 C6 **Mauld** Highld
74 F6 **Maulden** C Beds
138 F4 **Maulds Meaburn** Cumb
132 E3 **Maunby** N York
25 G5 **Maundown** Somset
93 K2 **Mautby** Norfk
85 J1 **Mavesyn Ridware** Staffs
118 E7 **Mavis Enderby** Lincs
147 J5 **Mawbray** Cumb
121 G7 **Mawdesley** Lancs
36 C4 **Mawdlam** Brdgnd
3 J6 **Mawgan** Cnwll
4 D3 **Mawgan Porth** Cnwll
3 J3 **Mawla** Cnwll
3 K5 **Mawnan** Cnwll
3 K5 **Mawnan Smith** Cnwll
88 B7 **Mawsley** Nhants
89 G2 **Maxey** C Pete
86 B6 **Maxstoke** Warwks
167 J4 **Maxton** Border
35 J6 **Maxton** Kent
155 G6 **Maxwell Town** D & G
9 H6 **Maxworthy** Cnwll
99 J3 **May Bank** Staffs
163 H7 **Maybole** S Ayrs
43 G8 **Maybury** Surrey
33 G7 **Mayfield** E Susx
177 K5 **Mayfield** Mdloth
100 D4 **Mayfield** Staffs
31 G1 **Mayford** Surrey
55 G4 **May Hill** Gloucs
61 L7 **Mayland** Essex
61 L7 **Maylandsea** Essex
20 C3 **Maynard's Green** E Susx
93 J4 **Maypole Green** Norfk
77 K3 **Maypole Green** Suffk
39 G8 **Meadgate** BaNES
58 D6 **Meadle** Bucks
151 G6 **Meadowfield** Dur
9 K8 **Meadwell** Devon
123 K3 **Meanwood** Leeds
26 C3 **Meare** Somset
25 L6 **Meare Green** Somset
25 M6 **Meare Green** Somset
174 F7 **Mearns** E Rens
74 B2 **Mears Ashby** Nhants
86 D2 **Measham** Leics
129 J4 **Meathop** Cumb
6 D3 **Meavy** Devon
88 B5 **Medbourne** Leics
9 H2 **Meddon** Devon
115 L7 **Meden Vale** Notts
42 D4 **Medmenham** Bucks
150 E4 **Medomsley** Dur
30 A4 **Medstead** Hants
46 C7 **Medway Crematorium** Kent
46 D7 **Medway Services** Medway
99 M1 **Meerbrook** Staffs
60 C2 **Meesden** Herts
10 E3 **Meeth** Devon
107 G6 **Meeting House Hill** Norfk
50 C2 **Meidrim** Carmth
82 D2 **Meifod** Powys
195 L7 **Meigle** P & K
164 F6 **Meikle Carco** D & G
175 J7 **Meikle Earnock** S Lans
173 H6 **Meikle Kilmory** Ag & B
195 G8 **Meikle Obney** P & K
195 J7 **Meikleour** P & K
216 D7 **Meikle Wartle** Abers
50 F4 **Meinciau** Carmth
99 L4 **Meir** C Stke
75 L5 **Melbourn** Cambs
101 G7 **Melbourne** Derbys
125 H2 **Melbourne** E R Yk
27 K7 **Melbury Abbas** Dorset
14 B2 **Melbury Bubb** Dorset
14 B2 **Melbury Osmond** Dorset
74 E2 **Melchbourne** Bed
14 E2 **Melcombe Bingham** Dorset
10 E6 **Meldon** Devon
158 E5 **Meldon** Nthumb
75 L5 **Meldreth** Cambs
184 F7 **Meldrum** Stirlg
182 B5 **Melfort** Ag & B
110 E5 **Meliden** Denbgs
97 G3 **Melin-y-wig** Denbgs
138 D3 **Melkinthorpe** Cumb
149 J3 **Melkridge** Nthumb
39 K7 **Melksham** Wilts
130 B5 **Melling** Lancs
111 L2 **Melling** Sefton
92 C8 **Mellis** Suffk
219 K3 **Mellon Charles** Highld
219 K3 **Mellon Udrigle** Highld
121 J4 **Mellor** Lancs
113 M4 **Mellor** Stockp
121 J4 **Mellor Brook** Lancs
27 G2 **Mells** Somset
149 G7 **Melmerby** Cumb
131 K3 **Melmerby** N York
132 E4 **Melmerby** N York
229 J3 **Melness** Highld
13 L3 **Melplash** Dorset
167 H3 **Melrose** Border
234 b7 **Melsetter** Ork
140 F5 **Melsonby** N York
123 G7 **Meltham** Kirk
126 B5 **Melton** E R Yk
79 G4 **Melton** Suffk
106 C6 **Melton Constable** Norfk
102 C8 **Melton Mowbray** Leics
126 D7 **Melton Ross** N Linc
219 H4 **Melvaig** Highld
83 G1 **Melverley** Shrops
230 C3 **Melvich** Highld
13 H2 **Membury** Devon
40 F5 **Membury Services** W Berk
217 H2 **Memsie** Abers
196 C5 **Memus** Angus
109 H6 **Menai Bridge** IoA
92 F6 **Mendham** Suffk
26 E3 **Mendip Crematorium** Somset
26 D2 **Mendip Hills**
78 D2 **Mendlesham** Suffk
78 D2 **Mendlesham Green** Suffk
5 L4 **Menheniot** Cnwll
164 F7 **Mennock** D & G
123 H2 **Menston** C Brad
185 H7 **Menstrie** Clacks
58 E4 **Mentmore** Bucks
200 C7 **Meoble** Highld
83 J2 **Meole Brace** Shrops
29 L7 **Meonstoke** Hants
45 M6 **Meopham** Kent
90 B7 **Mepal** Cambs
75 G7 **Meppershall** C Beds
113 G5 **Mere** Ches E
27 J5 **Mere** Wilts
120 F6 **Mere Brow** Lancs
122 C4 **Mereclough** Lancs
33 H3 **Mereworth** Kent
86 B6 **Meriden** Solhll
208 F7 **Merkadale** Highld
15 J3 **Merley** Poole
48 F7 **Merrion** Pembks
26 C8 **Merriott** Somset
31 G2 **Merrow** Surrey
43 J2 **Merry Hill** Herts
84 F4 **Merryhill** Wolves
5 L3 **Merrymeet** Cnwll
62 B5 **Mersea Island** Essex
34 E6 **Mersham** Kent
32 B3 **Merstham** Surrey
18 B5 **Merston** W Susx
17 G5 **Merstone** IoW
67 L6 **Merthyr Cynog** Powys
36 D5 **Merthyr Mawr** Brdgnd
53 G6 **Merthyr Tydfil** Myr Td
53 G7 **Merthyr Vale** Myr Td
10 D3 **Merton** Devon
44 E6 **Merton** Gt Lon
91 K4 **Merton** Norfk
57 L4 **Merton** Oxon
24 B7 **Meshaw** Devon
61 L4 **Messing** Essex
116 E2 **Messingham** N Linc
93 G7 **Metfield** Suffk
6 B3 **Metherell** Cnwll
103 H1 **Metheringham** Lincs
186 F7 **Methil** Fife
186 F7 **Methilhill** Fife
217 G6 **Methlick** Abers
185 L3 **Methven** P & K
91 G4 **Methwold** Norfk
91 G4 **Methwold Hythe** Norfk
93 H5 **Mettingham** Suffk
106 E5 **Metton** Norfk
4 F6 **Mevagissey** Cnwll
115 J2 **Mexborough** Donc
231 K2 **Mey** Highld
94 D6 **Meyllteyrn** Gwynd
56 C7 **Meysey Hampton** Gloucs
232 d2 **Miabhig** W Isls
232 d2 **Miavaig** W Isls
54 D3 **Michaelchurch** Herefs
69 G7 **Michaelchurch Escley** Herefs
37 K4 **Michaelstone-y-Fedw** Newpt
37 J5 **Michaelston-le-Pit** V Glam
5 G1 **Michaelstow** Cnwll
39 G2 **Michaelwood Services** Gloucs
29 K4 **Micheldever** Hants
29 K3 **Micheldever Station** Hants
29 G6 **Michelmersh** Hants
78 D3 **Mickfield** Suffk
115 K3 **Micklebring** Donc
143 G5 **Mickleby** N York
124 C4 **Micklefield** Leeds
31 K2 **Mickleham** Surrey
100 F5 **Mickleover** C Derb
140 B3 **Mickleton** Dur
71 L5 **Mickleton** Gloucs
124 B5 **Mickletown** Leeds
112 C7 **Mickle Trafford** Ches W
132 C4 **Mickley** N York
150 D3 **Mickley Square** Nthumb
217 H2 **Mid Ardlaw** Abers
234 c4 **Midbea** Ork
206 C5 **Mid Beltie** Abers
176 E5 **Mid Calder** W Loth
231 K7 **Mid Clyth** Highld
216 C3 **Mid Culbeuchly** Abers
57 J3 **Middle Aston** Oxon
57 H3 **Middle Barton** Oxon
155 L6 **Middlebie** D & G
194 D3 **Middlebridge** P & K
26 C8 **Middle Chinnock** Somset
58 B3 **Middle Claydon** Bucks
131 L3 **Middleham** N York
115 H6 **Middle Handley** Derbys
39 J6 **Middlehill** Wilts
83 K5 **Middlehope** Shrops
172 F1 **Middle Kames** Ag & B
71 J5 **Middle Littleton** Worcs
14 C2 **Middlemarsh** Dorset
100 C4 **Middle Mayfield** Staffs
117 H4 **Middle Rasen** Lincs
7 K2 **Middle Rocombe** Devon
141 L4 **Middlesbrough** Middsb
129 L2 **Middleshaw** Cumb
131 K5 **Middlesmoor** N York
46 D5 **Middle Stoke** Medway
141 G2 **Middlestone** Dur
123 K6 **Middlestown** Wakefd
167 K2 **Middlethird** Border
188 B7 **Middleton** Ag & B
100 F2 **Middleton** Derbys
114 D8 **Middleton** Derbys
77 K6 **Middleton** Essex
29 H3 **Middleton** Hants
69 K1 **Middleton** Herefs
123 L5 **Middleton** Leeds
123 G2 **Middleton** N York
134 B3 **Middleton** N York
88 B5 **Middleton** Nhants
90 F1 **Middleton** Norfk
158 D5 **Middleton** Nthumb
186 B6 **Middleton** P & K
113 K1 **Middleton** Rochdl
83 K7 **Middleton** Shrops
79 J2 **Middleton** Suffk
50 E7 **Middleton** Swans
85 L4 **Middleton** Warwks
73 G6 **Middleton Cheney** Nhants
113 K1 **Middleton Crematorium** Rochdl
139 L3 **Middleton-in-Teesdale** Dur
79 J2 **Middleton Moor** Suffk
141 J5 **Middleton One Row** Darltn
18 C5 **Middleton-on-Sea** W Susx
69 K2 **Middleton on the Hill** Herefs
125 L2 **Middleton on the Wolds** E R Yk
207 H3 **Middleton Park** C Aber
132 E4 **Middleton Quernhow** N York
141 J5 **Middleton St George** Darltn
84 C6 **Middleton Scriven** Shrops
57 K4 **Middleton Stoney** Oxon
141 G6 **Middleton Tyas** N York
2 a2 **Middle Town** IoS
82 F2 **Middletown** Powys
72 D5 **Middle Tysoe** Warwks
28 F4 **Middle Wallop** Hants
113 G7 **Middlewich** Ches E
28 E5 **Middle Winterslow** Wilts
5 L2 **Middlewood** Cnwll
28 C4 **Middle Woodford** Wilts
78 D3 **Middlewood Green** Suffk
163 M3 **Middleyard** E Ayrs
26 B5 **Middlezoy** Somset
39 H7 **Midford** BaNES
41 K6 **Midgham** W Berk
122 F5 **Midgley** Calder
123 K7 **Midgley** Wakefd
114 E2 **Midhopestones** Sheff

30 E6 **Midhurst** W Susx
18 B4 **Mid Lavant** W Susx
167 H4 **Midlem** Border
212 C6 **Mid Mains** Highld
173 H6 **Midpark** Ag & B
26 F1 **Midsomer Norton** BaNES
229 J4 **Midtown** Highld
72 C3 **Mid Warwickshire Crematorium** Warwks
235 d3 **Mid Yell** Shet
205 K4 **Migvie** Abers
26 F7 **Milborne Port** Somset
14 F3 **Milborne St Andrew** Dorset
26 F7 **Milborne Wick** Somset
158 E6 **Milbourne** Nthumb
39 L3 **Milbourne** Wilts
138 F2 **Milburn** Cumb
38 F3 **Milbury Heath** S Glos
132 F6 **Milby** N York
72 E7 **Milcombe** Oxon
77 L5 **Milden** Suffk
91 G8 **Mildenhall** Suffk
40 E6 **Mildenhall** Wilts
105 L8 **Mileham** Norfk
19 H4 **Mile Oak** Br & H
176 E2 **Milesmark** Fife
113 J2 **Miles Platting** Manch
46 F5 **Mile Town** Kent
168 D3 **Milfield** Nthumb
101 G4 **Milford** Derbys
22 C6 **Milford** Devon
99 L7 **Milford** Staffs
30 F3 **Milford** Surrey
48 F6 **Milford Haven** Pembks
16 C4 **Milford on Sea** Hants
54 E6 **Milkwall** Gloucs
30 D5 **Milland** W Susx
122 F6 **Mill Bank** Calder
217 J5 **Millbreck** Abers
30 D3 **Millbridge** Surrey
74 E6 **Millbrook** C Beds
29 G8 **Millbrook** C Sotn
6 B5 **Millbrook** Cnwll
236 c7 **Millbrook** Jersey
113 L4 **Mill Brow** Stockp
206 F4 **Millbuie** Abers
212 E4 **Millbuie** Highld
21 G2 **Millcorner** E Susx
222 E7 **Millcraig** Highld
100 C2 **Milldale** Staffs
42 C4 **Mill End** Bucks
60 B2 **Mill End** Herts
177 J4 **Millerhill** Mdloth
114 C6 **Miller's Dale** Derbys
175 H5 **Millerston** C Glas
76 F5 **Mill Green** Cambs
61 G7 **Mill Green** Essex
103 L7 **Mill Green** Lincs
77 L6 **Mill Green** Suffk
78 B3 **Mill Green** Suffk
78 D3 **Mill Green** Suffk
68 F5 **Millhalf** Herefs
175 K7 **Millheugh** S Lans
44 E2 **Mill Hill** Gt Lon
173 G4 **Millhouse** Ag & B
155 K5 **Millhousebridge** D & G
114 E2 **Millhouse Green** Barns
115 G5 **Millhouses** Sheff
174 D6 **Milliken Park** Rens
125 J1 **Millington** E R Yk
99 J5 **Millmeece** Staffs
185 H4 **Mill of Drummond** P & K
174 D2 **Mill of Haldane** W Duns
128 E4 **Millom** Cumb
173 K7 **Millport** N Ayrs
78 C1 **Mill Street** Suffk
130 C2 **Millthrop** Cumb
207 G5 **Milltimber** C Aber
205 G4 **Milltown** Abers
205 K3 **Milltown** Abers
156 C6 **Milltown** D & G
23 J4 **Milltown** Devon
206 C5 **Milltown of Campfield** Abers
215 G6 **Milltown of Edinvillie** Moray
206 C5 **Milltown of Learney** Abers
186 B6 **Milnathort** P & K
175 G4 **Milngavie** E Duns
122 D7 **Milnrow** Rochdl
129 K3 **Milnthorpe** Cumb
208 B4 **Milovaig** Highld
84 B8 **Milson** Shrops
34 B3 **Milstead** Kent
28 D3 **Milston** Wilts
73 H5 **Milthorpe** Nhants
76 C2 **Milton** Cambs
148 F3 **Milton** Cumb
144 F4 **Milton** D & G
154 E7 **Milton** D & G
100 F7 **Milton** Derbys
209 L5 **Milton** Highld
212 D7 **Milton** Highld
212 E4 **Milton** Highld
223 G6 **Milton** Highld
231 L5 **Milton** Highld
174 C5 **Milton** Inver
46 A5 **Milton** Kent
204 E2 **Milton** Moray
215 L2 **Milton** Moray
37 M7 **Milton** N Som
116 B6 **Milton** Notts
41 J3 **Milton** Oxon
72 F7 **Milton** Oxon
195 G4 **Milton** P & K
49 H6 **Milton** Pembks
26 C6 **Milton** Somset
184 B6 **Milton** Stirlg
174 D4 **Milton** W Duns
14 F3 **Milton Abbas** Dorset
9 K8 **Milton Abbot** Devon
177 H5 **Milton Bridge** Mdloth
58 F3 **Milton Bryan** C Beds
26 F4 **Milton Clevedon** Somset
6 D3 **Milton Combe** Devon
9 K3 **Milton Damerel** Devon
74 E4 **Milton Ernest** Bed
98 C2 **Milton Green** Ches W
41 J3 **Milton Hill** Oxon
74 C6 **Milton Keynes** M Keyn
40 D7 **Milton Lilbourne** Wilts
73 K4 **Milton Malsor** Nhants
184 D1 **Milton Morenish** P & K
206 B5 **Milton of Auchinhove** Abers
186 E7 **Milton of Balgonie** Fife
174 E1 **Milton of Buchanan** Stirlg
175 H3 **Milton of Campsie** E Duns
213 G6 **Milton of Leys** Highld
207 G5 **Milton of Murtle** C Aber
205 J6 **Milton of Tullich** Abers
27 J5 **Milton on Stour** Dorset
46 E6 **Milton Regis** Kent
56 E4 **Milton-under-Wychwood** Oxon
25 H6 **Milverton** Somset
72 C2 **Milverton** Warwks
99 L6 **Milwich** Staffs
182 D7 **Minard** Ag & B
55 K7 **Minchinhampton** Gloucs
24 F3 **Minehead** Somset
97 L3 **Minera** Wrexhm
40 A3 **Minety** Wilts
95 K5 **Minffordd** Gwynd
190 D3 **Mingarrypark** Highld
118 D8 **Miningsby** Lincs
5 L2 **Minions** Cnwll
163 J6 **Minishant** S Ayrs
81 J2 **Minllyn** Gwynd
145 J2 **Minnigaff** D & G
216 E3 **Minnonie** Abers
132 F6 **Minskip** N York
16 C1 **Minstead** Hants
30 D7 **Minsted** W Susx
35 J2 **Minster** Kent
46 F5 **Minster** Kent
83 G3 **Minsterley** Shrops
56 F5 **Minster Lovell** Oxon
55 H5 **Minsterworth** Gloucs
14 C2 **Minterne Magna** Dorset
117 K6 **Minting** Lincs
217 J5 **Mintlaw** Abers
105 G8 **Mintlyn Crematorium** Norfk
167 H5 **Minto** Border
83 H5 **Minton** Shrops
136 D4 **Mirehouse** Cumb
231 K4 **Mireland** Highld
123 J6 **Mirfield** Kirk
55 L6 **Miserden** Gloucs
37 G4 **Miskin** Rhondd
116 B3 **Misson** Notts
87 G6 **Misterton** Leics
116 C3 **Misterton** Notts
13 L2 **Misterton** Somset
62 D2 **Mistley** Essex
44 F6 **Mitcham** Gt Lon
54 F4 **Mitcheldean** Gloucs
4 D5 **Mitchell** Cnwll
155 G3 **Mitchellslacks** D & G
54 C6 **Mitchel Troy** Mons
158 F5 **Mitford** Nthumb
3 J2 **Mithian** Cnwll
73 H7 **Mixbury** Oxon
113 H5 **Mobberley** Ches E
100 A4 **Mobberley** Staffs
82 B5 **Mochdre** Powys
145 H5 **Mochrum** D & G
33 J4 **Mockbeggar** Kent
136 F3 **Mockerkin** Cumb
6 F5 **Modbury** Devon
99 L5 **Moddershall** Staffs
109 G4 **Moelfre** IoA
97 J6 **Moelfre** Powys
155 J2 **Moffat** D & G
75 G5 **Moggerhanger** C Beds
86 C1 **Moira** Leics
34 D4 **Molash** Kent
199 G3 **Mol-chlach** Highld
111 H8 **Mold** Flints
123 H7 **Moldgreen** Kirk
60 E3 **Molehill Green** Essex
126 C3 **Molescroft** E R Yk
88 F7 **Molesworth** Cambs
24 C5 **Molland** Devon
111 L7 **Mollington** Ches W
72 F5 **Mollington** Oxon
175 J4 **Mollinsburn** N Lans
197 J1 **Mondynes** Abers
78 F3 **Monewden** Suffk
185 M2 **Moneydie** P & K
154 D4 **Moniaive** D & G
187 H2 **Monifieth** Angus
196 E8 **Monikie** Angus
186 E5 **Monimail** Fife
44 E1 **Monken Hadley** Gt Lon
124 D5 **Monk Fryston** N York
70 B5 **Monkhide** Herefs
148 C3 **Monkhill** Cumb
84 B5 **Monkhopton** Shrops
69 J3 **Monkland** Herefs
23 G7 **Monkleigh** Devon
36 E6 **Monknash** V Glam
10 E4 **Monkokehampton** Devon
159 H7 **Monkseaton** N Tyne
77 L5 **Monks Eleigh** Suffk
31 K6 **Monk's Gate** W Susx
113 J6 **Monks Heath** Ches E
29 L1 **Monk Sherborne** Hants
25 G4 **Monksilver** Somset
86 F6 **Monks Kirby** Warwks
78 E2 **Monk Soham** Suffk
58 D6 **Monks Risborough** Bucks
118 F7 **Monksthorpe** Lincs
60 F3 **Monk Street** Essex
53 M7 **Monkswood** Mons
12 F2 **Monkton** Devon
47 M6 **Monkton** Kent
163 J4 **Monkton** S Ayrs
151 H3 **Monkton** S Tyne
39 H7 **Monkton Combe** BaNES
27 J4 **Monkton Deverill** Wilts
39 J7 **Monkton Farleigh** Wilts
25 K6 **Monkton Heathfield** Somset
13 J3 **Monkton Wyld** Dorset
151 J4 **Monkwearmouth** Sundld
30 A5 **Monkwood** Hants
85 G4 **Monmore Green** Wolves
54 D5 **Monmouth** Mons
69 G5 **Monnington on Wye** Herefs
145 H6 **Monreith** D & G
26 D7 **Montacute** Somset
83 H1 **Montford** Shrops
83 H1 **Montford Bridge** Shrops
206 B2 **Montgarrie** Abers
82 E4 **Montgomery** Powys
197 H5 **Montrose** Angus
236 b3 **Mont Saint** Guern
28 F3 **Monxton** Hants
114 D7 **Monyash** Derbys
206 D3 **Monymusk** Abers
185 H3 **Monzie** P & K
175 J4 **Moodiesburn** N Lans
186 E4 **Moonzie** Fife
123 L3 **Moor Allerton** Leeds
118 D8 **Moorby** Lincs
15 J2 **Moor Crichel** Dorset
15 K4 **Moordown** Bmouth
112 E5 **Moore** Halton
122 F5 **Moor End** Calder
125 G7 **Moorends** Donc
123 H3 **Moorhead** C Brad
148 B4 **Moorhouse** Cumb
116 C7 **Moorhouse** Notts
32 D3 **Moorhouse Bank** Surrey
26 B4 **Moorlinch** Somset
133 H7 **Moor Monkton** N York
142 E4 **Moorsholm** R & Cl
27 H7 **Moorside** Dorset
5 K3 **Moorswater** Cnwll
124 C7 **Moorthorpe** Wakefd
123 K3 **Moortown** Leeds
117 H2 **Moortown** Lincs
223 G5 **Morangie** Highld
199 L6 **Morar** Highld
215 J3 **Moray Crematorium** Moray
89 G5 **Morborne** Cambs
11 H4 **Morchard Bishop** Devon
13 K4 **Morcombelake** Dorset
88 D4 **Morcott** Rutlnd
97 L6 **Morda** Shrops
15 H4 **Morden** Dorset
44 E6 **Morden** Gt Lon
69 L6 **Mordiford** Herefs

141 H2 **Mordon** Dur
83 G5 **More** Shrops
24 E6 **Morebath** Devon
168 B4 **Morebattle** Border
129 J6 **Morecambe** Lancs
40 C3 **Moredon** Swindn
220 E3 **Morefield** Highld
35 G7 **Morehall** Kent
7 H5 **Moreleigh** Devon
184 D1 **Morenish** P & K
29 K6 **Morestead** Hants
14 F4 **Moreton** Dorset
60 E6 **Moreton** Essex
69 K2 **Moreton** Herefs
58 B6 **Moreton** Oxon
111 J4 **Moreton** Wirral
98 E7 **Moreton Corbet** Shrops
11 H7 **Moretonhampstead** Devon
56 D2 **Moreton-in-Marsh** Gloucs
69 L5 **Moreton Jeffries** Herefs
72 C4 **Moreton Morrell** Warwks
69 K5 **Moreton on Lugg** Herefs
73 H5 **Moreton Pinkney** Nhants
98 F5 **Moreton Say** Shrops
55 H6 **Moreton Valence** Gloucs
94 E4 **Morfa Nefyn** Gwynd
178 C4 **Morham** E Loth
138 E3 **Morland** Cumb
113 J5 **Morley** Ches E
101 H4 **Morley** Derbys
123 K5 **Morley** Leeds
113 J5 **Morley Green** Ches E
92 C4 **Morley St Botolph** Norfk
177 H4 **Morningside** C Edin
175 L7 **Morningside** N Lans
92 F5 **Morningthorpe** Norfk
158 F5 **Morpeth** Nthumb
197 H4 **Morphie** Abers
100 C8 **Morrey** Staffs
51 J6 **Morriston** Swans
106 B4 **Morston** Norfk
23 G3 **Mortehoe** Devon
115 J4 **Morthen** Rothm
41 M7 **Mortimer** W Berk
41 M7 **Mortimer West End** Hants
44 E5 **Mortlake** Gt Lon
44 D5 **Mortlake Crematorium** Gt Lon
148 C4 **Morton** Cumb
101 H1 **Morton** Derbys
103 H7 **Morton** Lincs
116 D3 **Morton** Lincs
102 B3 **Morton** Notts
97 L7 **Morton** Shrops
177 H5 **Mortonhall Crematorium** C Edin
132 E2 **Morton-on-Swale** N York
92 D1 **Morton on the Hill** Norfk
2 D4 **Morvah** Cnwll
200 E2 **Morvich** Highld
84 C5 **Morville** Shrops
6 C3 **Morwellham Quay** Devon
9 G2 **Morwenstow** Cnwll
115 H5 **Mosborough** Sheff
163 L2 **Moscow** E Ayrs
85 J6 **Moseley** Birm
85 G4 **Moseley** Wolves
70 E3 **Moseley** Worcs
188 B7 **Moss** Ag & B
124 F7 **Moss** Donc
205 K2 **Mossat** Abers
235 d4 **Mossbank** Shet
112 D3 **Moss Bank** St Hel
136 D2 **Mossbay** Cumb
163 K4 **Mossblown** S Ayrs
167 K6 **Mossburnford** Border
154 B7 **Mossdale** D & G
153 K2 **Mossdale** E Ayrs
120 F2 **Moss Edge** Lancs
175 K6 **Mossend** N Lans
113 L2 **Mossley** Tamesd
156 D3 **Mosspaul Hotel** Border
213 K4 **Moss-side** Highld
215 H3 **Mosstodloch** Moray
145 L5 **Mossyard** D & G
121 H7 **Mossy Lea** Lancs
13 L2 **Mosterton** Dorset
113 K2 **Moston** Manch
111 G5 **Mostyn** Flints
27 J6 **Motcombe** Dorset
6 F6 **Mothecombe** Devon
138 B2 **Motherby** Cumb
175 K6 **Motherwell** N Lans
44 E6 **Motspur Park** Gt Lon
45 H5 **Mottingham** Gt Lon
28 F6 **Mottisfont** Hants
16 E5 **Mottistone** IoW
113 M3 **Mottram in Longdendale** Tamesd
113 K5 **Mottram St Andrew** Ches E
112 D7 **Mouldsworth** Ches W
194 E4 **Moulin** P & K
19 J4 **Moulsecoomb** Br & H
41 L4 **Moulsford** Oxon
74 C6 **Moulsoe** M Keyn
222 E7 **Moultavie** Highld
112 F7 **Moulton** Ches W
104 A7 **Moulton** Lincs
141 G6 **Moulton** N York
73 L2 **Moulton** Nhants
77 G2 **Moulton** Suffk
37 G6 **Moulton** V Glam
103 M8 **Moulton Chapel** Lincs
93 H3 **Moulton St Mary** Norfk
104 A6 **Moulton Seas End** Lincs
5 J3 **Mount** Cnwll
123 G4 **Mountain** C Brad
53 G7 **Mountain Ash** Rhondd
176 F8 **Mountain Cross** Border
3 J3 **Mount Ambrose** Cnwll
61 L2 **Mount Bures** Essex
20 E2 **Mountfield** E Susx
212 E3 **Mountgerald House** Highld
3 J2 **Mount Hawke** Cnwll
4 D4 **Mountjoy** Cnwll
177 H6 **Mount Lothian** Mdloth
60 F8 **Mountnessing** Essex
38 D2 **Mounton** Mons
101 G3 **Mount Pleasant** Derbys
77 G5 **Mount Pleasant** Suffk
150 E4 **Mountsett Crematorium** Dur
87 H2 **Mountsorrel** Leics
122 F5 **Mount Tabor** Calder
30 F3 **Mousehill** Surrey
2 E6 **Mousehole** Cnwll
155 J7 **Mouswald** D & G
99 J2 **Mow Cop** Ches E
168 B5 **Mowhaugh** Border
87 J5 **Mowsley** Leics
202 C8 **Moy** Highld
213 J7 **Moy** Highld
200 D2 **Moyle** Highld
64 F5 **Moylegrove** Pembks
161 H2 **Muasdale** Ag & B
207 G6 **Muchalls** Abers
54 D3 **Much Birch** Herefs
70 B5 **Much Cowarne** Herefs
54 C2 **Much Dewchurch** Herefs
26 B6 **Muchelney** Somset
26 C6 **Muchelney Ham** Somset
60 C4 **Much Hadham** Herts
120 F6 **Much Hoole** Lancs
5 K5 **Muchlarnick** Cnwll
54 F2 **Much Marcle** Herefs
84 B4 **Much Wenlock** Shrops
189 K1 **Muck** Highld
106 D4 **Muckleburgh Collection** Norfk
99 G5 **Mucklestone** Staffs
118 E5 **Muckton** Lincs
23 J4 **Muddiford** Devon
20 B3 **Muddles Green** E Susx
16 A4 **Mudeford** Dorset
26 E7 **Mudford** Somset
26 E7 **Mudford Sock** Somset
175 G3 **Mugdock** Stirlg
209 G6 **Mugeary** Highld
100 F4 **Mugginton** Derbys
216 D4 **Muirden** Abers
196 F8 **Muirdrum** Angus
216 D5 **Muiresk** Abers
186 E1 **Muirhead** Angus
186 E6 **Muirhead** Fife
175 J4 **Muirhead** N Lans
164 D4 **Muirkirk** E Ayrs
175 J2 **Muirmill** Stirlg
206 B3 **Muir of Fowlis** Abers
214 E3 **Muir of Miltonduff** Moray
212 E4 **Muir of Ord** Highld
192 B1 **Muirshearlich** Highld
217 J6 **Muirtack** Abers
185 J5 **Muirton** P & K
212 C4 **Muirton Mains** Highld
195 J7 **Muirton of Ardblair** P & K
139 K7 **Muker** N York
92 E4 **Mulbarton** Norfk
215 H4 **Mulben** Moray
181 J1 **Mull** Ag & B
3 H7 **Mullion** Cnwll
3 H7 **Mullion Cove** Cnwll
119 G6 **Mumby** Lincs
70 B4 **Munderfield Row** Herefs
70 B4 **Munderfield Stocks** Herefs
107 G5 **Mundesley** Norfk
91 H5 **Mundford** Norfk
93 G4 **Mundham** Norfk
61 K7 **Mundon Hill** Essex
137 K2 **Mungrisdale** Cumb
213 G4 **Munlochy** Highld
174 B8 **Munnoch** N Ayrs
70 B6 **Munsley** Herefs
83 K6 **Munslow** Shrops
11 G7 **Murchington** Devon
57 L5 **Murcott** Oxon
231 H2 **Murkle** Highld
200 F6 **Murlaggan** Highld
187 G1 **Murroes** Angus
89 L3 **Murrow** Cambs
58 D3 **Mursley** Bucks
196 D5 **Murthill** Angus
195 H8 **Murthly** P & K
133 K8 **Murton** C York
139 G3 **Murton** Cumb
151 J5 **Murton** Dur
179 K8 **Murton** Nthumb
13 H4 **Musbury** Devon
177 K4 **Musselburgh** E Loth
102 D5 **Muston** Leics
135 H4 **Muston** N York
44 F3 **Muswell Hill** Gt Lon
146 C5 **Mutehill** D & G
93 K6 **Mutford** Suffk
185 H4 **Muthill** P & K
231 H5 **Mybster** Highld
52 B3 **Myddfai** Carmth
98 C7 **Myddle** Shrops
66 B4 **Mydroilyn** Cerdgn
4 C8 **Mylor** Cnwll
4 C8 **Mylor Bridge** Cnwll
49 K2 **Mynachlog ddu** Pembks
38 C2 **Mynydd-bach** Mons
51 J6 **Mynydd-Bach** Swans
50 E4 **Mynyddgarreg** Carmth
111 J8 **Mynydd Isa** Flints
206 E5 **Myrebird** Abers
157 G3 **Myredykes** Border
30 E1 **Mytchett** Surrey
122 E5 **Mytholm** Calder
122 F5 **Mytholmroyd** Calder
132 F6 **Myton-on-Swale** N York

N

219 J5 **Naast** Highld
232 d4 **Na Buirgh** W Isls
124 F2 **Naburn** C York
123 H3 **Nab Wood Crematorium** C Brad
34 F4 **Nackington** Kent
78 F6 **Nacton** Suffk
135 G7 **Nafferton** E R Yk
25 K5 **Nailsbourne** Somset
38 C6 **Nailsea** N Som
86 E3 **Nailstone** Leics
55 J7 **Nailsworth** Gloucs
213 K3 **Nairn** Highld
111 G7 **Nannerch** Flints
87 G1 **Nanpantan** Leics
4 F5 **Nanpean** Cnwll
5 G3 **Nanstallon** Cnwll
65 L3 **Nanternis** Cerdgn
50 F2 **Nantgaredig** Carmth
96 F1 **Nantglyn** Denbgs
68 B2 **Nantmel** Powys
95 K4 **Nantmor** Gwynd
95 K2 **Nant Peris** Gwynd
98 F3 **Nantwich** Ches E
53 J6 **Nantyglo** Blae G
36 E2 **Nant-y-moel** Brdgnd
42 D2 **Naphill** Bucks
72 F3 **Napton on the Hill** Warwks
49 J4 **Narberth** Pembks
87 G4 **Narborough** Leics
91 H2 **Narborough** Norfk
95 H3 **Nasareth** Gwynd
87 K7 **Naseby** Nhants
73 L7 **Nash** Bucks
37 M4 **Nash** Newpt
69 L1 **Nash** Shrops
88 F4 **Nassington** Nhants
139 H6 **Nateby** Cumb
120 F2 **Nateby** Lancs
85 L1 **National Memorial Arboretum** Staffs
87 H3 **National Space Science Centre** C Leic
129 L2 **Natland** Cumb
78 B5 **Naughton** Suffk
56 C4 **Naunton** Gloucs
70 F6 **Naunton** Worcs
71 G4 **Naunton Beauchamp** Worcs
103 G2 **Navenby** Lincs
45 K1 **Navestock** Essex
60 E8 **Navestock Side** Essex
227 J5 **Navidale House Hotel** Highld
213 J2 **Navity** Highld
133 K3 **Nawton** N York
77 L7 **Nayland** Suffk
60 C6 **Nazeing** Essex
235 d5 **Neap** Shet
100 B4 **Near Cotton** Staffs
137 K7 **Near Sawrey** Cumb
44 E3 **Neasden** Gt Lon
141 H5 **Neasham** Darltn

51 L6 **Neath** Neath
30 C4 **Neatham** Hants
107 H7 **Neatishead** Norfk
66 D2 **Nebo** Cerdgn
96 C2 **Nebo** Conwy
95 H3 **Nebo** Gwynd
108 F4 **Nebo** IoA
91 K2 **Necton** Norfk
224 D3 **Nedd** Highld
78 B5 **Nedging** Suffk
78 B4 **Nedging Tye** Suffk
92 F6 **Needham** Norfk
78 C4 **Needham Market** Suffk
75 L1 **Needingworth** Cambs
84 C7 **Neen Savage** Shrops
84 B8 **Neen Sollars** Shrops
84 B6 **Neenton** Shrops
94 E4 **Nefyn** Gwynd
174 E6 **Neilston** E Rens
37 H2 **Nelson** Caerph
122 C3 **Nelson** Lancs
165 G1 **Nemphlar** S Lans
38 D7 **Nempnett Thrubwell** BaNES
149 K6 **Nenthead** Cumb
167 K2 **Nenthorn** Border
97 K1 **Nercwys** Flints
170 E7 **Nereabolls** Ag & B
175 H6 **Nerston** S Lans
168 E3 **Nesbit** Nthumb
123 G1 **Nesfield** N York
111 J6 **Ness Botanic Gardens** Ches W
98 B8 **Nesscliffe** Shrops
111 J6 **Neston** Ches W
39 K6 **Neston** Wilts
84 B5 **Netchwood** Shrops
113 J6 **Nether Alderley** Ches E
28 D2 **Netheravon** Wilts
167 H2 **Nether Blainslie** Border
216 F3 **Netherbrae** Abers
102 B7 **Nether Broughton** Leics
175 L8 **Netherburn** S Lans
13 L3 **Netherbury** Dorset
123 L2 **Netherby** N York
14 C3 **Nether Cerne** Dorset
155 K5 **Nethercleuch** D & G
26 E7 **Nether Compton** Dorset
206 F2 **Nether Crimond** Abers
215 H2 **Nether Dallachy** Moray
54 E7 **Netherend** Gloucs
20 E2 **Netherfield** E Susx
165 H7 **Nether Fingland** S Lans
28 C5 **Netherhampton** Wilts
196 B7 **Nether Handwick** Angus
115 H3 **Nether Haugh** Rothm
13 K2 **Netherhay** Dorset
116 C6 **Nether Headon** Notts
101 G3 **Nether Heage** Derbys
73 J3 **Nether Heyford** Nhants
165 K6 **Nether Howcleugh** S Lans
129 K6 **Nether Kellet** Lancs
217 K5 **Nether Kinmundy** Abers
115 K7 **Nether Langwith** Notts
146 C6 **Netherlaw** D & G
207 G6 **Netherley** Abers
155 H5 **Nethermill** D & G
217 G5 **Nethermuir** Abers
32 B3 **Netherne-on-the-Hill** Surrey
123 H6 **Netheroyd Hill** Kirk
114 E6 **Nether Padley** Derbys
174 F7 **Netherplace** E Rens
133 J8 **Nether Poppleton** C York
86 C2 **Netherseal** Derbys
133 G2 **Nether Silton** N York
25 J4 **Nether Stowey** Somset
123 H8 **Netherthong** Kirk
196 E5 **Netherton** Angus
7 K2 **Netherton** Devon
85 G6 **Netherton** Dudley
123 H7 **Netherton** Kirk
175 K7 **Netherton** N Lans
168 E7 **Netherton** Nthumb
195 J6 **Netherton** P & K
175 G3 **Netherton** Stirlg
123 K6 **Netherton** Wakefd
136 D5 **Nethertown** Cumb
231 L1 **Nethertown** Highld
100 C8 **Nethertown** Staffs
165 L1 **Netherurd** Border
28 F4 **Nether Wallop** Hants
136 F6 **Nether Wasdale** Cumb
56 E4 **Nether Westcote** Gloucs
86 B5 **Nether Whitacre** Warwks
165 G5 **Nether Whitecleuch** S Lans
58 B5 **Nether Winchendon** Bucks
158 D4 **Netherwitton** Nthumb
204 B2 **Nethy Bridge** Highld
16 F2 **Netley** Hants
29 G8 **Netley Marsh** Hants
42 B3 **Nettlebed** Oxon
26 F2 **Nettlebridge** Somset
13 M4 **Nettlecombe** Dorset
59 G6 **Nettleden** Herts
117 G6 **Nettleham** Lincs
33 H3 **Nettlestead** Kent
33 H3 **Nettlestead Green** Kent
17 H4 **Nettlestone** IoW
151 G5 **Nettlesworth** Dur
117 J2 **Nettleton** Lincs
39 J5 **Nettleton** Wilts
28 C4 **Netton** Wilts
64 F6 **Nevern** Pembks
88 B5 **Nevill Holt** Leics
147 G2 **New Abbey** D & G
217 G2 **New Aberdour** Abers
45 G7 **New Addington** Gt Lon
123 J2 **Newall** Leeds
29 L5 **New Alresford** Hants
195 K6 **New Alyth** P & K
234 e4 **Newark** Ork
102 D2 **Newark-on-Trent** Notts
175 K6 **Newarthill** N Lans
45 L6 **New Ash Green** Kent
102 D3 **New Balderton** Notts
45 L6 **New Barn** Kent
44 F2 **New Barnet** Gt Lon
177 J5 **Newbattle** Mdloth
169 G5 **New Bewick** Nthumb
147 L3 **Newbie** D & G
138 C2 **Newbiggin** Cumb
138 F2 **Newbiggin** Cumb
148 F5 **Newbiggin** Cumb
139 K2 **Newbiggin** Dur
131 J3 **Newbiggin** N York
159 H5 **Newbiggin-by-the-Sea** Nthumb
187 H1 **Newbigging** Angus
195 L7 **Newbigging** Angus
196 C8 **Newbigging** Angus
165 K1 **Newbigging** S Lans
139 G6 **Newbiggin-on-Lune** Cumb
86 F7 **New Bilton** Warwks
115 G6 **Newbold** Derbys
86 F7 **Newbold on Avon** Warwks
72 B5 **Newbold on Stour** Warwks
72 C3 **Newbold Pacey** Warwks
86 F3 **Newbold Verdon** Leics
104 A2 **New Bolingbroke** Lincs
89 H3 **Newborough** C Pete
108 E7 **Newborough** IoA
100 C7 **Newborough** Staffs
116 F7 **New Boultham** Lincs
78 F6 **Newbourne** Suffk
74 B6 **New Bradwell** M Keyn
115 G7 **New Brampton** Derbys
151 G6 **New Brancepeth** Dur
176 F4 **Newbridge** C Edin
37 K2 **Newbridge** Caerph
2 D5 **Newbridge** Cnwll
155 G6 **Newbridge** D & G
28 F7 **Newbridge** Hants
16 E5 **Newbridge** IoW
70 E6 **Newbridge Green** Worcs
67 L3 **Newbridge on Wye** Powys
111 J3 **New Brighton** Wirral
149 L2 **Newbrough** Nthumb
92 C5 **New Buckenham** Norfk
11 J4 **Newbuildings** Devon
207 J1 **Newburgh** Abers
217 H3 **Newburgh** Abers
186 D4 **Newburgh** Fife
121 G7 **Newburgh** Lancs
133 H4 **Newburgh Priory** N York
150 F2 **Newburn** N u Ty
27 G2 **Newbury** Somset
41 J6 **Newbury** W Berk
45 J3 **Newbury Park** Gt Lon
138 E3 **Newby** Cumb
122 B2 **Newby** Lancs
130 D5 **Newby** N York
142 B5 **Newby** N York
129 H3 **Newby Bridge** Cumb
148 E4 **Newby East** Cumb
216 F4 **New Byth** Abers
148 C4 **Newby West** Cumb
54 C5 **Newcastle** Mons
82 E6 **Newcastle** Shrops
158 F7 *Newcastle Airport* Nthumb
65 J6 **Newcastle Emlyn** Carmth
156 E5 **Newcastleton** Border
99 J4 **Newcastle-under-Lyme** Staffs
151 G3 **Newcastle upon Tyne** N u Ty
65 H6 **Newchapel** Pembks
32 C5 **Newchapel** Surrey
17 G5 **Newchurch** IoW
34 E7 **Newchurch** Kent
38 C2 **Newchurch** Mons
68 E4 **Newchurch** Powys
100 D7 **Newchurch** Staffs
92 E2 **New Costessey** Norfk
177 J4 **Newcraighall** C Edin
124 B6 **New Crofton** Wakefd
45 G5 **New Cross** Gt Lon
26 B7 **New Cross** Somset
164 C6 **New Cumnock** E Ayrs
217 G5 **New Deer** Abers
43 H4 **New Denham** Bucks
31 K3 **Newdigate** Surrey
73 K3 **New Duston** Nhants
133 J7 **New Earswick** C York
115 K2 **New Edlington** Donc
214 F3 **New Elgin** Moray
126 E3 **New Ellerby** E R Yk
42 E6 **Newell Green** Br For
45 H5 **New Eltham** Gt Lon
71 J3 **New End** Worcs
33 L7 **Newenden** Kent
89 H4 **New England** C Pete
55 G3 **Newent** Gloucs
150 F7 **Newfield** Dur
223 H6 **Newfield** Highld
89 H4 **New Fletton** C Pete
16 C2 **New Forest National Park**
48 E3 **Newgale** Pembks
154 B6 **New Galloway** D & G
59 M6 **Newgate Street** Herts
187 G5 **New Gilston** Fife
2 a1 **New Grimsby** IoS
98 E4 **Newhall** Ches E
159 H6 **New Hartley** Nthumb
177 H3 **Newhaven** C Edin
19 L5 **Newhaven** E Susx
43 H7 **New Haw** Surrey
49 J6 **New Hedges** Pembks
126 D5 **New Holland** N Linc
143 H5 **Newholm** N York
115 J7 **New Houghton** Derbys
105 J6 **New Houghton** Norfk
175 L6 **Newhouse** N Lans
130 B2 **New Hutton** Cumb
19 L2 **Newick** E Susx
35 G7 **Newington** Kent
46 E6 **Newington** Kent
41 L2 **Newington** Oxon
66 B6 **New Inn** Carmth
53 L7 **New Inn** Torfn
82 F7 **New Invention** Shrops
92 F3 **New Lakenham** Norfk
165 G2 **New Lanark** S Lans
126 D4 **Newland** C KuH
54 D6 **Newland** Gloucs
125 G5 **Newland** N York
24 C4 **Newland** Somset
70 E5 **Newland** Worcs
177 K6 **Newlandrig** Mdloth
156 E4 **Newlands** Border
150 D4 **Newlands** Nthumb
215 G4 **Newlands of Dundurcas** Moray
156 C5 **New Langholm** D & G
104 C2 **New Leake** Lincs
217 J4 **New Leeds** Abers
123 L8 **New Lodge** Barns
121 G5 **New Longton** Lancs
144 E3 **New Luce** D & G
2 E5 **Newlyn** Cnwll
4 C5 **Newlyn East** Cnwll
207 G2 **Newmachar** Abers
175 L6 **Newmains** N Lans
44 E6 **New Malden** Gt Lon
77 K5 **Newman's Green** Suffk
76 F2 **Newmarket** Suffk
232 f2 **Newmarket** W Isls
142 D3 **New Marske** R & Cl
57 K6 **New Marston** Oxon
206 E8 **New Mill** Abers
167 G7 **Newmill** Border
2 E4 **New Mill** Cnwll
123 H8 **New Mill** Kirk
215 K4 **Newmill** Moray
123 L7 **Newmillerdam** Wakefd
196 C4 **Newmill of Inshewan** Angus
177 G5 **Newmills** C Edin
113 M4 **New Mills** Derbys
176 D2 **Newmills** Fife
54 D6 **Newmills** Mons
82 C4 **New Mills** Powys
186 B2 **Newmiln** P & K
164 B2 **Newmilns** E Ayrs
16 B4 **New Milton** Hants
62 D2 **New Mistley** Essex
49 H3 **New Moat** Pembks
61 G6 **Newney Green** Essex
55 G5 **Newnham** Gloucs
30 B2 **Newnham** Hants

75 J6 **Newnham** Herts
34 C3 **Newnham** Kent
73 H3 **Newnham** Nhants
70 B2 **Newnham** Worcs
116 A7 **New Ollerton** Notts
217 G3 **New Pitsligo** Abers
9 J7 **Newport** Cnwll
125 K4 **Newport** E R Yk
76 D7 **Newport** Essex
39 G2 **Newport** Gloucs
227 K4 **Newport** Highld
16 F5 **Newport** IoW
37 L3 **Newport** Newpt
64 E6 **Newport** Pembks
99 H8 **Newport** Wrekin
187 G2 **Newport-on-Tay** Fife
74 C5 **Newport Pagnell** M Keyn
74 C5 **Newport Pagnell Services** M Keyn
163 J4 **New Prestwick** S Ayrs
65 L3 **New Quay** Cerdgn
4 C4 **Newquay** Cnwll
4 D3 *Newquay Airport* Cnwll
93 G2 **New Rackheath** Norfk
68 E3 **New Radnor** Powys
150 D3 **New Ridley** Nthumb
21 L2 **New Romney** Kent
115 L2 **New Rossington** Donc
185 J7 **New Sauchie** Clacks
216 D7 **Newseat** Abers
121 G4 **Newsham** Lancs
132 E3 **Newsham** N York
140 E5 **Newsham** N York
159 H6 **Newsham** Nthumb
124 B6 **New Sharlston** Wakefd
125 H5 **Newsholme** E R Yk
151 J4 **New Silksworth** Sundld
123 H7 **Newsome** Kirk
102 F5 **New Somerby** Lincs
44 F2 **New Southgate Crematorium** Gt Lon
167 H3 **Newstead** Border
101 K3 **Newstead** Notts
169 H4 **Newstead** Nthumb
175 K6 **New Stevenston** N Lans
101 J4 **Newthorpe** Notts
182 F7 **Newton** Ag & B
167 J5 **Newton** Border
36 C5 **Newton** Brdgnd
75 J5 **Newton** C Beds
76 B5 **Newton** Cambs
90 B1 **Newton** Cambs
98 D1 **Newton** Ches W
112 B7 **Newton** Ches W
128 F5 **Newton** Cumb
101 H2 **Newton** Derbys
53 M2 **Newton** Herefs
69 K4 **Newton** Herefs
212 F4 **Newton** Highld
213 H5 **Newton** Highld
213 J2 **Newton** Highld
231 L5 **Newton** Highld
103 H5 **Newton** Lincs
177 J4 **Newton** Mdloth
214 E2 **Newton** Moray
215 H2 **Newton** Moray
88 C6 **Newton** Nhants
91 J1 **Newton** Norfk
102 B4 **Newton** Notts
150 C3 **Newton** Nthumb
165 H3 **Newton** S Lans
175 H6 **Newton** S Lans
100 B7 **Newton** Staffs
77 K6 **Newton** Suffk
176 E3 **Newton** W Loth
87 G7 **Newton** Warwks
7 K2 **Newton Abbot** Devon
147 L4 **Newton Arlosh** Cumb
141 G3 **Newton Aycliffe** Dur
141 K2 **Newton Bewley** Hartpl
74 D4 **Newton Blossomville** M Keyn
74 E2 **Newton Bromswold** Nhants
86 D2 **Newton Burgoland** Leics
169 J4 **Newton-by-the-Sea** Nthumb
117 H4 **Newton by Toft** Lincs
6 A3 **Newton Ferrers** Cnwll
6 E6 **Newton Ferrers** Devon
232 c5 **Newton Ferry** W Isls
92 E4 **Newton Flotman** Norfk
177 J5 **Newtongrange** Mdloth
38 D3 **Newton Green** Mons
87 J4 **Newton Harcourt** Leics
113 K2 **Newton Heath** Manch
207 G6 **Newtonhill** Abers
121 K1 **Newton-in-Bowland** Lancs
124 C2 **Newton Kyme** N York
132 C2 **Newton-le-Willows** N York
112 E3 **Newton-le-Willows** St Hel
177 J5 **Newtonloan** Mdloth
58 D2 **Newton Longville** Bucks
174 F7 **Newton Mearns** E Rens
196 F4 **Newtonmill** Angus
203 H5 **Newtonmore** Highld
141 G5 **Newton Morrell** N York
186 B5 **Newton of Balcanquhal** P & K
187 H6 **Newton of Balcormo** Fife
133 H7 **Newton on Ouse** N York
134 C2 **Newton-on-Rawcliffe** N York
158 F2 **Newton-on-the-Moor** Nthumb
116 D6 **Newton on Trent** Lincs
12 E4 **Newton Poppleford** Devon
57 L3 **Newton Purcell** Oxon
86 C3 **Newton Regis** Warwks
138 C2 **Newton Reigny** Cumb
11 K5 **Newton St Cyres** Devon
92 F1 **Newton St Faith** Norfk
39 G7 **Newton St Loe** BaNES
9 K3 **Newton St Petrock** Devon
100 F7 **Newton Solney** Derbys
29 H4 **Newton Stacey** Hants
145 J3 **Newton Stewart** D & G
28 E4 **Newton Tony** Wilts
23 H6 **Newton Tracey** Devon
142 C5 **Newton under Roseberry** R & Cl
125 H2 **Newton upon Derwent** E R Yk
30 B5 **Newton Valence** Hants
155 K3 **Newton Wamphray** D & G
120 F4 **Newton with Scales** Lancs
147 J5 **Newtown** Cumb
148 E3 **Newtown** Cumb
164 F7 **Newtown** D & G
12 D3 **Newtown** Devon
24 B6 **Newtown** Devon
27 L7 **New Town** Dorset
27 M7 **New Town** Dorset
19 M2 **New Town** E Susx
54 F7 **Newtown** Gloucs
29 L8 **Newtown** Hants
70 B5 **Newtown** Herefs
70 C6 **Newtown** Herefs
202 B4 **Newtown** Highld
16 E4 **Newtown** IoW
168 F4 **Newtown** Nthumb
15 K4 **Newtown** Poole
82 C5 **Newtown** Powys
98 B7 **Newtown** Shrops
98 C6 **Newtown** Shrops
25 L8 **Newtown** Somset
99 K1 **Newtown** Staffs
112 E1 **Newtown** Wigan
70 F4 **Newtown** Worcs
87 G2 **Newtown Linford** Leics
174 D6 **Newtown of Beltrees** Rens
167 J3 **Newtown St Boswells** Border
53 H7 **New Tredegar** Caerph
164 F2 **New Trows** S Lans
195 L7 **Newtyle** Angus
90 C2 **New Walsoken** Cambs
118 C1 **New Waltham** NE Lin
177 L4 **New Winton** E Loth
182 D5 **Newyork** Ag & B
103 L2 **New York** Lincs
49 G6 **Neyland** Pembks
25 H7 **Nicholashayne** Devon
51 G7 **Nicholaston** Swans
132 D7 **Nidd** N York
207 H5 **Nigg** C Aber
223 H6 **Nigg** Highld
223 H7 **Nigg Ferry** Highld
149 K4 **Ninebanks** Nthumb
40 C3 **Nine Elms** Swindn
20 E3 **Ninfield** E Susx
16 E5 **Ningwood** IoW
167 K4 **Nisbet** Border
179 G7 **Nisbet Hill** Border
17 F6 **Niton** IoW
174 F6 **Nitshill** C Glas
117 H8 **Nocton** Lincs
57 K5 **Noke** Oxon
48 E4 **Nolton** Pembks
48 E4 **Nolton Haven** Pembks
98 D3 **No Man's Heath** Ches W
86 C2 **No Man's Heath** Warwks
11 J3 **Nomansland** Devon
28 E7 **Nomansland** Wilts
98 C6 **Noneley** Shrops
35 H4 **Nonington** Kent
129 L3 **Nook** Cumb
44 D6 **Norbiton** Gt Lon
98 E3 **Norbury** Ches E
100 C4 **Norbury** Derbys
44 F6 **Norbury** Gt Lon
83 G5 **Norbury** Shrops
99 H7 **Norbury** Staffs
70 F2 **Norchard** Worcs
90 D4 **Nordelph** Norfk
84 C4 **Nordley** Shrops
93 K2 **Norfolk Broads** Norfk
179 J8 **Norham** Nthumb
112 E6 **Norley** Ches W
16 D3 **Norleywood** Hants
117 G4 **Normanby** Lincs
125 K7 **Normanby** N Linc
134 B3 **Normanby** N York
142 C4 **Normanby** R & Cl
117 J3 **Normanby le Wold** Lincs
30 F2 **Normandy** Surrey
12 D2 **Norman's Green** Devon
101 G5 **Normanton** C Derb
102 D4 **Normanton** Leics
102 F4 **Normanton** Lincs
102 B2 **Normanton** Notts
124 B6 **Normanton** Wakefd
86 D2 **Normanton le Heath** Leics
101 K7 **Normanton on Soar** Notts
101 L6 **Normanton on the Wolds** Notts
116 C7 **Normanton on Trent** Notts
111 L3 **Norris Green** Lpool
86 D1 **Norris Hill** Leics
123 J6 **Norristhorpe** Kirk
58 F4 **Northall** Bucks
141 J7 **Northallerton** N York
29 H8 **Northam** C Sotn
23 G5 **Northam** Devon
73 L3 **Northampton** Nhants
70 E2 **Northampton** Worcs
115 K5 **North Anston** Rothm
42 E6 **North Ascot** Br For
57 J3 **North Aston** Oxon
59 L7 **Northaw** Herts
13 H1 **Northay** Somset
29 H7 **North Baddesley** Hants
191 L4 **North Ballachulish** Highld
26 E5 **North Barrow** Somset
105 L5 **North Barsham** Norfk
46 C3 **North Benfleet** Essex
18 C5 **North Bersted** W Susx
178 C2 **North Berwick** E Loth
17 H1 **North Boarhunt** Hants
89 H3 **Northborough** C Pete
35 J4 **Northbourne** Kent
11 H7 **North Bovey** Devon
27 J1 **North Bradley** Wilts
10 C8 **North Brentor** Devon
27 G4 **North Brewham** Somset
29 K4 **Northbrook** Hants
23 G4 **North Buckland** Devon
93 H2 **North Burlingham** Norfk
26 F6 **North Cadbury** Somset
116 F6 **North Carlton** Lincs
115 L4 **North Carlton** Notts
125 K4 **North Cave** E R Yk
56 A6 **North Cerney** Gloucs
19 K2 **North Chailey** E Susx
30 F5 **Northchapel** W Susx
28 D7 **North Charford** Hants
169 H5 **North Charlton** Nthumb
44 E6 **North Cheam** Gt Lon
27 G6 **North Cheriton** Somset
13 K4 **North Chideock** Dorset
58 F6 **Northchurch** Herts
125 K3 **North Cliffe** E R Yk
116 D6 **North Clifton** Notts
118 E4 **North Cockerington** Lincs
182 C1 **North Connel** Ag & B
36 C4 **North Cornelly** Brdgnd
118 E2 **North Cotes** Lincs
9 J6 **Northcott** Devon
57 J7 **Northcourt** Oxon
93 K5 **North Cove** Suffk
141 G6 **North Cowton** N York
74 D5 **North Crawley** M Keyn
105 K5 **North Creake** Norfk
25 L6 **North Curry** Somset
125 L1 **North Dalton** E R Yk

124 B1 **North Deighton** N York
23 H5 **North Devon Crematorium** Devon
35 K2 **Northdown** Kent
34 B4 **North Downs**
125 G3 **North Duffield** N York
218 C6 **North Duntulm** Highld
44 E6 **North East Surrey Crematorium** Gt Lon
106 B7 **North Elmham** Norfk
124 D7 **North Elmsall** Wakefd
17 J3 **North End** C Port
61 G4 **North End** Essex
28 C7 **North End** Hants
74 D2 **North End** Nhants
18 D5 **North End** W Susx
72 E4 **Northend** Warwks
113 J4 **Northenden** Manch
219 H5 **North Erradale** Highld
87 J3 **North Evington** C Leic
61 K7 **North Fambridge** Essex
126 B5 **North Ferriby** E R Yk
85 H7 **Northfield** Birm
207 G4 **Northfield** C Aber
126 C5 **Northfield** E R Yk
88 E2 **Northfields** Lincs
45 M5 **Northfleet** Kent
135 H8 **North Frodingham** E R Yk
15 M1 **North Gorley** Hants
79 G3 **North Green** Suffk
117 G6 **North Greetwell** Lincs
134 C6 **North Grimston** N York
17 K2 **North Hayling** Hants
5 L1 **North Hill** Cnwll
43 H4 **North Hillingdon** Gt Lon
57 J6 **North Hinksey Village** Oxon
31 K3 **North Holmwood** Surrey
7 G5 **North Huish** Devon
116 F7 **North Hykeham** Lincs
21 G2 **Northiam** E Susx
75 G5 **Northill** C Beds
29 K4 **Northington** Hants
117 H2 **North Kelsey** Lincs
213 G5 **North Kessock** Highld
126 E6 **North Killingholme** N Linc
132 F3 **North Kilvington** N York
87 H6 **North Kilworth** Leics
103 J3 **North Kyme** Lincs
135 K5 **North Landing** E R Yk
104 B2 **Northlands** Lincs
56 C5 **Northleach** Gloucs
58 D6 **North Lee** Bucks
12 F3 **Northleigh** Devon
57 H5 **North Leigh** Oxon
116 C5 **North Leverton with Habblesthorpe** Notts
10 D5 **Northlew** Devon
71 J5 **North Littleton** Worcs
92 C6 **North Lopham** Norfk
88 D3 **North Luffenham** Rutlnd
30 D7 **North Marden** W Susx
58 C4 **North Marston** Bucks
177 K6 **North Middleton** Mdloth
216 F5 **North Millbrex** Abers
144 C4 **North Milmain** D & G
24 B5 **North Molton** Devon
57 H7 **Northmoor** Oxon
41 K3 **North Moreton** Oxon
196 C5 **Northmuir** Angus
18 B5 **North Mundham** W Susx
102 D2 **North Muskham** Notts
125 L3 **North Newbald** E R Yk
72 E6 **North Newington** Oxon
40 C8 **North Newnton** Wilts
25 L5 **North Newton** Somset
17 K2 **Northney** Hants
39 H2 **North Nibley** Gloucs
43 J4 **Northolt** Gt Lon
111 H7 **Northop** Flints
111 J7 **Northop Hall** Flints
142 B4 **North Ormesby** Middsb
118 C3 **North Ormsby** Lincs
123 J6 **Northorpe** Kirk
103 K5 **Northorpe** Lincs
116 E3 **Northorpe** Lincs
132 E2 **North Otterington** N York
117 H3 **North Owersby** Lincs
123 G5 **Northowram** Calder
13 L1 **North Perrott** Somset
25 L5 **North Petherton** Somset
9 H6 **North Petherwin** Cnwll
91 J3 **North Pickenham** Norfk
71 G4 **North Piddle** Worcs
13 M3 **North Poorton** Dorset
15 H5 **Northport** Dorset
176 F3 **North Queensferry** Fife
103 G3 **North Rauceby** Lincs
106 F5 **Northrepps** Norfk
118 E5 **North Reston** Lincs
123 K1 **North Rigton** N York
113 K7 **North Rode** Ches E
234 e3 **North Ronaldsay** Ork
234 e3 *North Ronaldsay Airport* Ork
90 F1 **North Runcton** Norfk
116 D7 **North Scarle** Lincs
191 H7 **North Shian** Ag & B
151 J2 **North Shields** N Tyne
46 F3 **North Shoebury** Sthend
120 D3 **North Shore** Bpool
89 K4 **North Side** C Pete
118 F3 **North Somercotes** Lincs
132 D4 **North Stainley** N York
45 L4 **North Stifford** Thurr
39 G6 **North Stoke** BaNES
41 L3 **North Stoke** Oxon
18 D4 **North Stoke** W Susx
34 D3 **North Street** Kent
41 M6 **North Street** W Berk
169 J3 **North Sunderland** Nthumb
9 J5 **North Tamerton** Cnwll
10 F4 **North Tawton** Devon
175 K1 **North Third** Stirlg
118 D2 **North Thoresby** Lincs
232 d5 **Northton** W Isls
10 D3 **North Town** Devon
26 E3 **North Town** Somset
42 E4 **North Town** W & M
92 C2 **North Tuddenham** Norfk
233 b6 **North Uist** W Isls
157 L3 **Northumberland National Park** Nthumb
107 G6 **North Walsham** Norfk
29 K3 **North Waltham** Hants
30 B2 **North Warnborough** Hants
60 D7 **North Weald Bassett** Essex
116 C4 **North Wheatley** Notts
112 F6 **Northwich** Ches W
70 E3 **Northwick** Worcs
38 E8 **North Widcombe** BaNES
117 K4 **North Willingham** Lincs
115 H8 **North Wingfield** Derbys
102 F7 **North Witham** Lincs
91 H4 **Northwold** Norfk
43 H3 **Northwood** Gt Lon
16 F4 **Northwood** IoW
98 C6 **Northwood** Shrops
55 G5 **Northwood Green** Gloucs
26 F8 **North Wootton** Dorset
105 G7 **North Wootton** Norfk
26 E3 **North Wootton** Somset
39 J5 **North Wraxall** Wilts
142 F6 **North York Moors National Park**
124 E7 **Norton** Donc
19 M5 **Norton** E Susx
55 J3 **Norton** Gloucs
112 D5 **Norton** Halton
134 C5 **Norton** N York
73 H2 **Norton** Nhants
115 L6 **Norton** Notts
68 F2 **Norton** Powys
141 K3 **Norton** S on T
84 D4 **Norton** Shrops
77 L2 **Norton** Suffk
18 C4 **Norton** W Susx
39 K4 **Norton** Wilts
70 F4 **Norton** Worcs
71 J5 **Norton** Worcs
27 K3 **Norton Bavant** Wilts
99 K6 **Norton Bridge** Staffs
85 H2 **Norton Canes** Staffs
85 H3 **Norton Canes Services** Staffs
69 H5 **Norton Canon** Herefs
102 E2 **Norton Disney** Lincs
25 J6 **Norton Fitzwarren** Somset
16 D5 **Norton Green** IoW
38 E7 **Norton Hawkfield** BaNES
60 F6 **Norton Heath** Essex
99 G5 **Norton in Hales** Shrops
86 D3 **Norton-Juxta-Twycross** Leics
132 F5 **Norton-le-Clay** N York
72 B2 **Norton Lindsey** Warwks
77 L2 **Norton Little Green** Suffk
38 E7 **Norton Malreward** BaNES
27 H1 **Norton St Philip** Somset
93 J4 **Norton Subcourse** Norfk
26 C7 **Norton sub Hamdon** Somset
102 C1 **Norwell** Notts
116 B8 **Norwell Woodhouse** Notts
92 F2 **Norwich** Norfk
92 E2 *Norwich Airport* Norfk
92 F2 **Norwich Cathedral** Norfk
92 F1 **Norwich (St Faith) Crematorium** Norfk
235 e1 **Norwick** Shet
185 J8 **Norwood** Clacks
43 J5 **Norwood Green** Gt Lon
31 L3 **Norwood Hill** Surrey
6 E6 **Noss Mayo** Devon
132 D4 **Nosterfield** N York
210 D8 **Nostie** Highld
56 C4 **Notgrove** Gloucs
36 C5 **Nottage** Brdgnd
101 L5 **Nottingham** C Nott
123 L7 **Notton** Wakefd
39 K6 **Notton** Wilts
70 E2 **Noutard's Green** Worcs
42 A3 **Nuffield** Oxon
125 K2 **Nunburnholme** E R Yk
86 D5 **Nuneaton** Warwks
45 G5 **Nunhead** Gt Lon
133 H7 **Nun Monkton** N York
27 G3 **Nunney** Somset
133 K4 **Nunnington** N York
127 G8 **Nunsthorpe** NE Lin
124 F1 **Nunthorpe** C York
142 C4 **Nunthorpe** Middsb
142 C5 **Nunthorpe Village** Middsb
28 D6 **Nunton** Wilts
132 E5 **Nunwick** N York
29 G7 **Nursling** Hants
17 L2 **Nutbourne** W Susx
18 E3 **Nutbourne** W Susx
32 B3 **Nutfield** Surrey
101 K4 **Nuthall** Notts
76 B7 **Nuthampstead** Herts
31 K6 **Nuthurst** W Susx
32 D7 **Nutley** E Susx
122 B7 **Nuttall** Bury
231 L3 **Nybster** Highld
18 B6 **Nyetimber** W Susx
30 D6 **Nyewood** W Susx
11 G4 **Nymet Rowland** Devon
11 G5 **Nymet Tracey** Devon
55 J7 **Nympsfield** Gloucs
25 H6 **Nynehead** Somset
18 C5 **Nyton** W Susx

O

87 J4 **Oadby** Leics
34 B3 **Oad Street** Kent
100 B4 **Oakamoor** Staffs
176 E5 **Oakbank** W Loth
10 D5 **Oak Cross** Devon
37 J2 **Oakdale** Caerph
25 J6 **Oake** Somset
84 F3 **Oaken** Staffs
121 H2 **Oakenclough** Lancs
84 C2 **Oakengates** Wrekin
150 F7 **Oakenshaw** Dur
123 H5 **Oakenshaw** Kirk
66 B3 **Oakford** Cerdgn
24 E6 **Oakford** Devon
88 C2 **Oakham** Rutlnd
30 C4 **Oakhanger** Hants
26 F3 **Oakhill** Somset
76 B2 **Oakington** Cambs
55 H4 **Oakle Street** Gloucs
74 E4 **Oakley** Bed
57 M5 **Oakley** Bucks
176 D1 **Oakley** Fife
29 K2 **Oakley** Hants
92 E7 **Oakley** Suffk
55 K7 **Oakridge** Gloucs
39 M2 **Oaksey** Wilts
86 D2 **Oakthorpe** Leics
101 G5 **Oakwood** C Derb
122 F3 **Oakworth** C Brad
34 D3 **Oare** Kent
24 C3 **Oare** Somset
40 D7 **Oare** Wilts
103 G5 **Oasby** Lincs
26 B6 **Oath** Somset
196 D5 **Oathlaw** Angus
43 H7 **Oatlands Park** Surrey
182 B2 **Oban** Ag & B
182 C1 *Oban Airport* Ag & B
83 G7 **Obley** Shrops
195 G8 **Obney** P & K
26 F7 **Oborne** Dorset
78 D1 **Occold** Suffk
231 J7 **Occumster** Highld
163 L5 **Ochiltree** E Ayrs

101 H5 Ockbrook Derbys
31 H1 Ockham Surrey
190 B3 Ockle Highld
31 J4 Ockley Surrey
69 L5 Ocle Pychard Herefs
26 D7 Odcombe Somset
39 H7 Odd Down BaNES
71 G3 Oddingley Worcs
56 E3 Oddington Gloucs
57 K5 Oddington Oxon
74 D3 Odell Bed
30 C2 Odiham Hants
123 H5 Odsal C Brad
75 K6 Odsey Cambs
28 D6 Odstock Wilts
86 E3 Odstone Leics
72 D2 Offchurch Warwks
71 J5 Offenham Worcs
113 K4 Offerton Stockp
19 L3 Offham E Susx
33 H2 Offham Kent
18 D4 Offham W Susx
75 J2 Offord Cluny Cambs
75 J2 Offord D'Arcy Cambs
78 C5 Offton Suffk
12 F3 Offwell Devon
40 D6 Ogbourne Maizey Wilts
40 D6 Ogbourne St Andrew Wilts
40 D5 Ogbourne St George Wilts
158 E6 Ogle Nthumb
112 C5 Oglet Lpool
36 D5 Ogmore V Glam
36 D5 Ogmore-by-Sea V Glam
36 E3 Ogmore Vale Brdgnd
14 F1 Okeford Fitzpaine Dorset
10 E5 Okehampton Devon
100 F1 Oker Side Derbys
31 J4 Okewood Hill Surrey
87 L8 Old Nhants
207 H4 Old Aberdeen C Aber
29 L5 Old Alresford Hants
224 D2 Oldany Highld
154 D3 Old Auchenbrack D & G
101 K4 Old Basford C Nott
30 A2 Old Basing Hants
106 A8 Old Beetley Norfk
71 K2 Oldberrow Warwks
169 G5 Old Bewick Nthumb
118 E8 Old Bolingbroke Lincs
123 J2 Old Bramhope Leeds
115 G6 Old Brampton Derbys
146 D2 Old Bridge of Urr D & G
92 C5 Old Buckenham Norfk
41 J8 Old Burghclere Hants
85 H5 Oldbury Sandw
84 C5 Oldbury Shrops
86 C5 Oldbury Warwks
38 E2 Oldbury-on-Severn S Glos
39 J3 Oldbury on the Hill Gloucs
133 H3 Old Byland N York
115 L2 Old Cantley Donc
53 L3 Oldcastle Mons
92 F2 Old Catton Norfk
127 G8 Old Clee NE Lin
25 G3 Old Cleeve Somset
115 L8 Old Clipstone Notts
110 B6 Old Colwyn Conwy
115 L4 Oldcotes Notts
152 F3 Old Dailly S Ayrs
102 A7 Old Dalby Leics
217 J5 Old Deer Abers
115 K3 Old Edlington Donc
126 E3 Old Ellerby E R Yk
79 G7 Old Felixstowe Suffk
70 E2 Oldfield Worcs
89 H4 Old Fletton C Pete
27 H2 Oldford Somset
54 E4 Old Forge Herefs
2 a1 Old Grimsby IoS
60 B4 Old Hall Green Herts
113 L1 Oldham Oldham
178 F4 Oldhamstocks E Loth
60 D5 Old Harlow Essex
105 G4 Old Hunstanton Norfk
89 K7 Old Hurst Cambs
130 B2 Old Hutton Cumb
174 E4 Old Kilpatrick W Duns
59 L4 Old Knebworth Herts
92 F3 Old Lakenham Norfk
38 F6 Oldland S Glos
121 K4 Old Langho Lancs
104 C3 Old Leake Lincs
134 C5 Old Malton N York
216 F8 Oldmeldrum Abers
6 B2 Oldmill Cnwll
72 C2 Old Milverton Warwks
37 M8 Oldmixon N Som
78 C3 Old Newton Suffk
68 E3 Old Radnor Powys
216 D8 Old Rayne Abers
21 K2 Old Romney Kent
19 G4 Old Shoreham W Susx
228 C4 Oldshoremore Highld
39 H4 Old Sodbury S Glos
102 F5 Old Somerby Lincs
133 H4 Oldstead N York
73 L6 Old Stratford Nhants
194 C4 Old Struan P & K
84 F6 Old Swinford Dudley
132 F3 Old Thirsk N York
130 B3 Old Town Cumb
20 C5 Old Town E Susx
2 b2 Old Town IoS
113 J3 Old Trafford Traffd
148 E3 Oldwall Cumb
50 F6 Oldwalls Swans
75 G5 Old Warden C Beds
89 G7 Old Weston Cambs
231 L5 Old Wick Highld
43 G5 Old Windsor W & M
34 E4 Old Wives Lees Kent
43 G8 Old Woking Surrey
231 G5 Olgrinmore Highld
100 C8 Olive Green Staffs
29 J6 Oliver's Battery Hants
235 c3 Ollaberry Shet
209 H6 Ollach Highld
113 H6 Ollerton Ches E
116 A7 Ollerton Notts
98 F7 Ollerton Shrops
74 C4 Olney M Keyn
231 H3 Olrig House Highld
85 K6 Olton Solhll
38 E3 Olveston S Glos
70 E2 Ombersley Worcs
116 B7 Ompton Notts
237 d5 Onchan IoM
100 B2 Onecote Staffs
83 J7 Onibury Shrops
191 K4 Onich Highld
52 C6 Onllwyn Neath
99 H4 Onneley Staffs
61 G4 Onslow Green Essex
31 G2 Onslow Village Surrey
112 E6 Onston Ches W
219 H6 Opinan Highld
215 G3 Orbliston Moray
208 D5 Orbost Highld
119 G7 Orby Lincs
25 K6 Orchard Portman Somset
28 B3 Orcheston Wilts
54 C3 Orcop Herefs
54 C3 Orcop Hill Herefs
216 C3 Ord Abers
206 C3 Ordhead Abers
205 K5 Ordie Abers
215 H3 Ordiequish Moray
116 B5 Ordsall Notts
21 G4 Ore E Susx
79 J4 Orford Suffk
112 E4 Orford Warrtn
15 H4 Organford Dorset
34 D7 Orlestone Kent
69 J2 Orleton Herefs
70 C2 Orleton Worcs
74 C1 Orlingbury Nhants
142 C4 Ormesby R & Cl
93 K1 Ormesby St Margaret Norfk
93 K1 Ormesby St Michael Norfk
219 K4 Ormiscaig Highld
177 L4 Ormiston E Loth
189 L4 Ormsaigmore Highld
172 C4 Ormsary Ag & B
120 F8 Ormskirk Lancs
171 G2 Oronsay Ag & B
234 b6 Orphir Ork
45 J6 Orpington Gt Lon
111 K3 Orrell Sefton
112 D2 Orrell Wigan
146 D5 Orroland D & G
45 M4 Orsett Thurr
84 E1 Orslow Staffs
102 C4 Orston Notts
138 F5 Orton Cumb
88 B7 Orton Nhants
84 F4 Orton Staffs
89 H4 Orton Longueville C Pete
86 C3 Orton-on-the-Hill Leics
89 H4 Orton Waterville C Pete
75 L4 Orwell Cambs
121 J4 Osbaldeston Lancs
124 F1 Osbaldwick C York
86 E3 Osbaston Leics
97 L7 Osbaston Shrops
17 G4 Osborne House IoW
103 H5 Osbournby Lincs
112 D7 Oscroft Ches W
208 E6 Ose Highld
101 H8 Osgathorpe Leics
117 H3 Osgodby Lincs
124 F4 Osgodby N York
135 G3 Osgodby N York
209 H6 Oskaig Highld
189 L7 Oskamull Ag & B
100 D4 Osmaston Derbys
14 D5 Osmington Dorset
14 E6 Osmington Mills Dorset
123 L4 Osmondthorpe Leeds
141 K7 Osmotherley N York
57 J6 Osney Oxon
34 D3 Ospringe Kent
123 K6 Ossett Wakefd
116 C8 Ossington Notts
44 D5 Osterley Gt Lon
133 K4 Oswaldkirk N York
121 L5 Oswaldtwistle Lancs
97 L6 Oswestry Shrops
32 F2 Otford Kent
33 K3 Otham Kent
26 B5 Othery Somset
123 J2 Otley Leeds
78 E4 Otley Suffk
29 J6 Otterbourne Hants
131 G7 Otterburn N York
157 M4 Otterburn Nthumb
172 F2 Otter Ferry Ag & B
8 F6 Otterham Cnwll
25 K3 Otterhampton Somset
232 c5 Otternish W Isls
43 G7 Ottershaw Surrey
235 d3 Otterswick Shet
12 E5 Otterton Devon
12 E4 Ottery St Mary Devon
34 F6 Ottinge Kent
127 G5 Ottringham E R Yk
147 K6 Oughterside Cumb
114 F3 Oughtibridge Sheff
113 G4 Oughtrington Warrtn
133 H5 Oulston N York
147 M5 Oulton Cumb
106 D6 Oulton Norfk
99 K5 Oulton Staffs
93 L5 Oulton Suffk
93 L5 Oulton Broad Suffk
106 D6 Oulton Street Norfk
88 F6 Oundle Nhants
84 F5 Ounsdale Staffs
149 G7 Ousby Cumb
77 G3 Ousden Suffk
125 K6 Ousefleet E R Yk
151 G4 Ouston Dur
137 K7 Outgate Cumb
139 H6 Outhgill Cumb
71 K2 Outhill Warwks
123 G6 Outlane Kirk
120 E3 Out Rawcliffe Lancs
90 D3 Outwell Norfk
32 B4 Outwood Surrey
99 H8 Outwoods Staffs
123 L5 Ouzlewell Green Leeds
75 L1 Over Cambs
71 G6 Overbury Worcs
14 D6 Overcombe Dorset
26 E7 Over Compton Dorset
121 K8 Overdale Crematorium Bolton
114 D7 Over Haddon Derbys
129 L5 Over Kellet Lancs
57 H4 Over Kiddington Oxon
26 C4 Overleigh Somset
56 F3 Over Norton Oxon
113 H6 Over Peover Ches E
111 L6 Overpool Ches W
225 J4 Overscaig Hotel Highld
86 C1 Overseal Derbys
133 G2 Over Silton N York
34 E3 Oversland Kent
74 B2 Overstone Nhants
25 J4 Over Stowey Somset
106 F4 Overstrand Norfk
26 B7 Over Stratton Somset
72 F6 Overthorpe Nhants
207 G3 Overton C Aber
29 K2 Overton Hants
129 J7 Overton Lancs
133 H7 Overton N York
69 K1 Overton Shrops
50 F7 Overton Swans
123 K7 Overton Wakefd
98 A4 Overton Wrexhm
175 L7 Overtown N Lans
28 F4 Over Wallop Hants
86 B5 Over Whitacre Warwks
57 H3 Over Worton Oxon
58 C4 Oving Bucks
18 B5 Oving W Susx
19 K5 Ovingdean Br & H
150 D3 Ovingham Nthumb
140 E4 Ovington Dur
77 H6 Ovington Essex
29 K5 Ovington Hants
91 K3 Ovington Norfk
150 D3 Ovington Nthumb
28 F7 Ower Hants
14 E5 Owermoigne Dorset
115 G4 Owlerton Sheff
42 D7 Owlsmoor Br For
58 C6 Owlswick Bucks
117 G4 Owmby Lincs
117 H1 Owmby Lincs
29 K6 Owslebury Hants
124 E7 Owston Donc
87 L3 Owston Leics
116 D2 Owston Ferry N Linc
127 G4 Owstwick E R Yk
127 H5 Owthorne E R Yk
102 A5 Owthorpe Notts
141 L2 Owton Manor Hartpl
91 G3 Oxborough Norfk
118 D6 Oxcombe Lincs
129 L2 Oxenholme Cumb

122 F4 **Oxenhope** C Brad
129 G3 **Oxen Park** Cumb
26 C3 **Oxenpill** Somset
55 L2 **Oxenton** Gloucs
40 F8 **Oxenwood** Wilts
57 K6 **Oxford** Oxon
57 J5 *Oxford Airport* Oxon
57 K6 **Oxford Crematorium** Oxon
57 L6 **Oxford Services** Oxon
43 J2 **Oxhey** Herts
72 C5 **Oxhill** Warwks
84 F3 **Oxley** Wolves
61 L5 **Oxley Green** Essex
90 C6 **Oxlode** Cambs
167 L5 **Oxnam** Border
106 F7 **Oxnead** Norfk
43 J7 **Oxshott** Surrey
114 F2 **Oxspring** Barns
32 C3 **Oxted** Surrey
178 B7 **Oxton** Border
124 D2 **Oxton** N York
101 M3 **Oxton** Notts
51 G7 **Oxwich** Swans
50 F7 **Oxwich Green** Swans
221 K2 **Oykel Bridge Hotel** Highld
206 D1 **Oyne** Abers
51 H7 **Oystermouth** Swans

P

232 g2 **Pabail** W Isls
86 D1 **Packington** Leics
196 C6 **Padanaram** Angus
58 B2 **Padbury** Bucks
44 F4 **Paddington** Gt Lon
35 G6 **Paddlesworth** Kent
46 B7 **Paddlesworth** Kent
33 H4 **Paddock Wood** Kent
122 B4 **Padiham** Lancs
132 B7 **Padside** N York
4 E2 **Padstow** Cnwll
41 L7 **Padworth** W Berk
18 B6 **Pagham** W Susx
46 F2 **Paglesham** Essex
7 K4 **Paignton** Torbay
86 F6 **Pailton** Warwks
68 D5 **Painscastle** Powys
150 D3 **Painshawfield** Nthumb
134 C7 **Painsthorpe** E R Yk
55 K6 **Painswick** Gloucs
34 D3 **Painter's Forstal** Kent
174 E5 **Paisley** Rens
174 E5 **Paisley Woodside Crematorium** Rens
93 L5 **Pakefield** Suffk
77 L2 **Pakenham** Suffk
42 E5 **Paley Street** W & M
85 H4 **Palfrey** Wsall
92 D7 **Palgrave** Suffk
14 E4 **Pallington** Dorset
163 L5 **Palmerston** E Ayrs
146 E4 **Palnackie** D & G
145 J3 **Palnure** D & G
115 J7 **Palterton** Derbys
41 L8 **Pamber End** Hants
41 L8 **Pamber Green** Hants
41 L7 **Pamber Heath** Hants
55 L2 **Pamington** Gloucs
15 J3 **Pamphill** Dorset
76 C5 **Pampisford** Cambs
187 J1 **Panbride** Angus
9 H4 **Pancrasweek** Devon
53 M4 **Pandy** Mons
110 B8 **Pandy Tudur** Conwy
61 H3 **Panfield** Essex
41 M5 **Pangbourne** W Berk
19 J4 **Pangdean** W Susx
123 L1 **Pannal** N York
132 D8 **Pannal Ash** N York
205 J6 **Pannanich Wells Hotel** Abers
97 L7 **Pant** Shrops
111 G6 **Pantasaph** Flints
36 E4 **Pant-ffrwyth** Brdgnd
95 H3 **Pant Glas** Gwynd
81 G4 **Pantglas** Powys
117 K5 **Panton** Lincs
81 L8 **Pant-y-dwr** Powys
111 H8 **Pant-y-mwyn** Flints
93 H2 **Panxworth** Norfk
234 c3 *Papa Westray Airport* Ork
136 F2 **Papcastle** Cumb
231 L5 **Papigoe** Highld
178 D4 **Papple** E Loth
101 K3 **Papplewick** Notts
75 K3 **Papworth Everard** Cambs
75 J2 **Papworth St Agnes** Cambs
5 G5 **Par** Cnwll
121 G7 **Parbold** Lancs
26 E4 **Parbrook** Somset
96 D5 **Parc** Gwynd
49 K5 **Parc Gwyn Crematorium** Pembks
38 B3 **Parc Seymour** Newpt
136 F3 **Pardshaw** Cumb
79 G3 **Parham** Suffk
154 F4 **Park** D & G
149 H3 **Park** Nthumb
42 B3 **Park Corner** Oxon
120 E5 **Park Crematorium** Lancs
54 E6 **Parkend** Gloucs
33 G4 **Parkers Green** Kent
34 D6 **Park Farm** Kent
111 J6 **Parkgate** Ches W
155 H4 **Parkgate** D & G
17 G2 **Park Gate** Hants
123 J3 **Park Gate** Leeds
31 K3 **Parkgate** Surrey
196 F6 **Parkgrove Crematorium** Angus
174 E4 **Parkhall** W Duns
22 F6 **Parkham** Devon
51 G7 **Parkmill** Swans
44 D4 **Park Royal** Gt Lon
151 K5 **Parkside** Dur
175 L6 **Parkside** N Lans
15 J4 **Parkstone** Poole
59 J6 **Park Street** Herts
123 G6 **Park Wood Crematorium** Calder
60 C6 **Parndon** Essex
60 C6 **Parndon Wood Crematorium** Essex
23 L3 **Parracombe** Devon
89 L2 **Parson Drove** Cambs
62 B3 **Parson's Heath** Essex
174 F5 **Partick** C Glas
113 G3 **Partington** Traffd
118 F7 **Partney** Lincs
136 D3 **Parton** Cumb
19 G2 **Partridge Green** W Susx
100 D2 **Parwich** Derbys
73 L6 **Passenham** Nhants
107 G5 **Paston** Norfk
19 J4 **Patcham** Br & H
18 E4 **Patching** W Susx
38 E4 **Patchway** S Glos
132 B6 **Pateley Bridge** N York
186 E8 **Pathhead** Fife
177 K5 **Pathhead** Mdloth
185 M5 **Path of Condie** P & K
163 K7 **Patna** E Ayrs
40 B8 **Patney** Wilts
237 b5 **Patrick** IoM
132 C2 **Patrick Brompton** N York
113 H2 **Patricroft** Salfd
127 H6 **Patrington** E R Yk
127 H6 **Patrington Haven** E R Yk
35 G4 **Patrixbourne** Kent
137 L4 **Patterdale** Cumb
84 E4 **Pattingham** Staffs
73 J4 **Pattishall** Nhants
61 K3 **Pattiswick Green** Essex
2 E5 **Paul** Cnwll
73 K5 **Paulerspury** Nhants
126 E5 **Paull** E R Yk
28 C5 **Paul's Dene** Wilts
26 F1 **Paulton** BaNES
158 D3 **Pauperhaugh** Nthumb
74 E4 **Pavenham** Bed
25 L3 **Pawlett** Somset
71 L6 **Paxford** Gloucs
179 J7 **Paxton** Border
12 E3 **Payhembury** Devon
122 C1 **Paythorne** Lancs
19 L5 **Peacehaven** E Susx
114 D3 **Peak District National Park**
114 C5 **Peak Forest** Derbys
89 H3 **Peakirk** C Pete
39 G8 **Peasedown St John** BaNES
92 C1 **Peaseland Green** Norfk
41 J5 **Peasemore** W Berk
79 H2 **Peasenhall** Suffk
31 L5 **Pease Pottage** W Susx
31 H3 **Peaslake** Surrey
112 D3 **Peasley Cross** St Hel
21 H2 **Peasmarsh** E Susx
217 H2 **Peathill** Abers
187 G5 **Peat Inn** Fife
87 H5 **Peatling Magna** Leics
87 H5 **Peatling Parva** Leics
77 J7 **Pebmarsh** Essex
71 K5 **Pebworth** Worcs
122 E5 **Pecket Well** Calder
98 D2 **Peckforton** Ches E
45 G5 **Peckham** Gt Lon
86 F4 **Peckleton** Leics
34 F7 **Pedlinge** Kent
85 G6 **Pedmore** Dudley
26 B4 **Pedwell** Somset
166 C2 **Peebles** Border
237 b4 **Peel** IoM
35 G6 **Peene** Kent
59 J2 **Pegsdon** C Beds
159 G5 **Pegswood** Nthumb
35 K2 **Pegwell** Kent
209 H7 **Peinchorran** Highld
208 F3 **Peinlich** Highld
62 B5 **Peldon** Essex
85 H3 **Pelsall** Wsall
151 G4 **Pelton** Dur
5 K5 **Pelynt** Cnwll
51 G5 **Pemberton** Carmth
112 D2 **Pemberton** Wigan
50 E5 **Pembrey** Carmth
69 H3 **Pembridge** Herefs
49 G7 **Pembroke** Pembks
49 G6 **Pembroke Dock** Pembks
48 E4 **Pembrokeshire Coast National Park** Pembks
33 G5 **Pembury** Kent
54 E3 **Pen-allt** Herefs
54 D6 **Penallt** Mons
49 J7 **Penally** Pembks
37 J6 **Penarth** V Glam
80 F6 **Pen-bont Rhydybeddau** Cerdgn
65 J4 **Penbryn** Cerdgn
66 B7 **Pencader** Carmth
177 L5 **Pencaitland** E Loth
108 D6 **Pencarnisiog** IoA
66 C5 **Pencarreg** Carmth
53 H3 **Pencelli** Powys
51 G6 **Penclawdd** Swans
36 E4 **Pencoed** Brdgnd
69 L4 **Pencombe** Herefs
54 E4 **Pencraig** Herefs
97 G6 **Pencraig** Powys
2 C4 **Pendeen** Cnwll
52 E6 **Penderyn** Rhondd
50 B4 **Pendine** Carmth
113 H2 **Pendlebury** Salfd
121 L3 **Pendleton** Lancs
55 H2 **Pendock** Worcs
8 D8 **Pendoggett** Cnwll
13 M1 **Pendomer** Somset
37 G5 **Pendoylan** V Glam
81 G4 **Penegoes** Powys
49 J3 **Pen-ffordd** Pembks
37 J2 **Pengam** Caerph
37 K5 **Pengam** Cardif
45 G6 **Penge** Gt Lon
8 E7 **Pengelly** Cnwll
3 K2 **Penhallow** Cnwll
3 J4 **Penhalvean** Cnwll
40 D3 **Penhill** Swindn
38 B3 **Penhow** Newpt
177 H6 **Penicuik** Mdloth
209 G6 **Penifiler** Highld
161 J4 **Peninver** Ag & B
114 E2 **Penistone** Barns
152 F3 **Penkill** S Ayrs
85 G2 **Penkridge** Staffs
98 B4 **Penley** Wrexhm
36 F5 **Penllyn** V Glam
96 C3 **Penmachno** Conwy
37 J2 **Penmaen** Caerph
51 G7 **Penmaen** Swans
109 K6 **Penmaenmawr** Conwy
95 M8 **Penmaenpool** Gwynd
37 G6 **Penmark** V Glam
4 C6 **Penmount Crematorium** Cnwll
109 G6 **Penmynydd** IoA
42 F2 **Penn** Bucks
80 F4 **Pennal** Gwynd
216 F2 **Pennan** Abers
81 J4 **Pennant** Powys
83 G4 **Pennerley** Shrops
122 E4 **Pennines**
128 F4 **Pennington** Cumb
53 H3 **Pennorth** Powys
42 F2 **Penn Street** Bucks
129 G3 **Penny Bridge** Cumb
181 G3 **Pennycross** Ag & B
181 H3 **Pennyghael** Ag & B
163 H7 **Pennyglen** S Ayrs
11 K3 **Pennymoor** Devon
151 J4 **Pennywell** Sundld
65 H5 **Penparc** Cerdgn
53 L6 **Penperlleni** Mons
5 J5 **Penpoll** Cnwll
3 H4 **Penponds** Cnwll
154 E4 **Penpont** D & G
65 H6 **Pen-rhiw** Pembks
37 G2 **Penrhiwceiber** Rhondd
51 L4 **Pen Rhiwfawr** Neath
65 K6 **Penrhiw-llan** Cerdgn
65 K5 **Penrhiw-pal** Cerdgn
94 F5 **Penrhos** Gwynd
54 B5 **Penrhos** Mons
110 A5 **Penrhyn Bay** Conwy
109 H6 **Penrhyn Castle** Gwynd
95 K5 **Penrhyndeudraeth** Gwynd
50 F7 **Penrice** Swans
161 L1 **Penrioch** N Ayrs
138 D2 **Penrith** Cumb
4 D2 **Penrose** Cnwll
138 B2 **Penruddock** Cumb
3 K4 **Penryn** Cnwll
110 C5 **Pensarn** Conwy
70 C2 **Pensax** Worcs
27 H5 **Penselwood** Somset
38 F7 **Pensford** BaNES
71 G5 **Pensham** Worcs
151 H4 **Penshaw** Sundld
32 F4 **Penshurst** Kent
5 L2 **Pensilva** Cnwll
4 F6 **Pentewan** Cnwll

109 H7 **Pentir** Gwynd
4 C4 **Pentire** Cnwll
77 J5 **Pentlow** Essex
91 G2 **Pentney** Norfk
156 D6 **Pentonbridge** Cumb
29 G3 **Penton Mewsey** Hants
109 G5 **Pentraeth** IoA
54 B7 **Pentre** Mons
36 F2 **Pentre** Rhondd
98 A8 **Pentre** Shrops
53 G7 **Pentrebach** Myr Td
52 E2 **Pentre-bach** Powys
108 F6 **Pentre Berw** IoA
97 L3 **Pentrebychan Crematorium** Wrexhm
97 J2 **Pentre-celyn** Denbgs
81 J3 **Pentre-celyn** Powys
51 J6 **Pentre-chwyth** Swans
65 L6 **Pentre-cwrt** Carmth
97 J3 **Pentredwr** Denbgs
95 J5 **Pentrefelin** Gwynd
96 D3 **Pentrefoelas** Conwy
65 K4 **Pentregat** Cerdgn
51 H3 **Pentre-Gwenlais** Carmth
83 G7 **Pentre Hodrey** Shrops
110 F8 **Pentre Llanrhaeadr** Denbgs
36 E5 **Pentre Meyrick** V Glam
96 C1 **Pentre-tafarn-y-fedw** Conwy
101 G3 **Pentrich** Derbys
28 B7 **Pentridge** Dorset
54 D6 **Pen-twyn** Mons
37 J2 **Pentwynmaur** Caerph
37 H4 **Pentyrch** Cardif
5 G5 **Penwithick** Cnwll
51 H2 **Penybanc** Carmth
68 C2 **Penybont** Powys
97 K7 **Pen-y-bont** Powys
97 G7 **Pen-y-bont-fawr** Powys
65 G6 **Pen-y-bryn** Pembks
97 L4 **Penycae** Wrexhm
54 C6 **Pen-y-clawdd** Mons
37 G3 **Pen-y-coedcae** Rhondd
48 E3 **Pen-y-cwn** Pembks
111 G7 **Pen-y-felin** Flints
97 L1 **Penyffordd** Flints
97 H7 **Pen-y-Garnedd** Powys
94 D5 **Pen-y-graig** Gwynd
36 F3 **Penygraig** Rhondd
51 H3 **Penygroes** Carmth
95 H2 **Penygroes** Gwynd
50 F5 **Pen-y-Mynydd** Carmth
97 L1 **Penymynydd** Flints
108 F4 **Penysarn** IoA
97 J3 **Pen-y-stryt** Denbgs
52 F6 **Penywaun** Rhondd
2 E5 **Penzance** Cnwll
2 E5 *Penzance Heliport* Cnwll
71 G4 **Peopleton** Worcs
98 F7 **Peplow** Shrops
163 J2 **Perceton** N Ayrs
217 H2 **Percyhorner** Abers
28 E2 **Perham Down** Wilts
24 E3 **Periton** Somset
44 D4 **Perivale** Gt Lon
12 D4 **Perkins Village** Devon
115 M7 **Perlethorpe** Notts
3 K4 **Perranarworthal** Cnwll
3 K1 **Perranporth** Cnwll
2 F5 **Perranuthnoe** Cnwll
3 K4 **Perranwell** Cnwll
3 K2 **Perranzabuloe** Cnwll
85 J5 **Perry Barr** Birm
85 J5 **Perry Barr Crematorium** Birm
39 L3 **Perry Green** Wilts
99 J6 **Pershall** Staffs
71 G5 **Pershore** Worcs
74 F2 **Pertenhall** Bed
186 B3 **Perth** P & K
186 A3 **Perth Crematorium** P & K
98 A5 **Perthy** Shrops
69 L6 **Perton** Herefs
84 F4 **Perton** Staffs
89 H4 **Peterborough** C Pete
89 H3 **Peterborough Crematorium** C Pete
89 G5 **Peterborough Services** Cambs
69 G6 **Peterchurch** Herefs
206 F5 **Peterculter** C Aber
217 L5 **Peterhead** Abers
151 K6 **Peterlee** Dur
30 C6 **Petersfield** Hants
59 J4 **Peter's Green** Herts
44 D5 **Petersham** Gt Lon
10 C3 **Peters Marland** Devon
37 K4 **Peterstone Wentlooge** Newpt
37 G5 **Peterston-super-Ely** V Glam
54 E3 **Peterstow** Herefs
6 D1 **Peter Tavy** Devon
34 F4 **Petham** Kent
9 H6 **Petherwin Gate** Cnwll
10 D3 **Petrockstow** Devon
21 H3 **Pett** E Susx
78 E3 **Pettaugh** Suffk
196 C7 **Petterden** Angus
165 J2 **Pettinain** S Lans
79 G4 **Pettistree** Suffk
24 F6 **Petton** Devon
45 J6 **Petts Wood** Gt Lon
177 H2 **Pettycur** Fife
207 G1 **Pettymuk** Abers
31 G6 **Petworth** W Susx
20 D5 **Pevensey** E Susx
20 D5 **Pevensey Bay** E Susx
40 D7 **Pewsey** Wilts
71 G3 **Phepson** Worcs
22 D6 **Philham** Devon
166 F4 **Philiphaugh** Border
2 F4 **Phillack** Cnwll
4 D7 **Philleigh** Cnwll
176 E3 **Philpstoun** W Loth
30 C1 **Phoenix Green** Hants
203 G6 **Phones** Highld
26 C6 **Pibsbury** Somset
115 K1 **Pickburn** Donc
134 C3 **Pickering** N York
86 C6 **Pickford** Covtry
132 E3 **Pickhill** N York
83 J4 **Picklescott** Shrops
113 G6 **Pickmere** Ches E
25 J5 **Pickney** Somset
87 L2 **Pickwell** Leics
103 H5 **Pickworth** Lincs
88 E2 **Pickworth** Rutlnd
112 B7 **Picton** Ches W
141 K5 **Picton** N York
19 L5 **Piddinghoe** E Susx
74 B4 **Piddington** Nhants
57 M5 **Piddington** Oxon
14 D3 **Piddlehinton** Dorset
14 D3 **Piddletrenthide** Dorset
89 K7 **Pidley** Cambs
140 F4 **Piercebridge** Darltn
234 c3 **Pierowall** Ork
45 L2 **Pilgrims Hatch** Essex
116 E3 **Pilham** Lincs
6 A3 **Pillaton** Cnwll
72 C5 **Pillerton Hersey** Warwks
72 C5 **Pillerton Priors** Warwks
115 G2 **Pilley** Barns
16 D3 **Pilley** Hants
120 E2 **Pilling** Lancs
38 D4 **Pilning** S Glos
114 C8 **Pilsbury** Derbys
13 K3 **Pilsdon** Dorset
101 H1 **Pilsley** Derbys
114 E7 **Pilsley** Derbys
93 H2 **Pilson Green** Norfk
19 L2 **Piltdown** E Susx
23 J5 **Pilton** Devon
88 E6 **Pilton** Nhants
88 D3 **Pilton** Rutlnd
26 E3 **Pilton** Somset
15 G1 **Pimperne** Dorset
103 L7 **Pinchbeck** Lincs
59 L3 **Pin Green** Herts
12 C4 **Pinhoe** Devon
72 B2 **Pinley Green** Warwks
152 E4 **Pinminnoch** S Ayrs
152 E4 **Pinmore** S Ayrs
12 E5 **Pinn** Devon
43 J3 **Pinner** Gt Lon
43 J3 **Pinner Green** Gt Lon
71 G5 **Pinvin** Worcs
152 E5 **Pinwherry** S Ayrs
101 J2 **Pinxton** Derbys
69 K5 **Pipe and Lyde** Herefs
69 J1 **Pipe Aston** Herefs
99 G4 **Pipe Gate** Shrops
213 K4 **Piperhill** Highld
88 B6 **Pipewell** Nhants
30 F1 **Pirbright** Surrey
167 K4 **Pirnie** Border
161 L1 **Pirnmill** N Ayrs
59 J2 **Pirton** Herts
42 B3 **Pishill** Oxon
94 F4 **Pistyll** Gwynd
194 C3 **Pitagowan** P & K
217 J2 **Pitblae** Abers
185 M3 **Pitcairngreen** P & K
223 H6 **Pitcalnie** Highld
206 D1 **Pitcaple** Abers
196 B4 **Pitcarity** Angus
55 J6 **Pitchcombe** Gloucs
58 C4 **Pitchcott** Bucks
83 K3 **Pitchford** Shrops
58 C7 **Pitch Green** Bucks
214 E6 **Pitchroy** Moray
26 F5 **Pitcombe** Somset
178 E4 **Pitcox** E Loth
206 D3 **Pitfichie** Abers
216 D5 **Pitglassie** Abers
223 H3 **Pitgrudy** Highld
186 E5 **Pitlessie** Fife
194 E5 **Pitlochry** P & K
216 C8 **Pitmachie** Abers
203 H5 **Pitmain** Highld
217 G8 **Pitmedden** Abers
217 G8 **Pitmedden Garden** Abers
25 K7 **Pitminster** Somset
196 F6 **Pitmuies** Angus
206 C3 **Pitmunie** Abers
26 C5 **Pitney** Somset
186 C3 **Pitroddie** P & K
187 G5 **Pitscottie** Fife
46 C3 **Pitsea** Essex
73 L2 **Pitsford** Nhants
58 F5 **Pitstone** Bucks
197 H2 **Pittarrow** Abers
187 J6 **Pittenweem** Fife
186 D7 **Pitteuchar** Fife
151 H6 **Pittington** Dur
206 D1 **Pittodrie House Hotel** Abers
28 E5 **Pitton** Wilts
217 H2 **Pittulie** Abers
151 G5 **Pity Me** Dur
31 K2 **Pixham** Surrey
175 L5 **Plains** N Lans
83 K4 **Plaish** Shrops
45 H4 **Plaistow** Gt Lon
31 G5 **Plaistow** W Susx
28 F7 **Plaitford** Hants
33 G2 **Platt** Kent
151 G5 **Plawsworth** Dur
33 G3 **Plaxtol** Kent
21 H2 **Playden** E Susx
78 F5 **Playford** Suffk
42 C5 **Play Hatch** Oxon
4 C7 **Playing Place** Cnwll
55 H2 **Playley Green** Gloucs
83 H3 **Plealey** Shrops
175 L2 **Plean** Stirlg
186 D5 **Pleasance** Fife
121 J5 **Pleasington** Bl w D
121 J5 **Pleasington Crematorium** Bl w D
115 J8 **Pleasley** Derbys
112 C7 **Plemstall** Ches W
61 G5 **Pleshey** Essex
210 C7 **Plockton** Highld
83 H6 **Plowden** Shrops
34 B5 **Pluckley** Kent
34 B5 **Pluckley Thorne** Kent
147 K6 **Plumbland** Cumb
113 G6 **Plumley** Ches E
148 E7 **Plumpton** Cumb
19 K3 **Plumpton** E Susx
73 H5 **Plumpton** Nhants
19 K3 **Plumpton Green** E Susx
45 J4 **Plumstead** Gt Lon
106 D5 **Plumstead** Norfk
101 L6 **Plumtree** Notts
102 C5 **Plungar** Leics
34 C7 **Plurenden** Kent
14 D3 **Plush** Dorset
65 K4 **Plwmp** Cerdgn
6 C5 **Plymouth** C Plym
6 D4 *Plymouth Airport* C Plym
6 D5 **Plympton** C Plym
6 D5 **Plymstock** C Plym
12 D2 **Plymtree** Devon
133 K3 **Pockley** N York
125 J2 **Pocklington** E R Yk
26 D6 **Podimore** Somset
74 D3 **Podington** Bed
99 H5 **Podmore** Staffs
103 J6 **Pointon** Lincs
15 L4 **Pokesdown** Bmouth
224 B6 **Polbain** Highld
6 A4 **Polbathic** Cnwll
176 D5 **Polbeth** W Loth
3 H5 **Poldark Mine** Cnwll
88 F6 **Polebrook** Nhants
20 C5 **Polegate** E Susx
86 C3 **Polesworth** Warwks
224 C6 **Polglass** Highld
4 F5 **Polgooth** Cnwll
154 C2 **Polgown** D & G
18 E5 **Poling** W Susx
18 E5 **Poling Corner** W Susx
5 H5 **Polkerris** Cnwll
124 F6 **Pollington** E R Yk
190 F3 **Polloch** Highld
175 G6 **Pollokshaws** C Glas
175 G5 **Pollokshields** C Glas
4 F6 **Polmassick** Cnwll
176 C3 **Polmont** Falk
200 B8 **Polnish** Highld
5 K5 **Polperro** Cnwll
5 H5 **Polruan** Cnwll
78 B6 **Polstead** Suffk
182 B7 **Poltalloch** Ag & B
12 C3 **Poltimore** Devon
177 J5 **Polton** Mdloth
178 F7 **Polwarth** Border
9 H7 **Polyphant** Cnwll
4 E1 **Polzeath** Cnwll
177 H6 **Pomathorn** Mdloth
89 J5 **Pondersbridge** Cambs
45 G2 **Ponders End** Gt Lon
3 K4 **Ponsanooth** Cnwll
7 G2 **Ponsworthy** Devon
51 H4 **Pont Abraham Services** Carmth
50 F3 **Pontantwn** Carmth
51 K5 **Pontardawe** Neath

51 H5 **Pontarddulais** Swans
51 G2 **Pont-ar-gothi** Carmth
66 B8 **Pontarsais** Carmth
97 L1 **Pontblyddyn** Flints
124 C6 **Pontefract** Wakefd
124 C6 **Pontefract Crematorium** Wakefd
158 F7 **Ponteland** Nthumb
81 G7 **Ponterwyd** Cerdgn
83 H3 **Pontesbury** Shrops
83 H3 **Pontesford** Shrops
97 K5 **Pontfadog** Wrexhm
64 E7 **Pontfaen** Pembks
67 L7 **Pont-faen** Powys
65 K4 **Pontgarreg** Cerdgn
50 F4 **Ponthenry** Carmth
37 M2 **Ponthir** Torfn
65 J5 **Ponthirwaun** Cerdgn
37 J2 **Pontllanfraith** Caerph
51 H5 **Pontlliw** Swans
53 H6 **Pontlottyn** Caerph
95 G3 **Pontlyfni** Gwynd
52 D6 **Pontneddfechan** Neath
37 L2 **Pontnewydd** Torfn
67 G2 **Pontrhydfendigaid** Cerdgn
36 C2 **Pont-rhyd-y-fen** Neath
81 G8 **Pontrhydygroes** Cerdgn
54 B3 **Pontrilas** Herefs
82 C2 **Pont Robert** Powys
66 B5 **Pontshaen** Cerdgn
53 G5 **Pontsticill** Myr Td
65 L6 **Pontwelly** Carmth
50 F4 **Pontyates** Carmth
51 G4 **Pontyberem** Carmth
97 L2 **Pontybodkin** Flints
37 G4 **Pontyclun** Rhondd
36 D3 **Pontycymer** Brdgnd
96 B2 **Pont-y-pant** Conwy
53 L7 **Pontypool** Torfn
37 G3 **Pontypridd** Rhondd
37 K2 **Pontywaun** Caerph
3 H3 **Pool** Cnwll
123 J2 **Pool** Leeds
15 J4 **Poole** Poole
15 J3 **Poole Crematorium** Poole
39 M2 **Poole Keynes** Gloucs
219 K5 **Poolewe** Highld
138 C3 **Pooley Bridge** Cumb
99 K1 **Poolfold** Staffs
55 G3 **Poolhill** Gloucs
185 L7 **Pool of Muckhart** Clacks
77 H6 **Pool Street** Essex
45 G4 **Poplar** Gt Lon
16 F4 **Porchfield** IoW
92 F3 **Poringland** Norfk
3 J5 **Porkellis** Cnwll
24 D3 **Porlock** Somset
24 D2 **Porlock Weir** Somset
172 C6 **Portachoillan** Ag & B
210 B7 **Port-an-Eorna** Highld
191 H7 **Port Appin** Ag & B
171 H5 **Port Askaig** Ag & B
172 F4 **Portavadie** Ag & B
173 J5 **Port Bannatyne** Ag & B
38 D5 **Portbury** N Som
147 M3 **Port Carlisle** Cumb
170 E6 **Port Charlotte** Ag & B
17 H2 **Portchester** Hants
17 H2 **Portchester Crematorium** Hants
173 G4 **Port Driseach** Ag & B
160 C1 **Port Ellen** Ag & B
206 E2 **Port Elphinstone** Abers
152 B7 **Portencalzie** D & G
173 K8 **Portencross** N Ayrs
237 a6 **Port Erin** IoM
14 B5 **Portesham** Dorset
215 K2 **Portessie** Moray
50 F7 **Port Eynon** Swans
48 F4 **Portfield Gate** Pembks
10 B7 **Portgate** Devon
8 D8 **Port Gaverne** Cnwll
174 C4 **Port Glasgow** Inver
215 J2 **Portgordon** Moray
227 H5 **Portgower** Highld
4 C4 **Porth** Cnwll
36 F3 **Porth** Rhondd
3 K6 **Porthallow** Cnwll
5 K5 **Porthallow** Cnwll
36 C5 **Porthcawl** Brdgnd
4 D2 **Porthcothan** Cnwll
2 C6 **Porthcurno** Cnwll
219 H6 **Port Henderson** Highld
64 A7 **Porthgain** Pembks
2 C6 **Porthgwarra** Cnwll
37 G6 **Porthkerry** V Glam
3 H6 **Porthleven** Cnwll
95 K5 **Porthmadog** Gwynd
3 K5 **Porth Navas** Cnwll
3 K6 **Porthoustock** Cnwll
5 G5 **Porthpean** Cnwll
3 J2 **Porthtowan** Cnwll
51 G3 **Porthyrhyd** Carmth
183 J8 **Portincaple** Ag & B
125 J4 **Portington** E R Yk
182 D5 **Portinnisherrich** Ag & B
137 H3 **Portinscale** Cumb
8 D8 **Port Isaac** Cnwll
38 C5 **Portishead** N Som
215 K2 **Portknockie** Moray
14 D7 **Portland** Dorset
207 H6 **Portlethen** Abers
146 F4 **Portling** D & G
4 E7 **Portloe** Cnwll
144 D6 **Port Logan** D & G
223 K5 **Portmahomack** Highld
95 K5 **Portmeirion** Gwynd
4 F6 **Portmellon** Cnwll
189 K1 **Port Mor** Highld
191 H6 **Portnacroish** Ag & B
232 g2 **Portnaguran** W Isls
170 D7 **Portnahaven** Ag & B
208 E7 **Portnalong** Highld
232 g2 **Port nan Giuran** W Isls
232 c5 **Port nan Long** W Isls
232 g1 **Port Nis** W Isls
177 J4 **Portobello** C Edin
85 G4 **Portobello** Wolves
184 D6 **Port of Menteith** Stirlg
232 g1 **Port of Ness** W Isls
28 D4 **Porton** Wilts
144 B4 **Portpatrick** D & G
8 C8 **Port Quin** Cnwll
191 H7 **Port Ramsay** Ag & B
3 H3 **Portreath** Cnwll
209 G5 **Portree** Highld
237 b7 **Port St Mary** IoM
4 D8 **Portscatho** Cnwll
17 J3 **Portsea** C Port
230 C3 **Portskerra** Highld
38 D3 **Portskewett** Mons
19 H4 **Portslade** Br & H
19 H5 **Portslade-by-Sea** Br & H
144 B3 **Portslogan** D & G
17 J3 **Portsmouth** C Port
122 D5 **Portsmouth** Calder
237 c6 **Port Soderick** IoM
182 F3 **Portsonachan Hotel** Ag & B
216 B2 **Portsoy** Abers
111 K5 **Port Sunlight** Wirral
29 H8 **Portswood** C Sotn
36 B3 **Port Talbot** Neath
189 K3 **Portuairk** Highld
85 J8 **Portway** Worcs
170 D7 **Port Wemyss** Ag & B
145 H6 **Port William** D & G
6 A5 **Portwrinkle** Cnwll
145 K7 **Portyerrock** D & G
77 H5 **Poslingford** Suffk
166 B3 **Posso** Border
10 F8 **Postbridge** Devon
58 B7 **Postcombe** Oxon
34 F6 **Postling** Kent
93 G2 **Postwick** Norfk
206 B6 **Potarch** Abers
59 G6 **Potten End** Herts
134 F4 **Potter Brompton** N York
117 H7 **Potterhanworth** Lincs
117 H7 **Potterhanworth Booths** Lincs
107 J8 **Potter Heigham** Norfk
39 M8 **Potterne** Wilts
39 M8 **Potterne Wick** Wilts
59 L7 **Potters Bar** Herts
59 J6 **Potters Crouch** Herts
86 D6 **Potters Green** Covtry
87 G4 **Potters Marston** Leics
73 L6 **Potterspury** Nhants
207 H3 **Potterton** Abers
141 L6 **Potto** N York
75 J5 **Potton** C Beds
113 L5 **Pott Shrigley** Ches E
9 G4 **Poughill** Cnwll
11 K3 **Poughill** Devon
15 M2 **Poulner** Hants
39 L7 **Poulshot** Wilts
56 C7 **Poulton** Gloucs
120 D3 **Poulton-le-Fylde** Lancs
51 H6 **Poundffald** Swans
20 B2 **Pound Green** E Susx
77 G4 **Pound Green** Suffk
32 B5 **Pound Hill** W Susx
57 M3 **Poundon** Bucks
7 G2 **Poundsgate** Devon
9 G5 **Poundstock** Cnwll
145 K5 **Pouton** D & G
31 L3 **Povey Cross** Surrey
168 F6 **Powburn** Nthumb
12 C5 **Powderham** Devon
13 M3 **Powerstock** Dorset
147 K2 **Powfoot** D & G
70 E4 **Powick** Worcs
185 L7 **Powmill** P & K
14 E5 **Poxwell** Dorset
43 G5 **Poyle** Slough
19 H4 **Poynings** W Susx
26 F7 **Poyntington** Dorset
113 L5 **Poynton** Ches E
98 E8 **Poynton Green** Wrekin
3 G5 **Praa Sands** Cnwll
45 J7 **Pratt's Bottom** Gt Lon
3 H4 **Praze-an-Beeble** Cnwll
98 D5 **Prees** Shrops
120 E2 **Preesall** Lancs
98 E6 **Prees Green** Shrops
98 E5 **Prees Heath** Shrops
98 E5 **Prees Higher Heath** Shrops
65 L5 **Pren-gwyn** Cerdgn
95 K4 **Prenteg** Gwynd
112 C3 **Prescot** Knows
25 H8 **Prescott** Devon
195 J3 **Presnerb** Angus
110 E5 **Prestatyn** Denbgs
113 K6 **Prestbury** Ches E
55 L4 **Prestbury** Gloucs
69 G2 **Presteigne** Powys
26 F4 **Prestleigh** Somset
179 G6 **Preston** Border
19 J4 **Preston** Br & H
7 K2 **Preston** Devon
14 D5 **Preston** Dorset
126 F4 **Preston** E R Yk
56 B7 **Preston** Gloucs
59 K3 **Preston** Herts
34 D3 **Preston** Kent
35 H3 **Preston** Kent
121 H4 **Preston** Lancs
169 H4 **Preston** Nthumb
88 C3 **Preston** Rutlnd
25 H4 **Preston** Somset
77 L4 **Preston** Suffk
7 K4 **Preston** Torbay
40 B5 **Preston** Wilts
71 L2 **Preston Bagot** Warwks
58 A3 **Preston Bissett** Bucks
25 H6 **Preston Bowyer** Somset
98 D7 **Preston Brockhurst** Shrops
112 E5 **Preston Brook** Halton
29 L3 **Preston Candover** Hants
73 H4 **Preston Capes** Nhants
121 H4 **Preston Crematorium** Lancs
71 L2 **Preston Green** Warwks
98 C8 **Preston Gubbals** Shrops
72 B4 **Preston on Stour** Warwks
112 E5 **Preston on the Hill** Halton
69 H6 **Preston on Wye** Herefs
177 K4 **Prestonpans** E Loth
129 L3 **Preston Patrick** Cumb
26 D7 **Preston Plucknett** Somset
131 K2 **Preston-under-Scar** N York
84 C1 **Preston upon the Weald Moors** Wrekin
69 L5 **Preston Wynne** Herefs
113 J1 **Prestwich** Bury
163 J4 **Prestwick** S Ayrs
163 J4 ***Prestwick Airport*** S Ayrs
58 E7 **Prestwood** Bucks
90 E6 **Prickwillow** Cambs
26 D2 **Priddy** Somset
129 L5 **Priest Hutton** Lancs
164 B2 **Priestland** E Ayrs
82 F4 **Priest Weston** Shrops
179 G6 **Primrosehill** Border
168 B4 **Primsidemill** Border
58 D7 **Princes Risborough** Bucks
72 E1 **Princethorpe** Warwks
6 E2 **Princetown** Devon
72 F4 **Priors Hardwick** Warwks
84 C2 **Priorslee** Wrekin
72 F3 **Priors Marston** Warwks
55 K3 **Priors Norton** Gloucs
40 C3 **Priory Vale** Swindn
39 G7 **Priston** BaNES
46 E3 **Prittlewell** Sthend
30 B6 **Privett** Hants
23 J4 **Prixford** Devon
4 E6 **Probus** Cnwll
178 C3 **Prora** E Loth
147 K6 **Prospect** Cumb
3 H5 **Prospidnick** Cnwll
216 F2 **Protstonhill** Abers
150 D3 **Prudhoe** Nthumb
38 F7 **Publow** BaNES
60 C4 **Puckeridge** Herts
26 B7 **Puckington** Somset
39 G5 **Pucklechurch** S Glos
111 K6 **Puddington** Ches W
11 J3 **Puddington** Devon
14 E4 **Puddletown** Dorset
123 J4 **Pudsey** Leeds
18 E3 **Pulborough** W Susx

98 A2 **Pulford** Ches W
14 D2 **Pulham** Dorset
92 E6 **Pulham Market** Norfk
92 E6 **Pulham St Mary** Norfk
74 F7 **Pulloxhill** C Beds
176 E4 **Pumpherston** W Loth
66 E6 **Pumsaint** Carmth
49 G2 **Puncheston** Pembks
14 A5 **Puncknowle** Dorset
20 C2 **Punnett's Town** E Susx
17 J2 **Purbrook** Hants
45 K4 **Purfleet** Thurr
25 L3 **Puriton** Somset
61 K7 **Purleigh** Essex
44 F7 **Purley** Gt Lon
42 A5 **Purley** W Berk
27 G7 **Purse Caundle** Dorset
13 K2 **Purtington** Somset
54 F6 **Purton** Gloucs
55 G7 **Purton** Gloucs
40 C3 **Purton** Wilts
40 C3 **Purton Stoke** Wilts
73 K5 **Pury End** Nhants
41 G2 **Pusey** Oxon
70 B6 **Putley** Herefs
70 B6 **Putley Green** Herefs
44 E5 **Putney** Gt Lon
44 E5 **Putney Vale Crematorium** Gt Lon
30 F2 **Puttenham** Surrey
73 L6 **Puxley** Nhants
38 B7 **Puxton** N Som
50 F5 **Pwll** Carmth
97 H2 **Pwll-glas** Denbgs
68 B7 **Pwllgloyw** Powys
94 F5 **Pwllheli** Gwynd
38 D2 **Pwllmeyric** Mons
50 C3 **Pwll Trap** Carmth
36 C2 **Pwll-y-glaw** Neath
101 H3 **Pye Bridge** Derbys
19 J3 **Pyecombe** W Susx
36 C4 **Pyle** Brdgnd
25 H5 **Pyleigh** Somset
26 E4 **Pylle** Somset
90 C6 **Pymoor** Cambs
13 L4 **Pymore** Dorset
43 H8 **Pyrford** Surrey
42 B2 **Pyrton** Oxon
88 C8 **Pytchley** Nhants
9 J4 **Pyworthy** Devon

Q

103 L6 **Quadring** Lincs
103 L5 **Quadring Eaudike** Lincs
58 C4 **Quainton** Bucks
25 J4 **Quantock Hills** Somset
235 c6 **Quarff** Shet
28 F3 **Quarley** Hants
101 G4 **Quarndon** Derbys
174 C5 **Quarrier's Village** Inver
103 H4 **Quarrington** Lincs
151 H7 **Quarrington Hill** Dur
85 G6 **Quarry Bank** Dudley
214 E2 **Quarrywood** Moray
173 L6 **Quarter** N Ayrs
175 J7 **Quarter** S Lans
84 D5 **Quatford** Shrops
84 D6 **Quatt** Shrops
150 F6 **Quebec** Dur
55 J5 **Quedgeley** Gloucs
90 E7 **Queen Adelaide** Cambs
46 E5 **Queenborough** Kent
26 E6 **Queen Camel** Somset
38 F6 **Queen Charlton** BaNES
184 B6 **Queen Elizabeth Forest Park** Stirlg
70 F6 **Queenhill** Worcs
27 H5 **Queen Oak** Dorset
17 H5 **Queen's Bower** IoW
123 G4 **Queensbury** C Brad
111 K7 **Queensferry** Flints
175 H5 **Queenslie** C Glas
175 J3 **Queenzieburn** N Lans
60 E3 **Quendon** Essex
87 J2 **Queniborough** Leics
56 C7 **Quenington** Gloucs
85 J4 **Queslett** Birm
5 L3 **Quethiock** Cnwll
92 B6 **Quidenham** Norfk
28 C5 **Quidhampton** Wilts
73 L4 **Quinton** Nhants
4 D4 **Quintrell Downs** Cnwll
179 G5 **Quixwood** Border
185 H3 **Quoig** P & K
87 H1 **Quorn** Leics
165 J2 **Quothquan** S Lans
234 c6 **Quoyburray** Ork
234 b5 **Quoyloo** Ork

R

209 J5 **Raasay** Highld
165 L3 **Rachan Mill** Border
109 J7 **Rachub** Gwynd
24 D7 **Rackenford** Devon
18 E3 **Rackham** W Susx
93 G1 **Rackheath** Norfk
155 H7 **Racks** D & G
234 a7 **Rackwick** Ork
100 F5 **Radbourne** Derbys
113 H1 **Radcliffe** Bury
101 M5 **Radcliffe on Trent** Notts
73 J7 **Radclive** Bucks
213 H3 **Raddery** Highld
187 G5 **Radernie** Fife
86 D7 **Radford** Covtry
72 D2 **Radford Semele** Warwks
59 K7 **Radlett** Herts
57 K7 **Radley** Oxon
60 F6 **Radley Green** Essex
42 C2 **Radnage** Bucks
27 G1 **Radstock** BaNES
73 H6 **Radstone** Nhants
72 D5 **Radway** Warwks
74 E3 **Radwell** Bed
75 J7 **Radwell** Herts
76 E6 **Radwinter** Essex
37 H4 **Radyr** Cardif
214 C3 **Rafford** Moray
102 A8 **Ragdale** Leics
54 B6 **Raglan** Mons
116 D6 **Ragnall** Notts
213 J8 **Raigbeg** Highld
70 F4 **Rainbow Hill** Worcs
112 C2 **Rainford** St Hel
45 K4 **Rainham** Gt Lon
46 D6 **Rainham** Medway
112 C4 **Rainhill** St Hel
112 D4 **Rainhill Stoops** St Hel
113 L6 **Rainow** Ches E
132 E4 **Rainton** N York
101 L2 **Rainworth** Notts
186 D3 **Rait** P & K
118 D5 **Raithby** Lincs
118 E7 **Raithby** Lincs
30 D5 **Rake** Hants
203 H5 **Ralia** Highld
208 B5 **Ramasaig** Highld
3 J4 **Rame** Cnwll
6 B6 **Rame** Cnwll
14 B3 **Rampisham** Dorset
128 F6 **Rampside** Cumb
76 B2 **Rampton** Cambs
116 D5 **Rampton** Notts
122 B6 **Ramsbottom** Bury
40 F6 **Ramsbury** Wilts
227 K3 **Ramscraigs** Highld
30 B6 **Ramsdean** Hants
41 L8 **Ramsdell** Hants
57 G5 **Ramsden** Oxon
46 B2 **Ramsden Bellhouse** Essex
89 K6 **Ramsey** Cambs
62 E2 **Ramsey** Essex
237 e3 **Ramsey** IoM
89 K6 **Ramsey Forty Foot** Cambs
89 J6 **Ramsey Heights** Cambs
61 M6 **Ramsey Island** Essex
48 B3 **Ramsey Island** Pembks
89 K5 **Ramsey Mereside** Cambs
89 J6 **Ramsey St Mary's** Cambs
35 K2 **Ramsgate** Kent
131 L5 **Ramsgill** N York
157 J2 **Ramshope** Nthumb
100 B4 **Ramshorn** Staffs
30 F5 **Ramsnest Common** Surrey
118 B5 **Ranby** Lincs
116 A5 **Ranby** Notts
117 J5 **Rand** Lincs
44 D8 **Randalls Park Crematorium** Surrey
55 J6 **Randwick** Gloucs
174 D5 **Ranfurly** Rens
100 D7 **Rangemore** Staffs
39 G3 **Rangeworthy** S Glos
163 L6 **Rankinston** E Ayrs
193 G5 **Rannoch Station** P & K
24 E3 **Ranscombe** Somset
116 A4 **Ranskill** Notts
99 J7 **Ranton** Staffs
99 J7 **Ranton Green** Staffs
93 H1 **Ranworth** Norfk
185 G7 **Raploch** Stirlg
234 c4 **Rapness** Ork
146 D5 **Rascarrel** D & G
173 K2 **Rashfield** Ag & B
71 G2 **Rashwood** Worcs
133 G5 **Raskelf** N York
123 H6 **Rastrick** Calder
200 E2 **Ratagan** Highld
87 G3 **Ratby** Leics
86 D4 **Ratcliffe Culey** Leics
101 J6 **Ratcliffe on Soar** Notts
87 J1 **Ratcliffe on the Wreake** Leics
217 J3 **Rathen** Abers
186 F3 **Rathillet** Fife
130 F7 **Rathmell** N York
176 F4 **Ratho** C Edin
176 F4 **Ratho Station** C Edin
215 K2 **Rathven** Moray
72 E5 **Ratley** Warwks
35 H4 **Ratling** Kent
83 H4 **Ratlinghope** Shrops
231 J2 **Rattar** Highld
7 H4 **Rattery** Devon
77 L3 **Rattlesden** Suffk
20 C5 **Ratton Village** E Susx
195 J7 **Rattray** P & K
88 E8 **Raunds** Nhants
115 J3 **Ravenfield** Rothm
136 F7 **Ravenglass** Cumb
93 H4 **Raveningham** Norfk
143 K6 **Ravenscar** N York
175 K6 **Ravenscraig** N Lans
74 F4 **Ravensden** Bed
101 K2 **Ravenshead** Notts
123 J6 **Ravensthorpe** Kirk
73 J1 **Ravensthorpe** Nhants
86 E2 **Ravenstone** Leics
74 B4 **Ravenstone** M Keyn
139 G6 **Ravenstonedale** Cumb
165 H1 **Ravenstruther** S Lans
140 E5 **Ravensworth** N York
133 J8 **Rawcliffe** C York
125 G6 **Rawcliffe** E R Yk
123 J3 **Rawdon** Leeds
123 J3 **Rawdon Crematorium** Leeds
34 B3 **Rawling Street** Kent
115 H3 **Rawmarsh** Rothm
46 C2 **Rawreth** Essex
12 F2 **Rawridge** Devon
122 B6 **Rawtenstall** Lancs
78 C6 **Raydon** Suffk
46 D2 **Rayleigh** Essex
61 H4 **Rayne** Essex
44 E6 **Raynes Park** Gt Lon
76 E2 **Reach** Cambs
122 B4 **Read** Lancs
42 B5 **Reading** Readg
42 B5 **Reading Crematorium** Readg
42 A6 **Reading Services** W Berk
34 B8 **Reading Street** Kent
35 K2 **Reading Street** Kent
138 E4 **Reagill** Cumb
3 G4 **Realwa** Cnwll
223 G3 **Rearquhar** Highld
87 J2 **Rearsby** Leics
230 D3 **Reay** Highld
47 L6 **Reculver** Kent
25 H7 **Red Ball** Devon
49 J6 **Redberth** Pembks
59 J5 **Redbourn** Herts
116 F2 **Redbourne** N Linc
54 D6 **Redbrook** Gloucs
98 D4 **Redbrook** Wrexhm
34 C7 **Redbrook Street** Kent
213 L5 **Redburn** Highld
142 D3 **Redcar** R & Cl
146 E2 **Redcastle** D & G
212 E4 **Redcastle** Highld
176 C3 **Redding** Falk
176 C3 **Reddingmuirhead** Falk
71 J2 **Redditch** Worcs
71 J2 **Redditch Crematorium** Worcs
77 J4 **Rede** Suffk
92 F6 **Redenhall** Norfk
157 L5 **Redesmouth** Nthumb
197 J3 **Redford** Abers
196 F7 **Redford** Angus
30 E6 **Redford** W Susx
166 E6 **Redfordgreen** Border
186 A2 **Redgorton** P & K
92 C7 **Redgrave** Suffk
206 E4 **Redhill** Abers
15 K4 **Red Hill** Bmouth
59 M2 **Redhill** Herts
38 D7 **Redhill** N Som
32 B3 **Redhill** Surrey
93 J6 **Redisham** Suffk
38 E5 **Redland** Bristl
234 b5 **Redland** Ork
78 E1 **Redlingfield** Suffk
78 E1 **Redlingfield Green** Suffk
77 G1 **Red Lodge** Suffk
27 G5 **Redlynch** Somset
28 D7 **Redlynch** Wilts
70 D2 **Redmarley** Worcs
55 H2 **Redmarley D'Abitot** Gloucs
141 J3 **Redmarshall** S on T
102 D5 **Redmile** Leics
131 K2 **Redmire** N York
197 J2 **Redmyre** Abers
98 A6 **Rednal** Shrops
167 J3 **Redpath** Border
219 H7 **Redpoint** Highld
49 L5 **Red Roses** Carmth
159 G3 **Red Row** Nthumb
3 J3 **Redruth** Cnwll
186 C1 **Redstone** P & K
109 G5 **Red Wharf Bay** IoA
38 B4 **Redwick** Newpt
38 D3 **Redwick** S Glos

141 G3 **Redworth** Darltn
75 L7 **Reed** Herts
93 J3 **Reedham** Norfk
125 J6 **Reedness** E R Yk
122 B5 **Reeds Holme** Lancs
117 H6 **Reepham** Lincs
106 D7 **Reepham** Norfk
140 C7 **Reeth** N York
86 C7 **Reeves Green** Solhll
38 D7 **Regil** N Som
224 B5 **Reiff** Highld
31 L2 **Reigate** Surrey
135 H4 **Reighton** N York
207 G2 **Reisque** Abers
231 L5 **Reiss** Highld
2 F5 **Relubbus** Cnwll
214 B5 **Relugas** Moray
42 C4 **Remenham** Wokham
42 C4 **Remenham Hill** Wokham
101 L7 **Rempstone** Notts
56 A6 **Rendcomb** Gloucs
79 H2 **Rendham** Suffk
79 H4 **Rendlesham** Suffk
174 F5 **Renfrew** Rens
74 F4 **Renhold** Bed
115 J6 **Renishaw** Derbys
169 J5 **Rennington** Nthumb
174 D3 **Renton** W Duns
149 G6 **Renwick** Cumb
93 J1 **Repps** Norfk
100 F6 **Repton** Derbys
213 H5 **Resaurie** Highld
190 E4 **Resipole** Highld
3 H3 **Reskadinnick** Cnwll
213 G2 **Resolis** Highld
52 C7 **Resolven** Neath
183 J6 **Rest and be thankful** Ag & B
179 H6 **Reston** Border
196 E6 **Reswallie** Angus
116 B5 **Retford** Notts
61 J7 **Rettendon** Essex
103 M1 **Revesby** Lincs
12 B3 **Rewe** Devon
16 F4 **Rew Street** IoW
93 K7 **Reydon** Suffk
92 B3 **Reymerston** Norfk
49 J5 **Reynalton** Pembks
50 F7 **Reynoldston** Swans
6 A1 **Rezare** Cnwll
67 H5 **Rhandirmwyn** Carmth
67 L2 **Rhayader** Powys
212 D5 **Rheindown** Highld
111 G7 **Rhes-y-cae** Flints
97 H1 **Rhewl** Denbgs
97 J4 **Rhewl** Denbgs
224 D4 **Rhicarn** Highld
228 C5 **Rhiconich** Highld
222 F6 **Rhicullen** Highld
52 E6 **Rhigos** Rhondd
220 D3 **Rhireavach** Highld
223 H2 **Rhives** Highld
37 J4 **Rhiwbina** Cardif
37 K3 **Rhiwderyn** Newpt
109 H7 **Rhiwlas** Gwynd
33 H4 **Rhoden Green** Kent
34 F6 **Rhodes Minnis** Kent
48 C3 **Rhodiad-y-brenin** Pembks
146 C3 **Rhonehouse** D & G
37 G6 **Rhoose** V Glam
65 L7 **Rhos** Carmth
51 L5 **Rhos** Neath
108 C6 **Rhoscolyn** IoA
48 F6 **Rhoscrowther** Pembks
111 H7 **Rhosesmor** Flints
68 D5 **Rhosgoch** Powys
65 H6 **Rhoshill** Pembks
94 D6 **Rhoshirwaun** Gwynd
80 D3 **Rhoslefain** Gwynd
97 L3 **Rhosllanerchrugog** Wrexhm
108 F6 **Rhosmeirch** IoA
108 D6 **Rhosneigr** IoA
97 M3 **Rhosnesni** Wrexhm
110 B5 **Rhôs-on-Sea** Conwy
50 E7 **Rhossili** Swans
95 H2 **Rhostryfan** Gwynd
97 L3 **Rhostyllen** Wrexhm
108 F4 **Rhosybol** IoA
96 E5 **Rhos-y-gwaliau** Gwynd
97 L4 **Rhosymedre** Wrexhm
174 B2 **Rhu** Ag & B
110 F6 **Rhuallt** Denbgs
173 H4 **Rhubodach** Ag & B
110 E6 **Rhuddlan** Denbgs
172 C8 **Rhunahaorine** Ag & B
95 L4 **Rhyd** Gwynd
50 F1 **Rhydargaeau** Carmth
66 D6 **Rhydcymerau** Carmth
95 K3 **Rhyd-Ddu** Gwynd
65 K5 **Rhydlewis** Cerdgn
66 B5 **Rhydowen** Cerdgn
96 D5 **Rhyd-uchaf** Gwynd
94 F5 **Rhyd-y-clafdy** Gwynd
110 C6 **Rhyd-y-foel** Conwy
51 K4 **Rhydyfro** Neath
109 H7 **Rhyd-y-groes** Gwynd
80 E6 **Rhyd-y pennau** Cerdgn
110 D5 **Rhyl** Denbgs
53 H6 **Rhymney** Caerph
186 B4 **Rhynd** P & K
215 L8 **Rhynie** Abers
223 J5 **Rhynie** Highld
84 D8 **Ribbesford** Worcs
121 H4 **Ribbleton** Lancs
121 J4 **Ribchester** Lancs
126 F8 **Riby** Lincs
124 F3 **Riccall** N York
156 F3 **Riccarton** Border
163 K3 **Riccarton** E Ayrs
69 J1 **Richards Castle** Herefs
44 D5 **Richmond** Gt Lon
140 F6 **Richmond** N York
115 H4 **Richmond** Sheff
99 L7 **Rickerscote** Staffs
38 C8 **Rickford** N Som
7 H7 **Rickham** Devon
92 C7 **Rickinghall** Suffk
60 E3 **Rickling Green** Essex
43 H2 **Rickmansworth** Herts
167 H4 **Riddell** Border
10 F3 **Riddlecombe** Devon
123 G3 **Riddlesden** C Brad
15 H5 **Ridge** Dorset
59 K7 **Ridge** Herts
27 L5 **Ridge** Wilts
86 C4 **Ridge Lane** Warwks
115 H5 **Ridgeway** Derbys
77 G6 **Ridgewell** Essex
19 M2 **Ridgewood** E Susx
74 E7 **Ridgmont** C Beds
150 C3 **Riding Mill** Nthumb
107 H6 **Ridlington** Norfk
88 B3 **Ridlington** Rutlnd
158 A5 **Ridsdale** Nthumb
133 J3 **Rievaulx** N York
133 J3 **Rievaulx Abbey** N York
148 B2 **Rigg** D & G
175 K4 **Riggend** N Lans
213 K4 **Righoul** Highld
118 F6 **Rigsby** Lincs
165 G3 **Rigside** S Lans
121 J5 **Riley Green** Lancs
5 L2 **Rilla Mill** Cnwll
134 D5 **Rillington** N York
122 B2 **Rimington** Lancs
26 E6 **Rimpton** Somset
127 H5 **Rimswell** E R Yk
49 G3 **Rinaston** Pembks
84 D4 **Rindleford** Shrops
146 C4 **Ringford** D & G
92 D2 **Ringland** Norfk
19 L3 **Ringmer** E Susx
6 F6 **Ringmore** Devon
7 L2 **Ringmore** Devon
215 G5 **Ringorm** Moray
93 J5 **Ringsfield** Suffk
93 J6 **Ringsfield Corner** Suffk
59 G5 **Ringshall** Herts
78 C4 **Ringshall** Suffk
78 C4 **Ringshall Stocks** Suffk
88 E7 **Ringstead** Nhants
105 H4 **Ringstead** Norfk
15 L2 **Ringwood** Hants
35 K5 **Ringwould** Kent
20 B4 **Ripe** E Susx
101 H3 **Ripley** Derbys
15 M3 **Ripley** Hants
132 D7 **Ripley** N York
31 H1 **Ripley** Surrey
30 A6 **Riplington** Hants
132 D5 **Ripon** N York
103 H6 **Rippingale** Lincs
35 J5 **Ripple** Kent
70 F6 **Ripple** Worcs
122 F6 **Ripponden** Calder
160 B2 **Risabus** Ag & B
69 K4 **Risbury** Herefs
77 H2 **Risby** Suffk
37 K3 **Risca** Caerph
126 E3 **Rise** E R Yk
103 K6 **Risegate** Lincs
74 F3 **Riseley** Bed
42 B7 **Riseley** Wokham
78 E2 **Rishangles** Suffk
121 L4 **Rishton** Lancs
122 F6 **Rishworth** Calder
101 J5 **Risley** Derbys
112 F3 **Risley** Warrtn
132 C5 **Risplith** N York
35 J6 **River** Kent
30 F6 **River** W Susx
212 E4 **Riverford** Highld
32 F3 **Riverhead** Kent
121 J7 **Rivington** Lancs
73 L4 **Roade** Nhants
176 B7 **Roadmeetings** S Lans
164 B5 **Roadside** E Ayrs
231 H4 **Roadside** Highld
25 G4 **Roadwater** Somset
208 D5 **Roag** Highld
153 G2 **Roan of Craigoch** S Ayrs
37 J5 **Roath** Cardif
166 F6 **Roberton** Border
165 H4 **Roberton** S Lans
20 E2 **Robertsbridge** E Susx
123 J6 **Roberttown** Kirk
49 J4 **Robeston Wathen** Pembks
155 M7 **Robgill Tower** D & G
85 K7 **Robin Hood Crematorium** Solhll
116 A2 *Robin Hood Doncaster Sheffield Airport* Donc
143 K6 **Robin Hood's Bay** N York
6 D4 **Roborough** Devon
10 E2 **Roborough** Devon
112 B4 **Roby** Knows
100 C5 **Rocester** Staffs
48 E3 **Roch** Pembks
122 D7 **Rochdale** Rochdl
122 C7 **Rochdale Crematorium** Rochdl
4 F4 **Roche** Cnwll
46 C6 **Rochester** Medway
157 L3 **Rochester** Nthumb
46 E3 **Rochford** Essex
70 B2 **Rochford** Worcs
4 E2 **Rock** Cnwll
169 J5 **Rock** Nthumb
70 D1 **Rock** Worcs
12 C4 **Rockbeare** Devon
28 C7 **Rockbourne** Hants
148 C3 **Rockcliffe** Cumb
146 E4 **Rockcliffe** D & G
7 L4 **Rockend** Torbay
111 K4 **Rock Ferry** Wirral
223 K5 **Rockfield** Highld
54 C5 **Rockfield** Mons
24 B2 **Rockford** Devon
38 F2 **Rockhampton** S Glos
82 F7 **Rockhill** Shrops
88 C5 **Rockingham** Nhants
92 B4 **Rockland All Saints** Norfk
93 G3 **Rockland St Mary** Norfk
92 B4 **Rockland St Peter** Norfk
116 B6 **Rockley** Notts
173 L1 **Rockville** Ag & B
42 D3 **Rockwell End** Bucks
55 J6 **Rodborough** Gloucs
40 C4 **Rodbourne** Swindn
39 L4 **Rodbourne** Wilts
14 B5 **Rodden** Dorset
27 J2 **Rode** Somset
99 J2 **Rode Heath** Ches E
232 d5 **Rodel** W Isls
83 L1 **Roden** Wrekin
24 F4 **Rodhuish** Somset
83 L1 **Rodington** Wrekin
83 L1 **Rodington Heath** Wrekin
55 H5 **Rodley** Gloucs
39 L2 **Rodmarton** Gloucs
19 L4 **Rodmell** E Susx
34 B3 **Rodmersham** Kent
34 B3 **Rodmersham Green** Kent
26 C2 **Rodney Stoke** Somset
100 D4 **Rodsley** Derbys
132 E6 **Roecliffe** N York
59 K6 **Roe Green** Herts
75 K7 **Roe Green** Herts
44 E5 **Roehampton** Gt Lon
31 K5 **Roffey** W Susx
226 C7 **Rogart** Highld
30 D6 **Rogate** W Susx
37 L3 **Rogerstone** Newpt
232 d5 **Roghadal** W Isls
38 C3 **Rogiet** Mons
41 L2 **Roke** Oxon
151 J3 **Roker** Sundld
93 J1 **Rollesby** Norfk
87 K4 **Rolleston** Leics
102 C3 **Rolleston** Notts
100 E6 **Rolleston on Dove** Staffs
126 F2 **Rolston** E R Yk
33 L6 **Rolvenden** Kent
33 L7 **Rolvenden Layne** Kent
140 C3 **Romaldkirk** Dur
39 H7 **Roman Baths & Pump Room** BaNES
132 E2 **Romanby** N York
177 G8 **Romanno Bridge** Border
24 B7 **Romansleigh** Devon
208 F4 **Romesdal** Highld
15 K1 **Romford** Dorset
45 K3 **Romford** Gt Lon
113 L4 **Romiley** Stockp
29 G6 **Romsey** Hants
84 D6 **Romsley** Shrops
85 G7 **Romsley** Worcs
209 K3 **Rona** Highld
172 C7 **Ronachan** Ag & B
150 B6 **Rookhope** Dur
17 G5 **Rookley** IoW
26 A2 **Rooks Bridge** Somset
25 H5 **Rooks Nest** Somset
132 C3 **Rookwith** N York
127 G4 **Roos** E R Yk
75 G3 **Roothams Green** Bed
29 M5 **Ropley** Hants
29 L5 **Ropley Dean** Hants

103 G5 **Ropsley** Lincs
217 K4 **Rora** Abers
82 F4 **Rorrington** Shrops
215 J4 **Rosarie** Moray
3 K1 **Rose** Cnwll
24 C6 **Rose Ash** Devon
175 L7 **Rosebank** S Lans
49 J2 **Rosebush** Pembks
142 F7 **Rosedale Abbey** N York
61 L3 **Rose Green** Essex
77 L5 **Rose Green** Suffk
77 L6 **Rose Green** Suffk
18 B5 **Rose Green** W Susx
225 K7 **Rosehall** Highld
217 H2 **Rosehearty** Abers
122 C4 **Rose Hill** Lancs
214 E2 **Roseisle** Moray
20 C5 **Roselands** E Susx
49 G5 **Rosemarket** Pembks
213 H3 **Rosemarkie** Highld
25 J7 **Rosemary Lane** Devon
195 J7 **Rosemount** P & K
4 E3 **Rosenannon** Cnwll
177 J6 **Rosewell** Mdloth
141 K3 **Roseworth** S on T
138 D4 **Rosgill** Cumb
208 D5 **Roskhill** Highld
148 B6 **Rosley** Cumb
177 H5 **Roslin** Mdloth
86 B1 **Rosliston** Derbys
174 B2 **Rosneath** Ag & B
146 B6 **Ross** D & G
98 A2 **Rossett** Wrexhm
132 D8 **Rossett Green** N York
115 L2 **Rossington** Donc
174 E4 **Rossland** Rens
54 E4 **Ross-on-Wye** Herefs
231 J7 **Roster** Highld
113 H5 **Rostherne** Ches E
137 H4 **Rosthwaite** Cumb
100 C4 **Roston** Derbys
176 F2 **Rosyth** Fife
158 D2 **Rothbury** Nthumb
87 J1 **Rotherby** Leics
32 F7 **Rotherfield** E Susx
42 B4 **Rotherfield Greys** Oxon
42 B4 **Rotherfield Peppard** Oxon
115 H3 **Rotherham** Rothm
115 J3 **Rotherham Crematorium** Rothm
73 K3 **Rothersthorpe** Nhants
73 K3 **Rothersthorpe Services** Nhants
30 B1 **Rotherwick** Hants
215 G4 **Rothes** Moray
173 J5 **Rothesay** Ag & B
216 E6 **Rothiebrisbane** Abers
215 M5 **Rothiemay** Moray
204 B4 **Rothiemurchus Lodge** Highld
216 D7 **Rothienorman** Abers
87 H2 **Rothley** Leics
216 D7 **Rothmaise** Abers
123 L5 **Rothwell** Leeds
117 J2 **Rothwell** Lincs
88 B7 **Rothwell** Nhants
196 B3 **Rottal Lodge** Angus
19 K5 **Rottingdean** Br & H
136 D5 **Rottington** Cumb
155 H6 **Roucan** D & G
155 H6 **Roucan Loch Crematorium** D & G
105 K7 **Rougham** Norfk
77 K3 **Rougham Green** Suffk
34 F3 **Rough Common** Kent
205 H3 **Roughpark** Abers
118 C8 **Roughton** Lincs
106 F5 **Roughton** Norfk
84 D5 **Roughton** Shrops
60 F5 **Roundbush Green** Essex
59 J4 **Round Green** Luton
13 K1 **Roundham** Somset
123 L3 **Roundhay** Leeds
40 A7 **Roundway** Wilts
196 C6 **Roundyhill** Angus
234 c4 **Rousay** Ork
13 H4 **Rousdon** Devon
57 J3 **Rousham** Oxon
71 H4 **Rous Lench** Worcs
173 L6 **Routenburn** N Ayrs
126 D3 **Routh** E R Yk
129 K2 **Row** Cumb
156 D6 **Rowanburn** D & G
183 L7 **Rowardennan** Stirlg
114 A4 **Rowarth** Derbys
38 C8 **Rowberrow** Somset
39 L7 **Rowde** Wilts
109 L6 **Rowen** Conwy
149 H3 **Rowfoot** Nthumb
62 B4 **Rowhedge** Essex
72 B2 **Rowington** Warwks
114 E6 **Rowland** Derbys
17 K1 **Rowland's Castle** Hants
150 E4 **Rowland's Gill** Gatesd
30 D3 **Rowledge** Surrey
150 D5 **Rowley** Dur
85 H6 **Rowley Regis** Sandw
85 G6 **Rowley Regis Crematorium** Sandw
54 A3 **Rowlstone** Herefs
31 H4 **Rowly** Surrey
17 H3 **Rowner** Hants
71 J1 **Rowney Green** Worcs
29 G7 **Rownhams** Hants
29 H7 **Rownhams Services** Hants
136 E4 **Rowrah** Cumb
58 D4 **Rowsham** Bucks
114 E7 **Rowsley** Derbys
103 H2 **Rowston** Lincs
112 C8 **Rowton** Ches W
98 E8 **Rowton** Wrekin
167 L4 **Roxburgh** Border
125 L6 **Roxby** N Linc
75 G4 **Roxton** Bed
61 G6 **Roxwell** Essex
44 D5 **Royal Botanic Gardens** Gt Lon
192 D1 **Roy Bridge** Highld
60 C6 **Roydon** Essex
92 D7 **Roydon** Norfk
105 H7 **Roydon** Norfk
60 C6 **Roydon Hamlet** Essex
124 B7 **Royston** Barns
75 L6 **Royston** Herts
122 D8 **Royton** Oldham
236 e6 **Rozel** Jersey
97 L4 **Ruabon** Wrexhm
188 D6 **Ruaig** Ag & B
4 D7 **Ruan Lanihorne** Cnwll
3 J7 **Ruan Major** Cnwll
3 J7 **Ruan Minor** Cnwll
54 F4 **Ruardean** Gloucs
54 F5 **Ruardean Hill** Gloucs
54 F5 **Ruardean Woodside** Gloucs
85 H7 **Rubery** Birm
233 c9 **Rubha Ban** W Isls
69 J6 **Ruckhall** Herefs
34 D7 **Ruckinge** Kent
83 K4 **Ruckley** Shrops
141 L6 **Rudby** N York
150 E2 **Rudchester** Nthumb
101 L6 **Ruddington** Notts
27 J2 **Rudge** Somset
38 F3 **Rudgeway** S Glos
31 H5 **Rudgwick** W Susx
112 F6 **Rudheath** Ches W
61 K7 **Rudley Green** Essex
39 J6 **Rudloe** Wilts
37 J3 **Rudry** Caerph
135 H6 **Rudston** E R Yk
99 L2 **Rudyard** Staffs
167 J5 **Ruecastle** Border
120 F7 **Rufford** Lancs
124 D1 **Rufforth** C York
87 G7 **Rugby** Warwks
100 B8 **Rugeley** Staffs
25 K6 **Ruishton** Somset
43 H3 **Ruislip** Gt Lon
198 F5 **Rùm** Highld
215 J4 **Rumbach** Moray
185 L7 **Rumbling Bridge** P & K
93 H7 **Rumburgh** Suffk
4 D2 **Rumford** Cnwll
176 C3 **Rumford** Falk
37 K5 **Rumney** Cardif
112 D5 **Runcorn** Halton
18 B5 **Runcton** W Susx
90 E2 **Runcton Holme** Norfk
30 E3 **Runfold** Surrey
92 C3 **Runhall** Norfk
93 K2 **Runham** Norfk
25 H6 **Runnington** Somset
143 G4 **Runswick** N York
195 L3 **Runtaleave** Angus
46 C2 **Runwell** Essex
42 D5 **Ruscombe** Wokham
70 B7 **Rushall** Herefs
92 E6 **Rushall** Norfk
28 C1 **Rushall** Wilts
77 K3 **Rushbrooke** Suffk
83 K5 **Rushbury** Shrops
60 A2 **Rushden** Herts
74 D2 **Rushden** Nhants
46 E5 **Rushenden** Kent
91 K7 **Rushford** Norfk
62 E5 **Rush Green** Essex
45 K3 **Rush Green** Gt Lon
113 G4 **Rush Green** Warrtn
20 D3 **Rushlake Green** E Susx
93 K6 **Rushmere** Suffk
30 E4 **Rushmoor** Surrey
70 F1 **Rushock** Worcs
113 J3 **Rusholme** Manch
88 B6 **Rushton** Nhants
113 L8 **Rushton Spencer** Staffs
70 E4 **Rushwick** Worcs
141 G2 **Rushyford** Dur
184 D7 **Ruskie** Stirlg
103 H3 **Ruskington** Lincs
129 H2 **Rusland Cross** Cumb
31 K4 **Rusper** W Susx
54 F5 **Ruspidge** Gloucs
42 B3 **Russell's Water** Oxon
31 L4 **Russ Hill** Surrey
32 F5 **Rusthall** Kent
18 E5 **Rustington** W Susx
134 E3 **Ruston** N York
135 G6 **Ruston Parva** E R Yk
143 H5 **Ruswarp** N York
167 K4 **Rutherford** Border
175 H6 **Rutherglen** S Lans
4 F3 **Ruthernbridge** Cnwll
97 H2 **Ruthin** Denbgs
207 H4 **Ruthrieston** C Aber
215 L5 **Ruthven** Abers
195 L6 **Ruthven** Angus
203 H5 **Ruthven** Highld
4 E4 **Ruthvoes** Cnwll
147 J2 **Ruthwell** D & G
98 B7 **Ruyton-XI-Towns** Shrops
158 C7 **Ryal** Nthumb
13 K4 **Ryall** Dorset
70 F6 **Ryall** Worcs
33 H2 **Ryarsh** Kent
137 K6 **Rydal** Cumb
17 H4 **Ryde** IoW
21 H2 **Rye** E Susx
21 H2 **Rye Foreign** E Susx
70 D7 **Rye Street** Worcs
88 F2 **Ryhall** Rutlnd
124 B7 **Ryhill** Wakefd
151 K4 **Ryhope** Sundld
117 G5 **Ryland** Lincs
101 K5 **Rylands** Notts
131 H7 **Rylstone** N York
14 B1 **Ryme Intrinseca** Dorset
124 E3 **Ryther** N York
150 E3 **Ryton** Gatesd
84 D3 **Ryton** Shrops
86 E8 **Ryton-on-Dunsmore** Warwks

S

122 B3 **Sabden** Lancs
60 B4 **Sacombe** Herts
151 G5 **Sacriston** Dur
141 H4 **Sadberge** Darltn
161 K3 **Saddell** Ag & B
87 J5 **Saddington** Leics
90 E1 **Saddle Bow** Norfk
19 H4 **Saddlescombe** W Susx
76 D6 **Saffron Walden** Essex
49 H6 **Sageston** Pembks
91 K3 **Saham Hills** Norfk
91 K3 **Saham Toney** Norfk
98 C1 **Saighton** Ches W
179 J5 **St Abbs** Border
178 E5 **St Agnes** Border
3 J2 **St Agnes** Cnwll
2 a2 **St Agnes** IoS
59 J6 **St Albans** Herts
4 C5 **St Allen** Cnwll
236 c3 **St Andrew** Guern
187 H4 **St Andrews** Fife
187 H4 **St Andrews Botanic Garden** Fife
37 H6 **St Andrew's Major** V Glam
13 L4 **St Andrews Well** Dorset
120 D5 **St Anne's** Lancs
155 J4 **St Ann's** D & G
6 B2 **St Ann's Chapel** Cnwll
6 F6 **St Ann's Chapel** Devon
3 K6 **St Anthony** Cnwll
20 D5 **St Anthony's Hill** E Susx
38 D2 **St Arvans** Mons
110 E6 **St Asaph** Denbgs
36 F6 **St Athan** V Glam
236 b7 **St Aubin** Jersey
4 F5 **St Austell** Cnwll
136 D5 **St Bees** Cumb
5 G5 **St Blazey** Cnwll
167 J3 **St Boswells** Border
236 b7 **St Brelade** Jersey
236 b7 **St Brelade's Bay** Jersey
4 F2 **St Breock** Cnwll
5 H1 **St Breward** Cnwll
54 E6 **St Briavels** Gloucs
36 D5 **St Bride's Major** V Glam
37 H5 **St Brides super-Ely** V Glam
37 L4 **St Brides Wentlooge** Newpt
6 C4 **St Budeaux** C Plym
71 K6 **Saintbury** Gloucs
2 D6 **St Buryan** Cnwll
183 G6 **St Catherines** Ag & B
55 J7 **St Chloe** Gloucs
50 C3 **St Clears** Carmth
5 K3 **St Cleer** Cnwll
4 D6 **St Clement** Cnwll
236 e8 **St Clement** Jersey
9 G7 **St Clether** Cnwll

173 H5 **St Colmac** Ag & B
4 E3 **St Columb Major** Cnwll
4 D4 **St Columb Minor** Cnwll
4 E4 **St Columb Road** Cnwll
217 K2 **St Combs** Abers
93 G6 **St Cross South Elmham** Suffk
197 J4 **St Cyrus** Abers
185 K4 **St David's** P & K
48 C3 **St David's** Pembks
3 J3 **St Day** Cnwll
4 E4 **St Dennis** Cnwll
65 G5 **St Dogmaels** Pembks
6 B3 **St Dominick** Cnwll
36 E6 **St Donats** V Glam
4 F1 **St Endellion** Cnwll
4 D4 **St Enoder** Cnwll
4 D6 **St Erme** Cnwll
6 B4 **St Erney** Cnwll
2 F4 **St Erth** Cnwll
3 G4 **St Erth Praze** Cnwll
4 D2 **St Ervan** Cnwll
4 D3 **St Eval** Cnwll
4 F6 **St Ewe** Cnwll
37 H5 **St Fagans** Cardif
37 H5 St Fagans Welsh Life Museum Cardif
217 K4 **St Fergus** Abers
184 F3 **St Fillans** P & K
49 J7 **St Florence** Pembks
8 F5 **St Gennys** Cnwll
110 D6 **St George** Conwy
38 B7 **St Georges** N Som
37 H5 **St George's** V Glam
6 A4 **St Germans** Cnwll
23 H7 **St Giles in the Wood** Devon
9 K6 **St Giles-on-the-Heath** Devon
81 L8 **St Harmon** Powys
140 F2 **St Helen Auckland** Dur
17 J5 **St Helens** IoW
112 D3 **St Helens** St Hel
112 C3 **St Helens Crematorium** St Hel
44 E6 **St Helier** Gt Lon
236 d7 **St Helier** Jersey
2 F5 **St Hilary** Cnwll
36 F5 **St Hilary** V Glam
59 K3 **St Ippollitts** Herts
48 E6 **St Ishmael's** Pembks
4 E2 **St Issey** Cnwll
5 L3 **St Ive** Cnwll
75 K1 **St Ives** Cambs
2 F3 **St Ives** Cnwll
73 L3 **St James's End** Nhants
93 G7 **St James South Elmham** Suffk
4 E3 **St Jidgey** Cnwll
6 B5 **St John** Cnwll
236 c5 **St John** Jersey
237 b5 **St John's** IoM
32 F3 **St Johns** Kent
43 G8 **St Johns** Surrey
70 E4 **St Johns** Worcs
23 H5 **St John's Chapel** Devon
149 M7 **St John's Chapel** Dur
90 D2 **St John's Fen End** Norfk
165 J3 **St John's Kirk** S Lans
154 B6 **St John's Town of Dalry** D & G
44 F4 **St John's Wood** Gt Lon
237 d3 **St Jude's** IoM
2 C5 **St Just** Cnwll
4 D8 **St Just-in-Roseland** Cnwll
216 E7 **St Katherines** Abers
3 K6 **St Keverne** Cnwll
5 G1 **St Kew** Cnwll
5 G2 **St Kew Highway** Cnwll
5 K4 **St Keyne** Cnwll
62 A6 **St Lawrence** Essex
17 G6 **St Lawrence** IoW
236 c6 **St Lawrence** Jersey
35 K2 **St Lawrence** Kent
58 E6 **St Leonards** Bucks
15 L2 **St Leonards** Dorset
20 F4 **St Leonards** E Susx
2 C6 **St Levan** Cnwll
37 H6 **St Lythans** V Glam
5 G2 **St Mabyn** Cnwll
186 C3 **St Madoes** P & K
69 G7 **St Margarets** Herefs
60 B5 **St Margarets** Herts
35 K5 **St Margaret's at Cliffe** Kent
234 c7 **St Margaret's Hope** Ork
93 G6 **St Margaret South Elmham** Suffk
237 c6 **St Marks** IoM
3 J6 **St Martin** Cnwll
5 K5 **St Martin** Cnwll
236 d3 **St Martin** Guern
236 e6 **St Martin** Jersey
2 b1 **St Martin's** IoS
186 B2 **St Martin's** P & K
97 L5 **St Martins** Shrops
236 b6 **St Mary** Jersey
29 H2 **St Mary Bourne** Hants
7 L3 **St Marychurch** Torbay
36 F6 **St Mary Church** V Glam
45 J6 **St Mary Cray** Gt Lon
21 L1 **St Mary in the Marsh** Kent
44 E3 **St Marylebone Crematorium** Gt Lon
2 b1 **St Mary's** IoS
234 c6 **St Mary's** Ork
21 L1 **St Mary's Bay** Kent
46 D5 **St Mary's Hoo** Medway
54 C5 **St Maughans Green** Mons
3 L5 **St Mawes** Cnwll
4 D3 **St Mawgan** Cnwll
6 B3 **St Mellion** Cnwll
37 K4 **St Mellons** Cardif
4 D2 **St Merryn** Cnwll
4 F7 **St Michael Caerhays** Cnwll
25 L5 **St Michael Church** Somset
4 D7 **St Michael Penkevil** Cnwll
34 B7 **St Michaels** Kent
69 L2 **St Michaels** Worcs
120 F3 **St Michael's on Wyre** Lancs
4 F1 **St Minver** Cnwll
187 H6 **St Monans** Fife
5 J3 **St Neot** Cnwll
75 H3 **St Neots** Cambs
64 C7 **St Nicholas** Pembks
37 H5 **St Nicholas** V Glam
47 L6 **St Nicholas at Wade** Kent
185 G8 **St Ninians** Stirlg
93 J4 **St Olaves** Norfk
62 D5 **St Osyth** Essex
236 b6 **St Ouen** Jersey
54 D3 **St Owens Cross** Herefs
45 J6 **St Pauls Cray** Gt Lon
59 K4 **St Paul's Walden** Herts
236 b6 **St Peter** Jersey
236 d3 **St Peter Port** Guern
236 b3 **St Peter's** Guern
35 K2 **St Peter's** Kent
5 J3 **St Pinnock** Cnwll
163 J5 **St Quivox** S Ayrs
236 d2 **St Sampson** Guern
236 c3 **St Saviour** Guern
236 d7 **St Saviour** Jersey
4 E5 **St Stephen** Cnwll
6 B4 **St Stephens** Cnwll
9 J7 **St Stephens** Cnwll
8 E8 **St Teath** Cnwll
5 G1 **St Tudy** Cnwll
48 F7 **St Twynnells** Pembks
5 J5 **St Veep** Cnwll
197 G7 **St Vigeans** Angus
4 F3 **St Wenn** Cnwll
54 D3 **St Weonards** Herefs
7 H7 **Salcombe** Devon
12 F5 **Salcombe Regis** Devon
61 M5 **Salcott-cum-Virley** Essex
113 H3 **Sale** Traffd
118 F5 **Saleby** Lincs
71 G3 **Sale Green** Worcs
20 F2 **Salehurst** E Susx
80 F6 **Salem** Cerdgn
190 C7 **Salen** Ag & B
190 D4 **Salen** Highld
74 D6 **Salford** C Beds
56 F3 **Salford** Oxon
113 J2 **Salford** Salfd
71 J4 **Salford Priors** Warwks
32 B4 **Salfords** Surrey
93 G1 **Salhouse** Norfk
185 L8 **Saline** Fife
28 C5 **Salisbury** Wilts
28 C5 Salisbury Cathedral Wilts
28 D5 **Salisbury Crematorium** Wilts
28 B3 **Salisbury Plain** Wilts
148 F7 **Salkeld Dykes** Cumb
106 D7 **Salle** Norfk
118 D6 **Salmonby** Lincs
56 B4 **Salperton** Gloucs
175 L5 **Salsburgh** N Lans
99 L6 **Salt** Staffs
123 H3 **Saltaire** C Brad
6 B4 **Saltash** Cnwll
223 G7 **Saltburn** Highld
142 E3 **Saltburn-by-the-Sea** R & Cl
102 D7 **Saltby** Leics
163 G2 **Saltcoats** N Ayrs
19 K5 **Saltdean** Br & H
136 D3 **Salterbeck** Cumb
122 D2 **Salterforth** Lancs
28 C4 **Salterton** Wilts
118 F3 **Saltfleet** Lincs
118 F4 **Saltfleetby All Saints** Lincs
118 F3 **Saltfleetby St Clement** Lincs
118 F4 **Saltfleetby St Peter** Lincs
39 G6 **Saltford** BaNES
106 C4 **Salthouse** Norfk
125 J5 **Saltmarshe** E R Yk
111 L8 **Saltney** Flints
133 L4 **Salton** N York
23 G6 **Saltrens** Devon
151 G3 **Saltwell Crematorium** Gatesd
34 F7 **Saltwood** Kent
18 F5 **Salvington** W Susx
70 F3 **Salwarpe** Worcs
13 L3 **Salway Ash** Dorset
71 J3 **Sambourne** Warwks
99 G7 **Sambrook** Wrekin
25 H7 **Sampford Arundel** Somset
25 G3 **Sampford Brett** Somset
10 F5 **Sampford Courtenay** Devon
25 H7 **Sampford Moor** Somset
25 G8 **Sampford Peverell** Devon
6 D2 **Sampford Spiney** Devon
234 d5 **Samsonlane** Ork
178 B4 **Samuelston** E Loth
170 E4 **Sanaigmore** Ag & B
2 D5 **Sancreed** Cnwll
125 L3 **Sancton** E R Yk
199 L5 **Sandaig** Highld
123 L6 **Sandal Magna** Wakefd
199 G7 **Sandavore** Highld
234 d4 **Sanday** Ork
234 d4 *Sanday Airport* Ork
99 H1 **Sandbach** Ches E
99 H1 Sandbach Services Ches E
173 K3 **Sandbank** Ag & B
15 K5 **Sandbanks** Poole
216 B2 **Sandend** Abers
45 G7 **Sanderstead** Gt Lon
139 G4 **Sandford** Cumb
11 J4 **Sandford** Devon
15 H5 **Sandford** Dorset
15 M3 **Sandford** Hants
17 G6 **Sandford** IoW
38 B8 **Sandford** N Som
164 E2 **Sandford** S Lans
57 K7 **Sandford-on-Thames** Oxon
26 F7 **Sandford Orcas** Dorset
57 H3 **Sandford St Martin** Oxon
35 G7 **Sandgate** Kent
217 H2 **Sandhaven** Abers
144 D5 **Sandhead** D & G
124 B3 **Sand Hills** Leeds
57 K6 **Sandhills** Oxon
30 F4 **Sandhills** Surrey
150 B2 **Sandhoe** Nthumb
182 E7 **Sandhole** Ag & B
125 J3 **Sand Hole** E R Yk
125 J4 **Sandholme** E R Yk
42 D7 **Sandhurst** Br For
55 J4 **Sandhurst** Gloucs
33 K7 **Sandhurst** Kent
132 F3 **Sandhutton** N York
133 L7 **Sand Hutton** N York
101 J5 **Sandiacre** Derbys
119 G5 **Sandilands** Lincs
28 C7 **Sandleheath** Hants
57 J7 **Sandleigh** Oxon
27 H6 **Sandley** Dorset
235 b5 **Sandness** Shet
61 H6 **Sandon** Essex
75 K7 **Sandon** Herts
99 L6 **Sandon** Staffs
99 L6 **Sandon Bank** Staffs
17 H5 **Sandown** IoW
5 K4 **Sandplace** Cnwll
59 K6 **Sandridge** Herts
105 H6 **Sandringham** Norfk
143 H5 **Sandsend** N York
125 H8 **Sandtoft** N Linc
34 B5 **Sandway** Kent
35 J3 **Sandwich** Kent
235 c7 **Sandwick** Shet
232 g2 **Sandwick** W Isls
136 D4 **Sandwith** Cumb
75 H5 **Sandy** C Beds
155 L4 **Sandyford** D & G
7 K2 **Sandygate** Devon
237 d3 **Sandygate** IoM
146 F4 **Sandyhills** D & G
129 J6 **Sandylands** Lancs
39 L6 **Sandy Lane** Wilts
11 G6 **Sandy Park** Devon
228 F3 **Sangobeg** Highld
228 F3 **Sangomore** Highld
70 E2 **Sankyn's Green** Worcs
189 K3 **Sanna Bay** Highld
232 g2 **Sanndabhaig** W Isls
162 C1 **Sannox** N Ayrs
164 F7 **Sanquhar** D & G
136 F6 **Santon Bridge** Cumb

91 J6 **Santon Downham** Suffk
86 F5 **Sapcote** Leics
70 C2 **Sapey Common** Herefs
91 K7 **Sapiston** Suffk
55 L7 **Sapperton** Gloucs
103 G5 **Sapperton** Lincs
104 B6 **Saracen's Head** Lincs
231 L6 **Sarclet** Highld
17 G2 **Sarisbury** Hants
94 D6 **Sarn** Gwynd
81 K4 **Sarn** Powys
82 E5 **Sarn** Powys
65 K4 **Sarnau** Cerdgn
82 E1 **Sarnau** Powys
36 D4 **Sarn Park Services** Brdgnd
51 H3 **Saron** Carmth
109 G7 **Saron** Gwynd
59 H7 **Sarratt** Herts
47 L6 **Sarre** Kent
56 F4 **Sarsden** Oxon
150 E6 **Satley** Dur
23 L6 **Satterleigh** Devon
129 H2 **Satterthwaite** Cumb
206 D3 **Sauchen** Abers
186 C2 **Saucher** P & K
197 G3 **Sauchieburn** Abers
55 H6 **Saul** Gloucs
116 C4 **Saundby** Notts
49 K6 **Saundersfoot** Pembks
58 C7 **Saunderton** Bucks
23 G4 **Saunton** Devon
118 E7 **Sausthorpe** Lincs
123 K6 **Savile Town** Kirk
73 G2 **Sawbridge** Warwks
60 D5 **Sawbridgeworth** Herts
134 E3 **Sawdon** N York
122 B2 **Sawley** Lancs
132 C6 **Sawley** N York
76 C5 **Sawston** Cambs
89 H6 **Sawtry** Cambs
102 D8 **Saxby** Leics
117 G4 **Saxby** Lincs
126 B7 **Saxby All Saints** N Linc
102 B7 **Saxelbye** Leics
78 C3 **Saxham Street** Suffk
116 E6 **Saxilby** Lincs
106 B5 **Saxlingham** Norfk
92 F4 **Saxlingham Green** Norfk
92 F4 **Saxlingham Nethergate** Norfk
92 E4 **Saxlingham Thorpe** Norfk
79 H2 **Saxmundham** Suffk
102 B4 **Saxondale** Notts
76 F3 **Saxon Street** Cambs
78 F2 **Saxtead** Suffk
78 F2 **Saxtead Green** Suffk
78 F2 **Saxtead Little Green** Suffk
106 D6 **Saxthorpe** Norfk
124 D3 **Saxton** N York
19 H3 **Sayers Common** W Susx
133 K5 **Scackleton** N York
137 H5 **Scafell Pike** Cumb
116 A3 **Scaftworth** Notts
134 C5 **Scagglethorpe** N York
180 E8 **Scalasaig** Ag & B
125 K5 **Scalby** E R Yk
134 F2 **Scalby** N York
73 L1 **Scaldwell** Nhants
148 D3 **Scaleby** Cumb
148 D3 **Scalebyhill** Cumb
129 G5 **Scales** Cumb
137 K2 **Scales** Cumb
102 C7 **Scalford** Leics
142 F4 **Scaling** N York
235 c6 **Scalloway** Shet
209 J7 **Scalpay** Highld
118 C5 **Scamblesby** Lincs
191 G2 **Scamodale** Highld
134 D4 **Scampston** N York
116 F5 **Scampton** Lincs
212 F6 **Scaniport** Highld
123 G7 **Scapegoat Hill** Kirk
181 K6 **Scarba** Ag & B
135 G2 **Scarborough** N York
4 E5 **Scarcewater** Cnwll
115 J7 **Scarcliffe** Derbys
124 B3 **Scarcroft** Leeds
231 J2 **Scarfskerry** Highld
188 D7 **Scarinish** Ag & B
120 E7 **Scarisbrick** Lancs
91 L2 **Scarning** Norfk
102 B4 **Scarrington** Notts
118 C1 **Scartho** NE Lin
235 c4 ***Scatsta Airport*** Shet
116 F1 **Scawby** N Linc
115 K1 **Scawsby** Donc
115 K1 **Scawthorpe** Donc
133 H3 **Scawton** N York
19 K2 **Scayne's Hill** W Susx
53 H3 **Scethrog** Powys
99 J2 **Scholar Green** Ches E
123 H4 **Scholemoor Crematorium** C Brad
123 H8 **Scholes** Kirk
124 B3 **Scholes** Leeds
115 H3 **Scholes** Rothm
112 E1 **Scholes** Wigan
123 K7 **Scissett** Kirk
64 C7 **Scleddau** Pembks
115 L5 **Scofton** Notts
92 D7 **Scole** Norfk
186 B3 **Scone** P & K
209 H7 **Sconser** Highld
186 F6 **Scoonie** Fife
103 H2 **Scopwick** Lincs
220 C3 **Scoraig** Highld
126 C2 **Scorborough** E R Yk
3 J3 **Scorrier** Cnwll
121 G2 **Scorton** Lancs
141 G7 **Scorton** N York
148 D4 **Scotby** Cumb
140 F6 **Scotch Corner** N York
129 K7 **Scotforth** Lancs
117 G6 **Scothern** Lincs
186 C6 **Scotlandwell** P & K
231 G4 **Scotscalder Station** Highld
158 C5 **Scot's Gap** Nthumb
206 B2 **Scotsmill** Abers
174 F5 **Scotstoun** C Glas
150 F3 **Scotswood** N u Ty
116 E2 **Scotter** Lincs
116 E2 **Scotterthorpe** Lincs
116 E2 **Scotton** Lincs
132 E7 **Scotton** N York
140 F7 **Scotton** N York
92 B4 **Scoulton** Norfk
228 B6 **Scourie** Highld
228 B6 **Scourie More** Highld
235 c7 **Scousburgh** Shet
231 G2 **Scrabster** Highld
167 K5 **Scraesburgh** Border
104 C4 **Scrane End** Lincs
87 J3 **Scraptoft** Leics
93 K1 **Scratby** Norfk
133 L7 **Scrayingham** N York
103 H4 **Scredington** Lincs
118 F7 **Scremby** Lincs
179 L8 **Scremerston** Nthumb
102 B4 **Screveton** Notts
132 E7 **Scriven** N York
115 M4 **Scrooby** Notts
100 D6 **Scropton** Derbys
103 L2 **Scrub Hill** Lincs
132 D2 **Scruton** N York
229 J4 **Scullomie** Highld
105 L6 **Sculthorpe** Norfk
125 K7 **Scunthorpe** N Linc
13 K2 **Seaborough** Dorset
35 G7 **Seabrook** Kent
151 J3 **Seaburn** Sundld
124 B4 **Seacroft** Leeds
209 G5 **Seafield** Highld
176 D5 **Seafield** W Loth
177 J4 **Seafield Crematorium** C Edin
20 A6 **Seaford** E Susx
111 K3 **Seaforth** Sefton
101 L8 **Seagrave** Leics
151 K5 **Seaham** Dur
169 J3 **Seahouses** Nthumb
32 F2 **Seal** Kent
30 E2 **Seale** Surrey
134 F3 **Seamer** N York
142 B5 **Seamer** N York
173 L8 **Seamill** N Ayrs
107 J6 **Sea Palling** Norfk
117 H1 **Searby** Lincs
47 H6 **Seasalter** Kent
136 E6 **Seascale** Cumb
137 H7 **Seathwaite** Cumb
137 H4 **Seatoller** Cumb
5 L5 **Seaton** Cnwll
136 E2 **Seaton** Cumb
13 G4 **Seaton** Devon
126 E2 **Seaton** E R Yk
35 G3 **Seaton** Kent
159 H6 **Seaton** Nthumb
88 C4 **Seaton** Rutlnd
142 B2 **Seaton Carew** Hartpl
159 H6 **Seaton Delaval** Nthumb
125 J3 **Seaton Ross** E R Yk
159 H6 **Seaton Sluice** Nthumb
13 K4 **Seatown** Dorset
142 C7 **Seave Green** N York
17 J4 **Seaview** IoW
147 K4 **Seaville** Cumb
26 B7 **Seavington St Mary** Somset
26 B7 **Seavington St Michael** Somset
148 C6 **Sebergham** Cumb
86 C3 **Seckington** Warwks
130 C2 **Sedbergh** Cumb
38 D2 **Sedbury** Gloucs
131 G2 **Sedbusk** N York
71 H6 **Sedgeberrow** Worcs
102 D5 **Sedgebrook** Lincs
141 J2 **Sedgefield** Dur
105 H5 **Sedgeford** Norfk
27 K5 **Sedgehill** Wilts
26 A2 **Sedgemoor Services** Somset
85 G5 **Sedgley** Dudley
129 L3 **Sedgwick** Cumb
20 F3 **Sedlescombe** E Susx
58 D5 **Sedrup** Bucks
39 L7 **Seend** Wilts
39 L7 **Seend Cleeve** Wilts
42 F3 **Seer Green** Bucks
93 G4 **Seething** Norfk
111 K2 **Sefton** Sefton
99 K7 **Seighford** Staffs
109 H7 **Seion** Gwynd
84 E4 **Seisdon** Staffs
97 K5 **Selattyn** Shrops
30 C5 **Selborne** Hants
124 F4 **Selby** N York
30 F7 **Selham** W Susx
45 G6 **Selhurst** Gt Lon
167 G4 **Selkirk** Border
54 E3 **Sellack** Herefs
235 d2 **Sellafirth** Shet
34 E6 **Sellindge** Kent
34 D4 **Selling** Kent
39 L7 **Sells Green** Wilts
85 J6 **Selly Oak** Birm
20 B4 **Selmeston** E Susx
45 G7 **Selsdon** Gt Lon
55 J7 **Selsey** Gloucs
18 B6 **Selsey** W Susx
130 E4 **Selside** N York
35 G5 **Selsted** Kent
101 J2 **Selston** Notts
24 E3 **Selworthy** Somset
78 B5 **Semer** Suffk
39 K7 **Semington** Wilts
27 K6 **Semley** Wilts
31 G1 **Send** Surrey
37 H3 **Senghenydd** Caerph
2 C6 **Sennen** Cnwll
2 C6 **Sennen Cove** Cnwll
52 E3 **Sennybridge** Powys
133 G4 **Sessay** N York
90 F2 **Setchey** Norfk
177 L4 **Seton Mains** E Loth
130 F6 **Settle** N York
134 C5 **Settrington** N York
56 B4 **Sevenhampton** Gloucs
40 E3 **Sevenhampton** Swindn
78 F6 **Seven Hills Crematorium** Suffk
45 J3 **Seven Kings** Gt Lon
32 F3 **Sevenoaks** Kent
32 F3 **Sevenoaks Weald** Kent
52 C6 **Seven Sisters** Neath
61 M3 **Seven Star Green** Essex
38 D4 **Severn Beach** S Glos
70 F5 **Severn Stoke** Worcs
38 E3 **Severn View Services** S Glos
34 D6 **Sevington** Kent
76 E6 **Sewards End** Essex
59 G4 **Sewell** C Beds
135 J5 **Sewerby** E R Yk
3 J5 **Seworgan** Cnwll
102 E7 **Sewstern** Leics
232 g1 **Sgiogarstaigh** W Isls
58 A6 **Shabbington** Bucks
86 D3 **Shackerstone** Leics
30 F3 **Shackleford** Surrey
232 f1 **Shader** W Isls
151 H6 **Shadforth** Dur
93 J6 **Shadingfield** Suffk
34 C7 **Shadoxhurst** Kent
91 L6 **Shadwell** Norfk
76 B6 **Shaftenhoe End** Herts
27 K6 **Shaftesbury** Dorset
124 B7 **Shafton** Barns
113 G2 **Shakerley** Wigan
40 F7 **Shalbourne** Wilts
30 B3 **Shalden** Hants
7 L2 **Shaldon** Devon
16 E5 **Shalfleet** IoW
61 H3 **Shalford** Essex
31 G3 **Shalford** Surrey
61 H3 **Shalford Green** Essex
34 E4 **Shalmsford Street** Kent
73 J7 **Shalstone** Bucks
31 G3 **Shamley Green** Surrey
196 D4 **Shandford** Angus
174 B2 **Shandon** Ag & B
223 J6 **Shandwick** Highld
87 K4 **Shangton** Leics
17 H6 **Shanklin** IoW
138 E4 **Shap** Cumb
234 c5 **Shapinsay** Ork
15 H3 **Shapwick** Dorset
26 B4 **Shapwick** Somset
101 H6 **Shardlow** Derbys
85 G3 **Shareshill** Staffs
124 B6 **Sharlston** Wakefd
74 E3 **Sharnbrook** Bed
86 F5 **Sharnford** Leics
121 G4 **Sharoe Green** Lancs
132 E5 **Sharow** N York
59 H2 **Sharpenhoe** C Beds
158 B2 **Sharperton** Nthumb
54 F7 **Sharpness** Gloucs
106 C5 **Sharrington** Norfk
84 E7 **Shatterford** Worcs
6 D3 **Shaugh Prior** Devon
99 G3 **Shavington** Ches E
122 D8 **Shaw** Oldham
41 J6 **Shaw** W Berk

39 K7 **Shaw** Wilts
84 B2 **Shawbirch** Wrekin
232 e2 **Shawbost** W Isls
98 E7 **Shawbury** Shrops
87 G7 **Shawell** Leics
29 J6 **Shawford** Hants
154 F6 **Shawhead** D & G
132 C6 **Shaw Mills** N York
175 K7 **Shawsburn** S Lans
147 H2 **Shearington** D & G
87 J5 **Shearsby** Leics
25 L5 **Shearston** Somset
10 C3 **Shebbear** Devon
99 H7 **Shebdon** Staffs
230 E3 **Shebster** Highld
175 G6 **Sheddens** E Rens
29 K8 **Shedfield** Hants
100 C1 **Sheen** Staffs
123 H6 **Sheepridge** Kirk
123 L4 **Sheepscar** Leeds
55 K6 **Sheepscombe** Gloucs
6 E3 **Sheepstor** Devon
10 C4 **Sheepwash** Devon
86 D3 **Sheepy Magna** Leics
86 D3 **Sheepy Parva** Leics
60 E5 **Sheering** Essex
46 F5 **Sheerness** Kent
43 H7 **Sheerwater** Surrey
30 C6 **Sheet** Hants
115 G4 **Sheffield** Sheff
115 G4 **Sheffield City Road Crematorium** Sheff
75 G6 **Shefford** C Beds
228 B4 **Sheigra** Highld
83 L3 **Sheinton** Shrops
83 H7 **Shelderton** Shrops
85 L6 **Sheldon** Birm
114 D7 **Sheldon** Derbys
12 E2 **Sheldon** Devon
34 D4 **Sheldwich** Kent
92 D6 **Shelfanger** Norfk
102 A4 **Shelford** Notts
123 J7 **Shelley** Kirk
78 B6 **Shelley** Suffk
40 F2 **Shellingford** Oxon
60 F6 **Shellow Bowells** Essex
70 D2 **Shelsley Beauchamp** Worcs
70 C2 **Shelsley Walsh** Worcs
74 F2 **Shelton** Bed
92 F5 **Shelton** Norfk
102 C4 **Shelton** Notts
99 J5 **Shelton Under Harley** Staffs
83 G4 **Shelve** Shrops
69 K6 **Shelwick** Herefs
45 L2 **Shenfield** Essex
72 D6 **Shenington** Oxon
59 K7 **Shenley** Herts
74 B7 **Shenley Brook End** M Keyn
74 B7 **Shenley Church End** M Keyn
69 H6 **Shenmore** Herefs
145 H3 **Shennanton** D & G
85 K3 **Shenstone** Staffs
84 F8 **Shenstone** Worcs
86 E4 **Shenton** Leics
214 F7 **Shenval** Moray
59 L4 **Shephall** Herts
44 E4 **Shepherd's Bush** Gt Lon
35 H5 **Shepherdswell** Kent
123 J8 **Shepley** Kirk
43 H6 **Shepperton** Surrey
76 B5 **Shepreth** Cambs
101 J8 **Shepshed** Leics
26 B7 **Shepton Beauchamp** Somset
26 F3 **Shepton Mallet** Somset
27 G5 **Shepton Montague** Somset
33 K3 **Shepway** Kent
151 K7 **Sheraton** Dur
26 F7 **Sherborne** Dorset
56 D5 **Sherborne** Gloucs
26 E1 **Sherborne** Somset
29 L1 **Sherborne St John** Hants
72 C3 **Sherbourne** Warwks
151 H6 **Sherburn** Dur
134 E4 **Sherburn** N York
151 H6 **Sherburn Hill** Dur
124 D4 **Sherburn in Elmet** N York
31 H2 **Shere** Surrey
105 L6 **Shereford** Norfk
28 F6 **Sherfield English** Hants
42 B8 **Sherfield on Loddon** Hants
7 H6 **Sherford** Devon
84 D2 **Sheriffhales** Shrops
133 K6 **Sheriff Hutton** N York
106 E4 **Sheringham** Norfk
74 C5 **Sherington** M Keyn
105 H6 **Shernborne** Norfk
27 L4 **Sherrington** Wilts
39 J3 **Sherston** Wilts
101 K4 **Sherwood** C Nott
101 L2 **Sherwood Forest** Notts
116 A7 **Sherwood Forest Crematorium** Notts
175 H5 **Shettleston** C Glas
121 H8 **Shevington** Wigan
6 B5 **Sheviock** Cnwll
123 G5 **Shibden Head** C Brad
16 F5 **Shide** IoW
168 B2 **Shidlaw** Nthumb
200 E2 **Shiel Bridge** Highld
210 C4 **Shieldaig** Highld
155 H5 **Shieldhill** D & G
176 B3 **Shieldhill** Falk
165 J2 **Shieldhill House Hotel** S Lans
175 K7 **Shields** N Lans
190 D3 **Shielfoot** Highld
196 C5 **Shielhill** Angus
173 L4 **Shielhill** Inver
84 D2 **Shifnal** Shrops
169 J7 **Shilbottle** Nthumb
141 G3 **Shildon** Dur
174 E6 **Shillford** E Rens
24 F6 **Shillingford** Devon
41 L2 **Shillingford** Oxon
11 K6 **Shillingford Abbot** Devon
11 K7 **Shillingford St George** Devon
14 F1 **Shillingstone** Dorset
75 G7 **Shillington** C Beds
56 E6 **Shilton** Oxon
86 E6 **Shilton** Warwks
92 D6 **Shimpling** Norfk
77 J4 **Shimpling** Suffk
77 K4 **Shimpling Street** Suffk
151 H6 **Shincliffe** Dur
151 H4 **Shiney Row** Sundld
42 B6 **Shinfield** Wokham
225 L5 **Shinness** Highld
33 G3 **Shipbourne** Kent
91 L3 **Shipdham** Norfk
38 C8 **Shipham** Somset
7 K3 **Shiphay** Torbay
42 C5 **Shiplake** Oxon
123 H3 **Shipley** C Brad
31 J6 **Shipley** W Susx
32 B5 **Shipley Bridge** Surrey
93 H5 **Shipmeadow** Suffk
41 J2 **Shippon** Oxon
72 B6 **Shipston on Stour** Warwks
56 B4 **Shipton** Gloucs
133 H7 **Shipton** N York
83 L5 **Shipton** Shrops
28 E3 **Shipton Bellinger** Hants
13 L4 **Shipton Gorge** Dorset
17 L3 **Shipton Green** W Susx
39 K3 **Shipton Moyne** Gloucs
57 J5 **Shipton-on-Cherwell** Oxon
125 K2 **Shiptonthorpe** E R Yk
56 F4 **Shipton-under-Wychwood** Oxon
42 B2 **Shirburn** Oxon
120 E7 **Shirdley Hill** Lancs
115 K7 **Shirebrook** Derbys
115 G3 **Shiregreen** Sheff
38 D5 **Shirehampton** Bristl
159 H7 **Shiremoor** N Tyne
38 C2 **Shirenewton** Mons
115 K5 **Shireoaks** Notts
101 H2 **Shirland** Derbys
29 H8 **Shirley** C Sotn
100 E4 **Shirley** Derbys
45 G6 **Shirley** Gt Lon
85 K7 **Shirley** Solhll
29 L8 **Shirrell Heath** Hants
172 E2 **Shirvan** Ag & B
23 J4 **Shirwell** Devon
162 B4 **Shiskine** N Ayrs
69 H3 **Shobdon** Herefs
11 K5 **Shobrooke** Devon
102 B7 **Shoby** Leics
98 C3 **Shocklach** Ches W
46 F3 **Shoeburyness** Sthend
35 K4 **Sholden** Kent
16 F1 **Sholing** C Sotn
9 G2 **Shop** Cnwll
45 G4 **Shoreditch** Gt Lon
25 K6 **Shoreditch** Somset
45 K7 **Shoreham** Kent
19 G5 *Shoreham Airport* W Susx
19 H5 **Shoreham-by-Sea** W Susx
29 L6 **Shorley** Hants
46 B6 **Shorne** Kent
20 A3 **Shortgate** E Susx
4 C6 **Shortlanesend** Cnwll
163 K3 **Shortlees** E Ayrs
74 F5 **Shortstown** Bed
16 F5 **Shorwell** IoW
27 G1 **Shoscombe** BaNES
92 F4 **Shotesham** Norfk
46 C2 **Shotgate** Essex
78 F7 **Shotley** Suffk
150 D4 **Shotley Bridge** Dur
78 F7 **Shotley Gate** Suffk
78 F7 **Shotley Street** Suffk
34 D4 **Shottenden** Kent
71 L4 **Shottery** Warwks
72 E5 **Shotteswell** Warwks
79 G5 **Shottisham** Suffk
100 F3 **Shottlegate** Derbys
151 K6 **Shotton** Dur
111 J7 **Shotton** Flints
151 J6 **Shotton Colliery** Dur
176 B6 **Shotts** N Lans
111 K6 **Shotwick** Ches W
214 F4 **Shougle** Moray
90 F2 **Shouldham** Norfk
90 F2 **Shouldham Thorpe** Norfk
70 E3 **Shoulton** Worcs
83 H1 **Shrawardine** Shrops
70 E2 **Shrawley** Worcs
72 B2 **Shrewley** Warwks
83 J2 **Shrewsbury** Shrops
28 B3 **Shrewton** Wilts
18 C5 **Shripney** W Susx
40 E3 **Shrivenham** Oxon
92 B5 **Shropham** Norfk
69 L6 **Shucknall** Herefs
76 E5 **Shudy Camps** Cambs
181 M5 **Shuna** Ag & B
55 L4 **Shurdington** Gloucs
42 D5 **Shurlock Row** W & M
230 F4 **Shurrery** Highld
230 F4 **Shurrery Lodge** Highld
25 J3 **Shurton** Somset
86 B5 **Shustoke** Warwks
11 K5 **Shute** Devon
13 G3 **Shute** Devon
72 E6 **Shutford** Oxon
99 K7 **Shut Heath** Staffs
70 F7 **Shuthonger** Gloucs
73 K4 **Shutlanger** Nhants
86 B3 **Shuttington** Warwks
115 J6 **Shuttlewood** Derbys
122 B6 **Shuttleworth** Bury
232 e2 **Siabost** W Isls
232 f1 **Siadar** W Isls
87 K6 **Sibbertoft** Nhants
72 D6 **Sibford Ferris** Oxon
72 D6 **Sibford Gower** Oxon
77 H7 **Sible Hedingham** Essex
60 F3 **Sibley's Green** Essex
104 B3 **Sibsey** Lincs
89 G4 **Sibson** Cambs
86 D4 **Sibson** Leics
231 K5 **Sibster** Highld
102 C4 **Sibthorpe** Notts
116 B6 **Sibthorpe** Notts
79 H1 **Sibton** Suffk
77 K3 **Sicklesmere** Suffk
124 B2 **Sicklinghall** N York
12 E4 **Sidbury** Devon
84 C6 **Sidbury** Shrops
38 B8 **Sidcot** N Som
45 J5 **Sidcup** Gt Lon
113 J7 **Siddington** Ches E
56 B7 **Siddington** Gloucs
106 F4 **Sidestrand** Norfk
12 E4 **Sidford** Devon
18 B6 **Sidlesham** W Susx
20 E4 **Sidley** E Susx
12 E5 **Sidmouth** Devon
126 E2 **Sigglesthorne** E R Yk
36 F6 **Sigingstone** V Glam
41 L7 **Silchester** Hants
87 H1 **Sileby** Leics
128 D3 **Silecroft** Cumb
92 D4 **Silfield** Norfk
114 F1 **Silkstone** Barns
114 F1 **Silkstone Common** Barns
103 H4 **Silk Willoughby** Lincs
147 K4 **Silloth** Cumb
134 E2 **Silpho** N York
122 F2 **Silsden** C Brad
74 F7 **Silsoe** C Beds
27 H5 **Silton** Dorset
177 G6 **Silverburn** Mdloth
129 K4 **Silverdale** Lancs
99 J3 **Silverdale** Staffs
61 K4 **Silver End** Essex
216 E2 **Silverford** Abers
73 J5 **Silverstone** Nhants
12 B2 **Silverton** Devon
84 B7 **Silvington** Shrops
157 L7 **Simonburn** Nthumb
24 B4 **Simonsbath** Somset
122 B4 **Simonstone** Lancs
168 C1 **Simprim** Border
74 C7 **Simpson** M Keyn
48 F4 **Simpson Cross** Pembks
179 G7 **Sinclair's Hill** Border
163 L6 **Sinclairston** E Ayrs
132 E3 **Sinderby** N York
113 G4 **Sinderland Green** Traffd
42 C6 **Sindlesham** Wokham
101 G6 **Sinfin** C Derb
34 D6 **Singleton** Kent
120 E3 **Singleton** Lancs
18 B3 **Singleton** W Susx
46 A6 **Singlewell** Kent
205 K3 **Sinnarhard** Abers
134 B3 **Sinnington** N York
70 E3 **Sinton** Worcs
70 F2 **Sinton** Worcs
70 E3 **Sinton Green** Worcs
33 K5 **Sissinghurst** Kent

39 G5 **Siston** S Glos
3 H5 **Sithney** Cnwll
34 B3 **Sittingbourne** Kent
84 E5 **Six Ashes** Shrops
117 K4 **Sixhills** Lincs
76 E3 **Six Mile Bottom** Cambs
27 M7 **Sixpenny Handley** Dorset
129 K3 **Sizergh Castle** Cumb
234 d6 **Skaill** Ork
164 B6 **Skares** E Ayrs
207 G6 **Skateraw** Abers
178 F4 **Skateraw** E Loth
208 F5 **Skeabost** Highld
140 F6 **Skeeby** N York
87 L3 **Skeffington** Leics
127 J6 **Skeffling** E R Yk
101 J1 **Skegby** Notts
116 C7 **Skegby** Notts
119 H8 **Skegness** Lincs
223 H3 **Skelbo** Highld
223 H3 **Skelbo Street** Highld
124 D7 **Skelbrooke** Donc
104 B5 **Skeldyke** Lincs
116 F6 **Skellingthorpe** Lincs
124 E7 **Skellow** Donc
123 J7 **Skelmanthorpe** Kirk
112 C1 **Skelmersdale** Lancs
173 L5 **Skelmorlie** N Ayrs
229 L4 **Skelpick** Highld
154 E5 **Skelston** D & G
133 J7 **Skelton** C York
148 D7 **Skelton** Cumb
125 H5 **Skelton** E R Yk
132 E5 **Skelton** N York
142 E4 **Skelton** R & Cl
137 K6 **Skelwith Bridge** Cumb
118 F7 **Skendleby** Lincs
206 E4 **Skene House** Abers
54 C4 **Skenfrith** Mons
135 G7 **Skerne** E R Yk
229 K3 **Skerray** Highld
228 C5 **Skerricha** Highld
129 K6 **Skerton** Lancs
86 E5 **Sketchley** Leics
51 J6 **Sketty** Swans
51 K6 **Skewen** Neath
133 K5 **Skewsby** N York
230 E3 **Skiall** Highld
126 C4 **Skidby** E R Yk
232 g1 **Skigersta** W Isls
24 F6 **Skilgate** Somset
102 E7 **Skillington** Lincs
147 K4 **Skinburness** Cumb
176 B2 **Skinflats** Falk
208 C5 **Skinidin** Highld
172 F6 **Skipness** Ag & B
156 C5 **Skipper's Bridge** D & G
135 J8 **Skipsea** E R Yk
122 E1 **Skipton** N York
132 E4 **Skipton-on-Swale** N York
125 G3 **Skipwith** N York
126 E3 **Skirlaugh** E R Yk
165 L2 **Skirling** Border
42 C3 **Skirmett** Bucks
134 B7 **Skirpenbeck** E R Yk
149 G7 **Skirwith** Cumb
231 L2 **Skirza** Highld
48 C6 **Skokholm Island** Pembks
48 C5 **Skomer Island** Pembks
199 K2 **Skulamus** Highld
61 L4 **Skye Green** Essex
204 B1 **Skye of Curr** Highld
122 E5 **Slack** Calder
216 F5 **Slacks of Cairnbanno** Abers
55 K6 **Slad** Gloucs
23 H3 **Slade** Devon
45 K5 **Slade Green** Gt Lon
115 K4 **Slade Hooton** Rothm
149 H4 **Slaggyford** Nthumb
130 D8 **Slaidburn** Lancs
123 G7 **Slaithwaite** Kirk
150 B4 **Slaley** Nthumb
176 B4 **Slamannan** Falk
58 F4 **Slapton** Bucks
7 J6 **Slapton** Devon
73 J5 **Slapton** Nhants
31 L5 **Slaugham** W Susx
39 J5 **Slaughterford** Wilts
87 L5 **Slawston** Leics
30 D4 **Sleaford** Hants
103 H4 **Sleaford** Lincs
138 E4 **Sleagill** Cumb
84 B1 **Sleapford** Wrekin
222 E3 **Sleasdairidh** Highld
134 E6 **Sledmere** E R Yk
156 E6 **Sleetbeck** Cumb
143 H5 **Sleights** N York
231 K3 **Slickly** Highld
162 B5 **Sliddery** N Ayrs
209 G7 **Sligachan** Highld
173 K1 **Sligrachan** Ag & B
55 H7 **Slimbridge** Gloucs
99 J6 **Slindon** Staffs
18 C4 **Slindon** W Susx
31 J5 **Slinfold** W Susx
133 L4 **Slingsby** N York
59 H4 **Slip End** C Beds
75 K6 **Slip End** Herts
88 D7 **Slipton** Nhants
100 B8 **Slitting Mill** Staffs
182 B7 **Slockavullin** Ag & B
11 H7 **Sloncombe** Devon
119 G7 **Sloothby** Lincs
43 G4 **Slough** Slough
43 G4 **Slough Crematorium** Bucks
25 L7 **Slough Green** Somset
210 D6 **Slumbay** Highld
129 K6 **Slyne** Lancs
167 K3 **Smailholm** Border
107 G7 **Smallburgh** Norfk
19 G3 **Small Dole** W Susx
101 H4 **Smalley** Derbys
32 B5 **Smallfield** Surrey
85 K6 **Small Heath** Birm
34 B8 **Small Hythe** Kent
13 H3 **Smallridge** Devon
92 B7 **Smallworth** Norfk
29 G2 **Smannell** Hants
34 B6 **Smarden** Kent
34 B6 **Smarden Bell** Kent
32 F5 **Smart's Hill** Kent
190 D2 **Smearisary** Highld
12 F1 **Smeatharpe** Devon
34 E6 **Smeeth** Kent
87 K5 **Smeeton Westerby** Leics
227 L2 **Smerral** Highld
84 F5 **Smestow** Staffs
85 H6 **Smethwick** Sandw
101 G8 **Smisby** Derbys
148 D2 **Smithfield** Cumb
76 F6 **Smith's Green** Essex
219 J6 **Smithstown** Highld
213 H5 **Smithton** Highld
228 F3 **Smoo** Highld
61 L4 **Smythe's Green** Essex
154 E5 **Snade** D & G
83 G3 **Snailbeach** Shrops
76 F2 **Snailwell** Cambs
134 E3 **Snainton** N York
124 F6 **Snaith** E R Yk
132 D3 **Snape** N York
79 H3 **Snape** Suffk
79 H3 **Snape Street** Suffk
45 H3 **Snaresbrook** Gt Lon
86 D2 **Snarestone** Leics
117 H5 **Snarford** Lincs
34 D8 **Snargate** Kent
34 D8 **Snave** Kent
143 J5 **Sneaton** N York
117 H5 **Snelland** Lincs
100 D4 **Snelston** Derbys
92 B5 **Snetterton** Norfk
105 G5 **Snettisham** Norfk
158 C2 **Snitter** Nthumb
117 G3 **Snitterby** Lincs
72 B3 **Snitterfield** Warwks
83 L7 **Snitton** Shrops
46 B7 **Snodland** Kent
95 K2 **Snowdon** Gwynd
96 C6 **Snowdonia National Park**
60 C2 **Snow End** Herts
71 K7 **Snowshill** Gloucs
17 J1 **Soake** Hants
199 G3 **Soay** Highld
29 L7 **Soberton** Hants
29 L8 **Soberton Heath** Hants
141 J5 **Sockburn** Darltn
90 E8 **Soham** Cambs
232 c5 **Solas** W Isls
29 M4 **Soldridge** Hants
34 E5 **Sole Street** Kent
46 A6 **Sole Street** Kent
85 L7 **Solihull** Solhll
69 H4 **Sollers Dilwyn** Herefs
54 E2 **Sollers Hope** Herefs
48 D3 **Solva** Pembks
156 B6 **Solwaybank** D & G
87 L2 **Somerby** Leics
117 H1 **Somerby** Lincs
101 H2 **Somercotes** Derbys
15 M4 **Somerford** Dorset
40 A2 **Somerford Keynes** Gloucs
17 M3 **Somerley** W Susx
93 K4 **Somerleyton** Suffk
100 C5 **Somersal Herbert** Derbys
118 D6 **Somersby** Lincs
89 L7 **Somersham** Cambs
78 C5 **Somersham** Suffk
57 J3 **Somerton** Oxon
26 C5 **Somerton** Somset
77 J4 **Somerton** Suffk
19 G5 **Sompting** W Susx
42 C5 **Sonning** Wokham
42 B4 **Sonning Common** Oxon
15 M3 **Sopley** Hants
39 J3 **Sopworth** Wilts
145 J5 **Sorbie** D & G
231 G3 **Sordale** Highld
189 H4 **Sorisdale** Ag & B
164 B4 **Sorn** E Ayrs
231 K3 **Sortat** Highld
117 K5 **Sotby** Lincs
93 J6 **Sotterley** Suffk
111 H7 **Soughton** Flints
58 E3 **Soulbury** Bucks
139 H5 **Soulby** Cumb
57 K2 **Souldern** Oxon
74 E3 **Souldrop** Bed
98 F3 **Sound** Ches E
215 H4 **Sound Muir** Moray
38 F5 **Soundwell** S Glos
10 D6 **Sourton** Devon
128 F3 **Soutergate** Cumb
91 J2 **South Acre** Norfk
35 H6 **South Alkham** Kent
43 J4 **Southall** Gt Lon
7 J7 **South Allington** Devon
185 J8 **South Alloa** Falk
55 L3 **Southam** Gloucs
72 E3 **Southam** Warwks
30 E7 **South Ambersham** W Susx
29 H8 **Southampton** C Sotn
29 J7 *Southampton Airport* Hants
29 H7 **Southampton Crematorium** Hants
115 K5 **South Anston** Rothm
34 D6 **South Ashford** Kent
16 D3 **South Baddesley** Hants
191 K5 **South Ballachulish** Highld
124 F1 **South Bank** C York
26 E5 **South Barrow** Somset
44 F7 **South Beddington** Gt Lon
46 C3 **South Benfleet** Essex
18 C5 **South Bersted** W Susx
45 H6 **Southborough** Gt Lon
33 G5 **Southborough** Kent
15 L4 **Southbourne** Bmouth
17 L2 **Southbourne** W Susx
124 F7 **South Bramwith** Donc
7 G4 **South Brent** Devon
27 G4 **South Brewham** Somset
38 E6 **South Bristol Crematorium** Bristl
159 G3 **South Broomhill** Nthumb
92 B3 **Southburgh** Norfk
93 H3 **South Burlingham** Norfk
134 F8 **Southburn** E R Yk
26 F6 **South Cadbury** Somset
116 F6 **South Carlton** Lincs
115 L5 **South Carlton** Notts
125 L4 **South Cave** E R Yk
40 B2 **South Cerney** Gloucs
19 K3 **South Chailey** E Susx
169 H5 **South Charlton** Nthumb
27 G6 **South Cheriton** Somset
140 F2 **South Church** Dur
46 E3 **Southchurch** Sthend
125 K4 **South Cliffe** E R Yk
116 D7 **South Clifton** Notts
118 E4 **South Cockerington** Lincs
36 C4 **South Cornelly** Brdgnd
9 G5 **Southcott** Cnwll
11 H8 **Southcott** Devon
58 D5 **Southcourt** Bucks
93 K7 **South Cove** Suffk
105 K5 **South Creake** Norfk
87 K2 **South Croxton** Leics
126 B2 **South Dalton** E R Yk
45 K6 **South Darenth** Kent
19 K4 **South Downs National Park**
125 G4 **South Duffield** N York
19 L5 **Southease** E Susx
118 D4 **South Elkington** Lincs
124 D7 **South Elmsall** Wakefd
161 H7 **Southend** Ag & B
46 E3 *Southend Airport* Essex
46 E3 **Southend Crematorium** Sthend
46 E3 **Southend-on-Sea** Sthend
36 D5 **Southerndown** V Glam
147 G4 **Southerness** D & G
219 H7 **South Erradale** Highld
12 D4 **Southerton** Devon
90 E5 **Southery** Norfk
45 L3 **South Essex Crematorium** Gt Lon
46 E2 **South Fambridge** Essex
126 B6 **South Ferriby** N Linc
126 C5 **South Field** E R Yk
175 L4 **Southfield** Falk
45 L5 **Southfleet** Kent
44 F2 **Southgate** Gt Lon
51 G7 **Southgate** Swans
15 M1 **South Gorley** Hants

151 G2 **South Gosforth** N u Ty
46 B2 **South Green** Essex
33 L2 **South Green** Kent
92 C2 **South Green** Norfk
177 G4 **South Gyle** C Edin
61 H8 **South Hanningfield** Essex
30 C7 **South Harting** W Susx
17 K3 **South Hayling** Hants
58 E7 **South Heath** Bucks
19 L5 **South Heighton** E Susx
151 J6 **South Hetton** Dur
124 B7 **South Hiendley** Wakefd
5 M2 **South Hill** Cnwll
57 K7 **South Hinksey** Oxon
31 K3 **South Holmwood** Surrey
45 K4 **South Hornchurch** Gt Lon
7 G7 **South Huish** Devon
116 F8 **South Hykeham** Lincs
151 J4 **South Hylton** Sundld
75 H6 **Southill** C Beds
29 J2 **Southington** Hants
117 H2 **South Kelsey** Lincs
213 G5 **South Kessock** Highld
126 E7 **South Killingholme** N Linc
132 F3 **South Kilvington** N York
87 H6 **South Kilworth** Leics
124 C7 **South Kirkby** Wakefd
103 K3 **South Kyme** Lincs
175 J7 **South Lanarkshire Crematorium** S Lans
12 F4 **Southleigh** Devon
57 H6 **South Leigh** Oxon
116 C5 **South Leverton** Notts
71 J5 **South Littleton** Worcs
44 F6 **South London Crematorium** Gt Lon
92 C7 **South Lopham** Norfk
88 D3 **South Luffenham** Rutlnd
19 L4 **South Malling** E Susx
40 D3 **South Marston** Swindn
32 B3 **South Merstham** Surrey
124 D4 **South Milford** N York
7 G7 **South Milton** Devon
59 L7 **South Mimms** Herts
59 L7 **South Mimms Services** Herts
62 A7 **Southminster** Essex
23 L6 **South Molton** Devon
150 F5 **South Moor** Dur
41 H2 **Southmoor** Oxon
41 K3 **South Moreton** Oxon
196 C5 **Southmuir** Angus
18 B5 **South Mundham** W Susx
125 L4 **South Newbald** E R Yk
57 H2 **South Newington** Oxon
28 C4 **South Newton** Wilts
101 H2 **South Normanton** Derbys
45 G6 **South Norwood** Gt Lon
45 L4 **South Ockendon** Thurr
75 H2 **Southoe** Cambs
78 E2 **Southolt** Suffk
118 E6 **South Ormsby** Lincs
88 F3 **Southorpe** C Pete
132 E3 **South Otterington** N York
14 C4 **Southover** Dorset
117 H3 **South Owersby** Lincs
123 G5 **Southowram** Calder
31 L2 **South Park** Surrey
13 L2 **South Perrott** Dorset
26 B7 **South Petherton** Somset
9 J8 **South Petherwin** Cnwll
91 J3 **South Pickenham** Norfk
6 B4 **South Pill** Cnwll
7 H7 **South Pool** Devon
13 M3 **South Poorton** Dorset
120 D6 **Southport** Sefton
120 E7 **Southport Crematorium** Lancs
176 F3 **South Queensferry** C Edin
103 G4 **South Rauceby** Lincs
105 L7 **South Raynham** Norfk
106 F5 **Southrepps** Norfk
118 E5 **South Reston** Lincs
117 J7 **Southrey** Lincs
234 c7 **South Ronaldsay** Ork
56 D7 **Southrop** Gloucs
30 A3 **Southrope** Hants
90 F2 **South Runcton** Norfk
116 D8 **South Scarle** Notts
17 J3 **Southsea** C Port
191 H7 **South Shian** Ag & B
151 J2 **South Shields** S Tyne
151 J3 **South Shields Crematorium** S Tyne
120 D4 **South Shore** Bpool
140 E2 **Southside** Dur
132 D6 **South Stainley** N York
39 H7 **South Stoke** BaNES
41 L4 **South Stoke** Oxon
18 D4 **South Stoke** W Susx
34 E3 **South Street** Kent
47 J6 **South Street** Kent
176 D7 **South Tarbrax** S Lans
10 F6 **South Tawton** Devon
3 H3 **South Tehidy** Cnwll
118 E6 **South Thoresby** Lincs
93 L3 **Southtown** Norfk
233 c8 **South Uist** W Isls
148 D6 **Southwaite** Cumb
148 D6 **Southwaite Services** Cumb
93 H2 **South Walsham** Norfk
44 F4 **Southwark** Gt Lon
30 B3 **South Warnborough** Hants
31 J6 **Southwater** W Susx
45 L2 **South Weald** Essex
102 B2 **Southwell** Notts
43 J5 **South West Middlesex Crematorium** Gt Lon
42 B2 **South Weston** Oxon
17 J2 **Southwick** Hants
88 E5 **Southwick** Nhants
151 J4 **Southwick** Sundld
19 H5 **Southwick** W Susx
27 J1 **Southwick** Wilts
38 E8 **South Widcombe** BaNES
87 H4 **South Wigston** Leics
34 D6 **South Willesborough** Kent
117 K5 **South Willingham** Lincs
101 G2 **South Wingfield** Derbys
102 F8 **South Witham** Lincs
93 K7 **Southwold** Suffk
61 J7 **South Woodham Ferrers** Essex
105 G7 **South Wootton** Norfk
39 J7 **South Wraxall** Wilts
10 F6 **South Zeal** Devon
122 F6 **Sowerby** Calder
132 F4 **Sowerby** N York
122 F5 **Sowerby Bridge** Calder
123 G6 **Sowood** Calder
6 D3 **Sowton** Devon
12 C4 **Sowton** Devon
122 F6 **Soyland Town** Calder
76 F6 **Spain's End** Essex
103 L7 **Spalding** Lincs
125 H4 **Spaldington** E R Yk
89 G8 **Spaldwick** Cambs
116 D7 **Spalford** Notts
103 H5 **Spanby** Lincs
106 C8 **Sparham** Norfk
129 G3 **Spark Bridge** Cumb
26 E6 **Sparkford** Somset
85 K6 **Sparkhill** Birm
6 E4 **Sparkwell** Devon
114 C5 **Sparrowpit** Derbys
33 H6 **Sparrows Green** E Susx
29 H5 **Sparsholt** Hants
41 G3 **Sparsholt** Oxon
133 L2 **Spaunton** N York
25 K4 **Spaxton** Somset
201 K8 **Spean Bridge** Highld
28 F6 **Spearywell** Hants
58 D7 **Speen** Bucks
41 J6 **Speen** W Berk
135 J5 **Speeton** N York
112 C5 **Speke** Lpool
32 F5 **Speldhurst** Kent
60 D4 **Spellbrook** Herts
42 B6 **Spencers Wood** Wokham
99 J1 **Spen Green** Ches E
131 L2 **Spennithorne** N York
151 G7 **Spennymoor** Dur
70 F4 **Spetchley** Worcs
15 G3 **Spetisbury** Dorset
93 H7 **Spexhall** Suffk
215 H2 **Spey Bay** Moray
204 C1 **Speybridge** Highld
215 G6 **Speyview** Moray
118 E7 **Spilsby** Lincs
115 J5 **Spinkhill** Derbys
222 F4 **Spinningdale** Highld
115 L3 **Spital Hill** Donc
178 B3 **Spittal** E Loth
231 H5 **Spittal** Highld
179 L7 **Spittal** Nthumb
49 G3 **Spittal** Pembks
195 H7 **Spittalfield** P & K
205 G7 **Spittal of Glenmuick** Abers
195 H3 **Spittal of Glenshee** P & K
167 J5 **Spittal-on-Rule** Border
92 F1 **Spixworth** Norfk
10 E4 **Splatt** Devon
19 L2 **Splayne's Green** E Susx
37 K5 **Splottlands** Cardif
124 B1 **Spofforth** N York
101 H5 **Spondon** C Derb
92 D4 **Spooner Row** Norfk
91 J2 **Sporle** Norfk
178 E4 **Spott** E Loth
178 D7 **Spottiswoode** Border
73 K1 **Spratton** Nhants
30 D3 **Spreakley** Surrey
11 G5 **Spreyton** Devon
6 D5 **Spriddlestone** Devon
117 G5 **Spridlington** Lincs
175 G5 **Springburn** C Glas
148 B2 **Springfield** D & G
61 H6 **Springfield** Essex
186 E5 **Springfield** Fife
154 E7 **Springholm** D & G
163 J2 **Springside** N Ayrs
116 E4 **Springthorpe** Lincs
151 H4 **Springwell** Sundld
112 B4 **Springwood Crematorium** Lpool
126 F4 **Sproatley** E R Yk
113 G7 **Sproston Green** Ches W
115 K2 **Sprotbrough** Donc
78 D5 **Sproughton** Suffk
168 A3 **Sprouston** Border
92 F2 **Sprowston** Norfk
102 D7 **Sproxton** Leics
133 J3 **Sproxton** N York
98 D2 **Spurstow** Ches E
14 A4 **Spyway** Dorset
84 D4 **Stableford** Shrops
114 F4 **Stacey Bank** Sheff
130 F6 **Stackhouse** N York
49 G7 **Stackpole** Pembks
6 D5 **Staddiscombe** C Plym
57 L7 **Stadhampton** Oxon
233 b7 **Stadhlaigearraidh** W Isls
148 F6 **Staffield** Cumb
218 D7 **Staffin** Highld
99 L7 **Stafford** Staffs
99 L7 **Stafford Crematorium** Staffs
99 K6 **Stafford Services (northbound)** Staffs
99 K6 **Stafford Services (southbound)** Staffs
74 E5 **Stagsden** Bed
136 E2 **Stainburn** Cumb
102 E7 **Stainby** Lincs
123 L7 **Staincross** Barns
140 E3 **Staindrop** Dur
43 G6 **Staines-upon-Thames** Surrey
124 F7 **Stainforth** Donc
130 F6 **Stainforth** N York
120 D4 **Staining** Lancs
123 G6 **Stainland** Calder
143 J5 **Stainsacre** N York
129 L3 **Stainton** Cumb
138 C2 **Stainton** Cumb
115 K3 **Stainton** Donc
140 D4 **Stainton** Dur
141 L4 **Stainton** Middsb
117 H6 **Stainton by Langworth** Lincs
143 K7 **Staintondale** N York
117 K3 **Stainton le Vale** Lincs
128 F5 **Stainton with Adgarley** Cumb
163 K5 **Stair** E Ayrs
144 E4 **Stairhaven** D & G
143 G4 **Staithes** N York
159 G5 **Stakeford** Nthumb
17 K2 **Stakes** Hants
27 G7 **Stalbridge** Dorset
27 G7 **Stalbridge Weston** Dorset
107 H7 **Stalham** Norfk
34 C4 **Stalisfield Green** Kent
26 E7 **Stallen** Dorset
126 F7 **Stallingborough** NE Lin
120 E2 **Stalmine** Lancs
113 L2 **Stalybridge** Tamesd
77 G6 **Stambourne** Essex
77 G6 **Stambourne Green** Essex
88 E3 **Stamford** Lincs
169 J5 **Stamford** Nthumb
112 C7 **Stamford Bridge** Ches W
133 L7 **Stamford Bridge** E R Yk
158 D7 **Stamfordham** Nthumb
45 G3 **Stamford Hill** Gt Lon
58 F3 **Stanbridge** C Beds
122 F3 **Stanbury** C Brad
175 K5 **Stand** N Lans
176 C4 **Standburn** Falk
85 G3 **Standeford** Staffs
33 L5 **Standen** Kent
27 J2 **Standerwick** Somset
30 D4 **Standford** Hants
147 J7 **Standingstone** Cumb

121 H7 **Standish** Wigan
57 H7 **Standlake** Oxon
29 H6 **Standon** Hants
60 C4 **Standon** Herts
99 J5 **Standon** Staffs
176 B6 **Stane** N Lans
105 M7 **Stanfield** Norfk
75 H6 **Stanford** C Beds
34 F6 **Stanford** Kent
70 C4 **Stanford Bishop** Herefs
70 C2 **Stanford Bridge** Worcs
41 L6 **Stanford Dingley** W Berk
41 G2 **Stanford in the Vale** Oxon
46 B4 **Stanford le Hope** Thurr
87 H7 **Stanford on Avon** Nhants
101 K7 **Stanford on Soar** Notts
70 C2 **Stanford on Teme** Worcs
115 J6 **Stanfree** Derbys
142 E4 **Stanghow** R & Cl
89 H4 **Stanground** C Pete
105 J5 **Stanhoe** Norfk
165 L4 **Stanhope** Border
150 C6 **Stanhope** Dur
34 D6 **Stanhope** Kent
88 D6 **Stanion** Nhants
101 H4 **Stanley** Derbys
150 F4 **Stanley** Dur
186 B2 **Stanley** P & K
99 L3 **Stanley** Staffs
150 E7 **Stanley Crook** Dur
55 M3 **Stanley Pontlarge** Gloucs
19 K4 **Stanmer** Br & H
44 D2 **Stanmore** Gt Lon
29 J5 **Stanmore** Hants
157 J5 **Stannersburn** Nthumb
77 K3 **Stanningfield** Suffk
158 F6 **Stannington** Nthumb
114 F4 **Stannington** Sheff
158 F5 **Stannington Station** Nthumb
69 G3 **Stansbatch** Herefs
77 H4 **Stansfield** Suffk
77 J5 **Stanstead** Suffk
60 C5 **Stanstead Abbotts** Herts
45 L7 **Stansted** Kent
60 E4 Stansted Airport Essex
60 E3 **Stansted Mountfitchet** Essex
71 J7 **Stanton** Gloucs
158 E4 **Stanton** Nthumb
100 C4 **Stanton** Staffs
91 L8 **Stanton** Suffk
101 G6 **Stanton by Bridge** Derbys
101 J5 **Stanton by Dale** Derbys
38 E7 **Stanton Drew** BaNES
40 D3 **Stanton Fitzwarren** Swindn
57 H6 **Stanton Harcourt** Oxon
114 E8 **Stanton in Peak** Derbys
83 K7 **Stanton Lacy** Shrops
114 E8 **Stanton Lees** Derbys
83 L5 **Stanton Long** Shrops
101 M6 **Stanton on the Wolds** Notts
39 G7 **Stanton Prior** BaNES
40 C7 **Stanton St Bernard** Wilts
57 L6 **Stanton St John** Oxon
39 K4 **Stanton St Quintin** Wilts
77 L2 **Stanton Street** Suffk
86 F2 **Stanton under Bardon** Leics
98 E7 **Stanton upon Hine Heath** Shrops
38 E7 **Stanton Wick** BaNES
61 M3 **Stanway** Essex
56 B2 **Stanway** Gloucs
43 H5 **Stanwell** Surrey
74 E1 **Stanwick** Nhants
148 D4 **Stanwix** Cumb
233 b8 **Staoinebrig** W Isls
143 G7 **Stape** N York
99 G3 **Stapeley** Ches E
100 E7 **Stapenhill** Staffs
35 H4 **Staple** Kent
25 G7 **Staple Cross** Devon
20 F2 **Staple Cross** E Susx
32 B7 **Staplefield** W Susx
25 K7 **Staple Fitzpaine** Somset
76 C4 **Stapleford** Cambs
60 A5 **Stapleford** Herts
102 D8 **Stapleford** Leics
102 E2 **Stapleford** Lincs
101 J5 **Stapleford** Notts
28 B4 **Stapleford** Wilts
45 K2 **Stapleford Abbotts** Essex
25 K6 **Staplegrove** Somset
25 K6 **Staplehay** Somset
33 K5 **Staplehurst** Kent
34 E3 **Staplestreet** Kent
69 G2 **Stapleton** Herefs
86 E4 **Stapleton** Leics
141 G5 **Stapleton** N York
83 J3 **Stapleton** Shrops
26 C7 **Stapleton** Somset
25 J8 **Stapley** Somset
75 G3 **Staploe** Bed
70 C6 **Staplow** Herefs
186 E6 **Star** Fife
65 H7 **Star** Pembks
38 C8 **Star** Somset
132 E7 **Starbeck** N York
131 H5 **Starbotton** N York
12 C6 **Starcross** Devon
72 D1 **Stareton** Warwks
60 D2 **Starlings Green** Essex
92 F6 **Starston** Norfk
140 D4 **Startforth** Dur
39 L4 **Startley** Wilts
35 J4 **Statenborough** Kent
112 F4 **Statham** Warrtn
26 A5 **Stathe** Somset
102 C6 **Stathern** Leics
75 G2 **Staughton Green** Cambs
54 D5 **Staunton** Gloucs
55 H3 **Staunton** Gloucs
69 G3 **Staunton on Arrow** Herefs
69 G5 **Staunton on Wye** Herefs
129 H3 **Staveley** Cumb
138 C7 **Staveley** Cumb
115 H6 **Staveley** Derbys
132 E6 **Staveley** N York
7 J3 **Staverton** Devon
55 K4 **Staverton** Gloucs
73 G3 **Staverton** Nhants
39 J7 **Staverton** Wilts
26 A4 **Stawell** Somset
25 G6 **Stawley** Somset
231 L5 **Staxigoe** Highld
134 F4 **Staxton** N York
120 E2 **Staynall** Lancs
131 K5 **Stean** N York
133 J5 **Stearsby** N York
25 L3 **Steart** Somset
61 G3 **Stebbing** Essex
30 E6 **Stedham** W Susx
185 L8 **Steelend** Fife
156 F4 **Steele Road** Border
69 K3 **Steen's Bridge** Herefs
30 C6 **Steep** Hants
122 F5 **Steep Lane** Calder
61 M7 **Steeple** Essex
27 K1 **Steeple Ashton** Wilts
57 J3 **Steeple Aston** Oxon
76 F6 **Steeple Bumpstead** Essex
58 B3 **Steeple Claydon** Bucks
89 G7 **Steeple Gidding** Cambs
28 B4 **Steeple Langford** Wilts
75 K6 **Steeple Morden** Cambs
122 F2 **Steeton** C Brad
208 D3 **Stein** Highld
34 F5 **Stelling Minnis** Kent
26 B7 **Stembridge** Somset
4 F4 **Stenalees** Cnwll
154 D4 **Stenhouse** D & G
176 B2 **Stenhousemuir** Falk
218 D7 **Stenscholl** Highld
101 G6 **Stenson Fields** Derbys
178 D4 **Stenton** E Loth
232 f2 **Steornabhagh** W Isls
49 K6 **Stepaside** Pembks
154 E5 **Stepford** D & G
45 G4 **Stepney** Gt Lon
74 E7 **Steppingley** C Beds
175 H5 **Stepps** N Lans
79 H3 **Sternfield** Suffk
40 B8 **Stert** Wilts
76 F3 **Stetchworth** Cambs
59 L3 **Stevenage** Herts
163 H2 **Stevenston** N Ayrs
29 K2 **Steventon** Hants
41 J3 **Steventon** Oxon
76 E6 **Steventon End** Essex
74 E4 **Stevington** Bed
74 E6 **Stewartby** Bed
175 H7 **Stewartfield** S Lans
163 K1 **Stewarton** E Ayrs
58 D3 **Stewkley** Bucks
25 L7 **Stewley** Somset
19 G4 **Steyning** W Susx
48 F6 **Steynton** Pembks
9 G3 **Stibb** Cnwll
106 B6 **Stibbard** Norfk
10 C2 **Stibb Cross** Devon
40 E7 **Stibb Green** Wilts
88 F4 **Stibbington** Cambs
167 L2 **Stichill** Border
4 F5 **Sticker** Cnwll
104 B1 **Stickford** Lincs
10 F6 **Sticklepath** Devon
104 B2 **Stickney** Lincs
106 A4 **Stiffkey** Norfk
233 b7 **Stilligarry** W Isls
124 F3 **Stillingfleet** N York
133 J6 **Stillington** N York
141 J3 **Stillington** S on T
89 H5 **Stilton** Cambs
55 G7 **Stinchcombe** Gloucs
14 D4 **Stinsford** Dorset
83 G4 **Stiperstones** Shrops
84 C3 **Stirchley** Wrekin
217 L6 **Stirling** Abers
185 G8 **Stirling** Stirlg
175 L2 **Stirling Services** Stirlg
75 H2 **Stirtloe** Cambs
131 H8 **Stirton** N York
61 J3 **Stisted** Essex
3 J4 **Stithians** Cnwll
86 D7 **Stivichall** Covtry
117 K7 **Stixwould** Lincs
112 B6 **Stoak** Ches W
166 B2 **Stobo** Border
15 H5 **Stoborough** Dorset
167 G7 **Stobs Castle** Border
158 F3 **Stobswood** Nthumb
61 H7 **Stock** Essex
38 C7 **Stock** N Som
29 G4 **Stockbridge** Hants
164 F3 **Stockbriggs** S Lans
46 D7 **Stockbury** Kent
41 H6 **Stockcross** W Berk
88 B4 **Stockerston** Leics
71 H3 **Stock Green** Worcs
54 F2 **Stocking** Herefs
86 D5 **Stockingford** Warwks
60 D3 **Stocking Pelham** Herts
13 G2 **Stockland** Devon
25 K3 **Stockland Bristol** Somset
11 K4 **Stockleigh English** Devon
11 K4 **Stockleigh Pomeroy** Devon
39 M6 **Stockley** Wilts
26 B7 **Stocklinch** Somset
113 K4 **Stockport** Stockp
113 K4 **Stockport Crematorium** Stockp
114 E2 **Stocksbridge** Sheff
150 D3 **Stocksfield** Nthumb
69 K3 **Stockton** Herefs
93 H5 **Stockton** Norfk
84 C4 **Stockton** Shrops
72 E2 **Stockton** Warwks
27 M4 **Stockton** Wilts
84 D1 **Stockton** Wrekin
112 E4 **Stockton Heath** Warrtn
141 K4 **Stockton-on-Tees** S on T
70 C2 **Stockton on Teme** Worcs
133 K7 **Stockton on the Forest** C York
38 F6 **Stockwood** Bristl
14 B2 **Stockwood** Dorset
71 H3 **Stock Wood** Worcs
35 G3 **Stodmarsh** Kent
106 C5 **Stody** Norfk
224 C3 **Stoer** Highld
26 E8 **Stoford** Somset
28 B4 **Stoford** Wilts
25 H4 **Stogumber** Somset
25 J3 **Stogursey** Somset
86 D7 **Stoke** Covtry
22 C6 **Stoke** Devon
17 K3 **Stoke** Hants
29 H2 **Stoke** Hants
46 D5 **Stoke** Medway
13 L3 **Stoke Abbott** Dorset
88 B5 **Stoke Albany** Nhants
78 D1 **Stoke Ash** Suffk
101 M4 **Stoke Bardolph** Notts
70 B2 **Stoke Bliss** Worcs
73 L4 **Stoke Bruerne** Nhants
77 G5 **Stoke by Clare** Suffk
78 B7 **Stoke-by-Nayland** Suffk
12 B3 **Stoke Canon** Devon
29 J4 **Stoke Charity** Hants
6 A2 **Stoke Climsland** Cnwll
70 B4 **Stoke Cross** Herefs
43 J8 **Stoke D'Abernon** Surrey
88 E6 **Stoke Doyle** Nhants
88 C4 **Stoke Dry** Rutlnd
69 L6 **Stoke Edith** Herefs
28 B6 **Stoke Farthing** Wilts
91 G4 **Stoke Ferry** Norfk
7 K6 **Stoke Fleming** Devon
15 G5 **Stokeford** Dorset
7 J4 **Stoke Gabriel** Devon
38 F4 **Stoke Gifford** S Glos
86 E4 **Stoke Golding** Leics
74 B5 **Stoke Goldington** M Keyn
116 C6 **Stokeham** Notts
58 E3 **Stoke Hammond** Bucks
92 F3 **Stoke Holy Cross** Norfk
7 L2 **Stokeinteignhead** Devon

70 B5 Stoke Lacy Herefs
57 K3 Stoke Lyne Oxon
58 D6 Stoke Mandeville Bucks
42 C2 Stokenchurch Bucks
45 G3 Stoke Newington Gt Lon
7 J7 Stokenham Devon
99 K3 Stoke-on-Trent C Stke
55 K3 Stoke Orchard Gloucs
42 F4 Stoke Poges Bucks
69 K3 Stoke Prior Herefs
71 G2 Stoke Prior Worcs
23 K4 Stoke Rivers Devon
102 F6 Stoke Rochford Lincs
42 B4 Stoke Row Oxon
25 M6 Stoke St Gregory Somset
25 K6 Stoke St Mary Somset
26 F3 Stoke St Michael Somset
83 L6 Stoke St Milborough Shrops
83 H6 Stokesay Castle Shrops
93 J2 Stokesby Norfk
142 B5 Stokesley N York
26 C7 Stoke sub Hamdon Somset
58 B7 Stoke Talmage Oxon
27 H5 Stoke Trister Somset
98 F6 Stoke upon Tern Shrops
99 K4 Stoke-upon-Trent C Stke
25 K3 Stolford Somset
60 F7 Stondon Massey Essex
58 C5 Stone Bucks
39 G2 Stone Gloucs
115 K4 Stone Rothm
99 K5 Stone Staffs
84 F7 Stone Worcs
26 B2 Stone Allerton Somset
26 F2 Ston Easton Somset
38 B7 Stonebridge N Som
86 B6 Stonebridge Warwks
101 H2 Stonebroom Derbys
35 J4 Stone Cross Kent
33 J6 Stonecrouch Kent
126 D4 Stoneferry C KuH
172 E4 Stonefield Castle Hotel Ag & B
33 H7 Stonegate E Susx
133 K4 Stonegrave N York
207 G7 Stonehaven Abers
28 C3 Stonehenge Wilts
6 C5 Stonehouse C Plym
55 J6 Stonehouse Gloucs
175 K8 Stonehouse S Lans
21 J1 Stone in Oxney Kent
86 D8 Stoneleigh Warwks
102 D7 Stonesby Leics
57 H4 Stonesfield Oxon
62 E3 Stones Green Essex
33 G3 Stone Street Kent
93 H6 Stone Street Suffk
215 G2 Stonewells Moray
233 b8 Stoneybridge W Isls
176 D5 Stoneyburn W Loth
87 H3 Stoneygate C Leic
144 C4 Stoneykirk D & G
114 E6 Stoney Middleton Derbys
86 F4 Stoney Stanton Leics
27 G5 Stoney Stoke Somset
26 F4 Stoney Stratton Somset
207 G3 Stoneywood C Aber
175 L2 Stoneywood Falk
78 D3 Stonham Aspal Suffk
85 J3 Stonnall Staffs
42 B3 Stonor Oxon
87 K4 Stonton Wyville Leics
115 J7 Stony Houghton Derbys
73 L6 Stony Stratford M Keyn
23 K5 Stoodleigh Devon
24 E7 Stoodleigh Devon
34 F7 Stop 24 Services Kent
18 D2 Stopham W Susx
59 J3 Stopsley Luton
232 f2 Stornoway W Isls
232 g2 Stornoway Airport W Isls
18 E3 Storrington W Susx
129 K4 Storth Cumb
125 H2 Storwood E R Yk
214 F1 Stotfield Moray
75 J7 Stotfold C Beds
84 C6 Stottesdon Shrops
87 J3 Stoughton Leics
31 G2 Stoughton Surrey
17 L1 Stoughton W Susx
70 F4 Stoulton Worcs
84 F6 Stourbridge Dudley
84 F6 Stourbridge Crematorium Dudley
15 G1 Stourpaine Dorset
70 E1 Stourport-on-Severn Worcs
27 H6 Stour Provost Dorset
27 J7 Stour Row Dorset
84 F6 Stourton Staffs
72 C6 Stourton Warwks
27 H5 Stourton Wilts
27 G7 Stourton Caundle Dorset
235 c7 Stove Shet
93 J6 Stoven Suffk
167 G1 Stow Border
116 E5 Stow Lincs
90 F3 Stow Bardolph Norfk
91 L4 Stow Bedon Norfk
90 E3 Stowbridge Norfk
76 D3 Stow-cum-Quy Cambs
82 F8 Stowe Shrops
100 A6 Stowe by Chartley Staffs
27 G6 Stowell Somset
38 E7 Stowey BaNES
10 C7 Stowford Devon
77 L2 Stowlangtoft Suffk
75 G1 Stow Longa Cambs
61 K7 Stow Maries Essex
78 C3 Stowmarket Suffk
56 D3 Stow-on-the-Wold Gloucs
34 F6 Stowting Kent
34 F6 Stowting Common Kent
78 C3 Stowupland Suffk
204 B3 Straanruie Highld
206 D6 Strachan Abers
182 F6 Strachur Ag & B
92 F8 Stradbroke Suffk
77 H4 Stradishall Suffk
90 F3 Stradsett Norfk
102 E3 Stragglethorpe Lincs
177 H5 Straiton Mdloth
153 H2 Straiton S Ayrs
207 G2 Straloch Abers
195 G4 Straloch P & K
100 B5 Stramshall Staffs
237 c5 Strang IoM
113 J2 Strangeways Salfd
54 E3 Strangford Herefs
144 C3 Stranraer D & G
42 A7 Stratfield Mortimer W Berk
42 B7 Stratfield Saye Hants
42 B7 Stratfield Turgis Hants
45 H3 Stratford Gt Lon
79 H3 Stratford St Andrew Suffk
78 C7 Stratford St Mary Suffk
28 C6 Stratford Tony Wilts
72 B4 Stratford-upon-Avon Warwks
219 J5 Strath Highld
224 D4 Strathan Highld
229 J3 Strathan Highld
164 D1 Strathaven S Lans
175 G3 Strathblane Stirlg
220 F2 Strathcanaird Highld
210 E6 Strathcarron Highld
181 K2 Strathcoil Ag & B
205 H3 Strathdon Abers
187 G4 Strathkinness Fife
176 C4 Strathloanhead W Loth
202 F6 Strathmashie House Highld
186 C5 Strathmiglo Fife
212 D3 Strathpeffer Highld
194 E5 Strathtay P & K
162 D3 Strathwhillan N Ayrs
230 B3 Strathy Highld
230 B3 Strathy Inn Highld
184 C4 Strathyre Stirlg
9 G4 Stratton Cnwll
14 C4 Stratton Dorset
56 A7 Stratton Gloucs
57 L3 Stratton Audley Oxon
26 F2 Stratton-on-the-Fosse Somset
40 D3 Stratton St Margaret Swindn
92 E5 Stratton St Michael Norfk
106 F7 Stratton Strawless Norfk
19 K3 Streat E Susx
44 F5 Streatham Gt Lon
59 H3 Streatley C Beds
41 L4 Streatley W Berk
12 F5 Street Devon
26 C4 Street Somset
86 F6 Street Ashton Warwks
97 M5 Street Dinas Shrops
34 F4 Street End Kent
18 A5 Street End W Susx
85 K2 Streethay Staffs
141 H7 Streetlam N York
85 J4 Streetly Crematorium Wsall
76 E5 Streetly End Cambs
26 F4 Street on the Fosse Somset
186 C1 Strelitz P & K
101 K4 Strelley Notts
133 K7 Strensall C York
70 F6 Strensham Services (northbound) Worcs
70 F6 Strensham Services (southbound) Worcs
25 L3 Stretcholt Somset
7 J6 Strete Devon
113 H3 Stretford Traffd
76 C6 Strethall Essex
90 D8 Stretham Cambs
18 B4 Strettington W Susx
101 H1 Stretton Derbys
88 D1 Stretton Rutlnd
84 F2 Stretton Staffs
100 E7 Stretton Staffs
112 F5 Stretton Warrtn
70 B5 Stretton Grandison Herefs
86 E8 Stretton-on-Dunsmore Warwks
72 B6 Stretton on Fosse Warwks
69 J6 Stretton Sugwas Herefs
86 F7 Stretton under Fosse Warwks
83 L4 Stretton Westwood Shrops
217 H4 Strichen Abers
25 J3 Stringston Somset
74 C3 Strixton Nhants
38 E2 Stroat Gloucs
231 L1 Stroma Highld
210 D7 Stromeferry Highld
234 b6 Stromness Ork
183 L5 Stronachlachar Stirlg
173 H3 Stronafian Ag & B
224 F5 Stronchrubie Highld
173 L3 Strone Ag & B
192 B1 Strone Highld
212 E8 Strone Highld
201 J8 Stronenaba Highld
183 G2 Stronmilchan Ag & B
234 d5 Stronsay Ork
234 d5 Stronsay Airport Ork
191 G4 Strontian Highld
46 B6 Strood Medway
55 J6 Stroud Gloucs
30 B6 Stroud Hants
55 J6 Stroud Green Gloucs
102 E6 Stroxton Lincs
208 E6 Struan Highld
194 C4 Struan P & K
93 H3 Strumpshaw Norfk
175 K7 Strutherhill S Lans
186 F5 Struthers Fife
212 B6 Struy Highld
217 H5 Stuartfield Abers
17 G2 Stubbington Hants
122 B6 Stubbins Lancs
102 E3 Stubton Lincs
28 D8 Stuckton Hants
59 G5 Studham C Beds
15 J6 Studland Dorset
71 J2 Studley Warwks
39 L6 Studley Wilts
132 D5 Studley Roger N York
132 D5 Studley Royal N York
90 D7 Stuntney Cambs
77 G5 Sturmer Essex
27 H8 Sturminster Common Dorset
15 H3 Sturminster Marshall Dorset
27 H8 Sturminster Newton Dorset
35 G3 Sturry Kent
116 F2 Sturton N Linc
116 E5 Sturton by Stow Lincs
116 C5 Sturton le Steeple Notts
92 D7 Stuston Suffk
124 D3 Stutton N York
78 D7 Stutton Suffk
113 J5 Styal Ches E
215 H3 Stynie Moray
115 L4 Styrrup Notts
183 K6 Succoth Ag & B
70 C4 Suckley Worcs
88 D6 Sudborough Nhants
79 J4 Sudbourne Suffk
102 F4 Sudbrook Lincs
38 D3 Sudbrook Mons
117 G6 Sudbrooke Lincs
100 D6 Sudbury Derbys
44 D3 Sudbury Gt Lon
77 K6 Sudbury Suffk
134 F2 Suffield N York
106 F6 Suffield Norfk
99 H6 Sugnall Staffs
69 J6 Sugwas Pool Herefs
199 J3 Suisnish Highld
237 d3 Sulby IoM
73 G5 Sulgrave Nhants
73 H5 Sulgrave Manor Nhants
41 M5 Sulham W Berk
41 M6 Sulhamstead W Berk
235 c4 Sullom Shet
235 c4 Sullom Voe Shet
37 J6 Sully V Glam
235 c8 Sumburgh Airport Shet
132 C6 Summerbridge N York

4 D5 **Summercourt** Cnwll
105 J5 **Summerfield** Norfk
49 K6 **Summerhill** Pembks
140 F4 **Summerhouse** Darltn
18 B4 **Summersdale** W Susx
122 B7 **Summerseat** Bury
57 K6 **Summertown** Oxon
43 J6 **Sunbury** Surrey
154 E5 **Sundaywell** D & G
170 E5 **Sunderland** Ag & B
147 L7 **Sunderland** Cumb
129 J7 **Sunderland** Lancs
151 J4 **Sunderland** Sundld
151 G7 **Sunderland Bridge** Dur
151 J4 **Sunderland Crematorium** Sundld
166 E4 **Sundhope** Border
59 H3 **Sundon Park** Luton
32 E3 **Sundridge** Kent
42 F6 **Sunningdale** W & M
42 F6 **Sunninghill** W & M
57 J7 **Sunningwell** Oxon
150 E7 **Sunniside** Dur
150 F3 **Sunniside** Gatesd
101 G6 **Sunnyhill** C Derb
121 K6 **Sunnyhurst** Bl w D
185 G7 **Sunnylaw** Stirlg
57 J6 **Sunnymead** Oxon
44 D6 **Surbiton** Gt Lon
103 L6 **Surfleet** Lincs
93 G3 **Surlingham** Norfk
61 L4 **Surrex** Essex
32 B5 **Surrey & Sussex Crematorium** W Susx
106 E5 **Sustead** Norfk
116 D2 **Susworth** Lincs
9 J3 **Sutcombe** Devon
9 J3 **Sutcombemill** Devon
118 E6 **Sutterby** Lincs
103 M5 **Sutterton** Lincs
75 J5 **Sutton** C Beds
89 G4 **Sutton** C Pete
90 C7 **Sutton** Cambs
7 G7 **Sutton** Devon
20 A5 **Sutton** E Susx
44 E7 **Sutton** Gt Lon
35 J5 **Sutton** Kent
124 D5 **Sutton** N York
107 H7 **Sutton** Norfk
102 C5 **Sutton** Notts
57 H6 **Sutton** Oxon
84 D6 **Sutton** Shrops
99 H7 **Sutton** Staffs
79 G5 **Sutton** Suffk
18 D3 **Sutton** W Susx
45 K6 **Sutton at Hone** Kent
87 L5 **Sutton Bassett** Nhants
39 L5 **Sutton Benger** Wilts
101 K7 **Sutton Bonington** Notts
104 D7 **Sutton Bridge** Lincs
86 E4 **Sutton Cheney** Leics
85 K4 **Sutton Coldfield** Birm
85 K4 **Sutton Coldfield Crematorium** Birm
41 J2 **Sutton Courtenay** Oxon
116 B5 **Sutton cum Lound** Notts
31 G1 **Sutton Green** Surrey
132 D4 **Sutton Howgrave** N York
101 J2 **Sutton in Ashfield** Notts
122 F2 **Sutton-in-Craven** N York
84 C3 **Sutton Maddock** Shrops
26 A4 **Sutton Mallet** Somset
27 M5 **Sutton Mandeville** Wilts
26 F6 **Sutton Montis** Somset
126 E4 **Sutton-on-Hull** C KuH
119 G5 **Sutton on Sea** Lincs
133 J6 **Sutton-on-the-Forest** N York
100 E5 **Sutton on the Hill** Derbys
116 D7 **Sutton on Trent** Notts
89 L2 **Sutton St Edmund** Lincs
104 C8 **Sutton St James** Lincs
69 K5 **Sutton St Nicholas** Herefs
29 J4 **Sutton Scotney** Hants
72 C6 **Sutton-under-Brailes** Warwks
133 G3 **Sutton-under-Whitestonecliffe** N York
125 G2 **Sutton upon Derwent** E R Yk
33 L4 **Sutton Valence** Kent
27 K3 **Sutton Veny** Wilts
27 K7 **Sutton Waldron** Dorset
112 D5 **Sutton Weaver** Ches W
38 E8 **Sutton Wick** BaNES
41 J2 **Sutton Wick** Oxon
118 E6 **Swaby** Lincs
100 F8 **Swadlincote** Derbys
91 J2 **Swaffham** Norfk
76 D3 **Swaffham Bulbeck** Cambs
76 E2 **Swaffham Prior** Cambs
107 G6 **Swafield** Norfk
141 L6 **Swainby** N York
92 F4 **Swainsthorpe** Norfk
39 H6 **Swainswick** BaNES
72 E6 **Swalcliffe** Oxon
47 J6 **Swalecliffe** Kent
117 K2 **Swallow** Lincs
116 F7 **Swallow Beck** Lincs
27 L6 **Swallowcliffe** Wilts
42 B7 **Swallowfield** Wokham
15 J6 **Swanage** Dorset
58 D3 **Swanbourne** Bucks
113 G6 **Swan Green** Ches W
126 B5 **Swanland** E R Yk
45 K6 **Swanley** Kent
45 K6 **Swanley Village** Kent
29 L7 **Swanmore** Hants
86 E1 **Swannington** Leics
106 D8 **Swannington** Norfk
116 F7 **Swanpool Garden Suburb** Lincs
45 L5 **Swanscombe** Kent
51 J6 **Swansea** Swans
51 H7 *Swansea Airport* Swans
51 J5 **Swansea Crematorium** Swans
51 J5 **Swansea West Services** Swans
106 F7 **Swanton Abbot** Norfk
92 B1 **Swanton Morley** Norfk
106 B6 **Swanton Novers** Norfk
101 H2 **Swanwick** Derbys
17 G1 **Swanwick** Hants
103 H4 **Swarby** Lincs
92 E3 **Swardeston** Norfk
101 G6 **Swarkestone** Derbys
158 F2 **Swarland** Nthumb
29 K4 **Swarraton** Hants
129 G4 **Swarthmoor** Cumb
103 J5 **Swaton** Lincs
75 L2 **Swavesey** Cambs
16 C3 **Sway** Hants
103 G7 **Swayfield** Lincs
29 H7 **Swaythling** C Sotn
11 K5 **Sweetham** Devon
32 E7 **Sweethaws** E Susx
8 F5 **Sweets** Cnwll
5 H4 **Sweetshouse** Cnwll
79 H2 **Swefling** Suffk
86 D2 **Swepstone** Leics
57 G2 **Swerford** Oxon
113 J7 **Swettenham** Ches E
78 E4 **Swilland** Suffk
124 B4 **Swillington** Leeds
23 K5 **Swimbridge** Devon
23 J5 **Swimbridge Newland** Devon
56 F5 **Swinbrook** Oxon
132 C7 **Swincliffe** N York
116 E8 **Swinderby** Lincs
55 L3 **Swindon** Gloucs
84 F5 **Swindon** Staffs
40 D4 **Swindon** Swindn
126 E4 **Swine** E R Yk
125 H6 **Swinefleet** E R Yk
74 F2 **Swineshead** Bed
103 L4 **Swineshead** Lincs
227 M2 **Swiney** Highld
87 H7 **Swinford** Leics
35 G6 **Swingfield Minnis** Kent
35 H6 **Swingfield Street** Kent
77 L5 **Swingleton Green** Suffk
169 J4 **Swinhoe** Nthumb
131 K2 **Swinithwaite** N York
137 H3 **Swinside** Cumb
103 G7 **Swinstead** Lincs
179 H8 **Swinton** Border
132 C4 **Swinton** N York
134 B5 **Swinton** N York
115 J2 **Swinton** Rothm
113 H2 **Swinton** Salfd
87 G2 **Swithland** Leics
212 E2 **Swordale** Highld
200 B6 **Swordland** Highld
229 M3 **Swordly** Highld
99 J5 **Swynnerton** Staffs
13 M5 **Swyre** Dorset
81 L3 **Sychtyn** Powys
55 L5 **Syde** Gloucs
45 G5 **Sydenham** Gt Lon
58 B7 **Sydenham** Oxon
6 B2 **Sydenham Damerel** Devon
105 K6 **Syderstone** Norfk
14 C3 **Sydling St Nicholas** Dorset
41 J8 **Sydmonton** Hants
102 C3 **Syerston** Notts
95 K3 **Sygun Copper Mine** Gwynd
124 F6 **Sykehouse** Donc
235 d4 **Symbister** Shet
163 J3 **Symington** S Ayrs
165 J3 **Symington** S Lans
13 K4 **Symondsbury** Dorset
54 E5 **Symonds Yat** Herefs
229 L6 **Syre** Highld
56 B4 **Syreford** Gloucs
73 J6 **Syresham** Nhants
87 J2 **Syston** Leics
102 F4 **Syston** Lincs
70 E2 **Sytchampton** Worcs
74 B2 **Sywell** Nhants

T

57 J4 **Tackley** Oxon
92 D4 **Tacolneston** Norfk
124 D2 **Tadcaster** N York
114 C7 **Taddington** Derbys
41 L7 **Tadley** Hants
75 K5 **Tadlow** Cambs
72 E6 **Tadmarton** Oxon
44 E8 **Tadworth** Surrey
37 H4 **Taff's Well** Rhondd
36 B3 **Taibach** Neath
223 G5 **Tain** Highld
231 J3 **Tain** Highld
232 e4 **Tairbeart** W Isls
60 F4 **Takeley** Essex
60 E4 **Takeley Street** Essex
12 D3 **Talaton** Devon
48 E5 **Talbenny** Pembks
12 E3 **Taleford** Devon
81 K4 **Talerddig** Powys
65 L4 **Talgarreg** Cerdgn
68 D7 **Talgarth** Powys
208 E7 **Talisker** Highld
99 J2 **Talke** Staffs
148 F4 **Talkin** Cumb
219 L7 **Talladale** Highld
165 M5 **Talla Linnfoots** Border
153 J3 **Tallaminnock** S Ayrs
98 C4 **Tallarn Green** Wrexhm
147 K7 **Tallentire** Cumb
66 E7 **Talley** Carmth
88 F2 **Tallington** Lincs
229 J3 **Talmine** Highld
50 D1 **Talog** Carmth
66 D4 **Talsarn** Cerdgn
95 K5 **Talsarnau** Gwynd
4 E3 **Talskiddy** Cnwll
109 G6 **Talwrn** IoA
80 E5 **Tal-y-bont** Cerdgn
109 L7 **Tal-y-Bont** Conwy
95 K7 **Tal-y-bont** Gwynd
109 J7 **Tal-y-bont** Gwynd
53 H4 **Talybont-on-Usk** Powys
109 M7 **Tal-y-Cafn** Conwy
54 B5 **Tal-y-coed** Mons
95 H2 **Talysarn** Gwynd
6 C4 **Tamerton Foliot** C Plym
86 B3 **Tamworth** Staffs
86 B4 **Tamworth Services** Warwks
32 C3 **Tandridge** Surrey
150 F4 **Tanfield** Dur
150 F4 **Tanfield Lea** Dur
28 F2 **Tangley** Hants
18 B4 **Tangmere** W Susx
233 b9 **Tangusdale** W Isls
234 c6 **Tankerness** Ork
115 G2 **Tankersley** Barns
47 J6 **Tankerton** Kent
231 K6 **Tannach** Highld
206 E8 **Tannachie** Abers
196 D5 **Tannadice** Angus
85 J8 **Tanner's Green** Worcs
78 F2 **Tannington** Suffk
175 J6 **Tannochside** N Lans
100 F1 **Tansley** Derbys
88 F5 **Tansor** Nhants
150 F4 **Tantobie** Dur
71 K1 **Tanworth in Arden** Warwks
65 J5 **Tan-y-groes** Cerdgn
232 d5 **Taobh Tuath** W Isls
42 E4 **Taplow** Bucks
172 B7 **Tarbert** Ag & B
172 E5 **Tarbert** Ag & B
232 e4 **Tarbert** W Isls
183 K6 **Tarbet** Ag & B
200 B6 **Tarbet** Highld
228 B5 **Tarbet** Highld
163 K4 **Tarbolton** S Ayrs
176 D7 **Tarbrax** S Lans
71 H2 **Tardebigge** Worcs
196 D1 **Tarfside** Angus
205 K4 **Tarland** Abers
120 F6 **Tarleton** Lancs
55 L7 **Tarlton** Gloucs
26 B2 **Tarnock** Somset
112 D8 **Tarporley** Ches W
15 H2 **Tarrant Crawford** Dorset
27 L8 **Tarrant Gunville** Dorset
15 H1 **Tarrant Hinton** Dorset

15 H2 **Tarrant Keyneston** Dorset
15 H1 **Tarrant Launceston** Dorset
15 H2 **Tarrant Monkton** Dorset
15 H2 **Tarrant Rawston** Dorset
15 H2 **Tarrant Rushton** Dorset
19 L5 **Tarring Neville** E Susx
70 B6 **Tarrington** Herefs
199 J4 **Tarskavaig** Highld
217 G7 **Tarves** Abers
112 C7 **Tarvin** Ches W
92 E4 **Tasburgh** Norfk
100 D7 **Tatenhill** Staffs
118 D5 **Tathwell** Lincs
32 D2 **Tatsfield** Surrey
98 C2 **Tattenhall** Ches W
105 K6 **Tatterford** Norfk
105 K6 **Tattersett** Norfk
103 K2 **Tattershall** Lincs
103 L1 **Tattershall Thorpe** Lincs
78 D6 **Tattingstone** Suffk
78 D6 **Tattingstone White Horse** Suffk
13 J2 **Tatworth** Somset
215 J4 **Tauchers** Moray
25 K6 **Taunton** Somset
25 J6 **Taunton Deane Crematorium** Somset
25 J7 **Taunton Deane Services** Somset
92 E2 **Taverham** Norfk
49 K5 **Tavernspite** Pembks
6 C2 **Tavistock** Devon
10 F5 **Taw Green** Devon
23 J5 **Tawstock** Devon
114 A5 **Taxal** Derbys
182 F3 **Taychreggan Hotel** Ag & B
194 C4 **Tay Forest Park** P & K
161 H1 **Tayinloan** Ag & B
55 G4 **Taynton** Gloucs
56 E5 **Taynton** Oxon
182 E2 **Taynuilt** Ag & B
187 G2 **Tayport** Fife
172 C2 **Tayvallich** Ag & B
117 J4 **Tealby** Lincs
196 C8 **Tealing** Angus
151 G3 **Team Valley** Gatesd
199 K4 **Teangue** Highld
212 F2 **Teanord** Highld
138 E6 **Tebay** Cumb
138 E6 **Tebay Services** Cumb
59 G3 **Tebworth** C Beds
11 J6 **Tedburn St Mary** Devon
55 L2 **Teddington** Gloucs
44 D6 **Teddington** Gt Lon
70 C3 **Tedstone Delamere** Herefs
70 C3 **Tedstone Wafer** Herefs
141 L4 **Teesside Crematorium** Middsb
73 K1 **Teeton** Nhants
27 M5 **Teffont Evias** Wilts
27 M5 **Teffont Magna** Wilts
65 H7 **Tegryn** Pembks
88 C1 **Teigh** Rutlnd
7 K2 **Teigngrace** Devon
12 B7 **Teignmouth** Devon
166 F7 **Teindside** Border
84 C2 **Telford** Wrekin
84 D2 **Telford Crematorium** Wrekin
84 D2 **Telford Services** Shrops
27 J1 **Tellisford** Somset
19 L5 **Telscombe** E Susx
193 L5 **Tempar** P & K
155 J5 **Templand** D & G
5 J2 **Temple** Cnwll
177 J6 **Temple** Mdloth
66 C4 **Temple Bar** Cerdgn
38 F8 **Temple Cloud** BaNES
27 G6 **Templecombe** Somset
35 H5 **Temple Ewell** Kent
71 K4 **Temple Grafton** Warwks
56 C3 **Temple Guiting** Gloucs
124 F5 **Temple Hirst** N York
115 H7 **Temple Normanton** Derbys
197 K1 **Temple of Fiddes** Abers
138 E2 **Temple Sowerby** Cumb
11 K3 **Templeton** Devon
49 J5 **Templeton** Pembks
150 E5 **Templetown** Dur
75 H4 **Tempsford** C Beds
69 L2 **Tenbury Wells** Worcs
49 J7 **Tenby** Pembks
62 D3 **Tendring** Essex
62 D3 **Tendring Green** Essex
62 D3 **Tendring Heath** Essex
90 E4 **Ten Mile Bank** Norfk
34 B7 **Tenterden** Kent
61 J5 **Terling** Essex
98 F6 **Ternhill** Shrops
155 G6 **Terregles** D & G
133 K5 **Terrington** N York
104 E7 **Terrington St Clement** Norfk
90 D2 **Terrington St John** Norfk
33 J3 **Teston** Kent
29 G8 **Testwood** Hants
39 K2 **Tetbury** Gloucs
98 B6 **Tetchill** Shrops
9 J5 **Tetcott** Devon
118 D6 **Tetford** Lincs
118 D2 **Tetney** Lincs
58 B7 **Tetsworth** Oxon
84 F4 **Tettenhall** Wolves
101 J1 **Teversal** Notts
76 C3 **Teversham** Cambs
156 D2 **Teviothead** Border
59 L5 **Tewin** Herts
55 K2 **Tewkesbury** Gloucs
34 C3 **Teynham** Kent
123 H3 **Thackley** C Brad
18 F3 **Thakeham** W Susx
58 B6 **Thame** Oxon
44 D6 **Thames Ditton** Surrey
45 J4 **Thamesmead** Gt Lon
35 K2 **Thanet Crematorium** Kent
34 F4 **Thanington** Kent
165 J2 **Thankerton** S Lans
92 E5 **Tharston** Norfk
41 K6 **Thatcham** W Berk
60 F2 **Thaxted** Essex
132 D3 **Theakston** N York
125 K6 **Thealby** N Linc
26 C3 **Theale** Somset
41 M6 **Theale** W Berk
126 D3 **Thearne** E R Yk
56 B7 **The Beeches** Gloucs
79 J2 **Theberton** Suffk
209 H7 **The Braes** Highld
178 E4 **The Brunt** E Loth
237 d4 **The Bungalow** IoM
70 E2 **The Burf** Worcs
55 K5 **The Butts** Gloucs
42 C2 **The City** Bucks
28 E5 **The Common** Wilts
73 K3 **The Counties Crematorium** Nhants
87 J6 **Theddingworth** Leics
118 F4 **Theddlethorpe All Saints** Lincs
119 G4 **Theddlethorpe St Helen** Lincs
174 C7 **The Den** N Ayrs
54 F5 **The Forest of Dean Crematorium** Gloucs
34 D6 **The Forstal** Kent
46 E6 **The Garden of England Crematorium** Kent
128 E3 **The Green** Cumb
61 J4 **The Green** Essex
143 G6 **The Green** N York
27 K5 **The Green** Wilts
151 M7 **The Headland** Hartpl
128 E3 **The Hill** Cumb
58 E6 **The Lee** Bucks
237 d2 **The Lhen** IoM
175 G6 **The Linn Crematorium** E Rens
92 B7 **Thelnetham** Suffk
215 G2 **The Lochs** Moray
92 E7 **Thelveton** Norfk
112 F4 **Thelwall** Warrtn
113 J3 **The Manchester Crematorium** Manch
106 C7 **Themelthorpe** Norfk
33 K7 **The Moor** Kent
51 J7 **The Mumbles** Swans
175 H7 **The Murray** S Lans
206 D5 **The Neuk** Abers
73 G6 **Thenford** Nhants
30 E2 **The Park Crematorium** Hants
55 K4 **The Reddings** Gloucs
75 L6 **Therfield** Herts
115 L2 **The Rose Hill Crematorium** Donc
185 G3 **The Ross** P & K
21 H1 **The Stocks** Kent
39 L8 **The Strand** Wilts
91 K6 **Thetford** Norfk
91 J5 **Thetford Forest Park**
59 J3 **The Vale Crematorium** Luton
60 D7 **Theydon Bois** Essex
39 J5 **Thickwood** Wilts
118 C7 **Thimbleby** Lincs
141 K7 **Thimbleby** N York
111 J5 **Thingwall** Wirral
133 G4 **Thirkleby** N York
133 G3 **Thirlby** N York
178 C8 **Thirlestane** Border
132 C3 **Thirn** N York
132 F3 **Thirsk** N York
120 E3 **Thistleton** Lancs
102 E8 **Thistleton** Rutlnd
90 F7 **Thistley Green** Suffk
134 C7 **Thixendale** N York
158 B6 **Thockrington** Nthumb
90 B3 **Tholomas Drove** Cambs
133 G6 **Tholthorpe** N York
216 B6 **Thomastown** Abers
91 K4 **Thompson** Norfk
131 J3 **Thoralby** N York
117 K3 **Thoresway** Lincs
117 K3 **Thorganby** Lincs
125 G3 **Thorganby** N York
142 E7 **Thorgill** N York
93 J8 **Thorington** Suffk
78 B7 **Thorington Street** Suffk
131 H8 **Thorlby** N York
60 D4 **Thorley** Herts
16 D5 **Thorley Street** IoW
133 G5 **Thormanby** N York
141 K4 **Thornaby-on-Tees** S on T
106 C5 **Thornage** Norfk
73 L7 **Thornborough** Bucks
132 D4 **Thornborough** N York
123 J4 **Thornbury** C Brad
9 K3 **Thornbury** Devon
70 B3 **Thornbury** Herefs
38 F3 **Thornbury** S Glos
87 J7 **Thornby** Nhants
100 A2 **Thorncliff** Staffs
128 E5 **Thorncliffe Crematorium** Cumb
13 J2 **Thorncombe** Dorset
78 D1 **Thorndon** Suffk
10 D6 **Thorndon Cross** Devon
125 G7 **Thorne** Donc
124 B3 **Thorner** Leeds
25 H7 **Thorne St Margaret** Somset
89 K3 **Thorney** C Pete
116 E6 **Thorney** Notts
26 B6 **Thorney** Somset
16 A3 **Thorney Hill** Hants
17 L2 **Thorney Island** W Susx
25 L6 **Thornfalcon** Somset
26 E8 **Thornford** Dorset
149 K2 **Thorngrafton** Nthumb
126 F5 **Thorngumbald** E R Yk
105 H4 **Thornham** Norfk
78 D1 **Thornham Magna** Suffk
92 D8 **Thornham Parva** Suffk
88 F4 **Thornhaugh** C Pete
29 J8 **Thornhill** C Sotn
136 D5 **Thornhill** Cumb
154 F3 **Thornhill** D & G
114 D5 **Thornhill** Derbys
123 K6 **Thornhill** Kirk
184 E7 **Thornhill** Stirlg
37 J4 **Thornhill Crematorium** Cardif
135 H6 **Thornholme** E R Yk
15 G2 **Thornicombe** Dorset
168 D3 **Thornington** Nthumb
150 E7 **Thornley** Dur
151 J6 **Thornley** Dur
174 F6 **Thornliebank** E Rens
77 G4 **Thorns** Suffk
114 A4 **Thornsett** Derbys
137 H3 **Thornthwaite** Cumb
132 B7 **Thornthwaite** N York
196 C6 **Thornton** Angus
73 L7 **Thornton** Bucks
123 G4 **Thornton** C Brad
125 H2 **Thornton** E R Yk
186 E7 **Thornton** Fife
120 D3 **Thornton** Lancs
86 F3 **Thornton** Leics
141 L4 **Thornton** Middsb
179 K8 **Thornton** Nthumb
126 D6 **Thornton Curtis** N Linc
111 K2 **Thornton Garden of Rest Crematorium** Sefton
175 G7 **Thorntonhall** S Lans
44 F6 **Thornton Heath** Gt Lon
111 J5 **Thornton Hough** Wirral
122 D2 **Thornton-in-Craven** N York
130 D5 **Thornton in Lonsdale** N York
132 F2 **Thornton-le-Beans** N York
133 L6 **Thornton-le-Clay** N York
134 C3 **Thornton le Dale** N York
117 H3 **Thornton le Moor** Lincs
132 F2 **Thornton-le-Moor** N York
112 C6 **Thornton-le-Moors** Ches W
132 F3 **Thornton-le-Street** N York
178 F4 **Thorntonloch** E Loth
131 H2 **Thornton Rust** N York
132 B3 **Thornton Steward** N York

132 C3 **Thornton Watlass** N York
178 D8 **Thornydykes** Border
137 L3 **Thornythwaite** Cumb
102 C4 **Thoroton** Notts
124 C2 **Thorp Arch** Leeds
100 D3 **Thorpe** Derbys
126 B2 **Thorpe** E R Yk
131 J6 **Thorpe** N York
102 C3 **Thorpe** Notts
43 G6 **Thorpe** Surrey
92 E7 **Thorpe Abbotts** Norfk
102 C7 **Thorpe Arnold** Leics
124 D7 **Thorpe Audlin** Wakefd
134 D5 **Thorpe Bassett** N York
46 E3 **Thorpe Bay** Sthend
88 C4 **Thorpe by Water** Rutlnd
86 C2 **Thorpe Constantine** Staffs
93 G2 **Thorpe End** Norfk
62 E4 **Thorpe Green** Essex
77 L4 **Thorpe Green** Suffk
115 G3 **Thorpe Hesley** Rothm
124 F7 **Thorpe in Balne** Donc
87 L5 **Thorpe Langton** Leics
43 G6 **Thorpe Lea** Surrey
62 E4 **Thorpe-le-Soken** Essex
125 K2 **Thorpe le Street** E R Yk
88 B7 **Thorpe Malsor** Nhants
73 G5 **Thorpe Mandeville** Nhants
106 F5 **Thorpe Market** Norfk
92 E1 **Thorpe Marriot** Norfk
77 L4 **Thorpe Morieux** Suffk
79 K3 **Thorpeness** Suffk
116 E7 **Thorpe on the Hill** Lincs
43 G6 **Thorpe Park** Surrey
92 F2 **Thorpe St Andrew** Norfk
104 D1 **Thorpe St Peter** Lincs
115 K5 **Thorpe Salvin** Rothm
87 K2 **Thorpe Satchville** Leics
141 J3 **Thorpe Thewles** S on T
103 J2 **Thorpe Tilney** Lincs
133 G7 **Thorpe Underwood** N York
88 E7 **Thorpe Waterville** Nhants
124 E4 **Thorpe Willoughby** N York
62 C4 **Thorrington** Essex
11 L4 **Thorverton** Devon
92 D7 **Thrandeston** Suffk
88 E7 **Thrapston** Nhants
98 C4 **Threapwood** Ches W
100 B4 **Threapwood** Staffs
163 J7 **Threave** S Ayrs
146 C3 **Threave Castle** D & G
32 B5 **Three Bridges** W Susx
33 L5 **Three Chimneys** Kent
68 D6 **Three Cocks** Powys
61 J3 **Three Counties Crematorium** Essex
51 H6 **Three Crosses** Swans
20 D2 **Three Cups Corner** E Susx
103 H5 **Threekingham** Lincs
33 H6 **Three Leg Cross** E Susx
15 K2 **Three Legged Cross** Dorset
42 B6 **Three Mile Cross** Wokham
3 K3 **Threemilestone** Cnwll
176 E3 **Three Miletown** W Loth
21 G3 **Three Oaks** E Susx
137 J3 **Threlkeld** Cumb
60 D6 **Threshers Bush** Essex
131 J6 **Threshfield** N York
93 K2 **Thrigby** Norfk
101 H8 **Thringstone** Leics
132 D2 **Thrintoft** N York
76 B5 **Thriplow** Cambs
60 B3 **Throcking** Herts
150 E2 **Throckley** N u Ty
71 H4 **Throckmorton** Worcs
15 L4 **Throop** Bmouth
158 C2 **Thropton** Nthumb
176 B1 **Throsk** Stirlg
154 F5 **Throughgate** D & G
11 G6 **Throwleigh** Devon
34 C4 **Throwley Forstal** Kent
101 J6 **Thrumpton** Notts
231 L6 **Thrumster** Highld
127 H8 **Thrunscoe** NE Lin
55 K7 **Thrupp** Gloucs
87 J1 **Thrussington** Leics
28 F3 **Thruxton** Hants
69 J7 **Thruxton** Herefs
115 J3 **Thrybergh** Rothm
101 H6 **Thulston** Derbys
46 C3 **Thundersley** Essex
87 H2 **Thurcaston** Leics
115 J4 **Thurcroft** Rothm
106 E5 **Thurgarton** Norfk
102 B3 **Thurgarton** Notts
114 F2 **Thurgoland** Barns
87 G4 **Thurlaston** Leics
72 F1 **Thurlaston** Warwks
25 K7 **Thurlbear** Somset
89 G1 **Thurlby** Lincs
102 E1 **Thurlby** Lincs
119 G6 **Thurlby** Lincs
74 F3 **Thurleigh** Bed
7 G7 **Thurlestone** Devon
25 L5 **Thurloxton** Somset
114 E2 **Thurlstone** Barns
93 J4 **Thurlton** Norfk
87 H2 **Thurmaston** Leics
87 J3 **Thurnby** Leics
93 J1 **Thurne** Norfk
33 K2 **Thurnham** Kent
88 F6 **Thurning** Nhants
106 C6 **Thurning** Norfk
115 J1 **Thurnscoe** Barns
45 L4 **Thurrock Services** Thurr
148 B5 **Thursby** Cumb
106 B5 **Thursford** Norfk
30 E4 **Thursley** Surrey
231 G2 **Thurso** Highld
111 H5 **Thurstaston** Wirral
77 L2 **Thurston** Suffk
148 B4 **Thurstonfield** Cumb
123 H7 **Thurstonland** Kirk
93 G4 **Thurton** Norfk
100 E5 **Thurvaston** Derbys
92 B3 **Thuxton** Norfk
139 K7 **Thwaite** N York
78 D2 **Thwaite** Suffk
129 H2 **Thwaite Head** Cumb
93 G4 **Thwaite St Mary** Norfk
135 G5 **Thwing** E R Yk
185 L3 **Tibbermore** P & K
154 E3 **Tibbers** D & G
55 H4 **Tibberton** Gloucs
70 F3 **Tibberton** Worcs
99 G7 **Tibberton** Wrekin
166 C5 **Tibbie Shiels Inn** Border
92 D5 **Tibenham** Norfk
101 H1 **Tibshelf** Derbys
134 E7 **Tibthorpe** E R Yk
33 H7 **Ticehurst** E Susx
29 L5 **Tichborne** Hants
88 E2 **Tickencote** Rutlnd
38 C6 **Tickenham** N Som
115 L3 **Tickhill** Donc
83 J5 **Ticklerton** Shrops
101 G7 **Ticknall** Derbys
126 D3 **Tickton** E R Yk
40 F8 **Tidcombe** Wilts
57 M6 **Tiddington** Oxon
72 B4 **Tiddington** Warwks
33 G7 **Tidebrook** E Susx
6 A4 **Tideford** Cnwll
38 E2 **Tidenham** Gloucs
114 D6 **Tideswell** Derbys
41 M5 **Tidmarsh** W Berk
72 C6 **Tidmington** Warwks
28 E2 **Tidworth** Wilts
48 F5 **Tiers Cross** Pembks
73 K4 **Tiffield** Nhants
196 E4 **Tigerton** Angus
233 b6 **Tigh a Ghearraidh** W Isls
233 b6 **Tigharry** W Isls
173 G4 **Tighnabruaich** Ag & B
7 H4 **Tigley** Devon
74 F2 **Tilbrook** Cambs
45 M5 **Tilbury** Thurr
86 C7 **Tile Hill** Covtry
42 A5 **Tilehurst** Readg
30 E3 **Tilford** Surrey
31 L4 **Tilgate** W Susx
26 E4 **Tilham Street** Somset
185 J7 **Tillicoultry** Clacks
164 F1 **Tillietudlem** S Lans
62 B7 **Tillingham** Essex
69 J5 **Tillington** Herefs
30 F6 **Tillington** W Susx
69 J5 **Tillington Common** Herefs
206 D4 **Tillybirloch** Abers
206 C3 **Tillyfourie** Abers
207 G2 **Tillygreig** Abers
186 B6 **Tillyrie** P & K
35 J4 **Tilmanstone** Kent
104 F8 **Tilney All Saints** Norfk
104 E8 **Tilney High End** Norfk
90 D2 **Tilney St Lawrence** Norfk
28 B2 **Tilshead** Wilts
98 D5 **Tilstock** Shrops
98 C3 **Tilston** Ches W
98 E1 **Tilstone Fearnall** Ches W
59 G3 **Tilsworth** C Beds
87 L3 **Tilton on the Hill** Leics
39 J2 **Tiltups End** Gloucs
103 J2 **Timberland** Lincs
113 K8 **Timbersbrook** Ches E
24 E3 **Timberscombe** Somset
132 B8 **Timble** N York
156 B7 **Timpanheck** D & G
113 H4 **Timperley** Traffd
38 F8 **Timsbury** BaNES
29 G6 **Timsbury** Hants
232 d2 **Timsgarry** W Isls
232 d2 **Timsgearraidh** W Isls
77 J2 **Timworth** Suffk
77 J2 **Timworth Green** Suffk
14 E4 **Tincleton** Dorset
149 G3 **Tindale** Cumb
140 F2 **Tindale Crescent** Dur
58 A2 **Tingewick** Bucks
59 G2 **Tingrith** C Beds
235 c6 *Tingwall Airport* Shet
9 K7 **Tinhay** Devon
115 H4 **Tinsley** Sheff
32 B5 **Tinsley Green** W Susx
8 E7 **Tintagel** Cnwll
8 D6 **Tintagel Castle** Cnwll
54 D7 **Tintern Abbey** Mons
54 D7 **Tintern Parva** Mons
26 D7 **Tintinhull** Somset
114 A3 **Tintwistle** Derbys
155 H5 **Tinwald** D & G
88 E3 **Tinwell** Rutlnd
85 G5 **Tipton** Sandw
12 E4 **Tipton St John** Devon
61 L5 **Tiptree** Essex
61 L5 **Tiptree Heath** Essex
67 J6 **Tirabad** Powys
188 D7 **Tiree** Ag & B
188 C7 *Tiree Airport* Ag & B
172 C6 **Tiretigan** Ag & B
55 J3 **Tirley** Gloucs
53 H7 **Tirphil** Caerph
138 D2 **Tirril** Cumb
27 L5 **Tisbury** Wilts
100 D3 **Tissington** Derbys
22 C6 **Titchberry** Devon
17 G2 **Titchfield** Hants
88 E7 **Titchmarsh** Nhants
105 J4 **Titchwell** Norfk
102 B5 **Tithby** Notts
69 G3 **Titley** Herefs
32 D3 **Titsey** Surrey
9 H5 **Titson** Cnwll
99 K5 **Tittensor** Staffs
105 L7 **Tittleshall** Norfk
70 E1 **Titton** Worcs
98 D1 **Tiverton** Ches W
24 E8 **Tiverton** Devon
92 E6 **Tivetshall St Margaret** Norfk
92 E6 **Tivetshall St Mary** Norfk
99 L7 **Tixall** Staffs
88 E4 **Tixover** Rutlnd
235 c8 **Toab** Shet
189 L5 **Tobermory** Ag & B
181 L5 **Toberonochy** Ag & B
233 b7 **Tobha Mor** W Isls
216 D7 **Tocher** Abers
215 L2 **Tochieneal** Moray
40 B4 **Tockenham** Wilts
121 K6 **Tockholes** Bl w D
38 E3 **Tockington** S Glos
133 G8 **Tockwith** N York
27 J7 **Todber** Dorset
59 G3 **Toddington** C Beds
56 B2 **Toddington** Gloucs
59 G3 **Toddington Services** C Beds
72 B7 **Todenham** Gloucs
196 C8 **Todhills** Angus
148 C3 **Todhills Services** Cumb
122 D5 **Todmorden** Calder
115 J5 **Todwick** Rothm
75 L4 **Toft** Cambs
88 F1 **Toft** Lincs
235 c3 **Toft** Shet
140 E2 **Toft Hill** Dur
93 J4 **Toft Monks** Norfk
117 H4 **Toft next Newton** Lincs
105 L6 **Toftrees** Norfk
159 G2 **Togston** Nthumb
199 J3 **Tokavaig** Highld
42 B5 **Tokers Green** Oxon
232 g2 **Tolastadh** W Isls
25 H5 **Tolland** Somset
27 L7 **Tollard Royal** Wilts
124 E8 **Toll Bar** Donc
14 B3 **Toller Fratrum** Dorset
14 B3 **Toller Porcorum** Dorset
133 H6 **Tollerton** N York
101 L5 **Tollerton** Notts
62 A6 **Tollesbury** Essex
61 L5 **Tolleshunt D'Arcy** Essex
61 L5 **Tolleshunt Knights** Essex
61 L5 **Tolleshunt Major** Essex
14 E4 **Tolpuddle** Dorset
232 g2 **Tolsta** W Isls
44 D6 **Tolworth** Gt Lon
213 J8 **Tomatin** Highld
201 K3 **Tomchrasky** Highld
201 H5 **Tomdoun** Highld
211 L8 **Tomich** Highld
212 E5 **Tomich** Highld
222 F7 **Tomich** Highld

226 A7 **Tomich** Highld
204 E2 **Tomintoul** Moray
212 D6 **Tomnacross** Highld
204 F1 **Tomnavoulin** Moray
33 G4 **Tonbridge** Kent
36 D4 **Tondu** Brdgnd
25 H6 **Tonedale** Somset
123 J4 **Tong** C Brad
34 C4 **Tong** Kent
84 E3 **Tong** Shrops
101 H7 **Tonge** Leics
30 E2 **Tongham** Surrey
146 C4 **Tongland** D & G
84 E2 **Tong Norton** Shrops
229 J4 **Tongue** Highld
37 H4 **Tongwynlais** Cardif
36 C2 **Tonmawr** Neath
52 B7 **Tonna** Neath
60 B5 **Tonwell** Herts
36 F3 **Tonypandy** Rhondd
36 F3 **Tonyrefail** Rhondd
57 K7 **Toot Baldon** Oxon
60 E7 **Toot Hill** Essex
40 C4 **Toothill** Swindn
44 F5 **Tooting** Gt Lon
44 F5 **Tooting Bec** Gt Lon
132 F4 **Topcliffe** N York
92 F5 **Topcroft** Norfk
92 F5 **Topcroft Street** Norfk
77 G6 **Toppesfield** Essex
92 E4 **Toprow** Norfk
12 C5 **Topsham** Devon
162 A4 **Torbeg** N Ayrs
223 G2 **Torboll** Highld
213 G6 **Torbreck** Highld
7 J3 **Torbryan** Devon
192 B2 **Torcastle** Highld
7 J7 **Torcross** Devon
212 F4 **Tore** Highld
172 D5 **Torinturk** Ag & B
116 D5 **Torksey** Lincs
39 H5 **Tormarton** S Glos
161 M3 **Tormore** N Ayrs
213 J4 **Tornagrain** Highld
206 C4 **Tornaveen** Abers
212 E8 **Torness** Highld
140 F2 **Toronto** Dur
147 L6 **Torpenhow** Cumb
176 C4 **Torphichen** W Loth
206 C5 **Torphins** Abers
6 C5 **Torpoint** Cnwll
7 L3 **Torquay** Torbay
7 K3 **Torquay Crematorium** Torbay
177 L8 **Torquhan** Border
209 J5 **Torran** Highld
175 H4 **Torrance** E Duns
163 J1 **Torranyard** N Ayrs
210 D3 **Torridon** Highld
210 D3 **Torridon House** Highld
199 J2 **Torrin** Highld
161 K3 **Torrisdale** Ag & B
229 K3 **Torrisdale** Highld
227 G5 **Torrish** Highld
129 K6 **Torrisholme** Lancs
226 A7 **Torrobull** Highld
207 H4 **Torry** C Aber
176 D2 **Torryburn** Fife
236 b4 **Torteval** Guern
155 H6 **Torthorwald** D & G
18 D5 **Tortington** W Susx
84 E8 **Torton** Worcs
39 G2 **Tortworth** S Glos
209 H5 **Torvaig** Highld
137 J7 **Torver** Cumb
175 L2 **Torwood** Falk
167 G2 **Torwoodlee** Border
116 A4 **Torworth** Notts
209 L6 **Toscaig** Highld
75 J3 **Toseland** Cambs
130 E7 **Tosside** Lancs
77 L2 **Tostock** Suffk
208 C4 **Totaig** Highld
208 F5 **Tote** Highld
209 H3 **Tote** Highld
16 D5 **Totland** IoW
114 F5 **Totley** Sheff
7 J4 **Totnes** Devon
101 J5 **Toton** Notts
188 F5 **Totronald** Ag & B
208 F2 **Totscore** Highld
45 G3 **Tottenham** Gt Lon
90 F2 **Tottenhill** Norfk
44 E2 **Totteridge** Gt Lon
59 G4 **Totternhoe** C Beds
122 B7 **Tottington** Bury
29 G8 **Totton** Hants
25 J5 **Toulton** Somset
223 J5 **Toulvaddie** Highld
33 K3 **Tovil** Kent
173 K5 **Toward** Ag & B
173 J5 **Toward Quay** Ag & B
73 K5 **Towcester** Nhants
2 E4 **Towednack** Cnwll
58 B6 **Towersey** Oxon
205 K3 **Towie** Abers
150 E6 **Tow Law** Dur
90 B4 **Town End** Cambs
174 D3 **Townend** W Duns
114 D2 **Townhead** Barns
155 H4 **Townhead** D & G
146 C3 **Townhead of Greenlaw** D & G
176 F1 **Townhill** Fife
19 L3 **Town Littleworth** E Susx
41 K8 **Towns End** Hants
3 G5 **Townshend** Cnwll
91 H6 **Town Street** Suffk
168 B4 **Town Yetholm** Border
133 K7 **Towthorpe** C York
124 D3 **Towton** N York
110 D5 **Towyn** Conwy
111 K4 **Toxteth** Lpool
118 E8 **Toynton All Saints** Lincs
32 E3 **Toy's Hill** Kent
163 K5 **Trabboch** E Ayrs
163 L5 **Trabbochburn** E Ayrs
213 K3 **Tradespark** Highld
52 E3 **Trallong** Powys
101 G2 **Tramway Museum** Derbys
177 L4 **Tranent** E Loth
111 J4 **Tranmere** Wirral
230 C5 **Trantelbeg** Highld
230 C5 **Trantlemore** Highld
51 J2 **Trapp** Carmth
178 D4 **Traprain** E Loth
166 E3 **Traquair** Border
122 D3 **Trawden** Lancs
96 A5 **Trawsfynydd** Gwynd
36 F3 **Trealaw** Rhondd
120 F4 **Treales** Lancs
108 C5 **Trearddur Bay** IoA
208 F4 **Treaslane** Highld
4 E1 **Trebetherick** Cnwll
24 F4 **Treborough** Somset
5 M1 **Trebullett** Cnwll
6 A1 **Treburley** Cnwll
52 D3 **Trecastle** Powys
64 D7 **Trecwn** Pembks
52 F7 **Trecynon** Rhondd
53 H6 **Tredegar** Blae G
55 K3 **Tredington** Gloucs
72 C5 **Tredington** Warwks
38 B2 **Tredunnock** Mons
2 D6 **Treen** Cnwll
115 H4 **Treeton** Rothm
64 C6 **Trefasser** Pembks
53 H2 **Trefecca** Powys
81 L5 **Trefeglwys** Powys
49 G3 **Treffgarne** Pembks
48 E3 **Treffgarne Owen** Pembks
37 G3 **Trefforest** Rhondd
66 D3 **Trefilan** Cerdgn
64 B7 **Trefin** Pembks
110 E7 **Trefnant** Denbgs
97 K6 **Trefonen** Shrops
94 F4 **Trefor** Gwynd
109 L8 **Trefriw** Conwy
9 H7 **Tregadillett** Cnwll
54 B6 **Tregare** Mons
66 F3 **Tregaron** Cerdgn
109 H7 **Tregarth** Gwynd
9 H7 **Tregeare** Cnwll
97 J5 **Tregeiriog** Wrexhm
108 D3 **Tregele** IoA
48 D2 **Treglemais** Pembks
4 E3 **Tregonetha** Cnwll
4 E6 **Tregony** Cnwll
4 F5 **Tregorrick** Cnwll
68 E6 **Tregoyd** Powys
65 L5 **Tre-groes** Cerdgn
82 C4 **Tregynon** Powys
50 E2 **Tre-gynwr** Carmth
37 G3 **Trehafod** Rhondd
6 B4 **Trehan** Cnwll
37 H2 **Treharris** Myr Td
52 E7 **Treherbert** Rhondd
6 A1 **Trekenner** Cnwll
8 D7 **Treknow** Cnwll
110 F5 **Trelawnyd** Flints
65 J7 **Trelech** Carmth
48 C2 **Treleddyd-fawr** Pembks
37 H2 **Trelewis** Myr Td
8 C8 **Trelights** Cnwll
5 G1 **Trelill** Cnwll
4 C7 **Trelissick Garden** Cnwll
54 D6 **Trellech** Mons
110 F5 **Trelogan** Flints
95 K4 **Tremadog** Gwynd
8 F7 **Tremail** Cnwll
65 H5 **Tremain** Cerdgn
9 G6 **Tremaine** Cnwll
5 K3 **Tremar** Cnwll
6 B4 **Trematon** Cnwll
110 F6 **Tremeirchion** Denbgs
4 D3 **Trenance** Cnwll
4 E2 **Trenance** Cnwll
84 C2 **Trench** Wrekin
3 H5 **Trenear** Cnwll
9 G7 **Treneglos** Cnwll
26 E7 **Trent** Dorset
99 K4 **Trentham** C Stke
23 K2 **Trentishoe** Devon
36 E5 **Treoes** V Glam
36 E2 **Treorchy** Rhondd
5 G1 **Trequite** Cnwll
36 F5 **Trerhyngyll** V Glam
5 M4 **Trerulefoot** Cnwll
65 J4 **Tresaith** Cerdgn
2 a1 **Tresco** IoS
2 a1 *Tresco Heliport* IoS
3 G5 **Trescowe** Cnwll
4 C4 **Tresean** Cnwll
39 H3 **Tresham** Gloucs
189 G7 **Treshnish Isles** Ag & B
4 D6 **Tresillian** Cnwll
9 G5 **Treskinnick Cross** Cnwll
9 G7 **Tresmeer** Cnwll
8 F6 **Tresparrett** Cnwll
194 C4 **Tressait** P & K
235 c5 **Tresta** Shet
235 e3 **Tresta** Shet
116 C5 **Treswell** Notts
3 H3 **Treswithian Downs Crematorium** Cnwll
80 E5 **Tre Taliesin** Cerdgn
8 E6 **Trethevey** Cnwll
2 C6 **Trethewey** Cnwll
5 G5 **Trethurgy** Cnwll
54 D4 **Tretire** Herefs
53 J4 **Tretower** Powys
97 K2 **Treuddyn** Flints
8 E6 **Trevalga** Cnwll
98 B2 **Trevalyn** Wrexhm
4 D3 **Trevarrian** Cnwll
4 C4 **Treveal** Cnwll
8 E8 **Treveighan** Cnwll
3 J2 **Trevellas Downs** Cnwll
5 K3 **Trevelmond** Cnwll
3 K5 **Treverva** Cnwll
2 C6 **Trevescan** Cnwll
4 E5 **Treviscoe** Cnwll
4 D2 **Trevone** Cnwll
97 L4 **Trevor** Wrexhm
8 E7 **Trewalder** Cnwll
8 E7 **Trewarmett** Cnwll
9 H7 **Trewen** Cnwll
9 G8 **Trewint** Cnwll
4 D7 **Trewithian** Cnwll
4 F5 **Trewoon** Cnwll
30 D7 **Treyford** W Susx
151 J7 **Trimdon** Dur
151 J7 **Trimdon Colliery** Dur
151 J7 **Trimdon Grange** Dur
107 G5 **Trimingham** Norfk
78 F6 **Trimley St Martin** Suffk
79 G7 **Trimley St Mary** Suffk
50 F5 **Trimsaran** Carmth
23 H3 **Trimstone** Devon
194 B4 **Trinafour** P & K
58 F5 **Tring** Herts
196 F4 **Trinity** Angus
236 d6 **Trinity** Jersey
185 K4 **Trinity Gask** P & K
25 J4 **Triscombe** Somset
191 L2 **Trislaig** Highld
4 D5 **Trispen** Cnwll
158 F4 **Tritlington** Nthumb
194 F7 **Trochry** P & K
65 K5 **Troedyraur** Cerdgn
53 G7 **Troedyrhiw** Myr Td
3 H4 **Troon** Cnwll
163 H3 **Troon** S Ayrs
123 L3 **Tropical World Roundhay Park** Leeds
184 B5 **Trossachs** Stirlg
184 B6 **Trossachs Pier** Stirlg
91 K8 **Troston** Suffk
70 F4 **Trotshill** Worcs
33 H2 **Trottiscliffe** Kent
30 D6 **Trotton** W Susx
137 L6 **Troutbeck** Cumb
137 L7 **Troutbeck Bridge** Cumb
115 H5 **Troway** Derbys
39 J8 **Trowbridge** Wilts
101 J4 **Trowell** Notts
101 J4 **Trowell Services** Notts
92 F3 **Trowse Newton** Norfk
27 H3 **Trudoxhill** Somset
25 K6 **Trull** Somset
208 C3 **Trumpan** Highld
70 B6 **Trumpet** Herefs
76 C4 **Trumpington** Cambs
107 G5 **Trunch** Norfk
4 C6 **Truro** Cnwll
4 C6 **Truro Cathedral** Cnwll
11 K7 **Trusham** Devon
100 E5 **Trusley** Derbys
119 G5 **Trusthorpe** Lincs
84 F5 **Trysull** Staffs
57 H7 **Tubney** Oxon
7 J5 **Tuckenhay** Devon
84 E6 **Tuckhill** Shrops
3 H3 **Tuckingmill** Cnwll
27 L5 **Tuckingmill** Wilts
15 L4 **Tuckton** Bmouth
77 G1 **Tuddenham** Suffk
78 E5 **Tuddenham** Suffk
33 G4 **Tudeley** Kent
151 G7 **Tudhoe** Dur
94 D5 **Tudweiliog** Gwynd
55 J5 **Tuffley** Gloucs
29 J3 **Tufton** Hants
49 H2 **Tufton** Pembks
87 L4 **Tugby** Leics
83 L6 **Tugford** Shrops
169 J4 **Tughall** Nthumb
185 H7 **Tullibody** Clacks
212 F8 **Tullich** Highld
223 J6 **Tullich** Highld

194 F5 **Tulliemet** P & K
216 F7 **Tulloch** Abers
182 D7 **Tullochgorm** Ag & B
192 F1 **Tulloch Station** Highld
195 J5 **Tullymurdoch** P & K
206 B2 **Tullynessle** Abers
44 F5 **Tulse Hill** Gt Lon
51 G3 **Tumble** Carmth
103 L1 **Tumby** Lincs
103 L2 **Tumby Woodside** Lincs
194 B5 **Tummel Bridge** P & K
33 G5 **Tunbridge Wells** Kent
155 L6 **Tundergarth** D & G
39 G8 **Tunley** BaNES
99 K3 **Tunstall** C Stke
127 H4 **Tunstall** E R Yk
34 B3 **Tunstall** Kent
130 B5 **Tunstall** Lancs
140 F7 **Tunstall** N York
93 J2 **Tunstall** Norfk
99 H6 **Tunstall** Staffs
79 H4 **Tunstall** Suffk
151 J4 **Tunstall** Sundld
114 C6 **Tunstead** Derbys
107 G7 **Tunstead** Norfk
114 B5 **Tunstead Milton** Derbys
42 B8 **Turgis Green** Hants
56 C4 **Turkdean** Gloucs
87 K5 **Tur Langton** Leics
39 J7 **Turleigh** Wilts
69 G7 **Turnastone** Herefs
152 E2 **Turnberry** S Ayrs
100 F3 **Turnditch** Derbys
32 C6 **Turner's Hill** W Susx
177 G4 **Turnhouse** C Edin
14 F2 **Turnworth** Dorset
216 D4 **Turriff** Abers
121 L7 **Turton Bottoms** Bl w D
89 L4 **Turves** Cambs
74 D4 **Turvey** Bed
42 C3 **Turville** Bucks
73 H6 **Turweston** Bucks
166 D5 **Tushielaw Inn** Border
100 E6 **Tutbury** Staffs
38 D2 **Tutshill** Gloucs
106 F6 **Tuttington** Norfk
116 C7 **Tuxford** Notts
234 b5 **Twatt** Ork
235 c5 **Twatt** Shet
175 J3 **Twechar** E Duns
167 H3 **Tweedbank** Border
179 K7 **Tweedmouth** Nthumb
165 L4 **Tweedsmuir** Border
3 K3 **Twelveheads** Cnwll
113 H7 **Twemlow Green** Ches E
103 J7 **Twenty** Lincs
39 G7 **Twerton** BaNES
44 D5 **Twickenham** Gt Lon
55 J4 **Twigworth** Gloucs
19 H2 **Twineham** W Susx
77 J6 **Twinstead** Essex
24 C5 **Twitchen** Devon
114 F8 **Two Dales** Derbys
86 B4 **Two Gates** Staffs
86 D3 **Twycross** Leics
86 C3 **Twycross Zoo** Leics
58 A3 **Twyford** Bucks
29 J6 **Twyford** Hants
87 K2 **Twyford** Leics
106 B7 **Twyford** Norfk
42 C5 **Twyford** Wokham
146 B4 **Twynholm** D & G
70 F6 **Twyning Green** Gloucs
51 L2 **Twynllanan** Carmth
88 D7 **Twywell** Nhants
69 H6 **Tyberton** Herefs
51 H4 **Tycroes** Carmth
97 H8 **Tycrwyn** Powys
104 D8 **Tydd Gote** Lincs
90 B1 **Tydd St Giles** Cambs
104 C8 **Tydd St Mary** Lincs
76 E7 **Tye Green** Essex
113 G2 **Tyldesley** Wigan
34 F3 **Tyler Hill** Kent
36 F2 **Tylorstown** Rhondd
96 F4 **Ty-nant** Conwy
183 K2 **Tyndrum** Stirlg
97 K4 **Ty'n-dwr** Denbgs
151 J2 **Tynemouth** N Tyne
151 J2 **Tynemouth Crematorium** N Tyne
178 D3 **Tyninghame** E Loth
154 E4 **Tynron** D & G
38 D6 **Tyntesfield** N Som
66 F1 **Tynygraig** Cerdgn
109 L7 **Ty'n-y-Groes** Conwy
37 G4 **Tyn-y-nant** Rhondd
74 C5 **Tyringham** M Keyn
36 D5 **Tythegston** Brdgnd
113 K6 **Tytherington** Ches E
38 F3 **Tytherington** S Glos
27 K3 **Tytherington** Wilts
13 H2 **Tytherleigh** Devon
39 L5 **Tytherton Lucas** Wilts
5 H5 **Tywardreath** Cnwll
80 D4 **Tywyn** Gwynd

U

79 G1 **Ubbeston Green** Suffk
38 D8 **Ubley** BaNES
19 M2 **Uckfield** E Susx
70 F6 **Uckinghall** Worcs
55 K3 **Uckington** Gloucs
175 J6 **Uddingston** S Lans
165 G3 **Uddington** S Lans
21 H2 **Udimore** E Susx
207 G1 **Udny Green** Abers
207 G1 **Udny Station** Abers
25 G8 **Uffculme** Devon
88 F3 **Uffington** Lincs
40 F3 **Uffington** Oxon
83 K2 **Uffington** Shrops
89 G3 **Ufford** C Pete
79 G4 **Ufford** Suffk
72 E3 **Ufton** Warwks
41 M6 **Ufton Nervet** W Berk
161 K4 **Ugadale** Ag & B
7 G5 **Ugborough** Devon
93 J7 **Uggeshall** Suffk
143 H5 **Ugglebarnby** N York
114 E4 **Ughill** Sheff
60 E3 **Ugley** Essex
60 E3 **Ugley Green** Essex
143 G5 **Ugthorpe** N York
233 c8 **Uibhist A Deas** W Isls
233 b6 **Uibhist A Tuath** W Isls
188 F5 **Uig** Ag & B
208 C4 **Uig** Highld
208 F2 **Uig** Highld
232 d2 **Uig** W Isls
209 G5 **Uigshader** Highld
180 E4 **Uisken** Ag & B
231 K7 **Ulbster** Highld
118 F6 **Ulceby** Lincs
126 D7 **Ulceby** N Linc
126 E7 **Ulceby Skitter** N Linc
33 L4 **Ulcombe** Kent
147 M7 **Uldale** Cumb
55 H7 **Uley** Gloucs
159 G4 **Ulgham** Nthumb
220 E3 **Ullapool** Highld
71 K2 **Ullenhall** Warwks
124 D3 **Ulleskelf** N York
87 G6 **Ullesthorpe** Leics
115 J4 **Ulley** Rothm
69 L4 **Ullingswick** Herefs
208 E6 **Ullinish Lodge Hotel** Highld
136 E3 **Ullock** Cumb
138 B3 **Ullswater** Cumb
128 E2 **Ulpha** Cumb
135 J7 **Ulrome** E R Yk
235 d3 **Ulsta** Shet
189 K7 **Ulva** Ag & B
129 G4 **Ulverston** Cumb
15 J6 **Ulwell** Dorset
164 F7 **Ulzieside** D & G
23 J6 **Umberleigh** Devon
224 F2 **Unapool** Highld
129 K2 **Underbarrow** Cumb
156 E5 **Under Burnmouth** Border
123 J4 **Undercliffe** C Brad
83 K2 **Underdale** Shrops
32 F3 **Under River** Kent
101 J3 **Underwood** Notts
38 C3 **Undy** Mons
237 c5 **Union Mills** IoM
235 d1 **Unst** Shet
115 G6 **Unstone** Derbys
28 C1 **Upavon** Wilts
46 D6 **Upchurch** Kent
24 B5 **Upcott** Devon
12 B2 **Up Exe** Devon
106 D8 **Upgate** Norfk
14 B2 **Uphall** Dorset
176 E4 **Uphall** W Loth
11 K3 **Upham** Devon
29 K7 **Upham** Hants
69 H2 **Uphampton** Herefs
70 E2 **Uphampton** Worcs
37 L8 **Uphill** N Som
112 D1 **Up Holland** Lancs
174 E7 **Uplawmoor** E Rens
55 H3 **Upleadon** Gloucs
142 D4 **Upleatham** R & Cl
13 L4 **Uploders** Dorset
24 F7 **Uplowman** Devon
13 H4 **Uplyme** Devon
30 D8 **Up Marden** W Susx
45 K3 **Upminster** Gt Lon
26 E7 **Up Mudford** Somset
30 B2 **Up Nately** Hants
12 F2 **Upottery** Devon
83 J6 **Upper Affcot** Shrops
222 E4 **Upper Ardchronie** Highld
84 D7 **Upper Arley** Worcs
41 L5 **Upper Basildon** W Berk
19 G4 **Upper Beeding** W Susx
88 E5 **Upper Benefield** Nhants
71 H2 **Upper Bentley** Worcs
230 C4 **Upper Bighouse** Highld
72 F4 **Upper Boddington** Nhants
72 C6 **Upper Brailes** Warwks
199 L2 **Upper Breakish** Highld
70 E4 **Upper Broadheath** Worcs
102 B7 **Upper Broughton** Notts
41 K6 **Upper Bucklebury** W Berk
28 D7 **Upper Burgate** Hants
148 D4 **Upperby** Cumb
75 H5 **Upper Caldecote** C Beds
67 L6 **Upper Chapel** Powys
27 L5 **Upper Chicksgrove** Wilts
28 F2 **Upper Chute** Wilts
45 G3 **Upper Clapton** Gt Lon
29 G3 **Upper Clatford** Hants
83 K3 **Upper Cound** Shrops
123 J8 **Upper Cumberworth** Kirk
215 H2 **Upper Dallachy** Moray
35 K4 **Upper Deal** Kent
74 F2 **Upper Dean** Bed
114 E1 **Upper Denby** Kirk
20 B4 **Upper Dicker** E Susx
230 E3 **Upper Dounreay** Highld
62 F2 **Upper Dovercourt** Essex
184 E6 **Upper Drumbane** Stirlg
133 G6 **Upper Dunsforth** N York
30 F3 **Upper Eashing** Surrey
213 J2 **Upper Eathie** Highld
70 B5 **Upper Egleton** Herefs
100 B2 **Upper Elkstone** Staffs
100 C4 **Upper Ellastone** Staffs
30 B4 **Upper Farringdon** Hants
55 H6 **Upper Framilode** Gloucs
30 C3 **Upper Froyle** Hants
208 E4 **Upperglen** Highld
26 C3 **Upper Godney** Somset
75 G7 **Upper Gravenhurst** C Beds
41 G7 **Upper Green** W Berk
54 E3 **Upper Grove Common** Herefs
30 D2 **Upper Hale** Surrey
43 H6 **Upper Halliford** Surrey
88 C3 **Upper Hambleton** Rutlnd
34 F3 **Upper Harbledown** Kent
32 E6 **Upper Hartfield** E Susx
55 L4 **Upper Hatherley** Gloucs
123 H6 **Upper Heaton** Kirk
133 L7 **Upper Helmsley** N York
68 F4 **Upper Hergest** Herefs
73 J3 **Upper Heyford** Nhants
57 J3 **Upper Heyford** Oxon
69 J4 **Upper Hill** Herefs
123 J6 **Upper Hopton** Kirk
100 A1 **Upper Hulme** Staffs
40 D2 **Upper Inglesham** Swindn
51 H6 **Upper Killay** Swans
183 G2 **Upper Kinchrackine** Ag & B
40 F4 **Upper Lambourn** W Berk
85 H3 **Upper Landywood** Staffs
38 C7 **Upper Langford** N Som
115 K7 **Upper Langwith** Derbys
187 G6 **Upper Largo** Fife
100 A5 **Upper Leigh** Staffs
206 D6 **Upper Lochton** Abers
85 J2 **Upper Longdon** Staffs
75 H7 **Upper & Lower Stondon** C Beds
231 J7 **Upper Lybster** Highld
54 E5 **Upper Lydbrook** Gloucs
69 H2 **Upper Lye** Herefs
113 M1 **Uppermill** Oldham
84 E8 **Upper Milton** Worcs
40 A3 **Upper Minety** Wilts
215 H4 **Upper Mulben** Moray
83 L5 **Upper Netchwood** Shrops
100 B5 **Upper Nobut** Staffs
18 C3 **Upper Norwood** W Susx
133 H8 **Upper Poppleton** C York
28 F6 **Upper Ratley** Hants
56 D4 **Upper Rissington** Gloucs

70 B2 **Upper Rochford** Worcs
145 L3 **Upper Ruscoe** D & G
70 C2 **Upper Sapey** Herefs
39 L4 **Upper Seagry** Wilts
74 E5 **Upper Shelton** C Beds
106 D4 **Upper Sheringham** Norfk
173 L5 **Upper Skelmorlie** N Ayrs
56 D4 **Upper Slaughter** Gloucs
54 F6 **Upper Soudley** Gloucs
35 H6 **Upper Standen** Kent
92 F3 **Upper Stoke** Norfk
73 J3 **Upper Stowe** Nhants
28 D7 **Upper Street** Hants
93 H1 **Upper Street** Norfk
107 G8 **Upper Street** Norfk
77 H4 **Upper Street** Suffk
78 D4 **Upper Street** Suffk
59 H3 **Upper Sundon** C Beds
56 D3 **Upper Swell** Gloucs
92 E4 **Upper Tasburgh** Norfk
100 A5 **Upper Tean** Staffs
123 H8 **Upperthong** Kirk
30 F6 **Upperton** W Susx
69 L5 **Upper Town** Herefs
231 L1 **Uppertown** Highld
38 D7 **Upper Town** N Som
77 K2 **Upper Town** Suffk
51 G3 **Upper Tumble** Carmth
72 D5 **Upper Tysoe** Warwks
187 J1 **Upper Victoria** Angus
72 F5 **Upper Wardington** Oxon
70 D6 **Upper Welland** Worcs
19 L3 **Upper Wellingham** E Susx
92 F7 **Upper Weybread** Suffk
29 L4 **Upper Wield** Hants
58 C5 **Upper Winchendon** Bucks
28 C4 **Upper Woodford** Wilts
39 J5 **Upper Wraxall** Wilts
88 C4 **Uppingham** Rutlnd
83 L2 **Uppington** Shrops
133 G3 **Upsall** N York
168 C1 **Upsettlington** Border
60 C7 **Upshire** Essex
29 H5 **Up Somborne** Hants
35 G3 **Upstreet** Kent
58 C5 **Upton** Bucks
89 G4 **Upton** C Pete
89 H7 **Upton** Cambs
112 B7 **Upton** Ches W
5 L2 **Upton** Cnwll
7 G7 **Upton** Devon
12 E2 **Upton** Devon
14 E5 **Upton** Dorset
15 J4 **Upton** Dorset
112 C4 **Upton** Halton
29 G1 **Upton** Hants
29 G7 **Upton** Hants
86 D4 **Upton** Leics
116 E4 **Upton** Lincs
93 H2 **Upton** Norfk
102 B2 **Upton** Notts
116 C6 **Upton** Notts
41 K3 **Upton** Oxon
43 G5 **Upton** Slough
24 F5 **Upton** Somset
26 C6 **Upton** Somset
124 D7 **Upton** Wakefd
111 J4 **Upton** Wirral
54 F3 **Upton Bishop** Herefs
39 G6 **Upton Cheyney** S Glos
84 B5 **Upton Cressett** Shrops
30 B2 **Upton Grey** Hants
11 J4 **Upton Hellions** Devon
27 L4 **Upton Lovell** Wilts
83 K2 **Upton Magna** Shrops
27 G4 **Upton Noble** Somset
11 L5 **Upton Pyne** Devon
55 K5 **Upton St Leonards** Gloucs
27 K2 **Upton Scudamore** Wilts
71 G4 **Upton Snodsbury** Worcs
70 F6 **Upton upon Severn** Worcs
71 G2 **Upton Warren** Worcs
18 C3 **Upwaltham** W Susx
90 C3 **Upwell** Norfk
89 J6 **Upwood** Cambs
40 B8 **Urchfont** Wilts
113 H3 **Urmston** Traffd
215 G2 **Urquhart** Moray
142 C6 **Urra** N York
212 D4 **Urray** Highld
197 H5 **Usan** Angus
151 G6 **Ushaw Moor** Dur
54 B7 **Usk** Mons
117 H3 **Usselby** Lincs
151 H4 **Usworth** Sundld
112 D7 **Utkinton** Ches W
122 F3 **Utley** C Brad
11 J5 **Uton** Devon
118 D3 **Utterby** Lincs
100 C5 **Uttoxeter** Staffs
43 H4 **Uxbridge** Gt Lon
235 d2 **Uyeasound** Shet
49 G5 **Uzmaston** Pembks

V

236 d2 **Vale** Guern
37 H6 **Vale of Glamorgan Crematorium** V Glam
80 F7 **Vale of Rheidol Railway** Cerdgn
108 C5 **Valley** IoA
209 H2 **Valtos** Highld
232 d2 **Valtos** W Isls
46 B3 **Vange** Essex
235 d3 **Vatsetter** Shet
208 D5 **Vatten** Highld
53 G6 **Vaynor** Myr Td
235 c6 **Veensgarth** Shet
68 D7 **Velindre** Powys
9 K3 **Venngreen** Devon
12 D4 **Venn Ottery** Devon
17 G6 **Ventnor** IoW
6 E4 **Venton** Devon
29 G1 **Vernham Dean** Hants
41 G8 **Vernham Street** Hants
15 K2 **Verwood** Dorset
4 E7 **Veryan** Cnwll
128 E5 **Vickerstown** Cumb
4 F4 **Victoria** Cnwll
235 d4 **Vidlin** Shet
215 G2 **Viewfield** Moray
175 J6 **Viewpark** N Lans
45 M7 **Vigo** Kent
236 d3 **Village de Putron** Guern
20 C3 **Vines Cross** E Susx
33 K2 **Vinters Park Crematorium** Kent
43 G6 **Virginia Water** Surrey
9 K6 **Virginstow** Devon
27 G2 **Vobster** Somset
235 c4 **Voe** Shet
69 G7 **Vowchurch** Herefs

W

128 D2 **Waberthwaite** Cumb
140 E3 **Wackerfield** Dur
92 E5 **Wacton** Norfk
70 F5 **Wadborough** Worcs
58 C5 **Waddesdon** Bucks
7 K4 **Waddeton** Devon
117 G3 **Waddingham** Lincs
121 L2 **Waddington** Lancs
116 F8 **Waddington** Lincs
4 F2 **Wadebridge** Cnwll
13 H1 **Wadeford** Somset
88 E6 **Wadenhoe** Nhants
60 B4 **Wadesmill** Herts
33 H6 **Wadhurst** E Susx
114 F7 **Wadshelf** Derbys
115 K3 **Wadworth** Donc
104 D2 **Wainfleet All Saints** Lincs
104 D2 **Wainfleet St Mary** Lincs
9 G5 **Wainhouse Corner** Cnwll
46 C6 **Wainscott** Medway
122 F5 **Wainstalls** Calder
139 H5 **Waitby** Cumb
118 C2 **Waithe** Lincs
123 L6 **Wakefield** Wakefd
123 L7 **Wakefield Crematorium** Wakefd
88 D4 **Wakerley** Nhants
61 L3 **Wakes Colne** Essex
93 K8 **Walberswick** Suffk
18 C4 **Walberton** W Susx
146 D2 **Walbutt** D & G
26 D3 **Walcombe** Somset
103 H5 **Walcot** Lincs
83 L2 **Walcot** Shrops
40 D4 **Walcot** Swindn
87 H6 **Walcote** Leics
92 D7 **Walcot Green** Norfk
103 J2 **Walcott** Lincs
107 H6 **Walcott** Norfk
124 E6 **Walden Stubbs** N York
46 C7 **Walderslade** Medway
17 L1 **Walderton** W Susx
13 L4 **Walditch** Dorset
151 G5 **Waldridge** Dur
79 G5 **Waldringfield** Suffk
20 B2 **Waldron** E Susx
115 J5 **Wales** Rothm
26 E6 **Wales** Somset
117 J3 **Walesby** Lincs
116 B7 **Walesby** Notts
54 E4 **Walford** Herefs
83 H8 **Walford** Herefs
98 C8 **Walford Heath** Shrops
99 G3 **Walgherton** Ches E
74 B1 **Walgrave** Nhants
113 G2 **Walkden** Salfd
151 H3 **Walker** N u Ty
166 E3 **Walkerburn** Border
116 C3 **Walkeringham** Notts
116 C3 **Walkerith** Lincs
59 M3 **Walkern** Herts
186 D6 **Walkerton** Fife
16 B4 **Walkford** Dorset
6 D2 **Walkhampton** Devon
126 B3 **Walkington** E R Yk
115 G4 **Walkley** Sheff
122 C5 **Walk Mill** Lancs
71 J2 **Walkwood** Worcs
150 A2 **Wall** Nthumb
85 K3 **Wall** Staffs
153 G2 **Wallacetown** S Ayrs
163 J5 **Wallacetown** S Ayrs
19 L4 **Wallands Park** E Susx
111 J3 **Wallasey** Wirral
41 L3 **Wallingford** Oxon
44 F6 **Wallington** Gt Lon
17 H2 **Wallington** Hants
75 K7 **Wallington** Herts
15 K4 **Wallisdown** Poole
235 b5 **Walls** Shet
151 H2 **Wallsend** N Tyne
177 K4 **Wallyford** E Loth
35 K5 **Walmer** Kent
121 G5 **Walmer Bridge** Lancs
85 K5 **Walmley** Birm
93 H8 **Walpole** Suffk
104 E8 **Walpole Cross Keys** Norfk
90 D2 **Walpole Highway** Norfk
104 D8 **Walpole St Andrew** Norfk
90 C1 **Walpole St Peter** Norfk
85 H4 **Walsall** Wsall
122 D6 **Walsden** Calder
86 E7 **Walsgrave on Sowe** Covtry
78 B1 **Walsham le Willows** Suffk
132 F8 **Walshford** N York
90 C2 **Walsoken** Norfk
165 K1 **Walston** S Lans
59 K3 **Walsworth** Herts
42 D2 **Walter's Ash** Bucks
34 E5 **Waltham** Kent
118 C2 **Waltham** NE Lin
60 C7 **Waltham Abbey** Essex
29 K7 **Waltham Chase** Hants
60 B7 **Waltham Cross** Herts
102 D7 **Waltham on the Wolds** Leics
42 D5 **Waltham St Lawrence** W & M
45 G3 **Walthamstow** Gt Lon
148 F3 **Walton** Cumb
115 G7 **Walton** Derbys
124 C2 **Walton** Leeds
87 H6 **Walton** Leics
74 C7 **Walton** M Keyn
68 F3 **Walton** Powys
26 C4 **Walton** Somset
79 G7 **Walton** Suffk
17 M2 **Walton** W Susx
123 L6 **Walton** Wakefd
98 E8 **Walton** Wrekin
55 K2 **Walton Cardiff** Gloucs
49 H3 **Walton East** Pembks
38 B5 **Walton-in-Gordano** N Som
112 E4 **Walton Lea Crematorium** Warrtn
121 H5 **Walton-le-Dale** Lancs
43 J6 **Walton-on-Thames** Surrey
99 L7 **Walton-on-the-Hill** Staffs
31 L1 **Walton on the Hill** Surrey
62 F4 **Walton on the Naze** Essex
101 L8 **Walton on the Wolds** Leics
100 E8 **Walton-on-Trent** Derbys
38 B6 **Walton Park** N Som
48 E5 **Walton West** Pembks
122 E1 **Waltonwrays Crematorium** N York
141 G4 **Walworth** Darltn
45 G4 **Walworth** Gt Lon
48 E5 **Walwyn's Castle** Pembks
13 H2 **Wambrook** Somset
30 F2 **Wanborough** Surrey
40 E4 **Wanborough** Swindn
44 E5 **Wandsworth** Gt Lon
93 K7 **Wangford** Suffk
87 H2 **Wanlip** Leics
165 G6 **Wanlockhead** D & G
20 C5 **Wannock** E Susx
88 F4 **Wansford** C Pete
135 G7 **Wansford** E R Yk
33 K4 **Wanshurst Green** Kent
45 H3 **Wanstead** Gt Lon
27 G3 **Wanstrow** Somset
55 G7 **Wanswell** Gloucs
41 H3 **Wantage** Oxon

72 E2 **Wappenbury** Warwks
73 J5 **Wappenham** Nhants
20 C3 **Warbleton** E Susx
41 L2 **Warborough** Oxon
89 K7 **Warboys** Cambs
120 D3 **Warbreck** Bpool
9 G6 **Warbstow** Cnwll
113 G4 **Warburton** Traffd
139 H4 **Warcop** Cumb
150 A2 **Warden** Nthumb
72 F5 **Wardington** Oxon
98 E2 **Wardle** Ches E
122 D6 **Wardle** Rochdl
151 H3 **Wardley** Gatesd
88 B4 **Wardley** Rutlnd
114 D6 **Wardlow** Derbys
90 C6 **Wardy Hill** Cambs
60 B5 **Ware** Herts
15 H5 **Wareham** Dorset
34 D7 **Warehorne** Kent
169 H4 **Warenford** Nthumb
60 C5 **Wareside** Herts
75 J4 **Waresley** Cambs
42 E6 **Warfield** Br For
7 K6 **Warfleet** Devon
42 C5 **Wargrave** Wokham
105 M4 **Warham All Saints** Norfk
105 M4 **Warham St Mary** Norfk
157 L6 **Wark** Nthumb
168 C2 **Wark** Nthumb
23 K6 **Warkleigh** Devon
88 C7 **Warkton** Nhants
72 F6 **Warkworth** Nhants
159 G2 **Warkworth** Nthumb
132 E2 **Warlaby** N York
5 J3 **Warleggan** Cnwll
122 F5 **Warley Town** Calder
32 C2 **Warlingham** Surrey
124 B6 **Warmfield** Wakefd
99 G1 **Warmingham** Ches E
88 F5 **Warmington** Nhants
72 E5 **Warmington** Warwks
27 K3 **Warminster** Wilts
38 F5 **Warmley** S Glos
115 K2 **Warmsworth** Donc
14 E5 **Warmwell** Dorset
29 L6 **Warnford** Hants
31 J5 **Warnham** W Susx
18 D4 **Warningcamp** W Susx
31 L6 **Warninglid** W Susx
113 K7 **Warren** Ches E
48 F7 **Warren** Pembks
165 J2 **Warrenhill** S Lans
42 D4 **Warren Row** W & M
34 C4 **Warren Street** Kent
74 C4 **Warrington** M Keyn
112 E4 **Warrington** Warrtn
177 H4 **Warriston** C Edin
177 H3 **Warriston Crematorium** C Edin
16 F2 **Warsash** Hants
100 C2 **Warslow** Staffs
125 K1 **Warter** E R Yk
132 C4 **Warthermaske** N York
133 K7 **Warthill** N York
20 D4 **Wartling** E Susx
102 B7 **Wartnaby** Leics
120 E5 **Warton** Lancs
129 K5 **Warton** Lancs
86 C3 **Warton** Warwks
72 C2 **Warwick** Warwks
148 E4 **Warwick Bridge** Cumb
72 C2 **Warwick Castle** Warwks
72 D3 **Warwick Services** Warwks
234 c4 **Wasbister** Ork
137 G5 **Wasdale Head** Cumb
5 G2 **Washaway** Cnwll
7 J5 **Washbourne** Devon
78 D6 **Washbrook** Suffk
11 L2 **Washfield** Devon
25 G3 **Washford** Somset
11 J3 **Washford Pyne** Devon
117 G7 **Washingborough** Lincs
151 H4 **Washington** Sundld
18 F3 **Washington** W Susx
151 G4 **Washington Services** Gatesd
72 C3 **Wasperton** Warwks
133 H4 **Wass** N York
25 G3 **Watchet** Somset
40 E3 **Watchfield** Oxon
138 D7 **Watchgate** Cumb
11 H8 **Water** Devon
76 C2 **Waterbeach** Cambs
18 B4 **Waterbeach** W Susx
155 M6 **Waterbeck** D & G
125 J3 **Water End** E R Yk
100 B3 **Waterfall** Staffs
175 G7 **Waterfoot** E Rens
60 A5 **Waterford** Herts
177 H7 **Waterheads** Border
100 B3 **Waterhouses** Staffs
33 H3 **Wateringbury** Kent
199 K2 **Waterloo** Highld
175 L7 **Waterloo** N Lans
195 G8 **Waterloo** P & K
49 G6 **Waterloo** Pembks
111 K2 **Waterloo** Sefton
17 J1 **Waterlooville** Hants
138 C3 **Watermillock** Cumb
89 G4 **Water Newton** Cambs
85 L5 **Water Orton** Warwks
57 L6 **Waterperry** Oxon
25 G6 **Waterrow** Somset
18 D3 **Watersfield** W Susx
121 K5 **Waterside** Bl w D
163 K7 **Waterside** E Ayrs
163 L2 **Waterside** E Ayrs
175 J4 **Waterside** E Duns
208 B5 **Waterstein** Highld
57 M6 **Waterstock** Oxon
48 F6 **Waterston** Pembks
73 J7 **Water Stratford** Bucks
98 F8 **Waters Upton** Wrekin
43 J2 **Watford** Herts
73 H2 **Watford** Nhants
73 H2 **Watford Gap Services** Nhants
132 B6 **Wath** N York
132 E4 **Wath** N York
115 H2 **Wath upon Dearne** Rothm
90 E2 **Watlington** Norfk
42 B2 **Watlington** Oxon
231 J5 **Watten** Highld
92 B8 **Wattisfield** Suffk
78 B4 **Wattisham** Suffk
13 L4 **Watton** Dorset
126 C1 **Watton** E R Yk
91 K4 **Watton** Norfk
60 A4 **Watton-at-Stone** Herts
175 K4 **Wattston** N Lans
37 J3 **Wattsville** Caerph
206 C6 **Waulkmill** Abers
51 H6 **Waunarlwydd** Swans
80 E6 **Waunfawr** Cerdgn
95 J2 **Waunfawr** Gwynd
74 C6 **Wavendon** M Keyn
147 L5 **Waverbridge** Cumb
112 C8 **Waverton** Ches W
147 L5 **Waverton** Cumb
126 D3 **Wawne** E R Yk
107 J7 **Waxham** Norfk
13 K2 **Wayford** Somset
13 L3 **Waytown** Dorset
11 K3 **Way Village** Devon
25 H4 **Weacombe** Somset
56 F7 **Weald** Oxon
44 D3 **Wealdstone** Gt Lon
123 K2 **Weardley** Leeds
26 B2 **Weare** Somset
23 G6 **Weare Giffard** Devon
149 L6 **Wearhead** Dur
26 B5 **Wearne** Somset
141 G2 **Wear Valley Crematorium** Dur
105 K7 **Weasenham All Saints** Norfk
105 K7 **Weasenham St Peter** Norfk
113 J2 **Weaste** Salfd
112 E6 **Weaverham** Ches W
134 E5 **Weaverthorpe** N York
71 H2 **Webheath** Worcs
216 F7 **Wedderlairs** Abers
86 D5 **Weddington** Warwks
40 B8 **Wedhampton** Wilts
26 C2 **Wedmore** Somset
85 H4 **Wednesbury** Sandw
85 G4 **Wednesfield** Wolves
58 D4 **Weedon** Bucks
73 J3 **Weedon** Nhants
73 H5 **Weedon Lois** Nhants
85 K3 **Weeford** Staffs
29 J5 **Weeke** Hants
88 C7 **Weekley** Nhants
9 H5 **Week St Mary** Cnwll
126 D3 **Weel** E R Yk
62 D4 **Weeley** Essex
62 D4 **Weeley Crematorium** Essex
62 D4 **Weeley Heath** Essex
194 D6 **Weem** P & K
71 J4 **Weethley** Warwks
91 H5 **Weeting** Norfk
127 H6 **Weeton** E R Yk
120 E4 **Weeton** Lancs
123 K2 **Weeton** N York
123 K3 **Weetwood** Leeds
122 C5 **Weir** Lancs
6 C3 **Weir Quay** Devon
235 c5 **Weisdale** Shet
92 C2 **Welborne** Norfk
102 F2 **Welbourn** Lincs
133 L6 **Welburn** N York
141 J6 **Welbury** N York
102 F5 **Welby** Lincs
22 C7 **Welcombe** Devon
87 J7 **Welford** Nhants
41 H5 **Welford** W Berk
71 K4 **Welford-on-Avon** Warwks
87 L5 **Welham** Leics
116 B5 **Welham** Notts
59 L6 **Welham Green** Herts
30 C3 **Well** Hants
118 F6 **Well** Lincs
132 D3 **Well** N York
70 E6 **Welland** Worcs
196 D8 **Wellbank** Angus
72 C4 **Wellesbourne** Warwks
59 K3 **Well Head** Herts
45 J5 **Welling** Gt Lon
74 C2 **Wellingborough** Nhants
105 L7 **Wellingham** Norfk
103 G2 **Wellingore** Lincs
136 F6 **Wellington** Cumb
69 K5 **Wellington** Herefs
25 H7 **Wellington** Somset
84 B2 **Wellington** Wrekin
70 C6 **Wellington Heath** Herefs
39 H8 **Wellow** BaNES
16 E5 **Wellow** IoW
116 A7 **Wellow** Notts
26 D3 **Wells** Somset
105 L4 **Wells-next-the-sea** Norfk
61 G4 **Wellstye Green** Essex
185 K3 **Welltree** P & K
176 E2 **Wellwood** Fife
90 D5 **Welney** Norfk
98 C5 **Welshampton** Shrops
98 A6 **Welsh Frankton** Shrops
54 D4 **Welsh Newton** Herefs
82 E3 **Welshpool** Powys
36 F5 **Welsh St Donats** V Glam
148 C6 **Welton** Cumb
126 B5 **Welton** E R Yk
117 G5 **Welton** Lincs
73 H2 **Welton** Nhants
119 G7 **Welton le Marsh** Lincs
118 C4 **Welton le Wold** Lincs
127 H6 **Welwick** E R Yk
59 L5 **Welwyn** Herts
59 L5 **Welwyn Garden City** Herts
98 D6 **Wem** Shrops
25 L4 **Wembdon** Somset
44 D3 **Wembley** Gt Lon
6 D6 **Wembury** Devon
10 F3 **Wembworthy** Devon
173 L4 **Wemyss Bay** Inver
76 D7 **Wendens Ambo** Essex
57 K4 **Wendlebury** Oxon
91 L2 **Wendling** Norfk
58 E6 **Wendover** Bucks
3 H5 **Wendron** Cnwll
75 K5 **Wendy** Cambs
93 J7 **Wenhaston** Suffk
89 J7 **Wennington** Cambs
45 K4 **Wennington** Gt Lon
130 C5 **Wennington** Lancs
100 E1 **Wensley** Derbys
131 K2 **Wensley** N York
124 D6 **Wentbridge** Wakefd
83 H5 **Wentnor** Shrops
90 C7 **Wentworth** Cambs
115 G2 **Wentworth** Rothm
37 H6 **Wenvoe** V Glam
69 H4 **Weobley** Herefs
18 E4 **Wepham** W Susx
90 F3 **Wereham** Norfk
89 H3 **Werrington** C Pete
9 J7 **Werrington** Cnwll
112 B6 **Wervin** Ches W
120 F4 **Wesham** Lancs
29 J7 **Wessex Vale Crematorium** Hants
101 G2 **Wessington** Derbys
91 H1 **West Acre** Norfk
7 G6 **West Alvington** Devon
24 D6 **West Anstey** Devon
118 C6 **West Ashby** Lincs
17 M2 **West Ashling** W Susx
27 K1 **West Ashton** Wilts
140 F3 **West Auckland** Dur
134 F3 **West Ayton** N York
25 J5 **West Bagborough** Somset
112 D5 **West Bank** Halton
117 K5 **West Barkwith** Lincs
143 G5 **West Barnby** N York
178 E3 **West Barns** E Loth
105 L5 **West Barsham** Norfk
13 L4 **West Bay** Dorset
106 D5 **West Beckham** Norfk
43 H5 **West Bedfont** Surrey
35 G3 **Westbere** Kent
62 A3 **West Bergholt** Essex
41 K6 **West Berkshire Crematorium** W Berk
14 A5 **West Bexington** Dorset
91 G1 **West Bilney** Norfk
19 J4 **West Blatchington** Br & H
151 J3 **West Boldon** S Tyne
102 D4 **Westborough** Lincs
15 K4 **Westbourne** Bmouth
17 L2 **Westbourne** W Susx
123 H4 **West Bowling** C Brad
91 K2 **West Bradenham** Norfk
121 L2 **West Bradford** Lancs
26 E4 **West Bradley** Somset
123 K7 **West Bretton** Wakefd
101 L5 **West Bridgford** Notts

85 H5 **West Bromwich** Sandw
85 H5 **West Bromwich Crematorium** Sandw
35 J2 **Westbrook** Kent
41 H6 **Westbrook** W Berk
23 K5 **West Buckland** Devon
25 J7 **West Buckland** Somset
131 J3 **West Burton** N York
73 J7 **Westbury** Bucks
83 G2 **Westbury** Shrops
27 K2 **Westbury** Wilts
27 K2 **Westbury Leigh** Wilts
55 G5 **Westbury on Severn** Gloucs
38 E5 **Westbury-on-Trym** Bristl
26 D2 **Westbury-sub-Mendip** Somset
116 D1 **West Butterwick** N Linc
120 E4 **Westby** Lancs
43 H7 **West Byfleet** Surrey
144 D8 **West Cairngaan** D & G
93 K2 **West Caister** Norfk
176 D5 **West Calder** W Loth
26 E6 **West Camel** Somset
14 E5 **West Chaldon** Dorset
41 G3 **West Challow** Oxon
7 H7 **West Charleton** Devon
18 E3 **West Chiltington** W Susx
26 C8 **West Chinnock** Somset
31 H2 **West Clandon** Surrey
35 J5 **West Cliffe** Kent
46 E3 **Westcliff-on-Sea** Sthend
26 D8 **West Coker** Somset
27 G4 **Westcombe** Somset
26 E3 **West Compton** Somset
14 B4 **West Compton Abbas** Dorset
56 E4 **Westcote** Gloucs
57 H3 **Westcote Barton** Oxon
58 B5 **Westcott** Bucks
12 C2 **Westcott** Devon
31 J2 **Westcott** Surrey
125 G3 **West Cottingwith** N York
40 E7 **Westcourt** Wilts
124 F6 **West Cowick** E R Yk
51 H7 **West Cross** Swans
148 B5 **West Curthwaite** Cumb
20 B5 **Westdean** E Susx
18 B3 **West Dean** W Susx
28 E6 **West Dean** Wilts
89 G2 **West Deeping** Lincs
111 L3 **West Derby** Lpool
90 F4 **West Dereham** Norfk
23 H3 **West Down** Devon
8 E7 **Westdowns** Cnwll
43 H4 **West Drayton** Gt Lon
116 B6 **West Drayton** Notts
231 J2 **West Dunnet** Highld
126 C5 **West Ella** E R Yk
74 E4 **West End** Bed
29 J8 **West End** Hants
38 C6 **West End** N Som
93 K2 **West End** Norfk
42 F7 **West End** Surrey
27 M6 **West End** Wilts
42 A7 **West End Green** Hants
231 G5 **Westerdale** Highld
142 E6 **Westerdale** N York
78 E5 **Westerfield** Suffk
18 C5 **Westergate** W Susx
32 D3 **Westerham** Kent
150 F2 **Westerhope** N u Ty
7 K4 **Westerland** Devon
39 G4 **Westerleigh** S Glos
39 G5 **Westerleigh Crematorium** S Glos
176 D4 **Wester Ochiltree** W Loth
187 J6 **Wester Pitkierie** Fife
220 C5 **Wester Ross** Highld
197 G5 **Westerton of Rossie** Angus
235 c6 **Westerwick** Shet
33 J3 **West Farleigh** Kent
73 G4 **West Farndon** Nhants
97 M7 **West Felton** Shrops
26 F2 **Westfield** BaNES
136 D2 **Westfield** Cumb
21 G3 **Westfield** E Susx
230 F3 **Westfield** Highld
175 J4 **Westfield** N Lans
92 B2 **Westfield** Norfk
176 C4 **Westfield** W Loth
195 J6 **Westfields of Rattray** P & K
150 A7 **Westgate** Dur
125 J8 **Westgate** N Linc
35 J2 **Westgate on Sea** Kent
40 E7 **West Grafton** Wilts
30 C1 **West Green** Hants
28 E6 **West Grimstead** Wilts
31 K6 **West Grinstead** W Susx
124 E5 **West Haddlesey** N York
73 J1 **West Haddon** Nhants
41 K3 **West Hagbourne** Oxon
84 F7 **West Hagley** Worcs
93 J7 **Westhall** Suffk
101 H4 **West Hallam** Derbys
125 L6 **West Halton** N Linc
14 C6 **Westham** Dorset
20 D5 **Westham** E Susx
45 H4 **West Ham** Gt Lon
26 B3 **Westham** Somset
18 B4 **Westhampnett** W Susx
115 H6 **West Handley** Derbys
41 H2 **West Hanney** Oxon
61 H7 **West Hanningfield** Essex
28 C5 **West Harnham** Wilts
38 E8 **West Harptree** BaNES
30 C7 **West Harting** W Susx
25 L7 **West Hatch** Somset
27 L5 **West Hatch** Wilts
187 J1 **West Haven** Angus
26 C3 **Westhay** Somset
85 J7 **West Heath** Birm
227 H5 **West Helmsdale** Highld
41 H3 **West Hendred** Oxon
59 J7 **West Hertfordshire Crematorium** Herts
134 E4 **West Heslerton** N York
38 B7 **West Hewish** N Som
69 L5 **Westhide** Herefs
206 F4 **Westhill** Abers
12 D4 **West Hill** Devon
32 C6 **West Hoathly** W Susx
15 G5 **West Holme** Dorset
69 J4 **Westhope** Herefs
83 J6 **Westhope** Shrops
45 M3 **West Horndon** Essex
103 L6 **Westhorpe** Lincs
78 C2 **Westhorpe** Suffk
26 E3 **West Horrington** Somset
31 H2 **West Horsley** Surrey
35 H6 **West Hougham** Kent
112 F1 **Westhoughton** Bolton
130 D5 **Westhouse** N York
101 H2 **Westhouses** Derbys
15 K4 **West Howe** Bmouth
31 K2 **Westhumble** Surrey
185 M3 **West Huntingtower** P & K
25 L3 **West Huntspill** Somset
34 F7 **West Hythe** Kent
41 J4 **West Ilsley** W Berk
17 L3 **West Itchenor** W Susx
40 C6 **West Kennett** Wilts
173 L8 **West Kilbride** N Ayrs
45 L7 **West Kingsdown** Kent
39 J5 **West Kington** Wilts
111 H4 **West Kirby** Wirral
134 D4 **West Knapton** N York
14 D5 **West Knighton** Dorset
27 K5 **West Knoyle** Wilts
6 F5 **Westlake** Devon
26 B7 **West Lambrook** Somset
35 J5 **West Langdon** Kent
30 E7 **West Lavington** W Susx
28 A2 **West Lavington** Wilts
140 E5 **West Layton** N York
101 K7 **West Leake** Notts
23 G5 **Westleigh** Devon
25 G7 **Westleigh** Devon
25 H5 **West Leigh** Somset
79 J2 **Westleton** Suffk
91 J1 **West Lexham** Norfk
77 J2 **Westley** Suffk
76 E3 **Westley Waterless** Cambs
133 K6 **West Lilling** N York
58 C6 **Westlington** Bucks
176 F7 **West Linton** Border
148 D3 **Westlinton** Cumb
39 H5 **West Littleton** S Glos
41 H3 **West Lockinge** Oxon
44 E4 **West London Crematorium** Gt Lon
14 F6 **West Lulworth** Dorset
134 E5 **West Lutton** N York
26 E5 **West Lydford** Somset
25 L5 **West Lyng** Somset
104 F7 **West Lynn** Norfk
33 H2 **West Malling** Kent
70 D5 **West Malvern** Worcs
30 C8 **West Marden** W Susx
116 B6 **West Markham** Notts
35 H3 **Westmarsh** Kent
127 G8 **West Marsh** NE Lin
122 D1 **West Marton** N York
27 K7 **West Melbury** Dorset
29 M6 **West Meon** Hants
62 B5 **West Mersea** Essex
19 K3 **Westmeston** E Susx
84 E7 **West Midland Safari Park** Worcs
60 B3 **Westmill** Herts
13 L3 **West Milton** Dorset
44 F4 **Westminster** Gt Lon
46 E5 **West Minster** Kent
43 J6 **West Molesey** Surrey
25 K5 **West Monkton** Somset
15 K2 **West Moors** Dorset
15 G4 **West Morden** Dorset
167 J2 **West Morriston** Border
26 E7 **West Mudford** Somset
196 B5 **Westmuir** Angus
133 L4 **West Ness** N York
147 K6 **Westnewton** Cumb
126 F3 **West Newton** E R Yk
105 H6 **West Newton** Norfk
25 L5 **West Newton** Somset
44 F5 **West Norwood** Gt Lon
44 F5 **West Norwood Crematorium** Gt Lon
151 J2 **Westoe** S Tyne
7 J2 **West Ogwell** Devon
39 G6 **Weston** BaNES
99 G3 **Weston** Ches E
12 E3 **Weston** Devon
12 F5 **Weston** Devon
30 B6 **Weston** Hants
59 L3 **Weston** Herts
103 M7 **Weston** Lincs
123 H2 **Weston** N York
73 H5 **Weston** Nhants
116 C7 **Weston** Notts
83 L5 **Weston** Shrops
97 L6 **Weston** Shrops
99 L6 **Weston** Staffs
41 H5 **Weston** W Berk
69 L6 **Weston Beggard** Herefs
39 J3 **Westonbirt** Gloucs
87 L5 **Weston by Welland** Nhants
76 E4 **Weston Colville** Cambs
30 B3 **Weston Corbett** Hants
99 L4 **Weston Coyney** C Stke
73 L3 **Weston Favell** Nhants
76 F4 **Weston Green** Cambs
84 D2 **Weston Heath** Shrops
59 G2 **Westoning** C Beds
38 C5 **Weston-in-Gordano** N Som
99 H7 **Weston Jones** Staffs
92 D1 **Weston Longville** Norfk
98 B7 **Weston Lullingfields** Shrops
6 C4 **Weston Mill Crematorium** C Plym
57 K4 **Weston-on-the-Green** Oxon
30 B3 **Weston Patrick** Hants
97 L5 **Weston Rhyn** Shrops
71 K6 **Weston-sub-Edge** Gloucs
37 L7 **Weston-super-Mare** N Som
38 A7 **Weston-super-Mare Crematorium** N Som
58 D6 **Weston Turville** Bucks
84 E2 **Weston-under-Lizard** Staffs
54 F4 **Weston under Penyard** Herefs
98 E6 **Weston-under-Redcastle** Shrops
72 D1 **Weston under Wetherley** Warwks
100 F4 **Weston Underwood** Derbys
74 C4 **Weston Underwood** M Keyn
101 H6 **Weston-upon-Trent** Derbys
25 M4 **Westonzoyland** Somset
27 J7 **West Orchard** Dorset
40 C6 **West Overton** Wilts
134 B6 **Westow** N York
206 E5 **West Park** Abers
15 K3 **West Parley** Dorset
33 H3 **West Peckham** Kent
151 G4 **West Pelton** Dur
26 D4 **West Pennard** Somset
4 B4 **West Pentire** Cnwll
75 G2 **West Perry** Cambs
24 D3 **West Porlock** Somset
26 B7 **Westport** Somset
9 K2 **West Putford** Devon
25 H3 **West Quantoxhead** Somset
176 B3 **Westquarter** Falk
151 H5 **West Rainton** Dur
117 H4 **West Rasen** Lincs
234 c3 **Westray** Ork
234 c3 *Westray Airport* Ork
105 L7 **West Raynham** Norfk

176 B5 **Westrigg** W Loth
150 F2 **West Road Crematorium** N u Ty
40 D2 **Westrop** Swindn
141 K6 **West Rounton** N York
90 F7 **West Row** Suffk
105 K6 **West Rudham** Norfk
106 E4 **West Runton** Norfk
178 D7 **Westruther** Border
90 B4 **Westry** Cambs
178 B5 **West Saltoun** E Loth
11 J4 **West Sandford** Devon
235 d3 **West Sandwick** Shet
131 K3 **West Scrafton** N York
14 D4 **West Stafford** Dorset
116 C3 **West Stockwith** Notts
17 M2 **West Stoke** W Susx
27 H6 **West Stour** Dorset
35 H3 **West Stourmouth** Kent
77 J1 **West Stow** Suffk
40 C7 **West Stowell** Wilts
78 B1 **West Street** Suffk
77 J2 **West Suffolk Crematorium** Suffk
132 D4 **West Tanfield** N York
5 J3 **West Taphouse** Cnwll
172 E5 **West Tarbert** Ag & B
18 F5 **West Tarring** W Susx
158 F3 **West Thirston** Nthumb
17 L3 **West Thorney** W Susx
101 L7 **West Thorpe** Notts
45 L4 **West Thurrock** Thurr
46 A4 **West Tilbury** Thurr
29 M5 **West Tisted** Hants
117 J5 **West Torrington** Lincs
17 K3 **West Town** Hants
38 C6 **West Town** N Som
28 F5 **West Tytherley** Hants
90 C2 **West Walton** Norfk
90 C2 **West Walton Highway** Norfk
148 B6 **Westward** Cumb
23 G5 **Westward Ho!** Devon
34 D5 **Westwell** Kent
56 E6 **Westwell** Oxon
34 C5 **Westwell Leacon** Kent
28 F7 **West Wellow** Hants
6 D6 **West Wembury** Devon
186 E7 **West Wemyss** Fife
76 B2 **Westwick** Cambs
76 E5 **West Wickham** Cambs
45 G6 **West Wickham** Gt Lon
49 H6 **West Williamston** Pembks
39 K7 **West Wiltshire Crematorium** Wilts
90 F1 **West Winch** Norfk
28 E5 **West Winterslow** Wilts
17 L3 **West Wittering** W Susx
131 K2 **West Witton** N York
12 C3 **Westwood** Devon
35 K2 **Westwood** Kent
39 J8 **Westwood** Wilts
157 M5 **West Woodburn** Nthumb
41 H7 **West Woodhay** W Berk
116 C2 **Westwoodside** N Linc
30 C4 **West Worldham** Hants
18 F5 **West Worthing** W Susx
76 E4 **West Wratting** Cambs
148 E4 **Wetheral** Cumb
124 B2 **Wetherby** Leeds
124 C1 **Wetherby Services** N York
78 B3 **Wetherden** Suffk
78 D2 **Wetheringsett** Suffk
61 H2 **Wethersfield** Essex
78 D2 **Wetherup Street** Suffk
99 L3 **Wetley Rocks** Staffs
98 F1 **Wettenhall** Ches E
100 C2 **Wetton** Staffs
134 E7 **Wetwang** E R Yk
99 H5 **Wetwood** Staffs
40 F8 **Wexcombe** Wilts
106 D4 **Weybourne** Norfk
30 D2 **Weybourne** Surrey
92 F7 **Weybread** Suffk
92 F7 **Weybread Street** Suffk
43 H7 **Weybridge** Surrey
13 H3 **Weycroft** Devon
231 H3 **Weydale** Highld
28 F3 **Weyhill** Hants
14 D6 **Weymouth** Dorset
14 C6 **Weymouth Crematorium** Dorset
74 B7 **Whaddon** Bucks
75 L5 **Whaddon** Cambs
55 J5 **Whaddon** Gloucs
28 D6 **Whaddon** Wilts
39 K7 **Whaddon** Wilts
115 K7 **Whaley** Derbys
114 A5 **Whaley Bridge** Derbys
115 K7 **Whaley Thorns** Derbys
231 K7 **Whaligoe** Highld
121 L4 **Whalley** Lancs
235 d4 **Whalsay** Shet
158 E6 **Whalton** Nthumb
104 A7 **Whaplode** Lincs
89 K2 **Whaplode Drove** Lincs
72 E4 **Wharf** Warwks
130 E5 **Wharfe** N York
120 F4 **Wharles** Lancs
74 D5 **Wharley End** C Beds
114 F3 **Wharncliffe Side** Sheff
134 D6 **Wharram-le-Street** N York
69 K4 **Wharton** Herefs
140 E6 **Whashton** N York
129 L4 **Whasset** Cumb
72 C5 **Whatcote** Warwks
86 B4 **Whateley** Warwks
78 B5 **Whatfield** Suffk
13 J2 **Whatley** Somset
27 G3 **Whatley** Somset
20 F3 **Whatlington** E Susx
102 C5 **Whatton** Notts
145 J5 **Whauphill** D & G
93 K5 **Wheatacre** Norfk
59 K5 **Wheathampstead** Herts
30 C4 **Wheatley** Hants
57 L6 **Wheatley** Oxon
151 J6 **Wheatley Hill** Dur
115 L1 **Wheatley Hills** Donc
84 F2 **Wheaton Aston** Staffs
24 E4 **Wheddon Cross** Somset
99 H2 **Wheelock** Ches E
121 J6 **Wheelton** Lancs
125 G2 **Wheldrake** C York
56 D7 **Whelford** Gloucs
59 G6 **Whelpley Hill** Bucks
60 A4 **Whempstead** Herts
133 K5 **Whenby** N York
77 J3 **Whepstead** Suffk
78 E6 **Wherstead** Suffk
29 H3 **Wherwell** Hants
114 C6 **Wheston** Derbys
33 H4 **Whetsted** Kent
87 G4 **Whetstone** Leics
128 D3 **Whicham** Cumb
72 C7 **Whichford** Warwks
150 F3 **Whickham** Gatesd
11 G6 **Whiddon Down** Devon
196 D7 **Whigstreet** Angus
73 J2 **Whilton** Nhants
12 D3 **Whimple** Devon
107 H6 **Whimpwell Green** Norfk
92 B2 **Whinburgh** Norfk
146 C4 **Whinnie Liggate** D & G
217 K7 **Whinnyfold** Abers
17 G4 **Whippingham** IoW
59 G4 **Whipsnade** C Beds
12 B4 **Whipton** Devon
116 E7 **Whisby** Lincs
88 B2 **Whissendine** Rutlnd
105 L7 **Whissonsett** Norfk
183 J8 **Whistlefield** Ag & B
183 G8 **Whistlefield Inn** Ag & B
42 C5 **Whistley Green** Wokham
112 C3 **Whiston** Knows
74 B3 **Whiston** Nhants
115 H4 **Whiston** Rothm
84 F2 **Whiston** Staffs
100 B3 **Whiston** Staffs
128 D3 **Whitbeck** Cumb
70 D3 **Whitbourne** Herefs
151 J3 **Whitburn** S Tyne
176 C5 **Whitburn** W Loth
143 J5 **Whitby** N York
178 F6 **Whitchester** Border
38 F6 **Whitchurch** BaNES
58 D4 **Whitchurch** Bucks
37 J4 **Whitchurch** Cardif
6 D2 **Whitchurch** Devon
29 J2 **Whitchurch** Hants
54 D4 **Whitchurch** Herefs
41 M5 **Whitchurch** Oxon
48 D3 **Whitchurch** Pembks
98 D4 **Whitchurch** Shrops
13 K4 **Whitchurch Canonicorum** Dorset
41 M5 **Whitchurch Hill** Oxon
14 D5 **Whitcombe** Dorset
83 H5 **Whitcot** Shrops
82 F6 **Whitcott Keysett** Shrops
86 B5 **Whiteacre Heath** Warwks
25 H7 **White Ball** Somset
202 D3 **Whitebridge** Highld
54 D6 **Whitebrook** Mons
207 H2 **Whitecairns** Abers
45 G4 **Whitechapel** Gt Lon
121 H3 **White Chapel** Lancs
54 E6 **Whitecliffe** Gloucs
61 L3 **White Colne** Essex
177 K4 **Whitecraig** E Loth
144 E4 **Whitecrook** D & G
3 H6 **White Cross** Cnwll
176 C3 **Whitecross** Falk
222 F4 **Whiteface** Highld
161 L2 **Whitefarland** N Ayrs
163 H7 **Whitefaulds** S Ayrs
113 J1 **Whitefield** Bury
25 G5 **Whitefield** Somset
206 D1 **Whiteford** Abers
112 F7 **Whitegate** Ches W
234 d5 **Whitehall** Ork
136 D4 **Whitehaven** Cumb
30 C5 **Whitehill and Bordon** Hants
216 C2 **Whitehills** Abers
206 C3 **Whitehouse** Abers
172 D6 **Whitehouse** Ag & B
178 D3 **Whitekirk** E Loth
14 D3 **White Lackington** Dorset
26 B7 **Whitelackington** Somset
71 G4 **White Ladies Aston** Worcs
58 D6 **Whiteleaf** Bucks
17 G1 **Whiteley** Hants
17 G6 **Whiteley Bank** IoW
214 B4 **Whitemire** Moray
101 K4 **Whitemoor** C Nott
4 F4 **Whitemoor** Cnwll
235 c6 **Whiteness** Shet
61 J4 **White Notley** Essex
28 E6 **Whiteparish** Wilts
118 E6 **White Pit** Lincs
206 F2 **Whiterashes** Abers
60 E5 **White Roding** Essex
231 L5 **Whiterow** Highld
214 C3 **Whiterow** Moray
55 J6 **Whiteshill** Gloucs
20 B3 **Whitesmith** E Susx
13 H1 **Whitestaunton** Somset
11 K6 **Whitestone Cross** Devon
42 D5 **White Waltham** W & M
121 K2 **Whitewell** Lancs
187 G2 **Whitfield** C Dund
35 J5 **Whitfield** Kent
73 H6 **Whitfield** Nhants
149 K4 **Whitfield** Nthumb
38 F3 **Whitfield** S Glos
13 G4 **Whitford** Devon
111 G5 **Whitford** Flints
125 J6 **Whitgift** E R Yk
99 K6 **Whitgreave** Staffs
145 J6 **Whithorn** D & G
162 D4 **Whiting Bay** N Ayrs
124 B4 **Whitkirk** Leeds
49 L4 **Whitland** Carmth
167 G6 **Whitlaw** Border
163 J5 **Whitletts** S Ayrs
124 E6 **Whitley** N York
42 B6 **Whitley** Readg
115 G3 **Whitley** Sheff
39 K6 **Whitley** Wilts
159 J7 **Whitley Bay** N Tyne
159 H7 **Whitley Bay Crematorium** N Tyne
150 B4 **Whitley Chapel** Nthumb
123 J6 **Whitley Lower** Kirk
55 H6 **Whitminster** Gloucs
99 J4 **Whitmore** Staffs
25 G7 **Whitnage** Devon
72 D2 **Whitnash** Warwks
68 F5 **Whitney-on-Wye** Herefs
28 C7 **Whitsbury** Hants
179 H7 **Whitsome** Border
38 B4 **Whitson** Newpt
47 J6 **Whitstable** Kent
9 H5 **Whitstone** Cnwll
168 F6 **Whittingham** Nthumb
83 H5 **Whittingslow** Shrops
115 G6 **Whittington** Derbys
56 A4 **Whittington** Gloucs
130 B4 **Whittington** Lancs
91 G4 **Whittington** Norfk
97 L6 **Whittington** Shrops
84 F6 **Whittington** Staffs
85 L2 **Whittington** Staffs
86 C4 **Whittington** Warwks
70 F4 **Whittington** Worcs
73 K5 **Whittlebury** Nhants
121 H6 **Whittle-le-Woods** Lancs
89 J4 **Whittlesey** Cambs
76 C5 **Whittlesford** Cambs
125 L5 **Whitton** N Linc
158 D3 **Whitton** Nthumb
68 F2 **Whitton** Powys
141 J3 **Whitton** S on T
83 L8 **Whitton** Shrops
150 D4 **Whittonstall** Nthumb
41 J8 **Whitway** Hants
115 K6 **Whitwell** Derbys
59 K4 **Whitwell** Herts
17 G6 **Whitwell** IoW
141 G7 **Whitwell** N York
88 D2 **Whitwell** Rutlnd
133 L6 **Whitwell-on-the-Hill** N York

106 D7 **Whitwell Street** Norfk
86 E1 **Whitwick** Leics
122 D6 **Whitworth** Lancs
98 D5 **Whixall** Shrops
133 G7 **Whixley** N York
140 E4 **Whorlton** Dur
69 L3 **Whyle** Herefs
32 C2 **Whyteleafe** Surrey
123 H4 **Wibsey** C Brad
86 F6 **Wibtoft** Warwks
70 D3 **Wichenford** Worcs
34 B4 **Wichling** Kent
15 L4 **Wick** Bmouth
231 L5 **Wick** Highld
39 G5 **Wick** S Glos
36 E6 **Wick** V Glam
18 D5 **Wick** W Susx
71 G5 **Wick** Worcs
231 L5 *Wick Airport* Highld
76 E1 **Wicken** Cambs
73 L6 **Wicken** Nhants
60 D2 **Wicken Bonhunt** Essex
117 H5 **Wickenby** Lincs
105 K6 **Wicken Green Village** Norfk
115 J3 **Wickersley** Rothm
77 L6 **Wicker Street Green** Suffk
46 C2 **Wickford** Essex
17 H1 **Wickham** Hants
41 H6 **Wickham** W Berk
61 K5 **Wickham Bishops** Essex
35 G3 **Wickhambreaux** Kent
77 H4 **Wickhambrook** Suffk
71 J6 **Wickhamford** Worcs
78 D2 **Wickham Green** Suffk
79 G4 **Wickham Market** Suffk
93 J3 **Wickhampton** Norfk
77 J7 **Wickham St Paul** Essex
78 C2 **Wickham Skeith** Suffk
78 C1 **Wickham Street** Suffk
92 C3 **Wicklewood** Norfk
106 E5 **Wickmere** Norfk
38 A7 **Wick St Lawrence** N Som
39 G3 **Wickwar** S Glos
60 E2 **Widdington** Essex
159 G3 **Widdrington** Nthumb
159 G4 **Widdrington Station** Nthumb
7 G1 **Widecombe in the Moor** Devon
5 L4 **Widegates** Cnwll
9 G4 **Widemouth Bay** Cnwll
159 G7 **Wide Open** N Tyne
61 H6 **Widford** Essex
60 C5 **Widford** Herts
42 E2 **Widmer End** Bucks
101 M6 **Widmerpool** Notts
45 H6 **Widmore** Gt Lon
112 D5 **Widnes** Halton
112 D4 **Widnes Crematorium** Halton
13 G3 **Widworthy** Devon
112 E1 **Wigan** Wigan
112 E2 **Wigan Crematorium** Wigan
26 C7 **Wigborough** Somset
12 E4 **Wiggaton** Devon
90 E2 **Wiggenhall St Germans** Norfk
90 E2 **Wiggenhall St Mary Magdalen** Norfk
90 E2 **Wiggenhall St Mary the Virgin** Norfk
133 J7 **Wigginton** C York
58 F6 **Wigginton** Herts
57 H2 **Wigginton** Oxon
86 B3 **Wigginton** Staffs
130 F7 **Wigglesworth** N York
148 B4 **Wiggonby** Cumb
124 D2 **Wighill** N York
105 M4 **Wighton** Norfk
84 F4 **Wightwick** Wolves
29 G7 **Wigley** Hants
69 H2 **Wigmore** Herefs
46 D6 **Wigmore** Medway
116 E7 **Wigsley** Notts
88 F6 **Wigsthorpe** Nhants
87 H4 **Wigston** Leics
86 F5 **Wigston Parva** Leics
115 L5 **Wigthorpe** Notts
103 L5 **Wigtoft** Lincs
148 A5 **Wigton** Cumb
145 J4 **Wigtown** D & G
123 L3 **Wike** Leeds
88 B5 **Wilbarston** Nhants
125 H1 **Wilberfoss** E R Yk
90 C7 **Wilburton** Cambs
74 C2 **Wilby** Nhants
92 B5 **Wilby** Norfk
78 F1 **Wilby** Suffk
40 C7 **Wilcot** Wilts
98 B8 **Wilcott** Shrops
113 M7 **Wildboarclough** Ches E
75 G4 **Wilden** Bed
84 E8 **Wilden** Worcs
175 L7 **Wildmanbridge** S Lans
85 G7 **Wildmoor** Worcs
116 D3 **Wildsworth** Lincs
101 L5 **Wilford Hill Crematorium** Notts
98 F4 **Wilkesley** Ches E
223 K4 **Wilkhaven** Highld
176 F5 **Wilkieston** W Loth
12 D1 **Willand** Devon
99 G3 **Willaston** Ches E
111 K6 **Willaston** Ches W
74 C6 **Willen** M Keyn
86 D7 **Willenhall** Covtry
85 H4 **Willenhall** Wsall
126 C4 **Willerby** E R Yk
134 F4 **Willerby** N York
71 K6 **Willersey** Gloucs
68 F5 **Willersley** Herefs
34 D6 **Willesborough** Kent
34 D6 **Willesborough Lees** Kent
44 E3 **Willesden** Gt Lon
39 J3 **Willesley** Wilts
25 H5 **Willett** Somset
84 C4 **Willey** Shrops
86 F6 **Willey** Warwks
30 F2 **Willey Green** Surrey
72 F5 **Williamscot** Oxon
59 L2 **Willian** Herts
60 F6 **Willingale** Essex
20 C5 **Willingdon** E Susx
76 B1 **Willingham** Cambs
116 E5 **Willingham by Stow** Lincs
75 G4 **Willington** Bed
100 F6 **Willington** Derbys
150 F7 **Willington** Dur
33 K3 **Willington** Kent
72 C6 **Willington** Warwks
151 H2 **Willington Quay** N Tyne
125 H4 **Willitoft** E R Yk
25 H4 **Williton** Somset
119 G6 **Willoughby** Lincs
73 G2 **Willoughby** Warwks
101 M7 **Willoughby-on-the-Wolds** Notts
87 H5 **Willoughby Waterleys** Leics
116 F3 **Willoughton** Lincs
61 H4 **Willows Green** Essex
26 B6 **Willtown** Somset
71 L3 **Wilmcote** Warwks
13 G3 **Wilmington** Devon
20 B5 **Wilmington** E Susx
45 K5 **Wilmington** Kent
113 J5 **Wilmslow** Ches E
121 K4 **Wilpshire** Lancs
123 G3 **Wilsden** C Brad
103 G4 **Wilsford** Lincs
28 C4 **Wilsford** Wilts
40 C8 **Wilsford** Wilts
123 G8 **Wilshaw** Kirk
132 B6 **Wilsill** N York
101 H7 **Wilson** Leics
176 C7 **Wilsontown** S Lans
74 F5 **Wilstead** Bed
88 F2 **Wilsthorpe** Lincs
58 E5 **Wilstone** Herts
54 E3 **Wilton** Herefs
134 D3 **Wilton** N York
142 C4 **Wilton** R & Cl
28 C5 **Wilton** Wilts
40 E7 **Wilton** Wilts
167 G6 **Wilton Dean** Border
76 E7 **Wimbish Green** Essex
44 E6 **Wimbledon** Gt Lon
90 B5 **Wimblington** Cambs
113 G8 **Wimboldsley** Ches W
15 J3 **Wimborne Minster** Dorset
28 B8 **Wimborne St Giles** Dorset
90 E3 **Wimbotsham** Norfk
75 L4 **Wimpole** Cambs
72 B5 **Wimpstone** Warwks
27 G5 **Wincanton** Somset
176 E4 **Winchburgh** W Loth
56 A3 **Winchcombe** Gloucs
21 H3 **Winchelsea** E Susx
29 J5 **Winchester** Hants
29 K4 **Winchester Services** Hants
33 J5 **Winchet Hill** Kent
30 C1 **Winchfield** Hants
42 F2 **Winchmore Hill** Bucks
44 F2 **Winchmore Hill** Gt Lon
113 L7 **Wincle** Ches E
115 G3 **Wincobank** Sheff
137 L7 **Windermere** Cumb
72 D6 **Winderton** Warwks
212 E5 **Windhill** Highld
42 F7 **Windlesham** Surrey
4 D2 **Windmill** Cnwll
20 D4 **Windmill Hill** E Susx
25 L7 **Windmill Hill** Somset
56 D5 **Windrush** Gloucs
216 B3 **Windsole** Abers
42 F5 **Windsor** W & M
42 F5 **Windsor Castle** W & M
55 J7 **Windsoredge** Gloucs
77 K4 **Windsor Green** Suffk
72 C1 **Windy Arbour** Warwks
186 E7 **Windygates** Fife
31 L7 **Wineham** W Susx
127 G5 **Winestead** E R Yk
92 D6 **Winfarthing** Norfk
17 G5 **Winford** IoW
38 D7 **Winford** N Som
68 F5 **Winforton** Herefs
14 F5 **Winfrith Newburgh** Dorset
58 E4 **Wing** Bucks
88 C3 **Wing** Rutlnd
151 J7 **Wingate** Dur
115 G7 **Wingerworth** Derbys
59 G3 **Wingfield** C Beds
92 F7 **Wingfield** Suffk
27 J1 **Wingfield** Wilts
35 H3 **Wingham** Kent
58 E4 **Wingrave** Bucks
102 B2 **Winkburn** Notts
42 E6 **Winkfield** Br For
42 E6 **Winkfield Row** Br For
100 B3 **Winkhill** Staffs
10 F4 **Winkleigh** Devon
132 C5 **Winksley** N York
150 F3 **Winlaton** Gatesd
231 K5 **Winless** Highld
120 F2 **Winmarleigh** Lancs
29 J5 **Winnall** Hants
42 C6 **Winnersh** Wokham
112 F6 **Winnington** Ches W
38 B8 **Winscombe** N Som
112 F7 **Winsford** Ches W
24 E4 **Winsford** Somset
13 J2 **Winsham** Somset
100 F7 **Winshill** Staffs
51 K6 **Winshwen** Swans
149 G7 **Winskill** Cumb
39 J7 **Winsley** Wilts
58 C3 **Winslow** Bucks
56 C6 **Winson** Gloucs
28 F8 **Winsor** Hants
129 J2 **Winster** Cumb
100 E1 **Winster** Derbys
140 E4 **Winston** Dur
78 E3 **Winston** Suffk
55 L6 **Winstone** Gloucs
10 D3 **Winswell** Devon
14 D5 **Winterborne Came** Dorset
14 F2 **Winterborne Clenston** Dorset
14 F2 **Winterborne Houghton** Dorset
15 G3 **Winterborne Kingston** Dorset
14 D5 **Winterborne Monkton** Dorset
14 F2 **Winterborne Stickland** Dorset
14 F3 **Winterborne Whitechurch** Dorset
15 G3 **Winterborne Zelston** Dorset
38 F4 **Winterbourne** S Glos
41 J6 **Winterbourne** W Berk
14 C4 **Winterbourne Abbas** Dorset
40 C5 **Winterbourne Bassett** Wilts
28 D4 **Winterbourne Dauntsey** Wilts
28 D5 **Winterbourne Earls** Wilts
28 D4 **Winterbourne Gunner** Wilts
40 C6 **Winterbourne Monkton** Wilts
14 C4 **Winterbourne Steepleton** Dorset
28 B3 **Winterbourne Stoke** Wilts
131 H7 **Winterburn** N York
125 L6 **Winteringham** N Linc
99 H2 **Winterley** Ches E
28 E5 **Winterslow** Wilts
125 L6 **Winterton** N Linc
107 K8 **Winterton-on-Sea** Norfk
102 D2 **Winthorpe** Notts
15 K4 **Winton** Bmouth
139 H5 **Winton** Cumb
134 D5 **Wintringham** N York
89 G7 **Winwick** Cambs
87 J8 **Winwick** Nhants
112 E3 **Winwick** Warrtn
100 F2 **Wirksworth** Derbys
111 J4 **Wirral**
98 D4 **Wirswall** Ches E
90 C2 **Wisbech** Cambs
90 B2 **Wisbech St Mary** Cambs
31 H6 **Wisborough Green** W Susx
49 K6 **Wiseman's Bridge** Pembks
116 B4 **Wiseton** Notts
175 L7 **Wishaw** N Lans
85 L5 **Wishaw** Warwks
43 H8 **Wisley Gardens** Surrey
117 K6 **Wispington** Lincs

93 H7 **Wissett** Suffk
62 A2 **Wissington** Suffk
83 H6 **Wistanstow** Shrops
98 F6 **Wistanswick** Shrops
99 G2 **Wistaston** Ches E
49 H4 **Wiston** Pembks
165 J3 **Wiston** S Lans
18 F3 **Wiston** W Susx
89 K7 **Wistow** Cambs
124 F4 **Wistow** N York
121 L3 **Wiswell** Lancs
90 C7 **Witcham** Cambs
15 J2 **Witchampton** Dorset
90 C7 **Witchford** Cambs
26 C6 **Witcombe** Somset
61 K5 **Witham** Essex
27 H3 **Witham Friary** Somset
88 F1 **Witham on the Hill** Lincs
118 C5 **Withcall** Lincs
19 J4 **Withdean** Br & H
33 H7 **Witherenden Hill** E Susx
11 J3 **Witheridge** Devon
86 D4 **Witherley** Leics
118 F5 **Withern** Lincs
127 H5 **Withernsea** E R Yk
126 F3 **Withernwick** E R Yk
92 F7 **Withersdale Street** Suffk
76 F5 **Withersfield** Suffk
129 J3 **Witherslack** Cumb
4 F3 **Withiel** Cnwll
24 F5 **Withiel Florey** Somset
56 B5 **Withington** Gloucs
69 L5 **Withington** Herefs
113 J3 **Withington** Manch
83 L2 **Withington** Shrops
100 B5 **Withington** Staffs
11 K3 **Withleigh** Devon
121 J6 **Withnell** Lancs
85 H8 **Withybed Green** Worcs
86 E6 **Withybrook** Warwks
24 F3 **Withycombe** Somset
32 E6 **Withyham** E Susx
24 D4 **Withypool** Somset
38 E6 **Withywood** Bristl
30 F4 **Witley** Surrey
78 E4 **Witnesham** Suffk
57 G6 **Witney** Oxon
88 F3 **Wittering** C Pete
21 H1 **Wittersham** Kent
85 J5 **Witton** Birm
93 G2 **Witton** Norfk
107 H6 **Witton** Norfk
151 G5 **Witton Gilbert** Dur
140 E2 **Witton le Wear** Dur
140 F2 **Witton Park** Dur
25 G5 **Wiveliscombe** Somset
30 A4 **Wivelrod** Hants
19 K2 **Wivelsfield** E Susx
19 K2 **Wivelsfield Green** E Susx
62 C4 **Wivenhoe** Essex
106 C4 **Wiveton** Norfk
62 E3 **Wix** Essex
71 K4 **Wixford** Warwks
77 G6 **Wixoe** Suffk
58 F2 **Woburn** C Beds
58 F2 **Woburn Abbey** C Beds
74 D7 **Woburn Sands** M Keyn
43 G8 **Woking** Surrey
42 F8 **Woking Crematorium** Surrey
42 D6 **Wokingham** Wokham
32 C3 **Woldingham** Surrey
135 G5 **Wold Newton** E R Yk
118 C3 **Wold Newton** NE Lin
165 K3 **Wolfclyde** S Lans
105 G6 **Wolferton** Norfk
186 B2 **Wolfhill** P & K
49 G3 **Wolf's Castle** Pembks
48 F3 **Wolfsdale** Pembks
84 F6 **Wollaston** Dudley
74 C2 **Wollaston** Nhants
83 G2 **Wollaston** Shrops
101 K4 **Wollaton** C Nott
98 F6 **Wollerton** Shrops
85 G6 **Wollescote** Dudley
100 A7 **Wolseley Bridge** Staffs
150 D7 **Wolsingham** Dur
99 J3 **Wolstanton** Staffs
86 E7 **Wolston** Warwks
57 J6 **Wolvercote** Oxon
85 G4 **Wolverhampton** Wolves
84 E5 *Wolverhampton Business Airport* Staffs
84 E7 **Wolverley** Worcs
41 K8 **Wolverton** Hants
74 B6 **Wolverton** M Keyn
72 B3 **Wolverton** Warwks
27 H5 **Wolverton** Wilts
54 C7 **Wolvesnewton** Mons
86 E6 **Wolvey** Warwks
86 E5 **Wolvey Heath** Warwks
141 K3 **Wolviston** S on T
133 K3 **Wombleton** N York
84 F5 **Wombourne** Staffs
115 H2 **Wombwell** Barns
35 G5 **Womenswold** Kent
124 E6 **Womersley** N York
31 G3 **Wonersh** Surrey
12 B4 **Wonford** Devon
14 E2 **Wonston** Dorset
29 J4 **Wonston** Hants
42 E3 **Wooburn** Bucks
42 E3 **Wooburn Green** Bucks
9 K4 **Woodacott** Devon
115 J5 **Woodall** Rothm
115 J5 **Woodall Services** Rothm
93 G1 **Woodbastwick** Norfk
71 J4 **Wood Bevington** Warwks
101 M3 **Woodborough** Notts
40 C7 **Woodborough** Wilts
78 F5 **Woodbridge** Suffk
12 C5 **Woodbury** Devon
12 C5 **Woodbury Salterton** Devon
55 J7 **Woodchester** Gloucs
34 C7 **Woodchurch** Kent
24 E3 **Woodcombe** Somset
44 F7 **Woodcote** Gt Lon
41 M4 **Woodcote** Oxon
84 D1 **Woodcote** Wrekin
38 D2 **Woodcroft** Gloucs
106 C6 **Wood Dalling** Norfk
76 F3 **Woodditton** Cambs
57 K5 **Woodeaton** Oxon
43 J4 **Wood End** Gt Lon
60 B3 **Wood End** Herts
190 F4 **Woodend** Highld
73 H5 **Woodend** Nhants
176 C4 **Woodend** W Loth
17 M2 **Woodend** W Susx
71 K1 **Wood End** Warwks
118 C8 **Wood Enderby** Lincs
28 D7 **Woodfalls** Wilts
9 G3 **Woodford** Cnwll
39 G2 **Woodford** Gloucs
45 H2 **Woodford** Gt Lon
88 D7 **Woodford** Nhants
113 K5 **Woodford** Stockp
45 H2 **Woodford Bridge** Gt Lon
73 G4 **Woodford Halse** Nhants
45 H2 **Woodford Wells** Gt Lon
85 H6 **Woodgate** Birm
25 H7 **Woodgate** Devon
18 C5 **Woodgate** W Susx
71 H2 **Woodgate** Worcs
44 F2 **Wood Green** Gt Lon
28 D7 **Woodgreen** Hants
131 J2 **Woodhall** N York
117 K8 **Woodhall Spa** Lincs
58 B4 **Woodham** Bucks
43 H7 **Woodham** Surrey
61 J7 **Woodham Ferrers** Essex
61 K6 **Woodham Mortimer** Essex
61 K6 **Woodham Walter** Essex
85 G3 **Wood Hayes** Wolves
216 E6 **Woodhead** Abers
84 D6 **Woodhill** Shrops
26 A6 **Woodhill** Somset
159 H4 **Woodhorn** Nthumb
123 K4 **Woodhouse** Leeds
87 G1 **Woodhouse** Leics
115 H4 **Woodhouse** Sheff
124 B6 **Woodhouse** Wakefd
87 G2 **Woodhouse Eaves** Leics
177 H5 **Woodhouselee** Mdloth
156 D6 **Woodhouselees** D & G
100 D8 **Woodhouses** Staffs
89 K7 **Woodhurst** Cambs
19 K5 **Woodingdean** Br & H
123 K5 **Woodkirk** Leeds
207 G2 **Woodland** Abers
6 F5 **Woodland** Devon
7 J3 **Woodland** Devon
140 D2 **Woodland** Dur
152 E3 **Woodland** S Ayrs
206 E6 **Woodlands** Abers
124 E8 **Woodlands** Donc
15 K2 **Woodlands** Dorset
16 C1 **Woodlands** Hants
132 E8 **Woodlands** N York
85 L5 **Woodlands (Coleshill) Crematorium** Warwks
42 E5 **Woodlands Park** W & M
134 F3 **Woodlands (Scarborough) Crematorium** N York
125 K7 **Woodlands (Scunthorpe) Crematorium** N Linc
7 H6 **Woodleigh** Devon
42 C5 **Woodley** Wokham
39 H2 **Woodmancote** Gloucs
55 L3 **Woodmancote** Gloucs
56 A6 **Woodmancote** Gloucs
17 L2 **Woodmancote** W Susx
19 H3 **Woodmancote** W Susx
29 K3 **Woodmancott** Hants
126 C3 **Woodmansey** E R Yk
30 E6 **Woodmansgreen** W Susx
32 B2 **Woodmansterne** Surrey
12 C5 **Woodmanton** Devon
35 J4 **Woodnesborough** Kent
88 F5 **Woodnewton** Nhants
106 B6 **Wood Norton** Norfk
121 G4 **Woodplumpton** Lancs
92 B3 **Woodrising** Norfk
20 D2 **Wood's Corner** E Susx
99 H7 **Woodseaves** Staffs
115 K5 **Woodsetts** Rothm
14 E4 **Woodsford** Dorset
33 H6 **Wood's Green** E Susx
42 F6 **Woodside** Br For
187 G5 **Woodside** Fife
45 G6 **Woodside** Gt Lon
195 K8 **Woodside** P & K
57 H5 **Woodstock** Oxon
89 H4 **Woodston** C Pete
107 H7 **Wood Street** Norfk
30 F2 **Wood Street Village** Surrey
93 G5 **Woodton** Norfk
22 F6 **Woodtown** Devon
19 J4 **Woodvale Crematorium** Br & H
89 J7 **Wood Walton** Cambs
69 K2 **Woofferton** Shrops
26 D3 **Wookey** Somset
26 D2 **Wookey Hole** Somset
14 F5 **Wool** Dorset
23 G3 **Woolacombe** Devon
35 H5 **Woolage Green** Kent
54 E7 **Woolaston** Gloucs
54 E7 **Woolaston Common** Gloucs
25 M3 **Woolavington** Somset
30 E6 **Woolbeding** W Susx
12 E5 **Woolbrook** Devon
168 E4 **Wooler** Nthumb
11 J3 **Woolfardisworthy** Devon
22 E7 **Woolfardisworthy** Devon
176 D6 **Woolfords** S Lans
41 L6 **Woolhampton** W Berk
69 L7 **Woolhope** Herefs
14 E2 **Woolland** Dorset
39 H6 **Woolley** BaNES
89 G8 **Woolley** Cambs
123 L7 **Woolley** Wakefd
123 K7 **Woolley Edge Services** Wakefd
71 G2 **Woolmere Green** Worcs
59 L4 **Woolmer Green** Herts
13 K2 **Woolminstone** Somset
77 L3 **Woolpit** Suffk
83 J4 **Woolstaston** Shrops
102 D5 **Woolsthorpe** Lincs
102 F7 **Woolsthorpe-by-Colsterworth** Lincs
16 E1 **Woolston** C Sotn
97 L7 **Woolston** Shrops
25 H4 **Woolston** Somset
26 F5 **Woolston** Somset
112 F4 **Woolston** Warrtn
55 L3 **Woolstone** Gloucs
74 C6 **Woolstone** M Keyn
40 F3 **Woolstone** Oxon
7 H3 **Woolston Green** Devon
112 B4 **Woolton** Lpool
41 H7 **Woolton Hill** Hants
78 E6 **Woolverstone** Suffk
27 H2 **Woolverton** Somset
45 H4 **Woolwich** Gt Lon
69 G4 **Woonton** Herefs
99 G4 **Woore** Shrops
92 F8 **Wootten Green** Suffk
74 E5 **Wootton** Bed
35 G5 **Wootton** Kent
126 D7 **Wootton** N Linc
73 L3 **Wootton** Nhants
57 H4 **Wootton** Oxon
57 J7 **Wootton** Oxon
100 C4 **Wootton** Staffs
40 B4 **Wootton Bassett** Wilts
17 G4 **Wootton Bridge** IoW
24 E3 **Wootton Courtenay** Somset
13 J4 **Wootton Fitzpaine** Dorset
40 D7 **Wootton Rivers** Wilts

29 L2 **Wootton St Lawrence** Hants
71 L2 **Wootton Wawen** Warwks
70 F4 **Worcester** Worcs
44 E6 **Worcester Park** Gt Lon
84 F6 **Wordsley** Dudley
84 D4 **Worfield** Shrops
136 D2 **Workington** Cumb
115 L5 **Worksop** Notts
126 C7 **Worlaby** N Linc
29 M8 **Worlds End** Hants
19 J2 **Worlds End** W Susx
38 A7 **Worle** N Som
98 F2 **Worleston** Ches E
93 J5 **Worlingham** Suffk
11 H3 **Worlington** Devon
91 G8 **Worlington** Suffk
78 F2 **Worlingworth** Suffk
54 B2 **Wormbridge** Herefs
90 F2 **Wormegay** Norfk
54 C3 **Wormelow Tump** Herefs
114 C6 **Wormhill** Derbys
61 M2 **Wormingford** Essex
57 M6 **Worminghall** Bucks
71 J7 **Wormington** Gloucs
186 F3 **Wormit** Fife
72 F4 **Wormleighton** Warwks
60 B6 **Wormley** Herts
30 F4 **Wormley** Surrey
34 B3 **Wormshill** Kent
69 H5 **Wormsley** Herefs
30 F2 **Worplesdon** Surrey
114 F3 **Worrall** Sheff
115 G2 **Worsbrough** Barns
115 G2 **Worsbrough Bridge** Barns
115 G2 **Worsbrough Dale** Barns
113 H2 **Worsley** Salfd
107 G7 **Worstead** Norfk
122 C4 **Worsthorne** Lancs
6 E5 **Worston** Devon
122 B3 **Worston** Lancs
35 J4 **Worth** Kent
92 C7 **Wortham** Suffk
83 G3 **Worthen** Shrops
98 B4 **Worthenbury** Wrexhm
106 B8 **Worthing** Norfk
18 F5 **Worthing** W Susx
18 F4 **Worthing Crematorium** W Susx
101 H7 **Worthington** Leics
15 H6 **Worth Matravers** Dorset
114 F2 **Wortley** Barns
123 K4 **Wortley** Leeds
131 H2 **Worton** N York
39 L8 **Worton** Wilts
92 F6 **Wortwell** Norfk
39 H2 **Wotton-under-Edge** Gloucs
58 B5 **Wotton Underwood** Bucks
74 C6 **Woughton on the Green** M Keyn
46 B7 **Wouldham** Kent
62 E2 **Wrabness** Essex
23 H4 **Wrafton** Devon
117 J6 **Wragby** Lincs
124 C6 **Wragby** Wakefd
7 G4 **Wrangaton** Devon
104 C3 **Wrangle** Lincs
25 H7 **Wrangway** Somset
25 L6 **Wrantage** Somset
126 C8 **Wrawby** N Linc
38 C6 **Wraxall** N Som
26 E4 **Wraxall** Somset
130 B6 **Wray** Lancs
43 G5 **Wraysbury** W & M
130 C5 **Wrayton** Lancs
120 E4 **Wrea Green** Lancs
148 D5 **Wreay** Cumb
30 D3 **Wrecclesham** Surrey
151 G3 **Wrekenton** Gatesd
134 B3 **Wrelton** N York
98 E3 **Wrenbury** Ches E
92 E4 **Wreningham** Norfk
93 K6 **Wrentham** Suffk
83 H3 **Wrentnall** Shrops
125 G4 **Wressle** E R Yk
126 B8 **Wressle** N Linc
75 J5 **Wrestlingworth** C Beds
91 G4 **Wretton** Norfk
97 M3 **Wrexham** Wrexhm
84 E7 **Wribbenhall** Worcs
99 H3 **Wrinehill** Staffs
38 C7 **Wrington** N Som
27 G1 **Writhlington** BaNES
61 G6 **Writtle** Essex
84 B2 **Wrockwardine** Wrekin
116 B2 **Wroot** N Linc
123 H3 **Wrose** C Brad
33 G2 **Wrotham** Kent
40 C4 **Wroughton** Swindn
17 G6 **Wroxall** IoW
72 B1 **Wroxall** Warwks
83 L2 **Wroxeter** Shrops
107 G8 **Wroxham** Norfk
72 E6 **Wroxton** Oxon
100 D4 **Wyaston** Derbys
104 B4 **Wyberton East** Lincs
75 H3 **Wyboston** Bed
99 G3 **Wybunbury** Ches E
71 G2 **Wychbold** Worcs
85 L1 **Wychnor** Staffs
56 D4 **Wyck Rissington** Gloucs
140 E4 **Wycliffe** Dur
122 D3 **Wycoller** Lancs
102 C7 **Wycomb** Leics
42 E3 **Wycombe Marsh** Bucks
60 B2 **Wyddial** Herts
34 E5 **Wye** Kent
123 H5 **Wyke** C Brad
27 H6 **Wyke** Dorset
26 F4 **Wyke Champflower** Somset
134 E3 **Wykeham** N York
86 D7 **Wyken** Covtry
84 D4 **Wyken** Shrops
14 C6 **Wyke Regis** Dorset
98 B7 **Wykey** Shrops
150 E3 **Wylam** Nthumb
85 K5 **Wylde Green** Birm
28 A4 **Wylye** Wilts
101 L7 **Wymeswold** Leics
74 D2 **Wymington** Bed
102 D8 **Wymondham** Leics
92 D3 **Wymondham** Norfk
14 B3 **Wynford Eagle** Dorset
84 E8 **Wyre Forest Crematorium** Worcs
71 G5 **Wyre Piddle** Worcs
101 L6 **Wysall** Notts
85 J7 **Wythall** Worcs
57 J6 **Wytham** Oxon
113 J4 **Wythenshawe** Manch
89 K8 **Wyton** Cambs
126 E4 **Wyton** E R Yk
78 C2 **Wyverstone** Suffk
78 B2 **Wyverstone Street** Suffk

Y

116 E1 **Yaddlethorpe** N Linc
141 H7 **Yafforth** N York
7 K4 **Yalberton** Torbay
33 J3 **Yalding** Kent
138 D2 **Yanwath** Cumb
56 B5 **Yanworth** Gloucs
125 J1 **Yapham** E R Yk
18 D5 **Yapton** W Susx
38 B8 **Yarborough** N Som
118 E3 **Yarburgh** Lincs
13 G2 **Yarcombe** Devon
24 B6 **Yard** Devon
85 K6 **Yardley** Birm
85 K6 **Yardley Crematorium** Birm
73 L5 **Yardley Gobion** Nhants
74 C3 **Yardley Hastings** Nhants
85 K7 **Yardley Wood** Birm
69 L6 **Yarkhill** Herefs
26 D3 **Yarley** Somset
26 F5 **Yarlington** Somset
141 K5 **Yarm** S on T
16 D4 **Yarmouth** IoW
27 K1 **Yarnbrook** Wilts
99 K6 **Yarnfield** Staffs
23 J6 **Yarnscombe** Devon
57 J5 **Yarnton** Oxon
69 J2 **Yarpole** Herefs
166 E4 **Yarrow** Border
166 E4 **Yarrow Feus** Border
166 F4 **Yarrowford** Border
88 F4 **Yarwell** Nhants
39 G4 **Yate** S Glos
42 D7 **Yateley** Hants
40 B6 **Yatesbury** Wilts
41 K5 **Yattendon** W Berk
69 H2 **Yatton** Herefs
38 B7 **Yatton** N Som
39 K5 **Yatton Keynell** Wilts
17 H5 **Yaverland** IoW
92 B2 **Yaxham** Norfk
89 H5 **Yaxley** Cambs
92 D8 **Yaxley** Suffk
69 H5 **Yazor** Herefs
43 J4 **Yeading** Gt Lon
123 J3 **Yeadon** Leeds
129 K5 **Yealand Conyers** Lancs
129 K4 **Yealand Redmayne** Lancs
6 E5 **Yealmpton** Devon
133 J5 **Yearsley** N York
98 B8 **Yeaton** Shrops
100 D4 **Yeaveley** Derbys
168 D4 **Yeavering** Nthumb
134 D4 **Yedingham** N York
57 G6 **Yelford** Oxon
235 d3 **Yell** Shet
75 J3 **Yelling** Cambs
87 H7 **Yelvertoft** Nhants
6 D3 **Yelverton** Devon
93 G3 **Yelverton** Norfk
27 G7 **Yenston** Somset
11 H5 **Yeoford** Devon
9 J7 **Yeolmbridge** Cnwll
26 D7 **Yeovil** Somset
26 D7 **Yeovil Crematorium** Somset
26 D7 **Yeovil Marsh** Somset
26 D6 **Yeovilton** Somset
26 D6 **Yeovilton Fleet Air Arm Museum** Somset
234 b5 **Yesnaby** Ork
14 B1 **Yetminster** Dorset
12 D5 **Yettington** Devon
185 L6 **Yetts o'Muckhart** Clacks
85 H4 **Yew Tree** Sandw
109 G7 **Y Felinheli** Gwynd
65 G5 **Y Ferwig** Cerdgn
95 G5 **Y Ffor** Gwynd
97 G2 **Y Gyffylliog** Denbgs
74 E2 **Yielden** Bed
176 B7 **Yieldshields** S Lans
43 H4 **Yiewsley** Gt Lon
96 F4 **Y Maerdy** Conwy
37 G2 **Ynysboeth** Rhondd
37 J2 **Ynysddu** Caerph
36 F3 **Ynyshir** Rhondd
51 K5 **Ynystawe** Swans
37 G2 **Ynysybwl** Rhondd
83 H2 **Yockleton** Shrops
125 J5 **Yokefleet** E R Yk
174 F5 **Yoker** C Glas
124 F1 **York** C York
124 F2 **York City Crematorium** C York
34 E3 **Yorkletts** Kent
54 F6 **Yorkley** Gloucs
124 F1 **York Minster** C York
131 G4 **Yorkshire Dales National Park**
42 E7 **York Town** Surrey
114 E8 **Youlgreave** Derbys
134 B7 **Youlthorpe** E R Yk
133 G6 **Youlton** N York
100 C8 **Yoxall** Staffs
79 H2 **Yoxford** Suffk
94 D6 **Y Rhiw** Gwynd
96 C3 **Ysbyty Ifan** Conwy
67 G1 **Ysbyty Ystwyth** Cerdgn
111 G7 **Ysceifiog** Flints
52 B6 **Ystalyfera** Neath
36 F2 **Ystrad** Rhondd
66 C4 **Ystrad Aeron** Cerdgn
52 E5 **Ystradfellte** Powys
52 C6 **Ystradgynlais** Powys
66 F2 **Ystrad Meurig** Cerdgn
37 H2 **Ystrad Mynach** Caerph
36 F5 **Ystradowen** V Glam
217 G7 **Ythanbank** Abers
216 C6 **Ythanwells** Abers
217 G7 **Ythsie** Abers

Z

11 G4 **Zeal Monachorum** Devon
27 H5 **Zeals** Wilts
4 C5 **Zelah** Cnwll
2 E4 **Zennor** Cnwll
101 J7 **Zouch** Notts
59 G4 **ZSL Whipsnade Zoo** C Beds

Ireland

NORTH ATLANTIC OCEAN
IRISH SEA
Celtic Sea
NORTHERN IRELAND
REPUBLIC OF IRELAND
Malin Head
Rathlin Island
Toraigh
Tory Island
Árainn Mhór
Aran Island
An Clochán Liath
Dunglow
Portrush
Ballycastle
Coleraine
Limavady
LONDONDERRY DERRY
Letterkenny
Ballybofey
Strabane
Ballymena
Larne
Maghera
SPERRIN MTS
Antrim
BELFAST
Bangor
Newtownards
Portaferry
Downpatrick
Newcastle
Donegal
Omagh
Cookstown
Dungannon
Ballyshannon
Bundoran
Donegal Bay
Portadown
Armagh
Enniskillen
Monaghan
Newry
MOURNE MTS
Sligo
Castleblayney
Carrickmacross
Dundalk
Béal an Mhuirthead
Belmullet
Bangor
Ballina
OX MTS
Oileán Acla
Achill Island
Charlestown
Foxford
Boyle
Carrick-on-Shannon
Cavan
Castlebar
Knock
Clare Island
Westport
Castlerea
Longford
Virginia
Kells
Slane
Drogheda
Navan
Inishturk
Claremorris
Roscommon
Balbriggan
Inishbofin
Mullingar
Kinnegad
Lambay
Tuam
Clifden
Athlone
DUBLIN
Oughterard
Tullamore
Dún Laoghaire
GALWAY
Garumna
Gorumna Island
Oranmore
Loughrea
Kildare
Naas
Bray
Galway Bay
Blessington
Oileáin Árann
Aran Islands
Portumna
Birr
SLIEVE BLOOM MTS
Portlaoise
Wicklow
Gort
Roscrea
WICKLOW MTS
Ennistymon
Carlow
Tullow
Arklow
Ennis
Newmarket-on-Fergus
Nenagh
Gorey
Kilkee
Kilrush
LIMERICK
Thurles
Kilkenny
Loop Head
Adare
Cashel
Enniscorthy
Tipperary
Abbeyfeale
GALTY MTS
Clonmel
New Ross
Wexford
Cahir
Rosslare
Charleville
KNOCKMEALDOWN MTS
Tralee
Castleisland
Mitchelstown
WATERFORD
Rosslare Harbour
Carnsore Point
An Daingean
Dingle
Mallow
Lismore
An Blascaod Mór
Great Blasket Island
Killorglin
Fermoy
Dungarvan
Dingle Bay
Killarney
BOGGERAGH MTS
Youghal
Cahersiveen
Parknasilla
Macroom
CORK
An Coireán
Waterville
Kenmare
Ringaskiddy
Glengarriff
Kinsale
Bantry
Dursey Island
Bantry Bay
Clonakilty
Skibbereen
Mizen Head
Clear Island
Troon, Cairnryan (Mar-Oct)
Cairnryan
Cairnryan
Douglas-(Apr-Sept)
Liverpool (Birkenhead)
Holyhead
Douglas-(Apr-Sept)
Liverpool
Holyhead
Holyhead (Apr-Sept)
Fishguard (July-Sept)
Fishguard
Pembroke
Cherbourg (Feb-Dec)
Roscoff (May-Sept)
Roscoff (Mar-Oct)
0 20 40 miles
0 20 40 60 kilometres

Map pages north

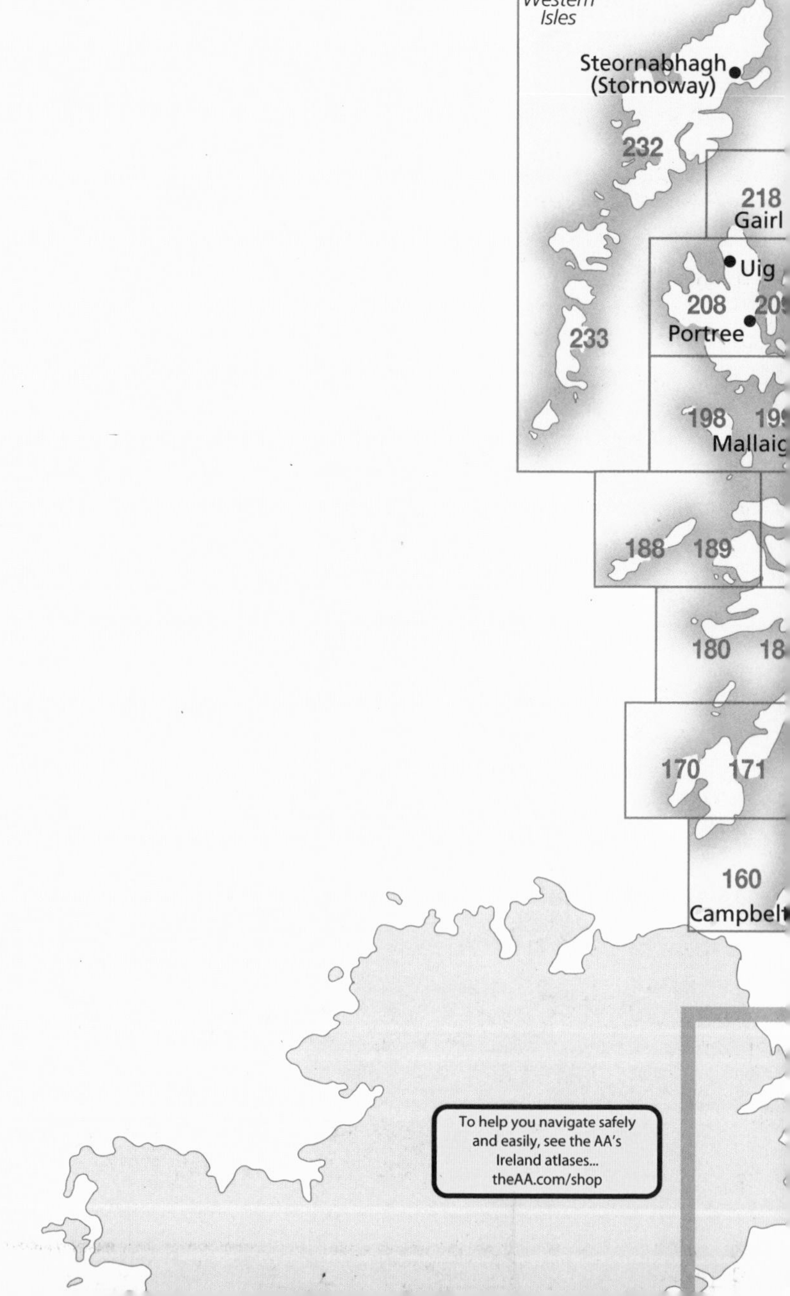